The Negro Leagues Book

A 1930s-vintage Homestead Grays bus.
Jeff Eastland

Cover

An imaginary scene set at Comiskey Park, home of the great East-West All-Star Games. In appropriate uniforms from left to right: Ray Dandridge, Buck Leonard, Pop Lloyd, Bill Foster, Rube Foster, Satchel Paige, Martin Dihigo, Oscar Charleston, Josh Gibson, Cool Papa Bell, and Cristobal Torriente.

Artist Jeff Suntala is a SABR member who specializes in historically accurate baseball illustrations. A poster of the cover art, entitled "Legends of the Black Diamond," is available. Contact SABR at P.O. Box 93183, Cleveland, OH 44101.

A never before published view of the 1925 Colored World Series teams. From the left for Hilldale are: Louis Santop, Nip Winters, Scrip Lee, Rube Currie, Biz Mackey, Tank Carr, Red Ryan, Judy Johnson, George Johnson, Zip Campbell, Phil Cockrell, Joe Lewis, Clint Thomas, Newt Robinson, Otto Briggs, Pete Washington, Jake Stephens, and Frank Warfield. The officials are: Ed Bolden, Charles Spedden, J.L. Wilkinson, and Rube Foster. For Kansas City are: Hurley McNair, Newt Joseph, Wade Johnston, Hooks Foreman, Jose Mendez, Newt Allen, Nelson Dean, Mule Hawkins, William Bell, Dobie Moore, Cliff Bell, Frank Duncan, Bill Drake, George Sweatt, and Chet Brewer.

Jeff Eastland

The Negro Leagues Book

Edited by Dick Clark and Larry Lester

A Monumental Work from the Negro Leagues Committee

of The Society for American Baseball Research

Published by The Society for American Baseball Research, P.O. Box 93183, Cleveland, Ohio 44101

Designed by Jeanne Criscola/Criscola Design, North Haven, Connecticut

The uniform used as the background on the cover is a modern replica, provided by the Negro Leagues Baseball Museum. It was photographed by Cathy Carver.

Printed and manufactured in the United States of America by EBSCO Media, Birmingham, Alabama

Funding for publication of *The Negro Leagues Book* was provided by dues-paying members of The Society for American Baseball Research and grants from The George Gund Foundation and The Pittsburgh National Bank Charitable Trust.

Contents

Dedicated to:

The men, the women, the photographers, and the writers associated with black baseball.
May they be remembered for their entrepreneurial abilities, their testimonial penmanship and most of all,
for how they played the game.

May we remember the intimidation of their fastballs, the grace of their glovework,
and the thunder of their homeruns.

Respect, Redemption, Recognition

Introduction

Andrew "Rube" Foster.
Chicago Historical Society

The baseball of the Negro Leagues and of black teams before the era of league play, was neglected in its time by the greater society, and has been largely forgotten since.

Organized Baseball has taken credit for a pioneering role in the modern civil rights movement and, indeed, it did provide us with such thoroughly admirable heroes and role models as Jackie Robinson and the equally strong, dignified, courageous, and talented men—Larry Doby, Monte Irvin, and others—who soon followed him.

But Organized Baseball was white baseball until 1946. An occasional "Cuban" or "Indian" may have slipped through the cracks in the owners' "Gentleman's Agreement," but virtually all of the great black ballplayers whose primes came before World War II were consigned to segregated play, their skills, their stories, and their personalities unknown even to most rabid fans.

We believe these men, their teams, and their feats deserve recognition. And we believe that most baseball fans who are given a chance to examine the record will find it fascinating and compelling.

Prior to the 1970 release of *Only The Ball Was White,* by Robert Peterson, baseball historians knew little about the subject, and there was no recognition of the black leagues within the mainstream story of our national pastime. Peterson's pioneering work, along with John Holway's oral history, *Voices From The Great Black Baseball Leagues,* began to expose historians and researchers to a world of great teams, wonderful players and the rich history of apartheid baseball in the United States. The founding of SABR in 1971, and the creation of the Negro Leagues Committee soon thereafter, fueled the research. A host of books on the leagues have appeared since 1970 and interest in black baseball has exploded. Only now, after more than two decades of concerted research by many dedicated students of the game (see the acknowledgments, below), does our accumulated data on the Negro Leagues allow us to offer this caliber of guide on the subject.

A Note on Statistics

Although there are plenty of Negro Leagues statistics in *The Negro Leagues Book*, it is not, and was never meant to be, a statistical encyclopedia.

Despite the publication of career statistics for some prominent Negro Leagues players in recent editions of *The Baseball Encyclopedia*, a complete statistical Negro Leagues encyclopedia is impossible at present, and won't become possible for years. In fact, many of the statistical lines in "the record" are dubious and subject to change. This is because of a fundamental difference between white major (and even most minor) league baseball and the best black baseball: for the Negro Leagues, nothing like a complete statistical record exists.

- Official Negro Leagues figures are limited to a few years and, for the most part, have not been checked and balanced for accuracy.
- Published season or career statistics in newspapers have more often than not proven to be unreliable.
- Most black newspapers were weeklies, and, since no wire services existed for black baseball, they relied on teams to send boxscores in. If information didn't arrive on time, it wasn't printed.
- Neutral-site games add to researchers' headaches.
- Common stats—RBIs and earned runs, for example—often weren't supplied in boxscores.

Therefore, instead of starting with largely correct league statistics, as we can do with all of the white major leagues, we have to reconstruct Negro Leagues statistics day by day. This is a mammoth task, and it is nowhere near complete.

One other point needs to be made about the statistics you'll see in this book. Virtually all Negro Leagues teams played many, many exhibition games each season, usually against inferior opposition, but sometimes against top-notch clubs, both black and white. Statistics garnered in such games "don't count" (although they should be considered when historians judge the greatness of Negro Leagues players). The relatively low season totals in homeruns or wins chalked up by Negro Leagues leaders have to be seen in the light of a much shorter "official" season than the one enjoyed by white major leaguers.

The Baseball Hall of Fame

It is our sincere hope that this book will help others in their search for truth about the Negro Leagues and their players. We trust that such research will, at long last, result in the proper recognition of great black players of the segregated era.

We hope that continuing education of the general public will result in the eventual selection of outstanding Negro Leaguers to the Baseball Hall of Fame at Cooperstown. We think that the Hall of Fame has been too slow in granting many great black players the honors they've earned.

In 1971, five years after Ted Williams said he hoped the greats of black baseball would get their proper recognition at Cooperstown, a special Negro Leagues Committee was formed. After selecting an "All-Star team" of Negro Leaguers, they were disbanded, and the standing Veterans Committee was charged with the obligation of choosing any future apartheid-era players. Of all the overlooked greats of the era, only Rube Foster (1981) and Ray Dandridge (1987) have been selected since.

Since Jackie Robinson's election in 1961 (he was the first black player eligible to be voted upon by the baseball writers), 42 players have been elected: 26 white (62%) and 16 black (38%). Since 1962, the Veterans Committee has chosen 77 players from the game's past: 75 white and two black (the other nine Negro Leaguers selected were chosen by the Special Committee). Based on our research, *we think there are at least 60 players from the Negro Leagues who deserve serious consideration for the Hall of Fame.*

The Veteran's Committee, like most of the baseball world, remains unaware of the staggering accomplishments of the great black players of the segregated era. We think it is time to reinstate the Special Negro Leagues Committee. Made up of veteran black players and historians, it could help redress the historic wrong that kept the finest black baseball players from competing with and against their white counterparts. Baseball is our greatest game, our national pastime. Its greats—*all* its greats—should share equal space on the walls of its Hall of Fame. Only in this way can we tell and understand—friend to friend, generation to generation—our sport's whole story.

A Note on Photos

Only a few of the photos in this book have been seen before, even by avid baseball fans, readers or researchers. Many of them have never been published in a book before, and some have never been published *at all* until now. Some shots are more than 90 years old, and many were taken from the original glass negatives. We obtained some of our pictures from the original photographer, some from historical societies, some from private collectors, and some from the families of Negro Leagues players themselves. We are grateful to those who provided photos for this book. We think they are one of the best parts of the book, and we hope they convey to you a compelling sense of the Negro Leagues, and of black baseball before there were Negro Leagues.

We thank the following for providing readers with the chance to buy some of the individual photos that appear here: Dick Clark, Jeff Eastland, Luis Munoz, and Jay Sanford. Interested readers may contact SABR.

Acknowledgments

The Negro Leagues Committee is indebted to many SABR members for their contributions. The families of the editors are gratefully acknowledged for giving up their quality time so their dads could spend the time needed to put this work together. Val Lester and Marilyn Taylor, wives of the editors, merit particular appreciation, for their supportive efforts.

The Rosters section would not have been possible without the efforts of Terry Baxter, Todd Bolton, Harry Conwell, Dick Cramer, Paul Doherty, Bob Gill, Jim Holway, John Holway Jr., Merl Kleinknecht, Jerry Malloy, Joe McGillen, Joe Overfield, Jim Overmyer, Mark Presswood, Jim Riley, Rob Ruck, Jay Sanford, Susan Scheller, Arthur Schott, A.D. Suehsdorf, Brad Sullivan, Edie Williams, and Charles Zarelli. All of these people have helped in the gathering of statistics which in turn provide rosters.

Special thanks to Leslie Heaphy for '50s rosters, Robert Eisen and Neil Lanctot for Eastern League rosters, and Bill Plott for his extensive research on Southern teams. Special, special thanks to John Holway for many things which have helped this project.

The Register section received assistance from Luis Alvelo, L. Robert Davids, Jim Riley, and Jay Sanford, and of course Robert Peterson whom without his original Register ours would not be possible.

Anecdotes were compiled by Jim Overmyer with input from Dick Clark, Larry Hogan, John Holway, and Larry Lester.

Team histories are by Dick Clark, Merl Kleinknecht, and Jerry Malloy.

All-Star records were supplied by Merl Kleinknecht.

The Records section was made possible by the terrific efforts of Baylor Butler and Bob Hoie, with assistance from Luis Alvelo, John Holway, and Jerry Vaughn.

The Bibliography section was put together by Leslie Heaphy and Larry Lester. Input was received from Tim Cary, Dick Clark, Larry Hogan, John Holway, Jerry Malloy, Frank Phelps, and Jim Riley.

We would be remiss if we didn't extend our sincere appreciation to Mark Alvarez, SABR Publications Director, and to former SABR president and long-time NLC member Lloyd Johnson for their great help. Also to Patrick Rock who provided his computer programming expertise.

SABR's Executive Director Morris Eckhouse's role in providing leadership for the NLC publication and actively seeking and getting grants cannot be understated.

To the past Negro Leagues Committee Chairmans, John Holway, Merl Kleinknecht, and Phil Lowry, thanks for showing the way.

To the players of the Negro Leagues, we hope you enjoy this book and we thank you for your pioneering efforts that made it all possible.

A Personal Note on Researching Negro Leagues Baseball History
Larry Lester

In the mid-seventies, the Rubik Cube came upon the scene. This multi-colored layer of small cubes, arranged in a systematic pattern of colors, amazed many Americans. The idea was to twist and rotate these colors, creating a seemingly impossible disarray of orderliness. Later to be rearranged until their original color sequence was retained. The solution to this puzzle has befuddled the inquisitive minds of many. Likewise, solutions to discovering the formula for accurately researching the Negro Baseball Leagues has puzzled many sport historians.

To the newcomer, the leagues appear to be simply a part of baseball history—yet to be researched. An unexplored territory with treasures of untold stories with unheralded stars. Some may say, "Undiscovered greatness!" But, the mystery surrounding the leagues, like the Rubik cube, is deceptively innocent in its appearance.

The Rubik cube includes only six colors: white, yellow, orange, red, green and blue. While, the Negro Leagues encompasses a kaleidoscope of every hue of the baseball rainbow. Normally, colors that appear to be primary and secondary in "regular" baseball, turn out to be many shades of gray in black baseball.

This simple, little cube is an ingeniously linked block of twenty-seven small cubes, with each layer of nine cubes forming an original uniform coloring of six colors. You could say, the Negro Leagues parallel this puzzle with each year representing a layer of the cube. As more and more layers (or years) are twisted and turned, the correct facts, the anecdotes become further and further from their origination or the simple truth.

Ready to play? Turn one level left and you'll find the local newspapers reported only the home games— no road games. And sometimes, the home box score did not report at bats, or pitching totals.

Turn another level of colors to the right, and you'll find that there is no report on the game, because it was played at a neutral site or in a non-league city. The newspapers in that town or city reveal minute information on the game—but you have to know enough to look for them.

Another turn of the cube reveals that the box scores are really just line scores, with no game detail listed. Traditionally, when double headers were played, only the first game was listed in any detail, with only a line score for the second game.

Turn the cube horizontally, and you'll find no earned runs, saves, or strikeouts for pitchers listed. Flip the cube vertically, and you'll find no game summary of extra bases, double plays, stolen bases and runs batted

in. You are at the mercy of the accompanying story to fill in the blanks.

After many turns, U-turns and detours, you finally reach post-season play. Surprisingly, you find little or no coverage—what happened? Many minority newspapers had one sports reporter to cover all sporting events. By October, the most popular sport in the country is College Football. Jackie Robinson is running touchdowns for UCLA, while the Homestead Grays are winning another championship. Result? Limited coverage of the Negro World Series is buried near the want ads.

Moving on, you now turn the cube clockwise for the editorials, league history and the player biographies. And you find little mention of vital personal data about a player's birth or death. Meanwhile, team histories are vague and incomplete. Turn the cube counter-clockwise and you discover the athlete played under a fictitious name to protect his identity or college eligibility. You also find teams folding in mid-season, with no announcement until the following year. Frustrated, you toss the cube in the air, as if you just don't care—but the challenge and the interest in this fascinating page of our national history remains.

Every turn of a layer of colors results in a different color pattern. Similarly, every discovery of a piece of Negro League history results in additional complexity before settling into a final and correct status. After many years of trial and error, one layer of the cube or one season (or team, or player) is successfully restored. You relax before continuing to the next level of effort. Once you master the research moves at one level, you try to produce the same results for the other levels. All the time knowing it will become more and more difficult to get every level of the cube's history back to its pristine state. Your work may involve temporarily changing a layer of history to complete the next layer, before completing all the layers simultaneously.

Yes, researching the men of color reflect a phenomenon of research or visual perception that has enabled many fans to differentiate otherwise identical and confusing facts, producing a kaleidoscope of Pandemonium. Thus, creating twentieth century's most incredible, challenging and fascinating sports puzzle— researching the Negro Baseball Leagues.

Key to

Abbreviations

We use many abbreviations throughout this book, especially in the Records and Leaders sections. Here is the key to them all.

Negro Leagues Teams

ABC	Indianapolis ABCs
AC	Atlantic City Bacharach Giants
ACT	Arkansas Claybrook Tigers
BBB	Birmingham Black Barons
BBS	Baltimore Black Sox
BC	Atlanta Black Crackers
BEG	Baltimore Elite Giants
BG	Bacharach Giants
BKE	Brooklyn Eagles
BRG	Brooklyn Royal Giants
CAG	Chicago American Giants
CB	Cleveland Bears
CBB	Columbia Blue Birds
CBE	Cleveland Buckeyes
CBN	Cleveland Browns
CC	Cincinnati Clowns
CEG	Columbus Elite Giants
CG	Chicago Giants
CH	Cleveland Hornets
CIB	Cincinnati Buckeyes
COB	Columbus Buckeyes
CRS	Cleveland Red Sox
CSE	Cuban Stars (East)
CSW	Cuban Stars (West)
CT	Cincinnati Tigers
CTS	Cleveland Tate Stars
CUB	Cleveland Cubs
CUG	Chicago Union Giants
DM	Dayton Marcos
DS	Detroit Stars
DW	Detroit Wolves
HBG	Harrisburg Giants
HE	Houston Eagles
HG	Homestead Grays
HIL	Philadelphia Hilldale Giants (Hilldale)
HOD	Cuban House of David
IC	Indianapolis Clowns

JRC	Jacksonville Red Caps
KCM	Kansas City Monarchs
LBC	Louisville Black Caps
MB	Milwaukee Bears
MM	Monroe Monarchs
MRS	Memphis Red Sox
NB	Newark Browns
NBY	New York Black Yankees
ND	Newark Dodgers
NE	Newark Eagles
NEG	Nashville Elite Giants
NHS	New York Harlem Stars
NLG	New York Lincoln Giants
NO	New Orleans Eagles
NYC	New York Cubans
PC	Pittsburgh Crawfords
PIL	Washington Pilots
PS	Philadelphia Stars
SLG	St. Louis Giants
SLS	St. Louis Stars
TC	Toledo Crawfords
TT	Toledo Tigers
WBS	Washington Black Senators
WEG	Washington Elite Giants
WM	Wilmington Potomacs
WP	Washington Potomacs

Other Negro Leagues

SLCB	Southern League of Colored Baseballists	1886
LCBBP	League of Colored Base Ball Players	1887
BAA	Baseball Association of America	1949
USL	United States Baseball League	1945

Winter Leagues

COLB	Colombia
CUBA	Cuban League
CWL	Cuban Winter League
DOM	Dominican League
MXPC	Mexican Pacific League
MXWL	Mexican Winter League
NICR	Nicaraguan Winter League
OCC	Occidental League
PANA	Panama League
PRWL	Puerto Rican Winter League
VENZ	Venezuelan Winter League

Negro Major Leagues

Six Negro Leagues were considered "major" over the life of league play, from 1920 through 1960. Here they are, with the abbreviations used to denote them throughout this book.

(*) indicates did not complete season.

(†) indicates not a major league during this season.

NNL	Negro National League	1920-1931, 1933-1948
SNL	Southern Negro League	1920
ECL	Eastern Colored League	1923-1928*
ANL	American Negro League	1929
EWL	East-West League	1932*
NSL	Negro Southern League	1932, 1926†, 1945†
NAL	Negro American League	1937-1960

Minor Leagues

AA	American Association
AZMX	Arizona-Mexico League
AZTX	Arizona-Texas League
BGST	Big State League
BORD	Border League
CAAM	Canadian-American League
CALF	California League
CARO	Carolina League
CENT	Central League
CMEX	Central Mexican League
COL	Colonial League
DMSL	Dominican Summer League
EAST	Eastern League
EVAG	Evangeline League
FINT	Florida International League
FLST	Florida State League
GCL	Gulf Coast League
III	Three I League League
INT	International League
INST	Interstate League

JAP	Japanese League
KITT	Kitty League
LGHN	Longhorn League
MADK	Manitoba-Dakota League
MATL	Mid-Atlantic League
MEX	Mexican League
MIDW	Midwest League
MOV	Mississippi-Ohio Valley League
MTST	Mountain States League
MXCT	Mexican Central League
MXSE	Mexican Southeast League
NATL	North Atlantic League
NDL	North Dakota League
NENG	New England League
NORL	Northern League
NWL	Northwest League
NYP	New York-Pennsylvania League
PCL	Pacific Coast League
PIED	Piedmont League
PION	Pioneer League
PONY	Pony League
PROV	Provincial League
SATL	South Atlantic (Sally) League
SOON	Sooner State League
SOU	Southern League
SOWS	Southwest League
SUN	Sunset League
SWIN	Southwest International League
SWL	Southwestern League
TEX	Texas League
WEST	Western League
WEAS	Western Association
WINT	Western International League
WISC	Wisconsin State League
WTNM	West Texas-New Mexico League

The Negro

Leagues:

A Brief History

Merl F. Kleinknecht

The first sustaining Negro Baseball League operated in 1920. It came about as the culmination of years of determined effort by Andrew (Rube) Foster to organize the best of the then independent black teams into a structure similar to that of white baseball's American and National Leagues. "Black" and "White" baseball had become an entrenched reality as a result of racial intolerance and misunderstanding that ran rampant throughout all levels of American society following the Civil War and into the Twentieth Century.

African Americans had proven their ability to compete at any level of baseball open to them as the game grew in popularity following the War between the States. Moses Fleetwood Walker had been a successful catcher with Toledo in the then-major league American Association in 1884. Walker's brother, Welday had also played for Toledo that season. However, they would be the first, last and only African Americans to compete in the white major leagues for another 63 years. Over six dozen other dark-skinned performers *did* play in the minor leagues during the nineteenth century, beginning with John (Bud) Fowler in 1878 and ending with Bill Galloway in 1899. Many of them starred under difficult circumstances. One, pitcher George Stovey, set the existing International League record with 34 wins in 1887.

The Cuban Giants, the first all-professional black team, competed successfully as a unit in the minor leagues from 1889 through 1891. In 1889 they represented Trenton (NJ) of the Mid-States League and posted a 55-17 record to finish as runners-up to Harrisburg (64-19). The all-black New York Gorhams (14-20) were also in the league. The following year the Cuban Giants moved to the Eastern Interstate League and represented York (PA). Their 40-16 record was the best in the league but they once again played second fiddle to Harrisburg. The Harrisburg club had also transferred to the Eastern Interstate League and were awarded the pennant despite finishing five games worse than York with a 39-25 record. Frank Grant, Harrisburg's second baseman, hit .325 and led the league with five homeruns. Grant may have been the greatest black baseball player of his time. He posted a .337 career average in six minor league seasons. The Cuban Giants performed for Ansonia in the 1891 Connecticut State League. The last all-black team in the minor leagues was the 1898 Celeron (NY) club of the Iron & Oil League. Winning but eight of 50 decisions they finished in the circuit's basement.

The remaining all-black teams of the nineteenth century had operated as traveling independents. Among the more distinguished clubs were the Adrian (MI) Page Fence Giants, Chicago Columbia Giants, Chicago Unions, New York Gorhams, Norfolk (VA) Red Stockings and the Philadelphia Orians. The Cuban Giants also operated independently throughout most of their existence. Their popularity resulted in the use of the Cuban Giant moniker by other teams of black players as well. This created confusion and even led to a court case. The original Cuban Giants then became known also as the Genuine Cuban Giants and another club as the Cuban X Giants. The Cuban X Giants became particularly successful and were generally regarded as the top black team in the East from 1897 through 1903. The original Cuban Giants did claim a championship in 1888 by winning a tournament that also included the Pittsburgh Keystones, New York Gorhams and Norfolk (VA) Red Stockings and were awarded a Silver Cup for their triumphant effort.

The Pittsburgh Keystones had been part of an unsuccessful attempt to organize a National Negro League in 1887. Baltimore, Boston, Cincinnati, Louisville, New York, Philadelphia and Washington were also awarded franchises. The league opened play on May 6 with six of the original eight clubs on board but folded within two weeks.

Black teams continued to operate independent of any league structure into the twentieth century. However, many of the better black performers were afforded the opportunity to play in Latin American Winter Leagues, often against white major leaguers, and continued to distinguish themselves with outstanding play. Black teams also competed against white major leaguers barnstorming for dollars after the regular season. Research has revealed that the blacks defeated their white major league counterparts 60 percent of the time in such contests.

As America moved into the new century the popularity of these all black teams continued to grow. African Americans performed on diamonds throughout much of the country with outstanding clubs blossoming along the Atlantic seaboard and well into the heartland of the Midwest. The Atlantic City Bacharach Giants, Brooklyn Royal Giants, Cuban X Giants, (Genuine) Cuban Giants, Hilldale Club of Philadelphia, Homestead (PA) Grays, New York Lincoln Giants, New York Lincoln Stars and Philadelphia Giants dominated the East. Among the best in the Midwest were the Algona (IA) Brownies, Indianapolis ABCs, St. Louis Giants and a variety of Chicago teams labeled American Giants, Columbia Giants, Leland Giants, Unions and Union Giants. One will note the popularity of the Giant label in particular. A number of teams also operated throughout

Peters Union Giants out of Chicago, circa 1915.
The Golda Meir Library, University of Wisconsin (Milwaukee)

the South, including Atlanta, Birmingham, Dallas, Ft. Worth, Houston, Jacksonville, Louisville, Memphis, Montgomery, Nashville, New Orleans, San Antonio and other cities. A league known as the Southern League of Colored Baseballists operated in major southern cities in 1886.

While no lasting Negro Leagues operated prior to 1920, a series billed as for the "Colored Championship of the World" was frequently played by the leading teams of a given year. In 1903 the Cuban X Giants claimed supremacy after taking five of seven games from the Philadelphia Giants. The Philadelphians countered by claiming themselves black baseball's best after then won two of three from the X Giants the following year. The Indianapolis ABCs won a disputed "Colored Championship Series", five games to four, over the Chicago American Giants in 1916. East versus West title confrontations saw the Chicago American Giants top the Brooklyn Royal Giants, four games to none, in 1914. A 1915 series between the American Giants and New York Lincoln Stars resulted in a standoff, with each team winning five times. The 1917 American Giants returned to black baseball's pinnacle with a four game to three conquest of the Lincoln Stars. The time for a major league of black teams to satisfy the desire to organize their enterprise and crown undisputed champions was on the horizon.

By 1920 Andrew (Rube) Foster had displayed exceptional baseball talent and knowledge as an outstanding pitcher, manager and team owner. Foster pitched the Cuban X Giants and Philadelphia Giants to their early titles and managed the Chicago American Giants to their conquests. He also owned the Chicago team and was anxious to see them and the other leading black teams operating in a single Negro League.

Foster's dream came true when he convinced owners of the Chicago Giants, Cuban Stars, Dayton Marcos, Detroit Stars, Indianapolis ABCs, Kansas City Monarchs and St. Louis Giants to join with his American Giants in formation of the Negro National League. The league operated from 1920 through 1931 and extended into the deep south when the Birmingham Black Barons and Memphis Red Sox joined the circuit in 1924. The Negro National League normally included eight teams in any given season. The American Giants, Cuban Stars and teams in Detroit, Kansas City and St. Louis were sustaining members while Cleveland, Milwaukee, Pittsburgh and Toledo also were represented on occasion.

The Eastern Colored League was organized in 1923, with teams in Atlantic City, Baltimore, Brooklyn, Philadelphia and New York, as well as an eastern edition of the Cuban Stars. The league survived into the spring of 1928 and added teams in Harrisburg and Washington its second season. The Homestead Grays joined with former Eastern Colored League clubs in Atlantic City, Baltimore, Philadelphia, New York and the eastern Cuban Stars to form the American Negro League in 1929. This circuit survived only its maiden season.

In 1932 the Baltimore Black Sox, Cleveland Stars, Cuban Stars, Detroit Wolves, Hilldale Club of Philadelphia, Homestead Grays of Pittsburgh and Newark Browns banded together as the East-West League. The East-West League failed to complete the season, and with its demise the Negro Southern League claimed the position of being a major black circuit. The Negro Southern League had operated since 1920 similar to a minor league in comparison to the Negro National League and the Eastern loops. The southern circuit had a fluid membership. Its claim to black major league status was unchallenged in 1932 with the failure of the East-West League and no other Negro Leagues operating. The presence of at least two former Negro National League teams, the Chicago American Giants and Memphis Red Sox, added to the Negro Southern League's status. While the Negro Southern League continued to operate sporadically, possibly into the fifties, its status as the supreme black loop lasted but a single season. Minor black circuits also operated as the Texas-Oklahoma-Louisiana League (in the late twenties and early thirties) and later with a Negro American Association, also in the south.

A second Negro National League came onto the scene in 1933, and included the Baltimore Black Sox, Chicago American Giants, Cleveland Giants, Columbus Blue Birds, Detroit Stars, Nashville Elite Giants and Pittsburgh Crawfords. Later members included the Brooklyn Eagles, New York Cubans, Newark Eagles and Philadelphia Stars. The Elite Giants traveled to Columbus in 1935 and on to Washington the following year. The new Negro National League operated as the sole black circuit through 1936.

In 1937 the Negro American League was organized from Midwestern and Southern teams, and the Negro National League became an Eastern loop. The Negro American League continued to operate through 1960. The Negro National League folded after the 1948 season. While they were both in business, each league normally numbered six teams. With the Negro National League's death in 1949 the Negro American League expanded to ten teams with East and West divisions. The league struggled to survive with fewer and fewer teams throughout the fifties. The Negro American League's final season saw it field but four teams: the Birmingham Black Barons, Detroit-New Orleans Stars, Kansas City Monarchs and Raleigh Tigers. Throughout its history the league had played with teams in Atlanta, Baltimore, Chicago, Cincinnati, Cleveland, Houston, Indianapolis, Jacksonville, Louisville, Memphis, Mobile, Newark, New York, Philadelphia, St. Louis and Toledo.

The Negro Leagues played an important role in stabilizing black baseball prior to the integration of Organized Baseball in 1946. It insured that when the racial ban was finally lifted there would be an instant pool of talent to take advantage of this. The Negro Leagues were also a source of income to the black community, and in their heyday, they were the second largest black owned business interest per capita next to insurance companies.

The biggest event for Negro Leagues teams was the East-West All-Star game, played annually in Chicago's Comiskey Park beginning in 1933. During baseball's apartheid era this game provided the prime showcase for the talents of African-American baseball stars. The event occurred in August and drew crowds of upwards of 50,000 fans. As integration overtook Organized Baseball, interest in the game as well as the Negro Leagues in general declined. Nevertheless, the East-West Game continued to be held into the fifties.

When Jackie Robinson became the first African American in 63 years to play in the major leagues In 1947, he opened the door for many Negro League performers to also get their chance in recognized Organized Baseball. Many, like Robinson, did become stars in both the American and National Leagues. Many more also went on to star at the minor league level.

Roy Campanella (Baltimore Elite Giants), Monte Irvin (Newark Eagles) and Sam Jethroe (Cleveland Buckeyes) achieved major league stardom after spending at least seven years in the Negro Leagues. Larry Doby (Newark Eagles), Luke Easter (Homestead Grays), Sam Jones (Cleveland Buckeyes), Minnie Minoso (New York Cubans), Don Newcombe (Newark Eagles), and Al Smith (Cleveland Buckeyes) all starred in the major leagues.

And two players that cannot be left out are the incomparable Satchel Paige (Kansas City Monarchs and others) and Ray Dandridge (Newark Eagles). Paige, of course, helped to pitch the 1948 Cleveland Indians into the World Series, and later enjoyed success with the St. Louis Browns. Dandridge, after years of starring in the Negro Leagues and Mexican League, was named the AAA American Association's Most Valuable Player after leading the 1950 Minneapolis Millers to the circuit's

Royal Poinciana Club of Palm Beach, Florida, circa 1905. Standing L to R: Emmett Bowman, unknown, Rube Foster, unknown, Mike Moore, and Grant Johnson. Sitting L to R: Pete Hill, John Hill, Sol White, unknown, and Charlie Grant.
Jay Sanford

regular season title, but he was considered too old to get a shot in the majors. Paige had debuted in the Negro Leagues in 1926. Dandridge played his first Negro League game in 1933.

In 1971 the National Baseball Hall of Fame opened its doors to former stars of the Negro Leagues and has enshrined Paige, Josh Gibson, Buck Leonard, Monte Irvin, Cool Papa Bell, Judy Johnson, Oscar Charleston, Martin Dihigo, John Henry Lloyd, Rube Foster and Dandridge on the basis of their accomplishments in the Negro Leagues.

Jackie Robinson (Kansas City Monarchs) and Roy Campanella were enshrined in the Hall of Fame in 1962 and 1969 respectively on the basis of their careers with the National League Brooklyn Dodgers. In 1977 Ernie Banks (Kansas City Monarchs) of the Chicago Cubs joined the Hall of Fame rolls. Willie Mays (Birmingham Black Barons) of the New York and San Francisco Giants and New York Mets was elected in 1979. And major league baseball's all-time homerun champion, Hank Aaron (Indianapolis Clowns), of the Milwaukee Braves and Brewers and Atlanta Braves was voted his plaque in 1982.

The Negro Leagues featured great players and they also featured great teams. The Kansas City Monarchs captured 17 Negro League pennants, followed by the Homestead Grays with 12, of which nine came consecutively, and the Chicago American Giants with another dozen championship flags. All three teams won Black World Championships as did the Cleveland Buckeyes, Newark Eagles, New York Cubans, Philadelphia Hilldale Club, Philadelphia Stars and Pittsburgh Crawfords.

All baseball fans can be glad the Negro Leagues existed in their time—and can be just as glad they eventually became unnecessary.

Barnstorming Accidents

Black ballclubs traveled thousands of miles each year to make well over a hundred playing dates outside their home cities, playing in two, and occasionally three towns in a day. With so much travel, there were bound to be some traffic accidents. It is perhaps miraculous that only one team, the Cleveland Buckeyes, suffered any fatalities. Two Buckeyes, Buster Brown and Raymond Owens, were killed in an accident in 1942 when a car returning team members to Ohio from a doubleheader in Buffalo, N.Y., was hit by a truck. Probably the second worst crash was in September 1944, when five members of the Birmingham Black Barons were badly hurt in a collision between the team bus and a car. The Philadelphia Stars' bus overturned after colliding with an auto enroute to a game in Cleveland, also in the late '30s. While several players suffered injuries, the team still made its way to Cleveland, and played in front of about 9,000 waiting fans. But the most unusual accident of all involved the Homestead Grays on their way north from spring training in a pair of new Buicks in 1930. Enroute to Shreveport, Louisiana, the drivers, outfielder Oscar Charleston and co-owner Charlie Walker, began to race to see who could make town first. Charleston's car, in the lead, kicked up so much dust that Walker lost control on the high-crowned dirt road and brought his Buick to a soft landing in a ditch. The players jumped out and righted the car with little damage. They hadn't gone far, however, when they came upon another accident—and found the lead Grays car in the ditch. Charleston, who suffered a minor head injury, emerged from the smash-up clutching pieces of the wooden steering wheel, which the powerful slugger had wrenched apart trying to keep the car on the road.

—Various, including Brashler's *Josh Gibson*, *New Jersey Afro-American* (9/12/42), *Black Diamonds*, and *Courier*, 9/16/44

Five years after the fatal accident (above), the Cleveland Buckeyes' bus is resting during the 1947 season, and five players take a break. From L to R: Johnnie Cowan, Jesse Williams, Clyde Williams, and Doc Bracken. Sam Jones is peering out the door.
Negro Leagues Baseball Museum

Great

Teams

F rom 1903 to 1953, there were no changes in the major league franchises of Organized Baseball. Negro Leagues ball, on the other hand, was a constantly shifting universe of leagues, cities and teams, much as "white" baseball had been in its early professional days. Through all of this change, some clubs stand out. Here are brief histories of some cities and their teams, followed by a complete listing of all clubs that played in recognized Negro Leagues.

Detroit

The Detroit Stars were formed in 1919 under the guidance of Rube Foster, as a prelude to his idea of establishing a full Negro League.

John T. "Tenny" Blount, a local gambler, was considered the owner of the team. This first year, Detroit played an independent schedule of black professional and various black and white semi-pro teams. It was an outstanding squad of players including Pete Hill, Jose Mendez, Bruce Petway, and Edgar Wesley. The Stars were allowed to play in the integrated Michigan Semi-Pro Championship tournament, and they won the championship five straight years, beginning in 1919.

In 1920, the first Negro National League was formed, and Detroit became a charter member, remaining in the league until it folded after 1931.

The Detroit Stars were much like their white counterparts, the Tigers; they had terrific hitting and suspect pitching throughout their existence. In 1920 they finished third at 35-23. The team always challenged for the top, but except for 1925 (playoff for second place), it could not make the playoffs until 1930. The Stars' records were: 1921, 32-32 (fourth); 1922, 43-32 (fourth); 1923, 41-29 (tie for second); 1924, 37-29 (third); 1925, 57-40 (third); 1926, 50-42 (fourth); 1927, 53-46 (fourth); 1928, 54-37 (third); 1929, 38-42 (fourth); 1930, 50-33 (second half winners, second overall) 1931, 25-26 (fourth).

During this time the club employed many outstanding players. Between 1920 and 1929, Andy Cooper was the team's pitching mainstay. He was always dependable, even with less than good pitching companions. Perhaps if Detroit had been able to keep Bill Holland from their 1920-22 teams (he jumped East), they could have won pennants. Jimmie Lyons had a superb 1920 season but was heisted by the Chicago American Giants. Edgar Wesley was a top homerun threat during his tenure (1919-27). Pete Hill, Bruce Petway and Bingo DeMoss played with and managed the Stars during this time. In 1923, the greatest black player in Detroit baseball history joined the Stars from the Montgomery Grey Sox. He was Norman "Turkey" Stearnes. Stearnes was the Number One slugger of this era, surpassing such greats as John Beckwith and Oscar Charleston. Turkey remained the heart and soul of the Stars until leaving prior to 1930, going East to the Lincoln Giants. Detroit played .500 ball the first half of 1930. Perking up considerably upon Stearnes return in July, they streaked to the second half pennant entitling them to play the St. Louis

Mack Park in Detroit the day after a grandstand fire ruined a July 6, 1929 doubleheader between Detroit and the Kansas City Monarchs. Dozens were injured but no deaths.
Richard Bak and THE DETROIT NEWS

Stars for the championship. Alas, they fell in seven games, despite Stearnes' hitting .481.

Upon the collapse of the NNL after 1931, a new Detroit team joined the newly formed East-West League. This was the Detroit Wolves, owned by "Cum" Posey, also owner of the Homestead Grays. With much of the team coming from the Kansas City Monarchs and St. Louis Stars, this was without question the greatest array of talent ever seen in Detroit. The Wolves roared to a huge lead in the race. However, the Depression was taking its toll, and with low attendance a problem everywhere, the Wolves were assimilated by Posey's Homestead Grays enabling them to be the power of the League. The Wolves were 29-13 when they disbanded.

The Detroit Stars replaced the Indianapolis franchise and rejoined the re-organized NNL in 1933. They did poorly, and when new backers could not be found, they folded prior to 1934. They returned for one season in 1937, in the Negro American League, (NAL) with Stearnes again leading the way. After 16 years, the Detroit Stars franchise, under Ted Rasberry, reentered the NAL in 1954 for its last hurrah.

The Stars played in Mack Park until it burned on July 6, 1929, and then in Hamtramack Stadium. The 1937 team played at Dequindre Park. During the 1940's many Negro League games were played at the Tigers' Briggs Stadium.

Chicago American Giants

The history of the Chicago American Giants is divided into two distinct parts: the Rube Foster years and the post-Foster years. The American Giants had been black baseball's most celebrated institution for a full decade before the ambitious and able Foster took on the most formidable challenge of his distinguished career: the creation of the first successful black baseball league, the Negro National League, in 1920.

Chicago, with its accessible transportation and the abundance of jobs occassioned by wartime labor shortages, provided hope and opportunity for a burgeoning African-American community lured from the South by the promise of a better life. In 1911 Foster, player-manager of Chicago's Leland Giants, struck off on his own and created the Chicago American Giants. Not coincidentally, he also embarked upon becoming the country's most successful African-American booking agent. Rube Foster capitalized on black Chicago's growth and prosperity, using baseball savvy, business accumen, and a forceful personality to build the greatest sporting institution that black America had ever seen.

Copies of the Chicago *Defender* were distributed throughout the South by the Illinois Central Railroad's African-American porters, and the American Giants (as the name implied) soon had a following of unrivaled breadth. Small Southern towns revelled in a carnival atmosphere whenever Rube Foster's ballplayers came to town, barnstorming their way to and from their winter playground in Palm Beach, Forida. Foster, in turn, fortified his already great team by recruiting talented Southern players. He made similar forays to such distant places as California and Cuba.

Foster had thus been a dominant force in black baseball for a full decade by the time of his Bismarkian deed of unifying the Midwest's strongest African-American teams into one great black league. Playing in the 5,000-seat stadium on 39th and Wentworth that Charles Comiskey foresook when he built the Baseball Palace of the World in 1910, the American

Giants' success continued in the Negro National League through most of the League's twelve seasons. The American Giants received Foster's most minute attention until he was stricken with mental illness in 1926. This despite his various obligations in overseeing both his own team and the entire league operations.

Foster's teams were famous for their pitching and defense, and their speed and guile. Every player (even power hitter Cristobal Torriente) was drilled to proficiency in bunting. Foster guided the American Giants to NNL championships in 1920, 1921, and 1922. They also won NNL championships and Negro League World Series crowns against Eastern Colored League champs in 1926 and 1927 under Foster's successor as team manager, Dave Malarcher.

Unable to withstand the Great Depression's withering blast, the American Giants suffered through the league's inglorious collapse in 1931. In 1932, the team, now called Cole's American Giants after new owner Robert A. Cole, won the Negro Southern League championship. The following year (1933) they joined the reorganized Negro National League created by the Pittsburgh Crawford's Gus Greenlee. In the first season, Cole's Giants had their rightful championship snatched from them by Greenlee, who declared his Crawfords the champs. In 1934, an unfavorable protest ruling proved fatal in losing the championship series, four games to three, to the Philadelphia Stars. Malarcher had piloted the club through the NSL title season and the new NNL's initial pair of campaigns before retiring after the 1935 schedule of play.

H.G. Hall, president of the American Giants, led the next reorganization of black baseball in 1937 by creating a western circuit, the Negro American League, with the Negro National League becoming an eastern league. The American Giants played in the Negro American League from 1937 through 1952. While continuing to be highly competitive in the NAL the American Giants were unable to capture another championship. They came close on three occasions but were defeated in NAL championship play-off series in 1937, 1943, and 1949.

The club featured many great players throughout the years including Hall-of-Famer John Henry Lloyd (ss), Preston (Pete) Hill and Cristobal Torriente (of), Bruce Petway (c) and Dave Brown (p) during Foster's reign. Malarcher (3b), and Rube's half brother Bill Foster. Webster McDonald (p) and Alec Radcliff (3b) starred for the post Rube American Giants. These and other American Giants provided countless rabid fans with the highest caliber of American baseball on the very cusp of the great black metropolis on Chicago's South Side.

Cleveland

Cleveland has enjoyed a long history of black teams in the city leagues as well as in the Negro Leagues. The Cleveland Tate Stars were the first professional black team organized in Cleveland, in 1918. Cleveland's first Negro National League team was the 1922 Tate Stars, who were 17-29 and did not finish the season. In 1924, it was the Browns, 15-34 and dead last. In 1926, the Elites were 7-41 and folded before the end of the season. In 1927, the Hornets were last at 16-38, and in 1928 the Tigers were worse at 19-53. All were unsuccessful due mainly to a lack of quality players. This in turn resulted in a lack of fan interest. Cleveland's black population and central location were important to the Negro Leagues, so various individuals and groups continued to seek the proper combination.

1947 Cleveland Buckeyes. Standing L to R: Archie Ware, Johnnie Cowans, Al Smith, Jesse Williams, Joe Atkins, Willie Grace, Clyde Nelson, Leon Kellman, and Sam Jethroe. Kneeling are Clyde Williams and Quincy Trouppe.
Negro Leagues Baseball Museum

Upon the demise of the Negro National League after 1931, Cleveland tried a team in each of the 1932 Leagues, The East-West, and Negro Southern League. The Cleveland Stars were a middle of the road team in the E-W League, while the NSL Cleveland Cubs were 22-18—not far from the lead when the league folded. The Cubs included Satchel Paige. In 1933, the Cleveland Giants evolved from the demise of the Akron and Columbus franchises but went nowhere. In 1934 another new team, the Cleveland Red Sox, were 4-25 and cellar dwellers when they gave up.

After four years of no league teams, the Cleveland Bears were formed, as members of the Negro American League. In 1939 and 1940, they were a .500 team but they were not financially successful. In 1942, Ernest Wright became the owner and established the Buckeyes. 1942 saw the team being shared by both Cleveland and Cincinnati. They were 35-15 and second overall, Cleveland's first successful team. The 1943 team was also second overall at 27-12, just missing out. They fell back to 40-41 and third in 1944, but were finally a solid franchise. In 1945, under the leadership of Quincy Trouppe and with the terrific play of Sam Jethroe (who was probably Cleveland's all-time best Negro Leagues player, and who would become the National League's Rookie of the Year in 1950), the Buckeyes blitzed the NAL with a 53-16 mark. They stunned the NNL champ Homestead Grays in a four-game sweep in the World Series. They struggled in 1946, but returned to the top of the NAL in 1947 at 54-23. They could not overcome the New York Cubans and lost in the World Series four games to one. They were a .500 team, 41-42 in 1948 and combined with the Cleveland Indians terrific championship

season and the presence of Larry Doby on the major league roster, attendance plummeted. They shifted to Louisville for 1949 but with basically a new team, finished a disappointing 15-51 and in fifth place. A disastrous attempt to revive the Buckeyes in Cleveland occurred in 1950. Cleveland folded in the second half with a 3-39 mark and 55 rotating players on the roster.

Cleveland teams played in a variety of parks through the years. Tate Park, Hooper Field, Cubs Stadium, Hareware Field, and Luna Bowl were all used. The Bears and Buckeyes played in League Park.

Indianapolis

The Indianapolis saga in the Negro Leagues is basically a story of two teams bearing unusual names. They are the Negro National League Indianapolis ABCs, named for the American Brewing Company, and the Negro American League Indianapolis Clowns, so titled due to their antics on the field.

The ABCs came to Indianapolis in 1914 from Birmingham, Alabama via West Baden, Indiana. Their field commander, Charles Isam Taylor, had become manager of the Birmingham Giants in 1904, and moved the club to West Baden, dubbing it the Sprudels, prior to settling in Indianapolis. The ABCs quickly became recognized as one of the top independent baseball teams in the Midwest and claimed the "Colored World's Championship" after edging past Rube Foster's powerful Chicago American Giants in a late season series tainted by controversy in 1916.

Taylor, commonly known as C.I., utilized his disciplined

1950 Birmingham Black Barons. L to R back row: Joe Atkins (secretary), Sam Williams, Bill Greason, Pijo King, William Powell, Andy Watts, Ed Steele, Alonzo Perry, Vic Harris, Herman Bell, Charles Rudd (bus driver). Front row: Pepper Bassett, Curtis Hollingsworth, Jimmy Newberry, Norman Robinson, Johnnie Cowan, Henry Baylis, Roosevelt Adkins (trainer) and Frank Dixon.
Negro Leagues Baseball Museum

and persuasive manner to weld the ABCs into an effective and close-knit unit. His players reflected their manager's gentlemanly attitude, normally appearing in suit and tie. One demonstration of their camaraderie was the enlistment of several ABCs into the Army *en masse* in 1918.

After World War I, the ABCs became charter members of the Negro National League. Indianapolis hosted the circuits initial contest on May 2, 1920. Taylor was named a Vice-President of the fledgling circuit and continued to manage. However, the ABCs experienced limited success and failed to secure an NNL pennant. The 1922 season represented the club's high water mark in the league, as they finished in second place with a 46-33 log. They won 10 more games than the champion American Giants but also lost 10 more. But a single game separated the top four teams in an unbalanced schedule. The ABCs (35-38) had finished fifth the previous season. In 1923 they wound up fourth at 45-34.

Taylor had passed away just prior to the 1922 season, and by 1924 the ABCs were struggling under his wife's leadership to compete in the NNL. They withdrew from the league early in the campaign, but rejoined it in 1925 and suffered through a horrendous 17-57 last place performance. 1926 saw the club improve to 43-45, but it choose not to return for the 1927 NNL schedule. A revived version of the ABCs reentered the NNL for the loop's final season in 1931 and competed in the Negro Southern League in 1932. A third incarnation of the ABCs joined the Negro American League for 1938 and 1939. Indianapolis was also represented in the NAL by the 1937 Athletics and the 1940 Crawfords.

As various Negro Leagues struggled through the '30s, more and more of the black clubs were returning to barnstorming with no league affiliation. One such team was Syd Pollock's Ethiopian Clowns. Operating out of Miami, Florida, Pollock's charges went to extremes to attract crowds. The Clowns' comic endeavors were deplored by much of the black ball community. However, the team was also stocked with skilled and talented players. The team was good enough to win the prestigious Denver Post Baseball Tournament crown in 1940. The tournament was a marathon 16-team double elimination affair drawing top clubs from around the country.

As times changed during World War II, Pollock sought to trade the Clowns' independence for the security of a spot in the Negro American League. In 1943, the team was accepted into the NAL on the condition that its undignified field behavior cease. Pollock accepted the requirements of the league and located in Cincinnati. The newest NAL entry claimed both Cincinnati and Indianapolis as home turf the following season. By 1946, the Clowns were operating exclusively out of Indianapolis and represented the city in the NAL thru 1954. While the 1944 Clowns (40-31) finished as the league's runners-up, the team normally finished in the second division throughout the '40s.

However, the Clowns became a dominant force in the constantly realigning Negro American League of the early '50s. They topped the circuit's Eastern Division in 1950 and 1951, and claimed the NAL pennant both seasons. These claims to league supremacy remain unsubstantiated as no record of a League Championship Series involving Indianapolis and the

Western Division leader has been discovered for either season. The Clowns clearly captured the circuit crown in 1952 by defeating the Birmingham Black Barons in a lengthly LCS, seven games to five. After dropping to 31-43 in 1953 they recaptured the NAL title with a 43-22 mark in 1954.

Foreseeing the inevitable demise of the Negro American League and race baseball, the Clowns withdrew from the circuit and returned to their barnstorming ways. The club integrated, and may continue to be active to this day. Still billed as the Indianapolis Clowns, the 1973 edition played 70 games in the Eastern half of the country. In their heyday, as many as 180 contests had dotted their schedule. Of the 70 games played in 1973, none was played in Indianapolis and but two were held in Indiana. The club had become the Indianapolis Clowns in name only.

A number of outstanding players performed for the Indianapolis Negro Leagues entries. Of particular note during the ABCs' tenure are C.I. Taylor's younger brothers: James, a third baseman, and Ben, a first baseman. Both enjoyed long and distinguised baseball careers. William "Dizzy" Dismukes was a successful pitcher and later manager for the ABCs.

The Clowns featured a variety of interesting figures during their existence including Harlem Globetrotter basketball star Goose Tatum; Toni Stone in 1953; Connie Morgan in 1954; a pair of feminine performers; 2' 7" Dero Austin during the club's later years; the major leagues' all-time homerun leader, Hank Aaron, in his initial professional season (1952), and baseball's best known pitcher, Satchel Paige, in his last year as a player (1967). Ray Neil was a Clown mainstay, hitting NAL pitching at a .329 clip from 1948 through 1954. Neil was the league batting champion in 1953 and twice topped the NAL in hits. And of particular note is Indianapolis native and National Baseball Hall of Famer Oscar Charleston. Charleston began his stat-studded professional baseball career with the 1915 Indianapolis ABCs and ended it managing the 1954 Indianapolis Clowns to their final NAL championship. Buster Haywood piloted them to the 1952 title. ABCs' Field, located at Route 40, was the home field for the ABCs, Athletics, and Crawfords. Victory Field, now known as Bush Stadium, was the Indianapolis home of the Clowns.

Birmingham

The Birmingham Black Barons were the most successful of the many Southern teams that played Negro Leagues baseball in the Jim Crow era. Organized in 1920 as an entry in the Negro Southern League, Birmingham had its first taste of "major league" baseball in 1923, when Birmingham and Memphis played as "associate" members of the Negro National League. Birmingham was 15-23-5 against NNL teams. They became official members of the NNL in 1924 and finished fifth with a 34-44 record. Harry Salmon, Sam Streeter, and Mule Suttles were the top players on the team. They were seventh (24-49) in 1925. Finances kept the team in the "minor" Negro Southern League for 1926 but they rejoined the NNL in 1927 and—led by rookie pitcher Satchel Paige—won the second half championship. However, they lost in four straight games to the Chicago American Giants for the NNL title. In 1928 they were 44-54 and fifth. Fifth in 1929 (29-51) and fourth (44-48) in 1930.

With the Depression going full force, the Black Barons returned to the Southern League in 1931. They were part of the 1932 major league NSL but stayed in the "minors" until joining the new Negro American League in 1937. The '37 and '38 teams were not good. They dropped out after 1938, but returned in 1940 and were a strong team throughout the remainer of their history. In 1943 they were NAL champions topping Chicago in the playoffs. They battled the Homestead Grays to a seventh game before losing 8-4. Some of the stars were Lyman Bostock, Sr., Lorenzo "Piper" Davis, Lester Lockett, Ed Steele, and Jesse Walker. In 1944, the Black Barons took both half pennants and were 48-22 overall. Unfortunately, the Grays beat them in five games in the Series. They were 39-30 in 1945, finishing second. They were near the top also in 1946 and 1947 before grabbing the championship of the NAL in 1948. They defeated the Kansas City Monarchs in seven games but again they could not beat the Homestead Grays, losing in five games. When the two leagues merged following the season, Birmingham became a Western Division power in the NAL. In 1950, they were 52-25, but trailed Kansas City at 52-21. During the '50s the Black Barons continued to field formidable teams and provide future major leaguers with a starting point, as they had for Willie Mays in 1948.

Mays must be considered the greatest player who ever donned a Black Baron uniform, but the top longtime Baron was certainly "Piper" Davis. Other outstanding players were Sam Hairston and Tommy Sampson. The Black Barons, who played their home games at Rickwood Field, home of the white Birmingham Barons, finally ceased to exist after the 1960 season.

Memphis

The Memphis Red Sox were an original member of the Negro Southern League, which began play in 1920. They joined with the Birmingham Black Barons as "associate" members of the Negro National League in 1923, and Memphis compiled a 13-6 mark against NNL teams that season. The Red Sox finished sixth their first two seasons as official members, in 1924 (29-37) and 1925 (30-48). They rejoined the NSL in 1926, and then returned to the NNL in 1927, but they remained a second division team through 1930.

They played well in the "major" Negro Southern League of 1932, their only major league affilation from 1931 to 1936. They joined the new Negro American League in 1937, finishing in the middle of the pack. Finally, in 1938, the Sox won the NAL first half with a 21-4 record. They stumbled during the second half, but won the only two games played in a hotly disputed championship series with the Atlanta Black Crackers. This team was managed by Ted "Double Duty" Radcliffe. The Red Sox remained a viable, competitive franchise through the '40s, but fell short of a championship. They finally called it quits in 1960.

Memphis was controlled over the years by the Martin brothers, all doctors: J.B., also a NAL official, A.T., B.B., and W.S. The club's home games were played at Martin Park. Many great players toiled for Memphis over the years, the best being Bob Boyd, Larry Brown, Marlin Carter, Chin Evans, Cowan Hyde, Clinton Jones, Verdell Mathis, Neil Robinson, and Nat Rogers.

St. Louis

The first professional black team in St. Louis was the Giants, in 1910. The Giants became charter members of the Negro National League, organized by Rube Foster, in 1920.

1949 Memphis Red Sox. Standing L to R: Clyde Martin (secretary), Bubba Hyde, Verdell Mathis, Neil Robinson, Orlando Varona, Willie Brooks Wells, Johnnie Cowans, Willie Wells, Harry Barnes, Joe B. Scott, and Chin Evans. Kneeling L to R: Spoon Carter, Larry Brown, Lionel Hampton, Bill Morgan, Bob Boyd, Casey Jones, "Big George" (road manager for Lionel Hampton Band).
Negro Leagues Baseball Museum

They finished sixth that initial season, with a 25-32 record. Led by Oscar Charlesto, they were third in 1921, at 40-28.

A change of ownership and name occurred after 1921. James "Cool Papa" Bell joined the St. Louis Stars in 1922. They were 35-26 and finished fourth that year. In 1923 they dropped to 25-40 (sixth), but rebounded to 42-34 (fourth) in 1924. The 1925 entry, including Bell and Willie Wells, finished one game behind Kansas City the first half and won the second half. Overall, they had a terrific record of 69-27. They fell to the defending World's Champion Monarchs in a seven game playoff.

The Stars dropped back to fourth in 1926, at 49-30. In 1927, they suffered a sub-par season. Their star hitter, George "Mule" Suttles, was out with a broken ankle much of the season. They were the champions of the NNL in 1928, under Candy Jim Taylor. Their overall record was 66-26, but the Colored World Series was no longer being played. In 1929, the Stars had the second best record at 59-33, as Kansas City took both halves. The 1930 team won the first half flag and finished 65-22, defeating Detroit in seven games for the title. Again, no World Series was played. In 1931, with the Depression in full swing, the Stars disbanded before the end of the year. Many outstanding Stars went on to form the heart of fine future Negro Leagues teams. The best were Cool Papa Bell, Dewey Creacy, Slap Hensley, Wilson Redus, Branch Russell, Mule Suttles, Ted Trent, and Willie Wells.

St. Louis played at Stars Park, a strange field where a trolley car barn was located in left field about 250 feet away. Ground rule doubles were the norm. But this power hitting squad had plenty of firepower and hit many more homeruns than any other NNL team during this period.

St. Louis rejoined the "majors" four times after 1931. A new club joined the newly formed Negro American League in 1937, finishing way back. In 1939, it returned and jelled after a miserable first half to take the second half crown, eventually losing to Kansas City in a five game post-season series. Dropping out again, the Stars returned in 1941, splitting home games between St. Louis and New Orleans. Out of league play in 1942, they rejoined the NNL as the Harrisburg-St. Louis Stars, but only played in the first half as they were suspended for going on a barnstorming tour. This was a sad ending for a proud black baseball tradition.

Atlantic City

The Duval Giants of Jacksonville, Florida, were lured to Atlantic City, New Jersey by Mayor Harry Bacharach in 1916, and thus acquired their unique name of the Bacharach Giants. They played at Bacharach Park on South Carolina Avenue until the mid '30s.

They were one of the strongest Eastern clubs of the pre-league era, and they were associate members of the Negro National League from 1920 to 1922. In fact, in 1922 there were two Bacharach teams, one in New York City, the other still based in Atlantic City. Most of the great black players were with the Bacharachs at one time or another.

The Bacharach Giants joined the Eastern Colored League in 1923. They finished fourth at 19-23 that first year. They were

1926 St. Louis Stars. Standing L to R: Mule Suttles, Willie Wells, Mitch Murray, Slap Hensley, E. Patton, John Henry Russell, Branch Russell, Henry Williams, Dizzy Dismukes. Sitting: Rosey Davis, John Reese, Willie Bobo, Dewey Creacy, William Ross, Cool Papa Bell, Percy Miller, G. Brown, and Wilson Redus.
Jay Sanford

again fourth in 1924 (30-29) and 1925 (26-27). In 1926, led by the hitting of "King Richard" Lundy and Oliver "Ghost" Marcelle, and the pitching of Arthur "Rats" Henderson, Claude "Red" Grier, and Luther Farrell, the Giants won the ECL flag with a 34-20 record. They then played 11 games against the Chicago American Giants to determine a World's Champion. Despite a third game 10-0 no-hitter by Grier, Chicago prevailed five games to three.

1927 was an even better year. The Giants took both halves and finished 54-35. In game five of the World Series, Luther Farrell pitched a no-hitter but again Chicago won five games to three, with one tie. In 1928, the ECL broke up and the Bacharach Giants were a poor 19-45 in the 1929 American Negro League. From 1930 to 1933 they played independently. The Bacharachs briefly rejoined the newly organized NNL during the second half of 1934, and then became a semi-pro local entry in Eastern circles. In fact, the 1934 team was based in Philadelphia. Some of the stars who played with the Bacharachs during the glory years were, Nap Cummings, Lundy, Marcelle, Roy Roberts, and Chaney White.

Baltimore

The Baltimore Black Sox came into existence in 1913 as a club team. A change in ownership in 1918 upgraded their status to semi-pro, and they continually improved and became charter members of the Eastern Colored League in 1923. In their first seasons, the Black Sox finished last at 19-30, but they were second at 30-19 in 1924. They were 31-19 and third the following season before falling to sixth in 1926. The

1927 team was just 35-35. There was no ECL in 1928, but the 1929 Black Sox, anchored by their "Million Dollar" infield of Jud Wilson, Frank Warfield, Dick Lundy, and Oliver Marcelle, swept to pennants in both halves. Overall, they were 49-21. Unfortunately, there was no World Series held from 1928 to 1941. This was easily the greatest Black Sox squad with Rap Dixon, Robert Clarke, and pitchers Red Ryan, Pud Flournoy, and Laymon Yokeley adding their talents to those of the terrific infield.

The Black Sox played independently in 1930 and 1931. They joined the East-West League in 1932, and were battling for the top spot when the curcuit folded. In 1933, the second Negro National League was founded with Baltimore as a member. The team dropped out after the season but returned for the second half in 1934. This was the Black Sox's swan song. Unable to keep quality players during the Depression, the Black Sox reverted to a semi-pro local basis and "major league" ball left Baltimore for several years.

Richard Powell was instrumental in getting top-flight baseball back to Baltimore. He got the Nashville Elite Giants, founded by Tom Wilson in 1918, to play several NNL games in Baltimore during 1936 and 1937. Finally, in 1938, the Nashville team transferred to Crab Town, and the Baltimore Elite Giants came into being. The 1938 entry was mediocre. However, after placing third the first half of the 1939 season, Baltimore had the best second half record. An elimination tournament was held, and the Elite Giants knocked off the Newark Eagles and the Homestead Grays two games to none. They were declared champions, despite Homestead's having the best overall record.

Homestead Grays of 1939

1939 Homestead Grays. Standing L to R: Josh Gibson, Edsall Walker, Dave Whatley, Roy Welamker, Arnold Waite, Henry Spearman, Ray Brown, Tom Parker, Rab Roy Gaston, and Roy Partlow. Kneeling: Jerry Benjamin, Speck Roberts, Louis Dula, Vic Harris, Buck Leonard, Sam Bankhead, Jelly Jackson.
Negro Leagues Baseball Museum

The Elite Giants finished second in 1940 (25-14), third in 1941 (22-18) and had a 37-15 record in 1942, which was the league's best overall. In a reversal of the 1939 elimination series, they finished second to Homestead. The 1943 and 1944 entries were second division teams, but Baltimore rebounded to second in 1945 at 25-17. In 1946 and 1947 the club was again in the middle of the pack. The Elite Giants took the first half flag in 1948, but lost to the Homestead Grays in the playoffs. This was a prelude to a World Title the next year.

In 1949, the two Negro Leagues merged into the Negro American League with East and West divisions. The Elite Giants cruised to the Eastern Title and then beat the Chicago American Giants in four straight games for the championship. They were 24-20 in 1950. Stadium problems forced Baltimore to give up the ghost after the 1951 season.

The Black Sox and Elite Giants had many superb players over the course of their existence. They included Joe Black, Bill Byrd, "Pee Wee" Butts, Roy Campanella, "Junior" Gilliam, Sammy T. Hughes, Henry Kimbro, Andy Porter, Felton Snow, Jud Wilson, Laymon Yokeley, and Robert Clarke, who caught for both Baltimore teams.

Newark

Newark's first "major" team was the short-lived 1926 Stars of the ECL. They disbanded after starting 1-10. A second entry was the Browns in the 1932 East-West League. The 1934

and '35 Newark Dodgers brought up the rear in the Negro National League.

The team that brought glory to Newark began as the Brooklyn Eagles in 1935. The club was owned by Abe Manley but was run by his wife, Effa Manley. After one year and a 28-31 record in Brooklyn, the Manleys moved the team, replacing the defunct Newark Dodgers. The Eagles would be a first division club until their transfer to Houston after the 1948 season.

The team was just 30-29 that first season, and second in 1937. After a fourth in 1938 the Eagles were second in 1939, but lost to Baltimore in the playoffs. Nosed out for second in 1940, Newark finished second in 1941, then third in 1942 and '43. With the heart of the team in the service, the 1944 and 1945 squads were middle of the pack. With the return of Leon Day and Monte Irvin, the 1946 club, managed by "Biz" Mackey, finally reached the pinnacle, winning both halves and going 47-16 overall. Leon Day pitched an opening day no-hitter and they never looked back. The Eagles then beat the Kansas Ciy Monarchs in a tough seven game series, winning the final 3-2. They again won the first half in 1947, but the New York Cubans were named NNL champs without a playoff. In 1948, decimated by raids from Organized Baseball, Newark finished out the schedule and left for Houston. The long-overdue integration of Organized Baseball quickly destroyed this once proud franchise.

Some of the greats who toiled for the Eagles through the

years were Ray Dandridge, Johnny Davis, Leon Day, Larry Doby, Monte Irvin, Max Manning, Lennie Pearson, Ed Stone, and Mule Suttles.

Pittsburgh Crawfords

The Pittsburgh Crawfords came into being in the 1920s. They were named after the Crawford Bath House on Crawford Avenue in Pittsburgh's black area. They were a local amateur team and their leaders were Harold Tinker, Johnny Moore, and the Harris brothers. Josh Gibson started his career with the 1928 team. The Crawfords became professional in 1930, after Gus Greenlee, a local numbers king, took over the ownership. Greenlee's goal was to surpass the Homestead Grays as Pittsburgh's best team, and he would succeed for a time. After playing strong independent schedules during 1930 and 1931, the Crawfords joined the East-West League in 1932. Known records show a 32-26 record for that season.

Greenlee was the main force in starting the second Negro National League in 1933 and Pittsburgh went 20-8 during the first half schedule, just one game behind the Chicago American Giants. The second half schedule was not completed, but Chicago claimed the NNL pennant. Months later, President Greenlee awarded the flag to the Crawfords. In 1934 they went 29-17 for third place. Greenlee continued to raid Cum Posey's Grays and in 1935 put together arguably the greatest black team in history. Five future Hall of Famers anchored it. They were James "Cool Papa" Bell, Oscar Charleston, Josh Gibson, Judy Johnson, and Satchel Paige. The Crawfords went 39-15 and defeated the New York Cubans four games to three in the playoff for the title.

The 1936 team was 36-24, again the best in the NNL. 1937 found most of the Crawford stars leaving to play for dictator Rafael Trujillo's team in what is now the Dominican Republic. Coupled with other business failures in Greenlee's enterprises, the team did poorly in 1937 and 1938. Following 1938, the team left Pittsburgh for Toledo, OH, and in 1940 moved to Indianapolis. Greenlee resurrected the Crawfords for the USL League in the mid '40s.

The Crawfords were only in existence for a brief time, but their star shined brightly. They played at Greenlee Field, built for $100,000 in 1932. Outfielder Jimmy Crutchfield and pitcher Sam Streeter were other outstanding stars lured to the Crawfords during their glory years.

Homestead Grays

This famous team began as a group of black Pittsburgh steelworkers. They became the Homestead Grays in 1910. Cumberland Posey joined the Grays in 1911 and became captain in 1916. Posey owned the team by the '20s. They became the strongest non-League team playing during that decade, with stars like Oscar Owens, Charles "Lefty" Williams, "Smokey Joe" Williams, Willis Moody, Ralph Mellix, and Vic Harris.

The Grays' first league appearance was in the 1929 American Negro League. They were so-so at 34-29. In 1930, they again played independently, but had a 28-8 record against NNL outfits. In 1931, they were 29-18 against top-flight black competition. Homestead joined the 1932 East-West League and had a 29-19 record when the EWL broke up. Consistently raided by Gus Greenlee's Crawfords, Posey

briefly joined, then dropped out of, the 1933 NNL. The team rejoined the NNL in 1935, going 23-23, and following with a 22-27 record in 1936. In 1937, Posey began to split his home games between Pittsburgh and Washington D.C. With the rival Crawfords raided by dictator Rafael Truillo and suffering because of Greenlee's financial woes, Posey was able to put together a strong team that would win the first of nine straight NNL pennants. (Some of these championships were disputed. For example, in 1939 Baltimore had beaten Homestead two games to none in the playoffs after the Grays had fashioned the best seasonal record.)

In 1942, the Colored World Series was started up again, and the Grays lost out to the Kansas City Monarchs. In 1943, the Grays defeated Birmingham in seven games. In 1944 they again beat the Black Barons, this time in five games. They lost the world title to the Cleveland Buckeyes in 1945. These Homestead teams featured the "Black Ruth and Gehrig", Josh Gibson and Buck Leonard. The Grays slumped to 27-28 in 1946, the result of the rise of the Newark Eagles and the death of Cum Posey in March of 1946. Josh Gibson died in January, 1947, and the Grays' season was played out without enthusiasm.

In 1948, they bounced back, winning the second half title and sweeping the Baltimore Elite Giants in three straight. They then defeated Birmingham in five games for Homestead's last World Championship. The NNL merged with the NAL in 1949, but the Grays joined the BAA, winning the flag there. However, continued fan interest in the major leagues' intregation caused the Homestead Grays to go back to barnstorming for 1950, and out of existence after the season.

Some additional greats that spent many years with the Grays were Sam Bankhead, Jerry Benjamin, Ray Brown, Lick Carlisle, Wilmer Fields, Rab Roy Gaston, Edsall Walker, and Jud Wilson. Throughout the years, the Grays drew great crowds for their home games in Pittsburgh's Forbes Field and Washington's Griffith Stadium.

Philadelphia

Philadelphia has one of the longest histories of Negro Baseball of any city in the country, beginning with the Philadelphia Pythians of 1867. The Philadelphia Giants were a dominant team in the early part of this century, being Colored World Champions in 1902, 1904, and 1906. Some great players toiled for the Giants, including, Sol White, Grant Johnson, Pete Hill, John Henry Lloyd, Frank Grant, and Rube Foster.

The Hilldale Giant team was first formed in 1910 as a local club team. Usually referred to simply as "Hilldale" or "the Hilldales," they became professional in 1917. After playing strong independent and NNL teams through the years, they joined the Eastern Colored League in 1923 and won the first three championships. In 1923, they were 32-17. In 1924, they were 47-22 and played the Kansas City Monarchs in the first official Colored World Series, falling five games to four with one tie. They were a brilliant 52-15 in 1925, and beat the Monarchs in six games for the world title. The Bacharach Giants ended Hilldale's ECL reign in 1926, Hilldale finishing third at 34-24. They fell further in 1927, to 36-45. The ECL disbanded after this year and the Hilldales played an independent schedule. They rejoined the American Negro League for 1929, going 39-35 and finishing fourth. There was no league in the East in 1930 and 1931, but Hilldale's 1931 team was 42-13 against black professional clubs, and was generally considered Eastern champs.

Hilldale ceased to exist after this season. However, Ed Bolden formed a new entry that joined the second Negro National League in 1933—the Philadelphia Stars. The Stars would be a strong black team until falling victim to intregation and finances following the 1952 season.

The 1934 Stars were 23-13, and they won the second half championship and a hotly disputed seven game playoff against the Chicago American Giants. They were 28-27 in 1935, 25-30 in 1936, and in the middle of the pack from 1937 to 1948, but never pennant winners. They joined the Negro American League after the merger of the leagues following the 1948 season.

Over the years, the Philadelphia teams played in Darby and Yeadon, Pennsylvania, and at Passon Field and Pennar Park in Philadelphia.

The great Hilldale stars were Otto Briggs, Phil Cockrell, Nip Winters, George Johnson, Judy Johnson, Biz Mackey, Red Ryan, and Louis Santop. Some of the top Philadelphia Stars players were Gene Benson, Barney Brown, Bill Cash, "Slim" Jones, Webster McDonald, and Red Parnell.

Kansas City

Arguably the greatest franchise in black baseball history, the Kansas City Monarchs trace their beginnings back to J.L. Wilkinson's famous All Nations of Des Moines, Iowa in 1912. A powerful force in the Midwest, led by ace pitcher, John Donaldson, the club moved to Kansas City in 1915.

When Rube Foster was organizing the Negro National League, he wanted only black owners, but allowed Wilkinson to be involved because of Wilinson's color-blindness. It was, as most of Foster's were, an excellent decision. The Kansas City Monarchs became charter members of the NNL, and over the years were perhaps black baseball's most successful team both on the field and in the box office.

In 1920, the initial Monarchs team drew players from the 1919 Detroit Stars and recruits from the great army squads. It included Bullet Joe Rogan, Dobie Moore, John Donaldson, Hurley McNair, Rube Currie, Sam Crawford, Dink Mothell, and George Carr. Kansas City finished in a tie for second, with a 41-29 record. The 1921 squad went 50-31, a half-game behind Chicago in a mildly disputed campaign. The Monarchs tied for third in 1922 at 46-33, and cruised to the first of three straight NNL titles in 1923, finishing at 57-33. In 1924, they were 55-22, and they represented the NNL in the first official Colored World Series against the Eastern Colored League Champions, Hilldale. Tied at four games apiece, with one tie, Monarchs manager Jose Mendez, the great Cuban veteran, pitched a three-hit 5-0 shutout to take the title. They again were best in the NNL overall in 1925 at 62-23, but had to defeat the heavy hitting St. Louis Stars in a seven game playoff in order to again meet Hilldale. This time, with ace Wilber "Bullet Joe" Rogan sidelined by a freak accident, Kansas City fell five games to one.

In 1926, Kansas City had the best overall record again at 57-21. The Monarchs won the first half ,and played second half winners the Chicago American Giants in a rousing playoff. Ahead four games to three in a best of nine series, youngster Willie Foster outduelled Bullet Joe in both games of a doubleheader, ending KC's string of titles. 1927 saw a terrific five team race in the NNL, with Kansas City finishing out of the money even with a 54-29 record. In 1928 they were 50-31, again second best.

The 1929 entry won both halves finishing 62-17. But the ECL had folded and no World Series was played with American Negro League Champion Baltimore. In 1930, the Monarchs were nosed out by St. Louis for the first half title despite a 31-14 mark. During the second half they scheduled a long country-wide barnstorming tour with the Homestead Grays. During the trip, the team cars were involved in a nasty accident. Rogan and others were lost to the Monarchs. Upon returning to NNL play, still missing these important members, the team fell out of pennant contention.

Kansas City dropped out of the NNL for 1931, and the league itself folded later that year. Between 1930 and 1937, Kansas City would often rejoin the league for a brief time, but the Monarchs were mainly barnstorming around the country, playing many night games under their new portable lighting system.

When the Negro American League was started in 1937, Kansas City returned officially and was first half winner and NAL titlist after beating Chicago four games to one in the playoff. In 1938, th Monarchs were 32-15, but not champions. In 1939, they were again NAL champs, beating St. Louis three games to two in a playoff. Again champions in 1940, they won a disputed title in 1941. This made four flags in five years, unfortunately during a period when no World Series was being played. Kansas City continued its dominance by winning both halves in 1942 and topping the Homestead Grays in four games to none in the first Colored World Series since 1927.

The Monarchs' great run was ended by the Birmingham Black Barons in 1943, as World War II player losses combined with Mexican League defections to weaken the Kansas City club. The 1944 team was only 23-42, the 1945 version, 32-30. The 1946 squad, bolstered by returning war veterans, won the NAL flag again before falling 3-2 to the Newark Eagles in the seventh game of the World Series. In 1947, the Monarchs trailed the Cleveland Buckeyes, but in 1948 they took the second half pennant and met Birmingham for the right to face the Homestead Grays. Birmingham beat them in seven games.

In 1949, the Monarchs took the first half championship of the Western Division of the reorganized Negro American League, but because so many of their players had been picked off by Organized Baseball, they declined to meet second half winner Chicago. In 1950, the Monarchs were Western Champs in both halves finishing 51-20 overall.

Kansas City continued as a dominant team throughout the '50s, finally folding in 1960. Dozens of Monarchs went into Organized Baseball, including Gene Baker, Ernie Banks, Willard Brown, Elston Howard, Connie Johnson, Booker McDaniels, and Satchel Paige.

Because the Monarchs were such a stable franchise, they had a vast array of talent over the years. The list of greats who spent the bulk of their careers with Kansas City reads like a Who's Who of black baseball greats: Newt Allen, William Bell, Chet Brewer, Andy Cooper, Frank Duncan, Newt Joseph, Hurley McNair, Dobie Moore, Buck O'Neil, Paige, Rogan, Hilton Smith, and Tom Young. Jackie Robinson spent his Negro Leagues time with the Monarchs.

Through the years, the Kansas City Monarchs played in Muelebach Field or Blues Stadium, then in Municipal Stadium.

Teams and

their Cities

1886-1955

Over the decades, several dozen cities served as home base for teams in the various Negro Leagues. Presented here are teams that were members of formally organized leagues dating back to 1886. Teams are listed alphabetically by city, and in chronological order with their league affiliation. This format allows you to follow the path of teams in a given city year-by-year and league-to-league.

Team	Years	League
Akron, Ohio		
Akron Black Tyrites	1933	NNL
Albany, Georgia		
Albany Giants	1926	NSL
Asheville, North Carolina		
Asheville Blues	1945	NSL
Atlanta, Georgia		
Georgia Champions	1886	SLCB
Atlanta Black Crackers	1920	SNL
Atlanta Black Crackers	1926	NSL
Atlanta Black Crackers	1932	NSL
Atlanta Black Crackers	1938	NAL
Atlanta Black Crackers	1945	NSL
Atlantic City, New Jersey		
Bacharach Giants	1923-28	ECL
Bacharach Giants	1929	ANL
Bacharach Giants	1934	NNL
Baltimore, Maryland		
Lord Baltimores	1887	LCBBP
Baltimore Black Sox	1923-28	ECL
Baltimore Black Sox	1929	ANL
Baltimore Black Sox	1932	EWL
Baltimore Black Sox	1933-34	NNL
Baltimore Elite Giants	1938-51	NNL
Birmingham, Alabama		
Birmingham Black Barons	1920	SNL
Birmingham Black Barons	1923-25	NNL
Birmingham Black Barons	1926	NSL
Birmingham Black Barons	1927-30	NNL
Birmingham Black Barons	1932	NSL
Birmingham Black Barons	1937-38	NAL
Birmingham Black Barons	1940-55	NAL
Boston, Massachusetts		
Boston Resolutes	1887	LCBBP

Team	Years	League	Team	Years	League
Brooklyn, New York			**Harrisburg, Pennsylvania**		
Brooklyn Royal Giants	1923-27	ECL	Harrisburg Giants	1924-27	ECL
Brooklyn Eagles	1935	NNL	Harrisburg-St. Louis Stars	1943	NNL
Brooklyn Brown Dodgers	1945	USL			
			Houston, Texas		
Charleston, South Carolina			Houston Eagles	1949-50	NAL
Charleston Fultons	1886	SLCB			
			Indianapolis, Indiana		
Chattanooga, Tennessee			Indianapolis ABCs	1920-26	NNL
Chattanooga Black Lookouts	1920	SNL	Indianapolis ABCs	1931	NNL
Chattanooga White Sox	1926	NSL	Indianapolis ABCs	1932	NSL
Chattanooga Choo-Choos	1945	NSL	Indianapolis ABCs	1933	NNL
			Indianapolis Athletics	1937	NAL
Chicago, Illinois			Indianapolis ABCs	1938-39	NAL
Chicago Giants	1920-21	NNL	Indianapolis-Toledo Crawfords	1939-40	NAL
Chicago American Giants	1920-31	NNL	Indianapolis-Cincinnati Clowns	1944-45	NAL
Cole's American Giants	1932	NSL	Indianapolis Clowns	1946-55	NAL
Cole's American Giants	1933-35	NNL			
Chicago American Giants	1937-52	NAL	**Jacksonville, Florida**		
Chicago Brown Bombers	1945	USL	Florida Clippers	1886	SLCB
			Jacksonville Athletics	1886	SLCB
Cincinnati, Ohio			Jacksonville Macedonias	1886	SLCB
Cincinnati Browns	1887	LCBBP	Roman Cities	1886	SCLB
Cincinnati Cubans	1921	NAL	Jacksonville Red Caps	1920	SNL
Cincinnati Tigers	1937	NAL	Jacksonville Red Caps	1938	NAL
Cincinnati Buckeyes	1942	NAL	Jacksonville Red Caps	1941-42	NAL
Cincinnati Clowns	1943	NAL			
Cincinnati-Indianapolis Clowns	1944-45	NAL	**Kansas City, Missouri**		
			Kansas City Monarchs	1920-30	NNL
Cleveland, Ohio			Kansas City Monarchs	1932	NSL
Cleveland Tate Stars	1922	NNL	Kansas City Monarchs	1937-55	NAL
Cleveland Browns	1924	NNL			
Cleveland Elites	1926	NNL	**Knoxville, Tennessee**		
Cleveland Hornets	1927	NNL	Knoxville Grays or Smokies	1945	NSL
Cleveland Tigers	1928	NNL			
Cleveland Cubs	1931	NNL	**Little Rock, Arkansas**		
Cleveland Cubs	1932	NSL	Little Rock Greys	1932	NSL
Cleveland Stars	1932	EWL	Little Rock Black Travelers	1945	NSL
Cleveland Giants	1933	NNL			
Cleveland Red Sox	1934	NNL	**Louisville, Kentucky**		
Cleveland Bears	1939-40	NAL	Fall Citys	1887	LCBBP
Cincinnati-Cleveland Buckeyes	1942	NAL	Louisville White Caps	1930	NNL
Cleveland Buckeyes	1943-48	NAL	Louisville White Sox	1931	NAL
Cleveland Buckeyes	1950	NAL	Louisville Black Caps	1932	NSL
			Louisville Buckeyes	1949	NAL
Columbus, Ohio			Louisville Black Colonels	1954	NAL
Columbus Buckeyes	1921	NNL			
Columbus Turfs	1932	NSL	**Memphis, Tennessee**		
Columbus Blue Birds	1933	NNL	Memphis Eclipses	1886	SCLB
Columbus Elite Giants	1935	NNL	Memphis Eurekas	1886	SLCB
			Memphis Red Sox	1923-25	NNL
Dayton, Ohio			Memphis Red Sox	1926	NSL
Dayton Marcos	1920	NNL	Memphis Red Sox	1927-30	NNL
Dayton Marcos	1926	NNL	Memphis Red Sox	1932	NSL
			Memphis Red Sox	1937-55	NAL
Detroit, Michigan			Memphis Grey Sox	1945	NSL
Detroit Stars	1920-31	NNL			
Detroit Wolves	1932	EWL	**Milwaukee, Wisconsin**		
Detroit Stars	1937	NAL	Milwaukee Bears	1923	NNL
Motor City Giants	1945	USL			
Detroit Stars	1954-55	NAL			

Team	Years	League	Team	Years	League
Mobile, Alabama			**Newark, New Jersey**		
Mobile Black Bears or Shippers	1945	NSL	Newark Stars	1926	ECL
			Newark Browns	1932	EWL
Monroe, Louisiana			Newark Dodgers	1934-35	NNL
Monroe Monarchs	1932	NSL	Newark Eagles	1936-48	NNL
Montgomery, Alabama			**Palmyra, New Jersey**		
Montgomery Blues	1886	SCLB	Riverton-Palmyra Athletics	1906	ILIP
Montgomery Grey Sox	1926	NSL			
Montgomery Grey Sox	1932	NSL	**Philadelphia, Pennsylvania**		
			Philadelphia Pythians	1887	LCBBP
Nashville, Tennessee			Philadelphia Giants	1906	ILIP
Nashville Giants	1920	SNL	Philadelphia Professionals	1906	ILIP
Nashville Elite Giants	1926	NSL	Hilldale Giants	1923-27	ECL
Nashville Elite Giants	1930	NNL	Philadelphia Tigers	1928	ECL
Nashville Elite Giants	1932	NSL	Hilldale Giants	1929	ANL
Nashville Elite Giants	1933-34	NNL	Hilldale Giants	1932	EWL
Nashville Black Vols	1945	NSL	Philadelphia Stars	1933-52	NNL
			Hilldale Giants	1945	USL
New Orleans, Louisiana					
New Orleans Unions	1886	SLCB	**Pittsburgh, Pennsylvania**		
New Orleans Black Pelicans	1920	SNL	Pittsburgh Keystones	1887	LCBBP
New Orleans-St. Louis Stars	1941	NAL	Pittsburgh Keystones	1922	NNL
New Orleans Black Pelicans	1945	NSL	Homestead Grays	1929	ANL
New Orleans Eagles	1951	NAL	Homestead Grays	1930	NNL
			Homestead Grays	1932	EWL
New York, New York			Pittsburgh Crawfords	1932	EWL
New York Cubans	1887	LCBBP	Homestead Grays	1933	NNL
New York Gorhams	1887	LCBBP	Pittsburgh Crawfords	1933-38	NNL
Cuban Stars	1906	ILIP	Homestead Grays	1935-37	NNL
Cuban X-Giants	1906	ILIP	Homestead-Washington Grays	1937-48	NNL
Havana Stars	1906	ILIP	Pittsburgh Crawfords	1945	USL
Quaker Giants	1906	ILIP			
Lincoln Giants	1923-26	ECL	**Savannah, Georgia**		
Cuban Stars (East)	1923-28	ECL	Savannah Broads	1886	SLCB
Lincoln Giants	1927-28	ECL	Savannah Jerseys	1886	SCLB
Cuban Stars (East)	1929	ANL	Savannah Lafayettes	1886	SLCB
Lincoln Giants	1929	ANL			
Cuban Stars (East)	1932	EWL	**St. Louis, Missouri**		
New York Black Yankees	1932	EWL	St. Louis Giants	1920-21	NNL
New York Cubans	1935-36	NNL	St. Louis Stars	1922-31	NNL
New York Black Yankees	1937-48	NNL	St. Louis Stars	1937	NAL
New York Cubans	1939-50	NNL	St. Louis Stars	1939	NAL
			St. Louis-New Orleans Stars	1941	NAL
			St. Louis-Harrisburg Stars	1943	NAL
			Toledo, Ohio		
			Toledo Tigers	1923	NNL
			Toledo-Indianapolis Crawfords	1939-40	NAL
			Toledo Rays	1945	USL
			Washington, D.C.		
			Capital Citys	1887	LCBBP
			Washington Potomacs	1924	ECL
			Washington Pilots	1932	EWL
			Washington Elite Giants	1935-37	NNL
			Washington-Homestead Grays	1937-48	NNL
			Washington Black Senators	1938	NNL
			Wilmington, Delaware		
			Wilmington Giants	1906	ILIP
			Wilmington Potomacs	1925	ECL

The Umpire Strikes Back

Discipline on the field was a frequent problem in the Negro Leagues, which had an understaffed, and sometimes underqualified, umpire corps not always able to make the more obstreperous players behave. Unfortunately, there were instances where players physically assaulted umps over what they thought were bad calls. At least once, however, the umpire got satisfaction. The *Pittsburgh Courier* reported in 1940 that an otherwise humdrum 8-1 win by the Homestead Grays over the Newark Eagles was "enlivened in the eighth inning" when Eagle manager Dick Lundy and umpire E.C. "Pop" Turner came to blows, "and Lundy was felled by a right to the jaw."

Hall Of Fame

Players

Larry Lester

"The other day Willie Mays hit his 522nd home run. He has gone past me, and he's pushing, and I say to him, 'Go get 'em, Willie.' Baseball gives every American boy a chance to excel. This is the nature of man and the name of the game. I hope that someday Satchel Paige and Josh Gibson will be voted into the Hall of Fame as symbols of the great Negro players who are not here only because they weren't given the chance."

—from Ted Williams' induction speech into the Hall of Fame, 1966.

In 1971, twenty-four years after Jackie Robinson first took the field for the Brooklyn Dodgers and well over a hundred years after the first black men began to play what would become the National Pastime, the National Baseball Hall of Fame created a special committee to recognize African-American athletes who played during baseball's segregated period. Subjected to the Jim Crow laws and attitudes of the times, these players were never given the opportunity to showcase their talents in the white major leagues.

This "Hall of Fame Committee on Negro Baseball Leagues" selected only a representative nine players to illustrate the accomplishments of many great but unrecognized black players. The token team of ebony stars included: Satchel Paige, pitcher; Josh Gibson, catcher; Buck Leonard, first baseman; Martin Dihigo, second baseman; Judy Johnson, third baseman; Pop Lloyd, shortstop; Cool Papa Bell, leftfield; Oscar Charleston, centerfield, and Monte Irvin, rightfield.

In the nearly two decades since the special committee disbanded after creating its "All-Star team," the Hall of Fame's Committee on Baseball Veterans has selected only two more Negro Leaguers: Andrew "Rube" Foster, who founded the first league and was unaccountably overlooked in the initial process, and Ray Dandridge, the marvelous third baseman, who won most of his fame with the Newark Eagles.

The Negro Leagues, therefore, are represented at Cooperstown by a single player at eight positions, two third basemen and an organizational figure. This is a good start, but common sense (not to mention the memories of many fans and baseball figures) dictates that there were many more Hall-of-Fame-worthy Negro League players. The message received, for example, is that only one pitcher from the black leagues was worthy of selection. I would expect this phenomenal individual's record to show all wins and no loses, because of his total domination. Without argument, Paige was a great pitcher, but he was not alone, as he reminded everyone during the induction ceremonies, saying: "There were many Satches and many Joshes." He later added, with homespun wisdom: "Oh, we had men by the hundreds who could have made the big leagues, by the hundreds, not by the fours, twos or threes. We had a lot of Satchel Paiges out there—men who could throw the ball as hard as me. Ain't no maybe so about it."

This section includes brief biographies of the chosen eleven Negro League veterans. We hope these essays will encourage more people to study the glorious history of this dark chapter of our national pastime. As Buck Leonard once said, "We were not disorganized, just unrecognized."

James "Cool Papa" Bell.
Moorland-Spingarn Library

JAMES THOMAS (COOL PAPA) BELL

Born May 17, 1903 at Starkville, Mississippi. Died March 7, 1991 at St. Louis, Missouri. Height: 6' 0". Weight: 145-170 lbs. Threw left. Batted both. Position(s) p, of.

Hall Of Fame Induction: 1974
Teams: 1922 to 1946, St. Louis Stars, Pittsburgh Crawfords, Detroit Wolves, Kansas City Monarchs, Chicago American Giants, and the Homestead Grays.

With daring speed and cunning game awareness, coupled with finesse at the bat, Cool Papa Bell epitomized the game of "tricky" baseball. He raised the once-conservative game to an art form that revolutionized modern day baseball.

His Hall of Fame plaque reads in part "….Contemporaries rated him the fastest man on the base paths." His critics claimed he cheated, sometimes sneaking from first to third base without touching second. Bell once scored from first on an infield bunt. Another time, he stole two bases on a single pitch. If you didn't see it, you didn't believe it. "Quick as a wink, fast as a blink" describes the unbridled speed of Cool Papa Bell.

He was born James Nichols to Mary Nichols and Jonas Bell. In 1920, he moved to St. Louis with his five brothers and two sisters and adopted his father's name. In August, he went to work for the Independent (later Swift) Packing Company at a weekly wage of $21.20—53 cents an hour. After hours, he joined the all-black semi-pro Compton Hill Cubs in the city league, before going across the river to play for the East St. Louis Cubs.

When the Cubs played the St. Louis Stars of the Negro National League (NNL) in an exhibition game in 1922, Bell's baseball career received a kick-start. The Stars signed him

for $90 a month as a left-handed pitcher with a wicked curve and a fade-away knuckler. After he beat the Chicago American Giants' Jimmy Lyons in a match race to claim the league's fastest man title, the Stars assigned Bell to patrol centerfield. In 1924, the switch-hitting Bell became the starting centerfielder for the Stars. He stayed with them until 1931, when the Great Depression killed off the NNL. In ten years with the Stars, he led them to league titles in 1928, 1930 and 1931.

In 1932, Bell joined the talented-rich Detroit Wolves of the East-West League, which collapsed in mid-season.

When the Wolves folded, he joined the Kansas City Monarchs for the remainder of the season. Dissatisfied with playing for a percentage of the gate with the barn-storming Monarchs, he felt the lure of the Mexican peso. After his first winter tour south of the border, he joined the Pittsburgh Crawfords in 1933. There he joined other future Cooperstown players like Judy Johnson, Josh Gibson, Oscar Charleston and Satchel Paige. Under manager Charleston they won the NNL championship in 1935. The 1935 squad featured one of the fleetest outfields in Negro League history with Bell, Sam Bankhead and Jimmie Crutchfield. Bell stayed with the Crawfords until 1937, when dictator Rafael Trujillo raided Pittsburgh of its stars to stock his all-star team in Santo Domingo (now Dominican Republic).

The Trujillo club later played in the popular *Denver Post* Tournament, where Bell batted .450, with five extra base hits and 11 stolen bases in 13 games. This prompted the sports editor of the *Denver Post* to write: "All these years I've been looking for a player who could steal first base. I've found my man: his name is Cool Papa Bell."

Bell was quiet, low-key, and unassuming, with the sleek build of a high school basketball point guard. Always calm under pressure, Bell recalled, "I was only nineteen and they thought I'd be afraid of big crowds...I took it so cool, they (teammates) began to call me 'Cool.' But that wasn't enough, they [actually manager Bill Gatewood] added 'Papa' to it."

Bell played briefly with the Pittsburgh Crawfords in 1938 before touring Mexico with the Tampico, Torreon, Veracruz and Monterrey clubs, earning personal salary highs of $450 per month. In 1940 he led the southern Mexican League in runs (119), hits (167), triples (15), home runs (12), RBIs (79) and slugging percentage (.685) in a 90 game season. Surprisingly, Bell lost the stolen base title to compadre Sam Bankhead.

At the age of 39, Bell returned to the States in 1942 to played with old friend Crutchfield and the Chicago American Giants. The following season Cum Posey lured Bell to join his power-packed Homestead Grays which included sluggers Sam Bankhead, Jerry Benjamin, Josh Gibson, Vic Harris, Buck Leonard and Jud Wilson. The Grays won three straight league titles with Bell anchoring centerfield. They defeated the Birmingham Black Barons for the World Series championship in 1943 and 1944 before relinquishing the title to Quincy Trouppe's Cleveland Buckeye team in 1945. Trouppe claims: "Cool Papa ran like he stole something."

Bell's speed was legendary. He transformed sacrifice bunts into hits and hits into doubles and doubles into triples. He was once timed on a wet field blazing the bases in a record 13.1 seconds, beating Evar Swanson's time by two-fifths of a second. The tan cheetah claimed that in 1924 he circled the bases in twelve seconds flat on a dry field, with a time of 3.1 from home to first.

Turning 43 years old, Bell retired from pro ball and joined the Detroit Senators, a black semi-pro independent team, for his last hurrah. In 1948, Tom Baird and J.L. Wilkinson, co-owners of the Kansas City Monarchs, hired Bell to managed their B Team. The contract called for Bell's team to be called the Kansas City Stars or the Travelers when they played in Monarch territory and the Kansas City Monarchs when they played outside the Midwestern states. Bell managed for three season, tutoring future major league stars Ernie Banks, Elston Howard and others before his final farewell to baseball.

After his baseball career ended, Bell worked as a custodian and night watchman at St. Louis City Hall for the next 21 years, retiring in 1973. He enjoyed his remaining years in a solid red-brick duplex at 3034 Dickson Street. The city of St. Louis, in recognition of this pioneer athlete, renamed the street "James 'Cool Papa' Bell Avenue." There he lived for more than 35 years.

Bell claimed much of his athletic inspiration came from his wife Clara. Clarabelle Thompson and James Bell were married on September 8, 1928 in East St. Louis, Missouri. They celebrated 62 years of marital bliss before Clara died on January 20, 1991. Already suffering from glaucoma in one eye, Bell endured a heart attack February 27 and was hospitalized at St. Louis University Hospital. He died a week later. The Bells had no children. He was laid to rest in St. Peter's Cemetery in St. Louis, Missouri.

Former teammate Satchel Paige summed up Bell's great career in his autobiography, *Maybe I'll Pitch Forever*, saying: "If Cool Papa had known about colleges or if colleges had known about Cool Papa, Jesse Owens would have looked like he was walking."

OSCAR McKINLEY CHARLESTON

Born October 14, 1896 at Indianapolis, Indiana. Died October 5, 1954 at Philadelphia, Pennsylvania. Height: 6' 1". Weight: 180-230 lbs. Threw left. Batted left. Position(s) of, 1b, mgr.

Hall Of Fame Induction: 1976
Teams: 1915 to 1954, Indianapolis ABCs, Lincoln Stars, Chicago American Giants, St. Louis Giants, Harrisburg Giants, Hilldale Giants, Homestead Grays, Pittsburgh Crawfords, Philadelphia Stars, Brooklyn Brown Dodgers, and the Indianapolis Clowns.

Oscar Charleston was a chubby-cheeked, barrel-chested Terminator with a penchant for fighting. He was famous for his temper, and his encounters with players and umpires were celebrated. Legend has it that he once ripped the hood off a white-robed Klansman and dared him to speak. Often feared and always respected, Charleston focused his fury into a fiery desire to win on the ball

Oscar Charleston.
Luis Munoz Collection

responsibility was to make sure of balls hit down the line and those in foul territory."

Charleston's rookie season did not pass without discord. On a barnstorming tour in Cuba, teammate Elwood "Bingo" DeMoss and Charleston attacked umpire James Scanlon during a heated discussion on October 24. Charleston and DeMoss were held under $1,000 bond on charges of assault and battery. When the volatile Charleston failed to show for the court appearance, owner Tom Bowser promptly suspended him.

Charleston responded with an apologetic letter to the public, stating in part: "The fact is that I could not overcome my temper as often times ball players can not...I consider the incident highly unwise...I am aware of the fact that some one has said that they presume I am actuated by mania, but my mind teaches me to judge not, for fear you may be judged."

Charleston was an explosively aggressive player, who ignited his peers to a higher level of play. With an occasional stop with the Lincoln Stars of New York City, Charleston stayed with the ABCs until the middle of 1918, before joining the Chicago American Giants. The Giants were owned by the eminent Andrew "Rube" Foster, who started the first league to survive a full season in 1920. Foster's Giants were loaded with quality players, so the benevolent Foster traded Charleston back to the ABCs to balance the power within the league. The next season, Foster moved Charleston to Charley Mills' St. Louis Giants, before returning him to the ABCs for the 1922 season.

After the season, on November 27, 1922, Charleston married the lovely Jane B. Howard from Harrisburg, Pennsylvania. When the Giants joined the one-year-old Eastern Colored League in 1924, the Charlestons relocated to her home town. The following year, 1925, records show that Charleston lead the Eastern Colored League with a monstrous .445 batting average. As a player-manager, he spent four seasons with Harrisburg. After a dismal second division finish in the first year, he lead the Giants to three consecutive second place finishes.

Economic conditions caused the Eastern Colored League to collapse. Charleston joined the Philadelphia Hilldale Club out of Darby, Pennsylvania. The next year, he joined the newly organized American Negro League and hit .396.

In 1930, he joined Cumberland Posey's independent Homestead Grays in Pittsburgh. There, he teamed with such legendary stars as Smokey Joe Williams, Vic Harris, George Scales, Josh Gibson and Judy Johnson. This powerhouse won a grueling 10-game World Series with the Lincoln Giants, claiming rights to the eastern seaboard championship. Charleston's combustive energy was the power behind many championship teams.

In 1932, financier and numbers runner Gus Greenlee raided the Grays team of its top stars, grabbing Charleston, Ted Page, Ted "Double Duty" Radcliffe, and Josh Gibson.

field. He commanded a dazzling array of baseball powers. He was a player's player—swift on the base paths, elegant in the field and possessed of tremendous power. This total package has been called by many the greatest centerfielder—black or white—in the history of the game.

Charleston was the son of Tom Charleston, a Sioux Indian and construction worker, and the former Mary Jeannette Thomas. He was raised in Indianapolis and served as a batboy for the powerful independent ABCs team, owned then by "Ran" Butler. In 1910, at the age of fourteen, he joined the U.S. Army.

Discharged from the service in 1915, he realized his boyhood dream and joined the hometown Indianapolis ABCs, now owned by the renown C.I. Taylor and Tom Bowser. His speed allowed him to play shallow and command outfield play. Once teammate Dave Malarcher claimed, "Some people ask me, 'Why are you playing so close to the right field foul line?' What they didn't know was that Charleston covered all three fields and my

His Pittsburgh Crawfords team would eventually be stocked with five future Hall of Famers: Charleston, Gibson, Judy Johnson, Cool Papa Bell and Satchel Paige. Although, now advanced in age, Charleston appeared in the first three East-West All-Star classics: 1933 through 1935. In 1935, he managed the Crawfords to the Negro National League title over the tough New York Cubans, lead by Martin Dihigo. Down three games to one, player-manager Charleston rallied his team, smashing out three home runs in the seven-game series for the league title.

Dominican Republic dictator, Rafael Trujillo, played Greenlee's own game by raiding Gus's club for its prime-time players. In 1937, he snatched up the Satchel Paige and Josh Gibson battery, eventually breaking up the team. In 1939 the Pittsburgh team with Charleston, reorganized as the Toledo Crawfords before moving on to Indianapolis the following season.

From 1941 to 1950, Charleston managed Ed Bolden's Philadelphia Stars team. There, he was influential in the development of future stars like Frank Austin, Gene Benson, Bill Cash, Mahlon Duckett, James "Bus" Clarkson, and Harry "Suitcase" Simpson.

In the sunset of his career, Charleton scouted for the Brooklyn Brown Dodgers of the United States League. This was an experimental circuit of six teams formed by Branch Rickey to indoctrinate black players for possible moves into the major leagues. The league failed and Charleston completed his managerial career with the Indianapolis Clowns. In 1954, his final year in pro ball, he led them to a league championship.

Charleston's career spanned five decades. He is among only a few who played both before the Negro leagues started and after the major leagues entertained an interest in black players. In 1949, the Philadelphia *Evening Bulletin* asked the great Oscar to pick his all-time all-star team. He chose: Ben Taylor (1b), Bingo DeMoss (2b), John Henry "Pop" Lloyd (ss), Oliver Marcelle (3b), Cristobal Torriente (lf), Rap Dixon (cf), Martin Dihigo (rf) with Josh Gibson and Louis Santop catching. His pitchers were Julio LeBlanc, Satchel Paige, Wilber "Bullet" Rogan, Pat Dougherty and William "Dizzy" Dismukes.

In October of 1954, Charleston suffered a stroke and lost his balance walking down a flight of stairs. He died a few days later. He was survived by his wife, Jane; they had no children. He was buried in Floral Park in Indianapolis.

Ray Dandridge.
Luis Munoz Collection

RAYMOND EMMETT (DANDY or HOOKS), DANDRIDGE, SR.

Born August 31, 1913 at Richmond, Virginia. Died February 12, 1994 at Palm Bay, FL. Height: 5' 7". Weight: 170-180 lbs. Threw right. Batted right. Position(s) 2b, ss, 3b.

Hall Of Fame Induction: 1987
Teams: 1933 to 1953, Detroit Stars, Nashville Elite Giants, Newark Dodgers, Newark Eagles, New York Cubans, Minneapolis Millers (AA), Sacramento Solons (PCL), Oakland Oaks (PCL).

Built low to the ground on bowed legs, Ray Dandridge's gift to the game was his spectacular defense at the hot corner. Despite the screaming, look-out line drives that made him one of baseball's greatest hitters, he was best known for his skills with the glove. Roy Campanella once said, "I never saw anyone better as a fielder."

"He was fantastic, the best I've ever seen at third," said former teammate Monte Irvin. Irvin added, "I saw all the greats—Brooks (Robinson), (Graig) Nettles—but I've never seen a better third baseman than Dandridge."

The son of the former Alberta Thompson and former semi-pro catcher, Archie Dandridge, Ray Dandridge's trademarks were his horseshoe-shaped legs, his pillow-sized glove, and his ability to swallow up bunts and toss out runners just before they stepped on first base. The standard joke was that a train would stand a better chance of going through Dandy's legs than a baseball. He was, as one writer said, "A third base Houdini."

Dandridge's career began in 1933 with the Detroit Stars, managed by the disciplinarian Candy Jim Taylor. Dandridge had been the captain of the semi-pro Richmond All-Stars when they played a game against the Stars. Taylor liked what he saw, enticed Dandridge's father with a $25 bonus, and the Stars had a third baseman. Taylor paid his new player only $15 a week, but added hitting instructions as a bonus. Taylor tossed away Dandridge's light stick, stepped into the batting cage, and told him to look and listen. Dandridge, a former home run hitter, was given a 37-ounce bat by Candy Jim and taught how to hit line drives to all fields. It was a lesson Dandridge never forgot.

The 1933 season was not a profitable one for the Stars. Forced to sell the team bus, Taylor sent the players packing back home. Dandridge finished the season with the Nashville Elite Giants. The next spring he signed with the Newark Dodgers and made his first appearance in the East-West All-Star classic. In 1936, the Newark team was sold to Abe and Effa Manley and renamed the Eagles. There he joined the great shortstop Willie "The Devil" Wells. Together, they formed a barrier on the left side of the infield more solid then the great wall of China. In 1937, Dandy and the Devil represented the East squad in the All-Star game. Clark Griffith, then owner of the Washington Senators begged, "Let me know when those two bowlegged men are coming to Washington. Please don't let me miss them."

After three productive seasons with the Eagles, Dandridge said adios and grabbed the grand peso from millionaire Jorge Pasquel of Mexico. Baseball-crazed Mexicans were willing to double and sometimes triple stateside salaries. Dandridge made about $10,000 a season with the Veracruz Diablos, plus living expenses and a maid. He, his first wife Florence, their two sons and a daughter enjoyed the Mexican hospitality. And it wasn't just the money they liked. There was another attraction for black players—being treated as first-class citizens.

Dandridge was well worth his salary, smashing the offerings of major league pitchers like Dizzy Dean, Sal Maglie, Whitey Ford, Max Lanier, Vic Raschi, Allie Reynolds and others. In 1948, he established a league record by hitting in 32 consecutive games. Dandridge was a bonafide hero in Mexico, hitting .331 in eight seasons. And his love of the game kept him playing all winter, too—either in Mexico, Venezuela, Puerto Rico or Cuba. In 11 seasons, he compiled a .282 lifetime batting average in the traditionally tough Cuban league.

In 1942, he returned to the Newark Eagles. Two years later, he re-signed with the Eagles for a stateside personal high of $360 a month. Dandridge had another fine season,

hitting .369 and was selected to his third East-West All-Star game. Cum Posey, owner of the Homestead Grays, placed him on his all-time all-star team in 1944, commenting, ". . . there was never a smoother functioning master at third base than Dandridge, and he can hit that apple, too." Rollo Wilson, sportswriter and later commissioner of the league claimed, "As far as I can recall there has been but one real third baseman developed in colored baseball since Judy (Johnson) passed from the game. His name is Ray Dandridge."

When the '44 season ended, Dandridge was off to Mexico once again, where he continued his rough treatment of pitchers for the next three seasons. In 1948, Dandy's benefactor Pasquel was killed in an airplane crash, and Dandridge came back to the U.S. to become manager of the New York Cubans. While he was managing the Cubans, the New York Giants plucked him and pitcher Dave Barnhill from the club, leaving unheralded Minnie Minoso behind. The Giants assigned Barnhill and Dandridge to their Triple-A Minneapolis Millers farm team.

At 36, his best years behind him, Dandridge hit .362 for the Millers in 1949. He missed the American Association batting championship by two points. The next year, a young fellow from Alabama named Willie Mays joined the Millers. Mays was hitting .477 when he got the call from the big leagues, leaving old man Dandridge behind to entertain the fans. Dandy didn't let them down, in 150 games he led the league in, at bats (627) and hits (195), while hitting .311. The American Association honored Dandridge with the Silver Ball Award as its Most Valuable Player.

With such outstanding credentials, Dandridge thought he would be next. But Dandridge never got his passport to prime time. Horace Stoneham, owner of the Giants, refused to bring him to New York or sell him to another major league team, supposedly because of his popularity in Minnesota. He closed out his third season with the Millers at the age of 38, hitting .324. Nearly forty years old, Dandridge played one more season with Minneapolis, hitting .291 in 618 at bats, and added a career high 27 doubles.

He moved to the Pacific Coast League with the Sacramento and Oakland teams, before finally hanging his gold glove up with Bismarck of North Dakota, where he hit .360. He never made it to the big time. Some said he was too old, while others whispered that the owners thought there were already too many black players in the majors.

After his playing days were over, Dandridge scouted briefly for the San Francisco Giants. He later became supervisor of a recreation center in Newark, New Jersey. He was honored when Newark renamed West Side Baseball Park Ray Dandridge, Sr. Field. In 1984, Dandridge moved with his second wife, Henrietta, to Palm Bay, Florida, where he was honored with the naming of Dandridge Avenue.

MARTIN (EL MAESTRO) DIHIGO

Born May 25, 1906 at Matanzas, Cuba. Died May 20, 1971 at Cienfuegos, Cuba. Height: 6' 3-1/2". Weight: 190-225 lbs. Threw right. Batted both. Position(s) p, inf, of, mgr.

Hall Of Fame Induction: 1977

Teams: 1923 to 1945, Cuban Stars (East), Homestead Grays, Hilldale, Baltimore Black Sox, Stars of Cuba, and the New York Cubans.

A superstar in every regard. Dihigo was a superb pitcher and a brilliant hitter who played every position except catcher. For more than a quarter of a century, he was the ace of many pitching staffs, and a league leader in home runs and batting average. He was the maestro of versatility. Roy Campanella recalled, "Dihigo was one of the greatest I ever saw. He was a tremendous hitter, had great power, could hit for an average, everything."

Dihigo started his career with the barnstorming Cuban Stars of the newly organized Eastern Colored League (ECL). He started out as a first baseman under owner Alex Pompez. Another first baseman, Hall of Famer Buck Leonard, claimed: "Dihigo was the best all-around baseball player I have ever seen. He could run, hit, throw, think, pitch and manage. He both knew the game and could play it. I was in the game for 23 years and I never saw anyone better than he was."

Dihigo played in Venezuela, Puerto Rico, Mexico, Cuba and the United States, where he was better known for his offense than his pitching. He batted .421 in 1926 and .370 in 1927 for the stateside Cuban Stars.

The great manager Cumberland Posey once said, "Dihigo's gifts afield have not been approached by any man—black or white." The Cuban also became the only player in the world, black or white, elected to baseball Halls of Fame in three countries; the United States, Cuba and Mexico.

The following year, Dihigo joined an unknown independent team based in the steel-mining town of Homestead, PA, located just outside of Pittsburgh. The team, owned by Posey, a former college basketball star, was called the Grays and would become one of the reigning teams of the East. Dihigo teamed with other marvelous hitters like John Beckwith and Vic Harris and splendid pitchers like Smokey Joe Williams and Sam Streeter.

In 1929, the Grays made their entrance into league play under the banner of the American Negro League. But Dihigo had settled in with the Hilldale Giants, a club from the Philadelphia suburb of Darby. He enjoyed his new surroundings, batting a royal .386. But his lofty average did not win him a crown. Teammates Oscar Charleston and Judy Johnson batted .396 and .390, respectively. The Hilldales of 1929 were loaded with speed and power. Crush Holloway led the league with 29 steals, while Johnson had

Martin Dihigo.
Jerry Malloy

23, Charleston 22, and Dihigo and Eggie Dallard had 18. With Crush and Eggie, batting in the number one and two slots, followed by Johnson, Charleston and Dihigo, they presented a most fearsome lineup. Dihigo also added 18 homeruns, second in the league only to Chino Smith (also batting champ), who had 23.

The great catcher Biz Mackey joined the team in late June. He had been suspended for taking an unauthorized Oriental junket with the Philadelphia Royal Giants. With Mackey inserted in the heart of the lineup, and able to play either catcher or shortstop, the Hilldale club dominated league play, but failed to catch the front running Baltimore Black Sox, who featured the Million Dollar Infield of Jud Wilson (1b), Frank Warfield (2b), Dick Lundy (ss) and Oliver Marcelle (3b).

After spending two seasons with the New York Cubans (1934-35) and losing an electrifying seven game series to the powerhouse Pittsburgh Crawfords, Dihigo began spending his summer seasons in the Mexican League (1937-44, 1946-47, 1950). He was primarily a pitcher down south, where he blazed to glory with a 119-57 record (.676) in eleven seasons. At the same time, he established a lifetime batting average of .317. His magical performances included a six-for-six effort in a 1937 contest. In 1938, he bewitched the Mexican League with 18 wins against only two loses, with a minuscule 0.90 ERA, meanwhile winning the batting crown with a .387 average. In 1942, he notched another ERA title to his championship belt with a 2.53 ERA. In Mexico, he threw his first no-hitter, later notching one each in Puerto Rico and Venezuela.

Dihigo also enjoyed his winters in Cuba. For 24 seasons (1922-29, 1931-46), he hit over .300 nine times for the island teams, accumulating a winter lifetime average of .291. He also put together a phenomenal 115-60 won-lost (.657) pitching performance.

After seeing Dihigo play in the winter leagues, former major league slugger Johnny Mize with a tone of admiration: "The greatest player I ever saw was a black man. He's in the Hall of Fame, although not a lot of people have heard of him. His name is Martin Dihigo. I played with him in Santo Domingo in winter ball in 1943. He was the manager. He was the only guy I ever saw who could play all nine positions, run and was a switch hitter. I though I was havin' a pretty good year myself down there and they were walkin' him to get to me."

Martin Dihigo, El Maestro, served as the Minister of Sports in Cuba, until his death at age 65. Baseball's magic man is buried in Cienfuegos, Cuba. A manager's dream, an opponent's nightmare, he remains today one of few players in baseball history who could truly do it all.

ANDREW (RUBE) FOSTER

Born September 17, 1879 at Calvert, Texas. Died December 9, 1930 at Kankakee, Illinois. Height: 6' 4". Weight: 225-260 lbs. Threw right. Batted right. Position(s) p, mgr, of.

Hall Of Fame Induction: 1981
Teams: 1898 to 1926, Waco Yellowjackets, Fort Worth Colts, Chicago Union Giants, Cuban X Giants, Philadelphia Giants, Leland Giants, Chicago American Giants.

Folks who knew Rube called him a pitcher, a cheater, a ticket taker, a popcorn maker, a showmaker, a showstopper, a money maker and, of course, a game breaker. He could do it all. The ultimate baseball attraction in one package—this was Rube Foster.

Reared in Texas by a preaching father and gospel-singing mother, Foster disobeyed his parents to pursue a career between the white foul lines. He had the God-given ability to organize and promote teams, but much credit goes to Frank Leland, a product of Fisk University, who tutored a young Rube to immortal stardom.

Young Rube's career began in 1897 with the Austin Reds of Tillotson College. The following year, he joined the semi-pro Yellowjackets in nearby Waco. The new century found Foster signing with Frank Leland's Chicago Union Giants for $40 a month and 15 cents meal money. Here, he developed a nasty screwball, thrown from an unique submarine delivery.

In 1903, he headed East to played for the Cuban X-Giants. That fall, he posted four victories in a seven-game series against the Philadelphia Giants for the so-called "Colored Championship of the World." The wandering Foster switched over to the Philly team the next season and met his old teammates for bragging rights to the "colored" title. Foster accounted for both victories in the best-of-three series. He struck out 18 batters in one game, beating the major league record of 15 set by Fred Glade of the St. Louis Browns.

Andrew Foster's reputation as a fine pitcher continue to expand with a victory over Rube Waddell and the Philadelphia Athletics in 1904, earning the nickname Rube. He also assisted John McGraw, New York Giants manager, with a few pitching tips for Christy Mathewson. Until 1903, Christy's won-lost record was 33 wins and 37 losses. After a sermon from Foster, Mathewson won 30, 33 and 31 games, and led the league in strikeouts the next three season.

In 1907, he returned to Chicago and the Leland Giants, leading them to a 110-10 record, including 48 straight wins. In 1909, the Giants enter the tough integrated city league. In Foster's first eleven starts, he won eleven games, with four shutouts. Such a dominating force that season, that after one commanding victory an Indianapolis newspaper's headlines simply stated: "FOSTER PITCHED, THAT'S ALL."

By 1910, the Leland Giants were the talk of the Midwest. They christened a ball park in an all-white neighborhood near 69th and Halsted as the Leland Giants Base Ball Park. Foster now serving as player-manager, amassed in his opinion the greatest team of all time. Featuring such stars as John Henry "Pop" Lloyd, the notorious streak hitter Pete Hill, Grant "Home Run" Johnson, catcher extraordinaire Bruce Petway and great pitchers like Frank Wickware and Pat Dougherty, the Leland team won 123 of 129 games. This impelled McGraw of the Giants to announce, "If I had a bucket of whitewash that wouldn't wash off, you wouldn't have five players left tomorrow."

The following season, Foster formed a partnership with John Schorling, a white businessman. Together they purchased the old ball park (Old Roman's) at 30th and Wentworth, from White Sox owner Charlie Comiskey. The park became home of one of black baseball's finest teams, the Chicago American Giants. Foster billed his team as "THE GREATEST AGGREGATION OF COLORED BASEBALL PLAYERS IN THE WORLD." The Giants normally played semi-pro teams for a guarantee of $60, rain or shine, with a fifty percent of the gross receipts if their ace, Rube Foster would pitch.

The Giants creative style of play epitomize black baseball. With a merciless assault on the rule book, his teams exploited every trick to its maximum advantage. Speed and quickness, gambling and risk were signature trademarks of the Midwest team, as they consistently defeated high-powered slugging teams.

Although an outstanding player, a dependable team owner and a brilliant manager, perhaps Rube Foster's most impressive fulfillment was the creation of the Negro National League (NNL) in Kansas City (1920). Foster was able to accomplish what other black entrepreneurs had been unable to achieve in 1887, 1906, and more recently in 1911. The league motto's "We Are The Ship, All Else The Sea" was symbolic of its relationship with major league baseball. Going against the tide of segregation, Rube's voyage became an obsession. For many years, Captain Rube struggled without a life preserver in his attempts to keep the league afloat.

From his throne in Chicago, Foster ran the NNL as a noble emperor. He realized the need for balance competition, as he moved players from team to team, even sending his star Oscar Charleston to the Indianapolis ABCs to help their cause. He often lent money to failing franchise to help meet their payroll and advanced monies to his own players. With unparalleled influence, Foster was the undisputed kingpin of black baseball in the Midwest.

In 1926, the czar-like, baritone-voiced Foster succumbed to mental illness and was institutionalize in Kankakee, Illinois. One of baseball's greatest minds was suddenly torn from the game. Four years later, the son of Sarah Watts and Rev. Andrew Foster, Sr., was buried in Lincoln Memorial Park in Chicago, Illinois. Foster with his dedicated, high-minded approach to baseball was the force behind all subsequent Negro Leagues.

Renowned sportswriter Frank (Fay) Young of the Chicago *Defender* testified in behalf of the late legend, "One of the most brilliant figures that the great national sports has ever produced. Rube knew every technicality of the game, how to play it, and how to make his men play it. A true master of the game."

He redefined the art of base running, hit and run techniques and the do-or-die sacrifice play. He used creative ways to "stretch" a hit, to "steal" a run and eventually "swipe" a victory. In 1981, justice was served; Foster was found guilty of larceny and sentenced to a life term, without parole, in Cooperstown's Hall of Fame.

Rube was a phenomenal pitcher, a magnificent manager, a powerful organizer, and even a greater humanitarian. He had the face of a teddy bear, the heart of Rocky Balboa, the legendary strength of John Henry, the soul of Malcolm X, the vision of Dr. Martin Luther King, the oratorical skills of James Earl Jones and the genius of Ray Charles. Rube Foster was the most perfect blend of baseball expertise ever assembled.

Josh Gibson.
Luis Alvelo

JOSHUA (JOSH) GIBSON

Born December 21, 1911 at Buena Vista, Georgia. Died January 20, 1947 at Pittsburgh, Pennsylvania. Height: 6' 2". Weight: 210-235 lbs. Threw right. Batted right. Position(s) c, of.

Hall Of Fame Induction: 1972
Teams: 1930 to 1946, Homestead Grays, Pittsburgh Crawfords

Gibson's batting feats were mythical, his power was legendary. His stroke blended the power of a piston with the smoothness of a cue ball. He was the king of swing, he mastered the masters, from Ruth to Reggie.

"There's a couple of million dollars worth of baseball talent on the loose, ready for the big leagues, yet unsigned by any major league. There are pitchers who would win twenty games a season…and outfielders who could hit .350, infielders who could win recognition as stars, and there's at least one catcher who at this writing is probably superior to Bill Dickey—Josh Gibson. Only one thing is keeping them out of the big leagues, the pigmentation of their skin." So wrote Shirley Povich of the Washington *Post* in 1941.

Gibson was the product of Mark Gibson, a steelworker and the former Nancy Woodlock. He attended public school in Buena Vista, GA, before studying at the Allegheny Pre-Vocational School in Pittsburgh to learn the electrician's trade. When he was seventeen, he married 18-year-old Helen Mason, who died in labor, delivering their twins, Josh, Jr. and Helen.

Gibson's legendary career began in 1927, with the semi-pro Pittsburgh Crawfords of Compton Hill. Three years later, while attending a Homestead Grays game, young Josh suddenly got his first chance at pro ball. The Grays catcher Buck Ewing had to leave the game with a split thumb. Some of the Grays players had seen Gibson play, and they asked him to take Ewing's place behind the plate. Unpolished as a catcher, but country-boy strong, he made a lasting impression on the Grays and the host team, the Kansas City Monarchs. He stayed with the Grays for two seasons (1930-31) and then jumped to the flash of cash from Gus Greenlee, to play for the cross-town rival Crawfords. He won homerun titles in 1932, 1934, and 1936 while wearing Crawford red. Gibson rejoined the Grays and Buck Leonard in 1937. The '37 edition of the Grays split their home games between Washington DC and Pittsburgh. Before the season ended, Gibson along with several teammates ran off to play for the Santo Domingo dictator, Rafael Trujillo. The 1937 edition of Trujillo's team was stacked with superstars of the Negro Leagues. Held under armed guard, the team won the championship and the dictator won re-election.

Gibson returned to the Homestead Grays and picked up where he left off. He won homerun crowns in 1938 and 1939, and his first batting title in 1938 with a stunning .440. Gibson was noted for his long distance drives. Teammate Buck Leonard said, "Nobody hit the ball as far as Gibson. I didn't see the one he is supposed to have hit out of Yankee Stadium. But I saw him hit a ball one night in the Polo Grounds that went between the upper deck and lower deck and out of the stadium. Later the night watchman came in and said, 'Who hit the damned ball out there?' He said it landed on the El. It must have gone 600 feet."

Gibson played briefly in Mexico and Puerto Rico, winning the Puerto Rican batting title in 1941 with an incredible .480 average and being named Most Valuable Player. After becoming very ill in Mexico, he returned to the Grays in 1942. Despite intermittent health problems, Gibson won homerun crowns in 1942, 1943, and 1946, plus a batting title in 1943, hitting .521.

Gibson didn't just destroy Negro League pitchers, he also beat up on white major leaguers. In a recorded 60 at bats against the likes of Dizzy and Daffy Dean, Johnny Vander Meer, and others, Josh hit .426, including five home runs. His bat was an equal opportunity banger.

Monte Irvin recalls a day in the life of Josh. "On opening day in Newark of 1941, we were leading the Grays 2-0 in the ninth inning with two outs. Jimmy Hill walked (Sam) Bankhead and (Buck) Leonard with Josh Gibson coming up. Leon Day was in the bullpen. He got two quick strikes on Josh and tried to slip the third one by him. He hit it in the center field bleachers to beat us 3-2, before 22,000 disappointed fans. Mrs. Effa Manley after the game said to Josh, 'You should be ashamed of yourself for spoiling our opener.' Josh replied, 'Mrs. Manley, I break hearts all over the country every summer. If you don't believe me just ask any pitcher.'"

Breaking pitchers' hearts was Gibson's business. In 1943, the unromantic Josh hit 10 home runs out of spacious Griffith Stadium, a feat never duplicated by any major leaguer. The back wall of the left field bleachers was cleared only three times. Mickey Mantle did it once, with a 565 foot blast, and Josh did it twice. Historian John Coates credits Gibson with 823 home runs in 22 years, including the pro winter leagues. Considering Gibson played the majority of his career in Forbes Field (center field 457 ft.) and Griffith Stadium (421 in center), his homerun totals could have been higher had he played in some of the band boxes in the league.

Max Manning, former ace of the Newark Eagles pitching staff recalled: "I never saw Josh take a leaving-the-ground swing. It was always a smooth, quick stroke. A lot of guys would swing, the ground would shake, the air would move, and their hats would fly off. But he'd just take that short, quick stroke, and that ball would leave any ballpark."

Gibson was the ultimate hitter. He hit with power, for a high average, and seldom struck out. He was a blue-collar slugger without the glitz and glamour of his major league counterparts. Gibson was simply known as Josh—no nicknames, no monikers, no labels.

In late 1942, Gibson begun to suffer from recurring headaches and dizzy spells. On New Year's Day of 1943, he was hospitalized for 10 days after doctors discovered a brain tumor. The man-child Josh refused to allow an operation. He returned to baseball, while the headaches and blackouts continued, eventually eroding his mythical skills. Gibson died at the age of 35. He was buried in Allegheny Cemetery in Pittsburgh, PA.

Gibson will be the eternal monarch of homerun kings. He dominated the game with majestic power like none before him. Former Crawford teammate Judy Johnson boasted, "If Josh Gibson had been in the big leagues in his prime, Babe Ruth and Hank Aaron would still be chasing him for the home run record."

MONFORD MERRILL (MONTE) IRVIN

Born February 25, 1919 at Columbia, Alabama. Height: 6' 2". Weight: 190-195 lbs. Threw right. Batted right. Position(s) 3b, ss, of.

Hall Of Fame Induction: 1973
Teams: 1937 to 1957, Newark Eagles, New Jersey Giants (INT), New York Giants (NL), Minneapolis Millers (AA), Chicago Cubs (NL) and the Los Angeles Angeles (PCL).

A high-energy player with vitality, vigor and vim, shortstop Irvin was the anchor of the Newark Eagles championship infield. When Effa Manley owner of the Newark Eagles lost Monte Irvin to the big leagues, she voiced her opinion of Branch Rickey initial selection to integrate baseball, "Monte was the choice of all Negro National and American League club owners to serve as the No. 1 player to join a white major league team. We all agreed, in meetings, he was the best qualified by tempera-ment, character, ability, sense of loyalty, morals, age, experience and physique to represent us as the first black player to enter the white majors since the Walker brothers (Moses and Weldy) back in the late 1880's. Of course, Branch Rickey lifted Jackie Robinson of the Negro ball and made him the first, and it turned out fine."

Monte Irvin was the seventh of ten children born to farmer Cupid Irvin and the former Mary Eliza Henderson. When Irvin was eight, the family of six boys and four girls migrated to Orange, NJ were Irvin lettered in four sports, earning all-state honors for East Orange High School and setting a state record for the javelin throw. An all-state football player with speed and agility, he declined a football scholarship to the University of Michigan. Instead, Irvin joined future teammate Max Manning at Lincoln University in Oxford, PA, where he majored in political science for two years.

In 1937, at the age of 18, Irvin joined the Newark Eagles under the assumed name of Jimmy Nelson, to protect his amateur collegiate status. After two years under the management of Willie Wells, Irvin matured into a fine shortstop earning his first berth to the 1941 East All-Star team. (After serving in the military, he also played in Negro League all-star games in 1946, 1947 and 1948).

Irvin was a terrific hitter, batting .422 in 1940 and leading the Negro National League the next year with a .396 average. Irvin recalls one of the highlights of his career: "In 1941, on a road trip with the (Homestead) Grays we beat them three games in one day. We beat (Terris) McDuffie and (Roy) Welmaker in Columbus (Ohio) and defeated Ray Brown in Dayton that night to complete the sweep."

He had signed a contract in 1941 for $165 a month. When Irvin asked for a $25 raise, owner Effa Manley rejected his offer, sending Monte packing his bat and glove for Mexico. In 68 games, Irvin slammed 30 homeruns and hit .398 to win the Mexican League triple crown. Irvin was at the top of his game when Uncle Sam called for him to serve in the U.S. Army for the next three years, and this possibly preventing him from being the first African American to break baseball's apartheid system.

"Monte was our best young ballplayer at the time," remembered James "Cool Papa" Bell. "He could do everything. You see, we wanted men who could go there and hit the ball over the fence, and Monte could do that. He could hit that long ball, he had a great arm, he could field, he could run. Yes, he could do everything. It's not that Jackie Robinson wasn't a good ballplayer; but we wanted Monte because we knew what he could do. But after Monte Irvin went to the Army and came back, he was sick (inner ear problem), and then they passed him up and looked for somebody else."

Although Irvin never regained the athletic form of his pre-service days, he earned the 1945-46 Puerto Rican Most Valuable Player Award. In 1946, he returned to his homeland and joined forces with Larry Doby, Leon Day, and Lennie Pearson under the management of Biz Mackey to lead the Eagles to a Negro National League pennant.

Monte Irvin.
Moorland-Spingarn Library

He hit .389 for the season and was instrumental in beating the Kansas City Monarchs in a seven game series with three round-trippers and hitting a flashy .462.

Irvin played two more seasons with Newark despite Brooklyn Dodger executive Branch Rickey's many attempts to sign him. After the 1948-49 season in Cuba, the New York Giants paid the Newark Eagles $5,000 for Irvin's services. Assigned to the Jersey City club of the International League, he proceeded to terrorized pitchers with a .373 batting average.

In the heat of a pennant race, the Giants called for Irvin in mid-July. Irvin failed to stick with the parent club, but immediately proved the Giants wrong, hitting .510 with 10 homers in only 18 games after being sent back down, and the team recalled him.

Irvin played in 764 major leagues games and become the first product of the Negro Leagues to led the majors in RBIs, with 121 in 1951. He teamed that year with Hank Thompson and Willie Mays to form major league baseball's first all-black outfield. The '51 season was the pinnacle of his major league career. He hit .312 with 24 homeruns and finished third in the MVP voting, while leading the team to the World Series. Although the Giants lost to the Yankees in six games, Irvin hit .458 and flashed some of the old speed with a steal of home plate against Allie Reynolds.

Tragedy struck the next year when Irvin broke his ankle in spring training. After four months of rehabilitation, he hit .310, but his speed had vanished. In 1953, he was hitting .329 when he re-injured the ankle, and he never regained his stellar form, batting only .262 during the Giants World Championship season of 1954. In 1955, after a .253 start in his first 51 games, he was demoted to Minneapolis, where he hit .352 in 75 games. After the season, the Giants traded Irvin to the Chicago Cubs. At the age of 39, Irvin's contract was sold to Chicago's Los Angeles Angels farm club. He finished his major league career with a .293 average, 97 doubles, 99 homeruns, and 443 runs scored. Irvin added a dazzling .394 average to his list of credits for two World Series performances.

After the 1956 season, the cerebral Monte traded his bat for a pen. He scouted for the New York Mets in 1967-68, and later spent 16 years (1968-1984) as a public relations specialist for the commissioner's office. Today, Irvin serves on the Veterans' Committee of the Hall of Fame and actively campaigns for recognition of baseball's forgotten pioneers.

William Julius "Judy" Johnson.
Todd Bolton

WILLIAM JULIUS (JUDY) JOHNSON

Born October 26, 1899 at Snow Hill, Maryland. Died June 15, 1989 at Wilmington, Delaware. Height: 5' 11". Weight: 145-165 lbs. Threw right. Batted right. Position(s) 3b, ss, mgr.

Hall Of Fame Induction: 1975
Teams: 1918, 1921 to 1938, Bacharach Giants, Hilldale Giants, Homestead Grays, and the Pittsburgh Crawfords.

The ultimate clutch-hitter, Johnson shamelessly indulged in game-winning hits and rally-killing catches. Judy Johnson was a bashful, quiet player with an astonishing ability to perform under pressure. He was respected for his intellectual approach to the game, excelling with grace and poise; providing a positive influence on teammates and opponents.

Ted Page, a former outfielder for the Crawfords, bragged, "Judy Johnson was the smartest third baseman I ever came across. A scientific ball player, did everything with grace and poise. You talk about playing third base—heck, he was better than anybody I saw. And I saw Brooks Robinson, Mike Schmidt and even Pie Traynor. He had a powerful, accurate arm. He could do anything, come in for a ball, cut if off at the line, or range way over toward the shortstop hole. He was really something."

Johnson was the son of William Henry Johnson and Annie Lee Johnson. His father was a sailor, a licensed boxing coach and the athletic director of the Negro

Settlement House in Wilmington. Judy learn to box from his older sister Emma, meanwhile playing baseball for the local Royal Blues. His pro career started with Tom Jackson's Bacharach Giants in 1918 for five bucks a game. The following year, he tried out for Ed Bolden's Hilldale team, the premier team in the area. He was considered too small and failed to make the cut. He joined the local Chester Stars to develop his skills. In 1921, he signed with the semi-pro Madison Stars before finally hooking up with the Hilldale club.

In his first pro season, he played behind Bill Francis at third, hitting a modest .227. Judy credits John Henry "Pop" Lloyd with his early development. "He's the man I gave the credit to for polishing my skills. He taught me how to play third base and how to protect myself. John taught me more baseball than anyone else." The well-schooled disciple of "Pop" developed into a full-time star leading the Hilldales to their first Eastern Colored League pennant, in 1923, with a .391 average. The following season, Hilldale behind Johnson's .324 average hosted the Kansas City Monarchs in the first official Colored World Series. Johnson led all batters in hitting .364, and slugging .614. He led the series in RBIs (8), hits (16), and added an inside-the-park home run in a thrilling nine-game series lost to the Monarchs.

Judy continued to punch in over .300 every season until he suffered a beaning in August 1926, in Atlantic City. It affected his confidence, and he slumped to .268 (1927) and .224 (1928). In 1929, Johnson shook off the wraps and proceeded to hit a hefty .390. This prompted sportswriter Rollo Wilson of the Pittsburgh Courier to name Johnson the league's Most Valuable Player. Lloyd Thompson, writer and former scorekeeper for the Hilldale Club recalled, "Judy could do all that is required to make up a sterling third baseman and do it better than the rest of the field. A right handed hitter, Judy developed a peculiar stance at the plate and hit the ball hard to all corners of the lot. Slight of build, this Hilldale luminary was a fielding gem, whose breath-taking plays on bunts and hard smashes are treasured among many fans memoirs."

After such a great comeback, Johnson's services were in much demand. Johnson left Hilldale and became a player-manager for the Homestead Grays in 1930 and then returned to the Darby Daises, a spin-off of the Hilldales, in 1931. He was back with the Grays at the start of the 1932 season, but midway through the season he jumped to the Pittsburgh Crawfords, where he finished his fine career in 1936.

In 1935, the Crawfords named Judy Johnson captain of their team over such stellar stars as Paige, Gibson, and Bell. This star-studded team, managed by Oscar Charleston, won 39 games and lost 15, defeating the New York Cubans and Luis Tiant, Sr., in a seven-game series for the Negro National League pennant.

Following his retirement from the Crawfords, he

traveled with them to Mexico to play against major league all-stars like Jimmie Foxx and Rogers Hornsby. In twenty games against white major league talent, he batted .263. He spent six seasons in the Cuban Winter Leagues (1923-1930) and hit .331 in 499 at bats.

After Johnson retired from baseball, he coached the Alco Flashes, a semi-pro basketball team. They became the Delaware State Champions in 1937, featuring former pitcher Bill Campbell at guard and shortstop Bill Yancey at forward. Meanwhile, he drove a cab for the Continental Cab Company in Wilmington before becoming a major league scout.

Johnson was renowned as a fine teacher of baseball art and worked as a scout for the Connie Mack's Philadelphia Athletics. Mack told him, "If you were a white boy, you could name your own price." He later scouted for the Milwaukee Braves and the Philadelphia Phillies. He is credited with signing slugger Richie Allen and Billy Bruton, later to become his son-in-law. "Judy could have done the major leagues a lot more good as somebody who could help develop ball players," said Crawford teammate Ted Page. "He should have been in the majors 15 to 20 years ago as a coach. They talk about Negro managers. I always thought Judy would have made a perfect major league manager."

The articulate Cool Papa Bell once bragged: "Johnson was the best hitter among the four top third basemen in the Negro Leagues, but no one would drive in as many clutch runs as he would. He was a solid ballplayer, real smart, but he was the kind of fellow who could 'just get it done.' He was dependable, quiet, not flashy at all, but could handle anything that came up. No matter how much the pressure, no matter how important the play or the throw or the hit, Judy could do it when it counted."

After election to Cooperstown glory, in November of 1975, the city of Wilmington in recognition of his contribution to baseball and the improved quality of life for young adults named the park on Second and du Pont Streets "Judy Johnson Park."

The patriotic Johnson died on Flag Day. Half-masted flags flew for a full pledge pressure performer. His wife, the former Anita T. Irons, a school teacher, had died earlier in 1986. They had been married for 63 years and had one daughter, Loretta.

WALTER FENNER (BUCK) LEONARD

Born September 8, 1907 at Rocky Mount, North Carolina. Height: 5' 10". Weight: 180-195 lbs. Threw left. Batted left. Position(s) 1b, of.

Hall Of Fame Induction: 1972
Teams: 1933 to 1953, Baltimore Stars, Brooklyn Royal Giants, Homestead Grays, Portsmouth (Piedmont League).

Leonard hit pitchers like a tropical storm. With a strong turbulent stroke, he uprooted pitchers, knocked-down fielders and destroyed teams from town to town. A powerful pull-hitter, Buck was a torrential terror at the plate. He normally proceeded another storm in the line-up named Josh Gibson. Together, Buck and Josh were the twin twisters of the Homestead dynasties in the late 30s and 40s.

A superb first baseman, Leonard was a model of consistency, digging throws out of the dirt, seizing bunts, and showcasing an accurate and powerful throwing arm. He was often compared to George Sisler because of his smooth style of play. Eastern booking agent, Eddie Gottlieb recalled, "Buck Leonard was as smooth a first baseman as I ever saw. In those days, the first baseman on a team in the Negro League often played the clown. They had a funny way of catching the ball so the fans would laugh, but

Buck Leonard.
Robert H. Mc Neill

Leonard was strictly baseball: a great glove, a hell of a hitter, and drove in runs."

The rock-steady, dependable, quiet, easy going Buck was named captain of the Grays team and served in that capacity until they folded in 1950. Leonard was the son of John Leonard, a railroad fireman and Emma. He left school at age 14 to work as a shoeshine boy and a mill hand for the Atlantic Coast Railroad. He played semi-pro ball until he lost his job during the Depression, when professional baseball proved to be his only alternative. At the age of 25, Leonard left the sandlots of Rocky Mount to become one of the finest first baseman in the game.

Leonard and his brother Charley (a pitcher) received their initial training with the semi-pro Rocky Mount Elks, the Black Swans and Dougherty's Black Revels. In 1933, Buck went to Portsmouth, Virginia, to play for the Firefighters, where he was discovered by the legendary first baseman Ben Taylor, manager of the Baltimore Stars. Taylor signed Leonard and taught him the art of first sacking and power hitting. When the Stars went bankrupt later that year, he caught the eye of manager Cannonball Dick Redding and signed with the Brooklyn Royal Giants, an independent team.

A close friend of Redding's, another former pitcher, now a bartender, Smokey Joe Williams recommended Leonard to Cum Posey, owner and manager of the Homestead Grays. Leonard joined Posey's Grays in 1934 and stayed for 17 years, anchored at first base. The next year, he was voted to his first of twelve East-West All-Star squads. His All-Star average was .317, with a record three All-Star home runs.

Teaming with Josh Gibson, Vic Harris, Howard Easterling, Cool Papa Bell, Jud Wilson and others, he and the Grays won nine straight league championships from 1937 to 1945, with a repeat performance in 1948. In 1948, now 40, and without the late Gibson batting behind him, pitchers still respected Leonard. He tied with teammate Luke Easter for the NNL home run crown with 13 and grabbed the batting title with a .395 average.

The 1948 edition of the Grays were Buck's favorite team. They featured Easter, Sam Bankhead, Luis Marquez with Wilmer "Red" Fields as their ace. They defeated an up and coming Birmingham Black Barons team, which featured rookie Willie Mays, for a unprecedented third Negro World Series championship.

At the time of the Grays' demise, Leonard was earning $1,000 a month and $2 a day for meal money. By 1948, Leonard claimed he was earning about $10,000 annually, including winter league ball. When he retired, it was reported that he was the third highest paid player in Negro League history behind Satchel Paige and Gibson.

The raiding of Negro League players by the majors caused the Grays to break up in 1950. Leonard went south to Mexico and played three years with Torreon and two years with Durango. He played 12 winters in Puerto Rico,

Cuba, Venezuela, and Mexico and with the Satchel Paige All-Stars in the California winter league against the Major League All-Stars in 1943. He batted .500 in eight games before commissioner Judge Landis halted the exhibitions.

Buck Leonard retired with an unofficial lifetime average of .324 and hit .419 in 27 post game appearances. In 1936 and 1943, in seven exhibition games against major league pitchers, Leonard hit .421 .

On December 31, 1937, he married Sarah Wroten, from Hertford, NC. They were married until her death on February 22, 1966. They had no children.

At age 46, Leonard made his only appearance in Organized Baseball with a 10-game stint, in 1953, with the Portsmouth club, hitting .333. He played two years in Mexico with Durango and retired at age 48. Later in 1962, the generous Leonard helped organize the Rocky Mount club in the Class-A Carolina League, serving as vice-president. Later, in 1966, he became a probation officer and athletic director for the school district and opened up his own real estate company in Rocky Mount were he lives today with his second wife, Lugenia.

When the color line was broken, Bill Veeck tried to sign the 40-year old Leonard. Looking back on his career, Leonard admits, "I was not 'bitter' by not being allowed to play in the major leagues. I just said, 'The time has not come.' I only wish I could have played in the big leagues when I was young enough to show what I could do. When an offer was given me to join up, I was too old and I knew it."

JOHN HENRY (POP) LLOYD

Born April 25, 1884 at Gainesville, Florida. Died March 19, 1965 at Atlantic City, New Jersey. Height: 6' 0". Weight: 170-185 lbs. Threw right. Batted left. Position(s) 1b, 2b, ss, of, mgr.

Hall Of Fame Induction: 1977
Teams: 1905 to 1931, Cuban X Giants, Philadelphia Giants, Leland Giants, Lincoln Giants, Chicago American Giants, Brooklyn Royal Giants, Columbus Buckeyes, Bacharach Giants, Kansas City Monarchs, Hilldale Giants, New York Black Yankees, Harlem Stars, and the Lincoln Stars.

The quintessential shortstop—great hands, an accurate arm, Lloyd could perform the double play with ballerina grace and slug for average and power. They called him "Pop," for he was the granddaddy of them all. He tutored the best and beat the rest.

Lloyd has been described as a left-handed, line-drive hitter, who used a closed stance. He held the bat in the cradle of his left elbow, and would uncoiled from his comfortable stance to unleash a controlled swing. Lloyd ran with long smooth strides, deceiving oppoRobert H. McNeillnents who did not realize his dangerous speed, until it was too late.

The tall, angular man with the Dick Tracy chin was a non-drinker who never cursed and was viewed as a gentleman. His peers claimed Pop was a complete professional, on and off the field. Cum Posey, owner of the Homestead Grays, added: "Lloyd is the Jekyll and Hyde of baseball—a fierce competitor on the field, but a gentle, considerate man off the field."

John Henry "Pop" Lloyd.
National Baseball Library, Cooperstown, NY

The nomadic Lloyd started his barnstorming career with the semi-pro Macon Acmes in Georgia, as a catcher. The following season, he joined the Cuban X-Giants of Philadelphia as a second baseman. The highlight of the season was a game against Connie Mack's Philadelphia Athletics for the city title. The Giants lost, but Pop spanked Mack's pitchers for four hits. Lloyd was often compared to Honus Wagner. Connie Mack, who saw some of the best players during 50 years of active ownership was quoted as saying, "You could put Wagner and Lloyd in a bag together, and whichever one you pulled out you couldn't go wrong."

After one season with the Cuban X-Giants, he joined the Philadelphia Giants under the mentorship of Sol White for the next three years. In 1910, he joined Rube Foster's powerhouse Leland Giants, who compiled a 123-6 record. He later went to the Lincoln Giants, where he hit .475 (1911) and .376 (1912). In 1910, Lloyd played in Cuba with the Havana Reds, along with stateside stars Bruce Petway, Grant "Home Run" Johnson and Pete Hill. The Reds played a series of exhibition games against Ty Cobb and the Detroit Tigers. Cobb hit .369 in five games, but was unable to steal a base against catcher Petway, claiming he would never played against blacks again. Meanwhile, Cobb's average was surpassed by Pop Lloyd at .500 (11 for 22), Grant Johnson at .412 and Petway at .388.

The popular Lloyd spent 12 seasons in Cuba, playing for the Reds, Havana, Fe, and the Almendares teams. In Cuba, he earned the nickname "El Cuchara," the shovel, because of his propensity to scoop up handfuls of dirt when charging for grounders. In a dozen seasons of winter ball, he compiled a batting average of .331 and led the leagues in triples twice and stolen bases once.

Foster enticed Lloyd to join his Chicago American Giants team in 1914. From 1914 to 1917, Lloyd batted clean-up for one of the dominate independent teams of the Midwest. These teams consisted of some of the greatest players ever to play America's game: Oscar Charleston, Bingo DeMoss, Louis Santop, Pete Hill, Ben Taylor, Bruce Petway, Bill Monroe and pitchers, Cyclone Joe Williams, Cannonball Dick Redding, and Frank Wickware. The Giants won the colored championship honors in 1914 and 1917.

Approaching the age of 35, the old man signed with the Brooklyn Royal Giants as player-manager. Lloyd played three abbreviated seasons for the Royal Giants, before going to the Columbus Buckeyes in 1921. Now 37, Lloyd led the new Columbus franchise in game played, hits, doubles and stolen bases, while hitting a solid .336.

The eternal youngster, Lloyd hit .387 (1922) with the Bacharach Giants, before moving on the Hilldale Giants to hit .386 (1923). Back with the Bacharachs in 1924, he led the league with an astonishing .433 average, setting a league record with 11 consecutive hits. He re-joined the Lincoln Giants out of New York in 1926. There, Old Man River just kept flowing with averages of .349, .375 and an

incredible .564 average at the age of 44, to win another batting title.

In 1931, now 47, Pop finished his career with his old friends, Clint Thomas and Red Ryan on the New York Black Yankees. He retired the following year with the hometown Bacharach Giants, playing mostly at first base.

How did Lloyd perform against major leaguer pitching? In 29 recorded games, he hit for a .321 average against 20-game winners like Addie Joss, Wabash George Mullin, Chief Bender, Gettysburg Eddie Plank and Rube Marquard.

In 1938, many years after Lloyd's career was over, Ted Harlow, a St. Louis sportswriter paid Lloyd the ultimate compliment, when asked "Who was the best baseball player in the history of the sport?" He replied, "If you mean in organized baseball, my answer would be Babe Ruth; but if you mean in all baseball, organized and unorganized, I would have to say it is a colored man named John Henry Lloyd."

After retiring from professional baseball, Lloyd coached and played semi-pro ball with the Johnson Stars, later known as the Farley Stars, (named after State Senator "Hap" Farley) until 1942, when he turned 58. In his later years, Lloyd worked as a janitor at the Atlantic City post office and school system. Always having a love for children, he served as the Little League commissioner for many years. On October 2, 1949, as Jackie Robinson was being named the Most Valuable Player in the National League, Atlantic City rewarded its foster father with the dedication of a $125,000 stadium at Indiana and Huron Avenues. It bears the name "'Pop' Henry Lloyd" and an inscribed plaque: "To a great ball player and a fine man."

After a two-year illness, suffering from arteriosclerosis, he died in 1965. His wife Nan was the only surviving family member. He was buried in Atlantic City, New Jersey. Ask the graybeards of baseball history and they will tell you that the popular "Pop" was the paternal player. Former diamond star and basketball magician Bill Yancey said, with a bit of awe in his voice, "Pop Lloyd was the greatest player, the greatest manager, the greatest teacher. He had ability and knowledge and, above all, patience. I did not know what baseball was until I played under him on the Lincoln Giants."

LEROY ROBERT (SATCHEL) PAIGE

Born July 7, 1906 at Mobile, Alabama. Died June 8, 1982 in Kansas City, Missouri. Height: 6' 3-1/2". Weight: 175-180 lbs. Threw right Batted right. Position(s) p, coach.

Hall Of Fame Induction: 1971
Teams: 1924 to 1967, Birmingham Black Barons, Baltimore Black Sox, Nashville Elite Giants, Cleveland Cubs, St. Louis Stars, Pittsburgh Crawfords, Trujillo All-

Stars, Kansas City Monarchs, Memphis Red Sox, New York Black Yankees, Paige's All-Stars, Philadelphia Stars, Chicago American Giants, Cleveland Indians (AL), St. Louis Browns (AL), Kansas City Athletics (AL), Miami Marlins (IL), Portland Beavers (PCL), Springfield Redbirds (AA), Atlanta Braves (NL), Indianapolis Clowns, and many more short stops with local, exhibition, and semi-pro squads.

The great Satch was known as much for his crowd-pleasing charisma and his phenomenal longevity and resiliency as for his legendary athletic achievements on pitchers mounds all over the Western Hemisphere. During his heyday of the thirties and forties, he was perhaps baseball's greatest gate attraction.

He was born the sixth child of twelve (including a set of twins) to John Paige, a gardener, and the former Lula Coleman, a domestic worker. At age 12, he was sent to the Industrial School for Negro Children in Mount Meigs,

Alabama, for shoplifting and truancy from W.C. Council School. There, he developed his pitching skills and, in 1924, joined the semi-pro Mobile Tigers.

On May 1, 1926, Paige made his professional pitching debut with the Chattanooga Black Lookouts of the Negro Southern League. In 1928, the Birmingham Black Barons purchased Paige's contract, paying him a phenomenal $275 a month. He jumped from the Black Barons to the Black Sox of Baltimore to the Nashville Elite Giants and finally the Cleveland Cubs, before settling with the Crawfords of Pittsburgh, in 1932. Three years later, he teamed with four other future Hall of Famers: Charleston, Bell, Johnson and Gibson, to win the Crawfords a league championship. He stayed with the Crawfords until 1937, when the Dominican Republic dictator, Rafael Trujillo, enticed him and other prominent stars of the Negro Leagues to stock his politically motivated team.

When Paige returned to the United States, his Crawfords contract was sold to one of baseball's few women owners: Effa Manley of the Newark Eagles. He refused to report to the Eagles and headed to Mexico, were

Satchel Paige.
Alvelo Collection

he promptly developed a sore arm that put his baseball career in jeopardy.

Paige returned to the U.S. and began to rehabilitate his arm by playing first base and pitching short stretches for the Kansas City Monarchs B-team, called either the Stars or the Travelers. He gradually worked his arm back to good health and became the ace of the Monarch pitching staff, leading them to the Negro World Series in 1942 and 1946. In the first series, the Monarchs swept the Homestead Grays in four games. Paige appeared in all four contests, winning three.

On Paige's forty-second birthday, he signed with Bill Veeck, owner of the Cleveland Indians. A record crowd of 78,383 for a night game watched Paige make his first major league appearance. Later, in his first starting role, he drew 72,434 fans in Cleveland's Municipal Stadium. As the oldest rookie in baseball, he won six times against one loss, helping the Indians to a pennant and earning a World Series appearance against the Boston Braves.

In 1949, Veeck sold his controlling interest in the Indians, forcing Paige to seek employment elsewhere. When Veeck purchased the lowly St. Louis Browns in 1951, he promptly signed old Satchel again. Incredibly, the following year, at the age of 46, Paige enjoyed one of his finest major league seasons. He won twelve games and was selected to the All-Star team, achieving another honor as baseball's oldest selection.

After Veeck became vice-president of the Miami Marlins of the International League, he signed Paige. In three years, Paige only walked 54 batters in 340 innings. Quite a feat for a player over fifty years old.

Paige briefly returned to the baseball scene in 1965, with a three-inning appearance with the Kansas City Athletics. When his two-month contract for $4,000 expired, the 59-year-old legend retired from baseball. He was later hired as a coach for the Atlanta Braves to complete the 158 days he needed to qualify for his major league pension.

On June 5, 1982, Paige, 75, suffering from the lingering illness of emphysema made his last public appearance. Speaking from a wheelchair, he graciously received recognition at the dedication of a $250,000 renovated park, to be called the Satchel Paige Memorial Stadium, in Kansas City, Missouri. Paige died three days later and was buried in Forest Hill Memorial Park Cemetery in Kansas City, Missouri. He was survived by his wife of nearly 35 years, the former Lahoma Jean Brown, and eight children.

Despite the lack of a formal education, the great Satchel Paige was honored with the dedication of a new magnet school on October 9, 1991, called the Leroy "Satchel" Paige Classical Greek Academy. The academy promotes the Greek philosophy of "body and spirit", symbolizing Paige as one of the most physically talented and spirited bodies to play the sport.

His homespun philosophy characterizes his impact on our national pastime: (1) Avoid fried foods which anger the blood, (2) If your stomach disputes you, lie down and pacify it with cooling thoughts, (3) Keep the juices flowing by jangling around gently as you move, (4) Go very lightly on the vices, such as carrying on in society—the social ramble ain't restful, (5) Avoid running at all times and (6) Don't look back. Something might be gaining on you.

Fittingly, on August 9, 1971, he became the first player from the Negro Leagues elected to Cooperstown's National Baseball Hall of Fame. When he accepted his award, he told the admirers that in the Negro Leagues, "there were many Satchels and many Joshes." Paige was the ultimate showman whose only major league counterpart was Gashouse Gang Cardinal pitcher, Dizzy Dean. Dean once boasted, "If Satch and me was pitching on the same team, we'd clinch the pennant by the fourth of July and go fishing until World Series time."

Hero's Welcome

One of the best of the small group of black players in organized baseball in the late 1800s was an infielder named Frank Grant, who was well known in the Northeastern United States as an outstanding ballplayer. When he joined the Harrisburg, PA, team in the Interstate League in May 1890, he got a welcome that most players, of any race and era, could only dream about. From the May 6 *Harrisburg Patriot:* "Long before it was time for the game to begin, it was whispered around the crowd that Grant would arrive on the 3.20 train and play third base. Everybody was anxious to see him come and there was a general stretch of necks towards the new bridge, all being eager to get a sight of the most famous colored ball player in the business. At 3.45 o'clock an open carriage was seen coming over the bridge with two men in it. Jim Russ' famous trotter was drawing it at a 2.20 speed and as it approached nearer, the face of Grant was recognized as being one of the men. 'There he comes,' went through the crowd like magnetism and three cheers went up. Grant was soon in the players' dressing room and in five minuets *(sic)* he appeared on the diamond in a Harrisburg uniform. A great shout went up from the immense crowd to receive him, in recognition of which he politely raised his cap. Grant's splendid work at the bat and on the bag pleased the 'fans', and he was greeted with applause each time he came to the bat."

—*Malloy*

Rosters

1862–1955

These are the most complete and accurate Negro Leagues rosters available, the culmination of over 25 years of research. Most of the rosters are taken from actual box scores, professional and semi-pro. We occasionally found yearly rosters and/or Spring rosters for various clubs. We have included teams back to 1862 because we did not want to ignore the prominent black professional teams prior to the formation of leagues. Some names that appear in this section are *not* listed in the Register. Generally this occurs when we have only a common last name, like Johnson, Smith, or Williams. To help researchers follow the careers of certain players, we have also included the rosters of many non-league teams.

In the rosters, we use the names most commonly associated with individual players. We use a four-column position system. The first column shows the positions played by the starters. The second column shows where reserves most often played, or where first-stringers sometimes filled in. The third column shows a starter's third position or a reserve's second. The fourth column contains an "M" for managers, or, more rarely, the notation "coach."

We have printed rosters by years, rather than by team. This makes it easy to compare rosters, and also to follow players who played for several teams in a single season. Teams are listed alphabetically by city, with those without a city affiliation first.

The front and back of a 1945 season ticket for the Washington Homestead Grays at Griffith Stadium.
Negro Leagues Baseball Museum

Player	1	2	3	Player	1	2	3	Player	1	2	3

1862

Brooklyn Monitor

Player	1	2	3
G. Abrams	p		
J. Abrams	cf		
? Brown	c		
W. Cook	rf		
? Cook	lf		
? Dudley	1b		
? Marshall	3b		
? Orater	2b		
? Williams	ss		

Weeksville Unknown

Player	1	2	3
? Durant	rf		
? Harvey	ss		
? Johnson	c		
? Pole	3b		
? Smith	cf		
V. Thompson	lf		
J. Thompson	p		
A. Thompson	1b		
? Wright	2b		

1870

Boston Resolutes

Player	1	2	3
? Banfield	ss		
? Churchill	2b		
? Cruckendie	cf		
? Gregory	p		
? Humphrey	1b		
? Molineaux	3b		
? Shepard	lf		
W. Taylor	c		
J. Taylor	rf		

1883

Cleveland Blue Stockings

Player	1	2	3
? Doctor	1b		
? Dorton	3b	p	
? Milligan	lf		
? Sabb	rf	2b	
? Smith	p		
Sam Smith	cf		
? Stanley	c		
? Tripp	2b		
? Wilson	ss		
? Wilson		rf	2b

St. Louis Black Stockings

Player	1	2	3
? Bracy	cf		
? Canter	ss		
Art Carter (Ike)	2b		
? Davis	p		
? Gordon	lf		
? Hannis		c	
? Obauvon	3b		
? Rodgers	1b		
William Smith (Big Bill)	rf	2b	c
? Sutton		c	

1884

Baltimore Atlantics

Player	1	2	3
George Burrell	p	c	
F. Call	3b		
F.T. Dorsey	2b		
William Gray	of		
James Harris	of		
Joe Johnson	p	c	
James Proctor	p	c	
J. Raine	of		
C. Slaughter	inf		
Joe Stuart	p		
L. Washington	ss		
Solomon Williams (Sol)	of		

Philadelphia Mutual BB Club

Player	1	2	3
J. Butler			
J. Cisco			
C. Cooper			
A. Fisher			
F. Fisher			
W. Fisher			
E. Harris			
D. Jones			
A. Mitchell			

1885

Babylon (NY) Argyle Hotel

Player	1	2	3
John F. Lang			M
Ben Boyd	cf	2b	
Milton Dabney	rf	lf	
Guy Day	c		
William Eggleston		ss	
Frank Harris	p		
Abe Harrison		ss	
Ben Holmes	3b		
R. Martin	p		
Charles Nichols	lf	rf	
George Parego	p		
Andrew Randolph	1b		
Shep Trusty	p		
George Williams	2b	1b	

Baltimore Atlantics

Player	1	2	3
George Burrell	p	c	
F. Call	3b		
F.T. Dorsey	2b		
William Gray	of		
James Harris	of		
Joe Johnson	p	c	
James Proctor	p		
J. Raine	of		
C. Slaughter	inf		
Joe Stuart	p	c	
L. Washington	ss		
Solomon Williams (Sol)	of		

Brooklyn Remsens

Player	1	2	3
C. Williams			M
G.W. Batum	2b		
John Coleman	of		
George Douglas	of		
W. Hancock	p		
W.R. Hill	ss		
John Oliver	3b		
Henry Paine		of	
L. Peterson	1b		
Hy Smith	of		
O.H. Smith	p		
James Williams	c		

1886

Cuban Giants

Player	1	2	3
John F. Lang			M
Ben Boyd	cf	2b	ss
Charles Brown	p		
Milton Dabney	of		
? Forbes	of	1b	
John H. Frye (Jack)	1b	2b	
Abe Harrison	ss		
Ben Holmes	3b		
George Jackson	of	p	
Harry Johnson	2b	cf	
George Parego	rf	p	of
Andrew Randolph	1b	of	
Richmond Robinson	of		
? Shadney	cf		
H. Simpson	1b		
James Simpson	cf	of	
George W. Stovey	p		
Arthur Thomas	of	c	1b
Shep Trusty	p	1b	
John Vactor	p	of	
William T. Whyte	p	of	
Clarence Williams	c	lf	of
George Williams	2b	1b	p

Unions of New Orleans

Player	1	2	3
James Arnold	p		
W. Davis	3b		
G. Irwin	ss		
P. Johnson	c		
C. Moise	lf		
G. Ogden	utl		
J. Recasner	2b		
W.J. Turner	1b		
J. Walker	rf		
T. Walker	cf		

New York Gorhams

Player	1	2	3
Ambrose Davis	rf		
Pete Fisher (The Wonder)	c		
? Garmer	3b		
? Hamilton	2b		
? Johnson	cf		
? Patterson	lf		
Richmond Robinson	1b		
? Smoot	ss		
M. White	p		

York Colored Monarchs

Player	1	2	3
Ben Boyd	cf		
John H. Frye (Jack)	1b		
Abe Harrison	ss		
Bob Jackson	c	rf	
William H. Malone	p		
William H. Selden	lf	p	
Arthur Thomas	rf	c	
Solomon White (Sol)	2b		
George Williams	3b		

1887

Baltimore Lord Baltimores

Player	1	2	3
J. Joseph Callis			M
Hugh S. Cumming			M
James Brooks			
A.C. Crain			
William Gray	of		

Player	1	2	3
James Harris	of		
J.H. Hordy			
James J. Horns			
James Payne			
James Proctor	p		
J.R. Simmons			
J.B. Weyman			
J.H. Wilson			

Boston Resolutes

Player	1	2	3
A.A. Selden			M
Marshall Thompson			M
Robert Brown			
Bennie Cross	of		
Ambrose Davis	2b	inf	
Joseph Harris			
? Lewis			
Dan Penno	inf		
? Pluno			
William H. Selden	p	of	
Ed Smith			
H.C. Taylor			
Windsor W. Terrill (George)			
R.A. Walker	inf		
George Waters			
Charles Williams	inf		

Chicago Unions

Player	1	2	3
Abe Jones	c		M
Grant Campbell	2b		
Joe Campbell	p		
Darby Cottman	3b		
Orange Fox	rf		
Albert Hackley	lf		
Frank C. Leland	cf		
William S. Peters	1b		
Frank Scott	ss		

Cincinnati Browns

Player	1	2	3
Horace McGee			M
William Allen			
John Austin			
William Blackstone			
Hal Carroll			
Joseph W. Chapman			
John Chapman			
Ellsworth Downs			
Al Garrett (Hal)			
George Matthews			
W.E. Owens			
George Rankin			
Sid Rogers			
Lee Stark			

Louisville Falls City

Player	1	2	3
William B. Franklin			M
C.W. Hines, Sr.			M
? Brooks			
? Clark	c		
Lafayette Condon			
Frank Garrett			
H. Gillespie			
W. Jessie			
? Keiger	p		
John Kinkeide			
Fred Mayfield			
Napoleon Ricks			
J. Thomas			
William Thompson	c		

New York Gorhams

Player	1	2	3
Benjamin Butler			M
George Evans			
John Evans			
John H. Frye (Jack)	1b	utl	
Bob Jackson	c	1b	
Oscar Jackson	of		
Andrew Jackson		3b	
John Nelson	p		
Joseph Palmer	utl		
Thomas Ray			
Samuel Sheppard			
B.B.H. Smith (Babe)	p		
M. White	p		
S. Willas			

Philadelphia Pythians

Player	1	2	3
Herman Close			M
S.K. Govern			M
James Aylor			
? Bowers	of		
? Forbes	3b		
Emory Hall	2b		
Yook Hargett			
George Jackson			
Walter James			
William H. Malone		p	
C.H. Norwood			
John Paine	of		
? Scudder	c		
James Simpson		of	
Bobby Still			
Joe Still			
Charles Stinson			
J.O. Turner			
John Vactor	p	of	
William Woods	ss		

Pittsburgh Keystones

Player	1	2	3
Walter S. Brown			M
David Allen	1b		
John Brady	of		
Charles Brown	p		
William H. Brown	1b		
Henry Byers	2b		
Al Card	3b		
? Gant		3b	
Ben Gross, Jr.	rf		
? Hart		c	
Sam Jackson	c		
James Lindsey		of	
William H. Malone	p		
James Mason	p		
Frank Miller		p	
William Saunders		of	
? Starmand		of	
Charles Thornton	p		
Weldy W. Walker		of	
Solomon White (Sol)		lf	
William H. Wilson	ss		
George Zimmerman	c		

Trenton (NJ) Cuban Giants

Player	1	2	3
S.K. Govern			M
David Allen	c		
Ben Boyd	cf		
Harry Cato	of		
Oscar J. Curry		p	
Abe Harrison	ss		
Ben Holmes	3b		

Player	1	2	3
George Jackson		p	
Harry Johnson		inf	c
? Jupiter	p		
Frank Miller	p	of	
George Parego	p	1b	of
William H. Selden		p	
Arthur Thomas	c	1b	
Shep Trusty	p	of	
William T. Whyte	p	of	
Clarence Williams	c	of	
George Williams	2b		

Washington Capital Citys

Player	1	2	3
Joseph Brown			M
Nelson M. Williams			M
Jesse Binga			
Thomas Findell			
Frank C. Leland	of		
George Lettlers			
J.G. Loving			
Ed Perry			
Jerome Thomas			
R.W. White			
Solomon White (Sol)	of		
E.J. Williams			
Joseph Wilson			

1888

Cuban Giants

Player	1	2	3
Ben Boyd	cf	2b	
Harry Cato	ss		
? Forbes	of		
John H. Frye (Jack)	1b		
Abe Harrison	ss		
Ben Holmes	3b		
Oscar Jackson	of		
Harry Johnson	2b	utl	
William H. Malone	p	ss	
George Parego	p	ss	
James Payne	of		
Andrew Randolph	lf	of	
William H. Selden	p	of	
? Seruby	of		
George W. Stovey	p	cf	
Arthur Thomas	rf	c	
Shep Trusty	p	of	
William T. Whyte	p	of	
Clarence Williams	c	rf	
George Williams	1b	2b	

Chicago Unions

Player	1	2	3
Abe Jones	c		M
Grant Campbell	lf		
Joe Campbell	p		
William Freeman	3b		
Albert Hackley	cf		
William Lee	ss		
Frank C. Leland	rf		
William S. Peters	1b		
Frank Scott	2b		

New York Gorhams

Player	1	2	3
Frank Bell	of		
Fred Collins (Nat)	p		
Ambrose Davis	2b	inf	
John Evans			
Andrew Jackson	3b		
Bob Jackson	c		

Player	1	2	3
Oscar Jackson	of		
John Nelson	p	of	
John Vactor	p	of	

1889

Chicago Unions

Player	1	2	3
R.R. Jackson			M
Grant Campbell	lf		
Joe Campbell	p		
Marshall Coffey	2b		
William Freeman	3b		
Albert Hackley	ss		
Abe Jones	c		
Frank C. Leland	cf		
William S. Peters	1b		
William Ramsay	rf		
William Smith (Big Bill)	p		

Philadelphia New York Gorhams

Player	1	2	3
Frank Bell	of		
Harry Cato		2b	p
? Chamberlain	1b		
Fred Collins (Nat)	p		
? Emory		c	
Ross Garrison	ss		
Andrew Jackson	3b		
Oscar Jackson	of		
Bob Jackson	c		
Frank Miller	p		
John Nelson		p	of
Solomon White (Sol)	2b	3b	

Trenton (NJ) Cuban Giants

Player	1	2	3
Ben Boyd	of		
John H. Frye (Jack)		1b	p
Frank Grant	2b		
Abe Harrison	ss		
Ben Holmes		3b	
Harry Johnson	of		
William H. Malone		p	1b
John Nelson	p	of	
William H. Selden		p	of
George W. Stovey		p	of
Arthur Thomas		1b	of
Shep Trusty	p	of	
William T. Whyte		p	of
Clarence Williams	c	3b	
George Williams	1b	3b	

1890

Chicago Unions

Player	1	2	3
William Baskin	2b		
Peter Burns		c	
Grant Campbell	lf		
Joe Campbell	p		
Darby Cottman	3b		
Albert Hackley	rf		
George Hopkins	p		
Abe Jones		c	
William King	ss		
? Parker	cf		
William S. Peters	1b		
William Smith (Big Bill)	p		

Lincoln (NEB) Giants

Player	1	2	3
Jesse Brown		2b	ss

Player	1	2	3
? Bullock		p	of
Ed Carr	rf	of	
William Castone	p	of	
? English	utl		
James Hightower	1b		
George Hughbanks			utl
Hugh Hughbanks	2b		
? Jackson	c		
? Lewis		of	
James Lincoln	ss	2b	
Frank Maupin	c	3b	
Joe Miller	p		
? Newman	c		
John W. Patterson (Pat)		cf	3b
John Reeves		p	3b
George Taylor	lf	1b	

York Cuban Giants

Player	1	2	3
J.Monroe Krider			M
Ben Boyd		of	
John H. Frye (Jack)		1b	p
Ross Garrison		ss	of
? Good		of	
Abe Harrison	ss	of	
Andrew Jackson	3b		
Oscar Jackson	of		
William Jackson	c	2b	of
William H. Malone	p	3b	of
William H. Selden	p	of	
Windsor W. Terrill (George)		utl	
Arthur Thomas	c	1b	
Solomon White (Sol)	2b	3b	
William T. Whyte	p	of	
George Williams	1b	3b	

1891

Ansonia Cuban Giants

Player	1	2	3
Frank Bell	of		
Ben Boyd	of		
? Cam		of	
George Douglas		of	
John H. Frye (Jack)	1b	p	
Frank Grant	2b		
Bob Jackson	of		
William Jackson		2b	of
John Nelson	p	of	
George W. Stovey		p	of
Solomon White (Sol)	3b		
Clarence Williams	c		

Chicago Unions

Player	1	2	3
William S. Peters	1b		M
William Baskin	2b		
Peter Burns		c	
Grant Campbell	cf		
Joe Campbell	p		
Darby Cottman	3b		
Albert Hackley	rf		
George Hopkins	p		
Abe Jones		c	
William King	ss		
? Parker	lf		
William Smith (Big Bill)	p		

New York Big Gorhams

Player	1	2	3
Ambrose Davis			M
Frank Grant	ss		
Andrew Jackson	3b		

Player	1	2	3
Oscar Jackson	cf		
William H. Malone	p	of	
William H. Selden	p	of	
George W. Stovey	p	of	
Arthur Thomas	of	c	
Solomon White (Sol)	2b		
Clarence Williams	c	of	
George Williams	1b		

1892

Chicago Unions

Player	1	2	3
William S. Peters	1b		M
William Baskin	2b		
Peter Burns		c	
Grant Campbell	lf		
Joe Campbell	p		
Darby Cottman	3b		
Albert Hackley	rf		
George Hopkins	p		
Abe Jones		c	
William King	ss		
William Smith (Big Bill)	cf		

1893

Cuban Giants

Player	1	2	3
Harry Cato	rf		
Frank Grant	2b	ss	
Abe Harrison	ss	lf	
Andrew Jackson	3b		
Oscar Jackson		of	
William Jackson	1b		
John Nelson	p	cf	
John W. Patterson (Pat)		2b	
Dan Penno	cf	p	
James Robinson	p		
George W. Stovey	p		
Solomon White (Sol)		2b	
Clarence Williams	c		

Chicago Unions

Player	1	2	3
William S. Peters	1b		M
Peter Burns		c	
Grant Campbell	2b		
Joe Campbell	p		
Darby Cottman	3b		
Albert Hackley	lf		
George Hopkins	p		
Abe Jones		c	
William Joyner	ss		
William Smith (Big Bill)	cf		

1894

Cuban Giants

Player	1	2	3
Frank Grant	ss		
Andrew Jackson	3b		
Oscar Jackson	1b		
John Nelson	p		
John W. Patterson (Pat)	lf		
William H. Selden	rf	p	
? Sneeden	cf		
William T. Whyte	2b		
Clarence Williams	c		

Chicago Unions

Player	1	2	3
William S. Peters	1b		M
Gus Brooks		of	
Peter Burns		c	
Frank Butler	rf		
Albert Hackley	cf		
Billy Holland	p		
George Hopkins	p		
Abe Jones		c	
William Joyner	ss		
Harry Moore (Mike)	lf		
Frank Scott	2b		
William Smith (Big Bill)	3b		

1895

Adrian (MI) Page Fence Giants

Player	1	2	3
A.S. Parsons			M
William Binga		c	
Gus Brooks	of		
Peter Burns		c	of
? Chavous		of	
John W. Fowler (Bud)	2b	of	
Vasco Graham	of		
Billy Holland	of	3b	p
George Hopkins		of	
Grant Johnson	ss		
James Lincoln		3b	
William H. Malone		p	of
Joe Miller		p	of
John Nelson		of	
John W. Patterson (Pat)	3b		
George Taylor	1b	ss	3b
Fred Van Dyke	p	of	
Solomon White (Sol)		2b	
George Wilson	p	of	

Chicago Unions

Player	1	2	3
William S. Peters			M
Frank Butler	p		
Robert Footes	c		
Albert Hackley	3b		
George Hopkins	2b		
Willis Jones	rf		
William Joyner	ss		
Harry Moore (Mike)	lf		
William Smith (Big Bill)	p		
Ed Woods	p	1b	

1896

Adrian (MI) Page Fence Giants

Player	1	2	3
A.S. Parsons			M
William Binga	c	of	3b
Peter Burns	rf	c	
? Chavous		p	
Vasco Graham		of	c
Charles Grant		2b	
Billy Holland	p	2b	of
Grant Johnson	ss		
George Johnson (Chappie)		of	
George Taylor	1b		
Fred Van Dyke		p	of
? Walker		of	
George Wilson	p	of	

Cuban Giants

Player	1	2	3
J.M. Bright			M

(Cuban Giants continued)

Player	1	2	3
William Cole		c	
John H. Frye (Jack)	1b		
Frank Grant	ss		
Robert Higgins		p	
Frank Hinson		p	
William Jackson	rf	c	
Robert Jordan		c	
Frank Miller		p	
John W. Patterson (Pat)	lf		
James Robinson		p	
Jim Taylor	cf		
Job Trusty	3b		
Solomon White (Sol)		2b	
Clarence Williams		c	

Cuban X Giants

Player	1	2	3
S.K. Govern			M
? Banks		p	
Harry Cato		of	
Milton Dabney	of	p	
Frank Hinson		p	
Andrew Jackson	3b		
Bob Jackson	c	1b	
Oscar Jackson		of	
? James		p	
Frank Miller		of	p
John Nelson	p	ss	
Dan Penno		2b	
William H. Selden	p		
? Singleton		c	
George W. Stovey		p	
Windsor W. Terrill (George)		ss	
Solomon White (Sol)	2b		
T. Williams		c	of
Ed Wilson	1b		

Chicago Unions

Player	1	2	3
William S. Peters			M
Harry Buckner	p		
Robert Footes	c		
Albert Hackley	lf		
George Hopkins	2b	p	
William Horn		p	
Harry Hyde	3b		
Willis Jones	rf		
William Joyner	ss		
Harry Moore (Mike)	p	1b	
William Smith (Big Bill)	cf		
Ed Woods	p	1b	
David Wyatt		inf	

1897

Adrian (MI) Page Fence Giants

Player	1	2	3
A.S. Parsons			M
William Binga	c	of	
Peter Burns	of	c	
Charles Grant		2b	
Billy Holland		2b	
George Johnson (Chappie)	1b	c	
Grant Johnson	ss		
Joe Miller	p	of	
John W. Patterson (Pat)	3b		
R. Shaw		p	
George Taylor	1b		
Fred Van Dyke		p	of
Ed Wilson	lf		
Ed Woods	cf	p	

Cuban Giants

Player	1	2	3
? Carter	p		
? Galey		1b	of
Ross Garrison	3b	of	
Frank Grant	2b	ss	
Abe Harrison	ss		
Charles Howard		p	2b
Robert Jordan	c		
William H. Malone	cf		
? McKeg		ss	
Frank Miller	rf	p	
James Robinson	lf	p	of
William Smith (Big Bill)	1b	2b	of

Chicago Unions

Player	1	2	3
William S. Peters			M
Harry Buckner	p		
Robert Footes		c	
Billy Holland	p		
George Hopkins	2b		
Harry Hyde	3b		
Robert Jackson		c	
Willis Jones	rf		
William Joyner	ss		
Harry Moore (Mike)	lf		
Louis Reynolds	1b		
R. Shaw		p	
William Smith (Big Bill)	cf		
Ed Woods	p		

1898

Adrian (MI) Page Fence Giants

Player	1	2	3
Sherman Barton	p		
William Binga	3b		
Peter Burns	c	lf	
Charles Grant	2b		
George Johnson (Chappie)	c		
James Johnson		rf	c
Joe Miller	cf		
John W. Patterson (Pat)	ss		
George Taylor	1b		
George Wilson	lf	p	

Cuban X Giants

Player	1	2	3
E.B. Lamar			M
Frank Grant	ss		
Charles Howard	p	of	
Andrew Jackson	lf		
Robert Jordan		c	
John Nelson	p	rf	
William H. Selden	p		
Solomon White (Sol)	2b		
Clarence Williams	c	of	
Ed Wilson	1b		

Celeron (NY) Acme Colored Giants

Player	1	2	3
Harry Curtis			M
Al Baxter	lf		
Billy Booker	2b		
Eddie Day	ss		
George Edsall	rf		
William Kelly	3b		
John Mickey	p		
William Payne	cf		
John Southall	c		
Walter Williams	p		
Edward Wilson	p		
Clarence Wright	1b		

Chicago Unions

Player	1	2	3
William S. Peters		M	
Harry Buckner	p		
Robert Footes	c		
Billy Holland	p		
George Hopkins	2b		
William Horn	p		
Harry Hyde	3b		
Robert Jackson	c		
Bert Jones	p		
Willis Jones	rf		
William Joyner		utl	
Harry Moore (Mike)	lf		
Louis Reynolds	1b		
William Smith (Big Bill)	cf		
Ed Woods	p		
David Wyatt	ss		

1899

Cuban Giants

Player	1	2	3
? Baxter	ss		
Ben Brown	rf		
? Carter	cf		
William Cole	p		
? Drew	3b		
Vasco Graham		c	
? Grey	2b		
? Sampson	p	rf	
William Smith (Big Bill)	c	p	
F. Watkins (Pop)	1b		

Cuban X Giants

Player	1	2	3
Frank Grant	2b	ss	
Charles Howard		utl	
Andrew Jackson	3b		
William Jackson	of	c	
Robert Jordan	c	1b	
John Nelson	p		
William H. Selden	p	of	
Solomon White (Sol)	inf		
Bill Williams	p		
Ed Wilson	1b		

Baltimore Giants

Player	1	2	3
William F. Jordan		M	
William Banks		3b	
? Dennis		p	
? Duvall	p		
? Green		c	
John Hill	ss		
? Jenks	1b		
? Johnson	p	rf	
? Pinder		c	
? Reynolds	2b		
? Rodgers	lf		
? Savoy	cf		
? Washington	p	rf	
? Wilson		3b	

Chicago Columbia Giants

Player	1	2	3
Al Garrett (Hal)		M	
Sherman Barton	cf		
William Binga	3b		
Harry Buckner	p		
Peter Burns	c		
Charles Grant	2b		
George Johnson (Chappie)	1b		
Grant Johnson	ss		

Player	1	2	3
Joe Miller	p		
John W. Patterson (Pat)	lf		
Louis Reynolds	rf		
George Wilson	p		

Chicago Unions

Player	1	2	3
William S. Peters		M	
Robert Footes	c		
Billy Holland	p		
George Hopkins	2b		
William Horn	p		
Harry Hyde	3b		
Robert Jackson	c		
Bert Jones	p		
Willis Jones	rf		
William Joyner	utl		
William Monroe	ss		
Harry Moore (Mike)	lf		
Bert Wakefield	1b		

1900

Cuban X Giants

Player	1	2	3
Bill Galloway	lf		
William Jackson	cf		
Robert Jordan	3b		
William Monroe	2b		
John Nelson	rf	p	
James Robinson	p		
William Smith (Big Bill)	1b		
? Stuart	ss		
T. Williams	c		

Genuine Cuban Giants

Player	1	2	3
Ben Brown	cf	p	
Frank Grant	2b		
John Hill	3b		
? Kelley	ss		
? Parker	lf		
? Rogers		p	
William Smith (Big Bill)		c	
William Thompson		c	
F. Watkins (Pop)	1b		
Bill Williams	p		

Chicago Columbia Giants

Player	1	2	3
Al Garrett (Hal)		M	
Sherman Barton	rf		
William Binga	3b		
Harry Buckner	p		
Peter Burns	c		
Charles Grant	2b		
Billy Holland	cf		
George Johnson (Chappie)	1b		
Joe Miller	p		
John W. Patterson (Pat)	lf		
Solomon White (Sol)	ss		
George Wilson	p		

Chicago Unions

Player	1	2	3
William S. Peters		M	
Robert Footes	c		
William Horn	p		
Harry Hyde	3b		
Robert Jackson	c		
Grant Johnson	ss		
Bert Jones	p		
Willis Jones	rf		
William Joyner	utl		

Player	1	2	3
Thomas Means	p		
William Monroe	2b		
Harry Moore (Mike)	lf		
Dangerfield Talbert			3b
Bert Wakefield	1b		

1901

Chicago Union Giants

Player	1	2	3
Frank C. Leland			M
Bert Jones	p		
Willis Jones	lf		
William Joyner	rf		
Clarence Lytle	p		
Joe Miller	p		
? Mitchell	c		
Harry Moore (Mike)	2b		
George Richardson	ss		
Dangerfield Talbert	3b		
Albert Toney	cf		
Bert Wakefield	1b		

1902

Algona (IA) Brownies

Player	1	2	3
Sherman Barton	of		
Peter Burns	c		
? Heiskell	p		
George Hopkins	2b		
William Horn	p		
Bert Jones	p	of	
Harry Moore (Mike)	of		
George Richardson	ss		
Albert Toney	3b		
Bert Wakefield	1b		
Robert Woods	p		

Chicago Union Giants

Player	1	2	3
Frank C. Leland			M
William Binga	3b		
Robert Footes	c		
Andrew Foster (Rube)	p		
Harry Hyde	1b		
George Johnson (Chappie)	c		
Willis Jones	rf		
William Joyner	cf		
Clarence Lytle	p		
Joe Miller	p		
John W. Patterson (Pat)	lf		
Dangerfield Talbert	ss		
David Wyatt	2b		

Philadelphia Giants

Player	1	2	3
Walter Schlichter			M
William Bell	p	of	
? Brown		3b	
Peter Burns	c		
Charles Carter (Kid)	p	of	
? Day		lf	
? Devereaux		1b	
? Devoe		c	rf
? Farrell		1b	c
Frank Grant	2b		
E. Griffin		p	rf
John Hill	3b		
George Johnson (Chappie)		c	
John Manning	cf		
? Martin		p	

Player	1	2	3
Dan McClellan		p	rf
? Nebon		ss	
John Nelson	p	3b	
Andrew Payne (Jap)	lf	cf	
Harry Smith	1b		
Shep Trusty		cf	
? Warwick		p	of
Solomon White (Sol)	ss		
Clarence Williams	c		
George Williams		1b	
Ray Wilson		3b	

1903

Cuban X-Giants

Player	1	2	3
Bill Bowman	p	c	3b
Andrew Foster (Rube)	p	1b	rf
Charles Grant	2b		
John Hill	3b		
Oscar Jackson		of	
William Jackson	lf		
George Johnson (Chappie)		c	
Grant Johnson	ss		
Robert Jordan		1b	c
Dan McClellan	p	rf	
Harry Moore (Mike)		of	1b
Andrew Payne (Jap)	cf		
James Robinson	p		
William Smith (Big Bill)		c	
Solomon White (Sol)		1b	
Clarence Williams		c	
Ed Wilson		of	
Ray Wilson	1b		

Algona (IA) Brownies

Player	1	2	3
Sherman Barton	lf		
John Davis	p		
Billy Holland	p		
William Horn	p		
George Johnson (Chappie)	c		
Bert Jones	p		
Willis Jones	rf		
Harry Moore (Mike)	cf		

1903 Cuban X Giants.
National Baseball Library, Cooperstown, NY

Player	1	2	3
George Richardson	2b		
? Robinson	1b		
Dangerfield Talbert	3b		
Albert Toney	ss		

Chicago Union Giants

Player	1	2	3
Frank C. Leland			M
George Ball (Walter)	p		
Andrew Campbell		c	
John Davis	p		
Robert Footes	c		
Charles Green (Joe)	cf		
Harry Hyde	3b		
Joe Miller	p		
Eugene Milliner	lf		
Fred Roberts	2b		
Arthur Ross	p		
James Smith	ss		
George Taylor	1b		
David Wyatt	rf		

Philadelphia Giants

Player	1	2	3
Walter Schlichter			M
William Bell	of	p	
William Binga	3b		
James Booker (Pete)		c	
Emmett Bowman		utl	
Harry Buckner	p	of	
Charles Carter (Kid)	p	rf	
William Evans		c	rf
Robert Footes	c		
Andrew Foster (Rube)		p	
Charles Grant	2b		
E. Griffin	p	cf	
Preston Hill (Pete)		of	
George Johnson (Chappie)		c	
Grant Johnson		ss	
? Madison		ss	
John Manning		cf	
Dan McClellan		p	
William Monroe	ss	1b	
John Nelson	cf	ss	
John W. Patterson (Pat)	lf		
? Pearson			lf

Player	1	2	3
? Thompson		rf	c
? Warwick		p	lf
Solomon White (Sol)	1b	ss	
Ray Wilson		1b	

1904

All Cubans

Player	1	2	3
Rafael Almeida	ss		
? Borges		2b	
Luis Bustamente	2b		
B. Carrillo	1b		
Jose Figarola	lf	1b	c
S. Garcia	cf		
Antonio Garcia		1b	
Joseito Munoz (Joe)	p		
Emilio Palomino	rf		
Gonzalo Sanchez	c		

Cuban X Giants

Player	1	2	3
George Ball (Walter)	p		
Bill Bowman		rf	p
Harry Buckner	p		
William Jackson	lf		
Grant Johnson	ss		
Robert Jordan		cf	c
Dan McClellan	p		
Harry Moore (Mike)		cf	ss
John W. Patterson (Pat)	2b		
James Robinson	p	rf	
James Smith	3b		
William Smith (Big Bill)		rf	
Clarence Williams	c		
J. Wilson		1b	
L. Wilson		p	

Chicago Union Giants

Player	1	2	3
Frank C. Leland			M
Sherman Barton	lf		
William Binga	c		
William Dewberry		c	
Charles Green (Joe)	cf		
Harry Hyde	3b		
Dell Matthews	p		
Thomas Means	p		
Arthur Ross	p		
Dangerfield Talbert	2b		
George Taylor	1b		
Albert Toney	ss		

Philadelphia Giants

Player	1	2	3
Walter Schlichter			M
William Bell	p	rf	
Emmett Bowman		of	p
Charles Carter (Kid)	p	c	
? Collender		cf	
Eddy Darby		cf	
? Devoe		1b	c
Robert Footes	c	rf	
Andrew Foster (Rube)	p	1b	rf
Bill Francis		3b	
? Fritz		rf	
Charles Grant	2b		
Charles Green (Joe)		utl	
E. Griffin		p	cf
John Hill	3b		
Preston Hill (Pete)	lf		
William Horn	p		
B. Johnson		inf	

Player	1	2	3
George Johnson (Chapple)	c		
John Manning	cf		
William Monroe	ss	1b	
Andrew Payne (Jap)	cf		
James Robinson		rf	p
Charles Thomas		1b	of
Albert Toney		3b	
Tom Washington	c		
? Wharton	p		
Solomon White (Sol)	1b		
W. Woodson		of	

1905

All Cubans

Player	1	2	3
Rafael Almeida	3b		
? Borges		2b	
Luis Bustamente	ss	3b	
Alfredo Cabrera	1b		
B. Carrillo		p	1b
? DeMeza	p		
Antonio Garcia		1b	c
Regino Garcia	c		
S. Garcia		cf	
? Garren	c		
Heliodoro Hidalgo		cf	
Armando Marsans	lf		
Joseito Munoz (Joe)	p	lf	
Emilio Palomino	rf		
Gonzalo Sanchez		c	
Rogelio Valdes	2b		

Cuban X Giants

Player	1	2	3
? Aubury		1b	
George Ball (Walter)	p	cf	
Harry Buckner	p	of	
John Hill	3b		
William Jackson	cf		
Robert Jordan	c		
John W. Patterson (Pat)	lf		
Dangerfield Talbert	2b		
Rogelio Valdes	ss		
T. Williams		c	
Ed Wilson	rf		
Ray Wilson	1b		

Brooklyn Royal Giants

Player	1	2	3
? Andrews (Pop)	p		
? Browcow		inf	
? Brown	rf		
? Hawk		c	
? Haynes		lf	
? Ingersoll		2b	
W. James (Nux)		3b	
George Johnson (Chappie)		c	
U. Johnson		3b	
B. Merritt	p		
Andrew Payne (Jap)	lf		
J. Robinson	cf		
Al Robinson	1b		
William Smith (Big Bill)		c	
? Walker		c	
? Warwick	p		
George Wright	ss		

Chicago Leland Giants

Player	1	2	3
Frank C. Leland			M
Sherman Barton	lf		
William Binga	3b		

Player	1	2	3
John Davis	p		
Charles Green (Joe)	cf		
Nathan Harris	2b		
Billy Holland	p		
William Horn	p		
Dell Matthews	rf		
William Prim			c
Bob Robinson			c
Arthur Ross	p		
James Smith	ss		
George Taylor	1b		

Famous Cuban Giants

Player	1	2	3
J.M. Bright			M
R. Best	p		
Phil Bradley	c		
Bill Galloway	2b		
Sam Gordon	3b		
? Kelley	lf		
Chase Lyons	p		
? Rawlins	rf		
? Sampson	p		
? Satterfield	ss		
F. Watkins (Pop)	1b		
Clarence Williams	cf		

Philadelphia Giants

Player	1	2	3
Walter Schlichter			M
James Booker (Pete)	c		
Emmett Bowman	p	rf	
? Devoe		c	
Andrew Foster (Rube)	p	rf	
Bill Francis		3b	
Charles Grant	2b		
Preston Hill (Pete)	lf		
George Johnson (Chappie)		c	
Grant Johnson	ss		
Dan McClellan	p	rf	
William Monroe	3b		
Harry Moore (Mike)	cf		
? Osborne		p	
? Thompson		c	
Tom Washington		c	
Solomon White (Sol)	1b		
Clarence Winston (Bobby)		of	

1906

Cuban X Giants

Player	1	2	3
Sherman Barton		cf	
Harry Buckner	p		
Antonio Garcia		c	
Bill Gatewood		p	
John Hill		ss	
W. James (Nux)		3b	
? Lee		2b	
John Henry Lloyd (Pop)		2b	
? Mayo		p	
Joseito Munoz (Joe)	p		
Emilio Palomino		cf	
? Perez		p	
Bruce Petway		c	
James Robinson	1b	p	
William Smith (Big Bill)		rf	
Rogelio Valdes		ss	
Tom Washington		rf	
? Weaver		1b	
Clarence Williams		c	
T. Williams		c	

Player	1	2	3
Ray Wilson		1b	
Clarence Winston (Bobby)	lf		

Famous Cuban Giants

Player	1	2	3
J.M. Bright			M
? Abbott	p		
R. Best	p		
Phil Bradley	c		
Bill Galloway	lf		
Sam Gordon	3b		
William Jackson	cf		
? Kelley	cf		
? Sampson	p		
? Satterfield	2b		
? Thompson	p		
Felix Wallace	ss		
F. Watkins (Pop)	1b		
L. Williams	rf		

Brooklyn Royal Giants

Player	1	2	3
? Abbott		p	
? Andrews (Pop)	p	rf	
? Browcow		2b	
? Brown		of	
Jack Emery		p	
Robert Footes		c	
Billy Holland	3b		
W. James (Nux)	2b	c	
Grant Johnson		ss	
B. Merritt	p		
? Miller	p		
William Monroe		3b	
John W. Patterson (Pat)		lf	
Andrew Payne (Jap)	lf		
Al Robinson	1b		
J. Robinson	cf	of	
James Robinson	p	cf	
William Smith (Big Bill)		c	
George Wright		ss	

Chicago Leland Giants

Player	1	2	3
Frank C. Leland			M
Sherman Barton	lf		
Andrew Campbell		c	
John Davis	p		
Bill Gatewood	p		
Charles Green (Joe)	cf		
William Irvin	3b		
Clarence Lytle	p		
Bruce Petway	c		
Howard Petway	p		
James Smith	rf		
Dangerfield Talbert	2b		
George Taylor	1b		
Albert Toney	ss		

Philadelphia Giants

Player	1	2	3
Solomon White (Sol)	1b		M
? Andrews (Pop)		p	
? Barnes		3b	
James Booker (Pete)	c		
Emmett Bowman		p	cf
Harry Buckner		rf	p
Andrew Foster (Rube)	p	of	
Bill Francis	3b		
Charles Grant	2b		
Nathan Harris	ss		
Preston Hill (Pete)	of		
George Johnson (Chappie)		c	
Grant Johnson		ss	

Player	1	2	3
Robert Jordan		1b	rf
Dan McClellan	p	of	
William Monroe		2b	
Harry Moore (Mike)		of	
Ray Wilson		p	

1907

Brooklyn Royal Giants

Player	1	2	3
Phil Bradley		c	
Harry Buckner	p	cf	
Luis Bustamente		2b	ss
John Hill		3b	
Billy Holland	p	cf	
W. James (Nux)		2b	rf
George Johnson (Chappie)		c	
Grant Johnson	ss		
Robert Jordan	1b		
B. Merritt		cf	p
Eugene Milliner	rf		
Bill Monroe		3b	
John W. Patterson (Pat)	lf		

Chicago Leland Giants

Player	1	2	3
Andrew Foster (Rube)	p	M	
Frank C. Leland			M
George Ball (Walter)	p		
James Booker (Pete)	c		
Bill Gatewood	p		
Nathan Harris	2b		
Preston Hill (Pete)	cf		
Harry Moore (Mike)	1b		
William Norman	p		
Andrew Payne (Jap)	rf	cf	
Haywood Rose		c	
Sam Strothers		c	
Dangerfield Talbert	3b		
Clarence Winston (Bobby)	lf		
George Wright	ss		

Havana Cuban Stars

Player	1	2	3
Rafael Almeida	3b		
Luis Bustamente	ss		
? Carvallo	1b		
Jose Figarola	c		
Hector Magrinat	lf		
Pedro Medina	p	c	
Joseito Munoz (Joe)	cf	p	
E. Pratz	rf		
? Ramos	2b		

Philadelphia Giants

Player	1	2	3
William Binga	rf		
Emmett Bowman		cf	of
Phil Bradley		c	
Harry Buckner	p		
Bill Francis		3b	
Charles Grant	2b		
E. Griffin	p		
John Hill		ss	
Preston Hill (Pete)		lf	of
John Henry Lloyd (Pop)	ss		
Dan McClellan	p	of	
Sam Mongin		3b	
Bruce Petway	c		
James Robinson		lf	of
Solomon White (Sol)		of	
Clarence Williams		c	

Player	1	2	3
E. Wilson	p		
Ray Wilson	1b		

1908

Pop Watkins Stars

Player	1	2	3
F. Watkins (Pop)	1b		M
? Boots	cf		
Phil Bradley		c	
? Brown		lf	
? Cobb	2b		
Frank Duncan (Pete)		rf	
Leroy Grant	1b		
? Hannon	3b		
Billy Holland	p	3b	
W. James (Nux)		2b	
? McFarland		of	
? Myers (Lefty)	ss		
Joe Scotland		lf	
? Tome	p		
? Williams		c	

Brooklyn Colored Giants

Player	1	2	3
? Clark	2b		
Jack Emery	p		
? Franklin	ss		
W.W. Fuller (Chick)	3b		
James Gardner	2b	3b	
Peter Green (Ed)	p		
? Hanks	c		
? Hudson	rf		
Grant Johnson	ss		
Lee Jones	rf		
C. Meyers	lf		
L. Meyers	2b		
? Murphy	cf		
? Paul	ss		
? Reeves	cf		
? Richardson	lf	rf	

Chicago Leland Giants

Player	1	2	3
Andrew Foster (Rube)	p	M	
George Ball (Walter)	p		
James Booker (Pete)	c		
Emmett Bowman	p		
? Davis (Dago)		p	
Nathan Harris	2b		
Preston Hill (Pete)	cf		
Frank C. Leland			
Harry Moore (Mike)	1b		
William Norman	p		
Andrew Payne (Jap)	rf		
Haywood Rose		c	
Sam Strothers		c	
Dangerfield Talbert	3b		
Clarence Winston (Bobby)	lf		
George Wright	ss		

Cleveland

Player	1	2	3
? Bowman	ss		
? Follis	c		
? Garrison	p		
? Glover	cf		
? Johnson	3b		
? Mosby		rf	
? Nelson		rf	
? Parks (Judy)	1b		
? Silkerson	2b		

Player	1	2	3
? Sloan	p		
? Turner	lf		

Columbus Black Tourist

Player	1	2	3
? Settles			M
? Allen	1b		
? Barnett		rf	
? Boyd	p		
? Green	lf		
? James		cf	
? Lewis		3b	
? Lindsay	ss		
? Nease		cf	
? Reed	p		
? Russell	3b		
? Scott	p		
? Seiden	2b		
? Thomas	c		
Lee Wade	p		
? White		cf	rf
? Winter		rf	

Genuine Cuban Giants

Player	1	2	3
? Abbott	rf	p	
? Batson	cf		
Jesse Bragg	3b		
? Lavelle	c		
? Nelson	2b		
? Parson	p		
? Satterfield	ss		
? Schiff	lf		
Harry Smith	1b		

Kansas City (KA) Giants

Player	1	2	3
Frank Evans	3b	of	
Fred Lee			
Robert Lindsay (Frog)	ss		
Bill Lindsay	p		
Dudley McAdoo (Tully)	1b		
Ernest McCampbell			
Tom McCampbell			
Chick Pulliam	c		
Tom Stearman	of		
Bert Wakefield	of		
Wesley Wilkins	of		

New York Colored Giants

Player	1	2	3
? Dawson	p		
? Devean	c		
W.W. Fuller (Chick)	ss		
? Kelly	3b		
? Land	1b		
? Parker	lf		
Jesse Shipp	rf	p	
? Smith	cf		
? Turner	2b		

Philadelphia Giants

Player	1	2	3
Frank Dunbar		lf	
? Fisher	rf		
William Francis (Bill)	3b		
W. James (Nux)		2b	
John Henry Lloyd (Pop)	ss		
Danny McClellan	p	cf	
Sam Mongin		cf	
? Patton	p		
Bruce Petway		c	
Spottswood Poles (Spots)	rf	cf	lf
Tom Washington		rf	
?Wildon	1b		

Player	1	2	3

1909

Cuban Stars

Player	1	2	3
Luis Bustamente	ss		
Antonio Garcia	c		
Manuel Govantes	2b		
Ricardo Hernandez (Chico)	3b		
Hector Magrinat	lf		
Jose Mendez (Joe)	p		
Joseito Munoz (Joe)	p		
Juan Padrone	p		
Augustin Parpetti	1b		
Eugenio Santa Cruz	cf		

Quaker Giants

Player	1	2	3
Jess Barbour	3b		
? Brown	lf		
Charles Carter (Kid)	rf	p	
? Govens		of	
Charles Grant	ss		
John Hill	2b		
? Hyman	p		
? Johnson	cf	p	
? Jones	p		

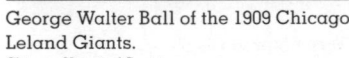

George Walter Ball of the 1909 Chicago Leland Giants.
Chicago Historical Society

Andrew "Rube" Foster of the 1909 Chicago Leland Giants
Chicago Historical Society

Player	1	2	3
? Shartz	c		
? Swicket	p		
Solomon White (Sol)	1b		

Brooklyn Royal Giants

Player	1	2	3
Phil Bradley	c		
? Brown	utl		
Harry Buckner	p		
? Clark	cf		
Ashby Dunbar	lf		
Charles Earle (Frank)		of	
W. James (Nux)	rf		
Grant Johnson	ss		
Sam Mongin	3b		
William Monroe	2b		
Al Robinson	1b		
Jules Thomas	p	of	

Chicago Leland Giants

Player	1	2	3
Andrew Foster (Rube)	p		M
George Ball (Walter)	p	of	
James Booker (Pete)	c	1b	
Charles Dougherty (Pat)	p	rf	
Bill Gatewood	p		
Charles Green (Joe)	lf	rf	
Nathan Harris	2b		
Preston Hill (Pete)	cf		
George Johnson (Chappie)		1b	c
Frank C. Leland			
Harry Moore (Mike)	1b	of	
? Newman		p	
William Norman	p		
Andrew Payne (Jap)	rf		
? Shawler		of	
Sam Strothers		c	
Dangerfield Talbert	3b	1b	
Clarence Winston (Bobby)	lf		
George Wright	ss		

Harrisburg Giants

Player	1	2	3
C.W. Strothers (Colonel)			M
? Bactory			
? Carpenter			
? Felks			
? Hampton			
? Jones			
John Manning		of	

The catcher is Gonzalo Sanchez, the batter is the superb Preston "Pete" Hill.
Chicago Historical Society

Player	1	2	3
? Moore			
? Porter			
? Tolin			
? Wilcox			

Kansas City (MO) Royal Giants

Player	1	2	3
Dan Booker	p		
Cody Buckley	p		
Charles Childs	p		
? Dougherty	1b		
Jack Johnson	rf		
Lown Lee	p		
S. Meckling		c	
Eugene Milliner	cf		
Jim Norman		inf	
Chick Pulliam	c		
? Smith	3b		
Tom Stearman	lf		
? Stopughers	ss		
T. Taylor	2b		

Philadelphia Giants

Player	1	2	3
? Batson		of	
Frank Duncan (Pete)	lf		
Jack Emery	p		
? Fisher	p		
Bill Francis	3b		
? Hannon		rf	
Charles Hayman (Bugs)	p	1b	
W. James (Nux)	2b		
John Henry Lloyd (Pop)	ss		
Dan McClellan	p	1b	
? Patton		rf	p
Bruce Petway	c		
Spottswood Poles (Spot)	cf		
William Smith (Big Bill)		c	
Ray Wilson	1b		

1910

Cuban Stars

Player	1	2	3
Luis Bustamente	ss		
Antonio Garcia	rf	c	
A. Gonzales	p		
Gervasio Gonzalez	c		
Luis Gonzalez	p		

Player	1	2	3
Ricardo Hernandez (Chico)		3b	
Hector Magrinat	lf		
Jesus Mederos (Frank)	p		
Agustin Molina	p	1b	
Eugenio Morin		3b	
Juan Padrone	2b	p	of
Augustin Parpetti	1b		
Eustaquio Pedroso	p	ss	
Eugenio Santa Cruz	cf		

Stars of Cuba

Player	1	2	3
Armando Cabanas	2b		
Pelayo Chacon	ss		
Jose Figarola	c		
Manuel Govantes	3b		
Juan Guerra	1b		
Heliodoro Hidalgo	cf		
Jose Mendez (Joe)	p		
Joseito Munoz (Joe)	p	of	
H. Pareda (Monk)	p		
Pablo Valdez (Tony)	lf		
Roberto Villa (Bobby)	rf		

Brooklyn Royal Giants

Player	1	2	3
Emmett Bowman		1b	p
Phil Bradley	ss		
Jesse Bragg	3b		
Harry Buckner		p	
? Delaney		inf	
W. James (Nux)		2b	
? Land	lf		
Dan McClellan		p	
? Myers (Lefty)		ss	
Al Robinson		p	1b
Jesse Shipp	rf	p	
Harry Smith		1b	
Jules Thomas	cf	rf	
Clarence Williams	c		

Chicago Giants

Player	1	2	3
Howard Baker			
George Ball (Walter)	p		
Otto Bolden		c	p
Charles Green (Joe)	rf		
? Harper		p	
Nathan Harris	2b	rf	
George Johnson (Chappie)	c		
Bobby Marshall	1b		
Harry Moore (Mike)	cf		
William Norman	p		
William Pettus (Zack)		c	1b
? Seldom	ss		
A. Skinner		c	
Dangerfield Talbert	3b		
Candy Jim Taylor		3b	
John Taylor (Steel Arm)	p		
Felix Wallace	2b		
James Webb		c	
Smokey Joe Williams	p		
Clarence Winston (Bobby)	lf		
George Wright	ss		

Chicago Leland Giants

Player	1	2	3
James Booker (Pete)		1b	c
E. Cooper		1b	
Charles Dougherty (Pat)	p		
Frank Duncan (Pete)	lf		
Andrew Foster (Rube)	p		
Preston Hill (Pete)	cf		
Fred Hutchinson			rf

Player	1	2	3
Grant Johnson	2b		
Bill Lindsay		p	
John Henry Lloyd (Pop)	ss		
Andrew Payne (Jap)	rf		
Bruce Petway	c		
Wes Pryor	3b		
Sam Strothers		1b	c
Frank Wickware	p		

Kansas City (KA) Giants

Player	1	2	3
Jim Norman			M
William Binga		3b	
Elwood DeMoss (Bingo)		2b	
Albert Foster (Red)	1b		
William Jackson (Ashes)		3b	
Bill Lindsay	p	of	
Merf Lindsay		cf	
P. Lindsay		cf	
Robert Lindsay (Frog)	ss		
George Neal		2b	
J. Robinson	rf		
? Taylor	p		
William Tenney	c		
Wesley Wilkins	lf		

Philadelphia Giants

Player	1	2	3
J. Addison		c	
Jess Barbour	lf		
? Fisher	p		
Bill Francis	3b		
Charles Hayman (Bugs)	p		
W. James (Nux)	2b		
Dan McClellan	p	of	
G. McDonald		p	utl
Joe Parks		c	1b
William Parks	ss	utl	
Bill Pierce		c	1b
Spottswood Poles (Spot)	rf	of	

Player	1	2	3
? Shartz		c	
Charles Thomas	cf	1b	
Lee Wade		p	1b
Ray Wilson		1b	

St. Louis Stars

Player	1	2	3
? Boone		cf	
Willie Green		c	
? Hannon		3b	
? Harrison		2b	cf
Joe Hewitt	ss		
Charley Hill (Lefty)		3b	
? Holden	rf		
? Jones	lf		
? Knight		cf	
Jimmie Lyons	p		
William McMurray		1b	
? Mims		cf	
William Prim		c	
? Stevenson	p		
? Tabor	2b		
H. Warmack		1b	
? Washington	p		
? Williams		2b	

West Baden (IND) Sprudels

Player	1	2	3
C.I. Taylor	2b	p	M
? Bingham (Bingo)	rf	of	
George Brown	cf		
Morten Clark	p	ss	
William Dismukes (Dizzy)	p		
? Foster			
William Houston	ss	c	
Jerome Lewis		1b	
L. Moore	lf		
? O'Neill	p		
? Stanford			
Sam Strothers		c	utl

1910 Stars of Cuba. In the middle of the back row is Bobby Villa. Middle row, second from left is Pelayo Chacon, with Jose Mendez to his left. First on the right in that row is Monk Pareda. Far right in the first row is Jose Figarola.
Luis Munoz Collection

1910

Player	1	2	3
Ben Taylor		1b	p
John Taylor (Steel Arm)	p		
Wabishaw Wiley (Doc)		c	1b

1911

All Cubans
Player	1	2	3
Luis Bustamente	ss		
Julian Castillo		1b	
? Costello	1b		
Antonio Garcia	c		
Hector Magrinat	lf		
? Marlotica	rf		
Jesus Mederos (Frank)		p	
Francisco Moran	cf		
Eustaquio Pedroso	p		
Jaime Rovira	3b		
Rogelio Valdes	2b	of	

Cuban Stars
Player	1	2	3
Luis Bustamente		ss	
Pelayo Chacon	rf	ss	
Jose Figarola	1b		
Gervasio Gonzalez		c	
Miguel Gonzalez (Mike)	c		
Ricardo Hernandez (Chico)	lf		
Heliodoro Hidalgo	cf		
Jesus Mederos (Frank)		p	
Jose Mendez (Joe)	p		
Eugenio Morin	3b		
Juan Padrone		of	p
Eustaquio Pedroso	p	utl	
Pablo Valdez		of	
Roberto Villa (Bobby)	2b		

Lincoln Giants of New York
Player	1	2	3
James Booker (Pete)		c	1b
Phil Bradley	1b	c	of
Harry Buckner	p		
Bill Francis	3b		
Robert Gans (Jude)	lf	cf	

Player	1	2	3
Sam Gordon	ss		
? Johnson		p	
John Henry Lloyd (Pop)	ss		
Jimmie Lyons	rf		
Dan McClellan	p		
Spottswood Poles (Spot)	cf	lf	
Dick Redding (Cannonball)	p		
Louis Santop	c	rf	
George Wright	2b		

Brooklyn Royal Giants
Player	1	2	3
? Andrews (Pop)	p	rf	
Jesse Bragg	3b		
? Brown	of		
Sam Crawford		p	
Ashby Dunbar	rf		
Charles Earle (Frank)	lf		
Bill Handy	ss		
Bill Kindle	2b	3b	
Hudson Oliver (Huddy)		2b	
Al Robinson		1b	p
? Satterfield		2b	
Jesse Shipp		p	
William Smith (Big Bill)		c	
Jules Thomas	cf	p	of
Wabishaw Wiley (Doc)		c	
Hank Williams			3b
? Wills			3b

Chicago American Giants
Player	1	2	3
Andrew Foster (Rube)	p		M
Jess Barbour	ss		
Charles Dougherty (Pat)	p		
Frank Duncan (Pete)	lf		
Leroy Grant	1b		
Preston Hill (Pete)	cf		
Fred Hutchinson		ss	
William Lain		ss	
Bill Lindsay	p		
William Monroe	2b		
William Parks		rf	2b
Andrew Payne (Jap)	rf	lf	

Player	1	2	3
William Pettus (Zack)	1b	c	
Bruce Petway		c	
Bill Pierce		c	
Wes Pryor	3b		
William Webster (Speck)	c		
Frank Wickware		p	

Chicago Giants
Player	1	2	3
George Ball (Walter)	p		
Jess Barbour	2b	3b	
Sherman Barton	cf		
Bill Gatewood		p	
Charles Green (Joe)	rf		
Grant Johnson		ss	
William Lain			3b
Harry Moore (Mike)	1b		
George Neal		2b	
William Parks		2b	ss
Archie Pate		c	
William Pettus (Zack)	c		
Sam Strothers		c	
Bobby Thurston		of	
Tom Washington		c	
Smokey Joe Williams		p	
Clarence Winston (Bobby)	lf		

Chicago Leland Giants
Player	1	2	3
George Ball (Walter)	p		
Sherman Barton	cf		
Frank Duncan (Pete)		of	
Bill Gatewood	p	1b	
? Johnston	ss		
Harry Moore (Mike)	3b		
A.W. Ormes			
William Parks	2b		
Tom Redmon			
Charles Rolls			
Tom Washington	c		
William Webster (Speck)		c	
Clarence Winston (Bobby)	lf		

Chicago Union Giants
Player	1	2	3
Theo Brown		3b	
Robert Gilkerson	1b		
Sam Gordon	3b		
James Harvey	c		
Guy Jackson	ss		
Horace Jenkins	cf		
Charles Jessup	p		
Willis Jones	rf		
Ed Lee		inf	
William Parks		2b	of
Mack Ramsey	lf		
Charles Reese	p		

Indianapolis ABCs
Player	1	2	3
G. Abrams			M
Todd Allen	3b		
Howard Bartlett (Hop)	p		
? Board	1b		
Del Francis	ss		
? Herron	cf		
? Highbee	p		
? Lolla	lf		
? Morris	2b		
William Prim	c		
? Sibley		c	
B. Turner (Aggie)	rf		
? Williams	p		

1911 Lincoln Giants. Standing L to R: Dan McClellan, John Henry "Pop" Lloyd, Bill Francis, Spot Poles, unknown, Dick Redding, Louis Santop, Jude Gans, Pete Booker. Kneeling: Phil Bradley, Grant Johnson, Harry Buckner, and George Wright.

Jeff Eastland

Player	1	2	3
Philadelphia Giants			
J. Addison		c	
K. Addison	3b		
T. Addison	ss		
? Dow		p	
Joe Forbes		3b	
? Gorham	rf		
W. James (Nux)	2b		
? Murphy		rf	
? Shartz	c		
Charles Thomas	1b	p	
Lee Wade	p	1b	
? Yancy	cf		
Pittsburgh Giants			
? Andrews (Pop)	1b	cf	
Charles Bradford	lf	p	
? Collins		1b	
? Delaney	2b		
Peter Green (Ed)	cf		
Willie Green	p	of	
James Griffin (Horse)	3b		
? Johnstone	c		
? Miller	rf	lf	
Leonard Oliver	ss		
St. Louis Giants			
Sam Bennett	cf	of	
Albert Gillard (Hamp)	p		
Willie Green		of	
Joe Hewitt	ss		
George Johnson (Chappie)		c	
Jimmie Lyons	lf		
Dudley McAdoo (Tully)	1b		
William McMurray		c	
Sam Mongin		3b	
L. Moore	rf	of	
John Taylor (Steel Arm)	p		
Candy Jim Taylor	3b		
Ben Taylor		p	1b
Felix Wallace	2b		
H. Warmack		1b	
West Baden (IND) Sprudels			
C.I. Taylor	2b		M
? Bingham (Bingo)	rf		
George Brown	cf		
? Dickenson			

Player	1	2	3
William Dismukes (Dizzy)	p		
? Ellis	ss		
Jerome Lewis	1b		
Bennie Lyons		of	1b
Pleas Miller (Hub)	p		
George Shively	lf		
? Sutton	3b		
Jack Watts	c		

1912

Player	1	2	3
Cuban Stars			
Luis Bustamente	3b		
Julian Castillo		1b	
Jose Figarola	1b		
Antonio Garcia		c	
A. Gonzales	p		
Miguel Gonzalez (Mike)		c	
Heliodoro Hidalgo	cf		
? Lavelle		1b	
Dolf Luque	p	cf	of
Hector Magrinat	lf		
Jose Mendez (Joe)	p		
Inocente Mendieta	2b		
Eustaquio Pedroso	p		
? Ramos		p	
Lincoln Giants of New York			
? Bernard		of	
James Booker (Pete)	c		
Ashby Dunbar		of	
Bill Francis	3b		
Robert Gans (Jude)	lf		
Leroy Grant	1b		
? Lindsey		of	
John Henry Lloyd (Pop)	ss		
Harry Moore (Mike)	rf		
William Pettus (Zack)		utl	
Spottswood Poles (Spot)	of		
Dick Redding (Cannonball)	p		
Louis Santop	c		
Ben Taylor	p	1b	
Smokey Joe Williams	p		
George Wright	2b		
Brooklyn Royal Giants			
? Andrews (Pop)	p	rf	

Player	1	2	3
Jesse Bragg	2b		
? Brown	cf		
Charles Earle (Frank)	lf	of	p
Bill Handy	2b		
W. James (Nux)	rf		
Grant Johnson		ss	
Bill Kindle	ss		
Jesse Shipp	p		
Pearl Webster		c	1b
Frank Wickware	p		
Wabishaw Wiley (Doc)	c		
Chicago American Giants			
Andrew Foster (Rube)	p		M
Jess Barbour		rf	3b
Charles Dougherty (Pat)	p		
Frank Duncan (Pete)	rf		
Bill Gatewood	p		
Charles Green (Joe)	lf		
Preston Hill (Pete)	cf		
Fred Hutchinson	2b		
Louis Johnson (Dicta)	p		
Bill Lindsay	p		
William Monroe	ss	2b	
William Parks		1b	rf
Andrew Payne (Jap)		rf	
Bruce Petway	c		
Bill Pierce		1b	
Sam Strothers		1b	
Candy Jim Taylor	3b		
Albert Toney		ss	
Frank Wickware	p		
Indianapolis ABCs			
Todd Allen	3b		
Howard Bartlett (Hop)	p		
? Board	1b		
? Herron	cf		
Fred Hutchinson	ss		
? Martin	lf		
? Seldom	2b		
? Sibley	c		
B. Turner (Aggie)	rf		
St. Louis Giants			
George Ball (Walter)	p	of	
Sam Bennett	cf		
William Dismukes (Dizzy)	p		
Frank Harvey		p	
Joe Hewitt	ss		
George Johnson (Chappie)	c		
? Langford (Ad)		p	
Jimmie Lyons	rf		
Dudley McAdoo (Tully)	1b		
Sam Mongin		2b	3b
Wes Pryor	3b		
Jules Thomas	lf		
Lee Wade	p		
Felix Wallace	2b		
William Webster (Speck)		c	
West Baden (IND) Sprudels			
? Bingham (Bingo)	rf		
George Brown	cf		
Morten Clark	ss		
Elwood DeMoss (Bingo)	2b		
Jerome Lewis	1b		
William McMurray	c		
Pleas Miller (Hub)	p		
? O'Neill		c	

1911 West Baden, Indiana Sprudels. #1 Jack Watts, #2 Bennie Lyons, #3 Bingo Bingham, #4 Dizzy Dismukes, #5 Pleas Miller, #6 George Shively, #7 Ellis, #8 C.I. Taylor, #9 Dickenson, #10 George Brown, #11 Sutton, #12 Jerome Lewis.
Dick Clark

Player	1	2	3
George Shively	lf		
Candy Jim Taylor	3b		
C.I. Taylor		rf	
John Taylor (Steel Arm)	p		

1913

Breaker's Hotel (Winter)

Player	1	2	3
Sam Bennett	cf		
James Booker (Pete)		c	
Phil Bradley		c	
Joe Hewitt	rf		
W. James (Nux)	2b		
Jimmie Lyons	lf		
Dudley McAdoo (Tully)	1b		
Sam Mongin	3b		
Ben Taylor		1b	
Lee Wade	p		
Felix Wallace		ss	2b
Frank Wickware	p		
George Wright	ss		

Cuban Stars

Player	1	2	3
Bernardo Baro		p	
Luis Bustamente		inf	
Pelayo Chacon	ss		
Jose Figarola	c		
Heliodoro Hidalgo	lf		
Jose Junco	p	rf	
Hector Magrinat	rf		
Francisco Moran	3b		
H. Pareda (Monk)	p		
Augustin Parpetti	1b		
Eustaquio Pedroso	p		
Jose Rodriquez		c	
Cristobal Torriente	cf		
Roberto Villa (Bobby)	2b	ss	

Lincoln Giants of New York

Player	1	2	3
Sam Bennett		of	
? Edwards (Smokey)	p		
Bill Francis	3b		

Player	1	2	3
Robert Gans (Jude)	lf		
Leroy Grant	1b		
Joe Hewitt		of	
Grant Johnson	2b		
John Henry Lloyd (Pop)	ss		
Andrew Payne (Jap)		of	
Spottswood Poles (Spot)	cf		
Dick Redding (Cannonball)	p		
Louis Santop	c	rf	
Lee Wade	p		
Wabishaw Wiley (Doc)		c	rf
Smokey Joe Williams	p		

Royal Ponciana Hotel (Winter)

Player	1	2	3
Jesse Bragg	2b		
W. Brown (Mike)		1b	
William Dismukes (Dizzy)	p		
Charles Earle (Frank)	lf		
? Gruber		1b	
Bill Handy		inf	
Frank Harvey	p		
Grant Johnson	ss		
George Johnson (Chappie)	c	1b	
? Pall		p	
Andrew Payne (Jap)	rf		
Wes Pryor	3b		
Jules Thomas	cf		
Pearl Webster		c	1b

Brooklyn Royal Giants

Player	1	2	3
George Ball (Walter)	rf	p	
James Booker (Pete)		1b	
William Dismukes (Dizzy)	p		
Charles Earle (Frank)	lf		
Bill Handy	ss		
Frank Harvey	p		
? Hatchett	2b		
William Pettus (Zack)	1b		
Wes Pryor	3b		
Jules Thomas	cf		
Lee Wade		p	of
Pearl Webster	c		
Frank Wickware		p	

Chicago American Giants

Player	1	2	3
Jess Barbour		of	1b
James Booker (Pete)		c	1b
Elwood DeMoss (Bingo)		2b	
Charles Dougherty (Pat)	p		
Frank Duncan (Pete)	lf		
Andrew Foster (Rube)	p		
Bill Gatewood	p		
Preston Hill (Pete)	cf		
Fred Hutchinson		ss	
Louis Johnson (Dicta)	p		
Bill Lindsay	p		
William Monroe		2b	
William Parks	rf		
Bruce Petway	c		
Bill Pierce		c	1b
? Strong		p	
Candy Jim Taylor	3b		
Ben Taylor	1b		
John Taylor (Steel Arm)		p	
? Watkins		p	
Smokey Joe Williams		p	

Chicago Giants

Player	1	2	3
? Alexander (Hub)		c	
? Armstrong		c	
Harry Bauchman		ss	
? Buford	p		
Sam Crawford	p		
Elwood DeMoss (Bingo)		2b	
Charles Green (Joe)	cf		
Guy Jackson		2b	3b
? Martin		p	
? McCune		3b	
Hurley McNair		p	
William Monroe		3b	
Harry Moore (Mike)	1b		
William Parks	ss		
Archie Pate		c	
Andrew Payne (Jap)	rf		
Sam Strothers	c		
Clarence Winston (Bobby)	lf		

French Lick (IN) Plutos

Player	1	2	3
W. Cobb		c	
? Cunningham	ss		
Elwood DeMoss (Bingo)		2b	
Albert Gillard (Hamp)		p	
Sam Gordon	1b		
? Hannon	cf		
Dan Kennard	c		
Thomas Lynch	2b		
Jimmie Lyons		rf	
? McLaughlin	p		
Harry Moore (Mike)		1b	
? Norman	3b		
? Patton		lf	
Joe Scotland		cf	

Havana Red Sox

Player	1	2	3
? Andrews (Pop)	1b		
? Ashport	3b		
? Brown	lf		
Ralph Burgin	rf		
? Hayes (Buddy)	c		
? Jackson	cf		
? Mankins	ss		
G. McDonald	p		
? Tudell	2b		

Bill Gatewood.
Chicago Historical Society

Spottswood Poles of the 1913 Lincoln
Giants of New York.
Chicago Historical Society

Indianapolis ABCs

Player	1	2	3
Todd Allen	3b		
Howard Bartlett (Hop)	p		
? Briscoe		cf	
? Connell		p	
Harry Cornett		c	
? Davis (Quack)	lf		
? Dupree	cf		
? Floyd		rf	
? Griffin		cf	
? Hannibal		rf	
? Highbee	p	of	
Fred Hutchinson	ss		
James Jeffries		rf	
Bennie Lyons		c	
Oscar Owens		p	
? Satterfield		2b	
? Seldom	2b		
? Shawler		lf	
? Sibley		c	
B. Turner (Aggie)	1b		
Jack Watts		c	
? West		rf	p
? Williams		p	

Philadelphia Giants

Player	1	2	3
? Andrews (Pop)		2b	
? Bernard		cf	
James Booker (Pete)	lf		
Charles Bradford	p		
W. Brown (Mike)	cf		
? Collins		c	
Joe Forbes	3b		
Charles Grant	2b		
Frank Harvey	p		
? Hawks		3b	
? Hayes		ss	
A. Johnson (Sampson)		c	
? Johnstone		c	
G. McDonald		rf	
? Miller	3b		
Leonard Oliver	ss		
Joe Parks	c		
? Sanchez		rf	1b
? Sisco		lf	
Franklin Sykes (Doc)	1b	p	

Schenectady Mohawk Giants

Player	1	2	3
Phil Bradley	c	cf	inf M
George Ball (Walter)	p	of	
James Booker (Pete)	c		
Jesse Bragg		of	3b
H. Brown	p		
W. Brown (Mike)	p	1b	of
Harry Buckner	p	of	
? Burton			
Ashby Dunbar		rf	
? Edwards (Smokey)	p		
Bill Francis	3b		
Robert Gans (Jude)	lf	of	
Leroy Grant	1b		
Blainey Hall	of		
W. James (Nux)	2b		
George Johnson (Chappie)	1b	c	
Grant Johnson	ss		
? Land	of		
? Langford (Ad)	p		
Floyd Lawyer	of		
? Mollett	ss		
Bill Pierce	c		

Player	1	2	3
Wes Pryor			3b
Johnny Pugh	cf	inf	
William Smith (Big Bill)	lf	c	1b
? White		p	
Frank Wickware	p	of	
Wabishaw Wiley (Doc)		c	
Hank Williams	3b	2b	
Smokey Joe Williams	p		

St. Louis Giants

Player	1	2	3
Sam Bennett	cf		
Elwood DeMoss (Bingo)		2b	
? Hannon	c		
Joe Hewitt	ss		
? Jones	p		
Dudley McAdoo (Tully)		1b	
Sam Mongin	3b		
L. Moore	lf		
? Smith	p	rf	
Felix Wallace		1b	utl

West Baden (IND) Sprudels

Player	1	2	3
C.I. Taylor		2b	M
George Brown	rf	cf	
Morten Clark	ss		
Elwood DeMoss (Bingo)		2b	
Charley Hill (Lefty)	cf		
Bruce Hocker		1b	
Bill Kindle	2b		
Jerome Lewis		2b	3b
William McMurray		c	1b
Pleas Miller (Hub)	p		
? O'Neill	c		
George Shively	lf		
Lawrence Simpson	p	of	
Ben Taylor	1b		
John Taylor (Steel Arm)	p		
? Williams	p		

1914

Cuban Giants

Player	1	2	3
William Smith (Big Bill)	1b		M
E. Brown	p		
Sam Gordon	lf		
A. Johnson	cf		
Bill Kindle		3b	
? Matthews	2b		
Fred Meade (Chick)	ss		
? Pannell	c		
Charles Reese	rf	p	
Hank Williams	1b		

Cuban Stars

Player	1	2	3
Pelayo Chacon		ss	
Jose Figarola		c	1b
Miguel Gonzalez (Mike)	1b	c	
Ricardo Hernandez (Chico)	3b	of	
Jose Junco		p	of
Hector Magrinat	lf	rf	
Francisco Moran		3b	
Eugenio Morin	ss	3b	
H. Pareda (Monk)	p		
Eustaquio Pedroso	p	rf	
Jose Rodriquez	c		
Cristobal Torriente	cf	rf	p
Roberto Villa (Bobby)	2b		

Lincoln Giants of New York

Player	1	2	3
George Ball (Walter)		p	
Sam Bennett		of	
Dell Clark		ss	
William Dismukes (Dizzy)	p		
Joe Forbes	p		
Bill Gatewood	p		of
Ernest Gatewood		c	
Leroy Grant	1b	3b	
Blainey Hall		lf	
Frank Harvey	p		
Joe Hewitt		3b	of
W. James (Nux)		2b	
A. Johnson		2b	
L. Moore		rf	
William Parks		lf	
Spottswood Poles (Spot)	cf	2b	p
Johnny Pugh		3b	
Dick Redding (Cannonball)	p	1b	rf
Louis Santop		c	rf
? Tate	p		
Jules Thomas		cf	
Felix Wallace	ss		
William Webster (Speck)		1b	
Wabishaw Wiley (Doc)		rf	c
Smokey Joe Williams	p		

Lincoln Stars of New York

Player	1	2	3
George Ball (Walter)	cf		
? Brown	rf		
Joe Forbes	ss		
Joe Hewitt		inf	
? Jackson	3b		
Bill Kindle		ss	3b
? Langford (Ad)	p		
William Parks	2b		
Andrew Payne (Jap)	lf		
William Pettus (Zack)	1b		
Bill Pierce	c		
? Thompson (Gunboat)	p		

Brooklyn All-Stars

Player	1	2	3
B. Brown	p		
E. Brown		p	
Sam Gordon	lf		
B. Johnson (Monk)	cf		
Bill Kindle	2b		
Fred Meade (Chick)	ss		
? Pannell		c	1b
? Pinto	p		
Charles Reese	rf	p	
William Smith (Big Bill)		1b	c
Hank Williams	3b		
L. Williams	p		

Brooklyn Royal Giants

Player	1	2	3
? Andrews (Pop)		rf	of
Phil Bradley	1b		
Jesse Bragg	3b		
Dell Clark	ss		
William Dismukes (Dizzy)	p		
Charles Earle (Frank)	rf		
Ernest Gatewood		c	of
Bill Handy	2b		
Frank Harvey	p		
Joe Hewitt		ss	
Bill Kindle		3b	
Jimmie Lyons	lf		
Andrew Payne (Jap)		3b	
Johnny Pugh		of	

Player	1	2	3
Louis Santop		c	
? Shirley		of	
Franklin Sykes (Doc)		p	
Jules Thomas	cf		
Pearl Webster	c		
Frank Wickware		p	
S. Williams		p	

Chicago American Giants

Player	1	2	3
Andrew Foster (Rube)		p	M
? Banton		p	
Jess Barbour	1b		
James Booker (Pete)	c		
Charles Dougherty (Pat)		p	
Frank Duncan (Pete)	rf	cf	
Bill Francis	3b		
Robert Gans (Jude)	lf		
Albert Gillard (Hamp)		p	
Charley Hill (Lefty)	of	p	
Preston Hill (Pete)	cf		
Horace Jenkins		rf	p
George Johnson (Chappie)		c	
Louis Johnson (Dicta)		p	
? Klondyke		c	
Bill Lindsay		p	lf
John Henry Lloyd (Pop)	ss		
? Maxwell		rf	
William Monroe	2b		
? Peterson		p	
Bruce Petway		c	1b
? Scott		p	
Walter Speedy		inf	
Lee Wade	p		
Jack Watts		c	
Frank Wickware		p	
Smokey Joe Williams		p	

Chicago Giants

Player	1	2	3
? Bilgar		c	
? Buckner	ss		
? Buford		p	
Sam Crawford	p		
? Dixon		p	
Charles Green (Joe)	cf		
Thurman Jennings	2b		
Jimmie Lyons		cf	
Dudley McAdoo (Tully)	1b		
Sam Mongin	3b		
Sam Strothers	c		
Albert Toney		rf	
Clarence Winston (Bobby)	lf		

French Lick (IN) Plutos

Player	1	2	3
Todd Allen	1b		
? Bingham (Bingo)		cf	
? Crew		c	
? Davis (Quack)	lf		
Elwood DeMoss (Bingo)	2b		
Albert Gillard (Hamp)	p		
Sam Gordon		c	
? Graham	p		
? Hannon		cf	
? Health	rf		
Thomas Lynch	ss		
? McLaughlin	p		
? Norman	3b		

Indianapolis ABCs

Player	1	2	3
C.I. Taylor			M
Howard Bartlett (Hop)		p	

Player	1	2	3
George Brown		of	
L. Brown		2b	
Alonzo Burch	p		
W. Cobb	c		lf
? Collins	c		
Sam Gordon		of	2b
? Hannibal		rf	
Fred Hutchinson	ss	2b	
James Jeffries		lf	rf
Louis Johnson (Dicta)	p		
? Leach		c	
L. Moore	of		
Russell Powell	c		
Joe Scotland	cf		
? Seldom		2b	ss
George Shively	lf		
? Simmons		rf	
Lawrence Simpson		p	
? Stallard		p	
Ben Taylor	1b		
Candy Jim Taylor	3b		
John Taylor (Steel Arm)	p		
B. Turner (Aggie)	2b	1b	
Frank Warfield		ss	
Jack Watts		c	
Andrew Williams (Stringbean)		p	

Louisville White Sox

Player	1	2	3
Todd Allen		1b	c
Sam Bennett		cf	
? Briscoe	cf		
Harry Buckner		rf	p
? Carter	ss		
E. Cooper		1b	
? Davis (Quack)		lf	
Ashby Dunbar		lf	
? Edwards (Smokey)		c	
Andrew Foster (Rube)		p	
? Hannibal		lf	
? Houston		rf	
W. James (Nux)		2b	
George Johnson (Chappie)		c	
Louis Johnson (Dicta)		p	
? McLaughlin		2b	p
Shirley Moore	p		
? Norman	3b		
? O'Neill		c	
Wes Pryor		3b	
? Pryor		p	
? Rogers		2b	
? Wallace		rf	
? Watson	1b	c	
Jack Watts		c	
? West	p	1b	
Frank Wickware		p	

New York Stars

Player	1	2	3
B. Brown	p		
E. Brown		1b	p
Sam Gordon	3b	rf	
B. Johnson (Monk)	cf	lf	
Bill Kindle	2b		
Fred Meade (Chick)	ss		
? Pannell		c	
Archie Pate	rf		
? Patton	lf	c	
? Pinto	p		
Charles Reese	p	lf	
William Smith (Big Bill)		c	
Hank Williams	1b	3b	

Philadelphia Giants

Player	1	2	3
G. Banks	p		
? Barnhard		cf	
Charles Bradford	cf		
W. Brown (Mike)	p		
Harry Despert (Denny)	lf		
Jimmy Fuller	c		
? Greene		rf	
D. Johnson (Dud)	2b		
Fred Meade (Chick)		rf	
? Miller		ss	
? Ping	1b		
? Williams		ss	

Schenectady Mohawk Giants

Player	1	2	3
Sam Bennett	cf		
Harry Buckner	rf	p	
E. Cooper	1b		
Ashby Dunbar	ss	of	1b
Ernest Gatewood		c	1b
Armour Henderson		p	
W. James (Nux)		2b	ss
George Johnson (Chappie)	c	1b	
Tom Johnson	p		
? Land		lf	
? Morris		2b	
Wes Pryor	3b		
C.L. Scott			
? Seldom		ss	
Lawrence Simpson		p	
Frank Wickware		p	

West Baden (IND) Sprudels

Player	1	2	3
? Banton	p		
George Brown	cf	3b	
W. Cobb		c	
Elwood DeMoss (Bingo)	2b		
? Harrison	1b	2b	
Bruce Hocker		of	1b
? Jones	rf	p	cf
Dan Kennard	c	lf	
Arthur Kimbro (Jess)	ss		
? Lindsey		of	
Thomas Lynch	3b		
William McMurray		rf	3b
Pleas Miller (Hub)	p	of	
? O'Neill		c	
? Williams	p		

1915

Cuban Stars

Player	1	2	3
Agustin Molina			M
Tatica Campos		of	
Pelayo Chacon	ss		
Jose Figarola		c	
Bienvenido Jimenez (Hooks)	2b		
Jose Junco	p	rf	
Hector Magrinat		lf	of
Juan Padrone	p		
H. Pareda (Monk)	p		
Augustin Parpetti	1b		
? Peda		of	
Eustaquio Pedroso	rf	lf	p
Herman Rios	3b		
C. Rodriquez		p	
Jose Rodriquez	c		
Cristobal Torriente	cf		
Roberto Villa (Bobby)	lf	2b	

Brooklyn Royal Giants

Player	1	2	3
H. Brown		p	
Charles Earle (Frank)		cf	
Ernest Gatewood	1b	c	
Bill Handy		2b	
Joe Hewitt		ss	
Bill Kindle		3b	
Johnny Pugh	rf		
Louis Santop		c	1b
Pearl Webster		lf	c
S. Williams	p	of	

Chicago American Giants

Player	1	2	3
Andrew Foster (Rube)	p	1b	M
? Allison	c		
George Ball (Walter)	p		
Jess Barbour	1b		
Harry Bauchman	2b		
Clarkson Brazelton	c		
Sam Crawford	p		
Frank Duncan (Pete)	cf		
Bill Francis	3b	ss	2b
Robert Gans (Jude)	of		
Bill Gatewood	p	1b	
? Hanson	ss		
Preston Hill (Pete)	lf		
Fred Hutchinson	ss		
Horace Jenkins	of	p	
Tom Johnson	p		
William Jones (Fox)	c		
Edward Jones	c		
John Henry Lloyd (Pop)	ss		
Hurley McNair	rf		
? Murphy	of		
William Parks	1b	ss	
Bruce Petway	c		
Louis Santop	c		
Edgar Washington (Blue)	p		
Jack Watts	c		
Dick Whitworth	p		
Frank Wickware	p		
Robert Wright			c

Chicago Giants

Player	1	2	3
Clarkson Brazelton	c		
Harry Buckner	rf	p	
? Dixon	p		
Charles Dougherty (Pat)		p	
Charles Green (Joe)	cf	c	
William Green	3b		
Guy Jackson	ss		
Thurman Jennings	2b		
Sam Strothers	1b		
Clarence Winston (Bobby)	lf		

Indianapolis ABCs

Player	1	2	3
C.I. Taylor			M
Todd Allen	3b		
Otto Briggs		2b	
Oscar Charleston	cf	p	
? Christian		cf	
Morten Clark	ss	p	
Elwood DeMoss (Bingo)	2b		
William Dismukes (Dizzy)	p		
Charles Goines		c	
Sam Gordon		of	
Fred Hutchinson		3b	ss
James Jeffries	rf	p	
Louis Johnson (Dicta)	p		
Tom Johnson	p		
Dan Kennard		c	
Jimmie Lyons		of	
Russell Powell	c		
Dick Redding (Cannonball)		p	
George Shively	lf		
Ben Taylor	1b	p	
Frank Warfield		of	

Louisville Sox

Player	1	2	3
McKinley Downs (Bunny)	ss		
Ashby Dunbar	lf		
Bruce Hocker	1b		
? Jones	c		
Arthur Kimbro (Jess)	2b		
L. Moore	rf		
Shirley Moore	p		
Joe Scotland	cf		
John Taylor (Steel Arm)	p		
Candy Jim Taylor	3b		

New York Lincoln Giants

Player	1	2	3
G. Banks		p	
S. Banks		c	
Jesse Bragg	3b		
Charles Earle (Frank)	rf		
Ernest Gatewood		c	
Leroy Grant	1b		
Blainey Hall	lf		
W. James (Nux)	2b		
? Langford (Ad)	p		
? Powell		p	
Dick Redding (Cannonball)	p		
Jules Thomas	cf		
Wabishaw Wiley (Doc)		c	
Smokey Joe Williams	p		

New York Lincoln Stars

Player	1	2	3
? Bernard		of	
Robert Gans (Jude)	lf		
Frank Harvey	p	of	
Bill Kindle	2b		
John Henry Lloyd (Pop)	ss		
L. Miller		of	inf
Sam Mongin	3b		
Juan Padrone		p	
William Parks	ss		
William Pettus (Zack)	1b		
Bill Pierce	c	of	
Spottswood Poles (Spot)	cf		
Dick Redding (Cannonball)	p		
Louis Santop	rf	c	of
Franklin Sykes (Doc)	p		
Lee Wade		p	

Philadelphia Giants

Player	1	2	3
Phil Bradley	c		
W. Brown (Mike)	1b		
Jack Emery	p		
James Griffin (Horse)	2b		
D. Johnson (Dud)	ss	2b	
Jesse Scragg	p		
? Valentine	rf		

St. Louis Giants

Player	1	2	3
Sam Bennett	cf		
W. Cobb		c	
Bill Gatewood	p	of	
Bill Handy	2b		
Joe Hewitt	rf	2b	
Arthur Kimbro (Jess)	3b		
Jimmie Lyons	lf	of	
Dudley McAdoo (Tully)	1b		
Felix Wallace	ss		
William Webster (Speck)	c	of	
Andrew Williams (Stringbean)	p		

West Baden (IND) Sprudels

Player	1	2	3
Charles Blackwell	lf		

1915 Breakers Hotel team of Palm Beach, Florida in their Sunday best. Back Row L to R: unknown, Dick Redding, Pop Lloyd, Jude Gans, Louis Santop, Leroy Grant. Middle: unknown, Dicta Johnson, Smokey Joe Williams, Zack Pettus, Bill Francis. Front: Pete Hill, unknown, unknown, Spotswood Poles.

Reid Poles

Player	1	2	3
Otto Briggs	rf		
George Brown	cf		
McKinley Downs (Bunny)	ss		
? Harrison	3b		
Charley Hill (Lefty)	2b		
? Keene	1b		
Pleas Miller (Hub)	p		
Burlin White	c		

1916

All Nations

Player	1	2	3
Frank Blukoi	2b		
Clarence Coleman		c	
John Donaldson	p	lf	
Frank Evans	rf	3b	
Ricardo Hernandez (Chico)	1b		
? Kennedy	lf		
? Kramer	3b		
? Lyles		p	
Jose Mendez (Joe)	ss	p	
Cristobal Torriente	cf		
? Weidel		p	
Wesley Wilkins		p	
J.L. Wilkinson		p	

Bacharach Giants

Player	1	2	3
Frank Crockett	cf	ss	
Willis Crump	rf	c	
Nap Cummings (Chance)	1b	of	
James Deas (Yank)	c	of	
Arthur Dilworth	p	lf	
W.W. Fuller (Chick)		ss	3b
W. James (Nux)		2b	
A. Johnson (Sampson)		c	
Dan Johnson (Shang)	p	of	
Dick Lundy	ss	3b	2b
Paul Mack	3b		
Elihu Roberts		2b	of
Henry Tucker	rf		
Felix Wallace		2b	
? Walsh		2b	
Smokey Joe Williams		p	
A. Williams	lf		
Tom Williams		p	

Bowser's ABCs

Player	1	2	3
Todd Allen	3b		
Howard Bartlett (Hop)		p	
Charles Blackwell		of	
? Chandler		p	
Oscar Charleston		cf	
? Christian		of	
Clarence Coleman		p	
Elwood DeMoss (Bingo)	2b		
? Floyd		of	
Charles Goines		of	
? Hannibal		cf	
? Harrison		lf	
Bruce Hocker	1b		
Fred Hutchinson	ss		
Louis Johnson (Dicta)	p		
Edward Jones		c	
? Keene		1b	
Dan Kennard		c	
Bennie Lyons		of	1b
? McReynolds	p	of	
Shirley Moore		p	
Archie Pate		of	3b

Player	1	2	3
? Pryor	p		
Cornelius Rhoades (Neal)		of	
George Shively		lf	
Lawrence Simpson		rf	p
Frank Warfield		of	
Jack Watts		c	
Burlin White		of	c

Cuban Stars of Havana

Player	1	2	3
Tatica Campos	3b	p	1b
Pelayo Chacon		ss	
Gervasio Gonzalez	1b	c	
Bienvenido Jimenez (Hooks)	2b		
Jose Junco	p	of	
Hector Magrinat	lf	cf	
P. Miranda			
Juan Padrone	p		
Eustaquio Pedroso	cf	lf	p
Herman Rios	ss	3b	
Jose Rodriquez	c		
Cristobal Torriente		of	
Roberto Villa (Bobby)	rf		

Cuban X Giants

Player	1	2	3
Frank Baynard	lf		
? Brown	p		
James Griffin (Horse)	3b		
Cecil Johnson (Sess)	1b		
H. Johnson	2b		
P. Johnson	c		
W. Jones	rf		
? Terrell	cf		
? Thomas	ss		

Baltimore Black Sox

Player	1	2	3
H.C. Harris			M
? Brown		p	
? Evans	ss		
Roy Ford	p	of	
? Fullman		of	
? Ganggang		of	p
George Greyer	1b		
J.B. Hairstone	rf	cf	
J. Johnson	cf		
? Matthews	2b		
? Ridgely (Buck)	3b	ss	
Charley Thomas	c		

Brooklyn Royal Giants

Player	1	2	3
Denny Despert	lf		
Ashby Dunbar		of	
Charles Earle (Frank)	cf	p	of
Ernest Gatewood	1b	c	of
Bill Handy	2b	3b	
Frank Harvey	p	of	
Joe Hewitt	ss		
Othello Johnson		rf	
Bill Kindle		3b	2b
L. Miller		3b	
Johnny Pugh		rf	3b
Dick Redding (Cannonball)		p	
Louis Santop		c	rf
R. Smith (Red)		p	
Franklin Sykes (Doc)		p	
Pearl Webster	c	1b	of
Andrew Williams (Stringbean)	p	of	

Pittsburgh Stars of Buffalo

Player	1	2	3
? Andrews (Pop)	1b	p	
Frank Baynard	cf		

Player	1	2	3
Phil Bradley	c		
? Collins	p	c	
Jack Emery	p		
W. James (Nux)	2b		
Grant Johnson	ss		
George Mayo	rf		
Fred Meade (Chick)	3b		

Chicago American Giants

Player	1	2	3
Andrew Foster (Rube)		p	M
Jess Barbour	3b	2b	
Harry Bauchman	2b		
? Biran		inf	
Emmett Bowman		2b	
Clarkson Brazelton		c	
? Carlson		c	
? Davis (Dago)		p	
William Dismukes (Dizzy)		p	
? Dixon		p	
Ashby Dunbar		of	
Frank Duncan (Pete)	rf	lf	
Bill Francis	3b		
Robert Gans (Jude)	lf	p	of
Leroy Grant	1b		
? Hayes (Buddy)		c	
Preston Hill (Pete)	cf	rf	
Tom Johnson	p		
John Henry Lloyd (Pop)	ss		
Dudley McAdoo (Tully)		1b	
Hurley McNair		rf	of
Bruce Petway	c		
? Scott		p	
Ruby Tyree		p	
Edgar Washington (Blue)		p	
Dick Whitworth	p		
Frank Wickware		p	
Tom Williams		p	
? Woods		p	

Chicago Giants

Player	1	2	3
James Booker (Pete)		c	
? Borter		1b	
Harry Buckner	p	rf	
Charles Green (Joe)	cf	rf	
William Green		3b	
Horace Jenkins	p	cf	
Thurman Jennings		2b	ss
William Jones (Fox)	c	3b	
Palmer Kelley	p		
Ed Lee		ss	
? Lewis (Tuck)		2b	
? Scott		p	
Sam Strothers	1b		
Albert Toney		2b	
B. Turner (Aggie)		1b	2b
? Walton		ss	
Ted Waters		inf	
Clarence Winston (Bobby)	lf		

Chicago Union Giants

Player	1	2	3
? Bennett		2b	
? Bingham (Bingo)		cf	
Virgil Blueitt		2b	
E. Brown	p		
Alonzo Burch		p	
Clarence Coleman		c	
? Greene	3b		
? Harper		p	
Edward Jones		c	
? Majors		p	

Player	1	2	3
Dudley McAdoo (Tully)		1b	
Hurley McNair		p	
Andrew Payne (Jap)	rf		
Frank Peters	ss		
Mack Ramsey	lf		
Lawrence Simpson		p	
? Turner		c	
? White		p	

Indianapolis ABCs

Player	1	2	3
C.I. Taylor			M
Jess Barbour		cf	rf
George Brown	rf	lf	
Oscar Charleston		cf	
Morten Clark	ss		
Elwood DeMoss (Bingo)		2b	
William Dismukes (Dizzy)	p		
McKinley Downs (Bunny)		ss	
Ashby Dunbar		of	
James Jeffries	p	of	
Louis Johnson (Dicta)		p	
Dan Kennard		c	
Dave Malarcher	2b	ss	
Fred Meade (Chick)	2b	of	
Russell Powell	c		
? Pryor		p	
George Shively		lf	cf
Ben Taylor	1b	p	
John Taylor (Steel Arm)		p	
Candy Jim Taylor	3b		
Jack Watts		c	
Frank Wickware		p	

Kansas City Tigers

Player	1	2	3
Floyd Webb			M
Troy Black	p	of	
Othello Countee	ss		
Reuben Currie (Rube)	p		
Arthur Davis		of	
Frank Duncan	c	1b	
Eddie Dwight	cf		
Dorsey Ewing		of	
William Ewing (Buck)	rf	of	
Roosevelt Gray (Chappy)	1b	c	
Arthur Henderson (Rats)	2b		
R.J. Nealy		of	
Hurland Ragland	p		
Eugene Redd	3b		
Leander Smith	lf	of	
Raymond Smith		utl	

Montgomery Grey Sox

Player	1	2	3
John Beckwith	c		
S. Brown	rf		
C. Brown	p		
? Cotton	p		
H. Cunningham (Rounder)	ss		
Marion Cunningham	1b		
McKinley Downs (Bunny)		2b	
? Hannon	lf		
? McCormack	3b		
? Patton	cf		
? Street	2b		

New York Cuban Stars

Player	1	2	3
Juan Almenteros	p		
Bernardo Baro	lf	p	of
Julian Fabelo	ss		
Rodolfo Fernandez		lf	p
Jose Fernandez	c		
Juan Guerra	1b		
Agipito Lazaga	rf	p	1b
? Manolo	1b		
Bartolo Portuando	3b	of	
Ramiro Ramirez	cf		
Julio Rojo		3b	c
? Suarez	p		
Recurvon Teran	2b		

New York Lincoln Giants

Player	1	2	3
G. Banks	p		
Jesse Bragg	2b	ss	
Joe Forbes	ss		
Blainey Hall	lf	rf	
Frank Harvey		of	p
? Langford (Ad)	p	rf	
? McNeil		ss	
Sam Mongin	3b		
? Payne		p	
William Pettus (Zack)	1b		
Bill Pierce	c	2b	
Spottswood Poles (Spot)	cf	2b	
Dick Redding (Cannonball)	p	rf	
Louis Santop	c		
Jules Thomas	rf	1b	of
? Thompson (Gunboat)	1b	p	
Wabishaw Wiley (Doc)	c	1b	
Smokey Joe Williams	p	of	1b

New York Lincoln Stars

Player	1	2	3
D. Bailey	3b	ss	
? Brown	cf		
Oscar Charleston	cf		
? Christian	cf		
E. Cooper	rf	lf	
? Culver	rf	ss	
Ashby Dunbar	of		
? Edwards (Smokey)	rf	p	
Jimmy Fuller	c		
Ernest Gatewood	c		
? Good	c	rf	
Peter Green (Ed)	of		
? Harper	1b		
Bruce Hocker	of		
? Jackson	c		
A. Johnson	2b	3b	
C. Johnston	2b	3b	ss
? Langford (Ad)	p	cf	
L. Miller	3b		
? Mollett	2b		
? Murphy	p		
William Parks	ss		
? Parks	p		
? Peters	c		
William Pettus (Zack)	1b	c	p
? Post	of		
Johnny Pugh	cf	of	
Louis Santop	c	of	
? Shields	p		
? Slawson	3b	2b	
R. Smith (Red)	p	of	
Franklin Sykes (Doc)	p	of	
? Thompson (Gunboat)	p	of	
Oscar Twyman	rf		
Lee Wade	p		

Philadelphia Giants

Player	1	2	3
S. Banks	c		
Charles Bradford	of		
Jesse Bragg	2b		
E. Cooper	1b		
Peter Green (Ed)	of		
Charles Hayman (Bugs)		p	
Othello Johnson		of	
? Lee	ss		
? Murphy	p		
William Pettus (Zack)		of	
? Tate	p		
Charles Thomas	3b		

St. Louis Giants

Player	1	2	3
Dick Waters			M
Sam Bennett	rf	of	
Charles Blackwell	lf		
? Carey	rf	ss	
W. Cobb	c		
McKinley Downs (Bunny)		2b	
Bill Drake	p		
Bill Gatewood		p	
Bill Handy		2b	
? Hayes (Buddy)		c	
Joe Hewitt		rf	ss
Dan Kennard		c	
Arthur Kimbro (Jess)	2b	3b	
Jimmie Lyons	cf	lf	
Dudley McAdoo (Tully)	1b		
? Melton		p	
Pleas Miller (Hub)	p		
? Nolan	c		
? Pryor		p	
Lee Wade	p		
Felix Wallace	3b	ss	
Frank Warfield		ss	of
William Webster (Speck)		c	
Andrew Williams (Stringbean)	p		

1917

All Nations

Player	1	2	3
Frank Blukoi	2b		
Clarence Coleman	c		
Sam Crow	3b		
John Donaldson	p	of	
? Kinnon	lf		
Hurley McNair	cf		
Wilber Rogan (Bullet Joe)	ss	lf	p
? Steno	rf		
B. Turner (Aggie)	1b		

Cuban Giants

Player	1	2	3
? Bernard	cf		
Tom Fiall	lf		
W.W. Fuller (Chick)	ss		
Jimmy Fuller	c		
Robert Gans (Jude)		rf	
James Griffin (Horse)	2b		
? Panier	p		
? Thompson (Gunboat)		1b	
? Valos	3b		

Cuban Stars (East)

Player	1	2	3
? Calderin	p		
Pelayo Chacon	ss		
Julian Fabelo	3b	inf	of
Jose Fernandez	c		
? Leon		c	
Alejandro Oms	lf		
Augustin Parpetti	1b		
Ramiro Ramirez	cf		

Player	1	2	3
? Rivas	2b		
Julio Rojo	rf	c	p
? Suarez		rf	p

Cuban Stars (West)

Player	1	2	3
Bernardo Baro	cf	p	
Tatica Campos	rf		
Gervasio Gonzalez	1b	c	
Juan Guerra	lf		
Bienvenido Jimenez (Hooks)	2b		
Jose Junco	p		
Juan Padrone	p		
Eustaquio Pedroso	p	of	inf
Bartolo Portuando	3b		
Herman Rios	ss		
Jose Rodriquez	c		

Hilldale

Player	1	2	3
? Bernard			cf
Otto Briggs	rf		
Louis Burgee			2b
McKinley Downs (Bunny)			2b
Frank Ford			c
Charlie Freeman			
W.W. Fuller (Chick)			inf
Andy Harris	3b		
Tom Jenkins			
Dan Johnson (Shang)	p		
George Kemp			rf
Arthur Kimbro (Jess)			3b
Dick Lundy	ss		
George Mayo	1b	of	
William Pettus (Zack)			1b
Fred Pinder	ss		
Spottswood Poles (Spot)			cf
Cornelius Rhoades (Neal)	c		
Louis Santop			c
Franklin Sykes (Doc)			p
John Taylor (Steel Arm)	p		
Jules Thomas			lf
? Triplett			cf
? Valentine	of		
Pearl Webster		rf	c
Smokey Joe Williams			p

Jewell's ABCs

Player	1	2	3
Charles Blackwell	lf		
? Branham (Slim)	p		
George Brown	rf		
W. Cobb	c		
? Lynn	p		
Bennie Lyons	1b		
? McLaughlin	p		
? Pryor	p		
William Webster (Speck)		c	
Frank Wickware		p	

Bacharach Giants

Player	1	2	3
? Banks		of	
Frank Baynard		rf	of
? Clinton		3b	
Nap Cummings (Chance)	1b		
James Deas (Yank)		c	
Arthur Dilworth		p	of
McKinley Downs (Bunny)	rf	inf	
Henry Gillespie		p	
Bill Handy	2b		
Ben Johnson		p	
Dick Lundy	ss		
Paul Mack		3b	of

Player	1	2	3
G. McDonald			p
L. Miller	3b		
William Pettus (Zack)		1b	
Elihu Roberts	lf		
Roy Roberts	p		
R. Smith (Red)		rf	
Jules Thomas		cf	
? Tomm		cf	of
Felix Wallace		cf	
? Wheatherspoon		p	
Burlin White		c	
? Wilson		ss	

Baltimore Black Sox

Player	1	2	3
? Bell		rf	
? Burrell	lf		
? Evans	2b		
Roy Ford		rf	
George Greyer	1b		
J.B. Hairstone	cf		
William Hodges	p		
Willie Parker	p		
? Ridgely (Buck)	ss		
Charley Thomas	c		
Harry Williams	3b		

Brooklyn Royal Giants

Player	1	2	3
Jesse Bragg			3b
Tom Brown		p	
Charles Earle (Frank)	cf		
Ernest Gatewood	c	1b	
Bill Handy		ss	2b
Frank Harvey	p		
Joe Hewitt		ss	
W. James (Nux)		of	
Bill Kindle		3b	
? Langford (Ad)	rf	p	of
L. Miller		3b	
Johnny Pugh	2b	of	
Louis Santop		1b	c
Franklin Sykes (Doc)		p	
Pearl Webster	lf	c	1b
S. Williams		p	
A. Williams	of		

Pittsburgh Stars of Buffalo

Player	1	2	3
Toussaint Allen (Tom)	1b		
Phil Bradley	cf	c	
? Collins	c	p	
? Gamp	rf		
W. James (Nux)	2b		
Grant Johnson	ss		
Fred Meade (Chick)	3b		
? Miller	p		
? Ransome	lf		

Chicago American Giants

Player	1	2	3	M
Andrew Foster (Rube)				M
Jess Barbour	rf	3b	2b	
Harry Bauchman		2b		
Clarkson Brazelton		c		
? Brenner		p		
Elwood DeMoss (Bingo)	2b			
George Dixon		c		
Frank Duncan (Pete)	lf			
Bill Francis	3b			
Robert Gans (Jude)		of	p	
Leroy Grant	1b			
Preston Hill (Pete)	cf			
Tom Johnson	p			
John Henry Lloyd (Pop)	ss			
Juan Padrone		p		
Bruce Petway		c	of	
Dick Redding (Cannonball)		p		
Ruby Tyree		p		
Burlin White		c		
Dick Whitworth		p		
Frank Wickware		p		
Tom Williams	p			

Chicago Giants

Player	1	2	3
George Ball (Walter)	p	of	
John Beckwith	ss		
James Booker (Pete)	1b		
Robert Gans (Jude)		lf	of
Charles Green (Joe)	rf	cf	
William Green		3b	
Frank Jeffreys		2b	
Thurman Jennings	2b	ss	
William Jones (Fox)	c		
Jimmie Lyons	cf	1b	
? Madert		2b	
Archie Pate		of	
Andrew Reed		3b	
Frank Wickware	p		
Clarence Winston (Bobby)		lf	

Chicago Union Giants

Player	1	2	3
? Allison	1b	c	
Harry Bauchman	2b		
? Bingham (Bingo)	rf		
Virgil Blueitt		2b	
Clarence Coleman	c		
William Green	3b		
Horace Jenkins	cf		
Palmer Kelley	p		
Dick Lee		of	
Andrew Payne (Jap)	lf		
Frank Peters	ss		

Havana Cubans

Player	1	2	3	M
Toney Soto				M
Miguel Clemente	c			
? Cordova (Pete)	3b			
Bienvenido Jimenez (Hooks)		ss		
Juan Padrone	p			
Augustin Parpetti		1b		
Jose Pillar	p			
? Rivas		2b		
Cristobal Torriente	cf	p		
Pablo Valdez (Tony)	rf	p		

Havana Red Sox

Player	1	2	3
Frank Baynard	lf		
John Cason	c		
Phil Cockrell	p	of	
? Dandridge (Ping)	3b		
? Forrest	rf		
Dick Lundy		ss	
? Morton	2b		
? O'May	1b		
? Thomas	cf		

Indianapolis ABCs

Player	1	2	3	M
C.I. Taylor				M
Charles Blackwell		of		
? Briggs		p		
Oscar Charleston	cf	p		
Morten Clark	ss			
W. Cobb		c		

Player	1	2	3	Player	1	2	3	Player	1	2	3
William Dismukes (Dizzy)	p			**Kansas City Tigers**				Arthur Kimbro (Jess)			3b
Bill Gatewood		p		Floyd Webb			M	George Lewis (Peaches)		p	
James Jeffries		p	rf	Troy Black	p	of		? Maywood		p	
Louis Johnson (Dicta)	p			Othello Countee	ss			G. McDonald		p	
John Landers		p		Reuben Currie (Rube)	p			? McLaughlin		p	
Dave Malarcher		rf	inf	Arthur Davis		of		B. Merritt		p	
Lemuel McDougal (Lem)	p			Frank Duncan	c	1b		Sam Mongin	3b		
Russell Powell	c			Eddie Dwight	cf			Bill Pierce	1b	c	
George Shively	lf			Dorsey Ewing		of		Spottswood Poles (Spot)	cf		
Ben Taylor	1b	p		William Ewing (Buck)	rf	of		Jules Thomas	rf		
Candy Jim Taylor	3b	2b		Roosevelt Gray (Chappy)	1b	c		Lee Wade	p		
Frank Warfield	2b	ss		Arthur Henderson (Rats)	2b			Felix Wallace	ss		
Jack Watts		c		R.J. Nealy		of		? Webb		p	
Andrew Williams (Stringbean)	p			Hurland Ragland	p			Wabishaw Wiley (Doc)	c		
				Eugene Redd	3b			Smokey Joe Williams	p		
Kansas City Colored Giants				Leander Smith	lf	of					
? Gorden	1b			Raymond Smith		utl		**New York Lincoln Stars**			
? Gray	rf							Ashby Dunbar	lf		
? Guinea	lf			**New York Lincoln Giants**				Peter Green (Ed)	rf		
William Jackson (Ashes)	3b			Jesse Bragg	2b			Bruce Hocker	cf	1b	
Robert Lindsay (Frog)	ss			? Dandridge (Ping)		p		A. Johnson		2b	
? Mansfield	2b			Joe Forbes		ss		Grant Johnson		2b	
? Moss	cf			Robert Gans (Jude)		of		? Langford (Ad)		p	
? Nolan	c			Blainey Hall	lf			L. Miller	3b		
Wilber Rogan (Bullet Joe)	p			W. James (Nux)		2b		William Parks	ss		
Floyd Skinner		utl		Dan Kennard	c			William Pettus (Zack)			1b

1917 Brooklyn Royal Giants. Back Row L to R: Nat Strong, Franklin "Doc" Sykes, Max Rosner. Middle: Ernest Gatewood, Charles Earle, Bill Kindle, Bill Handy, Johnny Pugh. Front: Louis Santop, Pearl Webster, Andrew Williams, Joe Hewitt, and Bill Harvey.
Bennett Rosner and Robert Eisen

Player	1	2	3
Louis Santop	c		
Franklin Sykes (Doc)		p	
? Thompson (Gunboat)	1b		

Pennsylvania Red Caps of NY

Player	1	2	3
D. Bailey	3b		
? Culver	cf		
Ashby Dunbar	lf		
? Edwards (Smokey)	p	c	
Joe Forbes	ss		
? Langford (Ad)	rf	p	
William Parks	2b		
Joe Parks	1b		
Bill Pierce	c		
? Smith (Gunboat)		of	
? Thompson (Gunboat)		p	

St. Louis Giants

Player	1	2	3
Sam Bennett	1b		
Charles Blackwell	lf		
? Carey	2b		
Frank Carter		p	
W. Cobb	rf	c	
Bill Drake	p		
Bill Gatewood	p		
Dan Kennard	c		
Arthur Kimbro (Jess)	3b		
Jimmie Lyons	cf		
William Pettus (Zack)	ss	1b	

1918

Cuban Stars (East)

Player	1	2	3
? Alderette		p	
? Barbette		1b	
? Calderin	rf	p	
Pelayo Chacon	ss		
Alejandro Crespo	3b	2b	
Isidro Fabre	p	of	
Jose Fernandez	c	1b	
Bienvenido Jimenez (Hooks)		2b	
Agipito Lazaga	1b		
? Leon		c	
Eustaquio Pedroso		p	of
Ramiro Ramirez	cf	of	
Julio Rojo	lf	c	
Recurvon Teran	3b		
Cristobal Torriente		of	

Cuban Stars (West)

Player	1	2	3
Bernardo Baro	lf	p	
Tatica Campos	3b	p	ss
? Gaideria		p	
Juan Guerra	c		
Bienvenido Jimenez (Hooks)	2b		
Jose Junco	p	of	
Eustaquio Pedroso	1b		
Bartolo Portuando	ss	3b	
Jose Rodriquez		c	
Cristobal Torriente	cf	p	
Roberto Villa (Bobby)	rf	p	

Grand Central Terminal

Player	1	2	3
E. Cooper		of	
Charles Earle (Frank)	c		
Bill Handy	2b		
Joe Hewitt	ss		
B. Johnson (Monk)	p	rf	
Arthur Kimbro (Jess)	3b		

Player	1	2	3
William Pettus (Zack)	1b		
Lee Wade		p	
William Webster (Speck)		c	of
William Young (Pep)	lf		

Bacharach Giants

Player	1	2	3
Frank Bennett			M
M. Brown	rf		
Nap Cummings (Chance)	1b		
James Deas (Yank)		lf	c
McKinley Downs (Bunny)		2b	
Bill Handy		2b	3b
Henry Howell		c	
Dick Lundy		ss	
John Reese	cf		
J.D. Roberts		2b	
Roy Roberts	p		
George Robinson	p		
? Smith			3b
William Webster (Speck)		c	

Baltimore Black Sox

Player	1	2	3
? Bell	cf		
? Burrell	lf		
? Evans	2b		
Roy Ford	rf		
George Greyer	1b		
J.B. Hairstone		c	
William Hodges	p		
Willie Parker	p		
? Ridgely (Buck)	ss		
Charley Thomas		c	
Harry Williams	3b		

Brooklyn Royal Giants

Player	1	2	3
Jesse Bragg		3b	
Beattie Brooks	2b	c	
Chester Brooks		2b	of
Irving Brooks	p		
John Cason		c	of
Frank Crockett		of	
John Donaldson		p	
Edward Douglass	1b		
Tom Fiall	cf	of	c
Ernest Gatewood		1b	
Joe Hewitt		ss	2b
Dan Johnson (Shang)		p	
George Johnson (Dibo)	lf		
John Henry Lloyd (Pop)	ss		
Oliver Marcelle	3b		
Joe Parks		c	
Johnny Pugh	rf	of	
Dick Redding (Cannonball)	p		
Louis Santop	c		
? Tomm		of	
Tom Williams		p	
A. Williams		of	2b

Chicago American Giants

Player	1	2	3
Andrew Foster (Rube)			M
Jess Barbour		cf	
Dave Brown		p	
Oscar Charleston		cf	
Sam Crawford	p		
Elwood DeMoss (Bingo)	2b		
George Dixon		c	
Frank Duncan (Pete)	lf		
? Fields		p	
Bill Francis	3b		
Robert Gans (Jude)		rf	

Player	1	2	3
Leroy Grant		1b	
Preston Hill (Pete)	rf		
Tom Johnson		p	
Jimmie Lyons		of	
Jose Mendez (Joe)		ss	p
Bruce Petway	c		
Dick Redding (Cannonball)		p	
Cristobal Torriente	cf		
Edgar Wesley		1b	
Dick Whitworth	p		
Frank Wickware	p		
Bobby Williams		ss	
Tom Williams		p	

Chicago Union Giants

Player	1	2	3
? Bingham (Bingo)	lf		
Virgil Blueitt		2b	
F. Brown	2b		
E. Brown	3b		
Clarence Coleman	c		
Ralph Jefferson	rf		
Palmer Kelley	p		
Dick Lee	cf		
? Mann		1b	
Earl Palmer		of	
Frank Peters	ss		
Sam Strothers	1b		
? Sullivan		of	

Dayton Marcos

Player	1	2	3
? Alexander		of	
George Brown	cf		
? Carr	1b		
? Cunningham	ss		
William Dismukes (Dizzy)		p	
? Dock	2b		
? Gibson	p		
? Gonzales		3b	
Thomas Lynch	rf		
? McNeil	c		
? Pettiford	lf		
? Thomas		3b	
? Wans		c	1b

Hilldale

Player	1	2	3
Elias Brown (Country)		rf	
Phil Cockrell	p	3b	
Nap Cummings (Chance)		1b	
Arthur Dilworth		p	
McKinley Downs (Bunny)	3b		
Tom Fiall		of	
W.W. Fuller (Chick)	2b		
? Hargett		p	
Bruce Hocker	1b		
Cecil Johnson (Sess)		3b	p
Dan Johnson (Shang)	p		
George Johnson (Dibo)		rf	
William Johnson (Judy)		3b	
Dick Lundy	ss		
William Pettus (Zack)	1b	3b	
John Reese	cf	lf	
Cornelius Rhoades (Neal)		c	
Louis Santop	c		
Franklin Sykes (Doc)		p	
? Triplett		of	
? Valentine		of	
Pearl Webster	c		
Tom Williams		p	

1919

Indianapolis ABCs

Player	1	2	3
C.I. Taylor			M
Oscar Charleston	cf		
Morten Clark	ss		
Clarence Coleman		c	
William Dismukes (Dizzy)	p		
John Donaldson		p	
James Jeffries	p		
Jimmie Lyons	rf		
Dave Malarcher	3b		
Russell Powell	c		
? Ross		p	
George Shively	lf		
Candy Jim Taylor		3b	2b
Ben Taylor	1b		
Frank Warfield	2b		
Andrew Williams (Stringbean)		p	

New York Lincoln Giants

Player	1	2	3
Todd Allen	3b		
Elmore Brown (Scrappy)		3b	
W. Cobb		c	
Phil Cockrell		p	
? Collins		c	2b
E. Cooper		1b	
? Culver		of	
James Deas (Yank)	c		
Arthur Dilworth		rf	
John Donaldson		p	
George Fiall		ss	
Joe Forbes		of	
Blainey Hall	lf		
Bill Handy		2b	
? Hendricks	p		
B. Johnson (Monk)		of	
Arthur Kimbro (Jess)		3b	
? Langford (Ad)	p		
John Henry Lloyd (Pop)		ss	
? McLaughlin		p	
Sam Mongin	2b		
William Parks	rf		
William Pettus (Zack)		1b	
Bill Pierce	1b		
Louis Santop		c	of
Jules Thomas	cf		
Felix Wallace	ss		
William Webster (Speck)		1b	c
Wabishaw Wiley (Doc)		c	
Smokey Joe Williams	p		
Tom Williams		p	

Pennsylvania Red Caps of NY

Player	1	2	3
D. Bailey	3b		
? Collins	c		
? Culver		cf	of
Ashby Dunbar	lf		
Joe Forbes	ss		
? Langford (Ad)		p	rf
? Malloy		rf	of
William Parks		2b	
Joe Parks		rf	c
Bill Pierce		1b	
Andrew Williams (Stringbean)	p		

Pennsylvania Giants

Player	1	2	3
? Cheatham		lf	
? Daley	ss		
James Deas (Yank)		c	
? Draper		cf	
W.E. Ferrell	1b		

Player	1	2	3
Frank Ford			c
C. Ford			p
W.W. Fuller (Chick)			2b
Henry Gillespie	lf		p
? Hall			1b
Wade Hampton			p
Andy Harris			3b
? Harts			p
? Horner	3b		
Henry Howell	p		
A. Johnson (Sampson)			c
? Kelly			1b
? Law			cf
? Richardson	rf		
J.D. Roberts		ss	3b
? Shrewsberry			of
R. Smith (Red)			p
? Warren			ss
E. Weeks			2b
? Weller	cf		
C. Wells			c

Philadelphia Giants

Player	1	2	3
Jesse Bragg	3b		
Beattie Brooks	2b		
Blainey Hall	lf		
Joe Hewitt	ss		
John Henry Lloyd (Pop)	1b		
Webster McDonald	p		
Johnny Pugh	rf		
? Tomm	cf		
Wabishaw Wiley (Doc)	c		
Andrew Williams (Stringbean)	p		
S. Williams			p

1919

Cuban Stars

Player	1	2	3
Eufemio Abreu	c		
Bernardo Baro	cf		
Tatica Campos		rf	
Bienvenido Jimenez (Hooks)		inf	
Jose Junco	p	rf	
? Lavera		c	
Julio LeBlanc (Jose)	p		
Eustaquio Pedroso	1b	p	
Bartolo Portuando	3b		
Herman Rios	2b		
Roberto Villa (Bobby)	lf		

Cuban Stars of Havana

Player	1	2	3
? Calderin	rf		
Pelayo Chacon	ss		
Alejandro Crespo		2b	
Valentin Dreke	lf		
Jose Fernandez	1b	c	
? Gonzales	3b		
Miles Lucas	p	1b	
Juan Padrone	p		
Ramiro Ramirez	cf		
Julio Rojo	c		
? Suarez		p	rf
Recurvon Teran	2b		

Atlantic City Bacharach Giants

Player	1	2	3
? Brown	p		
Joe Forbes		3b	rf
Ernest Gatewood	c		
Bill Handy	2b		

Player	1	2	3
Jesse Hubbard		p	
Fred Hutchinson	3b		
Ben Johnson		p	
Cecil Johnson (Sess)		lf	
George Johnson (Chappie)		c	
P. Johnson		c	
John Henry Lloyd (Pop)	ss		
L. Miller		lf	
Joe Parks		lf	
Spottswood Poles (Spot)		cf	
Johnny Pugh	lf		
Dick Redding (Cannonball)	p		
Roy Roberts	p		
George Shively	rf		
John Taylor (Steel Arm)		p	1b
Ben Taylor		1b	
? Thompson (Gunboat)		rf	
Dick Whitworth	p		
Wabishaw Wiley (Doc)		c	

Baltimore Black Sox

Player	1	2	3
? Boardley		of	
Kenneth Gardner (Ping)	p		
George Greyer	1b		
J.B. Hairstone		of	c
William Hodges	p		
? Johnson (Stonewall)	p		
Joseph Lewis	c		
? Ridgely (Buck)	ss		
Charley Thomas		c	

Brooklyn Royal Giants

Player	1	2	3
Chester Brooks	cf	of	inf
John Cason		c	
Edward Douglass	1b		
Peter Green (Ed)	p	of	
Jesse Hubbard	p	of	
Claude Johnson (Hooks)	rf		
D. Johnson (Dud)		ss	
W. Johnson		lf	
Harry Kenyon	2b		
Bill Kindle		2b	
John Henry Lloyd (Pop)		ss	
Oliver Marcelle	3b		
Johnny Pugh		3b	
Merven Ryan (Red)	p		
Louis Santop	c		
Robert Sloan	lf		
William Woods		rf	

Pittsburgh Stars of Buffalo

Player	1	2	3
? Allen		lf	
? Andrews (Pop)	rf	p	
Phil Bradley	c		
? Garry	cf		
Andy Harris	2b		
Grant Johnson	ss		
Fred Meade (Chick)	3b		
? Thompson (Gunboat)	p	1b	

Chicago American Giants

Player	1	2	3
Andrew Foster (Rube)			M
Jess Barbour	rf		
John Beckwith		c	inf
Dave Brown	p		
Jim Brown	c		
Oscar Charleston	lf		
Sam Crawford		p	
Elwood DeMoss (Bingo)	2b		
George Dixon	c		

Player	1	2	3
Bill Francis	3b		
Robert Gans (Jude)	p	of	
Leroy Grant	1b		
Tom Johnson		p	
Jimmie Lyons		of	
Dave Malarcher		inf	
Lemuel McDougal (Lem)	p		
John Reese		of	
Cristobal Torriente	cf		
? Turner (Tuck)		p	
Dick Whitworth		p	
Frank Wickware		p	
Andrew Williams (Stringbean)		p	
Bobby Williams	ss		

Chicago Giants

Player	1	2	3
George Ball (Walter)	p		
Harry Bauchman	ss		
John Beckwith	c		
Luther Brewer	1b		
William Green	3b		
Charles Green (Joe)	lf		
Frank Jeffreys	rf		
Horace Jenkins	cf		
Thurman Jennings	2b		

Dayton Marcos

Player	1	2	3
? Alexander		cf	
George Brown	cf	1b	
Albert Clark		p	

Player	1	2	3
? Cunningham		2b	
S.R. Dewitt (Eddie)	3b		
William Dismukes (Dizzy)	p		
Mack Eggleston		rf	c
Charley Hill (Lefty)	1b	lf	
Mitch Murray		c	
Ed Rile	p		
? Taylor		2b	
Frank Warfield	ss		
Jack Watts		c	
Andrew Williams (Stringbean)		p	

Detroit Stars

Player	1	2	3
? Chilton		of	
Sam Crawford		p	
? Dodson		lf	
John Donaldson	p	of	
Frank Duncan (Pete)		lf	
Floyd Gardner (Jelly)		rf	1b
Joe Hewitt		ss	3b
Preston Hill (Pete)	cf		
Louis Johnson (Dicta)		p	
Dave Malarcher		3b	
Oliver Marcelle		3b	
Hurley McNair		rf	
Jose Mendez (Joe)	ss	p	3b
Bruce Petway	c	1b	
Andrew Reed	3b		
Jose Rodriquez		c	
Frank Warfield		2b	3b

Player	1	2	3
Edgar Wesley	1b		
Frank Wickware	p		
? Wiley			1b

Hilldale

Player	1	2	3
Toussaint Allen (Tom)	1b		
Randolph Berkeley		c	
Otto Briggs		of	
Phil Cockrell		p	1b
Nap Cummings (Chance)		1b	
James Deas (Yank)	c		
McKinley Downs (Bunny)	2b	3b	
Willis Flournoy (Pud)		p	
Jesse Hubbard		p	
George Johnson (Dibo)	lf		
Dick Lundy	ss		
Fred Meade (Chick)	3b		
William Pettus (Zack)		1b	
Spottswood Poles (Spot)		cf	
John Reese	rf		
Elihu Roberts		2b	of
E. Ross	lf		
Louis Santop		c	
R. Smith (Red)		rf	
Otis Starks	p		
Ben Taylor	1b		
Felix Wallace		3b	
Burlin White		c	
Tom Williams	p		
Jim York		c	

1919 Detroit Stars. From the L: unknown, Joe Hewitt, Frank Warfield, Andrew Reed, Pete Hill, Jose Mendez, Tenny Blount, Frank Wickware, Jose Rodriquez, Edgar Wesley, Bruce Petway, John Donaldson, and Sam Crawford.
Richard Bak

Player	1	2	3

Indianapolis ABCs

Player	1	2	3
James Booker (Pete)	1b		
Luther Farrell	p		
Del Francis	3b		
? Goldie	rf		
? Houston	2b		
Thomas Lynch	lf		
? Ryle	ss		
Joe Scotland	cf		
William Webster (Speck)	c		

New York Lincoln Giants

Player	1	2	3
M. Allen	2b	ss	
Todd Allen	3b		
? Archer	p		
Frank Baynard	rf		
Tom Brown	p		
Dell Clark	ss		
Phil Cockrell	p		
? Dandridge (Ping)	ss		
? Forrest	c		
Blainey Hall	lf		
? Harris	of		
? Maywood	p		
? McLaughlin	rf	p	
Sam Mongin	2b		
Earl Palmer	rf		
Willie Parker	p		
William Pettus (Zack)	1b	c	
Bill Pierce	c		
Jules Thomas	cf		
M. Thomas	p		
Harold Treadwell	p		
? Webb	p		
Wabishaw Wiley (Doc)	c		
Smokey Joe Williams	p		

Pennsylvania Red Caps of NY

Player	1	2	3
D. Bailey	3b		
Jesse Bragg		3b	
E. Cooper		of	1b
? Culver		ss	
Ashby Dunbar	lf		
Charles Earle (Frank)		of	
Tom Fiall	cf		
Joe Forbes	ss		
W.W. Fuller (Chick)		ss	
? Jackson		c	
B. Johnson (Monk)		p	
? Langford (Ad)		p	
William Parks	2b		
Joe Parks	rf		
Andrew Payne (Jap)		2b	ss
Bill Pierce		1b	
? Thomas	1b		
Lee Wade	p		

St. Louis Giants

Player	1	2	3
Sam Bennett	rf		
Charles Blackwell	cf		
Charles Brooks		3b	
? Carey		rf	
Clarence Coleman	2b		
Fred Daniels		p	
John Finner	p		
Bill Gatewood	p		
Eddie Holtz		ss	
Ollie Jones	3b		
Dan Kennard	c		
Jimmie Lyons			lf

Player	1	2	3
Dudley McAdoo (Tully)	1b		
Charles Scott	lf		
Felix Wallace	ss		

1920

Cuban Stars (East)

Player	1	2	3
Tatica Campos	3b		
Pelayo Chacon	ss		
Julian Fabelo	1b	3b	
Isidro Fabre	rf	cf	p
Jose Fernandez	c		
E. Jimenez		of	
Jose Junco	p		
Miles Lucas	p	rf	lf
Armando Massip		1b	
Juan Padrone		p	
Ramiro Ramirez	cf		
Tomas Romanach	lf		
Recurvon Teran	2b		

Cuban Stars (West)

Player	1	2	3
Eufemio Abreu	c		
Bernardo Baro	cf		
Valentin Dreke	lf		
Juan Guerra	rf	1b	
Jose Hernandez	p	rf	
Ramon Herrera	3b	2b	ss
Bienvenido Jimenez (Hooks)	2b		
Julio LeBlanc (Jose)	p	rf	
Cando Lopez		2b	3b
Pasquel Martinez	p		
Eustaquio Pedroso	1b	c	p
Herman Rios	ss	3b	
Pablo Valdez (Tony)		p	rf

Bacharach Giants

Player	1	2	3
Jess Barbour	rf		
Elias Brown (Country)	lf		
James Deas (Yank)		c	
Bill Handy	2b		
Dick Lundy	ss		
Oliver Marcelle	3b		
Fred Meade (Chick)		rf	
Lewis Means		2b	
Jesus Mederos (Frank)	cf		
Bill Pierce	1b		
Johnny Pugh		cf	
Dick Redding (Cannonball)	p		
? Rims		p	
Julio Rojo	c		
Merven Ryan (Red)	p		
Harold Treadwell	p		
Andrew Williams (Stringbean)		p	

Baltimore Black Sox

Player	1	2	3
Elmore Brown (Scrappy)		3b	
J. Brown		ss	
? Bunel		c	
? Burrell		lf	
W.P. Evans	lf	rf	
? Fenton		ss	
Roy Ford	ss		
? Gardner		3b	
Art Grant		c	
George Greyer	1b		
J.B. Hairstone		c	
Blainey Hall		of	
William Hodges	p		

Player	1	2	3
Pearley Johnson (Tubby)		cf	
? Lewis		ss	
Nick Logan	p		
? Minor		lf	of
Willie Parker	p		
? Ridgely (Buck)	2b		
Wyman Smith		of	
F. Smith (Lefty)		p	
? Stricker		p	
Franklin Sykes (Doc)	p		
Charley Thomas	c		
Harry Williams	3b	2b	
Jesse Winters (Nip)		p	

Brooklyn Royal Giants

Player	1	2	3
M. Allen		2b	
Beattie Brooks	2b	c	
Edward Douglass	1b		
Tom Fiall	cf		
Kenneth Gardner (Ping)		p	
Ernest Gatewood	c	rf	
Peter Green (Ed)		of	
Bill Handy		2b	
Jesse Hubbard	p		
Harry Kenyon	p	2b	rf
John Henry Lloyd (Pop)	ss		
L. Miller	3b		
Juan Padrone	p		
Neil Pullen		c	
Ramiro Ramirez		lf	
Roy Roberts		p	
Robert Scott	rf		
Clint Thomas		of	

Pittsburgh Stars of Buffalo

Player	1	2	3
? Aldrath		cf	
Phil Bradley	c		
? Brown	1b		
Andy Harris		cf	
Grant Johnson	2b		
? Keating	p		
Bill Monroe	3b		
? Parker	rf		
R. Smith (Red)	p	rf	
? Thomas	ss		
? Thompson (Gunboat)	p		
? Weeks	lf		

Chicago American Giants

Player	1	2	3	
Andrew Foster (Rube)				M
Rudolph Ash		of		
Fred Boyd		ss		
Dave Brown	p			
Jim Brown		c	1b	
Elwood DeMoss (Bingo)	2b			
George Dixon	c			
William Ewing (Buck)		c		
Robert Gans (Jude)	lf			
Floyd Gardner (Jelly)	rf			
Leroy Grant	1b			
Tom Johnson		p		
Dave Malarcher	3b			
Jack Marshall		p		
Ralph Moore (Squire)		p		
Carroll Mothell (Dink)		c		
John Reese	lf			
Orville Riggins	ss			
Otis Starks		p		
John Taylor (Red)		p		
? Taylor		1b		

Player	1	2	3
Cristobal Torriente	cf		
Frank Wickware	p		
Maurice Wiggins		ss	
Bobby Williams	ss		
Tom Williams	p		

Chicago Giants

Player	1	2	3
Bobby Anderson	ss	2b	
George Ball (Walter)	p		
Harry Bauchman		2b	
John Beckwith	c	ss	p
Otto Bolden		p	
? Chase		p	
Clarence Coleman		p	c
James Davis		p	
Frank Duncan (Pete)	rf		
Frank Duncan		c	
Luther Farrell	p		
Fred Goliath		of	
Charles Green (Joe)		c	of
William Green	3b		
Frank Jeffreys		of	
Harry Jeffries		1b	2b
Horace Jenkins	cf	p	
Thurman Jennings	2b		
Lemuel McDougal (Lem)	p		
J.D. Roberts		ss	
John Taylor (Steel Arm)		p	
John Taylor (Red)		p	
Ted Waters		p	
Butler White	1b		
Carter Wilson		of	
Clarence Winston (Bobby)	lf		

Dayton Marcos

Player	1	2	3
? Alexander	lf		
? Branham (Slim)		p	
George Britt (Chippy)	p	2b	c
George Brown	of	1b	
Clarence Coleman		p	rf
? Cunningham	ss		
S.R. Dewitt (Eddie)		2b	
? Gardner		of	
G.E. Gray (Dolly)		p	
Bruce Hocker	1b	of	
William Johnson (Wise)		c	rf
I.S. Lane		p	rf
? Leary		p	
Edward McClain (Boots)		ss	
? McNeil		1b	c
Mitch Murray		c	
Hurland Ragland	p		
Curtiss Ricks		1b	
? Rutledge		p	
? Shelton		c	
Candy Jim Taylor	3b	2b	
? Thompkins		of	
James Thompson (Sandy)	rf		
William Webster (Speck)	c		
Charles Wilson	p		
? Wingfield	2b	of	

Detroit Stars

Player	1	2	3
Edward Brown		p	
William Carter		c	
? Chase		p	
Andrew Cooper (Andy)		p	
Mack Eggleston		c	
William Force		p	
Bill Gatewood	p		

Player	1	2	3
? Green		p	
Chick Harper		of	p
Joe Hewitt	3b	ss	2b
Charley Hill (Lefty)		of	
Preston Hill (Pete)	cf	of	
Bill Holland	p		
Louis Johnson (Dicta)		p	
? Long		of	
? Longware		2b	3b
Jimmie Lyons	lf	1b	p
Webster McDonald		p	
N. Moore		lf	
Bruce Petway		c	
Orville Riggins	ss	3b	
? Scott		c	
? Thompson (Gunboat)		p	
Frank Warfield	2b	3b	
Edgar Wesley	1b		

Hilldale

Player	1	2	3
Toussaint Allen (Tom)	1b		
? Barber (Bull)	2b		
Otto Briggs		cf	
Elmore Brown (Scrappy)		ss	
Arnold Brown		ss	
John Cason		lf	c
Phil Cockrell	p	rf	
McKinley Downs (Bunny)	ss	2b	
Willis Flournoy (Pud)	p		
Bill Francis	3b		
Henry Gillespie	p		
Chick Harper		ss	
Cecil Johnson (Sess)		ss	
George Johnson (Dibo)	rf	cf	
Dick Lundy		ss	
Cornelius Rector (Connie)		p	rf
Elihu Roberts		c	lf
Louis Santop	c		
Otis Starks		p	
Chaney White		lf	
Dick Whitworth	p		
Jim York		rf	c

Indianapolis ABCs

Player	1	2	3
C.I. Taylor			M
Henry Blackman		3b	
Edward Brown		p	
Oscar Charleston	cf	p	
Morten Clark	ss	2b	
Wilson Day (Connie)		2b	3b
S.R. Dewitt (Eddie)		inf	
William Dismukes (Dizzy)	p		
Del Francis		2b	
? Haines		p	
? Houston		p	
Robert Hudspeth (Highpocket)		1b	rf
Ralph Jefferson	rf		
James Jeffries		p	rf
Louis Johnson (Dicta)	p		
? Jones		p	
Raleigh Mackey (Biz)		c	p
Edward McClain (Boots)		inf	
Bob McClure	p		
Mitch Murray		c	
Russell Powell	c	rf	2b
Hurland Ragland		p	
Ed Rile		p	
George Shively	lf		
Ben Taylor	1b	p	
John Taylor (Steel Arm)		p	

Player	1	2	3
Namon Washington		of	
Morris Williams		p	

Kansas City Monarchs

Player	1	2	3
Jose Mendez (Joe)	p	2b	ss M
Clifford Alsop		p	
? Arumis		2b	
? Atame	p		
Bernardo Baro		of	
Hugh Blackburn		p	1b
Frank Blukoi		2b	
George Carr (Tank)	1b	2b	rf
Sam Crawford	p		
Reuben Currie (Rube)	p		
John Donaldson	cf	p	
Frank Evans		p	of
Bob Fagan		2b	
? Fern		p	
Slyvester Foreman (Hooks)		rf	c
Herman Gordon		2b	
Roosevelt Gray (Chappy)		2b	
Chick Harper		of	
? Houston		2b	
Roy Johnson		2b	
? Lightner		p	
Hurley McNair	lf		
Walter Moore (Dobie)		ss	
Carroll Mothell (Dink)		2b	3b
? Nolan		1b	
Bartolo Portuando	3b		
Otto Ray	c		of
Jose Rodriquez	c		
Wilber Rogan (Bullet Joe)	p	rf	cf
? Smith (Lefty)		p	
Edgar Washington (Blue)		1b	

Lincoln Giants (Winter)

Player	1	2	3
Henry Blackman		3b	
McKinley Downs (Bunny)	ss		
Kenneth Gardner (Ping)	p		
Alfred Goodwin (Lon)			
Johnson Hill (Fred)		3b	
Jesse Hubbard	p		
Raleigh Mackey (Biz)	c		
Carl Perry	2b		
William Pettus (Zack)	1b		
Spottswood Poles (Spot)	lf		
Neil Pullen		c	
Robert Scott	rf		
Jules Thomas	cf		
Jesse Winters (Nip)		p	

Los Angeles White Sox (Winter)

Player	1	2	3
George Carr (Tank)	1b		
Reuben Currie (Rube)	p		
Bob Fagan	2b		
Bill Foote	3b		
Lemuel Hawkins (Hawk)	rf		
Hurley McNair	lf		
Walter Moore (Dobie)	ss		
Otto Ray	c		
Wilber Rogan (Bullet Joe)	p	of	
William Woods	cf		

Madison Stars

Player	1	2	3
M. Allen		2b	
? Banks		3b	
Randolph Berkeley		c	
? Berry		1b	
Otto Briggs		of	

Player	1	2	3
George Britt (Chippy)		p	
Elias Brown (Country)		of	
Elmore Brown (Scrappy)		ss	
Louis Burgee		ss	
? Carey		1b	
? Coley		of	
? Crowder	p		
Nap Cummings (Chance)		1b	
William Dallard (Eggie)		c	
Robert Finch		p	
? Foreman		ss	
? Gallup		lf	
Henry Gillespie		p	
George Henderson (Rube)		p	
? Hilton		3b	
? Howard		p	
D. Johnson (Dud)		ss	
H. Johnson		3b	
Eugene Keeton		p	
Milton Lewis	2b		
? McDonnell		p	
? Parker		of	
Jose Perez		2b	
Carl Perry		3b	
Don Perry		p	
? Purgen		ss	
Roy Roberts		p	
? Russell		2b	
? Scott		c	
Marshall Smith (Darknight)		p	
? Swiggett		p	
? Truitt		1b	
Jack Watts		c	
E. Weeks		inf	
Leon Weldon		cf	
Burlin White		c	
? White		3b	
? Wicks		3b	
? Wills		3b	

Nashville Giants

Player	1	2	3
? Allison	ss	2b	rf
? Crowder	p		
? Dixon	rf	ss	2b
Columbus Ewing		of	
V. Johnson	c		
E. Johnson	1b		
? McCarver	2b	ss	
? Meyers	cf		
Eddie Noel	p		
Amos Otis		of	
Norman Stearnes (Turkey)	lf		
Leroy Stratton	3b	p	
Joe Ware	of		

New York Lincoln Giants

Player	1	2	3
M. Allen		2b	
? Archer		p	
? Crowder	p		
James Davis	p		
George Fiall		ss	
W. James (Nux)		of	
Clarence Jenkins (Fats)	rf		
? Kendall		2b	
Charles Lindsay (Clarence)	ss		
Sam Mongin	3b		
Alton Norman		ss	
William Pettus (Zack)	1b		
Spottswood Poles (Spot)	lf		
W. Reavis	p		

Player	1	2	3
Ed Rile		p	
Jules Thomas	cf		
Wabishaw Wiley (Doc)	c		
Smokey Joe Williams	p	1b	

Pennsylvania Red Caps of NY

Player	1	2	3
D. Bailey	cf		
Frank Baynard	c		
George Crossen		ss	
Ashby Dunbar		lf	
Joe Forbes	ss		
Andy Harris	1b		
J. Johnson		of	
Wade Johnston	p		
? Langford (Ad)	p		
William Parks	lf		
? Riley		p	
? Thomas		1b	
F. Wiley	rf	p	

Norfolk All-Stars

Player	1	2	3
John Cason		c	
? Chaffle		p	
Frank Crockett	cf		
? Croesant		p	
James Crump		3b	
Nap Cummings (Chance)	1b		
Chick Harper		ss	
? Howard		ss	
Cecil Johnson (Sess)		ss	
? Jones		p	
Ed Kemp		of	
Tony Mahoney	p		
Webster McDonald		p	
L. Miller		3b	
? Morgan	rf		
Carl Perry		2b	
? Rhodes		p	
Harry Roberts (Raggs)	lf		
? Stricker	p		
Frank Wickware		p	
Jesse Winters (Nip)		p	

Philadelphia Giants of NY

Player	1	2	3
E. Cooper		rf	
Jimmy Fuller	c		
Peter Green (Ed)	lf		
? Hatchett	2b		
E. Jimenez		rf	
J. Johnson		of	
N. Johnson		cf	
Charles Lindsay (Clarence)	ss		
? Panier	p		
Andrew Payne (Jap)	3b		

St. Louis Giants

Player	1	2	3
Sam Bennett		c	rf
Charles Blackwell	cf		
Charles Brooks	rf	2b	
? Burgett		of	
Wayne Carr	p		
Joe Casey		p	
W. Cobb		c	
? Dandridge (Ping)	2b	3b	
Bill Drake	p		
C.A. Dudley	lf		
Luther Farrell		p	
John Finner	p		
Charles Forest			
? Herring		3b	

Player	1	2	3
Johnson Hill (Fred)		lf	rf
Eddie Holtz	ss		
? Hutt		1b	rf
Roy Johnson		1b	
Dan Kennard	c		
Dudley McAdoo (Tully)	1b		
L. Moore		rf	
Jimmy Oldham		p	
? Rollins		rf	
George Scales		inf	
Charles Scott		lf	
? Shaw		rf	
? Stewart		p	ss
? Torrin		p	
Felix Wallace	3b	2b	

1921

All Cubans (East)

Player	1	2	3
? Borsel		p	
Tatica Campos		of	
Isidro Fabre		p	
Jose Fernandez	c		
? Jones		p	
Oscar Levis		p	
? Manolo	3b		
? Marcello		p	
Pasquel Martinez	p		
Pablo Mesa		of	
Alejandro Oms		cf	
Juan Padrone		p	
Eustaquio Pedroso	1b	p	
Ramiro Ramirez		cf	
Jose Ramos	rf		
? Redoud		c	
Jose Rodriquez		c	
Felipe Sierra	2b		
Pedro Silva		p	1b
Antonio Susini	ss	2b	
Roberto Villa (Bobby)	lf		

Bacharach Giants

Player	1	2	3
Dick Redding (Cannonball)	p		M
? Arnet		p	
Jess Barbour	cf		
Elias Brown (Country)	of	2b	3b
Maurice Busby		p	
Phil Cockrell		p	
James Deas (Yank)		c	
Jimmy Fuller		c	
Ernest Gatewood		c	
Dennis Graham		rf	
? Grimm		rf	
Bill Handy	2b	rf	
Frank Harvey		p	
? Hughes		p	
Fred Hutchinson		ss	2b
Richard Jackson		ss	2b
Ralph Jefferson		of	
George Johnson (Dibo)		of	
Dick Lundy	ss		
Oliver Marcelle	3b	ss	
? McDonnell		p	
? Merril		of	
Alonzo Mitchell (Hooks)		p	
Sam Mongin		2b	
William Pettus (Zack)	1b		
Bill Pierce		1b	
Johnny Pugh		rf	

Player	1	2	3
? Rich		of	
Henry Richardson	p		
Julio Rojo	c	3b	
Merven Ryan (Red)	p		
George Shively	lf		
H. Smith		of	p
George Suttles (Mule)	c		
Harold Treadwell	p		
Andrew Williams (Stringbean)	p		
Jesse Winters (Nip)	p		
Baltimore Black Sox			
Charley Thomas	c		M
Elmore Brown (Scrappy)	ss		
Charles Evans (Alexander)		p	
Roy Ford		inf	
George Greyer	1b		
J.B. Hairstone		of	c
Blainey Hall	cf		
William Hodges	p		
Joseph Lewis		c	
Nick Logan	p		

Player	1	2	3
Fred Meade (Chick)	of		
Willie Parker		p	
? Ridgely (Buck)	2b	inf	
Marshall Smith (Darknight)		p	
F. Smith (Lefty)		p	
Franklin Sykes (Doc)	p		
Joseph Wheeler		p	
Brooklyn Royal Giants			
Beattie Brooks	ss	2b	
Wayne Carr		p	
John Cason		c	1b
Edward Douglass	1b		
Tom Fiall	cf		
Ernest Gatewood		2b	c
Ananias Harris	p		
Henry Howell	p		
Jesse Hubbard	p		
Tony Mahoney		p	
L. Miller	3b		
Robert Scott	lf		
Robert Sloan	rf		

Player	1	2	3
Charles Spearman	c		
Bill Wagner		ss	
Andrew Williams (Stringbean)	p		
Pittsburgh Stars of Buffalo			
Phil Bradley	c		
? Brooks	p		
? Brown	1b		
? Coleman	rf		
Grant Johnson	2b		
J. Johnston	ss		
Henry Jordan	p	c	
? Thomas	3b		
E. Weeks	lf		
Chicago American Giants			
Andrew Foster (Rube)			M
Jim Brown	c	1b	of
Dave Brown	p		
Elwood DeMoss (Bingo)	2b		
George Dixon		c	
Floyd Gardner (Jelly)	rf		

1921 Kansas City Monarchs. Back row L to R: Rube Currie, John Donaldson, Frank Blatnner, Sam Crawford, Tank Carr, and Dobie Moore. Middle row L to R: Bullet Joe Rogan, Bartolo Portuando, Zack Foreman, Hurley McNair, Lem Hawkins, and Otto Ray. In front are Hooks Foreman and Bob Fagan.

Negro Leagues Baseball Museum

Player	1	2	3
Willie Gisentaner (Lefty)		p	
Leroy Grant	1b		
? Harris		p	
Bill Holland		p	
Tom Johnson	p		
Jimmie Lyons	lf		
Dave Malarcher	3b		
Jack Marshall	p		
John Reese		of	
? Smith		of	
Otis Starks	p		
Sam Streeter	p		
Cristobal Torriente	cf	p	
Frank Wickware		p	
Bobby Williams	ss		
Poindexter Williams		c	
Tom Williams	p		
William Woods		of	

Chicago Giants

Player	1	2	3
Charles Green (Joe)	of	c	M
? Alexander		of	
George Ball (Walter)	p		
Harry Bauchman	2b		
John Beckwith	ss		
? Bingham (Bingo)		of	
Luther Brewer		of	
Edward Brown		p	
? Byrd		1b	
Frank Duncan		c	
Luther Farrell	p	rf	
William Green	3b		
? Hamilton		rf	
Lemuel Hawkins (Hawk)	cf	1b	
George Henderson (Rube)		p	
Harry Jeffries	1b	c	of
Horace Jenkins		of	
Thurman Jennings	lf	2b	ss
Percy Miller		p	
Otto Ray	rf	c	
? Smith (Lefty)		p	
George Sweatt		of	
John Taylor (Steel Arm)	p		
Butler White		c	1b
Frank Wickware		p	
Carter Wilson		of	
Clarence Winston (Bobby)		of	

Cincinnati Cubans

Player	1	2	3
Eufemio Abreu	c		
Bernardo Baro	cf		
Lucas Boada	p	1b	of
Valentin Dreke	lf		
Rodolfo Fernandez		p	
Juan Guerra	rf		
? Guilleu		p	
Ramon Herrera	2b	3b	
Bienvenido Jimenez (Hooks)	3b	2b	
E. Jimenez		of	
Julio LeBlanc (Jose)	p	of	
? Manolo		p	
? Marcello		rf	
Agustin Molina			
Eugenio Morin		c	2b
Juan Padrone		p	
H. Pareda (Monk)	1b	p	
? Pohea		p	
? Porter		rf	
Herman Rios	ss	3b	

Player	1	2	3
? Suarez		p	rf
? Swallis		p	

Colored All-Stars (Winter)

Player	1	2	3
James P. White			M
Johnny Baugh	p		
Henry Blackman	3b	c	
George Carr (Tank)	rf	3b	c
Oscar Charleston		cf	
Bob Fagan	2b		
Bill Foote		of	3b
Lemuel Hawkins (Hawk)	1b		
James Jeffries	p	rf	
Raleigh Mackey (Biz)	cf	c	rf
Hurley McNair	lf	p	
Jose Mendez (Joe)		ss	p
Walter Moore (Dobie)	ss		
Neil Pullen	c		
Carl Sawyer		inf	
John Taylor (Steel Arm)	p	rf	
Tom Ward		of	

Columbus Buckeyes

Player	1	2	3
George Brown	lf		M
John Henry Lloyd (Pop)	ss		M
? Alexander	cf		
George Bennette		of	
George Britt (Chippy)	p	of	
Walter Cannady (Rev)		p	
Clarence Coleman		1b	
? Cunningham		ss	
Saul Davis		3b	
S.R. Dewitt (Eddie)	3b		
Mack Eggleston	c		
William Ewing (Buck)		c	p
? Gamble		p	
Willie Gisentaner (Lefty)		p	
G.E. Gray (Dolly)		of	
Lewis Hampton		p	
? Harris			p
Robert Hudspeth (Highpocket)	1b		
J. Johnson		of	
I.S. Lane		p	3b

Hilldale's Judy Johnson.
Todd Bolton

Player	1	2	3
Edward McClain (Boots)		2b	
? McNeil		c	
Mitch Murray		c	
Charles O'Neill		c	
Hurland Ragland		p	
Ed Rile		p	
Roy Roberts	p		
Clarence Smith		of	
Clint Thomas	2b		
? Thompkins		of	
Charles Wesley (Connie)		of	
? Williams		c	
Charles Wilson	p		
? Wingfield		utl	
William Woods	rf		

Detroit Stars

Player	1	2	3
Preston Hill (Pete)	cf	1b	M
George Brown		of	
? Chase		p	
Andrew Cooper (Andy)	p		
Leon Daniels (Pepper)		c	
William Force	p	of	
Bill Gatewood	p		
Perry Hall		p	
James Henderson		p	
Charley Hill (Lefty)	rf	of	
Johnson Hill (Fred)	3b		
Bill Holland	p		
? Howard		3b	p
Dave Knight		p	
I.S. Lane		p	
? LeRue		c	
? Long		of	
Percy Miller		p	
N. Moore		of	
Carl Perry		2b	
Bruce Petway	c	1b	
Andrew Reed		of	
John Reese		of	
Orville Riggins	ss		
? Scott		c	
? Smith		cf	
Frank Warfield	2b	3b	cf
William Webster (Speck)		c	
Edgar Wesley	1b		
Poindexter Williams		c	of
Charles Wilson		p	of
Elmer Wilson		2b	
? Wingfield		of	
William Ziegler (Doc)		p	

Hilldale

Player	1	2	3
Ed Bolden			M
Alex Albritton		p	
Toussaint Allen (Tom)	1b		
Otto Briggs	cf		
? Brooks		p	
Arnold Brown		ss	2b
Ralph Burgin		2b	
Phil Cockrell	p	rf	lf
James Crump		2b	ss
Nap Cummings (Chance)		2b	1b
William Dallard (Eggie)		c	lf
Lou Dickerson		p	
Nat Dobbins		2b	
McKinley Downs (Bunny)		2b	ss
? Flammer		of	
Willis Flournoy (Pud)	p		
? Foreman		ss	

Player	1	2	3
Bill Francis	3b	ss	
? Gaston		ss	
Henry Gillespie		p	
? Holland		1b	
George Johnson (Dibo)	rf	of	
William Johnson (Judy)		3b	ss
? Kenner		ss	
W. Prichett		p	
? Purgen		ss	
Cornelius Rector (Connie)	p	rf	
Louis Santop	c	3b	
W. Smith		ss	3b
Paul Stephens (Jake)		ss	
E. Weeks		ss	
Burlin White		c	
Chaney White	lf		
Dick Whitworth	p		
? Wicks		inf	
Jim York		c	rf

Indianapolis ABCs

Player	1	2	3
C.I. Taylor			M
George Bennette		of	
Henry Blackman		3b	
Larry Brown		c	
Maywood Brown		p	
Morten Clark	ss	3b	
Wilson Day (Connie)	2b	3b	
William Dismukes (Dizzy)		p	
? Fifer			p
? Harris		p	
Crush Holloway	rf		
Robert Hudspeth (Highpocket)		1b	
? Jackson		p	
Ralph Jefferson	cf		
James Jeffries	p		
Louis Johnson (Dicta)	p		
? Jones		p	
Harry Kenyon	lf	p	
? Latimer		p	
William Lowe		3b	
Raleigh Mackey (Biz)	c	2b	p
Tony Mahoney		p	
Bob McClure	p		
Carl Perry		inf	
Russell Powell		c	
? Reggie		p	
Ed Rile		p	
George Shively		of	
Frank Stevens		p	
Ben Taylor	1b		
Dan Thomas		1b	inf
Namon Washington	3b	of	c
Morris Williams		p	
Gerard Williams		ss	2b
William Woods		of	

Kansas City Monarchs

Player	1	2	3
Jose Mendez (Joe)	of	ss	p M
? Barr		3b	ss
Clifford Bell (Cliff)		p	
Frank Blattner		2b	1b
George Carr (Tank)	1b	of	
? Coffee		p	
? Cordova (Pete)		3b	
Sam Crawford	p	1b	
Reuben Currie (Rube)	p	rf	
James Davis		p	
John Donaldson	cf	p	
Frank Duncan	c	rf	

Player	1	2	3
Bob Fagan	2b	rf	
Slyvester Foreman (Hooks)		c	
Zack Foreman		p	
? Hamilton		p	
Chick Harper		of	p
Lemuel Hawkins (Hawk)		1b	of
? Hoard		p	
Roy Johnson		2b	
Leonard King		of	
John Henry Lloyd (Pop)		ss	
Mike McAllister		1b	
Hurley McNair	lf		
Walter Moore (Dobie)	ss		
Carroll Mothell (Dink)		utl	
Augustin Parpetti		1b	
Bartolo Portuando	3b		
? Potter		c	
Hurland Ragland		p	
Otto Ray		c	rf
Ed Rile		p	
Wilber Rogan (Bullet Joe)	p	of	2b
Percy Segula		p	
? Smith (Lefty)		p	of
George Sweatt		of	
John Taylor (Red)		p	
? Wharton		of	

Madison Stars

Player	1	2	3
? Banks		3b	
? Brown (Baldy)		of	
Tom Brown		rf	
Frank Crockett		of	
William Dallard (Eggie)		of	c
L. Dixon		p	
? Doyle		p	
Robert Finch		p	
? Flammer		lf	
? Foreman		ss	
? Fuller		p	
Henry Gillespie		p	
? Hearns		c	
William Johnson (Judy)		3b	ss
? Jones		1b	
? Kenner		ss	
Webster McDonald		p	
? O'Donnell		lf	
Earl Palmer		of	
Don Perry		1b	
? Purgen		ss	
Cornelius Rhoades (Neal)		c	
J.D. Roberts		inf	
? Swiggett		lf	p
? Valentine		of	
E. Weeks		inf	
Leon Weldon		p	
? White		2b	

Montgomery Grey Sox

Player	1	2	3
John Staples			M
? Barker	cf		
? Cardina		c	
? Charleston (Red)	c		
Marion Cunningham	1b		
James Cunningham	2b		
H. Cunningham (Rounder)	ss		
John Dickey (Steel Arm)	p		
? Mason (Big)	p		
? McCarver		utl	
? McGavock	lf		
George Meyers		p	

Player	1	2	3
? Parker		p	
? Preston		c	
? Russell	3b		
? Sallee (Slim)	p		
Norman Stearnes (Turkey)	rf		

New Orleans Caulfield Ads

Player	1	2	3
George Collins	2b		
? Durand	3b		
Glover Gardner (Gus)	rf	c	
John George	ss		
? Harris	lf		
? Lewis	c		
? Moffett	1b	p	
Aubrey Owens	p		
? Platt	p		
? Robertson	p		
Percy Segula	cf	p	

New York Lincoln Giants

Player	1	2	3
George Crossen		c	
George Fiall	ss	3b	
Robert Gans (Jude)	rf		
Kenneth Gardner (Ping)		p	
Dan Johnson (Shang)		p	
Othello Johnson		lf	of
Bill Pierce		c	1b
Spottswood Poles (Spot)	lf	cf	
W. Reavis		p	
Ed Rile		p	
? Southy		ss	
? Thomas		cf	of
Burlin White		c	
Wabishaw Wiley (Doc)	c		
Smokey Joe Williams		p	

Norfolk Stars

Player	1	2	3
? Brown		rf	3b
? Churchill		c	
James Crump		2b	
? Howard	ss		
Cecil Johnson (Sess)		1b	
George Johnson (Chappie)		c	1b
Ed Kemp	cf		
Holsey Lee (Scrip)	p	rf	
Milton Lewis	2b		
? Moore		of	
Bill Pierce		1b	
Harry Roberts (Raggs)	lf		
E. Smith	3b		
? Snowden		rf	
Jesse Winters (Nip)	p		
Jim York		c	

Pelham Silk Sox

Player	1	2	3
? Ayles	1b		
? Bibbs		p	rf
Chuck Bowers		cf	
Louis Burgee	2b		
? Farrell	c		
Robert Finch	p		
? Haney		cf	rf
Jimmie Jones	p		
? Jones	rf		
? Phillips		2b	
Eddie Pinder		cf	
? Trusty	ss		
Etwood Turner	lf		
Bill Yancey	3b		

Player	1	2	3
Pittsburgh Keystones			
William Dismukes (Dizzy)	p		M
Todd Allen		3b	of
? Bullock	p		
Fred Burnett (Tex)	c		
Albert Clark	ss	p	
? Clay	2b		
Charles Corbett	p		
Fred Downer	lf		
? Gilmore (Speed)	p		
Ernest Gooden	3b		
Herman Gordon	rf		
? Hayes (Buddy)		c	
Harold Martin		p	
Willie Miles	2b		
Willis Moody	rf		
Benjamin Pace (Brother)		c	
George Scales	1b		
? Spencer		of	
? Tolliver	p		
Jack Watts		c	
Mathis Williams (Matt)	ss		
St. Louis Giants			
Felix Wallace	ss		M
Sam Bennett		c	
? Bix		p	
Charles Blackwell	rf		
Charles Brooks		1b	of
Wayne Carr		p	
Oscar Charleston	cf		
Dell Clark		2b	
? Danage		2b	
John Dickey (Steel Arm)		p	
Bill Drake	p		
C.A. Dudley	lf		
? Fields		p	
John Finner	p		
Carl Glass		p	
Perry Hall		p	
Charley Hancock		c	
Joe Hewitt	ss		
Eddie Holtz	2b		
Dan Kennard	c		
Dudley McAdoo (Tully)	1b		
George Meyers		p	
Sam Mongin	3b		
Jimmy Oldham	p		
? Porsee		p	
George Scales		3b	
? Smith		of	
Otis Starks		p	
Washington Black Sox			
? Jones	2b		
? Lee	ss		
? Lyle	rf		
? Pryor	1b		
? Shelton	cf		
Cleveland Smith (Cleo)	3b		
A. Smith	p		
? Vanderhill	p		
Ted Waters	lf		
? Wrighter	c		
Washington Braves			
Alex Albritton		p	
M. Allen	3b		
? Arthur			3b
Arnold Brown	ss		

Player	1	2	3
? Burrell		ss	
James Crump	2b		
Jack Davis		3b	
Nat Dobbins		rf	
George Fisher		of	
William Johnson (Wise)	rf		
? Kenner		ss	2b
Don Perry		1b	
Herbert Pratt		rf	
Cornelius Rhoades (Neal)		c	
S. Smith	p		
? Stephen		cf	
? Street		3b	
? Wheatherspo		p	
Joseph Wheeler		p	
? Wingfield		of	
Jesse Winters (Nip)	p		lf
1922			
Cuban Stars (East)			
Bernardo Baro	lf		
Tatica Campos	1b		3b
Pelayo Chacon	ss		
Julian Fabelo		3b	2b
Isidro Fabre	p	of	
Jose Fernandez	c		
Pedro Ferrer		ss	
Bienvenido Jimenez (Hooks)	2b		
Jose Junco		p	
Oscar Levis	p		
? Manolo		p	
Pablo Mesa	rf		
Juanelo Mirabel		p	
Alejandro Oms	cf		
Juan Padrone	p		
Jose Perez		1b	3b
Recurvon Teran		2b	3b
Cuban Stars (West)			
? Barr		ss	3b
Lucas Boada	p	of	
Basilio Cuerira		p	of
? Culver		3b	
Valentin Dreke	cf		
Isidro Fabre		p	
Juan Guerra		1b	lf
Jose Hernandez		p	
Agipito Lazaga		p	
Eugenio Morin	c	1b	
Eustaquio Pedroso	1b	p	
? Rigal	ss		
Herman Rios	3b		
B. Conrado Rodriquez		p	
Jose Rodriquez		c	
Felipe Sierra	2b		
Pedro Silva	p	of	
Roberto Villa (Bobby)	rf		
Atlantic City Bacharach Giants			
Elias Brown (Country)		rf	
Arnold Brown		2b	
Frank Crockett		lf	
Nap Cummings (Chance)	1b		
Jack Davis		3b	
James Deas (Yank)	c		
Tom Finley	2b		
? Friely		2b	
J.B. Hairstone		rf	

Player	1	2	3
Nate Johnson		p	
William Jones (Fox)		c	2b
? Koop			
Andy Kyle		p	
Milton Lewis		2b	
George Lewis (Peaches)		p	
Dick Lundy	ss		
Lewis Means		c	
? Molloy		p	
Charles O'Neill		c	
? Quincy			
Ambrose Reed	cf		
George Shively		lf	
H. Smith		p	
J. Smith		inf	of
Sam Streeter	p		
Joseph Wheeler		p	
Tom Williams		p	
Jesse Winters (Nip)	p		
Berdell Young		cf	
Baltimore Black Sox			
Alex Albritton		p	
M. Allen		2b	
? Archer	p		
George Britt (Chippy)		utl	
Elmore Brown (Scrappy)		ss	
Maurice Busby		p	
Fred Downer		lf	
W.P. Evans		of	
Roy Ford		2b	
George Greyer		1b	
Blainey Hall	cf		
? Hendricks		p	
William Hodges		p	
Cecil Johnson (Sess)	3b		
James Johnson		ss	
Dave Knight		p	
Andy Kyle		p	of
Holsey Lee (Scrip)		p	
Joseph Lewis	c		
Nick Logan	p		
G. McDonald		p	
L. Miller		of	
? Parker		of	
Bill Pierce		1b	
E. Poles (Possum)		ss	
? Punch		p	
Henry Richardson		p	
? Ridgely (Buck)	ss		
Harry Roberts (Raggs)	rf		
Cleveland Smith (Cleo)	2b		
Marshall Smith (Darknight)	p		
L. Smith		of	
Wyman Smith	lf		
Franklin Sykes (Doc)	p		
Charley Thomas		c	
Wade Thompson		p	
Joseph Wheeler		p	
Harry Williams		3b	
Jud Wilson	1b		
Brooklyn Royal Giants			
Chester Brooks	cf		
John Cason		c	
Edward Douglass	1b		
Tom Fiall	rf		
Johnson Hill (Fred)	3b		
Jesse Hubbard	p		of
Sam Mongin	2b		

Player	1	2	3
Cornelius Rector (Connie)		p	of
Robert Scott	lf		
Charles Spearman		c	
? Spebbin		p	
Otis Starks	p		
Bill Wagner	ss		
Fred Williams		c	

Buffalo Stars

Player	1	2	3
Phil Bradley	c	rf	
? Brown	1b		
Jack Emery	p		
William Ewing (Buck)		c	
? Garry	of		
? Jimerson	p		
Grant Johnson	2b		
? Keating	p		
? Land	rf		
? Rhone	3b		
? Thomas	ss		
? Washington		of	
? Williams	p		
Benny Wilson	of		

Chicago American Giants

Player	1	2	3
Andrew Foster (Rube)			M
John Beckwith	3b		
Dave Brown	p		
Edward Brown		p	
Jim Brown	c		
Elwood DeMoss (Bingo)	2b		
George Dixon		c	
Floyd Gardner (Jelly)	rf		
John George		ss	
Leroy Grant	1b		
Joe Hewitt		ss	
Eddie Holtz		2b	
James Jeffries		p	
Harry Jeffries		3b	
Tom Johnson		p	
Jimmie Lyons	lf		
Dave Malarcher		3b	ss
Aubrey Owens		p	
Juan Padrone	p		
John Reese		of	
Ed Rile		p	
Cristobal Torriente	cf	p	
? Tyms		cf	
Dick Whitworth	p		
Bobby Williams	ss		

Cleveland Tate Stars

Player	1	2	3
Candy Jim Taylor	3b	p	M
John Barnes (Fat)	c		
George Boggs		p	
Robert Bonner	1b		
Fred Boyd		rf	
Finis Branahan	p		
? Branham (Slim)		p	
Walter Cannady (Rev)		p	of
? Chatman		p	
Eppie Hampton	c		
George Henderson (Rube)		rf	ss
? Howard		p	
Claude Johnson (Hooks)	2b		
John Wesley Johnson		p	
Wade Johnston	lf	p	
Eugene Keeton		p	
James Leonard (Bobo)	cf		
Edward McClain (Boots)		ss	

Player	1	2	3
Bob McClure	p		
Mitch Murray		c	
Alton Norman		ss	
Eugene Redd		ss	
Curtiss Ricks		p	of
Fulton Strong		p	

Detroit Stars

Player	1	2	3
Jess Barbour		of	
George Bennette		of	
Jack Combs		p	
Andrew Cooper (Andy)	p		
Leon Daniels (Pepper)		c	
William Force	p	of	
Chick Harper		p	
Bill Holland	p		
? Johnson		lf	
John Jones	lf	of	
I.S. Lane	3b		
Jack Marshall		p	
Everett Nelson		p	
Bruce Petway		c	
Orville Riggins	ss		
Clarence Smith	rf	of	
Clint Thomas	cf	2b	
Frank Warfield	2b	3b	
Johnny Watson		of	
Edgar Wesley	1b		
Poindexter Williams	c	rf	
Charles Wilson		p	of

Harrisburg Giants

Player	1	2	3
Jess Barbour		cf	
George Britt (Chippy)		p	c
Arnold Brown	ss		
Herbert Dixon (Rap)	rf		
Henry Jordan	c		
Milton Lewis	2b		
Fred Meade (Chick)	3b		
Don Perry	1b		
? Raymond		p	
Merven Ryan (Red)		p	
? Taylor		p	
E. Weeks		of	inf

Hilldale

Player	1	2	3
Toussaint Allen (Tom)	1b		
Otto Briggs	rf		
Phil Cockrell		p	of
James Crump	inf		
McKinley Downs (Bunny)	2b		
Willis Flournoy (Pud)		p	
Bill Francis	3b		
Kenneth Gardner (Ping)		p	
Henry Gillespie	p		
Ananias Harris		p	
Willie Haynes	p		
Charlie Henry	p		
George Johnson (Dibo)	cf		
William Johnson (Judy)	ss		
Harry Kenyon		p	
E.E. Muse	p		
Cornelius Rector (Connie)		p	
Dewey Richardson		c	
Merven Ryan (Red)		p	
Louis Santop	c		
Paul Stephens (Jake)		ss	
Franklin Sykes (Doc)		p	
Chaney White	lf		
Jesse Winters (Nip)		p	

Indianapolis ABCs

Player	1	2	3
C.I. Taylor			M
Henry Blackman	3b		
Wayne Carr		p	
Oscar Charleston	cf		
Morten Clark	ss		
Daltie Cooper		p	
Wilson Day (Connie)	2b		
William Dismukes (Dizzy)		p	
George Dixon		c	
Mack Eggleston		c	
Lewis Hampton	p	of	
Crush Holloway	rf		
James Jeffries	p	of	
Louis Johnson (Dicta)		p	
Raleigh Mackey (Biz)	c	ss	of
Tony Mahoney	p		
Harold Ross		p	
George Shively		of	
Ben Taylor	1b		
Namon Washington	lf	ss	
Charles Wesley (Connie)		of	

Kansas City Monarchs

Player	1	2	3
Sam Crawford	p		M
Newton Allen (Newt)		2b	3b
Clifford Alsop		p	
Theodore Anderson (Bubbles)		2b	
Clifford Bell (Cliff)		p	
George Bennette		of	
George Carr (Tank)		1b	3b
William Carter		c	
Reuben Currie (Rube)	p		
Fred Dewitt		c	
John Donaldson		of	p
Bill Drake	p		
Frank Duncan	c		
Bob Fagan		inf	
Slyvester Foreman (Hooks)		c	
Willie Gisentaner (Lefty)		p	
Lemuel Hawkins (Hawk)	1b		
Oscar Johnson (Heavy)	rf	c	
Roy Johnson		2b	
Newton Joseph (Newt)	3b	ss	
? Lightner		p	
Jack Marshall		p	
Hurley McNair	lf		
Jose Mendez (Joe)		p	ss
Percy Miller		p	
Walter Moore (Dobie)	ss		
? Murphy		p	
Charles O'Neill		c	
Bartolo Portuando		3b	
Otto Ray		c	
Eugene Redd		3b	
Wilber Rogan (Bullet Joe)	cf	p	
Branch Russell		of	3b
William Sheppard		p	
George Sweatt		2b	lf
John Taylor (Red)		p	
Dan Thomas		2b	
Henry Williams		c	
? Yokum		p	

New Orleans Crescent Stars

Player	1	2	3
Calvin Alexander	p		
George Collins	2b		
Richard Gee	c		
? Harris	lf		
? Jackson (Gumbo)	3b		

Player	1	2	3
Milt Laurent		utl	
Miles Lucas	p		
Anderson Pryor	ss		
? Wilcox		p	
Andrew Wilson	cf		
George Wilson	rf		
Percy Wilson	1b		

New York Bacharach Giants

Player	1	2	3
Elias Brown (Country)		rf	
Warren Duncan		lf	of
Ernest Gatewood		c	
Dennis Graham		rf	
Robert Hudspeth (Highpocket)	1b		
Fred Hutchinson		inf	
Richard Jackson	2b		
Clarence Jenkins (Fats)		cf	
John Henry Lloyd (Pop)	ss		
Oliver Marcelle	3b		
Charles Mason	lf		
Alonzo Mitchell (Hooks)		p	
Charles O'Neill		c	
Ramiro Ramirez		cf	
Dick Redding (Cannonball)	p		
Roy Roberts	p		
Julio Rojo	c	3b	
George Shively		of	
Harold Treadwell	p		
Andrew Williams (Stringbean)	p		

New York Lincoln Giants

Player	1	2	3
Charles Bradford	p		
George Fiall	ss		
Robert Gans (Jude)	cf		
Ernest Gatewood		c	
Othello Johnson		lf	of
Carl Perry		3b	
Bill Pierce	1b		
Spottswood Poles (Spot)	cf		
Orville Singer	2b		
F. Wiley	p		
Wabishaw Wiley (Doc)		c	
Tom Williams	p		

Philadelphia Giants

Player	1	2	3
? Edwards (Smokey)	p	rf	
Joe Forbes	ss		
Jimmy Fuller	1b	c	
? Gaynor	3b		
? Gilson	lf		
? Jackson	c	of	
? Leary	p	rf	
Webster McDonald	p	of	
Andrew Payne (Jap)	cf	rf	
Leslie Stewart	c		

Pittsburgh Keystones

Player	1	2	3
Jess Barbour	1b		
Fred Burnett (Tex)	c	of	
Joseph Campbell (Joe)		3b	
Albert Clark		p	
Charles Corbett	p		
William Dismukes (Dizzy)		p	
Ernest Gooden	2b		
G.E. Gray (Dolly)	cf		
? Hayes (Buddy)		c	
Johnny Holt		of	
William McCall (Bill)	p		
Oscar Owens	p	of	
Benjamin Pace (Brother)	c		

Player	1	2	3
? Price		of	
? Spencer	lf		
Jasper Washington (Jap)		3b	of
Robert White		2b	
Mathis Williams (Matt)	ss		

Richmond Giants

Player	1	2	3
Robert Clarke		c	
George Fisher	cf		
? Fletcher		2b	
Art Grant		c	
John Harper		p	
Arthur Henderson (Rats)	p		
Charles Hobson (Johnny)		2b	
Charles Lindsay (Clarence)	ss		
Charles Mason		lf	
Webster McDonald		p	
L. North		of	
Carl Perry	3b		
William Pettus (Zack)	1b		
Henry Richardson		p	
W.A. Smith		c	
Wade Thompson		p	
Sam Warmack	rf		

St. Louis Stars

Player	1	2	3
Joe Hewitt	inf		M
James Bell (Cool Papa)		p	
Sam Bennett		c	of
Charles Blackwell	rf		
Charles Brooks		2b	
John Dickey (Steel Arm)		p	
Eddie Douglas		cf	
Bill Drake	p		
C.A. Dudley		cf	
John Finner	p		
Bill Gatewood		p	
Dennis Graham		of	
James Gurley		p	
Logan Hensley (Slap)		p	
Eddie Holtz	ss	2b	
Dan Kennard	c		
Dudley McAdoo (Tully)	1b		
George Meyers	p		
Percy Miller		p	of
Jimmy Oldham		p	
Otto Ray		c	
Branch Russell	lf	3b	2b
George Scales		3b	
Charles Wesley (Connie)		of	1b
Robert White		2b	
William Woods		of	

1923

Cuban Stars (East)

Player	1	2	3
Bernardo Baro	rf		
Pelayo Chacon	ss		
Martin Dihigo	1b	p	
Julian Fabelo		inf	of
Isidro Fabre	p	of	
Jose Fernandez	c		
Oscar Levis	p		
Vidal Lopez	p		
? Maravale		p	
Armando Marsans		of	
Pablo Mesa	lf		
Juanelo Mirabel	p		
Estaban Montalvo		1b	

Player	1	2	3
Alejandro Oms	cf		
Juan Padrone		p	
Jose Perez		1b	2b
Bartolo Portuando	3b	2b	
Recurvon Teran	2b		

Cuban Stars (West)

Player	1	2	3
Eufemio Abreu	c	ss	
Lucas Boada	p	3b	rf
Tatica Campos	lf	rf	p
Pedro Dibut	p		
Valentin Dreke	cf	lf	
? Durvant		p	
Rodolfo Fernandez		p	
Juan Guerra	1b	of	
Estaban Montalvo	rf	1b	p
Eugenio Morin		c	
? Nirsa		of	
Juan Padrone	p		
Eustaquio Pedroso		of	1b
? Pellas		p	
? Rigal	ss		
Herman Rios	3b		
Jose Rodriquez	c		
Felipe Sierra	2b		

Bacharach Giants

Player	1	2	3
Thomas Jackson			M
Alex Albritton		p	
? Baptiste		of	
Clifford Carter		p	
Frank Crockett		cf	
Willis Crump		2b	
Nap Cummings (Chance)	1b		
James Deas (Yank)		c	
McKinley Downs (Bunny)	2b		
Bill Francis	3b		
? Gilender		p	
? Hamilton		p	
Lewis Hampton		p	
John Harper	p		
Willie Haynes		p	
Arthur Henderson (Rats)	p		
Charles Hobson (Johnny)		p	
Eddie Huff		rf	c
Nate Johnson		p	
William Jones (Fox)	c	rf	
Hubert Lockhart	p	rf	
Dick Lundy	ss		
Charles Mason	lf	rf	
Augustin Parpetti		rf	
Ambrose Reed	rf	cf	1b
Roy Roberts	p		
George Robinson		p	
? Smith		rf	
Harold Treadwell		p	
William Webster (Speck)		c	
Chaney White	cf	lf	
Burlin White		c	
? Wright		of	
Jim York		c	

Baltimore Black Sox

Player	1	2	3
Alex Albritton		p	
George Britt (Chippy)		c	p
Wayne Carr		p	
Clifford Carter	1b		
Morten Clark		2b	
Robert Clarke		c	rf
Daltie Cooper		p	

Player	1	2	3
Roy Ford		2b	lf
? Gordon	p		
Blainey Hall	lf	rf	
Willie Haynes	p		
? Heath	p		
? Jagers	p		
Henry Jordan		of	c
Ed Kemp	cf	lf	
Joseph Lewis		c	
Charles Lindsay (Clarence)		ss	
Nick Logan	p		
Tony Mahoney	p		
L. Miller		ss	
Alonzo Mitchell (Hooks)		p	of
Carl Perry		3b	
E. Poles (Possum)	ss	3b	
Ramiro Ramirez		of	
Henry Richardson		p	lf
Harry Roberts (Raggs)	rf	of	
Julio Rojo	c	1b	
Cleveland Smith (Cleo)	3b	of	
L. Smith		of	
Wyman Smith		of	
F. Smith (Lefty)		p	
Marshall Smith (Darknight)		p	
Franklin Sykes (Doc)	p		
Cyrus Taylor		of	
Joseph Wheeler		p	
Jud Wilson	1b	2b	

Birmingham Black Barons

Player	1	2	3
Poindexter Williams	c		M
Fred Bell		of	
A. Brown		c	
? Buck		p	
John Cason		c	
? Charleston (Red)		c	
Fred Daniels		p	
Jesse Edwards		p	utl
Carl Glass		p	
Curtis Green	p		
Walter Harper		c	
Stanford Jackson		ss	
Reuben Jones		of	
B. Juran (Johnny)	p		
Eli Juran		p	
John Kemp		cf	
? Maddox (One Wing)		p	of
George McAllister	1b		
Lewis Means	c	2b	
Buford Meredith (Geetchie)	ss	2b	
Bob Miller (Ruby)	3b		
Robert Mitchell	rf		
Ralph Moore (Squire)		p	rf
Juan Padrone		p	
Charles Robertson		p	
Harry Salmon	p	of	
Leroy Stratton		3b	
Sam Streeter		p	
George Suttles (Mule)	lf		
? Tubbs			
David Watson		p	
Charles Wesley (Connie)	2b		

Brooklyn Royal Giants

Player	1	2	3
Chester Brooks	2b	of	
John Cason		2b	c
Edward Douglass	1b		
McKinley Downs (Bunny)		ss	
Tom Fiall	rf	of	

Player	1	2	3
Willis Flournoy (Pud)	p		
Johnson Hill (Fred)	3b		
Jesse Hubbard		p	of
Nate Johnson		p	
Cornelius Rector (Connie)		p	of
Dick Redding (Cannonball)	p		
William Rogers (Nat)		3b	
Robert Scott	lf	of	
Charles Spearman	c		
Otis Starks		p	
Bill Wagner	ss		
E. Weeks		3b	
Andrew Williams (Stringbean)		p	
William Woods	cf		

Chicago American Giants

Player	1	2	3
Andrew Foster (Rube)			M
John Beckwith	p	3b	c
Edward Brown		p	
Jim Brown	c	1b	
Elwood DeMoss (Bingo)	2b		
Luther Farrell		p	
Willie Foster		p	
Floyd Gardner (Jelly)	rf		
Glover Gardner (Gus)		c	
John George		ss	
Leroy Grant		1b	
George Harney		p	
Tom Johnson		p	
Harry Kenyon		of	p
Jimmie Lyons	lf		
Dave Malarcher	3b	ss	
Jack Marshall	p		
Charles O'Neill		c	
Aubrey Owens		p	
Curtiss Ricks		p	
Ed Rile	p		
Herman Roth (Bobby)		c	
Fulton Strong		p	
Cristobal Torriente	cf	p	
Dick Whitworth		p	
Bobby Williams	ss		
Tom Williams	p		
Lewis Wolfolk		p	

Cleveland Tate Stars

Player	1	2	3
Robert Baldwin		ss	
John Barnes (Fat)		c	1b
Finis Branahan		p	
? Branham (Slim)		p	
? Cordova (Pete)	ss		
Ernest Gooden		2b	ss
G.E. Gray (Dolly)	1b		
Don Hammond	3b		
Vic Harris	rf	lf	
George Henderson (Rube)		of	
Logan Hensley (Slap)	p		
Harry Jeffries		3b	
Claude Johnson (Hooks)	2b		
James Leonard (Bobo)	cf		
William McCall (Bill)	p		
Bob McClure	p		
Willie Miles	lf		
Otto Ray	c	of	
Mathis Williams (Matt)		3b	

Detroit Stars

Player	1	2	3
Bruce Petway	c		M
Grover Alexander (Buck)	p		
George Boggs		p	

Player	1	2	3
Jack Combs		p	
Andrew Cooper (Andy)	p		
Leon Daniels (Pepper)	c		
Walter Davis (Steel Arm)		of	p
William Force	p	of	
Ernest Gooden		3b	
? Haley	p		
? Holcomb	p		
Harry Jeffries	3b		
John Jones	2b	of	
Harry Kenyon	p		
E. Manese		inf	
Edward McClain (Boots)		3b	
? Phillips	2b	3b	
Anderson Pryor		2b	
Orville Riggins	ss		
Clarence Smith	rf	of	
Norman Stearnes (Turkey)	cf		p
Johnny Watson	lf	of	
Edgar Wesley	1b		

Harrisburg Giants

Player	1	2	3
? Barber (Bull)		2b	
? Curtis		p	
Herbert Dixon (Rap)	rf		
George Fiall	ss		
George Fisher	lf		
? Gibbons		3b	
Lawrence Graves		p	
Ananias Harris		p	
Charlie Henry	p		
Richard Jackson	2b		
Clarence Jenkins (Fats)	cf		
Nate Johnson		p	
Dan Johnson (Shang)		p	
Henry Jordan	c		
William Pettus (Zack)	1b		
Sam Ross		p	
H. Smith		p	
Wade Thompson		p	
Harold Treadwell		p	
E. Weeks	3b		
Burlin White		1b	c
? Wisher		of	

Hilldale

Player	1	2	3
Toussaint Allen (Tom)		1b	
Otto Briggs	rf		
George Carr (Tank)	1b	of	
Phil Cockrell	p		
? Cottrell		c	
? Easte		p	
Willis Flournoy (Pud)		p	
Kenneth Gardner (Ping)		p	
Wade Hampton		p	
George Johnson (Dibo)	cf		
William Johnson (Judy)	3b		
Holsey Lee (Scrip)		p	
John Henry Lloyd (Pop)	ss		
Raleigh Mackey (Biz)	c	ss	
Sam Ross		p	
Merven Ryan (Red)	p		
Louis Santop		c	
Paul Stephens (Jake)		ss	
Franklin Sykes (Doc)		p	
Clint Thomas	lf		
Frank Warfield	2b		
Jesse Winters (Nip)	p		

Homestead Grays

Player	1	2	3	
Cumberland Posey (Cum)				M
Elmore Brown (Scrappy)	ss			
Walter Cannady (Rev)		p		
Maceo Clark (Marty)		p		
Raymond Harris (Mo)	2b			
Win Harris	1b			
William Johnson (Wise)		c		
Joseph Lewis		c		
Willis Moody	lf			
Oscar Owens	p	of		
Harry Roberts (Raggs)		of		
Pete Walker (Lottie)		3b	2b	
Jasper Washington (Jap)	3b	1b		
Charles Williams (Lefty)	p			
? Williams	rf			
William Young (Pep)	c			

Indianapolis ABCs

Player	1	2	3	
William Dismukes (Dizzy)	p			M
Henry Blackman	3b	1b		
Larry Brown		c		
Fred Burnett (Tex)		c	1b	
Oscar Charleston	1b	cf	p	
Albert Clark		p		
Daltie Cooper	p	of	ss	
Charles Corbett	p	of		
Wilson Day (Connie)	2b			
George Dixon	c			
Leroy Grant		1b		
Crush Holloway	rf	of	1b	
James Jeffries		p	of	
Earl Lewis		p		
Ralph Moore (Squire)		p		
Omer Newsome	p			
Harold Ross		p		
George Shively	lf			
Namon Washington		of	ss	
Gerard Williams	ss			

Kansas City Monarchs

Player	1	2	3	
Sam Crawford	p			M
Newton Allen (Newt)		2b	ss	
Theodore Anderson (Bubbles)		2b		
William Bell		p		
? Coley		p		
Alfred Cooper (Army)		p		
Reuben Currie (Rube)	p			
John Donaldson		of		
Bill Drake	p			
Frank Duncan	c			
Willie Gisentaner (Lefty)		p		
Lemuel Hawkins (Hawk)	1b			
Oscar Johnson (Heavy)	rf			
Wade Johnston		of		
Newton Joseph (Newt)	3b			
? Lightner		p		
Hurley McNair	cf			
Jose Mendez (Joe)		p		
Walter Moore (Dobie)	ss			
Wilber Rogan (Bullet Joe)	p	lf		
George Sweatt		of		
? Wharton		cf		
Henry Williams		c	1b	

Memphis Red Sox

Player	1	2	3	
Larry Brown		c		
? Carpenter		of		
Jesse Edwards		p	of	
James Ellis	1b	ss		
Willie Foster	p			
Carl Glass	p	lf	1b	
George Hamilton	c			
L. Hamilton	3b			
? Howard		3b		
Stanford Jackson	ss			
Ralph Moore (Squire)		p	lf	
Garrett Norman	rf			
? Parker		1b	lf	
John Henry Russell	2b			
William Spearman		p		
John Young	p			

Milwaukee Bears

Player	1	2	3	
George Boggs	p	of		
George Collins		p	of	
Frank Duncan (Pete)		of		
John Finner	p			
Slyvester Foreman (Hooks)		c		
Bill Gatewood		p		
Perry Hall		p		
? Hayes (Buddy)	c			
Joe Hewitt	ss	cf	inf	
Johnson Hill (Fred)		ss		
Preston Hill (Pete)	rf	of	1b	
? Horner		of		
Charles Hudson		p		
Louis Johnson (Dicta)	p			
Anderson Pryor	2b			
Eugene Redd		3b		
Herman Roth (Bobby)		c		
Percy Segula		p		
Louis Smallwood		2b	of	
Leroy Stratton	3b	ss		
Fulton Strong	p			
James Thompson (Sandy)	lf	rf	1b	
A. Walker		p		
? Walters		p		
Percy Wilson	1b	of		
Andrew Wilson	cf	p		

New York Lincoln Giants

Player	1	2	3	
Smokey Joe Williams	p			M
Dave Brown	p			
Richard Gee		c		
Fred Harpson		inf		
Charley Hill (Lefty)		of		
Charles Hobson (Johnny)		ss		
Bill Holland		p		
Eddie Holtz		ss		
Robert Hudspeth (Highpocket)	1b			
Oliver Marcelle	3b			
Carl Perry		ss	2b	
Bill Pierce	c	1b	of	
Spottswood Poles (Spot)	lf			
Ed Rile		p		
George Scales		2b	3b	
Orville Singer		2b		
Sam Streeter		p		
Jules Thomas	cf			
F. Wiley		p	of	
Wabishaw Wiley (Doc)		c		
Pete Willett		ss	of	
Benny Wilson	rf			

Richmond Giants

Player	1	2	3	
? Brown (Babe)	cf			
William Campbell (Zip)		p		
Paul Carter		p		
Robert Clarke		c		
? Coates	3b			
? Cook		p		
Sam Cooper		p		
James Deas (Yank)		c		
McKinley Downs (Bunny)		inf		
? Garfield	2b			
? Hearns		c	of	
Arthur Henderson (Rats)		p		
Charley Hill (Lefty)		of		
Charles Hobson (Johnny)		utl		
? Hooper		3b		
Milton Lewis		2b		
Charles Lindsay (Clarence)	ss			
Jack Matthews	ss			
? Maynard		p		
? Miller		3b		
L. North		rf	of	
? O'Dell	lf			
Augustin Parpetti	1b			
Carl Perry		3b	2b	
Spottswood Poles (Spot)		lf		
? Punch		p		
Ramiro Ramirez		cf		
Bill Rankin		p	c	
? Read	c			
? Rhone		of		
J.D. Roberts		ss		
W.A. Smith		c		
Marshall Smith (Darknight)		p		
F. Smith (Lefty)		p		
Sam Warmack	cf			
James Womack	2b			

St. Louis Stars

Player	1	2	3	
Joe Hewitt	ss	inf	of	M
Candy Jim Taylor	3b	ss		M
Fred Bell	p			
James Bell (Cool Papa)		of	p	
Sam Bennett		of		
Charles Blackwell	rf	of		
Robert Bonner		1b		
Charles Brooks		of	1b	
C.A. Dudley		of		
Bob Fagan		2b		
John Finner		p		
? Gardner		of		
Herman Gordon		p		
James Gurley		p		
Logan Hensley (Slap)		p		
Eddie Holtz		ss	2b	
Ray Johnson		of		
Dan Kennard	c			
Dudley McAdoo (Tully)	1b			
? McCabb		p		
George Meyers		p		
Percy Miller		p	of	
Mitch Murray		c		
Jimmy Oldham	p			
Otto Ray		c	lf	
John Reese		of		
Branch Russell		of	inf	
George Scales		inf	of	
? Sharpe		ss		
? Stewart	p			
Dan Thomas		2b	ss	
? Turner (Tuck)		p		
John Young		p		

Toledo Tigers

Player	1	2	3	
Candy Jim Taylor	3b			M

Player	1	2	3
Abe Atkins		ss	3b
? Banles		c	
Fred Bell			
Robert Bonner	1b	2b	c
Jim Calhoun		2b	
? Chase		p	
? Coley	p		
George Collins		p	
S.R. Dewitt (Eddie)	2b		
Frank Duncan (Pete)	rf		
? Fox		of	
? Gardner		of	
Bill Gatewood	p		
Ernest Gooden		2b	3b
Herman Gordon		p	lf
Don Hammond		inf	
? Hayes (Buddy)		c	
Johnny Holt	lf		
? Hutt		1b	
Louis Johnson (Dicta)	p		
Jack Matthews		3b	
Edward McClain (Boots)	ss		
George Meyers		1b	p
Mitch Murray	c		
Charles O'Neill		c	
Jimmy Reel		of	
John Reese		of	
Frank Stevens	p		
Smith Summers (Tack)	cf		
Etwood Turner		rf	
Robert White		2b	
? Wingfield		p	

Washington Potomacs

Player	1	2	3
Ben Taylor	1b		M
Alex Albritton	p		
Elias Brown (Country)		rf	
William Campbell (Zip)		p	
Wayne Carr	p		
Maceo Clark (Marty)	p		
Dell Clark	2b	ss	
Mack Eggleston	c		
Tom Finley	3b		
Willie Gisentaner (Lefty)		p	
Joe Goodrich	ss	3b	
Ralph Jefferson	lf	cf	
Harry Jeffries		3b	
Joseph Lewis	c	of	
William Owens		2b	ss
Carl Perry		2b	
Bill Rankin	p		
? Ridgely (Buck)		ss	
Sam Ross	p		
H. Smith	p		
? Spike		of	p
C. Ward (Pinky)		cf	
Peter Washington		of	
Andrew Williams (Stringbean)	p		
William Woods		cf	

1924

Cuban Stars (East)

Player	1	2	3
Alex Pompez			M
Bernardo Baro	1b	of	c
Lucas Boada		p	
? Calderin		p	
P. Cardenas		c	rf
Pelayo Chacon	ss		

Player	1	2	3
Martin Dihigo		ss	2b
Oscar Estrada		p	of
Isidro Fabre	rf	1b	p
Jose Fernandez	c	1b	
Bienvenido Jimenez (Hooks)	2b		
Oscar Levis	p		
? Manolo			p
Pablo Mesa	lf		
Juanelo Mirabel	p		
Alejandro Oms	cf		
Bartolo Portuando	3b	2b	
? Salvat		p	
? Tevera		2b	

Cuban Stars (West)

Player	1	2	3
Eufemio Abreu	c		
Angel Alfonso	ss		
Raul Alvarez		p	
Lucas Boada	p	rf	
Valentin Dreke	cf		
Juan Guerra	lf		
Pasquel Martinez		p	
Estaban Montalvo	rf	1b	p
? Pastoria		p	
Eustaquio Pedroso	p	lf	1b
Jose Perez	1b		
? Petricola		p	
Herman Rios		3b	ss
Lazaro Salazar	p		
Felipe Sierra	2b		
Recurvon Teran	3b		

Atlanta Black Crackers

Player	1	2	3
? Bosch	c		
? Butler	1b		
? Daniel	p	lf	
? Harrell	ss		
? Jackson	cf		
? Jennings	p		
? Murden	2b		
? Tinker	3b		
? Wright	rf		
? Young	lf		

Bacharach Giants

Player	1	2	3
Elias Brown (Country)		of	
Wayne Carr	p		
Clifford Carter		p	
Nap Cummings (Chance)	1b		
Charles Evans (Alexander)		p	
Luther Farrell		p	
Tom Finley		3b	
Ernest Gatewood	c		
John George		ss	
Henry Gillespie		p	
Claude Grier (Red)		p	
John Harper	p		
Arthur Henderson (Rats)	p		
Charles Hobson (Johnny)		p	
William Jones (Fox)		c	
James Leonard (Bobo)		of	
? Levins		p	
Milton Lewis		2b	rf
John Henry Lloyd (Pop)	2b	ss	3b
Hubert Lockhart	p		
? Lowell		p	
Dick Lundy	ss		
Oliver Marcelle		3b	
Charles Mason	rf		
Alonzo Mitchell (Hooks)		p	

Player	1	2	3
H. Nuttall (Bill)		p	
Ramiro Ramirez	cf	lf	2b
Ambrose Reed	3b	lf	
Roy Roberts		p	
George Shively		cf	lf
Otis Starks		p	
Chaney White	lf	cf	
Andrew Williams (Stringbean)		p	
Berdell Young		of	

Baltimore Black Sox

Player	1	2	3
John Beckwith	ss	3b	
Henry Blackman	3b		
George Britt (Chippy)		p	lf
Robert Clarke		c	
William Dallard (Eggie)		of	
Wilson Day (Connie)	2b	3b	
George Fiall		3b	
William Force	p		
Roy Ford		2b	ss
Preston Hill (Pete)		cf	lf
Crush Holloway	rf		
James Jeffries		p	
M. Jeffries	3b	lf	
Wade Johnston	cf		
James Leonard (Bobo)		lf	
Charles Lindsay (Clarence)		ss	2b
Bob McClure	p		
E. Poles (Possum)		lf	2b
Neil Pullen		c	
Julio Rojo	c	lf	1b
F. Smith (Lefty)		p	
Wyman Smith		lf	
Joe Strong	p		
Franklin Sykes (Doc)		p	
Jud Wilson	1b	lf	2b
Pete Wilson		1b	

Birmingham Black Barons

Player	1	2	3
Joe Hewitt	2b		M
Theodore Anderson (Bubbles)		2b	
Fred Daniels		p	rf
William Dismukes (Dizzy)		p	
George Dixon		c	
Reuben Jones	rf	of	
Eli Juran		p	
George McAllister	1b		
William McCall (Bill)	p		
Lewis Means		c	2b
Buford Meredith (Geetchie)	ss		
Robert Poindexter	p		
John Richardson		p	2b
Harry Salmon		p	rf
Ray Sheppard		ss	rf
Leroy Stratton	3b		
Sam Streeter	p		
George Suttles (Mule)	lf		
James Thompson (Sandy)	cf		
Charles Wesley (Connie)	2b	3b	rf
Poindexter Williams	c	1b	

Brooklyn Royal Giants

Player	1	2	3
Chester Brooks		rf	ss
Irving Brooks		of	2b
John Cason	c	1b	2b
Edward Douglass	1b		
McKinley Downs (Bunny)		2b	ss
Willis Flournoy (Pud)	p		
Johnson Hill (Fred)	3b		
Jesse Hubbard		p	rf

Player	1	2	3
Cornelius Rector (Connie)	p	rf	cf
Dick Redding (Cannonball)	p		
Robert Scott	lf		
George Shively		of	
J. Smith		ss	
Charles Spearman		c	ss
Jules Thomas	cf	of	
Bill Wagner	ss		
William Watson		of	
Smokey Joe Williams	p		

Chicago American Giants

Player	1	2	3
Andrew Foster (Rube)			M
Jim Brown	c	rf	
Walter Davis (Steel Arm)		rf	
Elwood DeMoss (Bingo)	2b		
George Dixon		c	
Willie Foster		p	
Floyd Gardner (Jelly)	cf		
Leroy Grant		1b	
George Harney	p		
Vic Harris		rf	
Joe Hewitt		2b	3b
John Hines	c	of	
James Leonard (Bobo)		of	
Jimmie Lyons		of	
Dave Malarcher	3b		
Eddie Miller (Buck)		p	rf
Aubrey Owens		p	
Juan Padrone	p		
Ed Rile		p	1b
Harold Ross	p		
Herman Roth (Bobby)		c	
? Stewart		ss	
Cristobal Torriente	lf		
Harold Treadwell		p	
William Ware		1b	
Dick Whitworth	p		
Bobby Williams	ss		
Tom Williams	p		
Lewis Wolfolk		p	

Cleveland Browns

Player	1	2	3
Solomon White (Sol)			M
John Barnes (Fat)		c	
Charles Beverly		p	
Robert Bonner		2b	
? Browne (Hap)		p	
Albert Clark		p	
James Ellis		ss	
? Fields	p		
Slyvester Foreman (Hooks)		c	
Bill Francis		3b	
Herman Gordon	p	of	
Leroy Grant		1b	
? Hamilton	p		
Don Hammond		ss	p
Vic Harris	lf		
? Hayes (Buddy)		c	
Logan Hensley (Slap)	p		
Eugene Hunter	p		
Harry Jeffries		of	
John Wesley Johnson	p		
William Joseph	ss		
James Leonard (Bobo)		cf	
Dudley McAdoo (Tully)	1b		
Edward McClain (Boots)	cf	2b	ss
Willie Miles		cf	
W. Morrison		1b	
Carl Perry	2b	ss	3b

Player	1	2	3
Otto Ray	c	1b	p
Wilson Redus		rf	
Curtiss Ricks		1b	
Harold Ross		p	
John Shackleford		3b	
Orville Singer		rf	cf
? Stovall		p	
Harold Treadwell		p	
Ruby Tyree		p	rf
? Walters		p	

Detroit Stars

Player	1	2	3
Bruce Petway	c	1b	M
Grover Alexander (Buck)	p		
John Barnes (Fat)		c	
Julian Bell		p	
Charles Brooks		p	
? Coley		p	
Jack Combs	p		
Andrew Cooper (Andy)	p	of	
Leon Daniels (Pepper)		c	
Harry Jeffries	3b		
John Jones	lf	of	2b
I.S. Lane		3b	
William Lowe	3b		
N. Moore		of	
Bill Pierce	1b	rf	
Anderson Pryor	2b	3b	
Orville Riggins	ss		
Herman Roth (Bobby)		c	
Carl Sawyer		2b	
Clarence Smith	rf	of	3b
Norman Stearnes (Turkey)	cf		
Lawrence Terrell	p		
Harold Treadwell		p	
Johnny Watson		of	
Tom Williams		p	

Harrisburg Giants

Player	1	2	3
Henry Jordan	c		M
Jess Barbour		lf	
? Battles		c	3b
Fred Bell	p		
Finis Branahan		p	
? Brigham		p	
Earl Brown		p	
Clifford Carter		p	
Oscar Charleston	cf		
Daltie Cooper	p		
Charles Corbett	p		
Leon Daniels (Pepper)		c	
Herbert Dixon (Rap)	rf		
? Face		3b	
George Fiall	3b	ss	
Kenneth Gardner (Ping)	p		
John George	ss		
Willie Haynes		p	
Charlie Henry		p	
Richard Jackson	2b	lf	
James Jeffries		p	
Harry Jeffries		3b	
Clarence Jenkins (Fats)	lf		
Oscar Johnson (Heavy)		rf	2b
Claude Johnson (Hooks)		2b	c
E. Poles (Possum)		3b	
William Rogers (Nat)	c	1b	
E. Russell		3b	of
J. Smith	ss		inf
Cyrus Taylor		of	

Player	1	2	3
E. Weeks		3b	
Edgar Wesley	1b		

Hilldale

Player	1	2	3
Charley Akers		ss	
Toussaint Allen (Tom)		1b	
Otto Briggs	rf		
William Campbell (Zip)		p	
George Carr (Tank)	1b		
Paul Carter	p		
Clifford Carter		p	
John Cason		c	
Phil Cockrell	p		
Reuben Currie (Rube)	p		
Wade Hampton		p	
George Johnson (Dibo)	cf		
William Johnson (Judy)	3b		
Holsey Lee (Scrip)		p	
Joseph Lewis		c	
Raleigh Mackey (Biz)	ss	c	1b
Wilbur Pritchett		p	
Merven Ryan (Red)		p	
Louis Santop	c		
Paul Stephens (Jake)		ss	
Clint Thomas	lf		
? Tischman			
Bob Underhill		p	
Frank Warfield	2b		
Jesse Winters (Nip)	p		

Homestead Grays

Player	1	2	3
Cumberland Posey (Cum)			M
John Beckwith	c		
Finis Branahan		p	
Charles Brooks		2b	3b
Elmore Brown (Scrappy)	ss		
Walter Cannady (Rev)	1b		
Slyvester Foreman (Hooks)		c	
Dennis Graham		rf	of
G.E. Gray (Dolly)	cf		
Raymond Harris (Mo)	2b		
Win Harris		1b	
Willie Miles		of	
Willis Moody		of	
Oscar Owens	p	rf	
Ed Rile		p	
Harry Roberts (Raggs)	lf		
H. Smith		p	
Marshall Smith (Darknight)		p	
Jasper Washington (Jap)	3b		
Joseph Wheeler		p	
Charles Williams (Lefty)	p		
William Young (Pep)		c	

Indianapolis ABCs

Player	1	2	3
Howard Bartlett (Hop)		p	
A.L. Davis		ss	lf
? Davis (Goldie)		p	
William Dismukes (Dizzy)	p		
George Dixon	c		
? Emmett		p	
Bill Evans	p	of	1b
James Jeffries		p	
William Joseph	3b	ss	
James Leonard (Bobo)	rf	of	
? Murdock		p	
Wilson Redus	cf		
Curtiss Ricks	1b		
Ray Sheppard	ss	2b	
Hulan Stamps	p		

Player	1	2	3
? Strickland			p
? Swancy			p
? Trabue			p
C. Ward (Pinky)		lf	3b
Namon Washington	2b	3b	
Henry Williams	c		

Kansas City Monarchs

Player	1	2	3
Newton Allen (Newt)	2b		
Howard Bartlett (Hop)		p	
William Bell	p		
Clifford Bell (Cliff)		p	
Willie Bobo		1b	
Dewey Creacy		3b	
John Donaldson		of	
Bill Drake	p		
Frank Duncan	c		
Lemuel Hawkins (Hawk)	1b		
Oscar Johnson (Heavy)	lf	rf	1b
Newton Joseph (Newt)	3b		
E. Manese		2b	
Jack Marshall	p		
William McCall (Bill)	p		
Hurley McNair	rf	of	p
Jose Mendez (Joe)		p	cf
Walter Moore (Dobie)	ss		
Harold Morris	p		
Carroll Mothell (Dink)		1b	3b
Wilber Rogan (Bullet Joe)	p	cf	of
George Sweatt		of	1b

Memphis Red Sox

Player	1	2	3
Larry Brown	c		
? Charleston (Red)		c	
Albert Clark	p		
Marion Cunningham	1b		
Jesse Edwards		2b	ss
Willie Foster	p		
Carl Glass	p	rf	lf
James Gurley	lf	p	
George Hamilton		c	
L. Hamilton		2b	lf
Eugene Hunter	p		
Stanford Jackson	ss		
John Kemp		cf	rf
B. McIntyre	p		
Bob Miller (Ruby)	2b	3b	
Ralph Moore (Squire)	p		
Garrett Norman		of	
John Henry Russell	3b	ss	
Harry Salmon	p		
William Sheppard	p		
William Spearman	p		
Hulan Stamps	p		
C. Ward (Pinky)		rf	cf
Charles Williams	ss		
John Young	p		

Milwaukee Giants

Player	1	2	3
? Austin (Tank)	p		
? Biggs	lf		
? Chistian	rf		
? Jackson	c		
? Lewis	2b		
A. Mitchell	cf		
C. Mitchell	3b		
? Pewe	ss		
? Shelton	1b		
? Terry	p		

New Orleans Stars

Player	1	2	3
? Benjamin	lf	rf	
George Collins	ss		
? Phillips	cf	lf	
? Platt	p		
? Prichard		2b	
? Richards	2b		
? Riley	rf	1b	
? Roussell	1b		
Percy Segula		lf	cf
? Thomas	p		
? Tives	c		
? Winberry	3b		

New York Lincoln Giants

Player	1	2	3
Robert Gans (Jude)	of	p	M
Finis Branahan		p	
Dave Brown	p		
Earl Brown		p	
Fred Burnett (Tex)	c	rf	
Fred Daniels	p		
Edward Douglass	1b		
W.P. Evans	p		
Kenneth Gardner (Ping)	p		
Richard Gee	c		
Bill Holland	p		
Robert Hudspeth (Highpocket)	1b		
Ed Kemp		of	
Harry Kenyon	cf	p	
James Leonard (Bobo)		cf	lf
Oliver Marcelle	3b		
George Scales	2b		
Orville Singer		of	
Cleveland Smith (Cleo)		ss	2b
Otis Starks		p	
John Taylor (Red)	p		
William Webster (Speck)		c	
Gerard Williams	ss		
Benny Wilson	lf	rf	

Philadelphia Giants

Player	1	2	3
Dan McClellan			M
? Archer		c	
? Baptiste		of	
William Campbell (Zip)	p		
? Cordova (Pete)	2b	3b	
? Crudup (Zeke)		p	
James Crump		2b	
William Dallard (Eggie)	cf		
Henry Gillespie	p	of	
Willie Gisentaner (Lefty)	rf	p	
Ralph Jefferson		of	
William Johnson (Wise)	c		
A.J. Lockhart (Joe)	3b		
Webster McDonald		p	
? Peacock		2b	
Pender Ricks	1b		
William Rogers (Nat)		c	
Charles Smith (Chino)		of	
Paul Stephens (Jake)	ss		
Berdell Young	lf		

Pittsburgh Crawfords

Player	1	2	3
Abe Atkins		1b	
Don Hammond	ss		
C. Harris	rf	c	
? Hermon	2b		
Johnny Holt	lf		
? Jackson (Lefty)	p		
? Matlin	p		

Player	1	2	3
? Morlin	p		
Melvin Sykes	3b		
H. Williams	1b	c	
N. Williams	c	1b	
Mathis Williams (Matt)	cf		

Pittsburgh Giants

Player	1	2	3
Alex Albritton	p		
M. Allen	3b		
? Anderson	rf	c	
Jess Flood		c	
Ernest Gooden	ss		
Claude Grier (Red)	p		
Don Hammond		2b	
Johnny Holt	rf	of	
Ralph Mellix (Lefty)	p		
? Miller		of	
Willis Moody	cf		
? Moore		2b	
? Owens	1b		
Ed Rile		c	
? Spencer	lf		
Pete Walker (Lottie)	p		
? Williams		2b	
William Young (Pep)	c		

St. Louis Giants

Player	1	2	3
Sam Bennett	lf	rf	
Charles Blackwell		of	
? Bostick		of	
Charles Brooks	2b	3b	
E. Cooper		of	
? Ducey	3b		
John Finner	p		
Charley Hill (Lefty)		rf	
? Hutt	1b		
Dan Kennard	c		
Percy Miller	p	lf	
? Nelson		2b	
? Rich		3b	
Willie Wells	ss		
Elmer Wilson		2b	

St. Louis Stars

Player	1	2	3
Candy Jim Taylor	3b		M
Fred Bell		p	
James Bell (Cool Papa)	cf	p	
Charles Blackwell	lf		
Willie Bobo	1b	p	
Ralph Cleage		lf	
Sam Crawford		p	
Dewey Creacy	3b		
Roosevelt Davis (Rosey)	p		
John Finner		p	
? Hamilton		p	
Logan Hensley (Slap)		p	
Eddie Holtz		2b	
Tom Jackson		p	
George Meyers	p		
Percy Miller		p	
George Mitchell		p	lf
Robert Mitchell		c	of
Mitch Murray	c		
Wilson Redus		lf	of
John Reese	rf	of	
Charles Robertson		p	
Cecil Rose		p	
William Ross	p		
Branch Russell	2b	ss	3b
Dan Thomas		3b	

Player	1	2	3
Eddie Watts		2b	ss
Willie Wells	ss		
Washington Potomacs			
Alex Albritton	p		
Theodore Anderson (Bubbles)	2b	c	
Fred Bell		p	
Elias Brown (Country)	rf	of	2b
Wayne Carr	p		
Arthur Chambers (Rube)	p		
Maceo Clark (Marty)		1b	p
Willie Creek		c	
William Dallard (Eggie)		lf	
Mack Eggleston	c	3b	2b
Tom Finley	ss	3b	
Joe Goodrich	3b	1b	
? Grady		p	
Claude Grier (Red)	p		
J.H. Hamilton (John)		ss	2b
Lewis Hampton		p	
? Jenkins		p	
William Johnson (Wise)		c	
Bill Lindsey		ss	
Jimmie Lyons		cf	
Omer Newsome		p	
William Owens		ss	
Leonard Pierce		p	
George Shively	cf	lf	
H. Smith		p	
Ben Taylor	1b		
Peter Washington	lf	cf	
Chaney White		cf	rf
? Willas		p	
Andrew Williams (Stringbean)		p	
Fred Williams		c	
? Williamson		p	
William Woods		of	

1925

Chappie Johnson's Stars

Player	1	2	3
George Johnson (Chappie)			M
Elmore Brown (Scrappy)	ss		
Paul Carter		p	
? Cooper		p	
William Ewing (Buck)	c		
? Johnson	cf		
Ed Kemp	rf		
Don Perry	1b		
? Ridgely (Buck)	3b		
Cleveland Smith (Cleo)		utl	
Marshall Smith (Darknight)	p		
Sam Warmack		of	
Joseph Wheeler	p		

Cuban Stars (East)

Player	1	2	3
Alex Pompez			M
Bernardo Baro	1b	of	
P. Cardenas		c	
Pelayo Chacon	ss		
Martin Dihigo	p	2b	3b
Oscar Estrada		p	
Isidro Fabre	rf	p	
Jose Fernandez	c	1b	
Pedro Ferrer	2b		
Sijo Gomez (Joe)		p	
Oscar Levis	p		
Armando Massip		1b	
Pablo Mesa	lf		

Player	1	2	3
Juanelo Mirabel	p		
Alejandro Oms	cf		
Bartolo Portuando	3b		
? Salvat		p	
Cuban Stars (West)			
Eufemio Abreu	c	1b	
Angel Alfonso	ss	2b	
? Almas		p	
Raul Alvarez	p		
Luis Arango	3b		
Lucas Boada		p	
? Bomes		3b	
? Dominguez		p	rf
Valentin Dreke	cf		
Juan Eckelson		p	
? Fumes	lf	3b	
? Garey		c	
David Gomez	p	3b	
Pasquel Martinez		p	
? Mexio		p	
Estaban Montalvo	rf	p	
Eustaquio Pedroso		p	1b
Jose Perez	1b	c	
Felipe Sierra	2b	ss	
Bacharach Giants			
Elias Brown (Country)		3b	rf
Fred Burnett (Tex)		c	
Maceo Clark (Marty)		p	
Nap Cummings (Chance)	1b		
Charles Evans (Alexander)		p	
Luther Farrell	p		
Tom Finley	3b	2b	rf
Ernest Gatewood		c	
John George		ss	
Henry Gillespie	p		
Claude Grier (Red)		p	
John Harper		p	
Arthur Henderson (Rats)	p		
Louis Henderson		p	
Charles Hobson (Johnny)		p	
William Jones (Fox)	c		

Player	1	2	3
James Leonard (Bobo)		rf	
Milton Lewis		2b	3b
John Henry Lloyd (Pop)	2b		
Hubert Lockhart		p	
Dick Lundy	ss		
Oliver Marcelle		3b	
Charles Mason	rf		
Alonzo Mitchell (Hooks)		p	
H. Nuttall (Bill)		p	
Ambrose Reed	cf	3b	
Roy Roberts		p	
? Savage		p	
George Shively	lf		
Otis Starks		p	
Ted Waters		p	of
Chaney White		lf	of
Andrew Williams (Stringbean)		p	
Benny Wilson		of	
William Woods		cf	
Berdell Young	lf		
Baltimore Black Sox			
Ben Taylor		1b	M
John Beckwith	ss		
George Britt (Chippy)	p	lf	cf
Earl Brown		p	
Wayne Carr		p	
Robert Clarke		c	
William Dallard (Eggie)		of	
Wilson Day (Connie)	2b		
W.P. Evans		p	
George Fiall		ss	
William Force		p	
Roy Ford		2b	
Blainey Hall		of	
Preston Hill (Pete)		of	
Crush Holloway	rf		
James Jeffries		p	
Harry Jeffries		1b	3b
Oscar Johnson (Heavy)	lf		
James Leonard (Bobo)		of	
Nick Logan		p	
Bob McClure	p		

Three 1925 Wilmington Potomacs, L to R: Peter Washington, Toussaint "Tom" Allen, Chaney White.

Larry Shane

Player	1	2	3
J. Mungin		p	
Julio Rojo	c	1b	
H. Smith		p	
Wyman Smith		of	
Joe Strong	p		
Jud Wilson	3b	1b	ss

Birmingham Black Barons

Player	1	2	3
Charles Beverly		p	
Charles Blackwell	lf	rf	
Sam Crawford	p	2b	
Fred Daniels		p	of
Saul Davis		ss	lf
Jesse Edwards		inf	of
John Finner		p	
Willie Foster		p	
L. Hamilton		lf	
Eppie Hampton		c	
? Henderson		c	
? Horn		2b	
Arthur Jones		ss	
Reuben Jones	rf	of	p
William Joseph		2b	ss
? Lillie		utl	
Buford Meredith (Geetchie)	2b	ss	c
Ralph Moore (Squire)		p	
Grady Orange	ss	2b	
? Pardee	c		
Robert Poindexter	p	1b	of
Charles Robertson		p	
Herman Roth (Bobby)		c	
Harry Salmon	p		
? Stevenson (Lefty)		p	
Leroy Stratton	3b	p	
Sam Streeter		p	
George Suttles (Mule)	1b	p	
James Thompson (Sandy)	cf		
Poindexter Williams	c	1b	

Brooklyn Royal Giants

Player	1	2	3
Chester Brooks		cf	
Irving Brooks		of	
C. Brown		of	
John Cason	c	1b	
? Collins		p	
Edward Douglass	1b		
McKinley Downs (Bunny)	2b		
Willis Flournoy (Pud)	p		
Johnson Hill (Fred)	3b		
Bill Holland	p		
Jesse Hubbard	rf	p	1b
Cornelius Rector (Connie)	p		
Dick Redding (Cannonball)	p		
Robert Scott	lf		
Charles Smith (Chino)	cf		
Charles Spearman		c	
E.C. Turner (Pop)		2b	3b
Bill Wagner	ss		
William Watson		of	

Chicago American Giants

Player	1	2	3
Andrew Foster (Rube)			M
Bobby Anderson		3b	
Eugene Bragg		c	
James Bray		c	
Jim Brown	c	1b	of
? Buddles		inf	
Sam Crawford	p		
Elwood DeMoss (Bingo)	rf	2b	of
Oland Dials (Lou)		of	

Player	1	2	3
George Dixon		c	
Willie Foster	p		
Bill Francis		3b	
Floyd Gardner (Jelly)	cf	rf	
Leroy Grant		1b	
James Gurley		lf	p
George Harney	p		
Vic Harris		of	
John Hines		rf	c
Dave Malarcher	2b	3b	
William McCall (Bill)	p		
Webster McDonald		p	
Eddie Miller (Buck)		p	lf
George Mitchell		p	
Aubrey Owens		p	
Juan Padrone	p		
Willie Powell		p	
William Ross		p	
Herman Roth (Bobby)		c	
Frank Stevens		p	
Leroy Stratton	3b		
Albert Streets		inf	
Leroy Taylor		lf	of
Cristobal Torriente	lf	cf	
Roy Tyler		rf	
William Ware	1b		
Bobby Williams	ss		
Tom Williams		p	

Detroit Stars

Player	1	2	3
Bruce Petway		c	1b M
Grover Alexander (Buck)		p	
Fred Bell	p	of	
Finis Branahan		p	
Jack Combs	p		
Andrew Cooper (Andy)	p		
Leon Daniels (Pepper)	c		
Saul Davis		3b	
Lewis Hampton		p	of
Chick Harper		lf	
Joe Hewitt		3b	2b
John Jones	lf	2b	of
Dan Kennard		c	
Harry Kenyon	p	of	
George McAllister		1b	
Harold Morris		p	
Omer Newsome		p	
Anderson Pryor	2b	3b	
Orville Riggins	ss		
Ray Sheppard	3b		
Clarence Smith	rf	of	1b
James Smith (Jim)		ss	
Norman Stearnes (Turkey)	cf		
Lawrence Terrell		p	
Edgar Wesley	1b		

Harrisburg Giants

Player	1	2	3
Oscar Charleston	cf		M
Fred Bell		p	
Fred Burnett (Tex)	c		
Walter Cannady (Rev)	ss		
Daltie Cooper	p		
Charles Corbett	p		
? Curtis		p	
Herbert Dixon (Rap)	rf		
McKinley Downs (Bunny)		2b	
Mack Eggleston		c	3b
George Fiall	3b		
Kenneth Gardner (Ping)	p		
Willie Gisentaner (Lefty)		p	

Player	1	2	3
Charlie Henry		p	
Richard Jackson	2b		
Clarence Jenkins (Fats)	lf		
William Johnson (Wise)		c	
Edward Jones		c	
Henry Jordan		c	
Miles Lucas		p	
Wilbur Pritchett		p	
William Rogers (Nat)		c	
E. Russell		3b	of
? Sanford		c	
John Shackleford		3b	
Ben Taylor	1b		

Hilldale

Player	1	2	3
Otto Briggs	rf		
William Campbell (Zip)		p	
George Carr (Tank)	1b		
Phil Cockrell	p		
Reuben Currie (Rube)	p		
Luther Farrell			p
William Johnson (Judy)	3b		
George Johnson (Dibo)	cf		
Holsey Lee (Scrip)			p
Joseph Lewis		c	
Raleigh Mackey (Biz)	c	ss	
Walter Robinson (Newt)		ss	
Merven Ryan (Red)			p
Louis Santop		c	
Paul Stephens (Jake)	ss	2b	
Clint Thomas	lf	cf	
Frank Warfield	2b	3b	
Namon Washington		of	ss
Jesse Winters (Nip)	p		

Homestead Grays

Player	1	2	3
Cumberland Posey (Cum)			M
Dennis Graham	rf		
G.E. Gray (Dolly)	1b		
Raymond Harris (Mo)	2b		
Vic Harris	lf		
Willis Moody	cf		
Oscar Owens	p		
Benjamin Pace (Brother)		c	
Herbert Pierce		c	
Harry Roberts (Raggs)		c	of
George Scales		3b	
Sam Streeter	p		
Pete Walker (Lottie)		p	
Jasper Washington (Jap)	3b		
Pete Willett		3b	
Charles Williams (Lefty)	p		
Gerard Williams	ss		
Smokey Joe Williams		p	
William Young (Pep)	c		

Houston Black Buffaloes

Player	1	2	3
? Alexander (Chuffy)	rf	2b	
J. Burdine	p		
? Calloway	lf		
? Curtis	1b		
? Danage	2b		
S.R. Dewitt (Eddie)	3b	ss	
? Henderson		c	
? McChaney	ss	2b	3b
D. O'Brien	p	lf	
Roy Parnell (Red)	cf		
Herman Roth (Bobby)		c	
? Williams		p	

Indianapolis ABCs

Player	1	2	3
Todd Allen	of		M
Grover Alexander (Buck)	p		
? Allison		2b	
Theodore Anderson (Bubbles)		2b	
Henry Baker	rf	of	1b
Robert Baldwin		inf	
Howard Bartlett (Hop)	p		
Maywood Brown	p		
George Collins	ss		
A.L. Davis	of		
? Davis (Goldie)	p		
George Dixon	c		
Ernest Duff	of		
Eddie Dwight	of	2b	
Wilmer Ewell	c		
Bill Freeman	p		
James Gurley	lf	p	1b
J.H. Hamilton (John)	2b	ss	
? Hitchman		3b	
Fred Hutchinson	2b	ss	
Eugene Keeton	p		
? Long	cf	rf	
William Martin (Stack)	c	2b	p
George McAllister	1b		
George Mitchell		p	rf
Omer Newsome		p	
Mose Offert	p		
William Owens	ss		
Ed Rile	p		
William Robinson (Bobby)	3b		
Harold Ross		p	
? Rowe			
Frank Stevens		p	
? Stevenson (Lefty)		p	lf
Harold Treadwell	p		
? White			
Henry Williams	c		
Fred Williams	c		

Kansas City Monarchs

Player	1	2	3
Newton Allen (Newt)	2b	3b	
? Barber (Bull)		2b	
? Barnes	p		
Howard Bartlett (Hop)	p		
William Bell	p	lf	
Clifford Bell (Cliff)	p		
Chet Brewer	p		
? Butler (Sol)	p		
Nelson Dean	p		
Fred Dewitt	1b		
Bill Drake	p		
Frank Duncan	c		
Slyvester Foreman (Hooks)		c	
Lemuel Hawkins (Hawk)	1b	lf	rf
Oscar Johnson (Heavy)		of	
Wade Johnston	cf	lf	
Newton Joseph (Newt)	3b		
Louis LaFlora		of	
Hurley McNair	lf		rf
Jose Mendez (Joe)		p	
Walter Moore (Dobie)	ss		
Carroll Mothell (Dink)		3b	1b
A. Mullin		inf	
Wilber Rogan (Bullet Joe)	p	cf	1b
George Sweatt	rf	lf	1b
Henry Williams	c		
Tom Young	c		

Memphis Red Sox

Player	1	2	3
Larry Brown	c		
Marion Cunningham	1b		
Earl C. Curley		of	
William Dismukes (Dizzy)		p	1b
Bill Gatewood		p	
Carl Glass		p	1b
George Hamilton		c	
Stanford Jackson	cf	rf	3b
John Kemp		of	
William Lowe		2b	3b
Bob Miller (Ruby)	2b		
Ralph Moore (Squire)	p		
Pythias Russ		c	1b
John Henry Russell	3b		
William Sheppard		p	
William Spearman		p	
Hulan Stamps		p	
Bill Tyler	p		
C. Ward (Pinky)	lf	of	
Charles Wesley (Connie)	rf	of	
Charles Williams	ss		

New York Lincoln Giants

Player	1	2	3
Dave Brown		p	
Arthur Chambers (Rube)	p		
William Dallard (Eggie)		of	
Robert Dean	ss		
Edward Dudley		p	
W.P. Evans		p	
William Ewing (Buck)	c		
Luther Farrell		p	
Tom Fiall	lf		
Tom Finley		3b	
? Forrest		of	
Robert Gans (Jude)	rf		
Richard Gee	c		
Tom Gee	c	of	
Henry Gillespie	p		
John Harper	p		
Charlie Heywood (Dobie)	p		
William Hodges	p		
Robert Hudspeth (Highpocket)	1b		
Bill Jackman		p	
John Wesley Johnson		p	
B. Johnson (Monk)		p	
Dan Johnson (Shang)		p	
? Kendall		2b	ss
Charles Lindsay (Clarence)		ss	2b
Oliver Marcelle		3b	
Charles Mason		of	p
H. Nuttall (Bill)	p		
Edward Pryor	2b		
Roy Roberts		p	
George Scales	3b	2b	of
Orville Singer		of	
Cleveland Smith (Cleo)		ss	
H. Smith	p		
W. Smith	ss		
Cyrus Taylor		of	
John Taylor (Red)	p		
Jules Thomas	cf		
Peter Washington		of	
F. Wiley		p	
Gerard Williams		ss	
Andrew Williams (Stringbean)	p		
Smokey Joe Williams	p		
Benny Wilson		of	
Berdell Young		of	

Pennsylvania Red Caps of NY

Player	1	2	3
? Banot	c		
Frank Baynard		c	of
Eddie Bryant		2b	
Andy Harris	3b		
? Johnson	1b		
? Lair			rf
? Leah			of
? Leary	ss		
Edward Pryor		2b	
W. Reavis	p		
? Saunders		c	
Richard Seay (Dick)		ss	
? Stock	p		
Jules Thomas	lf		
F. Wiley		p	
Benny Wilson	cf		

Philadelphia Giants

Player	1	2	3
Jess Barbour	cf		
Clay Carpenter		3b	
? Cephus (Goldie)	lf		
? Crudup (Zeke)		p	
Jack Davis	2b		
? Fethum	rf		
Bill Jackman		p	
Ralph Jefferson	rf		
Clarence Jenkins (Barney)		c	
Charles Lewis (Babe)	2b		
A.J. Lockhart (Joe)	3b		
Leonard Pierce	p		
Pender Ricks	1b		
Remy Scott		of	
Richard Seay (Dick)		inf	
Burlin White	c	3b	
Bill Yancey	ss		

Philadelphia Royal Giants (Winter)

Player	1	2	3
George Britt (Chippy)	p	ss	
George Carr (Tank)	lf	3b	
Reuben Currie (Rube)	p		
Wilson Day (Connie)	2b		
Herbert Dixon (Rap)	cf		
Crush Holloway	rf	lf	
Jesse Hubbard	p	rf	
Robert Hudspeth (Highpocket)	1b		
Raleigh Mackey (Biz)	ss	3b	c
Neil Pullen	c		

St. Louis Stars

Player	1	2	3
Candy Jim Taylor	3b	rf	p	M
John Barnes (Fat)		c	
James Bell (Cool Papa)	cf	1b	
Willie Bobo	1b		
Finis Branahan		p	
G. Brown		p	
D. Brown		p	
? Broyles		p	
Dewey Creacy	3b	2b	rf
Roosevelt Davis (Rosey)	p		
Logan Hensley (Slap)	p		
George Meyers		p	
Percy Miller	p	of	
Mitch Murray	c		
Wilson Redus	lf		
John Reese		lf	rf
William Ross			p
Dick Ross	lf		
Branch Russell	rf	2b	
? Smith	c		

Player	1	2	3
Edward Tyler	rf		
Eddie Walls	p		
Eddie Watts		2b	
Willie Wells	ss		
Elmer Wilson		2b	

Wilmington Potomacs

Player	1	2	3
Dan McClellan			M
Alex Albritton		p	
Toussaint Allen (Tom)	1b	3b	
Elias Brown (Country)	3b	of	
Wayne Carr	p		
Arthur Chambers (Rube)		p	
Maceo Clark (Marty)		1b	
William Dallard (Eggie)	cf	1b	
Mack Eggleston	c		
Tom Finley		ss	3b
Joe Goodrich		3b	
Claude Grier (Red)	p		
J.H. Hamilton (John)	2b	3b	
Lewis Hampton	p		
William Johnson (Wise)		c	
Milton Lewis		2b	
Charles Lindsay (Clarence)	ss		
A.J. Lockhart (Joe)		3b	p
Hubert Lockhart		p	
William Martin (Stack)		of	
Webster McDonald		p	
Omer Newsome		p	
William Owens		ss	
? Savage		p	
Peter Washington	lf		
? West		1b	
Joseph Wheeler		p	
Chaney White	rf	of	

1926

Chappie Johnson's Stars

Player	1	2	3
George Johnson (Chappie)			M
Elmore Brown (Scrappy)	ss		
William Ewing (Buck)	c		
Robert Gans (Jude)		p	of
Charles Hobson (Johnny)	3b		
? Jackson (Lefty)	p		
Ed Kemp	cf		
Don Perry	1b		
? Ridgely (Buck)	2b		
Marshall Smith (Darknight)		rf	p
Sam Warmack	lf		
Joseph Wheeler		p	
? Wise	p		

Cuban Stars (East)

Player	1	2	3
Bernardo Baro	rf	p	
P. Cardenas		c	1b
Pelayo Chacon	ss		
Alejandro Crespo	2b		
Martin Dihigo	1b	p	ss
Isidro Fabre		p	lf
Jose Fernandez	c		
Oscar Levis	p		
Pablo Mesa	lf		
Juanelo Mirabel	p		
Alejandro Oms	cf		
Eustaquio Pedroso		1b	p
Bartolo Portuando	3b	1b	
Pedro San (Eli)	p		

Cuban Stars (West)

Player	1	2	3
Angel Alfonso	3b		
Luis Arango	1b	3b	
Benito Calderon	c	lf	
Marceline Correra (Cho Cho)	ss		
Edolfo Diaz (Yo Yo)	p		
Valentin Dreke	lf		
Manuel Garcia (Cocaina)		p	
David Gomez	p	of	
Luis Guiterrez	rf		
Cando Lopez	cf		
Juan Padrone		p	lf
? Pedemonte		p	2b
Eustaquio Pedroso		1b	c
Basilio Roselle	p		
Felipe Sierra	2b		

Bacharach Giants

Player	1	2	3
Elias Brown (Country)		rf	3b
Nap Cummings (Chance)	1b		
William Dallard (Eggie)		1b	rf
Luther Farrell	rf	p	
Romando Garcia	2b		
? Garrett		of	
Ernest Gatewood		c	
Claude Grier (Red)	p		
Arthur Henderson (Rats)	p		
William Jones (Fox)	c		
Joseph Lewis		c	
Hubert Lockhart		p	
Dick Lundy	ss		
Oliver Marcelle	3b		
Alonzo Mitchell (Hooks)		p	
Ambrose Reed	lf		
Roy Roberts		p	
Jack Wallace		2b	rf
Chaney White	cf		

Baltimore Black Sox

Player	1	2	3
John Beckwith		3b	ss
Chuck Bowers	p	ss	
George Britt (Chippy)	p	c	
Clay Carpenter	p		
Robert Clarke	c		
Sam Cooper		p	
William Dallard (Eggie)		of	
Wilson Day (Connie)	2b		
Mack Eggleston		rf	c
George Fiall		ss	3b
William Force		p	
Crush Holloway	cf		
Oscar Johnson (Heavy)	lf		
Pearley Johnson (Tubby)		ss	2b
Bob McClure	p		
Alonzo Mitchell (Hooks)		p	
J. Mungin		p	
Wilbur Pritchett		p	
Julio Rojo	3b	c	
Richard Seay (Dick)	ss	2b	
Joe Strong	p		
Ben Taylor	1b		
Jud Wilson	rf	cf	1b
Laymon Yokeley	p		

Brooklyn Royal Giants

Player	1	2	3
Chester Brooks	cf		
Fred Burnett (Tex)		1b	c
John Cason	1b	c	
? Ecora			
Willis Flournoy (Pud)	p		

Player	1	2	3
Johnson Hill (Fred)	3b		
Bill Holland	p		
Jesse Hubbard	rf	p	
Cornelius Rector (Connie)	p		
Dick Redding (Cannonball)	p		
Robert Scott	lf		
Charles Smith (Chino)	c	of	
Charles Spearman	c		
Jules Thomas		of	
Bill Wagner	ss		
William Woods		of	

Chattanoogna Black Lookouts

Player	1	2	3
Ralph Cleage	rf		
Anthony Cooper	lf		
James Gurley	cf		
? Herman	2b		
? Levanshown	1b		
William Lowe	3b		
Leonard Mitchell (Otto)	ss		
Leroy Paige (Satchel)	p		
? Stine	c		

Chicago American Giants

Player	1	2	3
Andrew Foster (Rube)			M
Jim Brown	1b	c	
Sam Crawford		of	
Reuben Currie (Rube)	p	lf	
Oland Dials (Lou)		of	
Willie Foster	p		
Floyd Gardner (Jelly)	rf	of	
George Harney	p		
John Hines		cf	rf
Stanford Jackson	ss	3b	of
Dave Malarcher	3b	2b	
Webster McDonald	p		
Eddie Miller (Buck)		p	
Aubrey Owens		p	
Robert Poindexter		p	
Willie Powell		p	
Pythias Russ	c		
John Shackleford		3b	
George Sweatt	cf	1b	2b
James Thompson (Sandy)	lf	of	
Roy Tyler	lf		
William Ware		1b	
Charles Williams	2b	ss	

Cleveland Elites

Player	1	2	3
Frank Duncan (Pete)	rf		M
Candy Jim Taylor	3b	p	M
Grover Alexander (Buck)	p		
Robert Baldwin		2b	ss
John Barnes (Fat)		c	
Howard Black		p	
Robert Bonner	c	1b	
Finis Branahan	p		
George Brannigan		p	
Ernest Duff		c	2b
? Fields		p	
? Goldie		1b	
J.H. Hamilton (John)		3b	2b
Art Hancock		p	
Andy Harris		3b	
Sam Jackson		c	
John Wesley Johnson	p		
James Leonard (Bobo)		cf	
Willie Miles		cf	lf
Dempsey Miller (Dimp)		p	
Edward Milton		cf	of

Player	1	2	3
Ralph Moore (Squire)		p	
? Nehf		of	
Alton Norman		ss	
William Owens		ss	3b
Joe Ransom		c	
? Redwine		p	
William Robinson (Bobby)		lf	ss
Jerry Ross		p	
Charles Spearman		3b	of
William Spearman		p	rf
Smith Summers (Tack)	lf	of	
Roy Tyler		of	
Eddie Walls		p	
Eddie Watts		1b	
Edward Woolridge		ss	
Charles Zomphier	2b	rf	p

Dayton Marcos

Player	1	2	3
Henry Baker		1b	
Don Bennett		2b	
Howard Black		p	
Chester Blanchard		2b	ss
George Boggs		of	
? Bradshaw		of	
Charles Brooks		of	inf
Albert Clark		p	
Troy Dandridge		ss	
S.R. Dewitt (Eddie)		3b	
? Dimes		lf	
? Ducey	rf	lf	
Bill Evans		cf	
? Fields		p	
Joe Hewitt		2b	ss
? Hinkey		of	
Eddie Huff	c	rf	
Eugene Keeton		p	
? Kirksey		c	2b
Bill Lindsey		ss	lf
William Marshall (Jack)		2b	
William Martin (Stack)	p	lf	
Edward McClain (Boots)		2b	ss
George Meyers	p	ss	
Omer Newsome		p	1b
William Owens		ss	2b
Leon Palmer		2b	
Everett Radcliffe (Red)		ss	
Curtiss Ricks		1b	
E. Russell	3b		
? Smith		p	
? Taylor		1b	
Harold Treadwell	p	rf	
? Whitlock	1b		
John Williams (Big Boy)	p	1b	
Elmer Wilson		2b	

Detroit Stars

Player	1	2	3	M
Candy Jim Taylor	3b	p		M
Robert Baldwin		2b		
Fred Bell		p	of	
Charles Blackwell	rf	of		
Larry Brown		c		
Jack Combs		p		
Andrew Cooper (Andy)	p			
Leon Daniels (Pepper)		c		
John Dixon (Johnny Bob)		p		
Perry Hall		2b		
Lewis Hampton	p			
Joe Hewitt		2b	3b	
Harry Jeffries	3b	p		
John Jones		lf		

Player	1	2	3
Harry Kenyon		of	1b
? Long		rf	
Harold Morris	p		
Omer Newsome		p	
Anderson Pryor	2b		
Orville Riggins	ss		
Bob Saunders		p	
Ray Sheppard		3b	ss
Norman Stearnes (Turkey)	cf		
Harold Treadwell		p	
Johnny Watson	lf		
Edgar Wesley	1b		

Harrisburg Giants

Player	1	2	3	M
Oscar Charleston	cf	1b	p	M
John Beckwith	3b	ss		
Walter Cannady (Rev)	ss			
Clifford Carter	p			
? Chester		of		
Sam Cooper	p			
Charles Corbett	p	rf		
Wilson Day (Connie)		2b		
Herbert Dixon (Rap)	rf	cf		
Mack Eggleston		c	inf	
Kenneth Gardner (Ping)	p			
? Garrett		of		
? Gaston		ss		
Henry Gillespie		p		
Domingo Gomez (Harry)	c	rf		
Joe Goodrich		3b	2b	
Richard Jackson	2b			
Clarence Jenkins (Fats)	lf			
William Johnson (Wise)		c	of	
Alonzo Mitchell (Hooks)		p		
Jose Perez	1b			
Wilbur Pritchett		p		
? Robbins		of		
? Royce			3b	
E. Russell			3b	
Wade Thompson		p		

Hilldale

Player	1	2	3
Paul Arnold			lf
Rudolph Ash			of
Otto Briggs	rf		
William Campbell (Zip)	p		
George Carr (Tank)	1b	lf	
Phil Cockrell		p	lf
Rube Ellis (Rocky)		of	
Charlie Henry		p	
William Johnson (Judy)	3b	ss	p
Holsey Lee (Scrip)	p	lf	rf
Raleigh Mackey (Biz)	c	lf	1b
Carl Perry		3b	
Hank Perry		p	
Dewey Rivers		lf	cf
Walter Robinson (Newt)		ss	2b
Merven Ryan (Red)	p		
Louis Santop		c	
Paul Stephens (Jake)		ss	2b
Melvin Sykes		lf	rf
Clint Thomas	cf	lf	
Edward Tyler		p	
Frank Warfield	2b	cf	
Namon Washington	lf	c	
Jesse Winters (Nip)	p	1b	cf

Homestead Grays

Player	1	2	3	M
Cumberland Posey (Cum)				M
George Britt (Chippy)		p		

Player	1	2	3
Charles Craig		p	
Dennis Graham	rf		
G.E. Gray (Dolly)	cf		
Raymond Harris (Mo)	2b		
Vic Harris	lf		
Willis Moody		of	
Oscar Owens	p		
Herbert Pierce	c		
Harry Roberts (Raggs)		of	c
Cleveland Smith (Cleo)	3b		
Sam Streeter	p		
Pete Walker (Lottie)		utl	
Jasper Washington (Jap)	1b		
Bobby Williams	ss		
Charles Williams (Lefty)	p		
Gerard Williams		ss	
Smokey Joe Williams	p		
William Young (Pep)		c	

Indianapolis ABCs

Player	1	2	3
John Barnes (Fat)		c	
Elwood DeMoss (Bingo)	2b		
George Dixon		c	
Bill Drake		p	
Ernest Duff		of	
Bill Evans		of	
Slyvester Foreman (Hooks)	c		
Hallie Harding	ss		
John Jones	lf	rf	
Reuben Jones	rf	lf	
E. Manese		inf	
William Martin (Stack)		inf	of
William McCall (Bill)	p		
Eddie Miller (Buck)	p	3b	rf
George Mitchell	p		
Mose Offert	p		
Juan Padrone	p		
Ed Rile	1b	p	
William Robinson (Bobby)	3b		
Frank Stevens	p	lf	
? Sturm			
Leroy Taylor	cf		
Raymond Williams (Red)		ss	

Kansas City Monarchs

Player	1	2	3	M
Wilber Rogan (Bullet Joe)	p	1b	2b	M
Newton Allen (Newt)	ss	2b		
William Bell	p			
Clifford Bell (Cliff)		p		
Chet Brewer	p			
Nelson Dean		p		
Frank Duncan	c			
Lemuel Hawkins (Hawk)	1b			
Wade Johnston	lf	p		
Newton Joseph (Newt)	3b			
Tom Long		c		
Hurley McNair	rf			
Jose Mendez (Joe)		p		
Dempsey Miller (Dimp)	p			
Walter Moore (Dobie)	ss			
Carroll Mothell (Dink)	2b	lf	cf	
Grady Orange		2b		
Randolph Primm	p			
Bob Saunders	p			
Cristobal Torriente	cf	rf		
Harold Vaughn		cf		
Tom Young	c			

Memphis Red Sox

Player	1	2	3
? Augustus		p	

Player	1	2	3
Black Bottom Buford	3b		
J.C. McHaskell	1b		
Bob Miller (Ruby)	2b		
N. Moore	lf		
Pythias Russ	ss		
H. Walker	c		
C. Ward (Pinky)	cf		
Charles Wesley (Connie)	rf		

New York Lincoln Giants

Player	1	2	3
Charles Bradford		p	
Walter Cannady (Rev)		3b	
Arthur Chambers (Rube)	p		
Daltie Cooper		p	
Charles Craig		p	
Edward Dudley		p	
Mack Eggleston		c	
Robert Finch		p	
Tom Finley	3b		
Richard Gee	c		
Tom Gee		c	
? Gilmore (Speed)	p		
Willie Gisentaner (Lefty)	p	rf	
? Harris	1b		
Charlie Heywood (Dobie)		p	
? Howard		p	
Robert Hudspeth (Highpocket)	1b		
George Johnson (Dibo)	cf		
? Kennedy		3b	
Charles Lewis (Babe)		ss	
Joseph Lewis	c		
Bill Lindsey		ss	
John Henry Lloyd (Pop)	2b		
Charles Mason	lf		
Jace Nestor		of	
H. Nuttall (Bill)		p	
George Scales	ss		
Robert Scott		lf	
? Simmons (Si)	p		
Orville Singer	rf		
? Stammore	p		
Melvin Sykes		of	
Berdell Young	rf	lf	

Pennsylvania Red Caps of NY

Player	1	2	3
D. Bailey	3b		
Frank Baynard	rf		
? Cunningham		2b	
B. Johnson (Monk)	1b	p	
? Johnson	1b		
Charles Lindsay (Clarence)	ss		
Edward Pryor	2b		
W. Reavis	p	of	
? Saunders	c		
John Taylor (Red)	p		
Jules Thomas	cf		
Jack Wallace	ss		
William Watson	lf		
F. Wiley	p		
Benny Wilson	lf		

Newark Stars

Player	1	2	3
Toussaint Allen (Tom)	1b		
Rudolph Ash		rf	
Frank Baynard		rf	
Wayne Carr	p		
? Gackles			
Tom Gee	c		
Willie Gisentaner (Lefty)	p	lf	
? Gumbs			

Player	1	2	3
? Hammerod			
Andy Harris	3b		
? Jackson		utl	
Cecil Johnson (Sess)	p		
Eli Juran	p		
Charles Mason	lf		
? Mitchell	p	rf	
? Mitchell (Bud)		p	of
Ted Page	cf		
? Payne	p		
George Scales		2b	
Richard Seay (Dick)	ss		
Cleveland Smith (Cleo)		2b	of
Otis Starks	p		

Philadelphia Giants

Player	1	2	3
Jess Barbour	lf	cf	
Clay Carpenter		2b	utl
? Cephus (Goldie)	rf	1b	
? Crudup (Zeke)	p		
Willie Gisentaner (Lefty)		p	of
Bill Jackman	p		
? Jackson (Lefty)		p	
Ralph Jefferson	cf	rf	
Clarence Jenkins (Barney)	c		
Holsey Lee (Scrip)		p	
Milton Lewis	2b		
A.J. Lockhart (Joe)	3b		
Leonard Pierce		p	
Bill Pierce		1b	
Bill Rankin		p	
Pender Ricks		1b	
Burlin White	1b	c	
Bill Yancey	ss		

St. Louis Stars

Player	1	2	3
James Bell (Cool Papa)	cf		
Willie Bobo		1b	rf
G. Brown		p	
Dewey Creacy	3b		
Roosevelt Davis (Rosey)	p		
William Dismukes (Dizzy)		p	
Carl Glass		p	
Logan Hensley (Slap)	p		
Tom Jackson	p		
Percy Miller		p	
Mitch Murray	c		
E. Patton		p	
Wilson Redus	lf	rf	
John Reese		of	
William Ross	p		
John Henry Russell	2b		
Branch Russell	rf	2b	ss
George Suttles (Mule)	1b	lf	
Willie Wells	ss		
Henry Williams		c	

1927

Chappie Johnson's Stars

Player	1	2	3
George Johnson (Chappie)			M
Rudolph Ash	lf		
Elmore Brown (Scrappy)	3b		
Gilbert Coleman	2b	ss	
McKinley Downs (Bunny)	ss	3b	
Edward Dudley	p		
Fred Flournoy	c		
Joe Forbes	2b		
Robert Gans (Jude)	p		

Player	1	2	3
Charles Hobson (Johnny)		ss	
? Hopkins		p	
? Jackson (Lefty)		p	
Earl Jackson	1b		
Alphonso Lattimore		c	
? Lovett		p	
? Morton		rf	
Ted Page		cf	
Don Perry	1b		
Dewey Rivers		cf	
Marshall Smith (Darknight)	p		
Edward Tyler		p	
Jack Wallace	3b		
Ted Waters		lf	
? Williams	p		
William Woods		rf	

Cuban Stars (East)

Player	1	2	3
Angel Alfonso	2b	ss	3b
Raul Alvarez		p	
Bernardo Baro	rf	p	
Pelayo Chacon		ss	1b
Alejandro Crespo	3b	2b	
Martin Dihigo	ss	p	1b
Isidro Fabre	lf	p	
Jose Fernandez	c		
? Lau		p	
Oscar Levis	p	lf	1b
Pablo Mesa		lf	
Juanelo Mirabel		p	
Alejandro Oms	cf		
? Pontello		p	
Bartolo Portuando	1b	ss	2b
B. Conrado Rodriquez		p	
? Saabin		p	
Pedro San (Eli)	p		
Jose Vargas (Tetelo)		ss	2b

Cuban Stars (West)

Player	1	2	3
Rogelio Alonso	rf	of	p
Benito Calderon	c	3b	
P. Cardenas		c	
Marceline Correra (Cho Cho)	ss		
Edolfo Diaz (Yo Yo)	p		
Valentin Dreke	lf	cf	
? Estenza		3b	2b
Manuel Garcia (Cocaina)	p	rf	
David Gomez	p	1b	
Cando Lopez	cf	lf	
Eustaquio Pedroso	1b	c	
? Rigal	3b		
Basilio Roselle	p	1b	
Felipe Sierra	2b		
Charles Zomphier		2b	

Bacharach Giants

Player	1	2	3
Edward Jones	c		M
? Bundy			
Sam Cooper		p	
William Dallard (Eggie)	1b	c	
Joe Duncan	c		
Warren Duncan		of	
Luther Farrell	p	lf	
Ernest Gatewood		c	
Henry Gillespie		p	
Claude Grier (Red)		p	
Bill Handy			2b
Arthur Henderson (Rats)	p		
Jesse Hubbard	p	rf	
Jack Jackson			of

Player	1	2	3
Milton Lewis	2b		
Hubert Lockhart		p	
Dick Lundy	ss		
Oliver Marcelle	3b		
Lewis Means		c	
Ambrose Reed	lf	3b	ss
Roy Roberts		p	c
Clarence Smith	rf		
J. Wagner		2b	
Chaney White	cf		

Baltimore Black Sox

Player	1	2	3
Percy Bailey (Bill)		p	
Elmore Brown (Scrappy)	ss		
Robert Clarke	c		
Mack Eggleston		c	of
William Force		p	
Crush Holloway	lf	rf	
Richard Jackson	2b		
Pearley Johnson (Tubby)	rf	lf	p
? Mason		3b	
Bob McClure	p		
Bill Monroe		ss	3b
Wilbur Pritchett		p	
Joe Strong	p		
Ben Taylor	1b		
Peter Washington	cf		
Jud Wilson		3b	inf
Laymon Yokeley	p		

Birmingham Black Barons

Player	1	2	3
? Alexander (Chuffy)		inf	of
J. Burdine	p	lf	
Fred Daniels	p	rf	
Nelson Dean	p		
Bill Gatewood	p		
James Gurley		rf	
J.H. Hamilton (John)		inf	
James Jeffries		p	
Reuben Jones	rf	of	
George McAllister	1b		
Buford Meredith (Geetchie)	2b		
Bob Miller (Ruby)		2b	
J. Webb Oden		3b	
William Owens	ss	3b	
Leroy Paige (Satchel)	p		
Clarence Palm (Spoony)		c	
Roy Parnell (Red)	lf	of	p
? Phillips		p	
Robert Poindexter	p		
William Robinson (Bobby)		3b	
Harry Salmon	p	of	
Hank Shanks		1b	
Sam Streeter	p	lf	rf
James Thompson (Sandy)	cf	of	
Columbus Vance		p	
C. Ward (Pinky)		cf	
F. Williams		rf	
Poindexter Williams	c	1b	
Charles Zomphier		3b	lf

Brooklyn Royal Giants

Player	1	2	3
Dick Redding (Cannonball)	p		M
Paul Arnold	lf		
Chester Brooks	cf		
Elias Brown (Country)	2b	rf	
Fred Burnett (Tex)	c		
William Campbell (Zip)		p	
Wayne Carr	p		
John Cason		c	

Player	1	2	3
Tom Finley	3b	ss	
Willis Flournoy (Pud)	p		
? Henley		3b	
Johnson Hill (Fred)		3b	2b
Bill Holland	p		
Robert Hudspeth (Highpocket)	1b		
? Johnson		p	
William Owens		ss	
Richard Seay (Dick)		ss	3b
Charles Smith (Chino)	rf	of	inf
J. Smith		3b	
Otis Starks	p		
Bill Wagner		2b	

Chicago American Giants

Player	1	2	3
Dave Malarcher	3b		M
James Bray		c	lf
Jim Brown	1b	c	rf
Larry Brown		c	
Sam Crawford			p
Reuben Currie (Rube)		p	lf
Walter Davis (Steel Arm)	lf	rf	
Oland Dials (Lou)		of	
Willie Foster	p	lf	
James Gurley		p	of
George Harney	p	rf	
John Hines	rf	c	
Stanford Jackson	cf	ss	
George Kobek		of	
Webster McDonald	p		
Eddie Miller (Buck)		p	of
Willie Powell	p		
William Robinson (Bobby)		3b	
William Rogers (Nat)		lf	rf
Pythias Russ	ss	c	
Ted Shaw	p		
George Sweatt	cf	rf	1b
Charles Williams	2b		

Cleveland Hornets

Player	1	2	3
Frank Duncan (Pete)	cf		M
John Barnes (Fat)		c	
? Bonds		c	
George Brannigan	p		
Nelson Dean	p		
George Dixon	c		
Ernest Duff	rf	of	
Bill Evans	cf	ss	
B. Gibson		p	
? Givens		ss	
? Goldie		1b	
James Gurley		p	
Art Hancock		1b	lf
James Leonard (Bobo)		of	1b
Willie Miles	3b	of	
Dempsey Miller (Dimp)	p	lf	
Ralph Moore (Squire)		p	
Orville Riggins	ss	1b	
William Ross		p	
Bob Saunders		3b	
William Spearman		p	
Frank Stevens		p	1b
Theodore Stockard		3b	
Smith Summers (Tack)	lf		
Dan Thomas		3b	
Eddie Watts		ss	2b
Edgar Wesley	1b		
Charles Zomphier	2b	3b	1b

Detroit Stars

Player	1	2	3
Elwood DeMoss (Bingo)	2b	1b	M
Fred Bell		p	
Edward Chapman		p	
Andrew Cooper (Andy)		p	
Leon Daniels (Pepper)	c		
Albert Davis		p	
Bill Drake		p	
Clarence Everett		ss	of
Lewis Hampton		p	
Hallie Harding	ss	of	
Harry Jeffries	3b	c	
Claude Johnson (Hooks)	2b	3b	
John Jones		lf	
Harry Kenyon		lf	p
William Martin (Stack)		c	1b
Harold Morris	p	of	
Anderson Pryor		3b	
Ed Rile	1b	p	
William Ross		p	
Norman Stearnes (Turkey)	cf		
? Stevens		c	
Cristobal Torriente	rf	p	
Edgar Wesley		1b	

Harrisburg Giants

Player	1	2	3
Oscar Charleston	cf	p	M
John Beckwith	3b	ss	c
Walter Cannady (Rev)	ss	3b	1b
Clifford Carter	p		
Alex Cooper		of	
Daltie Cooper	p		
Sam Cooper	p		
Charles Corbett		p	
Charles Craig		p	
Wilson Day (Connie)	2b		
Herbert Dixon (Rap)		rf	3b
George Fiall		ss	3b
Kenneth Gardner (Ping)		p	
Domingo Gomez (Harry)	c		
James Gurley		p	
Clarence Jenkins (Fats)	lf		
Oscar Johnson (Heavy)	rf	cf	c
Miles Lucas		p	
J. Mungin		p	
William Owens		ss	
Jose Perez	1b	3b	
Walter Robinson (Newt)		ss	
Robert Scott		lf	rf
Cleveland Smith (Cleo)		inf	

Hilldale

Player	1	2	3
Otto Briggs	rf		
William Campbell (Zip)		p	
George Carr (Tank)	1b	lf	3b
Porter Charleston		p	
Phil Cockrell	p	lf	
Charles Corbett		p	
Bill Holland		p	
William Johnson (Wise)		c	1b
William Johnson (Judy)	3b		
George Johnson (Dibo)		of	
? Kenwood		p	
Holsey Lee (Scrip)		p	
Joseph Lewis	c		
Raleigh Mackey (Biz)		c	
Walter Robinson (Newt)		3b	ss
Merven Ryan (Red)	p		
Robert Scott		lf	
Paul Stephens (Jake)	ss		

Player	1	2	3	
Clint Thomas	cf	lf		
J. Wagner		1b		
Frank Warfield	2b			
Namon Washington		lf	cf	
Ted Waters		of		
Jesse Winters (Nip)	p	1b		
Bill Yancey		inf	of	

Homestead Grays

Player	1	2	3	
George Britt (Chippy)		c	p	
Dennis Graham	rf			
G.E. Gray (Dolly)	cf			
Vic Harris	lf			
Win Harris	2b			
Oscar Owens	p	of		
Orville Riggins		3b		
Merven Ryan (Red)		p		
Charles Spearman		c		
Jasper Washington (Jap)	1b			
Bobby Williams	ss			
Smokey Joe Williams	p			
Charles Williams (Lefty)	p			

Kansas City Monarchs

Player	1	2	3	
Wilber Rogan (Bullet Joe)	p	rf	1b	M
Newton Allen (Newt)	ss			
Clifford Bell (Cliff)		p		
William Bell	p	cf	rf	
Chet Brewer	p			
G. Brown		p		
Fred Dewitt		1b		
Frank Duncan		c		
? Evans		c		
Clarence Everett		inf		
Slyvester Foreman (Hooks)		c		
George Giles	1b			
Carl Glass		p	1b	
? Grant				
Lemuel Hawkins (Hawk)	cf	1b	lf	
A. Hughes		of		
Wade Johnston	lf	rf		
Newton Joseph (Newt)	3b			
Hurley McNair	rf	of		
George Mitchell		p		
Carroll Mothell (Dink)	2b	cf	lf	
Grady Orange		2b	3b	
Owen Smaulding		p		
Bill Tyler		p		
Harold Vaughn		cf		
A. Walker		p		
F. Williams		cf		
Maurice Young		p		
Tom Young	c			
William Young		p		

Memphis Red Sox

Player	1	2	3	
? Augustus		p		
Clifford Bell (Cliff)	p	of		
Julian Bell		p	of	
? Brown		1b	lf	
Larry Brown	c			
J. Burdine		of		
Saul Davis		3b	ss	
Carl Glass	p	of		
Perry Hall		of	3b	
George Hamilton		c		
Eppie Hampton		c		
Wesley Hicks		lf	rf	
? Howard	p			
Cowan Hyde (Bubber)		rf	cf	

Player	1	2	3	
Tom Jackson		p	cf	
William Lowe		2b	3b	
J.C. McHaskell	1b			
Buford Meredith (Geetchie)		2b		
Willie Miles		3b	of	
A. Miller		lf		
Bob Miller (Ruby)	ss	2b		
J. Webb Oden		3b		
Bill Pryor		p	of	
William Robinson (Bobby)	3b	ss		
William Rogers (Nat)	lf	rf		
Willie Lee Scott (Joe)		1b		
? Smith		rf		
Hulan Stamps	p			
Leslie Starks		cf		
Bill Tyler		p	rf	
C. Ward (Pinky)	cf			
Charles Wesley (Connie)	2b	rf	cf	

Nashville Elite Giants

Player	1	2	3	
Joe Hewitt				M
William Anderson	rf			
Ralph Anderson		of		
Charles Beverly	p			
Black Bottom Buford	3b			
? Carpenter	cf			
? Charleston (Red)		c		
George Collins		2b		
James Gurley	lf	p		
Al Morris	2b	lf		
Jack Ridley	1b			
? Root		of		
William Spearman		p		
Leroy Stratton	ss			
Nish Williams	c			
Jim Willis	p			
? Wilson	p			

New York Lincoln Giants

Player	1	2	3	
Arthur Chambers (Rube)		p		
Charles Craig	p			
? Dillard		p		
Edward Dudley		p		
George Fiall		3b		
Romando Garcia		3b		
Willie Gisentaner (Lefty)	p	rf		
? Harris		1b		
Bill Holland		p		
George Johnson (Dibo)	cf			
John Henry Lloyd (Pop)	2b			
Charles Mason	lf	p		
Estaban Montalvo		rf		
Neil Pullen		c		
Cornelius Rector (Connie)	p	rf		
Walter Robinson (Newt)	ss			
Julio Rojo	c			
George Scales	3b			
F. Wiley		p		
Berdell Young	1b	rf		

Pennsylvania Red Caps of NY

Player	1	2	3	
Frank Baynard	rf			
? Cunningham	2b			
Charles Evans (Alexander)		p		
William Johnson (Wise)	1b			
C. Johnson		c		
Charles Lindsay (Clarence)	ss			
Edward Pryor		3b	2b	
W. Reavis	p			
? Saunders		c	3b	

Player	1	2	3	
John Taylor (Red)	p			
Jules Thomas	lf			
F. Wiley		p		
Benny Wilson	cf			

Philadelphia Giants

Player	1	2	3	
? Cephus (Goldie)	lf			
? Concepcion		3b		
? Cordova (Pete)		2b		
Earl Davis (Hawk)		ss	3b	
Bill Jackman	p	of		
Ralph Jefferson		cf		
Obie Lackey	ss			
Milton Lewis		2b		
Leonard Pierce	rf	p		
Bill Rankin	p			
Pender Ricks	1b			
Burlin White	c			

St. Louis Giants

Player	1	2	3	
Felix Wallace	3b			M
Fred Bell	p			
Sam Bennett	of			
Charles Brooks	3b			
Henry Harris	ss			
Charley Hill (Lefty)		of		
? Hutt	lf	of		
Dan Kennard	c			
Dudley McAdoo (Tully)	1b			
Willie Miles		cf	2b	
Percy Miller	p	of		
Elmer Wilson	2b			

St. Louis Stars

Player	1	2	3	
Candy Jim Taylor	3b	of	p	M
James Bell (Cool Papa)	cf	1b		
Willie Bobo	1b			
G. Brown		p		
Dewey Creacy	3b	2b		
Roosevelt Davis (Rosey)	p			
William Dismukes (Dizzy)		p		
Bill Gatewood		p		
Tomlini Harrison		p		
Logan Hensley (Slap)		p		
Tom Jackson		p		
? Johnson		p		
Luther McDonald (Vet)	p			
Mitch Murray	c			
Wilson Redus	lf	of		
John Henry Russell	2b	3b		
Branch Russell	rf	3b	2b	
William Spearman		p		
Frank Stevens		p	of	
George Suttles (Mule)	1b	2b		
Ted Trent	p			
Willie Wells	ss			
Henry Williams		c	2b	
John Williams (Big Boy)	p	lf		
Charles Zomphier		2b	3b	

1928

Cuban Stars (East)

Player	1	2	3	
Angel Alfonso	ss			
Bernardo Baro	rf			
Augustin Bejerano		of		
Ramon Bragana		p		
? Bregan	3b			
Isidro Fabre	p	of		

Player	1	2	3
Jose Fernandez	c		
Ramon Herrera		2b	
Ramon Herrera		2b	3b
Oscar Levis	p		
Juanelo Mirabel	p		
Emilio Navarro		inf	
Alejandro Oms	cf		
Jose Perez	1b		
Silvino Ruiz	p		
Pedro San (Eli)	p		
Miguel L. Solis		3b	

Cuban Stars (West)

Player	1	2	3
Rogelio Alonso	rf	lf	p
? Borges		ss	3b
? Celada		ss	
Marceline Correra (Cho Cho)	ss		
Aurelio Cortez	c		
Edolfo Diaz (Yo Yo)	p		
Valentin Dreke		of	
? Estenza	3b	c	
? Gainez		p	
? Galbae		p	
Cuneo Galvez	p		
Manuel Garcia (Cocaina)	p	lf	
David Gomez		p	
Bienvenido Jimenez (Hooks)	2b		
Cando Lopez	cf		
Vidal Lopez		p	
Jesus Lorenzo		p	
Pasquel Martinez		p	
C. Martinez	c		
Jose Martini		p	
Estaban Montalvo	lf	rf	
Busta Quintana		2b	3b
B. Conrado Rodriquez		2b	3b
Jacinto Roque (Siki)		of	
Basilio Roselle	p		
Felipe Sierra	1b		

Ewing's All-Stars

Player	1	2	3
William Ewing (Buck)	c		M
? Buckridge	cf		
Knowlington Burbage (Buddy)		rf	
? Corley	c		
Charles Craig	p		
Robert Dean	3b		
? Durant		1b	
Curtis Green		1b	
? Jackson (Lefty)	p		
Frankie Johnson	ss		
Ed Kemp	lf		
Bill Pierce		rf	
? Ridgely (Buck)		2b	
H. Smith	p		
Sam Warmack	lf		
? Wise		p	

Bacharach Giants

Player	1	2	3
R. Albrecht		p	
George Carr (Tank)	1b		
John Cason		c	
? Collier		c	
Nap Cummings (Chance)		2b	1b
Luther Farrell	p	rf	
Kenneth Gardner (Ping)	p		
Walter Greene		of	1b
Claude Grier (Red)	p		
Arthur Henderson (Rats)	p		
Jesse Hubbard	p		

Player	1	2	3
Clarence Jenkins (Fats)	lf		
Edward Jones	c		
Hubert Lockhart		p	
Dick Lundy	ss		
Oliver Marcelle	3b		
Alonzo Mitchell (Hooks)		p	
Ambrose Reed	2b		
Jimmy Shields		p	
Clint Thomas	rf		
Chaney White	cf		

Baltimore Black Sox

Player	1	2	3
George Boggs		p	
Robert Clarke	c		
? Collins		p	
Herbert Dixon (Rap)	cf		
Mack Eggleston		c	
Kenneth Gardner (Ping)		p	
Crush Holloway	rf		
Jesse Hubbard		p	
Jack Jackson		of	
Ben Taylor	1b		
Jud Wilson	3b		
Laymon Yokeley	p		

Birmingham Black Barons

Player	1	2	3
? Alexander (Chuffy)	rf		
J. Burdine	p	of	
Anthony Cooper		of	
Nelson Dean		p	
Oland Dials (Lou)		of	
? Gilers		cf	
? Haley (Red)		2b	3b
Perry Hall		of	3b
James Jeffries		p	of
? Johnson		of	
Reuben Jones		of	
George McAllister	1b		
Lewis Means		c	
Buford Meredith (Geetchie)	2b	of	
A. Miller		of	
? Morgan		of	
A. Mullen		of	
William Nash		p	
J. Webb Oden		3b	
William Owens		ss	
Leroy Paige (Satchel)		p	
Roy Parnell (Red)		cf	
? Payne		of	
Bill Perkins	c		
Robert Pipkin (Lefty)		p	
Robert Poindexter		p	
Harry Salmon	p	of	
Ray Sheppard	3b	2b	ss
Owen Smaulding		p	
Sam Streeter	p		
James Thompson (Sandy)		of	
Charles Wesley (Connie)		2b	of
Poindexter Williams		c	
Jim Willis	p		

Brooklyn Cuban Giants

Player	1	2	3
John B. Johnson			M
Howard Black	2b		
Gilbert Coleman		inf	
Charles Craig		p	
McKinley Downs (Bunny)		ss	
Fred Flournoy	c		
Curtis Green		1b	of
Walter Greene	1b	of	

Player	1	2	3
Fred Harpson	3b		
Joseph Holt	of		
Robert Johnson (Bob)		3b	ss
Elbert Melton		of	
Wilbur Pritchett	p		
Edward Tyler		p	
Namon Washington	of		
William Webster (Speck)		c	
Joseph Wheeler	p		
Craig Williams (Stringbean)	p		

Chicago American Giants

Player	1	2	3
Dave Malarcher	3b		M
Jim Brown	1b	c	lf
Walter Davis (Steel Arm)	rf	1b	
Oland Dials (Lou)		of	
Tommy Dukes		c	
Willie Foster	p		
Floyd Gardner (Jelly)	cf		
George Harney	p	of	
Lemuel Hawkins (Hawk)		1b	2b
John Hines	c	of	
Robert Holsey (Frog)		p	
Stanford Jackson	3b	cf	
Reuben Jones		rf	
Eddie Miller (Buck)		p	1b
Mitch Murray		c	
Willie Powell	p		
William Rogers (Nat)		lf	of
Pythias Russ	ss	c	
Owen Smaulding		p	
George Sweatt		of	
James Thompson (Sandy)	lf		
Harold Treadwell		p	
Bobby Williams		ss	3b
Charles Williams	2b		

Cleveland Tigers

Player	1	2	3
Sam Crawford		p	M
Frank Duncan (Pete)			M
Perry Hall		2b	3b M
John Barnes (Fat)		c	
George Boggs		p	
Tom Cox		p	
Homer Curry (Goose)	p	lf	
Saul Davis		ss	2b
A.C. Davis		inf	
Nelson Dean	p		
S.R. Dewitt (Eddie)		1b	
George Dixon		c	
John Dixon (Johnny Bob)		p	
Ernest Duff		1b	cf
Chancellor Edwards (Jack)		c	
Robert Gans (Jude)	p		
Eppie Hampton	c		
Tom Jackson		p	
? Jauron		p	
Harry Jeffries	3b		
John Wesley Johnson		p	
Oscar Johnson (Heavy)	rf	1b	
? Kirby		p	
James Leonard (Bobo)	1b		
Edward Milton	2b	cf	1b
Ralph Moore (Squire)		p	of
Grady Orange		of	
A. Owens		ss	
William Ross		p	
Orville Singer		cf	
Owen Smaulding		p	
Frank Stevens	p	cf	rf

Player	1	2	3
? Stevenson (Lefty)		p	
Theodore Stockard	ss		
Smith Summers (Tack)	lf	rf	2b
Pete Willett		3b	ss
George Williams	ss		
Raymond Williams (Red)	ss		
James Womack	1b		
? Woodard	inf		
Edward Woolridge	1b	lf	
Charles Zomphier	3b	2b	

Detroit Stars

Player	1	2	3
Elwood DeMoss (Bingo)	2b		M
Reuben Currie (Rube)		p	
Albert Davis		p	
Hallie Harding	ss		
Claude Johnson (Hooks)	3b	2b	
Wade Johnston	lf		
Jack Marshall	p		
William Martin (Stack)		c	
Hurley McNair	rf		
George Mitchell	p		
Grady Orange	2b	ss	3b
Ted Radcliffe (Double Duty)	c		
Ed Rile	1b	p	
Ted Shaw	p		
Norman Stearnes (Turkey)	cf		
Cristobal Torriente		rf	p

Hilldale

Player	1	2	3
Otto Briggs	rf		
William Campbell (Zip)		p	
Walter Cannady (Rev)		ss	3b
George Carr (Tank)		1b	
Porter Charleston	p		
Oscar Charleston	cf		
Phil Cockrell	p		

Player	1	2	3
Ray Cooper	p		
William Dallard (Eggie)		lf	
William Johnson (Judy)	3b		
Joseph Lewis		c	
Raleigh Mackey (Biz)	c		
Merven Ryan (Red)		p	
John Stanley (Neck)		p	
Paul Stephens (Jake)	ss		
Joe Strong	p		
Clint Thomas		lf	
Clarence Thorpe		p	
Frank Warfield	2b		

Homestead Grays

Player	1	2	3
Cumberland Posey (Cum)			M
John Beckwith	ss		
George Britt (Chippy)		p	3b
Benito Calderon		c	
Martin Dihigo	inf	p	of
Dennis Graham	rf		
Raymond Harris (Mo)	2b		
Vic Harris	lf		
Win Harris		1b	
James Leonard (Bobo)		of	
Grover Lewis		3b	
Webster McDonald		p	
Oscar Owens		p	
William Ross		p	
Sam Streeter	p		
Jasper Washington (Jap)	1b		
Charles Williams (Lefty)	p		
Smokey Joe Williams	p		

Kansas City Monarchs

Player	1	2	3
Newton Allen (Newt)	ss		
William Bell	p	rf	
Chet Brewer	p	1b	rf

Player	1	2	3
G. Brown		p	
Roy Brown		p	
Alfred Cooper (Army)	p		
Andrew Cooper (Andy)	p		
Frank Duncan	c		
Eddie Dwight	cf		
George Giles	1b		
Hallie Harding		lf	cf
? Hopwood		of	
Newton Joseph (Newt)	3b		
Harry Kenyon		p	rf
L.D. Livingston	lf		
Carroll Mothell (Dink)	2b	1b	lf
Wilber Rogan (Bullet Joe)		p	1b
Leroy Taylor	rf		
Herbert Wilson (Herb)		p	
Tom Young		c	

Memphis Red Sox

Player	1	2	3
Clifford Bell (Cliff)	p		
Julian Bell		p	
Willie Broadnax		p	
Ameal Brooks		c	
Larry Brown	c		
William Clark (Eggie)		c	
Saul Davis		2b	ss
Oland Dials (Lou)		of	
Carl Glass	p	of	
James Gurley	lf	rf	
George Hamilton		c	
Eppie Hampton		p	
Henry Harris	ss		
Wesley Hicks	rf	lf	p
Tom Jackson		p	
Oscar Johnson (Heavy)		rf	
John Kemp		of	
Harry Kenyon		p	

1928 Cuban Stars of the Negro National League. Among the many Cubans on the team are, back row, left, Estaban Montalvo; fourth from left, Hooks Jimenez; fourth from right, Agustin Molina; second from right, Pedro Arango, and last on right, Aurelio Cortez. The front row includes first on left, Rogelio Alonzo, next to Cando Lopez. Third from right is Yoyo Diaz, and far right is Cho Cho Correra.

Luis Munoz Collection

Player	1	2	3
William Lowe		ss	3b
Elliott Mayweather		p	
J.C. McHaskell	1b		
Bob Miller (Ruby)		2b	
William Robinson (Bobby)	3b		
William Rogers (Nat)		lf	
Hulan Stamps		p	
Dan Thomas	2b	ss	of
Bill Tyler	p		
C. Ward (Pinky)	cf		
Clarence White (Red)		p	

Nashville Elite Giants

Player	1	2	3
Charles Blackwell		of	
Willie Bobo		1b	
Black Bottom Buford	ss		
Willie Cornelius (Sug)	p		
Fred Daniels		p	
Jesse Edwards	2b		
James Gurley		p	of
Tom Jackson	p		
Al Morris	cf		
Jack Ridley	lf		
? Ronsell	rf		
Leroy Stratton	3b		
L. Thomas	1b		
Nish Williams	c		
Jim Willis	p		
Henry Wright (Red)		p	

New York Lincoln Giants

Player	1	2	3
William Campbell (Zip)		p	
Walter Cannady (Rev)	3b		
George Carr (Tank)		rf	1b
? Gilmore (Speed)		p	
Clarence Jenkins (Fats)		lf	
John Henry Lloyd (Pop)	2b		
Cornelius Rector (Connie)	p		
Julio Rojo	c		
George Scales	ss		
Dave Thomas	1b		
Jules Thomas	cf		
Jesse Winters (Nip)	p		
Berdell Young		of	

Pennsylvania Red Caps of NY

Player	1	2	3
D. Bailey	3b		
Frank Baynard		3b	
George Fiall	ss		
Fred Flournoy		c	
? Johnson	1b		
James Leonard (Bobo)		lf	
Edward Pryor	2b		
W. Reavis	p		
? Saunders		c	
? Scurly		rf	
John Taylor (Red)	p		
Henry Thomas	cf		
Benny Wilson	rf		

Philadelphia Colored Giants of NY

Player	1	2	3
Charles Bradford	p		
E. Cooper	1b		
James Deas (Yank)	c		
? Forrest	lf		
? Harvey	cf		
Johnson Hill (Fred)	3b		
Omer Newsome	p	rf	
? Payne	2b		
Jack Wallace	ss		

Philadelphia Quaker City Giants

Player	1	2	3
? Andrews		rf	
Frank Baynard		cf	
? Crudup (Zeke)	p	lf	
Jesse Hubbard		p	1b
Bill Jackman	p		
Milton Lewis			2b
? Monceville		2b	
Pender Ricks		3b	
Burlin White		c	
Bill Yancey		ss	

Philadelphia Tigers

Player	1	2	3
? Breen		1b	
Clifford Carter		p	
Alex Cooper			of
McKinley Downs (Bunny)		ss	
Edward Dudley		p	
Henry Gillespie		p	rf
Cecil Johnson (Sess)		lf	
Robert Johnson (Bob)		3b	
? Thomas		2b	
? Thornton		c	
Ted Waters		cf	

Pittsburgh Crawfords

Player	1	2	3
Josh Gibson		c	
William Harris (Bill)		3b	
Neal Harris (Nate)		lf	
Gilbert Hill		p	
Charlie Hughes		2b	
Claude Johnson		ss	
Howard Kimbro (Howdy)		p	
Johnny Moore		1b	
Jimmy Stills		rf	
Allie Thompkins			of
Harold Tinker		cf	

St. Louis Giants

Player	1	2	3
Bill Gatewood	p		M
? Augustus	p		
Charles Blackwell	rf		
Ameal Brooks	c		
? Chapman	lf		
Alex Clark	2b		
James Ellis	ss		
Ben Henderson	p		
? Holsey	3b		
? Hyde	1b		
Taft Newman	cf		

St. Louis Stars

Player	1	2	3
Candy Jim Taylor	3b	p	M
James Bell (Cool Papa)	cf		
Willie Bobo		1b	
Richard Cannon		p	
W. Cobb		c	
Dewey Creacy	3b	2b	rf
Roosevelt Davis (Rosey)		p	
? Hastings		p	
Logan Hensley (Slap)	p		
Luther McDonald (Vet)		p	
Mitch Murray		c	
Clarence Palm (Spoony)		c	
Wilson Redus	lf		
John Reese		of	
John Henry Russell	2b	3b	
Branch Russell	rf		
George Suttles (Mule)	1b	rf	
Ted Trent	p		

Player	1	2	3
? Turner (Tuck)		p	
Willie Wells	ss		
John Williams (Big Boy)	p	lf	
Henry Williams	c		

1929

Cuban Stars (East)

Player	1	2	3
Angel Alfonso		3b	2b
Bernardo Baro	lf	rf	
Augustin Bejerano	cf	of	
Antonio Castro		c	
Marceline Correra (Cho Cho)	ss		
Isidro Fabre		cf	rf
Jose Fernandez	c		
Willie Gisentaner (Lefty)	p		
Sijo Gomez (Joe)		p	c
? Lamberto		of	
Oscar Levis	p		
Juanelo Mirabel	p		
Emilio Navarro		inf	
Jose Perez	1b		
Jose Ramos	3b	lf	
Basilio Roselle		p	
Silvino Ruiz		p	
? Seto		of	
Miguel L. Solis	2b	3b	
Jose Vargas (Tetelo)		ss	rf

Cuban Stars (West)

Player	1	2	3
Rogelio Alonso	lf	p	
? Bema		of	
? Celada		ss	3b
Aurelio Cortez	1b	c	
Edolfo Diaz (Yo Yo)	p		
Cuneo Galvez	p		
Ramon Hernandez	3b		
Bienvenido Jimenez (Hooks)	2b		
Cando Lopez	cf		
Vidal Lopez		p	
Jesus Lorenzo	p		
? Molina	p		
? Pena	c	1b	
B. Conrado Rodriquez		p	
Jacinto Roque (Siki)	rf	p	
Felipe Sierra	ss	1b	
? Ventura		p	

Bacharach Giants

Player	1	2	3
Mack Eggleston	c	3b	M
R. Albrecht		p	
Otto Briggs		of	
Joe Cade		of	p
George Carr (Tank)		1b	2b
Sam Cooper	p		
Nap Cummings (Chance)		1b	
Wilson Day (Connie)	2b		
Luther Farrell	p	cf	
Kenneth Gardner (Ping)			p
Arthur Henderson (Rats)	p		
Clarence Jenkins (Fats)	lf	rf	
Edward Jones		c	
Ben Lindsey	3b	ss	
Bob McClure	p		
? Mitchell (Bud)		p	
Ambrose Reed		2b	of
Jimmy Shields		p	2b
? Stevens		p	
Ben Taylor	1b		

Player	1	2	3
Clint Thomas	rf	lf	
Jesse Walker (Hoss)	ss	3b	
Chaney White	cf		
? Williams (Willie)		ss	
James Wilson (Chubby)		of	

Baltimore Black Sox

Player	1	2	3
Knowlington Burbage (Buddy)		rf	
Robert Clarke	c		
James Cooke (Jay)		p	
Herbert Dixon (Rap)	cf	lf	
Willis Flournoy (Pud)	p		
William Force		p	rf
Domingo Gomez (Harry)		c	
Burnalle Hayes (Bun)		p	rf
Jesse Hubbard	rf	p	
Alphonso Lattimore		c	inf
Holsey Lee (Scrip)		p	rf
Dick Lundy	ss		
Oliver Marcelle	3b		
Elbert Melton		rf	
Merven Ryan (Red)	p		
H. Smith		p	
Frank Warfield	2b		
Namon Washington		of	
Peter Washington	lf	cf	
T. Wilson		lf	cf
Jud Wilson	1b	lf	
Jesse Winters (Nip)		p	1b
Laymon Yokeley	p		

Birmingham Black Barons

Player	1	2	3
Julian Bell		p	lf
J. Burdine	p	lf	
Anthony Cooper		ss	of
Porter Dallas (Big Boy)	3b	of	
A. Dykes		2b	
George Fiall		ss	
James Gurley		lf	
George Hamilton		c	
Eppie Hampton		c	
Claude Johnson (Hooks)		3b	c
Jack Marshall		p	
George McAllister	1b	inf	lf
Buford Meredith (Geetchie)	2b	of	
John Moore		ss	
J. Webb Oden		3b	
Leroy Paige (Satchel)	p		
Robert Pipkin (Lefty)		p	
? Ronsell	cf		
Harry Salmon	p	lf	
Ray Sheppard		ss	
Clarence Smith	rf		
L. Thomas	lf	1b	p
Charles Wesley (Connie)		of	2b
Poindexter Williams	c		

Chicago American Giants

Player	1	2	3
Jim Brown	1b	c	
Larry Brown		c	
Saul Davis	2b		
Walter Davis (Steel Arm)	rf	1b	
Willie Foster	p		
Floyd Gardner (Jelly)	cf	rf	
Herbert Gay		p	
W. Gay		p	
John Hines		utl	
Robert Holsey (Frog)	p		
Stanford Jackson		cf	
Harry Jeffries	3b	c	

Player	1	2	3
Hubert Lockhart		p	
Jack Marshall		p	
Webster McDonald		p	
Eddie Miller (Buck)		ss	p
Harold Morris	p		
Mitch Murray		c	
? Nance		ss	
Robert Poindexter		p	
Willie Powell		p	rf
Pythias Russ	c	ss	of
Smith Summers (Tack)		of	
James Thompson (Sandy)	lf		
Charles Williams	ss	3b	2b
James Winston (Lefty)		p	

Detroit Stars

Player	1	2	3
Elwood DeMoss (Bingo)	2b		M
Albert Davis	p		
Jesse Edwards		p	
Louis English		c	
? Foote		c	
Charlie Henry	p		
Clarence Jenkins (Barney)		c	
Claude Johnson (Hooks)	3b		
Wade Johnston	lf		
John Jones	rf		
George Mitchell		p	1b
Grady Orange	2b		
Ted Radcliffe (Double Duty)		c	
Ed Rile	1b	p	
William Robinson (Bobby)	ss		
Ted Shaw	p		
Norman Stearnes (Turkey)	cf		
? Stevens		c	
? Stevenson		c	
Bill Tyler	p		
? Wyatt		c	

Hilldale

Player	1	2	3
George Britt (Chippy)		c	p
William Campbell (Zip)		p	
Clifford Carter		p	
Paul Carter		p	
Oscar Charleston	cf	1b	
Porter Charleston	p		
Phil Cockrell	p		
Ray Cooper	p	rf	
William Dallard (Eggie)		lf	of
Martin Dihigo	ss	inf	of
Crush Holloway	rf	lf	
Robert Hudspeth (Highpocket)	1b		
Richard Jackson	2b		
William Johnson (Judy)	3b	ss	
Obie Lackey		ss	
Joseph Lewis		c	
Raleigh Mackey (Biz)	c	ss	3b
? Mitchell (Bud)		1b	c
Wilbur Pritchett		p	
? Reeves		c	
Merven Ryan (Red)		p	
John Stanley (Neck)		p	
Paul Stephens (Jake)		ss	
Joe Strong		p	
Sam Warmack		of	

Homestead Grays

Player	1	2	3
Cumberland Posey (Cum)			M
John Beckwith		3b	ss
George Britt (Chippy)	p	c	
Walter Cannady (Rev)	2b	ss	1b

Player	1	2	3
Martin Dihigo		utl	
William Ewing (Buck)	c		
Dennis Graham	rf		
Raymond Harris (Mo)		2b	
Vic Harris	lf	cf	
William Harris (Bill)		3b	
C. Jackson	cf	3b	ss
Obie Lackey		ss	
Charles Mason	lf	rf	
Eddie Miller (Buck)	p	ss	
Willis Moody	of		
Oscar Owens	p	rf	
Herbert Pierce	c		
William Ross	p		
George Scales	3b		
Sam Streeter	p		
E.C. Turner (Pop)	ss	3b	2b
Jasper Washington (Jap)	1b		
Charles Williams (Lefty)	p	rf	
Graham H. Williams		utl	
Smokey Joe Williams	p		

Kansas City Monarchs

Player	1	2	3
Wilber Rogan (Bullet Joe)	cf	rf	3b M
Newton Allen (Newt)	2b		
William Bell	p		
Chet Brewer	p	1b	lf
Andrew Cooper (Andy)	p		
Alfred Cooper (Army)	p		
Frank Duncan		c	1b
Eddie Dwight		of	
George Giles		1b	
Hallie Harding	ss		
Newton Joseph (Newt)	3b		
L.D. Livingston	lf		
Carroll Mothell (Dink)	1b		
Leroy Taylor	rf		
Herbert Wilson (Herb)		p	
Tom Young	c		

Los Angeles Royal Giants (Winter)

Player	1	2	3
Alfred Goodwin (Lon)			M
Newton Allen (Newt)	2b		
Andrew Cooper (Andy)	p		
Crush Holloway	of		
Newton Joseph (Newt)	3b		
L.D. Livingston	of		
Raleigh Mackey (Biz)	ss	c	
Carroll Mothell (Dink)		utl	
Neil Pullen	c	1b	
Wilber Rogan (Bullet Joe)	p		
Tom Young		c	

Memphis Red Sox

Player	1	2	3
Clifford Bell (Cliff)	p		
Alonzo Boone		p	
Willie Broadnax		p	
Larry Brown	c		
Anthony Cooper		cf	
Willie Cornelius (Sug)		p	lf
Homer Curry (Goose)	p	2b	
Nelson Dean		p	2b
S.R. Dewitt (Eddie)		1b	
Oland Dials (Lou)		of	
Carl Glass	p	1b	of
Julius Green	cf	1b	p
Henry Harris		ss	
J. Johnson (Lefty)		p	
Harry Kenyon		p	
Alto Lane		p	

Player	1	2	3
Milt Laurent	2b	p	inf
William Lowe	ss	2b	
Elliott Mayweather	p		
J.C. McHaskell	1b		
William Nash	p		
Omer Newsome	p		
J. Webb Oden	3b		
William Owens	ss	2b	
Tom Parker	of		
Robert Poindexter	p		
William Rogers (Nat)	rf	lf	
C. Ward (Pinky)	lf	rf	
Charles Wesley (Connie)	inf	of	

Nashville Elite Giants

Player	1	2	3
Charles Blackwell	cf		
Willie Bobo	1b		
Black Bottom Buford	3b		
? Charleston (Red)	c		
Willie Cornelius (Sug)	p		
Jesse Edwards	2b	rf	
Tom Jackson	p		
Al Morris	of		
? Pennington	p		
Jack Ridley	lf		
? Singlong	2b	rf	
William Spearman	p		
Leroy Stratton	ss		
? Sutton			
Clarence Trealkill (Harvey)	ss	of	
? Washington	c		
Clarence White (Red)	p		
Jim Williams (Bullet)	p		
Nish Williams	rf	c	
Jim Willis	p		
Henry Wright (Red)	p		

New York Lincoln Giants

Player	1	2	3
John Beckwith	3b		
William Campbell (Zip)	p		
Dean Everett	p		
G.E. Gray (Dolly)	cf		
Bill Harland	p		
Bill Holland	p		
Frank Holmes	p		
? Howard	p		
Robert Hudspeth (Highpocket)	1b		
John Henry Lloyd (Pop)	1b		
Elbert Melton	of		
Cornelius Rector (Connie)	p	rf	
Orville Riggins	3b	2b	ss
Julio Rojo	c	1b	
George Scales	2b		
Charles Smith (Chino)	rf		
Charles Spearman	c		
John Stanley (Neck)	p		
George Suttles (Mule)	lf		
Herb Thomas	p	rf	
Namon Washington	lf	2b	
Jesse Winters (Nip)	p		
Bill Yancey	ss		

Pittsburgh Crawfords

Player	1	2	3
? Burton (Lefty)	p		
Josh Gibson	c		
Neal Harris (Nate)	lf		
William Harris (Bill)	3b		
Gilbert Hill	p		
Charlie Hughes	2b		
Claude Johnson	ss		

Player	1	2	3
Howard Kimbro (Howdy)	p		
Harry Kincannon	p		
Johnny Moore	1b		
Jimmy Stills	rf		
Allie Thompkins		of	
Harold Tinker	cf		

Schenectady Mohawk Giants

Player	1	2	3
Robert Dean	ss		
? Durant	rf		
Curtis Green	1b		
? Jackson		utl	
Ed Kemp	cf		
Alphonso Lattimore	c		
? Ridgely (Buck)	3b		
Cleveland Smith (Cleo)	2b		
E. Smith	p		
Sam Warmack	lf		
? Wright	p		

St. Louis Stars

Player	1	2	3
Candy Jim Taylor	p		M
James Bell (Cool Papa)	cf	1b	p
Richard Cannon		p	
Dewey Creacy	3b	2b	
Roosevelt Davis (Rosey)	p		
Bill Harris		c	
Logan Hensley (Slap)	p		
Leroy Matlock		p	
Luther McDonald (Vet)		p	
Clarence Palm (Spoony)	c		
Wilson Redus	lf	rf	
John Henry Russell	2b		
Branch Russell	rf	2b	
George Suttles (Mule)	1b	3b	
Ted Trent	p		
? Vivens		p	
Willie Wells	ss		
Henry Williams		c	of
John Williams (Big Boy)	p	lf	
V. Williams		c	

1930

Cuban Stars (East)

Player	1	2	3
Eufemio Abreu	p	c	
? Ahrens		rf	
Raul Alvarez	p		
? Avill		p	
Bernardo Baro		of	
Ramon Bragana	p	rf	
Tatica Campos		3b	
Pelayo Chacon	ss		
? Cruz		p	
Martin Dihigo	3b	inf	of
Carlos Etchegoyen	rf		
? Fumes	lf		
Armando Massip	1b		
Alejandro Oms	cf		
Eustaquio Pedroso	c		
Miguel L. Solis	2b		

Cuban Stars (West)

Player	1	2	3
? Aballi		p	
Angel Alfonso	2b		
Rogelio Alonso	rf	p	
Marcelline Bauza	ss		
Aurelio Cortez	c		
Pablo Diaz		c	1b

Player	1	2	3
Edolfo Diaz (Yo Yo)	p	of	
Ramon Hernandez	3b		
Cando Lopez	cf		
Jesus Lorenzo	p	1b	rf
? Molina		p	
? Palma		p	
Lazaro Salazar	lf	rf	p
Felipe Sierra	1b	of	
Luis Tiant, Sr.	p		

Baltimore Black Sox

Player	1	2	3
Ralph Burgin		3b	
William Casey (Mickey)		c	
? Cheatham		p	
Robert Clarke	c	rf	
Reuben Currie (Rube)		p	rf
Herbert Dixon (Rap)		of	
Mack Eggleston	rf	3b	c
Willis Flournoy (Pud)	p	rf	
Herbert Gay		p	
Burnalle Hayes (Bun)	p		
Clarence Jenkins (Fats)		lf	
Holsey Lee (Scrip)	p	rf	1b
Dick Lundy	ss		
Webster McDonald		p	
? McNeil		lf	
Leroy Paige (Satchel)		p	
Clarence Smith	lf		
Sam Streeter		p	
George Suttles (Mule)	1b	cf	
Dave Thomas		1b	
Orval Tucker		2b	
? Walton (Fuzzy)		cf	
Frank Warfield	2b		
Peter Washington	cf	lf	
? Williams		1b	
Jud Wilson	3b	1b	2b
Laymon Yokeley	p		

Birmingham Black Barons

Player	1	2	3
Herman Andrews (Jabo)		rf	lf
? Austin (Tank)		p	
Julian Bell	p		
Don Bennett		of	
John Bennett		of	
J. Burdine		p	
Elmer Carter (Willie)		ss	
Anthony Cooper	ss	2b	lf
Willie Cornelius (Sug)		p	
Jimmy Crutchfield	cf		
Herbert Gay		p	
Cowan Hyde (Bubber)		2b	lf
Claude Johnson (Hooks)		3b	
Terris McDuffie	lf	rf	p
Leonard Mitchell (Otto)		2b	
? Murphy			
William Owens		ss	2b
Leroy Paige (Satchel)		p	
Bill Perkins	c		
William Rogers (Nat)		rf	lf
Harry Salmon		p	rf
John Shackleford	2b	3b	
Robert Smith		c	rf
Clarence Smith		of	2b
Sam Streeter	p		
L. Thomas	1b		
Nat Trammel		1b	
E.C. Turner (Pop)	3b		
Columbus Vance	p		
Jim West		1b	

Player	1	2	3		Player	1	2	3		Player	1	2	3
Brooklyn Royal Giants					Harold Morris		p			Willie Powell	p		
Dick Redding (Cannonball)	p		M		Mitch Murray	c				Ed Rile	1b	2b	p
Chester Brooks	cf				Melvin Powell (Putt)		of	1b		William Robinson (Bobby)	3b		
Elmore Brown (Scrappy)	ss				? Smith		p			Ted Shaw	p		
C. Brown		of	2b		James Thompson (Sandy)	lf	rf			James Smith (Jim)		ss	
John Cason	c				Charles Williams	2b				Norman Stearnes (Turkey)	cf		
Willie Creek		c			Chester Williams		ss			Bill Tyler		p	of
William Force	p												
Robert Hudspeth (Highpocket)	1b				**Columbus Keystones**					**Gilkerson's Union Giants**			
Oliver Marcelle	3b				J. Dennis		inf			Charley Akers	ss		
Bob McClure	p				George Fisher	lf	of			Alejandro Crespo	2b		
? Mirall		3b			Dennis Gilcrest	2b	c			Eddie Dwight	cf		
Ted Page	rf				Don Hammond	ss	3b			Jose Fernandez	c		
Richard Seay (Dick)	2b				Joe Hinton	p				? Haley (Red)	3b		
John Stanley (Neck)	p				Dana Hoyt	1b				Perry Hall	1b		
Otis Starks		p			M. Jeffries		3b			? Johnson	p		
Dave Thomas		1b			John Kearns	rf	of			Hurley McNair	lf		
Namon Washington	lf				Alphonso Lattimore	c				Harold Morris	p		
					Jack Matthews	3b				Cristobal Torriente	rf		
Chicago American Giants					Dennis Petree		of						
Lewis Anderson		c			Wayman Smith	cf	of			**Hilldale**			
James Bray		c			Roy Williams	p				? Banks		2b	
Jim Brown	1b	c			Claude Wilson	p				? Bram		p	
? Clarke		lf	cf		James Womack		1b	3b		Otto Briggs	rf	of	
Saul Davis		2b	3b							? Brown		p	
Walter Davis (Steel Arm)	rf	1b	p		**Detroit Stars**					Knowlington Burbage (Buddy)		lf	of 2b
Herbert Dixon (Rap)	cf	lf			Elwood DeMoss (Bingo)	2b		M		Ralph Burgin		3b	
Jose Fernandez		c	1b		E. Berry		inf			Clifford Carter		p	
Joseph Fleet		p			Andrew Cooper (Andy)	p				Paul Carter		p	
Willie Foster	p				Leon Daniels (Pepper)		c	1b		William Casey (Mickey)		c	
Floyd Gardner (Jelly)		of			Albert Davis	p				Phil Cockrell	p	lf	of
George Harney		p			Dwight Davis		p			Reuben Currie (Rube)		rf	
John Hines		lf	c		Nelson Dean	p				William Dallard (Eggie)	1b	p	
Robert Holsey (Frog)		p			Oland Dials (Lou)		1b	of		Earl Davis (Hawk)		2b	ss
Stanford Jackson		3b	cf		Joseph Dunn (Jake)	ss				Wilson Day (Connie)		2b	
Harry Jeffries	3b	c			Julius Green		of			Fred Dewitt		3b	
John Wesley Johnson		p			Crush Holloway	cf	rf			Martin Dihigo		3b	
Dave Knight		p			Wade Johnston	lf				Kenneth Gardner (Ping)	p		
Webster McDonald	p				William Love (Andy)		2b	1b		Henry Gillespie		p	
Eddie Miller (Buck)	ss	3b	p		Grady Orange	2b	ss			Jesse Hubbard	p	lf	rf
George Mitchell	p	1b			Clarence Palm (Spoony)		c	3b		Richard Jackson		2b	lf
										William Jones (Fox)		c	1b
										Obie Lackey		2b	ss
										Holsey Lee (Scrip)		3b	cf
										Oscar Levis	p	1b	lf
										Joseph Lewis		c	
										Raleigh Mackey (Biz)	ss	3b	c
										Webster McDonald		p	
										? Mitchell (Bud)		p	lf
										Wilbur Pritchett		p	
										Ambrose Reed	3b	2b	rf
										Roy Roberts		p	
										Herb Smith		p	
										Felton Stratton		c	
										Herb Thomas		p	
										Orval Tucker		2b	ss
										? Weston		p	
										Chaney White		cf	

1930 Homestead Grays. Standing L to R: Charlie Walker Jr (official), Raymond "Mo" Harris, William Ross, William "Buck" Ewing, Smokey Joe Williams, George Scales, Judy Johnson, and Cum Posey. Kneeling L to R: Vic Harris, Jake Stephens, Oscar Owens, Charles "Lefty" Williams, George "Chippy" Britt, Bennie Charleston, and Oscar Charleston.

Jeff Eastland

Player	1	2	3
Homestead Grays			
Cumberland Posey (Cum)			M
George Britt (Chippy)	p		
Bennie Charleston		of	
Oscar Charleston	1b		
Sam Cooper		p	
Bill Evans	rf		
William Ewing (Buck)	c		
Josh Gibson		c	
Raymond Harris	2b		
Vic Harris	lf		
William Johnson (Judy)	3b		
Oscar Owens		p	

Player	1	2	3
William Ross		p	
George Scales	2b		
Paul Stephens (Jake)	ss		
Chaney White	cf		
Smokey Joe Williams	p		
Charles Williams (Lefty)	p		

Kansas City Monarchs

Player	1	2	3
Wilber Rogan (Bullet Joe)	cf	rf	M
Newton Allen (Newt)	ss	2b	
William Bell	p	lf	rf
Chet Brewer	p	1b	cf
Alfred Cooper (Army)	p		
Roosevelt Davis (Rosey)		p	
Frank Duncan	1b	c	lf
Hallie Harding	of	ss	3b
Tomlini Harrison		p	
Newton Joseph (Newt)	3b		
L.D. Livingston	lf	of	
John Markham		p	
Henry McHenry	p		
Carroll Mothell (Dink)	2b	1b	3b
Wilson Redus		lf	
Leroy Taylor	rf	cf	1b
? Turner		1b	
Tom Young	c		

Louisville White Sox

Player	1	2	3
? Ballew		p	lf
Julian Bell		p	
? Cable		cf	
Richard Cannon	p		
? Capers (Lefty)	p		
Louis English		c	1b
Rowland Ewing (Monk)		rf	
Willie Gisentaner (Lefty)		p	of
Carl Glass		p	
Henry Harris	ss		
Charles Hudson	p		
Sammy T. Hughes	2b		
? Johnson		rf	c
? Massey	rf	of	
? McAfee		2b	
William McNeil (Red)	lf	p	
Al Morris		of	2b
? Norris (Slim)	3b		
Leon Palmer		of	
Willie Lee Scott (Joe)	1b		
Charles Wesley (Connie)	cf	of	2b
Clarence White (Red)		p	2b
Poindexter Williams	c		

Memphis Red Sox

Player	1	2	3
Candy Jim Taylor	3b	p	M
Herman Andrews (Jabo)		rf	of
John Barnes (Fat)	c		
Clifford Bell (Cliff)	p		
E. Berry		2b	ss
Jimmy Binder	3b		
J. Burdine		p	
Willie Cornelius (Sug)		p	
Harry Cunningham	p	rf	
Homer Curry (Goose)	p	of	
Saul Davis		2b	
Benny Fields		2b	
Murray Gillespie		p	rf
Carl Glass		p	1b
Bill Harris		c	
Jess Houston		p	inf
? Huber		c	

Player	1	2	3
Oscar Johnson (Heavy)		lf	rf
J. Johnson (Lefty)		p	
Milt Laurent		of	c
William Love (Andy)		1b	of
William Lowe		inf	of
George McAllister	1b		
Jasper Miller		p	of
Jimmy Morrison		inf	of
Martin Oliver		c	
Johnny Robinson	lf		
William Rogers (Nat)		of	
? Ronsell	cf		
Harry Salmon		p	rf
? Simpson		c	
Dan Tye		3b	
Jim West		1b	2b
Chester Williams	ss		
Charles Zomphier		2b	3b

Nashville Elite Giants

Player	1	2	3
William Anderson		of	
? Austin (Tank)		p	
Willie Bobo	1b		
Black Bottom Buford	2b	3b	ss
? Campbell		lf	
? Charleston (Red)		c	2b
Comer Cox (Hannibal)	rf	of	3b
Andrew Drake		p	
Jesse Edwards		2b	3b
Louis English		c	lf
Lenon Henderson		3b	lf
Joe Hewitt		ss	of
William Lowe		3b	
? McCauley		p	rf
Buford Meredith (Geetchie)		2b	
Dempsey Miller (Dimp)		p	
Al Morris		lf	
Albert Owens		p	
Ed Pace		of	
Jack Ridley	cf	lf	1b
Leroy Stratton	ss	2b	3b
Jim West		1b	
Clarence White (Red)		p	
Joe Wiggins		3b	ss
? Wigware		ss	3b
Nish Williams	c	lf	
Norm Williams		of	
Poindexter Williams		c	
Jim Willis	p	lf	
Henry Wright (Red)	p	lf	rf

New York Lincoln Giants

Player	1	2	3
John Beckwith		1b	3b
Larry Brown	c		
Walter Cannady (Rev)	2b		
Tom Cox		p	
Luther Farrell	p		
Bill Holland	p		
Clarence Jenkins (Fats)		of	
John Henry Lloyd (Pop)	1b		
Cornelius Rector (Connie)	p		
Orville Riggins	3b		
Julio Rojo		c	
Merven Ryan (Red)		p	
Charles Smith (Chino)	rf		
Norman Stearnes (Turkey)	cf	lf	
Clint Thomas	lf	cf	
Bill Yancey	ss		
? Young		ss	

Pennsylvania Red Caps of NY

Player	1	2	3
Robert Dean	3b		
Tom Finley	3b		
G.E. Gray (Dolly)	lf	of	
James Leonard (Bobo)	cf	of	
Charles Lindsay (Clarence)	ss		
Charles Spearman	c		
Jules Thomas	1b		

Pittsburgh Crawfords

Player	1	2	3
? Burton (Lefty)		p	
Josh Gibson	c		
William Harris (Bill)	3b		
Neal Harris (Nate)	lf		
Clarence Horton		p	
Charlie Hughes	2b		
Claude Johnson		inf	
Howard Kimbro (Howdy)	p		
Harry Kincannon	p		
Ralph Mellix (Lefty)	p		
Johnny Moore	1b		
Gus Nevelle		p	
Ormby Roy	ss		
Jimmy Stills	rf		
Harold Tinker	cf		
Wright Turner		c	
Harry Williams		3b	of
Roy Williams		p	
? Williams (Bucky)		p	

St. Louis Stars

Player	1	2	3
James Bell (Cool Papa)	cf		
Dewey Creacy	3b		
Roosevelt Davis (Rosey)		p	
Bill Drake		p	
George Giles	1b		
Logan Hensley (Slap)	p		
Leroy Matlock		p	
Ted Radcliffe (Double Duty)	p	c	
Wilson Redus		lf	cf
John Reese		of	
John Henry Russell	2b		
Branch Russell	rf	lf	
Joe Strong		p	
George Suttles (Mule)		lf	rf
Ted Trent	p		
Quincy Trouppe		p	
Willie Wells	ss		
Henry Williams	c	lf	
John Williams (Big Boy)		p	lf

Wilmington Quaker Giants

Player	1	2	3
Dan McClellan			M
Otto Briggs	lf		
William Dallard (Eggie)	2b		
Henry Gillespie	rf	p	
Bill Jackman	p		
? Lewis	3b		
? Monceville	ss		
? Page	1b		
John Stanley (Neck)	p		
Burlin White	c		
B. White	cf		

1931

Cuban Stars (East)

Player	1	2	3
Raul Alvarez	p		
Luis Arango	3b		

Player	1	2	3
? Arbans		of	
Pelayo Chacon	ss		
Aurelio Cortez		c	1b
Pablo Diaz		1b	c
Isidro Fabre	p		
Jose Fernandez	c		
Manuel Garcia (Cocaina)		rf	p
? Goshen		rf	
? Hortis		p	
? Kin		c	
Oscar Levis		p	
Cando Lopez		lf	ss
Armando Massip		rf	
? Monceville	rf		
Alejandro Oms	cf		
Jose Perez	1b	c	
Jacinto Roque (Siki)	lf		
Miguel L. Solis	2b		

Cuban Stars (West)

Player	1	2	3
Barney Brown	p	of	
John Dixon (Johnny Bob)		p	
Tommy Dukes		c	
Oscar Estrada		p	
Carlos Etchegoyen	3b		
? Haddad		of	p
? Holmes		rf	
Pedro Lanuza	c		
Jim Mason	cf	of	
? Nimin		1b	
Ramiro Ramirez	rf	of	
Henry Richardson	p		
Jacinto Roque (Siki)		cf	
Frank Stevens		p	
Luis Tiant, Sr.	p		
Strico Valdez	2b		
Jose Vargas (Tetelo)	ss		
Woodrow Wilson (Lefty)		p	

Santop's Broncos

Player	1	2	3
Louis Santop			M
Ralph Anderson		rf	
? Banks		of	
? Bluford		of	
? Bonner		c	
Otto Briggs		rf	
? Brown		c	
Chester Buchanan (Buck)		p	
? Clark		3b	
Leroy Clayton (Zack)		1b	
? Ducey		lf	
? Gordon		p	
Frank Holmes	p		
? Jefferson		p	
? Johnson		ss	
Obie Lackey	ss		
P. Lee		c	
W. Lee	p		
Bill Norman	cf		
Walter Robinson (Newt)	3b		
Richard Tutt (King)		1b	
? Washington		of	
Johnny Watson		2b	c
? Wilkerson		2b	ss

Bacharach Giants

Player	1	2	3
Otto Briggs		lf	
Irving Brooks		2b	
Chester Buchanan (Buck)		p	
Walter Burch		c	

Player	1	2	3
Ralph Burgin		3b	
Robert Campbell (Buddy)		c	
? Cephus (Goldie)		lf	
? Crawley		3b	
Paul Dixon		of	
Rube Ellis (Rocky)		p	
? Galloway		2b	
Henry Gillespie		rf	p
Hallie Harding		3b	
Charlie Henry	p		
Frank Holmes		p	
? Jefferson		p	
George Johnson (Dibo)		of	
John Jones		cf	
? Keeler		lf	
Obie Layton	p		
Charles Lindsay (Clarence)	ss		
? McHenry		ss	
Bob Saunders	2b		
Ed Stone	cf		
Richard Tutt (King)		1b	
William Watson	rf	1b	
Edgar Wesley	1b		
? Wilkerson		2b	
Jesse Winters (Nip)	p		
Howard Wright		p	

Baltimore Black Sox

Player	1	2	3
John Beckwith	rf	3b	
William Casey (Mickey)		c	of
Robert Clarke	c	1b	
Daltie Cooper	p	of	
Albert Davis		p	
Martin Dihigo		inf	of
Herbert Dixon (Rap)		of	
Willis Flournoy (Pud)		p	
Henry Gillespie		p	
Hallie Harding		2b	p
Crush Holloway	lf		
Richard Jackson	3b	2b	ss
Holsey Lee (Scrip)	p	1b	
Dick Lundy	ss		
John Stanley (Neck)	p		
Dave Thomas	1b		
Frank Warfield	2b	3b	
Peter Washington	cf		
Phil Williams (Pete)		3b	
Laymon Yokeley		p	

Birmingham Black Barons

Player	1	2	3
William Anderson	rf		
Sam Bankhead		2b	
? Bremble		2b	
Black Bottom Buford	3b	ss	
J. Burdine	p	rf	cf
Walter Calhoun		of	p
Matthew Carlisle (Lick)		ss	
Elmer Carter (Willie)		p	
Walter Cooley		c	3b
Tommy Dukes	c		
Jesse Edwards	ss	2b	
William Howard		1b	
? Huber		of	3b
? Jeffery		lf	
Hurley Jones		p	
George McAllister	1b		
Terris McDuffie	cf	lf	
Buford Meredith (Geetchie)	2b	c	
Dempsey Miller (Dimp)		p	lf
? Mott		3b	

Player	1	2	3
Harry Salmon		p	
Leroy Stratton		cf	
Columbus Vance	p		
? Veal		p	rf
Charley Wright	p		

Brooklyn Royal Giants

Player	1	2	3
Dick Redding (Cannonball)	p		M
Elmore Brown (Scrappy)	ss		
Elias Brown (Country)		of	
Willie Creek	c		
Tom Fiall	3b		
Kenneth Gardner (Ping)	p		
? Jackson (Lefty)	p		
? Payne	2b		
Wilbur Pritchett	p		
Ed Rile	1b		
? Ruson		ss	
Richard Seay (Dick)		inf	
Charles Smith (Chino)		of	
Namon Washington		of	

Chattanooga Black Lookouts

Player	1	2	3
William Lowe	3b		M
? Coley	p		
L. Cunningham	lf		
Andrew Drake	c		
Jesse Edwards	2b		
? Flipping	ss		
Lenon Henderson	rf		
H. Henderson (Long)	1b		
A. Owens		of	
Claude Rhodes (Dusty)	p		
Ely Underwood	cf		
Zarlie White		of	p
? Willis		of	

Chicago Giants

Player	1	2	3
Charles Green (Joe)			M
T. Childs		ss	
William Clay (Lefty)	p		
Saul Davis	2b		
? Jackson		ss	
Harry Jeffries	3b		
Dave Knight	p		
Melvin Powell (Putt)		lf	
J. Smith	1b		
A. Smith	c		
Roy Tyler	cf		
William Ziegler (Doc)	rf		

Cincinnati Giants

Player	1	2	3
Wilmer Ewell	c		
Dennis Gilcrest	ss		
? Hunter	cf		
Bill Johnson	3b		
J. Kerner	lf		
William Owens		inf	
? Payton	rf		
J. Thomas	2b		
Irving Waddy (Lefty)	p		
James Womack	1b		

Cleveland Cubs

Player	1	2	3
Clifford Bell (Cliff)	p		
Alonzo Boone		p	
Black Bottom Buford		2b	
Richard Cannon		p	
Comer Cox (Hannibal)	rf	lf	
George Dixon		c	

Player	1	2	3
A. Gillespie		p	
Joe Hewitt	2b	of	
Milt Laurent	2b	utl	p
Dempsey Miller (Dimp)	p		
J. Owens		of	
Leroy Paige (Satchel)		p	
Bill Perkins		c	
Robert Pipkin (Lefty)		p	
Jack Ridley	cf		
Branch Russell		2b	
Orville Singer	lf		
Robert Smith		c	lf
Zack Spencer		p	
Sam Streeter		p	
E.C. Turner (Pop)		3b	
Jesse Walker (Hoss)	ss		
Jack Wallace		3b	
Jim West	1b		
Joe Wiggins	3b		
Nish Williams	c	rf	
Jim Willis	p		
Henry Wright (Red)		p	
Charles Zomphier		2b	

Columbia CAG

Player	1	2	3
Sam Crawford	p		M
Dave Malarcher	3b		M
James Bray		c	
Jim Brown		1b	c
Edward Chapman		p	
Leon Daniels (Pepper)		c	
Robert Griffin		p	
Perry Hall		2b	
Hallie Harding	2b		
George Harney		p	
Walter Harper		c	
Robert Holsey (Frog)	p		
Stanford Jackson	cf		
Harry Jeffries		c	3b
William Marshall (Jack)		1b	3b
Luther McDonald (Vet)	p		
Eddie Miller (Buck)		p	
Guy Ousley		ss	
Melvin Powell (Putt)	p		
Harry Roberts (Raggs)		c	
William Rogers (Nat)	rf		
Clarence Smith	1b	2b	c
Zack Spencer	p		
James Thompson (Sandy)	lf		
C. Ward (Pinky)		lf	cf
Charles Williams		ss	
James Winston (Lefty)	p		

Detroit Giants

Player	1	2	3
? Briggs	rf		
Knowlington Burbage (Buddy)		of	
James Crump	2b		
? Curtis		3b	
? Evans	1b	p	
Charlie Henry	p		
? Hicks	c		
John Jones	cf	ss	
? Mahoney	ss		
Juan Padrone	p		
Johnny Robinson	3b		
Johnny Watson	lf		

Detroit Stars

Player	1	2	3
Saul Davis		ss	
Nelson Dean	p		

Player	1	2	3
Oland Dials (Lou)	1b	of	
John Dixon (Johnny Bob)		p	
? Gales		1b	
Floyd Gardner (Jelly)	rf	of	2b
William Gill		1b	
Arthur Henderson (Rats)		p	
? Jackson		p	
Wade Johnston	lf		
? Kelly		p	
William Love (Andy)		1b	c
William McCall (Bill)	p		
Luther McDonald (Vet)		p	
Grady Orange		2b	
William Owens		ss	
Clarence Palm (Spoony)	c		
Willie Powell	p		
Bill Pryor		p	
Anderson Pryor		ss	2b
Ted Radcliffe (Double Duty)		p	
William Robinson (Bobby)	3b		
Bob Saunders		2b	
Zack Spencer		p	
Norman Stearnes (Turkey)	cf	1b	
Elbert Williams		p	
James Winston (Lefty)		p	

Hilldale

Player	1	2	3
Walter Cannady (Rev)	2b		
Paul Carter	p		
Porter Charleston	p		
Phil Cockrell		p	of
William Dallard (Eggie)	1b		
Martin Dihigo	rf	p	
Herbert Dixon (Rap)	lf	p	
William Johnson (Judy)	3b		
Obie Layton		p	
Oscar Levis	p	of	
Joseph Lewis		c	
Raleigh Mackey (Biz)	c	1b	3b
Webster McDonald		p	
? Mitchell (Bud)		p	
Merven Ryan (Red)		p	of
Ed Sherkliff		p	
Paul Stephens (Jake)		ss	
? Taylor (Rip)		of	
Chaney White	cf		
Jesse Winters (Nip)		p	
Bill Yancey	ss		

Homestead Grays

Player	1	2	3
Cumberland Posey (Cum)			M
George Britt (Chippy)		p	lf
Fred Burnett (Tex)		c	
Oscar Charleston	1b		
Bill Evans	ss	cf	
Willie Foster		p	
Josh Gibson	c		
? Green		of	
Vic Harris	lf	cf	
John Jones	cf		
Oscar Owens		p	lf
Ted Page	rf		
Ted Radcliffe (Double Duty)	p	c	
Ambrose Reed		of	
George Scales	2b		
Paul Stephens (Jake)		ss	
Jasper Washington (Jap)	1b		
Charles Williams (Lefty)		p	
Smokey Joe Williams	p		

Player	1	2	3
Roy Williams		p	
Jud Wilson	3b		

Indianapolis ABCs

Player	1	2	3
Candy Jim Taylor	3b	p	M
Herman Andrews (Jabo)	rf	lf	p
? Berno		of	
Jimmy Binder	3b		
Finis Branahan		p	
Ray Brown	p	of	
Jimmy Crutchfield	cf		
Roosevelt Davis (Rosey)		p	
John Dixon (Johnny Bob)		p	
Dennis Gilcrest		c	
? Gray		c	
Bill Harris		c	
Lenon Henderson		ss	
J. Kerner		of	
Alto Lane		p	
Robert Lindsey		p	lf
Fred McBride	1b		
George Mitchell	p	1b	lf
Mitch Murray	c		
Tom Parker	p		
Ed Rile		p	
John Henry Russell	2b		
John Terry		2b	
Dan Thomas		2b	
Charles Williams	ss		
Henry Williams		2b	c
John Williams (Big Boy)	lf	rf	
James Womack		1b	

Kansas City Monarchs

Player	1	2	3
Wilber Rogan (Bullet Joe)	of		M
Newton Allen (Newt)		ss	2b
Charles Beverly	p		
Chet Brewer	p		
Roy Brown		p	of
Richard Byas (Subby)		of	
? Clark		p	
Alfred Cooper (Army)		p	
John Donaldson	rf	cf	
Frank Duncan		c	lf
Willie Foster		p	
Hallie Harding		ss	
Chick Harris (Popsickle)	lf	p	
Wesley Hicks		lf	
Newton Joseph (Newt)	3b		
Alto Lane		p	
L.D. Livingston		1b	
Henry McHenry	p		
Carroll Mothell (Dink)	1b	2b	
Grady Orange	2b	ss	1b
William Rogers (Nat)		of	
Ray Sheppard		of	
Norman Stearnes (Turkey)		cf	
Samuel Thompson (Sad Sam)		p	
Tom Young	c		

Knoxville Giants

Player	1	2	3
? Allen	1b		
Jerry Benjamin	3b		
? Borden	c		
? Crook	p		
? Dawson	p		
? Denson	2b		
? Eagle	cf		
Luther Green		of	
? Jackson	p		

Player	1	2	3
Clarence Keith	rf		
? Lynch		c	
J. Webb Oden	ss		
Roosevelt Tate (Speed)	lf		

Louisville White Sox

Player	1	2	3
Julian Bell	p		
? Capers (Lefty)	p	1b	
Joe Cates		2b	ss
? Clark	lf	cf	
Anthony Cooper	ss	cf	
Louis English	c	lf	
Willie Gisentaner (Lefty)	p	lf	rf
Sammy T. Hughes	2b	ss	
Robert Hughes	p		
Tom Jackson	p		
? Johnson		cf	rf
William McNeil (Red)	cf	of	
Leonard Mitchell (Otto)		2b	
James Pope	p		
Edward Robinson		of	
Willie Lee Scott (Joe)	1b		
Felton Snow	3b	lf	
Clarence White (Red)	p		
Poindexter Williams		c	
Elbert Williams		p	

Memphis Red Sox

Player	1	2	3
Larry Brown	c		
Willie Cornelius (Sug)	p		
Harry Cunningham	p		
Homer Curry (Goose)	lf	p	
Jimmy Ford		3b	
Murray Gillespie	p		
Otis Henry		3b	lf
J. Johnson (Lefty)	1b	p	
Oscar Johnson (Heavy)	rf		
Reuben Jones		of	
Clarence Lewis (Foots)	ss		
William Lowe	3b		
? Moody		ss	
Elvin Powell	2b		
? Rookie	cf		
Ted Shaw		p	
Raymond Taylor	c		
Sammy Thompson (Runt)	2b		
Bill Van Buren		of	
? Wingfield		ss	

Monroe Monarchs

Player	1	2	3
Porter Dallas (Big Boy)	2b		
Harry Else	c		
? Heller	1b		
? Johnson	lf		
Zearlee Maxwell	3b		
Leroy Morney	ss		
Bob Sloan	p		
W. Walker	cf		
Zollie Wright	rf		

Montgomery Grey Sox

Player	1	2	3
Frank Bradley		p	
? Burns	2b		
H. Cunningham (Rounder)	ss		
Paul Hardy	c		
? Manning	1b		
Alonzo Mitchell (Hooks)	lf	p	
Everett Nelson	p		
? Peaks	p		
Harvey Peterson	cf		

Player	1	2	3
Otto Scott	3b		
B. Williams	rf		

Nashville Elite Giants

Player	1	2	3
Clarence Adkins		of	
Clifford Bell (Cliff)		p	
Black Bottom Buford		2b	
Richard Cannon	p		
? Charleston (Red)	c		
? Coley		of	
Comer Cox (Hannibal)		2b	rf
Jesse Edwards		2b	
? Gray		3b	
Lenon Henderson		of	
? Huber		cf	of
Claude Johnson (Hooks)		3b	
William Lowe		ss	
Granville Lyons	1b		
Dempsey Miller (Dimp)	p		
Albert Owens		p	
? Petway	ss	2b	
Jack Ridley		of	
? Ronsell	lf	of	
Leroy Stratton	3b		
Clarence Trealkill (Harvey)	rf	of	
Jesse Walker (Hoss)		ss	
Joe Wiggins		3b	
Nish Williams		c	
Jim Willis		p	rf
Henry Wright (Red)	p		

New York Black Yankees

Player	1	2	3
William Bell		p	
Larry Brown	c		
Ralph Burgin		ss	
Fred Burnett (Tex)		c	
Frank Duncan		c	
Mack Eggleston		c	3b
Tom Finley	3b		
Henry Gillespie		p	
Bill Holland	p		
Clarence Jenkins (Fats)	lf		
L.D. Livingston	rf		
John Henry Lloyd (Pop)	1b		
Webster McDonald		p	
Henry McHenry		p	
Cornelius Rector (Connie)	p		
Orville Riggins	2b	ss	3b
Walter Robinson (Newt)		ss	
Merven Ryan (Red)	p		
? Smith		rf	
Henry Thomas		of	
Clint Thomas	cf		
E.C. Turner (Pop)	ss	2b	
Bill Wagner		3b	

Pennsylvania Red Caps of NY

Player	1	2	3
Robert Dean		3b	
Jimmy Everett	p		
Tom Finley		ss	
G.E. Gray (Dolly)	cf		
Pearley Johnson (Tubby)	1b		
James Leonard (Bobo)	lf		
Charles Lindsay (Clarence)		3b	p
Edward Pryor	2b		
Charles Spearman	c		
Jules Thomas	rf		

Newark Browns

Player	1	2	3
Paul Arnold	cf		

Player	1	2	3
John Beckwith		3b	
? Bluford		cf	
? Bradley			lf
Benny Brown	ss		
Gilbert Coleman	rf		
Earl Davis (Hawk)	2b		
? Defrid		c	
Paul Dixon		lf	
Jimmy Everett		p	
? Hareway		p	
? Herndon	p		
? Hickson		2b	
? Johnson	1b		
Cecil Johnson (Sess)		2b	
? Lumpkins (Lefty)		p	
Frank McCoy	c		
? Monceville		3b	
? Pedrero		2b	c
Kenneth Robinson		3b	lf
Ray Vaughn (Slim)		p	lf
Jesse Winters (Nip)	p		

Pittsburgh Crawfords

Player	1	2	3	M
Ernest Terry				M
Bobby Williams	2b	cf		M
Knowlington Burbage (Buddy)	lf	of		
Robert Campbell (Buddy)		c		
Jimmy Crutchfield		cf		
Dwight Davis		p		
Dennis Graham		rf		
Raymond Harris (Mo)	2b			
Neal Harris (Nate)		of		
Curtis Harris (Popeye)		of		
William Harris (Bill)		3b	of	
Burnalle Hayes (Bun)		p		
Charlie Hughes		ss		
Claude Johnson		2b		
Howard Kimbro (Howdy)		p		
Harry Kincannon	p			
Leroy Paige (Satchel)	p			
Bill Perkins	c	of		
Dick Redding (Cannonball)		p		
Ambrose Reed	rf	ss	3b	
Harry Roberts (Raggs)		ss		
Ormby Roy		ss		
John Henry Russell		2b		
Jimmy Stills		of		
Sam Streeter	p			
Harold Tinker		of		
Wright Turner		c		
Jasper Washington (Jap)	1b			
Chester Williams	ss			
Harry Williams		c	3b	
M. Williams		ss		
Roy Williams		p		
? Williams (Bucky)		p		

St. Louis Stars

Player	1	2	3
Newton Allen (Newt)	2b		
Henry Baker		of	
John Barnes (Fat)		c	
James Bell (Cool Papa)	cf		
Dewey Creacy	3b		
Roosevelt Davis (Rosey)		p	
George Giles	1b		
Logan Hensley (Slap)	p		
Bertrum Hunter	p		
Leroy Matlock		p	
Wilson Redus		of	
John Reese		of	

Player	1	2	3
Branch Russell	rf	2b	
Joe Strong		p	
George Suttles (Mule)	lf		
Ted Trent	p		
Quincy Trouppe		c	p
Willie Wells	ss		
John Williams (Big Boy)		p	
Tom Young	c		

Wilmington Quaker Giants

Player	1	2	3
Dan McClellan			M
? Banks	lf		
Joe Baylor	c		
? Cephus (Goldie)	cf		
Earl Davis (Hawk)	2b		
? Ferguson	ss		
? Jetter	rf		
Joseph Johnson (Joe)	p		
? Williams	1b		
Bill Yancey			3b

1932

Cuban Stars (East)

Player	1	2	3
Eufemio Abreu	3b	c	
? Albertus		p	
Raul Alvarez	p		
Luis Arango		3b	
? Davis (Big Boy)		p	
Pablo Diaz	c		
Isidro Fabre		p	
Jose Fernandez	c		
Rodolfo Fernandez (Rudy)	p		
David Gomez		p	
Oscar Levis	p		
Cando Lopez	lf		
Armando Massip	1b		
Juanelo Mirabel	p		
? Monceville		p	rf
Ismael Morales	rf		
Alejandro Oms	cf		
Jose Perez		1b	
Felipe Sierra	ss		
Miguel L. Solis	2b		

Cubans (West)

Player	1	2	3
Barney Brown	p	of	
James E. Claxton		p	
Marceline Correra (Cho Cho)	ss		
Pablo Diaz		c	
John Dixon (Johnny Bob)		p	
Ernest Duff		of	
Carlos Etchegoyen	3b		
Cuneo Galvez	p		
? Golder		2b	
Pedro Lanuza		c	
Jim Mason	1b		
George McAllister		1b	
Terris McDuffie		cf	
Lou Mosley	p		
? Neely	p		
? O'Meada		inf	
Ramiro Ramirez	rf		
Jacinto Roque (Siki)	lf		
Lazaro Salazar	cf	p	
? Soldero		p	
Luis Tiant, Sr.	p		
Strico Valdez	2b	p	
James Womack		1b	

Foster Memorial Giants

Player	1	2	3
George Bennette	of		
Al Brooks	2b		
Jim Brown		utl	
Richard Byas (Subby)		c	
Robert Holsey (Frog)	p		
Albert Morehead		c	
Clarence Ora	of		
Guy Ousley	ss		
Andrew Porter	p		
Cristobal Torriente	1b		
Ed Williams	p		
James Winston (Lefty)	p		

Gilkerson Union Giants

Player	1	2	3
Charley Akers	ss		
Alejandro Crespo	2b		
Leon Daniels (Pepper)	c		
William Gill	1b		
? Hickok	p		
Al Morris	cf		
? Page	lf		
Bob Saunders	3b		
? Shanahan	rf		

Atlanta Black Crackers

Player	1	2	3
Hipolito Arenas (Torrento)	cf	3b	
? Austin (Tank)		p	
Bo Briggery	ss	1b	
James Greene (Joe)	1b		
Herman Howard (Red)	p		
Emory Long (Bang)	3b		
D. Potter	p	of	
Ambrose Reed	lf	rf	
? Robertson	p		
? Robinson		p	
Ormond Sampson		ss	
? Stinson		cf	
Jack Thornton	p		
Strico Valdez	2b		
Roy Welmaker		p	
James Winston (Lefty)	rf	lf	
? Yarbrough	c		

Bacharach Giants

Player	1	2	3
Clifford Allen		p	
? Bell		c	2b
? Bowman		of	
Otto Briggs	lf		
Benny Brown		ss	
Walter Burch		c	
Ralph Burgin		2b	
Clifford Carter	p		
Leroy Clayton (Zack)	1b		
Phil Cockrell	1b	p	
Gilbert Coleman	rf	of	
? Colley	c		
Daltie Cooper	p		
Hubert Crawford	2b		
Willie Creek	c		
Earl Davis (Hawk)	2b		
? Dillard	p		
A. Dotson	p		
Jim Elam	p		
Rube Ellis (Rocky)	p		
Henry Gillespie	p		
Sijo Gomez (Joe)	p	rf	
? Hackett	p		
Julius Hogan	of	c	
Dana Hoyt	1b		

Player	1	2	3
? Jackson	c		
Ralph Jefferson	of		
Harry Jeffries	c		
John Jones	of		
? Kelley	p		
Obie Lackey	3b		
? Lambert	ss		
Joseph Lewis	c		
Charles Lindsay (Clarence)	ss		
John Henry Lloyd (Pop)	1b		
? Loatman	2b		
? Maiden	c		
Frank McCoy	c		
Terris McDuffie	of		
? Moore	3b		
Lou Mosley	p		
Wilbur Pritchett	p		
Walter Robinson (Newt)		3b	
? Sinclair	of		
Otis Starks	p		
Ed Stone	of		
? Talley	p		
C. Ward (Pinky)		cf	of
? Wharton	p		
Joe Wiggins	3b		
Jesse Winters (Nip)	p		
James Womack	3b		

Baltimore Black Sox

Player	1	2	3
Clifford Allen	p		
Frank Blake	p		
Knowlington Burbage (Buddy)	lf	of	
William Casey (Mickey)		c	3b
John Cason		of	
Robert Clarke	c		
James Cooke (Jay)		p	
William Dallard (Eggie)		1b	
Paul Dixon		of	
? Durant		of	
Tom Finley	3b	2b	
Willis Flournoy (Pud)	p		
Crush Holloway		rf	
Eddie Holmes		p	
Harry Jeffries		3b	
Stuart Jones (Slim)		p	
Charles Lindsay (Clarence)		ss	
Dick Lundy	ss		
Terris McDuffie		p	
Richard Seay (Dick)	2b	ss	
H. Smith		p	
Dave Thomas	1b		
Peter Washington	cf		
Chaney White		rf	of
Joe Wiggins		3b	
Laymon Yokeley	p		

Birmingham Black Barons

Player	1	2	3
Poindexter Williams		c	M
Sam Bankhead	p		
Alonzo Boone	p		
J. Borden		of	p
Richard Cannon	p		
Ernest Carter (Spoon)	p		
Harry Cunningham	p		
Andrew Drake	c		
Lenon Henderson	3b		
? Jasper	p		
Milt Laurent	2b		
George McAllister	1b		
William Nash		p	

Player	1	2	3
Martin Oliver	rf		
Harvey Peterson	lf		
? Petway		ss	
Harry Salmon	p		
? Smith (Buster)		1b	
Roosevelt Tate (Speed)		cf	
Jim West	of	1b	

Brooklyn Royal Giants

Player	1	2	3
Dick Redding (Cannonball)	p		M
Chester Brooks	cf		
Elmore Brown (Scrappy)	3b		
Elias Brown (Country)	lf		
Sam Crawford		p	
Willie Creek	c		
Al Fennar		ss	
? Jones (Country)		c	
Orville Riggins		ss	
Ed Rile	1b		
Ormond Sampson		ss	
Otis Starks	p		
Nat Trammel	rf		

Cleveland Cubs

Player	1	2	3
Don Bennett	rf		
Ameal Brooks	cf		
Jim Brown	1b		
Roy Brown		p	
Tom Cox		p	
Benny Fields	3b		
Albert Morehead	c		
Clarence Ora	lf		
Guy Ousley	ss		
Andrew Porter	p		
Sammy Thompson (Runt)	2b		
Cristobal Torriente		p	1b
Jim Williams (Bullet)	p		

Cleveland Stars

Player	1	2	3
? Case		rf	
Alfred Cooper (Army)	p		
Anthony Cooper	ss		
? Davis (Big Boy)		p	
Nelson Dean	p		
Benny Fields		of	
Chick Harris (Popsickle)	1b		
George Mitchell	p		
Carroll Mothell (Dink)	2b	p	
Bill Perkins		c	
Wilson Redus	lf		
William Robinson (Bobby)	3b		
Branch Russell	rf	2b	
Orville Singer	cf		
Joe Ware		lf	cf
Fietman Wilson		c	

Cole's CAG

Player	1	2	3
Dave Malarcher	3b		M
Ameal Brooks		c	
Robert Campbell (Buddy)		c	
Norman Cross		p	
Walter Davis (Steel Arm)	1b		
Kermit Dial		2b	1b
John Dixon (Johnny Bob)		p	
Andrew Drake		c	p
Willie Foster	p		
Walter Harper		1b	
John Hines	c	lf	
? Lightner		p	
Joe Lillard		p	1b

Player	1	2	3
? Lyda	p		
Jimmie Lyons	c		
William Marshall (Jack)	2b		
Luther McDonald (Vet)	p		
Clarence Palm (Spoony)	c		
Willie Powell	p		
Melvin Powell (Putt)	p	lf	
Alex Radcliff	3b		
William Rogers (Nat)	rf		
Norman Stearnes (Turkey)	cf		
James Thompson (Sandy)	lf		
E.C. Turner (Pop)	ss		
Bill Tyler		p	
? Wash		2b	

Detroit Wolves

Player	1	2	3
William Dismukes (Dizzy)	p		M
Newton Allen (Newt)		2b	
William Bell		p	
James Bell (Cool Papa)	cf		
George Britt (Chippy)		p	
Ray Brown	p	of	
Dewey Creacy	3b		
George Giles		1b	
Vic Harris	lf		
Bertrum Hunter	p		
Leroy Matlock		p	
John Henry Russell		2b	
Harry Salmon	p		
Ray Sheppard		2b	
George Suttles (Mule)	1b		
Leroy Taylor		rf	
Ted Trent	p		
Quincy Trouppe	rf	c	of
Willie Wells	ss		
Charles Williams (Lefty)	p		
Smokey Joe Williams		p	
Jim Williams (Bullet)		p	
Tom Young	c		

Harrisburg Giants

Player	1	2	3
? Bluford	lf		
James Crump	2b		
? Durant	1b		
Ralph Jefferson	cf		
? Johnson	rf		
Bill Lindsey	ss		
? Mitchell (Bud)		c	
Arthur White		p	
James Womack	3b		

Hilldale

Player	1	2	3
Clifford Allen		p	
Bob Bailey		of	
? Capers (Lefty)		p	
Clifford Carter		p	
Paul Carter	p		
Porter Charleston	p		
Phil Cockrell	p		
William Dallard (Eggie)		1b	
Oland Dials (Lou)	lf	rf	
Tom Dixon		p	
? Durant		of	
Gus Gadsden		of	
George Giles		1b	
Crush Holloway		rf	
M. Jeffries		3b	
Claude Johnson (Hooks)		3b	
Jim Johnson	ss		
William Johnson (Judy)		3b	ss

Player	1	2	3
Benny Jones (Hoghead)		3b	
Obie Lackey	2b		
Joseph Lewis	c		
Terris McDuffie		of	
? Mitchell (Bud)		of	
Sam Warmack		of	
Chaney White	cf		
Joe Wiggins		3b	

Homestead Grays

Player	1	2	3
Cumberland Posey (Cum)			M
Newton Allen (Newt)		2b	
Ralph Anderson		rf	
Herman Andrews (Jabo)		cf	rf
William Bell	p		
James Bell (Cool Papa)		cf	
George Britt (Chippy)	p	rf	c
Ray Brown		p	cf
Walter Cannady (Rev)		3b	
Anthony Cooper		of	ss
Oland Dials (Lou)		rf	
Frank Duncan	c		
Mack Eggleston		c	rf
Bill Evans		cf	
Robert Gaston	c		
George Giles		1b	
Vic Harris	lf		
Dixon Harris			
Bertrum Hunter		p	
? Jameson		p	
Leroy Matlock		p	
Clarence Palm (Spoony)		c	
Bill Perkins		c	
Harry Salmon	p	rf	
Paul Stephens (Jake)		ss	
Joe Strong	p	rf	cf
Leroy Taylor		rf	lf
John Terry		2b	
Quincy Trouppe		of	
Columbus Vance		p	
Jasper Washington (Jap)		1b	
Willie Wells		ss	
Charles Williams (Lefty)		p	
Chester Williams		ss	
Graham H. Williams		3b	
Smokey Joe Williams		p	
Jud Wilson		3b	
Tom Young		c	

Indianapolis ABCs

Player	1	2	3	
Candy Jim Taylor		3b		M
Ralph Anderson		of		
Herman Andrews (Jabo)		of		
Henry Baker	rf	lf		
? Bashum		c		
Jimmy Binder	3b	cf		
? Brammell	c			
J. Burdine		3b		
Roosevelt Davis (Rosey)		p		
? Davis (Big Boy)		p		
Wilson Day (Connie)	2b	ss		
Charles Decker (Dusty)		ss	3b	
John Dixon (Johnny Bob)		p		
Eddie Dwight		of		
? Gladney		ss		
Bob Graves		p		
Jack Hannibal		p		
Lenon Henderson		3b		
Logan Hensley (Slap)		p		
? Jackson		cf	c	

Player	1	2	3
John Lyles		ss	c
Henry Milton		ss	
Mitch Murray	c		
William Owens		ss	p
Willie Lee Scott (Joe)	1b		
? Smart	p	lf	
J. Thomas		2b	
Samuel Thompson (Sad Sam)	p	lf	
Columbus Vance		p	lf
Irving Waddy (Lefty)	p		
B. Williams		of	
C. Williams		ss	
John Williams (Big Boy)	lf	rf	
Kansas City Monarchs			
Newton Allen (Newt)	2b		
Clifford Bell (Cliff)		p	
William Bell			
James Bell (Cool Papa)	cf		
Charles Beverly	p		
Chet Brewer	p		
Maceo Brodnax		p	
William Clay (Lefty)		p	
Andrew Cooper (Andy)		p	
Reuben Currie (Rube)		p	
Nelson Dean		p	
Frank Duncan		c	
George Giles	1b		
Chick Harris (Popsickle)		rf	lf
Bertrum Hunter		p	
Newton Joseph (Newt)		3b	
Carroll Mothell (Dink)	3b	inf	of
Leroy Taylor		of	
Samuel Thompson (Sad Sam)		p	
Ted Trent		p	
Quincy Trouppe	lf	rf	p
Willie Wells	ss		
Tom Young		c	
Little Rock Grays			
S. Taylor			M
? Blevins	3b		
? Buford		1b	
? Carr		of	
William Carter	2b		
? Cobb		c	
? Coss	ss		
? Faison		ss	
? Haines	p		
? Haynes		1b	
Herman Howard (Red)	p		
Edgar Jackson		c	
S. Jones	1b		
Reuben Jones	lf	c	
James Liggons	p	lf	
Wayman Longley (Red)		utl	
Pete McQueen	rf		
? Overton	p		
Johnny Robinson	cf		
Louisville Black Caps			
Sam Bankhead		p	
John Bennett		of	
Jim Brown		lf	rf
Richard Cannon		p	
Ernest Carter (Spoon)		p	
? Cummings		c	
? Curtis		c	
Andrew Drake		c	
Louis English	c		
Willie Gisentaner (Lefty)		p	rf
Henry Harris	ss		
George Harris		2b	
Lenon Henderson		3b	
Alto Lane		p	
Granville Lyons	1b		
Jimmie Lyons		cf	
William McNeil (Red)	rf	of	
Charlie Miller		2b	
? Neely		p	
J. Webb Oden		of	
Martin Oliver	cf	2b	
? Petway		lf	c
Andrew Porter		p	
Claude Rhodes (Dusty)	p		
Felton Snow	3b	cf	
Roosevelt Tate (Speed)		of	
Jim Thurman		of	p
C. Ward (Pinky)		lf	
Memphis Red Sox			
Emery Adams (Ace)		p	lf
Herman Andrews (Jabo)		rf	p
Jerry Benjamin	2b	rf	
Walter Calhoun		p	
Ernest Carter (Spoon)		p	
? Cosa		rf	1b
Harry Cunningham	p	cf	
Homer Curry (Goose)	lf	p	rf
Tommy Dukes	c		
Murray Gillespie		p	rf
David Harvey (Bill)	p	rf	
? Hawley		c	
Otis Henry	3b		
J. Johnson (Lefty)		1b	p
Reuben Jones		cf	3b
Clarence Lewis (Foots)	ss		
Guy Ousley		2b	3b
Harvey Peterson		of	
? Taylor		of	
Jim West	1b		
Monroe Monarchs			
? Alexander (Chuffy)	1b		
Homer Allen		p	
Willie Burnham		p	
Marlin Cater (Mel)		ss	
Homer Curry (Goose)		of	
Porter Dallas (Big Boy)	3b		
Harry Else	c		
Leland Foster		p	
Murray Gillespie		p	
Samuel Harris		of	p
Bill Harris	c		
David Harvey (Bill)		p	
Frank Johnson		of	
James Liggons		p	
Dick Matthews	p		
P.D. Moore		c	
Leroy Morney	ss		
Barney Morris	p		
Harold Morris		p	
? Murray		p	
Roy Parnell (Red)	cf	p	
? Pervis		p	
Bob Saunders		2b	
Ray Sheppard		1b	3b
Hilton Smith		p	
Samuel Thompson (Sad Sam)		p	
H. Walker		c	lf
W. Walker		of	
Graham H. Williams	p		
Zollie Wright	rf	lf	
Montgomery Grey Sox			
James Bell (Steel Arm)		c	
Jim Brown		utl	
Walter Calhoun	p	cf	
Matthew Carlisle (Lick)	ss	lf	
Charles Decker (Dusty)		ss	3b
? Felix		p	
Albert Frazier	2b		
? Goins	p		
James Gurley	1b	p	
Paul Hardy		c	1b
A. Jackson (Matthew)	3b		
F. Lewis	lf	rf	
? Manning		1b	
John Mitchell	c	cf	
George Mitchell	p		
Everett Nelson	p		
James Pope		p	
John Ray	rf	lf	
Clarence White (Red)		p	
Nashville Elite Giants			
Joe Hewitt			M
Sam Bankhead		p	cf
Black Bottom Buford	2b	3b	
Richard Cannon		p	
? Charleston (Red)		c	
Tommy Dukes		c	
H. Henderson (Long)	1b		
Lenon Henderson		3b	
Robert Holsey (Frog)	p		
? Hovley		p	
? Lamont		rf	
Milt Laurent		rf	1b
? Lester		p	
Granville Lyons		1b	
? Marsh		rf	
Charlie Miller		2b	3b
William Nash		p	
? Petway		ss	
Andrew Porter		p	
Jack Ridley	cf	1b	
? Rowe		p	
Robert Smith		c	
Leroy Stratton	lf		
Roosevelt Tate (Speed)		cf	rf
Jesse Walker (Hoss)	ss		
Joe Wiggins		3b	
M. Williams		of	
Nish Williams	c	rf	
Jim Willis	p	lf	
Burnis Wright (Bill)	rf	lf	
Henry Wright (Red)	p		
L. Wright		rf	
New York Black Yankees			
Larry Brown	c		
Fred Burnett (Tex)		c	3b
Luther Farrell		p	
Bill Holland	p		
Crush Holloway		rf	
Jesse Hubbard		p	
Robert Hudspeth (Highpocket)		1b	
Clarence Jenkins (Fats)	lf		
Ted Page		rf	
Cornelius Rector (Connie)	p		

Player	1	2	3
Orville Riggins		3b	
George Scales	2b		
John Stanley (Neck)	p		
Clint Thomas	cf		
Dave Thomas		1b	
Harry Williams		3b	
Bill Yancey	ss		

Pennsylvania Red Caps of NY

Player	1	2	3
Robert Dean	3b		
G.E. Gray (Dolly)		1b	
James Leonard (Bobo)	lf		
Charles Lindsay (Clarence)	ss		
L.D. Livingston	rf	of	
Henry McHenry	p		
? Penoy	c		
Edward Pryor	2b		
W. Reavis		p	

Newark Browns

Player	1	2	3
Paul Arnold	lf		
John Beckwith	3b		
Benny Brown	ss		
Gilbert Coleman	rf		
Earl Davis (Hawk)	2b		
Kenneth Gardner (Ping)	p		
G.E. Gray (Dolly)	cf		
? Hinson		p	
? Kearney		p	
? Lumpkins (Lefty)		p	
Frank McCoy	c		
Henry McHenry		p	

Player	1	2	3
Dempsey Miller (Dimp)		p	
Richard Seay (Dick)		3b	
Jasper Washington (Jap)	1b		

Philadelphia Royal Giants (Winter)

Player	1	2	3
Henry Baker		utl	
Alfred Bland	3b		
George Carr (Tank)	1b		
V. Checo	rf		
Andrew Cooper (Andy)	p		
Clemente Delgardo	cf		
? Evans (Show Time)		p	
Hallie Harding	ss		
Raleigh Mackey (Biz)	c		
William Martin (Stack)	lf		
Jose Perez	2b		
William Ross	p		

Pittsburgh Crawfords

Player	1	2	3
Herman Andrews (Jabo)		cf	rf
William Bell	p		rf
James Bell (Cool Papa)		cf	
Charles Beverly	p		
Walter Cannady (Rev)		2b	3b
Oscar Charleston	1b		
Jimmy Crutchfield	cf	lf	
Herbert Dixon (Rap)	rf	cf	
Frank Duncan	c	lf	
Josh Gibson	lf	c	
Willie Gisentaner (Lefty)		p	lf
Clarence Jenkins (Fats)		of	
William Johnson (Judy)	3b		

Player	1	2	3
Benny Jones (Hoghead)		inf	
Howard Kimbro (Howdy)		p	
Harry Kincannon	p		
L.D. Livingston		of	
? Milhouse		lf	
Ted Page		rf	
Leroy Paige (Satchel)	p		
Bill Perkins		c	1b
Ted Radcliffe (Double Duty)	p	c	
John Ray		2b	
Harry Roberts (Raggs)		c	
John Henry Russell	2b		
? Shannon		lf	
Clyde Spearman		rf	
Paul Stephens (Jake)	ss		
Sam Streeter		p	
Ely Underwood		of	
Joe Ware		rf	
Bobby Williams		3b	
Chester Williams		ss	
Harry Williams		c	3b
Roy Williams		p	
T. Williams		3b	
Jud Wilson		lf	3b

Washington Pilots

Player	1	2	3
Chet Brewer	p		
Walter Burch		c	
Ted Carney		c	inf
Daltie Cooper		p	
Dewey Creacy	3b		
Paul Dixon		of	

1932 Philadelphia Royal Giants in Manila. Back row left is Andy Cooper, next to William Ross. Second from right is George "Tank" Carr, and far right is Biz Mackey.

Player	1	2	3
Joseph Dunn (Jake)	ss		
? Durant		of	
Mack Eggleston	c		
Bill Evans	cf		
Slyvester Foreman (Hooks)		c	
? Hackett	p		
George Hamilton	c		
Eppie Hampton	c		
Burnalle Hayes (Bun)	p		
Charlie Hughes	2b		
Robert Johnson (Bob)	rf	lf	
Bert Johnston		of	
John Jones		lf	
Roosevelt Kinard		2b	
Charles Lindsay (Clarence)		ss	
Jim Mason		1b	
Leroy Matlock	p		
Webster McDonald	p		
? Meagher		of	
Willie O'Bryant	lf	ss	
Henry Richardson	p		
Theodore Scott		c	
? Smith		3b	
George Suttles (Mule)	1b		
Ted Trent	p		
Frank Warfield	2b		
Sam Warmack		lf	
Jesse Winters (Nip)		p	

1933

Cuban Stars

Player	1	2	3
Luis Arango	3b		
? Calarai		p	
Marceline Correra (Cho Cho)	ss		
Edolfo Diaz (Yo Yo)	p		
Isidro Fabre	p	rf	
Jose Fernandez	c		
Rodolfo Fernandez (Rudy)		p	
Bill Freeman		p	
Manuel Garcia (Cocaina)	p	lf	
Cando Lopez	cf		
Alejandro Oms		cf	of
Jose Perez	1b		
? Pla		p	
Lazaro Salazar	rf		
Miguel L. Solis	2b		
? Sowen		ss	

Cuban Stars (East)

Player	1	2	3
Raul Alvarez		p	
John Cowan		ss	
L. Cunningham	rf		
? Haley (Red)	3b		
Lincoln Jackson	1b		
Busta Quintana	2b		
Nenene Rivera	ss		
Carlos Rivero (Charley)	cf		
? Storts	p		
James Thompson (Sandy)	lf		
S. Thompson	p		
Burlin White	c		

Akron Tyrites

Player	1	2	3
Ernest Carter (Spoon)	p		
Oland Dials (Lou)	rf		
? Dimes		of	
Willie Hunter	p		
Bill Johnson		3b	

Player	1	2	3
Charley Justice	p		
Clarence Lewis (Foots)	2b	lf	
Charlie Looney		2b	
Alonzo Mitchell (Hooks)		1b	
Clarence Palm (Spoony)	c		
Willie Powell		p	
? Simpson		of	
? Swan		ss	
John Tapley	3b		
Townsend Tapley	ss		
Alfred Taylor		1b	
Joe Ware	cf		
Bobby Williams	3b		
Woodrow Williams		p	
Fietman Wilson		c	

Bacharach Giants

Player	1	2	3
Gene Benson		cf	
Otto Briggs	rf		
Knowlington Burbage (Buddy)	cf		
George Carr (Tank)	1b		
Clifford Carter		p	
Phil Cockrell	p		
James Cooke (Jay)		p	
Daltie Cooper	p	rf	
Leon Daniels (Pepper)		c	
Willis Flournoy (Pud)		p	
Sijo Gomez (Joe)		p	
Joe Harris		p	
Harry Jeffries		3b	
Jim Johnson		ss	3b
Obie Lackey		ss	
Holsey Lee (Scrip)		p	
Joseph Lewis	c		
? Mitchell (Bud)		c	p
William Pelham (Don)		of	
Jose Perez	2b		
? Robinson (Babe)		p	
Ed Stone	lf		
Sam Warmack		of	
Joe Wiggins		3b	
Jesse Winters (Nip)		p	

Baltimore Black Sox

Player	1	2	3
Lewis Anderson		c	
Fred Burnett (Tex)	c	lf	1b
Anthony Cooper		ss	
Joseph Dunn (Jake)		ss	
Mack Eggleston		c	
George Giles		of	
Burnalle Hayes (Bun)		p	
Crush Holloway	cf	of	
Jesse Hubbard	lf	of	p
Bert Johnston	rf		
Stuart Jones (Slim)	p		
Obie Lackey		3b	2b
Holsey Lee (Scrip)		p	
Joseph Lewis	c	1b	
Tom Payne		of	
Henry Richardson	p		
Dewey Rivers		of	
Richard Seay (Dick)	2b		
? Simpson		1b	
? Washington		1b	
Roy Williams		p	
Harry Williams	3b	1b	ss
James Womack		1b	
Laymon Yokeley	p		

Baltimore Stars

Player	1	2	3	M
Ben Taylor				M
Clifford Allen		p	of	
Robert Evans	p			
William Force	p	rf		
? Harrison		lf	3b	
? Lee		3b		
Walter Leonard (Buck)	1b			
? Plummer	p	rf		
W. Taylor	cf			
Howard Wallace	ss			
Phil Williams (Pete)	2b			
J. Williams	c			

Birmingham Black Barons

Player	1	2	3
J. Borden		ss	
? Caldwell		cf	
Walter Calhoun	p		
William Howard		2b	
H. Johnson (Hamp)		rf	
William Nash	lf	p	
? Smith (Buster)		1b	
Carl Smith	c		

Chicago American Giants

Player	1	2	3	M
Dave Malarcher	3b			M
Larry Brown	c			
Willie Cornelius (Sug)	p			
Walter Davis (Steel Arm)	lf			
Willie Foster	p			
Willie Jordan		p		
Joe Lillard		p	lf	
William Marshall (Jack)	2b	ss		
Melvin Powell (Putt)		p	of	
Willie Powell	p			
Alex Radcliff	3b			
William Rogers (Nat)	rf			
William Spencer (Pee Wee)		utl		
Norman Stearnes (Turkey)	cf			
George Suttles (Mule)	1b	2b		
Quincy Trouppe		c	2b	
Willie Wells	ss			

Cleveland Giants

Player	1	2	3
Ernest Carter (Spoon)	p		
Dewey Creacy	3b		
Oland Dials (Lou)	rf		
David Harvey (Bill)	p		
Clarence Lewis (Foots)	1b		
Leroy Morney	ss		
Clarence Palm (Spoony)	c		
Wilson Redus	lf		
? Simpson	cf		
Bobby Williams	2b		

Columbus Blue Birds

Player	1	2	3	M
William Dismukes (Dizzy)				M
Herman Andrews (Jabo)	cf			
Ameal Brooks	c	lf		
Bill Byrd	p	cf		
Dewey Creacy	3b			
Roosevelt Davis (Rosey)	p			
Kermit Dial	2b	ss	cf	
Dennis Gilcrest		c	2b	
C.B. Griffin (Clarence)	lf			
Charlie Hughes		2b		
Don Jarmon	p			
J. Kerner	of			
Alphonso Lattimore	c			
Edward McClain (Boots)		inf		

Player	1	2	3
Bill McLain		p	
C. Milton		inf	
Leroy Morney	ss		
James Pope		p	
Ted Radcliffe (Double Duty)		c	p
Wilson Redus	rf	lf	
Claude Rhodes (Dusty)		p	
Willie Lee Scott (Joe)	1b		
Zack Spencer		p	
Jim Thurman		p	
Roy Tyler		of	
Sam Warmack		of	
Bobby Williams		2b	
Roy Williams	p		

Detroit Stars

Player	1	2	3
Candy Jim Taylor	p		M
? Armour		3b	p
Percy Bailey (Bill)	p		
Jerry Benjamin	cf		
Rainey Bibbs		1b	
Jimmy Binder	3b		
Black Bottom Buford	ss	2b	
? Busby		3b	of
Ray Dandridge		ss	
William Gill		3b	
Paul Hardy	c	1b	
Logan Hensley (Slap)		p	
? Jackson		2b	
Wade Johnston		lf	
J. Kerner		rf	
Granville Lyons	1b	p	
George Mitchell		p	rf
Everett Nelson		p	rf
William Owens		ss	
Clarence Palm (Spoony)		c	
Anderson Pryor	2b		
Clarence Smith	rf	of	
? Snowden	p		
Hulan Stamps		p	
? Stokes		p	
Leroy Taylor		rf	
Samuel Thompson (Sad Sam)		p	
Columbus Vance	p	of	
Irving Waddy (Lefty)		p	
Jim Webster (Double Duty)		c	
John Williams (Big Boy)		lf	

Homestead Grays

Player	1	2	3
Cumberland Posey (Cum)			M
Jimmy Binder		3b	
George Britt (Chippy)	p	3b	
Ameal Brooks		c	
Ray Brown	p	cf	
Louis Dula		p	
Bill Evans	cf	ss	
Robert Gaston		c	
William Gill		of	1b
Vic Harris	lf		
Charlie Hughes		2b	
George McAllister		1b	
Leroy Morney		ss	
Tom Payne		of	
? Peacock		3b	
? Pierson		2b	3b
Ted Radcliffe (Double Duty)		c	p
Harry Salmon	p	lf	
Willie Lee Scott (Joe)		1b	
Joe Strong		p	of
John Terry	2b		

Player	1	2	3
Jasper Washington (Jap)	1b	3b	
Charles Williams (Lefty)	p		
Chester Williams		ss	
John Williams (Big Boy)	rf	cf	
Poindexter Williams		1b	

Kansas City Monarchs

Player	1	2	3
Newton Allen (Newt)	ss		
Charles Beverly	p		
Ollie Boyd (Turk)		of	
Chet Brewer	p		
Andrew Cooper (Andy)	p		
? Dooley		of	
Frank Duncan	c		
Eddie Dwight	cf		
Slyvester Foreman (Hooks)		c	
George Giles	1b		
Newton Joseph (Newt)	3b		
Carroll Mothell (Dink)	2b	inf	of
Garrett Norman		of	
Wilber Rogan (Bullet Joe)	lf		
Leslie Starks		of	
Tom Young	rf	c	

Louisville Red Caps

Player	1	2	3
Richard Cannon	p		
Joe Cates	ss		
W.M. Charter (Bill)	rf		
Louis English	c	3b	
? Evans	p		
Ulysses Evans		p	
George Harris	2b		
? Lewis	p		
William McNeil (Red)	cf	p	
R. Miller	1b		
A. Miller	lf		
P.D. Moore		c	
Jack Ridley		of	
D. Wright	3b		

Memphis Red Sox

Player	1	2	3
Matthew Carlisle (Lick)	ss		
Marlin Carter (Mel)		3b	2b
Ernest Carter (Spoon)		p	
Homer Curry (Goose)	cf		
Louis English		rf	c
Jimmy Ford	3b		
David Harvey (Bill)		p	
Herman Howard (Red)		p	
? Jasper		p	
J. Johnson (Lefty)	1b		
P. Johnson		p	
Robert Jones	lf		
Reuben Jones		of	
William Lowe		3b	
Jim Mason	rf		
Eddie Peoples		p	
Harvey Peterson		2b	3b
Bob Saunders		2b	
Robert Smith		c	
Raymond Taylor		c	

Nashville Elite Giants

Player	1	2	3
Candy Jim Taylor			M
Percy Bailey (Bill)		p	
Sam Bankhead	cf	ss	
Willie Collins		of	
Homer Curry (Goose)		of	
Ray Dandridge		ss	
Tommy Dukes	c		

Player	1	2	3
Joseph Dunn (Jake)		2b	ss
? Finch			
Willie Gisentaner (Lefty)		p	lf
Sammy T. Hughes	2b		
Percy Miller	p		
Andrew Porter		p	
Jack Ridley		of	
Robert Smith		c	rf
? Smith		rf	
Felton Snow	3b		
Leroy Stratton	lf	2b	ss
Jesse Walker (Hoss)	ss		
Jim West	1b		
Clarence White (Red)		p	
E. Williams		c	
Nish Williams		c	lf
Poindexter Williams		c	
Jim Willis	p		
Burnis Wright (Bill)	rf		
Henry Wright (Red)	p	of	
Howard Wright		p	

New Orleans Crescent Stars

Player	1	2	3
George Collins	2b		
Harry Else	c		
Eppie Hampton		c	
Chick Harris (Popsickle)	rf		
Milt Laurent		2b	ss
Dick Matthews	p		
Charlie Miller		ss	3b
Jasper Miller		p	
Barney Morris	p		
E.E. Muse		ss	2b
Roy Parnell (Red)	cf		
Robert Pipkin (Lefty)		p	
? Sias	3b		
Hilton Smith	p		
Morris Smith		p	
Percy Wilson	1b		
Zollie Wright	lf		

New York Black Yankees

Player	1	2	3
John Beckwith	3b		
Walter Cannady (Rev)	2b		
Robert Clarke	c		
Luther Farrell		p	
Bill Holland	p		
Clarence Jenkins (Fats)	lf		
Ted Radcliffe (Double Duty)		p	c
Cornelius Rector (Connie)	p		
George Scales	rf		
John Stanley (Neck)	p		
Dave Thomas	1b		
Clint Thomas	cf		
Ted Trent		p	
Joe Wiggins		3b	
Ray Williams	p		
Bill Yancey	ss		

Pennsylvania Red Caps of NY

Player	1	2	3
Robert Dean	3b		
Fred Flournoy	c		
G.E. Gray (Dolly)	cf		
William Johnson (Wise)	1b		
James Leonard (Bobo)	lf		
Charles Lindsay (Clarence)	ss		
L.D. Livingston	rf		
Henry McHenry	p		
Edward Pryor	2b		

Player	1	2	3
Newark Dodgers			
Walter Burch	3b	c	
Gilbert Coleman	rf		
Robert Evans	p		
Harry Jeffries		c	3b
Jim Johnson		ss	
Benny Jones (Hoghead)	lf		
? Sinclair	2b		
? Smith		1b	
Ray Vaughn (Slim)	p		
A. Walker	cf		
James Wilson (Chubby)		of	
Philadelphia Stars			
Clifford Allen		p	
? Bounds		p	
Clifford Carter	p		
Paul Carter		p	
William Casey (Mickey)		c	3b
Porter Charleston	p		
William Dallard (Eggie)	1b		
? Devon		of	
Herbert Dixon (Rap)	rf	lf	
Tom Finley		3b	
Dick Lundy	ss		
Raleigh Mackey (Biz)	c		
Webster McDonald	p		
? Mitchell (Bud)		of	
? Schmidt		p	
Lindsay Silvers		inf	
Herb Smith	p		
Paul Stephens (Jake)	2b		
Jim Stevens		ss	
Peter Washington	cf		
Chaney White	lf	rf	
? Willetts		p	
Elbert Williams		p	
Jim Willis		p	
Jud Wilson	3b	1b	
Pittsburgh Crawfords			
James Bell (Cool Papa)	cf		
William Bell		p	
Ernest Carter (Spoon)		p	
Oscar Charleston	1b	p	
Anthony Cooper		rf	2b
Jimmy Crutchfield	lf		
Josh Gibson	c	3b	
David Harvey (Bill)		p	
Bertrum Hunter	p		
William Johnson (Judy)	3b		
Harry Kincannon		p	1b
Obie Lackey		ss	
Clarence Lewis (Foots)		ss	
Leroy Matlock	p		
Ted Page	rf		
Leroy Paige (Satchel)	p		
Tom Payne		of	
Bill Perkins		c	lf
John Henry Russell	2b	1b	
Sam Streeter		p	
Chester Williams	ss		

1934

Player	1	2	3
Cuban Stars (East)			
Eufemio Abreu	3b	c	of
Edolfo Diaz (Yo Yo)	p		
Isidro Fabre	p	of	

Player	1	2	3
Al Fennar		ss	
Jose Fernandez	c	1b	
Rodolfo Fernandez (Rudy)		p	
Oscar Levis	p		
Cando Lopez	lf	of	
Armando Massip	1b		
Juanelo Mirabel		p	
Jose Perez	3b	ss	2b
Ramiro Ramirez	rf		
B. Conrado Rodriquez		p	
Lazaro Salazar	cf	of	p
Miguel L. Solis	2b	3b	
Padrone's Cuban Giants			
Juan Padrone	p		M
Albert Davis	p		
Carl Edmond	p		
Bob Farmer		lf	
Charlie Groves		p	
Carl Hannibal		p	
Logan Hensley (Slap)	p		
Wade Johnston	lf	p	
Obie Layton		utl	
John Lyles	3b		
William McCall (Bill)	p		
George Mitchell	rf	p	
Mitch Murray		c	
Clarence Palm (Spoony)		c	
Bobby Robertson		inf	
Johnny Robinson	cf		
Cornelius Robinson (Neil)		of	
Townsend Tapley	ss		
Olan Taylor (Jelly)	1b		
David Thomas	inf	of	
Ely Underwood	2b		
? Watkins		c	
Wilson's Elite Giants (Winter)			
James Bell (Cool Papa)	cf		
Larry Brown	c		
Ernest Carter (Spoon)	p		
Sammy T. Hughes	2b		
Leroy Paige (Satchel)	p		
Andrew Porter	p		
Felton Snow	3b		
Norman Stearnes (Turkey)	lf		
George Suttles (Mule)	1b		
Candy Jim Taylor	3b		
Willie Wells	ss		
Chester Williams		2b	
Burnis Wright (Bill)	rf		
Tom Young	c	of	
Bacharach Giants			
Otto Briggs			M
Clifford Allen		p	
Gene Benson	cf		
Chester Buchanan (Buck)	p		
Knowlington Burbage (Buddy)		lf	
George Carr (Tank)		3b	rf
Clifford Carter		p	
Leroy Clayton (Zack)	1b		
? Collins (Sonny)		p	rf
Daltie Cooper	p		
Mack Eggleston		c	
Luther Farrell	p	of	
Al Fennar		ss	
? Garrison	1b		
? Haines		c	
Crush Holloway	rf	cf	

Player	1	2	3
Jesse Hubbard	p	rf	
? Jackson		ss	
Harry Jeffries		3b	c
Jim Johnson		utl	
Robert Johnson (Bob)		3b	
Obie Lackey	3b	ss	
Joseph Lewis	c		
Charles Lindsay (Clarence)		ss	
Maurice Lisby		p	
Carl Logan		ss	
? Marshall		c	
Henry McHenry		p	
? Monceville		p	
Roy Morrison		p	
Clay Murray		p	
? Parnell		p	
Jose Perez	2b		
Willie Prophet		rf	
Henry Richardson		p	
Bing Robelson		p	
Bill Sadler		ss	
? Smith		of	
Ed Stone	lf		
Clarence Thorpe		p	
? Tuck		of	
Joe Wiggins	ss		
Laymon Yokeley	p		
Baltimore Black Sox			
Clifford Allen		p	
Walter Burch		2b	
George Carr (Tank)		3b	
L. Cunningham		cf	
Leon Day		p	
Paul Dixon		2b	lf
Tom Dixon		c	lf
Herbert Dixon (Rap)		of	
Richard Harris		2b	
Burnalle Hayes (Bun)		p	
? Hughes		ss	
Lincoln Jackson		1b	
Robert Johnson (Bob)		3b	
John Jones		rf	
? Mitchell (Bud)		of	
Birmingham Black Barons			
Matthew Carlisle (Lick)		2b	
Frank Collins	p		
Anthony Cooper		cf	ss
John Cowan	3b	2b	
Willie Crawford		of	
Felix Evans (Chin)		p	of
Paul Hardy	c		
A. Jackson (Matthew)	ss		
? Johnson	rf		
H. Johnson (Hamp)		of	
Arthur Jones	p		
W. Jones		of	
Harvey Peterson	lf	utl	
Columbus Vance	p	of	
John Washington	1b		
Chicago American Giants			
Dave Malarcher	3b		M
Percy Bailey (Bill)		p	
Larry Brown	c		
Ossie Brown		p	
Willie Cornelius (Sug)	p		
Willie Foster	p		
John Hines	rf	lf	

Player	1	2	3
Joe Lillard	lf	p	
William Marshall (Jack)	2b	rf	
Tom Miles	p		
Jack Miles	of		
Melvin Powell (Putt)	p	of	
Alex Radcliff	3b		
Everett Radcliffe (Red)	utl		
Ted Radcliffe (Double Duty)	p	c	
Wilson Redus	of		
John Reed	p		
William Rogers (Nat)	rf		
Willie Lee Scott (Joe)	1b	of	
Norman Stearnes (Turkey)	cf		
George Suttles (Mule)	1b		
Ted Trent	p		
Willie Wells	ss		

Cincinnati Tigers

Player	1	2	3
Bert Blakely	c		
? Dunson	3b		
Bill Evans	3b	of	
Jess Houston	ss		
F. Jackson	1b		
Alto Lane	p		
Helburn Meadows	cf		
Porter Moss	p		
Roy Partlow	lf	p	
? Postell	2b		
? Redden	c		
? Rogers	of		
John Terry	3b		
C. Ward (Pinky)	rf		

Cleveland Red Sox

Player	1	2	3
Bobby Williams			M
Jesse Brooks	3b	c	
Bill Byrd	p		
Anthony Cooper	ss	3b	
S. Davidson	3b		
John Dixon (Johnny Bob)	p		
Dennis Gilcrest	rf	c	
Thomas Glover	p		
C.B. Griffin (Clarence)	of		
Charlie Hughes	2b		
? Hurd	of		
Norman Jackson (Jelly)	rf	ss	
Bill Johnson	ss		
B. Jones	c	of	
Reuben Jones	rf	lf	
Holsey Lee (Scrip)	p		
Clarence Lewis (Foots)	ss		
George McAllister	1b		
C. Milton	inf		
Andrew Patterson (Pat)	2b		
Willie Powell	p		
Wilson Redus	lf		
James Reese	p		
Roy Roberts	p		
William Robinson (Bobby)	3b		
? Robinson (Babe)	p		
John Henry Russell	2b		
? See	rf	p	
Felton Snow	3b		
Leroy Taylor	cf	lf	
Guy Williams	3b		

Homestead Grays

Player	1	2	3
Herman Andrews (Jabo)	of		
Jimmy Binder	3b		
Ray Brown	p		

Player	1	2	3
Knowlington Burbage (Buddy)	rf		
Fred Burnett (Tex)	c		
? Cheatham	p		
Louis Dula	p	lf	
Robert Evans	p		
Paul Gibson	p		
Dennis Gilcrest	ss	c	
Willie Gisentaner (Lefty)	p		
? Jarnagin	of		
Josh Johnson	c		
Walter Leonard (Buck)	1b		
John Lyles	ss		
Clarence Palm (Spoony)	rf	c	
Andrew Patterson (Pat)	2b		
? Robinson	lf	cf	
John Henry Russell	2b		
Harry Salmon	p		
Joe Strong	p	rf	
Charles Williams (Lefty)	p		
James Williams (Jim)	2b	lf	
Smokey Joe Williams	p		
Harry Williams	ss		

Jacksonville Red Caps

Player	1	2	3
Alonzo Mitchell (Hooks)	p	of	M
James Bell (Steel Arm)	c		
Thad Christopher	lf		
Rube Ellis (Rocky)	p		
Albert Frazier	cf	utl	
Leroy Holmes (Phillie)	ss		
Ernest Jones (Mint)	1b		
Kenneth Robinson	2b		
Lacey Thomas	rf	p	
Phil Williams (Pete)	3b		

Kansas City Monarchs

Player	1	2	3
Sam Crawford			M
Wilber Rogan (Bullet Joe)	of		M
Newton Allen (Newt)	2b	ss	
Sam Bankhead	2b	3b	
James Bell (Cool Papa)	cf		
Charles Beverly	p		
Chet Brewer	p		
Andrew Cooper (Andy)	p		
? Davis	of		
John Donaldson	p		
Frank Duncan	c		
Eddie Dwight	cf	of	
Willie Foster	p		
George Giles	1b		
Chick Harris (Popsickle)	lf		
Bertrum Hunter	p		
Newton Joseph (Newt)	3b		
Hurley McNair	rf		
Carroll Mothell (Dink)	3b	2b	
Norman Stearnes (Turkey)	cf		
Leroy Taylor	rf		
Quincy Trouppe	lf		
Willie Wells	ss		
Tom Young	c		

Memphis Red Sox

Player	1	2	3
Don Bennett	2b		
Homer Curry (Goose)	cf		
Luther Gillard	of		
Eppie Hampton	c		
David Harvey (Bill)	p		
Herman Howard (Red)	p		
Reuben Jones	lf		
Wayman Longley (Red)	ss		

Player	1	2	3
Jim Mason	rf		
Beauford Nunley	1b		
? Smittie	3b		

Nashville Elite Giants

Player	1	2	3
Candy Jim Taylor	3b		M
Sam Bankhead	cf	p	ss
Alfred Carter	of		
Walter Davis (Steel Arm)	of		
Tommy Dukes	c		
Mack Eggleston	c		
Jimmy Ford	2b		
Robert Griffith	p		
Paul Hardy	c		
Stokes Hendrix	p		
Sammy T. Hughes	2b		
Clarence Lewis (Foots)	2b	ss	
Granville Lyons	1b		
Percy Miller	p		
Dempsey Miller (Dimp)	p		
Tom Parker	p		
Roy Parnell (Red)	of		
Andrew Porter	p		
? Roberson (Charley)	ss		
? Scott	2b		
Felton Snow	3b	ss	
Jesse Walker (Hoss)	ss		
Jim West	1b		
Nish Williams	c	rf	
Jim Willis	p		
Burnis Wright (Bill)	rf	cf	
Henry Wright (Red)	p	lf	
Zollie Wright	of		

New Orleans Crescent Stars

Player	1	2	3
Lloyd Bassett (Pepper)	c		
Charles Beverly	p	lf	
Matthew Carlisle (Lick)	2b		
Lloyd Davenport	cf	lf	
Chick Harris (Popsickle)	1b		
Milt Laurent	2b		
John Markham	p		
? Marsley	rf		
Charlie Miller	3b	ss	
C.D. Mosley	p		
Roy Parnell (Red)	cf		
? Sims	3b		
? Sis	3b		
Felton Snow	3b		
? Vassetti	c		
Graham H. Williams	p		
? Wright	ss		
? Wrother	1b		

New York Black Yankees

Player	1	2	3
Percy Bailey (Bill)	p		
John Beckwith	of	inf	
Frank Blake	p		
Walter Cannady (Rev)	2b		
Robert Clarke	c		
Bill Holland	p		
Clarence Jenkins (Fats)	lf		
Cornelius Rector (Connie)	p		
George Scales	3b		
Clyde Spearman	rf		
John Stanley (Neck)	p		
? Talley	p		
Dave Thomas	1b		
Clint Thomas	cf		
Ted Trent	p		

Player	1	2	3
Ray Williams		p	
Bill Yancey	ss		

Pennsylvania Red Caps of NY

Player	1	2	3
Ben Mulvey			M
Tom Cox	p		
Robert Dean	3b		
Jimmy Everett	p		
Al Fennar		2b	
Willis Flournoy (Pud)	p		
G.E. Gray (Dolly)	cf		
Curtis Henderson	ss		
William Johnson (Wise)	c		
Co Johnson		of	
James Leonard (Bobo)	lf		
Terris McDuffie	p		
Henry McHenry	p		
Edward Pryor	1b		
Merven Ryan (Red)		p	

Newark Dodgers

Player	1	2	3
Paul Arnold	cf		
Percy Bailey (Bill)		p	
Alonza Bailey		p	
John Beckwith		1b	
George Britt (Chippy)	p	c	
Knowlington Burbage (Buddy)		lf	
Richard Byas (Subby)	2b	1b	
? Cephus (Goldie)		inf	
Roy Clark		p	
Homer Craig		p	
Ray Dandridge	3b		
Hy Davis	of		2b
Robert Evans	p		
? Hairston (Rap)		utl	
John Hayes	c		
Bert Johnston	rf		
Maurice Lisby		p	
Dick Lundy	ss		
Frank McCoy		c	
Ralph Mellix (Lefty)	p		
Schute Merritt		utl	
? Owens		p	
Hank Perry	p		
Busta Quintana		3b	2b
Ormond Sampson		ss	
Leslie Starks	1b	utl	
Ray Vaughn (Slim)	p		
Arthur White		p	
Jim Williams		of	

Philadelphia Stars

Player	1	2	3
? Blackwell		p	
Alex Brooks		of	
Ameal Brooks		c	
George Carr (Tank)	1b		
Paul Carter		p	
William Casey (Mickey)	c		
Phil Cockrell		p	
? Coleman		p	
Dewey Creacy	3b		
Joseph Dunn (Jake)	rf		
Rube Ellis (Rocky)	p		
Tom Finley		3b	
John Hayes	c		
Frank Holmes	p		
Stuart Jones (Slim)	p		
Raleigh Mackey (Biz)		c	1b
Webster McDonald	p		
Tom Miles		1b	of

Player	1	2	3
Jim Richardson		p	
Richard Seay (Dick)	2b		
Paul Stephens (Jake)	ss		
Peter Washington	cf		
Chaney White	lf		
Jud Wilson	1b		

Pittsburgh Crawfords

Player	1	2	3
James Bell (Cool Papa)	cf		
William Bell		p	
? Brooks		p	
Oscar Charleston	1b		
? Cheatham			
Jimmy Crutchfield	rf		
Roosevelt Davis (Rosey)		p	
Herbert Dixon (Rap)		of	
Josh Gibson	c	1b	
Curtis Harris (Popeye)		lf	c
Vic Harris	lf		
John Hayes		c	
Bertrum Hunter	p		
William Johnson (Judy)	3b		
Harry Kincannon		p	
Leroy Matlock	p		
Leroy Morney	ss	2b	
Ted Page		rf	
Leroy Paige (Satchel)	p		
Clarence Palm (Spoony)		c	
Bill Perkins		c	
Sam Streeter		p	
Irving Vincent (Lefty)		p	
Jasper Washington (Jap)		3b	
Joe Wiggins		2b	
Chester Williams	2b	ss	

Washington Pilots

Player	1	2	3
Walter Burch	c	ss	
George Carr (Tank)		3b	
L. Cunningham	cf	of	
Paul Dixon	lf		
Tom Dixon		c	
Thomas Hall	ss		
Burnalle Hayes (Bun)	p	rf	
Lincoln Jackson	1b		
John Jones		rf	of
L.B. Lawson (Flash)		p	
? Mitchell (Bud)	p		
? O'Lee		c	
Ed Sherkliff		p	
? Stack		c	

1935

Royal Giants (Winter)

Player	1	2	3
Candy Jim Taylor			M
Chet Brewer	p		
Robert Griffin	p		
John Hines	c		
Sammy T. Hughes	2b		
Raleigh Mackey (Biz)		c	ss
Leroy Paige (Satchel)	p		
Felton Snow	ss		
Norman Stearnes (Turkey)	lf		
George Suttles (Mule)	3b		
Jim West	1b		
Burnis Wright (Bill)	cf		
Zollie Wright	rf		

Bacharach Giants

Player	1	2	3
Clifford Allen			p
Gene Benson		cf	
Knowlington Burbage (Buddy)		of	
Phil Cockrell	p		
Anthony Cooper		lf	
Daltie Cooper			p
W. Cooper	rf		
Earl Davis (Hawk)		2b	
Tom Dixon	c		
Lincoln Jackson		1b	
Leaman Johnson	2b		
N. Johnson		2b	
Charles Lindsay (Clarence)		ss	
Eudie Napier		c	
? Richards	3b		
? Robbins		p	
Roy Roberts	p		
Johnny Taylor		p	
Laymon Yokeley	p		

Brooklyn Eagles

Player	1	2	3
Ben Taylor			M
Jimmy Binder	3b		
Fred Burnett (Tex)		3b	c
Leroy Clayton (Zack)		1b	
Lawrence Copeland		inf	
Leon Daniels (Pepper)		c	
Walter Davis (Steel Arm)		1b	
Spencer Davis (Babe)		utl	
Leon Day	p		
Herbert Dixon (Rap)	cf		
Leon Dougherty		p	
? Floyd		p	
? Gavin		p	
Dennis Gilcrest		2b	ss
George Giles	1b		
C.B. Griffin (Clarence)		of	
Burnalle Hayes (Bun)		p	
Albert Haywood (Buster)		c	
Leroy Holmes (Phillie)		ss	
Bill Jackman	p		
Clarence Jenkins (Fats)		lf	
Benny Jones (Hoghead)		inf	
? Lewis		ss	
Melvin Markham		p	
Jim Martin (Pepper)		inf	
Eldridge Mayweather (Ed)		1b	
Terris McDuffie		p	
Henry Milton		of	
John Morton		of	
William Nicholas		p	
Ted Page		of	
Clarence Palm (Spoony)	c		
Jose Perez		2b	3b
Ted Radcliffe (Double Duty)	p	c	
James Reese		p	
William Rogers (Nat)		of	
Leon Ruffin		c	
Bill Sadler		ss	
Ed Stone	rf		
S. Thompson		p	
C. Ward (Pinky)		rf	
Eugene White		3b	
Roy Williams		p	
Harry Williams	3b	2b	
Elbert Williams		p	
Bill Yancey	ss		
Laymon Yokeley		p	

Chicago American Giants

Player	1	2	3
Jim Brown	1b		
Larry Brown	c		
Ossie Brown	p		
Richard Byas (Subby)	2b		
Leroy Clayton (Zack)	1b		
Willie Cornelius (Sug)	p		
Walter Davis (Steel Arm)	1b		
Willie Foster	p		
? Hyne	c		
William Marshall (Jack)	2b		
Luther McDonald (Vet)	p		
Melvin Powell (Putt)	p		
Alex Radcliff	3b		
Wilson Redus	rf		
Norman Stearnes (Turkey)	cf		
George Suttles (Mule)	lf		
Hazel Thomas	p		
Lacey Thomas	of	p	
Ted Trent	p		
Quincy Trouppe	c		
Willie Wells	ss		

Cincinnati Tigers

Player	1	2	3
Carl Glass	M		
Marlin Carter (Mel)	3b		
A. Gibson (Jerry)	p		
Virgil Harris	of	p	
J. Harris (Sonny)	of		
Jess Houston	p		
Josh Johnson	c		
Arthur Maddox	p		
Helburn Meadows	of		
Charlie Miller	inf		
Porter Moss	p		
Harvey Peterson	of		
Miller Rice	of		
Cornelius Robinson (Neil)	of		
Ewing Russell	c		

Player	1	2	3
Bill Simms	of		
Robert Smith	c		
Olan Taylor (Jelly)	1b		
? Wolf	p		

Columbus Elite Giants

Player	1	2	3
Candy Jim Taylor			M
Bill Byrd	p	rf	cf
Tommy Dukes	c		
Thomas Glover	p		
C.B. Griffin (Clarence)	of		
Robert Griffith	p		
Paul Hardy	c		
Sammy T. Hughes	2b		
Leroy Morney	ss		
Tom Parker	of		
Roy Parnell (Red)	lf		
Andrew Porter	p		
Felton Snow	3b	ss	
O. Taylor	p		
Samuel Thompson (Sad Sam)	p		
Jesse Walker (Hoss)	ss		
Jim West	1b		
John Williams (Big Boy)	3b		
Nish Williams	c		
Jim Willis	p		
Burnis Wright (Bill)	cf	rf	
Henry Wright (Red)	p		
Zollie Wright	rf	ss	

Detroit Cubs

Player	1	2	3
? Booker	utl		
A. Clarr	utl		
Richard Dennard (Dick)	lf		
William Dudley	p		
William Friday	3b		
E. Hale (Red)	ss		
Clarence Jenkins (Barney)	c		
D. Jenkins	2b		

Player	1	2	3
Oscar Johnson (Heavy)	of		
Charley Justice	p		
William Love (Andy)	rf		
James Trapp	cf		
T. Wells (Lou)	p		
Robert Wiggins (Bob)	lf		
Felton Wilson	c		

Havana Cubans

Player	1	2	3
Hipolito Arenas (Torrento)	3b	of	
? Darlo	2b		
P. Jimenez	lf	of	
M. Jimenez	p		
Enrique Lantiqua	c		
Horacio Martinez (Rabbit)	ss		
Ismael Morales	cf		
? Pla	rf	p	
Joe Rodriquez	1b		

Homestead Grays

Player	1	2	3
Cumberland Posey (Cum)			M
Clifford Allen	p		
Jerry Benjamin	cf		
Jimmy Binder	3b	2b	
Ray Brown	p	of	
Knowlington Burbage (Buddy)	rf	lf	2b
Fred Burnett (Tex)	c		
Matthew Carlisle (Lick)	2b		
Tommy Dukes	c		
Louis Dula	p		
Robert Gaston	c		
Willie Gisentaner (Lefty)	p		
Vic Harris	lf		
Norman Jackson (Jelly)	ss	c	
Benny Jones (Hoghead)	utl		
Walter Leonard (Buck)	1b		
C.D. Mosley	p		
Tom Parker	p		
John Henry Russell	2b		
Harry Salmon	p		
George Scales	3b	2b	
Joe Strong	p		
Harry Williams	inf		

Kansas City Monarchs

Player	1	2	3
Sam Crawford			M
Newton Allen (Newt)	ss	2b	
John Paul Berry	p		
Charles Beverly	p		
Chet Brewer	p		
Willard Brown	ss	3b	
Andrew Cooper (Andy)	p		
Eddie Dwight	cf		
Newton Joseph (Newt)	3b		
Floyd Kranson	p		
Robert Madison	p	ss	
Eldridge Mayweather (Ed)	1b		
Henry Milton	2b	of	
Leroy Paige (Satchel)	p		
Wilber Rogan (Bullet Joe)	of		
Leroy Taylor	rf		
Quincy Trouppe	lf		
Tom Young	c		

New York Cubans

Player	1	2	3
A. Anas	p		
Luis Arango	3b		
Frank Blake	p		
Ramon Bragana	p		
Marceline Correra (Cho Cho)	lf	ss	

1935 Pittsburgh Crawfords. Back row L to R: Jelly Taylor, Judy Johnson, Leroy Matlock, unknown, Josh Gibson, trainer Hood Whitton. Middle row L to R: Cool Papa Bell, Sam Bankhead, Oscar Charleston, Spoony Palm, Jimmy Crutchfield, Spoon Carter, Bill Perkins. Front row L to R: Tim Bond, Carl Howard, Bertrum Hunter, Sam Streeter, Harry Kincannon, and Rosy Davis.

Jimmy Crutchfield

Player	1	2	3
? Delugo		p	
Edolfo Diaz (Yo Yo)		c	p
Pablo Diaz		c	
Martin Dihigo	cf	p	of
Paul Dixon	rf	lf	
Frank Duncan	c		
Rodolfo Fernandez (Rudy)		p	
Manuel Garcia (Cocaina)		rf	p
Enrique Lantiqua		c	
Cando Lopez		cf	of
Dick Lundy	2b		
Horacio Martinez (Rabbit)	ss	3b	
Jose Martini		p	
Alejandro Oms	lf	rf	
Jose Perez		2b	lf
Basilio Roselle		p	
Lazaro Salazar	1b	p	
Anastacio Santaella (Tacho)		2b	3b
Clyde Spearman		rf	cf
John Stanley (Neck)	p		
Johnny Taylor	p		
Dave Thomas		1b	
Luis Tiant, Sr.	p		
Strico Valdez		inf	
Bill Yancey		ss	

Newark Dodgers

Player	1	2	3
Dick Lundy	2b		M
Paul Arnold	cf		
Alonza Bailey	p		
Marvin Barker		lf	of
William Bell		p	
Timothy Bond		ss	
Fred Burnett (Tex)		c	
Willie Burns		p	
Roy Clark		p	
Anthony Cooper		ss	
Homer Craig	p		
Ray Dandridge	3b		
? Daniels		p	
Roosevelt Davis (Rosey)		p	
Robert Evans	p		
Paul Gibson		p	
? Hairston (Rap)		utl	
Burnalle Hayes (Bun)	p		
John Hayes	c	lf	
Willie Hubert		p	
? Jameson		p	
Bert Johnston		rf	
Raleigh Mackey (Biz)		of	c
Frank McCoy		c	
Terris McDuffie	p		
Schute Merritt		utl	
Leroy Miller (Flash)		2b	
Leslie Starks	1b		
John Terry		2b	
Casey Walker		c	
Joe Ware		1b	
Jim Williams	ss		

Philadelphia Stars

Player	1	2	3
Paul Carter		p	
William Casey (Mickey)		c	
Porter Charleston		p	
Dewey Creacy	3b	lf	
Lloyd Davenport		of	
Joseph Dunn (Jake)	cf	rf	
Rube Ellis (Rocky)		p	
Frank Holmes	p		
Stuart Jones (Slim)	p		

Player	1	2	3
Obie Lackey		inf	
Granville Lyons		1b	
Raleigh Mackey (Biz)		c	1b
Webster McDonald	p		
? Moles (Lefty)		p	
Ted Page		lf	of
Joe Reynolds		p	
Richard Seay (Dick)	2b	p	
Paul Stephens (Jake)	ss		
? Washington		p	
Peter Washington		of	
Chaney White	rf	lf	
Jud Wilson	1b	rf	lf

Pittsburgh Crawfords

Player	1	2	3
Sam Bankhead	lf		
James Bell (Cool Papa)	cf	1b	
William Bell		p	
Timothy Bond		ss	3b
W. Breen		of	
Ernest Carter (Spoon)		p	
Alfred Carter		of	
Oscar Charleston	1b		
Charlie Cook		p	
Jimmy Crutchfield	rf	lf	
Roosevelt Davis (Rosey)	p		
Josh Gibson	c	1b	
Curtis Harris (Popeye)		rf	2b
Robert Harris		of	
David Harvey (Bill)		p	
Carl Howard		of	
Bertrum Hunter	p		
Norman Jackson (Jelly)		ss	
William Johnson (Judy)	3b		
Harry Kincannon		p	
Leroy Matlock	p		
Leroy Paige (Satchel)		p	
Clarence Palm (Spoony)		c	
Andrew Patterson (Pat)	2b		
Bill Perkins		c	
Sam Streeter		p	
Olan Taylor (Jelly)		p	
Irving Vincent (Lefty)		p	
Chester Williams	ss		

1936

NNL All-Stars (Winter)

Player	1	2	3
Lloyd Bassett (Pepper)	c		
James Bell (Cool Papa)	cf		
Oscar Charleston	1b		
Bob Griffith	p		
David Harvey (Bill)	p		
Leroy Morney	ss		
Bill Perkins	rf	c	
Felton Snow	3b		
Jud Wilson	2b		
Burnis Wright (Bill)	lf		

Bacharach Giants

Player	1	2	3
Paul Arnold		of	
Marvin Barker		of	
Gene Benson	cf		
Alex Brooks		of	
Chester Buchanan (Buck)	p		
Knowlington Burbage (Buddy)	lf		
Leroy Clayton (Zack)	1b		
Earl Davis (Hawk)	2b		
Paul Dixon	rf		

Player	1	2	3
Tom Dixon	c		
? Garrett		lf	
? Getty		c	
Frank Holmes		p	
? Jackson		p	
Larnie Jordan	ss		
Obie Lackey	3b		
Sarah Roberts (Mutt)		p	
Kenneth Robinson		3b	
Bill Sadler		ss	
J. White		p	
Bill Yancey		ss	

Birmingham Black Barons

Player	1	2	3
Fred Bankhead	ss		
Harry Barnes	c		
? Brewton	p		
James Canada	1b		
Benny Fields	cf		
? Hollins	p		
Carl Howard	lf		
? Kimbroe		c	
Dewitt Owens	2b		
Armand Tyson		c	
David Whatley	rf		
Parnell Woods	3b		

Brooklyn Royal Giants

Player	1	2	3
Johnny Albertson		ss	
John Beckwith		1b	
? Berger		utl	
George Britt (Chippy)		c	3b
Curtis Henderson	ss	2b	
Crush Holloway	lf		
Robert Johnson (Bob)	3b	of	
James Leonard (Bobo)		of	
Joseph Lewis	c		
Elbert Melton		of	
Ted Page	rf		
Dick Redding (Cannonball)		p	
Orville Riggins	2b		
Ed Rile	1b	p	
Otis Starks	p		
Peter Washington	cf		
Chaney White		of	
Roy Williams	p		

Chicago American Giants

Player	1	2	3
Richard Byas (Subby)	c		
Willie Cornelius (Sug)	p		
Norman Cross		p	
Kermit Dial	2b	rf	
Oland Dials (Lou)		of	
Herman Dunlop	rf	cf	
? Ivory		1b	
A. Jackson (Matthew)		ss	
Livingston James (Winky)		ss	
Floyd Kranson	p		
? LeBeaux	ss		
Emory Long (Bang)		2b	3b
? McCall (Butch)	1b		
Melvin Powell (Putt)	p	of	
? Prince		3b	
Alex Radcliff	3b		
Wilson Redus	lf		
Henry Strong		ss	
Dan Thomas		p	of
Ted Trent	p		
James Wilson		of	
Edward Young (Pep)		c	

Player	1	2	3
Cincinnati Tigers			
Carl Glass			M
Rainey Bibbs	2b		
Marlin Carter (Mel)	3b	ss	
Wolf Childers		c	
Howard Easterling		3b	
Frank Edwards		ss	utl
A. Gibson (Jerry)		of	p
J. Harris (Sonny)		of	
Virgil Harris	p	of	
Jess Houston	p		
Josh Johnson	c		
Arthur Maddox		p	
Jasper Miller		p	
Charlie Miller		inf	
Porter Moss	p		
Al Murphy		p	
Harvey Peterson	rf	of	
Miller Rice		of	
Cornelius Robinson (Neil)	lf	of	
Ewing Russell		c	
? Russell		ss	3b
Bill Simms	cf	of	
? Smith (Turkey)		c	
Olan Taylor (Jelly)	1b		
Dan Tye		3b	
Homestead Grays			
Cumberland Posey (Cum)			M
Lloyd Bassett (Pepper)		c	
Jerry Benjamin	cf		
Jimmy Binder		3b	
Fox Blavis		3b	
Ray Brown	p	of	
Walter Burch		inf	
Matthew Carlisle (Lick)	2b	ss	3b
Herbert Dixon (Rap)		of	
Tommy Dukes	c		
Louis Dula		p	rf
Willie Gisentaner (Lefty)		p	rf

Player	1	2	3
Vic Harris	lf		
Curtis Henderson		ss	
Norman Jackson (Jelly)	ss		
Walter Leonard (Buck)	1b		
Tom Parker	p		
? Perry		1b	2b
Henry Spearman		3b	
Joe Strong		p	of
John Terry		2b	
Arnold Waite		p	
Edsall Walker	p		
Roy Welmaker		p	
Kansas City Monarchs			
Andrew Cooper (Andy)	p		M
Wilber Rogan (Bullet Joe)	1b		M
Newton Allen (Newt)	2b		
John Paul Berry		p	
E. Brooks		p	
Willard Brown	ss		
Eddie Dwight	cf		
Harry Else	c		
Chick Harris (Popsickle)		of	
Curtis Harris (Popeye)	1b		
Floyd Kranson		p	
Robert Madison		p	
Eldridge Mayweather (Ed)		1b	
Henry Milton	lf		
Harold Morris		p	
Leroy Paige (Satchel)		p	
Andrew Patterson (Pat)	3b		
Leroy Taylor	rf		
Walter Thomas		p	
Ted Trent		p	
Quincy Trouppe		of	c
Jim Webster (Double Duty)	p	c	
Woodrow Wilson (Lefty)		p	
Memphis Red Sox			
? Allen		ss	

Player	1	2	3
Roosevelt Cox		c	
Charles Decker (Dusty)	3b	2b	
? Easley	lf		
Bill Evans		of	
Felix Evans (Chin)		p	
Jimmy Everett	p		
Jimmy Ford	2b		
Eppie Hampton		p	c
Claude Haslett	p		
Otis Henry	1b		
Herman Howard (Red)	p		
? Humphries	rf		
Livingston James (Winky)	ss		
William Rogers (Nat)		of	
Willie Sanders		p	
Robert Smith	c	1b	
Joe Ware	cf		
New York Black Yankees			
Robert Clarke	c		M
Ramiro Ramirez			M
Marvin Barker	cf		
Alex Brooks		of	
Barney Brown	p		
Willie Burns		p	
Walter Cannady (Rev)	3b	ss	
? Collins (Sonny)		p	
Roosevelt Davis (Rosey)	p		
Oland Dials (Lou)		of	1b
George Giles	1b		
Bill Holland	p		
Clarence Jenkins (Fats)	lf		
Henry McHenry		p	
Clarence Palm (Spoony)		c	
Cornelius Rector (Connie)		p	
George Scales	2b		
Richard Seay (Dick)		2b	ss
Paul Stephens (Jake)	ss		
Jim Williams	rf		

1936 New York Black Yankees. Back row L to R: George Giles, Jim Williams, Willie Burns, Henry McHenry, Rev Cannady, George Scales, Barney Brown, and Robert Clarke. Front row L to R: Clarence Palm, Rosey Davis, Bill Holland, Fats Jenkins, Marvin Barker, and Jake Stephens.
Dick Clark

New York Cubans

Player	1	2	3
Thomas Albright		p	
Raul Alvarez		p	of
Herman Andrews (Jabo)		lf	
Chet Brewer	p		
Marceline Correra (Cho Cho)		2b	ss
Felix Delgado (Felle)		of	
Edolfo Diaz (Yo Yo)		p	
Martin Dihigo		p	of
Frank Duncan	c		
Jose Fernandez		c	
Manuel Garcia (Cocaina)		1b	2b
Cando Lopez		cf	
Horacio Martinez (Rabbit)	2b	ss	
Armando Massip		1b	
Eddie Powell		c	
Alex Radcliff		3b	
? Rodriquez		3b	
Julio Rojo		c	1b
Lazaro Salazar	lf	cf	p
Anastacio Santaella (Tacho)	ss	of	2b
Miguel L. Solis		2b	
Clyde Spearman	rf		
John Stanley (Neck)		p	
Johnny Taylor	p		
C. Thomas		c	
C. Thomas		c	
Dave Thomas	1b		
Clint Thomas		of	
Luis Tiant, Sr.	p		
Chaney White	cf		

Newark Eagles

Player	1	2	3
William Bell	p		M
Charles Beverly		p	
Fred Burnett (Tex)		c	
Thad Christopher	cf	of	
? Crawford		ss	
Ray Dandridge		3b	
Leon Day	p		
Herbert Dixon (Rap)		of	
? Duffey		3b	
Robert Evans	p		
Jimmy Everett		p	
John Hayes	c		
Bill Jackman		p	
Melvin Markham		p	
Terris McDuffie	p		
James Moore (Red)		1b	
Barney Morris		p	
William Nicholas		p	
Ted Page		cf	
Leonard Pearson (Lennie)		of	
Leon Ruffin		c	
Henry Spearman		3b	
Ed Stone	lf	of	
George Suttles (Mule)	1b	lf	
Clint Thomas	rf	of	
? Walsh		p	
Willie Wells	ss		
Eugene White		3b	inf
Harry Williams	2b		

Philadelphia Stars

Player	1	2	3
Charles Beverly		p	
Larry Brown	c		
Ralph Burgin		3b	
William Casey (Mickey)		c	
Dewey Creacy	3b		
Lloyd Davenport	lf	of	

Pittsburgh Crawfords

Player	1	2	3
Joseph Dunn (Jake)	ss	2b	lf
Rube Ellis (Rocky)	p		
Bertrum Hunter		p	
Stuart Jones (Slim)	p		
Obie Lackey		inf	
William Marshall (Jack)	2b		
Webster McDonald	p		
Ted Page		of	
Roy Parnell (Red)	rf	of	
? Scott		of	1b
Richard Seay (Dick)		2b	
Norman Stearnes (Turkey)	cf	of	
Samuel Thompson (Sad Sam)		p	
Jud Wilson	1b		
Bill Yancey		ss	2b
Laymon Yokeley		p	

Pittsburgh Crawfords

Player	1	2	3
Sam Bankhead	lf	cf	
James Bell (Cool Papa)	cf		
Ralph Burgin		rf	
Ernest Carter (Spoon)		p	
Paul Carter		p	
Oscar Charleston		1b	
Jimmy Crutchfield	rf	lf	
Ishkooda Dunkin		p	
Willie Foster		p	
Josh Gibson	c		
David Harvey (Bill)		p	
Bertrum Hunter		p	
William Johnson (Judy)	3b		
Harry Kincannon		p	
Rufus Lewis		p	
Leroy Matlock	p		
Pete McQueen		of	
Leroy Paige (Satchel)	p		
Bill Perkins		c	
Richard Seay (Dick)	2b		
Theolic Smith		p	
Ed Stone		rf	
Sam Streeter	p		
John Washington		1b	2b
Chester Williams	ss		
Harry Williams	1b	lf	
S. Williams		3b	
Emmett Wilson		of	

St. Louis Stars

Player	1	2	3
Jesse Askew	ss		
Andy Childs	2b		
Frank Edwards	3b	c	
Ben Henderson	p		
Clarence Palm (Spoony)	c		
Al Pinkston	1b		
? Pollard	cf		
Eddie Powell		c	
William Robinson (Bobby)		3b	
? Russell	lf		
? Simerson	p		
Fred Smith	p	rf	
William Summerall		p	

Washington Elite Giants

Player	1	2	3
Candy Jim Taylor			M
Jimmy Binder	ss	3b	
Bill Byrd	p		
Thad Christopher		of	
Homer Curry (Goose)	lf	of	
Thomas Glover		p	
Robert Griffith	p		

Player	1	2	3
Frank Holmes		p	
Sammy T. Hughes	2b		
Wayman Longley (Red)		2b	c
Raleigh Mackey (Biz)	c		
Leroy Morney		ss	2b
Andrew Porter	p		
Felton Snow	3b	ss	2b
Frank Stewart		p	
Jesse Walker (Hoss)		ss	3b
Jim West	1b		
Nish Williams		c	
Jim Willis		p	
Burnis Wright (Bill)	cf	of	
Zollie Wright	rf	of	

1937

Atlanta Black Crackers

Player	1	2	3
Ormond Sampson	ss		M
? Burke (Ping)	p		
W.T. Cooper (Bill)	c		
Spencer Davis (Babe)	lf	of	
Oscar Glenn	3b		
James Greene (Joe)		c	
? Hadley (Red)	rf	of	
Frank Hughes		p	
James Kemp	2b		
William Pelham (Don)	cf		
James Reese	p		
Jack Thornton	1b		

Birmingham Black Barons

Player	1	2	3
A.M. Walker			M
? Bames		c	
Fred Bankhead	2b		
? Barnes	p		
Harry Barnes		c	
Charles Bruton (Jack)		p	1b
James Canada	1b		
Elmer Carter (Willie)		1b	
Melvin Coleman	ss	c	
? Eatmon		p	
? Fellows		p	
Willie Ferrell (Truehart)		p	
Ben Henderson		p	
Herman Howard (Red)		p	of
Clarence Lamar		ss	
A.D. Lewis		1b	
Alonzo Mitchell (Hooks)		p	
Al Murphy		p	
Dewitt Owens	rf	of	2b
? Pervis	p		
? Quicksley		lf	
John Ray	lf	of	
C. Scott	p		
? Sullivan		p	
David Whatley	cf	of	
Nish Williams		c	of
Parnell Woods	3b	2b	

Chicago American Giants

Player	1	2	3
Candy Jim Taylor			M
Tobias Barnes		3b	
Clifford Blackman		p	
Timothy Bond	ss	3b	
Richard Byas (Subby)	c		
Leroy Clayton (Zack)	1b		
Willie Cornelius (Sug)	p		
Herman Dunlop	rf	cf	

Player	1	2	3
Willie Foster	p		
Luther Gillard		1b	of
Paul Hardy		c	
Bill Hoskins		of	
Joe Lillard		p	
William Marshall (Jack)	2b	c	of
? McCall (Butch)		1b	
Jack Miles		cf	
Melvin Powell (Putt)		p	of
Alex Radcliff	3b	ss	
Wilson Redus	lf		
Ernest Smith		c	
Joe Sparks		2b	lf
Norman Stearnes (Turkey)		of	
Roosevelt Tate (Speed)		cf	rf
Dan Thomas	p		
Ted Trent	p		

Cincinnati Tigers

Player	1	2	3
Ted Radcliffe (Double Duty)	c	p	of M
? Bagley		c	
? Balley		p	
Rainey Bibbs	ss	2b	
Frank Bradley		p	2b
Eugene Bremmer	p		
Marlin Carter (Mel)	2b	3b	
Lloyd Davenport	cf	rf	
Howard Easterling	3b	ss	
Frank Edwards		ss	
J. Harris (Sonny)		2b	
Virgil Harris	rf	of	
Jess Houston	p		
William Hudson		p	1b
Cowan Hyde (Bubber)		of	
Willie Jefferson		p	
Josh Johnson		c	
Hurley McNair		of	
Porter Moss	p		
? Moten		c	
Roy Partlow		p	
Ernest Payne (Rusty)		lf	of
Harvey Peterson		of	
Miller Rice		of	
Cornelius Robinson (Neil)	lf		
Bill Simms		of	
Roosevelt Tate (Speed)		of	
Olan Taylor (Jelly)	1b		

Detroit Stars

Player	1	2	3
Larry Bleach		2b	
Roosevelt Cox	3b	ss	2b
Albert Davis	p		
Charles Decker (Dusty)		2b	
Kermit Dial		of	inf
Alphonse Dunn (Blue)	1b		
E. Hale (Red)	ss		
Sam Hill		of	
Bill Hoskins		of	
Charles House (Red)		3b	2b
Earl Jones		inf	
Charley Justice	p	of	
Jimmy McIntosh		c	
Dempsey Miller (Dimp)		p	
Sherley Petway (Charlie)		c	
Edward Salters		rf	
Bob Saunders		inf	
Norman Stearnes (Turkey)	cf		
? Stiles		of	
J. Thomas		ss	
Orel Thomas (Dean)		p	

Player	1	2	3
Walter Thomas		p	
Ely Underwood	lf	rf	
Ray Underwood		p	
Jim Webster (Double Duty)	p	c	
Felton Wilson		c	

Homestead Grays

Player	1	2	3
Clifford Allen		p	
Lloyd Bassett (Pepper)		c	
Jerry Benjamin	cf		
Ray Brown	p	of	3b
Matthew Carlisle (Lick)	2b		
Tommy Dukes		c	1b
Louis Dula		p	
Josh Gibson	c		
Vic Harris	lf	1b	
Norman Jackson (Jelly)	ss		
Walter Leonard (Buck)	1b		
Tom Parker	p		
Jose Perez	3b	ss	
Henry Spearman		3b	
Joe Strong		p	
Arnold Waite		p	
Edsall Walker	p		
George Walker		p	
Roy Welmaker		p	
James Williams (Jim)	rf	of	

Indianapolis Athletics

Player	1	2	3
? Benning		2b	
Chuck Bowen		of	
Ossie Brown		p	
Charles Burke		ss	of
Andy Childs	2b		
Howard Cook (Johnny)		p	
Homer Curry (Goose)		of	
? Dunbar (Vet)	c	inf	
? Floyd		p	
William Gill		1b	
Bob Graves	rf	p	
Perry Hall		3b	of
Jack Hannibal		p	
Claude Haslett	p		
Otis Henry	lf		
Herman Howard (Red)	p		
Frank Hughes		p	
Cowan Hyde (Bubber)		rf	lf
? Legrove		of	
Emory Long (Bang)	3b	of	
Robert Madison		p	
? McCall (Butch)		1b	
Ned Miller		1b	
John Morgan		of	
Al Murphy		p	
Tom Parker	p		
John Reed		p	
Joseph Royall (John)		p	
? Seagraves		of	
T.R. Strong (Ted)	cf	ss	p
Casey Walker		c	

Kansas City Monarchs

Player	1	2	3
Andrew Cooper (Andy)	p		M
Newton Allen (Newt)	2b		
Ed Barnes		p	
Frank Bradley		p	
Eugene Bremmer		p	
Chet Brewer	p		
Jesse Brooks	3b		
Willard Brown	cf	lf	ss

Player	1	2	3
? Clark			rf
Jesse Douglas		2b	
Frank Duncan	c		
Eddie Dwight	rf	cf	
Harry Else		c	
Bryon Johnson (Mex)	ss		
Floyd Kranson		p	
John Markham	p		
Dave Mays		of	
Eldridge Mayweather (Ed)	1b	3b	
Henry McHenry		p	
Henry Milton	lf	rf	
Wilber Rogan (Bullet Joe)		1b	of
Bill Simms		rf	cf
Hilton Smith	p		
Theodore Stockard		2b	
T.R. Strong (Ted)		inf	of
Woodrow Wilson (Lefty)		p	

Memphis Red Sox

Player	1	2	3
Frank Johnson			M
Emery Adams (Ace)	p		
Allen Bryant (Lefty)	p		
R.B. Bryant	ss		
Samuel Burris		p	
Homer Curry (Goose)	cf		
Felix Evans (Chin)		p	
Jimmy Ford	3b	2b	
Luther Gillard		1b	of
Thomas Glover	p		
Eppie Hampton		c	
Floyd Kranson		p	
Wayman Longley (Red)	2b	of	
Granville Lyons	1b		
Robert Madison		p	of
Zearlee Maxwell		3b	
? Mays		p	
Luther McDonald (Vet)		p	
John Morgan		rf	
John O'Neil (Buck)		1b	
William Rogers (Nat)	lf		
Bob Saunders		ss	
Robert Smith		c	3b
? Stedgrass		p	
Zachary Taylor		p	
Raymond Taylor	c		
Woodrow Wilson (Lefty)		p	

New York Black Yankees

Player	1	2	3
Johnny Albertson		ss	
? Allison		ss	
Norman Baker		p	
Lamb Barbee (Bud)		1b	p
Marvin Barker	rf	cf	p
William Barnes (Jimmy)		p	
Barney Brown		p	of
Ralph Burgin		3b	ss
Walter Cannady (Rev)	2b	3b	
Robert Clarke	c		
Alex Crumbley		of	
Roosevelt Davis (Rosey)		p	
George Giles	1b		
Curtis Henderson	3b	ss	
Bill Holland	p		
Clarence Jenkins (Fats)	lf		
Harry Kincannon	p	of	
? Kinson			
Eddie Powell		c	
John Stanley (Neck)	p		
Paul Stephens (Jake)	ss	2b	

Player	1	2	3
Clint Thomas	cf	rf	
Ray Williams		p	
Newark Eagles			
Dick Lundy	2b	ss	M
Norman Baker		p	
William Bell		p	
Ulysses Brown (Buster)		c	
Fred Burnett (Tex)		c	
Jimmy Crutchfield	cf		
Ray Dandridge	3b		
Leon Day	p		
Robert Evans	p		
Jonas Gaines		p	
Cleveland Good		p	
John Hayes	c		
John Humes		p	
Monte Irvin		ss	
Terris McDuffie	p		
James Moore (Red)		1b	3b
? Owens		p	
Leonard Pearson (Lennie)	lf	1b	
Richard Seay (Dick)	2b		
Ed Stone	rf		
George Suttles (Mule)	1b	of	
Willie Wells	ss		
John Wright		p	
Philadelphia Stars			
Gene Benson	cf		
Barney Brown		p	
Larry Brown	c		
William Casey (Mickey)		c	
Dewey Creacy	3b		
Paul Dixon		rf	
Joseph Dunn (Jake)	ss	2b	of
Rube Ellis (Rocky)	p		
Roy Harding		p	
Curtis Harris (Popeye)	2b	inf	of
A. Harvey		ss	
Bill Holland		p	

Player	1	2	3
Bertrum Hunter		p	
Stuart Jones (Slim)	p		
Ernest Jones (Mint)		1b	
Obie Lackey		inf	
Webster McDonald	p		
Jim Missouri		p	
Albert Overton		p	
Ted Page		rf	
Roy Parnell (Red)	lf		
? Rauze			
Sarah Roberts (Mutt)		p	
Ed Stone		rf	
? Stumm			
Samuel Thompson (Sad Sam)		p	
Jim Williams		of	
Walter Williams			
Jud Wilson	1b	3b	
Laymon Yokeley		p	
Pittsburgh Crawfords			
Herman Andrews (Jabo)		lf	
Lloyd Bassett (Pepper)	c		
Jimmy Binder		3b	
James Brown		p	
Knowlington Burbage (Buddy)		rf	
? Butler		3b	
Marion Cain (Sugar)		p	
Oscar Charleston	1b		
James Clarkson (Bus)		inf	
Roosevelt Davis (Rosey)		p	
Herbert Dixon (Rap)		lf	
Ishkooda Dunkin		p	
? Eacy		p	
Claude Evans		lf	
David Harvey (Bill)	p		
Rufus Lewis		p	
Barney Morris		p	
John Morton		of	
Andrew Patterson (Pat)		2b	
Leon Ruffin		c	
Pete Smith	cf		

Player	1	2	3
Theolic Smith	p		
Henry Spearman	3b		
James Starks		1b	2b
John Washington		1b	of
Harry Williams		2b	
Chester Williams	ss		
Emmett Wilson		cf	
Dan Wilson	rf	2b	
Tom Young		c	
St. Louis Stars			
John Paul Berry		p	
? Bledsloe		of	
Ossie Brown		p	
William Carter		3b	
Elijah Chism (Eli)		3b	
William Davis	lf	of	
Bob Dean		p	
? Dillard			
Glenn Dixon	p	of	
Frank Edwards	c		
Felix Evans (Chin)		p	
Luther Gillard	1b		
Robert Griffin	p		
? Hardiman		p	
Johnathan Hill		of	p
Bill Hoskins		lf	of
Tommy Johnson		p	
Clarence Lamar		ss	
Lester Lockett		2b	
? Mays		p	
Jasper Miller		p	
Leroy Paige (Satchel)		p	
Leonard Pearson (Lennie)		rf	
? Phiffer		3b	
Curtis Reed		of	
John Reed	p		
Marshall Riddle		ss	
William Robinson (Bobby)		3b	
? Shropshire		c	
? Siebert		of	
Joe Sparks		2b	
? Thurman		1b	
William Walker		cf	
B. Williams		of	
Lemuel Williams		p	
Washington Elite Giants			
Augusta Benson		p	
Bill Byrd	p		
Jimmy Direaux		p	
Jonas Gaines		p	
Thomas Glover	p		
Robert Griffith		p	
Sammy T. Hughes	2b	3b	
Norman Jackson (Jelly)		ss	
Henry Kimbro	lf		
Raleigh Mackey (Biz)	c		
Leroy Morney	ss	3b	lf
Andrew Porter	p		
Harvey Smith		p	
Felton Snow	3b	p	
Arnold Waite		p	
Jesse Walker (Hoss)		ss	
Jim West	1b		
Nish Williams		c	
Willie Williams		p	
Jim Willis		p	
Burnis Wright (Bill)	cf		
Zollie Wright	rf		

Rafael Trujillo's great 1937 club. Standing L to R: Bill Perkins, Enrique Latiqua, Cool Papa Bell, Toni Costano, Josh Gibson, Rodolfo Fernandez, Bob Griffith, and Satchel Paige. Kneeling from the left: Lazaro Salazar, Tetelo Vargas, S. Alvarado, Silvio Garcia, Sam Bankhead, Harry Williams, and Perucho Cepeda (Orlando's dad).

Luiz Munoz Collection

Player	1	2	3

1938

Atlanta Black Crackers

Player	1	2	3
Nish Williams			M
? Bubbles	p		
Thomas Butts (Pee Wee)	ss		
James Canada	1b		
Marlin Carter (Mel)	3b		
James Cooper	p		
W.T. Cooper (Bill)	c		
Alex Crumbley	of		
Clarence Darden	3b		
Spencer Davis (Babe)	3b		
William Davis	of		
Eddie Lee Dixon	p		
Charlie Duncan	p		
Felix Evans (Chin)	p		
Bernard Fernandez	p		
Leonard Foster	inf		
Oscar Glenn	3b		
James Greene (Joe)	c		
? Hadley (Red)	of	c	
Charles Holliday	lf	rf	
Herman Howard (Red)	p		
James Kemp	2b		
Alonzo Mitchell (Hooks)	p		
James Moore (Red)	1b		
William Pelham (Don)	cf	of	ss
Edgar Pope	of		
John Reed	p		
Donald Reeves	rf	lf	
Ormond Sampson	ss		
? Shamberger			
Leo Sims	ss		
Sammy Thompson (Runt)	2b		

Bacharach Giants

Player	1	2	3
Clifford Allen	p		
Marion Cain (Sugar)	p		
Earl Davis (Hawk)	2b		
Tom Dixon	c		
Rick Johnson	lf		
H. Johnson	rf		
Larnie Jordan	ss		
Obie Lackey	3b		
Nathaniel Nix	p		
Bill Sadler	1b		
? Waters	cf		

Baltimore Elite Giants

Player	1	2	3
George Scales	2b	3b	M
Bill Byrd	p	of	
Roy Campanella	c		
Homer Curry (Goose)	p	of	
Jimmy Direaux	p		
Jimmy Ford	3b		
Jonas Gaines	p		
Thomas Glover	p		
Robert Griffith	p		
Bill Hoskins	lf		
Sammy T. Hughes	2b		
Henry Kimbro	rf		
Granville Lyons	of		
Raleigh Mackey (Biz)	c		
Andrew Porter	p		
Felton Snow	3b	ss	2b
Lonnie Summers	of		
Jesse Walker (Hoss)	ss		
Jim West	1b		
Willie Williams	p		

Player	1	2	3
Woodrow Wilson (Lefty)		p	
Burnis Wright (Bill)	cf		

Birmingham Black Barons

Player	1	2	3
Sam Crawford	p		M
William Dismukes (Dizzy)			M
Fred Bankhead	2b		
Harry Barnes		c	
Clifford Blackman	p		
Charles Bruton (Jack)	p		
Samuel Burris		p	
? Cephus (Goldie)	ss		
? Eatmon		p	
Bert Johnston		of	
Lester Lockett		ss	
? McCall (Butch)	1b		
Alonzo Mitchell (Hooks)		p	
? Osley		p	
Dewitt Owens	rf	cf	
Carl Smith	c		
? Thurston		p	
David Whatley	cf	rf	
B. Williams		of	1b
Parnell Woods	3b		

Chicago American Giants

Player	1	2	3
Candy Jim Taylor			M
Rainey Bibbs	2b	ss	3b
Richard Byas (Subby)	1b	c	
Willie Cornelius (Sug)	p		
? Davis		p	
Frank Duncan		c	
Herman Dunlop	rf		
Percy Forrest		p	
Luther Gillard		lf	
Billy Horne	ss		
Jess Houston	p		
Bill Johnson (Willie)		c	
Tommy Johnson		p	
Jack Miles		rf	
Alex Radcliff	3b		
Wilson Redus	lf		
John Reed		p	
Tommy Sampson		ss	
Bill Simms	cf		
Robert Smith		c	3b
Joe Sparks		2b	ss
Norman Stearnes (Turkey)		cf	
Ted Trent	p		
Edward Young (Pep)	c	of	1b

Homestead Grays

Player	1	2	3
Jerry Benjamin	cf		
Ray Brown	p	of	
Matthew Carlisle (Lick)	2b		
Tommy Dukes		c	3b
Louis Dula		p	of
Josh Gibson	c		
Jack Hannibal		p	
Vic Harris	lf		
Norman Jackson (Jelly)	ss		
Jack Johnson		3b	2b
Josh Johnson		c	
Obie Lackey		ss	
Walter Leonard (Buck)	1b		
Tom Parker	p	of	
Roy Partlow		p	
Henry Spearman		3b	
Edsall Walker	p		
George Walker		p	

Player	1	2	3
Roy Welmaker		p	
Harry Williams		rf	
James Williams (Jim)	rf		

House of David

Player	1	2	3
Ollie Boyd (Turk)	cf		
Maceo Breelove (Suitcase)	rf		
Worley Coleman (Wimpy)	lf		
Rowland Ewing (Monk)	1b		
C.D. Gatewood	p		
Albert McCray (Black Goo)	c		
Rogers Pierre	p		
Walmon Sampson (Steel Arm)	p		
Lester Saunders (Youngblood)	2b		
Theodore Stockard	3b		
Edward Williams (Froggie)	p		

Indianapolis ABCs

Player	1	2	3
Ted Alexander		p	
Alfred Armour (Buddy)	ss		
Jimmie Armstead		of	
Bill Bradford	rf		
Ossie Brown		p	
Walter Calhoun	p		
Andy Childs		2b	
Jack Hannibal		p	
Monroe Lockett		p	
Willie Lockett		of	
John Lyles	cf		
Frank McAllister (Chip)	p		
George Mitchell		p	
John Reed	p		
Marshall Riddle	2b		
William Robinson (Bobby)	3b		
Willie Lee Scott (Joe)		1b	
? Shepard		lf	
Harry Steel		p	
Frank Stewart		p	
T.R. Strong (Ted)	1b	lf	
Robert Taylor	c		
Quincy Trouppe	lf	c	

Jacksonville Red Caps

Player	1	2	3
Alonzo Mitchell (Hooks)	p	1b	M
Herbert Barnhill	c		
Dave Barnhill (Impo)		p	
Howard Cleveland (Duke)	cf	lf	
M.D. Cox (Alphonse)		p	
Robert Evans	p		
Willie Ferrell (Truehart)		p	
Albert Frazier	2b	3b	
Leo Henry (Preacher)	ss		
Leroy Holmes (Phillie)	ss		
Ernest Jones (Mint)	1b		
James Kemp	3b		
Joseph Royall (John)	rf		
Dan Thomas	lf		
Lacey Thomas		p	
Henry Turner		c	
John Williams (Big Boy)		of	

Kansas City Monarchs

Player	1	2	3
Andrew Cooper (Andy)	p		M
Packinghouse Adams		3b	
Newton Allen (Newt)	2b		
Ed Barnes		p	
? Betts		of	
Rainey Bibbs		3b	
? Blackburn		p	
Randolph Bowe (Bob)		p	

Player	1	2	3
Frank Bradley	p		
Willard Brown	cf	of	
Roosevelt Cox	3b	c	
Johnny Dawson		c	
Frank Duncan		c	
Harry Else	c		
Luther Gillard		of	
W. Jackson (Big Train)		p	
Bryon Johnson (Mex)	ss		
Floyd Kranson	p		
John Markham	p		
William Marshall (Jack)		2b	
Alfred Marvin		p	
Eldridge Mayweather (Ed)		of	1b
Henry Milton	rf	of	
C. Moses		p	
C.D. Mosley		p	
John O'Neil (Buck)	1b	rf	
Wilber Rogan (Bullet Joe)		p	
Bill Simms		of	
Hilton Smith		p	
Norman Stearnes (Turkey)		cf	
T.R. Strong (Ted)		ss	
Raymond Taylor		c	

Louisville Black Colonels

Player	1	2	3
Charles Decker (Dusty)	inf		M
Leonard Mitchell (Otto)			M
Walter Calhoun		p	
Joe Cates	ss		
W.M. Charter (Bill)	rf		
Howard Gay		3b	
George Harris	2b		
Willie Jordan	p		
A.D. Lewis	1b		
Charlie Looney		2b	
? Manuel (Clown)	lf		
Sam Warmack	cf		
Jim Webster (Double Duty)	c		

Memphis Red Sox

Player	1	2	3
Clifford Allen		p	
Eugene Bremmer		p	
Larry Brown	c		
Marlin Carter (Mel)	3b		
Andy Childs		2b	
Lloyd Davenport	lf	cf	
Eppie Hampton		c	p
Cowan Hyde (Bubber)	cf	lf	3b
Willie Jefferson	p		
Wayman Longley (Red)	2b	inf	of
Robert Madison		3b	of
Zearlee Maxwell		3b	2b
? Mays		p	
Porter Moss	p		
Ted Radcliffe (Double Duty)	p	c	
Cornelius Robinson (Neil)	ss	3b	
William Rogers (Nat)	rf	lf	
Robert Smith		c	
Olan Taylor (Jelly)	1b		
? Walker		ss	
David Whatley		of	
Woodrow Wilson (Lefty)		p	

New York Black Yankees

Player	1	2	3
Marvin Barker		of	3b
Alex Brooks	rf	3b	
Barney Brown	p		
Jesse Brown		p	of
Dave Campbell	2b	1b	

Player	1	2	3
Walter Cannady (Rev)	3b	ss	1b
Thad Christopher		of	c
Robert Clarke		c	
Homer Curry (Goose)		p	of
Roosevelt Davis (Rosey)		p	
Jesse Douglas		ss	
Bill Holland	p		
Clarence Jenkins (Fats)		lf	
Jimmy Johnson (Slim)		p	
Josh Johnson		c	
Terris McDuffie		p	
Leroy Miller (Flash)		ss	
Leroy Morney	ss	of	
Clarence Palm (Spoony)	c	of	
Jack Parker		3b	
Eddie Powell		c	
Cornelius Rector (Connie)		p	
Henry Spearman		3b	
John Stanley (Neck)	p		
James Starks	1b		
Clint Thomas		cf	
John Washington		1b	
Roy Williams		p	
Fred Wilson		of	
Zollie Wright		cf	of

New York Cubans

Player	1	2	3
Carlos Blanco	1b		
Ameal Brooks	rf		
Clemente Cabrera (Sungo)	3b		
Rafael Echevarria	2b		
Isidro Fabre		p	of
Jose Fernandez	c		
? Jiminez		p	
Pedro Lopez	cf		
Cando Lopez		of	
Cornelius Rector (Connie)	p		
Julio Rojo		c	
Silvino Ruiz	p		
Strico Valdez	ss		
Jose Vargas (Tetelo)	lf		

Newark Eagles

Player	1	2	3
Dick Lundy			M
Jesse Brown		p	
Ulysses Brown (Buster)		c	
Jimmy Crutchfield	cf		
Ray Dandridge	3b		
Roosevelt Davis (Rosey)		p	
Leon Day	p		
Felix Evans (Chin)		p	
Robert Evans	p		
John Hayes	c		
Jimmy Hill		p	
Monte Irvin		ss	
Lester Jackson		p	
Jimmy Johnson (Slim)		p	
Bert Johnston		3b	of
Maxwell Manning (Max)		p	
Francis Matthews (Fran)		1b	
Terris McDuffie	p		
Henry Miller		p	
Leonard Pearson (Lennie)	lf		
? Robinson		p	
Richard Seay (Dick)	2b		
William Smith		2b	ss
Charlie Smith		ss	
Ed Stone	rf		
George Suttles (Mule)	1b		

Player	1	2	3
Willie Wells	ss		
John Wright		p	

Philadelphia Stars

Player	1	2	3
Gene Benson	cf		
Larry Brown		c	
Charles Bruton (Jack)		p	
Ernest Carter (Spoon)		p	
Jimmy Carter		p	
Dewey Creacy	3b		
Paul Dixon		of	
Joseph Dunn (Jake)	ss		
Rube Ellis (Rocky)	p		
George Giles		1b	
Curtis Harris (Popeye)		inf	of
Ernest Jones (Mint)		1b	of
Stuart Jones (Slim)		p	
Webster McDonald	p		
Henry McHenry			p
Henry Miller			p
Jim Missouri			p
Roy Parnell (Red)	lf		
Andrew Patterson (Pat)	2b		
Bill Perkins	c		
Clyde Spearman	rf		
Samuel Thompson (Sad Sam)			p
Jud Wilson	1b	3b	

Pittsburgh Crawfords

Player	1	2	3
Sam Bankhead	cf		
Leroy Bass (Red)		c	
Lloyd Bassett (Pepper)	c		
James Bell (Cool Papa)		of	
Gene Benson		cf	
Marion Cain (Sugar)		p	
William Casey (Mickey)		c	
Oscar Charleston		1b	
James Clarkson (Bus)	2b	ss	3b
Alex Crumbley		cf	
George Giles	1b		
Napoleon Hairston	lf		
David Harvey (Bill)		p	
Clarence Jenkins (Fats)		lf	
Leroy Matlock		p	
Barney Morris	p		
Jack Parker		inf	
Henry Richardson		p	
Leon Ruffin		c	
Carl Smith		3b	
Harvey Smith		p	
Theolic Smith	p		
Johnny Taylor	p		
? Walton (Fuzzy)		rf	
John Washington		1b	
Chester Williams	ss		
Harry Williams	3b	2b	
Dan Wilson	rf	2b	3b
Emmett Wilson		rf	

Washington Black Senators

Player	1	2	3
Ben Taylor			M
Herman Andrews (Jabo)	lf		
George Britt (Chippy)		p	
Knowlington Burbage (Buddy)	cf		
Rowland Calhan		p	
William Casey (Mickey)	c		
? Clarke (Allie)	2b	of	c
Alex Crumbley		of	
? Finley			
Jimmy Ford		2b	

Player	1	2	3
Curtis Henderson		inf	
Frank Holmes	p		
Bill Hoskins		of	
Charlie Hughes	ss		
Al Johnson	p		
? Johnson		2b	
Harry Kincannon	p		
Emory Long (Bang)		3b	
Eddie Powell	c		
Henry Richardson	p		
Charley Roberts	p		
Tom Roberts (Speck)	p		
Bill Sadler		ss	
Charlie Smith		inf	
Henry Spearman	3b		
Dave Thomas	1b		
Clarence Williams		p	
Walter Williams		p	
Zollie Wright	rf		
Laymon Yokeley	p		

1939

Paige All-Stars (Winter)

Player	1	2	3
Newton Joseph (Newt)	3b		M
Ed Barnes		p	
Bill Brown		of	
Fred Daniels	rf		
Jesse Douglas	2b		
George Giles	1b		
Paul Hardy	c		
? Jackson (Big Train)		p	
Bryon Johnson (Mex)	ss		
Everett Marcell	lf		
John Markham	p		
Leroy Paige (Satchel)	p		
Norman Robinson (Bobby)	cf		
Henry Robinson (Frazier)		c	
Herb Souell	3b		
Leandy Young		of	

Bacharach Giants

Player	1	2	3
Tom Cain		of	
? Dick	p		
Tom Dixon	3b	c	
? Gamble	p		
Robert Johnson (Bob)	ss		
Bill Sadler	2b		
R. Smith	1b		
Pete Sunkett	rf	p	
? Washington	cf		
? Waters	lf		
Willie Wynn	c		

Baltimore Elite Giants

Player	1	2	3
Emery Adams (Ace)		p	
Ed Barnes		p	
? Beverie		3b	
Oscar Boone		c	
George Britt (Chippy)		p	c
Thomas Butts (Pee Wee)		ss	
Bill Byrd	p		
Roy Campanella	c		
Jimmy Direaux		p	
Tom Dixon		p	
Jonas Gaines	p		
Thomas Glover		p	
Crush Holloway		of	
Bill Hoskins	lf		

Player	1	2	3
Willie Hubert	p		
Sammy T. Hughes	2b		
Al Johnson	p		
John Johnson (Johnny)	p		
Henry Kimbro	cf	of	
Raleigh Mackey (Biz)		c	
Francis Matthews (Fran)		1b	
James Moore (Red)		1b	of
John Phillips	p		
Andrew Porter	p		
Carlos Rivero (Charley)		2b	3b
Sarah Roberts (Mutt)	p		
Norman Robinson (Bobby)		of	
Felton Snow	3b	2b	
Jesse Walker (Hoss)	ss		
Jim West	1b		
Clarence Williams		p	
G. Williams		utl	
M. Williams		p	
Willie Williams		p	
Jim Willis		p	
Burnis Wright (Bill)	rf	of	
Zollie Wright		of	

Baltimore Elite Giants (Winter)

Player	1	2	3
Lloyd Bassett (Pepper)	c		
Marlin Carter (Mel)	3b		
Joseph Dunn (Jake)	lf		
Thomas Glover	p		
David Harvey (Bill)	p		
Bill Hoskins	cf		
Terris McDuffie	p		
? Mitchell		p	
Lonnie Summers	rf		
John Terry	2b		
Jesse Walker (Hoss)	ss		
Jim West	1b		
John Wright	p		

Brooklyn Royal Giants

Player	1	2	3
Johnny Albertson		3b	
Lamb Barbee (Bud)		of	p
John Beckwith		utl	
? Berger		of	
Raymond Brown		c	
Chester Buchanan (Buck)	p		
Knowlington Burbage (Buddy)	cf		
Marion Cain (Sugar)	p		
Leroy Clayton (Zack)		1b	
Dewey Creacy	3b		
Willie Gisentaner (Lefty)		p	of
Clarence Jenkins (Fats)	lf		
Josh Johnson	rf	c	
Robert Johnson		of	
Larnie Jordan	ss		
Obie Lackey		c	of
Leroy Miller (Flash)		ss	
Nathaniel Nix	p		
Kenneth Robinson		2b	
Otis Starks	p	of	
Dave Thomas	1b		

Chicago American Giants

Player	1	2	3
Lloyd Bassett (Pepper)	c		
John Bissant		of	
Randolph Bowe (Bob)	p		
Richard Byas (Subby)	rf		
Willie Cornelius (Sug)	p		
Herman Dunlop		rf	
Luther Gillard		1b	

Player	1	2	3
E. Hale (Red)		ss	
Logan Hensley (Slap)	p		
Billy Horne	2b		
Jess Houston	p	2b	
Tommy Johnson	p		
Jack Miles		of	
Rogers Pierre	p		
Alex Radcliff	3b	p	
Wilson Redus	lf		
Donald Reeves		cf	
Charles Robinson		of	
Bill Simms	cf	p	
Ernest Smith		c	of
John Ford Smith		lf	p
Joe Sparks		ss	3b
Ted Trent	p		
Joe Williams		ss	
Lemuel Williams		p	
Edward Young (Pep)	1b		

Cleveland Bears

Player	1	2	3
Alonzo Mitchell (Hooks)	1b	p	M
Herman Andrews (Jabo)		p	
Herbert Barnhill		c	
Alonzo Boone		p	
Charles Bruton (Jack)		p	of
Walter Burch	c	of	
Howard Cleveland (Duke)	cf		
Ralph Cole	rf		
M.D. Cox (Alphonse)		p	
Willie Ferrell (Truehart)	p		
Albert Frazier	2b		
? Green (Honey)		p	
Leo Henry (Preacher)	p		
Leroy Holmes (Phillie)		ss	
Herman Howard (Red)		p	
Ernest Jones (Mint)		1b	
Clarence Lamar		ss	
John Lyles	ss	of	
Jack Moore		of	
Raymond Owens (Smokey)	p		
John Ray		of	
Joseph Royall (John)		lf	
Lacey Thomas		p	of
Henry Turner	lf	c	
? Tyler		of	
David Whatley		lf	
Parnell Woods	3b		

Homestead Grays

Player	1	2	3
Sam Bankhead		2b	ss
Jerry Benjamin	cf		
J. Brown		p	
Ray Brown	p	of	
Matthew Carlisle (Lick)		2b	
? Davis		of	
Tommy Dukes		c	
Louis Dula		p	
Willie Ferrell (Truehart)		p	
Wilmer Fields		p	
Robert Gaston		c	
Josh Gibson	c		
J.C. Hamilton (John)		p	
Vic Harris	lf		
Norman Jackson (Jelly)	ss	2b	
Josh Johnson		p	
Jack Johnson		3b	
Walter Leonard (Buck)	1b		
? Levitt		1b	
Tom Parker	p		

Player	1	2	3	Player	1	2	3	Player	1	2	3
Roy Partlow		p		C. Moses		p		Esterio Carabello	rf		
Tom Roberts (Speck)		p		John O'Neil (Buck)	1b			William Casey (Mickey)	c		
? Smith		p		Leroy Paige (Satchel)		p		Edolfo Diaz (Yo Yo)		p	
Henry Spearman	3b			Hilton Smith		p		Isidro Fabre		p	of
Edsall Walker		p		Norman Stearnes (Turkey)	cf			Jose Fernandez		c	
David Whatley		rf		T.R. Strong (Ted)	ss			Rodolfo Fernandez (Rudy)	p		
? Winthrop		rf		Elbert Treadway			p	Ramon Heredia	ss	2b	
				George Walker			p	Archie Jones		p	
Indianapolis ABCs				Jesse Williams (H.)		3b	of	Justo Lopez	1b		
Wilson Day (Connie)			M					Pedro Lopez	cf	lf	
Alonzo Mitchell (Hooks)	p		M	**Memphis Red Sox**				Vidal Lopez		p	
Herman Andrews (Jabo)	lf			Fred Bankhead	3b			Francisco Martinez	p		
Clifford Blackman		p		Warren Blackman		p		Autorio Mirable		c	of
Oscar Boone		c	1b	Frank Bradley		p	ss	Pedro Pages		1b	
Thomas Butts (Pee Wee)	ss			Eugene Bremmer		p		? Rabbar			
Jimmy Cockerham		1b		H. Brown		ss		Cornelius Rector (Connie)		p	1b
Spencer Davis (Babe)	3b			Larry Brown	c			Antonio Rodriquez	p		
William Davis		of		T.J. Brown (Tom)	ss			? Rodriquez		ss	
? Dejernett		p		W. Brown		ss		Silvino Ruiz		p	
Eddie Lee Dixon	p			Marlin Carter (Mel)		2b		Luis Tiant, Sr.		p	
P. Drew	p	of		Lloyd Davenport	rf			Armando Torres		p	
Felix Evans (Chin)	p			William Davis		lf	p	Strico Valdez	2b	ss	
Herman Howard (Red)		p		Cowan Hyde (Bubber)	2b			Jose Vargas (Tetelo)	lf	of	
R. Jefferson		3b		Willie Jefferson	p						
James Kemp		2b	ss	Wayman Longley (Red)		of	I	**Newark Eagles**			
Clarence Lamar	2b			Jasper Miller		p		Dick Lundy			M
James Moore (Red)	1b			Porter Moss	p			Charles Biot		of	
Clyde Nelson		3b		Ted Radcliffe (Double Duty)	p	c		Ulysses Brown (Buster)		c	
Dewitt Owens	cf	of	p	Cornelius Robinson (Neil)	cf			James Brown		p	
Donald Reeves	rf			William Rogers (Nat)		lf	cf	Jesse Brown		p	
John Ford Smith		p	of	Frank Ross		p		Haywood Cozart (Harry)		p	
B. Williams		of		Olan Taylor (Jelly)	1b			Leon Day	p		
Nish Williams	c			Woodrow Wilson (Lefty)		p		Joe Echols		of	
								Robert Evans		p	
Jacksonville Red Caps				**New York Black Yankees**				John Hayes	c		
Bernard Fernandez		p		Ted Alexander		p		Jimmy Hill	p		
Willie Ferrell (Truehart)	p			Marvin Barker		of		Willie Hubert		p	
Albert Frazier	2b			Charles Biot		of		Monte Irvin	3b	of	
Leo Henry (Preacher)	p			Alex Brooks	lf	of		? Johnson (Pee Wee)		2b	
Leroy Holmes (Phillie)	ss			Barney Brown	p			Raleigh Mackey (Biz)		c	1b
Ernest Jones (Mint)	1b			Charles Bruton (Jack)		p		Maxwell Manning (Max)	p		
Clarence Lamar		2b	ss	Ralph Burgin	ss	3b	of	Leonard Pearson (Lennie)	lf	3b	cf
Alonzo Mitchell (Hooks)	p			Marion Cain (Sugar)		p		Vernon Riddick		2b	ss
John Ray		of		Dave Campbell	2b	of		Leon Ruffin		c	
Joseph Royall (John)	cf			Walter Cannady (Rev)		inf		Richard Seay (Dick)	2b		
Andrew Sarvis		p		Robert Clarke		c		Ed Stone	rf	3b	
Dan Thomas	lf			Homer Curry (Goose)	cf	p		George Suttles (Mule)	1b	rf	
Henry Turner	c			Charles Davidson		p		Willie Wells	ss		
David Whatley		rf		Charlie Gordon		of		Walter Williams		p	
Parnell Woods	3b			Bill Holland	p			Fred Wilson	cf	lf	p
				Robert Johnson		of					
Kansas City Monarchs				Bill Johnson (Willie)		c		**Philadelphia Stars**			
Andrew Cooper (Andy)	p		M	Terris McDuffie		p		Gene Benson	cf		
Newton Allen (Newt)	2b			Leroy Miller (Flash)		ss	2b	Chet Brewer		p	
Rainey Bibbs	3b			Arthur Mitchell		inf		Ernest Carter (Spoon)		p	
Randolph Bowe (Bob)		p		Clarence Palm (Spoony)	c			Jimmy Carter		p	
Frank Bradley		p		John Parks		c	of	W.T. Cooper (Bill)		of	c
Willard Brown	lf			Robert Poinsette		of		Joseph Dunn (Jake)	ss	rf	
Lionel Decuir		c		Jim Richardson		p		? Duval			
James Greene (Joe)	c			Joshua Robinson		of		Rube Ellis (Rocky)	p		
Paul Hardy		c		Joseph Royall (John)		p		Tom Evans		p	
Willie Hutchinson		p		George Scales	3b			Curtis Harris (Popeye)	3b	2b	1b
W. Jackson (Big Train)		p		John Stanley (Neck)	p			Webster McDonald	p		
Bryon Johnson (Mex)	ss			John Washington	1b			Henry McHenry	p		
Floyd Kranson	p			Roy Williams		p		Henry Miller		p	
? Langram		2b	of	Alec Wilson		of		? Mincey		p	
Everett Marcell		c	p	Zollie Wright	rf			Jim Missouri		p	
John Markham	p							Leroy Morney		inf	
? Metz				**New York Cubans**				Clarence Palm (Spoony)		c	
Henry Milton	rf			Luis Arango	3b			Roy Parnell (Red)	lf		

Player	1	2	3
Andrew Patterson (Pat)		3b	inf
Bill Perkins	c		
Leon Ruffin		c	
Clyde Spearman	rf		
Samuel Thompson (Sad Sam)	p		
Roy Welmaker	p		
Jim West	1b		
Chester Williams		2b	ss
Jud Wilson	1b	3b	of

St. Louis Stars

Player	1	2	3
Alfred Armour (Buddy)	ss		
Jimmie Armstead		p	
Bill Bradford	rf		
Ossie Brown		p	
Walter Calhoun	p		
Bob Dean		p	
Jimmy Ford		inf	
Leslie Green (Chin)	cf		
John Lyles		3b	
Eldridge Mayweather (Ed)	1b		
Frank McAllister (Chip)		p	of
George Mitchell	p		
Marshall Riddle	2b		
Johnny Robinson			
William Robinson (Bobby)	3b		
Eugene Smith		p	
P. Smith		p	
Robert Smith		c	
Theolic Smith	p	of	
Robert Taylor	c		

Player	1	2	3
Quincy Trouppe		c	
Dan Wilson	lf		

Toledo Crawfords

Player	1	2	3
Oscar Charleston	1b		M
Sam Bankhead	cf		
Lloyd Bassett (Pepper)	c		
Jerry Benjamin		of	
? Boswell		p	
Ernest Carter (Spoon)		p	
? Chapel		of	
James Clarkson (Bus)	ss	lf	
Jimmy Crutchfield		of	
Tommy Dukes		c	
Napoleon Hairston	rf		
David Harvey (Bill)	p		
Curtis Henderson		2b	
? Henson		ss	
? Hill		3b	
Clarence Jenkins (Fats)	lf		
Jimmy Johnson (Slim)		p	
Jack Johnson		3b	
Harry Kincannon	p		
Leroy Morney		ss	
Barney Morris		p	
Tom Parker		p	
Robert Poinsette		p	
Leon Ruffin		c	
Theolic Smith		p	
William Spencer (Pee Wee)		c	3b
? Taylor (Shine)		of	

Player	1	2	3
Johnny Taylor		p	
Elbert Treadway		p	
Chester Williams		2b	ss
Harry Williams		3b	
Phil Williams (Pete)		2b	
James Williams (Jim)		3b	rf
Harvey Wilson		inf	
John Wright		p	

1940

Bacharach Giants

Player	1	2	3
Alex Brooks	3b		
Raymond Brown		c	
Chester Buchanan (Buck)	p		
T. Childs	2b		
Carl Childs		of	
Tom Dixon		c	
Rick Johnson		of	
? Mitchell		of	
John Reed	p		
? Russell		of	
Pete Sunkett	p	of	
Clarence Thorpe	1b	rf	
? Wilson	ss		

Baltimore Elite Giants

Player	1	2	3
Emery Adams (Ace)	p		
Jimmie Armstead		rf	
Tom Baker		p	

1939 Newark Eagles. Standing L to R: Monte Irvin, Fred Wilson, Lennie Pearson, Mule Suttles, Max Manning, Harry Cozart, Ed Stone, James Brown, and Johnny Hayes. Sitting: Leon Day, Dick Seay, Dick Lundy, Willie Wells, Leon Ruffin, Jimmy Hill, and Vernon Riddick.
Negro Leagues Baseball Museum

Player	1	2	3
Lamb Barbee (Bud)		p	
Ed Barnes		p	
Charles Biot		of	
Jesse Brown		p	
Thomas Butts (Pee Wee)	ss		
Bill Byrd	p		
Roy Campanella	c		
Homer Curry (Goose)		of	p
Roosevelt Davis (Rosey)		p	
Jonas Gaines		p	
Bill Hoskins	lf		
Willie Hubert	p		
Sammy T. Hughes	2b		
Al Johnson		p	
Henry Kimbro	cf		
James Moore (Red)	1b		
Nate Moreland		p	
Bill Perkins	c	of	
John Phillips		p	
James Reese		p	
Norman Robinson (Bobby)		rf	
George Scales	3b	ss	
Felton Snow	3b		
Samuel Thompson (Sad Sam)		p	
Clarence Williams		p	
Roy Williams		p	

Birmingham Black Barons

Player	1	2	3
Candy Jim Taylor			M
? Allen	of		
Herman Andrews (Jabo)	lf	rf	
Dan Bankhead	inf	p	
John Bissant	rf		
Oscar Boone	c		
Lyman Bostock, Sr.	1b		
Charles Bruton (Jack)	lf	3b	
Samuel Burris	p		
Rossie Dalton	c	inf	
Robert Fulcher	p		
? Gregory	p		
Paul Hardy	c		
Samuel Harris	p		
Albert Haywood (Buster)	c		
Herman Howard (Red)	p		
Gentry Jessup	p		
? Jones			
Fred McBride	3b	1b	
James Mickey	3b	ss	
Frank Moody	p		
Bill Nixon	rf		
Robert Pipkin (Lefty)	p		
Ulysses Redd	ss		
Tommy Sampson	2b		
Leo Saunders	ss	p	
Eddie Sneed	p		
Dan Thomas	cf		
Armand Tyson	3b		
Eddie Vines	1b	3b	
James Wilson	of		
Parnell Woods	3b		

Brooklyn Royal Giants

Player	1	2	3
Bill Anderson	p		
Ameal Brooks	c		
Ralph Burgin	rf		
Marion Cain (Sugar)	p		
Walter Cannady (Rev)	2b		
Dewey Creacy	3b		
A. Davis	ss		
? Shamberger	lf		

Player	1	2	3
Dave Thomas	1b		
? Wilkie	cf		

Chicago American Giants

Player	1	2	3
Timothy Bond	3b		
Randolph Bowe (Bob)	p		
Raymond Brown		c	
Ulysses Brown (Buster)		c	
Lloyd Bruce	p		
Walter Burch		c	
Willie Cornelius (Sug)	p		
Rossie Dalton		c	
Johnny Dawson		c	
Frank Duncan		c	
Harry Else		c	
Billy Horne	2b		
William Hudson	p	of	
Tommy Johnson	p		
? McKinley		p	
Henry Merchant	cf	p	
W. Miller		p	
Leroy Morney	ss		
Art Pennington		of	
Wilson Redus	lf		
Donald Reeves	rf		
Leo Saunders		ss	
Bill Simms		of	
Ernest Smith		c	
L. Smith		of	
Joe Sparks	3b	ss	
Archie Ware	1b		
Edward Young (Pep)	1b		

Cincinnati Buckeyes

Player	1	2	3
Kermit Dial		inf	
A. Gibson (Jerry)	p		
Ted Gibson		c	
Jack Johnson	3b		
Nora Listach	of		
Lester Lockett	ss		
? McFall	cf	of	
Jonas Miles		p	
Alfred Saylor	1b		
? Scott	of		
Howard Wallace	2b		

Cleveland Bears

Player	1	2	3
James Williams (Jim)	of		M
Ted Alexander		p	
Herbert Barnhill	c		
Ed Bordes	ss	inf	
? Broom		p	
Howard Cleveland (Duke)	rf		
Ralph Cole	lf		
Albert Frazier		2b	
Leo Henry (Preacher)	p		
Clarence Lamar		ss	
? Manuel (Clown)		of	
Alonzo Mitchell (Hooks)		p	
Raymond Owens (Smokey)	p		
John Ray	cf		
Walter Robinson (Skin Down)	3b		
Kenneth Robinson	1b		
Sam Sampson	2b	of	
Andrew Sarvis	p		
Henry Turner		c	of
Henry White	p		
Parnell Woods	3b		

Homestead Grays

Player	1	2	3
Leroy Bass (Red)		c	
Jerry Benjamin		cf	
George Britt (Chippy)		c	
Ray Brown	p	of	
Matthew Carlisle (Lick)	2b		
Howard Easterling	3b		
Rube Ellis (Rocky)	p		
Willie Ferrell (Truehart)		p	
Wilmer Fields		p	3b
Robert Gaston	c		
J.C. Hamilton (John)		p	
Vic Harris	lf		
Eugene Hicks (Jimmy)		p	
Norman Jackson (Jelly)	ss		
Jeff Jeffries		p	
Josh Johnson		c	
Walter Leonard (Buck)	1b		
Everett Marcell		c	
Alonzo Perry		p	
Tom Roberts (Speck)		p	
Willie Stevenson		p	
Edsall Walker	p		
David Whatley	rf		
Jud Wilson		3b	1b

Indianapolis Crawfords

Player	1	2	3
Oscar Charleston	1b		M
James Bell (Steel Arm)		c	
Rainey Bibbs		2b	
Ernest Carter (Spoon)	p		
James Clarkson (Bus)		ss	
Dick Craig		1b	
Joe Craig		of	
Jimmy Crutchfield	cf		
Tommy Dukes		c	
Luther Gillard		1b	
Napoleon Hairston	lf		
? Hall (Bad News)		3b	
Tom Harding	rf		
David Harvey (Bill)		p	
Curtis Henderson	ss	of	
Clifford Johnson (Connie)		p	
Jimmy Johnson (Slim)	p		
Steve Keyes (Zeke)	p		
? Norman (Bud)		p	
Dewitt Owens		of	
Ernest Payne (Rusty)		of	
Jimmy Reynolds	3b		
? Shamberger		ss	
John Ford Smith	p	1b	
William Spencer (Pee Wee)	c		
? Turner (Lefty)		1b	
James Wilson	2b	of	
Russell Wise		1b	
John Wright	p		

Kansas City Monarchs

Player	1	2	3
Andrew Cooper (Andy)	p		M
Newton Allen (Newt)		2b	
V. Barnes		of	
Rainey Bibbs		2b	
Frank Bradley		p	
Chet Brewer		p	
Willard Brown		of	
Allen Bryant (Lefty)		p	
Lionel Decuir		c	
Jesse Douglas		2b	
James Greene (Joe)	c		
Clifford Johnson (Connie)		p	

Player	1	2	3
Bryon Johnson (Mex)		ss	
Floyd Kranson		p	
John Markham	p		
Jack Matchett		p	
Booker McDaniels		lf	
Henry Milton	rf		
C. Moses		p	
John O'Neil (Buck)	1b		
Leroy Paige (Satchel)	p		
Hilton Smith	p		
Herb Souell	3b		
Norman Stearnes (Turkey)	cf		
Elbert Treadway		p	
George Walker		p	
Jesse Williams (H.)	ss		
Leandy Young		of	

Memphis Red Sox

Player	1	2	3
Fred Bankhead	2b		
Augusta Benson		p	
Steve Boone		p	
Bill Bradford		of	
Eugene Bremmer		p	
Larry Brown	c		
T.J. Brown (Tom)	ss		
Marlin Carter (Mel)		3b	
William Davis	lf		
Johnny Dawson		c	
Jim Dumas	p		
Felix Evans (Chin)		p	
Leslie Green (Chin)		rf	
Willie Hutchinson		p	
Cowan Hyde (Bubber)		of	
W. Jackson (Big Train)	p		
Clinton Jones (Casey)		c	
Wayman Longley (Red)	rf		
Verdell Mathis (Lefty)		cf	of
Fred McDaniels		of	
Jasper Miller	p		
? Nears (Red)	c		
? Newman	p		
Alex Radcliff	3b		
Ted Radcliffe (Double Duty)	c		
Cornelius Robinson (Neil)	3b	lf	cf
William Rogers (Nat)	of		
Bill Savage (Junior)	p		
Robert Sharpe	p		
Frank Stewart	p		
William Summerall	p		
Olan Taylor (Jelly)	1b		
Jesse Warren		3b	
Willie Wells	ss		
Woodrow Wilson (Lefty)	p		

N.O.-St. Louis Stars

Player	1	2	3
George Mitchell	p		M
Alfred Armour (Buddy)	ss	rf	
Bradford Bennett	rf	lf	
Charles Boone (Lefty)	p		
Herbert Bracken (Doc)		p	
Bill Bradford		of	
John Britton		3b	
Charles Bruton (Jack)	p		
Walter Burch	c		
Walter Calhoun	p		
Bob Dean		p	
Charlie Duncan	p		
Jimmy Ford	2b	ss	
Leslie Green (Chin)	lf	cf	
John Lyles	cf	3b	

Player	1	2	3
Eldridge Mayweather (Ed)	1b		
Frank McAllister (Chip)	p		
? Oakley		p	
Marshall Riddle		2b	
William Robinson (Bobby)	3b		
Eugene Smith		p	
Robert Smith	c		
Leroy Sutton		p	
Robert Taylor		c	
Lafayette Washington (Fay)		p	
Dan Wilson		cf	

New York Black Yankees

Player	1	2	3
Fred Burnett (Tex)			M
Lamb Barbee (Bud)	p		
Marvin Barker		of	2b
Bill Bea		of	
Charles Biot	lf	cf	
Jesse Brown		p	
Robert Clarke		c	
Homer Curry (Goose)	cf	lf	
Roy Debran		of	
Robert Evans		p	
John Hawkins		ss	
John Hayes		c	
Bill Holland	p		
Lester Jackson		p	
Robert Johnson		of	
Leroy Miller (Flash)	2b		
Richard Seay (Dick)		2b	
Henry Spearman	3b		
John Stanley (Neck)	p		
James Starks		1b	of
Jesse Walker (Hoss)	ss		
John Washington	1b	2b	
James Williams (Jim)		of	
Roy Williams		p	
Zollie Wright	rf		

New York Cubans

Player	1	2	3
Russell Awkard	rf		
Clemente Cabrera (Sungo)	2b		
Alfred Carter		of	
William Casey (Mickey)	c		
Francisco Coimbre (Pancho)	cf	rf	
Alejandro Crespo (Alex)	lf		
Jose Fernandez		c	
Jose Figueroa (Tito)		p	
Silvio Garcia		ss	2b
? Gilbert		1b	
Juan Guilbe		p	
Ramon Heredia	3b		
Carranza Howard		p	
? Juillo	p		
Rogelio Linares	1b		
Horacio Martinez (Rabbit)	ss		
Autorio Mirable		c	
Silvino Ruiz	p		
? Sigenero		p	
Johnny Taylor	p		
Luis Tiant, Sr.	p		

Newark Eagles

Player	1	2	3
Dick Lundy			M
Spencer Alexander		of	
Ernest Carter (Spoon)		p	
James Clarkson (Bus)	ss		
Daltie Cooper		p	
Johnny Davis		p	
Jimmy Everett		p	

Player	1	2	3
Jimmy Hill	p		
Lenial Hooker (Len)	p		
Monte Irvin	cf	ss	
Clarence Israel (Pint)	2b	3b	
Raleigh Mackey (Biz)	c		
Maxwell Manning (Max)	p		
Francis Matthews (Fran)	1b		
? Mincey		p	
Charles Parks		c	
Leonard Pearson (Lennie)	3b	cf	
Richard Seay (Dick)		2b	
Leon Stewart		p	
Ed Stone	rf		
George Suttles (Mule)	lf	of	1b
Jack Walker		p	

Philadelphia Stars

Player	1	2	3
Webster McDonald	p		M
Bill Bea		rf	
Gene Benson	cf		
Charles Biot		1b	
Chester Buchanan (Buck)	p		
Knowlington Burbage (Buddy)		of	
Dave Campbell		2b	3b
Alfred Carter		ss	
W.T. Cooper (Bill)		c	
James Cooper		p	
? Dean		of	
Mahlon Duckett	3b		
Joseph Dunn (Jake)	ss	inf	of
Rube Ellis (Rocky)	p	of	
? Green		2b	
Curtis Harris (Popeye)	2b	3b	
John W. Hayes		ss	2b
Clarence Jenkins (Fats)		rf	
Ralph Johnson		p	
Archie Jones		p	
Larnie Jordan		ss	
L.B. Lawson (Flash)		p	
Carl Logan		inf	
Emory Long (Bang)		3b	
Terris McDuffie		p	
Henry McHenry	p		
Henry Miller	p		
Jim Missouri		p	
Sidney Morton (Sy)		3b	ss
Clarence Palm (Spoony)		c	
Roy Parnell (Red)	lf		
Ed Pitts		c	
Leon Ruffin	c		
? Samuels		p	
George Scales		inf	of
Samuel Thompson (Sad Sam)		p	
Roy Welmaker		p	
Jim West	1b		
Chester Williams		3b	ss

1941

Otto Briggs All-Stars

Player	1	2	3
Otto Briggs			M
Bill Bea	rf		
? Bell		2b	
Gene Benson		1b	
Knowlington Burbage (Buddy)	lf		
Bill Cash (Ready)		c	
? Cisco		2b	
Dick Craig		1b	
? Dorsey	cf		

Player	1	2	3
? Gamble	p		
? Hinson		rf	
Lincoln Jackson	1b		
? Jenkins		ss	2b
Pearley Johnson (Tubby)		1b	
Webster McDonald	p		
Henry Miller		p	
Sidney Morton (Sy)	ss	2b	
? Wilder		c	
? Williams		1b	

Baltimore Elite Giants

Player	1	2	3
Emery Adams (Ace)	p		
William Barnes (Jimmy)		p	
Charles Biot	cf	rf	
Jesse Brown		p	
Thomas Butts (Pee Wee)	ss		
Bill Byrd	p	of	
Roy Campanella	c		
Robert Clarke		c	
Homer Curry (Goose)	rf	cf	
Jonas Gaines		p	
Robert Griffith		p	
Bill Hoskins	lf		
George Scales	2b	ss	3b
Felton Snow	3b	2b	
Henry Spearman		3b	1b
John Washington	1b		
Roy Williams	p		

Birmingham Black Barons

Player	1	2	3
Wingfield Welch			M
Dan Bankhead	p		
Lyman Bostock, Sr.	1b	lf	
Lloyd Davenport	cf		
Johnny Dawson		c	
Jesse Douglas		of	
Alvin Gipson	p		
Paul Hardy		c	
Lee Johnson		c	
Nora Listach		of	
Lester Lockett	3b		
John Markham		p	
Gready McKinnis		p	
Bill Nixon		of	
Melvin Powell (Putt)		lf	
Ulysses Redd	ss		
Emanual Sampson (Eddie)		of	
Tommy Sampson	2b		
Alfred Saylor	c	1b	p
Willie Spencer	rf		
Ed Steele		of	
Reece Tatum (Goose)		1b	
Jesse Walker (Hoss)	ss		
Willie Wells		ss	
Willie Williams	p		

Chicago American Giants

Player	1	2	3
Candy Jim Taylor			M
Ted Alexander	p		
Lloyd Bassett (Pepper)	c		
Oscar Boone		c	
Bill Bradford		2b	
Willie Cornelius (Sug)	p		
Jimmy Crutchfield	cf		
Willie Ferrell (Trueheart)		p	
Jonas Gaines		p	
Alvin Gipson		p	3b
Curtis Henderson		ss	3b
Billy Horne	2b	ss	3b

Player	1	2	3
William Hudson	p	of	
Livingston James (Winky)		ss	
Gentry Jessup	p		
John Lyles		ss	
Henry Merchant	lf	of	p
Art Pennington		lf	
Alex Radcliff	3b		
Ted Radcliffe (Double Duty)		c	
Donald Reeves	rf		
William Serrell (Bonnie)		3b	
Charlie Shields	p		
Clyde Spearman		of	
Ralph Wyatt		ss	
Edward Young (Pep)	1b		

Detroit Black Sox

Player	1	2	3
Charlie Henry			M
W.M. Charter (Bill)	3b		
Emmett Davis		p	
Louis Hick		p	
Charles House (Red)	lf		
Sam Jones	p		
Curtis Jones (Bud)		p	
Obie Layton	p		
A.D. Lewis		1b	
Mark McCloud	rf		
George Mitchell	2b		
Johnny Robinson	cf		
O. Robinson		p	
Sam Warmack	ss		

Homestead Grays

Player	1	2	3
Jerry Benjamin	cf		
Clifford Blackman		p	
Ameal Brooks		c	
Ray Brown	p	of	
Matthew Carlisle (Lick)	2b		
Howard Easterling	3b		
Wilmer Fields		p	3b
Robert Gaston	c		
J.C. Hamilton (John)		p	
Vic Harris	lf		
Bill Houston		p	
Walter Leonard (Buck)	1b		
Terris McDuffie		p	of
Clarence Palm (Spoony)		c	
Roy Partlow		p	
Edsall Walker	p		
David Whatley	rf		
Chester Williams	ss		
Joe Williams		ss	
Jud Wilson		3b	1b
John Wright		p	

Jacksonville Red Caps

Player	1	2	3
Alonzo Mitchell (Hooks)	1b		M
? Broom		p	
Howard Cleveland (Duke)	rf		
Leo Henry (Preacher)	p		
? Kelly		p	
Clarence Lamar	ss		
Bill Nixon	lf		
John Ray	cf		
Walter Robinson (Skin Down)	2b		
Sam Sampson		2b	
Henry Turner	c		
Parnell Woods	3b		

Kansas City Monarchs

Player	1	2	3
Newton Allen (Newt)	2b	ss	3b M

Player	1	2	3
William Dismukes (Dizzy)			M
Rainey Bibbs	3b	2b	
Frank Bradley		p	
Chet Brewer	p		
Willard Brown	lf	cf	
Allen Bryant (Lefty)		p	
Jesse Douglas		2b	
Frank Duncan		c	
Frank Duncan III		p	
James Greene (Joe)	c		
Willie Hutchinson		p	
Clifford Johnson (Connie)		p	
Jack Matchett		p	
Booker McDaniels		p	
John O'Neil (Buck)	1b		
Leroy Paige (Satchel)	p		
Andrew Patterson (Pat)		2b	3b
Bill Simms	cf	lf	p
Hilton Smith	p		
Eugene Smith		p	
John Ford Smith		p	
Sylvester Snead		of	
Herb Souell		3b	
T.R. Strong (Ted)	rf	3b	
Samuel Thompson (Sad Sam)		p	
George Walker		p	
Jesse Williams (H.)	ss	cf	3b
Tom Young		c	

Memphis Red Sox

Player	1	2	3
Fred Bankhead	3b		
T.J. Brown (Tom)	ss		
Larry Brown		c	
Richard Byas (Subby)		p	of
Marlin Carter (Mel)	2b		
Jim Dumas		p	
Felix Evans (Chin)		p	
? Green (Honey)		p	
Willie Hutchinson	p		
Cowan Hyde (Bubber)	rf		
Livingston James (Winky)		inf	
Clinton Jones (Casey)	c		
Steve Keyes (Zeke)		p	
Robert Keyes		p	
Wayman Longley (Red)	c	of	
Verdell Mathis (Lefty)	p		
Porter Moss	p		
Ted Radcliffe (Double Duty)		c	p
Cornelius Robinson (Neil)	cf		
William Rogers (Nat)	lf		
Olan Taylor (Jelly)	1b		

N.O.-St. Louis Stars

Player	1	2	3
George Mitchell	p		M
Alfred Armour (Buddy)	cf		
Bradford Bennett	rf		
? Berkley		p	
Clifford Blackman		p	
Charles Boone (Lefty)		p	
Charles Bruton (Jack)		of	inf
Walter Calhoun	p		
Jimmy Ford	2b		
John Lyles		ss	of
Eldridge Mayweather (Ed)	1b		
Frank McAllister (Chip)	p		
Tom Parker		of	p
Marshall Riddle	ss		
William Robinson (Bobby)		3b	
? Rooney		p	
Eugene Smith	p		

Player	1	2	3
Robert Smith		c	
Leroy Sutton		p	
Robert Taylor	c		
Jesse Warren	3b	2b	
Lafayette Washington (Fay)		p	
Dan Wilson	lf	of	

New York Black Yankees

Player	1	2	3
Fred Burnett (Tex)			M
Lamb Barbee (Bud)		p	
Marvin Barker	3b	lf	of
Knowlington Burbage (Buddy)		of	
Anthony Cooper	ss		
Spencer Davis (Babe)		ss	3b
Russ Dedeaux		p	
Robert Evans		p	
Johnny Flowers (Jake)		3b	ss
John Hayes	c		
Bill Holland	p		
Henry Kimbro	cf		
Everett Marcell		c	
David Marsellas		c	
Leroy Paige (Satchel)		p	
Tom Parker	p		
Gabriel Patterson		of	
Guillermo Pillot (Guido)		p	
Cornelius Rector (Connie)	p		
Tom Roberts (Speck)		p	
Richard Seay (Dick)	2b	ss	
William Shinn		2b	
John Stanley (Neck)	p		
James Starks	1b		
George Suttles (Mule)	lf		
Jesse Walker (Hoss)		ss	
Herman Watts		p	
Harry Williams		2b	
James Williams (Jim)	rf		
M. Williams		3b	
Ray Williams		p	
Norman Young (Harvey)		3b	

New York Cubans

Player	1	2	3
Bill Anderson	p		
Dave Barnhill (Impo)	p		
Blacedo Bernal		p	
Clifford Blackman		p	
Carlos Blanco	1b		
Heberto Blanco (Harry)	lf	2b	
Clemente Cabrera (Sungo)	2b	3b	
? Canton		p	
Pedro Cepeda (Perucho)		lf	
Francisco Coimbre (Pancho)	cf	rf	
Carlos Colas (Charlie)	c		
Felix Delgado (Felle)		1b	of
Jose Fernandez		c	
T. Fernandez		p	of
Emanuel Fernandez		of	p
? Green		p	
? Harris (Lefty)		p	
Ramon Heredia	3b	1b	of
Alberto Hernandez		rf	
Eugene Hicks (Jimmy)		p	
Carranza Howard		p	
John Johnson (Johnny)		p	
Horacio Martinez (Rabbit)	ss		
Silvino Ruiz	p		
? Valez		cf	
Jose Vargas (Tetelo)	rf	cf	

Newark Eagles

Player	1	2	3
Raleigh Mackey (Biz)	c	3b	M
Spencer Alexander		of	
Russell Awkard		of	
James Brown		p	
Thad Christopher	cf	rf	
Johnny Davis		rf	
Leon Day	p	of	inf
Russ Dedeaux		p	
Jimmy Hill		p	
Freddie Hobgood		p	
Lenial Hooker (Len)	p		
Monte Irvin	ss	of	
Clarence Israel (Pint)	3b	lf	
Leaman Johnson	2b	ss	
Maxwell Manning (Max)	p		
Francis Matthews (Fran)	1b		
Charles Parks	c		
Leonard Pearson (Lennie)	lf	3b	
Vernon Riddick		inf	
Ray Robinson		p	
Charles Thomason		cf	rf
Tom Young		c	

Philadelphia Stars

Player	1	2	3
Oscar Charleston	1b		M
Gene Benson	cf		
Chet Brewer		p	
Chester Buchanan (Buck)	p		
Dave Campbell		ss	2b
W.T. Cooper (Bill)		c	
? Darcy		of	
Mahlon Duckett	3b	2b	c
Joseph Dunn (Jake)		rf	
Joe Fillmore		p	
John Gibbons		p	
Charlie Gordon		of	
Curtis Henderson		3b	
John Huber		c	
Willie Hubert		p	
Ralph Johnson		p	
Archie Jones		p	
Larnie Jordan		ss	
Lester Lockett		ss	
Henry McHenry	p		
Henry Miller		p	
Jim Missouri		p	
Dewitt Owens		of	1b
Clarence Palm (Spoony)		c	
Roy Parnell (Red)	lf		
Andrew Patterson (Pat)	2b	ss	3b
Hiawatha Shelby		of	
Jack Walker	p		
Edsall Walker		p	
Jim West	1b		
Chester Williams		ss	
Zollie Wright		rf	

1942

Baltimore Elite Giants

Player	1	2	3
Emery Adams (Ace)		p	
William Barnes (Jimmy)		p	
Jesse Brown		p	
Thomas Butts (Pee Wee)	ss		
Bill Byrd	p		
Roy Campanella	c		
William Casey (Mickey)		c	
Robert Clarke		c	

Player	1	2	3
Thomas Fabors		p	
Jonas Gaines		p	
Thomas Glover	p		
David Harvey (Bill)	p		
Bill Hoskins	lf	rf	
Sammy T. Hughes	2b	2b	
Henry Kimbro	cf		
Granville Lyons		1b	
Andrew Porter	p		
George Scales		3b	ss
Felton Snow	3b		
Henry Spearman	1b	3b	
? Turner (Lefty)		1b	
Burnis Wright (Bill)	rf	lf	

Birmingham Black Barons

Player	1	2	3
Wingfield Welch			M
Dan Bankhead		p	
Harry Barnes		c	
Bradford Bennett		of	
Lyman Bostock, Sr.		1b	
Bill Bradford	rf	lf	
Lloyd Davenport		cf	
Lorenzo Davis (Piper)		inf	
Ross Davis	p		
Jesse Douglas		inf	
Alphonse Dunn (Blue)		1b	of
Ted Gibson		c	
Luther Gillard	1b		
Alvin Gipson	p		
Paul Hardy	c		
Roger Harris		inf	
Lester Lockett	3b		
Robert Madison		p	
John Markham		p	
Jesse Matthews		inf	
Gready McKinnis	p		
Felix McLaurin		of	
Leroy Morney		ss	lf
Robert Pipkin (Lefty)	p		
Alex Radcliff		3b	
Ted Radcliffe (Double Duty)		c	p
Tommy Sampson	2b		
Alfred Saylor		1b	
Herbert Simpson		of	
John Smith		of	
Eddie Sneed	p		
Joe Spencer		ss	2b
Ed Steele		of	
Leon Stewart		of	
Reece Tatum (Goose)		of	1b
? Tipton			
Jesse Walker (Hoss)		ss	
Jesse Warren		lf	of
Charlie West		of	

Boston Royal Giants

Player	1	2	3
Burlin White	c		M
Billy Burke	3b		
? Faulk		c	
? Green (Honey)		p	
Bill Jackman	p		
Pearley Johnson (Tubby)	rf		
Ernest Jones (Mint)		1b	
Dick Mapp	ss		
Francis Matthews (Fran)	1b		
Charlie Mitchell		c	
? Mitchell		p	
Elmer Munroe	p		
? Reddick		cf	of

Player	1	2	3
? Robinson (Babe)	p		
Charlie Thomas	cf		
Orval Tucker	2b		
? Ward		p	
Jesse Warren		3b	
? West		3b	

Chicago American Giants

Player	1	2	3
Herman Andrews (Jabo)		lf	
James Bell (Cool Papa)	cf	1b	
John Bissant		lf	
George Britt (Chippy)		c	
Ameal Brooks		c	
? Burgess	p		
Willie Burns	p		
Jesse Cannady (Hoss)	2b		
Willie Cornelius (Sug)	p		
Jimmy Crutchfield	rf		
Willie Ferrell (Truehart)		p	
John Huber	c	p	
William Hudson		p	
Samuel Jackson		p	
Gentry Jessup	p		
Tommy Johnson		p	
Lester Lockett	2b		
Henry Merchant		p	of
W. Miller		p	
Art Pennington	1b	lf	
Alex Radcliff	3b		
Harry Rhodes		1b	
Charlie Shields	p		
Robert Smith	c		
Henry Smith	c		
John Ford Smith		of	
Clyde Spearman		rf	
Leroy Sutton	p		
Samuel Thompson (Sad Sam)		p	
Ollie West		p	
Ralph Wyatt	ss		
Edward Young (Pep)		c	

Chicago Brown Bombers

Player	1	2	3
Elwood DeMoss (Bingo)			M
John Bissant	cf		
Roosevelt Davis (Rosey)	p		
Jimmy Longest	1b		
Bernell Longest (Chick)	2b		
? Parker (Sonny)		p	
Sherley Petway (Charlie)	c		
Melvin Powell (Putt)	lf	p	
John Reed	p		
? Thompson (Buddy)		c	
Eugene Tyler	3b	c	
Robert Wiggins (Bob)	ss		
Bilbo Williams (Biggie)		rf	
Johnny Williams	p		

Cincinnati Clowns

Player	1	2	3
McKinley Downs (Bunny)			M
Lamb Barbee (Bud)		p	
Lloyd Bassett (Pepper)	c		
Ameal Brooks		c	
Ralph Cole	rf		
Livingston James (Winky)	2b		
Steve Keyes (Zeke)	p		
Leonard Lindsay	1b		
Lou Montgomery		p	
Raymond Owens (Smokey)	p		
Rogers Pierre	p		
Joe Sykes		of	

Player	1	2	3
? Thompson (Copperknee)	3b	ss	2b
Jesse Walker (Hoss)	ss		
Art Wilbert	lf		
Fred Wilson	cf		

Cincinnati-Cleveland Buckeyes

Player	1	2	3
Alonzo Boone		p	
Charles Boone (Lefty)		p	
Eugene Bremmer	p		
Chet Brewer		p	
George Britt (Chippy)		c	
George Brown		of	
Ulysses Brown (Buster)	c		
Walter Burch		c	p
Thad Christopher		lf	rf
Howard Cleveland (Duke)		of	
Willie Cornelius (Sug)		p	
John Cowan	3b		
Lloyd Davenport		of	
Willie Grace		of	
J. Harris (Sonny)		of	
Billy Horne	2b		
Willie Hubert		p	
Livingston James (Winky)	ss	2b	
Willie Jefferson	p		
Sam Jethroe	cf	lf	
John Lyles		ss	2b
Fred McKelvin		p	
Raymond Owens (Smokey)	p		
Ray Robinson		p	
Dode Smith		p	
Eugene Smith (Gene)		3b	
Raymond Taylor		c	
Archie Ware	1b		
Herman Watts		p	
Jesse Williams		c	
Emmett Wilson		of	
Parnell Woods	3b		

Homestead Grays

Player	1	2	3
Sam Bankhead	rf	ss	
Jerry Benjamin	cf		
Ray Brown	p	of	
Matthew Carlisle (Lick)	2b	of	
Ernest Carter (Spoon)	p		
Tom Corcoran		p	
Howard Easterling	3b	of	inf
Wilmer Fields		p	3b
Robert Gaston		c	
Josh Gibson	c		
J.C. Hamilton (John)		p	
Vic Harris	lf		
Bill Houston		p	
Josh Johnson		c	
Walter Leonard (Buck)	1b		
Roy Partlow	p	of	
Roy Welmaker		p	
David Whatley		rf	
Frank Williams		of	
Harry Williams		3b	
Chester Williams	ss	2b	
Jud Wilson		1b	3b
John Wright	p		

Jacksonville Red Caps

Player	1	2	3
Hoses Allen (Buster)	p		
Herman Andrews (Jabo)		of	
Herbert Barnhill		c	
Charles Boone (Lefty)	p		
? Broom		p	

Player	1	2	3
? Butt			
James Canada	1b		
Howard Cleveland (Duke)		rf	
Lloyd Davenport		of	
Willie Dunn	p		
? Dykes			
Gervis Fagan		ss	2b
Greene Farmer		of	
Leo Henry (Preacher)	p		
Alfred Ingram		p	
George Jefferson		p	
? Kelly		p	
Clarence Lamar	ss		
? Lockhart			
Fred McKelvin		p	
Felix McLaurin	cf		
Raymond Owens (Smokey)	p	rf	
John Ray	lf		
Marshall Riddle		2b	
Walter Robinson (Skin Down)		2b	
Joseph Royall (John)		of	
Sam Sampson		2b	
Andrew Sarvis	p		
? Seavers		p	
Eugene Smith (Gene)	3b		
Henry Smith	2b		
L. Smith		c	
Parnell Woods		3b	

Kansas City Monarchs

Player	1	2	3
William Dismukes (Dizzy)			M
Frank Duncan	c	rf	M
Newton Allen (Newt)	3b	2b	
Frank Bradley	p		
Willard Brown	cf		
Johnny Dawson		c	
James Greene (Joe)	c		
Paul Hardy	c	rf	
Clifford Johnson (Connie)	p		
Jim LaMarque	p	cf	
Jack Matchett	p		
Booker McDaniels		p	
John O'Neil (Buck)	1b		
Leroy Paige (Satchel)	p		
Norris Phillips		p	
Henry Robinson (Frazier)	c		
William Serrell (Bonnie)	2b	rf	
Bill Simms	lf	cf	
Hilton Smith	p		
I. Smith		p	
Herb Souell	3b		
T.R. Strong (Ted)	rf	3b	
George Walker		p	
Jesse Williams (H.)	ss		

Memphis Red Sox

Player	1	2	3
William Dismukes (Dizzy)			M
Fred Bankhead	2b		
Bill Bradford		of	
John Brooks		p	
T.J. Brown (Tom)	ss		
Larry Brown	c		
Richard Byas (Subby)		c	
Marlin Carter (Mel)	3b		
Felix Evans (Chin)		p	
? Hatten		p	
Willie Hutchinson		p	
Cowan Hyde (Bubber)	rf		
Steve Keyes (Zeke)		p	
Robert Keyes		p	

Player	1	2	3
Henry Lipsey		p	
Verdell Mathis (Lefty)	p	cf	
Jesse Matthews		inf	
Fred McDaniels	lf		
Porter Moss	p		
Norris Phillips	p		
Ted Radcliffe (Double Duty)		c	
Cornelius Robinson (Neil)	cf		
William Rogers (Nat)		of	
Robert Smith		c	
Olan Taylor (Jelly)	1b		
Leandy Young		of	

New York Black Yankees

Player	1	2	3
Fred Burnett (Tex)			M
Bradford Bennett	1b		
Charles Boone (Lefty)	p		
Walter Calhoun	p		
Spencer Davis (Babe)		ss	
Robert Evans		p	
Greene Farmer		of	
Johnny Flowers (Jake)		3b	
Jimmy Ford		3b	2b
Chesley Gray (Chester)		c	lf
Leslie Green (Chin)	cf		
Robert Griffith		p	
John Hayes	c		
Curtis Henderson		ss	3b
Leaman Johnson		ss	
Josh Johnson		c	
Larnie Jordan		ss	
Eldridge Mayweather (Ed)		1b	
Frank McAllister (Chip)	p		
Tom Parker	rf	p	
Richard Seay (Dick)	2b		
Eugene Smith		p	
John Stanley (Neck)		p	
James Starks		1b	
Raymond Taylor		c	
Jack Walker		p	
Carl Whitney		of	
Harry Williams		3b	1b
Dan Wilson	lf		

New York Cubans

Player	1	2	3
Bill Anderson	p		
Dave Barnhill (Impo)	p		
Heberto Blanco (Harry)	2b	ss	
Roosevelt Cox	ss	3b	2b
Martin Crue (Matty)		p	
Alphonse Dunn (Blue)	rf	1b	
Jose Fernandez		c	
Alphonse Green		of	
Albert Haywood (Buster)	c		
Carranza Howard		p	
Louis Louden (Tommy)	lf	c	
Horacio Martinez (Rabbit)		ss	
Leroy Matlock		p	
Barney Morris	p		
Javier Perez (Blue)	3b	2b	
Alex Pompez			
Silvino Ruiz		p	
John Sampson		of	
Thomas Saxton (Lefty)		p	
Dave Thomas	1b		
Jose Vargas (Tetelo)		of	
L.C. Williams	cf		

Newark Eagles

Player	1	2	3
James Brown		p	of
James Clarkson (Bus)		2b	ss
Ray Dandridge	3b	2b	
Johnny Davis		lf	of
Leon Day	p	of	inf
Larry Doby		2b	3b
Jimmy Hill		p	
Freddie Hobgood		p	
Lenial Hooker (Len)	p		
Monte Irvin	cf		
Clarence Israel (Pint)		3b	2b
Maxwell Manning (Max)	p		
Francis Matthews (Fran)		1b	
Charles Parks		c	
Leonard Pearson (Lennie)		lf	of
Leon Ruffin	c		
Ed Stone	rf		
George Suttles (Mule)	1b		
Charles Thomason		of	
Willie Wells	ss		

Philadelphia Daisies

Player	1	2	3
Clarence Jenkins (Fats)	of		M
Bill Bea	rf		
? Bell		3b	
? Brooks		2b	
Knowlington Burbage (Buddy)	p	of	
? Campbell		c	
Bill Cash (Ready)		c	
? Dorsey	cf		
? Hinson	lf		
? Jenkins	ss		
Jack Johnson		3b	
Webster McDonald	p		
Henry Miller	p		
James Moore (Red)		1b	
R. Smith		1b	

Philadelphia Stars

Player	1	2	3
Oscar Charleston	1b		M
Marvin Barker		3b	
Gene Benson	cf		
Barney Brown	p		
Chester Buchanan (Buck)		p	
Walter Calhoun		p	
James Clarkson (Bus)		ss	
W.T. Cooper (Bill)		p	
Homer Curry (Goose)	rf		
Mahlon Duckett	2b		
Robert Evans	p		
Joe Fillmore		p	
Leedell Garvin		p	
Eddie Jefferson		p	
Larry Kimbrough		p	
Terris McDuffie	p		
Clarence Palm (Spoony)		c	
Roy Parnell (Red)	lf		
Henry Spearman	3b		
Jim West	1b		

1943

NNL All-Stars (Winter)

Player	1	2	3
Homer Curry (Goose)	of		M
Gene Benson	cf		
George Brown	lf		
Barney Brown	p		
Bill Cash (Ready)	c		
Leon Day	p	utl	
Lenial Hooker (Len)	p		

Player	1	2	3
Sidney Morton (Sy)	2b		
Roy Parnell (Red)		3b	of
Felton Snow	3b		
Ed Stone	rf		
Pete Sunkett	p	1b	
Dave Thomas	1b		
Chester Williams	ss		

Baltimore Elite Giants

Player	1	2	3
Lamb Barbee (Bud)		1b	p
Mike Berry (Red)		p	
Joe Black		p	
George Brown		of	
Willie Burns		p	
Bill Byrd	p	of	
Charles Carter		p	
Robert Clarke	c		
Wesley Dennis (Doc)			1b
Thomas Glover	p		
David Harvey (Bill)		p	of
Bill Hoskins	lf		
Eugene Jones		p	
Henry Kimbro	cf		
Andrew Porter	p		
Norman Robinson (Bobby)		of	
Frank Russell (Junior)		2b	
George Scales	2b	inf	
Felton Snow	3b		
Joe Spencer		3b	
Manuel Stewart		p	
Bilbo Williams (Biggie)		of	
Norman Young (Harvey)	ss		

Baltimore Giants (Winter)

Player	1	2	3
James Bell (Cool Papa)	cf		
Howard Easterling	3b		
Cowan Hyde (Bubber)	rf		
Walter Leonard (Buck)	1b		
John Markham	p		
Booker McDaniels	p		
Tom Moss	p		
Leroy Paige (Satchel)	p		
Ted Radcliffe (Double Duty)	c		
Sam Sampson	2b		
Clyde Spearman	lf		
Jesse Walker (Hoss)	ss		

Birmingham Black Barons

Player	1	2	3
Wingfield Welch			M
Herman Bell		c	
Lyman Bostock, Sr.		1b	of
Jim Daniels	p		
Lorenzo Davis (Piper)		ss	
Alphonse Dunn (Blue)		1b	of
Alvin Gipson	p		
Paul Hardy	c		
John Huber	p	c	
Leaman Johnson		3b	
James Lindsay		inf	
Leonard Lindsay		1b	
Lester Lockett	lf		
John Markham	p		
Gready McKinnis		p	
Felix McLaurin	cf		
Leroy Morney		3b	
Jimmy Newberry		p	
Emanual Sampson (Eddie)		of	
Tommy Sampson	2b		
Alfred Saylor		p	c
Clyde Spearman	rf		

Player	1	2	3
Ed Steele		of	
John Taylor		of	
Jesse Walker (Hoss)		3b	
Chicago American Giants			
Ted Radcliffe (Double Duty)	c	p	M
John Bissant	rf	lf	
Herbert Buster		ss	2b
W.M. Charter (Bill)	1b	2b	
Willie Cornelius (Sug)	p		
Lloyd Davenport	cf		
Gentry Jessup	p		
Art Pennington	lf	rf	
Alex Radcliff	3b		
Charlie Shields		p	
Henry Smith	2b	of	
Lonnie Summers		c	
Leroy Sutton	p		
Ralph Wyatt	ss		
Edward Young (Pep)	c	1b	
Chicago Brown Bombers			
Elwood DeMoss (Bingo)			M
Chuck Bowen	lf		
Leroy Clayton (Zack)	1b		
Ulysses Evans		p	
Charlie Harris		ss	
Jim Lewis	p		
Albert Morehead	c		
Clyde Nelson	3b		
Melvin Powell (Putt)	rf	p	
? Presby		p	
Richard Ray	ss	of	
William Rowe (Schoolboy)	p	inf	
William Thomas	cf		
Oliver Turner		p	
Eugene Tyler		c	inf
George Waller	2b		
Johnny Williams	p		
Cincinnati Clowns			
Fred Wilson	p	of	M
Hoses Allen (Buster)		p	
Lloyd Bassett (Pepper)		c	
John Britton	3b		
Willie Burns		p	
Jesse Cannady (Hoss)	3b		
Thad Christopher		rf	lf
Roosevelt Davis (Rosey)		p	
Eddie Davis (Nyasses)	p		
Jimmy Everett	p		
Willie Ferrell (Truehart)	p		
A. Gibson (Jerry)	p		
Charlie Harris	2b	inf	
Albert Haywood (Buster)	c		
Leo Henry (Preacher)	p		
Barney Higdon		p	
Collins Jones		2b	3b
Brennan King		p	
Roger Lett		p	
Leonard Lindsay		1b	
Eddie Locke	p		
Levingelo Lugo (Leo)		lf	
Leroy Morney	ss		
James Oliver (Pee Wee)		ss	
Alex Radcliff		3b	
John Ray	cf		
Alfred Saylor		p	1b

Player	1	2	3
Sylvester Snead		ss	2b
Reece Tatum (Goose)	1b	rf	
Emmett Wilson	lf		
Cleveland Buckeyes			
Sam Barber		p	
Alonzo Boone	p		
Eugene Bremmer	p		
Chet Brewer	p		
George Britt (Chippy)		c	
Thad Christopher	rf	c	
Howard Cleveland (Duke)	lf		
Ross Davis		p	
Willie Grace		of	
? Grimes		of	
Napoleon Gulley		p	
Lovell Harden		p	
Billy Horne	ss		
Johnny Lee Hundley	c	of	
Willie Jefferson		p	
Sam Jethroe	cf	3b	
Johnny Johnson		p	of
John Lyles		inf	
Willie McCarey		p	
Marshall Riddle	2b		
Quincy Smith		of	
Theolic Smith	p	of	
Raymond Taylor		c	
Henry Turner		c	of
Archie Ware	1b		
Parnell Woods	3b		
Harrisburg–St. L Stars			
George Mitchell			M
Alfred Armour (Buddy)	cf		
Charles Boone (Lefty)	p		
Ronnie Brown		1b	
T.J. Brown (Tom)		ss	
Walter Calhoun	p	of	
William Carter	3b		
Jimmy Ford		2b	
Chesley Gray (Chester)		c	utl
? Grimes		p	
Billy Horne		2b	
? Jones		ss	
Frank McAllister (Chip)	p	of	
Frank McCoy	c		
? Parker (Sonny)		p	
Tom Parker	rf	of	
? Shelton		of	
James Starks	1b		
Henry Turner		1b	
Jack Walker		p	
Eli Williams (Eddie)	lf		
Harry Williams		ss	2b
Dan Wilson	2b	lf	
Homestead Grays			
Candy Jim Taylor			M
Bill Anderson		p	
Sam Bankhead	ss		
James Bell (Cool Papa)	cf		
Jerry Benjamin	rf	lf	
James Boyd		p	
Ray Brown	p	of	
Matthew Carlisle (Lick)		2b	
Charles Carter	p		
Ted Christopher		of	c
Martin Crue (Matty)	p		
Howard Easterling	3b	of	

Player	1	2	3
Robert Gaston		c	
Josh Gibson	c		
Vic Harris		lf	
Eugene Jones		p	
Walter Leonard (Buck)	1b		
? Lynn		p	
Ralph Mellix (Lefty)		p	
Roy Partlow	p		
Charlie Shields		p	
Herbert Simpson		p	
Joe Spencer	2b		
Willie Stevenson		p	
Edsall Walker	p		
Ollie West		p	
Frank Williams		of	
Jud Wilson		of	3b
John Wright	p		
Ralph Wyatt		ss	
Kansas City Monarchs			
Frank Duncan	c		M
Ted Alexander		p	
Newton Allen (Newt)		inf	
Herbert Barnhill		c	
Willard Brown	cf		
Allen Bryant (Lefty)		p	
James Greene (Joe)		c	
Sammy Haynes		c	
Bill Hoskins		of	
Jack Matchett	p		
Booker McDaniels		p	
John O'Neil (Buck)	1b		
Leroy Paige (Satchel)	p		
? Parker (Sonny)		p	
Norris Phillips	p		
Henry Robinson (Frazier)		c	1b
William Serrell (Bonnie)	2b	of	
Bill Simms	lf		
Hilton Smith		p	of
R. Smith		of	
Herb Souell	3b		
Henry Thompson (Hank)	rf		
Eugene Tyler		3b	ss
George Walker		p	
Jesse Williams (H.)	ss		
Memphis Red Sox			
Fred Bankhead	2b		
William Barnes (Jimmy)		p	
Larry Brown	c		
James Canada	1b		
Felix Evans (Chin)		p	
Willie Hutchinson		p	
Cowan Hyde (Bubber)	cf	of	
Clinton Jones (Casey)		c	
Robert Keyes		p	
Wayman Longley (Red)	3b	of	inf
Verdell Mathis (Lefty)	p	of	
Fred McDaniels	rf	lf	
Porter Moss	p		
Leroy Paige (Satchel)		p	
Cornelius Robinson (Neil)	lf	of	
William Rogers (Nat)		of	
New York Black Yankees			
Emery Adams (Ace)	p	of	
? Allen		of	
? Averett		of	
Rufus Baker		inf	
Marvin Barker	lf	3b	2b

Player	1	2	3
Bill Bradford	cf	lf	
Leroy Clayton (Zack)	1b		
Howard Carranza	p		
Charlie Dean	p		
Robert Evans	p		
Johnny Flowers (Jake)	inf		
Percy Forrest	p		
Robert Griffith	p	of	
? Kemp	c		
Obie Lackey	of		
? Lenox	1b		
? Leonard			
George McCrary	p		
Leroy Miller (Flash)	2b	3b	ss
Henry Milton	of		
Clarence Palm (Spoony)	c		
Gabriel Patterson	of		
Albert Preston	p		
Tom Roberts (Speck)	p		
Kenneth Robinson	3b	of	
? Robinson	c		
Joe Spencer	2b		
John Stanley (Neck)	p		
Ed Stone	rf	cf	
Harry Williams	3b	2b	
Sidney Williams (Al)	p		
Zollie Wright	rf		

New York Cubans

Player	1	2	3
Jose Fernandez	c		M
Bill Anderson	p		
Dave Barnhill (Impo)	p		
Ameal Brooks	c	of	
Francisco Coimbre (Pancho)	cf	rf	
Roosevelt Cox	2b	3b	
Martin Crue (Matty)	p		
Pedro Diaz (Manny)	p		
? Dieckert	3b		
Rodolfo Fernandez (Rudy)	p		
Vic Greenidge	p		
Carranza Howard	p		
Rogelio Linares	lf	1b	
Louis Louden (Tommy)	lf	c	
? Lougary	of		
Horacio Martinez (Rabbit)	ss		
Barney Morris	p		
Javier Perez (Blue)	3b	2b	
Carlos Rivero (Charley)	3b	2b	
Charlie Shields	p		
? Snyder	of		
Dave Thomas	1b		
Luis Tiant, Sr.	p		
? Tynor	of		
Jose Vargas (Tetelo)	rf	cf	

Newark Eagles

Player	1	2	3
George Suttles (Mule)	1b		M
James Brown	p	of	
? Butler			
Haywood Cozart (Harry)	p		
Johnny Davis	lf	of	p
A. Davis	ss	3b	
Leon Day	p	of	inf
Larry Doby	2b		
Jim Elam	p		
Bob Harvey	of		
Jimmy Hill	p		
Freddie Hobgood	p		
Lenial Hooker (Len)	p		
Leonard Pearson (Lennie)	1b		

Player	1	2	3
Earl Richardson		ss	
Leon Ruffin	c		
? Spencer			
Larry St. Thomas		c	
Ed Stone	rf		
Charles Thomason		of	
Murray Watkins		3b	ss
Albert Williams	p		
Eli Williams (Eddie)	of		
M. Williams	ss		
Robert Williams (Cotton)	ss	3b	
Sidney Williams (Al)	p		
Wilmore Williams	of		

Philadelphia Stars

Player	1	2	3
Homer Curry (Goose)	rf	of	M
Herman Andrews (Jabo)		of	
Gene Benson	cf		
Barney Brown		p	of
Chester Buchanan (Buck)	p		
Knowlington Burbage (Buddy)	of		
Willie Burns	p		
Bill Cash (Ready)	c		
Oscar Charleston			coach
Robert Clarke	c		
? Dua			
Mahlon Duckett		2b	inf
Robert Evans	p		
Gervis Fagan	ss	inf	
Jimmy Ford	inf		
Stanley Glenn	c		
Hubert Glenn	p		
Dave Harper	p		
Ben Hill	p		
B. Jackson (Bozo)	3b		
Jimmy Johnson (Slim)	p		
Steve Keyes (Zeke)	p		
Garvin Keyes	inf		
Henry Kimbro	lf		
Larry Kimbrough	p		
Verdell Mathis (Lefty)	p		
Henry Miller	p		
Sidney Morton (Sy)	inf		
Roy Parnell (Red)	lf		
Felton Snow	ss		
Henry Spearman	3b		
Pete Sunkett	p		
Jim West	1b		
Marvin Williams		2b	

1944

Baltimore Elite Giants

Player	1	2	3
Robert Clarke	c		M
Joe Black	p		
Thomas Butts (Pee Wee)	ss		
Bill Byrd	p		
Roy Campanella	c		
? Chapman		1b	
Wesley Dennis (Doc)	1b		
Jonas Gaines		p	
Thomas Glover	p		
David Harvey (Bill)	p		
Bill Hoskins	lf		
Henry Kimbro	cf		
Lester Lockett		of	
Andrew Porter	p		
Norman Robinson (Bobby)			rf
Frank Russell (Junior)	of		

Player	1	2	3
George Scales		2b	
Felton Snow	3b		
Donald Troy	p		
Edsall Walker	p		
Laymon Yokeley	p		

Birmingham Black Barons

Player	1	2	3
Wingfield Welch			M
Lloyd Bassett (Pepper)	c		
Alonzo Boone	p		
John Britton	3b		
Earl Bumpus		p	
Lorenzo Davis (Piper)	1b	2b	
Rube Ellis (Rocky)		p	
Alvin Gipson	p		
Clyde Harriston		c	inf
John Huber	p	c	
Collins Jones		of	
Joe Lillard		utl	p
Lester Lockett	lf		
John Markham	p		
Felix McLaurin	cf	rf	
Leroy Morney		1b	utl
Jimmy Newberry	p		
Ted Radcliffe (Double Duty)		c	p
Tommy Sampson	2b		
Alfred Saylor	p		
John Scott		of	
Ed Steele	rf	cf	
Lafayette Washington (Fay)	p		
Arthur Wilson (Artie)	ss		
Leandy Young		of	

Chicago American Giants

Player	1	2	3
Elwood DeMoss (Bingo)			M
Herbert Barnhill	c		
Rainey Bibbs		ss	3b
John Bissant	2b	of	
Jimmy Crutchfield	rf	of	
Lloyd Davenport	cf	of	
Jesse Douglas	1b	ss	
Kendall Felder		2b	3b
Samuel Jackson		p	
Gentry Jessup	p		
Albert Jones (Alonzo)		p	
Gready McKinnis	p		
George Minor		of	
Clyde Nelson	1b		
Art Pennington	lf	of	
Alex Radcliff		3b	
William Rogers (Nat)		of	
Robert Sharpe	p		
John Ford Smith		of	p
Robert Smith	c		
Leroy Sutton	p		
Alfred Thomas (Buck)		p	
Ollie Waldon		of	
Willie Wells (Brooks)		ss	3b
Ralph Wyatt	ss		

Cleveland Buckeyes

Player	1	2	3
Alfred Armour (Buddy)	lf		
Rainey Bibbs		inf	
Eugene Bremmer	p		
George Britt (Chippy)		c	
John Brown	p		
Walter Burch		c	2b
Frank Carswell	p		
John Cowan		2b	3b
Jimmy Crutchfield		of	

Player	1	2	3	Player	1	2	3	Player	1	2	3
Lloyd Davenport		rf		Edsall Walker	p			Sammy Haynes		c	
Willie Grace	of			Roy Welmaker		p		Robert Johnson		p	
Jefferson Guiwn		c		Edward White (Eddie)		p		Jim LaMarque		p	
Lovell Harden	p			Jud Wilson		utl		Eddie Locke	p		
Billy Horne	ss							Jack Matchett	p		
George Jefferson	p			**Indy-Cincy Clowns**				Booker McDaniels	p		
Willie Jefferson	p			Lloyd Bassett (Pepper)		c		Fred McDaniels		of	
Sam Jethroe	cf			Willie Burns		p		Lee Moody	1b		
Wilbur King (Dolly)		inf		Rafael Cabrera	1b	p		Julio Arango Ortiz (Bill)		utl	
? McCreary		lf		Jesse Cannady (Hoss)		inf		Leroy Paige (Satchel)		p	
Sherley Petway (Charlie)		c		Roosevelt Davis (Rosey)	p			? Perkins		1b	
Harmon Purcell		3b		Clyde Harriston		inf		Bill Rivers		of	
William Rowe (Schoolboy)		p		Albert Haywood (Buster)	c			Clarence Rochelle		p	
Archie Ware	1b			James Jenkins		p		William Serrell (Bonnie)	2b	3b	
Jesse Williams		c		Levingelo Lugo (Leo)	of			Hilton Smith		p	
Parnell Woods	3b			William Marshall (Jack)		inf		Monroe Smith (Mance)		of	
Norman Young (Harvey)		ss		Lazarus Medina		p		Herb Souell	3b	inf	
				Henry Merchant		cf	of	Raymond Taylor		c	
Homestead Grays				Albert Overton		p		Walter Thomas		p	of
Candy Jim Taylor			M	Rogers Pierre		p		Bobby Vanever		inf	
Sam Bankhead	ss			Alex Radcliff		3b		Ollie Waldon		of	
Ray Battle		inf		John Ray	rf	of		Britt Ward		c	
James Bell (Cool Papa)	lf			Antonio Ruiz	p			Jesse Williams (H.)	ss		
Jerry Benjamin	cf			Henry Smith		2b	ss	? Wingo (Doc)		c	
Ray Brown	p	of		Fermin Valdes	2b			Enloe Wylie		p	
Jesse Cannady (Hoss)	3b			Armando Vasquez	1b	of		Edward Young (Pep)		c	
Ernest Carter (Spoon)	p			Jesse Walker (Hoss)	ss						
Robert Gaston		c		Johnny Williams	p			**Memphis Red Sox**			
Josh Gibson	c							Larry Brown	c		M
Vic Harris		of		**Kansas City Monarchs**				Fred Bankhead	2b	inf	
Dave Hoskins	of	p		Frank Duncan	c		M	T.J. Brown (Tom)		ss	
Norman Jackson (Jelly)		2b	inf	Ted Alexander		p		James Canada	1b		
John Johnson (Johnny)		p		Newton Allen (Newt)		2b		Edgar Chatman		p	
Walter Leonard (Buck)	1b			Earl Bumpus		p	rf	Felix Evans (Chin)		p	
Roy Partlow		p		William Edwards		p		Kendall Felder		inf	
Joe Spencer		inf		Dave Harper		of		Jimmy Ford	3b		

1944 Washington Homestead Grays. Front L to R: Jelly Jackson, Ray Battle, Edward Robinson, Sam Bankhead, Josh Gibson, Buck Leonard, Dave Hoskins, Jerry Benjamin, and Cool Papa Bell.
Negro Leagues Baseball Museum

Player	1	2	3
Willie Hutchinson	p		
Cowan Hyde (Bubber)	rf	of	
W. Johnson	p		
Clinton Jones (Casey)		c	
Albert Jones (Alonzo)		p	
Robert Keyes		p	
Wilbur King (Dolly)	ss		
Rufus Ligon	p		
Wayman Longley (Red)	of		inf
Verdell Mathis (Lefty)	p	of	
Fred McDaniels	cf	of	
Porter Moss	p		
Cornelius Robinson (Neil)	lf	of	
William Rogers (Nat)		of	
Joseph Burt Scott		of	
Robert Sharpe	p		
Willie Wells	ss		3b
Willie Wells (Brooks)	ss		
Enloe Wylie	p		

New York Black Yankees

Player	1	2	3
John Stanley (Neck)	p		M
Rufus Baker	2b	ss	3b
Lamb Barbee (Bud)		of	
Marvin Barker	3b	of	
Thad Christopher	rf	of	1b
Leroy Clayton (Zack)	1b		
Percy Forrest		p	
William Kelly		c	
Wilbur King (Dolly)		of	
John McFarland	p		
Cornelius Rector (Connie)	p		
Carlos Rivero (Charley)	ss		3b
Joseph Royall (John)		c	

Player	1	2	3
? Spencer		of	
James Starks		1b	
? Sydney		cf	
James Williams (Jim)	cf	of	
Harry Williams		c	
Dan Wilson	lf	of	

New York Cubans

Player	1	2	3
Jose Fernandez			M
Bill Anderson		p	
Dave Barnhill (Impo)		p	
Ameal Brooks		c	utl
Francisco Coimbre (Pancho)	lf	of	
Roosevelt Cox		c	
Claro Duany	cf	of	
Rodolfo Fernandez (Rudy)		p	
Gil Garrido	2b		
Victor Greenidge		p	
Carranza Howard	p		
Rogelio Linares	1b	of	
Louis Louden (Tommy)	c		
Horacio Martinez (Rabbit)	ss		
Barney Morris	p		
Javier Perez (Blue)		2b	3b
Hector Rodriguez (Antonio)	3b		
Pat Scantlebury		p	
Dave Thomas	1b		
Luis Tiant, Sr.		p	
Jose Vargas (Tetelo)	rf	of	

Newark Eagles

Player	1	2	3
George Suttles (Mule)	1b		M
Alonzo Braithwaite (Archie)	cf		
Fred Burnett (Tex)		c	

Player	1	2	3
Haywood Cozart (Harry)		p	
Ray Dandridge	ss	3b	
Johnny Davis	lf	p	
Bob Harvey	rf		
Jimmy Hill	p		
Lenial Hooker (Len)	p		
? Jacob		p	
Frank Makell		c	
Terris McDuffie	p		
Sidney Morton (Sy)		ss	2b
Don Newcombe		p	
Leonard Pearson (Lennie)	3b	1b	of
Charles Thomason		of	
Henry Turner		of	
Murray Watkins	2b	3b	
Albert Williams		p	
Willie Wynn	c		

Philadelphia Stars

Player	1	2	3
Homer Curry (Goose)	rf	of	M
Frank Austin	ss		
Gene Benson	cf		
Charles Boone (Lefty)		p	
Barney Brown	p		
Bill Cash (Ready)	c		
Oscar Charleston			coach
Mahlon Duckett		3b	2b
Stanley Glenn		c	
Hubert Glenn		p	
Garrel Hartman		utl	
Freddie Hobgood		p	
Ulysses Mahoney		p	
Henry Miller	p		
Clarence Palm (Spoony)		c	

1944 Philadelphia Stars. Standing L to R: Stan Glenn, Garrel Hartman, Bill Ricks, Henry Miller, Marvin Williams, Ed Bolden, Ed Stone, Goose Curry, Jim West, Hubert Glenn, Spoony Palm, and Oscar Charleston. Kneeling: Frank Austin, Charles Boone, Mahlon Duckett, Barney Brown, Ulysses Mahoney, Gene Benson, and Bill Cash.

Negro Leagues Baseball Museum

Player	1	2	3	Player	1	2	3	Player	1	2	3
Bill Ricks	p			Jay Wilson	inf			Napoleon Gulley		p	
Clyde Spearman		of	3b	Leandy Young	of			Lovell Harden	p		
Henry Spearman		3b	of	Wilbur Young	p			Billy Horne		2b	ss
Ed Stone	lf	of		Willie Young	p			George Jefferson	p		
Pete Sunkett		p						Willie Jefferson	p		
Jim West	1b			**Chicago American Giants**				Sam Jethroe	cf		
Marvin Williams	2b			Candy Jim Taylor			M	Willie McCarey		p	
				Herbert Barnhill		c		Quincy Trouppe	c		
1945				John Bissant	lf			Archie Ware	1b		
				Willie Cornelius (Sug)		p		Jesse Williams		c	
Baltimore Elite Giants				Jimmy Crutchfield	cf			Parnell Woods	3b		
Joe Black		p		Martin Davis		p					
Thomas Butts (Pee Wee)	ss			Jesse Douglas	2b			**Harlem Globetrotters**			
Bill Byrd	p			Tommy Dukes	c			Ted Radcliffe (Double Duty)	c	p	M
Roy Campanella	c			Gentry Jessup	p			Wesley Barrow		c	
Robert Clarke		c		Wilbur King (Dolly)		ss		Mike Berry (Red)		p	
Wesley Dennis (Doc)	1b			Clarence Locke		p	1b	Norman Cross		p	
Frank Duncan III		p		Henry McCall		of		John Gibbons	p		
Thomas Glover	p			Walter McCoy	p			Napoleon Gulley	p	of	
David Harvey (Bill)		p		Gready McKinnis	p			Stamp Holly	of		
Roland Hinton (Archie)		inf		Willie McMeans		p		Collins Jones	2b		
Bill Hoskins	lf			Clyde McNeal		ss		Everett Marcell	c	of	
Henry Kimbro	cf			Clyde Nelson	3b			Rogers Pierre	p		
Nate Moreland		p		Art Pennington	1b	of		Bobby Robinson	of		
William Morgan		p		Charlie Shields		p		Joe Spencer	ss		
Andrew Porter	p			John Ford Smith	rf			Bundy Treherno	1b		
Norman Robinson (Bobby)	3b			Ollie West		p		Bruce Wright	3b		
Felton Snow	s	s		Ralph Wyatt	ss						
Donald Troy		p						**Homestead Grays**			
Tom Walker (Tony)		p		**Cincy-Indy Clowns**				Vic Harris	of		M
Harry Williams	2b			Jesse Walker (Hoss)	inf		M	Sam Bankhead	ss		
Burnis Wright (Bill)	rf			Hoses Allen (Buster)		p		Ray Battle		3b	
				Lamb Barbee (Bud)		of	p	James Bell (Cool Papa)	cf	lf	
Birmingham Black Barons				Jim Bennett		p		Jerry Benjamin	rf	cf	
Wingfield Welch			M	Leroy Cromartie		inf		Garnet Blair		p	
Lloyd Bassett (Pepper)		c		Roosevelt Davis (Rosey)		p		Ray Brown	p	of	
Herman Bell		c		? Dickins		p		? Butts		3b	
Alonzo Boone		p		Reynaldo Drake (Verdes)	lf			Ernest Carter (Spoon)		p	
John Britton	3b			Atires Garcia (Angel)		p		A. Davis		3b	
Earl Bumpus	p			Sam Hairston	c	inf		Robert Gaston		c	
Lorenzo Davis (Piper)	1b			Albert Haywood (Buster)		c		Josh Gibson	c		
Kendall Felder		inf		Leroy Holmes (Phillie)		ss		Dave Hoskins	lf	rf	p
Alvin Gipson	p			Lazarus Medina	p			B. Jackson (Bozo)		2b	
Paul Hardy		c		Henry Merchant	cf			Norman Jackson (Jelly)	2b		
John Huber		p	c	Raymond Navarro (Raul)		c	of	Cecil Kaiser		p	
Lester Lockett	lf			Julio Arango Ortiz (Bill)	ss	of		Wilbur King (Dolly)		utl	
Louis Louden (Tommy)		c		Alex Radcliff	3b			John Leftwich		p	
John Markham		p		John Ray		of		Walter Leonard (Buck)	1b		
Felix McLaurin		cf		Henry Smith	2b	ss		Edward Robinson (Robbie)		3b	ss
Jimmy Newberry	p			Oliver Smith		p		Joe Spencer		2b	
Tom Parker		of		Leroy Sutton		p		Edsall Walker		p	
Art Pennington		lf		Reece Tatum (Goose)		1b		Robert Walker (R.T.)		p	
Bill Perkins		c		Armando Vasquez	1b			Roy Welmaker	p		
Ted Radcliffe (Double Duty)	c	p		Lafayette Washington (Fay)		p		David Whatley		of	
John Ray		of		Amos Watson		p		Jud Wilson		3b	
Jim Riley	2b			Johnny Williams	p			John Wright	p		
Tommy Sampson		2b		Fred Wilson		of	p				
Alfred Saylor	p							**Kansas City Monarchs**			
Tommy Shepard		of		**Cleveland Buckeyes**				Frank Duncan	c		M
Fred Shepard	p			Alfred Armour (Buddy)	lf			James Abernathy		cf	
Quincy Smith		of		Earl Ashby		c		John Paul Berry		1b	
Joe Spencer		2b		Eugene Bremmer	p			Sylvester Carlyle (Junius)		inf	
Ed Steele	rf			George Brown		p		Lee Davis		p	
John Taylor		of		Avelino Canizares	ss			Chesley Gray (Chester)		c	
Frank Thomas	p			Frank Carswell		p		Dave Harper		of	
Frank Thompson (Groundhog)	p			John Cowan	2b	3b		Sammy Haynes		c	
Lafayette Washington (Fay)	p			Lloyd Davenport	rf			Dozier Hood		c	
Jim West	1b			Roosevelt Davis (Rosey)		p		Jim LaMarque	p		
Arthur Wilson (Artie)	ss			Willie Grace		of		Eddie Locke		p	
				Jefferson Guiwn		c		Emory Long (Bang)		of	

Player	1	2	3
John Mack		p	
? Massingale		of	
Jack Matchett		p	
Booker McDaniels	p		
Clarence McMullin		of	
Lee Moody	1b	3b	
Nate Moreland		p	
Leroy Paige (Satchel)		p	
Ted Radcliffe (Double Duty)		c	
John Ray		of	
Othello Renfroe (Chico)	lf	inf	of
Jackie Robinson	ss		
John Scott	cf	of	
William Serrell (Bonnie)		1b	
Hilton Smith	p		
Theolic Smith		p	
Herb Souell	3b	inf	
Walter Thomas		of	p
Henry Thompson (Hank)		2b	
George Walker		p	
Lafayette Washington (Fay)		p	
Jesse Williams (H.)	2b	ss	
Eli Williams (Eddie)		of	
Enloe Wylie		p	
Leandy Young		of	

Major League All Stars (Winter)

Player	1	2	3
Raleigh Mackey (Biz)	c		M
Frank Austin	2b		
Bill Byrd	p		
Roy Campanella	c		
Johnny Davis	lf		
Bob Harvey	rf		

Player	1	2	3
Lenial Hooker (Len)	p		
Monte Irvin	cf		
Don Newcombe	p		
Roy Partlow	p		
Leonard Pearson (Lennie)		1b	3b
Dave Thomas	1b		
Murray Watkins	3b		
Willie Wells	ss		

Memphis Red Sox

Player	1	2	3
Larry Brown	c		M
Edgar Baker		p	
Fred Bankhead	2b	inf	
T.J. Brown (Tom)		ss	
B.L. Brown		p	
James Canada		1b	
Edgar Chatman		p	
Andy Childs		2b	
Felix Evans (Chin)		p	
Kendall Felder		inf	
Jimmy Ford	3b		
Cowan Hyde (Bubber)		rf	of
W. Johnson		p	
Leaman Johnson		ss	
Albert Jones (Alonzo)		p	
Clinton Jones (Casey)		c	
Robert Keyes	p		
Rufus Ligon	p		
Wayman Longley (Red)		inf	of
Verdell Mathis (Lefty)	p		
Fred McDaniels	cf	of	
John Henry Oliver		ss	
Frank Pearson		p	

Player	1	2	3
Cornelius Robinson (Neil)	lf	of	
William Rogers (Nat)		of	
Joseph Burt Scott		of	
Robert Sharpe		p	
Olan Taylor (Jelly)	1b		
Willie Wells (Brooks)		3b	ss

New Orleans Black Pelicans

Player	1	2	3
Wesley Barrow			M
? Beverly (Nunnie)	lf		
Bob Bissant	ss		
? Davis (Tutt)	rf		
Clarence Fernandez		2b	
? Hardin (Mule)	1b		
? Hicks (Pee Wee)	2b		
Thompson Luther (Jitterbug)		p	
Clifford Matthews	of		
Joseph Medice		inf	
? Moffit (Lefty)		p	
James Murphy (Jimmy)		p	
Rogers Pierre		p	
English Robb	c		
Douglas Rome		p	
? Saucier (Popeye)	cf		
? Stamps (Jelly)		3b	
Frank Thompson (Groundhog)		p	
Joe Wiley	3b		
Britt Wood	c		

New York Black Yankees

Player	1	2	3
George Scales	2b		M
Emery Adams (Ace)	p		
Rufus Baker		inf	

1945 Kansas City Monarchs. Back row L to R: Hilton Smith, Enloe Wylie, Lee Davis, Satchel Paige, Frank Duncan, Jim LaMarque, George Walker, unknown, unknown. Front row L to R: Lee Moody, Eddie Locke, Emory Long, Jesse Williams, John Scott, Dave Harper, Walter Thomas, Herb Souell, Chico Renfoe, and Jackie Robinson.
Larry Lester

Player	1	2	3	Player	1	2	3	Player	1	2	3
Marvin Barker	3b			Murray Watkins	3b			**1946**			
Ted Christopher	c	1b	of	Willie Wells	ss						
Roosevelt Davis (Rosey)		p		James Wilkes (Jimmy)			of	**Satchel Paige All-Stars (Winter)**			
Percy Forrest	p			Albert Williams		p		Frank Austin	2b	ss	
Alphonso Gerrard		inf		Robert Williams (Cotton)		p		Dan Bankhead	p		
Walter Hardy		ss		Sidney Williams (Al)		p		Gene Benson		of	
Leroy Holmes (Phillie)	2b			Willie C. Williams (Curley)		2b	ss	Willard Brown	of		
John Johnson (Johnny)		p		Willie Wynn	c			Barney Brown	p		
William Kelly		c						Frank Duncan		c	
Robert Mack		p		**Philadelphia Stars**				Howard Easterling	3b		
Luis Marquez		of		Frank Austin	ss			John Hayes		c	
Felix McLaurin	cf			Gene Benson	cf			Monte Irvin		of	
Pete McQueen	lf			Barney Brown	p			Gentry Jessup	p		
Clarence Palm (Spoony)		c		Bill Cash (Ready)		c		Sam Jethroe	of		
Bill Perkins		c		Joe Chisholm		p		Rufus Lewis	p		
Claude Poole		p		Homer Curry (Goose)	rf			Maxwell Manning (Max)	p		
Henry Spearman	3b			Bill Davis		p		John O'Neil (Buck)	1b		
John Stanley (Neck)	p			Mahlon Duckett	inf			Leroy Paige (Satchel)	p		
James Starks		1b		Joe Fillmore		p		Leonard Pearson (Lennie)		1b	of
? Tyson		1b		Stanley Glenn		c		Hilton Smith	p		
Lawrence Washington		1b		Hubert Glenn		p		Henry Thompson (Hank)	of		
Willie Wells		ss		Wilmer Harris		p		Quincy Trouppe	c		
David Whatley	rf			Eddie Jefferson		p		Arthur Wilson (Artie)	ss		
				Ralph Johnson		p					
New York Cubans				Willie Johnson		c		**Asheville Blues**			
Jose Fernandez			M	Larry Kimbrough		p		C.L. Moore			M
Bill Anderson		p		Jim Kimbrough		p		Spencer Alexander	lf		
Dave Barnhill (Impo)	p			? McClaren		p		? Banks		c	
Ameal Brooks		c		Henry Miller		p		Bob Bowman	p		
Jesse Cannady (Hoss)		3b		Clarence Palm (Spoony)		c		? Brannon		1b	
Chifian Clark (Cleveland)	cf			Roy Partlow	p			Ed Bryon		2b	
Martin Dihigo	rf	of	p	Bill Ricks	p			Waldo Dunlap	p		
Greene Farmer		p		Raymond Smith		p		Frank Flemming	p		
Gil Garrido	2b			Clyde Spearman		of		? Hatten		c	
Victor Greenidge		p		Ed Stone	lf			Arthur Hefner	cf		
Ramon Heredia		3b		Pete Sunkett		p		A.C. Neely	rf		
Carranza Howard	p			Jim West	1b			Vernon Phillips	p		
Rogelio Linares	lf			Marvin Williams	2b			Herman Taylor	3b		
Louis Louden (Tommy)	c			Tom Woods			3b	Fred Worthy	ss		
Horacio Martinez (Rabbit)	ss										
Orestes Minoso (Minnie)		3b		**Pittsburgh Crawfords**				**Atlanta Black Crackers**			
Barney Morris	p			Fred Burnett (Tex)			M	Bill Bradford	rf		
Rafael Noble (Ray)		c		Jorge Almagro	lf			Robert Branson	p		
Tom Parker	of			Joe Atkins	3b			Robert Davis (Butch)	lf		
Fernando Pedroso (Diaz)	3b			Charles Boone (Lefty)	p			? Ellison (Early-Bird)		c	
Javier Perez (Blue)		of	2b	Jose Luis Cuella	rf			Thomas Favors (Monk)	1b		
Santos Salazar		utl		Cecil Kaiser	p			Charles Glenn	cf		
Carlos Santiago		2b		Howard Kimbro (Howdy)		p		Sammy Haynes		c	
Pat Scantlebury		p		Fernando Marvarez	ss			B. Jackson (Bozo)		ss	
Johnny Taylor		p		Gready McKinnis		p		Brennan King	p		
Dave Thomas	1b			Fred Morefield		of		Early King	p		
Luis Tiant, Sr.		p		Sidney Morton (Sy)		inf		? Owens (Dusty)	2b		
				Gabriel Patterson	cf			Johnny Richardson (Bob)	ss		
Newark Eagles				Willie Patterson		c		William Rowe (Schoolboy)	p		
Earl Banks	2b			Maurice Peatross		1b		Emanual Sampson (Eddie)		of	
Johnny Davis	lf	p		Willie Pope		p		Willie Terrell	3b		
? Gray		p		William Rowe (Schoolboy)	p			Leon Wyatt	p		
Bob Harvey	rf			Joe Spencer	2b						
Jimmy Hill	p							**Baltimore Elite Giants**			
Lenial Hooker (Len)		p		**Toledo Cubs**				Jimmie Armstead		of	
? Hopkins		p		? Finley	p			William Barnes (Jimmy)		p	
Tom Humber (Charlie)		2b		? Hoke (Bud)				Joe Black		p	
Monte Irvin		of	3b	William Love (Andy)		utl		Thomas Butts (Pee Wee)	ss		
Raleigh Mackey (Biz)		c		William Spencer (Pee Wee)		c		Bill Byrd	p		
Francis Matthews (Fran)	cf	1b		Norman Stearnes (Turkey)		of		Robert Clarke		c	
Terris McDuffie	p			Ron Teasley	1b	of		Jose Figueroa (Tito)		p	
Don Newcombe	p			Charley Williams		p		Enrique Figueroa		p	
Warren Peace		p						Jonas Gaines	p		
Leonard Pearson (Lennie)	1b							Jim Gilliam (Junior)	2b	inf	of
Tom Roberts (Speck)		p						Felix Guilbe		p	of

Player	1	2	3
Roland Hinton (Archie)		p	
Bill Hoskins	lf		
Sammy T. Hughes		2b	
Henry Kimbro	cf		
Luis Marquez		of	
Andrew Porter	p		
Henry Robinson (Frazier)		c	
Norman Robinson (Bobby)	rf		
Robert Romby		p	
Frank Russell (Junior)		2b	
George Scales		inf	of
Felton Snow	3b		
Manuel Stewart		ss	3b
Luis Villodas		c	
John Washington	1b		
Willie Wells		ss	
Stephen Zapp		3b	

Birmingham Black Barons

Player	1	2	3
Tommy Sampson	2b		M
Earl Ashby		c	
Lloyd Bassett (Pepper)	c		
Herman Bell		c	
Alonzo Boone		p	
Lyman Bostock, Sr.		1b	
John Britton	3b		
Lorenzo Davis (Piper)	2b		
Alvin Gipson	p		
Dave Harper		of	
Jehosie Heard	p		
Curtis Hollingsworth		p	
H. Johnson (Hamp)		cf	
Lester Lockett	lf		
? McNealy		of	
Lee Moody		of	
Jimmy Newberry	p		
Alonzo Perry		p	1b
Nat Pollard	p		
Bill Powell		p	
? Reynolds		1b	
Emanual Sampson (Eddie)		rf	
Fred Shepard		cf	
Quincy Smith		cf	
Ed Steele	rf		
J. Thomas		of	
Arthur Wilson (Artie)	ss		

Boston Blues

Player	1	2	3
Tom Parker	of		M
Robert Abernathy	lf		
Bradford Bennett	rf		
Charles Boone (Lefty)		p	
Joe Buckner		p	
Cloyce Burns		p	
George Cooper	p		
Ross Davis	p		
George Edwards	ss		
Chesley Gray (Chester)		c	utl
John Hayes	c		
Oziah Johnson		of	
Robert Kennedy	p		
Hiram Marshall		p	3b
Eldridge Mayweather (Ed)	1b		
Alexander Newkirk		p	
Robert Scott		1b	utl
Leroy Sutton	p		
Robert Walker (R.T.)		p	
Jesse Warren	3b		
Emmett Wilson		of	

Chicago American Giants

Player	1	2	3
Candy Jim Taylor			M
Herbert Barnhill	c		
John Bissant		2b	
Chet Brewer		p	
Joe Buckner		p	
W.M. Charter (Bill)		of	c
Willie Cornelius (Sug)		p	
Herman Howard (Red)	p		
Grover Hunt		c	
Gentry Jessup	p	ss	
Clarence Locke		p	
Bernell Longest (Chick)		2b	of
Walter McCoy	p		
Jim McCurine	rf	lf	
Clyde McNeal	2b	ss	
Harry Mello		ss	
John Miles (Mule)		lf	cf
Herald Millon		inf	
Clyde Nelson	3b		
Art Pennington		of	
Harry Rhodes	lf	p	
Jacob Robinson		3b	
Sam Seagraves		c	
Wardell Smith		p	
Walter Thomas	cf	p	rf
Ralph Wyatt	ss		
Edward Young (Pep)	1b		

Cincinnati Crescents (Winter)

Player	1	2	3
Wingfield Welch			M
Lorenzo Davis (Piper)	2b	utl	
Luke Easter	rf	1b	
Paul Hardy	c		
Leroy Paige (Satchel)	p		
Ted Radcliffe (Double Duty)	p	c	
Ed Steel	cf		
Reece Tatum (Goose)	1b		
Frank Thompson (Groundhog)	p		
Arthur Wilson (Artie)	ss		

Cleveland Buckeyes

Player	1	2	3
Hoses Allen (Buster)		p	
Alfred Armour (Buddy)	lf	3b	
Alonzo Boone	p		
Charles Boone (Lefty)		p	
Herbert Bracken (Doc)		p	
Eugene Bremmer	p		
Chet Brewer	p		
John Brown		p	
Walter Burch		c	
? Bush		p	
Walter Calhoun		p	
Frank Carswell		p	
Elijah Chism (Eli)		of	
Vibert Clarke	p		
John Cowan	2b	3b	ss
Frank Flemming		p	
Willie Grace	rf		
Tommy Harris		c	
Billy Horne	ss	2b	
Willie Jefferson		p	
George Jefferson		p	
Sam Jethroe	cf		
Curtis Jones (Bud)		p	
Leon Kellman	3b	c	p
Steve Keyes (Zeke)		p	
Eddie Klepp		p	
Perez Larrinago		2b	ss
Nath McClinnic		of	

[Chicago Stars / third column]

Player	1	2	3
George Minor		of	
John Henry Oliver		ss	
Jimmy Reynolds		3b	
Vicial Richardson		ss	
? Singleton		p	
Al Smith		3b	
Quincy Trouppe	c		
Archie Ware	1b		
Andy Watts		3b	
Jesse Williams		c	
Sam Woods		p	
Ralph Wyatt	ss		

Cleveland Clippers

Player	1	2	3
Jimmy Binder			M
John Shackleford			M
Leonard Ausbrook		c	
Edgar Baker	p		
Sam Barber	p		
Lee Boyd		3b	
Jack Bruce		rf	
Carl Childs		c	
Otis Davis	ss		
Leroy Greffenreed		2b	
William Hall	lf		
Jack Henderson	2b		
Lucious Holton	p		
Tommy Jackson		p	
Robert Johnson	1b		
Eddie Johnson		rf	2b
William Mason		utl	
Frank McAllister (Chip)		p	
Tom Miles	cf		
Harvey Peterson		p	of
Leroy Reed		utl	
Raymond Taylor	c		
Travis Taylor	3b		
Eli Williams (Eddie)		p	
Jesse Williams		c	

Colored Athletics

Player	1	2	3
? Baer		p	
Sherwood Brewer		3b	
? Clark		2b	
? Dawson		lf	
? Good		rf	
? Laboeu		ss	
Francis Matthews (Fran)		1b	
Bill Simms		cf	
? Wash		c	

Homestead Grays

Player	1	2	3
Vic Harris	of		M
Sam Bankhead	ss	2b	3b
James Bell (Cool Papa)	lf		
Jerry Benjamin	cf		
Garnet Blair		p	
Matthew Carlisle (Lick)		2b	
? Casper		p	
Howard Easterling	3b		
Tom Fields		p	
Wilmer Fields	p	3b	
Josh Gibson	c		
Harold Hairston		p	
? Harrison		p	
Dave Hoskins	rf	of	
Samuel Jones (Sad Sam)		p	
Walter Leonard (Buck)	1b		
Luis Marquez		of	2b
Eudie Napier		c	

Player	1	2	3
Ed Pape		of	
Alonzo Perry	p		
Dave Pope		utl	
Ted Radcliffe (Double Duty)	p	c	
Eugene Smith		p	
Frank Thompson (Groundhog)		p	
Bob Thurman		of	p
Robert Walker (R.T.)		p	
Cicero Warren		p	
Frank Williams		of	
Dan Wilson		3b	of

Indianapolis Clowns

Player	1	2	3
Jesse Walker (Hoss)		3b	M
Lamb Barbee (Bud)		rf	
Jim Bennett		p	
Julius Brown		p	
Howard Cleveland (Duke)		cf	rf
Ralph Cole		of	
Jim Colzie		p	
Eddie Davis (Nyasses)	p		
Reynaldo Drake (Verdes)		rf	cf
Efigenio Ferrer (Coco)		ss	
Atires Garcia (Angel)		p	
Manuel Godinez		p	
Sam Hairston	c		
Albert Haywood (Buster)		c	
Leo Henry (Preacher)	p		
Leonard Lindsay		1b	3b
Levingelo Lugo (Leo)	lf		
Lazarus Medina		p	
Henry Merchant	cf	of	
Raymond Navarro (Raul)		ss	
Ray Neil	2b		
James Oliver (Pee Wee)	ss		
Thomas Quinones		p	
Hiawatha Shelby		of	
Eugene Smith (Gene)		3b	ss
Reece Tatum (Goose)	1b		
Amos Watson		p	
Johnny Williams	p		
? Winkle		3b	

Kansas City Monarchs

Player	1	2	3
Frank Duncan			M
Ted Alexander		p	
Willard Brown	cf		
Allen Bryant (Lefty)		p	
Frank III Duncan		p	
James Greene (Joe)		c	of
Jim Hamilton		ss	
Larry Hubbard		inf	of
Clifford Johnson (Connie)		p	
Jim LaMarque	p		
? McKamey		ss	
Clarence McMullin		of	
Lee Moody		1b	3b
Larry Napoleon		p	
John O'Neil (Buck)	1b		
Leroy Paige (Satchel)	p		
Othello Renfroe (Chico)	ss	inf	
John Scott	lf		
Fred Smith		c	
Hilton Smith	p		
John Ford Smith		p	
Herb Souell	3b		
T.R. Strong (Ted)	rf		
Earl Taborn		c	
Henry Thompson (Hank)	2b		
Bob Turner		c	

Player	1	2	3
Amos Watson	p		
Jesse Williams (H.)		ss	
Enloe Wylie	p		

Kansas City Royals (Winter)

Player	1	2	3
Chet Brewer	p		M
Sam Hairston	c		
Bill Hoskins	cf		
Cowan Hyde (Bubber)	rf		
Verdell Mathis (Lefty)	p		
Lee Moody	1b		
Ray Neil	2b		
Clyde Nelson	3b		
Ed Steele	lf		
Johnny Williams	p		
Jesse Williams (H.)	ss		

Knoxville Giants

Player	1	2	3
William Rogers (Nat)	rf		M
? Armstrong	1b		
? Fine	c		
George Handy	2b		
? Harper	cf		
? Horne	lf		
? Long	3b		
? Smith	ss		

Memphis Red Sox

Player	1	2	3
Olan Taylor (Jelly)	1b		M
Dan Bankhead	p		
Fred Bankhead	2b		
Bob Boyd		1b	
Otis Branch			
Larry Brown			c
Marlin Carter (Mel)	3b		
Edgar Chatman		p	
Charles Davidson		p	
Felix Evans (Chin)		p	
Kendall Felder		inf	
Jimmy Ford	3b		
Leslie Green (Chin)	cf		
George Handy		inf	
John Huber	p		
Willie Hutchinson	p		
Cowan Hyde (Bubber)	rf	of	
Leaman Johnson		2b	ss
Albert Jones (Alonzo)	p		
Clinton Jones (Casey)	c		
Cecil Jordan			
Robert Keyes		p	
Rufus Ligon		p	
James Lockman (Tut)			
Wayman Longley (Red)		inf	of
? Mathew		of	
Verdell Mathis (Lefty)	p		
Fred McDaniels		of	
John Henry Oliver		of	
Frank Pearson	p		
Alex Radcliff	lf	of	3b
Cornelius Robinson (Neil)	ss	of	
William Rogers (Nat)		of	
Riley Stewart	p		
Walter Thomas	p	of	
Jesse Warren	p		
Willie Wells (Brooks)		ss	

Nashville Cubs

Player	1	2	3
Wesley Barrow			M
Fred Burnett (Tex)			M
Wilburn Atkinson	rf		

Player	1	2	3
Alfred Brown (Bomber)	p		
Claiborne Cartwright		2b	
Nathanial Edwards	p		
Tobey Farmer		3b	
Raymond Gaffney		c	
R.B. Jackson			
H.L. Johnson		3b	
Robert Lee Jones		c	
Clinton McCord (Butch)	1b		
Richard Murray		p	
Nathan Owen	c		
William Scott	ss		
Wilbur Waters	p		
Norman Young (Harvey)	2b		

New York Black Yankees

Player	1	2	3
Emery Adams (Ace)		p	
Carlos Ascanio	1b		
Rufus Baker		c	of
Lamb Barbee (Bud)		1b	p
Marvin Barker	3b	cf	1b
Ameal Brooks		rf	
W.T. Cooper (Bill)		c	
James Cooper		p	
Charles Davidson		p	
A. Davis		2b	
Russ Dedeaux		p	
Rodolfo Fernandez (Rudy)		p	
Percy Forrest		p	
Robert Griffith	p		
Walter Hardy		ss	2b
John Hayes		c	
Freddie Hobgood		p	
Bill Hoskins		of	
John Johnson (Johnny)	p		
Felix McLaurin	cf		
Calvin Medley		p	
Alexander Newkirk		p	
Clarence Palm (Spoony)			c
Clyde Parris		2b	3b
Bill Perkins		c	
Claude Poole		p	
Albert Preston		p	
Glemby Richardson		2b	
Richard Seay (Dick)		2b	of
John Ford Smith		rf	of
Sylvester Snead	rf	lf	2b
Clyde Spearman		lf	
Joe Spencer		3b	
John Stanley (Neck)	p		
Jake Tolbert		of	p
Willie Wells		ss	
Joe Williams		of	3b

New York Cubans

Player	1	2	3
Jose Fernandez			M
Bill Anderson	p		
Dave Barnhill (Impo)		p	
Chifian Clark (Cleveland)	rf	of	
Francisco Coimbre (Pancho)		of	
Alejandro Crespo (Alex)	cf		
Martin Crue (Matty)		p	
Eddie Daniels		p	
Silvio Garcia	ss		
Gil Garrido		2b	ss
Carranza Howard		p	
James Jenkins		p	
Rogelio Linares	lf		
Louis Louden (Tommy)	c		
Horacio Martinez (Rabbit)	2b		ss

Player	1	2	3
Orestes Minoso (Minnie)	3b		
Barney Morris		p	
Rafael Noble (Ray)	c		
Fernando Pedroso (Diaz)	rf	3b	2b
Carlos Santiago		2b	
Pat Scantlebury	p		
Dave Thomas	1b		
Luis Tiant, Sr.	p		
? Wright		3b	

Newark Eagles

Player	1	2	3
Raleigh Mackey (Biz)	c		M
James Boyd		p	
Cecil Cole		p	
Johnny Davis	lf	p	
Leon Day	p	of	
Larry Doby	2b		
William Felder (Benny)		3b	
Oscar Givens		ss	
? Harrison		2b	3b
Bob Harvey	rf	of	
Lenial Hooker (Len)	p		
Monte Irvin	ss	of	
Clarence Israel (Pint)		3b	ss
Rufus Lewis		p	
Maxwell Manning (Max)	p		
Charles Parks		c	1b
Andrew Patterson (Pat)	3b		
Warren Peace		p	
Leonard Pearson (Lennie)	1b	3b	
Leon Ruffin	c		
Murray Watkins		3b	
James Wilkes (Jimmy)	cf	of	
Robert Williams (Cotton)		p	

Philadelphia Stars

Player	1	2	3
Homer Curry (Goose)	rf	of	M
Leroy Dawson			M
Frank Austin	ss		
Gene Benson	cf		
Barney Brown	p		
George Brown		of	
Bill Cash (Ready)	c		
James Clarkson (Bus)	3b	rf	
Joe Craig		of	inf
Wesley Dennis (Doc)	1b		
Mahlon Duckett		inf	
Joe Fillmore		p	
Stanley Glenn		c	
Wilmer Harris	p		
Eddie Jefferson		p	
Tom Jones (Pete)		c	
Larry Kimbrough		p	
Henry McHenry	p		
Henry Miller		p	
Leroy Paige (Satchel)		p	
Bill Perkins		c	
Bill Ricks		p	
Harry Simpson (Suitcase)	lf	p	
Raymond Smith		p	
John Thorn		of	
Murray Watkins	2b	3b	
Alfred Wilmore		p	
? Wilson		c	

Pittsburgh Crawfords

Player	1	2	3
Roy Parnell (Red)			M
Robert Arthur		p	
Joe Atkins	3b		
John Barber		of	

Player	1	2	3
Ralph Crumbie		c	
Bernard Fernandez		p	
George Harris	c		
Ben Hill	p		
Frank Jarrett		p	
Fred Johnson	p		
Jimmy Johnson (Jeep)		ss	
Fred Morefield	rf		
Sidney Morton (Sy)		ss	
Gabriel Patterson	cf		
Willie Pope	p		
Henry Spearman	1b		
Ted Toles		p	
Ollie West		p	
David Whatley		of	

1947

Asheville Blues

Player	1	2	3
Spencer Alexander	rf		
? Banks	c		
Bob Bowman	p		
? Brannon	1b		
Arthur Heffner	cf		
Tom Humber (Charlie)	2b		
Jim Pendleton	ss		
? Stewart	lf		
Herman Taylor	3b		
Will Thompson (Gene)		p	

Baltimore Elite Giants

Player	1	2	3
Wesley Barrow			M
George Scales			M
Joe Black	p		
Ernest Burke		p	
Thomas Butts (Pee Wee)	ss		
Bill Byrd	p		
Robert Davis (Butch)	lf		
Jonas Gaines		p	
Jim Gilliam (Junior)		2b	
Felix Guilbe	rf	p	
? Jackson (Gen)		p	of
Henry Kimbro	cf		
Lester Lockett	3b	of	
Everett Marcell		c	
Clinton McCord (Butch)		1b	
Jose Pereira		p	
Bill Perkins		c	
Norman Robinson (Bobby)		of	
Henry Robinson (Frazier)		c	
Robert Romby	p		
Joe Spencer		inf	
Manuel Stewart		utl	
Luis Villodas		c	
John Washington	1b	3b	
Amos Watson		p	
Joe Wiley		2b	3b

Birmingham Black Barons

Player	1	2	3
Lloyd Bassett (Pepper)	c		
Herman Bell		c	
? Bizzle		inf	
John Britton	3b		
Elijah Chism (Eli)	lf		
Lorenzo Davis (Piper)	1b		
Alvin Gipson		p	
Jehosie Heard	p		
Curtis Hollingsworth		p	
Clarence King (Pijo)		of	

Player	1	2	3
Lee Moody		of	
Jimmy Newberry	p		
Alonzo Perry		p	
Nat Pollard		p	
Bill Powell	p		
Norman Robinson (Bobby)		of	
Tommy Sampson	2b		
Joe Scott		1b	
Ed Steele	rf		
J. Thomas	cf		
Walter Thomas		of	
Jim West		1b	
Sam Williams		p	
Arthur Wilson (Artie)	ss		

Chicago American Giants

Player	1	2	3
Candy Jim Taylor			M
Alfred Armour (Buddy)	lf	cf	
John Bissant	cf	lf	
Lyman Bostock, Sr.	1b		
Earl Bumpus	p		
Walter Collins		p	
Erwin Fowlkes		ss	
Sam Hill	rf	lf	
Samuel Jackson		p	1b
Gentry Jessup	p		
Leonard Johnson		p	
Clarence Locke		p	
Bernell Longest (Chick)	2b	3b	
Walter McCoy		p	
Jim McCurine		of	
Clyde McNeal	ss		
John Miles (Mule)	3b		
Herald Millon		ss	3b
Sidney Morton (Sy)		inf	
Henry Newberry		p	
Richard Newberry		ss	
Harry Rhodes	p		
John Ritchey	c		
Jacob Robinson		3b	
Riley Stewart		p	
James Talbert		c	
Thomas Turner		1b	
Jesse Warren		2b	

Cleveland Buckeyes

Player	1	2	3
Quincy Trouppe	c		M
Joe Atkins	lf	rf	
Alonzo Boone		p	
Herbert Bracken (Doc)		p	
Ramon Bragana		p	
Eugene Bremmer	p		
Chet Brewer	p		
Frank Caldwell		p	
Vibert Clarke	p		
John Cowan	2b		
Ross Davis		p	
Willie Grace	rf		
Tommy Harris		c	
Sam Jethroe	cf		
Samuel Jones (Sad Sam)	p		
Leon Kellman	3b		
Nath McClinnic		of	
George Minor		of	
Clyde Nelson		3b	
Al Smith	ss		
Eugene Smith		p	
Archie Ware	1b		
Jesse Williams		ss	of
Clyde Williams		p	

Detroit Senators

Player	1	2	3
Wingfield Welch			M
James Bell (Cool Papa)	cf		
William Blair, Jr.		p	
Alvin Gipson	p		
Napoleon Gulley		p	
John Markham	p		
Edward Napoleon		p	
Tom Parker	p		
Robert Pipkin (Lefty)		p	
Alex Radcliff	3b		
Joe Scott	1b		
Ben F. Smith		p	
Jesse Warren	2b		

Detroit Wolves

Player	1	2	3
? Baldwin (Tiny)	c		M
William Dismukes (Dizzy)			M
Luther Hughes (Yoatee)		p	
James Lane (Big Jim)	cf		
Rogers Logan		p	
Lawrence Mathews (Goatee)		p	
Charles Means	2b		
Warren O'Neil	c		
Porter Reed	lf		
Joseph Siddle		p	
Willie Smith	ss		
Fred Sourie		p	
Travis Taylor		c	
Joseph Thurman	1b		
Julius Wood	3b		

Harlem Globetrotters

Player	1	2	3
Paul Hardy	c		M
Joe Brooks		p	
Alphonse Dunn (Blue)	1b		
Howard Gay	3b		
Eugene Hardin		c	
? Holly (Stamp)	cf		
Louis Hutchinson	p		
Collins Jones	2b		
Albert Jones (Alonzo)	p		
Zell Miles	rf		
Rogers Pierre	p		
Ulysses Redd	ss		
Herbert Simpson	lf		
Sam Wheeler		cf	

Havana La Palomas

Player	1	2	3
Ramiro Ramirez		M	
Pedro Barrios	2b		
Jim Bennett	p		
Robustino Cabriales	3b		
Efigenio Ferrer (Coco)	ss		
Richard Jackson (Dick)	p		
Leonard Lindsay	1b	p	
Winslow Means		p	
Andres Mesa	lf		
Juan Noble (John)		p	
Leonard Pigg	c		
Claude Rhodes (Dusty)	p	of	
Eugene Smith (Gene)		3b	inf
Haney Smith	rf		
Armando Vasquez	cf	of	inf

Homestead Grays

Player	1	2	3
Vic Harris	of		M
Earl Ashby		c	
Sam Bankhead	ss		
Jerry Benjamin	cf		
Clarence Bruce		2b	
Robert Carter		p	
Luke Easter	lf		
Wilmer Fields	p	3b	of
Robert Gaston		c	
Harold Hairston		p	
James Harden		p	
Clarence Israel (Pint)	3b		
Jimmy Johnson (Jeep)		ss	
Cecil Kaiser		p	
William Kelly		c	
Wilbur King (Dolly)		2b	
Walter Leonard (Buck)		1b	
Luis Marquez	2b	3b	
Eudie Napier	c		
Gabriel Patterson		of	
Maurice Peatross	1b		
Willie Pope		p	
Eugene Smith		p	
Frank Thompson (Groundhog)		p	
Bob Thurman	rf	p	
Robert Walker (R.T.)	p		
Cicero Warren		p	
John Wright	p		
Edward Young (Pep)	1b	c	3b

Indianapolis Clowns

Player	1	2	3
Jesse Walker (Hoss)	3b		M
Willie Wells	ss		M
Robert Abernathy	lf		
Newton Allen (Newt)		3b	ss
Hoses Allen (Buster)		inf	of
William Barnes (Jimmy)	p		
Jim Bennett		p	
James Brown		p	of
T.J. Brown (Tom)	ss		
Jim Colzie	p		
Reynaldo Drake (Verdes)	cf		
? Espenosia		p	
Efigenio Ferrer (Coco)		inf	
Atires Garcia (Angel)		p	
Alphonso Gerrard		2b	
Manuel Godinez		p	
Juan Guilbe		p	of
Sam Hairston	3b	c	
Albert Haywood (Buster)	c		
Leo Henry (Preacher)	p		
Carranza Howard		p	
Henry Merchant	rf		
Ray Neil	2b		
Leonard Pigg		c	
Thomas Quinones		p	
Reece Tatum (Goose)	1b		
Vicente Villafane		c	inf
Johnny Williams	p		

Kansas City Monarchs

Player	1	2	3
Frank Duncan			M
Ted Alexander	p		
Mike Berry (Red)		p	
Willard Brown	cf		
Allen Bryant (Lefty)		p	
Gene Collins		p	
Tom Cooper		of	1b
Bill Duffy		c	
Thomas Favors (Monk)		inf	of
James Greene (Joe)	c		
Clifford Johnson (Connie)	p		
Jim LaMarque	p		
Booker McDaniels		p	
Lee Moody		of	ss
Larry Napoleon		p	
John O'Neil (Buck)	1b		
Leroy Paige (Satchel)		p	
Othello Renfroe (Chico)	ss		
Gene Richardson		p	
Curt Roberts	2b		
Johnny Sanderson		ss	
John Scott	lf	cf	
John Scroggins		p	of
Hilton Smith	p		
John Ford Smith		p	
Herb Souell	3b		
T.R. Strong (Ted)	rf		
Earl Taborn		c	
Henry Thompson (Hank)		2b	ss
Enloe Wylie	p		

Memphis Red Sox

Player	1	2	3
Larry Brown	c		M
Fred Bankhead	2b		
Dan Bankhead		p	
Bob Boyd	1b		
T.J. Brown (Tom)		ss	
Marlin Carter (Mel)	3b		
Jose Colas		of	
Felix Evans (Chin)	p		
Pedro Formenthal		of	
George Handy		inf	
Paul Hardy		c	
Chester Havis		p	
John Huber	p		
Willie Hutchinson		p	
Cowan Hyde (Bubber)		of	
Clinton Jones (Casey)	c		
Wayman Longley (Red)		rf	of
Verdell Mathis (Lefty)	p		
Frank Pearson	p		
Harmon Purcell		p	
Cornelius Robinson (Neil)	cf	of	
Joseph Burt Scott		of	
Robert Sharpe		p	
Willie Wells (Brooks)		ss	
? White (Ladd)		p	
James Wilson		p	

Nashville Cubs

Player	1	2	3
Felton Snow	3b		M
Jimmie Armstead	cf		
Gerald Jones	lf		
Brennan King	p		
Clinton McCord (Butch)	1b		
? Owens (Dusty)	2b		
Seared Russell	ss		
? Scott	rf		
? Swanson	c		

New York Black Yankees

Player	1	2	3
Rufus Baker		2b	
Lamb Barbee (Bud)	p	of	
Marvin Barker	3b		
Julius Bowers (Julie)		c	
J.B. Broome		of	
Curtis Brown	1b		
George Crowe	1b		
Charles Davidson	p		
Charlie Dean		p	
Alpheus Deane		p	
John Fallings		p	
Greene Farmer		cf	

Player	1	2	3
Alphonso Gerrard		ss	rf
Robert Griffith	p		
Walter Hardy	ss		
John Hayes	c		
Arthur Heffner		of	
Jim Lewis	p		
John McFarland	p		
Alexander Newkirk	p		
Clyde Parris		3b	
Clyde Parris	ss		
Gabriel Patterson		of	
Albert Preston	p		
Glemby Richardson		2b	
Richard Seay (Dick)		2b	
John Ford Smith	cf	of	
Joe Spencer		c	
Larry St. Thomas		c	
John Stanley (Neck)	p		
Benjamin Taylor	p		
Jim West		1b	

New York Cubans

Player	1	2	3
Jose Fernandez			M
Bill Anderson	p		
Homero Ariosa		of	
Dave Barnhill (Impo)	p		
Lorenzo Cabrera	1b		
Chifian Clark (Cleveland)	rf	lf	
Martin Crue (Matty)	p		
Eddie Daniels	p		
Lino Donoso	p		
Claro Duany	lf	rf	
Silvio Garcia	ss	3b	2b
James Jenkins	p		
Louis Louden (Tommy)	c		
Horacio Martinez (Rabbit)	2b	ss	
Orestes Minoso (Minnie)	3b		
Barney Morris	p		
Rafael Noble (Ray)	c		
Pedro Pages		of	
Fernando Pedroso (Diaz)	cf	of	2b
Jose Santiago	p		
Pat Scantlebury	p		
Francisco Sostre		p	
Luis Tiant, Sr.	p		

Newark Eagles

Player	1	2	3
Raleigh Mackey (Biz)	c		M
G. Beal (Lefty)		p	
Ameal Brooks		c	
James Cooper		p	
Johnny Davis	lf	p	
Larry Doby		2b	
Napoleon Gulley		p	
Bob Harvey	cf	rf	
Lenial Hooker (Len)	p		
Monte Irvin	ss	of	
Rufus Lewis	p		
Maxwell Manning (Max)	p		
Charles Parks		c	1b
John Parks		c	of
Andrew Patterson (Pat)	3b		
Warren Peace		p	
Leonard Pearson (Lennie)	1b		
Andrew Porter		p	
Nelson Thomas		p	
James Wilkes (Jimmy)	rf	of	
Leroy Williams		ss	inf
Robert Williams (Cotton)	p		
Willie C. Williams (Curley)		ss	

Player	1	2	3
Robert Wilson		of	3b
Willie Wynn		c	

Philadelphia Stars

Player	1	2	3
Homer Curry (Goose)	of		M
Frank Austin	ss		
Gene Benson	cf	lf	
Alonzo Braithwaite (Archie)	rf	of	
Barney Brown	p		
Arthur Carter			
Bill Cash (Ready)		c	
James Clarkson (Bus)		utl	
Bill Davis		p	
Wesley Dennis (Doc)	1b		
Mahlon Duckett	2b		
Joe Fillmore		p	
Frank Foster			
Stanley Glenn		c	
John Gould (Willie)		p	
Wilmer Harris	p		
Eddie Jefferson		p	
Frank Makell		c	
Henry McHenry	p		
Henry Miller		p	
Clyde Parris		of	
Roy Partlow		p	
Gabriel Patterson		of	
Bill Perkins		c	
Bill Ricks		p	
Ray Robinson		p	
Harry Simpson (Suitcase)		cf	of
Julius Tyus		p	
Mahlon Walls			
Murray Watkins	3b		
Alfred Wilmore		p	
Dan Wilson		of	inf

1948

Baltimore Elite Giants

Player	1	2	3
Joe Black	p		
Wallace Brooks		p	
Ernest Burke		p	
Thomas Butts (Pee Wee)	ss		
Bill Byrd	p		
Joe Campini		c	
James Dailey		p	
Leroy Ferrell		p	
Ed Finney	3b		
Jonas Gaines		p	
Jim Gilliam (Junior)	2b		
Henry Kimbro	cf		
Lester Lockett	lf		
Clinton McCord (Butch)		1b	of
Bill Perkins		c	
Henry Robinson (Frazier)	c		
Robert Romby	p		
Frank Russell (Junior)	rf		
Clyde Sowell		p	
John Washington	1b	3b	
Alfred Wilmore		p	
Henry Wright, Jr.		c	

Birmingham Black Barons

Player	1	2	3
Joe Bankhead		p	
Lloyd Bassett (Pepper)		c	
Herman Bell		c	
John Britton	3b		
Lorenzo Davis (Piper)	2b		

Player	1	2	3
Bill Greason	p		
Wiley Griggs		inf	
Jehosie Heard	p		
Clarence King (Pijo)		of	
Willie Mays		of	
William Morgan		p	
Jimmy Newberry	p		
Alonzo Perry	p	1b	
Nat Pollard		p	
Bill Powell	p		
Norman Robinson (Bobby)	cf		
Joe Scott	1b		
Ed Steele		lf	
Sam Williams		p	
Arthur Wilson (Artie)	ss		
Jay Wilson		3b	ss
Jim Zapp	rf		

Chicago American Giants

Player	1	2	3
Quincy Trouppe	c		M
Henry Bayliss		3b	
Earl Bumpus		p	
Marlin Carter (Mel)	3b		
Alphonso Gerrard		of	
Sam Hill	cf	of	
Gentry Jessup	p		
Leonard Johnson		p	
Clarence Locke		p	1b
Eddie Locke		p	
Walter McCoy		p	
Jim McCurine		lf	
Clyde McNeal	2b	ss	
John Miles (Mule)		of	
Rafaelito Ortiz		p	
Jim Pendleton	ss		
Harry Rhodes	p	1b	
Benvienido Rodriquez		of	c
Fred Shepard		p	
Taylor Smith		p	
Theolic Smith		p	
Riley Stewart	p		
Lonnie Summers		c	
James Talbert		c	
Roberto Vargas	p		
John Williams	1b		
Johnny Wilson		of	

Cleveland Buckeyes

Player	1	2	3
Alonzo Boone		p	
Eugene Bremmer		p	
Chet Brewer	p		
John Brown		p	
Frank Carswell		p	
Vibert Clarke	p		
Willie Grace	rf		
James Greene (Joe)		c	of
Tommy Harris	c		
George Jefferson			coach
Sam Jethroe	cf		
Samuel Jones (Sad Sam)	p		
Leon Kellman	3b	2b	
Earnest Long	p		
Nath McClinnic		of	
George Minor		of	
Clyde Nelson	3b	2b	
Henry Presswood		ss	
Othello Renfroe (Chico)	ss	2b	
William Reynolds (Bill)		2b	ss
Al Smith	lf		
Eugene Smith		p	

Player	1	2	3
Harold Thompson		p	
Archie Ware	1b		

Greensboro Red Wings

Player	1	2	3
Tom Alston	1b		
John Chandler	p		
Tutt Davis	rf		
Benny Hairston	p		
? Ledwell	lf		
John McInnis	p		
Charles Parks	c		
? Roach	3b		
Joseph Siddle		1b	2b
Dave Sims	cf		
Jim Tonkins	2b		
Orlando Varona	ss		

Harlem Globetrotters

Player	1	2	3
Joe Bankhead		p	
J. Bear		c	
W. Bear		of	
Mike Berry (Red)		p	
Sherwood Brewer	ss		
Joe Brooks		p	
Frank Carswell		p	
Johnny Cogdell		p	
Alphonse Dunn (Blue)		utl	
Jim Fishback		2b	
Howard Gay	cf		
Eugene Hardin		c	
Paul Hardy		c	
Louis Hutchington		p	
Dick Kittemer		ss	
Winslow Means		p	
Zell Miles	rf		
Rogers Pierre	p		
Laymon Ramsey		p	
Ulysses Redd	3b		
Herbert Simpson	1b		
? Smith (Sonny)		p	
Othello Strong	p		
Sam Wheeler	lf		
Jesse Williams (H.)	2b		
Johnny Williams		p	
Parnell Woods		3b	

Homestead Grays

Player	1	2	3
Vic Harris		M	
Ted Alexander		p	
Garnett Bankhead		p	
Sam Bankhead	ss		
Charles Bell		p	
? Billings		c	
Garnet Blair	p		
Bob Boston		3b	
Clarence Bruce	2b	3b	
Luther Clifford		c	
Luke Easter	lf		
Wilmer Fields	p	3b	
Erwin Fowlkes	ss		
Charles Gary	3b		
Robert Gaston		c	
Cecil Kaiser	p		
Jim Kimbrough		p	
Walter Leonard (Buck)	1b		
Ben Littles		rf	of
Luis Marquez	cf		
Eudie Napier	c		
Tom Parker		p	
A. Pope		of	

Player	1	2	3
Willie Pope		p	
Willie D. Smith		p	
Ramon Sosa		c	
Frank Thompson (Groundhog)		p	
Bob Thurman	rf	p	
Robert Trice (Bill)		p	
Robert Walker (R.T.)	p		
John Wright	p		

Indianapolis Clowns

Player	1	2	3
Albert Haywood (Buster)	c		M
Jim Bennett		p	
Luis Caballero (Perez)	3b		
Luis Raul Cabrera	p		
Villa Cabrera		of	
Willis Cathey (Bill)	p		
Jim Cohen	p		
? Colthirst		p	
Reynaldo Drake (Verdes)	cf		
James Felder		ss	
Efigenio Ferrer (Coco)		2b	ss
Atires Garcia (Angel)		p	
Walter Gibbons		p	
Manuel Godinez		p	
Sam Hairston	c	3b	1b
Henry Merchant		of	p
Andres Mesa	lf		
Ray Neil	2b		
Leonard Pigg		c	
Andrew Porter		p	
T.R. Strong (Ted)		rf	of
Reece Tatum (Goose)	1b		
Jose Laru Velasquez		p	
? Walton		inf	of
Artemis White (Art)		p	
Johnny Williams	p		
Charles Wilson		of	
Lester Witherspoon		p	

Kansas City Monarchs

Player	1	2	3
Gene Baker	ss		
Willard Brown	cf		
Gene Collins	p		
Tom Cooper		1b	c
Charley Hall		utl	
Herb Howard		of	p
Elston Howard		c	lf
L. Johnson		p	
Clifford Johnson (Connie)		p	
Leonard Johnson		p	
Jim LaMarque	p		
John O'Neil (Buck)	1b		
Gene Richardson	p		
Curt Roberts	2b	lf	
John Scott	rf	c	
John Ford Smith	p		
Hilton Smith		p	
Herb Souell	3b		
Mickey Stubblefiel		p	
Earl Taborn		c	
Henry Thompson (Hank)	lf	rf	2b
Bill Wright		of	

Memphis Red Sox

Player	1	2	3
Fred Bankhead		2b	
? Bivins		p	
Bob Boyd	1b		
Larry Brown		c	
Ernest Carter (Spoon)	p		
Jose Colas	cf		

Player	1	2	3
Walter Collins		p	
John Cowan	2b	3b	
Felix Evans (Chin)	p		
? Gaichey		p	
Cowan Hyde (Bubber)		lf	of
Clinton Jones (Casey)	c		
Steve Keyes (Zeke)		p	
Candido Mara		3b	
Verdell Mathis (Lefty)	p		
William Morgan		p	
Frank Pearson		p	
Cornelius Robinson (Neil)	lf	of	3b
Amando Sanchez		p	
Joseph Burt Scott	rf		
Robert Sharpe	p		
Orlando Varona		ss	3b
I. Wells		p	
Willie Wells (Brooks)	ss	2b	
Willie Wells		3b	
? White (Ladd)		p	
Sam Woods	p		

New York Black Yankees

Player	1	2	3
Ted Alexander		p	
Rufus Baker		c	
Lamb Barbee (Bud)	p	1b	
Marvin Barker	2b	3b	
George Crowe		1b	
Charles Davidson		p	
Willie Ervin		p	
Robert Griffith	p		
Walter Hardy	ss		
John Hayes	c		
Arthur Heffner	rf	cf	
Ben Littles		of	
Felix McLaurin	cf		
Alexander Newkirk		p	
Clyde Parris		3b	
Gabriel Patterson	lf		
Frank Pearson		p	
John Ford Smith		of	
Joe Spencer	3b		
John Stanley (Neck)	p		
Les Wesson		p	

New York Cubans

Player	1	2	3
Jose Fernandez			M
Louis Louden (Tommy)	c	M	
Edward Arencibia		of	
Homero Ariosa		of	
Miguel Ballestro (Pedro)	ss		
Dave Barnhill (Impo)	p		
Jerry Benjamin	cf		
Lyman Bostock, Sr.		1b	
Lorenzo Cabrera	1b		
Chifian Clark (Cleveland)	lf		
George Crowe		1b	
Martin Crue (Matty)		p	
Ray Dandridge		3b	
Jose Fernandez (Pepe)		c	
Martinano Garay (Jose)		p	
Walter Hardy		2b	
James Jenkins		p	
Isidore Leon		of	
Raul Lopez		p	
? Mangrum		of	
Orestes Minoso (Minnie)	3b		
Pedro Miro	2b		
Barney Morris	p		
Alexander Newkirk		p	

Player	1	2	3
Rafael Noble (Ray)		c	
Fernando Pedroso (Diaz)		of	
Wilfredo Salas		p	
Tommy Sampson		2b	
Jose Santiago		p	
Pat Scantlebury	p		
Armando Vasquez		2b	3b
Sam Wheeler		of	

Newark Eagles

Player	1	2	3
William Bell	p		M
Earl Ashby	c		
Bill Carter		p	
Johnny Davis	lf		
Oscar Givens	2b		
Clyde Golden		p	
Bob Harvey	rf		
Lenial Hooker (Len)		p	
Monte Irvin		of	
Wilbur Lansing		p	
Rufus Lewis	p		
Maxwell Manning (Max)	p		
? McLawn		c	
Warren Peace		p	
Leonard Pearson (Lennie)	1b		
? Skinner		c	
James Wilkes (Jimmy)	cf		
Leroy Williams	ss		
Robert Williams (Cotton)	p		
Willie C. Williams (Curley)		of	ss
Bill Wilson		3b	
Robert Wilson	3b		

Philadelphia Stars

Player	1	2	3
Oscar Charleston			M
Frank Austin	ss		
Gene Benson	cf		
Alonzo Braithwaite (Archie)	lf		
Barney Brown	p		
Bill Cash (Ready)	c		
Jimmy Dean		p	
Wesley Dennis (Doc)	1b		
Mahlon Duckett	2b		
Joe Fillmore		p	
Stanley Glenn		c	
John Gould (Willie)		p	
Wilmer Harris		p	
Henry McHenry		p	
Henry Miller	p		
Roy Partlow	p		
Bill Ricks		p	
Harry Simpson (Suitcase)	rf		
Murray Watkins	3b		

1949

Asheville Blues

Player	1	2	3
Charles Green			M
Spencer Alexander	cf		
Joe Anderson	p		
? Bramer	1b		
Eddie Davis (Nyasses)		p	
John Dickerson (Fount)	p		
Waldo Dunlap	p		
? Goins	rf		
? Greene	lf		
Harry Grier	ss		
Tom Humber (Charlie)	2b		
? Mangrum		2b	

Player	1	2	3
Grady Montgomery	3b		
C.L. Moore		of	
Charles Parks	c		
Jim Plummer		ss	
Gene Thompson (Will)		p	
LaVerna Washington	p		

Baltimore Elite Giants

Player	1	2	3
Jesse Walker (Hoss)			M
Henry Bayliss		inf	
Joe Black	p	3b	
Thomas Butts (Pee Wee)	ss		
Bill Byrd	p		
Charles Davidson		p	
Robert Davis (Butch)	lf	rf	
Leon Day		p	inf
Leroy Ferrell		p	
Ed Finney	3b		
Jim Gilliam (Junior)	2b		
Vic Harris			coach
John Hayes	c		
Henry Kimbro	cf		
Lester Lockett		of	
Frank Makell		p	
Clinton McCord (Butch)	1b	rf	
Leonard Pearson (Lennie)	rf	1b	of
Henry Robinson (Frazier)		c	
Silvester Rodgers		p	
Robert Romby	p		
Frank Russell (Junior)		3b	2b
Alfred Wilmore	p		

Birmingham Black Barons

Player	1	2	3
Ted Alexander		p	
Lloyd Bassett (Pepper)		c	
Henry Bayliss		inf	
Herman Bell		c	
Luther Branham		inf	of
John Britton	3b		
Jose Burgos	ss		
Ernest Carter (Spoon)		p	
Lorenzo Davis (Piper)	2b		
Felix Evans (Chin)		p	
Bill Greason	p		
Wiley Griggs		inf	
Clarence King (Pijo)		of	
Willie Mays	cf		
Jimmy Newberry		p	
Alonzo Perry	p	1b	of
Bill Powell	p		
Norman Robinson (Bobby)	lf		
Joe Scott	1b		
William Scruggs (Willie)		p	
Ed Steele	rf		
Dick Watts		p	
Sam Williams	p		

Chicago American Giants

Player	1	2	3
Wingfield Welch			M
Lyman Bostock, Sr.	1b		
George Brown		of	
Nat Clifton (Sweetwater)		1b	
Lloyd Davenport	rf		
Jesse Douglas	3b		
Alvin Gipson	p		
Gentry Jessup	p		
Jim McCurine		of	
Gready McKinnis	p		
Felix McLaurin	lf		
Clyde McNeal	ss		

Player	1	2	3
John Miles (Mule)		of	
Willie Patterson		c	3b
Art Pennington		of	
Ted Radcliffe (Double Duty)		c	p
Harry Rhodes	p		
Tommy Sampson	2b		
Eugene Smith		p	
Theolic Smith		p	
Taylor Smith		p	
Othello Strong		p	
Lonnie Summers	c		
Joe Taylor		c	
Alfred Thomas (Buck)		p	
Johnny Wilson	cf		

Homestead Grays

Player	1	2	3
Sam Bankhead	cf		
Lonnie Blair		p	
Mahlon Duckett	2b		
Clarence Evans		p	
Wilmer Fields	p	3b	
Charles Gary	3b		
Robert Gaston	c		
Josh Gibson, Jr.		3b	
Dan Jackson	lf		
Cecil Kaiser		p	
Walter Leonard (Buck)	1b		
Roy Partlow	p		
Johnny Richardson (Bob)	ss		
Robert Trice (Bill)		p	
Robert Walker (R.T.)		p	
Lester Witherspoon	rf		

Houston Eagles

Player	1	2	3
Eddie Brooks	2b		
Jerome Brown		inf	
John Brown		p	
John Dandridge		p	
Johnny Davis	lf	p	
Welda Gibson		p	
Clyde Golden		p	
George Handy		inf	
Bob Harvey	rf		
Jehosie Heard	p		
Lenial Hooker (Len)		p	
Raymond Lacy		of	
Wilbur Lansing		p	
Rufus Lewis	p		
Maxwell Manning (Max)	p		
Fred McDaniel		utl	
Clarence McMullin		of	
John O'Dell		p	
Andrew Patterson (Pat)		2b	3b
Porter Reid		of	
Leon Ruffin	c		
James Wallace		c	
John Washington	1b		
James Wilkes (Jimmy)	cf		
Felix Williams (Jeff)		utl	
Robert Williams (Cotton)		p	
Willie C. Williams (Curley)	ss		
Robert Wilson	3b		

Indianapolis Clowns

Player	1	2	3
Albert Haywood (Buster)	c		M
Sherwood Brewer	rf	of	inf
Harry Butts		p	
Willis Cathey (Bill)		p	
Jim Cohen	p		
Eddie Davis (Nyasses)	p		

Player	1	2	3
Reynaldo Drake (Verdes)	lf	cf	
Percy Forrest		p	
Raul Galata		p	
Horace Garner		rf	of
Alphonso Gerrard		inf	
Walter Gibbons		p	
Manuel Godinez		p	
Sam Hairston	3b	of	
Raydell Maddix		p	of
Henry Merchant	cf	of	inf
Ray Neil	2b		
Clyde Nelson		3b	
Leonard Pigg	c	1b	
Andrew Porter	p		
Othello Renfroe (Chico)		inf	
Reece Tatum (Goose)	1b		
Jesse Williams (H.)	ss		
Charles Wilson		lf	of
Lester Witherspoon		of	p

Kansas City Monarchs

Player	1	2	3
John O'Neil (Buck)	1b		M
Gene Baker	ss		
Quincy Barbee (Bud)		of	
Frank Barnes	p		
William Bell (Lefty)		p	
Jim Bergin	1b		
Willard Brown		lf	
Alfred Cartmill		2b	
Ernest Chretian		of	
Luther Clifford		c	
Gene Collins	p	of	
Tom Cooper		c	1b
Melvin Duncan		p	
Frank Duncan III		p	
Isaac Gaston		utl	
Samuel Goshay		of	
Jimmy Hayes		c	
James Henderson (Duke)		cf	of
Elston Howard	c	of	1b
Leonard Hunt		cf	of
Clifford Johnson (Connie)		p	
Ernest Johnson		p	
Jim LaMarque	p		
Robert Landers		p	
Eddie Locke		p	
Booker McDaniels		p	
Nat Peeples		of	
Merle Porter		1b	
Gene Richardson	p		
Curt Roberts	2b		
William Serrell (Bonnie)	3b	inf	
Theolic Smith		p	
Herb Souell	rf	inf	
Alfred Surratt (Slick)		inf	of
Earl Taborn		c	
Harold Thompson		p	
Bob Thurman		p	of
Felix Williams (Jeff)		of	

Louisville Buckeyes

Player	1	2	3
Quincy Barbee (Bud)		of	
Pablo Bernard	ss	inf	
Alonzo Boone		p	
Lincoln Boyd		of	
T.J. Brown (Tom)		ss	3b
Vibert Clarke	p		
Rayford Finch		p	
Willie Grace	cf	rf	
Tommy Harris	c		

Player	1	2	3
Dave Hoskins	lf	cf	
George Jefferson		p	
Paul Jones	p		
Leon Kellman	3b		
Earnest Long	p		
Charles Marvray		of	
George Minor		of	
Charles Murray			
Alberto Osorio		p	
Clyde Parris		3b	
William Reynolds (Bill)	2b		
John Scott	rf	lf	
William Scruggs (Willie)		p	
Eugene Smith		p	
Archie Ware	1b		
Isaac Weston (Deacon)		p	
Parnell Woods		3b	
Calvin Wynn		of	

Memphis Red Sox

Player	1	2	3
Larry Brown	c		M
Homer Curry (Goose)	of		M
Harry Barnes		c	
Bob Boyd	1b		
Ernest Carter (Spoon)		p	
Carlos Colas (Charlie)			c
Jose Colas	of		
John Cowan	3b		
Felix Evans (Chin)		p	
Pedro Formenthal	cf		
Isiah Harris	p		
Willie Hutchinson	p		
Cowan Hyde (Bubber)		of	
Charles Johnson		3b	
Clinton Jones (Casey)	c		
Verdell Mathis (Lefty)	p	of	
William Morgan		p	
Jose Piloto		p	
Cornelius Robinson (Neil)	rf		
Joseph Burt Scott	lf		
Robert Sharpe		p	
Frank Thompson (Groundhog)	p		
Orlando Varona	ss		
Willie Wells (Brooks)		ss	
Willie Wells		3b	
Sam Woods		p	

New York Black Yankees

Player	1	2	3
Marvin Barker	3b	lf	M
Lamb Barbee (Bud)	1b		
Roy Lee Chapman (Ray)		p	
Ted Christopher	c		
Albert Clay (Alton)	cf		
Bernard Fernandez		p	
Joe Forrest	p		
Carranza Howard		p	
Eddie Locke		3b	
Benjamin Lott (Honey)	ss		
Curtis Palmer		lf	of
Frank Pearson		p	
Albert Preston		p	
Glemby Richardson	2b		
John Ford Smith	rf	of	
Joe Spencer		inf	
John Stanley (Neck)		p	
Joe Stephens (Junior)		p	
Chris Vierira	lf	of	

New York Cubans

Player	1	2	3
Homero Ariosa	rf	of	

Player	1	2	3
Dave Barnhill (Impo)		p	
Lorenzo Cabrera	1b		
Chifian Clark (Cleveland)	lf		
George Crowe		1b	
Ray Dandridge		3b	
Lino Donoso		p	
Howard Easterling	3b		
Domingo Galata		p	
Walter Hardy	2b		
James Jenkins		p	
Raul Lopez	p		
Louis Louden (Tommy)	c		
Alexander Newkirk	p		
Rafael Noble (Ray)		c	
Juan Noble (John)		p	
Frank Pearson		p	
Fernando Pedroso (Diaz)	cf		
Pat Scantlebury	p		
Quincy Trouppe		c	
Guillermo Vargas		of	
Armando Yvanes	ss		

Philadelphia Stars

Player	1	2	3
Oscar Charleston			M
Jimmie Armstead		of	
Barney Brown		p	
Bill Cash (Ready)	c		
James Clarkson (Bus)	ss		
Nat Davis	1b		
Jimmy Dean		p	
Mahlon Duckett		inf	
Joe Fillmore		p	
Jonas Gaines		p	
Stanley Glenn		c	
Robert Griffith	p		
Wilmer Harris		p	
Arthur Heffner	lf	3b	p
Herb Hill		p	of
James Jones	cf	lf	
Ben Littles	rf		
Henry Miller	p		
Orlando O'Farrill		inf	of
Bill Ricks	p		
Milt Smith		2b	
Gene Thompson (Will)		p	
Murray Watkins		3b	2b
Marvin Williams		inf	

1950

Baltimore Elite Giants

Player	1	2	3
Clyde Agnew		p	
Thad Anthony		c	
James Bankes		p	
Joe Black	p		
Thomas Butts (Pee Wee)	ss		
Bill Byrd		p	
? Carrol (Sonny)		p	
John Coleman (Lefty)		p	
Floyd Darden		2b	of
Robert Davis (Butch)		lf	
Leon Day		p	of
Lacy Ellerbe		of	inf
? Fanell		p	
Leroy Ferrell		p	
Ed Finney	3b		
Jim Gilliam (Junior)	2b		
Dave Green		rf	
Alvin Green		3b	

Player	1	2	3
John Hayes	c	of	
Alfred Henry		rf	
Tom Humber (Charlie)		of	
Henry Kimbro	cf		
Hank Mainor		p	
Clinton McCord (Butch)		1b	of
Leonard Pearson (Lennie)	1b	of	
Robert Preston		p	
Albert Preston		p	
Fleming Reedy (Buddy)		inf	of
Henry Robinson (Frazier)		c	
Silvester Rodgers		p	
Robert Romby	p	1b	
William Saunders		c	
Kelly Searcy		p	
Hubert Simmons		p	
? Whitfield (Lefty)		p	
Alfred Wilmore	p		
Jim Zapp		of	

Birmingham Black Barons

Player	1	2	3	
Vic Harris				M
Lloyd Bassett (Pepper)		c		
Henry Bayliss	2b	inf		
Herman Bell		c		
William Bell (Lefty)		p		
Jose Burgos	ss			
Willie Collins (Rip)		p		
John Cowan		inf		
Lorenzo Davis (Piper)		1b	2b	
Frank Dixon		3b		
Bill Greason	p			
Wiley Griggs		inf		
Ulysses Hollimon		p		
Curtis Hollingsworth		p		
Leroy Johnson		p		
Fate Jones		of		
Clarence King (Pijo)	cf	of		
Willie Mays		cf		
Jimmy Newberry	p			
Alonzo Perry	1b	p		
Nat Pollard		p		
Bill Powell	p			
Norman Robinson (Bobby)	lf	of		
Kelly Searcy		p		
Ed Steele	rf			
Andy Watts	3b			
Dick Watts		p		
Charles Webster		of		
Sam Williams		p		

Chicago American Giants

Player	1	2	3
Stacy Atkins		p	
Sam Baker		p	
Luther Branham	2b	3b	
Louis Chirban		p	
Louis Clarizio		of	
Benny Coleman		p	
John Dixon		p	
Jesse Douglas	3b	2b	
Frank Dyll		ss	
Clifford Fields (Pete)		lf	
Alvin Gipson		p	
Harold Gordon		p	
John Huber	p		
Cowan Hyde (Bubber)		rf	
Walter Kennedy		rf	
Lester Lockett	lf		
Wayman Longley (Red)		c	
Clinton McCord (Butch)	rf	1b	

Player	1	2	3
Clyde McNeal	ss	lf	
Stanley Miarka		2b	p
Jackson Owens		p	
Frank Pearson	p		
Art Pennington	cf		
Curtis Pitts	c		
Marvin Price		1b	
Ted Radcliffe (Double Duty)		c	
Harry Rhodes	p	of	
Joe Scott	1b	rf	
Alvin Spearman		p	
Othello Strong	p		
Joe Taylor		c	
Lawrence White (Eugene)		2b	

Cleveland Buckeyes

Player	1	2	3	
Alonzo Boone	p			M
Otha Bailey (Bill)	c			
Sam Barber		p		
Pablo Bernard		2b		
Samuel Brewster		of		
T.J. Brown (Tom)	3b			
Charles Bruton (Jack)		3b	2b	
Johnnie Bryant		of		
Joseph Caffie (Clifford)	lf	rf		
Wesley Calhoun		rf		
Kenneth Carter		c		
Leonard Colliers		p		
Robert Cunningham		p		
Albert Ellis		p		
Frank Evans	cf			
Rayford Finch	p			
? Flourney		p		
Samuel Fowlkes		p		
Clyde Golden		p		
Willie Grace		of	p	
Wiley Griggs		3b		
? Hardy (Doc)		2b		
Charles Harvey		ss		
Dallas Jackson		ss		
Eddie Jamison		c		
George Jefferson		p	of	
Charles Johnson		2b	3b	
Rudolph Johnson (Rudy)		of		
Charles Jones		3b		
Paul Jones	p			
Walter Kelly		p		
Curtis Livingston		of		
Earnest Long		p		
? Lyons		p		
Lorenzo Marsh		c		
Charles Marvray		of	1b	
Bob Mitchell		p		
Excell Moore		p		
Charles Murray				
Leonard Pigg		c		
Curtis Pitts		c		
Henry Presswood		inf		
Marvin Price		1b		
William Reynolds (Bill)		3b	2b	
Thomas Russell		p		
Robert Scruggs		p		
William Scruggs (Willie)	p			
Eugene Smith		p		
Artis Stewart		p		
Norris Stiles		p		
Earl Suttles		1b		
John Thomas		p		
Joe Trawick		2b		
Willie Turnstall		p		

Player	1	2	3
Marvin Williams	2b		
Stuart Williams		ss	2b
Clyde Williams		p	
? Wilson		p	
Clarence Wynder		c	
Bob Young	ss	2b	3b

Homestead Grays

Player	1	2	3
Alfred Armour (Buddy)		lf	of
Sam Bankhead	2b		
Lonnie Blair		p	
Luther Clifford	c	of	
Mahlon Duckett		2b	3b
Wilmer Fields	p	cf	
Charles Gary		3b	
Josh Gibson, Jr.		3b	
Jackie Jackson		lf	of
Walter Leonard (Buck)	1b		
Eudie Napier		c	
Roy Partlow	p		
Gabriel Patterson		cf	of
Johnny Richardson (Bob)	ss		
Robert Trice (Bill)		p	

Houston Eagles

Player	1	2	3	
Roy Parnell (Red)				M
Lavance Anthony (Pete)		c		
Otha Bailey (Bill)		c		
Bill Beverly	p			
Eddie Brooks	2b			
? Budbill		p		
Larry Cunningham		of		
Johnny Davis		p	of	
? Devers		p		
Welda Gibson		p		
Clyde Golden		p		
Willie Grace		of		
Wiley Griggs		3b	ss	
Bob Harvey	rf			
Jehosie Heard	p			
Robert Herron		of		
John Jackson (Stony)		p		
Maynard Jordan		of		
? Keys		p		
Raymond Lacy		of		
Rufus Lewis		p		
John O'Dell		p		
? Parkinson (Parky)		p		
Leon Ruffin	c			
William Scruggs (Willie)		p		
Roy Spottsville (Bill)		p		
? Stevens		p		
Bob Turner		c		
John Washington	1b			
James Wilkes (Jimmy)		cf	of	
Robert Williams (Cotton)	lf	p		
Willie C. Williams (Curley)	ss			
Robert Wilson		3b		

Indianapolis Clowns

Player	1	2	3	
Albert Haywood (Buster)	c			M
? Bowen		p		
Sherwood Brewer		3b	of	
John Britton		3b		
Harry Butts	p			
Willis Cathey (Bill)		p		
Joe Chestnut		p		
Jim Cohen	p			
Eddie Davis (Nyasses)		p		
Carl Dent		ss		

Player	1	2	3
Reynaldo Drake (Verdes)	cf		
Bill Dumpson		p	
Raul Galata	p		
Atires Garcia (Angel)		p	
Granville Gladstone	rf	of	
Whitt Graves		p	
Sam Hairston	c		
Tommy F. Johnson		p	
Ralph Johnson (R.B.)		3b	ss
Benjamin Lott (Honey)	3b	ss	
Raydell Maddix		p	
Henry McHenry		p	
Henry Merchant	lf	of	
Pedro Naranjo		p	
Ray Neil	2b		
Nat Peeples		c	
Charles Peete		of	
Andrew Porter		p	
Othello Renfroe (Chico)		inf	of
Pablo Sama		3b	ss
Sam Sands (Piggy)		ss	
Leander Tugerson		p	
Archie Ware	1b		
Len Williams		1b	inf
Jesse Williams (H.)		ss	
Lester Witherspoon		of	

Kansas City Monarchs

Player	1	2	3
John O'Neil (Buck)		1b	M
Joe Alexander		c	
Gene Baker		ss	
Ernie Banks	ss		
Frank Barnes	p		
William Bell (Lefty)		p	
Russell Betts		p	
Bill Breda	lf	rf	
Willard Brown		of	
Ernest Chretian		rf	of
Gene Collins	cf	p	
Tom Cooper		c	of
Melvin Duncan		p	
Curtis Everett		of	c
Samuel Fowlkes		p	
Elston Howard	lf		
Lee Hughes		p	
Leonard Hunt		of	
Londell Jamerson (Tincy)		p	
Clifford Johnson (Connie)	p		
Curtis Johnson		p	
Ernest Johnson		of	
Jim LaMarque	p		
Leroy Paige (Satchel)		p	
Nat Peeples		c	of
Joseph Pierre		inf	
Robert Pointer		p	
Merle Porter		1b	
Gene Richardson		p	
Curt Roberts		2b	ss
William Serrell (Bonnie)	1b	2b	
Herb Souell	3b		
Alfred Surratt (Slick)		of	
Earl Taborn		c	
George Walker	p		
Felix Williams (Jeff)		3b	
Leroy Williams		ss	

Memphis Red Sox

Player	1	2	3
Homer Curry (Goose)	of		M
Joe Barnes		p	
Tom Barnes		p	

Player	1	2	3
? Benton		p	
John Billingsley		c	
Sam Billingsley		p	
Bob Boyd	1b		
Ollie Brantley		p	
Eddie Brooks		2b	
T.J. Brown (Tom)		2b	
? Butler (Doc)		c	
Marlin Carter (Mel)		3b	
Vibert Clarke		p	of
Jose Colas	cf		
Carlos Colas (Charlie)	lf	c	of
Larry Cunningham		of	
Pedro Formenthal		rf	
Isiah Harris		p	
Joe Henry	2b		
Willie Hutchinson	p		
Cowan Hyde (Bubber)		of	
Verdell Jackson		p	
Clinton Jones (Casey)	c		
Leon Kellman	3b		
Ernest Kennedy		inf	
? Long (Buck)	c		
Verdell Mathis (Lefty)	p		
Fred McDaniels		of	
Curtis McGowan		p	
Jose Piloto		p	
Cornelius Robinson (Neil)	lf		
Jimmy Scott		p	
Frank Thompson (Groundhog)	p		
Gilberto Varona	1b		
Orlando Varona	ss		
Richard Watkins		inf	
Willie Wells (Brooks)		ss	
Joe Wiley		2b	3b
Parnell Woods		3b	
Sam Woods	p		

New York Black Yankees

Player	1	2	3
Marvin Barker	of		M
Harry Williams			M
Lamar Baker		p	
Rufus Baker		c	
Julius Bowers (Julie)	c		
Curtis Brown	1b		
Roy Lee Chapman (Ray)	p		
Albert Clay (Alton)		of	
Major Dysoin		ss	
Osee Edwards	cf		
Soloman Garrett	2b		
Ellsworth Grace		2b	
James Green		3b	
Carranza Howard	p		
George Jackson		inf	
Ben Jones	ss		
Eddie Locke	p		
Fred Logan		of	
Benjamin Lott (Honey)	3b		
Herbert McKenzie		c	
Curtis Palmer		of	
Robert Scott (Bob)		p	
John Ford Smith	of	p	
Joe Spencer	2b		
Joe Stephens (Junior)	p		
Lawrence Stockley	lf		
Ed Stone	lf		
Ray Williams	p	of	

New York Cubans

Player	1	2	3
Jose Fernandez			M

Player	1	2	3
Edmundo Amoros (Sandy)	lf	1b	of
Lavance Anthony (Pete)		c	
Luis Caballero (Perez)	3b		
Lorenzo Cabrera		1b	
Chifian Clark (Cleveland)		cf	of
Renaldo Fernandez		of	
Jose Fernandez (Pepe)		c	
Domingo Galata	p		
Martinano Garay (Jose)		p	
Hiram Gonzalez (Rene)	1b	of	
Walter Hardy	2b	ss	
James Jenkins		p	
John Johnson		ss	3b
Raul Lopez		p	
Louis Louden (Tommy)	c		
Ramundo Navarrette		p	
Juan Noble (John)		p	
Carlos Noble		p	
Rafael Noble (Ray)		c	
Willie Patterson		c	
Fernando Pedroso (Diaz)	rf	of	
? Rotoret		p	
Pat Scantlebury	p		
Riley Stewart	p		
Robert Watson		p	
Willie Wynn		c	
Armando Yvanes	ss	2b	

Philadelphia Stars

Player	1	2	3
Oscar Charleston			M
Bill Cash (Ready)		c	
Joe Chestnut		p	
Ernest Chretian		of	3b
James Clarkson (Bus)	ss		
Nat Davis	1b		
Jimmy Dean	p		
Bill Dumpson		p	
Joe Fillmore		p	
Jonas Gaines	p		
Willy Gaines	p		
Stanley Glenn		c	
Wilmer Harris		p	
Elbert Israel		inf	
J.D. Johnson (James)		p	
James Jones		1b	of
Ben Littles	rf		
Ray Lott		cf	lf
Henry McHenry		p	
Leroy Paige (Satchel)		p	
Bill Ricks		p	
Bill Scott		lf	
John Scott		lf	of
Milt Smith	2b		
Gene Thompson (Will)		p	
Murray Watkins		3b	
Charlie White	3b	c	

1951

Baltimore Elite Giants

Player	1	2	3
? Brice		of	
Tom Coleman		p	
Wesley Dennis (Doc)	1b		
George Edwards		inf	
Jim Gilliam (Junior)		2b	inf
John Hayes	c		
Ulysses Hollimon	p		
Henry Kimbro	cf		
Orlando O'Farrill	ss		

Player	1	2	3
Fleming Reedy (Buddy)	3b		
Gene Richardson		p	
Kelly Searcy	p		
Frank Thompson (Hoss)	p		
Ennis Williams (Stew)		2b	
J. Williams	lf		
Jim Zapp	rf		

Birmingham Black Barons

Player	1	2	3
Lloyd Bassett (Pepper)		c	
? Blackmore		c	
James Canada	1b		
Irwin Castille	ss		
Elijah Chism (Eli)		inf	
Leonard Colliers	p		
Willie Collins (Rip)	p		
Ralph Gibson (Rufus)	2b		
Louis Gillis (Sea Boy)		c	
Bill Greason	p		
Wiley Griggs	cf		
Acie Griggs (Skeet)		of	
? Hubbie (Butch)	p		
Leroy Johnson	p		
Jim Kennedy	1b		
Roosevelt Lilly	p		
Willie Patterson	c		
Willie Price	p		
Norman Robinson (Bobby)	lf		
Eddie Stankie	rf		
Ed Steele	rf		
John Henry Williams	2b	3b	p

Chicago American Giants

Player	1	2	3
Wingfield Welch		M	
Andy Anderson		of	
Carl Coleman		1b	inf
Lloyd Davenport	cf		
Efigenio Ferrer (Coco)		ss	
Harold Gordon	p		
John Greene		inf	
Paul Hardy	c		
Robert Hinesman	p		
Cowan Hyde (Bubber)		lf	of
Don Johnson		2b	
Felix McLaurin	rf		
Zell Miles		lf	of
Joe Mitchell	p		
Alphonso Owens (Buddy)		inf	
Jackson Owens	p		
Leroy Paige (Satchel)	p		
? Palmer	p		
Willie Patterson		inf	
Art Pennington		of	
Curtis Pitts	ss	c	
Larry Raines	ss		
Laymon Ramsey	p		
Ulysses Redd	ss	2b	
Herbert Simpson	p		
? Smith (Sonny)		of	
Eugene Smith	p		
Theolic Smith	p		
Jim Spearman	p		
Alvin Spearman	p		
Charley Stewart		of	
T.R. Strong (Ted)	1b	3b	
Othello Strong	p		
Lonnie Summers	1b	c	
Joe Taylor	c		of
Leon Wheeler	p		
Lawrence White (Eugene)		2b	

Player	1	2	3
Johnny Williams			p
Parnell Woods	3b		
Danny Wright			p

Indianapolis Clowns

Player	1	2	3
Albert Haywood (Buster)	c		M
Lincoln Boyd	rf		
Sherwood Brewer	ss		
Harry Butts		p	
Frank Carswell	p		
Jim Cohen		p	
Walter Collins	p		
Herman Darnell		1b	
Reynaldo Drake (Verdes)	cf		
Erwin Ford		inf	
Raul Galata		p	
Whitt Graves		p	
Leo Henry (Preacher)		p	
? Hicks (Buddy)		inf	of
Benjamin Lott (Honey)	3b		
Henry Merchant		1b	of
Otto Miller		inf	
Pedro Naranjo		p	
Ray Neil	2b		
Nat Peeples	lf	c	
Leonard Pigg		c	
T.W. Richardson (Ted)		p	
Sam Sands (Piggy)		ss	c
Dewitt Smallwood (Woody)		of	
Toni Stone		2b	
Elzie Todd		p	
Leander Tugerson		p	
James Tugerson		p	
? Wallace		p	
Mickey Walls		p	
Archie Ware		1b	
Len Williams	p	1b	3b

Kansas City Monarchs

Player	1	2	3
John O'Neil (Buck)	1b		M
Ray Barnes		p	
Joe Barnes		p	
Henry Bayliss	2b		
William Bell (Lefty)		p	
Jerry Bennett		p	
Russell Betts		p	
Bill Breda	rf		
Willard Brown	lf		
Alfred Cartmill		2b	
Gene Collins	p	of	
Tom Cooper	c	1b	
? Dooley		p	
Melvin Duncan		p	
Curtis Everett		of	
Miller Guyton		inf	
John Head		of	
Herman Horn (Doc)		of	3b
Leonard Hunt		of	
Isiah Jackson (Ike)	cf	c	
John Jackson (Stony)		p	of
Londell Jamerson (Tincy)		p	
Jim LaMarque	p		
Robert Landers		p	
Eddie Locke		p	
Henry Mason (Hank)		p	
Pedro Naranjo		p	
Nat Peeples		c	
Lester Phiffer		ss	
Joseph Pierre		inf	
Gene Richardson		p	

Player	1	2	3
Bill Rowan		rf	
William Serrell (Bonnie)		of	inf
Herb Souell	3b		
Alfred Surratt (Slick)		of	
Earl Taborn		c	
James Tugerson		p	
George Walker		p	
Jesse Williams (H.)		ss	
Felix Williams (Jeff)		2b	
Leroy Williams		ss	
B. Wingate		3b	

Memphis Red Sox

Player	1	2	3
James Bankes	rf		
Joe Barnes		p	
Marshall Bridges	lf	p	
Vibert Clarke	p		
Jose Colas	cf		
Carlos Colas (Charlie)		c	
Isiah Harris	p		
Joe Henry	2b		
Clinton Jones (Casey)	c		
Frank Pearson		p	
Cornelius Robinson (Neil)	3b		
Felix Valdez (Manuel)	p		
Gilberto Varona	1b		
Orlando Varona	ss		

New Orleans Eagles

Player	1	2	3
Otha Bailey (Bill)		c	
Bill Beverly		p	
Eddie Brooks	2b		
Martin Crue (Matty)		p	
Larry Cunningham	cf		
Jesse Douglas	3b		
Russell Ewell		inf	
Clyde Golden		p	
Howard Gray		inf	
Wiley Griggs		inf	
Lacey Guice		of	c
John Hancock		inf	
Leroy Hancock		p	
Bob Harvey	lf		
Jehosie Heard		p	
Robert Herron		of	
Clyde Holder	p		
Vincent Husband		p	
John Jones (Edward)		p	
Bailey Jones		c	
Wayman Longley (Red)		c	
Fred McDaniels	rf		
Excell Moore		p	
J.W. Pirtle		p	
Marvin Price		1b	
Ewell Price		c	
? Prue		1b	
William Scruggs (Willie)	p		
Jack Sherber		inf	
Art Sherman		of	
Jack Shorter	3b		
Joseph Soto		c	
Roy Spottsville (Bill)		p	
Gerald Stearnes		c	
Oscar Vaughan		of	
John Washington	1b	p	
Willie Wells (Brooks)		ss	
Robert Williams (Cotton)	p		
Willie C. Williams (Curley)		ss	

1952

Player	1	2	3
Philadelphia Stars			
Carl Brown	ss		
? Canada		p	
Robbie Cartledge (Manny)	p		
Joe Chestnut		p	
Howard Coffey		p	
Carl Dent	2b		
Frank Evans		of	
William Felder (Benny)		3b	ss
Joe Fillmore		p	
Jonas Gaines		p	
Willy Gaines		p	
Robert Griffith	p		
Miller Guyton		3b	
Willie Harris		lf	of
Wilmer Harris	p		
Alfred Henry	rf		
James Jones	1b		
M. Kitchen		of	
Ben Littles	cf		
Hank Mainor		p	
Ed Martin		p	
Howard Rouse		rf	of
? Sails		c	
Bill Scott		cf	of
Harry Sims		c	1b
Milt Smith	2b	ss	3b
Bill Washington		ss	
? Watson		1b	
Robert Williams (Cotton)		lf	p
Adam Young		p	
Raleigh Tigers			
Lamb Barbee (Bud)	of		M
Haywood Cozart (Harry)	p	1b	
Leon Diggs	rf		
? Ford (Butch)	p		
? Heafner	lf		
? Kuckles	1b		
? Mangrum	2b		
? Miller	ss		
? Morgan		c	
Jim Parham	p		
Jason Stallings	cf		
Big Joe Williams	p		
Joe Winborne	3b		
? Yates		c	
Washington Pilots			
Fred Banks			M
Lou Bagby		p	
Johnny Banks	p		
Bill Bea	rf		
? Berry		2b	
Boyd Brown	p		
Knowlington Burbage (Buddy)	lf		
Ben Hill	p		
? Jolly		c	
Howard Kimbro (Howdy)	p		
? Looper		c	
? McGeters		2b	
Roscoe Price	3b		
? Staco	ss		
? Warfield	cf		

1952

Player	1	2	3
Birmingham Black Barons			
George Scales			M

Player	1	2	3
Otha Bailey (Bill)		c	
Lloyd Bassett (Pepper)	c		
Jim Bolden		p	
Eddie Brooks	2b		
William Brown		inf	
Thomas Butts (Pee Wee)	ss		
Robbie Cartledge (Manny)		p	
Irwin Castille	3b		
Joe Chestnut		p	
Wesley Dennis (Doc)	1b		
Hiram Gaston		p	
Wiley Griggs		inf	
James Jenkins		p	
J.D. Johnson (James)		p	
Henry Kimbro	cf		
Clarence King (Pijo)	lf		
Bill Powell	p		
T.W. Richardson (Ted)	p		
Norman Robinson (Bobby)		inf	
Frank Russell (Junior)		of	
William Scruggs (Willie)		p	
Taylor Smith	p		
Ed Steele	rf		
Frank Thompson (Hoss)		p	
Sam Williams		p	
Chicago American Giants			
Bill Beverly	p		
Rich Brown		inf	
Lonnie Davis		1b	
Ed Dobbins		2b	
Winn Durham		rf	of
James Felix		p	
Clyde Golden	p		
Lacey Guice	rf	of	
Leroy Hancock		rf	
Paul Hardy	c		
Vincent Husband		p	
Don Johnson		2b	
Johnny Keene		lf	of
James McDougal (John)	lf		
Felix McLaurin	cf		
Grady Montgomery		inf	
Jackson Owens		p	
Alphonso Owens (Buddy)		3b	
Willie Patterson		c	
Albert Preston		p	
Marvin Price		1b	
Larry Raines	ss		
Ulysses Redd		3b	
James Sheelor (Willie)		inf	
Othello Strong		p	
Clarence Williams		inf	
George Williams		c	
Jimmy Williams		p	
Johnny Williams		p	
Reuben Williams (Rube)		inf	
Roy Williams		3b	
Danny Wright	p		
Indianapolis Clowns			
Albert Haywood (Buster)	c		M
Hank Aaron	ss		
Joe Barnes		p	
Herbert Benson		1b	
Lincoln Boyd		lf	of
Frank Carswell		p	
Willis Cathey (Bill)		p	
Jim Cohen	p		
Walter Collins		p	

Player	1	2	3
Herman Donnell (Lee)		of	
Frank Ensley		cf	
Juan Garcia (Renee)		inf	
Robert Griffith	p		
Curtis Hardaway	3b		
Gordon Hopkins		2b	
James Jenkins		p	
Charlie Johnson		p	
Leon Kellman		lf	of
Henry Merchant	cf		
Excell Moore		p	
Johnny Murryall		p	
Ray Neil	2b		
Ernie Nimmons		of	
Lane Owens		inf	
T.W. Richardson (Ted)		p	
Gary Ross		of	
Sam Sands (Piggy)		ss	c
Dewitt Smallwood (Woody)		lf	of
Percy Smith		p	
Toni Stone		2b	
Elzie Todd		p	
Julio Toledo	1b		
James Tugerson	p		
Leander Tugerson		p	
Clarence Turner		p	
Armando Vasquez		1b	
Issac Welch		of	
James Wilkes (Jimmy)	rf		
Reuben Williams (Rube)		inf	
Kansas City Monarchs			
John O'Neil (Buck)	1b		M
Ben Banks		2b	
Henry Bayliss	2b		
Clyde Bennett		2b	
Willie Bennett		ss	
Rich Booker		of	
Willard Brown		of	
Tom Cooper	c	1b	
Miximo Diago		c	
Joe Douse		of	
Frank Ensley	cf		
? Green		lf	
James Henderson (Duke)	lf		
Francisco Herrera (Pancho)		c	
Carey Humphreys		rf	
Isiah Jackson (Ike)	rf	c	of
John Jackson (Stony)		p	
Ralph Johnson (R.B.)		3b	
J.D. Johnson (James)		p	
Robert Landers		p	
Henry Mason (Hank)	p		
Earl McCree		p	
Booker McDaniels	p		
? Murray		c	
Lester Phiffer		3b	
Dick Phillips		p	
Henry Presswood		3b	
Charles Rasberry		utl	
Gene Richardson		p	
Bill Rowan		of	
Henry Veadez		inf	
George Walker	p		
Bill White (Willie)		p	
Milton Woods		of	
Memphis Red Sox			
James Bankes		p	
Ollie Brantley		p	

Player	1	2	3	M
Marshall Bridges	p			
Vibert Clarke	p			
Jose Colas	cf			
Eddie Hancock		p		
Isiah Harris	p			
Joe Henry	2b			
Sam Hill	rf			
Clinton Jones (Casey)	c			
? Keeley		of		
Leon Kellman	3b			
Bennie Maben		inf		
Willie Neal		inf		
Cornelius Robinson (Neil)	lf			
Frank Thompson (Groundhog)		p		
Felix Valdez (Manuel)		p		
Gilberto Varona	1b			
Orlando Varona	ss			
Sherman Watrous		of		
Sam Woods		p		

Philadelphia Stars

Player	1	2	3	M
Oscar Charleston				M
John Barnes		p		
William Blake		p		
Robbie Cartledge (Manny)		p		
John Chaney		p		
Joe Chestnut		p		
Carl Dent	ss			
Bill Dumpson	p			
Joe Fillmore		p		
Willy Gaines		p		
Wilmer Harris	p			
James Jones	rf			
Carl Long		of		
Ed Martin	p			
Willie Parker		1b		
Willie Patterson	1b	c	of	
James Robinson		3b		
Bill Scott	cf			
Fate Simms		3b	c	
Harry Sims	of			
Dewitt Smallwood (Woody)	lf			
Ted Washington		ss		
Don Whittington	2b			
Clarence Willford		of		

1953

Birmingham Black Barons

Player	1	2	3	M
Jesse Walker (Hoss)				M
Otha Bailey (Bill)	c			
Eddie Brooks	2b			
Thomas Butts (Pee Wee)	ss			
Robbie Cartledge (Manny)	p			
Irwin Castille	3b	of		
Wesley Dennis (Doc)	1b			
Hiram Gaston		p		
Wiley Griggs		inf		
? Guthrie	p			
? Hair	3b			
Harold Hairston	p			
Tommy Jackson	p			
Donald Johnson	p			
Charles Johnson	c			
Walter Kelly	p			
Henry Kimbro	lf			
Clarence King (Pijo)		of		
Carl Long	cf			
Al Mobley (Johnny)		rf		

Player	1	2	3	M
T.W. Richardson (Ted)		p	of	
Frank Russell (Junior)		utl	p	
William Scott (Bill)		of		
Kelly Searcy		p		
Taylor Smith	p			
Ed Steele		of		
John Thomas		p		
Frank Thompson (Hoss)	p			
Danny Wright	p			

Indianapolis Clowns

Player	1	2	3	M
Albert Haywood (Buster)	c			M
Dave Amaro	p			
Charlie Bigby		of		
Carl Brown		p		
Willie Brown	ss			
Frank Carswell		p		
Luther Clifford		c		
Leon Diggs		of		
Reynaldo Drake (Verdes)	cf			
Frank Ensley	rf			
Willy Gaines	p			
Raul Galata		p		
Atires Garcia (Angel)		p		
Dick Hairston		p	of	
Arthur Lee Hamilton		c		
Curtis Hardaway	3b			
Bill Holder		ss		
Gordon Hopkins		2b	1b	
Jim Lewis		2b		
Raydell Maddix		p		
Raydell Maddix		p		
Rufus McNeal (Zippy)		p		
Henry Merchant	lf	p		
Ray Neil	ss	2b	of	
T.W. Richardson (Ted)	p			
James Robinson		3b		
Sam Sands (Piggy)	c			
Dewitt Smallwood (Woody)		of		
Percy Smith	p			
Toni Stone		2b		
Julio Toledo	1b			
James Tugerson		p		
Clarence Turner	p			
Vern Williams		p		
Reuben Williams (Rube)		ss		
John Wyatt		p		

Kansas City Monarchs

Player	1	2	3	M
John O'Neil (Buck)	1b			M
Juan Armenteros	c			
Ernie Banks	ss			
Henry Bayliss	3b			
William Bell (Lefty)		p		
Sherwood Brewer	2b			
Tom Cooper	of	c		
Bill Dickey		p		
Joe Douse		p		
James Gilmore		p		
James Henderson (Duke)	cf			
Francisco Herrera (Pancho)	1b			
Bill Holder		ss		
Herman Horn (Doc)		of		
Leonard Hunt		of		
Isiah Jackson (Ike)		c		
John Jackson (Stony)	p			
Ernest Johnson	lf			
J.D. Johnson (James)		p		
Ben McCauley		of		
Dagoberto Nunez	p			

Player	1	2	3	M
Dick Phillips	p			
Othello Renfroe (Chico)		utl		
Gene Richardson	p			
Willie Steele		rf		
Sam Taylor		c		
Felix Williams (Jeff)		of	ss	

Memphis Red Sox

Player	1	2	3	M
Homer Curry (Goose)	p			M
Ben Adams		p		
Lloyd Bassett (Pepper)	c			
? Berry		p		
Ollie Brantley		p		
Clay Cartwright		inf		
Joe Chisolm	2b			
Vibert Clarke		p		
Charley Davis	p			
Billy Ray Haggins	lf			
Eddie Hancock	p			
Isiah Harris	p	of		
Clinton Jones (Casey)		c		
Leon Kellman		3b		
Walter Kelly		p		
James Lewis		p		
Zeke Merrick		of		
Willie Patterson	1b			
Charley Pride		p		
Eddie Reed	cf			
T.W. Richardson (Ted)		p		
Frank Russell (Junior)		1b	of	
James Sheelor (Willie)	ss			
Fate Simms		c	of	
Don Whittington	3b			
Sam Woods	p			

1954

Birmingham Black Barons

Player	1	2	3	M
Jesse Walker (Hoss)				M M
Willie Wells	ss			M
Otha Bailey (Bill)	c			
Bill Beverly	p	1b	of	
Bill Breda	cf	of		
Eddie Brooks	2b			
Ralph Brown		ss	2b	
Sidney Bunch		of		
Marion Cain (Sugar)		p		
Robbie Cartledge (Manny)		p		
John Coleman (Lefty)		p		
Elliot Coleman	p			
Ralph Crosby	ss			
Alonzo Daniels		inf		
Wesley Dennis (Doc)	1b			
Wiley Griggs		inf		
Ulysses Hollimon		p		
William Holscroff		inf		
Michael Houleward		p		
Tommy Jackson		p		
James Jenkins		p		
John Kennedy		3b	ss	
Clarence King (Pijo)		of		
? Michaels		p		
Jessie Mitchell		cf		
Charley Pride	p	of		
R. Richardson		p		
Kelly Searcy	p			
Dewitt Smallwood (Woody)		of		
Frank Thompson (Hoss)	p			
Willie C. Williams (Curley)		ss	of	

Player	1	2	3
Danny Wright	p		
Richard Wright		c	
Jim Zapp		of	

Detroit Stars

Player	1	2	3
Ted Rasberry			M
Lloyd Bassett (Pepper)		c	
Carl Brown	p		
Andy Carpenter	p		
Clay Cartwright		of	
Carl Dancer		of	
? Dunn	ss		
James Earle		inf	
Irv Floyd	p		
Earle Floyd	1b		
? Galiton		p	
Harold Gordon	p		
? Gray		p	
Herman Green	cf		
Wally Griggs		inf	
Robert Hinesman	p		
? Ivory (Buddy)		inf	
Jimmy Jenkins	lf		
Aaron Jones		p	
Charles Longest		of	
? Lytle	p		
Ray Miller	1b		
Joe Montgomery		rf	
Pedro Naranjo	p		
Jackson Owens	p		
Arthot Owens		p	
? Palmer		p	
Willie Patterson	3b	c	
Felix Pine	p		
Wallace Porter	p		
Jack Robinson	p	of	
Bob Robinson		of	
Sammy Robinson	p		
Henry Salverson	2b		
Bob Smith		c	
Andrew Tolbert		2b	
Jake Tolbert		c	
Jim Underwood	ss		
Jimmy Valentine		3b	2b
Dewitt White (Carver)		c	
Walter Wilkins	p		

Indianapolis Clowns

Player	1	2	3
Oscar Charleston			M
Dave Amaro	p		
Willie Brown		ss	
Howard Coffey	p		
Celedonco Cos			
Reynaldo Drake (Verdes)	cf		
Joseph Duncan		1b	p
Frank Ensley	lf		
Johnny Evans		ss	
Erwin Ford	rf		
Willy Gaines	p		
Cornelius Giles			
Dick Hairston		p	
Arthur Lee Hamilton		c	
Bill Holder		inf	
Gordon Hopkins		2b	
Percy Howard		of	c
Vincent Husband	p		
Mamie Johnson	p		
Furman Johnson	p		
Gene Koger			
Philomeno Laduna (Phil)	p		

Player	1	2	3
Cliff Layton		p	
Orlando Luga		inf	
Rufus McNeal (Zippy)		of	p
Henry Merchant	1b	of	
Connie Morgan		2b	
Ray Neil	2b	ss	of
James Portier		c	
Pedro Quintana		inf	
T.W. Richardson (Ted)	p		
Percy Smith		p	
Sam Taylor		c	
George Wannamaker	3b		
John Williams		ss	1b
John Wright		p	
John Wyatt		p	

Kansas City Monarchs

Player	1	2	3
John O'Neil (Buck)	3b		M
Juan Armenteros	c		
Henry Bayliss	3b		
William Bell (Lefty)	p		
? Beltran		of	
Willie Blakemore		c	
Sherwood Brewer	2b	of	
? Connors (Dock)	ss		
Melvin Duncan		p	
Conrad Flores		p	
James Gilmore	p		
Leon Harris		p	
Francisco Herrera (Pancho)	1b		
Herman Horn (Doc)		rf	
Marvin Jones	p		
Ned Kennedy		p	
? Ketchum		of	
Enrique Maroto		lf	p
Henry Mason (Hank)	p		
Bob Mitchell		p	
Dick Mobley		ss	inf
Dagoberto Nunez		of	p
Dick Phillips	p		
Sam Sands (Piggy)		ss	c
Toni Stone		2b	
Sam Taylor		c	
Richard Thompson (Dick)		of	
James Walls		cf	
Ernest Webster	p		
Felix Williams (Jeff)		of	

Louisville Black Colonels

Player	1	2	3
Homer Curry (Goose)	p		M
Willie Blakemore		c	
? Brown		p	
Mark Carter		p	
Clay Cartwright	rf		
W. Curry		c	
? Dees	1b		
? Dunn		ss	
Joe Elliott		p	
Willie Forge		c	
Ralph Gibson (Rufus)	2b		
Wiley Griggs	3b		
Lonnie Harris	cf		
Willie Harris	cf		
? Ivory (Buddy)		ss	
Tommy Jackson		p	
Frank McCollum	p		
William McCray	p		
Willie Patterson		c	3b
Frank Pearson		p	
? Quidglay		p	

Player	1	2	3
T.W. Richardson (Ted)		p	
? Santiago		of	p
William Scruggs	p		
Jim Underwood		of	
Jimmy Valentine		3b	
Walter Wilkins	p		
John Henry Williams	lf		
Nate Wooten	p		

Memphis Red Sox

Player	1	2	3
Albert Haywood (Buster)	c		M
? Anderson		p	
Tom Barnes		p	
Willie Blakemore		c	
John Bridges		p	
Marshall Bridges		p	of
Thomas Butts (Pee Wee)		ss	
Clay Cartwright		of	
Frank Crossan	p		
Charley Davis	p		
Joe Elliott		p	
Billy Ray Haggins	cf		
Gene Hancock		lf	of
Leroy Hancock		p	
Isiah Harris	p		
Willie Harris		of	
Clinton Jones (Casey)	c		
? Meredith (Zeke)	rf		
Zeke Merrick		rf	
Frank Pearson		p	
Charley Pride		p	
Eddie Reed	lf		
Arzell Robinson (Ace)		p	
Frank Russell (Junior)	p	of	2b
James Sheelor (Willie)		2b	
Fate Simms		of	c
Frank Thompson (Groundhog)		p	
Jimmy Valentine		2b	3b
Gilberto Varona	1b		
Bill Washington	ss		
Don Whittington	3b	ss	
Sam Woods		p	

1955

Birmingham Black Barons

Player	1	2	3
James Canada			M
Homer Curry (Goose)			M
Otha Bailey (Bill)	c		
Bill Beverly	p		
Eddie Brooks	2b		
Robbie Cartledge (Manny)		p	
Elliot Coleman		p	
Joe Coleman		p	
Wesley Dennis (Doc)	1b		
Frank Evans		of	
Sam Fulton		p	
Ralph Gibson (Rufus)	ss	of	
Wiley Griggs		inf	
Fred Jackson		of	
John Kennedy	3b	ss	
Frank McCollum	p		
Jessie Mitchell	cf		
Joe Moses		c	
Willie Patterson		3b	c
Kelly Searcy	p		
John Williams		of	
Johnny Williams		p	
Roy Williams	lf		

Player	1	2	3
Stanley Williams	rf		

Detroit Stars

Player	1	2	3
Ed Steele			M
Jesse Walker (Hoss)			M
Andy Carpenter	p		
Warren Carruthers	p		
Mark Carter	p		
Earl Cunningham	2b	of	inf
John Daniels	p		
Melvin Duncan	p		
Mel Dunes	of		
Joe Elliott	p		
Earle Floyd	rf		
Sammy Gee		ss	
Herman Green	lf		
William Harris (Willie)	p		
James Hickle		of	
Percy Howard		c	
? Ivory (Buddy)		ss	
George Jenkins	p		
Aaron Jones	p		
Ezell King	1b		
Joe McRee		p	
Joe Mimes		p	
Joe Montgomery	cf		
Willie Patterson		c	
Ralph Rosado		c	
Henry Salverson			inf
Juan Soler			inf
Jimmy Valentine	3b		
John Winston		p	
Virgil Woods	p		
Danny Wright		p	

Indianapolis Clowns

Player	1	2	3
McKinley Downs (Bunny)			M
Dave Amaro	p		
Willy Gaines		p	
Philomeno Laduna (Phil)		p	
Rufus McNeal (Zippy)		p	
Jim Proctor	p		
T.W. Richardson (Ted)		p	
George Wannamaker	3b		
John Williams	lf		
John Wyatt	p		

Kansas City Monarchs

Player	1	2	3
John O'Neil (Buck)			M
George Altman		rf	of
Juan Armenteros	c		
Henry Bayliss	3b		
Willie Bennett		of	
Arthur Bennett		of	
Sherwood Brewer		inf	
Alfred Cartmill	2b		
Estaban Clark	1b		
Melvin Duncan	p		
Willie Forge		c	
John Gautier	p		
James Gilmore	p		
JC Hartman (Joe)	ss		
Bill Hill		p	
Victor Incera		of	
Lou Johnson		rf	of
Hank Jones		lf	of
Marvin Jones	p		
Willie Lee		utl	
Enrique Maroto		p	
Bob Mitchell		p	

Player	1	2	3
Leroy Paige (Satchel)		p	
Joe Patterson		cf	of
Dick Phillips	p		
James Sanders		of	
B.G. Stephens		p	
Milton Tiddle		c	
Don Vaughn		p	
Dave Whitley		lf	of
Larry Williams		cf	of

Memphis Red Sox

Player	1	2	3
Homer Curry (Goose)			M
Isaac Barnes		c	
Tom Barnes		p	
Charley Davis	p		
Billy Ray Haggins		lf	of
Eddie Hancock		p	
Willie Harris		lf	of
Lonnie Harris	cf	3b	
Isiah Harris	p		
Clinton Jones (Casey)		c	

Player	1	2	3
Paris King		c	
Eddie Reed	rf		
Arzell Robinson (Ace)		p	
Frank Russell	p		
James Sheelor (Willie)	2b		
Gilberto Varona	1b		
Orlando Varona	ss		
Bill Washington	3b		

"Kick, Mule"

Although he was far from the all-around best player, George "Mule" Suttles was one of the most feared homerun hitters in Negro Leagues history. A first baseman who sometimes played the outfield, the muscular Suttles played for 10 teams between 1923 and 1944. Fans had a special chant when Suttles came to bat—"Kick, Mule," they would beseech him, and he frequently delivered for them. The best statistics on his career credit him with 183 home runs in 830 games against Negro League competition, although he probably hit more. As a member of the Chicago American Giants in 1933, Suttles hit the first homerun in an East-West All-Star Game. Two years later, he hit the annual classic's most dramatic homer, a 475-foot clout with two men on and two out in the bottom of the eleventh inning to give the West an 11-8 victory.

—*Black Mac, Courier* (8/17/35), *Peterson*

Under the Lights

The need for black teams to barnstorm around the countryside to turn a profit, getting in as many games as possible against anyone who would play them, combined with the technology of electricity to produce the Kansas City Monarchs' traveling night baseball lighting system in 1929. J.L. Wilkinson, the Monarchs owner, decided that the only route to salvation for his team was to include night baseball among its attractions. This was, however, before even major league stadiums had lights. So, as Janet Bruce wrote in her book, *The Kansas City Monarchs*, Wilkinson ordered a lighting system which "consisted of telescoping poles, which elevated lights forty-five to fifty feet above the playing field." The poles were mounted on trucks, and they traveled with the team to the small towns where it played. The lighting was far from satisfactory so far as playing was concerned, but the Monarchs' caravan of ballplayers and equipment made it through the Depression, when other black clubs were foundering.

—*Bruce*

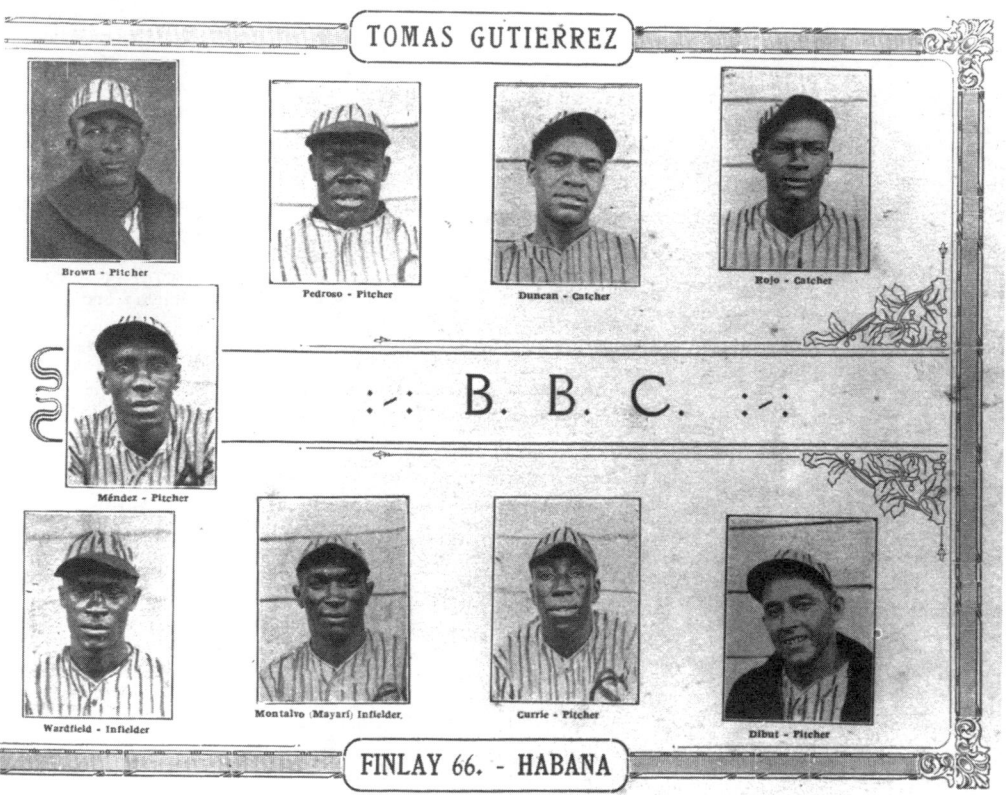

Santa Clara Base Ball Club, Cuban Winter League 1922-23. Clockwise from the top: The mysterious Dave Brown, Eustaquio Pedroso, Frank Duncan, Julio Rojo, Pedro Dibut (played in both Negro Leagues and Major Leagues), Rube Currie, Estaban Montalvo, Frank Warfield, and "The Black Diamond", Jose Mendez.
Luis Munoz Collection

Santa Clara Base Ball Club, Cuban Winter League 1922-23. Clockwise from the top: Oscar Charleston, Herman Rios, Walter "Dobie" Moore, Oliver "The Ghost" Marcelle, Agustin "Tinti" Molina, Alejandro Oms, Pablo Mesa, Bill Holland, and Oscar "Heavy" Johnson.
Luis Munoz Collection

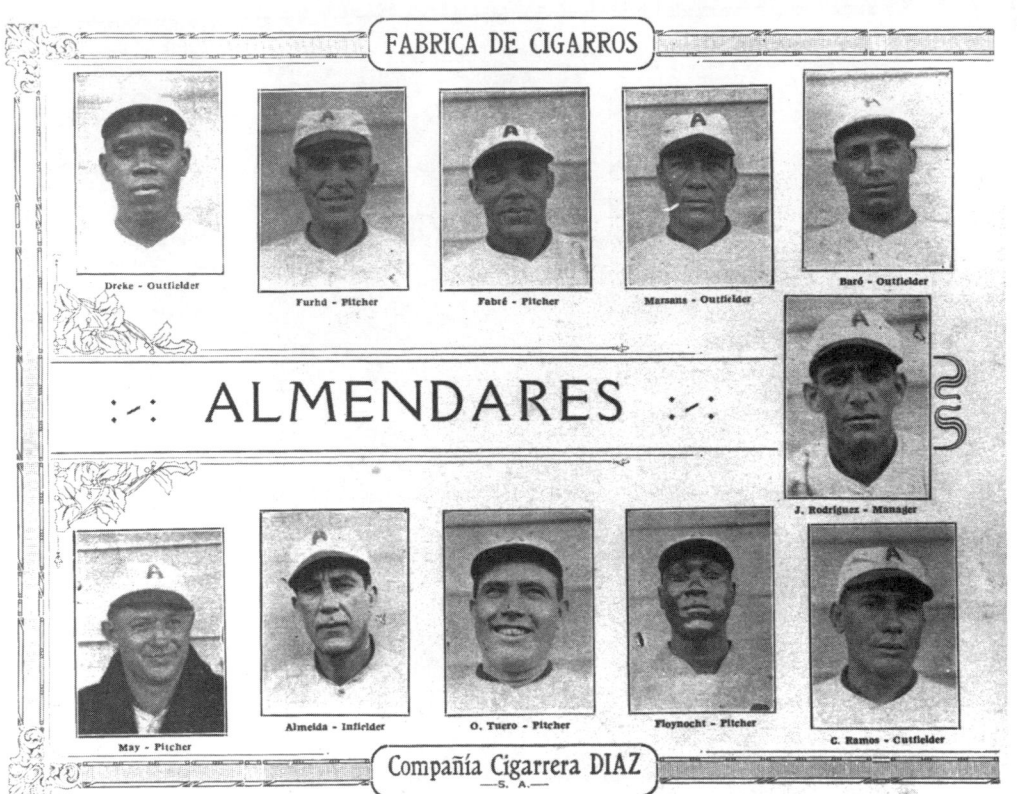

Almendares Base Ball Club, Cuban Winter League 1922-23. Clockwise from the top: Valentin Dreke, Oscar Fuhr, Isidro Fabre, Armando Marsans, Bernardo Baro, Jose Rodriquez, Jose "Cheo" Ramos, Willis "Pud" Flournoy, Oscar Tuero, Rafael Almeida, and Jakie May.
Luis Munoz Collection

Almendares Base Ball Club, Cuban Winter League 1922-23. Clockwise from the top: Gonzalez (Kakin), Jesse Hubbard, Manuel Cueto, "Snake" Henry, Eugenio Morin, Jose Fernandez, Oscar Rodriquez, Lucas Boada, Gonzalez (Papo), and Negro Leaguer and Major Leaguer Ramon "Mike" Herrera.
Luis Munoz Collection

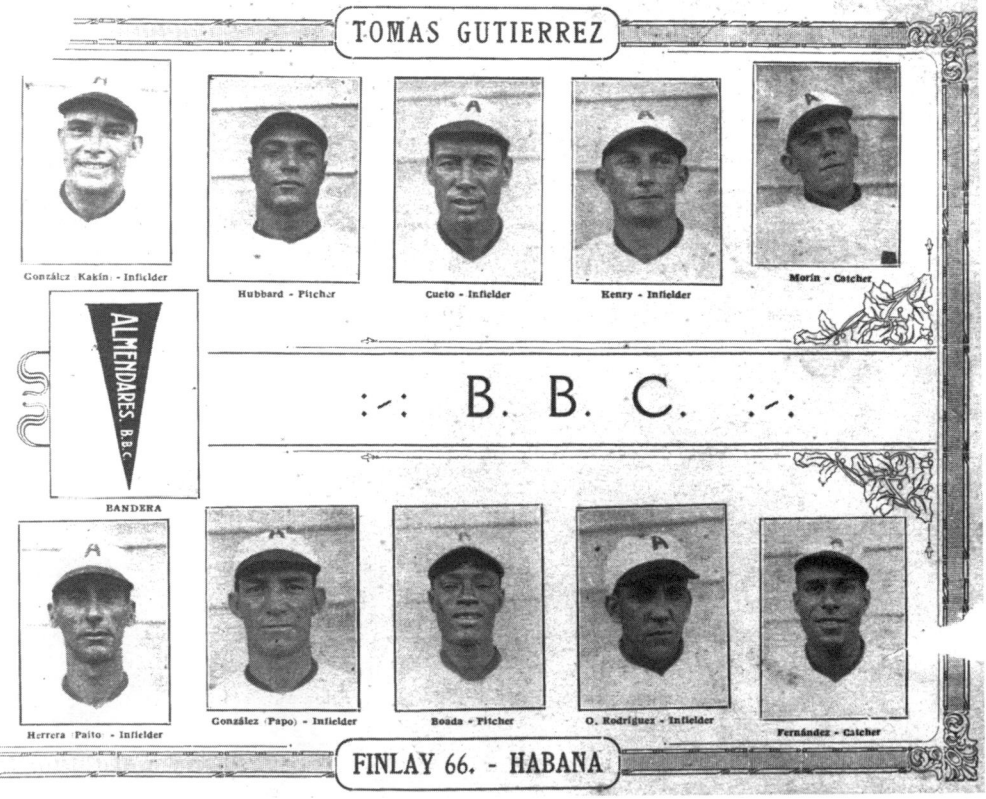

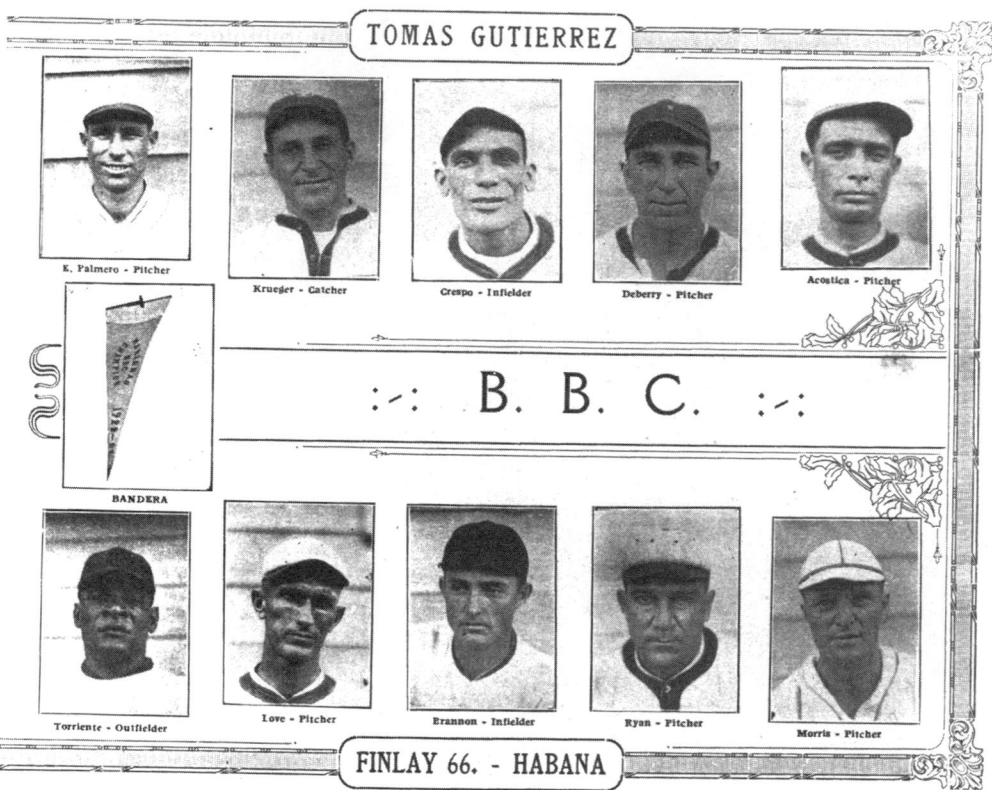

Marianao Base Ball Club, Cuban Winter League 1922-23. Clockwise from the top: Emilio Palmero, Otto Krueger, Rogelio Crespo, Harry Deberry, Acostica, Ed Morris, Rosy Ryan, Otis Brannan, Slim Love, and the superlative Cuban, Cristobal Torriente.
Luis Munoz Collection

Marianao Base Ball Club, Cuban Winter League 1922-23. Clockwise from the top: Jesse Petty, Jose "Pepin" Perez, Harry McCurdy, Charlie Dressen, Don Brown, Merito Acosta, Jimmy Cooney, Art Phelan, Hank Schreiber, Eddie Brown, and umpire and former player Hector Magrinat.
Luis Munoz Collection

Habana Base Ball Club, Cuban Winter League 1922-23. Clockwise from the top: Busta Quintana, Mac Eggleston, Tatica Campos, Eufemio Abreau, Pelayo Chacon, Merven "Red" Ryan, Buster Ross, Bienviendo "Hooks" Jimenez, Juanelo Mirabal, and Marcelino Guerra.
Luis Munoz Collection

Habana Base Ball Club, Cuban Winter League 1922-23. Clockwise from the top: Clarck, John Bischoff, Clint Thomas, Edgar Wesley, Andy Cooper, Adofo Luque, Bartolo Portuando, Jack Calvo, Oscar Levis, John Henry "Pop" Lloyd, and umpire and former player, Gervasio "Strike" Gonzalez.
Luis Munoz Collection

League Standings 1920-1954

The various Negro Leagues can be pretty hard to follow. Here's a quick rundown. The Negro National League, founded by Rube Foster, operated from 1920 through 1931. The Eastern Colored League was organized in 1923 and lasted into the spring of 1928. The American Negro League played only one season, in 1929.

In the hard times of 1932, some very good black teams banded together to form the East-West League, but the circuit failed before it could complete the regular season. In the absence of any other top-quality Negro Leagues, the Negro Southern League stepped forward to fill the void and claim major-league status for that single year.

The following year, 1933, a new Negro National League was formed, and it had no competition at the top of black baseball until 1937, when the Negro American League began operations. The modern NNL played through 1948, and the NAL hung on through 1960.

Fans usually thought of Negro Leagues baseball in terms of "Eastern" teams and "Western" teams. The first Negro National League, the Negro Southern League, and the Negro American League were considered "Western." The Eastern Colored League, the American Negro League, and the second Negro National League were considered "Eastern." The short-lived East-West League was also considered more "East" than "West." When the Negro American League absorbed the Negro National League after the 1948 season, it split into Eastern and Western divisions for a few years. We've kept NAL records in the West.

The standings printed here are incomplete, but they are the best we have for now. They are mostly based on actual game scores. No official standings were issued, and newspapers often did not publish their own unofficial final standings. The work of compiling complete statistics—which will eventually give us complete, balanced standings—goes on.

Negro National League

1920

Chicago American Giants	32-13
Detroit Stars	35-23
Kansas City Monarchs	41-29
Indianapolis ABCs	39-35
Cuban Stars	21-24
St. Louis Giants	25-32
Dayton Marcos	8-18
Chicago Giants	4-24

1921

Chicago American Giants	42-22
Kansas City Monarchs	50-31
St. Louis Giants	40-28
Detroit Stars	32-32
Indianapolis ABCs	35-38
Cincinnati Cubans	29-39
Columbus Buckeyes	25-38
Chicago Giants	10-32

1922

Chicago American Giants	36-23
Indianapolis ABCs	46-33
Kansas City Monarchs	46-33
St. Louis Stars	35-26
Detroit Stars	43-32
Pittsburgh Keystones	16-21
Cuban Stars	19-31
Cleveland Tate Stars	17-29

1923

Kansas City Monarchs	57-33
Detroit Stars	41-29
Chicago American Giants	41-29
Indianapolis ABCs	45-34
Cuban Stars	27-31
St. Louis Stars	25-40
Toledo Tigers	11-15
Milwaukee Bears	14-32
Birmingham Black Barons	15-23
Memphis Red Sox	13-6

1924

Kansas City Monarchs	55-22
Chicago American Giants	49-24
Detroit Stars	37-29
St. Louis Stars	42-34
Memphis Red Sox	29-37
Birmingham Black Barons	34-44
Cuban Stars	16-33
Cleveland Browns	15-34

1925

	1st Half	2nd Half	Total
Kansas City	31-12	31-11	62-23
St. Louis	31-14	38-12	69-27
Detroit	29-20	28-21	57-40
Chicago American Giants	26-22	28-18	54-40
Cubans	12-13	10-12	22-28

Memphis Red Sox	18-24	12-24	30-48
Indianapolis ABCs	13-24	4-33	17-57
Birmingham Black Barons	14-33	10-16	24-49

1926

	1st Half	2nd Half	Totals
Kansas City Monarchs	35-12	22-9	57-21
Chicago American Giants	28-16	29-70	57-23
St. Louis Stars	29-18	20-12	49-30
Detroit Stars	34-17	16-25	50-42
Indianapolis ABCs	28-18	15-27	43-45
Cuban Stars	6-27	13-20	19-47
Dayton Marcos	7-32	0-5	7-37
Cleveland Elites	5-32	2-9	7-41

1927

	1st Half	2nd Half	Totals
Chicago American Giants	32-14	24-15	56-29
Kansas City Monarchs	36-18	18-11	54-29
St. Louis Stars	32-19		
Detroit Stars	29-22	24-24	53-46
Birmingham Black Barons	25-29	29-15	54-44
Memphis Red Sox	19-25		
Cuban Stars	15-23		
Cleveland Hornets	16-38		

1928

	1st Half	2nd Half	Totals
St. Louis Stars	32-8	34-18	66-26
Kansas City Monarchs	24-15	26-16	50-31
Detroit Stars	29-13	25-24	54-37
Chicago American Giants	24-20	30-17	54-37
Birmingham Black Barons	19-28	25-26	44-54
Memphis Red Sox	16-25	14-23	30-48
Cleveland Tigers			19-53
Cuban Stars			12-37

1929

	1st Half	2nd Half	Totals
Kansas City Monarchs	28-11	34-6	62-17
St. Louis Stars	30-14	29-19	59-33
Chicago American Giants	22-29	27-11	49-40
Detroit Stars	25-18	13-24	38-42
Birmingham Black Barons	20-24	9-27	29-51
Cuban Stars	6-14	12-12	18-26
Memphis Red Sox	14-22	5-22	19-44
Nashville Elite Giants			10-20

1930

	1st Half	2nd Half	Totals
St. Louis Stars	41-15	24-7	65-22
Detroit Stars	26-26	24-7	50-33
Kansas City Monarchs	31-14	8-12	39-26
Birmingham Black Barons	30-27	14-21	44-48
Chicago American Giants	24-39	23-14	47-56
Memphis Red Sox	21-22	8-23	29-45
Cuban Stars	17-25	6-12	23-37
Nashville Elite Giants	13-35	7-16	20-51
Louisville White Caps			14-27

1931

	1st Half Only
Cleveland Cubs	24-22
Indianapolis ABCs	25-23
St. Louis Stars	11-11
Detroit Stars	25-26
Louisville White Sox	18-19
Chicago American Giants	10-11

1932

No Negro National League

1933

	1st Half Only
Cole's American Giants (Chicago)	21-7
Pittsburgh Crawfords	20-8
Baltimore Black Sox	10-9
Nashville Elite Giants	12-13
Detroit Stars	13-20
Columbus Blue Birds	11-18
Homestead (Dropped out 7/11)	11-9

1934

	1st Half	2nd Half
Cole's American Giants (Chicago)	17-6	11-9
Philadelphia Stars	12-9	11-4
Pittsburgh Crawfords	14-8	15-9
Newark Dodgers	6-5	5-9
Nashville Elite Giants	9-11	6-3
Cleveland Red Sox	2-22	2-3
Bacharach Giants		3-12
Baltimore Black Sox		1-6

1935

	1st Half	2nd Half
Pittsburgh Crawfords	26-6	13-9
New York Cubans	10-16	20-7
Columbus Elite Giants	17-11	10-10
Philadelphia Stars	14-17	14-10
Homestead Grays	14-13	9-10
Brooklyn Eagles	15-15	13-16
Cole's American Giants (Chicago)	14-16	7-13
Newark Dodgers	8-20	9-21

1936

	1st Half	2nd Half
Pittsburgh Crawfords	16-15	20-9
Newark Eagles	15-18	15-11
New York Cubans	9-11	13-12
Washington Elite Giants	14-10	7-14
Philadelphia Stars	15-12	10-18
Homestead Grays	10-13	12-14
New York Black Yankees		7-14

1937

	1st Half Only
Homestead Grays	21-9
Newark Eagles	19-14
Philadelphia Stars	12-11
Washington Elite Giants	11-15
Pittsburgh Crawfords	11-16
New York Black Yankees	11-17

1938

	1st Half Only
Homestead Grays	26-6
Philadelphia Stars	20-11
Pittsburgh Crawfords	14-14
Newark Eagles	11-11
Baltimore Elite Giants	12-14
New York Black Yankees	4-17
Washington Black Senators	1-20

1939

	Total
Homestead Grays	33-14
Newark Eagles	29-20
Baltimore Elite Giants	25-21
Philadelphia Stars	31-32
New York Black Yankees	15-21
New York Cubans	5-22

1940

Homestead Grays	28-13
Baltimore Elite Giants	25-14
Newark Eagles	25-17
New York Cubans	12-19
Philadelphia Stars	16-31
New York Black Yankees	10-22

1941

	1st Half	2nd Half
Homestead Grays	17-9	8-8
Newark Eagles	11-6	8-5
Baltimore Elite Giants	13-10	9-8
New York Cubans	7-10	4-2
New York Black Yankees	7-13	5-5
Philadelphia Stars	10-18	2-8

1942

	Totals
Baltimore Elite Giants	37-15
Homestead Grays	26-17
Philadelphia Stars	21-17
Newark Eagles	19-17
New York Black Yankees	7-19
New York Cubans	6-19

1943

	Totals
Homestead Grays	31-9
New York Cubans	20-9
Newark Eagles	19-14
Philadelphia Stars	21-18
Baltimore Elite Giants	17-24
New York Black Yankees	2-21

1944

	1st Half	2nd Half
Homestead Grays	15-8	12-4
Baltimore Elite Giants	12-11	12-9
New York Cubans	12-10	4-4
Philadelphia Stars	7-11	12-7
Newark Eagles	13-9	6-13
New York Black Yankees	2-13	2-11

1945

	1st Half	2nd Half
Homestead Grays	18-7	14-6
Philadelphia Stars	14-9	7-10
Baltimore Elite Giants	13-9	12-8
Newark Eagles	11-9	10-8
New York Cubans	3-11	3-9
New York Black Yankees	2-16	5-10

1946

	1st Half	2nd Half
Newark Eagles	25-9	22-7
New York Cubans	13-13	15-8
Homestead Grays	18-15	9-13
Philadelphia Stars	17-12	10-17
Baltimore Elite Giants	14-17	14-14
New York Black Yankees	3-24	5-16

1947

	1st Half Only
Newark Eagles	27-15
New York Cubans	20-12
Baltimore Elite Giants	23-20
Homestead Grays	19-20
Philadelphia Stars	13-16
New York Black Yankees	6-25

Eastern Colored League

1923

Hilldale	32-17
Cubans Stars (East)	23-17
Brooklyn Royal Giants	18-18
Bacharach Giants	19-23
Lincoln Giants	16-22
Baltimore Black Sox	19-30

1924

Hilldale	47-22
Baltimore Black Sox	30-19
Lincoln Giants	31-25
Bacharach Giants	30-29
Harrisburg Giants	26-28
Brooklyn Royal Giants	16-25
Washington Potomacs	21-37
Cuban Stars (East)	15-31

1925

Hilldale	52-15
Harrisburg Giants	37-19
Baltimore Black Sox	31-19
Bacharach Giants	26-27
Brooklyn Royal Giants	13-20
Wilmington	13-22 Out 7/18
Cuban Stars (East)	15-26
Lincoln Giants	7-39

1926

Bacharach Giants	34-20
Harrisburg Giants	25-17
Hilldale	34-24

Cuban Stars (East)	28-21
Lincoln Giants	19-22
Baltimore Black Sox	18-29
Brooklyn Royal Giants	7-20
Newark Stars	1-10*

*Disbanded in midseason.

1927

	1st Half	2nd Half
Bacharach Giants	29-17	25-18
Baltimore Black Sox	23-17	12-18
Cuban Stars (East)	24-19	9-13
Harrisburg Giants	25-20	16-12
Hilldale	17-28	19-17
Brooklyn Royal Giants	10-21	5-10

1929 American Negro League

	1st Half	2nd Half
Baltimore Black Sox	24-11	25-10
Lincoln Giants	22-11	18-15
Homestead Grays	15-13	19-16
Hilldale	15-20	24-15
Bacharach Giants	11-20	8-25
Cuban Stars (East)	6-16	9-23

1930

No League

1931

East - No League

Hilldale	42-13
Homestead Grays	29-18
Baltimore	18-31
Cubans	8-18

Negro American League

1937

	1st Half Only
Kansas City Monarchs	19-8
Chicago American Giants	18-8
Cincinnati Tigers	15-11
Memphis Red Sox	13-13
Detroit Stars	12-15
Birmingham Black Barons	10-17
Indianapolis Athletics	9-18
St. Louis Stars	5-22

1938

	1st Half	2nd Half
Memphis Red Sox	21-4	8-15
Kansas City Monarchs	19-5	13-10
Indianapolis ABC's	6-6	8-13
Atlanta Black Crackers	9-10	12-4
Chicago American Giants	8-13	17-7
Birmingham Black Barons	3-11	5-12
Jacksonville Red Caps	3-4	

1939

	1st Half Only
Kansas City Monarchs	17-7
Chicago American Giants	17-11
Memphis Red Sox	11-11
Cleveland Bears	9-9
St. Louis Stars	10-12

1940

	1st Half Only
Kansas City Monarchs	12-7
Cleveland Bears	10-10
Memphis Red Sox	12-12
Birmingham Black Barons	9-9
Chicago American Giants	9-15
Indianapolis Crawfords	3-5

1941, 1942: No published standings

1943

	2nd Half Only
Chicago American Giants	13-5
Birmingham Black Barons	5-3
Cleveland Buckeyes	8-5
Kansas City Monarchs	6-7
Cincinnati Clowns	3-7
Memphis Red Sox	4-11

1944

	1st Half	2nd Half
Birmingham Black Barons	24-9	24-13
Indianapolis-Cincinnati Clowns	18-13	22-18
Cleveland Buckeyes	20-20	20-21
Memphis Red Sox	20-23	24-28
Kansas City Monarchs	12-19	11-23
Chicago American Giants	10-20	22-19

1945

	1st Half	2nd Half
Cleveland Buckeyes	31-9	22-7
Birmingham Black Barons	26-11	13-19
Kansas City Monarchs	17-18	15-12
Chicago American Giants	17-24	22-11
Cincinnati Clowns	15-26	15-13
Memphis Red Sox	13-31	4-30

1946

	1st Half Only
Kansas City Monarchs	27-8
Birmingham Black Barons	22-15
Indianapolis Clowns	15-19
Cleveland Buckeyes	14-17
Memphis Red Sox	16-21
Chicago American Giants	14-28

1947: No published standings

1948

	1st Half	2nd Half	Total
Birmingham Black Barons	38-14	17-7	55-21
Kansas City Monarchs	24-18	19-7	43-25
Cleveland Buckeyes	31-21	10-21	41-42
Memphis Red Sox	13-29	20-15	33-44

Indianapolis Clowns	20-33	7-13	27-46
Chicago American Giants	20-31	7-17	27-48

1949 NAL East

	1st Half Only
Baltimore Elite Giants	24-12
New York Cubans	14-10
Philadelphia Stars	13-20
Indianapolis Clowns	14-23
Louisville Buckeyes	8-29

1949 NAL West: No published standings

1950 NAL East

	1st Half	2nd Half	Total
Indianapolis Clowns	29-17-1	18-21-1	47-38-2
Baltimore Elite Giants	10-9-1	14-11	24-20-1
New York Cubans	12-13-0	6-3	18-16
Philadelphia Stars	10-21-1	5-7	15-28-1
Cleveland Buckeyes	3-37	0-2	3-39

1950 NAL West

	1st Half	2nd Half	Total
Kansas City Monarchs	30-11	22-10	52-21
Birmingham Black Barons	38-14-1	14-11	52-25-1
Houston Eagles	18-21-1	5-20	23-41-1
Memphis Red Sox	19-23-1	23-9-1	42-32-2
Chicago American Giants	13-16	2-15	15-31

1951 NAL East

	1st Half	2nd Half	Total
Indianapolis Clowns	29-12	24-14	53-26
Birmingham Black Barons	15-21	9-19	24-40
Philadelphia Stars	12-17	6-11	18-28
Baltimore Elite Giants	13-24	15-12	28-36

1951 NAL West

	1st Half	2nd Half	Total
Kansas City Monarchs	28-15	14-13	42-28
Chicago American Giants	21-16	13-8	34-24
Memphis Red Sox	13-17	9-17	22-34
New Orleans	17-26	22-18	39-44

1952

	1st Half	2nd Half	Total
Indianapolis Stars	26-14	18-16	44-30
Birmingham Black Barons	28-21	23-15	51-36
Chicago American Giants	16-16	16-15	32-31
Kansas City Monarchs	12-12	11-14	23-26
Memphis Red Sox	15-22	14-18	29-40
Philadelphia Stars	11-23	11-15	22-38

1953

Kansas City Monarchs	56-21
Birmingham Black Barons	28-34
Indianapolis Clowns	31-43-1
Memphis Red Sox	20-37-1

1954

Indianapolis Stars	43-22
Memphis Red Sox	49-34-1
Birmingham Black Barons	41-38-1
Detroit Stars	23-31-1

| Louisville Black Colonels | 19-30-2 |
| Kansas City Monarchs | 23-43-1 |

East-West League (Broke up in late June)
1932

Baltimore Black Sox	20-9	
Homestead Grays	16-8	29-19
Cuban Stars	12-15	
Washington Pilots	13-18	
Hilldale	10-17	
Cleveland Stars (Cubs)	8-16	
Newark Browns	3-14	
Detroit Wolves		29-13
New York Black Yankees		
Pittsburgh Crawfords		32-16

Negro Southern League
1932

Chicago American Giants	34-7
Monroe Monarchs	33-7
Nashville Elite Giants	24-15
Montgomery Grey Sox	22-18
Memphis Red Sox	24-22
Louisville Black Caps	13-17
Indianapolis ABCs	14-19
Birmingham Black Barons	8-11
Little Rock Travelers	3-3
Atlanta Black Crackers	1-7
Cleveland Cubs	22-18

Playoff and World Series Results

NA   Not applicable (no team to play)

NP   Series not played

For team abbreviations, check the key near the beginning of the book.

Year	1st Half	2nd Half	Play-off Results	World Series	Play-off Results	2nd Half	1st Half	Year
			Negro National League		**Eastern Colored League**			
1920	CAG	NA						1920
1921			CAG	NA				1921
1922			CAG	NA				1922
1923			KCM	NP	HIL			1923
1924			KCM	5-4	HIL			1924
1925	KCM	SLS	KCM, 4-3	1-5	HIL			1925
1926	KCM	CAG	CAG, 5-4	5-3	BG			1926
1927	CAG	BBB	CAG, 4-0	5-3	BG			1927
1928	SLS	CAG	SLS, 5-4	NA				1928
			Negro National League		**American Negro League**			
1929	KCM	KCM	KCM	NP	BBS			1929
1930	SLS	DS	SLS, 4-3	NP	HG			1930
1931	SLS	SLS	SLS	NP	HG			1931
			Negro Southern League		**East-West League**			
1932	CAG	NEG	CAG, 4-3	NP	BBS			1932

Year	1st Half	2nd Half	Play-off Results	World Series	Play-off Results	2nd Half	1st Half	Year
	Negro American League				**Negro National League**			
1933					CAG, 0-0?	PC	CAG	1933
1934					PS, 4-3	PS	CAG	1934
1935					PC 4-3	NYC	PC	1935
1936					No Play-off	PC	WEG	1936
1937	KCM	CAG	No Play-off	NP	HG	HG	HG	1937
1938	MRS	BC	MRS, 2-0	NP	HHG	HG	HG	1938
1939	KCM	SLS	KCM, 3-2	NP	BEG, 2-0	HG	HG	1939
1940	KCM	KCM	KCM	NP	HG	HG	HG	1940
1941			KCM	NP	HG, 3-1	NYC	HG	1941
1942			KCM	4-0	HG	HG	HG	1942
1943	BBB	CAG	BBB, 3-2	3-4	HG	HG	HG	1943
1944	BBB	BBB	BBB	1-4	HG	HG	HG	1944
1945	CBE	CBE	CBE	4-0	HG	HG	HG	1945
1946	KCM	KCM	KCM	3-4	NE	NE	NE	1946
1947	CBE	CBE	CBE	1-4	NYC, 0-0?	NYC	NE	1947
1948	BBB	KCM	BBB, 4-3	1-4	HG, 3-0	HG	BEG	1948
1949	KCM	CAG	CAG -forfeit	0-4	BEG	BEG	BEG	1949
1950	KCM	KCM	KCM	NP	IC 0-0 ??	NYC	IC	1950
1951	KCM	IC	IC					1951
1952	IC	BBB	IC 0-0 ??					1952
1953	KCM	KCM	KCM					1953
1954	IC	IC	IC					1954
1955	KCM							1955

The Kansas City Monarchs won 17 pennants and two World Series: 1923, **'24**, '25, '26 (1/2), '29, '37 (1/2), '39, '40, '41, '42, **'46**, '48 (1/2), '49 (1/2), '50, '51 (1/2), '53, and '55.

The Homestead Grays won 12 pennants and three World Series: 1931, '31, '37, '38 '39 (1/2), '40, '41, '42, **'43, '44**, '45, and **'48**.

The Chicago American Giants won 12 pennants and two World Series: 1920, '21, '22, '26, **'27, '28** (1/2), '32, '33, '34 (1/2), '37 (1/2), '43 (1/2), and '49

Breaking the Color Line

Many baseball fans are dimly aware that Moses and Welday Walker, played in one major league season, late in the 1880s, "integrating" the game temporarily. Few, however, know that professional baseball was reintegrated in 1935, 11 years before Robinson took the field for the Montreal Royals. Canada also was the site when Alfred Wilson, a pitcher and outfielder from black barnstorming teams in the United States, joined the Granby Red Sox in the Quebec Provincial League. Wilson's presence in the Provincial League is a nearly invisible footnote to baseball history, because the league was at the time an "outlaw" circuit, not affiliated with Organized Baseball. And as students of the Negro leagues well know, the sport's power structure then was convinced that if it didn't happen in Organized Baseball, it didn't count.

—Merritt Clifton, 1984 BRJ

The Family Business

More than one set of relatives made Negro League baseball the family business. The apparent record is held by the five Bankhead brothers, who were Sam, a player and manager from 1930 to 1950; Fred, an infielder from 1937-48; Dan, a pitcher from 1940-47 (who then hurled in the white majors), and Garnett and Joe, who each pitched in 1948. Three families contributed four brothers each.

The first was the Taylors, with "Candy Jim" playing and managing from 1904-48; Charles "C.I." managing from 1904-22; "Steel Arm Johnny" pitching from 1903-25, and Ben playing and managing from 1913-40. The four Spearman brothers were Charles, a catcher and infielder from 1919-31; Clyde, an outfielder from 1932-46; Henry, an infielder from 1936-46, and William, a pitcher from 1924-27. The four Martin brothers, who all used initials instead of first and middle names, and who all were involved in medicine and used the honorific "doctor", were league and team officials between 1923 and 1950. One of them, J.B. Martin, was president of the Negro American League and the Southern League. W.S. Martin was also a Southern League president and a club official, as were B.B. and A.T. Martin.

—Clark

Negro Baseball

Register

Dick Clark and Larry Lester

A Negro Baseball Register appeared in Robert Peterson's landmark work *Only The Ball Was White* (Prentice-Hall 1970). Minor changes were made in the reprint by McGraw-Hill in 1984, and in the Oxford Press reissue of 1992. The immense task undertaken by Peterson is difficult for the average researcher to comprehend. He emphasizes the dilemma with his spaghetti theory:

"Tracing the course of the organized Negro Leagues is rather like trying to follow a single black strand through a ton of spaghetti. The footing is infirm, and the strand has a tendency to break off in one's hand and slither back into the amorphous mass."

We are extremely grateful for Bob Peterson's pioneering efforts in this field.

Aided by many players and an extensive research of microfilmed newspapers, Peterson provided future historians with a superb base to work from. Our goals were to add players, to find additional teams that many of them had played for, to fill in missing first names, and to verify the years that each played. The committee accomplished this with more newspaper research. Because first names do not normally appear in box scores, we interviewed players to fill this void. We estimate that we have made more than 5,000 changes to the original Peterson register. This includes extending the register years through 1955, from Peterson's original cut-off date of 1950. We hope that future updates of this publication will include years through 1960, the official league ending date.

We have attempted to provide the reader with the player's full legal name, and his nicknames. Some players have a name in brackets, to indicate that they appear in stories or boxscores under different names or under variations of one name. In a few entries, you will find, "see...." This is for players who were misidentified in earlier Registers. The years noted indicate the beginning and end dates of a player's career.

This project to include all former Negro League players is an on-going effort. We solicit your support for any additions or modifications. Please send any changes to the editors.

A

AARON, HENRY LOUIS (HANK)—1952—ss, Indianapolis Clowns

ABALLI,—1930—p, Cuban Stars (West)

ABBOTT,—1906-1908—p, of, Famous Cuban Giants, Genuine Cuban Giants, Brooklyn Royal Giants

ABERNATHY, JAMES—1945-47—of, Kansas City Monarchs

ABERNATHY, ROBERT W.—1946-47—of, Boston Blues, Indianapolis Clowns

ABRAMS, G.—1911—mgr., Indianapolis ABCs

ABREAU, EUFEMIO [ABREU]—1919-34—c, 1b, of, Cincinnati Cuban Stars Cuban Stars (NNL), Cuban Stars (ECL)

ACOSTA, JOSE y FERNANDEZ—1915—p, Long Branch N.J. Cubans

ADAMS, BEN—1953—p, Memphis Red Sox

ADAMS, EMERY (ACE)—1932-46—p, Memphis Red Sox, Baltimore Elite Giants, New York Black Yankees

ADAMS, MALACHI—1887—ump., LCBBP

ADAMS, (PACKINGHOUSE)—1938—3b, Kansas City Monarchs

ADDISON, J.—1910-11—c, Philadelphia Giants

ADDISON, K.—1911-12—3b, Philadelphia Giants, Pittsburgh Giants

ADDISON, T.—1911—ss, Philadelphia Giants

ADKINS, CLARENCE—1931—of, Nashville Elite Giants

ADKINS, STACY (See STACY ATKINS)

AGNEW, CLYDE—1950—p, Baltimore Elite Giants

AHRENS,—1930—of, p, Cuban Stars (East)

AKERS, CHARLEY—1924—ss, Hilldale

ALBERTSON, JOHNNY—1936-39—ss, New York Black Yankees, Brooklyn Royal Giants

ALBERTUS,—1932—p, Cuban Stars (East)

ALBRECHT, R.—1928-29—p, Bacharach Giants

ALBRIGHT, THOMAS (PISTOL PETE)—1936—p, New York Cubans

ALBRITTON, ALEXANDER (ALEX)—1921-25—p, Baltimore Black Sox, Washington Potomacs, Hilldale, Bacharach Giants, Wilmington Potomacs

ALDERETTE,—1918—p, Cuban Stars (East)

ALEXANDER,—1918-21—of, 1b, 2b, Dayton Marcos, Chicago Giants, Columbus Buckeyes

ALEXANDER, CALVIN—1922—p, New Orleans Crescent Stars

ALEXANDER, (CHUFFY)—1927-32—3b, of, 1b, Birmingham Black Barons, Monroe Monarchs

ALEXANDER, FREYL—1912—president, Homestead Grays

ALEXANDER, GROVER CLEVELAND (BUCK)—1923-26—p, Chicago Giants, Detroit Stars, Indianapolis ABCs, Cleveland Elites

ALEXANDER, (HUB)—1913—c, Chicago Giants

ALEXANDER, JOE—1950—c, Kansas City Monarchs

ALEXANDER, SPENCER—1940-41—of, Newark Eagles

ALEXANDER, TED (RED)—1938-49—p, Cleveland Bears, Chicago American Giants, Kansas City Monarchs, Birmingham Black Barons, Homestead Grays, New York Black Yankees, Indianapolis ABCs

ALFONSO, ANGEL—1924-30—ss, 3b, 2b, Cuban Stars (NNL), Cuban Stars (ECL), Cuban Stars (East)

ALLEN,—1936—ss, Memphis Red Sox

ALLEN,—1940, 1943—of, Birmingham Black Barons, New York Black Yankees

ALLEN, CLIFFORD (CROOKS, CLYDE)—1932-38—p, Hilldale, Baltimore Black Sox, Homestead Grays, Memphis Red Sox, Philadelphia Stars, Bacharach Giants

ALLEN, DAVE—1887—c, 1b, utl., Trenton Cuban Giants (Middle States Lg.), Pittsburgh Keystones

ALLEN, HOMER—1932—p, Monroe Monarchs

ALLEN, HOSES (BUSTER)—1942-47—p, utl., Jacksonville Red Caps, Cincinnati Clowns, Cincinnati-Indianapolis Clowns, Cleveland Buckeyes

ALLEN, M. —1919-22-2b, Lincoln Giants, Baltimore Black Sox, Brooklyn Royal Giants

ALLEN, NEWTON HENRY (NEWT, COLT)—1922-47—2b, ss, of, mgr., All Nations, Kansas City Monarchs, St. Louis Stars, Homestead Grays, Indianapolis Clowns

ALLEN, TODD—1911-25—3b, mgr., Bowser's ABCs, Indianapolis ABCs, Chicago American Giants, Lincoln Giants, Louisville White Sox

ALLEN, TOUSSAINT L'OUVERTURE (TOM)—1914-26—1b, Havana Red Sox, Hilldale, Wilmington Potomacs, Newark Stars

ALLEN, WILLIAM —1887—player, Cincinnati Browns

ALLISON,—1915-17, 21, 25—1b, 2b, c, Chicago Union Giants, Chicago American Giants, Nashville Giants, Indianapolis ABCs

ALLISON,—1937—ss, New York Black Yankees

ALMAGRO, JORGE—1945—of, Pittsburgh Crawfords

ALMAS,—1925—p, Cubans (NNL)

ALMEIDA, RAFAEL [ALMEYDA]—1904-07—3b, All Cubans, Havana Cuban Stars

ALMENTEROS, JUAN PABLO—1916—p, New York Cuban Stars

ALONSO, ROGELIO—1927-30—p, of, Cuban Stars (NNL)

ALSOP, CLIFFORD—1920-22—p, Kansas City Monarchs

ALSTON, TOM—1948—1b, Greensboro (NC) Red Wings

ALTMAN, GEORGE LEE—1955—of, Kansas City Monarchs

ALVAREZ, RAUL—1924-36—p, of, Cuban Stars (NNL), Cuban Stars (East), New York Cubans

AMARO, DIONISIO (DAVE)—1953-55—p, Indianapolis Clowns

AMOROS, EDMUNDO (SANDY)-1950—1b, of, New York Cubans

ANAS, A.—1935—p, New York Cubans

ANDERSON,—1908, 1912—p, 3b, Cuban Giants

ANDERSON,—1954—p, Memphis Red Sox

ANDERSON, ANDY—1951—of, Chicago American Giants

ANDERSON, ELIJAH—1887—ump., LCBBP

ANDERSON, LEWIS —1930-33—c, Chicago American Giants, Baltimore Black Sox

ANDERSON, RALPH—1932—of, Indianapolis ABCs, Homestead Grays

ANDERSON, ROBERT JAMES (BOBBY)—1915-25—ss, 2b, Peters' Union Giants, Chicago American Giants, Philadelphia Giants, Gilkerson's Union Giants, Chicago Giants

ANDERSON, THEODORE (BUBBLES)—1922-25—2b, c, Kansas City Monarchs, Birmingham Black Barons, Washington Potomacs, Wilmington Potomacs, Indianapolis ABCs

ANDERSON, WILLIAM—1927-1931—of, Nashville Elite Giants, Birmingham Black Barons

ANDERSON, WILLIAM (BILL)—1940-47—p, Brooklyn Royal Giants, New York Cubans, Philadelphia Stars, Homestead Grays

ANDREWS, HERMAN (JABO)—1930-43—of, p, 1b, mgr., Birmingham Black Barons, Memphis Red Sox, Indianapolis ABCs, Detroit Wolves, Homestead Grays, Columbus Blue Birds, Pittsburgh Crawfords, Washington Black Senators, Chicago American Giants, Jacksonville Red Caps, Cleveland Bears, Philadelphia Stars, New York Cubans

ANDREWS, (POP)—1905-19—p, of, 1b, 2b, Brooklyn Royal Giants, Pittsburgh Stars of Buffalo, Philadelphia Giants, Havana Red Sox, Pittsburgh Giants

ANTHONY, LAVANCE (PETE)—1950—c, Houston Eagles, New York Cubans

ANTHONY, THAD—1950—c, Baltimore Elite Giants

ARANGO, LUIS PEDRO [ORANGO]—1925-39—3b, 1b, Cuban Stars (East) (NNL), New York Cubans

ARBANS,—1931—of, Cuban Stars (East)

ARCHER,—1919-24—p, c, Lincoln Giants, Baltimore Black Sox, Philadelphia Giants

ARENAS, HIPOLITO (TORRENTO)—1932—of, 3b, Atlanta Black Crackers

ARENCIBIA, EDUARDO—1948—of, New York Cubans

ARGUELLES, MARTINANO, (See GARAY)

ARIOSA, HOMERO MARIO—1947-49—of, New York Cubans

ARMENTEROS, JUAN—1953-55—c, Kansas City Monarchs

ARMOUR,—1933—p, 3b, Detroit Stars

ARMOUR, ALFRED (BUDDY)—1936-50—of, ss, St. Louis Stars, Indianapolis ABCs, New Orleans-St. Louis Stars, Harrisburg-St.Louis Stars, Cleveland Buckeyes, Chicago American Giants, Homestead Grays

ARMSTEAD, JAMES (JIMMIE)—1938-49—p, of, Indianapolis ABCs, St.Louis Stars, Baltimore Elite Giants, Philadelphia Stars

ARMSTRONG,—1913—c, Chicago Giants

ARNET,—1921—p, Bacharach Giants

ARNOLD, PAUL—1926-36—of, Brooklyn Royal Giants, Newark Dodgers, Bacharach Giants, Hilldale, Newark Browns

ARTHUR, ROBERT—1946—p, Pittsburgh Crawfords

ARUMIS, (ARUMI)—1920—of, 2b, Kansas City Monarchs

ASBURY,—1918—p, Lincoln Giants

ASCANIO, CARLOS—1946—1b, New York Black Yankees

ASH, RUDOLPH [RUDOLPH]—1920, 1926—of, p, Chicago American Giants, Newark Stars, Hilldale

ASHBY, EARL—1945-48—c, Cleveland Buckeyes, Birmingham Black Barons, Homestead Grays, Newark Eagles

ASKEW, JESSE—1936—ss, St. Louis Stars

ASHPORT,—1913—3b, Havana Red Sox

ATAME,—1920—p, Kansas City Monarchs

ATKINS, ABE—1923—ss, 3b, Toledo Tigers

ATKINS, JOSEPH O. (JOE, LEROY)—1945-47—3b, of, Pittsburgh Crawfords, Cleveland Buckeyes

ATKINS, STACY—1950—p, Chicago American Giants

AUBURY,—1905—1b, Cuban X Giants

AUGUSTINE, LEON—1923—umpire, NNL

AUGUSTUS,—1927—p, Memphis Red Sox

AUSBROOK, DOUGLAS LEONARD—1946—c, Cleveland Clippers

AUSTIN, FRANK SAMUEL (JUNIOR)—1944-48—ss, Philadelphia Stars

AUSTIN, JOHN—1887—player, Cincinnati Browns

AUSTIN, (TANK)_—1930-32—p, Nashville Elite Giants, Birmingham Black Barons, Atlanta Black Crackers

AVERETT,—1943—of, New York Black Yankees

AVILL,—1930—p, Cuban Stars (East)

AWKARD, RUSSELL—1940-41—of, New York Cubans, Newark Eagles

AYLOR, JAMES—1887—player, Philadelphia Pythians

B

BAGLEY,—1937—c, Cincinnati Tigers

BAILEY,—1910—c, Chicago Giants

BAILEY, ALONZA—1934-35—p, Newark Dodgers

BAILEY, BOB—1932—of, Hilldale

BAILEY, D.—1916-28—of, 3b, Lincoln Stars, Pennsylvania Red Caps of New York

BAILEY, OTHA WILLIAM—1950-55—c, Cleveland Buckeyes, Houston Eagles, New Orleans Eagles, Birmingham Black Barons

BAILEY, PERCY (BILL)—1927-34—p, Baltimore Black Sox, Nashville Elite Giants, Detroit Stars, Cole's American Giants, New York Black Yankees, Newark Dodgers

BAIRD, THOMAS Y.—1938-50—officer, Kansas City Monarchs; booking agent for NAL exhibition games

BAKER, EDGAR—1945-46—p, Memphis Red Sox, Cleveland Clippers (USL)

BAKER, EUGENE WALTER (GENE)—1948-50—ss, Kansas City Monarchs

BAKER, HENRY—1925-32—of, Indianapolis ABCs, Dayton Marcos, St.Louis Stars

BAKER, HOWARD (HOME RUN)—1910—player, Chicago Leland Giants

BAKER, LAMAR—1950—p, New York Black Yankees

BAKER, NORMAN (BUD)—1937—p, Newark Eagles, New York Black Yankees

BAKER, RUFUS (SCOOP)—1943-50—inf, c, of, New York Black Yankees

BAKER, SAMMY—1950—p, Chicago American Giants

BAKER, TOM—1940—p, Baltimore Elite Giants

BAKER, WELTON B.—1937-38—bus. mgr., Atlanta Black Crackers

BALDWIN, ROBERT —1923-26—ss, 2b, Indianapolis ABCs, Cleveland Elites, Detroit Stars, Cleveland Tate Stars

BALL, GEORGE WALTER (GEORGIA RABBIT)—1902-23—p, of, Cuban X Giants, Augusta, (GA), Philadelphia Giants, Leland Giants, Chicago Giants, Chicago American Giants, St.Louis Giants, Mohawk Giants, Brooklyn Royal Giants, Chicago Union Giants, Milwaukee Giants, Lincoln Stars, Lincoln Giants

BALLARD,—1910—p, Chicago Giants

BALLESTEROS,—1916—p, of, Long Branch Cubans

BALLESTRO, MIGUEL (PEDRO BALLESTER)—1948—ss, New York Cubans

BALLEW,—1930—p, Louisville White Sox

BALLEY,—1937—p, Cincinnati Tigers

BAMES,—1937—c, Birmingham Black Barons

BANKES, JAMES—1950-52—p, of, Baltimore Elite Giants, Memphis Red Sox

BANKHEAD, DANIEL ROBERT (DAN)—1940-47—p, Chicago American Giants, Birmingham Black Barons, Memphis Red Sox

BANKHEAD, FRED—1936-48—2b, 3b, 1b, Birmingham Black Barons, Memphis Red Sox

BANKHEAD, GARNETT—1948—p, Homestead Grays

BANKHEAD, JOE—1948—p, Birmingham Black Barons

BANKHEAD, SAMUEL HOWARD (SAM)—1930-50—ss, of, 2b, p, mgr., Birmingham Black Barons, Nashville Elite Giants, Pittsburgh Crawfords, Toledo Crawfords, Homestead Grays, Louisville Black Caps, Kansas City Monarchs

BANKS,—1896—p, Cuban X Giants

BANKS,—1930—2b, Hilldale

BANKS, BEN—1952—2b, Kansas City Monarchs

BANKS, ERNEST (ERNIE)—1950, 53—ss, Kansas City Monarchs

BANKS, G.—1914-17-p, Lincoln Giants, Philadelphia Giants

BANKS, JOHNNY—1950—p, Philadelphia Stars

BANKS, NORMAN EARL—1945—2b, Newark Eagles

BANKS, S.—1915-19—c, Philadelphia Giants, Lincoln Giants

BANLES —1923—c, Toledo Tigers

BANTON,—1914—p, Chicago American Giants, West Baden (IN) Sprudels

BAPISTE,—1923-24—of, Bacharach Giants, Philadelphia Giants

BARANDA,—1915-16—3b, of, 1b, Long Branch N.J. Cubans, Jersey City Cubans

BARBEE, LAMB (BUD, BARBOO)—1937-49—p, 1b, mgr., New York Black Yankees, Cincinnati Clowns, Cincinnati-Indianapolis Clowns, Philadelphia Stars, Baltimore Elite Giants, Raleigh Tigers, Indianapolis Clowns, Brooklyn Royal Giants

BARBEE, QUINCY (BUD)—1949—of, Louisville Buckeyes, Kansas City Monarchs

BARBER, (BULL) —1920-1925—2b, Hilldale, Kansas City Monarchs, Harrisburg Giants

BARBER, JOHN—1946—of, Pittsburgh Crawfords

BARBER, SAM—1943-50—p, Cleveland Clippers (USL), Cleveland Buckeyes,

Sam Bankhead.
Robert H. McNeill

BARBETTE,—1918—1b, Cuban Stars (East)
BARBOUR, JESS [BARBER]—1909-1926—of, 1b, 3b, 2b,
    Philadelphia Giants, Chicago American Giants, Bacharach
    Giants, Detroit Stars, Pittsburgh Keystones, Harrisburg
    Giants, St. Louis Giants, Indianapolis ABCs, Quaker Giants,
    Chicago Giants
BARCELO,—1921—p, Cuban Stars (East)
BARKER, MARVIN (HACK)—1935-50—of, 2b, 3b, mgr., New York
    Black Yankees, Philadelphia Stars, Newark Dodgers,
    Bacharach Giants
BARKINS, W.C.—1928—officer, Cleveland Stars
BARLOW, TOM—1877—player, Mutuals of Washington
BARNES,—1906—3b, Philadelphia Giants
BARNES,—1925—p, Kansas City Monarchs
BARNES, ED—1937-40—p, Kansas City Monarchs, Baltimore
    Elite Giants
BARNES, FRANK—1949-50—p, Kansas City Monarchs
BARNES, HARRY (TACK HEAD, MOOCH)—1935-42, 1944-45,
    1949—c, Birmingham Black Barons, Memphis Red Sox,
    Atlanta Black Crackers
BARNES, ISAAC—1955—c, Memphis Red Sox
BARNES, JOE SR.—1950-52—p, Memphis Red Sox, Kansas City
    Monarchs, Indianapolis Clowns
BARNES, JOHN (TUBBY, FAT)—1921-31—c, Cleveland Tate
    Stars, Cleveland Browns, Detroit Stars, St. Louis Stars,
    Cleveland Hornets, Cleveland Tigers, Memphis Red Sox,
    Toledo Tigers, Indianapolis ABCs, Cleveland Elites

BARNES, JOHN—1952—p, Philadelphia Stars
BARNES, O.—1932—officer, New York Black Yankees
BARNES, RAY—1951—p, Kansas City Monarchs
BARNES, TOBIAS—1937—inf., Chicago American Giants
BARNES, TOM—1950-55—p, Memphis Red Sox
BARNES, V.—1940—of, Kansas City Monarchs
BARNES, WILLIAM H.—1887—officer, Baltimore Lord
    Baltimores
BARNES, WILLIAM (JIMMY, BILL)—1937-47—p, Baltimore Elite
    Giants, Memphis Red Sox, Indianapolis Clowns, New Yoirk
    Black Yankees
BARNHILL, DAVID (DAVE, IMPO)—1938-49—p, New Orleans-
    Jacksonville Red Caps, St. Louis Stars, New York Cubans
BARNHILL, HERBERT (HERB)—1938-46—c, Jacksonville Red
    Caps, Kansas City Monarchs, Chicago American Giants,
    Cleveland Bears
BARO, BERNARDO—1913-30—of, 1b, p, Cuban Stars (East),
    Cuban Stars (NNL), New York Cuban Stars, Kansas City
    Monarchs, Cuban Stars, Cincinnati Cubans
BARR,—1921-22—3b, ss, Kansas City Monarchs, Cuban Stars
    (West)
BARROW, WESLEY—1945-47—c, mgr., New Orleans Black
    Pelicans, Nashville Cubs, Baltimore Elite Giants
BARTAMINO,—1904—mgr., All Cubans
BARTLETT, HOWARD (HOMER, HOP, SAPHO)—1911-25—p,
    Indianapolis ABCs, Bowser's ABCs, Kansas City Monarchs
BARTON, SHERMAN—1896-1911—of, 3b, Chicago Unions,
    Columbia Giants, Quaker Giants of New York, Cuban X
    Giants, St. Paul Gophers, Chicago Giants, Chicago Union
    Giants, Leland Giants
Adrian (MI) Page Fence Giants, Algona (IA) Brownies
BASHUM,—1932—c, Indianapolis ABCs
BASKIN, WILLIAM—1890-92—2b, Chicago Unions
BASS, LEROY (RED)—1938-40—c, Homestead Grays, Pittsburgh
    Crawfords
BASSETT, LLOYD P. (PEPPER)—1934-54—c, New Orleans
    Crescent Stars, Philadelphia Stars, Chicago American
    Giants, Pittsburgh Crawfords, Cincinnati Clowns,
    Cincinnati-
Indianapolis Clowns, Birmingham Black Barons, Toledo
    Crawfords, Homestead Grays, Memphis Red Sox, Detroit
    Stars
BATSON,—1908-09—of, Genuine Cuban Giants, Philadelphia
    Giants
BATTLE(S), RAY—1944-45—3b, Homestead Grays
BATTLE, WILLIAM (BILL)—1947-49—p, Homestead Grays,
    Memphis Red Sox
BATTLES,—1924—inf., c, Harrisburg Giants
BATUM, G.W.—1885—2b, Brooklyn Remsens
BAUCHMAN, HARRY—1913-23—2b, ss, 1b, Chicago American
    Giants, Chicago Union Giants, Chicago Giants
BAUZA, MARCELINO —1930—ss, Cuban Stars (NNL)
BAXTER, AL—1898—of, Celeron Acme Colored Giants (Iron and
    Oil League)
BAYLIS(S), HENRY J.—1948-55—inf, c, Chicago American
    Giants, Baltimore Elite Giants, Birmingham Black Barons,
    Kansas City Monarchs
BAYNARD, FRANK —1913-28-of, c, Pennsylvania Red Caps of
    New York, Newark Stars, Hilldale, Bacharach Giants,
    Havana Red Sox, Lincoln Giants, Cuban X Giants
BEA, BILL—1940—of, New York Black Yankees, Philadelphia
    Stars
BEAL, G. (LEFTY)—1947—p, Newark Eagles
BEALE, HARRY—1926-30—p, officer, Pittsburgh Crawfords
BEBLEY,—1925—p, Birmingham Black Barons
BEBOP, RALPH (SPEC)—1950—mascot, Indianapolis Clowns
BECKWITH, JOHN—1916-39—ss, 3b, c, of, mgr., Chicago Giants,

William Bell, generally known as "W" Bell.
Luis Munoz Collection

Chicago American Giants, Baltimore Black Sox, Homestead Grays, Harrisburg Giants, Lincoln Giants, Bacharach Giants, New York Black Yankees, Newark Dodgers, Brooklyn Royal Giants, Newark Browns, Hilldale Daisies, Montgomery Grey Sox

BEJERANO, AGUSTIN—1928-29-of, Cuban Stars (ECL)

BELL,—1917-18—of, Baltimore Black Sox

BELL,—1946—utl., Philadelphia Stars

BELL, CHARLES (LEFTY)—1948—p, Homestead Grays

BELL, CLIFFORD (CLIFF, CHERRY)—1921-32—p, Kansas City Monarchs, Memphis Red Sox, Cleveland Cubs, Nashville Elite Giants

BELL, FRANK—1888-91-of, Cuban Giants, New York Gorhams (Middle States Lg.), Ansonia Cuban Giants (Connecticut St.Lg.), Philadelphia Giants

BELL, FRED (LEFTY)—1922-27—p, of, St. Louis Stars, Detroit Stars, Birmingham Black Barons, Toledo Tigers, Harrisburg Giants, Washington Potomacs

BELL, HERMAN—1943-50—c, Birmingham Black Barons

BELL, JAMES THOMAS (COOL PAPA)—1922-46—of, p, St. Louis Stars, Pittsburgh Crawfords, Detroit Wolves, Kansas City Monarchs, Chicago American Giants, Memphis Red Sox, Homestead Grays

BELL, JAMES (STEEL ARM)—1932-40—c, Montgomery Grey Sox, Indianapolis Crawfords, Jacksonville Red Caps

BELL, JULIAN (JUTE)—1923-31—p, Birmingham Black Barons, Memphis Red Sox, Detroit Stars, Louisville White Sox

BELL, WILLIAM—1902-04—p, of, Philadelphia Giants

BELL, WILLIAM SR. (W.)—1923-48—p, mgr., Kansas City Monarchs, Detroit Wolves, Homestead Grays, Pittsburgh Crawfords, Newark Dodgers, Newark Eagles, New York Black Yankees

BELL, WILLIAM R. JR.(LEFTY)—1949-54—p, Kansas City Monarchs, Birmingham Black Barons

BELTRAN,—1954—of, Kansas City Monarchs

BEMA,—1929—of, Cuban Stars (NNL)

BENJAMIN, JERRY CHARLES—1932-48—of, Memphis Red Sox, Detroit Stars, Birmingham Black Barons, Homestead Grays, Toledo Crawfords, New York Cubans

BENNETT,—1916—2b, Chicago Union Giants

BENNETT, ARTHUR—1955—of, Kansas City Monarchs

BENNETT, BRADFORD—1940-46—of, St. Louis Stars, New Orleans-St. Louis Stars, New York Black Yankees, Boston Blues, Birmingham Black Barons

BENNETT, CLYDE—1952—2b, Kansas City Monarchs

BENNETT, DON—1926, 1930-34—2b, Dayton Marcos, Cleveland Cubs, Memphis Red Sox, Birmingham Black Barons

BENNETT, FRANK—1918—mgr., Bacharach Giants

BENNETT, JERRY—1951—p, Kansas City Monarchs

BENNETT, JIM—1945-48—p, Cincinnati-Indianapolis Clowns, Indianapolis Clowns

BENNETT, JOHN—1930-32—of, Louisville Black Caps Birmingham Black Barons

BENNETT, SAM—1911-25—of, c, St. Louis Giants, St. Louis Stars, Mohawk Giants, Lincoln Giants

BENNETT, WILLIE—1952-55—ss, of, Kansas City Monarchs

BENNETTE, GEORGE CLIFFORD (JEW BABY)—1920-36—of, c, Columbus Buckeyes, Memphis Red Sox, Indianapolis ABCs, Detroit Stars, Chicago Giants, Chicago Union Giants, Pittsburgh Keystones, Kansas City Monarchs

BENNING,—1937—2b, Indianapolis Athletics

BENSON, AUGUSTA—1937-40—p, Memphis Red Sox, Washington Elite Giants

BENSON, EUGENE (GENE, SPIDER)—1933-48—of, Brooklyn Royal Giants Bacharach Giants, Pittsburgh Crawfords, Philadelphia Stars, Newark Eagles

BENSON, HERBERT—1952—1b, Indianapolis Clowns

BENTION, (See GENE BENSON)

BENTON,—1950—p, Memphis Red Sox

BENVENUTI, JULIUS—1939—vice-pres, Chicago American Giants

BERGIN, JIMMY—1949—1b, Kansas City Monarchs

BERKELEY, RANDOLPH—1919—c, Hilldale

BERKLEY,—1941—p, New Orleans-St. Louis Stars

BERNAL, BLACEDO (PABLO)—1941—p, New York Cuban Stars

BERNARD,—1911-17-c, of, Pittsburgh Giants, Lincoln Stars, Cuban Giants, Philadelphia Giants, Lincoln Giants, Hilldale

BERNARD, PABLO—1949-50—2b, ss, Louisville Buckeyes, Cleveland Buckeyes

BERNO,—1931—of, Indianapolis ABCs

BERRY,—1953—p, Memphis Red Sox

BERRY, E.—1930—ss, 2b, Memphis Red Sox, Detroit Stars

BERRY, JOHN PAUL—1935-37, 1945—p, 1b, Kansas City Monarchs, St. Louis Stars

BERRY, MIKE (RED)—1943-47—p, Kansas City Monarchs, Baltimore Elite Giants

BEST, R.—1904-06—p, Brooklyn Royal Giants, Cuban Giants

BETTS,—1938—of, Kansas City Monarchs

BETTS, RUSSELL BOB—1950-51—p, Kansas City Monarchs

BEVERIE,—1939—3b, Baltimore Elite Giants

BEVERLY, CHARLES (HOOKS)—1924-36—p, Cleveland Browns, Birmingham Black Barons, Kansas City Monarchs, Cleveland Stars, Pittsburgh Crawfords, New Orleans

Gene Benson.

Gene Benson

Crescent Stars, Newark Eagles, Nashville Elite Giants, Philadelphia Stars

BEVERLY, WILLIAM (FIREBALL)—1950-55—p, Houston Eagles, New Orleans Eagles, Chicago American Giants, Birmingham Black Barons

BIBBS, JUNIUS A.(RAINEY)—1933-44—2b, ss, 3b, Detroit Stars, Cincinnati Tigers, Chicago American Giants, Kansas City Monarchs, Indianapolis Crawfords, Cleveland Buckeyes

BIGBY, CHARLIE—1953—of, Indianapolis Clowns

BILGAR,—1914—c, Chicago Giants

BILLINGS,—1948—c, Homestead Grays

BILLINGS, WILLIAM—1921—p, Nashville Elite Giants

BILLINGSLEY, JOHN—1950—c, Memphis Red Sox

BILLINGSLEY, SAM—1950—p, Memphis Red Sox

BINDER, JAMES (JIMMY)—1930-46—3b, 2b, mgr., Memphis Red Sox, Brooklyn Eagles, Indianapolis ABCs, Detroit Stars, Homestead Grays, Washington Elite Giants, Pittsburgh Crawfords, Cleveland Clippers

BINGA, JESSE E.—1887—player, Washington Capital Citys

BINGA, WILLIAM—1895-1910—3b, c, Adrian Page Fence Giants, Columbia Giants, Philadelphia Giants, St. Paul Gophers, Chicago Union Giants, Kansas City (Ka) Giants, Adrian (Michigan State League)

BINGHAM, (BINGO)—1910-21—of, Chicago Union Giants, Chicago Giants, West Baden, (Ind) Sprudels

BIOT, CHARLES AUGUSTUS JR. (CHARLIE)—1939-41—of, Newark Eagles, New York Black Yankees, Baltimore Elite Giants, Philadelphia Stars

BIRAN,—1916—inf., Chicago American Giants

BISSANT, JOHN L.—1934-47—of, p, 2b, Cole's American Giants, Chicago American Giants, Birmingham Black Barons, Chicago Brown Bombers

BIVINS,—1948—p, Memphis Red Sox

BIX,—1921—p, St. Louis Giants

BIZZLE,—1947—p, Birmingham Black Barons

BLACK,—1926—p, Cleveland Elites, Dayton Marcos

BLACK, HOWARD—1928—inf, Brooklyn Cuban Giants

BLACK, JOSEPH (JOE)—1943-50—p, Baltimore Elite Giants

BLACKBURN,—1938—p, Kansas City Monarchs

BLACKBURN, HUGH—1920—p, Kansas City Monarchs

BLACKMAN, CLIFFORD (SPEED)—1937-41—p, Chicago American Giants, Birmingham Black Barons, Memphis Red Sox, New York Cubans, Indianapolis ABCs, Homestead Grays, New Orleans-St. Louis Stars

BLACKMAN, HENRY—1920-24—3b, Indianapolis ABCs, Baltimore Black Sox

BLACKMAN, WARREN—1939—p, Memphis Red Sox

BLACKMORE,—1951—c, Birmingham Black Barons

BLACKSTONE, WILLIAM—1887—player, Cincinnati Browns

BLACKWELL,—1934—p, Philadelphia Stars

BLACKWELL, CHARLES—1915-29—of, West Baden (IN) Sprudels, Bowser's ABCs, Jewell's ABCs, St. Louis Giants, St. Louis Stars, Birmingham Black Barons, Indianapolis ABCs, Detroit Stars, Nashville Elite Giants

BLAIR, GARNETT E. SR—1945-48—p, Homestead Grays

BLAIR, LONNIE J. (CHICO)—1949-50—p, 2b, Homestead Grays

BLAKE, FRANK (BIG RED)—1932-35—p, Baltimore Black Sox, New York Black Yankees, New York Cubans

BLAKE, WILLIAM—1952—p, Philadelphia Stars

BLAKELY, BERT —1934—c, Cincinnati Tigers

BLAKEMORE, WILLIAM (WILLIE)—1954—c, Memphis Red Sox, Kansas City Monarchs, Louisville Black Colonels

BLANCHARD, CHESTER—1926-33—ss, Dayton Marcos

BLANCO, CARLOS —1938-41—1b, New York Cubans

BLANCO, HEBERTO (HARRY, HENNY)—1941-42—2b, of, New York Cubans

BLATTNER, FRANK—1921—1b, of, Kansas City Monarchs

BLAVIS, FOX—1936—3b, Homestead Grays

BLEACH, LARRY —1937—2b, Detroit Stars

BLEDSLOE,—1937—of, St. Louis Stars

BLOUNT, JOHN T. (TENNY)—1919-33—officer, Detroit Stars; vice-pres, NNL

BLUEITT, VIRGIL—1916-18, 1937-49—2b, umpire, Chicago Union Giants, NAL

BLUKOI, FRANK—1916-20—2b, All Nations, Kansas City Monarchs

BOADA, LUCAS—1921-25—p, of, Cuban Stars (NNL), Cuban Stars (ECL) Cincinnati Cubans

BOARD,—1911-12—1b, Indianapolis ABCs

BOBO, J. see James Leonard

BOBO, WILLIE—1923-30—1b, All Nations, Kansas City Monarchs, St. Louis Stars, Nashville Elite Giants

BOGGS, GEORGE—1922-34—p, of, Milwaukee Bears, Detroit Stars, Dayton Marcos, Cleveland Tigers, Baltimore Black Sox, Cleveland Tate Stars

BOLDEN, EDWARD (ED, CHIEF)—1910-50—officer, Hilldale, Darby Phantoms, Philadelphia Stars; officer, ECL, ANL, NNL

BOLDEN, JIM (FIREBALL)—1952—p, Birmingham Black Barons

BOLDEN, L.W.—1885—player, Brooklyn Remsens

BOLDEN, OTTO—1910, 1920—c, p, Leland Giants, Chicago Giants

BOMES,—1925—3b, Cuban Stars (NNL)

BOND, TIMOTHY—1935-40—ss, 3b, Pittsburgh Crawfords, Newark Dodgers, Chicago American Giants

BONDS,—1927—c, Cleveland Hornets

BONNER, ROBERT—1921-26—1b, c, 2b, Cleveland Tate Stars, St. Louis Stars, Toledo Tigers, Cleveland Browns, Cleveland Elites

BOOKER, BILLY—1898—2b, Celeron (NY) Acme Colored Giants (Iron and Oil League)

BOOKER, DAN—1909—p, Kansas City (MO) Royal Giants

BOOKER, JAMES (PETE)—1903-19—c, 1b, Philadelphia Giants, Leland Giants, Lincoln Giants, Chicago American Giants, Chicago Giants, Mohawk Giants, Brooklyn Royal Giants, Indianapolis ABCs

BOOKER, RICH—1952—of, Kansas City Monarchs

BOONE, ALONZO D.(BUSTER)—1929-50—p, mgr., Cleveland Cubs, Birmingham Black Barons, Chicago American Giants, Cincinnati Buckeyes, Cleveland Buckeyes, Louisville Buckeyes, Memphis Red Sox, Cleveland Bears

BOONE, CHARLES (LEFTY, BOB, BULLET)—1940-46—p, New Orleans-St. Louis Stars, Harrisburg-St. Louis Stars, Pittsburgh Crawfords, Cincinnati Buckeyes, Jacksonville Red Caps, Cleveland Buckeyes, New York Black Yankees, Philadelphia Stars, Boston Blues

BOONE, OSCAR—1939-42—c, 1b, Indianapolis ABCs, Chicago American Giants, Birmingham Black Barons, Baltimore Elite Giants

BOONE, ROBERT—1923-28, 1946—umpire, NNL

BOONE, STEVE (LEFTY)—1940—p, Memphis Red Sox

BORDEN,—1912—cf, Pittsburgh Giants

BORDEN, J.—1932-33—ss, utl., Birmingham Black Barons

Joe Black.

BORDES, ED—1940—utl., Cleveland Bears

BORGES,—1904-05—2b, All Cubans

BORGES,—1928—inf, Cuban Stars (NNL)

BORSELO, [BOROTTO]—1921—p, c, Cuban Stars (East), All Cubans

BORTER,—1916—1b, Chicago Giants

BOSTICK,—1924—of, St. Louis Giants

BOSTOCK, LYMAN WESLEY SR.—1938-49—1b, of, Birmingham Black Barons, Chicago American Giants, Brooklyn Royal Giants, New York Cubans

BOSTON, BOB—1948—3b, Homestead Grays

BOSWELL,—1939—p, Toledo Crawfords

BOUNDS,—1933—p, Philadelphia Stars

BOWE, RANDOLPH (BOB, LEFTY)—1938-40—p, Kansas City Monarchs, Chicago American Giants

BOWEN,—1950—p, Indianapolis Clowns

BOWEN, (CHUCK)—1937-43—of, Indianapolis Athletics, Chicago Brown Bombers

BOWERS,—1887—of, Philadelphia Pythians

BOWERS, CHUCK—1926—p, ss, Baltimore Black Sox

BOWERS, JULIUS (JULIE)—1947-1950—c, New York Black Yankees

BOWMAN, BILL—1903-04—p, of, Cuban X Giants

BOWMAN, EMMETT (SCOTTY)—1903-16—3b, p, c, ss, of, Philadelphia Giants, Leland Giants, Brooklyn Royal Giants, Chicago American Giants

BOWSER, THOMAS—1914-17-owner, Indianapolis ABCs, Bowser's ABCs

BOYD, BENJAMIN—1885-91—2b, of, Argyle Hotel, Cuban Giants, York Cuban Giants, (Eastern Interstate Lg.), Trenton Cuban Giants (Middle States Lg.), Ansonia Cuban Giants (Connecticut St.Lg.), York Colored Monarchs

BOYD, FRED-1920-22—of, Chicago American Giants, Cleveland Tate Stars

BOYD, LINCOLN—1949-52—of, Louisville Buckeyes, Indianapolis Clowns

BOYD, OLLIE—1933—of, p, Kansas City Monarchs

BOYD, ROBERT RICHARD (BOB, ROPE)—1946-50—1b, Memphis Red Sox

BOYD, WILLIE JAMES—1943, 1946—p, Homestead Grays, Newark Eagles

BOYER,—1902—c, Philadelphia Giants

BRACKEN, HERB (DOC)—1940, 1946-47—p, New Orleans-St. Louis Stars, Cleveland Buckeyes, Brooklyn Brown Dodgers

BRADFORD, CHARLES—1910-28—p, of, 1b, coach, Pittsburgh Giants, Lincoln Giants, Philadelphia Giants

BRADFORD, WILLIAM (BILL)—1938-43—of, 2b, Indianapolis ABCs, St. Louis Stars, Memphis Red Sox, Birmingham Black Barons, New York Black Yankees, Chicago American Giants, New Orleans-St.Louis Stars

BRADLEY, PROVINCE FRANK (RED, DICK)—1937-43—p, Cincinnati Tigers, Kansas City Monarchs, Memphis Red Sox

BRADLEY, PHIL—1905-27—c, 1b, utl., Brooklyn Royal Giants, Lincoln Giants, Smart Set, Pittsburgh Colored Stars, Pittsburgh Stars of Buffalo, Mohawk Giants, Famous Cuban Giants, Philadelphia Giants, Pop Watkins Stars

BRADSHAW,—1926—of, Dayton Marcos

BRADY, JOHN—1887—of, Pittsburgh Keystones

BRADY, (LEFTY)—1921—p, Cleveland Tate Stars

BRAGANA, RAMON—1928-37, 1947—p, of, Cuban Stars (East), Stars of Cuba, New York Cubans, Cleveland Buckeyes

BRAGG, EUGENE—1925—c, Chicago American Giants

BRAGG, JESSE—1908-19—3b, ss, 2b, Genuine Cuban Giants, Cuban Giants, Brooklyn Royal Giants, Mohawk Giants, Lincoln Giants, Philadelphia Giants, Pennsylvania Red Caps of NY

James "Pete" Booker.
Chicago Historical Society

BRAITHWAITE, ALONZO—1948—2B, Philadelphia Stars
BRAITHWAITE, ARCHIE—1944-48—of, Newark Eagles, Philadelphia Stars
BRAM,—1930—p, Hilldale
BRAMMELL,—1932—c, Indianapolis ABCs
BRANAHAN, J. FINIS (SLIM)—1922-27, 1931—p, Cleveland Tate Stars, Harrisburg Giants, Detroit Stars, Cleveland Elites, Cleveland Hornets, St. Louis Stars, Toledo Tigers, Lincoln Giants, Indianapolis ABCs
BRANHAM, LUTHER H.—1949-50—inf, Birmingham Black Barons, Chicago American Giants
BRANHAM, (SLIM)—1917-23—p, Jewell's ABCs, Toledo Tigers, Dayton Marcos, Cleveland Elites, Cleveland Tate Stars
BRANNIGAN, GEORGE—1926-27—p, Cleveland Elites, Cleveland Hornets
BRANTLEY, OLLIE—1950-53—p, Memphis Red Sox
BRAY, JAMES—1922-31—c, of, Chicago Giants, Chicago American Giants, Chicago Columbia Giants
BRAZELTON, JOHN CLARKSON [CLARKSON]—1915-17—c, Chicago American Giants, Chicago Giants
BREDA, BILL—1950-54—of, Kansas City Monarchs, Birmingham Black Barons
BREEN, W.—1935—of, Pittsburgh Crawfords
BREGAN,—1928—3b, Cuban Stars (East)
BREMBLE,—1931—2b, Birmingham Black Barons
BREMMER, EUGENE (GENE)—1932-48—p, New Orleans Crescent Stars, Cincinnati Tigers, Memphis Red Sox, Kansas City Monarchs, Cincinnati Buckeyes, Cleveland Buckeyes

BRENNER,—1917—p, Chicago American Giants
BREWER, CHESTER ARTHUR (CHET)—1925-48—p, Kansas City Monarchs, Washington Pilots, New York Cubans, Philadelphia Stars, Chicago American Giants, Cleveland Buckeyes
BREWER, LUTHER—1918-21—1b, of, Chicago Giants
BREWER, SHERWOOD (SHERRY, WOODY)—1949-55—of, inf, Indianapolis Clowns, Kansas City Monarchs
BREWSTER, SAMUEL—1950—of, Cleveland Buckeyes
BREWTON,—1936—p, Birmingham Black Barons
BRICE,—1951—of, Baltimore Elite Giants
BRIDGEFORT, R. —1932—officer, Cleveland Cubs
BRIDGEFORTH, WILLIAM—1950-53—officer, Birmingham Black Barons, Baltimore Elite Giants
BRIDGES, JOHN—1954—p, Memphis Red Sox
BRIDGES, MARSHALL—1951-54—p, of, Memphis Red Sox
BRIGGERY, (BO)—1932—ss, Atlanta Black Crackers
BRIGGS,—1917—p, Indianapolis ABCs
BRIGGS, OTTO (MIRROR)—1914-34—of, mgr., West Baden (IN) Sprudels, Dayton Marcos, Hilldale, Quaker Giants, Bacharach Giants, Santop's Broncos
BRIGHAM,—1924—p, Harrisburg Giants
BRIGHT, JOHN M.—1888-1909—mgr., Cuban Giants
BRISCOE,—1913-14—of, Indianapolis ABCs, Louisville White Sox
BRISKER, WILLIAM—1950—gen mgr., Cleveland Buckeyes
BRITT, CHARLES (CHARLIE)—1927-33—3b, Homestead Grays
BRITT, GEORGE (CHIPPY)[BRITTON]—1920-44—p, c, inf, Dayton Marcos, Columbus Buckeyes, Baltimore Black Sox, Hilldale, Homestead Grays, Newark Dodgers, Columbus Elite Giants, Washington Black Senators, Jacksonville Red Caps, Brooklyn Royal Giants, Chicago American Giants, Detroit Wolves, Cincinnati-Cleveland Buckeyes, Harrisburg Giants
BRITTON, JOHN (JACK)—1940-50—3b, New Orleans-St. Louis Stars, Cincinnati Clowns, Birmingham Black Barons, Indianapolis Clowns
BROADNAX, WILLIE (BROADWAY)—1928-29—p, of, Memphis Red Sox
BROADNAX, MACEO (BABY BOY)—1932—p, Kansas City Monarchs
BROILES, (See BROYLES)
BROOKS,—1887—player, Louisville Falls City
BROOKS,—1934—p, Pittsburgh Crawfords
BROOKS, ALEX (ALVIN)—1934-40—of, New York Black Yankees, Brooklyn Royal Giants, Bacharach Giants, Philadelphia Stars
BROOKS, AMEAL (MACON)—1929-47—c, of, Chicago American Giants, Cleveland Cubs, Cole's American Giants, Columbus Blue Birds, Cincinnati Clowns, New York Black Yankees, New York Cubans, Homestead Grays, Newark Eagles, Philadelphia Stars, Memphis Red Sox
BROOKS, BEATTIE—1918-21—inf, c, Lincoln Giants, Brooklyn Royal Giants, Philadelphia Giants
BROOKS, CHARLES—1919-26—2b, p, of, St. Louis Giants, St. Louis Stars, Homestead Grays, Dayton Marcos, Detroit Stars
BROOKS, CHESTER—1918-33—of, Brooklyn Royal Giants
BROOKS, E.—1936—p, Kansas City Monarchs
BROOKS, EDWARD (EDDIE)—1949-55—2b, Houston Eagles, Memphis Red Sox, New Orleans Eagles, Birmingham Black Barons
BROOKS, GUS—1894-95—of, Page Fence Giants, Chicago Unions
BROOKS, IRVIN—1918-31—p, utl., Brooklyn Royal Giants, Bacharach Giants
BROOKS, JAMES—1887—player, Baltimore Lord Baltimores
BROOKS, JESSE—1934-37—3b, of, Cleveland Red Sox, Kansas City Monarchs

BROOKS, JOHN O.—1942—p, Memphis Red Sox
BROOKS, MOXIE—1945—p, Toledo Cubs (USL)
BROOKS, WALLACE—1948—p, Baltimore Elite Giants
BROOM,—1940-42—p, Cleveland Bears, Jacksonville Red Caps
BROOME, J.B.—1947—of, New York Black Yankees
BROWCOW,—1905-06—2b, Brooklyn Royal Giants
BROWN,—1905-12—of, Brooklyn Royal Giants
BROWN,—1949—player, Chicago American Giants
BROWN,—1954—p, Louisville Black Colonels
BROWN, A. —1923—c, Birmingham Black Barons
BROWN, ARNOLD—1920-22—ss, 2b, Hilldale, Bacharach Giants, Harrisburg Giants, Washington Braves
BROWN, B.—1914-18—of, New York Stars, Brooklyn All-Stars, Washington Red Caps
BROWN, BARNEY—1931-49—p, Cuban Stars (West), Philadelphia Stars, New York Black Yankees
BROWN, BEN—1899-1900—p, of, Genuine Cuban Giants
BROWN, BENNY—1931-32—ss, Newark Browns, Bacharach Giants
BROWN, C.—1925, 1930—of, Brooklyn Royal Giants
BROWN, CARL—1951-54—ss, p, Philadelphia Stars, Indianapolis Clowns, Detroit Stars
BROWN, CHARLES—1886-87—p, Cuban Giants, Pittsburgh Keystones
BROWN, CURTIS—1947, 1950—1b, New York Black Yankees
BROWN, DAVID (DAVE, LEFTY)—1918-25—p, Chicago American Giants, Lincoln Giants
BROWN, E. —1914-18—3b, p, Cuban Giants, New York Stars, Chicago Union Giants, Brooklyn All-Stars
BROWN, EARL—1923-26—p, of, Lincoln Giants, Baltimore Black Sox, Harrisburg Giants
BROWN, EDWARD—1920-23—p, Detroit Stars, Indianapolis ABCs, Chicago Giants, Chicago American Giants
BROWN, ELIAS (COUNTRY)—1918-33—3b, 2b, of, New York Bacharach Giants, Bacharach Giants, Brooklyn Royal Giants, Washington Potomacs, Wilmington Potomacs, Hilldale
BROWN, ELMORE (SCRAPPY)—1918-32—ss, Washington Red Caps, Lincoln Giants, Baltimore Black Sox, Brooklyn Royal Giants, Hilldale
BROWN, F.—1918—2b, Chicago Union Giants
BROWN, G. —1925-28—p, St. Louis Stars, Kansas City Monarchs
BROWN, GEORGE—1910-28—of, 3b, mgr., Jewell's ABCs, Indianapolis ABCs, St. Louis Giants, Dayton Marcos, Detroit Stars, Columbus Buckeyes, West Baden (IN) Sprudels
BROWN, GEORGE —1939-45—of, Cincy-Cleveland Buckeyes, Baltimore Elite Giants, Philadelphia Stars, Chicago American Giants
BROWN, H.—1913-15—p, Mohawk Giants, Brooklyn Royal Giants
BROWN, H.—1939—ss, Memphis Red Sox
BROWN, JAMES (JIM)—1918-42—c, 1b, mgr., Chicago American Giants, Louisville Black Caps, Cole's American Giants, Minneapolis-St. Paul Gophers, Chicago Columbia Giants, Cleveland Cubs, Montgomery Grey Sox
BROWN, JAMES PHILLIPS—1937-48—p, of Newark Eagles, Indianapolis Clowns, Pittsburgh Crawfords
BROWN, JEROME—1949—inf, Houston Eagles
BROWN, JESSE—1890—2b, ss, Lincoln (NEB) Giants
BROWN, JESSE J. (PROFESSOR, LEFTY)—1938-42—p, New York Black Yankees, Newark Eagles, Baltimore Elite Giants
BROWN, JIM (See WILLARD BROWN)
BROWN, JOHN W.—1942-49—p, Cleveland Buckeyes, Houston Eagles
BROWN, JOSEPH—1887—mgr., Washington Capital Citys

BROWN, JULIUS—1946—p, Indianapolis Clowns
BROWN, L.—1914—2b, Indianapolis ABCs
BROWN, L.A.—1926-27—officer, St. Louis Stars
BROWN, LARRY (IRON MAN)-1919-49—c, mgr., Birmingham Black Barons, Pittsburgh Keystones, Indianapolis ABCs, Memphis Red Sox, Detroit Stars, Chicago American Giants, Lincoln Giants, New York Black Yankees, Cole's American Giants, Philadelphia Stars
BROWN, LAWRENCE JAMES (LEFTY)—1931-40—p, Claybrook Tigers, Memphis Red Sox
BROWN, M.—1918—of, Bacharach Giants
BROWN, MAYWOOD—1921-25—p, Indianapolis ABCs
BROWN, OLIVER—1931-32—bus mgr., Newark Browns
BROWN, OSCAR—1939—c, Indianapolis ABCs, Baltimore Elite Giants
BROWN, OSSIE—1934-39—p, of, Cole's American Giants, Indianapolis Athletics, Indianapolis ABCs, St. Louis Stars
BROWN, RALPH—1954—ss, 2b, Birmingham Black Barons
BROWN, RAY—1939-40—c, Brooklyn Royal Giants, Chicago American Giants
BROWN, RAYMOND (RAY)—1930-48—p, of, Dayton Marcos, Indianapolis ABCs, Detroit Wolves, Homestead Grays
BROWN, RICH—1952—inf, Chicago American Giants
BROWN, ROBERT —1887—player, Boston Resolutes
BROWN, RONNIE—1943—1b, Harrisburg-St. Louis Stars
BROWN, ROY—1928-32—p, of, Kansas City Monarchs, Cleveland Cubs

Larry Brown.
Luis Munoz Collection

Ray Brown and Johnny Taylor.
Jeff Eastland

BROWN, T.J. (TOM)—1939-50—ss, 3b, Memphis Red Sox,
    Cleveland Buckeyes, Indianapolis Clowns, Harrisburg-
    St.Louis Stars, Louisville Buckeyes
BROWN, THEO—1911—3b, Chicago Union Giants
BROWN, TOM—1917-19—p, Brooklyn Royal Giants, Chicago
    American Giants, Lincoln Giants
BROWN, (TUTE)—1918—3b, Washington Red Caps
BROWN, ULYSSES (BUSTER, JOE)—1937-42—c, of, Newark
    Eagles, Jacksonville Red Caps, Cincinnati Buckeyes,
    Cleveland Buckeyes, Chicago American Giants
BROWN, W. (MIKE)—1910-15—p, 1b, of, Mohawk Giants,
    Philadelphia Giants, Cuban Giants
BROWN, WALTER S.—1887—mgr., pres, Pittsburgh Keystones,
    League of Colored Base Ball Clubs
BROWN, WILLARD JESSE (HOME RUN)—1934-52, 1958—of, ss,
    Monroe Monarchs, Kansas City Monarchs
BROWN, WILLIAM—1906—asst mgr., Leland Giants
BROWN, WILLIAM—1952—inf, Birmingham Black Barons
BROWN, WILLIAM H.—1887—1b, Pittsburgh Keystones
BROWN, WILLIAM M.—1931-32—officer, Montgomery Grey Sox
BROWN, WILLIE—1953-55—inf, Indianapolis Clowns
BROWNE, (HAP)—1924—p, Cleveland Browns
BROYLES, [BROILES]1925-27—p, St. Louis Stars
BRUCE, CLARENCE—1947-48—2b, Homestead Grays
BRUCE, LLOYD—1940—p, Chicago American Giants
BRUTON, CHARLES JOHN (JACK) [BURTON]—1928-41, 1950—p,
    of, inf, Cleveland Bears, Philadelphia Stars, New Orleans-
    St. Louis Stars, Birmingham Black Barons, Cleveland
    Buckeyes, New York Black Yankees
BRYANT, ALLEN JR. (LEFTY)—1937-47—p, All Nations, Kansas
    City Monarchs, Memphis Red Sox

BRYANT, EDDIE —1925-28—2b, Pennsylvania Red Caps of NY
    Harrisburg Giants
BRYANT, JOHNNIE—1950—of, Cleveland Buckeyes
BRYANT, R.B.—1937—ss, Memphis Red Sox
BUBBLES,—1938—p, Atlanta Black Crackers
BUCHANAN, CHESTER (BUCK)—1931-43—p, Philadelphia Stars,
    Bacharach Giants, Brooklyn Royal Giants
BUCHANAN, FLOYD (BUCK)—1914—p, Hilldale
BUCK,—1923—p, Birmingham Black Barons
BUCKNER,—1914—ss, Chicago Giants
BUCKNER, HARRY—1896-1918—p, of, Chicago Unions,
    Columbia Giants, Philadelphia Giants, Cuban X Giants,
    Brooklyn Royal Giants, Quaker Giants, Lincoln Giants,
    Smart Set, Chicago Giants, Mohawk Giants, Louisville
    White Sox
BUCKNER, JOSEPH JAMES (JOE)—1946—p, Chicago American
    Giants, Boston Blues
BUDBILL,—1950—p, Houston Eagles
BUDDLES,—1925—inf, Chicago American Giants
BUFORD,—1913-14—p, Chicago Giants
BUFORD, (BLACK BOTTOM)—1927-34—3b, ss, 2b, Nashville
    Elite Giants, Cleveland Cubs, Detroit Stars, Louisville Red
    Caps, Birmingham Black Barons
BULLOCK,—1890—p, Lincoln (NEB) Giants
BUMPUS, EARL—1944-48—p, of, Kansas City Monarchs,
    Birmingham Black Barons, Chicago American Giants
BUNCH, SIDNEY—1954—of, Birmingham Black Barons
BUNDY,—1927—player, Bacharach Giants
BURBAGE, KNOWLINGTON O.(BUDDY)—1928-51—of, Hilldale,
    Pittsburgh Crawfords, Baltimore Black Sox, Bacharach
    Giants, Newark Dodgers, Homestead Grays, Washington
    Black Senators, Brooklyn Royal Giants, Philadelphia Stars,
    New York Black Yankees
BURCH, ALONZO—1914-16—p, Indianapolis ABCs, Chicago
    Union Giants
BURCH, JOHN WALTER—1931-46—c, 2b, ss, mgr., Bacharach
    Giants, Baltimore Black Sox, Cleveland Bears, St. Louis
    Stars, New
Orleans-St. Louis Stars, Cincinnati Buckeyes, Cleveland
    Buckeyes, Chicago American Giants, Newark Dodgers,
    Washington Pilots
BURDINE, J.—1927-32—p, of, Birmingham Black Barons,
    Memphis Red Sox, Indianapolis ABCs
BURGEE, LOUIS—1910, 1917—p, 2b, Hilldale
BURGESS,—1942—p, Chicago American Giants
BURGETT,—1920—of, St. Louis Giants
BURGIN,—1913—rf, Havana Red Sox
BURGIN, RALPH [BERGIN]—1917-1943—2b, ss, 3b, of, Hilldale,
    New York Black Yankees, Philadelphia Stars, Brooklyn
    Royal Giants Baltimore Black Sox, Pittsburgh Crawfords,
    Bacharach Giants
BURGOS, JOSE ANTONIO—1949-50—ss, Birmingham Black
    Barons
BURKE, BILLY—1942—3b, Boston Royal Giants
BURKE, CHARLES —1937—ss, Indianapolis Athletics
BURKE, ERNEST—1947-48—p, Baltimore Elite Giants
BURKE, (PING)—1937—p, Atlanta Black Crackers
BURNETT, FRED (TEX)—1921-46—c, 1b of, coach, mgr.,
    Pittsburgh Keystones, Indianapolis ABCs, Lincoln Giants,
    Harrisburg Giants, Brooklyn Royal Giants, New York Black
    Yankees, Baltimore Black Sox, Homestead Grays, Brooklyn
    Eagles, Newark Eagles, Pittsburgh Crawfords, Bacharach
    Giants, Nashville Cubs, Newark Dodgers
BURNHAM, WILLIE (BEE)—1930-34—p, Monroe Monarchs
BURNS, CLOYCE—1946—p, Boston Blues

BURNS, PETE—1890-1902—c, of, Page Fence Giants, Columbia Giants Chicago Unions, Adrian (Mich. St. Lg.), Algona (IA) Brownies, Philadelphia Giants

BURNS, WILLIAM (BILL WILLIE)—1935-44—p, Memphis Red Sox, Cincinnati- Indianapolis Clowns, Newark Dodgers, Philadelphia Stars, Baltimore Elite Giants, Chicago American Giants, Atlanta Black Crackers, New York Black Yankees

BURRELL,—1917-20—of, Baltimore Black Sox

BURRELL, GEORGE—1884-85—p, c, Baltimore Atlantics

BURRIS, SAMUEL (SPEED)—1937-40—p, Memphis Red Sox, Birmingham Black Barons

BURTON, (SEE CHARLES BRUTON)

BURTON, (LEFTY)—1929-30—p, Pittsburgh Crawfords

BUSBY,—1933—of, Detroit Stars

BUSBY, MAURICE (LEFTY)—1920-22—p, Bacharach Giants, All Cubans, Baltimore Black Sox

BUSH,—1946—p, Cleveland Buckeyes

BUSTAMENTE, LUIS—1904-13—ss, 2b, of, Cuban Stars, All Cubans, Brooklyn Royal Giants, Havana Cuban Stars

BUSTER, HERBERT—1943—inf, Chicago American Giants

BUTLER,—1917—of, Lincoln Giants

BUTLER,—1937, 1943—3b, Pittsburgh Crawfords, Newark Eagles

BUTLER, BENJAMIN M.—1887—manager, New York Gorhams

BUTLER, (DOC)—1950—c, Memphis Red Sox

BUTLER, FRANK—1894-95—of, p, Chicago Unions

BUTLER, J. —1884—player, Philadelphia Mutual B.B.C.

BUTLER, (SOL)—1925—p, Kansas City Monarchs

BUTT,—1942—player, Jacksonville Red Caps

BUTTS, HARRY—1949-51—p, Indianapolis Clowns

BUTTS, ROBERT THOMAS (TOMMY, PEE WEE)—1938-54—ss, Atlanta Black Crackers, Indianapolis ABCs, Baltimore Elite Giants, Memphis Red Sox, Birmingham Black Barons

BYAS, RICHARD THOMAS (SUBBY)—1931-42—c, 1b, of, Kansas City Monarchs, Cole's American Giants, Chicago American Giants, Newark Dodgers, Memphis Red Sox

BYATT, (See CHARLES BIOT)

BYERS, HENRY [BYUS]—1887—2b, Pittsburgh Keystones

BYRD,—1921—1b, Chicago Giants

BYRD, JAMES F.—1927-30—officer, Hilldale

BYRD, PRENTICE—1934—officer, Cleveland Red Sox

BYRD, WILLIAM (BILL)—1932-50—p, of, Columbus Turfs, Columbus Blue Birds, Columbus Elite Giants, Washington Elite Giants, Baltimore Elite Giants, Nashville Elite Giants, Cleveland Red Sox

C

CABALLERO, LUIS PEREZ [LUIS PEREZ]—1948-50—3b, Indianapolis Clowns, New York Cubans

CABANAS, ARMANDO—1910—2b, Stars of Cuba

CABLE,—1930—of, Louisville White Sox

CABRERA, ALFREDO A.—1905—1b, All Cubans

CABRERA, CLEMENTE (SUNGO) [CARRERA]—1938-41—2b, of, 3b, New York Cubans

CABRERA, LORENZO (CHIQUITIN)—1947-50—1b, New York Cubans

CABRERA, LUIS RAUL—1948—p, Indianapolis Clowns

CABRERA, RAFAEL—1944-50—p, of, Indianapolis Clowns, Birmingham Black Barons

CABRERA, VILLA—1948—of, Indianapolis Clowns

CADE, JOE —1929—p, of, Bacharach Giants

CAFFIE, JOSEPH CLIFFORD (JOE, RABBITT)—1950—of, Cleveland Buckeyes

CAIN, MARION (SUGAR)—1937-55—p, Pittsburgh Crawfords, Brooklyn Royal Giants, Indianapolis Clowns, New York Black Yankees, Kansas City Monarchs, Birmingham Black Barons, Bacharach Giants

CALARAI,—1933—p, Cuban Stars

CALDERIN,—1917-19, 1924—p, of, Havana Stars, Cuban Stars (East), Cuban Stars of Havana

CALDERON, BENITO —1926-28—c, Cuban Stars (NNL), Homestead Grays

CALDWELL,—1933—of, Birmingham Black Barons

CALDWELL, FRANK—1947—p, Cleveland Buckeyes

CALHAN, ROWLAND—1938—p, Washington Black Senators

CALHOUN, JIM—1923—2b, Toledo Tigers

CALHOUN, WALTER (LEFTY)—1931-46—p, Birmingham Black Barons, Montgomery Grey Sox, Washington Black Senators, Pittsburgh Crawfords, Indianapolis ABCs, St. Louis Stars, New Orleans-St. Louis Stars, New York Black Yankees, Harrisburg-St. Louis Stars, Cleveland Buckeyes, Philadelphia Stars, Memphis Red Sox, Indianapolis Athletics, Louisville Black Colonels

CALHOUN, WESLEY—1950—inf, of, Cleveland Buckeyes

CALL, F.—1884-85—inf, Baltimore Atlantics

CALLIS, J. JOSEPH—1887—manager, Baltimore Lord Baltimore

CALVO, JACINTO y GONZALEZ (JACK)—1913-15—of, Long Branch, N.J. Cubans

CALVO, T.—1915-16—of, c, Long Branch, N.J. Cubans, Jersey City Cubans

CAM,—1891—of, Ansonia Cuban Giants (Connecticut St.Lg.)

CAMBRIA, JOE—1933—owner, officer, Baltimore Black Sox

CAMPANELLA, ROY—1937-45—c, Baltimore Elite Giants

CAMPBELL,—1930—of, Nashville Elite Giants

CAMPBELL, ANDREW—1903-06—c, Leland Giants, Chicago Union Giants

CAMPBELL, DAVID (DAVE)—1938-41—2b, New York Black Yankees, Philadelphia Stars

CAMPBELL, GRANT—1887-93—2b, of, Chicago Unions

CAMPBELL, HUNTER—1938-42—mgr, officer, Ethiopian Clowns, Cincinnati Clowns

CAMPBELL, JOE—1887-93—p, Chicago Unions

CAMPBELL, JOSEPH—1922—of, 3b, Pittsburgh Keystones

CAMPBELL, ROBERT (BUDDY)—1931-32—c, Cole's American Giants, Bacharach Giants, Pittsburgh Crawfords

CAMPBELL, WILLIAM (ZIP)—1923-29—p, Washington Potomacs, Philadelphia Giants, Hilldale, Lincoln Giants, Richmond Giants Brooklyn Royal Giants

CAMPINI, JOE—1948—c, Baltimore Elite Giants

CAMPOS, MANUEL—1905—mgr., Cuban Stars of Santiago

CAMPOS, TATICA—1915-23, 1930—p, of, 1b, 2b, 3b, New York Cuban Stars, Cuban Stars (East), Cuban Stars (NNL), All Cubans

CANADA,—1951—p, Philadelphia Stars

CANADA, JAMES (CAT)-1936-45, 51-55-1b, mgr Birmingham Black Barons, Memphis Red Sox, Baltimore Elite Giants, Jacksonville Red Caps, Atlanta Black Crackers

CANIZARES, AVELINO—1945—ss, Cleveland Buckeyes

CANNADY, JESSE (HOSS)—1942-45—3b, 2b, Chicago American Giants, Indianapolis-Cincinnati Clowns, Homestead Grays, New York Cubans

CANNADY, WALTER (REV)—1921-40—2b, ss, of, 3b, 1b, p, mgr, Columbus Buckeyes, Dayton Marcos, Cleveland Tate Stars, Homestead Grays, Harrisburg Giants, Hilldale, Lincoln Giants, Darby Daisies, Pittsburgh Crawfords, New York Black Yankees, Philadelphia Stars, Brooklyn Royal Giants

CANNON, RICHARD (SPEED BALL)—1928-34—p, St. Louis Stars, Nashville Elite Giants, Birmingham Black Barons, Louisville Red Caps, Cleveland Cubs, Louisville Blacks Caps

CANTON,—1941—p, New York Cubans

CAPER,—1912—ss, Pittsburgh Giants

CAPERS, (LEFTY)—1930-32—p, Louisville White Sox, Hilldale

CARABELLO, ESTERIO—1939—of, New York Cubans

CARD, AL [CURD]—1887—3b, Pittsburgh Keystones

CARDENAS, P.—1924-27—c, of, Cuban Stars (ECL), Cuban Stars (NNL)

CAREY, [CARRY]—1916-1921—3b, 2b, St. Louis Giants, Dayton Marcos

CARLISLE, MATTHEW (LICK)—1931-46—2b, ss, Birmingham Black Barons, Montgomery Grey Sox, Memphis Red Sox, Homestead Grays, New Orleans Crescent Stars

CARLSON,—1916—c, Chicago American Giants

CARLYLE, SYLVESTER JUNIUS—1945—inf, Kansas City Monarchs

CARMICHAEL, LUTHER—1948—sec, NSL

CARNEY, TED—1932—c, inf, Washington Pilots

CARPENTER,—1923, 1927—of, Memphis Red Sox, Nashville Elite Giants

CARPENTER, ANDREW (ANDY)—1954-55—p, Detroit Stars

CARPENTER, CLAY—1925-26—p, 3b, Baltimore Black Sox, Philadelphia Giants

CARR, ED—1890—of, Lincoln (NEB) Giants

CARR, GEORGE HENRY (TANK)—1912-1934—1b, 3b, of, c, Los Angeles White Sox, Kansas City Monarchs, Hilldale, Bacharach Giants, Philadelphia Stars, Lincoln Giants, Washington Pilots, Baltimore Black Sox

CARR, WAYNE—1920-28—p, St. Louis Giants, Indianapolis ABCs, Baltimore Black Sox, Washington Potomacs, Bacharach Giants, Wilmington Potomacs, Newark Stars, Brooklyn Royal Giants, Lincoln Giants

CARRERA, (See SUNGO CABRERA)

CARRILLO, B.—1904-06—1b, p, All Cubans

CARROLL, HAL—1887—player, Cincinnati Browns

CARROLL, (SONNY)—1950—p, Baltimore Elite Giants

CARRY, (See CAREY)

CARRUTHERS, WARREN—1955—p, Detroit Stars

CARSWELL, FRANK—1944-53—p, Cleveland Buckeyes, Indianapolis Clowns

CARTER,—1897-99—p, Cuban Giants

CARTER,—1914-18—2b, ss, Louisville White Sox, Chicago Giants

CARTER, ALFRED—1934-40—of, utl., Pittsburgh Crawfords, New York Cubans, Nashville Elite Giants, Philadelphia Stars

CARTER, ART (IKE)—1884—2b, St. Louis Black Stockings

CARTER, ARTHUR—1947—player, Philadelphhia Stars

CARTER, BILL—1948—p, Newark Eagles

CARTER, (BO)—1931—president, Chattanooga Black Lookouts

CARTER, CHARLES (KID)—1902-13—p, Philadelphia Giants, Wilmington Giants, Brooklyn Royal Giants, Quaker Giants

CARTER, CHARLES—1943—p, Baltimore Elite Giants, Homestead Grays

CARTER, CLIFFORD—1923-34—p, Baltimore Black Sox, Bacharach Giants, Harrisburg Giants, Philadelphia Tigers, Hilldale, Philadelphia Stars

CARTER, DR. A.B.—1933—vice-pres, NSL

CARTER, ELMER (WILLIE)-1930-32, 1937—c, ss, 1b, Birmingham Black Barons

CARTER, ERNEST C. (SPOON, WHIP)—1932-49—p, mgr., Pittsburgh Crawfords, Memphis Red Sox, Cleveland Red Sox, Toledo Crawfords, Indianapolis Crawfords, Newark Eagles, Philadelphia Stars, Homestead Grays, Birmingham Black Barons, Louisville Black Caps, Akron Tyrites, Cleveland Giants, Montgomery Dodgers

CARTER, FRANK—1917—p, St. Louis Giants

CARTER, JIMMY—1938-39—p, Philadelphia Stars

CARTER, KENNETH—1950—c, Cleveland Buckeyes

CARTER, MARK—1954-55—p, Detroit Stars, Louisville Black Colonels

CARTER, MARLIN THEODORE (MEL, PEE WEE)—1932-50—3b, 2b, Cincinnati Tigers, Atlanta Black Crackers, Memphis Red Sox, Chicago American Giants, Monroe Monarchs

CARTER, PAUL (NICK)—1924-36—p, Hilldale, Darby Daisies, Philadelphia Stars, New York Black Yankees, Pittsburgh Crawfords

CARTER, ROBERT—1947—p, Homestead Grays

CARTER, WILLIAM —1920-22—c, Detroit Stars, Kansas City Monarchs

CARTER, WILLIAM—1937, 1943—3b, St. Louis Stars, Harrisburg-St. Louis Stars

CARTLEDGE, MENSKE (ROBBIE, MANNY)—1951-55—p, Philadelphia Stars, Birmingham Black Barons

CARTMILL, ALFRED JR.—1949-51, 1955—2b, Kansas City Monarchs

CARTWRIGHT, CLAIBORNE (CLAY)—1953-54—utl., Memphis Red Sox, Louisville Black Colonels, Detroit Stars

CARVALLO,—1907—1b, Cuban Stars

CARY,—1927—p, Brooklyn Royal Giants

CASE,—1932—of, Cleveland Stars

CASEY, JOE—1920—p, St. Louis Giants

CASEY, WILLIAM (MICKEY)—1930-43—c, mgr., Baltimore Black Sox, Bacharach Giants, Philadelphia Stars, Washington Black Senators, New York Cubans, Baltimore Grays, New York Black Yankees, Hilldale, Pittsburgh Crawfords, Baltimore Elite Giants

CASH, WILLIAM WALKER (BILL, READY)—1943-50—c, of, 3b, Philadelphia Stars

CASON, JOHN—1917-32—c, of, 2b, ss, Brooklyn Royal Giants, Norfolk Stars, Hilldale, Lincoln Giants, Bacharach Giants, Baltimore Black Sox, Birmingham Black Barons, Havana Red Sox

CASPER,—1946—p, Homestead Grays

CASTILLE, IRWIN—1951-53—ss, 3b, Birmingham Black Barons

CASTILLO, JULIAN —1911-12—1b, All Cubans, Cuban Stars

CASTONE, WILLIAM—1889-92—p, of, Lincoln-Kearney (Nebraska State League), Lincoln (NEB) Giants, Aspen (Colorado St.Lg.)

CASTRO, ANTONIO —1929—c, Cuban Stars (East)

CATES, JOE (RABBIT)—1931-38—ss, Louisville White Sox, Louisville Red Caps, Louisville Black Colonels

CATHEY, WILLIS (JIM, BILL)—1948-52—p, Indianapolis Clowns

CATLING, CHARLES—1887—ump., LCBBP

CATO, HARRY —1887-96—2b, p, of, ss, Cuban X Giants, Cuban Giants New York Gorhams (Middle States Lg.), Philadelphia Giants, Trenton (NJ) Cuban Giants

CAULFIELD, FRED—1926—mgr., New Orleans Ads

CELADA,—1928-29—ss, Cuban Stars (NNL)

CEPEDA, PEDRO ANIBAL (PERUCHO)—1941—of, New York Cubans

CEPHUS, (GOLDIE)—1925-38—of, ss, Philadelphia Giants, Bacharach Giants, Birmingham Black Barons, Newark Dodgers

CHACON, PELAYO—1910-31—ss, mgr., Stars of Cuba, Cuban Stars, Havana Stars, Cuban Stars (ECL), Cuban Stars of Havana

CHAMBERLAIN,—1889—1b, New York Gorhams (Middle States Lg.)

CHAMBERS, ARTHUR (RUBE)—1924-27—p, Lincoln Giants, Wilmington Potomacs, Washington Potomacs

CHANDLER,—1916—p, Bowser's ABCs

CHANEY, JOHN—1952—p, Philadelphia Stars

CHAPEL,—1939—of, Toledo Crawfords

CHAPMAN,—1944—1b, Baltimore Elite Giants

CHAPMAN, EDWARD—1927, 1931—p, Detroit Stars, Chicago Columbia Giants

CHAPMAN, JOSEPH W.—1887—player, Cincinnati Browns

CHAPMAN, JOHN—1887—player, Cincinnati Browns

CHAPMAN, ROY LEE (RAY)—1949-50—p, New York Black
Yankees

CHARLESTON,—1942—c, Cincinnati Buckeyes

CHARLESTON, BENNY—1930—of, Homestead Grays

CHARLESTON, OSCAR McKINLEY (CHARLIE)—1915-54—of, 1b,
mgr., Bowser's ABCs, Indianapolis ABCs, Lincoln Stars,
Chicago American Giants, St. Louis Giants, Harrisburg
Giants, Hilldale, Homestead Grays, Pittsburgh Crawfords,
Toledo Crawfords, Indianapolis Crawfords, Philadelphia
Stars, Brooklyn Brown Dodgers, Indianapolis Clowns

CHARLESTON, PORTER—1927-35—p, Hilldale, Darby Daisies,
Philadelphia Stars

CHARLESTON, (RED)—1921-32—c, Nashville Elite Giants,
Birmingham Black Barons, Memphis Red Sox, Montgomery
Grey Sox

CHARTER, WILLIAM M.(BABY, BILL)—1933-46—of, 1b, c, 3b,
Louisville Red Caps, Chicago American Giants, Detroit
Black Sox. Louisville Black Colonels

CHASE,—1920-23—of, p, Detroit Stars, Chicago Giants, Toledo
Tigers

CHATMAN,—1922—p, Cleveland Tate Stars

CHATMAN, EDGAR—1944-46—p, Memphis Red Sox

CHAVOUS,—1895-96—p, of, Adrian (MI) Page Fence Giants

CHEATHAM,—1930-34—p, Baltimore Black Sox, Pittsburgh
Crawfords, Homestead Grays

CHERRY, HUGH—1949—officer, Houston Eagles

CHESTER,—1926—of, Harrisburg Giants

CHESTNUT, HENRY (JOE)—1950-52—p, Indianapolis Clowns,
Philadelphia Stars, Birmingham Black Barons

CHILDERS, WOLF—1936—c, Cincinnati Tigers

CHILDS, ANDY—1936-45—2b, p, Indianapolis Athletics,
Memphis Red Sox, St. Louis Stars, Indianapolis ABCs

CHILTON,—1919—of, Detroit Stars

CHIRBAN, LOUIS—1950—p, Chicago American Giants

CHISHOLM, JOE—1945—p, Philadelphia Stars

CHISM, ELIJAH (ELI, LITTLE CHIS)—1937, 1946-51—of, St. Louis
Stars, Birmingham Black Barons, Cleveland Buckeyes

CHISOLM, JOE—1953—p, Memphis Red Sox

CHRETIAN, ERNEST—1949-50—of, inf, Kansas City Monarchs,
Philadelphia Stars

CHRISTIAN,—1915-16—of, Indianapolis ABCs, Bowser's ABCs,
Lincoln Stars

CHRISTOPHER, TED—1943, 1949—c, Homestead Grays, New
York Black Yankees

CHRISTOPHER, THADIST (THAD)—1935-45—of, 1b, Newark
Eagles, Pittsburgh Crawfords, New York Black Yankees,
Cincy-Cleveland Buckeyes, Cincinnati Clowns, Cleveland
Buckeyes, Nashville Elite Giants, Washington Elite Giants,
Jacksonville Red Caps

CISCO, J. [SISCO]—1884—player, Philadelphia Mutual B.B.C.

CLARIZIO, LOUIS—1950—of, Chicago American Giants

CLARK,—1887—c, Louisville Falls City

CLARK,—1908—2b, Brooklyn Colored Giants

CLARK,—1909—of, Brooklyn Royal Giants

CLARK—1931—of, Louisville White Sox

CLARK,—1931—p, Kansas City Monarchs

CLARK,—1937—of, Kansas City Monarchs

CLARK, ALBERT—1919-26—p, Dayton Marcos, Cleveland Tate
Stars, Pittsburgh Keystones, Indianapolis ABCs, Cleveland
Browns, Memphis Red Sox

CLARK, CHIFIAN CLEVELAND—1945-50—of, New York Cubans

CLARK, DELL—1914-23—ss, Brooklyn Royal Giants, Indianapolis
ABCs, Lincoln Giants, Washington Potomacs, St. Louis
Giants

CLARK, ESTABAN—1955—1b, Kansas City Monarchs

CLARK, HARRY (LEFTY)—1922-25—p, Brooklyn Royal Giants,
Hilldale Bacharach Giants

CLARK, JOHN L.—1932-46—bus. mgr., Pittsburgh Crawfords;
public relations man, Homestead Grays; sec, NNL

CLARK, MACEO (MARTY)—1923-25—1b, p, Washington
Potomacs, Wilmington Potamacs, Indianapolis ABCs,
Bacharach Giants

CLARK, MILTON J., JR.—1937—sec, Chicago American Giants

CLARK, MORTEN (SPECS)—1910-23—ss, 3b, of, Indianapolis
ABCs, Baltimore Black Sox, West Baden (IN) Sprudels

CLARK, ROY—1934-35—p, Newark Dodgers

CLARK, WILLIAM (EGGIE, BIFF)—1928—of, Memphis Red Sox

CLARKE,—1930—of, Chicago American Giants

CLARKE, (ALLIE)—1938—1b, 2b, c, of, Washington Black
Senators

CLARKE, ROBERT (KIKE, EGGIE)-1922-48—c, mgr., Richmond
Giants, Baltimore Black Sox, New York Black Yankees,
Philadelphia Stars, Baltimore Elite Giants

CLARKE, VIBERT ERNESTO (WEBBO)—1946-53—p, Cleveland
Buckeyes, Louisville Buckeyes, Memphis Red Sox

CLARKSON, (See JOHN BRAZELTON)

CLARKSON, JAMES BUSTER (BUS, BUZZ)—1937-50—ss, of, 2b,
Pittsburgh Crawfords, Toledo Crawfords, Indianapolis
Crawfords, Newark Eagles, Philadelphia Stars, Baltimore
Elite Giants

CLAXTON, JAMES E.—1916, 1932—p, Oakland Oaks (PCL),
Cuban Stars

CLAY, ALBERT (ALTON)—1949-50—of, New York Black Yankees

CLAY, WILLIAM (LEFTY) —1932—p, Kansas City Monarchs

CLAYTON, LEROY WATKINS (ZACK)—1932-44—1b, c,
Bacharach Giants, Cole's American Giants, Chicago
American Giants, New York Black Yankees, Chicago Brown
Bombers, Brooklyn Eagles, Brooklyn Royal Giants

CLEAGE, RALPH (PETE)—1924, 1936—of, St. Louis Stars, ump.,
NNL

CLEMENTE, MIQUEL—1917—c, Havana Cubans

CLEVELAND, HOWARD (DUKE)[DUKE]—1938-46—of, Jacksonville Red Caps, Cleveland Bears, Cincinnati Buckeyes,
Cleveland Buckeyes, Indianapolis Clowns

CLIFFORD, LUTHER—1948-53—c, of, Homestead Grays, Kansas
City Monarchs, Indianapolis Clowns

CLIFTON, NAT (SWEETWATER)—1949—1b, Chicago American
Giants

CLINTON,—1917—3b, Bacharach Giants

CLOSE, HERMAN—1887—manager, Philadelphia Pythians

COBB, L.S.N.—1920-34—officer, St. Louis Giants, Birmingham
Black Barons, Memphis Red Sox, Cleveland Elites; sec, NSL

COBB, W.—1914-20, 1928—c, of, St. Louis Giants, Lincoln Giants,
Jewell's ABCs, Indianapolis ABCs, St. Louis Stars, West
Baden (IN) Sprudels

COCKERELL, PHIL (See COCKRELL)

COCKERHAM, JIMMY—1939—1b, Indianapolis ABCs

COCKRELL, PHILIP (PHIL, FISH)—1913-46—p, of, Havana Red
Sox, Lincoln Giants, Hilldale, Darby Daisies, Bacharach
Giants, Philadelphia Stars; umpire, NNL

COFFEE,—1921—p, Kansas City Monarchs

COFFEY, HOWARD—1951-54—p, Philadelphia Stars, Indianapolis Clowns

COFFEY, MARSHALL—1889—2b, Chicago Unions

COFFIE, CLIFFORD (See JOE CAFFIE)

COHEN, JAMES CLARENCE (JIM, FIREBALL)—1948-52—p,
Indianapolis Clowns

COIMBRE, FRANCISCO ATILES (PANCHO, AL)-1940-46—of, 2b,
New York Cubans

COLAS, CARLOS (CHARLIE) —1941, 1949-51—c, New York
Cubans, Memphis Red Sox

COLAS, JOSE LUIS—1947-52—of, mgr., Memphis Red Sox
COLE, (See COLEY)
COLE, CECIL EDWARD—1946—p, Newark Eagles
COLE, RALPH (PUNJAB, ASKARI)—1939-46—of, Jacksonville Red Caps, Cleveland Bears, Cincinnati Clowns, Indianapolis Clowns
COLE, ROBERT A.—1932-35—officer, Chicago American Giants; tres, NNL; vice-pres, NSL
COLE, WILLIAM—1896-99—c, p, Cuban Giants
COLEMAN,—1934—p, Philadelphia Stars
COLEMAN, BENNY—1950—p, Chicago American Giants
COLEMAN, CARL—1951—1b, Chicago American Giants
COLEMAN, CLARENCE (POPS)—1913-26-p, c, of, 1b, 2b, Chicago Giants, Chicago Union Giants, Indianapolis ABCs, Cleveland Tate Stars, St. Louis Giants, Columbus Buckeyes, Dayton Marcos, Lincoln Giants, All Nations, Bowser's ABCs
COLEMAN, ELLIOT HOYT SR.(JUNIOR)—1954-55—p, Birmingham Black Barons
COLEMAN, GILBERT—1928-33—inf, of, Brooklyn Cuban Giants, Bacharach Giants, Newark Dodgers, Newark Browns
COLEMAN, JOE—1955—p, Birmingham Black Barons
COLEMAN, JOHN—1885—of, Brooklyn Remsens
COLEMAN, JOHN (LEFTY)—1950-54—p, Baltimore Elite Giants, Birmingham Black Barons
COLEMAN, MELVIN (SLICK)—1937-40—ss, c, p, Birmingham Black Barons
COLEMAN, TOM—1951—p, Baltimore Elite Giants
COLEY,—1923-24—p, Toledo Tigers, Kansas City Monarchs, Detroit Stars
COLEY,—1931—of, Nashville Elite Giants
COLLENDER,—1904—of, Philadelphia Giants
COLLIER,—1928—c, Bacharach Giants
COLLIERS, LEONARD—1950-51—p, Cleveland Buckeyes, Birmingham Black Barons
COLLINS,—1910-18—c, 1b, New York Black Sox, Brooklyn Royal Giants, Pennsylvania Red Caps of New York, Lincoln Giants, Pittsburgh Giants, Philadelphia Giants, Pittsburgh Stars of Buffalo
COLLINS,—1925-28—p, Brooklyn Royal Giants, Baltimore Black Sox
COLLINS, EUGENE (GENE)—1947-51—p, of, Kansas City Monarchs
COLLINS, FRANK—1934—p, Brimingham Black Barons
COLLINS, FRED (NAT)—1888-89—p, New York Gorhams (Middle States Lg.), Philadelphia Giants
COLLINS, GEORGE—1921-33—of, 2b, p, ss, New Orleans Crescent Stars, Milwaukee Bears, Toledo Tigers, Indianapolis ABCs, Nashville Elite Giants, New Orleans Caulfield Ads, Kansas City Monarchs
COLLINS, (SONNY)—1934-36—p, Bacharach Giants, New York Black Yankees
COLLINS, WALTER—1947-52—p, Chicago American Giants, Memphis Red Sox, Indianapolis Clowns
COLLINS, WILLIE—1933—of, Nashville Elite Giants
COLLINS, WILLIE P. (JAMES, RIP)—1950-51—p, Birmingham Black Barons
COLTHIRST,—1948—p, Indianapolis Clowns
COLZIE, JIM—1946-47—p, Indianapolis Clowns
COMBS, A. CLARK (JACK)—1922-26—p, Detroit Stars
CONDON, LAFAYETTE—1887—player, Louisville Falls Citys
CONNELL,—1913—p, Indianapolis ABCs
CONNERS, (DOCK)—1954—ss, Kansas City Monarchs
CONNORS, JOHN W.—1904-1922—owner, officer, Brooklyn Royal Giants, Bacharach Giants
COOK, CHARLIE—1935—p, Pittsburgh Crawfords
COOK, HOWARD (JOHNNY) —1937—p, Indianapolis Athletics

COOK, WALTER—1886-88—officer, Cuban Giants
COOKE, JAMES (JAY)—1929-33—p, Baltimore Black Sox, Bacharach Giants
COOLEY, WALTER—1931—c, 3b, Birmingham Black Barons
COOPER, ALEX—1927-28—of, Philadelphia Tigers, Harrisburg Giants
COOPER, ALFRED (ARMY)—1923-32—p, Kansas City Monarchs, Cleveland Stars
COOPER, ANDY (LEFTY)—1920-41—p, mgr., Detroit Stars, Chicago American Giants, St. Louis Stars, Kansas City Monarchs
COOPER, ANTHONY (ANT)—1928-35, 1941—ss, 2b, of, Birmingham Black Barons, Cleveland Stars, Baltimore Black Sox, Cleveland Red Sox, Louisville Red Sox, Pittsburgh Crawfords, Newark Dodgers, Homestead Grays, New York Black Yankees
COOPER, C.—1884—player, Philadelphia Mutual B.B.C.
COOPER, (CHIEF)—1928—umpire, NNL
COOPER, DALTIE—1921-40—p, Nashville Elite Giants, Indianapolis ABCs, Harrisburg Giants, Lincoln Giants, Hilldale, Bacharach Giants, Homestead Grays, Baltimore Black Sox, Newark Eagles, Washington Potomacs
COOPER, E.—1914-1928—1b, of, Lincoln Stars, Cleveland Tate Stars, St. Louis Giants, Mohawk Giants, Louisville White Sox, Lincoln Giants
COOPER, GEORGE—1946—p, Boston Blues
COOPER, JAMES—1938-47—p, Atlanta Black Crackers, New York Black Yankees, Newark Eagles, Philadelphia Stars
COOPER, RAY—1928-29—p, Hilldale
COOPER, SAM—1926-34—p, Harrisburg Giants, Baltimore Black Sox, Bacharach Giants, Homestead Grays
COOPER, THOMAS (TOM)—1947-53—c, of, 1b, Kansas City Monarchs
COOPER, W.T. (BILL, THOMAS)—1937-46—c, Atlanta Black Crackers, Philadelphia Stars, New York Black Yankees
COPELAND, LAWRENCE—1935—inf, Brooklyn Eagles
CORBETT, CHARLES—1921-28—p, Pittsburgh Keystones, Indianapolis ABCs, Harrisburg Giants, Hilldale
CORCORAN, TOM—1942—p, Homestead Grays
CORDOVA, (PETE)—1917-23—3b, ss, Kansas City Monarchs, Cleveland Tate Stars, Toledo Tigers, Havana Cubans
CORNELIUS, WILLIAM McKINLEY (WILLIE, SUG)—1928-46—p, Nashville Elite Giants, Memphis Red Sox, Chicago American Giants, Cole's American Giants, Birmingham Black Barons, Cleveland Elites, Cincinnati-Cleveland Buckeyes
CORNETT, HARRY—1913—c, Indianapolis ABCs
CORREA, MARCELINE FRANCISCO (CHO-CHO, CUCO)—1926-36—ss, Cuban Stars (NNL), Cuban Stars (East), New York Cubans
CORTEZ, AURELIO—1928-31—c, Cuban Stars (NNL), Cuban Stars (East)
COS, CELEDONCO—1954—p, Indianapolis Clowns
COSA,—1932—of, Memphis Red Sox
COSTELLO,—1911—1b, All Cubans
COTTMAN, DARBY—1887-93—3b, Chicago Unions
COTTON, (See ROBERT A. WILLIAMS)
COTTON, JAMES—1945-46—officer, Chattanooga Choo Choos
COTTRELL,—1923—c, Hilldale
COWAN, EDDIE—1919—ss, Cleveland Tate Stars
COWAN, JOHNNIE—1933-50—3b, 2b, Birmingham Black Barons, Cleveland Buckeyes, Memphis Red Sox, Cincinnati Buckeyes, Cuban Stars
COWANS, RUSS—1942—sec, Negro Baseball League of America
COX, COMER LANE (HANNIBAL, RUSS)—1930-31-of, Nashville Elite Giants, Cleveland Cubs

COX, M.D. ALPHONSE—1938-43—p, Memphis Red Sox, Jacksonville Red Caps, Cleveland Bears

COX, ROOSEVELT—1936-44—3b, 2b, ss, c, Detroit Stars, Kansas City Monarchs, New York Cubans, Memphis Red Sox

COX, TOM (LEFTY)—1928-32—p, Lincoln Giants, Cleveland Cubs, Cleveland Tigers

COZART, HAYWOOD (HARRY, BIG TRAIN, JEFF)—1939-44—p, Newark Eagles

CRAIG, CHARLES—1926-28—p, Lincoln Giants, Brooklyn Cuban Giants, Harrisburg Giants, Homestead Grays

CRAIG, DICK—1940—1b, Indianapolis Crawfords

CRAIG, HOMER—1934-35—p, Newark Dodgers

CRAIG, JOHN—1932-46—umpire, EWL, NNL

CRAIG, JOSEPH P. (JOE)—1940, 1946—1b, of, Indianapolis Crawfords, Philadelphia Stars

CRAIN, A.C.—1887—player, Baltimore Lord Baltimores

CRAWFORD,—1936—ss, Newark Eagles

CRAWFORD, JOHN—1943—umpire, NNL

CRAWFORD, SAM—1910-38—p, mgr., coach, New York Black Sox, Chicago Giants, Chicago American Giants, Chicago Union Giants, Detroit Stars, Kansas City Monarchs, Brooklyn Royal Giants, Birmingham Black Barons, Chicago Columbia Giants, Cole's American Giants, Indianapolis Athletics, St. Louis Stars, Cleveland Tate Stars

CRAWFORD, WILLIE WALKER—1934—of, Birmingham Black Barons

CRAWLEY,—1931—3b, Bacharach Giants

CREACY, A.D. (DEWEY)—1924-40—3b, Kansas City Monarchs, St. Louis Stars, Detroit Wolves, Washington Pilots, Columbus Blue Birds, Cleveland Giants, Philadelphia Stars, Brooklyn Royal Giants

CREEK, WILLIE—1924, 1930-32—c, ss, Washington Potomacs, Brooklyn Royal Giants, Bacharach Giants

CRELIN, WILBUR C.—1926—officer, Newark Stars

CRESPO, ALEJANDRO ROGELIO—1918-33—2b, 3b, Cuban Stars (East), Cuban Stars of Havana

CRESPO, ALEJANDRO (ALEX, HOME RUN)—1940-46—of, New York Cubans

CROCKETT, FRANK —1916-23—of, Bacharach Giants, Brooklyn Royal Giants, Norfolk Stars

CROMARTIE, LEROY (RAY)—1945—2b, Cincinnati-Indianapolis Clowns

CROSBY, RALPH—1954—inf, Birmingham Black Barons

CROSS, BENNIE—1887—of, Boston Resolutes

CROSS, NORMAN—1932-36—p, Cole's American Giants

CROSSAN, FRANK—1954—p, Memphis Red Sox

CROSSEN, GEORGE—1921—c, Lincoln Giants

CROWDER,—1920—p, Lincoln Stars

CROWE, GEORGE DANIEL—1947-49-1b, inf, New York Cubans, New York Black Yankees

CROXTON,—1908-09—p, c, Cuban Giants

CRUDUP, ZEKE—1924-28—p, Philadelphia Giants

CRUE, MARTIN (MATTY)—1942-51—p, New York Cubans, Homestead Grays, New Orleans Eagles

CRUMBIE, RALPH—1946—c, Pittsburgh Crawfords

CRUMBLEY, ALEX—1937-38—of, New York Black Yankees, Atlanta Black Crackers, Pittsburgh Crawfords, Washington Black Senators

CRUMP., JAMES—1920-38—2b, Norfolk Giants, Hilldale, Philadelphia Giants, Norfolk Stars; umpire, NNL

CRUMP., WILLIS—1916-23—of, 2b, Bacharach Giants

CRUTCHFIELD, JOHN WILLIAM (JIMMIE)—1930-45—of, Birmingham Black Barons, Indianapolis ABCs, Pittsburgh Crawfords, Newark Eagles, Toledo Crawfords, Indianapolis Crawfords, Chicago American Giants, Cleveland Buckeyes

CRUZ,—1930—p, Cuban Stars (East)

CUELLA, JOSE LUIS—1945—of, Pittsburgh Crawfords

CUERIRA, BASILO—1921-22—p, of, All Cubans, Cuban Stars (NNL)

CULVER, [CULCRA]—1916-22—3b, ss, of, Pittsburgh Stars of Buffalo Penn Red Caps of NY, Cuban Stars (NNL), Lincoln Stars

CUMMING, HUGH S.—1887—mgr., Baltimore Lord Baltimores

CUMMINGS,—1932—c, Louisville Black Caps

CUMMINGS, NAPOLEON (CHANCE)—1916-29—1b, 2b, Bacharach Giants, Hilldale, Norfolk Stars, Madison Stars

CUNNINGHAM,—1917-21—ss, St. Louis Giants, Dayton Marcos, Columbus Buckeyes

CUNNINGHAM,—1926-27—2b, Pennsylvania Red Caps of NY

CUNNINGHAM, EARL—1955—2b, of, Detroit Stars

CUNNINGHAM, H.(ROUNDER)—1916-31—ss, Montgomery Grey Sox

CUNNINGHAM, HARRY (BABY)—1930-37—p, Memphis Red Sox, Birmingham Black Barons

CUNNINGHAM, L.—1933—34-of, Baltimore Black Sox, Washington Pilots, Cuban Stars (East)

CUNNINGHAM, LARRY—1950-51—of, Memphis Red Sox, Houston Eagles, New Orleans Eagles

CUNNINGHAM, MARION (DADDY)—1916-26—1b, mgr., Memphis Red Sox, Montgomery Grey Sox

CUNNINGHAM, ROBERT (SLIM)—1950—p, Cleveland Buckeyes

CURLEY, EARL C.—1925—of, Memphis Red Sox

CURRIE, REUBEN (RUBE, BLACK SNAKE)—1919-32—p, Chicago Unions, Kansas City Monarchs, Hilldale, Chicago American Giants, Detroit Stars, Cleveland Red Sox, Baltimore Black Sox

CURRY, HOMER (GOOSE)—1928-55—of, p, mgr., Memphis Red Sox, Washington Elite Giants, New York Black Yankees, Newark Eagles, Baltimore Elite Giants, Philadelphia Stars, Nashville Elite Giants, Cleveland Tigers, Indianapolis Athletics, Monroe Monarchs, Louisville Black Colonels, Birmingham Black Barons

CURRY, OSCAR J.—1887—p, Cuban Giants

CURRY, W.—1954—c, Louisville Black Colonels

CURTIS, (See CURTISS RICKS)

CURTIS,—1923-25—p, Harrisburg Giants

CURTIS,—1932—c, Louisville Black Caps

CURTIS, HARRY—1898—mgr., Celeron Acme Colored Giants (Iron and Oil League)

CYRUS, HERB (See Herb Souell)

D

DABNEY, MILTON—1885-96—of, p, Argyle Hotel, Cuban X Giants, Cuban Giants

DAILEY, JAMES—1948—p, Baltimore Elite Giants

DALLARD, WILLIAM (EGGIE)—1920-33—1b, of, c, 2b, Wilmington Potomacs, Baltimore Black Sox, Bacharach Giants, Hilldale, Quaker Giants, Darby Daisies, Philadelphia Stars, Washington Potomacs, Madison Stars, Philadelphia Giants, Lincoln Giants

DALLAS, PORTER (BIG BOY)—1929-32—3b, Birmingham Black Barons, Monroe Monarchs

DALTON, ROSSIE—1940—utility, Chicago American Giants, Birmingham Black Barons

DANAGE,—1921—2b, St.Louis Giants

DANCER, CARL—1954—of, Detroit Stars

DANDRIDGE, JOHN—1949—p, Houston Eagles

DANDRIDGE, (PING, DANDY)—1917-20—inf, p, Havana Red Sox, Lincoln Giants, St.Louis Giants

DANDRIDGE, RAYMOND EMMETT (HOOKS, SQUATTY)—1933-49—3b, 2b, ss, Detroit Stars, Nashville Elite Giants, Newark Dodgers, Newark Eagles, New York Cubans

DANDRIDGE, TROY RASMUSSEN (DAN)—1926-29—3b, ss, Chicago Giants, Dayton Marcos

DANIELS,—1935—p, Newark Dodgers

DANIELS, ALONZO—1954—inf, Birmingham Black Barons

DANIELS, EDDIE—1946-47—p, New York Cubans

DANIELS, FRED—1919-28—p, St. Louis Giants, Hilldale, Birmingham Black Barons, Lincoln Giants, Nashville Elite Giants

DANIELS, HAMMOND—1924-26—officer, Bacharach Giants

DANIELS, JAMES GEORGE (JIM, SCHOOLBOY)—1943—p, Birmingham Black Barons

DANIELS, JOHN—1955—p, Detroit Stars

DANIELS, LEON (PEPPER)—1921-35—c, 1b, Detroit Stars, Harrisburg Giants, Cuban Stars, Brooklyn Eagles, Bacharach Giants, Chicago Columbia Giants

DARBY, EDDY—1904—of, Philadelphia Giants

DARCY,—1941—of, Philadelphia Stars

DARDEN, CLARENCE—1938—3b, Atlanta Black Crackers

DARDEN, FLOYD—1950—2b, of, Baltimore Elite Giants

DARNELL, HERMAN—1951—1b, Indianapolis Clowns

DAVENPORT, LLOYD (BEAR MAN, DUCKY)—1934-51—of, mgr., Monroe Monarchs, Philadelphia Stars, Cincinnati Tigers, Memphis Red Sox, Birmingham Black Barons, Chicago American Giants, Cleveland Buckeyes, Pittsburgh Crawfords, Louisville Buckeyes, Jacksonville Red Caps, New Orleans Crescent Stars Cincinnati-Cleveland Buckeyes

DAVIDSON, CHARLES (SPECKS, SLIM)—1939-40, 1946-49—p, New York Black Yankees, Brooklyn Royal Giants, Baltimore Elite Giants, Memphis Red Sox

DAVIDSON, S.—1934—3b, Cleveland Red Sox

DAVIS,—1934—of, Kansas City Monarchs

DAVIS,—1938—p, Chicago American Giants

DAVIS, A.—1943-46—ss, 3b, Newark Eagles, Homestead Grays, New York Black Yankees

DAVIS, A.C.—1928—ss, Cleveland Tigers

DAVIS, A.G.—1887—ump., LCBBP

DAVIS, A.L.—1924-25—ss, of, Indianapolis ABCs

DAVIS, ALBERT (GUNBOAT)—1927-37—p, Detroit Stars, Baltimore Black Sox

DAVIS, AMBROSE—1886-91—of, mgr., Boston Resolutes, New York Gorhams

DAVIS, (BIG BOY)—1932—p, Indianapolis ABCs, Cuban Stars (West), Cleveland Stars

DAVIS, CHARLEY—1953-55—p, Memphis Red Sox

DAVIS, (DAGO)—1908, 1916—p, Leland Giants, Chicago American Giants

DAVIS, DWIGHT—1930-31—p, Detroit Stars, Pittsburgh Crawfords

DAVIS, EARL (HAWK)—1927-38—2b, Indianapolis ABCs, Bacharach Giants, Newark Browns, Hilldale, Philadelphia Giants

DAVIS, EDWARD A. (EDDIE, PEANUTS, NYASSES)—1939-50—p, Cincinnati Clowns, Cincinnati-Indianapolis Clowns, Indianapolis Clowns

DAVIS, (GOLDIE, RED)—1924-25—p, of, Indianapolis ABCs

DAVIS, HY—1934—1b, of, Hilldale, Newark Dodgers

DAVIS, JACK—1922-25—3b, Bacharach Giants, Philadelphia Giants

DAVIS, JAMES—1920-21—p, Chicago Giants, Lincoln Giants, Kansas City Monarchs

DAVIS, JOHN—1903-10—p, Leland Giants, Cuban Giants, Philadelphia Giants, Chicago Union Giants, Cuban Stars, Algona (IA) Brownies

DAVIS, JOHN HOWARD (CHEROKEE)—1940-50—of, p, Newark Eagles, Houston Eagles

DAVIS, LEE—1945—p, Kansas City Monarchs

DAVIS, LONNIE—1952—1b, Chicago American Giants

DAVIS, LORENZO (PIPER)—1942-50—1b, 2b, ss, mgr., Birmingham Black Barons

DAVIS, MARTIN LUTHER—1945—p, Chicago American Giants

DAVIS, NATHANIEL—1947-50—1b, New York Black Yankees, Philadelphia Stars

DAVIS, (QUACK)—1913-14—of, Indianapolis ABCs, Louisville White Sox

DAVIS, ROBERT LOMAX (BUTCH)—1947-50—of, Baltimore Elite Giants

DAVIS, ROOSEVELT (ROSEY, DURO)—1924-45—p, St. Lous Stars, Columbus Blue Birds, Pittsburgh Crawfords, New York Black Yankees, Philadelphia Stars, Memphis Red Sox, Brooklyn Royal Giants, Baltimore Elite Giants, Chicago Brown Bombers, Cincinnati Clowns, Cincinnati-Indianapolis Clowns, Cleveland Buckeyes, Indianapolis ABCs, Newark Eagles, Kansas City Monarchs, Newark Dodgers

DAVIS, ROSS (SATCHEL, SCHOOLBOY)—1940, 1942-47—p, Cleveland Buckeyes, Boston Blues (USL), Birmingham Black Barons, Baltimore Elite Giants, New York Black Yankees

DAVIS, SAUL HENRY JR.(RAREBACK)-1921-31—3b, 2b, ss, Birmingham Black Barons, Cleveland Tigers, Memphis Red Sox, Chicago American Giants, Detroit Stars, Columbus Buckeyes

DAVIS, SPENCER (BABE)—1935-48—ss, of, 3b, mgr., Atlanta Black Crackers, Indianapolis ABCs, New York Black Yankees, Winston-Salem Giants, Brooklyn Eagles

DAVIS, WALTER (STEEL ARM)—1923-35—of, 1b, p, Detroit Stars, Chicago American Giants, Chicago Columbia Giants, Cole's American Giants, Nashville Elite Giants, Brooklyn Eagles

DAVIS, WILLIAM—1937-40—3b, of, St. Louis Stars, Indianapolis ABCs, Memphis Red Sox, Atlanta Black Crackers

DAVIS, WILLIAM N.(BILL)—1945-47—p, Philadelphia Stars

DAVIS, WILLIE—1945—officer, Mobile Black Shippers

DAWSON,—1908—p, New York Colored Giants

DAWSON, JOHNNY—1938-42—c, Memphis Red Sox, Kansas City Monarchs Chicago American Giants, Birmingham Black Barons

DAWSON, LEROY—1946—mgr., Philadelphia Stars

DAY,—1902—of, Philadelphia Giants

DAY, EDDIE—1898—ss, Celeron Acme Colored Giants (Iron and Oil League)

DAY, GUY—1885—c, Argyle Hotel

DAY, LEON—1934-50—p, Brooklyn Eagles, Newark Eagles, Baltimore Elite Giants

DAY, WILSON C. (CONNIE)—1920-32, 1939—2b, 3b, ss, Mgr, Indianapolis ABCs, Baltimore Black Sox, Harrisburg Giants, Bacharach Giants, Hilldale

DEAN,—1940—of, Philadelphia Stars

DEAN, BOB—1937-40—p, St. Louis Stars, New Orleans-St.Louis Stars

DEAN, CHARLIE—1943, 1947—p, New York Black Yankees

DEAN, JIMMY—1948-50—p, Philadelphia Stars

DEAN, NELSON—1925-32—p, Kansas City Monarchs, Cleveland Hornets, Cleveland Tigers, Detroit Stars, Cleveland Stars, Memphis Red Sox, Birmingham Black Barons

DEAN, ROBERT —1925-33—3b, 2b, Lincoln Giants, Pennsylvania Red Caps of New York DEANE, ALPHEUS—1947—p, New York Black Yankees

DEAS, JAMES ALVIN (YANK)[YANK]—1916-28—c, Bacharach Giants, Pennsylvania Giants, Lincoln Giants, Hilldale, Richmond Giants, Philadelphia Giants

DEBERRY, C.I.(CHARLIE)—1948—mgr., Greensboro Red Wings; vice-pres, Negro American Association

DEBRAN, ROY—1940—of, New York Black Yankees

DECKER, CHARLES (DUSTY)—1932-38—inf, mgr., Indianapolis ABCs, Montgomery Grey Sox, Detroit Stars, Memphis Red Sox, Louisville Black Colonels

DECUIR, LIONEL—1939-40—c, Kansas City Monarchs

DEDEAUX, RUSS—1941, 1946—p, Newark Eagles, New York Black Yankees

DEES,—1954—1b, Louisville Black Colonels

DEJERNETT,—1939—p, Indianapolis ABCs

DELANEY,—1910-11-inf, Brooklyn Royal Giants, Pittsburgh Giants

DELGADO, FELIX RAFAEL (FELLE) —1936-41—of, 1b, New York Cubans

DeLUGO,—1935—p, New York Cubans

DeMEZA,—1905—p, All Cubans

DeMOSS, ELWOOD (BINGO)—1905-44—2b, ss, p, mgr., Topeka Giants, Kansas City (Kan) Giants, Oklahoma Giants, Indianapolis ABCs, Chicago American Giants, Detroit Stars, Cleveland Giants, Chicago Brown Bombers, Bowser's ABCs, St. Louis Giants, West Baden (IN) Sprudels

DENNARD, DICK—1945—of, Toledo Cubs (USL)

DENNIS, WESLEY L. (DOC)—1943-55—1b, of, Baltimore Elite Giants, Philadelphia Stars, Birmingham Black Barons

DENT, CARL J.—1950-52—ss, Indianapolis Clowns, Philadelphia Stars

DERRICK, L.B.—1925-26—officer, Detroit Stars

DESPERT, HARRY (DENNY)—1914-16—of, Lincoln Giants, Brooklyn Royal Giants, Philadelphia Giants

DEVEAN,—1908—c, New York Colored Giants

DEVEREAUX,—1902—1b, Philadelphia Giants

DEVERS,—1950—p, Houston Eagles

DEVOE,—1902-18—c, Philadelphia Giants, Chicago Giants

DEVOE, J.R.—1922—bus. mgr., Cleveland Tate Stars

DEVON,—1933—of, Philadelphia Stars

DEWBERRY, WILLIAM—1904—c, Chicago Union Giants

DEWITT, FRED—1922-30—1b, inf, c, Kansas City Monarchs, Hilldale

DeWITT, S.R.(EDDIE)—1917-30—3b, Dayton Giants, Dayton Marcos, Indianapolis ABCs, Columbus Buckeyes, Toledo Tigers, Cleveland Tigers, Memphis Red Sox

DIAGO, MIXIMO—1952—c, Kansas City Monarchs

DIAL, KERMIT—1932-40—2b, p, Columbus Blue Birds, Cole's American Giants, Detroit Stars, Cincinnati Buckeyes

DIALS, OLAND CECIL (LOU)—1925-36—1b, of, Detroit Stars Chicago American Giants, Memphis Red Sox, Hilldale, Cleveland Giants Homestead Grays, Akron Tyrites, Birmingham Black Barons, New York Black Yankees

DIAMOND, (LEFTY), (See ROBERT PIPKIN)

DIAZ, FERNANDO, (See FERNANDO DIAZ PEDROSO)

DIAZ, HELIODORO (EDOLFO, YOYO)—1926-39—p, 1b, of, Cuban Stars (NNL), New York Cubans, Cuban Stars (East)

DIAZ, PABLO MESA—1930-35—c, 1b, Cuban Stars (NNL), Cuban Stars (East), New York Cubans, Cuban Stars (West)

DIAZ, PEDRO (MANNY)—1943—p, New York Cubans

DIBUT, PEDRO y VILLAFANA—1923—p, Cuban Stars (NNL)

DICKERSON, JOHN FOUNT (BABE) —1950—p, Homestead Grays, Chicago American Giants

DICKERSON, LOU—1921—p, Hilldale

DICKEY, BILL—1953—p, Kansas City Monarchs

DICKEY, JOHN (STEEL ARM)—1921-22—p, Montgomery Grey Sox, St. Louis Stars, St. Louis Giants

DICKINS,—1945—p, Cincinnati Clowns

DIECKERT,—1943—3b, New York Cubans

DIGGS, LEON—1953—of, Indianapolis Clowns

DIHIGO, MARTIN (EL MAESTRO)—1923-1945—2b, p, of, ss, 3b, 1b, c, mgr., Cuban Stars (East), New York Cubans, Homestead Grays, Hilldale, Darby Daisies, Baltimore Black Sox

DILLARD,—1927, 1932—p, Lincoln Giants, Bacharach Giants

DILLARD,—1937—player, St.Louis Stars

DILWORTH, ARTHUR—1916-18—p, of, c, Bacharach Giants, Hilldale, Lincoln Giants

DIMES,—1926, 1933—of, Dayton Marcos, Akron Tyrites

DIREAUX, JIMMY [DIREUX]—1937-39—p, Washington Elite Giants, Baltimore Elite Giants

DISMUKES, WILLIAM (DIZZY)—1910-52—p, mgr., NNL sec, club sec, Philadelphia Giants, Brooklyn Royal Giants, Mohawk Giants, Indianapolis ABCs, Chicago American Giants, Dayton Marcos, Pittsburgh Keystones, Memphis Red Sox, St. Louis Stars, Cincinnati Dismukes, Detroit Wolves, Homestead Grays, Columbus Blue Birds, Birmingham Black Barons, Kansas City Monarchs, West Baden (IN) Sprudels, Lincoln Giants, St. Louis Giants

DIXON,—1914-16—p, Chicago American Giants, Chicago Giants

DIXON, EDDIE LEE (ED)—1938-39—p, Atlanta Black Crackers, Indianapolis ABCs, Baltimore Elite Giants

DIXON, FRANK—1950—p, Birmingham Black Barons

DIXON, GEORGE (TUBBY)—1917-31—c, Chicago American Giants, Indianapolis ABCs, Birmingham Black Barons, Cleveland Hornets, Cleveland Tigers, Cleveland Cubs

DIXON, GLENN—1937—of, p, St. Louis Stars

DIXON, HERBERT ALBERT (RAP)—1922-37—of, mgr., Harrisburg Giants, Baltimore Black Sox, Chicago American Giants, Hilldale Darby Daisies, Pittsburgh Crawfords, Philadelphia Stars, Brooklyn Eagles, Homestead Grays, New York Cubans, Washington Potomacs

Saul Davis.
Saul Davis

DIXON, JOHN ROBERT(JOHNNY BOB)—1926-34—p, ss, Cleveland Tigers, Detroit Stars, Cuban Stars (West), Cleveland Giants, Cleveland Red Sox, Indianapolis ABCs, Chicago American Giants

DIXON, JOHN—1950—p, Chicago American Giants, Birmingham Black Barons

DIXON, PAUL PERRY (DICK)—1931-38—of, Bacharachs Giants, Baltimore Black Sox, Washington Pilots, New York Cubans, Philadelphia Stars, Newark Browns

DIXON, TOM—1932-40—c, p, Baltimore Black Sox, Bacharach Giants, Hilldale, Washington Pilots, Baltimore Elite Giants

DOBBINS, ED, 1952—2b, Chicago American Giants

DOBBINS, NAT —1921—ss, Hilldale

DOBY, LAWRENCE EUGENE (LARRY) [LARRY WALKER]—1942-47—2b, Newark Eagles

DODSON,—1919—of, Detroit Stars

DOMINGUEZ,—1925—p, Cuban Stars (NNL)

DONALDSON, JOHN WESLEY—1916-34—p, of, All Nations, Los Angeles White Sox, Chicago Giants, Indianapolis ABCs, Kansas City Monarchs, Detroit Stars, Brooklyn Royal Giants, Donaldson All-Stars, Lincoln Giants

DONALDSON, W.W. (BILLY)—1923-37—umpire, NNL

DONNELL, HERMAN (LEE)—1952—of, Indianapolis Clowns

DONOSO, LINO LUIS y GALATA—1947-49—p, New York Cubans

DOOLEY,—1933—of, Kansas City Monarchs

DOOLEY,—1951—p, Kansas City Monarchs

DORSEY, F.T.—1884-85—of, Baltimore Lord Baltimore

DOUGHERTY, CHARLES (PAT)—1909-15—p, Leland Giants, Chicago American Giants, Chicago Giants

DOUGHERTY, LEON—1935—p, Brooklyn Eagles

DOUGLAS, EDDIE—1922—of, St. Louis Stars

DOUGLAS, GEORGE—1885, 1891—of, p, Brooklyn Remsens, Ansonia Cuban Giants (Connecticut St.Lg.)

DOUGLAS, JESSE WARREN—1937-51—inf, of, Kansas City Monarchs, Birmingham Black Barons, Chicago American Giants, Memphis Red Sox, New York Black Yankees, New Orleans Eagles

DOUGLASS, EDWARD (EDDIE)—1918-29—1b, mgr., Brooklyn Royal Giants, Lincoln Giants

DOUSE, JOSEPH SOLOMON (JOE)—1952-53—p, of, Kansas City Monarchs

DOW,—1911—p, Philadelphia Giants

DOWNER, FRED—1921-22—of, Pittsburgh Keystones, Baltimore Black Sox

DOWNS, ELLSWORTH—1887—player, Cincinnati Browns

DOWNS, McKINLEY (BUNNY)—1915-43, 1955—2b, ss, 3b, mgr., St. Louis Giants, Bacharach Giants, Hilldale, Brooklyn Royal Giants, Brooklyn Cuban Giants, Philadelphia Tigers, Cincinnati Clowns, Indianapolis ABCs, West Baden (IN) Sprudels, Louisville Sox, Harrisburg Giants, Richmond Giants, Indianapolis Clowns

DRAKE, ANDREW—1930-32—c, p, Birmingham Black Barons, Chattanooga Black Lookouts, Cole's American Giants, Nashville Elite Giants, Louisville Black Caps

DRAKE, REYNALDO VERDES—1945-54—of, Cincinnati-Indianapolis Clowns, Indianapolis Clowns

DRAKE, WILLIAM P.(PLUNK)—1914-30—p, Brown's Tennessee Rats, St. Louis Giants, St. Louis Stars, Kansas City Monarchs, Indianapolis ABCs, Detroit Stars

DREKE, VALENTIN [DRAKE]—1919-28—of, Cuban Stars of Havana, Cuban Stars (NNL), Cincinnati Cubans

DREW, JOHN M.—1931-32—officer, Darby Daisies, Hilldale

DREW, P. —1939—of, p, Indianapolis ABCs

DRUMMER,—1948—p, Newark Eagles

DUA,—1943—player, Philadelphia Stars

DUANY, CLARO—1944-47—of, New York Cubans

DUBISSON, D.J.—1932—officer; Little Rock Grays

Leon Day.
Moorland-Spingarn Library

DUCEY,—1924-26—inf, of, St. Louis Giants, Dayton Marcos

DUCKETT, MAHLON NEWTON (JOHN, MAL, DUCK)—1940-50—3b, 2b, ss, Philadelphia Stars, Homestead Grays

DUCY, EDDIE—1947—2b, Homestead Grays

DUDLEY, C.A.—1920-23—of, St. Louis Giants, St. Louis Stars

DUDLEY, EDWARD—1925-28-p, Lincoln Giants, Brooklyn Royal Giants, Philadelphia Tigers

DUFF, ERNEST—1925-32—of, Indianapolis ABCs, Cleveland Elites, Cleveland Hornets, Cleveland Tigers, Cuban Stars

DUFFEY,—1936—3b, Newark Eagles

DUFFY, BILL—1947—c, Kansas City Monarchs

DUKES, TOMMY (DIXIE)—1928-45—c, 3b, Chicago American Giants, Memphis Red Sox, Nashville Elite Giants, Columbus Elite Giants, Homestead Grays, Toledo Crawfords, Indianapolis Crawfords, Birmingham Black Barons, Cuban Stars (West)

DULA, LOUIS—1933-39—p, Cincinnati Tigers, Homestead Grays

DUMAS, JIM—1940-41—p, Memphis Red Sox

DUMPSON, BILL—1950-52—p, Indianapolis Clowns, Philadelphia Stars

DUNBAR, ASHBY—1909-20—of, Brooklyn Royal Giants, Lincoln Stars, Indianapolis ABCs, Pennsylvania Red Caps of New York, Lincoln Giants, Louisville Sox, Mohawk Giants, Chicago American Giants, Louisville White Sox

DUNBAR, FRANK—1908—of, Philadelphia Giants

DUNBAR, (VET)—1937—inf, c, Memphis Red Sox, Indianapolis Athletics

DUNCAN, CHARLIE (SCOTTIE)—1938-40—p, Atlanta Black Crackers, Indianapolis ABCs, St. Louis Stars

DUNCAN, FRANK (PETE)—1909-28—of, mgr., Philadelphia Giants, Leland Giants, Chicago American Giants, Detroit Stars, Chicago Giants, Toledo Tigers, Cleveland Elites, Cleveland Hornets, Cleveland Tigers, Milwaukee Bears

DUNCAN, FRANK JR.—1920-48—c, of, mgr., Chicago Giants, Kansas City Monarchs, New York Black Yankees, Pittsburgh Crawfords, Homestead Grays, New York Cubans, Chicago American Giants

DUNCAN, FRANK, III—1941, 1945-49—p, Kansas City Monarchs, Baltimore Elite Giants

DUNCAN, JOE—1927—c, Bacharachs Giants

DUNCAN, JOSEPH—1954—1b, p, Indianapolis Clowns

DUNCAN, MELVIN L.—1949-55—p, Kansas City Monarchs, Detroit Stars

DUNCAN, WARREN—1922-1927—c, of, Bacharach Giants

DUNES, MEL—1955—of, Detroit Stars

DUNKIN, ISHKOODA (STRINGBEAN)—1936-37—p, Pittsburgh Crawfords

DUNLAP, HERMAN—1936-39—of, Chicago American Giants

DUNN,—1954—ss, Detroit Stars, Louisville Black Colonels

DUNN, ALPHONSE (BLUE)—1937-43—1b, of, Detroit Stars, New York Cubans, Birmingham Black Barons

DUNN, JOSEPH P. JR. (JAKE)—1930-41—ss, of, 2b, mgr., Detroit Stars, Washington Pilots, Nashville Elite Giants, Baltimore Black Sox, Philadelphia Stars

DUNN, WILLIE—1942—p, Jacksonville Red Caps

Elwood "Bingo" DeMoss.
Dick Clark

DUNSON,—1934—3b, Cincinnati Tigers

DUPREE,—1913—of, Indianapolis ABCs

DURANT,—1932—of, Washington Pilots, Baltimore Black Sox, Hilldale

DURHAM, WINN (VANN)—1952—of, Chicago American Giants

DURVANT,—1923—p, Cuban Stars (NNL)

DUVAL,—1939—player, Philadelphia Stars

DWIGHT, EDWARD JOSEPH (EDDIE, PEE WEE)—1924-37—of, Indianapolis ABCs, Kansas City Monarchs, Gilkerson's Union Giants

DYKES,—1942—player, Jacksonville Red Caps

DYKES, A.—1929—2b, Birmingham Black Barons

DYKES, JOHN—1932—officer, Washington Pilots

DYLL, FRANK R.—1950—ss, Chicago American Giants

DYSOIN, MAJOR—1950—ss, New York Black Yankees

E

EACY,—1937—p, Pittsburgh Crawfords

EARLE, CHARLES BABCOCK (FRANK, PELES)-1906-19-of, p, mgr., Wilmington Giants, Cuban Giants, Philadelphia Giants, Brooklyn Royal Giants, Lincoln Giants, Bacharach Giants, Pennsylvania Red Caps of NY

EARLE, JAMES—1954—inf, Detroit Stars

EASLEY,—1936—of, Memphis Red Sox

EASTE,—1923—p, Hilldale

EASTER, LUSCIOUS (LUKE)—1946-48—of, 1b, Cincinnati Crescents, Homestead Grays

EASTERLING, HOWARD—1936-49—3b, ss, 2b, Cincinnati Tigers, Chicago American Giants, Homestead Grays, New York Cubans

EATMON, [EATON]—1937-38—p, Birmingham Black Barons

ECHEVARRIA, RAFAEL—1938—2b, New York Cubans

ECHOLS, MELVIN JIM (SUNNY)—1943—p, of, Atlanta Black Crackers

ECHOLS, JOE—1939—of, Newark Eagles

ECKELSON, JUAN [EKELSON]—1925—p, Cuban Stars (NNL)

ECORA,—1926—p, Brooklyn Royal Giants

EDSALL, GEORGE—1898—of, Celeron Acme Colored Giants (Iron and Oil League)

EDWARDS, CHANCELLOR (JACK, PEP)—1928—c, Cleveland Tigers

EDWARDS, FRANK NUTINOUS (TEANNIE)—1936-37—2b, c, ss, St. Louis Stars, Cincinnati Tigers

EDWARDS, GEORGE—1946, 1951—ss, Boston Blues, Baltimore Elite Giants

EDWARDS, JAMES (SMOKEY)—1913-22—p, of, c, Mohawk Giants, Lincoln Stars, Pennsylvania Red Caps of New York, Philadelphia Giants, Louisville White Sox Bacharach Giants, Lincoln Giants

EDWARDS, JESSE (JOHNNY)—1923-31—2b, of, p, Nashville Elite Giants, Birmingham Black Barons, Memphis Red Sox, Detroit Stars

EDWARDS, OSEE—1950—cf, New York Black Yankees

EDWARDS, WILLIAM—1944—p, Kansas City Monarchs

EGGLESTON, MACAJAH MARCHAND (MACK, EGG)-1917-34—c, of, 3b, Dayton Giants, Dayton Marcos, Detroit Stars, Indianapolis ABCs, Washington Potomacs, Columbus Buckeyes, Wilmington Potomacs, Harrisburg Giants, Baltimore Black Sox, Bacharach Giants, New York Black Yankees, Washington Pilots, Homestead Grays, Nashville Elite Giants, Lincoln Giants

EGGLESTON, WILLIAM—1885—ss, Argyle Hotel

EKELSON, (See ECKELSON)

ELAM, JAMES (ED)[ELAN]—1932, 1943—p, inf, Bacharach Giants, Newark Eagles

ELLERBE, LACEY—1950—utl., Baltimore Elite Giants

Larry Doby.
Moorland-Spingarn Library

ELLIOTT, JOE—1954-55—p, Detroit Stars, Memphhis Red Sox, Louisville Black Colonels

ELLIS, ALBERT—1950—p, Cleveland Buckeyes

ELLIS, JAMES —1921-1925—1b, 3b, Memphis Red Sox, Dayton Marcos, Nashville Elite Giants, Cleveland Browns

ELLIS, (ROCKY, RUBE)[ROCKY]—1925-42—p, of, Hilldale, Philadelphia Stars, Homestead Grays, Jacksonville Red Caps, Baltimore Grays, Bacharach Giants, Birmingham Black Barons

ELSE, HARRY (SPEEDY)—1931-40—c, Monroe Monarchs, Kansas City Monarchs, Chicago American Giants, New Orleans Crescent Stars

EMBRY, WILLIAM R. (CAP)—1923—umpire, NNL

EMERY, JACK—1906-22—p, of, Brooklyn Colored Giants, Philadelphia Giants, Smart Set, Pittsburgh Colored Stars, Pittsburgh Stars of Buffalo, Brooklyn Royal Giants

EMERY SIMS V.—1887-89—c, 1b, New York Gorhams (Middle States Lg.), Philadelphia Pythians

EMMETT,—1924—p, Indianapolis ABCs

ENGLISH,—1890—utl., Lincoln (NEB) Giants

ENGLISH, H.D.—1932—officer, Monroe Monarchs

ENGLISH, LOUIS —1929-34—c, of, Louisville White Sox, Louisville Black Caps, Louisville Red Caps, Nashville Elite Giants, Detroit Stars, Memphis Red Sox

ENSLEY, FRANK—1952-54—of, Kansas City Monarchs, Indianapolis Clowns

ERVIN, WILLIE—1948—p, New York Black Yankees

ERYE, JOHN (See JOHN FRYE)

ESPENOSIA,—1947—p, Indianapolis Clowns

ESTENZA,—1927-28—p, of, 3b, c, Cuban Stars (NNL)

ESTRADA, OSCAR—1924-25, 1931—p, of, Cuban Stars (ECL), Cuban Stars (West)

ETCHEGOYEN, CARLOS —1930-32—of, 3b, Cuban Stars (East & West)

EVANS,—1916-18—2b, Baltimore Black Sox

EVANS,—1927—c, Kansas City Monarchs

EVANS, CHARLES ALEXANDER—1921-27—p, Bacharach Giants, Penn Red Caps of NY, Baltimore Black Sox

EVANS, CLARENCE—1949—p, Homestead Grays

EVANS, CLAUDE—1937—of, Pittsburgh Crawfords

EVANS, FELIX (CHIN)—1934-49—p, of, Atlanta Black Crackers, Indianapolis ABCs, Memphis Red Sox, Birmingham Black Barons Baltimore Elite Giants, Newark Eagles

EVANS, FRANK—1908, 1915-20—of, 3b, Kansas City (KAN) Giants, All Nations, Kansas City Monarchs

EVANS, FRANK—1950-55—of, Cleveland Buckeyes, Birmingham Black Barons, Philadelphia Stars

EVANS, GEORGE—1887—player, New York Gorhams

EVANS, JOHN—1887-88—player, New York Gorhams

EVANS, JOHNNY—1954—2b, Indianapolis Clowns

EVANS, ROBERT (BOB)—1933-43—p, Newark Dodgers, Newark Eagles, Jacksonville Red Caps, New York Black Yankees, Philadelphia Stars, Homestead Grays

EVANS, TOM—1939—p, Philadelphia Stars

EVANS, ULYSSES (COWBOY)—1933, 1943—p, Louisville Red Caps, Cincinnati Clowns, Chicago Brown Bombers

EVANS, WILLIAM—1903—c, of, Philadelphia Giants

EVANS, WILLIAM DEMONT II (BILL, HAPPY, GREY GHOST)— 1924-36—of, ss, 3b, p, Chicago American Giants, Brooklyn Royal Giants, Dayton Marcos, Cleveland Hornets, St. Louis Stars, Indianapolis ABCs, Homestead Grays, Washington Pilots, Detroit Wolves, Cincinnati Tigers, Memphis Red Sox

EVANS, W. P.—1920-25—of, p, Baltimore Black Sox, Chicago American Giants, Lincoln Stars

EVERETT, CLARENCE—1927—ss, Kansas City Monarchs, Detroit Stars

EVERETT, CURTIS—1950-51—c, of, Kansas City Monarchs

EVERETT, DEAN—1929—p, Lincoln Giants

EVERETT, JAMES W.—1931-43—p, of, Pennsylvania Red Caps of New York, Cincinnati Clowns, Newark Browns, Memphis Red Sox, Newark Eagles

EWELL, RUSSELL—1951—inf, New Orleans Eagles

EWELL, WILMER—1925-34—c, Indianapolis ABCs, Cincinnati Tigers

EWING, WILLIAM MONROE (BUCK) —1920-30—c, Chicago American Giants, Columbus Buckeyes, Indianapolis ABCs, Homestead Grays, Lincoln Giants, Cleveland Tate Stars

EYERS, HENRY, (See HENRY BYERS)

F

FABELO, JULIAN—1916-23—inf, of, Cuban Stars (East), Havana Stars, New York Cuban Stars, Cuban Stars (West)

FABRE, ISIDRO—1918-39—p, of, Cuban Stars (ECL), Cuban Stars (NNL), New York Cubans, All Cubans, Cuban Stars (East)

FABORS, THOMAS—1942—p, Baltimore Elite Giants

FACE,—1924—3b, Harrisburg Giants

FAGAN, GERVIS—1942-43—inf, Memphis Red Sox, Jacksonville Red Caps, Philadelphia Stars

FAGAN, R.W. (BOB)—1920-23—2b, Kansas City Monarchs, St. Louis Stars

FALLINGS, JOHN—1947—p, New York Black Yankees

FANELL,—1950—p, Baltimore Elite Giants

FARMER, GREENE JR.—1942-47—of, Cincinnati Clowns, New York Cubans, New York Black Yankees, Jacksonville Red Caps

FARRELL,—1902—1b, c, Philadelphia Giants

FARRELL, JACK—1934—owner, Baltimore Black Sox

FARRELL, LUTHER (RED, FATS)—1919-34—p, of, Bacharach Giants, Lincoln Giants, New York Black Yankees, Chicago Giants, Chicago American Giants, Hilldale, St. Louis Giants, Gilkerson's Union Giants, Indianapolis ABCs

FAULK,—1942—c, Boston Royal Giants

FAVORS, THOMAS (MONK)—1947—1b, of, Kansas City Monarchs

FELDER, JAMES—1948—ss, Indianapolis Clowns

FELDER, KENDALL (BUCK)—1944-46—3b, Memphis Red Sox, Chicago American Giants, Birmingham Black Barons

FELDER, WILLIAM (BENNY)—1946, 1951—3b, ss, Newark Eagles, Philadelphia Stars

FELIX,—1932—p, Montgomery Grey Sox

FELIX, JAMES—1952—p, Chicago American Giants

FELLOWS,—1937—p, c, Birmingham Black Barons

FENNAR, ALBERTUS AVANT (AL, CLEFFIE)—1932-34—ss, Brooklyn Royal Giants, Cuban Stars (East), Bacharach Giants, New York Black Yankees

FERN,—1920—p, Kansas City Monarchs

FERNANDEZ, BERNARD—1938-39, 1946-49—p, Atlanta Black Crackers, Jacksonville Red Caps, New York Cubans, New York Black Yankees, Pittsburgh Crawfords

FERNANDEZ, EMANUEL—1941—of, p, New York Cubans

FERNANDEZ, JOSE MARIA SR—1916-50—c, 1b, mgr., Havana Stars, Cuban Stars (East), New York Cubans, Chicago American Giants, New York Cuban Stars (West), Cuban Stars (ECL), Cuban Stars of Havana

FERNANDEZ, JOSE M. JR. (PEPE)—1948-50—c, New York Cubans

FERNANDEZ, RENALDO—1950—of, New York Cubans

FERNANDEZ, RODOLFO—1916-23—p, New York Cuban Stars, Cuban Stars (NNL), Cincinnati Cubans

FERNANDEZ, RODOLFO (RUDY, VEN PORDIOS)—1932-46—p, New York Cubans, Cuban Stars (East & West), New York Black Yankees

FERNANDEZ, T.—1941—p, New York Cubans

FERRELL, HOWARD LEROY JR.(TOOTS)—1948-50—p, Baltimore Elite Giants, Newark Eagles

FERRELL, W.E.—1918—1b, Pennsylvania Giants

FERRELL, WILLIE (TRUEHART, RED)—1937-43—p, Homestead Grays, Chicago American Giants, Cincinnati Clowns, Birmingham Black Barons, Jacksonville Red Caps, Cleveland Bears

FERRER, EFIGENIO (COCO, AL)—1946-51—2b, ss, Indianapolis Clowns, Chicago American Giants

FERRER, PEDRO —1922-25—2b, Cuban Stars (ECL)

FIALL, GEORGE—1918-29—ss, 3b, Lincoln Giants, Harrisburg Giants, Baltimore Black Sox, Birmingham Black Barons, Penn Red Caps of NY

FIALL, TOM—1917-25, 1931—of, c, 3b, Cuban Giants, Brooklyn Royal Giants, Lincoln Giants, Hilldale, Pennsylvania Red Caps of New York

FIELDS,—1918-26—p, Chicago American Giants, Cleveland Browns, St. Louis Giants, Dayton Marcos, Cleveland Elites

FIELDS, BENNY—1930-36—2b, of, Memphis Red Sox, Cleveland Cubs, Birmingham Black Barons, Cleveland Stars

FIELDS, CLIFFORD PETER—1950—of, Chicago American Giants

FIELDS, TOM—1946—p, Homestead Grays

FIELDS, WILMER LEON SR.(RED, BILL, CHINKY)—1939-50—p, 3b, of, Homestead Grays

FIFER,—1921—p, Indianapolis ABCs

FIGAROLA, JOSE RAFAEL—1904-15—c, 1b, Stars of Cuba, Cuban Stars, All Cubans

FIGUEROA, ENRIQUE (TITE)—1946—p, Baltimore Elite Giants

FIGUEROA, JOSE ANTONIO (TITO) —1940, 1946—p, Baltimore Elite Giants, New York Cubans

FILLMORE, JOE—1941-52—p, Philadelphia Stars

FINE, CHARLIE (See CHARLES HARMON)

FINCH,—1933—player, Nashville Elite Giants

FINCH, RAYFORD—1949-50—p, Cleveland Buckeyes, Louisville Buckeyes

FINCH, ROBERT [FITCH]—1926—p, Lincoln Giants

FINDELL, THOMAS [PINDELL]—1887—player, Washington Capital City

FINLEY,—1938—player, Washington Black Senators

FINLEY, THOMAS (TOM)—1922-34—3b, c, Bacharach Giants, Lincoln Giants, Brooklyn Royal Giants, Pennsylvania Red Caps of New York, Darby Daisies, New York Black Yankees, Baltimore Black Sox, Philadelphia Stars, Wilmington Potomacs, Washington Potomacs

FINNER, JOHN—1919-25—p, St. Louis Giants, St. Louis Stars, Milwaukee Bears, Birmingham Black Barons

FINNEY, ED—1948-50—3b, Baltimore Elite Giants

FISHER,—1909-10—p, Philadelphia Giants

FISHER,—1932—p, Columbus Turfs

FISHER, A.—1884—player, Philadelphia Mutual B.B.C.

FISHER, F.—1884—player, Philadelphia Mutual B.B.C.

FISHER, GEORGE—1922-23—of, Richmond Giants, Harrisburg Giants

FISHER, W.—1884—player, Philadelphia Mutual B.B.C.

FISHUE, PETE (THE WONDER)—1886—c, New York Gorhams

FLAMMER,—1921—of, Hilldale

FLEET, JOSEPH—1930—p, Chicago American Giants

FLEMING, BUDDY (SEE FLEMING REEDY)

FLEMMING, FRANK—1946—p, Cleveland Buckeyes

FLOOD, JESS—1919—c, Cleveland Tate Stars

FLORES, CONRAD—1954—p, Kansas City Monarchs

FLOURNEY,—1950—p, Cleveland Buckeyes

FLOURNOY, FRED—1928-33—c, Brooklyn Cuban Giants, Penn Red Caps of NY

FLOURNOY, WILLIS (PUD)—1919-34—p, Hilldale, Brooklyn Royal Giants, Baltimore Black Sox, Bacharach Giants, Penn Red Caps of NY

FLOWERS, JOHNNY (JAKE)—1941-43—inf, New York Black Yankees

FLOYD,—1913-16—of, Indianapolis ABCs, Bowser's ABCs

FLOYD,—1935-37—p, Brooklyn Eagles, Indianapolis Athletics

FLOYD, EARLE—1954-55—of, 1b, Detroit Stars

FLOYD, IRV—1954—p, of, Detroit Stars

FLOYD, J.J.—1932—officer, Little Rock Greys

FOOTE,—1929—c, Detroit Stars

FOOTES, ROBERT—1895-1909—c, Chicago Unions, Philadelphia Giants, Brooklyn Royal Giants, Chicago Union Giants

FORBES,—1886-88—of, 3b, Cuban Giants, Philadelphia Pythians

FORBES, FRANK—1929-43—umpire; bus mgr., New York Cubans; NNL promoter

FORBES, JOE—1911-27—ss, 3b, of, Lincoln Giants, Pennsylvania Red Caps of New York, Bacharach Giants, Brooklyn Royal Giants, Lincoln Stars, Philadelphia Giants

FORCE, WILLIAM—1920-30—p, Detroit Stars, Baltimore Black Sox, Brooklyn Royal Giants

FORD, (BUBBER)—1947—officer, Jacksonville Eagles

FORD, C. —1918—p, Pennsylvania Giants

FORD, CARL—1947—officer, Shreveport Tigers

FORD, ERWIN—1951-54—2b, Indianapolis Clowns

FORD, FRANK —1915-18—c, Pennsylvania Giants, Hilldale

FORD, JAMES (JIMMY)—1931-46—3b, 2b, Memphis Red Sox, St. Louis Stars, New Orleans-St. Louis Stars, New York Black Yankees, Cincinnati Clowns, Philadelphia Stars, Baltimore Elite Giants, Harrisburg-St.Louis Stars, Washington Black Senators Nashville Elite Giants

FORD, ROY —1916-25—2b, p, Baltimore Black Sox, Harrisburg Giants

FOREMAN,—1921—ss, Hilldale

FOREMAN, F. SYLVESTER (HOOKS)—1920-33—c, p, Kansas City Monarchs, Indianapolis ABCs, Washington Pilots, Milwaukee Bears. Homestead Grays, Cleveland Browns

FOREMAN, ZACK—1921—p, Kansas City Monarchs

FOREST, CHARLES—1920—player, St. Louis Giants

FORGE, WILLIE—1954-55—c, Louisville Black Colonels, Kansas City Monarchs

FORKINS, MARTY—1931—officer, New York Black Yankees

FORMENTHAL, PEDRO—1947-50—of, Memphis Red Sox

FORREST,—1917-28—of, c, Havana Red Sox, Lincoln Giants, Philadelphia Giants

FORREST, JOE—1949—p, New York Black Yankees

FORREST, PERCY (PETE)—1938-49—p, Chicago American Giants, Newark Eagles, New York Black Yankees, Indianapolis Clowns

FOSTER, ALBERT (RED)—1910—1b, Kansas City, Kan., Giants

FOSTER, ANDREW (RUBE)—1902-26—p, mgr., Chicago Union Giants, Cuban X Giants, Philadelphia Giants, Leland Giants, Chicago American Giants, Louisville White Sox; founder and pres, tres, NNL

FOSTER, FRANK—1947—player, Philadelphia Stars

FOSTER, JIM—1945—officer, Chicago Brown Bombers

FOSTER, LELAND—1932-36—p, Monroe Monarchs

FOSTER, LEONARD—1938—inf., Atlanta Black Crackers

FOSTER, WILLIE HENDRICK (BILL)—1923-37—p, mgr., Memphis Red Sox, Chicago American Giants, Homestead Grays, Kansas City Monarchs, Cole's American Giants, Birmingham Black Barons, Pittsburgh Crawfords

FOULKE,—1912—rf, Cuban Giants

FOWLER, J.W. (BUD)—(real name John Jackson)—1872-1899—2b, p, of, 3b, c, ss, mgr., New Castle, Pa.; Stillwater (Northwestern League); Keokuk and Topeka (Western League); Binghamton (International League); Crawfordsville, Terre Haute, and Galesburg (Central Interstate league); Lafayette, Indiana; Greenville (Michigan League); Sterling and Davenport (ILlinois-Iowa League); Evansville, New York Gorhams, All-American Black Tourists, Page Fence Giants Adrian (Michigan St. Lg.), Lansing (Michigan St. Lg.) Lynn (Int. Ass.), Lincoln-Kearney (Neb. St. Lg.), Galesburg (lll-Iowa Lg.), Burlington (Ill-Iowa Lg.), Pueblo (Colorado Lg.) Worcester (New England Assn.), Santa Fe (New Mexico Lg.), Montpelier (Vermont Lg.)

FOWLKES, ERWIN—1947-48—ss, Chicago American Giants, Homestead Grays

FOWLKES, SAMUEL—1950—p, Kansas City Monarchs, Cleveland Buckeyes

FOX,—1923—of, Toledo Tigers

FOX, ORANGE—1887—rf, Chicago Unions

FRANCIS, DEL—1911, 1917-20—2b, Indianapolis ABCs

FRANCIS, WILLIAM (BILLY, BRODIE)—1904-25—3b, ss, Wilmington Giants, Cuban Giants, Philadelphia Giants, Lincoln Giants, Chicago American Giants, Hilldale, Bacharach Giants, Cleveland Browns, Chicago Giants, Mohawk Giants

FRANKLIN,—1908—ss, Brooklyn Colored Giants

FRANKLIN, WILLIAM B.—1887—manager, Louisville Falls City

FRAZIER, ALBERT EDWIN (COOL PAPA)—1932-40—2b, 3b, Montgomery Grey Sox, Jacksonville Red Caps, Cleveland Bears

FRAZIER, J.—1932—ss, Atlanta Black Crackers

FRAZIER, ORAN—1932—inf, Montgomery Grey Sox

FRAZIER, SEVERN (SAM)—1932—utl., Montgomery Grey Sox

FREEMAN, BILL—1925, 1933—p, Indianapolis ABCs, Cuban Stars

FREEMAN, CHARLIE—1916-17, 1927-30—player, officer, Hilldale

FREEMAN, WILLIAM—1888-89—3b, Chicago Unions

FREIHOFER, WILLIAM—1906—pres, International League of Independent Professional Base Ball Clubs

FRIELY,—1922—2b, Bacharach Giants

FRITZ,—1904—of, Philadelphia Giants

FRYE, JOHN H.(JACK)—1883-96—1b, c, p, of, Cuban Giants, Reading, PA (Interstate Lg.), Lewiston, (Penn. St. Lg.) York Cuban Giants (Eastern Interstate Lg.), Trenton Cuban Giants (Middle States Lg.), Ansonia Cuban Giants (Connecticut St. Lg.), New York Gorhams, York Colored Monarchs

FULCUR, ROBERT—1940—p, Chicago American Giants, Birmingham Black Barons

FULLER, JIMMY—1912-22—c, Cuban Giants, Bacharach Giants, Philadelphia Giants, Lincoln Stars

FULLER, W.W. (CHICK)—1908-19—ss, 2b, Bacharach Giants, Cuban Giants, Pennsylvania Giants, Cleveland Tate Stars, Hilldale Brooklyn Colored Giants, New York Colored Giants, Pennsylvania Red Caps of NY

FULLMAN,—1916—of, Baltimore Black Sox

FULTON, SAM—1955—p, Birmingham Black Barons

FUMES,—1925-30—of, Cuban Stars (NNL), Cuban Stars (East)

G

GACKLES,—1926—player, Newark Stars

GADSDEN, GUS—1932—of, Hilldale

GAICHEY,—1948—p, Memphis Red Sox

GAIDERIA,—1918—p, Cuban Stars

GAINES, JONAS GEORGE (LEFTY)—1937-51—p, Newark Eagles, Baltimore Elite Giants, Philadelphia Stars, Washington Elite Giants, Chicago American Giants

GAINES, WILLY—1950-55—p, Philadelphia Stars, Indianapolis Clowns

GAINEZ,—1928—p, Cuban Stars (NNL)

GALATA, DOMINGO—1949-50—p, New York Cubans

GALATA, RAUL—1949-53—p, Indianapolis Clowns

GALBAE,—1928—p, Cuban Stars (NNL)

GALES,—1931—1b, Detroit Stars

GALEY,—1897—1b, of, Cuban Giants

GALITON,—1954—p, Detroit Stars

GALLOWAY,—1931—2b, Bacharach Giants

GALLOWAY, BILL (HIPPO)—1899-06—of, 2b, Cuban X Giants, Cuban Giants, Woodstock (Canadian Lg.), Famous Cuban Giants

GALVEZ, CUNEO—1928-32—p, Cuban Stars (NNL), Cuban Stars (East), Cuban House of David

GAMBLE,—1921—p, Columbus Buckeyes

GANGGANG,—1916—p, of, Baltimore Black Sox

GANS, ROBERT EDWARD (JUDE, JUDY)—1910-38—of, p, mgr., Cuban Giants, Smart Set, Lincoln Giants, Chicago American Giants, Chicago Giants, Lincoln Giants, Mohawk Giants, Cleveland Tigers; umpire, East-West League, NNL

GANT,—1887—3b, Pittsburgh Keystones

GANTZ, (See DOMINGO GOMEZ)

GARAY, MARTINIANO ARGUELLES (JOSE)[ARGUELLES]—1948-50-of, p, New York Cubans

GARCIA, ANTONIO MARIA—1904-12—c, 1b, Cuban Stars, All Cubans, Cuban X Giants

GARCIA, ATIRES (ANGEL)—1945-53—p, Cincinnati-Indianapolis Clowns, Indianapolis Clowns

GARCIA, JOHN—1904—c, Cuban Giants

GARCIA, JUAN—1952—inf, Indianapolis Clowns

GARCIA, MANUEL (COCAINA)—1926-36—p, of, Cuban Stars (NNL), New York Cubans

Wilmer Fields, Bob Thurman, and Garnet Blair.
Robert H. McNeil

GARCIA, REGINO—1905—c, All Cubans

GARCIA, ROMANDO (CHANO)—1926-27—2b, Bacharach Giants, Lincoln Giants

GARCIA, S.—1904-05—of, All Cubans

GARCIA, SILVIO—1940-47—inf, New York Cubans

GARDNER,—1920-23, 1926—of, Toledo Tigers, St. Louis Stars, Dayton Marcos, Baltimore Black Sox

GARDNER, FLOYD (JELLY)—1919-1933—of, 1b, Detroit Stars, Chicago American Giants, Lincoln Giants, Homestead Grays

GARDNER, GLOVER C. (GUS)—1921-23—c, of, New Orleans Caufield Ads, Chicago American Giants

GARDNER, JAMES (CHAPPY)—1908-17—2b, 3b, Brooklyn Royal Giants, Havana Red Sox, Cuban Giants, Brooklyn Colored Giants

GARDNER, KENNETH (PING, STEEL ARM)-1918-32—p, Washington Red Caps, Brooklyn Royal Giants, Hilldale, Philadelphia Royal Stars, Lincoln Giants, Harrisburg Giants, Bacharach Giants, Cleveland Tigers, Baltimore Black Sox, Newark Browns

GAREY,—1925—c, Cuban Stars (NNL)

GARMER,—1886—3b, New York Gorhams

GARNER, HORACE CHARLES—1949—of, Indianapolis Clowns

GARREN,—1905—c, All Cubans

GARRETT,—1926, 1936—of, Bacharach Giants, Harrisburg Giants

GARRETT, AL H.—1887, 1899-1910—player, mgr, officer, Cincinnati Browns, Columbia Giants, Chicago Leland Giants

GARRETT, FRANK—1887—player, Louisville Falls Citys

GARRETT, SOLOMAN—1950—2b, New York Black Yankees

GARRETT, WILLIAM—1943—officer, New York Black Yankees

GARRIDO, GIL—1944-46—inf, New York Cubans

GARRISON,—1934—1b, Bacharach Giants

GARRISON, ROBERT—1909—p, St. Paul Gophers

GARRISON, ROSS—1889-97—ss, 3b, York Cuban Giants (Eastern Interstate Lg.), New York Gorhams (Middle States Lg.), Cuban Giants

GARVIN, LEEDELL—1942—p, Philadelphia Stars

GARY, CHARLES—1948-50—3b, Homestead Grays

GASTON,—1921, 1926—ss, Hilldale, Harrisburg Giants

GASTON, HIRAM—1952-53—p, Birmingham Black Barons

GASTON, ISAAC—1949—utl., Kansas City Monarchs

GASTON, ROBERT (RAB ROY)—1932-49—c, Homestead Grays, Brooklyn Brown Dodgers

GATEWOOD, BILL—1905-28—p, mgr., Cuban X Giants, Philadelphia Giants, Brooklyn Royal Giants, Leland Giants, Chicago Giants, Chicago American Giants, St. Louis Giants, Detroit Stars, St. Louis Stars, Toledo Tigers, Albany, Ga. Giants, Birmingham Black Barons, Memphis Red Sox, Milwaukee Bears, Lincoln Giants, Indianapolis ABCs

GATEWOOD, ERNEST—1914-27—c, 1b, Lincoln Giants, Brookyn Royal Giants, Bacharach Giants, Harrisburg Giants, Lincoln Stars, Mohawk Giants

GAUTIER, JOHN—1955—p, Kansas City Monarchs

GAVIN,—1935—p, Brooklyn Eagles

GAY, HERBERT—1929-30—p, of, Chicago American Giants, Birmingham Black Barons, Baltimore Black Sox

GAY, W.—1929—p, Chicago American Giants

GEE, RICHARD (RICH)—1922-29—c, of, Lincoln Giants, New Orleans Crescent Stars

GEE, SAMMY—1955—ss, Detroit Stars

GEE, TOM—1925-26—c, Lincoln Giants, Newark Stars

GEORGE, JOHN—1921-25—ss, New Orleans Crescent Stars, Chicago Giants, Harrisburg Giants, Chicago American Giants, Bacharach Giants, New Orleans Caulfield Ads

GERALD, ALPHONSO [GERRARD]—1945-49—of, inf, New York Black Yankees, Chicago American Giants, Indianapolis Clowns

GETTY,—1936—c, Bacharach Giants

GHOLSTON, BERT E.—1923-43—umpire, NNL, East-West League

GIBBONS,—1923—3b, Harrisburg Giants

GIBBONS, JOHN—1941—p, Philadelphia Stars

GIBBONS, WALTER LEE—1948-49—p, Indianapolis Clowns

GIBSON, A. JERRY—1935-43—of, p, Cincinnati Tigers, Cincinnati Clowns, Cincinnati Buckeyes

GIBSON, B.—1927—p, Cleveland Hornets

GIBSON, JOSHUA, SR (JOSH)—1928-46—c, of, Homestead Grays, Pittsburgh Crawfords

GIBSON, JOSHUA, JR.(JOSH)—1949-50—inf, Homestead Grays

GIBSON, PAUL—1934-35—p, Homestead Grays, Newark Dodgers

GIBSON, RALPH (RUFUS)—1951-55—2b, ss, Birmingham Black Barons, Louisville Black Colonels, Memphis Red Sox

GIBSON, TED—1940-42—inf, c, Columbus Buckeyes, Chicago American Giants, Cincinnati Buckeyes, Birmingham Black Barons

GIBSON, WELDA H.—1949-50—p, Houston Eagles

GILBERT,—1940—1b, New York Cubans

GILCREST, DENNIS—1931-35—c, 2b, Indianapolis ABCs, Columbus Blue Birds, Cleveland Red Sox, Brooklyn Eagles, Homestead Grays

GILENDER,—1923—p, Bacharach Giants

GILERS,—1928—of, Birmingham Black Barons

GILES, CORNELIUS—1954—p, Indianapolis Clowns

GILES, GEORGE FRANKLIN SR.—1927-38—1b, Kansas City Monarchs, St.Louis Stars, Brooklyn Eagles, New York Black

Bill Foster.
Luis Munoz Collection

Yankees, Philadelphia Stars, Detroit Wolves, Homestead
    Grays, Pittsburgh Crawfords, Baltimore Black Sox
GILKERSON, ROBERT—1911—1b, Chicago Union Giants
GILL, WILLIAM—1931-37—1b, 3b, of, Detroit Stars, Louisville
    Red Caps, Indianapolis Athletics, Homestead Grays
GILLARD, ALBERT (HAMP)—1909-14—p, St. Louis Giants,
    Chicago American Giants, West Baden (IN) Sprudels,
    Birmingham Giants
GILLARD, LUTHER (PEN,)[GILYARD]-1934-42—of, 1b, Memphis
    Red Sox, Chicago American Giants, Indianapolis
    Crawfords, Birmingham Black Barons, St. Louis Stars,
    Kansas City Monarchs
GILLESPIE, A.—1931—p, Cleveland Cubs
GILLESPIE, H.—1887—p, Louisville Falls Citys
GILLESPIE, HENRY—1917-34—p, of, Pennsylvania Giants,
    Hilldale, Lincoln Giants, Bacharach Giants, Philadelphia
    Tigers, Quaker Giants, New York Black Yankees, Baltimore
    Black Sox Harrisburg Giants, Madison Stars
GILLESPIE, MURRAY (LEFTY)—1930-32—p, Memphis Red Sox,
    Nashville Elite Giants, Monroe Monarchs
GILLIAM, JAMES (JUNIOR, JIM)—1945-51—2b, Nashville Black
    Vols, Baltimore Elite Giants
GILLIS, LOUIS (SEABOY)—1951—c, Birmingham Black Barons
GILMORE, JAMES (SPEED)—1953-55-p, Kansas City Monarchs
GILMORE, QUINCY JORDAN—1922-37—bus mgr., Kansas City
    Monarchs; sec, tres, NNL; pres, Texas-Oklahoma-Louisiana
    League
GILMORE, (SPEED)—1926-28—p, Lincoln Giants
GILYARD, LUTHER (See LUTHER GILLARD)

GIPSON, ALVIN (BUBBER, SKEET)—1941-50—p, Chicago
    American Giants, Birmingham Black Barons, Houston
    Eagles
GISENTANER, WILLIE (LEFTY)—1921-39—p, of, Columbus
    Buckeyes, Washington Potomacs, Kansas City Monarchs,
    Harrisburg Giants, Newark Stars, Lincoln Giants, Cuban
    Stars (East), Louisville White Sox, Pittsburgh Crawfords,
    Nashville Elite Giants, Louisville Red Caps, Homestead
    Grays, Louisville Black Caps, Chicago American Giants,
    Philadelphia Giants, Brooklyn Royal Giants
GIVENS,—1927—ss, Cleveland Hornets
GIVENS, OSCAR—1946-48—ss, Newark Eagles
GLADNEY,—1932—ss, Indianapolis ABCs
GLADSTONE, GRANVILLE—1950—of, Indianapolis Clowns
GLASS, CARL LEE (BUTCH, LEFTY)—1921-36—p, mgr., Memphis
    Red Sox, Cincinnati Tigers, St. Louis Stars, Birmingham
    Black Barons, Chicago American Giants, Kansas City
    Monarchs, Louisville White Sox, St.Louis Giants
GLENN, HUBERT (COUNTRY)—1943-49—p, New York Black
    Yankees, Brooklyn Brown Dodgers, Indianapolis Clowns,
    Philadelphia Stars
GLENN, OSCAR (HAP)—1937-38—3b, Atlanta Black Crackers
GLENN, STANLEY RUDOLF (DOC)—1943-50—c, Philadelphia
    Stars
GLOVER, THOMAS MOSS (LEFTY)—1934-45—p, Birmingham
    Black Barons, Cleveland Red Sox, New Orleans Black
    Pelicans, Washington Elite Giants, Memphis Red Sox,
    Baltimore Elite Giants, Columbus Elite Giants
GODINEZ, MANUEL—1946-49—p, Cincinnati-Indianapolis
    Clowns, Indianapolis Clowns
GOINES, CHARLES—1915-16—c, of, Indianapolis ABCs, Bowser's
    ABCs
GOINS,—1932—p, Montgomery Grey Sox
GOLDEN, CLYDE—1948-52—p, Newark Eagles, Houston Eagles,
    Cleveland Buckeyes, New Orleans Eagles, Chicago
    American Giants
GOLDER,—1932—2b, Cuban Stars (West)
GOLDIE,—1919, 1926-28—1b, Indianapolis ABCs, Cleveland
    Tigers, Cleveland Elites, Cleveland Hornets
GOLIATH, FRED—1920—of, Chicago Giants
GOMEZ, DAVID—1925-28, 1932—p, Cuban Stars (NNL), Cuban
    Stars (East)
GOMEZ, DOMINGO (HARRY)—1926-29—c, Harrisburg Giants,
    Philadelphia Tigers, Baltimore Black Sox
GOMEZ, JOE—(SIJO)—1929-33—c, p, Cuban Stars (East),
    Bacharach Giants
GONZALES,—1916-19—3b, Long Branch NJ Cubans, Cuban Stars
    of Havana
GONZALES, A.—1910-12—p, Cuban Stars
GONZALEZ, GERVASIO (STRIKE)—1910-17—1b, c, Cuban Stars,
    Long Branch Cubans
GONZALEZ, HIRAM RENE—1950—of, New York Cubans
GONZALEZ, LUIS (CHICHO)—1910—p, Cuban Stars
GONZALEZ, MIGUEL ANGEL CORDERO (MIKE)—1911-14—c, 1b,
    Cuban Stars
GOOD,—1890—of, York Cuban Giants (Eastern Interstate Lg.)
GOOD,—1916—c, of, Lincoln Stars
GOOD, CLEVELAND—1937—p, Newark Eagles
GOODEN, ERNEST (PUD)—1922-23—2b, 3b, Pittsburgh
    Keystones, Toledo Tigers, Chicago American Giants,
    Cleveland Tate Stars, Detroit Stars
GOODGAME, JOHN—1917—p, Chicago Giants
GOODMAN,—1928—of, Harrisburg Giants
GOODRICH, JOE—1923-26—2b, ss, 3b, Washington Potomacs,
    Philadelphia Giants, Wilmington Potomacs, Harrisburg
    Giants
GOODSON, M.E.—1931-32—officer, New York Black Yankees

GORDON, CHARLES WILLIAM (CHARLIE, FLASH)—1939-41—of, New York Black Yankees, Philadelphia Stars

GORDON, HAROLD (BEEBOP)—1950-54—p, Chicago American Giants, Detroit Stars

GORDON, HERMAN—1920-24—p, of, 2b, Toledo Tigers, Birmingham Black Barons, Kansas City Monarchs, St. Louis Stars, Cleveland Browns

GORDON, SAM—1905-15—ss, 3b, of, 2b, Genuine Cuban Giants, Cuban Giants, Chicago Union Giants, Indianapolis ABCs, New York Stars, Brooklyn All-Stars, Lincoln Giants

GORHAM,—1911—rf, Philadelphia Giants

GOSHAY, SAMUEL—1949—of, Kansas City Monarchs

GOSHEN,—1931—of, Cuban Stars (East)

GOTTLIEB, EDDIE—1936-50—officer, Philadelphia Stars; sec, NNL; promoter and booking agent, Owner

GOULD, JOHN (WILLIE, HAL)—1947-48—p, Philadelphia Stars

GOVANTES, MANUEL—1909-10—2b, of, Cuban Stars, Stars of Cuba

GOVENS,—1909—of, Quaker Giants

GOVERN, S.K. (SIKI)—1887-88, 1896—mgr., Philadelphia Pythians, Cuban Giants

GRACE, ARTHUR—1889—p, 1b, Champaign (Ill.-Ind. Lg.)

GRACE, ELLSWORTH—1950—2b, New York Black Yankees

GRACE, WILLIE—1942-50—of, Cincinnati-Cleveland Buckeyes, Cleveland Buckeyes, Louisville Buckeyes, Houston Eagles

GRADY,—1924—p, Washington Potomacs

GRAHAM, DENNIS—1918-31—of, Washington Red Caps, Bacharach Giants St. Louis Stars, Homestead Grays, Pittsburgh Crawfords

GRAHAM, VASCO—1895-99—c, of, Lansing, Michigan, Colored Capital All-Americans, Adrian (MI) Page Fence Giants, Adrian (Michigan St. Lg.), Dubuque (IA), Cuban Giants

GRANSBERRY, BILL—1929—of, 1b, Chicago American Giants, Chicago Giants

GRANT, ART—1920-22—c, Baltimore Black Sox, Richmond Giants

GRANT, CHARLES—1896-1916—2b, Adrian (MI) Page Fence Giants, Columbia Giants, Cuban X Giants, Philadelphia Giants, New York Black Sox, Lincoln Giants, Quaker Giants, Cincinnati Stars

GRANT, FRANK—1886-1905—2b, ss, Meriden (Eastern League); Buffalo (International League); Cuban Giants, Harrisburg (Eastern Interstate League); Lansing, Michigan, Colored Capital All-Americans, New York Gorhams (Middle States Lg.), Ansonia Cuban Giants (Connecticut St.Lg.), Trenton Cuban Giants (Middle States Lg.), Philadelphia Giants, Genuine Cuban Giants Cuban X Giants

GRANT, LEROY—1911-25—1b, Chicago American Giants, Lincoln Giants, Indianapolis ABCs, Cleveland Browns, Mohawk Giants

GRANT, PHIL—1927—player, Kansas City Monarchs

GRAVES, BOB—1932-37—p, of, Indianapolis ABCs, Indianapolis Athletics

GRAVES, LAWRENCE (CANNON BALL)—1923—p, Harrisburg Giants

GRAVES, WESLEY—1946—owner, Little Rock Black Travelers

GRAVES, WHITT—1950-51—p, Indianapolis Clowns

GRAY,—1931—3b, Nashville Elite Giants

GRAY,—1931—c, Indianapolis ABCs

GRAY,—1954—p, Detroit Stars

GRAY, CHESLEY (CHESTER)—1940-46—c, St. Louis Stars, New York Black Yankees, Harrisburg-St. Louis Stars, Kansas City Monarchs, Toledo Cubs (USL), Boston Blues (USL)

GRAY, G.E.(WILLIE, DOLLY, GREY)—1920-33—of, p, Cleveland Tate Stars, Homestead Grays, Lincoln Giants, Pennnsylvania Red Caps of New York, Dayton Marcos, Pittsburgh Keystones, Newark Browns, Columbus Buckeyes

GRAY, HOWARD—1951—inf, New Orleans Eagles

GRAY, ROOSEVELT (CHAPPY)—1920-23—1b, p, Cleveland Tate Stars, Toledo Tigers, Dayton Marcos, Kansas City Monarchs

GRAY, WILLIAM—1884-87—of, Baltimore Atlantics, Baltimore Lord Baltimores

GREASON, WILLIAM HENRY (WILLIE, BILL)—1948-51—p, Birmingham Black Barons

GREEN,—1920—p, Detroit Stars

GREEN,—1940—2b, Philadelphia Stars

GREEN,—1941—p, New York Cubans

GREEN,—1952—of, Kansas City Monarchs

GREEN, ALPHONSE—1942—of New York Cubans

GREEN, ALVIN—1950—inf, Baltimore Elite Giants

GREEN, CHARLES (JOE)—1902-31—mgr., of, owner, Leland Giants, Chicago Giants, Chicago American Giants, Union Giants, Columbia Giants, Philadelphia Giants

GREEN, CURTIS—1923-28—1b, of, Birmingham Black Barons, Brooklyn Cuban Giants

GREEN, DAVE—1950—of, Baltimore Elite Giants

GREEN, HENRYENE P.—1949-50—owner, Baltimore Elite Giants

GREEN, HERMAN—1954-55—of, Detroit Stars

GREEN, (HONEY)—1939-42—p, Cleveland Bears, Memphis Red Sox, Boston Royal Giants

GREEN, JAMES [GREENE]—1950—3b, New York Black Yankees

GREEN, JULIUS—1929-30—of, Memphis Red Sox, Detroit Stars

GREEN, LESLIE (CHIN)—1939-46—of, St. Louis Stars, New York Black Yankees, Memphis Red Sox

GREEN, PETER (ED)—1908-20—of, p, Pittsburgh Giants Lincoln Stars, Brooklyn Royal Giants, Brooklyn Colored Giants, Philadelphia Giants

GREEN, VERNON (FAT, BABY)—1921, 1942-49—c, officer, Nashville Giants, Baltimore Elite Giants

GREEN, WILLIAM—1911-23—3b, of, Chicago Giants, Chicago Union Giants

GREEN, WILLIE—1910-12—c, p, Pittsburgh Giants, St. Louis Giants

GREENE,—1916—3b, Chicago Union Giants

GREENE, JAMES ELBERT (JOE)[JAMES GREEN]—1932-48—c, Kansas City Monarchs, Cleveland Buckeyes, Atlanta Black Crackers, Homestead Grays

GREENE, JOHN—1951—inf, Chicago American Giants

GREENE, WALTER—1928—of, 1b, Brooklyn Cuban Giants, Bacharach Giants

GREENE, WILL—1912—p, Pittsburgh Giants

GREENIDGE, VICTOR (SLICKER)—1941-45—p, New York Cubans

GREENLEE, WILLIAM AUGUSTUS (GUS, BIG RED)—1931-46—officer, Pittsburgh Crawfords; founder and pres, second NNL; founder, United States Baseball League

GREER, J.B.—1939-42—officer, Cleveland Bears, Knoxville Red Caps, Jacksonville Red Caps

GREGORY,—1940—p, Birmingham Black Barons

GREY, WILLIAM (See G.E. GRAY)

GREYER, GEORGE—1916-22—1b, Baltimore Black Sox

GRIER, CLAUDE (RED)—1924-28—p, Wilmington Potomacs, Bacharach Giants, Washington Potomacs

GRIFFIN,—1913—of, Indianapolis ABCs

GRIFFIN, C.B. (CLARENCE)—1933-35—of, Columbus Blue Birds, Cleveland Red Sox, Brooklyn Eagles, Columbus Elite Giants

GRIFFIN, E.—1902-07—p, Philadelphia Giants

GRIFFIN, JAMES (HORSE)-1911-21—2b, Cuban Giants, Nashville Elite Giants, Pittsburgh Giants, Philadelphia Giants, Cuban X Giants

GRIFFIN, ROBERT—1931-37—p, Chicago Columbia Giants, St. Louis Stars

GRIFFITH, ROBERT LEE (BIG BILL, SCHOOLBOY)—1934-52—p, Nashville Elite Giants, Columbus Elite Giants, Washington Elite Giants, Baltimore Elite Giants, New York Black Yankees, Philadelphia Stars, Indianapolis Clowns

GRIGGS, ACIE (SKEET)—1951—of, Birmingham Black Barons

GRIGGS, WALLY—1954—inf, Detroit Stars

GRIGGS, WILEY LEE (WILLIE)—1948-55—3b, inf., Birmingham Black Barons, Houston Eagles, Cleveland Buckeyes, New Orleans Eagles, Louisville Black Colonels

GRIMES,—1943—of, p, Cleveland Buckeyes, Harrisburg-St.Louis Stars

GRIMM,—1921—of, Bacharach Giants

GROSS, BEN, JR.—1887—of, Pittsburgh Keystones

GUERRA, JUAN—1910-24—of, 1b, c, Stars of Cuba, Cuban Stars (NNL), New York Cuban Stars, Cincinnati Cubans

GUERRA, MARCELINO—1916—1b, Cuban Stars

GUICE, LACEY—1951-52—of, New Orleans Eagles, Chicago American Giants

GUILBE, FELIX—1946-47—of, Baltimore Elite Giants

GUILBE, JUAN—1940-47—p, of, New York Cubans, Baltimore Elite Giants, Indianapolis Clowns

GUILLEU,—1921—p, Cincinnati Cubans

GUITERREZ, LUIS (JOE)—1926—of, Cuban Stars (NNL)

GUINN, JEFFERSON—1943-45—c, Cleveland Buckeyes

GULLEY, NAPOLEON (NAP, LEFTY, SCHOOL BOY)—1943-47—p, of, Cleveland Buckeyes, Newark Eagles

GUMBS,—1926—player, Newark Stars

GURLEY, JAMES—1922-32—of, p, 1b, St. Louis Stars, Memphis Red Sox, Chicago American Giants, Montgomery Grey Sox, Nashville Elite Giants, Birmingham Black Barons, Indianapolis ABCs, Cleveland Hornets, Harrisburg Giants

GUTHRIE,—1953—p, Birmingham Black Barons

GUY, WESLEY—1927-29—p, Chicago Giants

GUYTON, MILLER—1951—3b, Kansas City Monarchs, Philadelphia Stars

H

HACKETT,—1932—p, Washington Pilots, Bacharach Giants

HACKLEY, ALBERT—1887-96—of, inf., Chicago Unions

HADDAD,—1931—p, of, Cuban Stars (West)

HADLEY, (RED)—1937-38—c, of, Atlanta Black Crackers

HAGGINS, BILLY RAY [HIGGINS]—1953-55—of Memphis Red Sox

HAINES,—1920—p, Indianapolis ABCs

HAINES,—1934—c, Bacharach Giants

HAIR,—1953—3b, Birmingham Black Barons

HAIRSTON, HAROLD (HAL)—1946-47, 1953—p, Homestead Grays, Birmingham Black Barons

HAIRSTON, NAPOLEON—1938-40—of, Pittsburgh Crawfords, Indianapolis Crawfords, Toledo Crawfords

HAIRSTON, (RAP)—1934-35—utl., Newark Dodgers

HAIRSTON, RICHARD (DICK)—1953-54—p, of, Indianapolis Clowns

HAIRSTON, SAMUEL (SAM)—1945-50—c, 3b, Cincinnati-Indianapolis Clowns, Indianapolis Clowns

HAIRSTONE, J.BURKE (J.B.)—1916-22-mgr, of, c, Baltimore Black Sox, Bacharach Giants

HALE, E. (RED)—1937-39—ss, Detroit Stars, Chicago American Giants

HALEY,—1923—p, Detroit Stars

HALEY, (RED)—1928-33—2b, 3b, Chicago American Giants, Birmingham Black Barons, Cuban Stars (East)

HALL, (BAD NEWS)—1940—3b, Indianapolis Crawfords

HALL, BLAINEY—1913-25—of, Mohawk Giants, Lincoln Giants, Philadelphia Giants, Baltimore Black Sox

HALL, CHARLEY—1948—utl., Kansas City Monarchs

HALL, EMORY—1887—2b, Philadelphia Pythians

HALL, HORACE G.—1933-42—officer, Chicago American Giants; vice pres, NAL

HALL, JOSEPH W.—1945—officer, Hilldale Club of Philadelphia

HALL, PERRY—1921-37—p, 3b, of, St.Louis Giants, Milwaukee Bears, Memphis Red Sox, Cleveland Tigers, Chicago Giants, Indianapolis Athletics, Chicago Columbia Giants, Birmingham Black Barons, Detroit Stars

HALL, SELLERS McKEE (SELL)—1916-20—p, Pittsburgh Colored Giants, Homestead Grays, Chicago American Giants

HALL, THOMAS—1934—ss, Washington Pilots

HAMILTON,—1886—2b, New York Gorhams

HAMILTON,—1921—of, Chicago Giants

HAMILTON,—1921-24—p, Kansas City Monarchs, Cleveland Browns, St. Louis Stars, Bacharach Giants

HAMILTON, ARTHUR LEE—1953-54—c, Indianapolis Clowns

HAMILTON, GEORGE—1923-32—c, Memphis Red Sox, Birmingham Black Barons, Washington Pilots

HAMILTON, J.C. (JOHN, ED)—1939-42—p, Homestead Grays

HAMILTON, J.H. (JOHN)—1924-27—3b, inf, Washington Potomacs, Birmingham Black Barons, Indianapolis ABCs, Cleveland Elites, Wilmington Potomacs

HAMILTON, JIM—1946—ss, Kansas City Monarchs

HAMILTON, L.—1923-25—2b, of, Memphis Red Sox, Birmingham Black Barons

HAMILTON, THERON B.—1934—vice pres, Homestead Grays

HAMMEROD,—1926—of, Newark Stars

HAMMOND, DON—1923-24—3b, ss, Cleveland Tate Stars, Cleveland Browns, Toledo Tigers

HAMPTON, EPPIE—1922-38—c, p, Memphis Red Sox, Washington Pilots, New Orleans Crescent Stars, Birmingham Black Barons, Cleveland Tigers, Cleveland Tate Stars

HAMPTON, LEWIS—1921-28—p, Columbus Buckeyes, Indianapolis ABCs, Bacharach Giants, Washington Potomacs, Lincoln Giants, Detroit Stars, Wilmington Potomacs

HAMPTON, WADE—1918-24—p, Pennsylvania Giants, Hilldale

HANCOCK, ART—1926-27—1b, of, Cleveland Elites, Cleveland Hornets

HANCOCK, CHARLES WINSTON (CHARLEY)—1921—c, St. Louis Giants

HANCOCK, EDDIE—1952-55—p, Memphis Red Sox

HANCOCK, GENE—1954—of, Memphis Red Sox

HANCOCK, JOHN—1951—p, New Orleans Eagles

HANCOCK, LEROY—1951-54—p, of, New Orleans Eagles, Memphis Red Sox, Chicago American Giants

HANCOCK, W.—1885—p, Brooklyn Remsens

HANDY, GEORGE—1946-49—inf, Memphis Red Sox, Houston Eagles

HANDY, WILLIAM OSCAR (BILL, BUCK)—1910-27—2b, ss, 3b, New York Black Sox, Brooklyn Royal Giants, St. Louis Giants, Lincoln Giants, Bacharach Giants, Philadelphia Royal Giants

HANKS,—1908—c, Brooklyn Colored Giants

HANNIBAL,—1913-17—of, Bowser's ABCs, Indianapolis ABCs, Louisville White Sox

HANNIBAL, LEO JACK—1932, 1937-38—p, Indianapolis ABCs, Indianapolis Athletics, Homestead Grays

HANNON,—1908-13—of, 3b, Pop Watkins Stars, Philadelphia Giants, St.Louis Giants

HANSON,—1915—ss, Chicago American Giants

HANSON, HARRY—1926—vice pres, NSL

HARDAWAY, CURTIS—1952-53—3b, Indianapolis Clowns

HARDEN, JAMES—1947—p, Homestead Grays

HARDEN, JOHN H.—1939-48—officer, Atlanta Black Crackers, Indianapolis ABCs, New York Black Yankees; tres, NSL

HARDEN, LOVELL (BIG PITCH)—1943-45—p, Cleveland Buckeyes

HARDIMAN,—1937—p, St. Louis Stars

HARDING, A. HALLIE—1926-31—ss, 2b, 3b, Indianapolis ABCs, Detroit Stars, Kansas City Monarchs, Chicago Columbia Giants, Bacharach Giants, Baltimore Black Sox

HARDING, ROY—1937—p, Philadelphia Stars

HARDING, TOM—1940—of, Indianapolis Crawfords

HARDY, ARTHUR WESLEY (ART) [WILLIAM (SHIN) NORMAN]—1906-12—p, Topeka Giants, Kansas City (KS) Giants, Leland Giants, Union Giants

HARDY, (DOC)—1950—inf., Cleveland Buckeyes

HARDY, PAUL JAMES—1931-52—c, Montgomery Grey Sox, Detroit Stars, Birmingham Black Barons, Baltimore Elite Giants, Columbus Elite Giants, Chicago American Giants, Kansas City Monarchs, Memphis Red Sox, Nashville Elite Giants

HARDY, WALTER—1945-50—ss, 2b, New York Black Yankees, New York Cubans

HAREWAY,—1931—p, Newark Browns

HARGETT,—1918—p, Hilldale

HARGETT, YOOK—1887—player, Philadelphia Pythians

HARLAND, BILL—1929—p, Lincoln Giants

HARMON, CHARLES BYRON (CHUCK) [CHARLIE FINE]—1947—of, Indianapolis Clowns

HARNESS, ROBERT MARSEILLES (O)—1927-28—p, Chicago Giants

HARNEY, GEORGE—1923-31—p, Chicago Giants, Chicago Columbia Giants, Chicago American Giants

HARPER,—1910, 1916—p, Leland Giants, Chicago Union Giants

HARPER,—1916—1b, Lincoln Stars

HARPER, (CHICK, CHALKY)—1920-25—ss, of, p, Hilldale, Norfolk Stars, Kansas City Monarchs, Detroit Stars

HARPER, DAVID T. (DAVE)—1943-46—of, p, Kansas City Monarchs, Philadelphia Stars, Birmingham Black Barons

HARPER, JOHN—1922-26—p, Bacharach Giants, Lincoln Giants, Richmond Giants

HARPER, WALTER—1923, 1929-32—1b, c, Chicago American Giants, Birmingham Black Barons, Chicago Columbia Giants

HARPSON, FRED—1923, 1928—inf, Lincoln Giants, Brooklyn Cuban Giants

HARRELL, WILLIAM (BILLY)—1951—ss, Birmingham Black Barons

HARRIS,—1919—of, Lincoln Giants

HARRIS,—1921—p, Indianapolis ABCs, Columbus Buckeyes, Chicago American Giants

HARRIS,—1922—of, New Orleans Crescent Stars

HARRIS,—1926-27—1b, Lincoln Giants

HARRIS, ANANIAS—1921-23—p, Brooklyn Royal Giants, Hilldale, Harrisburg Giants

HARRIS, ANDY—1917-26—3b, mgr., Hilldale, Pennsylvania Giants, Pennsylvania Red Caps of New York, Newark Stars, Pittsburgh Stars of Buffalo, Cleveland Elites

HARRIS, BILL—1929-32—c, Memphis Red Sox, Indianapolis ABCs, Monroe Monarchs, St. Louis Stars

HARRIS, CHARLIE—1943—inf, Cincinnati Clowns, Chicago Brown Bombers

HARRIS, CHICK (POPSICKLE, MOOCHA)-1931-36—of, 1b, Detroit Wolves, Kansas City Monarchs, New Orleans Crescent Stars, Cleveland Stars

HARRIS, CORNELIUS (NEAL, NATE)—1928-31—of, 3b, Pittsburgh Crawfords

HARRIS, CURTIS (POPEYE)—1931-40—2b, ss, 1b, c, Pittsburgh Crawfords, Philadelphia Stars, Kansas City Monarchs

HARRIS, DIXON—1932—player, Homestead Grays

HARRIS, E.—1884—player, Philadelphia Mutual B.B.C.

HARRIS, ELANDER VICTOR (VIC)—1923-50—of, mgr., coach, Cleveland Tate Stars, Cleveland Browns, Chicago American Giants, Homestead Grays, Pittsburgh Crawfords,

Baltimore Elite Giants, Birmingham Black Barons, Toledo Tigers, Detroit Wolves

HARRIS, FRANK—1885—p, Argyle Hotel

HARRIS, GEORGE—1932-38—2b, Louisville Black Caps, Louisville Red Caps

HARRIS, GEORGE—1946—c, Pittsburgh Crawfords

HARRIS, H.B.—1919—bus mgr., Brooklyn Royal Giants

HARRIS, H.C.—1916—mgr., Baltimore Black Sox

HARRIS, HENRY—1928-34—ss, Memphis Red Sox, Louisville Black Caps, Baltimore Black Sox, Louisville White Sox

HARRIS, ISAIAH—1949-55—p, Memphis Red Sox

HARRIS, J. (SONNY)—1935-1942—of, inf, Cincinnati Tigers, Cincinnati-Cleveland Buckeyes,

HARRIS, JAMES R.—1884-87—of, mgr., Baltimore Atlantics, Baltimore Lord Baltimores

HARRIS, JOE—1933—p, Bacharach Giants

HARRIS, JOSEPH—1887—player, Boston Resolutes

HARRIS, (LEFTY)—1941—p, New York Cubans

HARRIS, LEON—1954—p, Kansas City Monarchs

HARRIS, LONNIE—1954-55—of, Louisville Black Colonels, Memphis Red Sox

HARRIS, NATHAN (NATE)—1901-11—2b, of, Philadelphia Giants, Leland Giants, Chicago Giants, Cuban Giants, Columbia Giants

HARRIS, RAYMOND M. (MO)—1916-43—2b, of, Homestead Grays, Pittsburgh Crawfords; umpire, East-West League, NNL

HARRIS, ROBERT (BOB)—1935—ph., Pittsburgh Crawfords

HARRIS, ROGER—1942—inf, Birmingham Black Barons

HARRIS, SAMUEL (SAM)—1932, 1940—p, of, Monroe Monarchs, Chicago American Giants, Birmingham Black Barons

HARRIS, TOMMY—1946-49—c, Cleveland Buckeyes, Louisville Buckeyes

HARRIS, VIRGIL (SCHOOLBOY)—1935-37—p, of, 2b, Cincinnati Tigers, Cincinnati-Cleveland Buckeyes

HARRIS, WILLIAM A.(WOOGIE, BILL)—1928-31—of, Pittsburgh Crawfords, Homestead Grays

HARRIS, WILLIAM (WILLIE)—1955—p, Detroit Stars

HARRIS, WILLIE—1951-55—of, Philadelphia Stars, Memphis Red Sox, Louisville Black Colonels

HARRIS, WILMER—1945-52—p, Philadelphia Stars

HARRIS, WIN—1922-28—1b, ss, Homestead Grays

HARRISON,—1910-16—1b, West Baden (IN) Sprudels, Bowser's ABCs, St.Louis Giants

HARRISON,—1946—p, Homestead Grays

HARRISON, ABRAHAM—1885-97—ss, Philadelphia Orions, Argyle Hotel, Cuban Giants, Trenton Cuban Giants (Middle States Lg.), York Cuban Giants (Eastern Interstate Lg.), York Colored Monarchs

HARRISON, TOMLINI—1927-30—p, St. Louis Stars, Kansas City Monarchs

HARRISTON, CLYDE—1944—inf., Birmingham Black Barons, Cincinnati-Indianapolis Clowns

HART,—1887—c, Pittsburgh Keystones

HART, FRANK—1884—ss, St. Louis Black Stockings

HARTMAN, GARREL—1944—utl., Philadelphia Stars

HARTMAN, J C—1955—ss, Kansas City Monarchs

HARVEY, A.—1937—ss, Philadelphia Stars

HARVEY, B.T.—1950—sec, NSL

HARVEY, CHARLES—1950—ss, Cleveland Buckeyes

HARVEY, DAVID WILLIAM (BILL)—1932-45—p, Memphis Red Sox, Pittsburgh Crawfords, Baltimore Elite Giants, Cleveland Red Sox, Toledo Crawfords, Indianapolis Crawfords, Cleveland Giants, Monroe Monarchs

HARVEY, FRANK-1912-24—p, of, St. Louis Giants, Brooklyn Royal Giants, Lincoln Stars, Lincoln Giants, Bacharach Giants, Philadelphia Giants

HARVEY, JAMES—1911—c, Chicago Union Giants

HARVEY, ROBERT A. (BOB)—1943-51—of, Newark Eagles, Houston Eagles, New Orleans Eagles

HASLETT, CLAUDE—1936-37—p, Memphis Red Sox, Indianapolis Athletics

HASTINGS,—1928—p, St.Louis Stars

HATCHETT,—1913—2b, Brooklyn Royal Giants

HAVIS, CHESTER—1947—p, Memphis Red Sox

HAWK,—1905—c, Brooklyn Royal Giants

HAWKS,—1913—3b, Philadelphia Giants

HAWKINS, JOHN—1940—ss, New York Black Yankees

HAWKINS, LEMUEL (HAWK)—1919-28—1b, of, Los Angeles White Sox, Kansas City Monarchs, Chicago Giants, Chicago American Giants

HAWLEY,—1932—c, Memphis Red Sox

HAYES,—1912-13—c, of, ss, Pittsburgh Giants, Philadelphia Giants, Havana Red Sox

HAYES, BUDDY—1916-24—c, Chicago American Giants, Indianapolis ABCs, Pittsburgh Keystones, Cleveland Browns, St. Louis Giants, Milwaukee Bears, Toledo Tigers

HAYES, BURNALLE JAMES (BUN)-1929-35—p, mgr., Baltimore Black Sox, Washington Pilots, Chicago American Giants, Newark Dodgers, Brooklyn Eagles, Jacksonville Red Caps, Pittsburgh Crawfords

HAYES, JIMMY—1949—c, Kansas City Monarchs

HAYES, JOHN WILLIAM—1934-51—c, Newark Dodgers, Newark Eagles, New York Black Yankees, Boston Blues, Baltimore Elite Giants, Pittsburgh Crawfords, Philadelphia Stars

HAYES, JOHN W.—1940—ss, 2b, Philadelphia Stars, St. Louis Stars

HAYES, THOMAS H. JR.—1939-50—officer, Birmingham Black Barons; vice pres, NAL

HAYES, WILBUR—1942-50—off., g.m., Cincinnati Buckeyes, Cleveland Buckeyes; sergeant-at-arms, NAL

HAYMAN, CHARLES (BUGS)—1909-16—p, 1b, Philadelphia Giants

HAYNES,—1905—of, Brooklyn Royal Giants

HAYNES, SAMMIE—1943-45—c, Kansas City Monarchs

HAYNES, BILL(WILLIE)—1921-24—p, Dallas Giants, Hilldale, Harrisburg Giants, Baltimore Black Sox, Bacharach Giants

HAYWOOD, ALBERT ELLIOTT (BUSTER)—1935-54—c, mgr., Birmingham Black Barons, New York Cubans, Cincinnati-Indianapolis Clowns, Indianapolis Clowns, Cincinnati Clowns, Memphis Red Sox, Brooklyn Eagles

HEAD, JOHN—1951—of, Kansas City Monarchs

HEARD, JEHOSIE (LITTLE, JAY)—1946-51—p, Birmingham Black Barons, Memphis Red Sox, Houston Eagles, New Orleans Eagles

HEAT,—1941—p, New York Cubans

HEATH,—1923—p, Baltimore Black Sox

HEFFNER, ARTHUR—1947-49—of, New York Black Yankees, Philadelphia Stars

HENDERSON,—1925—c, Birmingham Black Barons

HENDERSON, ARMOUR—1914-15—p, Mohawk Giants

HENDERSON, ARTHUR CHAUNCEY (RATS)—1922-31—p, Richmond Giants, Bacharach Giants, Detroit Stars

HENDERSON, BEN (RABBIT)—1936-37—p, St. Louis Stars, Birmingham Black Barons

HENDERSON, CURTIS (CURT)—1936-42—ss, 3b, Philadelphia Stars New York Black Yankees, Washington Black Senators, Toledo Crawfords, Indianapolis Crawfords, Chicago American Giants Homestead Grays, Brooklyn Royal Giants

HENDERSON, GEORGE (RUBE)—1920-23—of, 3b, p, Cleveland Tate Stars, Toledo Tigers, Detroit Stars, Chicago Giants

HENDERSON, H. (LONG)—1932—1b, Nashville Elite Giants

HENDERSON, JAMES (DUKE)—1949-53—of, Kansas City Monarchs

HENDERSON, LENON—1930-33—3b, ss, Nashville Elite Giants, Birmingham Black Barons, Montgomery Grey Sox, Louisville Black Caps, Indianapolis ABCs

HENDERSON, LOUIS—1925—p, of, Bacharach Giants

HENDERSON, NEALE, JR. (BOBO),—1949—if, Kansas City Monarchs

HENDRICKS,—1918, 1922—p, of, Lincoln Giants, Baltimore Black Sox

HENDRIX, STOKES—1934—p, Nashville Elite Giants

HENLEY,—1927—3b, Brooklyn Royal Giants

HENRY, ALFRED—1950-51—of, Baltimore Elite Giants, Philadelphia Stars

HENRY, CHARLES (CHARLIE)—1922-42—p, mgr., Hilldale, Harrisburg Giants, Detroit Stars, Bacharach Giants, Detroit Black Sox, Louisville Black Colonels

HENRY, JOE—1950-52—2b, Memphis Red Sox

HENRY, LEO (PREACHER)—1938-51—p, Jacksonville Red Caps, Cleveland Bears, Cincinnati Clowns, Indianapolis Clowns

HENRY, OTIS—1931-37—2b, 3b, Memphis Red Sox, Monroe Monarchs, Indianapolis Athletics

HENSLEY, LOGAN (EGGIE, SLAP)—1922-39—p, St. Louis Stars, Toledo Tigers, Indianapolis ABCs, Detroit Stars, Cleveland Giants, Chicago American Giants, Cleveland Tate Stars, Cleveland Browns

HENSON,—1939—ss, Toledo Crawfords

HERBERT, HARRY—1894—of, Pawtucket (New England Lg.)

HEREDIA, RAMON (NAPOLEON)—1939-45—3b, ss, New York Cubans

HERMAN, (See HERMAN ANDREWS)

HERNANDEZ, ALBERTO—1941—of, New York Cubans

HERNANDEZ, JOSE—1920-22—p, of, Cuban Stars (NNL)

HERNANDEZ, RAMON—1929-30—3b, Cuban Stars (NNL)

HERNANDEZ, RICARDO (CHICO)—1909-16—2b, 3b, Cuban Stars, All Cubans, All Nations

HERNDON,—1931—p, Newark Browns

HERRERA, JUAN FRANCISCO (PANCHO)—1952-54—c, 1b, Kansas City Monarchs

HERRERA, RAMON (PAITO, MIKE)—1916-28—2b, 3b, Jersey City Cubans, Cuban Stars (NNL), Cuban Stars (ECL), Long Branch Cubans, Cincinnati Cubans

HERRING,—1920—3b, St. Louis Giants

HERRON, 1911-12—of, Indianapolis ABCs

HERRON, ROBERT LEE—1950-51—of, Houston Eagles, New Orleans Eagles

HESLIP, JESSE—1945—Pres.; Toledo Cubs (USL)

HEWITT, JOE—1910-32—ss, of, 2b, mgr., St. Louis Giants, Brooklyn Royal Giants, Lincoln Giants, Philadelphia Giants, Detroit Stars, Chicago American Giants, St. Louis Stars, Cleveland Cubs, Dayton Marcos, Milwaukee Bears, Birmingham Black Barons, Nashville Elite Giants, Lincoln Stars

HEYWOOD, CHARLIE (DOBIE)—1925-26—p, Lincoln Giants

HICKLE, JAMES—1955—of, Detroit Stars

HICKS, (BUDDY)—1951—of, Indianapolis Clowns

HICKS, EUGENE (JIMMY)—1940-41—p, Homestead Grays, New York Cuban Stars

HICKS, WESLEY—1927-31—of, Chicago American Giants, Memphis Red Sox, Kansas City Monarchs

HICKSON,—1931—2b, Newark Browns

HIDALGO, HELIODORO—1905-13—of, 3b, Stars of Cuba, Cuban Stars, All Cubans

HIGDON, BARNEY—1943—p, Cincinnati Clowns

HIGGINS, ROBERT (BOB)—1887-88, 1896—p, Syracuse (International League), Cuban Giants

HIGGINS, N.—1887—c, Columbus (Ohio St. Lg.)

J. Preston "Pete" Hill.
Dick Clark

Grant "Home Run" Johnson.
Dick Clark

HIGHBEE,—1911-13—p, of, Indianapolis ABCs

HIGHTOWER, JAMES—1890—1b, Lincoln (NEB) Giants

HILL,—1939—3b, Toledo Crawfords

HILL, WILLIAM E. (BILL)—1955—p, Kansas City Monarchs

HILL, BEN—1943, 1946—p, Philadelphia Stars, Pittsburgh Crawfords

HILL, CHARLEY (LEFTY)—1910-24—of, p, Chicago Union Giants, Dayton Marcos, Detroit Stars, St. Louis Giants, Chicago American Giants, West Baden (IN) Sprudels

HILL, GILBERT—1928-29—p, Pittsburgh Crawfords

HILL, HERB—1949—of, p, Philadelphia Stars

HILL, J. PRESTON (PETE)—1903-25—of, 2b, mgr., bus mgr, Philadelphia Giants, Leland Giants, Chicago American Giants, Detroit Stars, Milwaukee Bears, Baltimore Black Sox, Cuban X Giants

HILL, JAMES (JIMMY, LEFTY, SQUAB)—1938-45—p, Newark Eagles

HILL, JOHN—1900-07—3b, ss, Genuine Cuban Giants, Philadelphia Giants, Cuban X Giants, Brooklyn Royal Giants

HILL, JOHNSON (FRED)—1920-28—2b, 3b, of, St. Louis Giants, Detroit Stars, Milwaukee Bears, Brooklyn Royal Giants

HILL, JONATHAN—1937—of, p, Atlanta Black Crackers, St. Louis Stars

HILL, SAMUEL (SAM)—1937, 1947-48, 1952—of, 1b, Detroit Stars, Chicago American Giants, Memphis Red Sox

HILL, W.R.—1885—ss, Brooklyn Remsens

HINES, C.W. SR.—1887—mgr., Louisville Falls City

HINES, JOHN—1924-34—c, of, Chicago American Giants, Cole's American Giants

HINESMAN, ROBERT—1951-54—p, Chicago American Giants, Detroit Stars

HINKEY,—1926—player, Dayton Marcos

HINSON,—1932—p, Newark Browns

HINSON, FRANK—1896—p, Cuban X Giants, Cuban Giants

HINTON, ROLAND (ARCHIE, CHARLIE)—1945-46—p, inf, Baltimore Elite Giants

HITCHMAN,—1925—3b, Indianapolis ABCs

HOAGLAND, F.B.—1885—sec, Brooklyn Remsens

HOARD,—1921—p, Kansas City Monarchs

HOBGOOD, FREDERICK (LEFTY, JOHN) [HOPGOOD]—1941-46-p, utl., Newark Eagles, New York Black Yankees, Philadelphia Stars

HOBSON, CHARLES (JOHNNY) [HOPSON]—1922-25—p, ss, of, Lincoln Giants, Bacharach Giants, Richmond Giants

HOCKER, BRUCE—1913-20—1b, of, Bowser's ABCs, Lincoln Stars Dayton Marcos, Louisville White Sox, Chicago American Giants, Hilldale, West Baden (IN) Sprudels

HODGES, WILLIAM (JIMMY)—1917-25—p, Lincoln Giants, Baltimore Black Sox

HOGAN, JULIUS—1932—c, of, Bacharach Giants

HOKE, (BUD)—1945—player, Toledo Cubs (USL)

HOLCOMB,—1923—p, Detroit Stars

HOLDER, CLYDE—1951—p, New Orleans Eagles

HOLDER, WILLIAM (BILL)—1953-54—ss, Indianapolis Clowns, Kansas City Monarchs

HOLLAND,—1921—1b, Hilldale

HOLLAND, ELVIS WILLIAM (BILL)—1920-41—p, mgr., Detroit Stars, Chicago American Giants, Lincoln Giants, Brooklyn Royal Giants, New York Black Yankees, Philadelphia Stars, Hilldale

HOLLAND, WILLIAM (BILLY)—1894-1908, 1923—p, of, 3b, Adrian (MI) Page Fence Giants, Chicago Unions, Brooklyn Royal Giants, Leland Giants, Pop Watkins Stars, Algona (IA) Brownies, Chicago Columbia Giants; umpire, NNL

HOLLIDAY, CHARLES DOURCHER (FLIT)—1938—of, p, Atlanta Black Crackers

HOLLIMON, ULYSSES—1950-54—p, Baltimore Elite Giants, Birmingham Black Barons

HOLLINGSWORTH, CURTIS—1946-50—p, Birmingham Black Barons

HOLLINS,—1936—p, Birmingham Black Barons

HOLLOWAY, CRUSH—1921-39—of, Indianapolis ABCs, Baltimore Black Sox, Hilldale, Detroit Stars, Bacharach Giants, Brooklyn Eagles, New York Black Yankees, Brooklyn Royal Giants, Baltimore Elite Giants

HOLMES,—1931—of, Cuban Stars (NNL)

HOLMES, BENJAMIN F. (BEN)—1885-89—3b, Argyle Hotel, Cuban Giants, Trenton Cuban Giants (Middle States Lg.)

HOLMES, EDDIE—1932—p, Baltimore Black Sox

HOLMES, FRANK (SONNY, DUCKY)—1929-38—p, Bacharach Giants, Philadelphia Stars, Lincoln Giants, Washington Elite Giants, Washington Black Senators

HOLMES, LEROY THOMAS (PHILLIE)—1934-45—ss, Jacksonville Red Caps, Cleveland Bears, Atlanta Black Crackers, Kansas City Monarchs, Cincinnnati-Indianapolis Clowns, New York Black Yankees, Brooklyn Eagles

HOLSCROFF, WILLIAM—1954—inf, Birmingham Black Barons

HOLSEY, ROBERT J. (FROG)—1928-32—p, Chicago American Giants, Chicago Columbia Giants, Cleveland Cubs, Nashville Elite Giants

HOLT, JOHNNY—1922-23—of, Pittsburgh Keystones, Toledo Tigers

HOLT, JOSEPH—1928—of, Brooklyn Cuban Giants

HOLTZ, EDDIE—1919-24—2b, ss, St. Louis Giants, Chicago American Giants, St. Louis Stars, Lincoln Giants

HOOD, DOZIER CHARLES—1945—c, Kansas City Monarchs

HOODS, WILLIAM (See WILLIAM WOODS)

HOOKER, (See BRUCE HOCKER)

HOOKER, LENIEL CHARLIE (LEN, ELBOW)—1940-49—p, Newark Eagles, Houston Eagles

HOPKINS,—1945—p, Newark Eagles

HOPKINS, GEORGE—1890-1902—p, 2b, Chicago Unions, Adrian Page Fence Giants, Algona (IA) Brownies

HOPKINS, GORDON DERRICK (HOPPY)—1952-54—2b, 1b, Indianapolis Clowns

HOPWOOD,—1928—of, Kansas City Monarchs

HORDY, J.H.—1887—player, Baltimore Lord Baltimores

HORN,—1925—2b, Birmingham Black Barons

HORN, HERMAN (DOC)—1951-54—of, Kansas City Monarchs

HORN, WILLIAM (WILL)—1896-1905—p, Chicago Unions, Philadelphia Giants, Leland Giants, Algona (IA) Brownies

HORNE, WILLIAM (BILLIE)—1938-46—ss, 2b, Monroe Monarchs, Chicago American Giants, Cincinnati Buckeyes, Cleveland Buckeyes, Harrisburg-St.Louis Stars

HORNER,—1923—of, Milwaukee Bears

HORNS, JAMES J.—1887—player, Boston Resolutes

HORTIS,—1931—p, Cuban Stars (East)

HORTON, CLARENCE (SLIM)—1930—p, Pittsburgh Crawfords

HOSKINS, DAVID TAYLOR (DAVE)—1942-49—of, p, Cincinnati Clowns, Chicago American Giants, Homestead Grays, Louisville Buckeyes

HOSKINS, WILLIAM (BILL)—1937-46—of, Detroit Stars, Memphis Red Sox, Baltimore Elite Giants, New York Black Yankees, St. Louis Stars, Kansas City Monarchs, Chicago American Giants, Washington Black Senators

HOULEWARD, MICHAEL—1954—p, Birmingham Black Barons

HOUSE, CHARLES (RED)—1937—3b, Detroit Stars

HOUSTON,—1914—of, Louisville White Sox

HOUSTON,—1919-20—p, 2b, Indianapolis ABCs, Kansas City Monarchs

HOUSTON, BILL—1941-42—p, Homestead Grays

HOUSTON, NATHANIAL (JESS)—1930-39—p, inf, Memphis Red Sox, Cincinnati Tigers, Chicago American Giants

HOUSTON, WILLIAM—1910—c, ss, West Baden (Ind) Sprudels

HOVLEY,—1932—p, Nashville Elite Giants

HOWARD,—1920-29—ss, p, Norfolk Giants, Harrisburg Giants, Baltimore Black Sox, Lincoln Giants, Norfolk Stars

HOWARD,—1921-23, 1927—p, 3b, Detroit Stars, Indianapolis ABCs, Memphis Red Sox, Cleveland Tate Stars

HOWARD, CARL—1935-36—of, Pittsburgh Crawfords, Birmingham Black Barons

HOWARD, CARRANZA (SCHOOLBOY)—1940-50—p, New York Cubans, Indianapolis Clowns, New York Black Yankees

HOWARD, CHARLES—1897-99—utl, p, Cuban Giants, Cuban X Giants

HOWARD, ELSTON GENE (ELLIE)—1948-50—of, c, Kansas City Monarchs

HOWARD, HERB—1948—p, of, Kansas City Monarchs

HOWARD, HERMAN (RED)—1932-46—p, Atlanta Black Crackers, Memphis Red Sox, Washington Elite Giants, Indianapolis Athletics, Jacksonville Red Caps, Indianapolis ABCs, Chicago American Giants, Birmingham Black Barons, Little Rock Black Travelers, Cleveland Bears, Little Rock Grays

HOWARD, PERCY—1954-55—c, of, Detroit Stars, Indianapolis Clowns

HOWARD, WILLIAM (BILL)—1931-33—1b, 3b, 2b, Birmingham Black Barons

HOWELL,—1908—of, Brooklyn Royal Giants

HOWELL, HENRY—1918-21—p, Pennsylvania Giants, Bacharach Giants, Pennsylvania Red Caps of New York, Brooklyn Royal Giants

HOYT, DANA—1932—1b, Bacharach Giants

HUBBARD, DeHART—1934-37, 1942—official, sec, Cincinnati Tigers, Cleveland-Cincinnati Buckeyes

HUBBARD, JESSE JAMES (MOUNTAIN)-1919-34—p, of, Bacharach Giants, Brooklyn Royal Giants, Baltimore Black Sox, Hilldale, Homestead Grays, New York Black Yankees

HUBBARD, LARRY—1946—utl., Kansas City Monarchs

HUBBIE, (BUTCH)—1951—p, Birmingham Black Barons

HUBER, [HUBERT]—1930-31—c, of, Memphis Red Sox, Nashville Elite Giants, Birmingham Black Barons

HUBER, JOHN MARSHALL [HUBERT]—1939-50—p, c, Chicago American Giants, Birmingham Black Barons, Cincinnati Clowns, Memphis Red Sox, Philadelphia Stars

HUBERT, WILLIE (BUBBER)—1935-46—p, Newark Eagles, Baltimore Elite Giants, Cincinnati Buckeyes, Baltimore Grays, Homestead Grays, Pittsburgh Crawfords, Brooklyn Brown Dodgers, Philadelphia Stars, Cleveland Buckeyes, New York Black Yankees, Newark Dodgers

HUDSON,—1908—rf, Brooklyn Colored Giants

HUDSON, CHARLES (KEEN LEGS)—1923, 1930—p, Milwaukee Bears, Louisville White Sox

HUDSON, WILLIAM HENRY—1937-42—p, Cincinnati Tigers, Chicago American Giants

HUDSPETH, ROBERT (HIGHPOCKETS)—1920-32—1b, Indianapolis ABCs, Columbus Buckeyes, Bacharach Giants, Lincoln Giants, Brooklyn Royal Giants, Hilldale, New York Black Yankees

HUESTON, WILLIAM C.—1926-31—pres, NNL

HUFF, EDDIE—1923-32—c, of, mgr., Bacharach Giants, Dayton Marcos

HUGHBANKS, GEORGE—1890—utl., Lincoln (NEB) Giants

HUGHBANKS, HUGH [HUBANKS]—1890—2b, Lincoln (NEB) Giants

HUGHES,—1921—p, Bacharach Giants

HUGHES, A.—1927—of, Kansas City Monarchs

HUGHES, CHARLIE—1928-38—2b, Cleveland Red Sox, Columbus Blue Birds, Washington Black Senators, Washington Pilots, Pittsburgh Crawfords, Homestead Grays

HUGHES, FRANK—1937—p, Indianapolis Athletics, Atlanta Black Crackers

HUGHES, LEE—1950—p, Kansas City Monarchs

HUGHES, ROBERT—1931—p, Louisville White Sox

HUGHES, SAMUEL THOMAS (SAMMY T.)—1930-46—2b, Louisville White Sox, Nashville Elite Giants, Columbus Elite Giants, Washington Elite Giants, Baltimore Elite Giants, Washington Pilots

HUMBER, TOM (CHARLIE)—1945, 1950—2b, Newark Eagles, Baltimore Elite Giants

HUMES, JOHN—1937—p, Newark Eagles

HUMPHRIES,—1936-37—of, Atlanta Black Crackers, Memphis Red Sox

HUMPHREYS, CAREY—1952—rf, Kansas City Monarchs

HUNDLEY, JOHNNY LEE—1943—c, of, Cleveland Buckeyes

HUNGO,—1916—1b, of, Long Branch Cubans

HUNT, GROVER—1946—c, Chicago American Giants

HUNT, LEONARD (LEN)—1949-53—of, Kansas City Monarchs

HUNTER, BERTRUM (NATE, BUFFALO)—1931-37—p, St. Louis Stars, Detroit Wolves, Pittsburgh Crawfords, Kansas City Monarchs, Philadelphia Stars, Homestead Grays

HUNTER, EUGENE—1924—p, Memphis Red Sox, Cleveland Browns

HUNTER, WILLIE—1933—p, Akron Black Tyrites

HUSBAND, VINCENT—1951-54—p, New Orleans Eagles, Chicago American Giants, Indianapolis Clowns

HUTCHINSON, FRED (HUTCH, PUGGEY)—1910-25—ss, 3b, 2b, Leland Giants, Chicago American Giants, Indianapolis ABCs, Bacharach Giants, Bowser's ABCs

HUTCHINSON, WILLIE (ACE)—1939-50—p, Kansas City Monarchs, Memphis Red Sox

HUTT,—1920-24—1b, of, Dayton Marcos, Toledo Tigers, St. Louis Giants

HYDE, COWAN F.(BUBBA, BUBBER)—1927-30, 1937-51—of, 2b, Cincinnati Tigers, Memphis Red Sox, Chicago American Giants, Indianapolis Athletics, Houston Eagles, Birmingham Black Barons

HYDE, HARRY—1896-1904—3b, 1b, Chicago Unions, Chicago Union Giants

HYMAN,—1909—p, Quaker Giants

HYNE,—1935—c, Chicago American Giants

I

INCERA, VICTOR—1955—of, Kansas City Monarchs

INGERSOLL,—1905—2b, Brooklyn Royal Giants

INGRAM, ALFRED—1942—p, Jacksonville Red Caps

IRVIN, IRWIN (BILL)—1906, 1919—3b, of, mgr., Leland Giants, Cleveland Tate Stars

IRVIN, MONFORD MERRILL (MONTE)—1937-48—of, ss, 3b, Newark Eagles

ISRAEL, CLARENCE CHARLES (PINT)—1940-47—3b, 2b, Newark Eagles, Homestead Grays

ISRAEL, ELBERT WILLIS—1950—inf., Philadelphia Stars

IVORY,—1936—p, 1b, Chicago American Giants

IVORY, (BUDDY)—1954-55—ss, Louisville Black Colonels, Detroit Stars

J

JACKMAN, BILL (EARL, CANNON BALL)—1925-42—p, Lincoln Giants, Philadelphia Giants, Quaker Giants, Brooklyn Eagles, Boston Royal Giants, Newark Eagles

JACKSON,—1890—c, Lincoln (NEB) Giants

JACKSON,—1916-26—c, of, Pennsylvania Red Caps of New York, Lincoln Giants, Lincoln Stars, Philadelphia Giants

JACKSON,—1921—p, Indianapolis ABCs

JACKSON,—1932—of, c, Indianapolis ABCs

JACKSON, A. MATTHEW—1932-36—3b, ss, Montgomery Grey Sox, Birmingham Black Barons, Cincinnati Tigers, Chicago American Giants

JACKSON, ANDREW (ANDY)—1887-99—3b, New York Gorhams, Cuban Giants, Lansing, (Mi) Colored Capital All-Americans, Cuban X Giants, York Cuban Giants (Eastern Interstate Lg.), New York Gorhams (Middle States Lg.)

JACKSON, B. (BOZO)—1943—45-3b, Philadelphia Stars, Homestead Grays

JACKSON, C.—1929—3b, Homestead Grays

JACKSON, CARLTON—1928—officer, Harrisburg Giants

JACKSON, DALLAS—1950—2b, inf, Cleveland Buckeyes

JACKSON, DANIEL M. (DAN, HATCHET)—1949—of, Homestead Grays

JACKSON, EDGAR S.—1932-37—c, Memphis Red Sox, Little Rock Grays

JACKSON, F.—1887—officer, Brooklyn Remsens

JACKSON, F.—1934—1b, Cincinnati Tigers

JACKSON, FRED—1955—of, Birmingham Black Barons

JACKSON, (GEN)—1947—of, p, Baltimore Elite Giants

JACKSON, GEORGE—1886-87—p, of, Philadelphia Pythians, Trenton Cuban Giants (Middle States Lg.), Cuban Giants

JACKSON, GEORGE—1950—inf., New York Black Yankees

JACKSON, (GUMBO)—1922—3b, New Orleans Crescent Stars

JACKSON, GUY—1911-15—ss, inf, Chicago Giants, Chicago Union Giants

JACKSON, ISIAH (IKE)—1951-53—c, of, Kansas City Monarchs

JACKSON, JACK—1927-28—of, Bacharach Giants, Baltimore Black Sox

JACKSON, JACKIE—1950—of, Homestead Grays

JACKSON, JOHN W. JR.(STONY)—1950-53—p, Houston Eagles, Kansas City Monarchs

JACKSON, (LEFTY)—1926-31—p, Philadelphia Giants, Brooklyn Royal Giants

JACKSON, LESTER E.—1938-41—p, of, Newark Eagles, New York Black Yankees

JACKSON, LINCOLN—1933-35—1b, Cuban Stars (East), Washington Pilots, Bacharach Giants, Baltimore Black Sox

JACKSON, NORMAN (JELLY)—1934-45—ss, 2b, Cleveland Red Sox, Homestead Grays, Washington Elite Giants, Pittsburgh Crawfords

JACKSON, OSCAR—1887-1903—of, 1b, New York Gorhams, Cuban Giants, Cuban X Giants, York Cuban Giants (Eastern Interstate Lg.), Philadelphia Giants

JACKSON, R.B.—1931-50—pres, vice pres, NSL; officer, owner, Nashville Black Vols, Nashville Cubs

JACKSON, R.T.—1928-31—officer, Birmingham Black Barons; pres, NSL

JACKSON, RANDOLPH—1887—2b, Oswego (International Lg.)

JACKSON, RICHARD—1921-31—2b, ss, 3b, Bacharach Giants, Harrisburg Giants, Baltimore Black Sox, Hilldale

JACKSON, ROBERT (BOB)—1886-96—c, 1b, of, New York Gorhams, Cuban X Giants, Ansonia Cuban Giants (Connecticut St. Lg.), York Colored Monarchs

JACKSON, ROBERT—1897-1900—c, Chicago Unions

JACKSON, ROBERT R.(MAJOR)—1889, 1939-42—mgr., commissioner; Chicago Unions, NAL

JACKSON, RUFUS (SONNYMAN)—1934-49—pres, tres, Homestead Grays

JACKSON, SAM—1887—c, Pittsburgh Keystones

JACKSON, SAM—1926—c, Cleveland Elites

JACKSON, SAMUEL—1942-47—p, 1b, Chicago American Giants

JACKSON, STANFORD (JAMBO)—1923-31—of, ss, 3b, 2b, Memphis Red Sox, Chicago American Giants, Chicago Columbia Giants, Birmingham Black Barons

JACKSON, THOMAS—1916-28—officer, Bacharach Giants

JACKSON, THOMAS WALTON (JACK)—1924-31—p, St. Louis Stars, Cleveland Tigers, Nashville Elite Giants, Memphis Red Sox, Louisville White Sox

JACKSON, TOMMY—1946, 1953-54—p, Cleveland Clippers (USL) Birmingham Black Barons, Louisville Black Colonels

JACKSON, VERDELL—1950—p, Memphis Red Sox

JACKSON, W.(BIG TRAIN)—1938-40—p, Kansas City Monarchs, Memphis Red Sox

JACKSON, WILLIAM—1890-1906—of, c, 2b, Cuban Giants, Cuban X Giants, York Cuban Giants (Eastern Interstate Lg.), Ansonia Cuban Giants (CT St. Lg.), Famous Cuban Giants

JACKSON, WILLIAM (ASHES)—1910-17—3b, Kansas City, (Ka) Giants, Kansas City Royal Giants, Kansas City Colored Giants

JACOB,—1944—p, Newark Eagles

JAMERSON, LONDELL (TINCY)—1950-51—p, Kansas City Monarchs

JAMES,—1896—p, Cuban X Giants

JAMES,—1925—p, Cuban Stars (ECL)

JAMES, J.—1912—1b, Smart Set

JAMES, LIVINGSTON (TICE, WINKY, TARZAN)—1936-42-ss, Cincinnati Buckeyes, Cincinnati Clowns, Chicago American Giants, Cleveland Buckeyes, Memphis Red Sox

JAMES, W. (GUS, NUX)—1905-20—2b, c, of, Philadelphia Giants, Smart Set, Mohawk N.Y. Giants, Lincoln Giants, Bacharach Giants, Brooklyn Royal Giants, Pop Watkins Stars, Pittsburgh Stars of Buffalo, Cuban X Giants, Louisville White Sox

JAMES, WILLIAM WALTER—1887—player, Philadelphia Pythians

JAMESON,—1932-35—p, Newark Dodgers, Homestead Grays

JAMISON, CAESAR—1923-32—umpire, NNL, East-West League

JAMISON, EDDIE—1950—c, Cleveland Buckeyes

JARMON, DON—1933—p, Columbus Blue Birds

JARNAGIN,—1934—of, Homestead Grays

JASPER,—1932-33—p, Birmingham Black Barons, Memphis Red Sox

JAURON—1928—p, Cleveland Tigers

JEFFERSON,—1931—p, Bacharach Giants

JEFFERSON, EDWARD L. (EDDIE)—1942-47—p, Philadelphia Stars

JEFFERSON, GEORGE LEO (JEFF)—1942-50—p, Jacksonville Red Caps, Cleveland Buckeyes, Louisville Buckeyes

JEFFERSON, R.—1939—3b, p, Indianapolis ABCs

JEFFERSON, RALPH—1918-32—of, Indianapolis ABCs, Bacharach Giants, Philadelphia Royal Stars, Washington Potomacs, Philadelphia Giants, Peter's Chicago Union Giants

JEFFERSON, WILLIE—1937-50—p, Cincinnati Tigers, Memphis Red Sox, Cincinniati Buckeyes, Cleveland Buckeyes

JEFFREYS, FRANK—1917-20—of, 2b, Chicago Giants

JEFFRIES, E.—1922—c, Chicago Giants

JEFFRIES, HARRY—1920-48—3b, c, ss, 1b, mgr., Chicago Giants, Chicago American Giants, Detroit Stars, Cleveland Tigers, Chicago Columbia Giants, Bacharach Giants, Knoxville Giants, Toledo Tigers, Baltimore Black Sox, Harrisburg Giants, Baltimore Panthers, Cleveland Browns, Newark Dodgers, Brooklyn Royal Giants, Cleveland Tate Stars, Washington Potomacs

JEFFRIES, JAMES C.—1913-31—p, of, Indianapolis ABCs, Baltimore Black Sox, Birmingham Black Barons, Harris-burg Giants, Chicago American Giants

JEFFRIES, JEFF—1940—p, Brooklyn Royal Giants, Homestead Grays

JEFFRIES, M.—1924, 1932—3b, Baltimore Black Sox, Hilldale

JENKINS,—1924—p, Washington Potomacs

JENKINS, CLARENCE (BARNEY)—1925-29—c, Philadelphia Giants, Detroit Stars

JENKINS, CLARENCE R.(FATS)—1920-40—of, mgr., Lincoln Giants, Harrisburg Giants, Bacharach Giants, Baltimore Black Sox, New York Black Yankees, Philadelphia Stars, Brooklyn Eagles, Brooklyn Royal Giants, Pittsburgh Crawfords, Toledo Crawfords, Penn Red Caps of NY

JENKINS, GEORGE—1955—p, Detroit Stars

JENKINS, HORACE—1911-25—of, p, Chicago American Giants, Chicago Giants, Chicago Unions Giants

JENKINS, JAMES EDWARD (PEE WEE)—1944-54—p, Cincinnati-Indianapolis Clowns, New York Cubans, Birmingham Black Barons, Indianapolis Clowns

JENKINS, JIMMY—1954—of, Detroit Stars

JENKINS, TOM—1916-17, 1928—player, sec, Hilldale

JENNINGS, THURMAN (JACK)—1914-27—2b, ss, of, Chicago Giants

JESSIE, W.—1887—player, Louisville Falls City

JESSUP, CHARLES—1911—p, Chicago Union Giants

JESSUP, GENTRY—1940-49—p, Chicago American Giants, Birmingham Black Barons

JETHROE, SAMUEL (SAM, THE JET)—1942-48—of, Cincinnati Buckeyes, Cleveland Buckeyes

JEWELL, WARNER—1917-26—owner, officer, Jewell's ABCs, Indianapolis ABCs

JIMENEZ, BIENVENIDO (HOOKS)—1915-29—2b, Cuban Stars (NNL), Cuban Stars (ECL), Cuban Stars, Cuban Stars (East), Havana Cubans, Cincinnati Cubans

JIMENEZ, EUGENIO—1920-21—of, Philadelphia Giants, Cuban Stars (NNL), Cuban Stars (East), Cincinnati Cubans

JIMINEZ,—1938—p, New York Cubans

JOHNSON,—1886—of, New York Gorhams

JOHNSON,—1922—of, Detroit Stars

JOHNSON,—1927—p, Brooklyn Royal Giants

JOHNSON,—1930-31—c, of, Louisville White Sox

JOHNSON,—1938—2b, Washington Black Senators

JOHNSON, A.—1914-17—2b, 3b, of, Lincoln Stars, Cuban Giants, Lincoln Giants

JOHNSON, A. (SAMPSON)—1913-22—c, Bacharach Giants, Pittsburgh Giants, Pennsylvania Giants, Homestead Grays, Philadelphia Giants

JOHNSON, AL—1938-40—p, Baltimore Elite Giants, Washington Black Senators

JOHNSON, ALLEN—1938-46—officer, owner, St. Louis Stars, New York Black Yankees, Harrisburg-St. Louis Stars, Boston Blues, Indianapolis ABCs

JOHNSON, B.—1904—inf, Philadelphia Giants

JOHNSON, B. (MONK)—1914-26—1b, 2b, p, of, Pennsylvania Red Caps of New York, Lincoln Giants, Brooklyn All-Srars, New York Stars

JOHNSON, B.—1940—ss, Brooklyn Royal Giants

JOHNSON, BEN—1916-23—p, Bacharach Giants

JOHNSON, BERT (See BERT JOHNSTON)

JOHNSON, BILL—1933—3b, Akron Tyrites, Cleveland Red Sox

JOHNSON, BILL (WILLIE)—1938-39—c, New York Black Yankees, Chicago American Giants

JOHNSON, BYRON (MEX)—1937-40—ss, Kansas City Monarchs

JOHNSON, C. (See G. CLAUDE JOHNSON)

JOHNSON, CECIL (SESS)—1916-31—1b, 3b, ss, p, Hilldale, Philadelphia Tigers, Philadelphia Royal Stars, Baltimore Black Sox, Newark Stars, Norfolk Stars, Newark Browns, Cuban X Giants, Bacharach Giants

JOHNSON, CHARLES—1949-50—3b, Cleveland Buckeyes, Memphis Red Sox

JOHNSON, CHARLES B.—1925-26—officer, Bacharach Giants

JOHNSON, CHARLIE—1952—p, Indianapolis Clowns

JOHNSON, CLAUDE—1928-31—inf, Pittsburgh Crawfords

JOHNSON, CLIFFORD JR. (CLIFF, CONNIE)—1940-50—p, Indianapolis Crawfords, Kansas City Monarchs

JOHNSON, CURTIS—1950—p, Kansas City Monarchs

JOHNSON, D.(DUD)—1914-19—of, ss, 2b, Philadelphia Giants, Brooklyn Royal Giants

JOHNSON, DAN (SHANG)—1916-25—p, Bacharach Giants, Brooklyn Royal Giants, Lincoln Giants, Hilldale, Indianapolis ABCs, Harrisburg Giants

JOHNSON, DON (GROUNDHOG)—1948-53—2b, 3b, Chicago American Giants, Birmingham Black Barons, Baltimore Elite Giants

JOHNSON, DONALD—1953—p, Birmingham Black Barons

JOHNSON, ERNEST (SCHOOLBOY)—1949-53—p, of, Kansas City Monarchs

JOHNSON, FRANK—1932-37—of, mgr., Monroe Monarchs, Memphis Red Sox

JOHNSON, FRED—1946—p, Pittsburgh Crawfords

JOHNSON, FURMAN—1954—p, Indianapolis Clowns

JOHNSON, G. CLAUDE (HOOKS)—1919-32—3b, 2b, ss, p, Baltimore Black Sox, Harrisburg Giants, Detroit Stars, Birmingham Black Barons, Memphis Red Sox, Cleveland Tate Stars, Hilldale, Brooklyn Royal Giants, Nashville Elite Giants

JOHNSON, GEORGE (CHAPPIE, JUNIOR)—1896-1939—c, 1b, mgr Columbia Giants, Chicago Unions Giants, Brooklyn Royal Giants, Leland Giants, Chicago Giants, St. Louis Giants, Dayton Chappies, Custer's Baseball Club of Columbus, Philadelphia Royal Stars, Norfolk Stars, Algona (IA) Brownies, Adrian (MI) Page Fence Giants, Mohawk N.Y. Giants, Philadelphia Giants, Pennsylvania Red Caps of N.Y., Chappie Johnson's Stars, Louisville White Sox, Quaker Giants, Cuban X Giants

JOHNSON, GEORGE WASHINGTON (DIBO)—1909-31—of, Fort Worth Wonders, Kansas City, Kan., Giants, Brooklyn Royal Giants, Hilldale, Lincoln Giants, Philadelphia Tigers, Bacharach Giants

JOHNSON, GRANT (HOME RUN)—1894-1922—ss, 2b, mgr., Adrian (MI) Page Fence Giants, Columbia Giants, Brooklyn Royal Giants, Cuban X Giants, Philadelphia Giants, Lincoln Giants, Lincoln Stars, Pittsburgh Colored Stars, Pittsburgh Stars of Buffalo, Chicago Unions, Findlay, Ohio, Mohawk Giants, Brooklyn Colored Giants, Chicago Giants

JOHNSON, H. (HAMP)—1933-34, 1946—of, Birmingham Black Barons

JOHNSON, HARRY A.—1886-89—2b, of, c, Cuban Giants, Trenton Cuban Giants (Middle States Lg.)

JOHNSON, J.—1916, 1921—of, Baltimore Black Sox, Columbus Buckeyes

JOHNSON, J. (LEFTY)—1929-33—1b, p, of, Memphis Red Sox

JOHNSON, JACK (TOPEKA JACK)—1903-04, 1909-10—1b, of, Philadelphia Giants, Kansas City (Mo.) Royal Giants, Kansas City (Kan) Giants

JOHNSON, JACK—1938-40—3b, Homestead Grays, Toledo Crawfords, Cincinnati Buckeyes

JOHNSON, JAMES—1898—rf, c, Adrian Page Fence Giants

JOHNSON, JAMES (J.D.)—1950-53—p, Philadelphia Stars, Kansas City Monarchs, Birmingham Black Barons

JOHNSON, JIM—1932-34—ss, Hilldale, Bacharach Giants, Newark Dodgers

JOHNSON, JIMMY (SLIM)—1938-43—p, Toledo Crawfords, Indianapolis Crawfords, Philadelphia Stars, Newark Eagles, New York Black Yankees

JOHNSON, JIMMY (JEEP)—1946-47—ss, Pittsburgh Crawfords, Homestead Grays

JOHNSON, JOE—1884-85—p, c, Baltimore Atlantics

JOHNSON, JOHN (JOHNNY)—1939-46—p, Birmingham Black Barons, Homestead Grays, New York Black Yankees, Baltimore Elite Giants, Cleveland Buckeyes, New York Cubans

JOHNSON, JOHN—1950—utl., New York Cubans

JOHNSON, JOHN B.—1925-28—pres, mgr., Brooklyn Cuban Giants

JOHNSON, REV. JOHN H.—1947-48—pres, NNL

JOHNSON, JOHN WESLEY (SMOKEY)—1922-30—p, Cleveland Tate Stars, Cleveland Elites, Cleveland Browns, Lincoln Giants, Cleveland Tigers, Chicago American Giants

JOHNSON, JOSEPH—1937—officer, Indianapolis Athletics

JOHNSON, JOSHUA (JOSH, BRUTE)—1934-42—c, p, of, Cincinnati Tigers, Homestead Grays, New York Black Yankees, Brooklyn Royal Giants

JOHNSON, JUDY—see Johnson, William J.

JOHNSON, JUNIOR; see George (Chappie) Johnson

JOHNSON, LEAMAN—1941-46—ss, inf., Memphis Red Sox, Newark Eagles, Birmingham Black Barons, New York Black Yankees

JOHNSON, LEE—1941—c, Birmingham Black Barons

JOHNSON, LEONARD—1947-48—p, Chicago American Giants, Kansas City Monarchs

JOHNSON, LEROY—1950-51—p, Birmingham Black Barons

JOHNSON, LOUIS BROWN (LOU, SLICK)—1955—of, Kansas City Monarchs

JOHNSON, LOUIS (DICTA)—1911-25—p, mgr., coach, Twin City Gophers, Chicago American Giants, Indianapolis ABCs, Detroit Stars, Toledo Tigers, Pittsburgh Keystones, Milwaukee Bears, Bowser's ABCs, Louisville White Sox

JOHNSON, M. (See B. (MONK) JOHNSON)

JOHNSON, MAMIE (PEANUT)—1954—p, Indianapolis Clowns

JOHNSON, (MONK) (See B. (MONK) JOHNSON)

JOHNSON, NATE—1922-24—p, Bacharach Giants, Cleveland Browns, Brooklyn Royal Giants, Harrisburg Giants

JOHNSON, OSCAR (HEAVY)—1922-33—of, c, 2b, Kansas City Monarchs, Baltimore Black Sox, Harrisburg Giants, Cleveland Tigers, Memphis Red Sox, Dayton Marcos

JOHNSON, OTHELLO—1916-22—p, of, Bacharach Giants, Brooklyn Royal Giants, Philadelphia Giants, Lincoln Giants, Penn Red Caps of NY

JOHNSON, OZIAH—1946—of, Boston Blues (USL)

JOHNSON, P.—1933—p, Memphis Red Sox

JOHNSON, (PEE WEE)—1939—2b, Newark Eagles

JOHNSON, PEARLEY (TUBBY, PETER)—1920-27, 1942—p, of, inf, Baltimore Black Sox, Boston Royal Giants

JOHNSON, RALPH—1940-41, 1945—p, Philadelphia Stars

JOHNSON, RALPH (R.B., ROB)—1950-52—ss, Indianapolis Clowns, Kansas City Monarchs

JOHNSON, (RAT)—1909—player, St. Paul Gophers

JOHNSON, RAY—1923—of, St. Louis Stars

JOHNSON, RICHARD—1887-90—c, of, Zanesville (Ohio State League, Tri-State League), Springfield and Peoria (Central Interstate League)

JOHNSON, ROBERT (BOB)—1928-37—3b, inf, of, Brooklyn Cuban Giants, Philadelphia Tigers, Brooklyn Royal Giants, Washington Pilots

JOHNSON, ROBERT—1939-40—of, New York Black Yankees

JOHNSON, ROBERT (BOB)—1944—p, Kansas City Monarchs

JOHNSON, ROY (BUBBLES)—1920-22—1b, 2b, St. Louis Giants, Kansas City Monarchs

JOHNSON, RUDOLPH (RUDY)—1950— of, Cleveland Buckeyes

JOHNSON, S. (See CECIL JOHNSON)

JOHNSON, TOM (TOMMY)—1937-42—p, St. Louis Stars, Chicago American Giants

JOHNSON, THOMAS (TOMMY)—1914-25—p, Indianapolis ABCs, Chicago American Giants, Pittsburgh Keystones, Mohawk Giants; umpire, NNL

JOHNSON, TOMMY F.—1950—p, Indianapolis Clowns

JOHNSON, U.—1905—3b, Brooklyn Royal Giants

JOHNSON, W.—1944-45—p, Memphis Red Sox

JOHNSON, W.,1925 (See WILLIAM H. JOHNSON)

JOHNSON, W.,1928 (See WADE JOHNSTON)

JOHNSON, WILLIAM H. (WISE, BILL, BIG C.)—1920-34—c, of, mgr., Homestead Grays, Hilldale, Philadelphia Tigers, Pennsylvania Red Caps of New York, Wilmington Potomacs, Harrisburg Giants, Washington Potomacs, Dayton Marcos

JOHNSON, WILLIAM JULIUS (JUDY)—1918-38—3b, ss, mgr., Hilldale, Homestead Grays, Darby Daisies, Pittsburgh Crawfords

JOHNSON, WILLIE—1945—c, Philadelphia Stars

JOHNSON, WILLIE JAMES—1952—p, Chicago American Giants

JOHNSTON, BERT (BUCKY) [JOHNSON]—1932-38—of, Newark Dodgers, Baltimore Black Sox, Birmingham Black Barons, Washington Pilots, Newark Eagles

JOHNSTON, C.—1916—2b, Lincoln Stars

JOHNSTON, TOM—1923—umpire, NNL

JOHNSTON, WADE [JOHNSON]—1920-33—of, p, Cleveland Tate Stars, Kansas City Monarchs, Baltimore Black Sox, Detroit Stars, Pennsylvania Red Caps of NY

JOHNSTONE,—1911-13—c, Pittsburgh Giants, Philadelphia Giants

JONES,—1920-21—ss, p, Indianapolis ABCs

JONES,—1921—p, Cuban Stars (East)

JONES, AARON—1954-55—p, Detroit Stars

JONES, ABE—1887-94—c, manager, Chicago Unions

JONES, ALBERT ALONZO—1944-46—p, Chicago American Giants, Memphis Red Sox

JONES, ALVIN—1928—officer, Harrisburg Giants

JONES, ARCHIE—1939-41—p, New York Cubans, Philadelphia Stars

JONES, ARTHUR BROWN (MUTT, DUMP)—1925, 1934—p, Birmingham Black Barons

JONES, B.—1934—c, of, Cleveland Red Sox

JONES, BAILEY—1951—c, New Orleans Eagles

JONES, BEN—1950—ss, New York Black Yankees

JONES, BENNY (HOGHEAD)—1932-35—of, c, inf, Newark
Dodgers, Cleveland Red Sox, Hilldale, Brooklyn Eagles,
Pittsburgh Crawfords

JONES, BERT—1896-1903—p, of, Chicago Unions, Atchison
(Kansas St. Lg.), Algona (IA) Brownies

JONES, CHARLES—1950—3b, Cleveland Buckeyes

JONES, CLINTON JR.(CASEY)—1940-55—c, Memphis Red Sox

JONES, COLLINS (COLLIS)—1943-45—utility, Cincinnati Clowns,
Birmingham Black Barons

JONES, (COUNTRY)—1932-33—2b, c, Brooklyn Royal Giants

JONES, CURTIS (BUD)—1946—p, Cleveland Buckeyes

JONES, D.—1884—player, Philadelphia Mutual B.B.C.

JONES, EDWARD—1915-29—c, Chicago American Giants,
Chicago Giants, Bacharach Giants, Bowser's ABCs,
Chicago Union Giants

JONES, ERNEST (MINT)—1934-42—1b, Jacksonville Red Caps,
Cleveland Bears, Philadelphia Stars, Boston Royal Giants

JONES, EUGENE—1943—p, Homestead Grays, Baltimore Elite
Giants

JONES, FATE—1950—of, Birmingham Black Barons

JONES, HANK—1955—of, Kansas City Monarchs

JONES, HURLEY—1931—p, Birmingham Black Barons

JONES, JAMES—1949-52—of, 1b, Philadelphia Stars

JONES, JOHN (EDWARD)—1951—p, New Orleans Eagles

JONES, JOHN (NIPPY)—1922-34—of, 1b, Detroit Stars, Indianapolis ABCs, Bacharach Giants, Washington Pilots,
Homestead Grays, Baltimore Black Sox

JONES, LEE—1908-22—of, Brooklyn Colored Giants, Brooklyn
Royal Giants, Dallas Giants

JONES, MARVIN—1954-55—p, Kansas City Monarchs

JONES, OLLIE—1919—3b, St. Louis Giants

JONES, PAUL—1949-50—p, Louisville Buckeyes, Cleveland
Buckeyes

JONES, REUBEN—1918-49—of, mgr., Dallas Giants, Birmingham
Black Barons, Indianapolis ABCs, Chicago American
Giants, Little Rock Black Travelers, Memphis Red Sox,
Houston Eagles, Cleveland Red Sox

JONES, ROBERT LEO (FOX)—1933-34—of, Memphis Red Sox

JONES, SAMUEL POND (RED, SAD SAM)—1946-48—p, Homestead Grays, Cleveland Buckeyes

JONES, STUART (SLIM, COUNTRY)—1932-38—p, Baltimore
Black Sox, Philadelphia Stars

JONES, TOM (PETE)—1946—c, Philadelphia Stars

JONES, W.—1910-16—p, of, Cuban Giants, West Baden (IN)
Sprudels, St.Louis Giants, Cuban X Giants

JONES, W.—1934—of, Birmingham Black Barons

JONES, WILLIAM (FOX)—1915-30—c, p, Chicago American
Giants, Chicago Giants, Bacharach Giants, Hilldale,
Chicago Union Giants

JONES, WILLIS (WILL)—1895-1911—ss, of, Chicago Unions,
Leland Giants, Chicago Union Giants, Algona (IA) Brownies

JORDAN, HENRY (HEN)—1921-25—c, of, Harrisburg Giants,
Pittsburg Stars of Buffalo, Baltimore Black Sox

JORDAN, LARNIE—1936-42—ss, Philadelphia Stars, New York
Black Yankees, Brooklyn Royal Giants, Bacharach Giants

JORDAN, MAYNARD—1950—of, Houston Eagles

JORDAN, ROBERT—1896-1907—c, 1b, Cuban Giants, Cuban X
Giants, Philadelphia Giants, Brooklyn Royal Giants

JORDAN WILLIAM F.—1899—mgr., Baltimore Giants

JORDAN, WILLIE—1933, 1938—p, Chicago American Giants,
Louisville Black Colonels

JOSEPH, WALTER LEE (NEWT)—1922-39—3b, 2b, mgr., Kansas
City Monarchs, Birmingham Black Barons, Satchel Paige's
All-Stars

JOSEPHS, WILLIAM—1924-25—ss, Birmingham Black Barons,
Cleveland Browns, Indianapolis ABCs

JOYNER, WILLIAM—1893-1902—ss, Chicago Unions, Chicago
Union Giants

JUANELO, see Juanelo Mirabel

JUILLO,—1940—p, New York Cubans

JUNCO(S), JOSE—1912-22—p, Cuban Stars, Cuban Stars (East)
Cuban Stars of Havana

JUPITER,—1887—p, Cuban Giants

JURAN, B. (JOHNNY)—1923—p, Birmingham Black Barons

JURAN, ELI—1923-1926—p, Birmingham Black Barons, Newark
Stars

JUSTICE, CHARLES P.(CHARLEY)—1933, 1937—p, Akron
Tyrites, Detroit Stars

K

KAISER, CECIL (MINUTE MAN)—1945-49—p, Pittsburgh
Crawfords, Homestead Grays

KEARNEY,—1932—p, Newark Browns

KEELER,—1931—of, Bacharach Giants

KEELEY,—1952—of, Memphis Red Sox

KEENE,—1915-16—3b, West Baden (IN) Sprudels, Bowser's
ABCs

KEENE, JOHNNY—1952—of, Chicago American Giants

KEETON, EUGENE—1921-26—p, Dayton Marcos, Cleveland Tate
Stars, Indianapolis ABCs

KECK, D.J.—1948—tres, Negro American Association

KEENAN, JAMES J.—1919-30—bus mgr., Lincoln Giants; sec-tres,
ECL

KEIGER,—1887—p, Louisville Falls City

KELLEY,—1900-08—ss, of, 3b, Genuine Cuban Giants, Famous
Cuban Giants, New York Colored Giants

KELLEY,—1932—p, Bacharach Giants

KELLEY, HOLLAND—1942—gen. sec., United States League

KELLEY, PALMER—1916-18—p, Chicago Giants, Chicago Union
Giants

KELLEY, RICHARD A.(CHARLES)—1889-91—1b, 2b, ss, Danville
(Illinois- Indiana League); Jamestown (Pennsylvania-New
York League)

KELLMAN, EDRIC (LEON)—1946-53—3b, Cleveland Buckeyes,
Louisville Buckeyes, Memphis Red Sox, Indianapolis
Clowns

KELLY,—1941-42—p, Jacksonville Red Caps

KELLY, (LEFTY) (See KELLY SEARCY)

KELLY, WALTER—1950-53—p, Cleveland Buckeyes, Memphis
Red Sox, Birmingham Black Barons

KELLY, WILLIAM—1898—3b, Celeron Acme Colored Giants
(Iron and Oil League)

KELLY, WILLIAM—1944-47—c, New York Black Yankees,
Homestead Grays

KEMP,—1943—c, New York Black Yankees

KEMP, ED (DUCKY)—1914-28—of, Philadelphia Royal Giants,
Norfolk Stars, Norfolk Giants, Baltimore Black Sox, Lincoln
Giants

KEMP, GEORGE—1917—of, Hilldale

KEMP, JAMES ALLEN (GABBY)—1937-39—2b, Atlanta Black
Crackers, Jacksonville Red Caps, Indianapolis ABCs

KEMP, JOHN—1923-28—of, Memphis Red Sox, Birmingham
Black Barons

KENDALL,—1920, 1925—2b, Lincoln Giants

KENDRICKS, L.H.(WILLIE)—1943—p, Atlanta Black Crackers

KENNARD, DAN—1914-25—c, Indianapolis ABCs, Chicago
American Giants, St. Louis Giants, Lincoln Giants, St. Louis
Stars, Detroit Stars, Bowser's ABCs, West Baden (IN)
Sprudels

KENNEDY,—1916—of, All Nations

KENNEDY,—1926—ss, Lincoln Giants

KENNEDY, ERNEST D.—1950—inf., Memphis Red Sox
KENNEDY, JIM—1951—1b, Birmingham Black Barons
KENNEDY, JOHN IRVIN—1954-55—3b, Birmingham Black
　　Barons
KENNEDY, NED—1954—p, Kansas City Monarchs
KENNEDY, ROBERT—1946—p, Boston Blues
KENNEDY, WALTER—1950—of, Chicago American Giants
KENNER,—1921—ss, 2b, Hilldale
KENT, RICHARD B.—1922-31—officer, St. Louis Stars
KENWOOD,—1927—p, Hilldale
KENYON, HARRY C.—1919-29—p, 2b, of, mgr., Brooklyn Royal
　　Giants, Hilldale, Indianapolis ABCs, Chicago American
　　Giants, Lincoln Giants, Detroit Stars, Kansas City Mon-
　　archs, Memphis Red Sox
KERNER, J.—1931-33—of, Columbus Blue Birds, Detroit Stars,
　　Indianapolis ABCs
KETCHUM,—1954—of, Kansas City Monarchs
KEY, LUDIE—1934—pres, Birmingham Black Barons
KEYES, GARVIN—1943—inf, Philadelphia Stars
KEYES, ROBERT—1941-46—p, Memphis Red Sox, Cleveland
　　Buckeyes
KEYES, STEVE (YOUNGIE, ZEKE, KHORA)—1940-48—p,
　　Memphis Red Sox, Philadelphia Stars, Indianapolis
　　Crawfords, Cincinnati Clowns, Cleveland Buckeyes
KEYS,—1950—p, Houston Eagles
KEYS, DR. GEORGE B.—1922-32—officer, St. Louis Stars; officer,
　　NNL
KIMBRO, ARTHUR (JESS, TED)—1914-18—3b, 2b, Bowser's
　　ABCs, St. Louis Giants, Lincoln Giants, Louisville Sox, West
　　Baden (IN) Sprudels, Hilldale
KIMBRO, HENRY ALLEN (KIMMIE, JUMBO)—1937-53—of, mgr.,
　　Washington Elite Giants, Baltimore Elite Giants, New York
　　Black Yankees Birmingham Black Barons, Philadelphia
　　Stars
KIMBRO, HOWARD (HOWDY)—1928-32, 1945—p, Pittsburgh
　　Crawfords
KIMBROUGH, JIM—1945-48—p, Philadelphia Stars, Homestead
　　Grays
KIMBROUGH, LARRY NATHANIEL (SCHOOLBOY)—1942-46—p,
　　Philadelphia Stars
KIN,—1931—c, Cuban Stars (East)
KINARD, ROOSEVELT—1932—3b, Washington Pilots
KINCAIDE, C.J.—1945-47—officer, NSL
KINCANNON, HARRY (TIN CAN) [TINCANER]—1929-39—p,
　　Pittsburgh Crawfords, Philadelphia Stars, New York Black
　　Yankees, Washington Black Senators, Toledo Crawfords
KINDLE, WILLIAM (BILL)—1911-20—ss, 2b, of, Brooklyn Royal
　　Giants, Indianapolis ABCs, Chicago American Giants,
　　Lincoln Stars, Lincoln Giants, Brooklyn All-Stars, New York
　　Stars, West Baden (IN) Sprudels, Cuban Giants
KING, BRENDAN L.—1943—p, Cincinnati Clowns
KING, CLARENCE EARL (CHARLEY, PIJO)—1947-54—of,
　　Birmingham Black Barons
KING, EZELL—1955—1b, Detroit Stars
KING, LEE (BABY)—1923—officer, Birmingham Black Barons
KING, LEONARD—1921—of, Kansas City Monarchs
KING, PARIS—1955—c, Memphis Red Sox
KING, WILBUR (DOLLY)—1944-47—ss, 2b Memphis Red Sox,
　　Cleveland Buckeyes, Chicago American Giants, Homestead
　　Grays, New York Black Yankees
KING, WILLIAM—1890-92—ss, Chicago Unions
KINKEIDE, JOHN—1887—player, Louisville Falls City
KINSON,—1937—p, New York Black Yankees
KIRBY,—1928—p, Cleveland Tigers
KIRKSEY,—1926—c, Dayton Marcos
KITCHEN, M.—1951—of, Philadelphia Stars
KLEPP, EDDIE—1946—p, Cleveland Buckeyes

KLONDYKE,—1914—c, Chicago American Giants
KNIGHT, DAVE (MULE)—1921-22, 1930—1b, of, p, Detroit Stars,
　　Baltimore Black Sox, Chicago American Giants
KNOX, ELWOOD C.—1920—co-drafter of constitution, NNL
KOBEK, GEORGE—1927—of, Chicago American Giants
KOGER, GENE—1954—utl., Indianapolis Clowns
KOOP,—1922—player, Bacharach Giants
KRAMER,—1916—3b, All Nations
KRANSON, FLOYD ARTHUR [KRANSTON]—1935-41—p, Kansas
　　City Monarchs, Memphis Red Sox, Chicago American
　　Giants
KRIDER, J. MONROE [KREITER]—1890—mgr., Cuban Giants,
　　Colored Monarchs of York (PA) (Eastern Interstate
　　League)
KYLE, ANDY—1922—of, p, Baltimore Black Sox, Bacharach
　　Giants

L

LACKEY, OBIE EZEKIEL [OBIE]—1927-43—ss, 2b, 3b, Philadel-
　　phia Giants, Hilldale, Bacharach Giants, Pittsburgh
　　Crawfords, Homestead Grays, Baltimore Black Sox,
　　Philadelphia Stars, Brooklyn Royal Giants, New York Black
　　Yankees, Santop's Broncos
LACY, RAYMOND—1949-50—of, Houston Eagles
LADUNA, PHILOMENO (PHIL)—1954-55—p, Indianapolis Clowns
LAFLORA, LOUIS—1925—of, Kansas City Monarchs
LAIN, WILLIAM—1911—3b, ss, Chicago Giants, Chicago
　　American Giants
LAIR,—1925—of, Pennsylvania Red Caps of New York
LAMAR, CLARENCE (LEMON)—1937-42—ss, 2b, St. Louis Stars,
　　Cleveland Bears, Jacksonville Red Caps, Indianapolis
　　ABCs, Birmingham Black Barons
LAMAR, E.B., JR.—1895-1926—mgr., club officer, booker, Cuban
　　X Giants, Cuban Stars, Bacharach Giants, Harrisburg
　　Giants, Brooklyn Cuban Giants
LaMARQUE, JAMES H.(JIM, LEFTY)—1942-51—p, Kansas City
　　Monarchs
LAMBERT,—1932—ss, Bacharach Giants
LAMBERTO,—1929—of, Cuban Stars (ECL)
LAMONT,—1932—of, Nashville Elite Giants
LAND, [LANG]—1908-22—of, 1b, New York Colored Giants,
　　Cuban Giants, Smart Set, Mohawk Giants, Brooklyn Royal
　　Giants
LANDERS, JOHN—1917—p, Indianapolis ABCs
LANDERS, ROBERT HENRY—1949-52—p, Kansas City Monarchs
LANE, ALTO (BIG TRAIN)—1929-34—p, Memphis Red Sox,
　　Indianapolis ABCs, Cincinnati Tigers, Louisville White Sox,
　　Kansas City Monarchs, Louisville Black Caps
LANE, ISAAC S.—1917-24—of, 3b, p, Dayton Giants, Dayton
　　Marcos, Columbus Buckeyes, Detroit Stars
LANG, JOHN F.—1885-86—mgr., Argyle Hotel, Cuban Giants
LANGFORD, (AD)—1912-20—p, of, St. Louis Giants, Lincoln
　　Stars, Brooklyn Royal Giants, Pennsylvania Red Caps of
　　New York, Lincoln Giants, Mohawk Giants
LANGRAM,—1939—2b, of, Kansas City Monarchs
LANGRUM, DR. E.L.—1934—officer, Cleveland Red Sox
LANIER, A.S.—1921—officer, Cuban Stars (NNL)
LANSING, WILBUR—1948-49—p, Newark Eagles, Houston Eagles
LANTIQUA, ENRIQUE—1935—c, New York Cubans
LANUZA, PEDRO—1931-32—c, Cuban Stars, House of David
　　Cubans
LARRINAGO, PEREZ—1946—2b, ss, Cleveland Buckeyes
LATIMER,—1921—p, Indianapolis ABCs
LATTIMORE, ALPHONSO—1929-33—c, Baltimore Black Sox,
　　Brooklyn Royal Giants, Columbus Blue Birds
LAU,—1927—p, Cubans (ECL)

Buck Leonard, Ray Brown, and Josh Gibson.
Jeff Eastland

LAURENT, MILFRED STEPHEN (MILT, RICK)—1922-35—3b, 1b, of, 2b, c, Memphis Red Sox, Cleveland Cubs, Birmingham Black Barons, Nashville Elite Giants, New Orleans Crescent Stars

LAVERA,—1919—c, Cuban Stars

LAWSON, L.B. (FLASH, CHICK)—1934, 1940—p, Washington Pilots, Philadelphia Stars

LAWYER, FLOYD—1913—rf, Mohawk Giants

LAYTON, CLIFF—1954—p, Indianapolis Clowns

LAYTON, OBIE—1931—p, Hilldale, Bacharach Giants

LAZAGA, AGIPITO—1916-22—of, p, Cuban Stars (NNL), New York Cuban Stars, Cuban Stars (East)

LEACH,—1914—c, Indianapolis ABCs

LEAK, CURTIS, A.—1940-48—officer, New York Black Yankees; sec, NNL

LEARY,—1920-25—3b, Dayton Marcos, Penn Red Caps of NY

LEAVELLE, HARRY—1908-12—c, 1b, Genuine Cuban Giants, Cuban Giants, Cuban Stars

LeBEAUX,—1936—ss, 2b, Chicago American Giants

LeBLANC,—1915—ss, Lincoln Giants

LeBLANC, JULIO (JOSE)—1919-21—p, of, Cuban Stars (NNL), Cincinnati Cubans

LEE,—1906—2b, Cuban X Giants

LEE, DICK—1917-18—of, Chicago Union Giants

LEE, ED—1911, 1916—ss, Chicago Giants, Chicago Union Giants

LEE, FRED—1908, 1915—of, Kansas City (KAN) Giants

LEE, HOLSEY SCRANTON SCRIPTUS(SCRIP)—1920-43—p, of, 1b, Norfolk Stars, Philadelphia Stars, Hilldale, Norfolk Giants, Richmond Giants, Baltimore Black Sox, Bacharach Giants, Cleveland Red Sox, Philadelphia Giants; umpire, NNL

LEE, LOWN—1909—p, Kansas City Royal Giants

LEE, WILLIAM—1888—ss, Chicago Unions

LEE, WILLIE—1955—p, of, Kansas City Monarchs

LEFTWICH, JOHN (HYMIE)—1945—p, Homestead Grays

LEGROVE,—1937—of, Indianapolis Athletics

LELAND, FRANK C.—1887-1912—of, mgr., Washington Capital Citys, Chicago Union Giants, Leland Giants, Chicago Giants

LEMON, (See CLARENCE LAMAR)

LENOX,—1943—1b, New York Black Yankees

LEON,—1917-18—of, p, c, Cuban Stars (East)

LEON, ISIDORE—1948—of, New York Cubans

LEONARD, JAMES (BOBO)—1919-36—p, of, 1b, Cleveland Tate Stars, Cleveland Browns, Cleveland Tigers, Cleveland Hornets, Toledo Tigers, Chicago American Giants, Bacharach Giants, Lincoln Giants, Baltimore Black Sox, Homestead Grays, Pennsylvania Red Caps of New York, Brooklyn Royal Giants, Indianapolis ABCs

LEONARD, WALTER FENNER (BUCK)—1933-50—1b, of, Brooklyn Royal Giants, Homestead Grays

LeRUE,—1921—c, Detroit Stars

LESTER,—1932—p, Nashville Elite Giants

LETT, ROGER—1943—p, Cincinnati Clowns

LETTLERS, GEORGE—1887—player, Washington Capital Citys

LEUSCHNER, W.A. (BILL)—1940-43—booking agent; officer, New York Black Yankees

LEVINS,—1924—p, Bacharach Giants

LEVIS, OSCAR [OSCAL]—1921-34—p, Cuban Stars (East), Hilldale, Darby Daisies, Baltimore Black Sox, All Cubans

LEVITT,—1939—1b, Homestead Grays

LEWIS,—1887—player, Boston Resolutes

LEWIS,—1890—c, Lincoln (NEB) Giants

LEWIS,—1935—ss, Brooklyn Eagles

LEWIS, A.D.—1937-38—1b, Birmingham Black Barons, Louisville Black Colonels

LEWIS, BERNARD—1943—p, Atlanta Black Crackers

LEWIS, CARY B.—1920—co-drafter, constitution of NNL; sec, NNL

LEWIS, CHARLES (BABE)—1925-26—ss, Lincoln Giants, Philadelphia Giants

LEWIS, CLARENCE (FOOTS)—1931-37—ss, Memphis Red Sox, Cleveland Red Sox, Nashville Elite Giants, Pittsburgh Crawfords, Akron Tyrites, Cleveland Giants

LEWIS, EARL—1923—p, Indianapolis ABCs

LEWIS, F.—1932—of, Montgomery Grey Sox

LEWIS, GEORGE (PEACHES)—1917-22—p, Lincoln Giants, Bacharach Giants

LEWIS, GROVER—1928—3b, Homestead Grays

LEWIS, HENRY N.—1943-45—mgr, officer, owner, Atlanta Black Crackers, Knoxville Black Smokies

LEWIS, IRA F.—1922—sec, Pittsburgh Keystones

LEWIS, JAMES—1953—p, Memphis Red Sox

LEWIS, JEROME—1910-13—1b, West Baden (IN) Sprudels

LEWIS, JIM (SLIM)—1943, 1947—p, Chicago Brown Bombers, New York Black Yankees

LEWIS, JIM—1953—2b, Indianapolis Clowns

LEWIS, JOSEPH HERMAN (SLEEPY)—1919-36, 1946—c, 3b, mgr., Baltimore Black Sox, Washington Potomacs, Homestead Grays, Hilldale, Lincoln Giants, Quaker Giants, Darby Daisies, Bacharach Giants, Norfolk-Newport News Royals, Brooklyn Royal Giants

LEWIS, MILTON—1922-28—2b, 1b, utl., Wilmington Potomacs, Bacharach Giants, Richmond Giants, Harrisburg Giants, Philadelphia Giants

LEWIS, ROBERT S. (BUBBLES, BUBBER)—1923-28—officer, Memphis Red Sox; vice pres, NNL

LEWIS, RUFUS (LEW)—1936-50—p, Pittsburgh Crawfords, Newark Eagles, Houston Eagles

LEWIS, (TUCK)—1916—2b, Chicago Giants

LIGGONS, JAMES—1932-34—p, of, Monroe Monarchs, Memphis Red Sox, Little Rock Black Travelers

LIGHTNER, [LINDER]—1920-23, 1932—p, Kansas City Monarchs, Cole's American Giants

LIGON, RUFUS C.—1944-46—p, Memphis Red Sox

LILLARD, JOE—1932-37, 1944—p, of, c, Cole's American Giants, Chicago American Giants, Cincinnati Tigers, Birmingham Black Barons

LILLIE,—1925—utility, Birmingham Black Barons

LINARES, ABEL—1911-21—owner, pres., All Cubans, Cuban Stars, Cincinnati Cubans

LINARES, ROGELIO (ICE CREAM)—1940-46—1b, of, Cuban Stars, New York Cubans

LINCOLN, JAMES—1890-95—ss, 3b, Lincoln (NEB) Giants, Adrian (MI) Page Fence Giants,

LINDSAY, BILL (THE KANSAS CYCLONE)—1908-14—p, Kansas City (Kan) Giants, Leland Giants, Chicago American Giants

LINDSAY, CHARLES CLARENCE-1920-35—ss, Richmond Giants, Bacharach Giants, Baltimore Black Sox, Wilmington Potomacs, Penn Red Caps of New York, Lincoln Giants, Philadelphia Giants, Washington Pilots

LINDSAY, JAMES—1943—inf, Birmingham Black Barons

LINDSAY, LEONARD (YAHOODI)—1942-46—1b, p, 3b, Cincinnati Clowns, Birmingham Black Barons, Indianapolis Clowns

LINDSAY, MERF—1910—of, Kansas City (Kan) Giants

LINDSAY, P.—1910—1b, of, Kansas City (Kan) Giants

LINDSAY, ROBERT (FROG)—1908-17—ss, Kansas City, (Kan.), Giants, Kansas City Colored Giants

LINDSEY,—1912-14—of, Lincoln Giants, West Baden (IN) Sprudels

LINDSEY, BEN—1929—ss, Bacharach Giants

LINDSEY, BILL—1924-26—ss, 2b, of, Washington Potomacs, Lincoln Giants, Dayton Marcos

LINDSEY, JAMES—1887—of, Pittsburgh Keystones

LINDSEY, ROBERT—1931—p, of, 1b, Indianapolis ABCs

LINTON, BENJAMIN—1945—officer, Detroit Giants

LIPSEY, HENRY—1942—p, Memphis Red Sox

LISBY, MAURICE C.—1934—p, Newark Dodgers, Bacharach Giants

LISTACH, NORA [LISTASH]—1940-41—of, Birmingham Black Barons, Cincinnati Buckeyes

LITTLE, WILLIAM—1937-50—officer, Chicago American Giants

LITTLES, BEN—1947-51—of, Homestead Grays, New York Black Yankees, Philadelphia Stars

LIVINGSTON, CURTIS—1950—of, Cleveland Buckeyes

LIVINGSTON, L.D. (LEE, GOO GOO)-1928-33—of, Kansas City Monarchs, New York Black Yankees, Pittsburgh Crawfords, Pennsylvania Red Caps of NY

LLOYD, JOHN HENRY (POP)—1905-32—ss, 1b, 2b, c, mgr., Macon Acmes, Cuban X Giants, Philadelphia Giants, Leland Giants, Lincoln Giants, Chicago American Giants, Brooklyn Royal Giants, Columbus Buckeyes, Bacharach Giants, Hilldale, New York Black Yankees, Lincoln Stars, Kansas City Monarchs

LOATMAN,—1932—2b, Bacharach Giants

LOCKE, CLARENCE VIRGIL (DAD)—1945-48—p, 1b, Chicago American Giants

LOCKE, EDDIE—1943-51—p, 3b, Cincinnati Clowns, Kansas City Monarchs, New York Black Yankees, Chicago American Giants

LOCKETT, LESTER (BUCK)—1937-50—2b, 3b, of, Chicago American Giants, Birmingham Black Barons, Cincinnati-

Indianapolis Clowns, Baltimore Elite Giants, Memphis Red Sox, St.Louis Stars, Cincinnati Buckeyes, Philadelphia Stars

LOCKETT, MONROE—1938—p, Indianapolis ABCs

LOCKETT, WILLIE—1938—of, Indianapolis ABCs

LOCKHART,—1942—player, Jacksonville Red Caps

LOCKHART, A.J.—1924-26—p, 3b, Wilmington Potomacs, Philadelphia Giants

LOCKHART, G.HUBERT (JOE)—1923-29—p, Bacharach Giants, Chicago American Giants, Wilmington Potomacs

LOFTIN, LOUIS SANTOP—see Santop, Louis

LOGAN, CARL—1934, 1940—inf, Bacharach Giants, Philadelphia Stars

LOGAN, FRED—1950—of, New York Black Yankees

LOGAN, NICK—1920-25—p, Baltimore Black Sox

LOLLA,—1911—of, Indianapolis ABCs

LONDO, JULIUS—1909—player, St. Paul Gophers

LONG,—1920-26—of, Detroit Stars, Indianapolis ABCs

LONG, (BUCK)—1950—c, Memphis Red Sox

LONG, CARL—1952-53—of, Birmingham Black Barons, Philadelphia Stars

LONG, EARNEST SYLVESTER (THE KID)—1948-50—p, Cleveland Buckeyes, Louisville Buckeyes

LONG, EMORY (BANG)—1932-40, 1945—3b, of, Atlanta Black Crackers, Chicago American Giants, Indianapolis Athletics, Philadelphia Stars, Kansas City Monarchs, Washington Black Senators

LONG, TOM—1926—c, Kansas City Monarchs

LONGEST, BERNELL (CHICK)—1942-47—2b, 3b, Chicago Brown Bombers, Chicago American Giants

LONGEST, CHARLES—1954—of, Detroit Stars

LONGEST, JIMMY—1942—1b, Chicago Brown Bombers

LONGLEY, WAYMAN (RED, RAY)—1932-51—2b, of, ss, c, 1b, 3b, Memphis Red Sox, Chicago American Giants, Little Rock Black Travelers, New Orleans Eagles, Washington Elite Giants

LONGWARE,—1920—2b, 3b, of, Detroit Stars

LOONEY, CHARLIE—1933, 1938—2b, Akron Tyrites, Louisville Black Colonels

LOPEZ, CANDO—1920-38—of, 3b, Cuban Stars (NNL), New York Cubans, Cuban Stars (East)

LOPEZ, JUSTO—1939—1b, Cuban Stars

LOPEZ, PEDRO—1938-39—of, Cuban Stars

LOPEZ, RAUL—1948-50—p, New York Cubans

LOPEZ, VIDAL—1923-39—p, Cuban Stars (ECL), Cuban Stars (NNL)

LORENZO, JESUS—1928-30—p, Cuban Stars (NNL)

LOTT, BENJAMIN (BENNY, HONEY)—1949-51-2b, 3b, Indianapolis Clowns, New York Black Yankees

LOTT, RAYMOND (RAY)—1950—of, Philadelphia Stars

LOUDEN, LOUIS OLIVER (TOMMY, LOU)—1942-50—c, New York Cubans Birmingham Black Barons

LOUGARY,—1943—player, New York Cubans

LOVE, WILLIAM ANDY—1930-31, 1945—c, of, Detroit Stars, Memphis Red Sox, Toledo Cubs (USL)

LOVING, J.G.—1887—player, Washington Capital Citys

LOWE, WILLIAM M.—1921-33—3b, ss, 2b, of, mgr., Indianapolis ABCs, Detroit Stars, Memphis Red Sox, Chattanooga Black Lookouts, Nashville Elite Giants

LOWELL,—1924—p, Bacharach Giants

LUCAS, MILES (PEPE)—1919-27—p, of, Cuban Stars of Havana, Cuban Stars (East), New Orleans Crescent Stars, Harrisburg Giants

LUCAS, (SCOTTY)—1928—officer, Philadelphia Tigers

LUGA, ORLANDO—1954—inf, Indianapolis Clowns

LUGO, LEVINGELO (LEO)—1943-46—of, Cincinnati-Indianapolis Clowns, Indianapolis Clowns

LUMPKINS, (LEFTY)—1931-32—p, Newark Browns

LUNDY, RICHARD (DICK, KING RICHARD)—1916-48—ss, 3b, 2b, mgr., Bacharach Giants, Lincoln Giants, Hilldale, Baltimore Black Sox, Philadelphia Stars, Newark Dodgers, New York Cubans, Newark Eagles, Jacksonville Eagles, Brooklyn Royal Giants, Havana Red Sox

LUQUE, ADOLFO (DOLF)—1912-13—p, of, Cuban Stars, Long Branch (NJ) Cubans

LUTHER, (See LUTHER FARRELL)

LYDA,—1932—p, Coles American Giants

LYLES,—1916—p, All Nations

LYLES, JOHN—1932-43—of, ss, 2b, 3b, c, Homestead Grays, Indianapolis ABCs, Cleveland Bears, St. Louis Stars, Chicago American Giants, Cincinnati Buckeyes, Cleveland Buckeyes, Indianapolis Clowns, New Orleans-St. Louis Stars

LYNCH, THOMAS—1914-19—of, 3b, 2b, Indianapolis ABCs, Dayton Marcos, West Baden (IN) Sprudels

LYNN,—1917—p, Jewell's ABCs

LYNN,—1943—p, Homestead Grays

LYONS,—1950—p, Cleveland Buckeyes

LYONS, BENNIE—1911-18—1b, of, c, Jewell's ABCs, Dayton Marcos, Bowser's ABCs, Indianapolis ABCs

LYONS, CHASE—1899-1905—p, Genuine Cuban Giants, Cuban Giants

LYONS, GRANVILLE—1931-42—1b, p, Nashville Elite Giants, Louisville Black Caps, Detroit Stars, Louisville Red Caps, Philadelphia Stars, Memphis Red Sox, Baltimore Elite Giants

LYONS, JAMES (JIMMIE)—1910-32—of, mgr., Lincoln Giants, St. Louis Giants, Chicago Giants, Brooklyn Royal Giants, Indianapolis ABCs, Chicago American Giants, Detroit Stars, Cleveland Browns, Louisville Black Caps, Washington Potomacs, Bowser's ABCs

LYTLE,—1954—p, Detroit Stars

LYTLE, CLARENCE—1901-06—p, Chicago Union Giants, Leland Giants

M

MABEN, BENNIE—1952—inf, Memphis Red Sox

MACK, JOHN H.—1945—p, Kansas City Monarchs

MACK, PAUL—1916-17—of, 3b, Bacharach Giants, Jersey City Colored Giants

MACK, ROBERT—1945—p, New York Black Yankees

MACKEY, RALEIGH (BIZ)—1918-47—c, ss, 3b, mgr., San Antonio Giants, Indianapolis ABCs, Hilldale, Darby Daisies, Philadelphia Stars, Washington Elite Giants, Baltimore Elite Giants, Newark Eagles, Newark Dodgers, Nashville Elite Giants

MACKLIN,—1924-29—3b, of, Chicago Giants

MADDIX, RAYDELL (RAY, BO)—1949-53—p, Indianapolis Clowns

MADDOX, ARTHUR—1935-36—p, Cincinnati Tigers

MADDOX, (ONE WING)—1923—p, of, Birmingham Black Barons

MADERT,—1917—2b, Chicago Giants

MADISON,—1903—ss, Philadelphia Giants

MADISON, ROBERT—1935-42—p, of, 3b, Kansas City Monarchs, Memphis Red Sox, Indianapolis Athletics, Birmingham Black Barons

MAGRINAT, HECTOR (KAKO)—1906-16—of, Cuban Stars, All Cubans, Cuban Stars of Havana

MAHONEY, TONY—1920-23—p, Norfolk Giants, Indianapolis ABCs, Baltimore Black Sox, Brooklyn Royal Giants, Norfolk Stars

MAHONEY, ULYSSES—1944—p, Philadelphia Stars

MAIDEN,—1932—c, Bacharach Giants

MAINOR, HANK—1950-51—p, Baltimore Elite Giants, Philadelphia Stars

"Gentleman" Dave Malarcher.
Negro Leagues Baseball Museum

MAJORS,—1916—p, Chicago Union Giants

MAKELL, WILLIAM FRANK—1944-49—c, Newark Eagles, Baltimore Elite Giants, Philadelphia Stars

MALARCHER, DAVID JULIUS (CAP, GENTLEMAN DAVE)—1916-34—3b, of, 2b, mgr., Indianapolis ABCs, Detroit Stars, Chicago American Giants, Cole's American Giants, Chicago Columbia Giants

MALLOY, [MALLORY]—1918-21—of, Pennsylvania Red Caps of New York, Nashville Elite Giants

MALONE, WILLIAM H.—1886-97—p, 1b, 3b, of, Cuban Giants, Pittsburgh Keystones, New York Gorhams (Middle States Lg.), Page Fence Giants, York Cuban Giants (Eastern Interstate Lg.), Trenton Cuban Giants (Middle States Lg.), Philadelphia Pythians, York Colored Monarchs

MANELLA, (See MANOLO)

MANESE, E.—1923-26—2b, Detroit Stars, Kansas City Monarchs, Indianapolis ABCs

MANGRUM,—1948—of, New York Cubans

MANLEY, ABRAHAM (ABE)—1935-46—officer, Brooklyn Eagles, Newark Eagles; vice pres, tres, NNL

MANLEY, EFFA (MRS. ABRAHAM)—1935-48—officer, Brooklyn Eagles, Newark Eagles, sec; NNL

MANN,—1918—1b, Chicago Union Giants

MANNING,—1931-32—1b, Montgomery Grey Sox

MANNING, JOHN—1902-04—of, Philadelphia Giants

MANNING, MAXWELL (MAX, DR. CYCLOPS)—1938-49—p, Newark Eagles, Houston Eagles

MANOLO, [MANELLA, MANNO]—1916-24—1b, p, Cuban Stars (East), New York Cuban Stars, Cincinnati Cubans, All

Cubans

MANUEL, (CLOWN)—1938-40—of, Louisville Black Colonels, Cleveland Bears

MAPP, DICK—1942—ss, Boston Royal Giants

MARA, CANDIDO—1948—3b, Memphis Red Sox

MARAVALE,—1923—p, Cuban Stars (ECL)

MARCELL, EVERETT (SAM, ZIGGY, JOE)—1939-48—c, Chicago American Giants, Newark Eagles, Baltimore Elite Giants, New York Black Yankees, Kansas City Monarchs, Homestead Grays

MARCELLE, OLIVER H. (GHOST) [MARCEL, MARCELL]—1918-32—3b, ss, Brooklyn Royal Giants, Bacharach Giants, Lincoln Giants, Detroit Stars, Baltimore Black Sox

MARCELLO,—1921—p, Cincinnati Cubans, All Cubans

MARINE, W.C.—officer, secretary, New Orleans Crescent Stars, NSL

MARKHAM, JOHN MATTHEW [MARCUM]—1930-45—p, Kansas City Monarchs, Monroe Monarchs, Birmingham Black Barons

MARKHAM, MELVIN—1935-36—p, Brooklyn Eagles, Newark Eagles

MARLOTICA,—1911—rf, All Cubans

MAROTO, ENRIQUE (RICKY)—1954-55—of, p, Kansas City Monarchs

MARQUEZ, LUIS ANGEL CANENA—1945-48—ss, 2b, 3b, of, New York Black Yankees, Homestead Grays, Baltimore Elite Giants

MARSANS, ARMANDO—1905, 1923—of, All Cubans, Cuban Stars

MARSELLAS, DAVID, JR.—1941—c, New York Black Yankees

MARSH,—1932—of, Nashville Elite Giants

MARSH, LORENZO—1950—c, Cleveland Buckeyes

MARSHALL,—1934—c, Bacharach Giants

MARSHALL, HIRAM—1946—p, 3b, Boston Blues

MARSHALL, JACK—1920-29—p, Chicago American Giants, Detroit Stars, Kansas City Monarchs, Birmingham Black Barons

MARSHALL, ROBERT W.(BOBBY)—1909-11—1b, mgr., St. Paul Gophers, Leland Giants, Twin City Gophers, Chicago Giants

MARSHALL, WILLIAM JAMES (JACK, BOISY)-1926-44—2b, 3b, 1b, Dayton Marcos, Gilkerson's Union Giants, Chicago Columbia Giants, Cole's American Giants, Chicago American Giants, Philadelphia Stars, Cincinnati-Indianapolis Clowns, Kansas City Monarchs

MARTIN,—1902—p, Philadelphia Giants

MARTIN,—1912—of, Indianapolis ABCs

MARTIN,—1913—p, Chicago Giants

MARTIN, ALEXANDER—1932—officer, Cleveland Cubs

MARTIN, DR. A.T.—1923-50—officer, Memphis Red Sox

MARTIN, DR. B.B.—1933-50—officer, Memphis Red Sox; officer, NSL

MARTIN, DR. JOHN B.—1929-50—officer, Memphis Red Sox, Chicago American Giants; pres, Negro Dixie League, NSL, NAL

MARTIN, DR. WILLIAM S.—1927-50—officer, Memphis Red Sox; pres, NSL, officer, NAL

MARTIN, ED—1951-52—p, Philadelphia Stars

MARTIN, JIM (PEPPER, BEANY)—1935—inf, Brooklyn Eagles

MARTIN, R.—1885—p, Argyle Hotel

MARTIN, WILLIAM (STACK)—1925-28—of, 1b, c, Indianapolis ABCs, Detroit Stars, Dayton Marcos, Wilmington Potomacs

MARTINEZ, C.—1928—c, Cubans (NNL)

MARTINEZ, FRANCISCO—1939—p, Cuban Stars

MARTINEZ, HORACIO (RABBIT)—1935-47—ss, 3b, New York Cubans

MARTINEZ, PASQUEL—1920-28—p, Cuban Stars (NNL), All Cubans

MARTINI, JOSE—1928, 1935—p, Cubans (NNL), New York Cubans

MARVAREZ, FERNANDO—1945—inf, Pittsburgh Crawfords

MARVIN, ALFRED—1938—p, Kansas City Monarchs

MARVRAY, CHARLES—1949-50—of, Louisville Buckeyes, Cleveland Buckeyes

MASON,—1927—3b, inf., Baltimore Black Sox

MASON, CHARLES (CORPORAL, SUITCASE)—1922-29—of, p, Richmond Giants, Bacharach Giants, Lincoln Giants, Newark Stars, Homestead Grays

MASON, HENRY (HANK, PISTOL)—1951-54—p, Kansas City Monarchs

MASON, JAMES—1887—p, Pittsburgh Keystones

MASON, JIM—1931-34—1b, of, Cuban Stars (West), Cubans (NNL), Memphis Red Sox, Washington Pilots

MASON, MARCELIUS—1939-40—officer, Cleveland Bears

MASON, WILLIAM—1946—utl., Cleveland Clippers (USL)

MASSEY,—1930—of, Louisville White Sox

MASSINGALE,—1945—of, Kansas City Monarchs

MASSIP, ARMANDO—1920-36—1b, of, Cuban Stars (ECL), Washington Pilots, Memphis Red Sox, Cuban Stars (East), New York Cubans

MATCHETT, CLARENCE (JACK)—1940-45—p, Kansas City Monarchs

MATHEW,—1946—of, Memphis Red Sox

MATHIS, VERDELL SR. (LEFTY)—1940-50—p, of, 1b, Memphis Red Sox, Philadelphia Stars

MATLOCK, LEROY—1929-42—p, St. Louis Stars, Detroit Wolves, Washington Pilots, Homestead Grays, Pittsburgh Crawfords, New York Cubans

MATTHEWS,—1914-16—2b, Baltimore Black Sox, Cuban Giants

MATTHEWS, CLIFFORD—1945—officer, owner, New Orleans Black Pelicans

MATTHEWS, DELL—1904-05—p, of, Chicago Union Giants, Leland Giants

MATTHEWS, DICK—1932-33—p, Monroe Monarchs, New Orleans Crescent Stars

Max Manning.
Max Manning

Horacio "Rabbit" Martinez.
Luis Munoz Collection

MATTHEWS, FRANCIS OLIVER (FRAN, MATTY)—1938-45—1b, Newark Eagles, Boston Royal Giants, Baltimore Elite Giants, New York Cubans

MATTHEWS, GEORGE—1887—player, Cincinnati Browns

MATTHEWS, JACK—1923—3b, Toledo Tigers

MATTHEWS, JESSE—1942—inf., Birmingham Black Barons

MATTHEWS, JOHN T.(BIG)—1919-33—owner, officer, Dayton Marcos

MATTHEWS, WILLIAM CLARENCE—1905-10—ss, 2b, Burlington (Vermont League); New York Black Sox

MAUPINS, FRANK—1890-92—c, 3b, Lincoln (NEB) Giants, Plattsmouth (Nebraska St. Lg.)

MAXWELL,—1914—of, Chicago American Giants

MAXWELL, ZEARLEE (JIGGS)—1931-38—3b, 2b, Monroe Monarchs, Memphis Red Sox

MAYARI, see Estaban Montalvo

MAYERS, GEORGE (See GEORGE MEYERS)

MAYFIELD, FRED—1887—player, Louisville Falls City

MAYO,—1906—p, Cuban X Giants

MAYO, GEORGE (HOT STUFF)—1911-17, 1928—1b, of, officer, Pittsburgh Giants, Pittsburgh Colored Stars, Hilldale, Pittsburgh Stars of Buffalo

MAYS,—1937-38—p, St. Louis Stars, Memphis Red Sox

MAYS, DAVE—1937—of, Kansas City Monarchs

MAYS, WILLIE HOWARD (BUCK)—1948-50—of, Birmingham Black Barons

MAYWEATHER, ELDRIDGE (CHILLIE, ED)—1934-46—1b, Monroe Monarchs, Kansas City Monarchs, St. Louis Stars, New Orleans-St. Louis Stars, New York Black Yankees, Boston Blues, Brooklyn Eagles

MAYWEATHER, ELLIOTT—1928-29—p, Memphis Red Sox

MAYWOOD,—1917-19—p, Lincoln Giants

MAZAAR, ROBERT—1945—officer, Hilldale Club of Philadelphia

McADOO, DUDLEY (TULLY)—1907-27—1b, Topeka Giants, Kansas City (Kan) Giants, St. Louis Giants, St. Louis Stars, Cleveland Browns, Chicago American Giants, Chicago Giants, Chicago Union Giants

McAFEE,—1930—2b, Louisville White Sox

McALLISTER, FRANK (CHIP, BUD)—1938-46—p, Indianapolis ABCs, St. Louis Stars, New Orleans-St. Louis Stars, New York Black Yankees, Harrisburg-St. Louis Stars, Brooklyn Brown Dodgers, Cleveland Clippers (USL)

McALLISTER, GEORGE—1923-34—1b, Birmingham Black Barons, Chicago American Giants, Indianapolis ABCs, Memphis Red Sox, Homestead Grays, Cleveland Red Sox, Detroit Stars, Cuban Stars (West)

McALLISTER, MIKE—1921—of, Kansas City Monarchs

McBRIDE, FRED—1931-40—1b, of, Indianapolis ABCs, Chicago American Giants, Birmingham Black Barons

McCABB,—1923—p, St. Louis Stars

McCALL, (BUTCH)—1936-38—1b, Chicago American Giants, Birmingham Black Barons, Indianapolis Athletics

McCALL, HENRY—1945—of, Chicago American Giants

McCALL, WILLIAM L. (BILL)—1922-31—p, Pittsburgh Keystones, Birmingham Black Barons, Kansas City Monarchs,

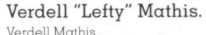

Verdell "Lefty" Mathis.
Verdell Mathis

Chicago American Giants, Indianapolis ABCs, Detroit Stars, Toledo Tigers, Cleveland Tigers, Cleveland Tate Stars

McCAMPBELL, ERNEST—1915—player, Kansas City (KAN) Giants

McCAMPBELL, TOM—1915—player, Kansas City (KAN) Giants

McCAREY, WILLIE—1943-45—p, Cleveland Buckeyes

McCARTHY, C.H.—1921—pres, SouthEastern Negro League

McCAULEY,—1930—p, Nashville Elite Giants

McCAULEY, BEN—1953—of, Kansas City Monarchs

McCLAIN, EDWARD (BOOTS) [McLAIN]—1920-33—inf p, Dayton Marcos, Cleveland Tate Stars, Toledo Tigers, Cleveland Browns, Detroit Stars, Indianapolis ABCs, Columbus Buckeyes, Columbus Blue Birds

McCLAREN,—1945—p, Philadelphia Stars

McCLINNIC, NATHANIEL (NAT)—1946-48—of, Cleveland Buckeyes

McCLELLAN, DAN—1902-31—p, mgr., Cuban X Giants, Philadelphia Giants, Smart Set, Lincoln Giants, Quaker Giants, Washington Potomacs, Wilmington Potomacs, Brooklyn Royal Giants

McCLELLAND, DR. J.W.—1922—officer, St. Louis Stars

McCLURE, ROBERT (BOB)—1920-30—p, Indianapolis ABCs, Cleveland Tate Stars, Baltimore Black Sox, Bacharach Giants, Brooklyn Royal Giants, Toledo Tigers

McCLURE, WILL—1947—officer, Chattanooga Choo Choos

McCOLLUM, FRANK—1954-55—p, Louisville Black Colonels, Birmingham Black Barons

Dan McClellan in 1907.
Dick Clark

McCORD, CLINTON HILL JR. (BUTCH)—1947-50—inf, 1b, Baltimore Elite Giants, Chicago American Giants

McCOY, FRANK (CHINK)—1931-43—c, Newark Browns, Newark Dodgers, Harrisburg-St.Louis Stars, Bacharach Giants

McCOY, ROY—1932—officer, Washington Pilots

McCOY, WALTER—1945-48—p, Chicago American Giants

McCRARY. GEORGE—1943—p, New York Black Yankees

McCRAY, WILLIAM—1954—p, Louisville Black Colonels

McCREARY, FRED—1938-49—umpire, NNL

McCREE, EARL—1952—p, Kansas City Monarchs

McCUNE,—1913—3b, Chicago Giants

McCURINE, JAMES (BIG JIM)—1946-49—of, Chicago American Giants

McDANIELS, BOOKER TALIAFERRO (CANNONBALL)—1940-52—p, of, Kansas City Monarchs, Memphis Red Sox

McDANIELS, FRED—1940-51—of, Memphis Red Sox, Kansas City Monarchs, New Orleans Eagles, Houston Eagles

McDEVITT, JOHN J.—1922—officer, Baltimore Black Sox

McDONALD, EARL—1938—officer, Washington Black Senators

McDONALD, G.—1910-17—p, of, Philadelphia Giants, Bacharach Giants, Lincoln Giants

McDONALD, LUTHER (VET, OLD SOUL)—1927-37—p, St. Louis Stars, Chicago American Giants, Chicago Columbia Giants, Cole's American Giants, Detroit Stars, Memphis Red Sox

McDONALD, WEBSTER (MAC)—1918-45—p, mgr., Philadelphia Giants, Richmond Giants, Chicago American Giants, Hilldale, Darby Daisies, Washington Pilots, Philadelphia Stars, Wilmington Potomacs, Detroit Stars, Homestead Grays, Lincoln Giants, Norfolk Stars, Baltimore Black Sox

McDONNELL,—1921—p, Bacharach Giants

McDOUGAL, JAMES (JOHN)—1952—of, Chicago American Giants

McDOUGAL, LEMUEL (LEM)—1917-20—p, Chicago American Giants, Indianapolis ABCs, Chicago Giants

McDUFFIE, TERRIS (THE GREAT)—1930-45—p, of Birmingham Black Barons, Baltimore Black Sox, New York Black Yankees, Newark Eagles, Homestead Grays, Philadelphia Stars, Newark Dodgers, Brooklyn Eagles, Pennsylvania Red Caps, Bacharach Giants, Hilldale, Cuban Stars (West)

McFALL,—1940—of, Cincinnati Buckeyes

McFARLAND, JOHN—1944-47—p, New York Black Yankees

McGEE, HORACE—1887—manager, Cincinnati Browns

McGOWAN, CURTIS—1950—p, Memphis Red Sox

McGOWAN, MALCOLM—1923-41—owner, officer, Bacharach Giants

McHASKELL, J.C.—1926-29—1b, Memphis Red Sox

McHENRY, HENRY (CREAM)—1930-50—p, Kansas City Monarchs, New York Black Yankees, Philadelphia Stars, Indianapolis Clowns, Pennsylvania Red Caps, Newark Browns, Bacharach Giants

McINTOSH, JIMMY—1937—c, Detroit Stars

McINTYRE, B.—1924—p, Memphis Red Sox

McKAMEY,—1946—ss, Kansas City Monarchs

McKEG,—1897—ss, Cuban Giants

McKELVIN, FRED [McKELLAM]—1942-p, Cincinnati- Cleveland Buckeyes, Jacksonville Red Caps

McKENZIE, HERBERT—1950—c, New York Black Yankees

McKINLEY,—1940—p, Chicago American Giants

McKINNIS, GREADY (LEFTY)—1941-49—p, Birmingham Black Barons, Chicago American Giants, Pittsburgh Crawfords

McLAIN, (See EDWARD McCLAIN)

McLAIN, BILL [McClAIN]—1933—p, Columbus Blue Birds

McLAUGHLIN,—1914-1919—p, 1b, of, Jewell's ABCs, Lincoln Giants, Louisville White Sox

McLAURIN, FELIX—1942-52—of, Jacksonville Red Caps, Birmingham Black Barons, New York Black Yankees, Chicago American Giants

Terris "The Great" McDuffie.
Moorland-Spingarn Library

McLAWN,—1948—c, Newark Eagles
McMAHON, JESS—1911-16—officer, owner, Lincoln Giants
McMAHON, ROD—1911-14—officer, Lincoln Giants
McMEANS, WILLIE—1945—p, Chicago American Giants
McMILLAN, EARL—1923—of, Toledo Tigers
McMULLIN, CLARENCE [McCULLIN]—1945-49—of, Kansas City
    Monarchs, Houston Eagles
McMURRAY, WILLIAM—1909-14—c, St. Paul Gophers, St. Louis
    Giants West Baden (IN) Sprudels
McNAIR, HURLEY ALLEN (BUGGER)—1911-46—of, p, Chicago
    Giants, Gilkerson's Union Giants, Chicago American
    Giants, Detroit Stars, Chicago Union Giants, Kansas City
    Monarchs, Cincinnati Tigers, All Nations; umpire, NAL
McNEAL, CLYDE (JUNIOR)—1945-50—ss, Chicago American
    Giants
McNEAL, RUFUS (ZIPPY)—1953-55—p, of, Indianapolis Clowns
McNEALY,—1946—of, Birmingham Black Barons
McNEIL,—1916—ss, Lincoln Giants
McNEIL,—1918-21—1b, c, Dayton Marcos, Columbus Buckeyes
McNEIL,—1930—of, Baltimore Black Sox
McNEIL, WILLIAM (RED)—1930-33—of, p, Louisville White Sox,
    Louisville Black Caps, Nashville Elite Giants, Louisville Red
    Caps
McQUEEN, PETE—1932-45—of, Memphis Red Sox, New York
    Black Yankees, Little Rock Grays, Pittsburgh Crawfords
McREE, JOE—1955—p, Detroit Stars
McREYNOLDS,—1916—of, p, Bowser's ABCs, Indianapolis ABCs

MEADE, FRED (CHICK)—1914-22-3b, ss, of, Pittsburgh Colored
    Stars, Hilldale, Pittsburgh Stars of Buffalo, Bacharach
    Giants, Baltimore Black Sox, Harrisburg Giants, Indianapo-
    lis ABCs, Brooklyn All-Stars, New York Stars, Cuban Giants,
    Philadelphia Giants
MEADOWS, HELBURN—1934-35—of, Cincinnati Tigers
MEADOWS, HILBURN—1952—of, Philadelphia Stars
MEAGHER,—1932—of, Washington Pilots
MEANS, LEWIS—1920-28—2b, 1b, c, Bacharach Giants,
    Birmingham Black Barons
MEANS, THOMAS—1900-04—p, Chicago Unions, Chicago Union
    Giants
MECKLING, S.—1909—c, Kansas City Royal Giants
MEDEROS, JESUS (FRANK)—1910-20—p, of, All Cubans,
    Bacharach Giants, Cuban Stars
MEDINA, LAZARUS (LAZARO)[CHAPMAN]—1944-46—p,
    Cincinnati-Indianapolis Clowns, Indianapolis Clowns
MEDINA, PEDRO—1905-07—c, p, Cuban Stars of Santiago,
    Cuban Stars
MEDLEY, CALVIN—1946—p, New York Black Yankees
MELLITO, (See EMILIO NAVARRO)
MELLIX, RALPH B.(GEORGE, LEFTY)—1922-34, 1943-46—p,
    mgr., Homestead Grays, Newark Browns, Brooklyn Brown
    Dodgers, Pittsburgh Crawfords, Newark Dodgers
MELLO, HARRY—1946—inf, Chicago American Giants
MELTON,—1916—p, St. Louis Giants
MELTON, ELBERT (BABE)—1928-29, 1936—of, Brooklyn Cuban
    Giants, Lincoln Giants, Baltimore Black Sox, Brooklyn
    Royal Giants
MENDEZ, JOSE De La CARIDAD (JOE, THE BLACK DIAMOND)—
    1908-26—p, ss, 3b, 2b, mgr., Cuban Stars, Stars of Cuba, All
    Nations, Los Angeles White Sox, Chicago American Giants,
    Detroit Stars, Kansas City Monarchs
MENDIETA, INOCENTE—1912-13—2b, Cuban Stars, Long
    Branch (NJ) Cubans
MERCHANT, HENRY L. (FRANK, SPEED)—1940-54—p, of,
    Chicago American Giants, Cincinnati-Indianapolis Clowns,
    Indianapolis Clowns
MEREDITH, BUFORD (GEETCHIE)—1923-31—ss, 2b, Birming-
    ham Black Barons, Nashville Elite Giants, Memphis Red
    Sox
MEREDITH, (ZEKE)—1954—of, Memphis Red Sox
MERRICK, ZEKE—1953-54—of, Memphis Red Sox
MERRIL,—1921—of, Bacharach Giants
MERRITT, SCHUTE—1934-35—utility, Newark Dodgers
MERRITT, WILLIAM (BILL)—1905-17—p, of, Brooklyn Royal
    Giants, Lincoln Giants
MESA, ANDRES ANARES—1948—of, Indianapolis Clowns
MESA, PABLO—1921-27—of, Cuban Stars (ECL), All Cubans
METZ,—1939—player, Kansas City Monarchs
MEXIO,—1925—p, Cuban Stars (NNL)
MEYERS, GEORGE (DEACON)[MYERS, MAYERS]—1921-26—p,
    1b, St. Louis Stars, Dayton Marcos, St. Louis Giants, Toledo
    Tigers
MEYERS, L.—1908—2b, Brooklyn Colored Giants
MIARKA, STANLEY V.—1950—2b, p, Chicago American Giants
MICHAELS,—1954—p, Birmingham Black Barons
MICKEY, JAMES—1940—ss, 3b, Chicago American Giants,
    Birmingham Black Barons
MICKEY, JOHN—1898—p, Celeron Acme Colored Giants (Iron
    and Oil League)
MILES, JACK (SONNY BOY)—1934-39—of, 3b, Chicago American
    Giants,
MILES, JOHN JR.(MULE)—1946-49—of, Chicago American
    Giants
MILES, JONAS—1940—p, Cincinnati Buckeyes

MILES, TOM (CHERRY)—1934, 1946—p, 1b, of, Philadelphia
    Stars, Chicago American Giants, Cleveland Clippers (USL)
MILES, WILLIE—1923-27—of, 1b, 3b, Toledo Tigers, Memphis
    Red Sox Cleveland Tate Stars, Cleveland Browns,
    Cleveland Elites, Cleveland Hornets, Homestead Grays
MILES, ZELL—1951—of, Chicago American Giants
MILHOUSE,—1932—of, Pittsburgh Crawfords
MILLER,—1911-20—c, of, Pittsburgh Giants, Dayton Marcos
MILLER, A.—1927-28—of, Memphis Red Sox, Birmingham Black
    Barons
MILLER, C.B.(RUBY BOB)—1923-28—2b, 3b, Memphis Red Sox,
    Birmingham Black Barons
MILLER, CHARLIE—1932-37—inf, p, Nashville Elite Giants, New
    Orleans Crescent Stars, Louisville Black Caps, Cincinnati
    Tigers, St.Louis Stars
MILLER, DEMPSEY (DIMP)—1926-45—p, mgr., Cleveland
    Hornets, Cleveland Tigers, Nashville Elite Giants, Detroit
    Stars, Detroit Giants, Cleveland Cubs, Birmingham Black
    Barons, Memphis Red Sox, Kansas City Monarchs, Newark
    Browns, Cleveland Elites
MILLER, EDDIE (BUCK)—1924-31—p, ss, 3b, Chicago American
    Giants, Indianapolis ABCs, Homestead Grays, Chicago
    Columbia Giants
MILLER, EUGENE—1909—of, St. Paul Gophers
MILLER, FRANK—1887-97—p, of, Pittsburgh Keystones, Cuban
    Giants, Cuban X Giants, New York Gorhams (Middle States
    Lg.), Philadelphia Giants, Trenton (NJ) Cuban Giants
MILLER, HENRY JOSEPH (HANK)—1938-49—p, Philadelphia
    Stars, Newark Eagles
MILLER, JASPER—1930-40—p, Memphis Red Sox, New Orleans
    Crescent Stars, St. Louis Stars
MILLER, JOSEPH (JOE, KID)—1890-03—p, of, Lincoln (NEB)
    Giants, Adrian (MI) Page Fence Giants, Columbia Giants,
    Adrian (Michigan State Lg), Chicago Union Giants
MILLER, L.—1912-23—3b, 2b, Smart Set, Lincoln Giants, Lincoln
    Stars, Brooklyn Royal Giants, Bacharach Giants, Baltimore
    Black Sox
MILLER, LEROY (FLASH)—1935-43—ss, 2b, Newark Dodgers,
    New York Black Yankees
MILLER, NED—1937—1b, Indianapolis Athletics
MILLER, OTTO—1951—inf, Indianapolis Clowns
MILLER, PERCY—1921-34—p, of, St. Louis Stars, St. Louis
    Giants, Nashville Elite Giants, Chicago Giants, Kansas City
    Monarchs Detroit Stars
MILLER, PLEAS (HUB)—1912-16—p, of, West Baden, (Ind)
    Sprudels, St. Louis Giants
MILLER, RAY—1954—1b, Detroit Stars
MILLER, W.—1940-42—p, Chicago American Giants
MILLINER, EUGENE J.(GABBIE)—1903-10—of, Chicago Union
    Giants, St. Paul Gophers, Kansas City Royal Giants,
    Brooklyn Royal Giants
MILLON, HERALD—1946-47—utility, Chicago American Giants
MILLS, CHARLES A.—1909-24—officer, St. Louis Giants, St. Louis
    Black Sox
MILTON, C.—1933-34—inf, Cleveland Red Sox, Columbus Blue
    Birds
MILTON, EDWARD—1926-28—of, 2b, Cleveland Elites, Cleveland
    Tigers
MILTON, HENRY—1932-43—of, Chicago Giants, Indianapolis
    ABCs, Chicago American Giants, Brooklyn Royal Giants,
    Kansas City Monarchs, New York Black Yankees, Brooklyn
    Eagles
MIMES, JOE—1955—p, Detroit Stars
MIMMS,—1932—p, Columbus Turfs
MINCEY,—1939-40—p, Philadelphia Stars, Newark Eagles
MINOR, GEORGE—1944-49—of, Chicago American Giants,
    Cleveland Buckeyes, Louisville Buckeyes

MINOSO, SATURNINO ORESTES ARRIETA ARMAS (MINNIE)—
    1945-48—3b, New York Cubans
MIRABEL, JUANELO,—1922-34, 1949-50—p, president, Cuban
    Stars (ECL) New York Cubans
MIRABLE, AUTORIO—1939-40—c, New York Cuban Stars
MIRAKA, STANLEY, (See STANLEY MIARKA)
MIRALL,—1930—3b, Brooklyn Royal Giants
MIRANDA, P.—1916—player, Cuban Stars
MIRO, PEDRO—1945-48—2b, New York Cubans
MISSOURI, JIM—1937-41—p, Philadelphia Stars
MITCHELL,—1901—c, Chicago Union Giants
MITCHELL,—1914—p, Pittsburgh Giants
MITCHELL, A.—1884—player, Philadelphia Mutual B.B.C.
MITCHELL, ALONZO (FLUKE, HOOKS)—1921-41—mgr.,1b, p,
    club officer, Jacksonville Red Caps, Cleveland Bears,
    Atlanta Black Crackers, Jacksonville Red Caps, Indianapo-
    lis ABCs, Baltimore Black Sox, Bacharach Giants, Harris-
    burg Giants, Birmingham Black Barons, Akron Tyrites
MITCHELL, ARTHUR HAROLD—1939—inf, New York Black
    Yankees
MITCHELL, (BUD)—1926-34—of, p, c, Hilldale, Darby Daisies,
    Bacharach Giants, Washington Pilots, Newark Stars,
    Baltimore Black Sox, Philadelphia Stars
MITCHELL, CHARLIE—1942—c, Boston Royal Giants
MITCHELL, GEORGE—1924-49—p, mgr., bus mgr., Chicago
    American Giants, Indianapolis ABCs, Montgomery Grey
    Sox, Cleveland Cubs, Mounds City, Illinois, Blues (became
    Indianapolis ABCs), St. Louis Stars, New Orleans-St. Louis
    Stars, New York Black Yankees, Harrisburg-St. Louis Stars,
    Houston Eagles, Cleveland Stars, Detroit Stars, Kansas City
    Monarchs
MITCHELL, JESSIE—1954-55—of, Birmingham Black Barons
MITCHELL, JOE—1951—p, Chicago American Giants
MITCHELL, JOHN—1932—c, of, Montgomery Grey Sox
MITCHELL, LEONARD OTTO—1930-38—2b, bus mgr., Birming-
    ham Black Barons, Louisville White Sox, Louisville Black
    Colonels
MITCHELL, ROBERT—1923-24—c, of, St. Louis Stars, Birming-
    ham Black Barons
MITCHELL, ROBERT L.(BOB, PEACHHEAD, MOONBEAM)—1950-
    55—p, Cleveland Buckeyes, Kansas City Monarchs
MOBLEY, AL (JOHNNY)—1953—of, Birmingham Black Barons
MOBLEY, IRA (DICK)—1954—ss, 2b, of, Kansas City Monarchs
MOLES, (LEFTY)—1935—p, Philadelphia Stars
MOLINA,—1929-30—p, Cuban Stars (NNL)
MOLINA, AGUSTIN (TINTI)—1906-31—1b, of, c, mgr., officer,
    Cuban Stars, Cuban Stars (NNL), Cuban Giants, Cincinnati
    Cubans
MOLLETT,—1913-16—2b, ss, Mohawk Giants, Lincoln Stars
MOLLOY,—1922—p, Bacharach Giants
MONCEVILLE, [MONCHILLE]—1930-32—of, 3b, Cuban Stars
    (East & West), Quaker Giants, Newark Browns
MONGIN, SAM—1907-22—3b, 2b, Brooklyn Royal Giants,
    Lincoln Stars, Lincoln Giants, Bacharach Giants, St. Louis
    Giants, Philadelphia Giants, Chicago GiantsMONROE, AL—
    1937—sec, NAL
MONROE, BILL—1920, 1927—3b, ss, Pittsburgh Stars of Buffalo
    Baltimore Black Sox
MONROE, WILLIAM (BILL, DIAMOND BILL)—1896-1914—2b, 3b,
    Chicago Unions, Philadelphia Giants, Brooklyn Royal
    Giants, Chicago American Giants, Cuban X Giants, Chicago
    Giants
MONTALVO, ESTABAN y MAYARI—1923-28—1b, of, Cuban
    Stars (NNL), Lincoln Giants, Cuban Stars (ECL)
MONTGOMERY, A.G.—1926—sec, NSL
MONTGOMERY, GRADY—1952—inf, Chicago American Giants
MONTGOMERY, JOE—1954-55—of, Detroit Stars

MONTGOMERY, LOU—1942—p, of, inf, Cincinnati Clowns

MOODY,—1931—ss, Memphis Red Sox

MOODY, FRANK—1940—p, Birmingham Black Barons

MOODY, LEE—1944-47—1b, Kansas City Monarchs, Birmingham Black Barons

MOODY, WILLIS—1921-29—of, Pittsburgh Keystones, Homestead Grays

MOORE,—1932—3b, Bacharach Giants

MOORE, CHARLES—1943—umpire, NNL

MOORE, CLARENCE LEE (C.L., COOL BREEZE, DAGO)—1945-48—mgr., officer, owner, Asheville Blues; pres. Negro American Association

MOORE, EXCELL—1950-52—p, Cleveland Buckeyes, New Orleans Eagles Indianapolis Clowns

MOORE, HARRY W.(MIKE)-1894-1913—of, 1b, 3b, Chicago Unions, Algona (IA) Brownies, Cuban X Giants, Philadelphia Giants, Leland Giants, Chicago Giants, Lincoln Giants, Chicago Union Giants

MOORE, HENRY L.—1937-38—officer, St. Louis Stars, Birmingham Black Barons

MOORE, JACK—1939—of, Cleveland Bears

MOORE, JAMES ROBERT (RED)—1936-40—1b, Newark Eagles, Atlanta Black Crackers, Baltimore Elite Giants, Indianapolis ABCs

MOORE, JOHN—1929—ss, Birmingham Black Barons

MOORE, JOHNNY—1928-30—1b, Pittsburgh Crawfords

MOORE, L.—1910-20—of, St. Louis Giants, Bowser's ABCs, West Baden (IN) Sprudels, Lincoln Giants, Louisville Sox, Indianapolis ABCs

MOORE, N.—1920-24—of, Detroit Stars

MOORE, P.D.—1932—c, Monroe Monarchs

MOORE, RALPH (SQUIRE, ROY, SQUARE)—1920-28—p, 1b, Memphis Red Sox, Kansas City Monarchs, Cleveland Hornets, Cleveland Tigers, Cleveland Tate Stars, Birmingham Black Barons, Chicago American Giants, Cleveland Elites

MOORE, SHIRLEY—1914-16—p, Bowser's ABCs, Louisville White Sox

MOORE, WALTER (DOBIE, THE BLACK CAT)—1920-26—ss, of, Kansas City Monarchs

MORALES, ISMAEL—1932—of, Cuban Stars

MORAN, FRANCISCO—1911-14—of, 3b, Cuban Stars, All Cubans

MOREFIELD, FRED (MUSCLES)—1945-46—of, Pittsburgh Crawfords

MOREHEAD, ALBERT [MOORHEAD]—1925, 1932, 1943—c, Chicago Giants, Cleveland Cubs, Birmingham Black Barons, Chicago Brown Bombers

MORELAND, NATE—1940-45—p, Baltimore Elite Giants, Kansas City Monarchs

MORGAN,—1928—of, Birmingham Black Barons

MORGAN, CONNIE—1954—inf, Indianapolis Clowns

MORGAN, JOHN.L.(PEPPER)—1937—of, Memphis Red Sox, Indianapolis Athletics

MORGAN, WILLIAM (WILD BILL, SACK)—1945-49—p, Memphis Red Sox, Baltimore Elite Giants, Birmingham Black Barons

MORIN, EUGENIO—1910-23—2b, 3b, c, Cuban Stars, Cuban Stars (NNL), Cincinnati Cubans

MORNEY, LEROY—1931-44—ss, 3b, 2b, Monroe Monarchs, Columbus Blue Birds, Cleveland Giants, Pittsburgh Crawfords, Columbus Elite Giants, Washington Elite Giants, New York Black Yankees, Philadelphia Stars, Chicago American Giants, Birmingham Black Barons, Cincinnati Clowns, Toledo Crawfords, Homestead Grays, Nashville Elite Giants

MORRIS,—1911-14—2b, Indianapolis ABCs, Mohawk Giants

MORRIS, AL—1927-30—of, 2b, Nashville Elite Giants, Louisville White Sox

MORRIS, BARNEY (BIG AD)—1932-48—p, Monroe Monarchs, Pittsburgh Crawfords, New York Cubans, Toledo Crawfords, Newark Eagles, New Orleans Crescent Stars

MORRIS, F.B.—1948—sec, Negro American Association

MORRIS, HAROLD (YELLOWHORSE)—1924-36—p, Kansas City Monarchs, Detroit Stars, Chicago American Giants, Monroe Monarchs

MORRISON, JIMMY—1930—utility, Memphis Red Sox

MORRISON, ROY—1934—p, Bacharach Giants

MORRISON, W.—1925—1b, Cleveland Browns

MORTIN, R.—1885—p, Argyle Giants

MORTON,—1917—2b, Havana Red Sox

MORTON, FERDINAND Q.—1935-38—commissioner, NNL

MORTON, JOHN—1935-37—of, Brooklyn Eagles, Pittsburgh Crawfords

MORTON, SIDNEY DOUGLAS (SY)—1940-47—ss, 2b, Philadelphia Stars, Pittsburgh Crawfords, Chicago American Giants, Newark Eagles

MOSELEY, BEAUREGARD F.—1910-11—officer, Leland Giants

MOSES, C.—1938-40—p, Kansas City Monarchs

MOSES, JOE—1955—c, Birmingham Black Barons

MOSLEY, C.D. (GATEWOOD)—1934-38—p, New Orleans Crescent Stars, Homestead Grays, Kansas City Monarchs

MOSLEY. LOU—1932—p, Bacharach Giants, Cuban Stars (West)

MOSLEY, WILLIAM—1928-33—officer, Detroit Stars

MOSS, PORTER (ANKLE BALL)—1934-44—p, Cincinnati Tigers, Memphis Red Sox

MOTEN,—1937—c, Cincinnati Tigers

MOTHELL, CARROLL RAY (DINK)—1918-34—of, 2b, 1b, ss, c, All Nations, Kansas City Monarchs, Cleveland Stars, Chicago American Giants, Topeka Giants

MOTT,—1931—3b, Birmingham Black Barons

MULLEN, A.—1925—28-of, Kansas City Monarchs, Birmingham Black Barons

MUNGIN, J.—1925-27—p, Baltimore Black Sox, Harrisburg Giants

MUNOZ, JOSEITO (JOE)—1904-16—p, of, Cuban Stars, Stars of Cuba, Jersey City Cubans, Long Branch Cubans, All Cubans, Cuban X Giants

MUNROE, ELMER—1942—p, Boston Royal Giants

MUNROE, WILLIAM, see William Monroe

MURDOCK,—1924—p, Indianapolis ABCs

MURPHY,—1908-11—cf, Brooklyn Colored Giants, Brooklyn Royal Giants, Philadelphia Giants

MURPHY,—1915—of, Chicago American Giants

MURPHY,—1916—p, Lincoln Stars, Philadelphia Giants

MURPHY,—1922—p, Kansas City Monarchs

MURPHY, AL—1936-37—p, Indianapolis Athletics, Birmingham Black Barons, Cincinnati Tigers

MURRAY,—1932—p, Monroe Monarchs

MURRAY,—1952—c, Kansas City Monarchs

MURRAY, CHARLES—1949-50—player, Louisville Buckeyes, Cleveland Buckeyes

MURRAY, CLAY—1934—p, Bacharach Giants

MURRAY, MITCHELL—1919-32—c, Indianapolis ABCs, Dayton Marcos, Cleveland Tate Stars, Toledo Tigers, St. Louis Stars, Chicago American Giants, Columbus Buckeyes

MURRYALL, JOHNNY—1952—p, Indianapolis Clowns

MUSE, E.E.—1922, 1933-34—p, New Orleans Crescent Stars, Hilldale, Monroe Monarchs

MYERS, (LEFTY)—1908-10—ss, c, Pop Watkins Stars, Brooklyn Royal Giants

N

NANCE,—1929—ss, Chicago American Giants

NAPIER, EUTHUMN (EUDIE)—1935-50—c, Homestead Grays, Pittsburgh Crawfords, Bacharach Giants

NAPOLEON, LAWRENCE (LARRY, LEFTY)—1946-47—p, Kansas City Monarchs

NARANJO, PEDRO—1950-54—p, Indianapolis Clowns, Kansas City Monarchs, Detroit Stars

NASH, WILLIAM—1928-34—p, of, Birmingham Black Barons, Memphis Red Sox, Nashville Elite Giants

NAVARRETTE, RAMUNDO—1950—p, New York Cubans

NAVARRO, EMILIO (MILLITO)—1928-29—inf, Cuban Stars (East)

NAVARRO, RAYMOND RAUL—1945-46—of, inf, c, Cincinnati-Indianapolis Clowns, Indianapolis Clowns

NEAL, CHARLES LENARD (CHARLIE)—1955—inf, Atlanta Black Crackers

NEAL, GEORGE—1910-11—2b, Chicago Giants, Kansas City Kan. Giants

NEAL, WILLIE—1952—inf, Memphis Red Sox

NEARS, (RED)—1940—c, of, Memphis Red Sox

NEBON,—1902—ss, Philadelphia Giants

NEELY,—1932-33—p, Louisville Black Caps, Cuban Stars

NEHF,—1926—of, Cleveland Elites

NEIL, RAY (AUSSA)—1942-54—2b, utl., Cincinnati Clowns, Indianapolis Clowns

NELSON, CLYDE—1939, 1943-49—3b, 2b, 1b, of, Chicago Brown Bombers, Chicago American Giants, Cleveland Buckeyes, Indianapolis Clowns, Indianapolis ABCs

NELSON, EVERETT (ACE)—1922, 1931-33—p, Montgomery Grey Sox, Detroit Stars

NELSON, JOHN—1887-1903—p, of, New York Gorhams, Cuban Giants, Cuban X Giants, Philadelphia Giants, Philadelphia Gorhams, (Middle States Lg.) Ansonia Cuban Giants (Connecticut St. Lg.), Trenton Cuban Giants (Middle States Lgg.), Adrian Page Fence Giants

NESBIT, DR. E.E.—1929—officer, Memphis Red Sox

NESTOR, S. JACE—1926—of, Lincoln Giants

NEVELLE, GUS—1930—p, Pittsburgh Crawfords

NEWBERRY, HENRY—1947—p, Chicago American Giants

NEWBERRY, JAMES LEE (JIMMIE)—1943-50—p, Birmingham Black Barons

NEWBERRY, RICHARD—1947—ss, Chicago American Giants

NEWCOMBE, DONALD (DON, BIG NEWK)—1944-45—p, Newark Eagles

NEWKIRK, ALEXANDER (ALEX, SLATS)—1946-49—p, New York Black Yankees, New York Cubans, Boston Blues (USL)

NEWMAN,—1890—c, Lincoln (NEB) Giants

NEWMAN,—1909—p, Leland Giants

NEWMAN,—1940—p, Memphis Red Sox

NEWSOME, OMER-1923-29—p, Indianapolis ABCs, Washington Potomacs, Detroit Stars, Dayton Marcos, Memphis Red Sox, Wilmington Potomacs

NEWSON,—1940—of, Newark Eagles

NICHOLAS, WILLIAM (BILL)—1935-36—p, Newark Eagles

NICHOLS, CHARLES—1885—of, Argyle Hotel

NIMIN, [MIMIN]—1931—1b, Cuban Stars (West)

NIMMONS, ERNIE—1952—of, Indianapolis Clowns

NIRSA,—1923—of, Cuban Stars (NNL)

NIX, NATHANIEL (TANK)—1938-39—p, Brooklyn Royal Giants, Bacharach Giants

NIXON, BILL—1940-41—of, Birmingham Black Barons, Jacksonville Red Sox

NOBLE, CARLOS—1950—p, New York Cubans

NOBLE, JUAN (JOHN, GYP)—1949-50—p, New York Cubans

NOBLE, RAFAEL MIGUEL (RAY, SAM)—1945-50—c, New York Cubans

NOEL, EDDIE—1920—p, Nashville Giants

NOLAN,—1916-20—c, 1b, St. Louis Giants, Kansas City Colored Giants, Kansas City Monarchs

NORMAN,—1914—3b, Louisville White Sox

NORMAN, ALTON (ED)—1920-26—ss, Lincoln Giants, Cleveland Elites Cleveland Tate Stars

NORMAN, (BUD, ACE)—1940—p, Indianapolis Crawfords

NORMAN, GARRETT—1923-24, 1933—of, Memphis Red Sox, Kansas City Monarchs

NORMAN, JIM—1907-10—inf, mgr., Kansas City, (Kan) Giants, Kansas City (MO) Royal Giants

NORMAN, WILLIAM (SHIN), See Arthur Hardy

John "Buck" O'Neil.
Buck O'Neil

NORRIS, (SLIM)—1930—3b, Louisville White Sox
NORWOOD, C.H.—1887—player, Philadelphia Pythians
NORWOOD, WALTER—1933—officer, Detroit Stars
NUNEZ, DAGOBERTO (BERTO)—1953-54—p, of, Kansas City
　　Monarchs
NUNLEY, BEAUFORD—1934—1b, Memphis Red Sox
NUTTALL, H. (BILL)—1924-26—p, Lincoln Giants, Bacharach
　　Giants
NUTTER, ISAAC H.—1927-28—officer, Bacharach Giants, pres.,
　　Eastern League

O

OAKLEY,—1940—p, New Orleans-St.Louis Stars
O'BRYANT, WILLIE [O'BRIEN]—1932—ss, of, Washington Pilots
O'DELL, JOHN WESLEY—1949-50—p, Houston Eagles
ODEN, JOHNNY WEBB—1927-32—ss, of, Birmingham Black
　　Barons, Knoxville Giants, Louisville Black Caps, Memphis
　　Red Sox
O'DONNELL, CHARLES K.—1887—mgr., officer, Pittsburgh
　　Keystones
O'FARRILL, ESTABAN ORLANDO y GARCIA—1949-51—ss,
　　Indianapolis Clowns, Philadelphia Stars, Baltimore Elite
　　Giants
OFFERT, MOSE—1925-26—p, Indianapolis ABCs
OLDHAM, JIMMY—1920-23—p, St. Louis Giants, St. Louis Stars
O'LEE,—1934—c, Washington Pilots
OLIVER, HUDSON (HUDDY)—1911—2b, Brooklyn Royal Giants
OLIVER, JAMES (PEE WEE, SELASSIE)—1943-46—ss, Cincinnati-
　　Indianapolis Clowns, Birmingham Black Barons, Indianapo-
　　lis Clowns
OLIVER, JOHN—1885—3b, Brooklyn Remsens
OLIVER, JOHN HENRY—1945-46—ss, Memphis Red Sox,
　　Cleveland Buckeyes
OLIVER, LEONARD E.—1911-13—ss, Philadelphia Giants,
　　Pittsburgh Giants
OLIVER, MARTIN—1930-34—c, of, Birmingham Black Barons,
　　Louisville Black Caps, Memphis Red Sox
O'MEADA,—1932—inf, Cuban Stars (West)
OMS, ALEJANDRO (WALLA WALLA)—1917-35—of, Cuban Stars
　　(ECL), New York Cubans, All Cubans, Cuban Stars (West)
O'NEIL, JOHN JORDAN JR.(BUCK)—1937-55—1b, mgr., Memphis
　　Red Sox, Kansas City Monarchs
O'NEILL,—1910-14—p, c, West Baden (IND.) Sprudels, Louisville
　　White Sox
O'NEILL, CHARLES-1921-23—c, Columbus Buckeyes, Bacharach
　　Giants, Toledo Tigers, Chicago American Giants, Kansas
　　City Monarchs
ORA, CLARENCE—1932—of, Cleveland Cubs
ORANGE, GRADY—1925-31—ss, 2b, 3b, Birmingham Black
　　Barons, Kansas City Monarchs, Detroit Stars, Cleveland
　　Tigers
ORMES, A.W.—1911—player Leland Giants
ORTIZ, JULIO ARANGO (ORTIE, BILL)—1944-45—of, ss,
　　Cincinnati-Indianapolis Clowns, Kansas City Monarchs
ORTIZ, RAFAELITO—1948—p, Chicago American Giants
OSBORNE,—1905—p, Philadelphia Giants
OSCAL, (See OSCAR LEVIS)
OSLEY,—1938—p, Birmingham Black Barons
OSORIO, ALBERTO—1949—p, Louisville Buckeyes
OTIS,—1930—p, Brooklyn Royal Giants
OTIS, AMOS—1920—of, Nashville Giants
OUSLEY, GUY C.—1931-32—ss, 2b, 3b, Chicago Columbia
　　Giants, Cleveland Cubs, Memphis Red Sox
OVERTON, ALBERT—1937, 1944—p, Philadelphia Stars,
　　Cincinnati-Indianapolis Clowns
OVERTON, JOHN—1925—officer, Indianapolis ABCs
OWENS,—1934, 1937—p, Newark Dodgers, Newark Eagles

OWENS, A. —1928—ss, Cleveland Tigers
OWENS, ALBERT—1930-31—p, Nashville Elite Giants
OWENS, ALPHONSO (BUDDY)—1951-52—3b, Chicago American
　　Giants
OWENS, ARTHOT C.—1954—p, Detroit Stars
OWENS, AUBREY—1920-26—p, Indianapolis ABCs, Chicago
　　American Giants, New Orleans Caulfield Ads, Chicago
　　Giants
OWENS, DEWITT—1936-42—of, 2b, Birmingham Black Barons,
　　Indianapolis ABCs, Indianapolis Crawfords, Philadelphia
　　Stars
OWENS, J.—1931—of, Cleveland Cubs
OWENS, JACKSON (JACK)—1950-54—p, Chicago American
　　Giants, Detroit Stars
OWENS, LANE—1952—inf, Indianapolis Clowns
OWENS, RAYMOND (SMOKEY, KANKOL)—1939-42—p, of,
　　Cleveland Bears, Cleveland Buckeyes, New Orleans-St.
　　Louis Stars, Cincinnati Clowns, Cincinnati Buckeyes,
　　Jacksonville Red Caps
OWENS, W.E.—1887—player, Cincinnati Browns
OWENS, W. OSCAR—1913-31—p, 1b, of, Homestead Grays,
　　Indianapolis ABCs, Pittsburgh Keystones
OWENS, WILLIAM JOHN (BILL)—1923-33—ss, 2b, p, Washington
　　Potomacs, Chicago American Giants, Indianapolis ABCs,
　　Dayton Marcos, Birmingham Black Barons, Memphis Red
　　Sox, Detroit Stars, Cleveland Elites, Harrisburg Giants,
　　Brooklyn Royal Giants, Wilmington Potomacs

P

PACE, BENJAMIN (BROTHER)—1921-25—c, Pittsburgh
　　Keystones, Homestead Grays
PACE, ED—1930—of, Nashville Elite Giants
PADRONE, JUAN—1909-26—p, 2b, of, Cuban Stars (ECL), Smart
　　Set, Long Branch (NJ) Cubans, Chicago American Giants,
　　Lincoln Stars, Cuban Stars (NNL), Indianapolis ABCs,
　　Brooklyn Royal Giants, Birmingham Black Barons, All
　　Cubans, Cuban Stars, Cuban Stars of Havana, Cuban Stars
　　(East), Havana Cubans, Cincinnati Cubans
PAGE, ALLEN—1945-50—vice pres, tres, NSL; officer, New
　　Orleans Creoles; promoter
PAGE, R.—1925—officer, Indianapolis ABCs
PAGE, THEODORE ROOSEVELT (TERRIBLE TED)—1926-37—of,
　　1b, Newark Stars, Homestead Grays, Pittsburgh Crawfords,
　　New York Black Yankees, Newark Eagles, Philadelphia
　　Stars, Brooklyn Royal Giants, Baltimore Black Sox, Quaker
　　Giants, Brooklyn Eagles PAGES, PEDRO—1939, 1947—of,
　　New York Cubans
PAIGE, ROBERT LeROY (SATCHEL)—1926-55—p, Chattanooga
　　Black Lookouts, Birmingham Black Barons, Cleveland
　　Cubs, Pittsburgh Crawfords, Kansas City Monarchs, New
　　York Black Yankees, Satchel Paige's All-Stars, Philadelphia
　　Stars, Memphis Red Sox, Baltimore Black Sox, St. Louis
　　Stars, Chicago American Giants
PAINE, HENRY—1885—of, Brooklyn Remsens
PAINE, JOHN—1887—of, Philadelphia Pythians
PALM, ROBERT CLARENCE (SPOONY)—1927-46—c, Birming-
　　ham Black Barons, St. Louis Stars, Detroit Stars, Cleveland
　　Giants, Homestead Grays, Brooklyn Eagles, New York
　　Black Yankees, Philadelphia Stars, Cole's American Giants,
　　Akron Tyrites, Pittsburgh Crawfords, Chicago American
　　Giants
PALMA,—1930—p, Cuban Stars (NNL)
PALMER,—1951-54—p, Chicago American Giants, Detroit Stars
PALMER, EARL—1918-19—of, Chicago Union Giants, Lincoln
　　Giants
PALMER, CURTIS—1949-50—of, New York Black Yankees
PALMER, JOSEPH—1887—utl., New York Gorhams

Andrew "Pap" Payne.
Chicago Historical Society

PALMER, LEON—1926, 1930—of, Dayton Marcos, Louisville White Sox

PALOMINO, EMILIO—1904-06—of, All Cubans, Cuban X Giants

PANIER,—1917-20—p, Cuban Giants, Philadelphia Giants

PANNELL,—1914—c, Cuban Giants, New York Stars, Brooklyn All-Stars

PAPE, ED—1946—of, Homestead Grays

PARDEE,—1925—c, Birmingham Black Barons

PAREDA, H.(MONK, PASTOR)—1910-21—p, 1b, Stars of Cuba, Cuban Stars, Cincinnati Cubans

PAREGO, GEORGE A.[PARAGO]—1885-88—p, of, 1b, Argyle Hotel, Cuban Giants, Trenton Cuban Giants (Middle States Lg.), Cuban Stars

PARKER,—1890-1908—of, Genuine Cuban Giants, Chicago Unions, New York Colored Giants

PARKER,—1921-23—1b, of, Pittsburgh Stars of Buffalo, Baltimore Black Sox, Memphis Red Sox

PARKER, JACK—1938—inf, Pittsburgh Crawfords, New York Black Yankees

PARKER, (SONNY)—1942-43—p, Chicago Brown Bombers, Kansas City Monarchs, Harrisburg-St.Louis Stars

PARKER, THOMAS (TOM, BIG TRAIN)—1929-48—p, of, mgr., Memphis Red Sox, Indianapolis ABCs, Monroe Monarchs, Homestead Grays, New Orleans-St. Louis Stars, New York Black Yankees, Harrisburg-St. Louis Stars, New York Cubans, Boston Blues, Indianapolis Athletics, Nashville Elite Giants, Columbus Elite Giants, Birmingham Black Barons, Toledo Crawfords

PARKER, WILLIE (LEFTY)—1917-20—p, Lincoln Giants, Baltimore Black Sox

PARKER, WILLIE—1952—1b, Philadelphia Stars

PARKINSON, (PARKY)—1950—p, Houston Eagles

PARKS,—1916—p, Lincoln Stars

PARKS, CHARLES EDISON (CHARLIE, HUNKY)—1940-47—c, Newark Eagles

PARKS, JOHN—1939-47—c, of, New York Black Yankees, Newark Eagles

PARKS, JOSEPH B.—1909-19—of, c, ss, Cuban Giants, Philadelphia Giants, Brooklyn Royal Giants, Pennsylvania Red Caps of New York, Bacharach Giants

PARKS, SAM—1945-46—officer, owner, Memphis Grey Sox, Little Rock Black Travelers

PARKS, WILLIAM (BUBBER)—1910-20—ss, 2b, of, Chicago Giants, Lincoln Giants, Chicago American Giants, Lincoln Stars, Pennsylvania Red Caps of New York, Philadelphia Giants, Chicago Union Giants

PARNELL,—1934—p, Bacharach Giants

PARNELL, ROY (RED)—1926-50—of, 1b, mgr., Birmingham Black Barons, Monroe Monarchs, New Orleans Crescent Stars, Columbus Elite Giants, Philadelphia Stars, Pittsburgh Crawfords, Houston Eagles, Nashville Elite Giants

PARPETTI, AUGUSTIN—1909-23—1b, of, Cuban Stars, Kansas City Monarchs, Bacharach Giants, Richmond Giants, Havana Cubans

PARRIS, JONATHAN CLYDE (THE DUDE)—1946-49—1b, 3b, of, New York Black Yankees, Louisville Buckeyes, Philadelphia Stars

PARSON,—1908—p, Genuine Cuban Giants

PARSONS, A.S.—1895-97—mgr., Adrian (MI) Page Fence Giants

PARTLOW, ROY (SILENT ROY)—1934-50—p, Cincinnati Tigers, Memphis Red Sox, Homestead Grays, Philadelphia Stars

PASSON, HARRY—1934—officer, Bacharach Giants

PASTORIA,—1924—p, Cuban Stars (NNL)

PATE, ARCHIE—1909-17—of, c, St.Paul Gophers, Chicago Giants, New York Stars, Bowser's ABCs

PATTERSON,—1886—of, New York Gorhams

PATTERSON, ANDREW L. (PAT)—1934-49—2b, 3b, of, Pennsylvania Red Caps Cleveland Red Sox, Pittsburgh Crawfords, Kansas City Monarchs, Philadelphia Stars, Newark Eagles, Houston Eagles, Homestead Grays

PATTERSON, GABRIEL—1941-50-of, c, Pittsburgh Crawfords, Homestead Grays, New York Black Yankees, Philadelphia Stars

PATTERSON, JOE—1955—of, Kansas City Monarchs

PATTERSON, JOHN W. (PAT)—1890-1907—2b, of, ss, mgr., Lincoln (NEB) Giants, Page Fence Giants, Columbia Giants of Chicago, Philadelphia Giants, Cuban X Giants, Cuban Giants, Quaker Giants, of New York, Brooklyn Royal Giants, Chicago Union Giants, Plattsmouth (Nebraska St. Lg.)

PATTERSON, WILLIE LEE JR. (ROY, PAT)—1945-55—c, 1b, 3b, New York Cubans, Birmingham Black Barons, Philadelphia Stars, Memphis Red Sox, Chicago American Giants, Louisville Black Colonels, Pittsburgh Crawfords (USL), Detroit Stars

PATTERSON, WILLIAM B.—1914-25—mgr., Houston Black Buffaloes, Austin Senators, Birmingham Black Barons

PATTON, E.—1909-14—of, p, Philadelphia Giants, New York Stars

PATTON,—1926—p, St. Louis Stars

PAUL,—1908—ss, Brooklyn Colored Giants

PAYNE,—1916—p, Lincoln Giants

PAYNE,—1926-31—2b, p, Brooklyn Royal Giants, Newark Stars, Philadelphia Giants

PAYNE,—1928—of, Birmingham Black Barons

PAYNE, ANDREW H. (JAP)—1902-22—of, Philadelphia Giants, Cuban X Giants, Leland Giants, Chicago American Giants, Chicago Union Giants, New York Central Red Caps, Brooklyn Royal Giants, Pennsylvania Red Caps of NY, Lincoln Stars, Chicago Giants, Lincoln Giants

PAYNE, ERNEST (RUSTY)—1937, 1940—of, Cincinnati Tigers, Indianapolis Crawfords

PAYNE, JAMES—1887-88—of, Baltimore Lord Baltimore, Cuban Giants

PAYNE, TOM—1933—of, Homestead Grays, Baltimore Black Sox, Pittsburgh Crawfords

PAYNE, WILLIAM (DOC)—1898—of, Celeron Acme Colored Giants (Iron and Oil League)

PEACE, WILLIAM WARREN—1945-48—p, Newark Eagles

PEACOCK,—1933—3b, Homestead Grays

PEAK, RUFUS—1931—officer, Detroit Stars

PEARSON,—1903—of, Philadelphia Giants

PEARSON, FRANK (IVY, WAHOO)—1945-54—p, Memphis Red Sox, Chicago American Giants, Louisville Black Colonels, New York Cubans, New York Black Yankees

PEARSON, JIMMY—1949—p, New York Cubans

PEARSON, LEONARD CURTIS (LENNIE, HOSS)—1936-50—of, 3b, ss, 1b, mgr., Newark Eagles, Baltimore Elite Giants, St. Louis Stars

PEARSON, RUTLEDGE—1952—1b, Chicago American Giants

PEATROS, MAURICE (BABY FACE)—1945-47—1b, Homestead Grays, Pittsburgh Crawfords

PEDA,—1915—of, Cuban Stars

PEDEMONTE,—1926—p, 3b, of, Cuban Stars (NNL)

PEDRERO,—1931—2b, c, Newark Browns

PEDROSO, EUSTAQUIO—1910-30—p, of, 1b, c, Cuban Stars, All Cubans, Cuban Stars (ECL), Cuban Stars (NNL)

PEDROSO, [FERNANDO DIAZ] (EL BICHO)—1945-50-inf, of, New York Cubans

PEEBLES, A.J.—1933—officer, Columbus Blue Birds

PEEKS, A.J.—1932—officer, Atlanta Black Crackers

PEEPLES, NATHANIEL (NAT)—1949-51—c, of, Kansas City Monarchs, Indianapolis Clowns

PEETE, CHARLES (MULE)—1950—of, Indianapolis Clowns

PELHAM, WILLIAM (DON)—1933-38—ss, of, Bacharach Giants, Atlanta Black Crackers

PELLAS,—1923—p, Cuban Stars (NNL)

PENA,—1929—c, 1b, Cuban Stars (NNL)

PENDLETON, JAMES (JIM)—1948—ss, Chicago American Giants

PENNINGTON,—1929—p, Nashville Elite Giants

PENNINGTON, ARTHUR DAVID (ART, SUPERMAN)—1940-51—of, 1b, 2b, Chicago American Giants, Pittsburgh Crawfords, Birmingham Black Barons

PENNO, DAN—1887-1896—p, of, 2b, Boston Resolutes, Cuban Giants, Cuban X Giants

PENOY,—1932—c, Pennsylvania Red Caps

PEOPLES, EDDIE—1933—p, Memphis Red Sox

PERDUE, FRANK M.—1920-34—pres, NSL; officer, Birmingham Black Barons

PEREIRA, JOSE (PEPIN)—1947—p, Baltimore Elite Giants

PEREZ,—1906—p, Cuban X Giants

PEREZ, JAVIER (BLUE)—1942-45—3b, New York Cubans

PEREZ, JOSE (PEPIN)—1911-37—p, 1b, c, 2b, ss, 3b, Cuban Stars (ECL), Cuban Stars (NNL), Harrisburg Giants, Bacharach Giants, Hilldale, New York Cubans, Homestead Grays, Brooklyn Eagles, Madison Stars

PEREZ, LUIS (See LUIS PEREZ CABALLERO)

PERKINS,—1944—1b, Kansas City Monarchs

PERKINS, WILLIAM GAMIEL (BILL, CY)—1928-48-c, of, mgr., Birmingham Black Barons, Cleveland Cubs, Pittsburgh Crawfords, Cleveland Stars, Philadelphia Stars, Baltimore Elite Giants, New York Black Yankees, Homestead Grays

PERRY,—1936—1b, 2b, Homestead Grays

PERRY, ALONZO THOMAS—1940-50—p, 1b, Homestead Grays, Birmingham Black Barons

PERRY, CARLISLE (CARL)—1920-26—2b, 3b, ss, Detroit Stars, Bacharach Giants, Washington Potomacs, Lincoln Giants, Cleveland Browns, Baltimore Black Sox, Indianapolis ABCs, Hilldale, Cleveland Tate Stars, Richmond Giants, Norfolk Stars

PERRY, DON—1920-27—1b, Madison Stars, Washington Braves, Harrisburg Giants

PERRY, ED—1887—player, Washington Capital City

PERRY, HANK—1926, 1934—p, Hilldale, Newark Dodgers

PERVIS,—1932, 1937—p, Monroe Monarchs, Birmingham Black Barons

PETERS,—1916—c, Lincoln Stars

PETERS, FRANK—1916-23—ss, Chicago Union Giants, Peters Union Giants

PETERS, WILLIAM S.—1887-1923—1b, owner, mgr., Chicago Unions, Peters Union Giants

PETERSON,—1914—p, Chicago American Giants

PETERSON, HARVEY (PETE)—1931-37, 1946—of, p, inf, Montgomery Grey Sox, Birmingham Black Barons, Memphis Red Sox, Cincinnati Tigers, Cleveland Clippers(USL)

PETERSON, L.—1885—1b, Brooklyn Remsens

PETRICOLA,—1924—p, Cuban Stars (NNL)

PETTUS, WILLIAM THOMAS (ZACK)—1909-23—c, 1b, 2b, ss, mgr., Kansas City Giants, Leland Giants, Chicago Giants,

Leonard "Hoss" Pearson.
Moorland-Spingarn Library

Lincoln Stars, Lincoln Giants, St. Louis Giants, Hilldale, Bacharach Giants, Richmond Giants, Harrisburg Giants, Brooklyn Royal Giants, Chicago American Giants

PETWAY,—1931-32—ss, 2b, Nashville Elite Giants, Birmingham Black Barons, Louisville Black Caps

PETWAY, BRUCE (BUDDY)—1906-25—c, of, mgr., Leland Giants, Brooklyn Royal Giants, Philadelphia Giants, Chicago American Giants, Detroit Stars, Cuban X Giants

PETWAY, HOWARD—1906—p, Leland Giants

PETWAY, SHERLEY (CHARLIE)—1937-44—c, mgr., Detroit Stars, Chicago Brown Bombers, Cleveland Buckeyes

PHIFFER,—1937—3b, ss, St. Louis Stars

PHIFFER, LESTER—1951-52—ss, 3b, Kansas City Monarchs

PHILLIPS,—1921-23—ss, 2b, Nashville Elite Giants, Detroit Stars

PHILLIPS,—1927—p, Birmingham Black Barons

PHILLIPS, JOHN—1939-40—p, Baltimore Elite Giants

PHILLIPS, NORRIS—1942-43—p, Kansas City Monarchs, Memphis Red Sox

PHILLIPS, RICHARD (DICK)—1952-55—p, Kansas City Monarchs

PIERCE, HERBERT—1925-29, 1932—c, Homestead Grays;umpire EWL

PIERCE, LEONARD—1924-27—p, Wilmington Potomacs, Philadelphia Giants

PIERCE, STEVE—1925-28—officer, Detroit Stars

PIERCE, WILLIAM H. (BILL)—1910-32—1b, c, of, Philadelphia Giants, Chicago American Giants, Lincoln Stars, Lincoln Giants, Pennsylvania Red Caps of New York, Bacharach Giants, Norfolk Giants, Detroit Stars, Baltimore Black Sox, Mohawk Giants; umpire, East-West League

PIERRE, JOSEPH—1950-51—inf, Kansas City Monarchs

PIERRE, ROGERS (SHAPE)—1934-45—p, Chicago American Giants, Colored House of David, Indianapolis- Cincinnati Clowns, Cincinnati Clowns, Cincinnati Tigers

PIERSON, 1937 (See LEN PEARSON)

PIERSON,—1933—3b, Homestead Grays

PIGG, LEONARD DANIEL (SHINE, LEN)—1947-53—c, of, Indianapolis Clowns, Cleveland Buckeyes

PILLAR, JOSE—1917—p, Havana Cubans

PILLOT, GUILLERMO LUIS (GUILLO)—1941-43—p, New York Black Yankees, Cincinnati Clowns

PILOTO, JOSE—1949-50—p, Memphis Red Sox

PINDER, EDDIE (POTATO)—1914-16—of, Hilldale

PINDER, FRED—1910-17—ss, Hilldale

PINDER, GEORGE (MONK)—1910—of, Hilldale

PINE, FELIX—1954—p, Detroit Stars

PINKSTON, AL—1936—1b, St. Louis Stars

PINTO,—1914—p, New York Stars, Brooklyn All-Stars

PIPKIN, ROBERT (LEFTY, BLACK DIAMOND)—1928-33, 1940-42—p, Birmingham Black Barons, Cleveland Cubs, New Orleans Crescent Stars

PIRTLE, J.W.—1951—p, New Orleans Eagles

PITTS, CURTIS—1950-51—c, ss, Chicago American Giants, Cleveland Buckeyes

PITTS, ED—1940—c, Philadelphia Stars

PLA,—1933—p, Cuban Stars

PLUNO,—1887—player, Boston Resolutes

POHEA,—1921—p, Cincinnati Cubans

POINDEXTER, ROBERT—1924-29—p, 1b, Birmingham Black Barons, Chicago American Giants, Memphis Red Sox

POINSETTE, ROBERT—1939—of, p, New York Black Yankees, Toledo Crawfords

POINTER, ROBERT LEE—1950—p, Kansas City Monarchs

POINTTER,—1887—p, 3b, Binghamton, N.Y.(Int. Lg.)

POLANCO, RAFAEL (RALPH)—1942—p, Philadelphia Stars

POLES, EDWARD (POSSUM, GOOGLES)—1922-28—ss, 3b, Baltimore Black Sox, Harrisburg Giants

POLES, SPOTTSWOOD (SPOT)—1909-23—of, Philadelphia Giants, Lincoln Giants, Brooklyn Royal Giants, Lincoln Stars, Hilldale, Bacharach Giants, Richmond Giants

POLLARD,—1936—of, St. Louis Stars

POLLARD, NATHANIEL (NAT)—1946-50—p, Birmingham Black Barons

POLLOCK, SYD—1926-50—off., owner, Havana Red Sox, Cuban House of David, Cuban Stars, Ethiopian Clowns, Cincinnati Clowns, Indianapolis Clowns

POMPEZ, ALEXANDRO (ALEX)—1922-50—officer, Cuban Stars (ECL), New York Cubans; vice-pres, NNL

PONTELLO,—1927—p, Cuban Stars (ECL)

POOLE, CLAUDE—1945-46—p, New York Black Yankees

POPE, A.—1948—of, Homestead Grays

POPE, DAVID (DAVE)—1946—utl., Homestead Grays

POPE, EDGAR—1938—of, Atlanta Black Crackers

POPE, JAMES—1931-33—p, Louisville White Sox, Montgomery Grey Sox, Columbus Blue Birds

POPE, WILLIE (BILL)—1945-48—p, Pittsburgh Crawfords, Homestead Grays

PORSEE,—1921—p, St. Louis Giants

PORTER,—1921—of, Cincinnati Cubans

PORTER, ANDREW (ANDY, PULLMAN)—1932-50—p, Cleveland Cubs, Nashville Elite Giants, Washington Elite Giants, Baltimore Elite Giants, Indianapolis Clowns, Columbus Elite Giants, Louisville White Sox, Newark Eagles, Louisville Black Caps

PORTER, MERLE—1949-50—1b, Kansas City Monarchs

PORTER, WALLACE—1954—p, Detroit Stars

PORTIER, JAMES—1954—c, Indianapolis Clowns

PORTUANDO, BARTOLO—1916-27—3b, 1b, Cuban Stars, Kansas City Monarchs, Cuban Stars (ECL), New York Cuban Stars

POSEY, CUMBERLAND WILLIS (CUM)—1911-46—of, officer, Homestead Grays, Detroit Wolves; founder, East-West League; sec, tres, NNL

POSEY, SEWARD HAYES (SEE, SEA)—1911-48—officer, bus mgr., Homestead Grays

POST,—1916—of, Lincoln Stars

POSTELL,—1934—2b, Cincinnati Tigers

POTTER,—1921—c, Kansas City Monarchs

POTTER, D.—1932—of, Atlanta Black Crackers

POWELL,—1914-15—p, Lincoln Giants

POWELL, EDWARD D.(EDDIE, BIG RED, BOCHE)—1936-38—c, New York Black Yankees, Washington Black Senators, New York Cubans, St.Louis Stars

POWELL, ELVIN (SHOELESS)—1931—2b, Memphis Red Sox

POWELL, J.J.—1931—officer, Little Rock Black Travelers

POWELL, MELVIN (PUTT)—1930-43—p, of, Cole's American Giants, Chicago American Giants, Chicago Brown Bombers, Chicago Columbia Giants, Birmingham Black Barons

POWELL, RICHARD D. (DICK)—1938-52—officer, owner, Baltimore Elite Giants, Nashville Elite Giants

POWELL, RUSSELL—1914-21—c, 2b, Indianapolis ABCs

POWELL, WILLIAM H. (BILL)—1946-52—p, Birmingham Black Barons

POWELL, WILLIE ERNEST (WEE WILLIE, PIGGY)—1925-35—p, Chicago American Giants, Detroit Stars, Cole's American Giants, Cleveland Red Sox, Akron Tyrites

PRATZ, E. [PRATS]—1907—of, Cuban Stars

PRESBY,—1945—p, Chicago Brown Bombers

PRESSWOOD, HENRY—1948-52—ss, 3b, Cleveland Buckeyes, Kansas City Monarchs

PRESTON, ALBERT WEBBER (AL)—1943-1952—p, New York Black Yankees, Chicago American Giants, Pittsburgh Crawfords (USL)

PRESTON, ROBERT—1950—p, Baltimore Elite Giants

PRICE,—1922—of, Pittsburgh Keystones

PRICE, EWELL—1951—c, New Orleans Eagles

PRICE, MARVIN—1950-52—1b, Cleveland Buckeyes, Chicago American Giants, New Orleans Eagles

PRICE, WILLIE—1951—p, Birmingham Black Barons

PRICHETT, W. —1921—p, Hilldale

PRIDE, CHARLEY FRANK—1953-54—p, of, Memphis Red Sox, Birmingham Black Barons

PRIM, WILLIAM {PRIMM}—1905-1911—c, Leland Giants, St.Louis Giants, Indianapolis ABCs

PRIMM, RANDOLPH—1926—p, Kansas City Monarchs

PRINCE,—1936—3b, Chicago American Giants

PRITCHETT, WILBUR—1924-32—p, Harrisburg Giants, Baltimore Black Sox, Brooklyn Royal Giants, Hilldale, Bacharach Giants, Brooklyn Cuban Giants

PROCTOR, JAMES (CUB)—1884-87—p, c, Baltimore Atlantics, Baltimore Lord Baltimores

PROCTOR, JAMES ARTHUR (JIM)—1955—p, Indianapolis Clowns

PROPHET, WILLIE—1934—of, Bacharach Giants

PRUE,—1951—1b, New Orleans Eagles

PRYOR,—1914-17—p, Indianapolis ABCs, St. Louis Giants, Jewell's ABCs, Bowser's ABCs, Louisville White Sox

PRYOR, ANDERSON—1922-33—2b, ss, Milwaukee Bears, Detroit Stars, Memphis Red Sox, New Orleans Crescent Stars

PRYOR, BILL—1927-31—p, Memphis Red Sox, Detroit Stars

PRYOR, EDWARD—1925-34—2b, Lincoln Giants, Penn Red Caps of NY

PRYOR, WES (WHIP)—1910-14—3b, Leland Giants, Chicago American Giants, St. Louis Giants, Chicago Giants, Mohawk Giants, Brooklyn Royal Giants, Louisville White Sox

PUGH, JOHNNY—1912-22—3b, 2b, of, Mohawk Giants, Brooklyn Royal Giants, Philadelphia Giants, Bacharach Giants, Harrisburg Giants, Lincoln Giants, Lincoln Stars

PULLEN, C. NEIL—1920-27—c, Brooklyn Royal Giants, Kansas City Monarchs, Baltimore Black Sox, Lincoln Giants

PULLIAM, ARTHUR (CHICK) {PULLIAM}—1908-15—c, Kansas City (KAN) Giants, Kansas City (MO) Royal Giants

PUNCH,—1922—p, Baltimore Black Sox

PURCELL, HARMON—1944-47—3b, p, Cleveland Buckeyes, Memphis Red Sox

PURGEN,—1920-21—ss, Madison Stars, Hilldale

Q

QUIDGLAY,—1954—p, Louisville Black Colonels

QUINCY,—1922—player, Bacharach Giants

QUINONES, THOMAS PLANCHARON—1946-47—p, Indianapolis Clowns

QUINTANA, BUSTA—1928-34—inf, Cuban Stars (NNL), Newark Dodgers, Cuban Stars (East)

QUINTANA, PEDRO—1954—inf, Indianapolis Clowns

R

RABBAR,—1939—player, New York Cubans

RADCLIFF, ALEXANDER (ALEX)—1927-46—ss, 3b, Chicago Giants, Cole's American Giants, Chicago American Giants, New York Cubans, Kansas City Monarchs, Cincinnati-Indianapolis Clowns, Memphis Red Sox, Birmingham Black Barons

RADCLIFFE, EVERETT (RED, RIP)—1926, 1934-37—ss, Dayton Marcos, Chicago American Giants

RADCLIFFE, THEODORE ROOSEVELT (DOUBLE DUTY)—1928-50—c, p, mgr., Detroit Stars, St. Louis Stars, Pittsburgh Crawfords, Homestead Grays, Columbus Blue Birds, New York Black Yankees, Brooklyn Eagles, Cincinnati Tigers, Memphis Red Sox, Birmingham Black Barons, Chicago American Giants, Louisville Buckeyes, Kansas City Monarchs, Harlem Globetrotters

RAGGS, HARRY(See HARRY ROBERTS)

RAGLAND, HURLAND EARL—1920-21—p, Indianapolis ABCs, Kansas City Monarchs, Columbus Buckeyes, Dayton Marcos

RAINE, J.—1884-85—of, Baltimore Atlantics

RAINES, LAWRENCE GLENN HOPE (LARRY)—1951-52—ss, Chicago American Giants

RAMIREZ, RAMIRO (ROME)—1916-48—of, mgr., Cuban Stars, Havana Stars, Cuban Stars (East), All Cubans, Bacharach Giants, Baltimore Black Sox, Havana Red Sox, Cuban House of David, Indianapolis Clowns, Brooklyn Royal Giants, New York Cuban Stars, Richmond Giants, Cuban Stars of Havana, Cuban Stars (ECL)

RAMOS,—1907-12—p, 2b, Cuban Stars, Long Branch (NJ) Cubans

RAMOS, JOSE (CHEO)—1921, 1929—of, All Cubans, Cuban Stars (East)

RAMSAY, WILLIAM—1889—of, Chicago Unions

RAMSEY, LAYMON—1951—p, Chicago American Giants

RAMSEY, MACK—1911-16—of, Chicago Union Giants

RANDOLPH, ANDREW G.—1882-88—1b, of, Argyle Hotel, Trenton (NJ) Cuban Giants, Boston Resolutes, Active of Philadelphia

RANKIN, BILL (BULLETS, SHORTY)—1923-27—p, c, Washington Potomacs, Richmond Giants, Philadelphia Giants

RANKIN, GEORGE—1887—player, Cincinnati Browns

RANSOM, JOE—1926—c, Cleveland Elites

RASBERRY, CHARLES—1952—utl. Kansas City Monarchs

Ramiro Ramirez.
Luis Munoz Collection

RASBERRY, TED—1954-55—owner, mgr., Detroit Stars, Kansas City Monarchs

RAUZE,—1937—player, Philadelphia Stars

RAWLINS,—1905—of, Cuban Giants

RAY, JOHN—1932-45—of, Montgomery Grey Sox, Birmingham Black Barons, Cleveland Bears, Jacksonville Red Caps, Cincinnati-Indianapolis Clowns, Kansas City Monarchs, Pittsburgh Crawfords

RAY, OTTO C.(JAYBIRD) —1920-24—p, c, of, Kansas City Monarchs, Chicago Giants, St. Louis Stars, Cleveland Tate Stars, Cleveland Browns, Toledo Tigers

RAY, RICHARD—1943—inf, of, Chicago Brown Bombers

RAY, THOMAS—1887—player, New York Gorhams

REAVIS, W.—1920-32—p, Lincoln Giants, Pennsylvania Red Caps of New York

RECTOR, CORNELIUS (CONNIE, BROADWAY)—1920-44—p, Hilldale, Brooklyn Royal Giants, Lincoln Giants, New York Black Yankees, New York Cubans

REDD, EUGENE—1922-23—3b, Pittsburgh Keystones, Milwaukee Bears New Orleans Crescent Stars, Kansas City Monarchs, Cleveland Tate Stars

REDD, ULYSSES ADOLPH (HICKEY, CHERRY)—1940-41, 1951-52—ss, Birmingham Black Barons, Chicago American Giants

REDDEN,—1934—c, Cincinnati Tigers

REDDICK,—1942—of, Boston Royal Giants

REDDING, RICHARD (DICK, CANNONBALL)—1911-38—p, of, mgr, Lincoln Giants, Lincoln Stars, Indianapolis ABCs, Chicago American Giants, Brooklyn Royal Giants, Bacharach Giants, Pittsburgh Crawfords

REDDON, BOB—1919—p, Cleveland Tate Stars

REDMON, TOM—1911—player, Leland Giants

REDUS, WILSON (FROG)—1924-40—of, mgr., coach, St. Louis Stars, Cleveland Stars, Columbus Blue Birds, Cleveland Giants, Kansas City Monarchs, Cleveland Red Sox, Chicago American Giants, Cleveland Browns, Indianapolis ABCs

REDWINE,—1926—p, Cleveland Elites

REED, AMBROSE—1922-32—of, 2b, 1b, 3b, Bacharach Giants, Hilldale, Pittsburgh Crawfords, Atlanta Black Crackers, Homestead Grays

REED, ANDREW—1917-21—3b, of, Chicago Union Giants, Detroit Stars, Chicago Giants

REED, CURTIS—1937—of, St. Louis Stars

REED, EDDIE—1953-55—of, Memphis Red Sox

REED, JOHN D.—1934-42—p, Cole's American Giants, Indianapolis ABCs, Chicago American Giants, Chicago Brown Bombers, Atlanta Black Crackers, Indianapolis Athletics, St. Louis Stars

REED, LEROY—1946—utl., Cleveland Clippers (USL)

REEDY, FLEMING (BUDDY)—1950-51—3b, Baltimore Elite Giants

REEL, JIMMY—1923—of, Toledo Tigers

REESE, CHARLES—1910-14—p, of, Cuban Giants, Chicago Union Giants New York Stars, Brooklyn All-Stars

REESE, JAMES (BIG JIM)—1934-40—p, Cleveland Red Sox, Brooklyn Eagles, Atlanta Black Crackers, Baltimore Elite Giants

REESE, JOHN E.—1918-31—of, Bacharach Giants, Hilldale, Chicago American Giants, Detroit Stars, Toledo Tigers, St. Louis Stars

REEVES,—1908—cf, Brooklyn Colored Giants

REEVES,—1929—c, Hilldale

REEVES, DONALD—1937-41—1b, of, Atlanta Black Crackers, Indianapolis ABCs, Chicago American Giants

REEVES, JOHN—1890-92—3b, of, p, Lincoln (NEB) Giants, Plattsmouth (Nebraska St. Lg.)

REGGIE,—1921—p, Indianapolis ABCs

REID, PORTER—1949—of, Houston Eagles

RENA, (See PENA)

RENFRO, WILLIAM—1887—p, Binghamton, N.Y.(Int. Lg.)

RENFROE, OTHELLO NELSON SR.(CHICO, CHAPPY)—1945-53—of, c, ss, Kansas City Monarchs, Cleveland Buckeyes, Indianapolis Clowns

REYNOLDS,—1946—1b, Birmingham Black Barons

REYNOLDS, JIMMY—1940, 1946—3b, Indianapolis Crawfords, Cleveland Buckeyes

REYNOLDS, JOE—1935—p, Philadelphia Stars

REYNOLDS, LOUIS THOMAS (LOU)—1897-99-of, 1b, Chicago Columbia Giants, Chicago Unions

REYNOLDS, WILLIAM ERNEST (BILL)—1948-50—2b, ss, Cleveland Buckeyes, Louisville Buckeyes

RHOADES, CORNELIUS (NEAL)—1910-18-c, of, Bowser's ABCs, Hilldale

RHODES, CLAUDE (DUSTY, SCHOOLBOY)—1931-33—p, Louisville Black Caps, Columbus Blue Birds, Chattanoonga Black Lookouts

RHODES, HARRY (LEFTY)—1942-50—p, 1b, Chicago American Giants

RICE, MILLER—1934-37—of, Cincinnati Tigers

RICH,—1924—3b, St. Louis Giants

RICHARDSON,—1908—of, Brooklyn Colored Giants

RICHARDSON, DEWEY—1922—c, Hilldale

RICHARDSON, EARL—1943—ss, Newark Eagles

RICHARDSON, GEORGE—1901-03—ss, Chicago Union Giants, Algona (IA) Brownies

RICHARDSON, GEORGE—1925—officer, Detroit Stars

RICHARDSON, GLEMBY (GLENN)—1946-49—2b, New York Black Yankees

RICHARDSON, HENRY (LONG TOM)—1921-38—p, of, Baltimore Black Sox, Washington Pilots, Bacharach Giants, Washington Black Senators, Pittsburgh Crawfords, Cuban Stars, Richmond Giants

RICHARDSON, JIM—1934, 1939—p, Philadelphia Stars, New York Black Yankees

RICHARDSON, JOHN—1924-25—p, Birmingham Black Barons

RICHARDSON, JOHNNY (BOB)—1949-50—ss, Homestead Grays

RICHARDSON, NORVAL EUGENE (GENE)—1947-53—p, Kansas City Monarchs, Baltimore Elite Giants, Birmingham Black Barons

RICHARDSON, R.—1954—p, Birmingham Black Barons

RICHARDSON, T.W. (TED, LEFTY)—1951-55—p, Indianapolis Clowns, Birmingham Black Barons, Memphis Red Sox, Louisville Black, Colonels

RICHARDSON, VICIAL—1946—ss, Cleveland Buckeyes

RICKS, CURTISS—1920-26-of, p, 1b, Dayton Marcos, Cleveland Tate Stars, Indianapolis ABCs, Chicago American Giants, Cleveland Browns

RICKS, NAPOLEON—1887—player, Louisville Falls City

RICKS, PENDER—1924-28-1b, Philadelphia Giants, Harrisburg Giants

RICKS, WILLIAM (BILL)—1944-50—p, Philadelphia Stars

RIDDICK, VERNON—1939-41—ss, Newark Eagles

RIDDLE, MARSHALL LEWIS (JIT)—1936-43—2b, ss, Indianapolis ABCs, St. Louis Stars, New Orleans-St. Louis Stars, Cleveland Buckeyes, Jacksonville Red Caps

RIDGELY, (BUCK)[RISLEY]—1916-23—ss, Lincoln Giants, Baltimore Black Sox, Harrisburg Giants, Washington Potomacs

RIDLEY, JACK—1927-34—of, 1b, Nashville Elite Giants, Cleveland Cubs, Louisville Red Caps

RIGAL,—1922-27—ss, 3b, Cuban Stars (NNL)

RIGGINS, ORVILLE (BO)—1920-36—ss, 3b, 2b, mgr., Detroit Stars, Cleveland Hornets, Homestead Grays, Lincoln

Wilber "Bullet Joe" Rogan.
Larry Lester

Giants, New York Black Yankees, Brooklyn Royal Giants, Chicago American Giants

RIGNEY, H.G. (HANK)—1939-45—officer, Toledo Crawfords, Indianapolis Crawfords, Toledo Cubs (USL)

RILE, EDWARD (ED, HUCK)—1919-36—p, 1b, Indianapolis ABCs, Chicago American Giants, Lincoln Giants, Columbus Buckeyes, Detroit Stars, Cole's American Giants, Brooklyn Royal Giants, Kansas City Monarchs, Dayton Marcos, Homestead Grays

RILEY, JIM (JACK)—1945—2b, Birmingham Black Barons

RIMS,—1920—p, Bacharach Giants

RIOS, HERMAN MATIAS—1915-24—3b, ss, Cuban Stars (NNL), Havana Stars, Cuban Stars, Cincinnati Cubans

RITCHEY, JOHN FRANKLIN (HOSS)—1947—c, Chicago American Giants

RIVAS,—1917-18—2b, Cuban Stars (East), Havana Cubans

RIVELL,—1934—umpire, NNL

RIVERA, NENENE ANICETO—1933—p, inf, Cuban Stars (East)

RIVERO, CARLOS (CHARLEY)-1933, 1939-44—ss, 3b, Cuban Stars, New York Black Yankees, Baltimore Elite Giants, Cuban Stars (East)

RIVERS, BILL (RIVERA)—1944—of, Kansas City Monarchs

RIVERS, DEWEY(DEEP)—1926, 1933—of, Hilldale, Baltimore Black Sox

ROBBINS,—1926, 1935—p, Harrisburg Giants, Bacharach Giants

ROBELSON, BING—1934—p, Bacharach Giants

ROBERSON, (CHARLEY)—1934—ss, Nashville Elite Giants

ROBERTS, CHARLEY—1938—p, Washington Black Senators

ROBERTS, CURTIS BENJAMIN SR.—1947-50—3b, 2b, Kansas City Monarchs

ROBERTS, ELIHU—1916-20—of, Bacharach Giants, Hilldale

ROBERTS, FRED P.—1903—2b, Chicago Union Giants

ROBERTS, HARRY (RAGGS)—1920-32—of, c, Norfolk Giants, Baltimore Black Sox, Harrisburg Giants, Homestead Grays, Chicago Columbia Giants, Pittsburgh Crawfords, Norfolk Stars

ROBERTS, J.D.—1918-24—ss, 3b, 2b, Pennsylvania Giants, Hilldale, Bacharach Giants, Richmond Giants, Chicago Giants

ROBERTS, LEROY (ROY, EVERREADY)—1916-35—p, Bacharach Giants, Columbus Buckeyes, Brooklyn Royal Giants, Lincoln Giants, Hilldale, Cleveland Giants, Cleveland Red Sox, Madison Stars

ROBERTS, SARAH MUTT—1936-39—p, Philadelphia Stars, Nashville Elite Giants, Baltimore Elite Giants, Bacharach Giants

ROBERTS, TOM (SPECK)—1937-45—p, Homestead Grays, New York Black Yankees, Newark Eagles, Philadelphia Stars, Washington Black Senators

ROBERTSON, BOBBIE (See WILLIAM ROBINSON)

ROBERTSON, CHARLES—1921-25—p, Birmingham Black Barons, St. Louis Stars, New Orleans Caulfield Ads

ROBINSON,—1932—p, Atlanta Black Crackers

ROBINSON,—1934—of, Homestead Grays

ROBINSON,—1943—c, New York Black Yankees

ROBINSON, AL—1905-12—1b, p, Brooklyn Royal Giants, New York Black Sox

ROBINSON, ARZELL, (ACE)—1954-55—p, Memphis Red Sox

ROBINSON, (BABE)—1933-34, 1942—p, Bacharach Giants, Cleveland Red Sox, Boston Royal Giants

ROBINSON, BILL (BOJANGLES)—1931—officer, New York Stars (Black Yankees)

ROBINSON, BOB—1905—c, Leland Giants

ROBINSON, CHARLES—1939—of, Chicago American Giants

ROBINSON, CORNELIUS RANDALL (NEIL, SHADOW)—1935-52—of, ss, Cincinnati Tigers, Homestead Grays, Memphis Red Sox

ROBINSON, EDWARD—1931—of, Louisville White Sox

ROBINSON, EDWARD (BOBBY, ROBBIE)—1945—utility, 3b, Homestead Grays

ROBINSON, GEORGE (SIS)—1918-23—p, Bacharach Giants

ROBINSON, GEORGE—1924—officer, Washington Potomacs

ROBINSON, HENRY FRAZIER (SLOE, HANK)—1942-50—c, Baltimore Grays, Baltimore Elite Giants, Kansas City Monarchs

ROBINSON, J.—1905-10—of, Kansas City, (Kan) Giants, Brooklyn Royal Giants

ROBINSON, JACK—1954—of, p, Detroit Stars

ROBINSON, JACOB (RED)—1946-47—3b, Chicago American Giants

ROBINSON, JAMES (BLACK RUSIE)—1893-1907—p, Lansing, Michigan, Colored Capital All-Americans, Cuban Giants, Cuban X Giants, Brooklyn Royal Giants, Pawtucket (New Eng. Lg.), Philadelphia Giants

ROBINSON, JAMES—1952-53—inf, 3b, Philadelphia Stars, Indianapolis Clowns

ROBINSON, JOHN ROOSEVELT (JACKIE)—1945—ss, Kansas City Monarchs

ROBINSON, JOHNNY—1930, 1938-42—inf, of, Memphis Red Sox, St.Louis Stars, Indianapolis ABCs

ROBINSON, JOSHUA—1939—of, New York Black Yankees

ROBINSON, KENNETH—1931-43—2b, 3b, of, Brooklyn Royal Giants, Newark Browns, Cleveland Bears, New York Black Yankees, Bacharach Giants

ROBINSON, NEIL (See CORNELIUS ROBINSON)
ROBINSON, NEWT (See WALTER ROBINSON)
ROBINSON, NORMAN WAYNE (BOBBY, NORM)—1939-52—of,
    ss, 3b, Baltimore Elite Giants, Birmingham Black Barons
ROBINSON, RAY (NOT SUGAR)—1941-47—p, Newark Eagles,
    Cincinnati Buckeyes, Philadelphia Stars, Cleveland
    Buckeyes
ROBINSON, RICHMOND (BLACK DIAMOND)—1883-86—of,
    St.Louis Black Stockings, Trenton (NJ) Cuban Giants, New
    York Gorhams
ROBINSON, ROBERT (BOB)—1954—of, Detroit Stars
ROBINSON, SAMMY—1954—p, Detroit Stars
ROBINSON, WALTER WILLIAM (NEWT, BILL)—1925-32—ss,
    Hilldale, Lincoln Giants, Harrisburg Giants, New York Black
    Yankees, Bacharach Giants
ROBINSON, WALTER (SKINDOWN)—1940-42—2b, Cleveland
    Bears, Jacksonville Red Caps
ROBINSON, WILLIAM (BOBBY)—1925-42—3b, ss, Indianapolis
    ABCs, Cleveland Elites, Memphis Red Sox, Detroit Stars,
    Cleveland Stars, Cleveland Red Sox, Birmingham Black
    Barons, Chicago American Giants, St.Louis Stars, New
    Orleans-St. Louis Stars
ROCHELLE, CLARENCE—1944—p, Kansas City Monarchs
RODDY, B.M.—1926—pres, NSL
RODGERS, SILVESTER CLIFFORD (SPEEDIE)—1949-50—p,
    Baltimore Elite Giants
RODRIGUEZ,—1936-39—ss, 3b, New York Cubans
RODRIGUEZ, ANTONIO—1939—p, Cuban Stars
RODRIGUEZ, B.CONRADO—1922, 1927-34—p, of, Cuban Stars
    (NNL), Cuban Stars (East)
RODRIGUEZ, BIENVIENIDO (BENNY) Y GARCIA—1946-48—of, c,
    Chicago American Giants

RODRIGUEZ, C.—1915—p, Cuban Stars
RODRIGUEZ, HECTOR ANTONIO—1944—3b, New York Cubans
RODRIGUEZ, HERRADO (See HECTOR ANTONIO RODRIGUEZ)
RODRIGUEZ, JOSE—1913-29—c, Cuban Stars, Cuban Stars
    (East), Detroit Stars, Kansas City Monarchs, Cuban Stars
    (NNL), All Cubans, Cuban Stars of Havana
RODRIGUEZ, OSCAR—1935—mgr., Havana Red Sox
RODOUD,—1921—c, Cuban Stars (East)
ROESINK, JOHN—1925-30—officer, owner, Detroit Stars
ROGAN, WILBER (BULLET JOE)—1917-46—p, of, 1b, 2b, 3b, ss,
    mgr., Kansas City Colored Giants, All Nations, Los Angeles
    White Sox, Kansas City Monarchs; umpire, NAL
ROGERS,—1900—p, Genuine Cuban Giants
ROGERS,—1914—2b, Louisville White Sox
ROGERS,—1934—of, Cincinnati Tigers
ROGERS, SID—1887—player, Cincinnati Browns
ROGERS, WILLIAM NATHANIEL (NAT)—1923-46—of, 1b, 3b, c,
    mgr., Harrisburg Giants, Brooklyn Royal Giants, Memphis
    Red Sox, Chicago Columbia Giants, Cole's American
    Giants, Chicago American Giants, Birmingham Black
    Barons, Kansas City Monarchs, Knoxville Giants, Brooklyn
    Eagles
ROJO, JULIO—1916-38—c, 3b, Cuban Stars (East), Havana Stars,
    Bacharach Giants, Baltimore Black Sox, Cuban Stars of
    Havana, Lincoln Giants, New York Cuban Stars, New York
    Cubans
ROLLINS,—1920—of, St. Louis Giants
ROLLS, CHARLES—1911—player, Leland Giants
ROMANACH, TOMAS—1916-20—ss, Long Branch Cubans,
    Cuban Stars (East)
ROMBY, ROBERT L.(BOB)—1946-50—p, Baltimore Elite Giants

Haywood Rose.
Chicago Historical Society

RONSELL,—1928-31—of, Birmingham Black Barons, Memphis Red Sox, Nashville Elite Giants

ROOKIE,—1931—of, Memphis Red Sox

ROONEY,—1941—p, New Orleans-St.Louis Stars

ROQUE, JACINTO (BATTLING SIKI)—1928-32—of, Cuban Stars (NNL), Cuba Stars (East)

ROSADO, RALPH—1955—c, Detroit Stars

ROSE, CECIL—1924—p, St. Louis Stars

ROSE, HAYWOOD—1907-08—c, Leland Giants

ROSELLE, BASILIO [ROSSELLE, ROSELLO]—1926-35—p, Cuban Stars (NNL), Cuban Stars (East), New York Cubans

ROSS,—1918—p, Indianapolis ABCs

ROSS, ALEX—1887-1889—3b, of, Greenville (Northern Mich. Lg.), and (Michigan St. Lg.)

ROSS, ARTHUR—1903-05—p, Chicago Union Giants, Leland Giants

ROSS, DICK—1925—of, St. Louis Stars

ROSS, E.—1919—of, Hilldale

ROSS, FRANK—1939—p, Memphis Red Sox

ROSS, GARY—1952—of, Indianapolis Clowns

ROSS, HAROLD—1922-25—p, Indianapolis ABCs, Chicago American Giants, Cleveland Browns

ROSS, JERRY—1926—p, Cleveland Elites

ROSS, SAM—1923—p, Hilldale, Harrisburg Giants, Washington Potomacs

ROSS, WILLIAM—1924-30—p, St. Louis Stars, Cleveland Hornets, Chicago American Giants, Homestead Grays, Cleveland Tigers, Detroit Stars

ROSSITER, GEORGE—1922-31—officer, owner, Baltimore Black Sox

ROTH, HERMAN JOSEPH (BOBBY)—1921-25—c, New Orleans Crescent Stars, Chicago American Giants, Milwaukee Bears, Detroit Stars, Birmingham Black Barons

ROTORET,—1950—p, New York Cubans

ROUSE, HOWARD—1951—of, Philadelphia Stars

ROVIRA, JAIME—1911—3b, All Cubans

ROWAN, BILL—1951-52—of, Kansas City Monarchs

ROWE,—1925, 1932—p, Indianapolis ABCs, Nashville Elite Giants

ROWE, WILLIAM (SCHOOLBOY)—1943-45—p, Chicago Brown Bombers, Pittsburgh Crawfords, Cleveland Buckeyes

ROY, ORMBY—1930-31—ss, Pittsburgh Crawfords

ROYALL, JOSEPH JOHN—1937-44—p, of, c, Indianapolis Athletics, Jacksonville Red Caps, New York Black Yankees, Cleveland Bears

ROYCE,—1926—player, Harrisburg Giants

RUFFIN, CHARLES LEON (LASSAS)—1935-50—c, mgr., Newark Eagles, Pittsburgh Crawfords, Philadelphia Stars, Houston Eagles, Brooklyn Eagles, Toledo Crawfords

RUIZ, ANTONIO (PEREZ)—1944—p, Cincinnati-Indianapolis Clowns

RUIZ, SILVINO (POPPA)—1928-42—p, Cuban Stars (ECL), New York Cubans

RUSH, JOE—1923-26—officer, owner, Birmingham Black Barons; sec, NNL; pres, NSL

RUSON,—1931—ss, Brooklyn Royal Giants

RUSS, PYTHIAS—1925-29—c, ss, Chicago American Giants, Memphis Red Sox

RUSSELL, 1929-31 (See RONSELL)

RUSSELL,—1933—p, Brooklyn Royal Giants

RUSSELL,—1936—ss, 3b, Cincinnati Tigers

RUSSELL, 1940 (See RUSSELL AWKARD)

RUSSELL, AARON A.—1913-20—3b, Homestead Grays

RUSSELL, BRANCH L.—1922-33—3b, of, Kansas City Monarchs, St. Louis Stars, Cleveland Stars, Cleveland Cubs

RUSSELL, E.—1924-26—3b, of, Harrisburg Giants, Dayton Marcos

RUSSELL, EWING—1935-36—c, Cincinnati Tigers

RUSSELL, FRANK (JUNIOR)—1943-54—2b, of, p, Baltimore Elite Giants, Memphis Red Sox, Birmingham Black Barons

RUSSELL, JOHN HENRY (PISTOL)—1923-34—2b, 3b, Memphis Red Sox, St. Louis Stars, Indianapolis ABCs, Pittsburgh Crawfords, Detroit Wolves, Cleveland Red Sox, Homestead Grays

RUSSELL, THOMAS—1950—p, Cleveland Buckeyes

RUTLEDGE,—1920-21—p, Dayton Marcos

RYAN, MERVEN J. (RED)—1915-34—p, Pittsburgh Stars of Buffalo, Brooklyn Royal Giants, Hilldale, Harrisburg Giants, Bacharach Giants, Baltimore Black Sox, Lincoln Stars, Newark Browns, Lincoln Giants, New York Black Yankees, Penn Red Caps of NY, Homestead Grays

RYLE,—1919—ss, Indianapolis ABCs

S

SAABIN,—1927—p, Cubin Stars (ECL)

SADLER, WILLIAM A.(BILL, BUBBY)—1934-39—ss, Brooklyn Eagles, Washington Black Senators, Bacharach Giants

SAILS,—1951—c, Philadelphia Stars

ST. THOMAS, LARRY—1943, 1947—c, Newark Eagles, New York Black Yankees

SALAS, WILFREDO—1948—p, New York Cubans

SALAZAR, LAZARO—1924-36—of, p, 1b, Cuban Stars (NNL), New York Cubans, Cuban Stars (East & West)

SALAZAR, SANTOS—1945—utility, New York Cubans

SALMON, HARRY—1923-35—p, Birmingham Black Barons, Homestead Grays, Memphis Red Sox, Detroit Wolves

SALTERS, EDWARD—1937—of, Detroit Stars

SALVAT,—1924-25—p, Cuban Stars (ECL)

SALVERSON, HENRY—1954-55—2b, Detroit Stars

SAMA, PABLO—1950—3b, Indianapolis Clowns

SAMPSON,—1899-1906—p, of, Genuine Cuban Giants, Cuban Giants

SAMPSON, EMANUAL (EDDIE, LEO)—1941-46—of, Birmingham Black Barons

SAMPSON, JOHN—1942—of, New York Cubans

SAMPSON, ORMOND LEONARD—1932-38—ss, Atlanta Black Crackers, Brooklyn Royal Giants, Newark Dodgers

SAMPSON, SAM—1940-41—2b, of, Cleveland Bears, Jacksonville Red Caps

SAMPSON, THOMAS (TOMMY, TOOTS)—1938-49—2b, 1b, mgr., Chicago American Giants, Birmingham Black Barons, New York Cubans

SAMUELS,—1940—p, Philadelphia Stars

SAN, PEDRO ALEJANDRO (ELI)—1926-28—p, Cuban Stars (ECL)

SANCHEZ,—1913—of, 1b, Philadelphia Giants

SANCHEZ, AMANDO—1948—p, Memphis Red Sox

SANCHEZ, GONZALO—1904-05—c, All Cubans

SANDERS, JAMES—1955—of, Kansas City Monarchs

SANDERS, WILLIE—1936—p, Memphis Red Sox

SANDERSON, JOHNNY—1947—ss, Kansas City Monarchs

SANDS, SAM (PIGGY)—1950-54—ss, c, Indianapolis Clowns, Kansas City Monarchs

SANFORD,—1925—c, Harrisburg Giants

SANTA CRUZ, EUGENIO (SANTA)—1909-10—of, Cuban Stars

SANTAELLA, ANASTACIO (JUAN, TACHO)—1935-36—2b, ss, New York Cubans

SANTIAGO,—1954, of, p, Louisville Black Colonels

SANTIAGO, CARLOS MANUEL—1946—2b, New York Cubans

SANTIAGO, JOSE GUILLERMO—1947-48—p, ss, New York Cubans

SANTOP, LOUIS (TOP, BIG BERTHA)—(real name Louis Santop Loftin)—1909-26—c, of, mgr., Fort Worth Wonders, Oklahoma Monarchs, Philadelphia Giants, Lincoln Giants,

Chicago American Giants, Lincoln Stars, Brooklyn Royal Giants, Hilldale

SAPERSTEIN, A.M. (ABE)—1932-50—booking agent; officer, Cleveland Cubs, Cincinnati Clowns, Chicago American Giants; pres, Negro Midwestern League, West Coast Negro Baseball Association

SARVIS, ANDREW (SMOKY)—1939-42—p, Cleveland Bears, Jacksonville Red Caps

SATTERFIELD,—1905-13—2b, ss, Cuban Giants, Genuine Cuban Giants, Brooklyn Royal Giants, Indianapolis ABCs

SAUNDERS,—1925-28—c, 3b, Pennsylvania Red Caps of NY

SAUNDERS, BOB—1926-37—2b, ss, p, Kansas City Monarchs, Detroit Stars, Bacharach Giants, Monroe Monarchs, Louisville Red Caps, Cleveland Hornets, Memphis Red Sox

SAUNDERS, LEO—1940—p, ss, Chicago American Giants, Birmingham Black Barons

SAUNDERS, WILLIAM—1887—of, Pittsburgh Keystones

SAUNDERS, WILLIAM—1950—c, Baltimore Elite Giants

SAVAGE,—1925—p, Bacharach Giants, Wilmington Potomacs

SAVAGE, ARTIE—1932—officer, Cleveland Stars

SAVAGE, BILL (JUNIOR)—1940—p, Memphis Red Sox

SAWYER, CARL—1924—2b, Detroit Stars

SAXON, THOMAS (LEFTY)—1942—p, New York Cubans

SAYLOR, ALFRED (GREYHOUND)—1940-45—p, 1b, c, Birmingham Black Barons, Cincinnati Buckeyes, Cincinnati Clowns

SCALES, GEORGE (TUBBY)—1920-52—2b, 3b, of, ss, mgr., St. Louis Giants, St. Louis Stars, Lincoln Giants, Newark Stars, Homestead Grays, New York Black Yankees, Philadelphia Stars, Baltimore Elite Giants, Pittsburgh Keystones, Birmingham Black Barons

SCANTLEBURY, PATRICIO ATHELSTAN (PAT)—1944-50—p, New York Cubans

SCHIFF,—1908—lf, Genuine Cuban Giants

SCHLICHTER, H. WALTER—1902-10—officer, mgr., Philadelphia Giants; pres, National Associaton of Colored Base Ball Clubs of the United States and Cuba

SCHMIDT,—1933—p, Philadelphia Stars

SCHORLING, JOHN M.—1911-27—officer, Chicago American Giants

SCOTLAND, JOE (OLD FORTY-FIVE)—1914-19—of, Chicago Union Giants, Indianapolis ABCs, Bowser's ABCs, Louisville Sox

SCOTT,—1914-16—p, Chicago Giants, Chicago American Giants

SCOTT,—1920-21—c, Detroit Stars

SCOTT,—1934—2b, Nashville Elite Giants

SCOTT,—1936—1b, of, Philadelphia Stars

SCOTT,—1940—of, Cincinnati Buckeyes

SCOTT, C.—1937—p, Birmingham Black Barons

SCOTT, C.L.—1915—player, Mohawk Giants

SCOTT, CHARLES—1919-20—of, St. Louis Giants

SCOTT, EDWARD—1952-55—officer, Indianapolis Clowns

SCOTT, ELISHA—1920—co-drafter, constitution of NNL

SCOTT, FRANK—1887-94—2b, ss, Chicago Unions

SCOTT, JIMMY—1950—p, Memphis Red Sox

SCOTT, JOHN—1944-50—of, 1b, Birmingham Black Barons, Kansas City Monarchs, Louisville Buckeyes, Chicago American Giants, Philadelphia Stars

SCOTT, JOSEPH (JOE)—1947-50—1b, Birmingham Black Barons, Chicago American Giants

SCOTT, JOSEPH BURT (JOE)—1944-49—of, Memphis Red Sox

SCOTT, ROBERT—1920-27—of, Brooklyn Royal Giants, Lincoln Giants Hilldale

SCOTT, ROBERT (BOB)—1946-50—p, 1b, Boston Blues (USL) New York Black Yankees

SCOTT, THEODORE—1932—c, Washington Pilots

SCOTT, WILLIAM—1932—officer, Louisville Black Caps

SCOTT, WILLIAM JR. (BILL)—1950-53—of, Philadelphia Stars, Birmingham Black Barons

SCOTT, WILLIE LEE (JOE)—1927-38—1b, Memphis Red Sox, Louisville White Sox, Indianapolis ABCs, Columbus Blue Birds, Homestead Grays, Chicago American Giants

SCRAGG, JESSE—1915—p, Philadelphia Giants

SCROGGINS, JOHN—1947—p, Kansas City Monarchs

SCRUGGS, ROBERT—1950—p, Cleveland Buckeyes

SCRUGGS, WILLIAM C. (WILLIE)—1949-54—p, Louisville Buckeyes, Cleveland Buckeyes, Houston Eagles, Birmingham Black Barons, Louisville Black Colonels, New Orleans Eagles

SCUDDER,—1887—c, Philadelphia Pythians

SEAGRAVES,—1937—of, Indianapolis Athletics

SEAGRAVES, SAMUEL—1946—c, Chicago American Giants

SEARCY, KELLY (LEFTY)—1950-55—p, Baltimore Elite Giants, Birmingham Black Barons

SEAVERS,—1942—p, Jacksonville Red Caps

SEAY, RICHARD WILLIAM (DICK, ERKIE)—1925-47—2b, ss, Pennsylvania Red Caps of New York, Newark Stars, Baltimore Black Sox, Brooklyn Royal Giants, Philadelphia Stars, Pittsburgh Crawfords, Newark Eagles, New York Black Yankees, Newark Browns

SEE,—1934—of, p, Cleveland Red Sox

SEGULA, PERCY—1921-23—p, New Orleans Caulfield Ads, Milwaukee Bears, Kansas City Monarchs

Bonnie Serrell.
Negro Leagues Baseball Museum

SELDEN, ALEXANDER A.—1887—mgr., Boston Resolutes

SELDEN, WILLIAM H.-1886-99—p, of, Boston Resolutes, Cuban Giants, New York Gorhams (Middle States Lg.), Lansing, Michigan Colored Capital All-Americans, Cuban X Giants, Trenton Cuban Giants (Middle States Lg.), York Cuban Giants (Eastern Interstate Lg.), York Colored Monarchs

SELDOM, {SELDEN}—1910-14—ss, 2b, Chicago Leland Giants, Indianapolis ABCs, Mohawk Giants

SELLER, (See GEORGE SUTTLES)

SEMLER, JAMES (SOLDIER BOY, BILL)—1932-48—officer, New York Black Yankees

SERRELL, WILLIAM C.(BONNIE, BARNEY)—1941-51—2b, 3b, Kansas City Monarchs, Chicago American Giants

SERUBY,—1888—of, Cuban X Giants

SETO,—1929—of, Cuban Stars (ECL)

SHACKLEFORD, JOHN G.—1924-46—3b, 2b, mgr., Cleveland Browns, Chicago American Giants, Birmingham Black Barons, Harrisburg Giants, Cleveland Clippers (USL), pres., United States League

SHADNEY,—1886—of, Trenton (NJ) Cuban Giants

SHAMBERGER—1938-40—ss, Atlanta Black Crackers, Indianapolis Crawfords

SHANKS, HANK—1927—1b, Birmingham Black Barons

SHANNON,—1932—of, Pittsburgh Crawfords

SHARPE,—1923—ss, St. Louis Stars

SHARPE, ROBERT (PEPPER)—1940-49—p, of, Memphis Red Sox, Chicago American Giants, Chicago Brown Bombers

SHARTZ,—1909-11—c, Quaker Giants, Philadelphia Giants

SHAW,—1920—of, St. Louis Giants

SHAW, R.—1897—p, Adrian (MI), Page Fence Giants, Chicago Unions

SHAW, THEODORE (TED)—1927-31—p, Chicago American Giants, Detroit Stars, Memphis Red Sox

SHAWLER,—1909-13—of, Leland Giants, Indianapolis ABCs

SHEELOR, JAMES (WILLIE)—1952-55—2b, ss, Chicago American Giants, Memphis Red Sox

SHEFFEY, DOUG—1910—p, Hilldale

SHELBY, HIAWATHA—1941-46—of, Philadelphia Stars, Indianapolis Clowns

SHELTON,—1920—c, Dayton Marcos

SHELTON,—1943—of, Harrisburg-St. Louis Stars

SHEPARD,—1938—of, Indianapolis ABCs

SHEPARD, FREDDIE—1945-48—p, of, Birmingham Black Barons, Chicago American Giants

SHEPARD, TOMMY—1945—2b, Birmingham Black Barons

SHEPPARD, RAY—1924-32—ss, Birmingham Black Barons, Detroit Wolves, Homestead Grays, Detroit Stars, Kansas City Monarchs Monroe Monarchs, Indianapolis ABCs

SHEPPARD, SAMUEL (SAM)—1887-1926—player, New York Gorhams; officer, St. Louis Stars, owner, Cleveland Elites

SHEPPARD, WILLIAM—1922-25—p, Kansas City Monarchs, Memphis Red Sox

SHERBER, JACK—1951—inf, New Orleans Eagles

SHERKLIFF, ROY (ED)—1931-34—p, Hilldale, Washington Pilots

SHERMAN, ART—1951—of, New Orleans Eagles

SHIELDS,—1916—p, Lincoln Giants

SHIELDS, CHARLIE (LEFTY)—1941-45—p, Chicago American Giants, Homestead Grays, New York Cubans

SHIELDS, JIMMY—1928-29—p, Bacharach Giants

SHINN, WILLIAM A.—1941-43—2b, New York Black Yankees, Louisville Black Caps

SHIPP, JESSE—1908-12—p, Brooklyn Royal Giants, New York Colored Giants

SHIRLEY,—1914—of, Brooklyn Royal Giants

SHIVELY, GEORGE (RABBIT)—1911-25—of, Indianapolis ABCs, Bacharach Giants, Washington Potomacs, Bowser's ABCs, Brooklyn Royal Giants, West Baden (IN) Sprudels

SHORTER, JACK—1951—3b, New Orleans Eagles

SHROPSHIRE,—1937—c, St. Louis Stars

SIBLEY,—1911-13—p, c, Indianapolis ABCs

SIEBERT,—1937—of, St. Louis Stars

SIERRA, FELIPE—1921-32—ss, 2b, 3b, of, All Cubans, Cuban Stars (NNL), Cuban Stars (East)

SIGENERO,—1940—p, New York Cubans

SIJO, (See SIJO GOMEZ)

SILVA, PEDRO—1921-22—p, of, All Cubans, Cuban Stars (NNL)

SILVERS, LINDSAY—1933—inf, Philadelphia Stars

SIMERSON,—1936—p, St. Louis Stars

SIMMONS—1914—of, Indianapolis ABCs

SIMMONS, (SI)—1926—p, Lincoln Giants

SIMMONS, HUBERT—1950—p, Baltimore Elite Giants

SIMMONS, J.R.—1887—player, Baltimore Lord Baltimores

SIMMONS, R.S.—1943-49—officer, Chicago American Giants; sec, NAL

SIMMS, FATE (PETE)—1952-54—3b, c, of, Philadelphia Stars, Memphis Red Sox

SIMMS, WILLIE (BILL, SIMMY)—1934-43—of, Monroe Monarchs, Cincinnati Tigers, Kansas City Monarchs, Chicago American Giants

SIMPSON,—1933—1b, of, Cleveland Giants, Baltimore Black Sox, Akron Tyrites

SIMPSON, H.—1886—1b, Trenton (NJ) Cuban Giants

SIMPSON, HARRY LEON (SUITCASE)—1946-48—of, Philadelphia Stars

SIMPSON, HERBERT HAROLD (HERB, BRIEFCASE)—1942-51—of, p, Birmingham Black Barons, Chicago American Giants, Homestead Grays

SIMPSON, JAMES—1886-87—of, Trenton (NJ) Cuban Giants, Philadelphia Pythians

SIMPSON, LAWRENCE—1910-20—p, of, Chicago Union Giants, Chicago Giants, Bowser's ABCs, Mohawk Giants, Indianapolis ABCs, West Baden (IN) Sprudels

SIMS, HARRY—1951-52—c, 1b, of, Philadelphia Stars

SIMS, LEO—1938—ss, Atlanta Black Crackers

SINCLAIR,—1932-33—3b, Bacharach Giants, Newark Dodgers

SINCLAIR, HARRY—1931—sec, NNL

SINGER, ORVILLE (RED)—1921-32—of, inf, Lincoln Giants, Cleveland Browns, Cleveland Tigers, Cleveland Cubs, Cleveland Stars

SINGLETON,—1896—c, Cuban X Giants

SINGLETON,—1946—p, Cleveland Buckeyes

SINGLONG,—1929—2b, of, Nashville Elite Giants

SIS—1934—of, New Orleans Crescent Stars

SISCO,—1913—lf, Philadelphia Giants

SKINNER,—1948—c, Newark Eagles

SKINNER, A.—1910—c, Leland Giants

SKINNER, FLOYD—1917—c, Kansas City Colored Giants

SLAUGHTER, C.—1884-85—inf, Baltimore Atlantics

SLAWSON,—1916—3b, 2b, Lincoln Stars

SLOAN, ROBERT—1919-21—of, Brooklyn Royal Giants

SMALLWOOD, DEWITT MARK (WOODY)—1951-54—of, New York Black Yankees, Philadelphia Stars, Indianapolis Clowns, Birmingham Black Barons

SMALLWOOD, LOUIS—1923-29—2b, Milwaukee Bears, Chicago Giants

SMART,—1932—p, Indianapolis ABCs

SMAULDING, OWEN BAZZ—1927-28—p, Kansas City Monarchs, Cleveland Tigers, Chicago American Giants, Birmingham Black Barons

SMITH,—1908—of, New York Colored Giants

SMITH,—1921—of, Chicago American Giants, St.Louis Giants

SMITH,—1923—of, Bacharach Giants

SMITH,—1925—c, St. Louis Stars

SMITH,—1926—p, Dayton Marcos

SMITH,—1927—of, Memphis Red Sox

SMITH,—1933—of, Nashville Elite Giants

SMITH, ALPHONSE EUGENE (AL, FUZZY)—1946-48—of, ss, Cleveland Buckeyes

SMITH, B.B.H. (BABE)—1887—p, New York Gorhams

SMITH, BOB—1954—c, Detroit Stars

SMITH, (BUSTER)—1932-33—p, 1b, Birmingham Black Barons

SMITH, C.—1931—1b, Chicago Columbia Giants

SMITH, CARL A. (CLYDE, BOOTNOSE)—1933-38—c, 3b, Birmingham Black Barons, Homestead Grays, Pittsburgh Crawfords

SMITH, CHARLES (CHINO)—1924-31—of, 2b, Philadelphia Giants, Brooklyn Royal Giants, Lincoln Giants

SMITH, CHARLIE—1938—inf, Washington Black Senators, Newark Eagles

SMITH, CLARENCE—1921-33—of, mgr., Columbus Buckeyes, Detroit Stars, Birmingham Black Barons, Baltimore Black Sox, Cleveland Cubs, Bacharach Giants, Chicago American Giants

SMITH, CLEVELAND (CLEO)—1922-28—2b, 3b, ss, Baltimore Black Sox, Lincoln Giants, Homestead Grays, Philadelphia Tigers, Harrisburg Giants, Newark Stars

SMITH, DODE—1942—p, Cincinnati-Cleveland Buckeyes

SMITH, DOUGLAS—1943—officer, Baltimore Elite Giants

SMITH, ED—1887—player, Boston Resolutes

SMITH, ERNEST—1934-40—c, Monroe Monarchs, Chicago American Giants

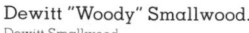

Dewitt "Woody" Smallwood.
Dewitt Smallwood

SMITH, EUGENE (GENIE)—1939-51—p, St. Louis Stars, New Orleans-St. Louis Stars, New York Black Yankees, Homestead Grays, Cleveland Buckeyes, Louisville Buckeyes, Chicago American Giants, Kansas City Monarchs

SMITH, EUGENE (GENE)—1942-46—3b, Jacksonville Red Caps, Cincinnati Buckeyes, Cleveland Buckeyes, Indianapolis Clowns

SMITH, F. (LEFTY)—1920-24—p, Richmond Giants, Baltimore Black Sox

SMITH, FORD (See JOHN FORD SMITH)

SMITH, FRED—1936, 1946—c, St.Louis Stars, Kansas City Monarchs

SMITH, GEORGE CORNELIUS—1952, 1956-57—2b, Indianapolis Clowns, Chicago American Giants

SMITH, H.—1921-32—p, Washington Potomacs, Baltimore Black Sox, Bacharach Giants, Homestead Grays, Lincoln Giants, Harrisburg Giants

SMITH, HARRY—1902-10—1b, of, Philadelphia Giants, Brooklyn Royal Giants, Genuine Cuban Giants

SMITH, HARVEY—1937-38—p, Pittsburgh Crawfords, Washington Elite Giants

SMITH, HENRY—1942-47—2b, ss, Jacksonville Red Caps, Chicago American Giants, Cincinnati Clowns, Cincinnati-Indianapolis Clowns, New York Black Yankees, Indianapolis Clowns

SMITH, HERB—1930-33—p, Hilldale, Philadelphia Stars

SMITH, I.—1942—p, Kansas City Monarchs

SMITH, HILTON LEE—1932-48—p, New Orleans Black Creoles, Monroe Monarchs, Kansas City Monarchs

SMITH, HY—1885—of, Brooklyn Remsens

SMITH, J.—1922-28—2b, ss, Brooklyn Royal Giants, Harrisburg Giants, Bacharach Giants

SMITH, JAMES—1903-06—3b, inf., Cuban X Giants, Leland Giants, Chicago Union Giants

SMITH, JAMES—1925, 1930—ss, Detroit Stars

SMITH, JOHN—1942—of, c, Birmingham Black Barons

SMITH, JOHN FORD (LEFTY, GERINOMO)—1939-50—of, p, Indianapolis Crawfords, Chicago American Giants, New York Black Yankees, Kansas City Monarchs, Indianapolis ABC's

SMITH, L.—1922-23—of, Baltimore Black Sox

SMITH, L.—1940-42—c, Cleveland Bears, Jacksonville Red Caps

SMITH, (LEFTY)—1920-21—p, of, Kansas City Monarchs, Chicago Giants

SMITH, (LEFTY)-1940-43-(See JOHN FORD SMITH)

SMITH, MARSHALL (DARKNIGHT)—1920-24—p, Baltimore Black Sox, Homestead Grays, Richmond Giants, Madison Stars

SMITH, MILTON (MILT)—1949-51—inf., Philadelphia Stars

SMITH, MONROE MANCE—1944—of, Kansas City Monarchs

SMITH, O.H.—1885—p, Brooklyn Remsens

SMITH, OLIVER (OLLIE)—1945—p, Cincinnati-Indianapolis Clowns

SMITH, P.—1939—p, St. Louis Stars

SMITH, PERCY—1952-54—p, Indianapolis Clowns

SMITH, PETE—1937—of, Pittsburgh Crawfords

SMITH, QUINCY—1943-46—of, Cleveland Buckeyes, Birmingham Black Barons

SMITH, R.—1943—of, Kansas City Monarchs

SMITH, RAYMOND D.—1945-46—p, Philadelphia Stars

SMITH, R. (RED)—1912-20—p, of, Lincoln Giants, Lincoln Stars, Bacharach Giants, Hilldale, Brooklyn Royal Giants

SMITH, ROBERT (JAKE)—1930-44—c, 3b, Birmingham Black Barons, Memphis Red Sox, Cincinnati Tigers, St. Louis Stars, New Orleans-St. Louis Stars, Chicago American Giants, Pittsburgh Crawfords, Cleveland Cubs, Nashville Elite Giants

SMITH, (SONNY)—1951—of, Chicago American Giants

SMITH, TAYLOR—1948-53—p, Chicago American Giants, Birmingham Black Barons

SMITH, THEOLIC (FIREBALL)—1936-51—p, Pittsburgh Crawfords, St. Louis Stars, New Orleans-St. Louis Stars, Cleveland Buckeyes, Kansas City Monarchs, Toledo Crawfords, Chicago American Giants

SMITH, TOBE—1907-14—owner, Kansas City (KAN) Giants

SMITH, (TURKEY)—1936—c, Cincinnati Tigers

SMITH, W.—1921, 1925—ss, p, Hilldale, Lincoln Giants

SMITH, WARDELL—1946—p, Chicago American Giants

SMITH, WILLIAM—1887—officer, Washington Capital Citys

SMITH, WILLIAM—1938—2b, ss, Newark Eagles

SMITH, WILLIAM T. (BIG BILL)—1883-16—c, of, mgr., Genuine Cuban Giants, Cuban X Giants, Philadelphia Giants, Brooklyn Royal Giants, Mohawk Giants, Chicago Unions, Memphis Giants, Cuban Giants, New York Stars, Brooklyn All-Stars, St.Louis Black Stockings

SMITH, WILLIE D.—1948—p, Homestead Grays

SMITH, WYMAN—1920-25—of, Baltimore Black Sox

SMOOT,—1886—ss, New York Gorhams

SNAER, LUCIAN—1923—umpire, NNL

SNEAD, SYLVESTER—1939-46—of, 2b, ss, Kansas City Monarchs, Cincinnati Clowns, New York Black Yankees

SNEED, EDDIE (LEFTY)—1940-42—p, Birmingham Black Barons

SNEEDEN,—1894—of, Cuban Giants

Ted Strong.
Moorland Spingarn Research Center

SNOW, FELTON (SKIPPER)—1931-47—3b, 2b, mgr., Louisville White Sox, Louisville Black Caps, Nashville Elite Giants, Columbus Elite Giants, Washington Elite Giants, Baltimore Elite Giants, Nashville Cubs, New Orleans Crescent Stars, Philadelphia Stars, Cleveland Red Sox

SNOWDEN,—1933—p, Detroit Stars

SNYDER,—1943—of, New York Cubans

SOCKARD, (See STOCKARD)

SOLDERO,—1932—p, Cuban Stars

SOLER, JUAN—1955—inf, Detroit Stars

SOLIS, MIGUEL L.—1928-36—2b, 3b, Cuban Stars (East), New York Cubans, Cuban Stars (NNL)

SOSA, RAMON—1948—c, Homestead Grays

SOSTRE, FRANCISCO—1947—p, New York Cubans

SOTO, JOSEPH—1951—c, New Orleans Eagles

SOTO, TONEY—1917—mgr., Havana Cubans

SOUELL, HERBERT (BALDY)[HERB CYRUS]—1940-51—inf, Kansas City Monarchs

SOUTHALL, JOHN—1898—c, Celeron Acme Colored Giants (Iron and Oil League)

SOUTHY,—1921—ss, Lincoln Giants

SOWELL, CLYDE—1948—p, Baltimore Elite Giants

SOWEN,—1933—ss, Cuban Stars

SPARKS, JOE—1937-40—2b, ss, St. Louis Stars, Chicago American Giants

SPARROW, ROY W.—1938—officer, Washington Black Senators

SPEARMAN, ALVIN—1950-51—p, Chicago American Giants

SPEARMAN, CHARLES—1919-31—c, 2b, 3b, ss, Brooklyn Royal Giants, Cleveland Elites, Homestead Grays, Lincoln Giants, Pennsylvania Red Caps of New York

SPEARMAN, CLYDE (BIG SPLO)-1932-46—of, Pittsburgh Crawfords, New York Black Yankees, New York Cubans, Newark Eagles, Philadelphia Stars, Chicago American Giants, Birmingham Black Barons

SPEARMAN, HENRY (JAKE, LITTLE SPLO)—1932-46—3b, 1b, Homestead Grays, Pittsburgh Crawfords, Washington Black Senators, New York Black Yankees, Baltimore Elite Giants, Philadelphia Stars, Newark Eagles

SPEARMAN, JIM—1951—p, Chicago American Giants

SPEARMAN, WILLIAM—1923-29—p, Memphis Red Sox, Cleveland Elites, Cleveland Hornets, Nashville Elite Giants, St. Louis Stars

SPEDDEN, CHARLES P.—1922-31—officer, owner, Baltimore Black Sox

SPEEDY, WALTER—1914—inf, Chicago American Giants

SPENCER,—1921-22—of, Pittsburgh Keystones

SPENCER,—1943—of, Newark Eagles, New York Black Yankees

SPENCER, J.C.(See JOSEPH SPENCER)

SPENCER, JOSEPH B.—1942-50—2b, ss, Birmingham Black Barons, Homestead Grays, Pittsburgh Crawfords, New York Cubans, Baltimore Elite Giants, New York Black Yankees

SPENCER, WILLIAM (PEE WEE)—1933-40, 1945—c, 3b, mgr., Chicago American Giants, Toledo Crawfords, Indianapolis Crawfords, Toledo Cubs (USL)

SPENCER, WILLIE—1941—of, Birmingham Black Barons

SPENCER, ZACK—1931-33—p, Chicago Columbia Giants, Columbus Blue Birds, Detroit Stars, Cleveland Cubs

SPIKE,—1923—p, Washington Potomacs

SPOTSVILLE, ROY (BILL)—1950-51—p, Houston Eagles, New Orleans Eagles

STACK,—1934—c, Washington Pilots

STAMMORE,—1926—p, Lincoln Giants

STAMPS, HULAN (LEFTY)—1924-33—p, Memphis Red Sox, Indianapolis ABCs, Detroit Stars

STANKIE, EDDIE—1951—of, Birmingham Black Barons

STANLEY, JOHN WESLEY (NECK)-1928-49—p, Bacharach Giants, Lincoln Giants, Quaker Giants, Brooklyn Royal Giants, Baltimore Black Sox, New York Black Yankees, New York Cubans, Philadelphia Stars, Hilldale

STAPLES, JOHN—1921—mgr., Montgomery Grey Sox

STARK, LEE—1887—player, Cincinnati Browns

STARKS, JAMES—1937-46—1b, New York Black Yankees, Harrisburg-St. Louis Stars, Pittsburgh Crawfords

STARKS, LESLIE—1927, 1933-35—of, Memphis Red Sox, Kansas City Monarchs, Newark Dodgers

STARKS, OTIS (LEFTY)—1919-1939—p, Hilldale, Chicago American Giants, Brooklyn Royal Giants, Lincoln Giants, Bacharach Giants, Newark Stars, St. Louis Giants

STARMAND,—1887—of, Pittsburgh Keystones

STEARMAN, TOM—1909, 1915—of, Kansas City (KAN) Giants

STEARNES, GERALD—1951—c, New Orleans Eagles

STEARNES, NORMAN THOMAS (TURKEY)—1920-42, 45-of, Nashville Giants, Montgomery Grey Sox, Detroit Stars, Lincoln Giants, Cole's American Giants, Chicago American Giants, Philadelphia Stars, Kansas City Monarchs, Detroit Black Sox, Toledo Cubs (USL)

STEDGRASS,—1937—p, Memphis Red Sox

STEEL, HARRY—1938—p, Indianapolis ABCs

STEELE, EDWARD (ED, STAINLESS)—1941-55—of, Birmingham Black Barons, Detroit Stars

STEELE, WILLIE—1953—of, Kansas City Monarchs

STEPHENS, (See FRANK STEVENS)

STEPHENS, B.G.—1955—p, Kansas City Monarchs

STEPHENS, JOE (JUNIOR)—1949-50—p, New York Black Yankees

STEPHENS, PAUL EUGENE (JAKE) [STEVENS]—1921-37—ss, Hilldale, Philadelphia Giants, Homestead Grays, Pittsburgh Crawfords, Philadelphia Stars, New York Black Yankees

STEVENS,—1927-29—c, Detroit Stars

STEVENS,—1929—p, Bacharach Giants

STEVENS,—1950—p, Houston Eagles

STEVENS, FRANK—1921-31—p, of, 1b, Chicago American Giants, Indianapolis ABCs, Cleveland Hornets, Toledo Tigers, St. Louis Stars, Cleveland Tigers, Cuban Stars (NNL)

STEVENS, (JAKE), see STEPHENS

STEVENS, JIM—1933—2b, Philadelphia Stars

STEVENS, L.(See FRANK STEVENS)

STEVENSON, (LEFTY)—1925-28—p, of, Cleveland Tigers, Indianapolis ABCs, Birmingham Black Barons

STEVENSON, WILLIE—1940, 1943—p, Homestead Grays

STEWART,—1920-24—p, ss, St. Louis Giants, St. Louis Stars, Chicago American Giants

STEWART, ARTIS—1950—p, Cleveland Buckeyes

STEWART, CHARLES W. (CHARLEY)—1951—of, Chicago American Giants

STEWART, FRANK—1936-40—p, Washington Elite Giants, Indianapolis ABCs, Memphis Red Sox

STEWART, LEONIEL (LEON)—1940-42—p, of, Newark Eagles, Birmingham Black Barons

STEWART, LESLIE—1922—c, Philadelphia Giants

STEWART, MANUEL—1943-47—3b, p, Baltimore Elite Giants

STEWART, RILEY A. SR.—1946-50—p, Chicago American Giants, New York Cubans, Memphis Red Sox

STILES,—1937—of, Detroit Stars

STILES, NORRIS—1950—p, Cleveland Buckeyes

STILL, BOBBY—1887—player, Philadelphia Pythians

STILL, JOE—1887—player, Philadelphia Pythians

STILLS, JIMMY—1928-31—of, Pittsburgh Crawfords

STINSON,—1932—of, Atlanta Black Crackers

STINSON, CHARLES P.—1887—player, Philadelphia Pythians

STITLER,—1922—p, Bacharach Giants

STOCKARD, THEODORE (LICKS)—1927-28, 1937—ss, 3b, Cleveland Hornets, Cleveland Tigers, Kansas City Monarchs

STOCKLEY, LAWRENCE—1950—of, New York Black Yankees

STOKES,—1933—p, Detroit Stars

STONE, ED—1931-50—of, Bacharach Giants, Brooklyn Eagles, Newark Eagles, Philadelphia Stars, Pittsburgh Crawfords, New York Black Yankees

STONE, MARCENIA (TONI)—1951-54—2b, Indianapolis Clowns, Kansas City Monarchs

STORTS,—1933—p, Cuban Stars (East)

STOVALL,—1924—p, Cleveland Browns

STOVALL, FRED—1930-35—officer, Monroe Monarchs

STOVEY, GEORGE WASHINGTON—1886-96—p, of, Jersey City (Eastern League); Newark (International League); Cuban Giants, New York Gorhams (Middle States Lg.), Cuban X Giants, Worchester (NorthEastern Lg.), Ansonia Cuban Giants Connecticut St. Lg.), Troy (NY St. Lg.), York Cuban Giants (Eastern Interstate Lg.), Trenton Cuban Giants (Middle States Lg.)

STRATTON, FELTON—1930—c, Hilldale

STRATTON, LEROY—1920-33—ss, 3b, 2b, mgr., Nashville Giants, Milwaukee Bears, Birmingham Black Barons, Chicago American Giants, Nashville Elite Giants

STREETER, SAMUEL (SAM, LEFTY)—1920-36—p, Montgomery Grey Sox, Atlanta Black Crackers, Chicago American Giants, Bacharach Giants, Lincoln Giants, Birmingham Black Barons, Homestead Grays, Cleveland Cubs, Pittsburgh Crawfords, Baltimore Black Sox

STREETS, ALBERT—1925—inf, Chicago American Giants

STRICKLAND,—1924—p, Indianapolis ABCs

STRONG,—1913—p, Chicago American Giants

STRONG, FULTON—1922-23—p, Cleveland Tate Stars, Chicago American Giants New Orleans Crescent Stars, Milwaukee Bears

STRONG, HENRY—1936—ss, Chicago American Giants

STRONG, JOSEPH TALTON (JOE, BABY FACE, J.T.)—1922-37—p, Hilldale, St. Louis Stars, Homestead Grays, Baltimore Black Sox

STRONG, NATHANIEL COLVIN (NAT)—1908-34—booking agent; officer, Brooklyn Royal Giants, New York Black Yankees, Cuban Stars

STRONG, OTHELLO L.—1949-52—p, Chicago American Giants

STRONG, T.R. (TED)—1937-51—of, inf, mgr., Indianapolis Athletics, Indianapolis ABCs, Kansas City Monarchs, Indianapolis Clowns, Chicago American Giants

STROTHERS, C.W. (COLONEL)—1924-27—officer, Harrisburg Giants

STROTHERS, TIMOTHY SAMUEL (SAM)—1907-18—c, 1b, 2b, Leland Giants, Chicago American Giants, Chicago Giants, Chicago Union Giants, West Baden (IN) Sprudels

STUART,—1900—ss, Cuban X Giants

STUART, JOE—1884-85—p, c, Brooklyn Atlantics

STUBBLEFIELD, MICKEY—1948—p, Kansas City Monarchs

STUMM,—1937—player, Philadelphia Stars

STURDEVEN, MARK—1916, 1928—player, treasurer, Hilldale

STURM,—1926—of, Indianapolis ABCs

SUAREZ,—1916-21—p, Cuban Stars, Havana Stars, Cuban Stars of Havana, Cuban Stars (NNL), New York Cuban Stars, Cincinnati Cubans

SULLIVAN,—1918—of, Chicago Union Giants

SULLIVAN,—1937—p, Birmingham Black Barons

SUMMERALL, WILLIAM (BIG, RED)—1936-40—p, St. Louis Stars, Memphis Red Sox

SUMMERS, LONNIE—1938-51—of, c, Baltimore Elite Giants, Chicago American Giants

SUMMERS, SMITH (TACK)—1923-29—of, Toledo Tigers,

Cleveland Browns, Cleveland Elites, Cleveland Hornets, Cleveland Tigers, Chicago American Giants

SUNKETT, PETE (GOLDEN)—1943-45—p, Philadelphia Stars

SURRATT, ALFRED (SLICK)—1949-51—of, Kansas City Monarchs

SUSINI, ANTONIO—1921—2b, ss, All Cubans

SUTTLES, EARL—1950—1b, Cleveland Buckeyes

SUTTLES, GEORGE (MULE)—1918-48—1b, of, mgr., Birmingham Black Barons, St. Louis Stars, Detroit Wolves, Washington Pilots, Chicago American Giants, Cole's American Giants, Newark Eagles, New York Black Yankees, Bacharach Giants Baltimore Black Sox, Lincoln Giants; umpire

SUTTLES, J.—1923—officer, Memphis Red Sox, Pres.;NSL

SUTTON,—1929—of, Nashville Elite Giants

SUTTON, LEROY—1940-46—p, New Orleans-St. Louis Stars, Chicago American Giants, Cincinnati-Indianapolis Clowns, Boston Blues

SWALLIS,—1921—p, Cincinnati Cubans

SWAN,—1933—ss, Akron Tyrites

SWANCY,—1924—p, Indianapolis ABCs

SWEATT, GEORGE ALEXANDER (NEVER, SHARKEY, THE TEACHER)—1921-28—3b, 2b, of, Chicago Giants, Kansas City Monarchs, Chicago American Giants

SWICKET,—1909—p, Quaker Giants

SYDNEY,—1944—of, New York Black Yankees

SYKES, FRANKLIN J.(DOC)—1913-26—p, Lincoln Stars, Hilldale, Baltimore Black Sox, Brooklyn Royal Giants, Philadelphia Giants

SYKES, JOE (SIKI)—1942—of, Cincinnati Clowns

SYKES, MELVIN—1926—of, Hilldale, Lincoln Giants

T

TABORN, EARL—1946-51—c, Kansas City Monarchs

TALBERT, DANGERFIELD—1900-11—3b, Leland Giants, Chicago Union Giants, Cuban X Giants, Chicago Unions, Algona (IA) Brownies

TALBERT, JAMES [TOLBERT]—1947-48—c, Chicago American Giants

TALLEY,—1932-34—p, Bacharach Giants, New York Black Yankees

TAPLEY, JOHN R.—1933—3b, Akron Tyrites

TAPLEY, TOWNSEND—1933—ss, Akron Tyrites

TATE,—1914-16—p, Lincoln Giants, Philadelphia Giants

TATE, GEORGE J.—1918-23—officer, Cleveland Tate Stars; vice pres, NNL

TATE, ROOSEVELT (SPEED)—1931-37—of, Birmingham Black Barons, Nashville Elite Giants, Memphis Red Sox, Cincinnati Tigers, Knoxville Giants, Louisville White Sox, Chicago American Giants, Louisville Black Caps

TATUM, REECE (GOOSE)—1941-49—of, 1b, Birmingham Black Barons, Minneapolis-St. Paul Gophers, Cincinnati Clowns, Cincinnati-Indianapolis Clowns, Indianapolis Clowns

TAYLOR,—1919—2b, Dayton Marcos

TAYLOR,—1926—1b, Dayton Marcos

TAYLOR, ALFRED—1933, 1936—1b, Akron Tyrites, Cincinnati Tigers

TAYLOR, BENJAMIN—1947—p, New York Black Yankees

TAYLOR, BENJAMIN H. (BEN)—1910-40—1b, mgr., Chicago American Giants, Indianapolis ABCs, St. Louis Giants, Bacharach Giants, Washington Potomacs, Harrisburg Giants, Baltimore Black Sox, Baltimore Stars, Brooklyn Eagles, Washington Black Senators, New York Cubans, West Baden (IN) Sprudels, Washington Pilots, Hilldale, Lincoln Giants; umpire NNL

TAYLOR, (BIG) (See JOHN TAYLOR)

TAYLOR, CHARLES ISHUM (C.I.)—1904-22—2b, mgr., Birmingham Giants, West Baden, (IN) Sprudels, Indianapolis ABCs; vice pres, NNL

TAYLOR, MRS. C.I.—1922-24—officer, Indianapolis ABCs

TAYLOR, CYRUS G.—1923-25—of, Lincoln Giants, Harrisburg Giants, Baltimore Black Sox

TAYLOR, GEORGE—1889-06—1b, c, inf.of, Aspen (Colo. St. Lg.), Denver (Colorado St. Lg.) Adrian (MI) Page Fence Giants, Chicago Union Giants, Leland Giants, Beatrice (Neb. St. Lg.), Lincoln (NEB) Giants

TAYLOR, H.C.—1887—player, Boston Resolutes

TAYLOR, JAMES ALLEN (CANDY JIM)—1904-48—3b, 2b, mgr., Birmingham Giants, St. Paul Gophers, Leland Giants, Indianapolis ABCs, St. Louis Giants, Chicago American Giants, Dayton Marcos, Cleveland Tate Stars, St. Louis Stars, Cleveland Elites, Memphis Red Sox, Detroit Stars, Nashville Elite Giants, Columbus Elite Giants, Homestead Grays, Baltimore Elite Giants, Bowser's ABCs, Toledo Tigers, Louisville Sox, Chicago Giants, West Baden (IN) Sprudels, Birmingham Black Barons, Washington Elite Giants; vice chairman, NNL

TAYLOR, JIM—1896—of, Cuban Giants

TAYLOR, JOHN (BIG, RED)-1920-28-p, Chicago Giants, Lincoln Giants, Kansas City Monarchs, Penn Red Caps of NY, Chicago American Giants

TAYLOR, JOHN A. JR (JOHNNY, SCHOOLBOY)—1935-45—p, New York Cubans, Pittsburgh Crawfords, Toledo Crawfords, Homestead Grays, Bacharach Giants

"Schoolboy" Johnny Taylor.
Larry Lester

TYLER, WILLIAM (STEEL ARM)—1925-32—p, Memphis Red Sox, Detroit Stars, Kansas City Monarchs, Cole's American Giants

TYMS,—1922—of, Chicago American Giants

TYNOR,—1943—of, New York Cubans

TYREE, RUBY—1916-24—p, All Nations, Chicago American Giants, Cleveland Browns

TYSON, ARMAND CUPREE (CAP)—1936-40—c, Birmingham Black Barons

TYUS, JULIUS JR—1947—p, Philadelphia Stars

U

UNDERHILL, BOB—1924—p, Hilldale

UNDERWOOD, ELY—1932, 1937—of, Pittsburgh Crawfords, Detroit Stars

UNDERWOOD, JIM—1954—ss, Detroit Stars, Louisville Black Colonels

UNDERWOOD, RAY—1937—p, Detroit Stars

V

VACTOR, JOHN—1886-88—p, Philadelphia Pythians, New York Gorhams, Trenton (NJ) Cuban Giants

VALDES, FERMIN—1944—2b, Cincinnati-Indianapolis Clowns

VALDES, ROGELIO—1905-11—of, 2b, All Cubans, Cuban X Giants

VALDEZ, FELIX (MANUEL)—1951-52—p, Memphis Red Sox

VALDEZ, PABLO (TONY)—1910-20—of, p, Stars of Cuba, Cuban Stars (NNL), Havana Cubans, Cuban Stars

VALDEZ, STRICO (SWAT)—1931-39—2b, ss, Cuban Stars, Atlanta Black Crackers, New York Cubans

VALENTINE,—1915-18—of, Hilldale, Philadelphia Giants

VALENTINE, JIMMY—1954-55—3b, 2b, Louisville Black Colonels, Detroit Stars, Memphis Red Sox

VALEZ,—1941—of, New York Cubans

VALOS,—1917—3b, Cuban Giants

VAN BUREN, BILL—1931—of, Memphis Red Sox

VANCE, COLUMBUS (LUKE)—1927-34—p, Birmingham Black Barons, Homestead Grays, Detroit Wolves, Detroit Stars, Indianapolis ABCs

VAN DYKE, FRED—1895-97—p, of, Adrian (MI) Page Fence Giants

VANEVER, BOBBY—1944—inf, Kansas City Monarchs

VARGAS, GUILLERMO—1949—of, New York Cubans

VARGAS, JUAN ESTEBAN (TETELO)[JOSE]—1927-44—of, ss, Cuban Stars (ECL) Cuban Stars (NNL), New York Cubans,

VARGAS, ROBERTO ENRIQUE—1948—p, Chicago American Giants

VARONA, GILBERTO—1950-55-1b, Memphis Red Sox

VARONA, ORLANDO CLEMENTE [VERONA]—1948-55—ss, Memphis Red Sox

VASQUEZ, ARMANDO BERNANDO—1944-52—utility, Cincinnati-Indianapolis Clowns, Indianapolis Clowns, New York Cubans

VAUGHAN, OSCAR—1951—of, New Orleans Eagles

VAUGHN, DON—1955—p, Kansas City Monarchs

VAUGHN, HAROLD—1926-27—of, Kansas City Monarchs

VAUGHN, JOE—1931—sec, NSL

VAUGHN, RAY (SLIM)—1931-34—p, Newark Dodgers, Newark Browns

VEADEZ, HENRY—1952—inf, Kansas City Monarchs

VEAL,—1931—p, of, Birmingham Black Barons

VELASQUEZ, JOSE LARU—1948-50—p, Indianapolis Clowns

VENEY, JEROME—1908-17—of, mgr., Homestead Grays

VENTURA,—1929—p, Cuban Stars (NNL)

VERNAL, (SLEEPY)—1941—p, New York Cubans

VERONA, ORLANDO (See ORLANDO VARONA)

VICTORY, GEORGE M.—1919-20—officer, Pennsylvania Giants

VIERIRA, CHRIS—1949—of, New York Black Yankees

VILLA, ROBERTO MANOLO (BOBBY)—1910-22—of, 2b, Stars of Cuba, Cuban Stars of Havana, All Cubans, Cuban Stars (NNL)

VILLAFANE, VINCETE—1947—utl., Indianapolis Clowns

VILLODAS, LUIS (KING KONG)—1946-47—c, Baltimore Elite Giants

VINCENT, IRVING B.(LEFTY)—1934-35—p, Pittsburgh Crawfords

VINES, EDDIE—1940—p, 3b, Chicago American Giants, Birmingham Black Barons

VIVENS,—1929—p, St. Louis Stars

W

WADDY, IRVING (LEFTY)—1932-33—p, Indianapolis ABCs, Detroit Stars

WADE, LEE—1909-19—p, of, 1b, Cuban Giants, Philadelphia Giants, St. Louis Giants, Lincoln Giants, Chicago American Giants, Lincoln Stars, Brooklyn Royal Giants, Pennsylvania Red Caps of New York

WAGNER, BILL—1921-31—ss, 2b, mgr., Lincoln Giants, Brooklyn Royal Giants, New York Black Yankees

WAGNER, J.—1927—2b, 1b, Bacharach Giants, Hilldale

WAITE, ARNOLD—1936-37—p, Homestead Grays, Washington Elite Giants

Juan Esteban "Tetelo" Vargas.
Luis Munoz Collection

WAKEFIELD, BERT—1895-1902, 1915—1b, 2b, Chicago Unions, Kansas City (KS) Giants, Salina and Emporia (Kansas St. Lg.), Algona (IA) Brownies, Chicago Union Giants

WALDON, (ALLIE, OLLIE)—1944—of, Chicago American Giants, Kansas City Monarchs

WALKER,—1896—of, Adrian Page Fence Giants

WALKER,—1905—c, Brooklyn Royal Giants

WALKER, A.—1923, 1927, 1933—p, of, Milwaukee Bears, Kansas City Monarchs, Newark Dodgers

WALKER, A.M.—1937—mgr., Birmingham Black Barons

WALKER, CASEY—1935-37-c, Newark Dodgers, Indianapolis Athletics

WALKER, CHARLIE JR.—1930-34—officer, Homestead Grays

WALKER, EDSALL (BIG)—1936-45—p, Homestead Grays, Philadelphia Stars, Baltimore Elite Giants

WALKER, GEORGE T.(LITTLE, SCHOOLBOY)—1937-52—p, Homestead Grays, Kansas City Monarchs

WALKER, H.—1932—c, Monroe Monarchs

WALKER, JACK (JIM)—1940-43—p, Newark Eagles, Philadelphia Stars, Harrisburg-St. Louis Stars, New York Black Yankees

WALKER, JESSE (HOSS, DEUCE, AUSSA)—1929-55—ss, 3b, mgr., officer Bacharach Giants, Cleveland Cubs, Nashville Elite Giants, Washington Elite Giants, Baltimore Elite Giants, New York Black Yankees, Birmingham Black Barons, Cincinnati Clowns, Cincinnati-Indianapolis Clowns, Nashville Cubs, Indianapolis Clowns, Columbus Elite Giants, Detroit Stars

WALKER, LARRY (See LARRY DOBY)

WALKER, MOSES FLEETWOOD (FLEET)—1883-89—c, of, 1b, Toledo (Northwestern League and American Association); Cleveland (Western League); Waterbury (Southern New England and Eastern Leagues); Newark and Syracuse (International League)

WALKER, MOSES L.—1928-31—officer, Detroit Stars

WALKER, PETE (LOTTIE)—1923-26—p, of, 2b, 3b, Homestead Grays

WALKER, R.A.—1887—inf, Boston Resolutes

WALKER, ROBERT TAYLOR (R.T.)—1945-49—p, Homestead Grays, Boston Blues

WALKER, TOM (TONY)—1945—p, Baltimore Elite Giants

WALKER, W.—1931-32—of, Monroe Monarchs

WALKER, WELDY WILBERFORCE—1884-87—of, c, 2b, Toledo (American Association); Akron (Ohio State League); Pittsburgh Keystones, Cleveland (Western League)

WALKER, WILLIAM—1937—0f, St.Louis Stars

WALLACE,—1914—of, Louisville White Sox

WALLACE,—1951—p, Indianapolis Clowns

WALLACE, FELIX (DICK)—1906-27—ss, 2b, 3b, mgr., St. Paul Gophers, Leland Giants, St. Louis Giants, Bacharach Giants, Lincoln Giants, Famous Cuban Giants, Hilldale

WALLACE, HOWARD—1940—2b, Cincinnati Buckeyes

WALLACE, JACK—1926-31—3b, 2b, Bacharach Giants, Cleveland Cubs, Philadelphia Giants, Pennsylvania Red Caps of NY

WALLACE, JAMES—1949—c, Houston Eagles

WALLER, GEORGE—1943—inf, Chicago Brown Bombers

WALLS, EDDIE [WALL]—1925-26—p, St. Louis Stars, Cleveland Hornets, Cleveland Elites

WALLS, (GREENIE)—1941-42—umpire

WALLS, JAMES—1954—of, Kansas City Monarchs

WALLS, MAHLON—1947—player, Philadelphia Stars

WALLS, MICKEY—1951—p, Indianapolis Clowns

WALSH,—1916—2b, Bacharach Giants

WALSH,—1936—p, Newark Eagles

WALTERS,—1923-24—p, Milwaukee Bears, Cleveland Browns

WALTON,—1916—ss, Chicago Giants

WALTON,—1948—utl., Indianapolis Clowns

WALTON, (FUZZY)—1930, 1938—of, Baltimore Black Sox, Pittsburgh Crawfords

WANNAMAKER, GEORGE—1954-55—3b, Indianapolis Clowns

WARD,—1942—p, Boston Royal Giants

WARD, BRITT—1944—c, Kansas City Monarchs

WARD, C. (PINKY)—1923-35—of, Memphis Red Sox, Chicago Columbia Giants, Louisville Black Caps, Cincinnati Tigers, Birmingham Black Barons, Brooklyn Eagles, Indianapolis ABCs Bacharach Giants, Washington Potomacs

WARD, IRA—1922-27—ss, 1b, Chicago Giants

WARE, ARCHIE V.—1940-51—1b, Chicago American Giants, Kansas City Monarchs, Cleveland Buckeyes, Louisville Buckeyes, Indianapolis Clowns, Cincinnati Buckeyes

WARE, JOE (SHOWBOAT)—1920, 1932-36—of, Nashville Giants Cleveland Stars, Cleveland Giants, Memphis Red Sox, Akron Tyrites, Pittsburgh Crawfords, Newark Dodgers

WARE, WILLIAM—1924-26—1b, Chicago American Giants

WARFIELD, FRANCIS XAVIER (FRANK)—1914-32—2b, ss, 3b, mgr., St. Louis Giants, Indianapolis ABCs, Kansas City Monarchs, Detroit Stars, Hilldale, Baltimore Black Sox, Washington Pilots, Bowser's ABCs, Dayton Marcos

WARMACK, H.—1910-11—1b, St. Louis Giants

WARMACK, SAM—1922-38—of, Richmond Giants, Hilldale, Bacharach Giants, Louisville Black Colonels, Washington Pilots, Columbus Blue Birds

WARREN, CICERO—1946-47—p, Homestead Grays

WARREN, JESSE—1940-47—2b, 3b, p, Memphis Red Sox, New Orleans-St. Louis Stars, Birmingham Black Barons, Chicago American Giants, Boston Blues, Boston Royal Giants

WARWICK, [WARRICK]—1903-05—p, of, Philadelphia Giants, Brooklyn Royal Giants

WASH,—1932—2b, Chicago American Giants

WASHINGTON,—1929—c, Nashville Elite Giants

WASHINGTON, BILL—1951-55—ss, 3b, Philadelphia Stars, Memphis Red Sox

WASHINGTON, EDGAR (ED, BLUE)—1915-20—p, 1b, Chicago American Giants, Kansas City Monarchs

WASHINGTON, I. JASPER (JAP)—1922-37—3b, 1b, of, Pittsburgh Keystones, Homestead Grays, Pittsburgh Crawfords, Newark Browns; umpire, NNL

WASHINGTON, ISAAC—1928—officer, Bacharach Giants

WASHINGTON, JOHN G. (JOHNNY)—1933-51—1b, 3b, Montgomery Grey Sox, Birmingham Black Barons, Pittsburgh Crawfords, New York Black Yankees, Baltimore Elite Giants, Houston Eagles, New Orleans Eagles

WASHINGTON, L.—1884-85—ss, Baltimore Atlantics

WASHINGTON, LAFAYETTE (FAY)—1940-45—p, Chicago American Giants, Birmingham Black Barons, Cincinnati-Indianapolis Clowns, Kansas City Monarchs, St. Louis Stars, New Orleans-St. Louis Stars

WASHINGTON, LAWRENCE—1945—1b, New York Black Yankees

WASHINGTON, NAMON (CY)—1920-31—of, ss, c, Indianapolis ABCs, Hilldale, Brooklyn Cuban Giants, Philadelphia Tigers, Lincoln Giants, Brooklyn Royal Giants, Baltimore Black Sox

WASHINGTON, PETER (PETE)—1923-36—of, Washington Potomacs, Wilmington Potomacs, Baltimore Black Sox, Philadelphia Stars, Lincoln Giants

WASHINGTON, TED—1952—ss, Philadelphia Stars

WASHINGTON, TOM—1904-11—c, of, Philadelphia Giants, Chicago Giants, Pittsburgh Giants, Cuban X Giants, Leland Giants

WATERS,—1938-39—of, Bacharach Giants

WATERS, DICK—1916—mgr., St. Louis Giants

WATERS, GEORGE—1887—player, Boston Resolutes

WATERS, THEODORE (TED)—1916-1928-p, of, Chicago Giants, Hilldale, Philadelphia Tigers, Bacharach Giants

WATKINS,—1913—p, Chicago American Giants

WATKINS, G.C.—1937—officer, Indianapolis Athletics

WATKINS, JOHN F.(POP)—1899-1922—1b, c, mgr., Genuine Cuban Giants, Cuban Giants, Havana Red Sox, Pop Watkins Stars, Famous Cuban Giants

WATKINS, MURRAY (SKEETER)—1943-50—3b, Newark Eagles, Philadelphia Stars

WATKINS, RICHARD—1950—inf, Memphis Red Sox

WATROUS, SHERMAN—1952—of, Memphis Red Sox

WATSON,—1914—1b, c, Louisville White Sox

WATSON,—1951—1b, Philadelphia Stars

WATSON, AMOS—1945-50—p, Cincinnati-Indianapolis Clowns, Baltimore Elite Giants, Indianapolis Clowns, Kansas City Monarchs

WATSON, DAVID—1923—p, Birmingham Black Barons

WATSON, EVERETT—1931—officer, Detroit Stars

WATSON, GEORGE JOHNNY—1922-26—of, Detroit Stars

WATSON, JIMMY—1950—p, New York Cubans

WATSON, ROBERT—1950—p, New York Cubans

WATSON, WILLIAM—1924-26, 1931—of, Brooklyn Royal Giants, Bacharach Giants, Penn Red Caps of NY

WATTERS, {WATERS}—1916—inf., Chicago Giants

WATTS, ANDREW (SONNY, BIG SIX)—1946-52—inf, Cleveland Buckeyes, Birmingham Black Barons, Indianapolis Clowns

WATTS, EDDIE—1924-27—2b, 1b, St. Louis Stars, Cleveland Hornets, Cleveland Elites

WATTS, HERMAN (LEFTY)—1941-42—p, Jacksonville Red Caps, Cincinnati-Cleveland Buckeyes, New York Black Yankees

WATTS, JACK—1911-19—c, Louisville Cubs, Chicago American Giants, Indianapolis ABCs, Dayton Marcos, Bowser's ABCs, West Baden (IN) Sprudels, Louisville White Sox

WATTS, RICHARD (DICK)—1949-50—p, Birmingham Black Barons

WEAVER,—1906—1b, Cuban X Giants

WEBB,—1917-19—p, Lincoln Giants

WEBB, JAMES (BABY)—1910—c, Leland Giants

WEBB, NORMAL (TWEED)—1926, 1931—inf, Ft. Wayne Pirates, St.Louis Pullmans

WEBSTER, CHARLES—1950—of, Birmingham Black Barons

WEBSTER, DANIEL JIM (DOUBLE DUTY)—1933-38—c, p, Detroit Stars, Kansas City Monarchs, Louisville Black Colonels

WEBSTER, ERNEST—1954—p, Kansas City Monarchs

WEBSTER, PEARL F.—1912-18—c, of, Brooklyn Royal Giants, Hilldale

WEBSTER, WILLIAM (WEST, SPECKS)—1911-28—c, 1b, of, St. Louis Giants, Chicago Giants, Mohawk Giants, Lincoln Giants, Detroit Stars, Dayton Marcos, Brooklyn Cuban Giants, Jewell's ABCs, Bacharach Giants, Chicago Leland Giants, Indianapolis ABCs, Chicago American Giants

WEEKS, E.—1918-24—2b, 3b, Pennsylvania Giants, Harrisburg Giants, Pittsburgh Stars of Buffalo, Brooklyn Royal Giants, Hilldale

WEEKS, WILLIAM—1922—officer, Bacharach Giants

WEEMS,—1936—of, Memphis Red Sox

WEIDEL,—1916—p, All Nations

WELCH, ISSAC—1952—of, Indianapolis Clowns

WELCH, WINGFIELD SCOTT (MOE, GUS)—1918-51—mgr., player, New Orleans Black Pelicans, Monroe Monarchs, Shreveport Giants, Cincinnati Buckeyes, Birmingham Black Barons, Cincinnati Crescents, New York Cubans, Chicago American Giants

WELLS, C.—1918—2b, c, Lincoln Giants, Pennsylvania Giants

WELLS, I.—1948—p, Memphis Red Sox

WELLS, WILLIE BROOKS—1944-51—ss, Memphis Red Sox, New Orleans Eagles

WELLS, WILLIE JAMES (THE DEVIL, CHICO)—1924-54—ss, 3b, mgr., St. Louis Stars, Detroit Wolves, Kansas City Monarchs, Chicago American Giants, Cole's American Giants, Newark Eagles, Memphis Red Sox, New York Black Yankees, Baltimore Elite Giants, Indianapolis Clowns, Homestead Grays, St. Louis Giants, Birmingham Black Barons

WELMAKER, ROY HORACE (SNOOK, LEFTY)—1932-45—p, Atlanta Black Crackers, Homestead Grays, Philadelphia Stars

WESLEY, CHARLES (CONNIE, TWO SIDES)—1921-30—of, 2b, manager, Columbus Buckeyes, Pittsburgh Keystones, Indianapolis ABCs, Memphis Red Sox, Birmingham Black Barons, St. Louis Stars, Louisville White Sox, Louisville Red Caps

WESLEY, EDGAR—1918-31—1b, Detroit Stars, Cleveland Hornets, Bacharach Giants, Chicago American Giants, Harrisburg Giants

WESSON, LES—1948-49—p, New York Black Yankees

WEST,—1913-14—of, p, 1b, Indianapolis ABCs, Louisville White Sox

WEST,—1925—1b, Wilmington Potomacs

WEST,—1942—3b, Boston Royal Giants

WEST, C.(See JAMES West)

WEST, CHARLIE—1942—of, Birmingham Black Barons

WEST, JAMES (JIM, SHIFTY)—1930-47—1b, Birmingham Black Barons, Cleveland Cubs, Memphis Red Sox, Nashville Elite Giants, Columbus Elite Giants, Washington Elite Giants, Baltimore Elite Giants, Philadelphia Stars, New York Black Yankees

WEST, OLLIE ERNEST—1942-46—p, Chicago American Giants, Pittsburgh Crawfords, Birmingham Black Barons, Homestead Grays

WESTON,—1930—p, Hilldale

WESTON, ISSAC (DEACON)—1949—p, Louisville Buckeyes

WEYMAN, J.B.—1887—player, Baltimore Lord Baltimores

WHARTON,—1904—p, Philadelphia Giants

WHARTON,—1921-23—of, Kansas City Monarchs

WHATLEY, DAVID (SPEED)—1936-46—of, Birmingham Black Barons, Homestead Grays, Pittsburgh Crawfords, Cleveland Bears, Jacksonville Red Caps, Memphis Red Sox, New York Black Yankees

WHEATHERSPOON,—1917—p, Bacharach Giants

WHEELER, JOE (JODIE)—1921-28—p, Bacharach Giants, Baltimore Black Sox, Brooklyn Cuban Giants, Wilmington Potomacs

WHEELER, LEON—1951—p, Chicago American Giants

WHEELER, SAM—1948—of, New York Cubans

WHITE,—1913-16—p, Mohawk Giants, Chicago Union Giants

WHITE, ARTEMIS (ART)—1948—p, Indianapolis Clowns

WHITE, ARTHUR—1934—p, Newark Dodgers

WHITE, BILL (WILLIE)—1952—p, Kansas City Monarchs

WHITE, BURLIN—1915-42—c, mgr., West Baden, Ind., Sprudels, Bacharach Giants, Lincoln Giants, Philadelphia Royal Stars, Harrisburg Giants, Philadelphia Giants, Quaker Giants, Boston Royal Giants, Bowser's ABCs, Hilldale, Madison Stars, Cuban Stars (East)

WHITE, BUTLER—1920-23—1b, Chicago Giants

WHITE, CHANEY (REINDEER)—1920-36—of, Hilldale, Bacharach Giants, Wilmington Potomacs, Quaker Giants, Homestead Grays, Darby Daisies, Philadelphia Stars, Baltimore Black Sox, New York Cubans, Brooklyn Royal Giants, Washington Potomacs

WHITE, CHARLES—1950—3b, Philadelphia Stars

WHITE, CLARENCE (RED)—1928-33—p, Nashville Elite Giants, Memphis Red Sox, Louisville White Sox, Monroe Monarchs, Montgomery Grey Sox

Frank "The Red Ant" Wickware.
Frank Keetz

WHITE, DEWITT (CARVER)—1954—c, Detroit Stars
WHITE, EDWARD—1944—p, Homestead Grays
WHITE, EUGENE—1935-36—3b, Brooklyn Eagles, Newark Eagles
WHITE, EUGENE (STINK)—1950-51—2b, Chicago American Giants
WHITE, HENRY (LEFTY)—1940—p, Cleveland Bears
WHITE, J.—1936—p, Bacharach Giants
WHITE, LAWRENCE (LADD)—1947-48—p, Memphis Red Sox
WHITE, M.—1886-87—p, New York Gorhams
WHITE, R.W.—1887—player, Washington Capital Citys, Cuban Giants
WHITE, (RED)(See CLARENCE WHITE)
WHITE, ROBERT—1922-23—2b, 3b, Pittsburgh Keystones, Toledo Tigers, St. Louis Stars
WHITE, SOLOMON(SOL)—1887-1926—2b, 3b, of, 1b, mgr., coach, Pittsburgh Keystones, Washington Capital Citys, Wheeling (Ohio State League); New York Gorhams (Middle States Lg.), York Monarchs (Eastern Interstate League); York Cuban Giants (Eastern Interstate Lg.), Genuine Cuban Giants, Fort Wayne (Western Interstate League); Page Fence Giants, Cuban X Giants, Columbia Giants, Philadelphia Giants, Lincoln Giants, Quaker Giants, Cleveland Browns, Newark Stars, Philadelphia Gorhams, Ansonia Cuban Giants (Connecticut St. Lg.), Cuban Giants
WHITE, ZARLIE—1934—of, Monroe Monarchs
WHITFIELD, (LEFTY)—1950—p, Baltimore Elite Giants
WHITLEY, DAVE—1955—of, Kansas City Monarchs

WHITLOCK,—1926—1b, Dayton Marcos
WHITNEY, CARL—1942—p, of, New York Black Yankees
WHITTINGTON, DON—1952-54—2b, 3b, Philadelphia Stars, Memphis Red Sox
WHITWORTH, RICHARD (BIG)—1915-24—p, Chicago American Giants, Chicago Giants, Hilldale, Bacharach Giants
WHYTE, WILLIAM T. (BILLY)-1883-1894—p, of, Cuban Giants, York Cuban Giants (Eastern Interstate Lg.), Trenton Cuban Giants (Middle States Lg.), St.Louis Black Stockings, Boston Resolutes
WICKERSON,—1931—2b, Bacharach Giants
WICKS,—1921—inf, Hilldale
WICKWARE, FRANK (SMILEY, SMOKEY, THE RED ANT)—1910-25—p, Leland Giants, St. Louis Giants, Philadelphia Giants, Mohawk Giants, Lincoln Stars, Chicago American Giants, Chicago Giants, Brooklyn Royal Giants, Detroit Stars, Norfolk Stars, Lincoln Giants, Jewell ABCs, Indianapolis ABCs, Louisville White Sox
WIGGINS, MAURICE—1920—ss, Chicago American Giants
WIGGINS, BOB—1942—ss, Chicago Brown Bombers
WIGGINS, JOE {CHEAVIER}—1930-34—3b, Nashville Elite Giants, Bacharach Giants, Baltimore Black Sox, New York Black Yankees, Hilldale, Cleveland Cubs, Pittsburgh Crawfords
WIGWARE,—1930—ss, 3b, Nashville Elite Giants
WILBERT, ART (MOFIKE)—1942—of, Cincinnati Clowns, Minneapolis-St. Paul Gophers
WILCOX,—1922—p, New Orleans Crescent Stars
WILDS,—1892—c, Stockton (California Lg.)
WILEY,—1919—1b, Detroit Stars
WILEY, F.—1920-27—2b, p, of, Lincoln Giants, Pennsylvania Red Caps of New York
WILEY, JOE—1947-50—3b, 2b, Baltimore Elite Giants, Memphis Red Sox
WILEY, WABISHAW SPENCER (DOC)—1910-23—c, 1b, of, Brooklyn Royal Giants, Lincoln Giants, Philadelphia Giants, West Baden (IN) Sprudels, Mohawk Giants, Bacharach Giants
WILKES, BARRON D.—1919-27—officer, New York Bacharach Giants
WILKES, JAMES EUGENE (JIMMY, SEABISCUIT)—1945-52—of, Newark Eagles, Houston Eagles, Indianapolis Clowns, Philadelphia Stars
WILKINS, S.B.—1932—sec. Washington Pilots
WILKINS, WALTER—1954—p, Detroit Stars, Louisville Black Colonels
WILKINS, WESLEY (West)—1908-16—of, p, Kansas City (KAN) Giants, All Nations
WILKINSON, JAMES LESLIE (J.L.)—1909-48—officer, All Nations, Kansas City Monarchs; sec, NNL; tres, NAL
WILLAS,—1924—p, Wilmington Potomacs, Washington Potomacs
WILLAS, S.—1887—player, New York Gorhams
WILLBURN,—1926—p, Baltimore Black Sox
WILLETT, PETE—1923-28—ss, of, Lincoln Giants, Cleveland Browns, Cleveland Tigers, Homestead Grays
WILLETTS,—1933—p, Philadelphia Stars
WILLFORD, CLARENCE—1952—of Philadelphia Stars
WILLIAMS,—1911-14—p, West Baden (IN) Sprudels, Indianapolis ABCs
WILLIAMS,—1921—c, Columbus Buckeyes
WILLIAMS, A.—1916-18—p, of, 2b, Brooklyn Royal Giants, Bacharach Giants
WILLIAMS, A.D.—1925—officer, Indianapolis ABCs
WILLIAMS, A.N.—1922—officer, Pittsburgh Keystones
WILLIAMS, ALBERT—1943-45—p, Newark Eagles
WILLIAMS, ANDREW (STRINGBEAN)—1914-25—p, mgr., St. Louis Giants, Pennsylvania Red Caps of New York,

Indianapolis ABCs, Chicago American Giants, Dayton Marcos, Bacharach Giants, Washington Potomacs, Lincoln Giants, Brooklyn Royal Giants, Philadelphia Giants

WILLIAMS, B.—1931-32, 1939—of, Montgomery Grey Sox, Indianapolis ABCs, St. Louis Stars, Birmingham Black Barons

WILLIAMS, BERT—1923—officer, Philadelphia Giants

WILLIAMS, BILBO (BIGGIE)—1942-43—of, Chicago Brown Bombers, Baltimore Elite Giants

WILLIAMS, BILL—1894-1900—p, Genuine Cuban Giants, Cuban X Giants

WILLIAMS, (BUCKY)—1930-31—inf, p, Pittsburgh Crawfords

WILLIAMS, C.—1885—mgr., Brooklyn Remsens

WILLIAMS, CHARLES—1887—inf, Boston Resolutes

WILLIAMS, CHARLES—1887—ump., LCBBP

WILLIAMS, CHARLES ARTHUR—1924-31—ss, 2b, Memphis Red Sox, Chicago American Giants, Indianapolis ABCs, Chicago Columbia Giants

WILLIAMS, CHARLES HENRY (LEFTY)—1915-34—p, Homestead Grays, Detroit Wolves

WILLIAMS, CHARLEY—1945—p, Toledo Cubs (USL)

WILLIAMS, CHESTER ARTHUR—1930-43—ss, 2b, Memphis Red Sox, Pittsburgh Crawfords, Homestead Grays, Philadelphia Stars, Chicago American Giants, Toledo Crawfords

WILLIAMS, CLARENCE—1886-1912—c, ss, 3b, of, mgr., Cuban Giants, New York Gorhams, Cuban X Giants, Philadelphia Giants, Lansing, Michigan Colored Capital All-Americans, Smart Set, Ansonia Cuban Giants (Connecticut St. Lg.), Trenton Cuban Giants, (Middle States Lg.) Harrisburg (Eastern Interstate Lg.)

WILLIAMS, CLARENCE—1938-40—p, of, Baltimore Elite Giants, Washington Black Senators

WILLIAMS, CLARENCE—1952—inf, Chicago American Giants

WILLIAMS, CLYDE (LEFTY)—1947-50—p, Cleveland Buckeyes

WILLIAMS, (COTTON) (See ROBERT WILLIAMS)

WILLIAMS, CRAIG (STRINGBEAN)—1928—p, Brooklyn Cuban Giants

WILLIAMS, (CURLY)(See WILLIE WILLIAMS)

WILLIAMS, E.—1933—c, Nashville Elite Giants

WILLIAMS, E.J.—1887—player, Washington Capital Citys

WILLIAMS, ELBERT—1931-35—p, Louisville White Sox, Monroe Monarchs, Brooklyn Eagles, Detroit Stars

WILLIAMS, ELI (EDDIE)—1943-46—of, Harrisburg-St. Louis Stars, Kansas City Monarchs, Newark Eagles, Cleveland Clippers (USL)

WILLIAMS, ENNIS (STEW)—1951—2b, Baltimore Elite Giants

WILLIAMS, F.—1927—of, Birmingham Black Barons, Kansas City Monarchs

WILLIAMS, FELIX (JEFF)—1949-54—2b, 3b, of, Houston Eagles, Kansas City Monarchs

WILLIAMS, FRANK (SHORTY)—1942-46—of, Homestead Grays

WILLIAMS, FRED—1922-25—c, Washington Potomacs, Harrisburg Giants, Brooklyn Royal Giants, Indianapolis ABCs

WILLIAMS, G.—1939—utl., Baltimore Elite Giants

WILLIAMS, GEORGE—1885-1902—2b, 1b, 3b Philadelphia Orions, Argyle Hotel, Cuban Giants, New York Gorhams, Cuban X Giants, York Cuban Giants (Eastern Interstate Lg.), Trenton Cuban Giants (Middle States Lg.), Philadelphia Giants, York Colored Monarchs

WILLIAMS, GEORGE—1928—ss, 3b, Cleveland Tigers

WILLIAMS, GEORGE—1952—c, Chicago American Giants

WILLIAMS, GERARD—1921-26—ss, Indianapolis ABCs, Homestead Grays, Lincoln Giants

WILLIAMS, GRAHAM H.—1929-34—p, Homestead Grays, Monroe Monarchs, New Orleans Crescent Stars

WILLIAMS, GUY—1934—3b, Cleveland Red Sox

WILLIAMS, HANK—1911-14—3b, 2b, 1b, Mohawk Giants, Brooklyn Royal Giants, Cuban Giants, New York Stars, Brooklyn All-Stars

WILLIAMS, HARRY—1917-22—3b, Baltimore Black Sox

WILLIAMS, HARRY—1930-50—3b, 2b, ss, mgr., Pittsburgh Crawfords, Toledo Crawfords, Baltimore Black Sox, Homestead Grays, Brooklyn Eagles, Newark Eagles, New York Black Yankees, Harrisburg-St. Louis Stars, Baltimore Elite Giants, New York Cubans, New Orleans Creoles

WILLIAMS, HENRY (FLICK)—1922-31—c, Kansas City Monarchs, St. Louis Stars, Indianapolis ABCs

WILLIAMS, J.—1951—of, Baltimore Elite Giants

WILLIAMS, JAMES—1885—c, Brooklyn Remsens

WILLIAMS, JAMES (BIG JIM)—1934-48—of, mgr., Homestead Grays, Toledo Crawfords, Cleveland Bears, New York Black Yankees, New York Cubans, Birmingham Black Barons, Durham Eagles, Atlanta Black Crackers

WILLIAMS, JESSE—1942-47—c, utl., Cleveland Buckeyes, Cleveland Clippers (USL)

WILLIAMS, JESSE HORACE (BILL)—1939-51—ss, 3b, Kansas City Monarchs, Indianapolis Clowns

WILLIAMS, JIM (BULLET)—1929-32—p, Nashville Elite Giants, Cleveland Cubs, Detroit Wolves

WILLIAMS, JIM—1934-37—of, 1b, Newark Dodgers, New York Black Yankees, Philadelphia Stars

WILLIAMS, JIMMY—1952—p, Chicago American Giants

WILLIAMS, JOE—1939-41—ss, Homestead Grays, Chicago American Giants

WILLIAMS, JOE—1946—of, New York Black Yankees

WILLIAMS, JOHN (BIG BOY)—1926-38—of, p, 1b, St. Louis Stars, Indianapolis ABCs, Detroit Stars, Homestead Grays, Dayton Marcos, Columbus Elite Giants, Jacksonville Red Caps

WILLIAMS, JOHN—1948-55—1b, of, Chicago American Giants, Indianapolis Clowns, Birmingham Black Barons

WILLIAMS, JOHN HENRY—1951-54—utl., Birmingham Black Barons, Louisville Black Colonels

WILLIAMS, JOHNNY—1942-55—p, Chicago Brown Bombers, Cincinnati-Indianapolis Clowns, Indianapolis Clowns, Chicago American Giants, Birmingham Black Barons

WILLIAMS, JOSEPH (CYCLONE, SMOKEY JOE)—1905-1934—p, mgr., San Antonio Bronchos, Leland Giants, Chicago Giants, Lincoln Giants, Chicago American Giants, Bacharach Giants, Brooklyn Royal Giants, Homestead Grays, Detroit Wolves, Hilldale, Mohawk Giants

WILLIAMS, L.C.—1939-42—of, New York Cubans

WILLIAMS, LARRY—1955—of, Kansas City Monarchs

WILLIAMS, LEM R.—1905-14—of, Cuban Giants, Brooklyn All-Stars; 1923, 1931—umpire, NNL, officer, Cleveland Stars

WILLIAMS, LEMUEL—1937-39—p, St.Louis Stars, Chicago American Giants

WILLIAMS, LEN—1950-51—inf, of, Indianapolis Clowns

WILLIAMS, LEROY—1945, 1947-51—ss, 2b, Newark Eagles, Kansas City Monarchs

WILLIAMS, M.—1931-32—ss, Pittsburgh Crawfords, Nashville Elite Giants

WILLIAMS, M.—1939—p, Baltimore Elite Giants

WILLIAMS, M.—1941-43—3b, New York Black Yankees, Newark Eagles

WILLIAMS, MARVIN (TEX)—1943-50—2b, Philadelphia Stars

WILLIAMS, MATHIS (MATT)—1921-23—ss, 3b, Pittsburgh Keystones, Cleveland Tate Stars

WILLIAMS, MORRIS—1920-21—p, Indianapolis ABCs

WILLIAMS, NELSON M.—1887—mgr., Washington Capital Citys

WILLIAMS, NISH (ZEKE, NATE)—1927-39—c, of, 3b, 1b, Nashville Elite Giants, Cleveland Cubs, Columbus Elite Giants, Washington Elite Giants, Birmingham Black Barons, Indianapolis ABCs, Atlanta Black Crackers

WILLIAMS, NORM—1930—of, Nashville Elite Giants

WILLIAMS, PHIL (PETE)—1931-39—2b, Baltimore Black Sox, Toledo Crawfords, Jacksonville Red Caps

WILLIAMS, POINDEXTER—1920-33—c, mgr., Chicago American Giants, Detroit Stars, Kansas City Monarchs, Birmingham Black Barons, Louisville White Sox, Nashville Elite Giants, Homestead Grays

WILLIAMS, RAY—1933-41—p, New York Black Yankees

WILLIAMS, RAYMOND (RAY)—1950—p, of, New York Black Yankees

WILLIAMS, (RED)—1926-28—ss, Indianapolis ABCs, Cleveland Tigers

WILLIAMS, REUBEN (RUBE)—1952-53—ss, Chicago American Giants, Indianapolis Clowns

WILLIAMS, ROBERT A.(COTTON)—1943-51—p, inf, Newark Eagles, Houston Eagles, New Orleans Eagles, Philadelphia Stars

WILLIAMS, ROBERT LAWNS (BOBBY)—1918-45—ss, 2b, 3b, mgr., Chicago American Giants, Indianapolis ABCs, Homestead Grays, Pittsburgh Crawfords, Cleveland Red Sox, Cleveland Tigers, Columbus Blue Birds, Akron Tyrites, Cleveland Giants

WILLIAMS, ROY K.—1929-41—p, Pittsburgh Crawfords, Columbus Blue Birds, Baltimore Black Sox, Brooklyn Royal Giants, Brooklyn Eagles, Philadelphia Stars, New York Black Yankees, Baltimore Elite Giants, Homestead Grays

WILLIAMS, ROY—1952-55—of, 3b, Birmingham Black Barons, Chicago American Giants

WILLIAMS, S.—1914-18—p, Brooklyn Royal Giants, Philadelphia Giants

WILLIAMS, S.—1936—3b, Pittsburgh Crawfords

WILLIAMS, SAMUEL C. (SAM)—1947-52—p, Birmingham Black Barons

WILLIAMS, SIDNEY (AL)—1943-45—p, Newark Eagles, New York Black Yankees

WILLIAMS, SOLOMON (SOL)—1884-85—of, Baltimore Atlantics

WILLIAMS, STANLEY—1955—of, Birmingham Black Barons

WILLIAMS, STUART—1950—2b, Cleveland Buckeyes

WILLIAMS, T.—1896-05—c, of, Cuban X Giants

WILLIAMS, T.—1932—3b, Pittsburgh Crawfords

WILLIAMS, THOMAS (TOM)—1916-25—p, Bacharach Giants, Chicago American Giants, Lincoln Giants, Brooklyn Royal Giants, Hilldale, Chicago Giants, Detroit Stars

WILLIAMS, V.—1929—c, St.Louis Stars

WILLIAMS, VERN—1953—p, Indianapolis Clowns

WILLIAMS, WALTER—1898—p, Celeron Acme Colored Giants (Iron andOil League)

WILLIAMS, WALTER—1937-39—p, Newark Eagles, Philadelphia Stars, Washington Black Senators

WILLIAMS, WIL—1902—1b, St. Cloud, MN

WILLIAMS, (WILLIE)—1929-33—ss, 2b, Bacharach Giants, Brooklyn Royal Giants

WILLIAMS, WILLIE—1937-41—p, Washington Elite Giants, Baltimore Elite Giants, Birmingham Black Barons

WILLIAMS, WILLIE C. (CURLEY)—1945-54—3b, ss, Newark Eagles, Houston Eagles, New Orleans Eagles, Birmingham Black Barons

WILLIAMS, WILMORE—1943—of, Newark Eagles

WILLIAMS, WOODROW—1933—p, Akron Tyrites

WILLIAMS, (ZEKE)(See NISH WILLIAMS)

WILLIAMSON,—1924—p, Washington Potomacs, Wilmington Potomacs

WILLIS, JIM (CANNONBALL)—1927-39—p, Birmingham Black Barons, Nashville Elite Giants, Cleveland Cubs, Philadelphia Stars, Columbus Elite Giants, Washington Elite Giants, Baltimore Elite Giants

WILLIS, S.—1887—player, New York Gorhams

WILLS,—1911—3b, Brooklyn Royal Giants

WILMORE, ALFRED G. (APPLES)—1946-50—p, Philadelphia Stars, Baltimore Elite Giants

WILSON,—1917—ss, Bacharach Giants

WILSON,—1927—c, Harrisburg Giants

WILSON,—1946—c, Philadelphia Stars

WILSON,—1950—p, Cleveland Buckeyes

WILSON, ALEC—1939—of, New York Black Yankees

WILSON, ANDREW—1922-27—of, p, New Orleans Crescent Stars, Milwaukee Bears, Chicago Giants

WILSON, ARTHUR LEE (ARTIE)—1944-48—ss, Birmingham Black Barons

WILSON, BENJAMIN (BENNY)—1923-28—of, Lincoln Giants, Pennsylvania Red Caps of New York, Bacharach Giants

WILSON, BILL—1948—3b, Newark Eagles

WILSON, CARTER (COLTIE)—1920-23—of, Gilkerson's Union Giants, Peters' Union Giants, Chicago Giants

WILSON, CHARLES—1917-22—p, of, Dayton Giants, Dayton Marcos Columbus Buckeyes, Detroit Stars

WILSON, CHARLES—1948-49—of, 3b, Indianapolis Clowns

WILSON, DANIEL RICHARD (DAN)—1937-47—of, 3b, 2b, ss, Pittsburgh Crawfords, St. Louis Stars, New Orleans-St. Louis Stars, New York Black Yankees, Harrisburg-St. Louis Stars, Homestead Grays, Philadelphia Stars

WILSON, ED—1896-1905—1b, of, Cuban X Giants, Lansing, Michigan, Colored Capital All-Americans, Adrian (MI) Page Fence Giants

Jesse H. Williams.
Elaine Williams

"Smokey" Joe Williams.
Jeff Eastland

WILSON, JOHN E. (JOHNNY)—1948-49—of, Chicago American Giants

WILSON, JOSEPH—1887—player, Washington Capital Citys

WILSON, JUDSON ERNEST (JUD, BOOJUM)—1922-45—3b, 1b, 2b, mgr., Baltimore Black Sox, Homestead Grays, Philadelphia Stars, Pittsburgh Crawfords

WILSON, L.—1904—p, Cuban X Giants

WILSON, (LEFTY) (See WOODROW WILSON)

WILSON, PERCY LAWRANCE—1922-24, 1933—1b, of, New Orleans Crescent Stars, Milwaukee Bears

WILSON, PETE—1924—1b, Baltimore Black Sox

WILSON, RAY—1902-10—1b, p, Cuban X Giants, Philadelphia Giants

WILSON, ROBERT (BOB)—1947-50—3b, Newark Eagles, Houston Eagles

WILSON, T.—1929—of, Baltimore Black Sox

WILSON, THOMAS T. (TOM)—1918-47—officer, Nashville Standard Giants, Nashville Elite Giants, Cleveland Cubs, Baltimore Elite Giants; vice-chairman, tres, pres, NNL; sec, pres, NSL

WILSON, W. ROLLO—1929-34—sec, ANL; commissioner, NNL

WILSON, WILLIAM H.—1887—ss, Pittsburgh Keystones

WILSON, WOODROW (LEFTY)—1931, 1936-40—p, Kansas City Monarchs, Memphis Red Sox, Baltimore Elite Giants, Cuban Stars (NNL)

WINGATE, B.—1951—3b, Kansas City Monarchs

Jud "Boojum" Wilson.
Moorland-Spingarn Library

WILSON, EDWARD—1898—p, Celeron Acme Colored Giants (Iron and Oil League)

WILSON, ELMER—1921-26—2b, 3b, Dayton Marcos, Detroit Stars, St. Louis Stars

WILSON, EMMETT DABNEY—1936-46—of, Pittsburgh Crawfords, Cincinnati Buckeyes, Cleveland Buckeyes, Cincinnati Clowns, Boston Blues

WILSON, FELTON—1937—c, Detroit Stars

WILSON, FIETMAN—1932-33—p, c, Akron Tyrites, Cleveland Stars

WILSON, FRED (SARDO)-1938-45—of, p, mgr., New York Black Yankees, Newark Eagles, Cincinnati Clowns, Cincinnati-Indianapolis Clowns

WILSON, GEORGE H.—1895-1905—p, of, Adrian (MI) Page Fence Giants, Columbia Giants, Chicago Union Giants, Adrian (Michigan St. Lg.)

WILSON, GEORGE—1922—of, New Orleans Crescent Stars

WILSON, HARVEY—1939—inf., Toledo Crawfords

WILSON, HERB—1928-29—p, Kansas City Monarchs

WILSON, J.—1904—1b, Cuban X Giants

WILSON, J.H.—1887—player, Baltimore Lord Baltimore

WILSON, JAMES (CHUBBY)—1929-33—of, Bacharach Giants, Newark Dodgers

WILSON, JAMES—1936-40—of, 2b, Birmingham Black Barons, Indianapolis Crawfords, Chicago American Giants

WILSON, JAMES—1947—p, Memphis Red Sox

WILSON, JAY—1945-1948—ss, Birmingham Black Barons

WINGFIELD,—1920-23, 1931—2b, of, ss, p, Dayton Marcos Detroit Stars, Toledo Tigers, Memphis Red Sox, Columbus Buckeyes

WINGO, (DOC)—1944—c, Kansas City Monarchs

WINKLE,—1946—3b, Indianapolis Clowns

WINSTON, CLARENCE (BOBBY)—1905-23—of, Philadelphia Giants, Leland Giants, Chicago Giants, Cuban X Giants

WINSTON, JAMES—1929-32—p, of, Chicago Giants, Chicago Columbia Giants, Atlanta Black Crackers, Detroit Stars

WINSTON, JOHN—1955—p, Detroit Stars

WINTERS, JESSE (NIP)—1919-33—p, Norfolk Stars, Bacharach Giants, Norfolk Giants, Hilldale, Philadelphia Stars, Harrisburg Giants, Lincoln Giants, Darby Daisies, Newark Browns, Washington Pilots, Baltimore Black Sox

WINTHROP,—1939—of, Homestead Grays

WISE, RUSSELL—1940—1b, Indianapolis Crawfords

WISHER,—1923—of, Harrisburg Giants

WITHERSPOON, LESTER—1948-49—p, of, Indianapolis Clowns, Homestead Grays

WOLFOLK, LEWIS—1923-24—p, Chicago American Giants

WOMACK, JAMES—1923-33—1b, 3b, Cleveland Tigers, Indianapolis ABCs, Cuban Stars (West), Columbus Turfs, Columbus Blue Birds, Baltimore Black Sox, Richmond Giants, Bacharach Giants

WOODARD,—1928—inf., Cleveland Tigers

WOODS,—1916—p, Chicago American Giants

WOODS, (DOGGY)—1904—p, Gray Eagle (MN)

WOODS, ED—1891-98-p, 1b, of Ansonia Cuban Giants (Connecticut St. Lg.), Chicago Unions, Adrian (MI) Page Fence Giants

WOODS, MILTON—1952—of, Kansas City Monarchs

WOODS, PARNELL—1933-51—3b, mgr., Birmingham Black Barons, Cleveland Bears, Jacksonville Red Caps, Cincinnati Buckeyes, Cleveland Buckeyes, Louisville Buckeyes, Memphis Red Sox, Chicago American Giants

WOODS, SAM (BUDDY)—1946-54—p, Cleveland Buckeyes, Memphis Red Sox, Kansas City Monarchs

WOODS, TOM—1945—3b, Philadelphia Stars

WOODS, VIRGIL—1955—p, Detroit Stars

WOODS, WILLIAM—1887—ss, Philadelphia Pythians

WOODS, WILLIAM J.—1919-26—of, Brooklyn Royal Giants, Indianapolis ABCs, Columbus Buckeyes, St. Louis Stars, Washington Potomacs, Bacharach Giants, Chicago American Giants, St. Louis Giants

WOODSON,—1904—of, Philadelphia Giants

WOOLRIDGE, CHARLES EDWARD—1926-28—ss, 1b, 0f, Cleveland Elites, Cleveland Tigers

WOOTEN, NATE—1954—p, Louisville Black Colonels

WRIGHT,—1908—1b, Brooklyn Colored Giants

WRIGHT,—1931—p, Bacharach Giants

WRIGHT, BILL—1948—of, Kansas City Monarchs

WRIGHT, BRUCE—1946—3b, New York Cubans

WRIGHT, BURNIS (WILD BILL)—1932-45—of, Nashville Elite Giants, Columbus Elite Giants, Washington Elite Giants, Baltimore Elite Giants, Philadelphia Stars

WRIGHT, CHARLEY—1931—p, Birmingham Black Barons

WRIGHT, CLARENCE (BUGGY)—1898—1b, Celeron Acme Colored Giants (Iron and Oil League)

WRIGHT, DANNY—1951-55—p, Chicago American Giants, Birmingham Black Barons, Detroit Stars

Clarence Lytle.
Chicago Historical Society

WRIGHT, ERNEST (ERNIE)—1941-49—off, owner, Cleveland White Sox, Cincinnati Buckeyes, Cleveland Buckeyes; vice-pres, NAL

WRIGHT, GEORGE (ED)—1905-13—ss, 2b, Quaker Giants, Brooklyn Royal Giants, Leland Giants, Chicago Giants, Lincoln Giants

WRIGHT, HENRY—1928-35—p, Nashville Elite Giants, Cleveland Cubs, Columbus Elite Giants, Birmingham Black Barons

WRIGHT, HENRY L. JR. (RED)—1948—c, Baltimore Elite Giants

WRIGHT, HOWARD—1931-33—p, Nashville Elite Giants, Bacharach Giants

WRIGHT, JOHN RICHARD SR (NEEDLE NOSE)—1937-54—p, Newark Eagles, Indianapolis Crawfords, Pittsburgh Crawfords, Homestead Grays, Toledo Crawfords, Indianapolis Clowns

WRIGHT, L.—1932—of, Nashville Elite Giants

WRIGHT, RICHARD—1954—c, Birmingham Black Barons

WRIGHT, ROBERT—1915—c, Chicago American Giants

WRIGHT, ZOLLIE—1931-43—of, Memphis Red Sox, Monroe Monarchs, New Orleans Crescent Stars, Columbus Elite Giants, Washington Elite Giants, Washington Black Senators, New York Black Yankees, Philadelphia Stars, Nashville Elite Giants, Baltimore Elite Giants

WYATT,—1929—c, Detroit Stars

WYATT, DAVID (DAVE)—1896-1920—of, 2b, ss, Chicago Unions, Chicago Union Giants; co-drafter, constitution of NNL

WYATT, JOHN THOMAS—1953-55—p, Indianapolis Clowns

WYATT, RALPH ARTHUR (PEPPER)—1941-46—ss, Chicago American Giants, Homestead Grays, Cleveland Buckeyes

WYLIE, STEVE ENLOE—1944-47—p, Kansas City Monarchs, Memphis Red Sox

WYNDER, CLARENCE—1950—c, Cleveland Buckeyes

WYNN, CALVIN—1949—of, Louisville Buckeyes

WYNN, WILLIAM W. (FOURTEEN, WILLIE)—1944-50—c, Newark Eagles, New York Cubans

Y

YANCEY, WILLIAM JAMES (BILL, YANK)—1923-36, 1946—ss, mgr., Philadelphia Giants, Hilldale, Philadelphia Tigers, Lincoln Giants, Darby Daisies, New York Black Yankees, Brooklyn Eagles, Philadelphia Stars, New York Cubans, Bacharach Giants, Atlanta Black Crackers

YANCY,—1911—cf, Philadelphia Giants

YARBROUGH,—1932—c, Atlanta Black Crackers

YOKELEY, LAYMON SAMUEL (NORMAN, CORNER POCKET)—1926-44—p, Baltimore Black Sox, Bacharach Giants, Philadelphia Stars, Washington Black Senators, Brooklyn Eagles, Baltimore Elite Giants

YOKUM,—1922—p, Kansas City Monarchs

YORK, JIM—1919-23—c, of, Norfolk Stars, Hilldale, Bacharach Giants

YOUNG,—1930—ss, New York Lincoln Giants

YOUNG,—1936—p, Washington Elite Giants

YOUNG, ADAM—1951—p, Philadelphia Stars

YOUNG, BERDELL—1922-28—of, Bacharach Giants, Lincoln Giants

YOUNG, BOB—1950—inf, Cleveland Buckeyes

YOUNG, EDWARD (PEP)—1936-47—c, 1b, 3b, Chicago American Giants, Kansas City Monarchs, Homestead Grays

YOUNG, FRANK A. (FAY)—1939-48—sec, NAL

YOUNG, JOHN—1923-24-p, St. Louis Stars, Memphis Red Sox

YOUNG, LEANDY—1940-45—of, Birmingham Black Barons, Kansas City Monarchs, Memphis Red Sox, Satchell Paige All-Stars

YOUNG, MAURICE (DOOLITTLE)—1927—p, Kansas City Monarchs

YOUNG, M.D.—1920—officer, Knoxville Giants

YOUNG, NORMAN HARVEY—1941-44—ss, Baltimore Elite Giants, Cleveland Buckeyes, New York Black Yankees

YOUNG, ROY—1942-45—umpire, NAL

YOUNG, THOMAS JEFFERSON (T.J., TOM)—1925-41—c, Kansas City Monarchs, St. Louis Stars, Detroit Wolves, New York Cubans, Pittsburgh Crawfords, Homestead Grays, Newark Eagles

YOUNG, DR. W.H.—1949-50—officer, Houston Eagles

YOUNG, WILBUR—1945—p, Birminghám Black Barons

YOUNG, WILLIAM P. (PEP)—1919-34—c, umpire, Homestead Grays, EWL

YOUNG, WILLIAM—1927—p, Kansas City Monarchs

YOUNG, WILLIE C. JR—1945—p, Birmingham Black Barons

YVANES, ARMANDO—1949-50—ss, New York Cubans

Z

ZAPP, JAMES (ZIPPER)—1948-54—of, Birmingham Black Barons, Baltimore Elite Giants

ZAPP, STEPHEN—1946—inf, Baltimore Elite Giants

ZIEGLER, WILLIAM (DOC)—1921, 1927-29—of, Detroit Stars, Chicago Giants

ZIMMERMAN, GEORGE—1887—c, Pittsburgh Keystones

ZOMPHIER, CHARLES (ZOMP)—1926-31—2b, 3b, ss, Cleveland Elites, Cleveland Hornets, Cleveland Tigers, Memphis Red Sox, Cleveland Cubs, Birmingham Black Barons, St. Louis Stars, Cuban Stars (NNL); umpire NAL

Chino Smith

Untimely death in 1931 robbed black baseball of what might have been its most awesome hitter, Charlie "Chino" Smith. Smith, an outfielder, played for the Brooklyn Royal Giants and the New York Lincoln Giants between 1925 and 1930, with a total average of .423 against other major black teams. In 1929 Smith, an outfielder, hit 20 home runs for the Lincoln Giants in only 60 games, while batting .454. Chino's totals, unfortunately, really were "lifetime" numbers. He went to Cuba after the 1930 season to play winter ball, contracted a disease that may have been yellow fever, and was dead by the time the Spring of 1931 rolled around. He wasn't yet 30.

—1978 BRJ

The Circular Trade

Andrew "Rube" Foster, founder and president of the first Negro National League, ruled the loop with an iron hand. Although he owned one of the teams, the Chicago American Giants, he wasn't averse to swapping players among the clubs to maintain as much balance, and thus fan interest, as possible. This led to a deal in 1920 that probably could only have occurred in Rube's baseball fiefdom. Shortly after the season ended, Foster swapped three players, veteran Jude Gans and youngsters Bill Force and Orville Riggins, to the Detroit Stars for outfielder Jimmie Lyons, the reigning batting champion. The thing was, Force and Riggins were already property of the American Giants—Foster had switched them to Detroit at the beginning of 1920 in one of his balancing moves.

—Clark

Seasonal

Leaders

Leaders are listed here league by league, with the Western leagues first. The Negro National League was considered "Western" during its first incarnation from 1920 through 1931. When it was reformed in 1933, it was considered "Eastern," so you'll find NNL records from 1933 through 1948 listed there.

Western Leagues

Batting Champions
Negro National League (NNL)

Year	Player	Team	Avg
1920	Cristobal Torriente	CAG	.411
1921	Charles Blackwell	SLG	.448
1922	Oscar "Heavy" Johnson	KCM	.389
1923	Cristobal Torriente	CAG	.412
1924	Walter "Dobie" Moore	KCM	.453
1925	Edgar Wesley	DS	.416
1926	George "Mule" Suttles	SLS	.418
1927	Roy "Red" Parnell	BBB	.426
1928	Pythias Russ	CAG	.405
1929	Pythias Russ	CAG	.391
1930	Willie Wells	SLS	.403
1931	Norman "Turkey" Stearnes	DS-KCM	.350

Negro Southern League (NSL)

1932	Insufficient Data		

Negro American League (NAL)

1937	Willard Brown	KCM	.371
1938	Willard Brown	KCM	.356
1939	Norman "Turkey" Stearnes	KCM	.350
1940	John "Buck" O'Neil	KCM	.345
1941	Willard Brown	KCM	.333
1942	William "Bonnie" Serrell	KCM	.400
1943	Alex Radcliff	CAG-CC	.354
1944	Sam Jethroe	CBE	.353
1945	Sam Jethroe	CBE	.393
1946	John "Buck" O'Neil	KCM	.350
1947	John Ritchey	CAG	.381
1948	Artie Wilson	BBB	.402
1949	Len Pigg	IC	.388
1950	Sam Hairston	IC	.424
1951	Henry Kimbro	BEG	.366
1952	Roy Williams	CAG	.347
1953	Ray Neil	IC	.397
1954	John Williams	IC	.388

Homerun Champions
Negro National League

Year	Player	Team	HR
1920	Edgar Wesley	DS	11
1921	Oscar Charleston	SLG	15

1922	Oscar Charleston	ABC	16
	Wilber "Bullet Joe" Rogan	KCM	16
1923	Oscar "Heavy" Johnson	KCM	18
1924	Norman "Turkey" Stearnes	DS	10
	Walter "Dobie" Moore	KCM	10
1925	Norman "Turkey" Stearnes	DS	18
	Edgar Wesley	DS	18
1926	George "Mule" Suttles	SLS	27
1927	Willie Wells	SLS	23
1928	Norman "Turkey" Stearnes	DS	24
1929	Willie Wells	SLS.	27
1930	Willie Wells	SLS	14
1931	Norman "Turkey" Stearnes	DS-KCM	8

Negro Southern League

1932	Norman "Turkey" Stearnes	CAG	5
	Alex Radcliff	CAG	5
	Walter Davis	CAG	5

Negro American League

1937	Willard Brown	KCM	8
1938	Willard Brown	KCM	6
1939	Insufficient Data		
1940	Norman "Turkey" Stearnes	KCM	5
1941	Willard Brown	KCM	3
1942	Willard Brown	KCM	9
1943	Willard Brown	KCM	6
1944	Alex Radcliff	IC-CC	7
1946	Willard Brown	KCM	13
1947	Bob Boyd	MRS	4
1948	Willard Brown	KCM	18

Negro American League (merged with Negro National League)

1949	Johnny Davis	HE	14
1950	Sam Hairston	IC	17
1951	Len Williams	IC	14
1952	Sherman Watrous	MRS	20
1953	Ernest Johnson	KC	11
1954	Bill Washington	MRS	18

Win Leaders
Negro National League

Year	Pitcher	Team	Wins
1920	Bill Gatewood	SLG	15–4
1921	Bill Drake	SLG.	20–10
1922	George Meyers	SLS	17–2
1923	Andy Cooper	DS	15–8
1924	Wilber "Bullet Joe" Rogan	KCM	16–5
1925	Wilber "Bullet Joe" Rogan	KCM	15–2
1926	William Bell	KCM	16–3
1927	Willie Foster	CAG	21–3
1928	Ted Trent	SLS	21–2
1929	John Williams	SLS	19–7
1930	Logan "Eggie" Hensley	SLS.	17–6
1931	Webster McDonald	CAG	8–2

Negro Southern League

1932	Willie Foster	CAG	15–8

Negro American League

1937	Ted Trent	CAG	8–2
1938	Hilton Smith	KCM	8–1
1939	Hilton Smith	KCM	8–2
1940	Hilton Smith	KCM	5–3
	Eugene Bremmer	MRS	5–2
1941	Hilton Smith	KCM	10–0
1942	Hilton Smith	KCM	8–3
1943	Chet Brewer	CBE	10–3
1944	Alfred Saylor	BBB	14–5
	Gentry Jessup	CAG	14–9
1945	Gentry Jessup	CAG	15–10
1946	Connie Johnson	KCM	9–3
1947	James LaMarque	KCM	12–2
	Chet Brewer	CBE	12–6
1948	James LaMarque	KCM	15–5

Negro American League (merged with Negro National League)

1949	Gene Richardson	KCM	14–5
1950	Bill Powell	BBB	15–4
1951	Jehosie Heard	NO	17-6
1952	Frank Thompson	BBB	13-6
1953	John Jackson	KC	15-3
1954	Isiah Harris	MRS	13-5

Eastern Leagues

Batting Champions
Eastern Colored League

Year	Player	Team	BA
1923	Jud Wilson	BBS	.373
1924	John Henry "Pop" Lloyd	BG	.433
1925	Oscar Charleston	HG	.445
1926	Robert Hudspeth	NLG	.365
1927	Jud Wilson	BBS	.469
1928	John Henry "Pop" Lloyd	NLG	.564

American Negro League

1929	Charles "Chino" Smith	NLG	.454

No Real League

1930	Charles "Chino" Smith	NLG	.492
1931	George Scales	HG	.389

East–West League

1932	Vic Harris	HG-DS	.348

Negro National League

1933	Oscar Charleston	PC	.372
1934	Ray Dandridge	NE	.436
1935	Norman "Turkey" Stearnes	CAG	.430
1936	Lazaro Salazar	NYC	.367
1937	Bill Wright	WEG	.410
1938	Jim West	BEG	.403
1939	Ed Stone	NE	.439
1940	Leonard Pearson	NE	.389
1941	Monte Irvin	NE	.382
1942	Larry Doby	NE	.392
1943	Josh Gibson	HG	.517
1944	Frank Austin	PS	.390

1945	Josh Gibson	HG	.398
1946	Monte Irvin	NE	.401
1947	Luis Marquez	HG	.417
1948	Walter "Buck" Leonard	HG	.395

Home Run Champions
Eastern Colored League

Year	Player	Team	HR
1923	Charlie Mason	BG	5
1924	Oscar Charleston	HG	14
	Dick Lundy	BG	14
1925	Oscar Charleston	HG	20
1926	Raleigh "Biz" Mackey	PHG	10
1927	Oscar Charleston	HG	11
1928	Luther Farrell	BG	13
1929	Charles "Chino" Smith	NLG	20

No Real League

1930	John Beckwith	NLG	19
1931	John Beckwith	BBS-NE	16

East-West League

1932	Josh Gibson	PC	7
1933	Oscar Charleston	PC	10
1934	Josh Gibson	PC	11

Negro National League

1935	Josh Gibson	PC	11
1936	Josh Gibson	PC	11
1937	George "Mule" Suttles	NE	12
1938	George "Mule" Suttles	NE	9
1939	Josh Gibson	HG	17
1940	Walter "Buck" Leonard	HG	9
1941	Monte Irvin	NE	6
1942	Josh Gibson	HG	15
1943	Josh Gibson	HG	16
1944	Walter "Buck" Leonard	HG	7
1945	Josh Gibson	HG	11
1946	Josh Gibson	HG	16
1947	Monte Irvin	NE	14
	Larry Doby	NE	14
1948	Walter "Buck" Leonard	HG	13
	Luke Easter	HG	13

Win Leaders
Eastern Colored League

Year	Pitcher	Team	Wins
1923	Arthur "Rats" Henderson	BG	8–6
1924	Jesse "Nip" Winters	PHG	19–5
1925	Jesse "Nip" Winters	PHG	21–10
1926	Jesse "Nip" Winters	PHG	15–5
1927	Arthur "Rats" Henderson	BG	19–7
1928	Laymon Yokeley	BBS	14–6

American Negro League

1929	Connie Rector	NLG	20–2

No Real League

1930	Bill Holland	NLG	12–1

1931	Charles "Lefty" Williams	HG	9–2
	Porter Charleston	PHG	9–3

East-West League

1932	Leroy "Satchel" Paige	PC	14–8

Negro National League

1933	Willie Foster	CAG	8–4
1934	Stuart "Slim" Jones	PS	22–3
1935	Leroy Matlock	PC	18–0
1936	William Byrd	WEG	8–4
1937	Terris McDuffie	NE	7–3
1938	Terris McDuffie	NE-NBY	12–5
1939	Leon Day	NE	14–7
1940	Ray Brown	HG	19–2
1941	Dave Barnhill	NYC	10–5
1942	Bill Byrd	BEG	15–4
1943	John Wright	HG	16–3
1944	Ray Brown	HG	12–3
1945	Roy Welmaker	HG	12–4
1946	Leon Day	NE	13–4
1947	Max Manning	NE	15–6
1948	Bill Byrd	BEG	11–6

All-Time Single-Season Leaders
Batting

Year	Player	Team	BA
1928	John Henry "Pop" Lloyd	NLG	.564
1943	Josh Gibson	Home	.517
1930	Charles "Chino" Smith	NLG	.492
1943	Tetelo Vargas	NYC	.479
1929	Charles "Chino" Smith	NLG	.462
1924	Walter "Dobie" Moore	KCM	.453
1921	Charles Blackwell	SLG	.448
1925	Oscar Charleston	HG	.445
1939	Ed Stone	NE	.439
1943	Francisco Coimbre	NYC	.438

Home Runs

Year	Player	Team	HR
1926	George "Mule" Suttles	SLS	27
1929	Willie Wells	SLS	27
1928	Norman "Turkey" Stearnes	DS	24
1926	Dewey Creacy	SLS	23
1927	Willie Wells	SLS	23
1928	Wilson Redus	SLS	21
1925	Oscar Charleston	HG	20
1929	Charles "Chino" Smith	NLG	20
1929	George "Mule" Suttles	SLS	20
1926	Norman "Turkey" Stearnes	DS	20
1927	Norman "Turkey" Stearnes	DS	20
1929	Norman "Turkey" Stearnes	DS	20

Wins

Year	Pitcher	Team	Wins
1934	Stuart "Slim" Jones	PS	22–3
1925	Jesse "Nip" Winters	PHG	21–10
1927	Willie Foster	CAG	21–3
1928	Ted Trent	SLS	21–2
1921	William Drake	SLS	20–10
1929	Connie Rector	NLG	20–2
1924	Jesse "Nip" Winters	PHG.	19–5
1927	Arthur "Rats" Henderson	AC, BG	19–7
1929	John Williams	SLS	19–7
1940	Ray Brown	HG	19–2

Newark's Larry Doby is called safe on this play. The Philadelphia Stars catcher is Bill Cash.
Moorland-Spingarn Library

Cash has already been ejected for arguing the call and "touching" the arbitor. Stars manager "Goose" Curry takes up the cause as Irvin looks on.
Moorland-Spingarn Library

East-West

All-Star Games

1933-1950

The grand pinnacle of any Negro League season, without question, was the East-West game. This was the black version of the major leagues' All-Star Game. Starting in 1933, the game was played annually at Comiskey Park. It brought thousands upon thousands of fans to the Grand Hotel in Chicago. It became the single most important black sporting event in America. Eventually, attendance grew to over 50,000, and the game outdrew its major league counterpart in the early forties. Many historians, players, and fans argued that the success of the Chicago All-Star games was the single most important factor in the integration of baseball.

The teams were chosen by the fans through voting in the two largest black newspapers, the *Chicago Defender* and the *Pittsburgh Courier*. Both papers were national weeklies that owed much of their success to excellent political and sports coverage. The East-West classics allowed fans across the country to discover many unheralded stars—the batting power of Buck Leonard, Mule Suttles, and Turkey Stearnes; the lightning speed of Cool Papa Bell, Willie Wells, and Sam Jethroe, and the pitching magic of Leon Day, Hilton Smith, and Satchel Paige. In 1941, a 22-year-old outfielder for the Newark Eagles, Monte Irvin, recalled the tingle that surrounded the game:

"Satch was the center of attention, and he knew it. As we stood around the batting cage, he'd say, 'Fellas, the East-West Game belongs to me. I don't have to pitch but two or three innings, so I'm gonna be very stingy today. In fact, I'm givin' up nothin'! When I get around to the Grand Hotel tonight, I'll buy you a beer. But today, nothin'! Zero!' He was right."

In the following section complete boxscores of every game from 1933 to 1950 are listed. Unpublished games are shown here for the first time, thanks to research done by Negro League historian Merl Kleinknecht. Also listed are the classic's all-time batting and pitching leaders.

1933

East	AB	R	H	E
Cool Papa Bell (Pittsburgh Crawfords), cf	5	1	0	0
Rap Dixon (Philadelphia Stars), rf	4	2	1	0

	AB	R	H	E
Oscar Charleston (Pittsburgh Crawfords), 1b	3	2	0	0
Biz Mackey (Philadelphia Stars), c	3	0	1	0
Josh Gibson (Pittsburgh Crawfords), c	2	0	1	1
Jud Wilson (Philadelphia Stars), 3b	3	1	2	0
Judy Johnson (Pittsburgh Crawfords), 3b	1	0	1	0
Dick Lundy (Philadelphia Stars), ss	3	0	0	1
Vic Harris (Homestead Grays), lf	2	0	0	1
Fats Jenkins (N.Y. Black Yankees), lf	2	0	0	0
John H. Russell (Pittsburgh Crawfords), 2b	3	0	0	0
Sam Streeter (Pittsburgh Crawfords), p	3	0	0	0
Bertrum Hunter (Pittsburgh Crawfords), p	0	0	0	0
George Britt (Homestead Grays), p	1	1	1	0
Totals	35	7	7	3

West	AB	R	H	E
Turkey Stearnes (Chicago American Giants), cf	5	1	2	0
Willie Wells (Chicago American Giants), ss	4	2	2	0
W. Davis (Chicago American Giants), lf	3	2	2	0
Alex Radcliffe (Chicago American Giants), 3b	4	1	2	0
Mule Suttles (Chicago American Giants), 1b	4	2	2	0
Leroy Morney (Cleveland Giants), 2b	4	0	1	3
Sam Bankhead (Nashville Elite Giants), rf	4	2	1	0
Larry Brown (Chicago American Giants), c	4	0	2	0
Willie Foster (Chicago American Giants), p	4	1	1	0
Totals	36	11	15	3

East	000	320	002-7
West	001	303	31x-11

2B-Stearnes, Wells, Davis (2), Radcliffe. 3B-Brown. HR-Suttles. SB-Dixon, Charleston, Bankhead. SH-Dixon, Gibson, Russell. DP-Wells, Morney, and Suttles; Bankhead and Radcliffe. SO-by Foster, 4; Streeter, 4; Britt, 1. BB-off Foster, 3. Hits-off Foster, 7 in 9 innings; off Streeter, 7 in 5 1/3 innings; Hunter, 4 in 2/3; Britt, 4 in 2. HBP-Foster, 2.

Winning pitcher-Foster; losing pitcher-Streeter. Attendance-19,568.

1934

East	AB	R	H	E
Cool Papa Bell (Pittsburgh Crawfords), cf	3	1	0	0
Jimmie Crutchfield (Pittsburgh Crawfords), rf	3	0	0	0
W. G. Perkins (Pittsburgh Crawfords), c	1	0	0	0
Oscar Charleston (Pittsburgh Crawfords), 1b	4	0	0	1
Jud Wilson (Philadelphia Stars), 3b	3	0	1	0
Josh Gibson (Pittsburgh Crawfords), c-lf	4	0	2	0
Vic Harris (Pittsburgh Crawfords), lf	2	0	1	0
Dick Lundy (Newark Dodgers), ss	4	0	0	0
Chester Williams (Pittsburgh Crawfords), 2b	4	0	3	0
Slim Jones (PHilsdelphia Stars), p	1	0	0	0
Harry Kincannon (Pittsburgh Crawfords), p	1	0	1	0
Satchel Paige (Pittsburgh Crawfords), p	2	0	0	0
Totals	32	1	8	1

West	AB	R	H	E
Willie Wells (Chicago American Giants), ss	3	0	1	0
Alex Radcliffe (Chicago American Giants), 3b	4	0	0	0
Turkey Stearnes (Chicago American Giants), cf	4	0	0	0
Mule Suttles (Chicago American Giants), 1b	4	0	3	1
Red Parnell (Nashville Elite Giants), lf	3	0	0	0
Sam Bankhead (Nashville Elite Giants), rf	3	0	1	0
Larry Brown (Chicago American Giants), c	3	0	1	0

	AB	R	H	E
Sammy T. Hughes (Nashville Elite Giants), 2b	2	0	0	0
Andy Patterson (Cleveland Red Sox), 2b	1	0	0	0
Theodore Trent (Chicago American Giants), p	1	0	0	0
Chet Brewer (Kansas City Monarchs), p	1	0	0	0
Willie Foster (Chicago American Giants), p	1	0	1	0
Totals	30	0	7	1

East	000	000	010-1
West	000	000	000-0

RBI-Wilson. 2B-Gibson, Williams, Wells. 3B-Suttles. SB-Bell. LOB-East, 8; West, 5. SO-by Jones, 4; Trent, 3; Brewer, 1; Paige, 5; Foster, 2. BB-off Brewer, 1; Jones, 1; Foster, 1.

Winning pitcher-Paige; losing pitcher-Foster. Attendance-30,000.

1935

East	AB	R	H	E
Paul Stephens (Philadelphia Stars), ss	6	1	2	1
George Giles (Brooklyn Eagles), 1b	5	1	0	0
Martin Dihigo (N.Y. Cubans), cf-p	5	1	1	2
Jud Wilson (Philadelphia Stars), 3b	5	1	2	0
Alejandro Oms (N.Y. Cubans), rf	4	1	2	0
Biz Mackey (Philadelphia Stars), c	5	1	0	0
Fats Jenkins (Brooklyn Eagles), lf	5	1	0	0
Dick Seay (Philadelphia Stars), 2b	3	0	1	2
Slim Jones (Philadelphia Stars), p	2	1	2	0
Leon Day (Brooklyn Eagles), p	1	0	0	0
*Ed Stone (Brooklyn Eagles)	1	0	0	0
Ray Dandridge (Newark Dodgers), 2b	1	0	1	0
Luis Tiant (N.Y. Cubans), p	2	0	0	0
Paul Arnold (Newark Dodgers), cf	0	0	0	0
Totals	45	8	11	5

*Batted for Seay in 8th.

West	AB	R	H	E
Cool Papa Bell (Pittsburgh Crawfords), cf	4	2	1	1
Sammy T. Hughes (Columbus Elite Giants), 2b	4	0	1	0
Willie Wells (Chicago American Giants), ss	3	0	0	1
Josh Gibson (Pittsburgh Crawfords), c	5	3	4	1
Mule Suttles (Chicago American Giants), lf	2	3	1	0
Oscar Charleston (Pittsburgh Crawfords), 1b	3	1	0	1
Alex Radcliffe (Chicago American Giants), 3b	5	1	2	0
Jimmie Crutchfield (Pittsburgh Crawfords), rf	2	0	0	0
Raymond Brown (Homestead Grays), p	1	0	0	0
Leroy Matlock (Pittsburgh Crawfords), p	2	0	0	0
*Turkey Stearnes (Chicago American Giants)	3	0	1	0
**Buck Leonard (Homestead Grays), 1b	3	0	0	0
Theodore Trent (Chicago American Giants), p	0	0	0	0
Chester Williams (Pittsburgh Crawfords), ss	2	1	0	1
***Bill Wright (Columbus Elite Giants)	1	0	0	0
Bob Griffith (Columbus Elite Giants), p	0	0	0	0
****Felton Snow (Columbus Elite Giants)	1	0	1	0
Willie Cornelius (Chicago American Giants), p	0	0	0	0
Totals	41	11	11	5

*Batted for Matlock in 6th.
**Batted for Crutchfield in 6th.
***Batted for Trent in 8th.
****Batted for Griffith in 10th.

East	200	110	000 40-8
West	000	003	100 43-11

There were two outs in the eleventh inning when Mule Suttles hit a home run with two men on base.

2B-Gibson (2). HR-Jones, Suttles. SB-Dihigo, Giles. SH-Hughes (2), Oms. DP-Wilson unassisted. SO-by Jones, 1; Brown, 1; Day, 3; Matlock, 1; Griffith, 3; Dihigo, 1. BB-off Jones, 2; Day, 2; Trent, 2; Griffith, 2; Tiant, 2; Dihigo, 1. PB-Gibson.

Winning pitcher-Cornelius; losing pitcher-Dihigo. Attendance-25,000.

1936

East	AB	R	H	E
Cool Papa Bell (Pittsburgh Crawfords), cf	3	1	3	0
Bill Wright (Washington Elite Giants), cf	2	0	0	0
Sammy T. Hughes (Washington Elite Giants), 2b	5	2	1	1
Sam Bankhead (Pittsburgh Crawfords), lf	4	1	2	0
Biz Mackey (Washington Elite Giants), c	2	0	2	0
Josh Gibson (Pittsburgh Crawfords), c	3	2	2	0
Jimmie Crutchfield (Pittsburgh Crawfords), rf	2	0	0	0
Zolley Wright (Washington Elite Giants), rf	1	2	1	0
Chester Williams (Pittsburgh Crawfords), ss	4	0	0	1
Jim West (Washington Elite Giants), 1b	3	1	1	1
John Washington (Pittsburgh Crawfords), 1b	1	0	0	1
Judy Johnson (Pittsburgh Crawfords), 3b	1	0	0	1
Felton Snow (Washington Elite Giants), 3b	2	1	1	0
Leroy Matlock (Pittsburgh Crawfords), p	1	0	0	0
Bill Byrd (Washington Elite Giants), p	3	0	0	0
Satchel Paige (Pittsburgh Crawfords), p	1	0	0	0
Totals	38	10	13	5

West	AB	R	H	E
Eddie Dwight (Kansas City Monarchs), cf	2	0	0	0
Henry Milton (Kansas City Monarchs), cf	2	0	0	0
Newt Allen (Kansas City Monarchs), 2b, ss	5	0	0	0
Wilson Redus (Chicago American Giants), rf	2	0	0	0
Lou Dials (Chicago American Giants), rf	2	0	0	1
Alex Radcliffe (Chicago American Giants), 3b	4	1	3	0
Bullet Rogan (Kansas City Monarchs), lf	1	0	0	0
Herman Dunlap (Chicago American Giants), lf	2	1	1	0
Harry Else (Kansas City Monarchs), c	0	0	0	0
Subby Byas (Chicago American Giants), c	3	0	1	0
Willard Brown (Kansas City Monarchs), ss	1	0	0	1
Pat Patterson (Kansas City Monarchs), 2b	2	0	2	0
Popsickle Harris (Kansas City Monarchs), 1b	4	0	1	0
Willie Cornelius (Chicago American Giants), p	1	0	0	0
Floyd Kranson (Kansas City Monarchs), p	0	0	0	0
Andy Cooper (Kansas City Monarchs), p	0	0	0	0
Theodore Trent (Chicago American Giants), p	0	0	0	0
Totals	31	2	8	2

East	200	130	220-10
West	000	001	010-2

RBI-Mackey (2), Bell, Z. Wright (2), Johnson, Gibson, Williams, Patterson. 2B-Bell, Hughes, Bankhead, Patterson. SB-Bell, Gibson, Snow. SO-by Cornelius, 2; Kranson, 1; Byrd, 4; Trent, 1. BB-off Cornelius, 1; Matlock, 1; Kranson, 1; Byrd, 1; Trent, 2. DP-Cornelius, Allen, and Harris. Hits-off Matlock, 2 in 3 innings; Cornelius, 5 in 3; Kranson, 4 in 2; Cooper, 1 in 1;

The Negro League All-Stars, 1936 *Denver Post* Tournament Champions. Back row L to R: See Posey, Sammy T. Hughes, Vic Harris, Bill Wright, and Hart (bus driver). Middle: Hood Whitton (trainer), Buck Leonard, Chester Williams, Cool Papa Bell, Felton Snow, Jack Marshall, Candy Jim Taylor. Front row: Paul Hardy, Bob Griffith, Satchel Paige, Ray Brown, Sam Streeter, Jossh Gibson, Horne (bat boy).
Jay Sanford

Byrd, 4 in 3; Trent, 3 in 3; Paige, 2 in 3. PB-Gibson. HP-by Kranson (West).

Winning pitcher-Matlock; loser-Cornelius.
Attendance-30,000.

1937

East

	AB	R	H	E
Jerry Benjamin (Homestead Grays), rf	5	0	1	0
Willie Wells (Newark Eagles), ss	5	2	1	0
Bill Wright (Washington Elite Giants), cf	5	1	3	0
Buck Leonard (Homestead Grays), 1b	4	1	2	1
Mule Suttles (Newark Eagles), lf	3	0	1	0
Chester Williams (Pittsburgh Crawfords), 2b	3	0	0	0
Jake Dunn (Philadelphia Stars), 2b	1	0	0	0
Ray Dandridge (Newark Eagles), 3b	5	2	1	0
Pepper Bassett (Pittsburgh Crawfords), c	3	0	0	0
Barney Morris (Pittsburgh Crawfords), p	2	0	0	0
Barney Brown (N.Y. Black Yankees), p	1	0	1	0
Leon Day (Newark Eagles), p	1	1	1	0
Totals	38	7	11	1

West

	AB	R	H	E
Newt Allen (Kansas City Monarchs), 2b-ss	4	0	0	0
Lloyd Davenport (Cincinnati Tigers), rf	4	1	1	0
Wilson Redus (Chicago American Giants), rf	0	0	0	0
Ted Strong (Indianapolis Athletics), 1b	4	1	2	2
Turkey Stearnes (Detroit Stars), cf	4	0	0	0
Willard Brown (Kansas City Monarchs), lf	2	0	0	0
Alex Radcliffe (Chicago American Giants), 3b	3	0	1	0
Howard Easterling (Cincinnati Tigers), ss	2	0	0	0
Rainey Bibbs (Cincinnati Tigers), 2b	1	0	1	0
Ted Radcliffe (Cincinnati Tigers), c	3	0	0	1
Theodore Trent (Chicago American Giants), p	0	0	0	0
Hilton Smith (Kansas City Monarchs), p	0	0	0	1
Porter Moss (Cincinnati Tigers), p	2	0	0	0
*Henry Milton (Kansas City Monarchs)	1	0	0	0
**Subby Byas (Chicago American Giants)	1	0	0	0
***Eldridge Mayweather (Kansas City Monarchs)	1	0	0	0
Totals	32	2	5	4

*Batted for W. Brown in 9th.
**Batted for T. Radcliffe in 9th.
***Batted for Trent in 3rd.

East	010	200	130-7
West	000	101	000-2

2B-Allen, Wright, Bibbs, Day. HR-Leonard, Strong. SB-Dandridge, Wright, Suttles. DP-Moss, T. Radcliffe, and Strong; Wells, Dunn and Leonard; Allen and Strong.

Winning pitcher-Morris; loser-Smith.
Attendance-20,000.

1938

East

	AB	R	H	E
Vic Harris (Homestead Grays), lf	5	1	1	0
Sammy T. Hughes (Baltimore Elite Giants), 2b	5	1	2	0
Willie Wells (Newark Eagles), ss	4	1	2	0
Buck Leonard (Homestead Grays), 1b	4	0	1	0
Rev Cannady (N.Y. Black Yankees), 3b	3	1	1	0
Sam Bankhead (Pittsburgh Crawfords), cf	4	0	2	0
Bill Wright (Baltimore Elite Giants), rf	4	0	0	0
Biz Mackey (Baltimore Elite Giants), c	4	0	0	0

	AB	R	H	E
Edsell Walker (Homestead Grays), p	0	0	0	0
Barney Brown (N.Y. Black Yankees), p	2	0	1	0
Johnny Taylor (Pittsburgh Crawfords), p	0	0	0	0
*Jake Dunn (Philadelphia Stars)	1	0	1	0
Totals	36	4	11	0

*Batted for Taylor in 9th.

West

	AB	R	H	E
Henry Milton (Kansas City Monarchs), rf	3	2	1	0
Newt Allen (Kansas City Monarchs), 2b	4	0	0	1
Alex Radcliffe (Chicago American Giants), 3b	4	1	2	0
Ted Strong (Indianapolis ABCs), 1b	3	1	0	0
Quincy Trouppe (Indianapolis ABCs), lf	4	0	0	0
Neil Robinson (Memphis Red Sox), cf	4	1	3	0
Frank Duncan (Chicago American Giants), c	1	0	0	0
Larry Brown (Memphis Red Sox), c	0	0	0	0
Byron Johnson (Kansas City Monarchs), ss	4	0	1	0
Willie Cornelius (Chicago American Giants), p	0	0	0	0
Hilton Smith (Kansas City Monarchs), p	2	0	1	0
Ted Radcliffe (Memphis Red Sox), p	2	0	1	0
Totals	31	5	9	1

East	300	010	000-4
West	104	000	00x-5

RBI-Wells, Cannady, Bankhead, A. Radcliffe (2), Robinson (3), Leonard. 2B-Harris, Cannady, Hughes. 3B-Wells. HR-Robinson. SH-Cannady. DP-Duncan and Radcliffe. LOB-East, 7; West, 8. Hits-off Cornelius, 5 in 1 inning; Walker, 4 in 3; Smith, 3 in 4; Brown, 2 in 3; Radcliffe, 3 in 4; Taylor, 3 in 2. SO-by Walker, 3; Smith, 3; Brown, 1; Taylor, 2. BB-off Smith, 1; Walker, 3; Taylor, 1. HP-by Smith. PB-Mackey.

Winning pitcher-Smith; loser-Walker.
Attendance-30,000.

1939

East

	AB	R	H	E
Bill Wright (Baltimore Elite Giants), cf	4	0	2	0
Willie Wells (Newark Eagles), ss	3	0	1	0
Josh Gibson (Homestead Grays), c	3	0	0	0
Mule Suttles (Newark Eagles), rf	4	0	0	0
Buck Leonard (Philadelphia Stars), 3b	3	1	0	0
Pat Patterson (Philadelphia Stars), 3b	4	1	1	0
Sammy T. Hughes (Baltimore Elite Giants), 2b	3	0	1	0
Roy Parnell (Philadelphia Stars), lf	3	0	0	0
Bill Byrd (Baltimore Elite Giants), p	1	0	0	0
Leon Day (Newark Eagles), p	1	0	0	0
Roy Partlow (Homestead Grays), p	1	0	0	0
Bill Holland (N.Y. Black Yankees), p	0	0	0	0
Totals	30	2	5	0

West

	AB	R	H	E
Henry Milton (Kansas City Monarchs), rf	3	0	1	0
Parnell Woods (Cleveland Bears), 3b	0	0	0	0
Dan Wilson (St. Louis Stars), lf	3	1	1	0
Alex Radcliffe (Chicago American Giants), 3b-ss	5	1	1	0
Neil Robinson (Memphis Red Sox), cf	4	1	3	0
Ted Strong (Kansas City Monarchs), ss-1b	2	0	0	1
Jelly Taylor (Memphis Red Sox), 1b	1	0	0	0
Billy Horn (Chicago American Giants), 2b	2	0	1	0
Leroy Morney (Toledo Crawfords), 2b-ss	1	0	0	0
Jim Williams (Toledo Crawfords), rf	2	0	0	0

	AB	R	H	E
Pepper Bassett (Chicago American Giants), c	1	0	0	0
Larry Brown (Memphis Red Sox), c	2	0	0	0
Theolic Smith (St. Louis Stars), p	0	0	0	0
Hilton Smith (Kansas City Monarchs), p	1	0	0	0
Ted Radcliffe (Memphis Red Sox), p	1	1	1	0
Totals	**28**	**4**	**8**	**1**

East	020	000	000-2	
West	000	000	13x-4	

RBI-Hughes (2), Wilson (2), Robinson, Horn. 2B-Wright, Robinson. HR-Wilson, Robinson. SB-Patterson. DP-T. Smith, Bassett, and Taylor. SO-by T. Smith, 1; T. Radcliffe, 1; H. Smith, 3; Byrd, 1; Day, 1. BB-off T. Smith, 1; T. Radcliffe, 2; Byrd, 1; Day, 2; Holland, 1. Hits-off T. Smith, 4 in 3 innings; H. Smith, 0 in 3 T. Radcliffe, 1 in 3; Byrd, 2 in 3; Day, 0 in 3; Partlow, 4 in 1 1/3; Holland, 2 in 2/3.

Winning pitcher-T. Radcliffe; loser-Partlow.
Attendance-40,000.

1940

East

	AB	R	H	E
Gene Benson (Philadelphia Stars), cf	6	1	2	0
Rabbit Martinez (N.Y. Cubans), ss	3	1	1	0
Bus Clarkson (Newark Eagles), ss	2	1	0	0
Ed Stone (Newark Eagles), rf	3	0	0	0
Alejandro Crespo (N.Y. Cubans), lf	2	2	1	0
Buck Leonard (Homestead Grays), 1b	4	2	2	0
Howard Easterling (Homestead Grays), 3b	5	1	2	0
Marvin Barker (N.Y. Black Yankees), cf-rf	5	1	2	0
W. G. Perkins (Baltimore Elite Giants), c	5	0	2	0
Robert Clarke (N.Y. Black Yankees), c	0	0	0	0
Dick Seay (N.Y. Black Yankees), 2b	4	1	0	0
Henry McHenry (Philadelphia Stars), p	0	0	0	0
Poppa Ruiz (N.Y. Cubans), p	2	1	0	0
Raymond Brown (Homestead Grays), p	2	0	0	0
Totals	**43**	**11**	**12**	**0**

West

	AB	R	H	E
Henry Milton (Kansas City Monarchs), rf	4	0	1	0
Parnell Woods (Birmingham Black Barons), 3b	4	0	1	0
Eldridge Mayweather (N.O.-St. L. Stars), 1b	3	0	1	0
Neil Robinson (Memphis Red Sox), cf	2	0	0	0
Leslie Green (N.O.-St. L. Stars), cf	2	0	1	0
Donald Reeves (Chicago American Giants), lf	4	0	0	0
James Green (Kansas City Monarchs), c	2	0	0	1
Larry Brown (Memphis Red Sox), c	1	0	1	0
Leroy Morney (Chicago American Giants), ss	2	0	0	4
Curt Henderson (Indianapolis Crawfords), ss	1	0	0	0
Tommy Sampson (Birmingham Black Barons), 2b	2	0	0	0
Marshall Riddle (N.O.-St. L. Stars), 2b	1	0	0	1

1936 All-Stars headed for Puerto Rico. From the left in the back row; Ed Stone, Slim Jones, Ray Brown, Rufus Lewis, Terris McDuffie, Buck Leonard, and Johnny Hayes. Front row; Ray Dandridge, Dick Seay, Bill Sadler, Leon Day, Frank Duncan, and Vic Harris.
Quincy Trouppe

	AB	R	H	E
Gene Bremmer (Memphis Red Sox), p	0	0	0	0
Walt Calhoun (N.O.-St. L. Stars), p	1	0	0	0
Connie Johnson (Indianapolis Crawfords), p	0	0	0	0
Hilton Smith (Kansas City Monarchs), p	1	0	0	0
*Jelly Taylor (Memphis Red Sox)	1	0	0	0
Totals	**31**	**0**	**5**	**6**

*Batted for Henderson in 9th.

East	200	114	030-11
West	000	000	000-0

2B-Benson. 3B-Crespo. SB-Leonard. DP-Seay, Clarkson, and Leonard; Morney, Sampson, and Mayweather. SO-by Bremmer, 2; Calhoun, 1; Johnson, 1; Smith, 3; McHenry, 1. BB-off Bremmer, 5; Johnson, 1; Smith, 4; McHenry, 1; Ruiz, 2.

Winning pitcher-McHenry; loser-Bremmer.

Attendance-25,000.

1941

East

	AB	R	H	E
Henry Kimbro (N.Y. Black Yankees), cf	3	1	1	0
Lennie Pearson (Newark Eagles), cf	2	0	0	0
Pancho Coimbre (N.Y. Cubans), rf	5	2	0	1
Bill Hoskins (Baltimore Elite Giants), lf	5	1	1	0
Buck Leonard (Homestead Grays), 1b	5	1	2	0
Monte Irvin (Newark Eagles), 3b	5	0	2	0
Roy Campanella (Baltimore Elite Giants), c	5	0	1	1
Horacio Martinez (N.Y. Cubans), ss	4	1	2	1
Dick Seay (N.Y. Black Yankees), 2b	4	1	0	1
Terris McDuffie (Homestead Grays), p	0	0	0	0
Dave Barnhill (N.Y. Cubans), p	2	1	2	0
Henry McHenry (Philadelphia Stars), p	0	0	0	0
Jimmy Hill (Newark Eagles), p	0	0	0	0
Bill Byrd (Baltimore Elite Giants), p	0	0	0	0
Totals	**40**	**8**	**11**	**4**

West

	AB	R	H	E
Dan Wilson (St. Louis Stars), lf	2	0	0	1
Jimmie Crutchfield (Chicago American Giants), lf	3	0	1	0
Newt Allen (Kansas City Monarchs), ss	2	0	0	2
Billy Horn (Chicago American Giants), ss	2	0	0	0
Neil Robinson (Memphis Red Sox), cf	2	1	1	0
Buddy Armour (St. Louis Stars), cf	2	1	1	0
Ted Strong (Kansas City Monarchs), rf	4	0	2	0
Jelly Taylor (Memphis Red Sox), 1b	2	0	1	0
Lyman Bostock (Birmingham Black Barons), 1b	2	1	1	0
Parnell Woods (Jacksonville Red Caps), 3b	4	0	0	0
Tommy Sampson (Birmingham Black Barons) 2b	0	0	0	1
Bill Ford (St. Louis Stars), 2b	3	0	0	0

1945 American All-Stars in Venezuela.

National Baseball Library, Cooperstown, NY

1948 West All-Stars. Standing L to R: Hornsby Howell (trainer), Gentry Jessup, John Williams, Clyde Nelson, Ed Steele, Dan Bankhead, Piper Davis, Chin Evans, Willie Grace, Quincy Trouppe, Joe Green, Alex Radcliff. Kneeling: (trainer), Candy Jim Taylor, Bubba Hyde, Archie Ware, Larry Brown, Artie Wilson, Chico Renfroe, Jesse Williams, Vibert Clarke, Sam Jethroe, Frank Duncan, and unknown.
Negro Leagues Baseball Museum

Pepper Bassett (Chicago American Giants), c	1	0	0	0
Larry Brown (Memphis Red Sox), c	3	0	0	1
Hllton Smith (Kansas City Monarchs), p	1	0	0	0
Ted Radcliffe (Memphis Red Sox), p	0	0	0	0
Leo Henry (Jacksonville Red Caps), p	0	0	0	0
Dan Bankhead (Memphis Red Sox), p	0	0	0	0
Satchel Paige (Kansas City Monarchs), p	1	0	0	0
*Verdell Mathis (Memphis Red Sox)	0	0	0	0
**Howard Cleveland (Jacksonville Red Caps)	1	0	1	0
***Henry Hudson (Chicago American Giants)	1	0	0	0
****George Mitchell (St. Louis Stars)	0	0	0	0
Totals	36	3	8	5

*Ran for Bassett in 2nd.
**Batted for Henry in 5th.
***Batted for Bankhead in 7th.
****Batted for Horn in 9th.

East	200	600	000-8	
West	100	000	020-3	

RBI-Kimbro, Coimbre, Hoskins, Leonard (3), Barnhill, Strong, Bostock, Woods. 2B-Strong, Irvin. 3B-Strong. HR-Leonard. SH-Leonard, Martinez, Barnhill. SB-Kimbro (2), Irvin, Martinez, Taylor. LOB-East, 10; West 7. DP-Campanella and Martinez. SO-by Barnhill, 2; Hill, 1; Smith, 1; Radcliffe, 1; Henry, 1; Paige, 2. BB-off Radcliffe, 1; Bankhead, 1; Paige, 1. Hits-off McDuffie, 3 in 2 innings; Barnhill, 2 in 3; McHenry, 2 in 2; Hill, 0 in 1; Byrd, 1 in 1; Smith, 2 in 3; Radcliffe, 4 in 2/3; Henry, 3 in 1 1/3; Bankhead, 1 in 2; Paige, 1 in 2. PB-Bassett.

Winning pitcher-McDuffie; loser-Smith.
Attendance-50,256.

1942

East	AB	R	H	E
Dan Wilson (N.Y. Black Yankees), lf	4	3	2	0
Sam Bankhead (Homestead Grays), 2b-cf	5	1	2	0
Willie Wells (Newark Eagles), ss	5	0	1	0
Josh Gibson (Homestead Grays), c	3	0	2	0
Bill Wright (Baltimore Elite Giants), rf	5	0	2	0
Jim West (Philadelphia Stars), 1b	4	0	0	0
Pat Patterson (Philadelphia Stars), 3b	3	0	0	2
Tetelo Vargas (N.Y. Cubans), cf	3	0	1	0
*Herberto Blanco (N.Y. Cubans), 2b	0	0	0	0
Jonas Gaines (Baltimore Elite Giants), p	1	0	0	0

	AB	R	H	E
**Vic Harris (Homestead Grays)	1	0	0	0
***Lennie Pearson (Newark Eagles)	1	1	1	0
Dave Barnhill (N.Y. Cubans), p	0	0	0	0
Barney Brown (Philadelphia Stars), p	0	0	0	0
Leon Day (Newark Eagles), p	1	0	0	0
Totals	36	5	11	2

*Ran for Vargas in 8th.
**Batted for Gaines in 4th.
***Batted for Barnhill in 7th.

West	AB	R	H	E
Cool Papa Bell (Chicago American Giants), cf	4	0	1	0
Parnell Woods (Cincinnati Buckeyes), 3b	3	1	1	0
Marlin Carter (Memphis Red Sox), 3b	1	0	0	0
Ted Strong (Kansas City Monarchs), rf	3	0	1	0
Willard Brown (Kansas City Monarchs), lf	4	0	1	0
Joe Greene (Kansas City Monarchs), c	4	0	0	0
John O'Neil (Kansas City Monarchs), 1b	4	0	0	1
Tommy Sampson (Birmingham Black Barons), 2b	3	0	0	1
*Art Pennington (Chicago American Giants)	1	0	0	0
T. J. Brown (Memphis Red Sox), ss	3	0	0	0
**Lloyd Davenport (Birmingham Black Barons)	1	0	0	0
Hilton Smith (Kansas City Monarchs), p	1	0	0	0
***Fred Bankhead (Memphis Red Sox)	0	1	0	0
Porter Moss (Memphis Red Sox), p	0	0	0	0
Eugene Bremmer (Cincinnati Buckeyes), p	0	0	0	0
Satchel Paige (Kansas City Monarchs), p	1	0	1	0
****Sam Jethroe (Cincinnati Buckeyes)	1	0	0	0
Totals	34	2	5	2

*Batted for Sampson in 9th.
**Batted for T. Brown in 9th.
***Ran for Smith in 3rd.
****Batted for Moss in 5th.

East	001	010	102-5
West	001	001	000-2

RBI-Wright (2), Bankhead (2), Gibson, Greene. 2B-Wilson, Bankhead, W. Brown, Pearson. 3B-Woods. SH-Wells. SB-Patterson, Wilson (2), Wells, Vargas. LOB-East, 8; West, 6. DP-Sampson, T. Brown, and O'Neil (2). SO-by H. Smith, 2; Moss, 2; Barnhill, 4; Bremmer, 1; Paige, 2; Day, 5. BB-off Moss, 2; Barnhill, 1; Paige, 1. Hits-off Smith, 4 in 3 innings; Moss, 2 in 2; Bremmer, 0 in 1; Paige, 5 in 3; Gaines, 1 in 3; Barnhill, 2 in 3; B. Brown, 2 in 2/3; Day, 0 in 2-1/3.
Winning pitcher-Day; loser-Paige.
Attendance-48,400.

1943

East	AB	R	H	E
Cool Papa Bell (Homestead Grays), lf	4	0	0	0
Henry Kimbro (Baltimore Elite Giants), cf	1	0	0	0
Juan Vargas (N.Y. Cubans), cf	2	0	0	0
Buck Leonard (Homestead Grays), 1b	4	1	1	0
Josh Gibson (Homestead Grays), c	3	0	1	0
Howard Easterling (Homestead Grays), 3b	4	0	1	0
Lennie Pearson (Newark Eagles), rf	3	0	0	0
Sam Bankhead (Homestead Grays), 2b	3	0	0	0
Horacio Martinez (N.Y. Cubans), ss	2	0	1	0
Dave Barnhill (N.Y. Cubans), p	1	0	0	0
John Wright (Homestead Grays), p	0	0	0	0
Bill Harvey (Baltimore Elite Giants), p	0	0	0	0
Leon Day (Newark Eagles), p	1	0	0	0

	AB	R	H	E
*George Scales (Baltimore Elite Giants)	1	0	0	0
**Jerry Benjamin (Homestead Grays)	1	0	0	0
***Vic Harris (Homestead Grays)	1	0	0	0
Totals	31	1	4	0

*Batted for Wright in 6th.
**Batted for Martinez in 9th.
***Batted for Pearson in 9th.

West	AB	R	H	E
Jesse Williams (Kansas City Monarchs), ss	3	0	2	0
Lloyd Davenport (Chicago American Giants), rf	2	0	0	0
Alex Radcliffe (Chicago American Giants), 3b	4	0	1	0
Willard Brown (Kansas City Monarchs), cf	3	1	1	0
Neil Robinson (Memphis Red Sox), lf	2	1	0	0
Lester Lockett (Birmingham Black Barons), lf	0	0	0	0
John O'Neil (Kansas City Monarchs), 1b	2	0	0	0
Tommy Sampson (Birmingham Black Barons), 2b	3	0	1	0
Ted Radcliffe (Chicago American Giants), c	3	0	0	0
Satchel Paige (Kansas City Monarchs), p	1	0	1	0
Gread McKinnis (Birmingham Black Barons), p	1	0	0	0
Theolic Smith (Cleveland Buckeyes), p	1	0	0	0
Porter Moss (Memphis Red Sox), p	0	0	0	0
*Bubber Hyde (Memphis Red Sox)	0	0	0	0
**Fred Wilson (Cincinnati Clowns)	1	0	0	0
Totals	26	2	6	0

*Ran for Paige in 3rd.
**Batted for Robinson in 8th.

East	000	000	001-1
West	010	100	00x-2

RBI-Leonard, Sampson. 2B-Paige. HR-Leonard. SB-Brown, Williams. LOB-East, 4; West 6. DP-Bankhead and Leonard; Pearson, Gibson, and Easterling. SO-Paige, 4; McKinnis, 1; Wright, 2; Smith, 1. BB-off Paige, 1; Smith, 1; Barnhill, 1; Day, 1.
Winning pitcher-Paige; loser-Barnhill.
Attendance-51,723.

1944

East	AB	R	H	E
Cool Papa Bell (Homestead Grays), lf	5	0	0	0
Ray Dandridge (Newark Eagles), 3b-2b	5	0	3	0
Pancho Coimbre (N.Y. Cubans), rf	5	0	0	0
Buck Leonard (Homestead Grays), 1b	3	1	1	1
Josh Gibson (Homestead Grays), c	3	1	2	0
John Davis (Newark Eagles), cf	3	0	2	0
Sam Bankhead (Homestead Grays), 2b-ss	3	1	1	1
Pee Wee Butts (Baltimore Elite Giants), ss	2	0	0	0
Horacio Martinez (N.Y. Cubans), ss	0	0	0	0
Terris McDuffie (Newark Eagles), p	1	0	1	0
Carranza Howard (N.Y. Cubans), p	1	0	0	0
Barney Morris (N.Y. Cubans), p	0	0	0	0
Bill Byrd (Baltimore Elite Giants), p	1	0	0	0
*Marvin Williams (Philadelphia Stars)	1	0	0	0
**Roy Campanella (Baltimore Elite Giants), 3b	1	1	1	0
***Henry Kimbro (Baltimore Elite Giants), rf	1	0	0	0
Totals	35	4	11	2

*Batted for Butts in 7th.
**Batted for Martinez in 8th.
***Batted for Morris in 7th.

West	AB	R	H	E
Sam Jethroe (Cleveland Buckeyes), cf	3	0	0	0
Neil Robinson (Memphis Red Sox), cf	2	0	0	0
Art Wilson (Birmingham Black Barons), ss	5	1	2	0
Lloyd Davenport (Chicago American Giants), rf	4	1	1	0
Buddy Armour (Cleveland Buckeyes), lf	4	2	2	0
Alex Radcliffe (Cincinnati Clowns), 3b	4	0	1	0
Bonnie Serrell (Kansas City Monarchs), 2b	3	1	2	0
Archie Ware (Cleveland Buckeyes), 1b	4	1	1	0
Ted Radcliffe (Birmingham Black Barons), c	4	1	2	0
Verdell Mathis (Memphis Red Sox), p	1	0	1	0
Gentry Jessup (Chicago American Giants), p	2	0	0	0
Gread McKinnis (Chicago American Giants), p	0	0	0	0
Gene Bremmer (Cleveland Buckeyes), p	0	0	0	0
Totals	**36**	**7**	**12**	**0**

East	010	100	200-4
West	101	050	00x-7

RBI-Bankhead, A. Radcliffe (2), Serrell, Ware, T. Radcliffe (2), Campanella, Dandridge, Davis. 2B-Gibson, Dandridge, Ware. 3B-Leonard, McDuffie, A. Radcliffe. HR-T. Radcliffe. SB-Armour. LOB-East, 8; West, 7. DP-Jethroe and T. Radcliffe; Wilson, Serrell, and Ware. SO-by McDuffie, 2; Morris, 1; McKinnis, 1; Bremmer, 2. BB-off Jessup, 2; McKinnis, 1; McDuffie, 1. Hits-off Mathis, 3 in 3 innings; McDuffie, 5 in 3; Howard, 4 in 1 2/3; Morris, 1 in 1 1/3; Jessup, 3 in 3; McKinnis, 4 in 1; Bremmer, 1 in 1 2/3; Byrd, 2 in 2. PB-T. Radcliffe.

Winning pitcher-Mathis; loser-Howard.

Attendance-46,247.

1945

East	AB	R	H	E
Jerry Benjamin (Homestead Grays), cf	5	1	1	0
Frank Austin (Philadephia Stars), ss	2	0	0	1
Horacio Martinez (N.Y. Cubans), ss	2	0	2	0
John Davis (Newark Eagles), lf	2	0	0	0
Gene Benson (Philadelphia Stars), lf	2	1	0	0
Buck Leonard (Homestead Grays), 1b	3	1	1	0
Roy Campanella (Baltimore Elite Giants), c	5	1	2	0
Willie Wells (Newark Eagles), 2b	5	0	1	0
Bill Wright (Baltimore Elite Giants), rf	1	0	0	0
Rogelio Linares (N.Y. Cubans), rf	3	1	0	0
Marvin Barker (N.Y. Black Yankees), 3b	2	0	1	0
Murray Watkins (Newark Eagles), 3b	2	0	2	0

1946 East All-Stars. Standing L to R: Felton Snow, Josh Gibson, Monte Irvin, Buck Leonard, Biz Mackey, Pat Scantlebury, Lennie Pearson, Larry Doby, Fernando Diaz Pedroso, Silvio Garcia, Vic Harris. Kneeling: Henry Kimbro, Jonas Gaines, Murray Watkins, Bill Ricks, Gene Benson, Leon Day, Sam Bankhead, and Howard Easterling.
Negro Leagues Baseball Museum

Tom Glover (Baltimore Elite Giants), p — 0 0 0 0
Bill Ricks (Philadelphia Stars), p — 0 0 0 0
Martin Dihigo (N.Y. Cubans), p — 1 0 0 0
Roy Welmaker (Homestead Grays), p — 0 0 0 0
*Lennie Pearson (Newark Eagles) — 1 0 0 0
**Bill Byrd (Baltimore Elite Giants) — 1 1 0 0

Totals — 37 6 10 1
*Batted for Dihigo in 7th.
**Batted for Welmaker in 9th.

West	AB	R	H	E
Jesse Williams (Kansas City Monarchs), 2b	5	0	2	0
Jackie Robinson (Kansas City Monarchs), ss	5	0	0	0
Lloyd Davenport (Cleveland Buckeyes), rf	4	1	1	0
Neil Robinson (Memphis Red Sox), cf	2	2	2	0
Alex Radcliffe (Cincinnati-Ind. Clowns), 3b	4	2	2	1
Lester Lockett (Birmingham Black Barons), lf	4	0	0	0
Archie Ware (Cleveland Buckeyes), 1b	4	1	2	0
Quincy Trouppe (Cleveland Buckeyes), c	1	2	1	0
Verdell Mathis (Memphis Red Sox), p	2	1	2	0
Gentry Jessup (Chicago American Giants), p	1	0	0	0
Booker McDaniels (Kansas City Monarchs), p	1	0	0	0
Gene Bremmer (Cleveland Buckeyes), p	0	0	0	0
Totals	33	9	12	1

East	000	000	105-6
West	044	100	00x-9

BRI-Benjamin, Martinez (3), Wells (2), Williams (4), Radcliffe, Lockett, Ware (3). 2B-Wells, Davenport, Radcliffe. 3B-Williams. SH-N. Robinson. LOB-West, 5; East, 10. SO-by Mathis, 4; Jessup, 1; McDonald, 1. BB-off Mathis, 1; Jessup, 2; McDaniels, 2; Glover, 1; Ricks, 1; Welmaker, 1.
Winning pitcher-Mathis; loser-Glover.
Attendance-31,714.

1946

(At Griffith Stadium, Washington)

West	AB	R	H	E
Art Wilson (Birmingham Black Barons), ss	3	1	1	0
Othello Renfroe (Kansas City Monarchs), ss	1	0	0	0
Archie Ware (Cleveland Buckeyes), 1b	4	0	0	0
Sam Jethroe (Cleveland Buckeyes), cf	4	1	0	0
Piper Davis (Birmingham Black Barons), 2b	4	1	2	0
Willie Grace (Cleveland Buckeyes), rf	4	0	1	0
Bubber Hyde (Memphis Red Sox), lf	3	0	1	0
John Scott (Kansas City Monarchs), lf	2	0	1	0
Alex Radcliffe (Memphis Red Sox), 3b	3	0	0	0
Quincy Trouppe (Cleveland Buckeyes), c	1	0	0	0
Buster Haywood (Cincinnati-Ind. Clowns), c	1	0	0	0
*John Brown (Cleveland Buckeyes)	1	0	0	0
Dan Bankhead (Memphis Red Sox), p	1	0	0	0
Vibert Clarke (Cleveland Buckeyes), p	0	0	0	0
Gentry Jessup (Chicago American Giants), p	1	0	0	0
Clyde Nelson (Chicago American Giants), 3b	1	0	0	0
John Williams (Cincinnati-Ind. Clowns), p	0	0	0	0
Totals	34	3	6	0

*Batted for Williams in 9th.

East	AB	R	H	E
Henry Kimbro (Baltimore Elite Giants), cf	2	1	1	0
Larry Doby (Newark Eagles), 2b	4	2	2	0
Howard Easterling (Homestead Grays), 3b	4	2	3	0
Buck Leonard (Homestead Grays), 1b	3	0	0	0
Monte Irvin (Newark Eagles), lf	3	0	0	0
Josh Gibson (Homestead Grays), c	2	0	1	0
Leon Ruffin (Newark Eagles), c	1	0	0	0
Louis Louden (N.Y. Cubans), c	1	0	0	0
*Murray Watkins (Philadelphia Stars)	0	0	0	0
Gene Benson (Philadelphia Stars), rf	1	0	1	0
Lennie Pearson (Newark Eagles), rf	3	0	1	0
Sam Bankhead (Homestead Grays), ss	2	0	0	0
Silvio Garcia (N.Y. Cubans), ss	2	0	0	0
Barney Brown (Philadelphia Stars), p	1	0	0	0
**Frank Austin (Philadelphia Stars)	0	0	0	0
Pat Scantlebury (N.Y. Cubans), p	0	0	0	0
Bill Byrd (Baltimore Elite Giants), p	1	0	0	0
***Pete Diaz (N.Y. Cubans)	1	0	0	0
Jonas Gaines (Baltimore Elite Giants), p	0	0	0	0
Leon Day (Newark Eagles), p	0	0	0	0
Totals	31	5	9	0

*Ran for Gibson in 4th
**Ran for Brown in 3rd.
***Batted for Byrd in 7th.

West	000	300	000-3
East	200	300	00x-5

BRI-Davis, Grace, Hyde, Easterling, Leonard, Irvin, Pearson. SB-Doby, Irvin. SH-Leonard. DP-Wilson, Ware, and Davis; Bankhead and Leonard. SO-by Bankhead, 2; Jessup, 1; Byrd, 4. BB-off Bankhead, 1; Jessup, 1; Byrd, 1. Hits-off Bankhead, 3 in 3 innings; Clark, 3 in 1/3; Jessup, 2 in 2 2/3; Williams 1 in 2; Brown, 0 in 2; Scantlebury, 3 in 1/3; Byrd, 1 in 2 2/3; Gaines, 1 in 2; Day, 1 in 1. PB-Trouppe, Haywood (2).
Winning pitcher-Byrd; loser-Clark.
Attendance-16,000.

(At Comiskey Park, Chicago)

East	AB	R	H	E
Henry Kimbro (Baltimore Elite Giants), cf	4	0	0	0
Larry Doby (Newark Eagles), 2b	3	0	1	0
Howard Easterling (Homestead Grays), 3b	4	0	0	0
Buck Leonard (Homestead Grays), 1b	4	0	1	0
Monte Irvin (Newark Eagles), lf	4	0	1	0
Josh Gibson (Homestead Grays), c	3	0	0	0
Gene Benson (Philadelphia Stars), rf	3	0	0	1
Silvio Garcia (N.Y. Cubans), ss	1	0	0	2
*Pat Scantlebury (N.Y. Cubans)	1	0	1	0
**Pee Wee Butts (Baltimore Elite Giants), ss	0	0	0	0
Barney Brown (Philadelphia Stars), p	1	0	0	0
Bill Byrd (Baltimore Elite Giants), p	1	0	0	0
Jonas Gaines (Baltimore Elite Giants), p	0	0	0	0
***Murray Watkins (Newark Eagles)	0	1	0	0
Leon Day (Newark Eagles), p	0	0	0	0
Totals	29	1	4	3

*Batted for Gaines in 8th.
**Ran for Scantlebury in 8th.
***Batted for Garcia in 8th.

West	A	R	H	E
Art Wilson (Birmingham Black Barons), ss	4	1	1	0
Archie Ware (Cleveland Buckeyes), 1b	2	0	0	0
Sam Jethroe (Cleveland Buckeyes), cf	3	1	0	0
Piper Davis (Birmingham Black Barons), 2b	3	1	1	0
Willie Grace (Cleveland Buckeyes), rf	4	1	3	0
Alex Radcliffe (Cincinnati Clowns), 3b	3	0	0	0
Bubber Hyde (Memphis Red Sox), lf	3	0	2	1
Quincy Trouppe (Cleveland Buckeyes), c	1	0	0	0
Felix Evans (Memphis Red Sox), p	1	0	0	0
Dan Bankhead (Hemphis Red Sox), p	1	0	0	0
John Williams (Cincinnati-Ind. Clowns), p	1	0	0	0
Totals	**26**	**4**	**7**	**1**

East	000	000	010-1
West	000	220	00x-4

RBI-Hyde, Davis, Doby. 2B-Hyde. SB-Wilson, Jethroe, Hyde. SH-Doby. DP-Davis, Wilson, and Ware. SO-by Brown, 3; Day, 1; Bankhead, 3; Gaines, 1; Evans 1. BB-off Evans, 2; Brown, 1; Bankhead, 3; Byrd, 2. Hits-off Brown, 2 in 3 innings; Gaines, 0 in 2 1/3; Byrd, 4 in 1 1/3; Day, 1 in 1; Evans, 1 in 3; Williams 2 in 3; Bankhead, 1 in 3. HP-by Bankhead (Garcia); Williams (Watkins); Brown (Jethroe).

Winning pitcher-Bankhead; loser-Byrd.
Attendance-45,474.

1947

East

	AB	R	H	E
Henry Kimbro (Baltimore Elite Giants), cf	4	0	0	0
Pee Wee Butts (Baltimore Elite Giants), ss	2	0	0	0
John Washington (Baltimore Elite Giants), 1b	4	0	0	0
Monte Irvin (Newark Eagles), lf	3	1	0	0
Silvio Garcia (N.Y. Cubans), 2b	3	0	0	0
Claro Duaney (N.Y. Cubans), rf	2	0	0	0
Orestes Minoso (N.Y. Cubans), 3b	3	0	0	0
John Hayes (N.Y. Black Yankees), c	1	0	0	0
Max Manning (Newark Eagles), p	2	0	1	0
Luis Tiant (N.Y. Cubans), p	1	0	0	0
Luis Marquez (Homestead Grays), rf	1	1	1	0
Louis Louden (N.Y. Cubans), c	1	0	1	0
Frank Austin (Philadelphia Stars), ss	2	0	0	0
Henry Miller (Philadelphia Stars), p	0	0	0	0
John Wright (Homestead Grays), p	0	0	0	0
*Bob Romby (Baltimore Elite Giants)	1	0	0	0
**Biz Mackey (Newark Eagles)	0	0	0	0
***Vic Harris (Homestead Grays)	0	0	0	0
Totals	**30**	**2**	**3**	**0**

*Flied out for Hayes in 6th.
**Walked for Miller in 8th.
***Ran for Mackey in 8th.

West

	AB	R	H	E
Art Wilson (Birmingham Black Barons), ss	4	0	0	0
Herb Souell (Kansas City Monarchs), 3b	5	1	1	0
Sam Jethroe (Cleveland Buckeyes), rf	3	1	1	0
Piper Davis (Birmingham Black Barons), 2b	3	1	2	0
Quincy Trouppe (Cleveland Buckeyes), c	2	1	1	0
Jose Colas (Memphis Red Sox), lf	4	0	2	0
Goose Tatum (Indianapolis Clowns), 1b	4	0	2	0
Buddy Armour (Chicago American Giants), rf	4	1	2	0
Dan Bankhead (Memphis Red Sox), p	2	0	0	0

Gentry Jessup (Chicago American Giants), p	1	0	0	0
Chet Brewer (Cleveland Buckeyes), p	1	0	1	0
Totals	**33**	**5**	**12**	**0**

East	010	000	010-2
West	211	000	01x-5

RBI-Davis, Colas (2), Duaney, Trouppe, Louden, Brewer. 2B-Davis, Armour (2), Marquez. 3B-Souell, Trouppe, Jethroe. SB-Jethroe, Davis. SH-Trouppe. DP-Wilson, Davis, and Tatum. SO-by Bankhead, 2; Manning, 3; Jessup, 1; Brewer, 1; Miller, 1. BB-off Manning, 2; Miller, 1; Brewer, 1. Hits-off Manning, 5 in 2 1/3 innings; Tiant, 2 in 2 2/3; Miller, 2 in 2; Wright, 3 in 1; Bankhead, 1 in 3; Jessup, 0 in 3; Brewer, 2 in 3. HP-by Bankhead (Irvin); Manning (Jethroe). PB-Louden.

Winning pitcher-Bankhead; loser-Manning.
Attendance-48,112.

1948

East

	AB	R	H	E
Luis Marquez (Homestead Grays), cf	4	0	0	0
Orestes Minoso (N.Y. Cubans), 3b	4	0	1	0
Luke Easter (Homestead Grays), lf	0	0	0	1
Lester Lockett (Baltimore Elite Giants), lf	2	0	0	0
Buck Leonard (Homestead Grays), 1b	4	0	1	0
Bob Harvey (Newark Eagles), rf	1	0	0	0
Monte Irvin (Newark Eagles), rf	2	0	0	0
Jim Gilliam (Baltimore Elite Giants), 2b	3	0	1	0
Louis Louden (N.Y. Cubans), c	3	0	0	0
Bill Cash (Philadelphia Stars), c	0	0	0	0
Pee Wee Butts (Baltimore Elite Giants), ss	2	0	0	1
Frank Austin (Philadelphia Stars), ss	1	0	0	0
Rufus Lewis (Newark Eagles), p	1	0	0	0
Wilmer Fields (Homestead Grays), p	1	0	0	0
Robert Griffith (N.Y. Black Yankees), p	1	0	0	0
Totals	**29**	**0**	**3**	**2**

West

	AB	R	H	E
Art Wilson (Birmingham Black Barons), ss	3	0	0	0
Herb Souell (Kansas City Monarchs), 3b	4	0	0	0
Piper Davis (Birmingham Black Barons), 2b	3	1	1	0
Willard Brown (Kansas City Monarchs), cf	4	1	2	0
Robert Boyd (Memphis Red Sox), 1b	4	1	2	1
Neil Robinson (Memphis Red Sox), lf	3	0	1	0
Quincy Trouppe (Chicago American Giants), c	3	0	0	0
Sam Hill (Chicago American Giants), rf	3	0	0	0
Bill Powell (Birmingham Black Barons), p	1	0	0	0
Jim LaMarque (Kansas City Monarchs), p	1	0	0	0
Gentry Jessup (Chicago American Giants), p	1	0	1	0
Totals	**30**	**3**	**7**	**1**

East	000	000	000-0
West	020	000	01x-3

RBI-Robinson, Hill, Boyd. 2B-Davis, Leonard. SB-Davis. DP-Gilliam, Louden, Minoso, Butts, and Minoso; Davis, Wilson, and Boyd. SO-by Powell, 2; Lewis, 4; LaMarque, 1; Fields, 2; Griffith, 2; Jessup, 1. BB-off Powell, 1; Lewis, 2; Fields, 1; Griffith, 1; Jessup, 1. Hits-off Powell, 1 in 3; Lewis, 3 in 3; LaMarque, 2 in 3; Fields, 1 in 3; Jessup, 0 in 3; Griffith, 3 in 2. WP-Powell.

Winning pitcher-Powell; loser-Lewis.
Attendance-42,000.

1949

East

	AB	R	H	E
Pee Wee Butts (Baltimore Elite Giants), ss	4	1	1	0
Pedro Diaz (N.Y. Cubans), cf	4	0	3	0
Lennie Pearson (Baltimore Elite Giants), 1b	5	0	0	0
Bus Clarkson (Philadelphia Stars), rf	2	0	1	0
Sherwood Brewer (Indianapolis Clowns), rf	2	1	1	0
Robert Davis (Baltimore Elite Giants), lf	4	1	1	1
Jim Gilliam (Baltimore Elite Giants), 2b	4	0	0	0
Howard Easterling (N.Y. Cubans), 3b	4	1	2	0
Bill Cash (Philadelphia Stars), c	4	0	1	0
Bob Griffith (Philadelphia Stars), p	1	0	1	0
*Dave Hoskins (Cleveland Buckeyes)	1	0	0	0
Andy Porter (Indianapolis Clowns), p	0	0	0	0
**Leon Kellman (Cleveland Buckeyes)	1	0	0	0
Pat Scantlebury (N.Y. Cubans), p	1	0	0	0
Totals	37	4	11	1

*Struck out for Griffith in 4th.
**Struck out for Porter in 7th.

West

	AB	R	H	E
Jose Burgos (Birmingham Black Barons), ss	2	0	0	0
Orlando Verona (Memphis Red Sox), ss	1	0	0	1
*Herman Bell (Birmingham Black Barons)	1	0	0	0
Bob Boyd (Memphis Red Sox), 1b	4	0	0	0
Pedro Formenthal (Memphis Red Sox), cf	1	0	0	0
John Davis (Houston Eagles), cf	2	0	0	0
Piper Davis (Birmingham Black Barons), 2b	4	0	1	0
Willard Brown (Kansas City Monarchs), lf-3b	3	0	0	0
Lonnie Summers (Chicago American Giants), c	3	0	1	2
Robert Wilson (Houston Eagles), ss-3b	3	0	0	0
Gene Richardson (Kansas City Monarchs), p	1	0	0	0
Willie Greason (Birmingham Black Barons), p	0	0	0	0
**John O'Neil (Kansas City Monarchs)	1	0	0	0
Gread McKinnis (Chicago American Giants), p	0	0	0	0
Willie Hutchinson (Memphis Red Sox), p	1	0	0	0
Jim LaMarque (Kansas City Monarchs), p	1	0	0	0
Totals	28	0	2	3

*Flied out for Verona in 6th.
**Struck out for Greason in 6th.

East	110	000	020-4
West	000	000	000-0

1946 West All-Stars. Standing L to R: Hornsby Howell (trainer), Gentry Jessup, John Williams, Clyde Nelson, Ed Steele, Dan Bankhead, Piper Davis, Chin Evans, Willie Grace, Quincy Trouppe, Joe Green, Alex Radcliff. Kneeling: (trainer), Candy Jim Taylor, Bubba Hyde, Archie Ware, Larry Brown, Artie Wilson, Chico Renfroe, Jesse Williams, Vibert Clarke, Sam Jethroe, Frank Duncan, and Jim LaMarque.

Negro Leagues Baseball Museum

RBI-Clarkson, Griffith, Gilliam, Easterling. 2B-P. Davis, Butts, Cash. SB-Easterling, Diaz, R. Davis. DP-Boyd and P. Davis; Easterling, Gilliam, and Pearson. SO-by Griffith, 1; Scantlebury, 1; Richardson, 2; Greason, 1. BB-off Richardson, 2; Griffith, 1; Porter, 1. Hits-off Griffith, 0 in 3; Porter, 0 in 3; Scantlebury, 2 in 3; Richardson, 4 in 3; Greason, 2 in 3; McKinnis, 4 in 1 2/3; Hutchinson, 0 in 1/3; LaMarque, 1 in 1.

    Winning pitcher-Griffith; loser-Richardson.

    Attendance-26,697.

1950

East

	AB	R	H	E
Henry Merchant (Indianapolis Clowns), lf	5	0	0	0
Pee Wee Putts (Baltimore Elite Giants), ss	3	1	0	0
Rene Gonzalez (N.Y. Cubans), 1b	3	0	2	0
Pedro Diaz (N.Y. Cubans), cf	5	0	1	0
Louis Louden (N.Y. Cubans), c	5	1	1	0
Jim Gilliam (Baltimore Elite Giants), 2b	3	1	1	0
Ben Little (Philadelphia Stars), rf	3	0	2	0
Charles White (Philadelphia Stars), 3b	1	0	0	0
Sherwood Brewer (Indianapolis Clowns), 3b-rf	3	0	0	1
Joe Black (Baltimore Elite Giants), p	1	0	0	0
Raul Galata (N.Y. Cubans), p	2	0	0	0
Jonas Gaines (Philadelphia Stars), p	0	0	0	0
Pat Scantlebury (N.Y. Cubans), p	1	0	0	0
Totals	**35**	**3**	**7**	**1**

West

	AB	R	H	E
Curley Williams (Houston Eagles), ss	1	1	0	0
Clyde McNeal (Chicago American Giants), ss	3	0	1	1
Herb Souell (Kansas City Monarchs), 3b	2	0	0	1
Leon Kellman (Memphis Red Sox), 3b	2	0	0	1
Jesse Douglas (Chicago American Giants), 3b	4	0	3	0
Alonzo Perry (Birmingham Black Barons), 1b	3	1	2	0
John Washington (Houston Eagles), 1b	2	0	0	1
Bob Harvey (Houston Eagles), rf	2	1	0	0
Pepper Bassett (Birmingham Black Barons), c	1	0	1	0
Art Pennington (Chicago American Giants), cf	3	1	1	0
Ed Steele (Birmingham Black Barons), lf	3	0	2	1
Casey Jones (Memphis Red Sox), c	2	0	0	0
Thomas Cooper (Kansas City Monarchs), c-rf	1	0	0	0
Vibert Clarke (Memphis Red Sox), p	1	0	0	0
Connie Johnson (Kansas City Monarchs), p	2	0	1	0
Bill Powell (Birmingham Black Barons), p	1	0	0	0
Totals	**32**	**5**	**11**	**4**

East	000	200	001-3
West	002	030	000-5

    RBI-Diaz, Little, Douglas (2), Pennington (2), Steele. 2B-Little, Diaz, Washington. 3B-Johnson, Pennington. HR-Gilliam. SB-Douglas (2), Butts. SH-Souell, Gilliam. SO-Clark, 3; Johnson, 3; Powell, 4; Galata, 1; Gaines, 3; Scantlebury, 1. BB-off Clark, 2; Johnson, 2; Black, 1; Galata, 1. HP-by Galata (Steele).

    Winning pitcher-Johnson; loser-Galata.

    Attendance-24,614.

All-Time East-West All-Star Records 1933 to 1948

Batting

Games
- Alex Radcliffe 11
- Buck Leonard 11
- Josh Gibson 9

At Bats
- Alex Radcliffe 44
- Buck Leonard 41
- Willie Wells 32

Runs Scored
- Buck Leonard 9
- Alex Radcliffe 7
- Josh Gibson 6

Hits
- Alex Radcliffe 15
- Josh Gibson 14
- Buck Leonard

Doubles
- Josh Gibson 4
- Willie Wells 3

Triples
- Thirteen players tied at 1

Homeruns
- Buck Leonard 3
- Neil Robinson 2
- Mule Suttles 2

RBIs
- Buck Leonard 11
- Alex Radcliffe 10
- Mule Suttles 6

Stolen Bases
- Seven players tied at 2

Batting Average (min. 15 at bats)
- Josh Gibson .483
- Neil Robinson .476
- Mule Suttles .412

Slugging Percentage (min. 15 at bats)
- Mule Suttles .882
- Neil Robinson .810
- Ray Dandridge .636

Pitching

Games Pitched
- Leon Day 6
- Hilton Smith 6
- Bill Byrd 5
- Satchel Paige 5

Complete Games
- Willie Foster 1

Games Won
- Verdell Mathis 2
- Satchel Paige 2

Games Lost
- Hilton Smith 2

Strikeouts
- Leon Day 14
- Satchel Paige 13
- Hilton Smith 13

Walks
- Leon Day 5
- Gentry Jessup 5
- Porter Moss 5
- Hilton Smith 5

From the
Negro Leagues
to the Majors

The next three sections give information about the players who moved from the Negro Leagues to the major leagues. Data is sorted so you can find (1) a chronological listing of players moving to the majors, (2) a list of players, based on their Negro League team, and (3) a list of players based on their major league team.

Most of this movement occurred during the 1940s and '50s, but you will notice a number of players listed before Jackie Robinson. Two of these, Fleet and Weldy Walker, were nineteenth century players who got a taste of the major leagues before attitudes hardened in the 1880s. The rest are Cuban players who played for black teams in the U.S., but were considered "white" by Organized Baseball.

Migration Dates to Major Leagues from Negro Leagues

Debut Date	Player	Major League Team	Negro League Team	Position
5-1-1884	Moses Fleet Walker	Toledo Blue Stockings	Newark Little Giants	c
7-1-1884	Weldy Walker	Toledo Blue Stockings	Pittsburgh Keystones	of
7-4-1911	Rafael Almieda	Cincinnati Reds	All Cubans	inf
7-4-1911	Armando Marsans	Cincinnati Reds	All Cubans	of
9-28-1912	Mike Gonzalez	Boston Braves	Cuban Stars	c
5-9-1913	Jack Calvo	Washington Senators	Long Branch (NJ) Cubans	of
5-16-1913	Alfredo Cabrera	St. Louis Cardinals	All Cubans	ss
5-20-1914	Dolf Luque	Boston Braves	Long Branch (NJ) Cubans	p
5-18-1920	Ricardo Torres	Washington Senators	Long Branch (NJ) Cubans	c
7-28-1920	Jose Acosta	Washington Senators	Long Branch (NJ) Cubans	p
5-1-1924	Pedro Dibut	Cincinnati Reds	Cuban Stars	p
9-22-1925	Ramon "Mike" Herrera	Boston Red Sox	Cuban Stars	if
4-21-1929	Oscar Estrada	St. Louis Browns	Cuban Stars	p
4-15-1947	Jackie Robinson	Brooklyn Dodgers	Kansas City Monarchs	1b
7-5-1947	Larry Doby	Cleveland Indians	Newark Eagles	2b
7-17-1947	Hank Thompson	St. Louis Browns	Kansas City Monarchs	2b
7-19-1947	Willard Brown	St. Louis Browns	Kansas City Monarchs	of
8-26-1947	Dan Bankhead	Brooklyn Dodgers	Memphis Red Sox	p
4-20-1948	Roy Campanella	Brooklyn Dodgers	Baltimore Elite Giants	c
7-9-1948	Satchel Paige	Cleveland Indians	Kansas City Monarchs	p
4-19-1949	Minnie Minoso	Cleveland Indians	New York Cubans	of
5-20-1949	Don Newcombe	Brooklyn Dodgers	Newark Eagles	p
7-8-1949	Monte Irvin	New York Giants	Newark Eagles	of
8-11-1949	Luke Easter	Cleveland Indians	Homestead Grays	of
4-18-1950	Sam Jethroe	Boston Braves	Cleveland Buckeyes	of
4-18-1951	Luis Marquez	Boston Braves	Homestead Grays	of
4-18-1951	Ray Noble	New York Giants	New York Cubans	c

Debut Date	Player	Major League Team	Negro League Team	Position
4-18-1951	Artie Wilson	New York Giants	Birmingham Black Barons	2b
4-21-1951	Harry Simpson	Cleveland Indians	Philadelphia Stars	of
5-25-1951	Willie Mays	New York Giants	Birmingham Black Barons	of
7-21-1951	Sam Hairston	Chicago White Sox	Indianapolis Clowns	c
9-8-1951	Bob Boyd	Chicago White Sox	Memphis Red Sox	1b
9-22-1951	Sam Jones	Cleveland Indians	Cleveland Buckeyes	p
4-15-1952	Hector Rodriquez	Chicago White Sox	New York Cubans	3b
4-16-1952	George Crowe	Boston Braves	New York Black Yankees	1b
4-30-1952	Buzz Clarkson	Boston Braves	Philadelphia Stars	ss
4-30-1952	Quincy Trouppe	Cleveland Indians	Cleveland Buckeyes	c
5-1-1952	Joe Black	Brooklyn Dodgers	Baltimore Elite Giants	p
7-1-1952	Dave Pope	Cleveland Indians	Homestead Grays	of
8-22-1952	Sandy Amoros	Brooklyn Dodgers	New York Cubans	of
4-14-1953	Jim Gilliam	Brooklyn Dodgers	Baltimore Elite Giants	2b
4-17-1953	Connie Johnson	Chicago White Sox	Kansas City Monarchs	p
4-17-1953	Jim Pendleton	Milwaukee Braves	Chicago American Giants	of
4-18-1953	Dave Hoskins	Cleveland Indians	Louisville Buckeyes	p
7-10-1953	Al Smith	Cleveland Indians	Cleveland Buckeyes	of
9-13-1953	Bob Trice	Philadelphia A's	Homestead Grays	p
9-17-1953	Ernie Banks	Chicago Cubs	Kansas City Monarchs	ss
9-20-1953	Gene Baker	Chicago Cubs	Kansas City Monarchs	2b
4-13-1954	Hank Aaron	Milwaukee Braves	Indianapolis Clowns	of
4-13-1954	Curt Roberts	Pittsburgh Pirates	Kansas City Monarchs	2b
4-17-1954	Chuck Harmon	Cincinnati Reds	Indianapolis Clowns	3b
4-17-1954	Jose Santiago	Cleveland Indians	New York Cubans	p
4-18-1954	Charlie White	Milwaukee Braves	Philadelphia Stars	c
4-24-1954	Jay Heard	Baltimore Orioles	New Orleans Eagles	p
5-31-1954	Bill Greason	St. Louis Cardinals	Birmingham Black Barons	p
8-26-1954	Joe Taylor	Philadelphia A's	Chicago American Giants	of
4-14-1955	Elston Howard	New York Yankees	Kansas City Monarchs	c
4-14-1955	Bob Thurman	Cincinnati Reds	Kansas City Monarchs	of
4-17-1955	Roberto Vargas	Milwaukee Braves	Chicago American Giants	p
6-18-1955	Lino Donoso	Pittsburgh Pirates	New York Cubans	p
7-21-1955	Milt Smith	Cincinnati Reds	Philadelphia Stars	3b
9-2-1955	Billy Harrell	Cleveland Indians	Birmingham Black Barrons	ss
9-4-1955	Vibert Clarke	Washington Senators	Memphis Red Sox	p
4-17-1956	Charlie Neal	Brooklyn Dodgers	Atlanta Black Crackers	2b
4-19-1956	Pat Scantlebury	Cincinnati Reds	New York Cubans	p
7-17-1956	Charles Peete	St. Louis Cardinals	Indianapolis Clowns	of
9-13-1956	Joe Caffie	Cleveland Indians	Cleveland Buckeyes	of
4-16-1957	Larry Raines	Cleveland Indians	Chicago American Giants	3b
4-22-1957	John Kennedy	Philadelphia Phillies	Birmingham Black Barons	inf
9-22-1957	Frank Barnes	St. Louis Cardinals	Kansas City Monarchs	p
4-15-1958	Pancho Herrera	Philadelphia Phillies	Kansas City Monarchs	1b
5-17-1958	Bob Wilson	Los Angeles Dodgers	Newark Eagles	of
9-12-1958	Hank Mason	Philadelphia Phillies	Kansas City Monarchs	p
4-11-1959	George Altman	Chicago Cubs	Kansas City Monarchs	of
6-17-1959	Marshall Bridges	St. Louis Cardinals	Memphis Red Sox	p
9-14-1959	Jim Proctor	Detroit Tigers	Indianapolis Clowns	p
4-17-1960	Lou Johnson	Chicago Cubs	Kansas City Monarchs	of
4-19-1960	Walt Bond	Cleveland Indians	Kansas City Monarchs	of
4-16-61	Choo-Choo Coleman	Philadelphia Phillies	Indianapolis Clowns	c
9-8-1961	John Wyatt	Kansas City A's	Indianapolis Clowns	p
7-21-1962	J.C. Hartman	Houston Colt .45s	Kansas City Monarchs	ss
6-18-1963	Willie Smith	Detroit Tigers	Birmingham Black Barons	p
8-4-1963	George Smith	Detroit Tigers	Indianapolis Clowns	2b
9-18-1965	Paul Casanova	Washington Senators	Indianapolis Clowns	c
6-17-1969	Ike Brown	Detroit Tigers	Kansas City Monarchs	of

Negro Leagues Teams of Players who Moved to the Major Leagues

Player's Name	Position	First Major League Team	Debut Date
All Cubans			
Rafael Almieda	3b	Cincinnati Reds	7-4-1911
Alfredo Cabrera	1b	St. Louis Cardinals	5-16-1913
Armando Marsans	of	Cincinnati Reds	7-4-1911
Atlanta Black Crackers			
Charlie Neal	2b	Brooklyn Dodgers	4-17-1956
Baltimore Elite Giants			
Joe Black	p	Brooklyn Dodgers	5-1-1952
Roy Campanella	c	Brooklyn Dodgers	4-20-1948
Jim Gilliam	2b	Brooklyn Dodgers	4-14-1953
Birmingham Black Barons			
Bill Greason	p	St. Louis Cardinals	5-31-1954
Billy Harrell	ss	Cleveland Indians	9-2-1955
John Kennedy	inf	Philadelphia Phillies	4-22-1957
Willie Mays	of	New York Giants	5-25-1951
Willie Smith	p	Detroit Tigers	6-18-1963
Artie Wilson	2b	New York Giants	4-18-1951
Chicago American Giants			
Jim Pendleton	of	Milwaukee Braves	4-17-1953
Larry Raines	3b	Cleveland Indians	4-16-1957
Joe Taylor	of	Philadelphia A's	8-26-1954
Roberto Vargas	p	Milwaukee Braves	4-17-1955
Cleveland Buckeyes			
Joe Caffie	of	Cleveland Indians	9-13-1956
Sam Jethroe	of	Boston Braves	4-18-1950
Sam Jones	p	Cleveland Indians	9-22-1951
Al Smith	of	Cleveland Indians	7-10-1953
Quincy Trouppe	c	Cleveland Indians	4-30-1952
Cuban Stars			
Pedro Dibut	p	Cincinnati Reds	5-1-1924
Oscar Estrada	p	St. Louis Browns	4-21-1929
Mike Gonzalez	c	Boston Braves	9-28-1912
Ramon "Mike" Herrera	2b	Boston Red Sox	9-22-1925
Homestead Grays			
Luke Easter	of	Cleveland Indians	8-11-1949
Luis Marquez	of	Boston Braves	4-18-1951
Dave Pope	of	Cleveland Indians	7-1-1952
Bob Trice	p	Philadelphia A's	9-13-1953
Indianapolis Clowns			
Hank Aaron	of	Milwaukee Braves	4-13-1954
Paul Casanova	c	Washington Senators	9-18-1965
Choo-Choo Coleman	c	Philadelphia Phillies	4-16-61
Sam Hairston	c	Chicago White Sox	7-21-1951
Chuck Harmon	3b	Cincinnati Reds	4-17-1954
Charles Peete	of	St. Louis Cardinals	7-17-1956
Jim Proctor	p	Detroit Tigers	9-14-1959
George Smith	2b	Detroit Tigers	8-4-1963
John Wyatt	p	Kansas City A's	9-8-1961
Kansas City Monarchs			
George Altman	of	Chicago Cubs	4-11-1959
Gene Baker	2b	Chicago Cubs	9-20-1953
Ernie Banks	ss	Chicago Cubs	9-17-1953
Frank Barnes	p	St. Louis Cardinals	9-22-1957
Walt Bond	of	Cleveland Indians	4-19-1960
Ike Brown	of	Detroit Tigers	6-17-1969
Willard Brown	of	St. Louis Browns	7-19-1947
J.C. Hartman	ss	Houston Colt .45s	7-21-1962
Pancho Herrera	1b	Philadelphia Phillies	4-15-1958

Player's Name	Position	First Major League Team	Debut Date
Elston Howard	c	New York Yankees	4-14-1955
Connie Johnson	p	Chicago White Sox	4-17-1953
Lou Johnson	of	Chicago Cubs	4-17-1960
Hank Mason	p	Philadelphia Phillies	9-12-1958
Satchel Paige	p	Cleveland Indians	7-9-1948
Curt Roberts	2b	Pittsburgh Pirates	4-13-1954
Jackie Robinson	1b	Brooklyn Dodgers	4-15-1947
Hank Thompson	2b	St. Louis Browns	7-17-1947
Bob Thurman	of	Cincinnati Reds	4-14-1955
Long Branch (NJ) Cubans			
Jose Acosta	p	Washington Senators	7-28-1920
Jack Calvo	of	Washington Senators	5-9-1913
Dolf Luque	p	Boston Braves	5-20-1914
Ricardo Torres	c	Washington Senators	5-18-1920
Louisville Buckeyes			
Dave Hoskins	p	Cleveland Indians	4-18-1953
Memphis Red Sox			
Dan Bankhead	p	Brooklyn Dodgers	8-26-1947
Bob Boyd	1b	Chicago White Sox	9-8-1951
Marshall Bridges	p	St. Louis Cardinals	6-17-1959
Vibert Clarke	p	Washington Senators	9-4-1955
New Orleans Eagles			
Jay Heard	p	Baltimore Orioles	4-24-1954
New York Black Yankees			
George Crowe	1b	Boston Braves	4-16-1952
New York Cubans			
Sandy Amoros	of	Brooklyn Dodgers	8-22-1952
Lino Donoso	p	Pittsburgh Pirates	6-18-1955
Minnie Minoso	of	Cleveland Indians	4-19-1949
Ray Noble	c	New York Giants	4-18-1951
Hector Rodriquez	3b	Chicago White Sox	4-15-1952
Jose Santiago	p	Cleveland Indians	4-17-1954
Pat Scantlebury	p	Cincinnati Reds	4-19-1956
Newark Eagles			
Larry Doby	2b	Cleveland Indians	7-5-1947
Monte Irvin	of	New York Giants	7-8-1949
Don Newcombe	p	Brooklyn Dodgers	5-20-1949
Bob Wilson	of	Los Angeles Dodgers	5-17-1958
Newark Little Giants			
Moses Fleet Walker	c	Toledo Blue Stockings	5-1-1884
Philadelphia Stars			
Buzz Clarkson	ss	Boston Braves	4-30-1952
Harry Simpson	of	Cleveland Indians	4-21-1951
Milt Smith	3b	Cincinnati Reds	7-21-1955
Charlie White	c	Milwaukee Braves	4-18-1954
Pittsburgh Keystones			
Weldy Walker	of	Toledo Blue Stockings	7-15-1884

Major League Teams of Players from the Negro Leagues

Player's Name	Position	Former Negro League Team	Debut Date
Baltimore Orioles			
Jay Heard	p	New Orleans Eagles	4-24-1954
Boston Braves			
Buzz Clarkson	ss	Philadelphia Stars	4-30-1952
George Crowe	1b	New York Black Yankees	4-16-1952

Player's Name	Position	Former Negro League Team	Debut Date
Mike Gonzalez	c	Cuban Stars	9-28-1912
Sam Jethroe	of	Cleveland Buckeyes	4-18-1950
Luis Marquez	of	Homestead Grays	4-18-1951
Boston Red Sox			
Ramon "Mike" Herrera	2b	Cuban Stars	9-22-1925
Luis Marquez	of	Homestead Grays	4-18-1951
Brooklyn Dodgers			
Sandy Amoros	of	New York Cubans	8-22-1952
Dan Bankhead	p	Memphis Red Sox	8-26-1947
Joe Black	p	Baltimore Elite Giants	5-1-1952
Roy Campanella	c	Baltimore Elite Giants	4-20-1948
Jim Gilliam	2b	Baltimore Elite Giants	4-14-1953
Charlie Neal	2b	Atlanta Black Crackers	4-17-1956
Don Newcombe	p	Newark Eagles	5-20-1949
Jackie Robinson	1b	Kansas City Monarchs	4-15-1947
Chicago Cubs			
George Altman	of	Kansas City Monarchs	4-11-1959
Gene Baker	2b	Kansas City Monarchs	9-20-1953
Ernie Banks	ss	Kansas City Monarchs	9-17-1953
Lou Johnson	of	Kansas City Monarchs	4-17-1960
Chicago White Sox			
Bob Boyd	1b	Memphis Red Sox	9-8-1951
Sam Hairston	c	Indianapolis Clowns	7-21-1951
Connie Johnson	p	Kansas City Monarchs	4-17-1953
Hector Rodriquez	3b	New York Cubans	4-15-1952
Cincinnati Reds			
Rafael Almieda	3b	All Cubans	7-4-1911
Pedro Dibut	p	Cuban Stars	5-1-1924
Chuck Harmon	3b	Indianapolis Clowns	4-17-1954
Armando Marsans	of	All Cubans	7-4-1911
Pat Scantlebury	p	New York Cubans	4-19-1956
Milt Smith	3b	Philadelphia Stars	7-21-1955
Bob Thurman	of	Kansas City Monarchs	4-14-1955
Cleveland Indians			
Walt Bond	of	Kansas City Monarchs	4-19-1960
Joe Caffie	of	Cleveland Buckeyes	9-13-1956
Larry Doby	2b	Newark Eagles	7-5-1947
Luke Easter	of	Homestead Grays	8-11-1949
Billy Harrell	ss	Birmingham Black Barons	9-2-1955
Dave Hoskins	p	Louisville Buckeyes	4-18-1953
Sam Jones	p	Cleveland Buckeyes	9-22-1951
Minnie Minoso	of	New York Cubans	4-19-1949
Satchel Paige	p	Kansas City Monarchs	7-9-1948
Dave Pope	of	Homestead Grays	7-1-1952
Larry Raines	3b	Chicago American Giants	4-16-1957
Jose Santiago	p	New York Cubans	4-17-1954
Harry Simpson	of	Philadelphia Stars	4-21-1951
Al Smith	of	Cleveland Buckeyes	7-10-1953
Quincy Trouppe	c	Cleveland Buckeyes	4-30-1952
Detroit Tigers			
Ike Brown	of	Kansas City Monarchs	6-17-1969
Jim Proctor	p	Indianapolis Clowns	9-14-1959
George Smith	2b	Indianapolis Clowns	8-4-1963
Willie Smith	p	Birmingham Black Barons	6-18-1963
Houston Colt .45s			
J.C. Hartman	ss	Kansas City Monarchs	7-21-1962
Kansas City A's			
John Wyatt	p	Indianapolis Clowns	9-8-1961
Los Angeles Dodgers			
Bob Wilson	of	Newark Eagles	5-17-1958

Player's Name	Position	Former Negro League Team	Debut Date
Milwaukee Braves			
Hank Aaron	of	Indianapolis Clowns	4-13-1954
Jim Pendleton	of	Chicago American Giants	4-17-1953
Roberto Vargas	p	Chicago American Giants	4-17-1955
Charlie White	c	Philadelphia Stars	4-18-1954
New York Giants			
Monte Irvin	of	Newark Eagles	7-8-1949
Willie Mays	of	Birmingham Black Barons	5-25-1951
Ray Noble	c	New York Cubans	4-18-1951
Artie Wilson	2b	Birmingham Black Barons	4-18-1951
New York Yankees			
Elston Howard	c	Kansas City Monarchs	4-14-1955
Philadelphia A's			
Joe Taylor	of	Chicago American Giants	8-26-1954
Bob Trice	p	Homestead Grays	9-13-1953
Philadelphia Phillies			
Choo-Choo Coleman	c	Indianapolis Clowns	4-16-61
Pancho Herrera	1b	Kansas City Monarchs	4-15-1958
John Kennedy	inf	Birmingham Black Barons	4-22-1957
Hank Mason	p	Kansas City Monarchs	9-12-1958
Pittsburgh Pirates			
Luis Donoso	p	New York Cubans	6-18-1955
Curt Roberts	2b	Kansas City Monarchs	4-13-1954
St. Louis Browns			
Willard Brown	of	Kansas City Monarchs	7-19-1947
Oscar Estrada	p	Cuban Stars	4-21-1929
Hank Thompson	2b	Kansas City Monarchs	7-17-1947
St. Louis Cardinals			
Frank Barnes	p	Kansas City Monarchs	9-22-1957
Marshall Bridges	p	Memphis Red Sox	6-17-1959
Alfredo Cabrera	1b	All Cubans	5-16-1913
Bill Greason	p	Birmingham Black Barons	5-31-1954
Charles Peete	of	Indianapolis Clowns	7-17-1956
Toledo Blue Stockings			
Moses Fleet Walker	c	Newark Little Giants	5-1-1884
Weldy Walker	of	Pittsburgh Keystones	7-15-1884
Washington Senators			
Jose Acosta	p	Long Branch (NJ) Cubans	7-28-1920
Jack Calvo	of	Long Branch (NJ) Cubans	5-9-1913
Paul Casanova	c	Indianapolis Clowns	9-18-1965
Vibert Clarke	p	Memphis Red Sox	9-4-1955
Ricardo Torres	c	Long Branch (NJ) Cubans	5-18-1920

Better than Satchel?

Satchel Paige was the first player elected to the Baseball Hall of Fame on the strength of a Negro League career. A master of self promotion as well as possessor of a blazing fastball and great control, he is thought of by the general baseball public as the greatest of the Negro Leagues pitchers.

But Negro League enthusiasts have other favorites, who have excellent credentials of their own for the top spot. "Smoky Joe" Williams, who pitched well into his 50s before retiring from the Homestead Grays in 1933, is often regarded as the greatest. A Texan who was part American Indian and who stood nearly six-and-a-half feet tall, Williams beat Hall of Famers Walter Johnson and Grover Cleveland Alexander in head-to-head competition, and threw a no-hitter against John McGraw's New York Giants in 1919.

When the *Pittsburgh Courier* sports department polled black baseball experts in 1952 to pick an all-time black team, Williams beat Paige for the top pitching spot by one vote. Wilber "Bullet" Rogan, who came in right behind Paige in that same voting, is also considered by many to have been the best. He spent 19 years with the Kansas City Monarchs, becoming the team's manager in addition to having been a star pitcher and hitter before retiring in 1938. Whoever might have been best, its clear that Williams and Rogan belong with Paige in the Hall of Fame.

—*various sources*

Organized

Baseball

Records

Many fans are aware of the black Hall of Famers who began their careers in the Negro Leagues, but few realize how many other fine major league and minor league players also got their start there.

This section presents many Organized Baseball records of pre-1951 Negro Leagues players. We have also included several prominent players who started in the Negro Leagues in the '50s before going into the major leagues. Where records are available, we have included the players' Negro League statistics, along with those from the Mexican League and, at the bottom of the listings, the winter leagues. Readers will see that many of the black players who were performing at the highest levels when Organized Baseball finally opened its doors still never got a shot at the majors.

Chet Brewer's passport to Panama.
Tina Brewer

FOTOGRAFIA

Chester A. Brewer
Firma del Portador

El infrascrito Secretario del Ministerio de Relaciones Exteriores

concede

Permiso Especial

al Sr. Chester Arthur Brewer

natural de Estados Unidos

para que pueda permanecer en el país en calidad de transeúnte por el tiempo que esté como jugador del equipo "CHESTERFIELD" de la Liga Profesional de Base Ball.

de conformidad con el Art. 5º del Decreto 663 de 20/11/1945

Panamá, 2 de Diciembre de 1948

ORIGINAL

Year	Club	League	Pos	G	AB	R	H	2B	3B	HR	RBI	SB	BA

Career Statistics by Individual Batter

Henry Louis "Hank" Aaron. Born February 5, 1934 at Mobile, AL. 6', 180 lbs. BR TR

Year	Club	League	Pos	G	AB	R	H	2B	3B	HR	RBI	SB	BA
1952	Eau Claire	NORL	SS	87	345	79	116	19	4	9	61	25	.336
1952	Indianapolis	NAL	SS	-	-	-	-	-	-	-	-	-	-
1953	Jacksonville	SATL	2B	137	574	**115**	**208**	**36**	14	22	**125**	13	**.362**
1954	Milwaukee	NL	OF	122	468	58	131	27	6	13	69	2	.280
1955	Milwaukee	NL	OF 2B	153	602	105	189	**37**	9	27	106	3	.314
1956	Milwaukee	NL	OF	153	609	106	**200**	34	14	26	92	2	**.328**
1957	Milwaukee	NL	OF	151	615	**118**	198	27	6	**44**	132	1	.322
1958	Milwaukee	NL	OF	153	601	109	196	34	4	30	95	4	.326
1959	Milwaukee	NL	OF 3B	154	629	116	**223**	46	7	39	123	8	**.355**
1960	Milwaukee	NL	OF 2B	153	590	102	172	20	11	40	**126**	16	.292
1961	Milwaukee	NL	OF 3B	**155**	603	115	197	**39**	10	34	120	21	.327
1962	Milwaukee	NL	OF 1B	156	592	127	191	28	6	45	128	15	.323
1963	Milwaukee	NL	OF	161	631	**121**	201	29	4	**44**	**130**	31	.319
1964	Milwaukee	NL	OF 2B	145	570	103	187	30	2	24	95	22	.328
1965	Milwaukee	NL	OF	150	570	109	181	**40**	1	32	89	24	.318
1966	Atlanta	NL	OF 2b	158	603	117	168	23	1	**44**	**127**	21	.279
1967	Atlanta	NL	OF 2B	155	600	**113**	184	37	3	**39**	109	17	.307
1968	Atlanta	NL	OF 1B	160	606	84	174	33	4	29	86	28	.287
1969	Atlanta	NL	OF 1B	147	547	100	164	30	3	44	97	9	.300
1970	Atlanta	NL	OF 1B	150	516	103	154	26	1	38	118	9	.298
1971	Atlanta	NL	1B OF	139	495	95	162	22	3	47	118	1	.327
1972	Atlanta	NL	1B OF	129	449	75	119	10	0	34	77	5	.265
1973	Atlanta	NL	OF	120	392	84	118	12	1	40	96	1	.301
1974	Atlanta	NL	OF	112	340	47	91	16	0	20	69	1	.268
1975	Milwaukee	AL	DH OF	137	465	45	109	16	2	12	60	0	.234
1976	Milwaukee	AL	DH OF	85	271	22	62	8	0	10	35	0	.229
53-4	Caguas	PRWL	OF	76	274	37	84	16	3	**9**	42	7	.307

Thomas Edison Alston. Born January 31, 1931 at Greensboro, NC. Died December 30, 1993 at Winston-Salem, NC. 6'5", 210 lbs. BL TR

Year	Club	League	Pos	G	AB	R	H	2B	3B	HR	RBI	SB	BA
1948	Greensboro	NSL	1B	-	-	-	-	-	-	-	-	-	-
1952	Porterville	SWIN	1B	54	224	54	79	18	5	12	69	15	.353
1952	San Diego	PCL	1B	78	258	29	63	10	1	2	26	0	.244
1953	San Diego	PCL	1B	**180**	697	101	207	25	5	23	101	8	.297
1954	Rochester	INT	1B	79	290	43	86	15	5	7	42	4	.297
1954	St. Louis	NL	1B	66	244	28	60	14	2	4	34	3	.246
1955	Omaha	AA	1B	117	430	68	118	21	9	6	59	7	.274
1955	St. Louis	NL	1B	13	8	0	1	0	0	0	0	0	.125
1956	Omaha	AA	1B	122	418	88	128	25	4	21	80	4	.306
1956	St. Louis	NL	1B	3	2	0	0	0	0	0	0	0	.000
1957	St. Louis	NL	1B	9	17	2	5	1	0	0	2	0	.294

George Lee Altman. Born March 20, 1933 at Goldsboro, NC. 6'4", 200 lbs. BL TR

Year	Club	League	Pos	G	AB	R	H	2B	3B	HR	RBI	SB	BA
1955	Kansas City	NAL	OF	-	-	-	-	-	-	-	-	-	-
1956	Burlington	III	OF	121	456	79	120	20	4	16	67	17	.263
1958	Pueblo	WEST	OF	89	345	72	112	9	11	14	78	7	.325
1959	Chicago	NL	OF	135	420	54	103	14	4	12	47	1	.245
1960	Chicago	NL	OF	119	334	50	89	16	4	13	51	4	.266
1961	Chicago	NL	OF	138	518	77	157	28	**12**	27	96	6	.303
1962	Chicago	NL	OF	147	534	74	170	27	5	22	74	19	.318
1963	St. Louis	NL	OF	135	464	62	127	18	7	9	47	13	.274
1964	New York	NL	OF	124	422	48	97	14	1	9	47	4	.230
1965	Chicago	NL	OF	90	196	24	46	7	1	4	23	3	.235
1966	Chicago	NL	OF	88	185	19	41	6	0	5	17	2	.222
1967	Chicago	NL	OF	15	18	1	2	2	0	0	1	0	.111
1967	Tacoma	PCL	OF	108	378	65	106	17	6	15	70	16	.280
1968	Lotte	JAP	OF	139	531	84	170	33	1	34	100	8	.320
1969	Lotte	JAP	OF	129	457	65	123	25	2	21	82	9	.269
1970	Lotte	JAP	OF	122	456	66	136	19	1	30	77	3	.298
1971	Lotte	JAP	OF	114	388	56	124	15	2	39	103	3	.320
1972	Lotte	JAP	OF	112	384	46	126	27	1	21	90	9	.328
1973	Lotte	JAP	OF	120	365	54	112	17	1	27	80	4	.307
1974	Lotte	JAP	OF	85	271	48	95	15	2	21	67	1	.351
1975	Hanshin	JAP	OF	114	361	33	99	12	1	12	57	0	.274

Year	Club	League	Pos	G	AB	R	H	2B	3B	HR	RBI	SB	BA
58-9		PANA	OF	-	147	-	44	-	-	9	26	-	.299
59-0	Cienfuegos	CWL	OF	-	219	41	55	5	1	14	32	3	.251

Edmundo "Sandy" Amoros y Isasi. Born January 30, 1930 at Havana, Cuba. Died June 27, 1992 in Miami, FL. 5'7 1/2", 170 lbs. BL TL

Year	Club	League	Pos	G	AB	R	H	2B	3B	HR	RBI	SB	BA
1950	New York	NAL	OF	34	136	28	46	8	6	4	17	4	.338
1951	Oriente	DMSL	OF	-	79	20	31	-	-	-	19	8	.392
1952	Brooklyn	NL	OF	20	44	10	11	3	1	0	3	1	.250
1952	St. Paul	AA		129	489	108	165	24	10	19	78	14	.337
1953	Montreal	INT		150	539	128	190	40	11	23	100	11	.353
1954	Brooklyn	NL	OF	79	263	44	72	18	6	9	34	1	.274
1954	Montreal	INT	OF	68	236	51	83	5	4	14	50	7	.352
1955	Brooklyn	NL	OF	119	388	59	96	16	7	10	51	10	.247
1956	Brooklyn	NL	OF	114	292	53	76	11	8	16	58	3	.260
1957	Brooklyn	NL	OF	106	238	40	66	7	1	7	26	3	.277
1958	Montreal	INT	OF	139	446	72	116	29	2	16	62	20	.260
1959	Los Angeles	NL	PH	5	5	1	1	0	0	0	1	0	.200
1959	Montreal	INT	OF	151	519	99	156	33	5	26	79	14	.301
1960	Detroit	AL	OF	65	67	7	10	0	0	1	7	0	.149
1960	Los Angeles	NL	OF	9	14	1	2	0	0	0	0	0	.143
1961	Denver	AA	OF	128	452	92	117	35	7	10	58	10	.259
1962	Mexico City	MEX	OF	111	403	78	123	19	7	13	71	13	.305
50-1	Havana	CWL	OF	41	42	13	12	4	1	1	8	1	.286
51-2	Havana	CWL	OF	53	165	23	55	10	4	3	27	4	.333
52-3	Havana	CWL	OF	64	220	38	82	16	2	2	38	5	.373
53-4	Havana	CWL	OF	73	283	39	91	11	4	9	39	11	.322
54-5	Havana	CWL	OF	65	241	53	74	8	3	5	40	9	.307
58-9	Almendares	CWL	OF	-	215	-	53	-	-	1	15	-	.247
59-0	Almendares	CWL	OF	-	221	-	52	-	-	6	24	-	.235
60-1	Almendares	CWL	OF	-	226	-	65	-	-	3	32	-	.288

Homero Mario Ariosa y Fernandez. Born September 12, 1920 at Remedios, Cuba. 6', 175 lbs. BR TR

Year	Club	League	Pos	G	AB	R	H	2B	3B	HR	RBI	SB	BA
1947	New York	NNL		-	36	6	7	1	0	0	-	0	.194
1947	Puebla	MEX	2B	6	4	0	0	0	0	0	0	0	.000
1948	New York	NNL		-	-	-	-	-	-	-	-	-	
1949	Aguila	MEX	2B	27	106	21	28	5	1	1	18	3	.264
1949	New York	NAL		41	146	22	38	-	-	-	-	-	.260
1950	Aguila	MEX	2B	91	369	66	119	16	10	3	52	10	.322
1951	Aguila	MEX	2B 3B	88	355	54	108	18	3	5	50	8	.304
1952	Aguila	MEX	2B	92	391	79	132	20	3	5	46	11	.338
1953	Aguila	MEX	2B	76	320	54	102	12	3	10	43	8	.319
1954	Aguila	MEX	2B	71	283	60	100	8	3	16	63	11	.353
1955	Aguila	MEX	3B SS	103	418	78	140	21	2	22	78	9	.335
1956	Aguila	MEX	OF 3B	123	479	59	149	26	4	3	52	11	.311
1957	Aguila	MEX	OF 2B 3B	119	475	82	144	21	4	11	79	16	.303
1958	Poza Rica, MC Reds	MEX	3B 2B	88	336	43	108	7	1	7	49	5	.321
1959	Poza Rica	MEX	OF	143	550	88	167	20	2	12	68	17	.304
1960	Aguila	MEX	3B OF	142	533	90	160	29	2	3	56	16	.300
1961	Aguila	MEX	OF 3B	110	386	58	108	15	2	3	47	5	.280
1962	Aguila	MEX	OF 3B	96	253	41	71	14	3	0	37	1	.281
1963	Aguila	MEX	OF INF	93	227	35	59	8	2	3	23	1	.260
1964	Aguila	MEX	OF INF	78	162	23	53	10	0	3	22	2	.327
1965	Aguila	MEX	OF INF	91	189	24	60	18	0	3	35	1	.317
1966	Aguila	MEX	1B OF	59	131	14	28	3	3	3	15	0	.214
1966	Campeche	MXSE	OF	1	4	1	1	0	0	0	0	0	.250
1968	Tabasco	MXSE	OF	27	41	5	14	2	1	0	7	0	.341
1972	Aguila	MEX	PH	1	1	0	0	0	0	0	0	0	.000

Alfred "Buddy" Armour. Born May 3, 1915 at Jackson, MS. 5'9", 170 lbs. BL TR

Year	Club	League	Pos	G	AB	R	H	2B	3B	HR	RBI	SB	BA
1938	Indianapolis	NAL	SS	-	-	-	-	-	-	-	-	-	
1939	St. Louis	NAL	SS	-	-	-	-	-	-	-	-	-	
1940	New Orleans-St. Lou	NAL	OF SS	5	19	6	9	3	-	-	-	2	.474
1941	New Orleans-St. Lou	NAL	OF	-	36	-	14	1	2	0	-	-	.389
1943	Harrisburg-St.Lou	NAL	CF	-	-	-	-	-	-	-	-	-	
1944	Cleveland	NAL	OF	63	231	40	69	10	8	1	23	14	.299
1945	Cleveland	NAL	OF	46	157	31	51	3	3	1	23	10	.325
1946	Cleveland	NAL	LF 3B	-	-	-	-	-	-	-	-	-	
1947	Chicago	NAL	OF	-	-	-	-	-	-	-	-	-	
1949	Farnham	PROV	OF	-	-	-	-	-	-	-	-	-	
1950	Farnham	PROV	OF	56	200	33	58	10	4	2	29	12	.290

Year	Club	League	Pos	G	AB	R	H	2B	3B	HR	RBI	SB	BA
1950	Homestead		OF	-	-	-	-	-	-	-	-	-	
1951	Farnham	PROV	CF	112	405	82	106	28	3	6	59	22	.262

Earl Ashby. Born 1921 at Havana, Cuba. 5'11, 170 lbs. BR TR

1945	Cleveland	NAL	C	17	35	6	10	3	0	0	2	1	.286
1946	Birmingham	NAL	C	-	-	-	-	-	-	-	-	-	
1946	VC, Pub. Mex.	MEX	C	7	9	2	2	-	-	-	1	-	.222
1947	Homestead	NNL	C	-	63	9	16	5	0	0	-	0	.254
1948	Newark	NNL	C	-	-	-	-	-	-	-	-	-	
1950	Drumm-St. Jean	PROV	C	22	65	14	19	3	0	2	9	2	.292

Joseph O. Atkins. Born 1922 at Pittsburgh, PA. 6'1", 193 lbs. BR TR

1946	Pittsburgh	USL	OF	-	-	-	-	-	-	-	-	-	
1947	Cleveland	NAL	3B OF	53	182	43	61	-	-	10	-	-	.335
1948	Farnham	PROV	OF	-	-	-	-	-	-	26	-	-	
1950	Fargo-Moorhead	NORL	OF 3B	26	89	16	21	3	0	5	19	0	.236
1951	Drummondville	PROV	OF 3B	113	407	55	109	25	0	18	73	7	.268
1952	Tampa	FINT	OF	31	100	11	21	5	0	0	11	0	.210
1953	Carman	MADK	OF	55	197	-	58	-	-	7	-	-	.294
1954	Escogido	DMSL	1B	-	19	4	6	-	-	-	2	-	.316
1954	Ottawa	INT		8	13	1	2	1	-	1	3	-	.154
48-9	Ponce	PRWL	OF 3B	-	120	25	39	7	-	6	25	2	.325

Frank Samuel Austin. Born May 22, 1922 in Panama. Died January, 15, 1960 in Panama City, Panama. 5'7", 168 lbs. BR TR

1944	Philadelphia	NNL	SS	34	136	34	53	7	4	0	16	3	**.390**
1945	Philadelphia	NNL	SS	39	161	29	**57**	10	0	2	21	9	.354
1946	Philadelphia	NNL	SS	**46**	174	34	57	11	1	0	20	3	.328
1947	Philadelphia	NNL	SS	-	218	32	62	10	-	0	-	8	.284
1948	Philadelphia	NNL	SS	-	-	-	-	-	-	0	-	-	
1949	Newark	INT	SS	19	71	13	20	2	0	1	6	2	.282
1949	Portland	PCL	SS	135	429	45	104	6	1	4	34	2	.242
1950	Portland	PCL	SS	160	523	54	145	17	3	3	55	3	.277
1951	Portland	PCL	SS	167	597	64	175	35	3	4	70	1	.293
1952	Portland	PCL	SS	177	702	87	186	23	2	4	38	17	.265
1953	Portland	PCL	SS	180	739	91	207	39	1	7	62	14	.280
1954	Portland	PCL	SS	166	661	77	178	31	4	4	53	3	.269
1955	Portland	PCL	SS	172	604	57	141	19	0	3	46	1	.233
1956	Vancouver	PCL	SS	120	281	32	80	14	0	0	27	0	.285
45-6	General Electric	PANA	SS	43	166	34	52	6	2	1	23	12	.313
46-7	Chesterfield	PANA	SS	32	182	44	65	6	5	2	23	25	.357
47-8	Chesterfield	PANA	SS	16	58	11	19	1	0	0	10	6	.328
48-9	Chesterfield	PANA	SS	37	147	28	46	4	0	0	10	5	.313
49-0	Chesterfield	PANA	SS	45	194	34	56	8	0	0	17	16	.289
50-1	Chesterfield	PANA	SS	32	126	18	40	7	1	0	14	6	.317
51-2	Chesterfield	PANA	SS	36	147	22	40	7	2	0	9	7	.272
52-3	Chesterfield	PANA	SS	36	143	24	41	18	2	3	30	0	.287
53-4	Chesterfield	PANA	SS	38	151	16	44	6	2	1	13	1	.291
54-5	Chesterfield	PANA	SS	40	157	24	52	9	2	0	9	3	**.331**

Eugene Walter "Gene" Baker. Born June 15, 1925 at Davenport, IA. 6'1", 177 lbs. BR TR

1948	Kansas City	NAL	SS	69	270	56	79	16	8	2	32	9	.293
1949	Kansas City	NAL	SS	88	347	47	82	-	-	-	-	-	.236
1950	Des Moines	WEST	SS	49	184	50	59	17	6	0	24	8	.321
1950	Kansas City	NAL	SS	-	-	-	-	-	-	-	-	-	
1950	Los Angeles	PCL	SS	100	375	64	105	16	5	2	16	12	.280
1950	Springfield	INT	SS	3	9	0	1	0	0	0	0	0	.111
1951	Los Angeles	PCL	SS	168	666	101	185	20	9	11	62	10	.278
1952	Los Angeles	PCL	SS	174	696	93	181	32	4	15	73	11	.260
1953	Chicago	NL	2B	7	22	1	5	1	0	0	0	1	.227
1953	Los Angeles	PCL	SS	162	595	89	169	26	5	20	99	20	.284
1954	Chicago	NL	2B	135	541	68	149	32	5	13	61	4	.275
1955	Chicago	NL	2B	154	609	82	163	29	7	11	52	9	.268
1956	Chicago	NL	2B	140	546	65	141	23	3	12	57	4	.258
1957	Chciago,Pittsburgh	NL	INF	123	409	40	108	22	5	3	46	3	.264
1958	Pittsburgh	NL	3B 2B	29	56	3	14	1	1	0	7	0	.250
1960	Pittsburgh	NL	3B 2B	33	37	5	9	0	0	0	4	0	.243
1961	Batavia	NYP	3B P	53	155	48	60	12	0	8	45	6	.387
1961	Pittsburgh	NL	3B	9	10	1	1	0	0	0	0	0	.100
1962	Columbus	INT	PH INF	22	52	3	6	2	-	-	2	-	.115

Year	Club	League	Pos	G	AB	R	H	2B	3B	HR	RBI	SB	BA
52-3	San Juan	PRWL	SS	-	261	-	80	-	-	3	30	-	.307
53-4	San Juan	PRWL	SS	-	226	-	60	-	-	3	28	-	.265

Miguel Ballestro "Pedro" Ballester. Born 1925. 5'8 1/2", 160 lbs. BR TR

Year	Club	League	Pos	G	AB	R	H	2B	3B	HR	RBI	SB	BA
1948	New York	NNL	SS	-	-	-	-	-	-	-	-	-	
1951	Sherbrooke	PROV	SS	123	472	69	133	24	3	23	93	4	.282
1952	Keokuk	III	INF	121	440	59	97	19	0	10	61	9	.220
1953	Fond Du Lac	WISC	SS	119	435	82	137	19	4	18	91	21	.315
1954	St. Jean-Drumm.	PROV	INF	107	379	58	108	34	2	12	60	0	.285
1955	Ne.L. Yucatan	MEX	SS 2B	70	278	48	78	13	2	3	48	2	.281
48-9	Mariano	CWL	SS	2	4	0	1	0	0	0	1	0	.250
50-1	Mariano-Cienfuegos	CWL	SS	35	59	4	13	1	0	1	5	0	.220

Daniel Robert Bankhead. Born May 3, 1920 at Empire, AL. Died May 2, 1976 in Houston, TX. 6'1", 184 lbs. BR TR

Year	Club	League	Pos	G	AB	R	H	2B	3B	HR	RBI	SB	BA
1940	Birmingham	NAL	P	-	-	-	-	-	-	-	-	-	
1941	Birmingham	NAL	P	-	-	-	-	-	-	-	-	-	
1942	Birmingham	NAL	P	-	-	-	-	-	-	-	-	-	
1946	Memphis	NAL	P	-	-	-	-	-	-	-	-	-	
1947	Brooklyn	NL	P	6	4	2	1	0	0	1	2	0	.250
1947	Memphis	NAL	P	-	-	-	-	-	-	-	-	-	
1948	Nashua	NENG	P	49	97	25	28	6	-	1	11	2	.289
1948	St. Paul	AA	P	6	18	4	9	-	-	-	2	-	.500
1949	Montreal	INT	P	57	127	21	41	7	3	1	26	0	.323
1950	Brooklyn	NL	P	41	39	2	9	1	0	0	1	0	.231
1951	Brooklyn	NL	P	15	2	3	0	0	0	0	0	0	.000
1951	Montreal	INT	P	14	22	3	8	0	0	1	2	0	.364
1952	Escogido	DMSL	P	-	62	4	16	0	0	0	8	1	.258
1952	Montreal	INT	P	12	9	2	1	0	0	0	0	0	.111
1953	Drummondville	PROV	P 1B 2B	47	167	22	46	8	3	3	28	2	.275
1953	Monterrey	MEX	1B P	28	96	15	27	5	1	3	12	0	.281
1954	Monterrey	MEX	1B P	58	198	40	54	10	3	7	33	3	.273
1955	Monterrey, Aguila	MEX	OF 1B P	81	297	54	94	16	4	9	46	10	.316
1956	Aguila, Mexico City	MEX	1B P	66	219	28	63	12	3	4	28	5	.288
1957	Aquascalientes	CMEX	2B SS 1B P	73	252	44	91	20	5	4	57	8	.361
1959	Aguila	MEX	1B OF P	28	45	5	11	2	0	0	6	1	.244
1960	Puebla	MEX	P OF	51	82	11	31	3	0	1	12	2	.378
1961	Puebla	MEX	OF 1B P	67	150	25	38	6	2	0	12	3	.253
1962	Puebla	MEX	P OF	69	87	10	27	2	0	0	9	0	.310
1963	Puebla	MEX	P OF	38	39	3	9	2	0	0	1	0	.231
1964	Leon	MXCT	OF P	38	102	35	45	4	3	4	31	4	.441
1966	Reynosa	MEX	P	11	14	3	6	-	0	-	2	-	.429
41-2	Mayaquez	PRWL		-	-	-	-	-	-	-	-	-	
46-7	Caguas	PRWL	P	-	249	40	80	-	-	-	29	-	.321
48-9	Caguas	PRWL	P	-	234	28	60	11	7	3	34	3	.256
49-0	Caguas	PRWL	P	-	140	-	42	-	-	2	-	-	.300
51-2	Santurce	PRWL	P OF	33	90	11	25	3	0	0	7	1	.278
52-3	Santurce	PRWL	OF	-	85	10	23	5	3	0	7	-	.271
62-3	Ponce, Aguas	PRWL	OF P	25	46	2	8	5	0	0	6	-	.174

Samuel Bankhead. Born September 18, 1905 at Empire, AL. Died July 24, 1976 at Pittsburgh, PA. 5'8", 175 lbs. BR TR

Year	Club	League	Pos	G	AB	R	H	2B	3B	HR	RBI	SB	BA
1931	Birmingham	NNL	2B	1	4	-	2	1	1	0	-	0	.500
1932	Louis.,Birm., Nash.	NSL	OF P	5	10	-	4	1	0	0	-	0	.400
1933	Nashville	NNL	SS OF	22	86	-	27	3	1	1	-	3	.314
1934	Nashville, KC	NNL	OF INF P	19	80	-	27	-	1	0	-	4	.338
1935	Pittsburgh	NNL	OF	59	235	-	79	14	6	1	-	4	.336
1936	Pittsburgh	NNL	2B OF	29	125	-	27	5	-	-	0	1	.216
1937	Ciudad Trujillo	DOM	OF	17	68	10	21	1	-	2	13	-	.309
1938	Pittsburgh	NNL	OF	14	50	-	10	3	-	1	-	3	.200
1939	Homestead, Toledo	NNL	2B SS OF	25	78	-	26	3	-	5	-	1	.333
1940	Monterrey	MEX	SS	93	384	80	122	19	11	8	74	32	.318
1941	Monterrey	MEX	SS	101	405	74	142	21	12	8	85	19	.351
1942	Homestead	NNL	SS RF	37	126	-	33	3	3	2	-	-	.262
1943	Homestead	NNL	SS	-	162	-	39	1	1	1	-	8	.241
1944	Homestead	NNL	SS	40	150	32	43	8	4	0	32	4	.287
1945	Homestead	NNL	SS	35	124	11	35	5	2	1	16	3	.282
1946	Homestead	NNL	INF	32	120	17	43	4	3	4	12	3	.358
1947	Homestead	NNL	SS	-	244	28	60	12	-	3	-	8	.246
1948	Homestead	NNL	SS	-	-	-	-	-	-	-	-	-	
1949	Homestead	BAA	SS CF	-	-	-	-	-	-	-	-	-	
1950	Homestead		2B	-	-	-	-	-	-	-	-	-	

Year	Club	League	Pos	G	AB	R	H	2B	3B	HR	RBI	SB	BA
1951	Farnham	PROV	SS 2B	122	435	46	119	20	2	2	51	12	.274
37-8	Santa Clara	CWL	UTL	-	**243**	**47**	**89**	6	**5**	2	34	-	**.366**
38-9	Santa Clara	CWL	UTL	-	227	42	52	7	2	5	44	5	.229
39-0	Santa Clara	CWL	UTL	-	**209**	**41**	**67**	8	2	3	29	7	.321
40-1	Almendares	CWL	UTL	-	123	9	30	3	1	0	16	2	.244
41-2	Ponce	PRWL	UTL	-	168	33	59	16	3	0	35	-	.351
44-5	Ponce	PRWL	UTL	-	144	21	39	-	-	0	23	-	.271
45-6	Ponce	PRWL	UTL	-	155	30	45	3	1	**3**	24	**12**	.290
46-7	Caguas, Guayama	PRWL	UTL	-	234	36	75	-	-	-	27	-	.321

Ernest "Ernie" Banks. Born January 31, 1931 at Dallas, TX. 6'1", 186 lbs. BR TR

Year	Club	League	Pos	G	AB	R	H	2B	3B	HR	RBI	SB	BA
1950	Kansas City	NAL	SS	53	196	27	50	11	1	1	20	3	.255
1953	Chicago	NL	SS	10	35	3	11	1	1	2	6	0	.314
1953	Kansas City	NAL	SS	46	173	26	60	16	2	7	47	7	.347
1954	Chicago	NL	SS	154	593	70	163	19	7	19	79	6	.275
1955	Chicago	NL	SS	154	596	98	176	29	9	44	117	9	.295
1956	Chicago	NL	SS	139	538	82	160	25	8	28	85	6	.297
1957	Chicago	NL	SS 3B	156	594	113	169	34	6	43	102	8	.285
1958	Chicago	NL	SS	154	617	119	193	23	11	**47**	**129**	4	.313
1959	Chicago	NL	SS	155	589	97	179	25	6	45	**143**	2	.304
1960	Chicago	NL	SS	156	597	94	162	32	7	**41**	117	1	.271
1961	Chicago	NL	SS OF 1B	138	511	75	142	22	4	29	80	1	.278
1962	Chicago	NL	1B 3B	154	610	87	164	20	6	37	104	5	.269
1963	Chicago	NL	1B	130	432	41	98	20	1	18	64	0	.227
1964	Chicago	NL	1B	157	591	67	156	29	6	23	95	1	.264
1965	Chicago	NL	1B	163	612	79	162	25	3	28	106	3	.265
1966	Chicago	NL	1B 3B	141	511	52	139	23	7	15	75	0	.272
1967	Chicago	NL	1B	151	573	68	158	26	4	23	95	2	.276
1968	Chicago	NL	1B	150	552	71	136	27	0	32	83	2	.246
1969	Chicago	NL	1B	155	565	60	143	19	2	23	106	0	.253
1970	Chicago	NL	1B	72	222	25	56	6	2	12	44	0	.252
1971	Chicago	NL	1B	39	83	4	16	2	0	3	6	0	.193

Henry Baylis. 5'9", 170 lbs. BR TR

Year	Club	League	Pos	G	AB	R	H	2B	3B	HR	RBI	SB	BA
1948	Chicago	NAL	3B	39	150	18	48	8	1	0	13	0	.320
1949	Birmingham, Balt.	NAL	2B 3B	31	92	12	25	-	-	-	-	-	.272
1950	Birmingham	NAL	2B 3B	78	318	53	86	11	2	0	25	8	.270
1951	Kansas City	NAL	2B	-	96	17	38	-	-	-	12	-	.396
1952	Kansas City	NAL	2B	-	-	-	-	-	-	-	-	-	
1953	Kansas City	NAL	3B	74	271	40	77	16	2	2	31	2	.284
1954	Kansas City	NAL	3B	-	-	-	-	-	-	-	-	-	
1954	Oriente	DMSL	3B	-	55	5	16	0	0	0	3	2	.291
1955	Kansas City	NAL	3B	-	-	-	-	-	-	-	-	-	
1956	El Paso	SOWS	3B	138	593	101	156	32	7	2	64	4	.263
1957	El Paso	SOWS	3B	8	25	-	6	-	-	-	-	-	.240
1957	Tucson	AZMX	2B 3B	57	243	50	70	6	2	3	32	12	.288
1957	Yakima	NWL	3B	20	76	4	16	3	0	0	5	0	.211

Pablo Bernard. Born 1927 in Panama. 5'11", 158 lbs. BR TR

Year	Club	League	Pos	G	AB	R	H	2B	3B	HR	RBI	SB	BA
1949	Louisville	NAL	SS INF	54	149	15	36	-	-	-	-	-	.242
1950	Cleveland	NAL	2B	-	-	-	-	-	-	-	-	-	
1950	Ventura	CALF	SS 2B	115	482	93	137	15	14	5	56	16	.284
1951	Denver	WEST	INF	13	30	7	5	0	0	1	4	1	.167
1951	Ventura	CALF	2B	67	273	39	82	13	9	4	45	10	.300
1952	Denver	WEST	2B SS	75	210	28	49	5	3	0	31	4	.233
1953	Billings	PION	SS	129	503	94	148	17	13	5	79	27	.294
1954	Billings	PION	SS 2B	120	473	95	158	33	4	6	64	40	.334
1955	Tulsa	TEX	SS	108	395	51	111	19	1	5	48	2	.281
1956	Havana	INT	SS 2B	143	506	53	137	23	3	3	40	0	.271
1957	Austin	TEX	2B	27	88	4	13	4	0	0	3	0	.148
1957	Havana	INT	2B	63	203	14	41	6	2	1	12	0	.202
1957	Indianapolis	AA	3B 2B	19	48	6	13	3	0	1	4	0	.271
1958	Nuevo Laredo	MEX	SS	118	490	**106**	**182**	27	4	12	56	10	**.371**
1959	N.L.-Vera Cruz	MEX	SS	136	515	82	153	26	5	4	48	6	.297
1960	Aguila	MEX	SS 2B	118	379	45	105	16	0	2	41	3	.277
1961	Aguila	MEX	SS	111	439	73	128	17	4	10	48	4	.292
57-8	Chesterfield	PANA	SS	-	115	-	29	-	-	1	5	-	.252
58-9	Marlboro	PANA	SS	-	132	-	41	-	-	1	15	-	.311
59-0	Marlboro	PANA	SS	-	115	-	30	-	-	-	9	-	.261
60-1	Marlboro	PANA	SS	-	112	-	27	-	-	-	7	-	.241

Year	Club	League	Pos	G	AB	R	H	2B	3B	HR	RBI	SB	BA

Heberto "Harry" Blanco. Born October 17, 1920 at Bayamo, Cuba. 5'7", 168 lbs. BR TR

Year	Club	League	Pos	G	AB	R	H	2B	3B	HR	RBI	SB	BA
1941	New York	NNL	2B	-	-	-	-	-	-	-	-	-	
1942	New York	NNL	2B	-	-	-	-	-	-	-	-	-	
1943	Monterrey	MEX	2B	90	354	54	93	16	7	0	34	12	.263
1944	Monterrey	MEX	2B	92	377	74	113	9	2	1	34	12	.300
1945	Monterrey	MEX	2B SS	93	397	87	131	15	5	0	40	19	.330
1946	Monterrey	MEX	2B SS	97	402	63	112	8	7	0	26	12	.279
1948	V.C. Monterrey	MEX	2B	60	250	42	65	10	4	0	24	1	.260
1950	Nuevo Laredo	MEX	2B	70	276	31	75	14	2	3	24	18	.272
1951	Licey	DMSL	2B	-	18	3	5	-	-	0	3	-	.278
1951	Nuevo Laredo	MEX	2B	42	167	31	44	8	1	3	24	7	.263
1952	Monterrey	MEX	2B	47	184	22	63	10	2	0	27	7	.342
1953	Torreon	MEX	2B	34	140	10	31	2	-	0	19	6	.221
1954	Aguila	MEX	2B	80	322	66	97	22	1	6	59	8	.301
1955	Aguila	MEX	2B	98	385	62	113	15	4	10	66	7	.294
1956	Roswell	SWL	2B	10	38	9	13	1	0	0	7	0	.342
44-5	Havana	CWL	2B	28	111	17	31	-	-	-	-	-	.279
48-9	Havana	CWL	2B	10	34	0	3	0	0	0	1	0	.088
50-1	Marianao	CWL	2B	35	57	4	11	1	1	-	10	1	.193

Lincoln Boyd. Born 1933?. 6'3", 180 lbs. BR TR

Year	Club	League	Pos	G	AB	R	H	2B	3B	HR	RBI	SB	BA
1949	Louisville	NAL	OF	-	-	-	-	-	-	-	-	-	
1951	Indianapolis	NAL	OF	-	-	-	-	-	-	-	81	-	
1952	Indianapolis	NAL	OF	-	-	-	-	-	-	-	-	-	
1952	Torreon	MEX	OF	54	185	17	36	10	1	5	36	1	.195
1953	Leesburg	FLST	OF	88	323	56	77	15	1	8	57	15	.238
1954	Clovis	WTNM	OF	130	438	110	138	23	4	30	112	4	.315
1955	Clovis	WTNM	OF	137	500	130	170	33	2	44	157	3	.340
1956	Clovis	WTNM	OF	71	268	61	81	17	1	21	69	2	.302

Robert Richard "The Rope" Boyd. Born October 1, 1925 at Potts Camp, MS. 5'9", 170 lbs. BL TL

Year	Club	League	Pos	G	AB	R	H	2B	3B	HR	RBI	SB	BA
1946	Memphis	NAL	1B	-	-	-	-	-	-	-	-	-	
1947	Memphis	NAL	1B	73	283	54	96	-	-	4	-	-	.339
1948	Memphis	NAL	1B	77	303	52	114	18	**9**	5	51	4	.376
1949	Memphis	NAL	1B	76	293	57	110	-	-	-	-	-	.375
1950	Colorado Springs	WEST	1B	42	158	39	59	6	5	9	39	3	.373
1950	Memphis	NAL	1B	63	250	54	89	27	8	7	58	9	.356
1951	Chicago	AL	1B	12	18	3	3	0	1	0	4	0	.167
1951	Sacramento	PCL	1B	145	555	82	190	32	11	5	64	**41**	.342
1952	Seattle	PCL	1B OF	161	641	100	205	29	18	3	75	33	**.320**
1953	Charleston	AA	OF	49	198	33	64	8	6	2	22	12	.323
1953	Chicago	AL	1B OF	55	165	20	49	6	2	3	23	1	.297
1953	Toronto	INT	OF	31	120	16	37	4	4	3	12	1	.308
1954	Chicago	AL	OG 1B	29	56	10	10	3	0	0	5	2	.179
1954	Houston	TEX	1B	94	358	59	115	22	2	7	68	3	.321
1955	Houston	TEX	1B	**163**	**635**	96	**197**	39	6	15	94	13	.310
1956	Baltimore	AL	1B OF	70	225	28	70	8	3	2	11	0	.311
1957	Baltimore	AL	1B OF	141	485	73	154	16	8	4	34	2	.318
1958	Baltimore	AL	1B	125	401	58	124	21	5	7	36	1	.309
1959	Baltimore	AL	1B	128	415	42	110	20	2	3	41	3	.265
1960	Baltimore	AL	1B	71	82	9	26	5	2	0	9	0	.317
1961	Kansas City	AL	1B	26	48	7	11	2	0	0	9	0	.229
1962	Louisville, OK Cty	AA	1B	117	368	56	120	18	12	5	42	1	.326
1962	Milwaukee	NL	1B	36	41	3	10	0	0	0	3	0	.244
1963	Oklahoma City	PCL	1B	67	223	19	56	12	1	2	23	0	.251
1963	San Antonio	TEX	1B	55	229	34	77	17	4	2	25	3	.336
1964	Oklahoma City	PCL	PH	9	8	1	0	0	0	0	0	0	.000
49-0	Havana	CWL	1B	9	36	2	9	1	0	0	4	4	.250
51-2	Ponce	PRWL	1B	72	305	55	**114**	18	5	2	43	3	**.374**
52-3	Ponce	PRWL	1B	-	293	46	82	10	3	6	44	11	.280
54-5	Cienfuegos	CWL	1B	70	**292**	38	**90**	8	4	5	31	3	.308
55-6	Cienfuegos	CWL	1B	-	285	43	89	11	2	5	42	5	.312
56-7	Cienfuegos	CWL	1B	-	38	2	8	1	0	0	3	-	.211

Ramon "El Professor" Bragana. Born May 11, 1909 at Havana, Cuba. Deceased. 5'10", 175 lbs. BR TR

Year	Club	League	Pos	G	AB	R	H	2B	3B	HR	RBI	SB	BA
1928	Cuban Stars	ECL	P	-	-	-	-	-	-	-	-	-	
1930	Cuban Stars	P	-	-	-	-	-	-	-	-	-	-	
1935	New York	NNL	P	-	-	-	-	-	-	-	-	-	
1938	Agrario	MEX	P INF OF	37	119	38	36	5	2	8	23	9	.303
1939	Anahuac	MEX	P C INF OF	44	119	18	28	6	2	2	17	1	.235

Year	Club	League	Pos	G	AB	R	H	2B	3B	HR	RBI	SB	BA
1940	Vera Cruz	MEX	P INF OF	56	150	37	40	7	2	3	24	1	.267
1941	Vera Cruz	MEX	P INF OF	65	175	28	48	9	1	4	24	4	.274
1942	Vera Cruz	MEX	P INF OF	88	314	57	94	12	3	17	82	7	.299
1943	Vera Cruz	MEX	P INF OF	84	255	35	61	6	5	6	40	2	.239
1944	Vera Cruz	MEX	P INF OF	80	264	53	73	9	3	5	44	3	.277
1945	Vera Cruz	MEX	P C INF OF	72	206	33	43	8	2	2	35	5	.209
1946	Vera Cruz	MEX	P C INF OF	60	123	12	21	3	-	1	13	1	.171
1947	Cleveland	NAL	P	-	-	-	-	-	-	-	-	-	-
1947	Vera Cruz	MEX	P OF	46	90	13	13	1	1	0	10	0	.144
1948	Vera Cruz	MEX	P	31	69	6	10	1	0	0	8	0	.145
1949	Vera Cruz	MEX	P	36	59	10	10	2	2	1	8	0	.169
1950	Vera Cruz	MEX	P	31	62	6	14	1	0	0	2	0	.226
1951	Vera Cruz	MEX	P 3B	47	116	10	25	4	0	0	14	1	.216
1952	Jalisco,Monterrey	MEX	P OF 1B	32	54	7	15	4	0	1	10	0	.278
1953	Monterrey	MEX	P	23	35	2	4	-	-	-	1	0	.114
1954	Mexico City	MEX	P	1	1	0	0	0	0	0	0	0	.000
1955	Yucatan, Vera Cruz	MEX	P	20	32	4	9	0	0	0	0	0	.281
36-7	Gavilanes	VENZ	P	-	44	-	14	-	-	-	-	-	.318
53-4		MEX	P	-	-	-	-	-	-	-	-	-	

Alonzo Braithwaite. Born in Panama. 5'11 1/2", 174 lbs. BR TR

Year	Club	League	Pos	G	AB	R	H	2B	3B	HR	RBI	SB	BA
1948	Philadelphia	NNL	2B	-	-	-	-	-	-	-	-	-	
1951	Farnham	PROV	2B	123	507	73	137	17	3	3	39	22	.270
1952	St. Hyacinthe	PROV	2B	129	531	109	126	27	1	12	75	20	.237
1953	St. Hyacinthe-Drum	PROV	2B SS	124	507	77	125	13	9	2	48	11	.247
1954	Drum., St. Jean	PROV	2B	31	115	10	23	5	1	1	7	1	.200
1955	Burlington	PROV	2B	93	385	66	128	19	7	2	47	5	.332
1955	Johnstown	EAST	2B 3B	28	98	18	18	0	1	1	5	1	.184
1956	Abilene	BGST	1B	48	205	33	56	10	0	3	14	5	.273
1956	Columbia	SATL	1B	83	332	55	89	10	7	2	29	4	.268
1957	Abilene	BGST	3B 1B	121	491	78	151	28	7	3	57	6	.308
1958	Roch.-Winona	III	INF	101	325	45	71	18	0	6	43	0	.218
1959	Mont., Poza Rica	MEX	1B 2B 3B	94	281	35	76	10	4	2	23	5	.270
45-6	General Electric	PANA	UTL	43	158	28	53	13	1	3	-	12	.335
46-7	General Electric	PANA	UTL	41	166	38	55	8	3	3	-	23	.331
47-8	Chesterfield	PANA	UTL	42	149	17	44	9	1	1	-	6	.295
48-9	Chesterfield	PANA	UTL	32	121	29	43	4	1	2	18	12	.355
49-0	Chesterfield	PANA	UTL	33	129	24	46	5	1	2	28	7	.357
50-1	Chesterfield	PANA	UTL	37	127	11	37	6	1	0	15	0	.291
51-2	Chesterfield	PANA	UTL	35	124	22	35	5	0	0	16	7	.282
52-3	Chesterfield	PANA	UTL	30	108	15	28	3	0	0	7	3	.259
53-4	Spur Cola	PANA	UTL	41	152	25	45	12	1	2	8	3	.296
54-5	Spur Cola	PANA	UTL	34	102	10	30	6	1	-	7	0	.294
57-8	Cer., Balboa	PANA	UTL	-	121	-	31	-	-	1	12	-	.256

Archie Braithwaite

Year	Club	League	Pos	G	AB	R	H	2B	3B	HR	RBI	SB	BA
1944	Newark	NNL	OF	31	103	13	29	5	2	2	19	1	.282
1947	Philadelphia	NNL	OF	-	188	36	52	7	-	0	-	11	.277
1951	Vera Cruz	MEX	OF	84	315	56	104	14	1	4	51	13	.330
1953	Anahuac, N.Laredo	MEX	OF	77	304	49	95	12	3	2	42	5	.313
1954	Mont., M.C. N.L.	MEX	OF	68	264	42	76	14	2	4	43	6	.288

Luther Branham. Born 1924. 5'6 1/2", 160 lbs. BR TR

Year	Club	League	Pos	G	AB	R	H	2B	3B	HR	RBI	SB	BA
1949	Birmingham	NAL	2B	-	-	-	-	-	-	-	-	-	
1950	Chicago	NAL	2B 3B	43	155	27	38	11	2	2	18	4	.245
1951	Drummondville	PROV	2B	47	167	25	34	5	0	0	10	3	.204
1952	Victoria	WINT	2B OF	120	438	89	126	16	2	3	41	21	.288
1953	Victoria	WINT	2B SS	129	496	81	132	24	4	2	43	19	.266

Sherwood "Woody" Brewer. Born August 16, 1923 at Clarksdale, MS. 5'8", 168 lbs. BR TR

Year	Club	League	Pos	G	AB	R	H	2B	3B	HR	RBI	SB	BA
1949	Indianapolis	NAL		81	323	40	90	-	-	-	-	-	.279
1950	Indianapolis	NAL	2B SS OF	81	322	53	96	18	5	1	34	11	.298
1951	Indianapolis	NAL	SS	-	-	-	-	-	-	-	-	-	
1952	Ardmore	SOON	2B	29	101	19	24	7	0	2	16	7	.238
1953	Kansas City	NAL	2B	76	301	52	66	10	2	6	30	7	.219
1954	Kansas City	NAL	2B	55	175	27	54	4	0	1	20	3	.309
1955	Kansas City	NAL	2B	-	-	-	-	-	-	-	-	-	
1955	San Angelo	LGHN	2B	131	545	109	157	17	4	6	54	22	.288
1956	San Angelo	SWL	2B	92	429	71	115	24	2	9	38	7	.268
1958	Detroit	NAL	3B	-	-	-	-	-	-	-	-	-	

Year	Club	League	Pos	G	AB	R	H	2B	3B	HR	RBI	SB	BA

Marshall Bridges. Born June 2, 1931 at Jackson, MS. Died September 7, 1990 in Jackson, MS. 6'1", 165 lbs. BB TL

Year	Club	League	Pos	G	AB	R	H	2B	3B	HR	RBI	SB	BA
1953	Sioux City	WEST	1B P	129	477	71	118	25	6	6	55	12	.247
1954	Danville	CARO	OF PH	15	38	4	8	2	0	1	5	0	.211
1954	Memphis	NAL	P OF	33	91	23	28	5	1	2	20	11	.308
1955	Amarillo	AZMX	P OF	45	120	25	28	7	2	9	33	0	.233
1955	Beaumont	TEX	P OF	12	9	0	1	0	1	0	0	0	.111
1956	Austin	TEX	P	1	3	0	0	0	0	0	0	0	.000
1956	Topeka	WEST	P PH	57	114	23	31	5	3	1	13	0	.272
1957	Sacramento	PCL	P OF PH	58	108	8	24	1	1	1	8	0	.222
1958	Sacramento	PCL	P PH	41	84	8	14	3	1	1	9	0	.167

Barney Brown. BL TL

Year	Club	League	Pos	G	AB	R	H	2B	3B	HR	RBI	SB	BA
1939	Vera Cruz	MEX	P OF	46	148	24	47	4	2	0	16	0	.318
1940	Vera Cruz	MEX	P OF	66	192	36	54	17	0	0	27	1	.281
1941	Vera Cruz	MEX	P OF	78	251	38	81	12	2	0	39	0	.323
1944	Philadelphia	NNL	P OF	30	71	6	14	3	0	-	12	0	.197
1945	Mexico City	MEX	P OF	47	129	32	41	2	6	0	18	0	.318
1945	Philadelphia	NNL	P	11	35	5	8	3	0	0	4	0	.229
1946	Philadelphia	NNL	P	36	70	8	12	2	0	0	7	1	.171
1947	Philadelphia	NNL	P	13	63	4	7	0	0	0	-	0	.111
1949	Philadelphia	NAL	P	20	39	5	13	0	0	0	-	0	.333
1950	Torreon	MEX	P OF	41	88	11	26	1	1	0	8	1	.295
1951	Torreon	MEX	P OF	45	102	11	28	3	0	0	7	0	.275
1952	Torreon	MEX	P	13	30	2	7	2	0	0	2	0	.233
1953	Brandon	MADK	P	18	49	-	15	-	-	0	10	0	.306
47-8	Ponce	PRWL	P	-	33	3	9	0	0	0	3	0	.273

Isaac (Ike) Brown. Born April 13, 1942 at Memphis, TN. 6'1", 200 lbs. BR TR

Year	Club	League	Pos	G	AB	R	H	2B	3B	HR	RBI	SB	BA
1960	Kansas City	NAL	SS	-	-	-	-	-	-	-	-	-	
1962	Duluth-Superior	NORL	SS	115	370	57	86	6	5	5	43	28	.232
1962	Jamestown	NYP	SS	9	33	6	9	1	0	1	6	2	.273
1963	Duluth-Superior	NORL	SS	115	394	71	96	14	3	9	59	17	.244
1964	Knoxville	SOU	SS 2B	98	290	56	88	11	8	5	38	6	.303
1965	Montg. Lynchburg	SOU	3B SS	113	383	39	90	10	4	6	37	17	.235
1965	Syracuse	INT	SS	19	63	10	15	3	0	0	6	0	.238
1966	Montgomery	SOU	OF	100	334	53	99	10	5	9	41	10	.296
1967	Toledo	INT	UTL	134	435	56	117	18	4	7	57	15	.269
1968	Toledo	INT	INF OF	110	350	52	92	12	1	13	54	6	.263
1969	Detroit	AL	INF OF	70	170	24	39	4	3	5	12	2	.229
1969	Toledo	INT	3B SS	53	180	43	64	14	3	11	38	9	.356
1970	Detroit	AL	2B 3B OF	56	94	17	27	5	0	4	15	0	.287
1971	Detroit	AL	INF OF	59	110	20	28	1	0	8	19	0	.255
1972	Detroit	AL	OF INF	51	84	12	21	3	0	2	10	1	.250
1973	Detroit	AL	UTL	42	75	12	22	2	1	1	9	0	.293
1974	Detroit	AL	3B	2	2	0	0	0	0	0	0	0	.000
1974	Evansville	AA	1B 3B	58	163	21	42	4	1	3	19	3	.258

Raymond Brown. Born February 23, 1908 at Ashland Grove, OH. Died in Dayton, OH. 6'1", 195 lbs. BB TR

Year	Club	League	Pos	G	AB	R	H	2B	3B	HR	RBI	SB	BA
1939	Homestead	NNL	P OF	27	91	-	29	-	-	0	-	0	.319
1940	Homestead	NNL	P OF	-	72	-	23	1	1	1	-	-	.319
1941	Homestead	NNL		-	-	-	-	-	-	-	-	-	
1942	Homestead	NNL		-	-	-	-	-	-	-	-	-	
1943	Homestead	NNL		-	-	-	-	-	-	-	-	-	
1944	Homestead	NNL	P	23	49	6	15	0	1	2	7	0	.306
1945	Homestead	NNL		-	-	-	-	-	-	-	-	-	
1946	Tampico	MEX	P OF	49	117	14	25	8	1	0	8	0	.214
1947	Tampico	MEX		-	-	-	-	-	-	-	-	-	
1948	Tampico, Vera Cruz	MEX		-	-	-	-	-	-	-	-	-	
1949	Mexico City	MEX	P OF	57	131	23	33	7	0	3	18	1	.252
1950	Sherbrooke	PROV	P	15	32	6	8	2	0	2	7	-	.250
1951	Sherbrooke	PROV	P	62	119	13	23	6	0	4	13	-	.193
1953	Thetford Mines	PROV		-	-	-	-	-	-	-	-	-	
36-7	Santa Clara	CWL	P OF	-	132	23	41	5	2	1	27	2	.311
37-8	Santa Clara	CWL	P	-	86	11	22	0	1	4	14	-	.256
38-9	San Juan	PRWL	P OF	-	57	-	23	-	-	-	-	-	.404
38-9	Santa Clara	CWL	P OF	-	135	17	31	4	2	1	23	1	.230
39-0	San Juan	PRWL	P OF	-	92	-	27	-	-	-	14	-	.293
40-1	Santurce	PRWL		-	-	-	-	-	-	-	-	-	
41-2	Ponce	PRWL	P	-	135	20	33	3	2	1	24	-	.244
44-5	San Juan	PRWL		-	-	-	-	-	-	-	-	-	

Year	Club	League	Pos	G	AB	R	H	2B	3B	HR	RBI	SB	BA
45-6	Almend., Marianao	CWL		-	-	-	-	-	-	-	-	-	
47-8	Santiago	CWL		-	-	-	-	-	-	-	-	-	

T.J. "Tom" Brown. BR TR

Year	Club	League	Pos	G	AB	R	H	2B	3B	HR	RBI	SB	BA
1940	Memphis	NAL	SS	12	39	7	12	1	0	0	-	1	.308
1942	Memphis	NAL	SS	14	54	-	17	2	3	1	-	0	.315
1944	Memphis	NAL	SS	46	161	9	34	8	1	0	-	4	.211
1945	Memphis	NAL	SS	12	19	2	2	-	0	0	2	0	.105
1949	Louisville	NAL	SS	-	-	-	-	-	-	-	-	-	
1950	Cleveland, Memphis	NAL	2B SS 3B	15	48	8	14	6	0	0	3	0	.292
1952	Danville	MOV	SS	66	253	31	61	8	0	0	24	2	.241
1953	Danville	MOV	3B	23	78	6	13	3	0	0	11	0	.167
1957	Lawton	SOON	SS 3B	125	440	70	108	21	2	17	70	2	.245

Willard Jessie "Home Run" Brown. Born June 26, 1911 at Shreveport, LA. 5'11 1/2", 200 lbs. BR TR

Year	Club	League	Pos	G	AB	R	H	2B	3B	HR	RBI	SB	BA
1935	Kansas City	NAL	SS	2	7	-	2	0	0	1	-	2	.286
1936	Kansas City	NAL	SS	6	30	-	11	0	0	1	-	2	.367
1937	Kansas City	NAL	SS	32	143	-	53	10	3	8	-	4	.371
1938	Kansas City	NAL	OF	29	104	-	37	3	3	6	-	10	.356
1939	Kansas City	NAL	OF	31	119	-	40	9	1	1	-	4	.336
1940	Kansas City	NAL	OF	2	7	-	0	0	0	0	-	0	.000
1940	Nuevo Laredo	MEX	OF	70	294	49	104	18	4	8	61	13	.354
1941	Kansas City	NAL	OF	23	89	-	30	5	4	3	-	2	.337
1941	Puebla	MEX	OF	28	125	20	32	7	0	2	24	5	.256
1942	Kansas City	NAL	OF	-	181	-	66	7	2	7	-	4	.365
1943	Kansas City	NAL	OF	-	113	-	39	6	2	6	-	-	.345
1946	Kansas City	NAL	OF	58	230	-	80	8	4	13	-	3	.348
1947	Kansas City	NAL	OF	50	211	38	71	-	-	-	-	-	.336
1947	St. Louis	AL	OF	21	67	4	12	3	0	1	6	2	.179
1948	Kansas City	NAL	OF	60	262	65	98	20	5	18	68	13	.374
1949	Kansas City	NAL	OF	83	291	67	108	22	10	12	83	-	.371
1950	Ottawa	BORD	OF	30	128	23	45	7	1	1	18	2	.352
1951	Escogido	DMSL	OF	-	91	11	23	-	-	-	17	2	.253
1951	Jalisco, N.L.	MEX	OF	7	24	1	4	2	0	0	1	1	.167
1951	Kansas City	NAL	OF	-	138	31	58	-	-	1	41	-	.420
1952	Escogido	DMSL	OF	-	183	27	55	-	-	-	28	8	.301
1953	Dallas	TEX	OF	138	522	91	162	36	2	23	108	3	.310
1954	Dallas, Houston	TEX	OF	144	583	92	183	36	4	35	120	2	.314
1955	Houston	TEX	OF	149	544	73	164	34	4	19	104	3	.301
1956	Austin, San Ant, Tuls	TEX	OF	104	351	50	105	17	0	14	73	2	.299
1956	Topeka	WEST	OF	23	85	11	25	2	0	3	14	0	.294
1958	Kansas City	NAL	OF	14	37	9	12	1	0	2	10	-	.324
37-8	Marianao	CWL	OF	-	55	5	8	1	0	0	3	-	.145
41-2	Humacao	PRWL	2B	-	122	22	50	12	4	4	26	-	.410
46-7	Santurce	PRWL	OF	-	254	44	99	25	4	9	50	-	.390
47-8	Santurce	PRWL	OF	-	234	79	101	20	5	27	86	-	.432
48-9	Santurce	PRWL	OF	-	294	59	95	20	3	18	69	-	.323
49-0	Santurce	PRWL	OF	-	331	65	117	21	6	16	97	-	.353
50-1	Santurce	PRWL	OF	-	305	56	99	20	3	14	76	-	.325
51-2	Santurce	PRWL	OF	-	112	14	33	4	1	4	20	-	.295
52-3	Santurce	PRWL	OF	-	114	20	39	7	0	3	20	-	.342
53-4	Santurce	PRWL	OF	-	151	16	40	6	1	4	22	-	.265
56-7	Santurce	PRWL	OF	-	23	2	6	-	-	2	5	-	.261

Clarence Bruce. Born September 26, 1926 at Pittsburgh, PA. Died January 23, 1990 in Pittsburgh, PA. 6'1", 170 lbs. BR TR

Year	Club	League	Pos	G	AB	R	H	2B	3B	HR	RBI	SB	BA
1947	Homestead	NAL	2B	-	138	18	34	4	0	3	-	1	.246
1948	Homestead	NAL	2B	-	-	-	-	-	-	-	-	-	
1950	Farnham	PROV	2B	14	54	4	12	1	0	-	6	0	.222

Jose A. Burgos. Born 1928. 5'6", 150 lbs. BR TR

Year	Club	League	Pos	G	AB	R	H	2B	3B	HR	RBI	SB	BA
1949	Birmingham	NAL	SS	84	312	40	70	-	-	-	-	-	.224
1950	Birmingham	NAL	SS	74	243	39	59	12	0	0	30	9	.243
1951	Lakeland	FLST	SS	77	286	53	61	6	1	0	14	6	.213
1951	Leesburg	FLST	INF	67	243	62	78	9	4	0	23	15	.321
1952	Lakeland	FLST	SS	154	583	63	129	8	4	0	33	13	.221
1953	Richmond	PIED	SS	123	470	75	114	22	4	1	36	2	.243
44-5	Ponce	PRWL	SS	-	17	2	4	-	-	0	4	-	.235
46-7	Ponce	PRWL	SS	-	206	25	44	-	-	0	26	-	.214
47-8	Ponce	PRWL	SS	-	191	22	47	3	8	1	20	-	.246
48-9	Ponce	PRWL	SS	-	285	52	53	13	0	1	20	0	.186

Year	Club	League	Pos	G	AB	R	H	2B	3B	HR	RBI	SB	BA
49-0	Ponce	PRWL	SS	-	188	35	40	7	1	-	17	-	.213
50-1	Ponce	PRWL	SS	-	240	38	62	4	5	1	30	8	.258
51-2	Ponce	PRWL	SS	72	284	43	56	7	2	0	17	6	.197
52-3	Ponce	PRWL	SS	-	255	31	61	6	1	0	21	0	.239
53-4	Ponce	PRWL	SS	68	214	22	40	4	0	0	13	2	.187
54-5	Ponce	PRWL	SS	5	6	0	1	0	0	0	-	0	.167

Ernest Burke. Born June 26, 1924 at Havre de Grace, MD. 6'1", 180 lbs. BL TR

Year	Club	League	Pos	G	AB	R	H	2B	3B	HR	RBI	SB	BA
1947	Baltimore	NNL	P	-	-	-	-	-	-	-	-	-	
1948	Baltimore	NNL	P	-	-	-	-	-	-	-	-	-	
1949	Pough.,Kingston	COL	P OF 3B	60	194	25	49	8	2	1	16	1	.253
1950	St. Jean	PROV	P OF 3B	74	169	32	52	11	1	2	22	0	.308
1951	St. Jean	PROV	P 3B	81	163	28	42	4	1	4	17	0	.258

Thomas "Pee Wee" Butts. Born August 27, 1919 at Sparta, GA. Died January, 1973 in Atlanta, GA. 5'7", 140 lbs. BR TR

Year	Club	League	Pos	G	AB	R	H	2B	3B	HR	RBI	SB	BA
1938	Atlanta	NAL	SS	6	21	-	8	-	1	-	-	0	.381
1939	Ind., Baltimore	NNL	SS	20	66	-	32	2	0	-	-	1	.485
1940	Baltimore	NNL	SS	44	176	-	63	10	1	1	-	2	.358
1941	Baltimore	NNL	SS	45	167	-	30	4	0	-	-	0	.180
1942	Baltimore	NNL	SS	40	151	-	34	3	2	-	-	4	.225
1943	Monterrey	MEX	SS	80	286	32	71	13	1	1	20	9	.248
1944	Baltimore	NNL	SS	41	143	24	44	4	4	0	14	1	.308
1945	Baltimore	NNL	SS	35	123	21	37	7	1	0	6	2	.301
1946	Baltimore	NNL	SS	**46**	164	26	47	6	4	2	20	6	.287
1947	Baltimore	NNL	SS	74	296	58	97	7	-	1	-	6	.328
1948	Baltimore	NNL	SS	-	-	-	-	-	-	-	-	-	
1949	Baltimore	NNL	SS	86	333	52	87	-	-	-	-	-	.261
1950	Baltimore	NNL	SS	39	151	34	40	5	1	0	16	4	.265
1951	Winnipeg	MADK	SS	61	245	-	70	-	-	1	26	-	.286
1952	Birmingham	NAL	SS	-	-	-	-	-	-	-	-	-	
1952	Lincoln	WEST	SS 2B	47	171	29	29	4	-	0	15	0	.170
1953	Birmingham	NAL	SS	54	192	28	46	5	2	0	12	5	.240
1954	Licey	DMSL	SS	-	132	12	28	-	0	-	8	1	.212
1954	Memphis	NAL	SS	-	-	-	-	-	-	-	-	-	
1955	Texas City	BGST	SS	28	98	8	26	2	0	0	8	1	.265
47-8	Almendares	CWL	SS	-	285	26	71	8	3	0	28	13	.249

Luis Perez Caballero. Born 1927. 5'8", 158 lbs. BR TR

Year	Club	League	Pos	G	AB	R	H	2B	3B	HR	RBI	SB	BA
1945	Vera Cruz	MEX	3B	25	43	6	9	2	1	0	4	1	.209
1948	Indianapolis	NAL	3B	38	113	20	28	7	1	0	18	0	.248
1950	New York	NAL	3B	32	115	9	24	4	0	0	12	1	.209
1954	Big Spring	LGHN	OF 3B SS	116	422	90	122	24	4	3	52	25	.289
1955	Big Spring	LGHN	3B SS	133	488	95	143	26	3	5	57	33	.293

Lorenzo Cabrera. Born April 30, 1920 at Cienfuegos, Cuba. 6', 195 lbs. BL TL

Year	Club	League	Pos	G	AB	R	H	2B	3B	HR	RBI	SB	BA
1947	New York	NNL	1B	-	230	54	81	16	-	4	-	2	.352
1948	New York	NNL	1B	-	-	-	-	-	-	-	-	-	
1949	New York	NAL	1B	29	114	29	43	-	-	-	-	-	.377
1950	Mexico City	MEX	1B	68	268	40	95	10	3	1	39	14	**.354**
1950	New York	NAL	1B	-	-	-	-	-	-	-	-	-	
1951	Oakland	PCL	1B	20	73	5	15	1	1	0	5	0	.205
1951	Ottawa	INT	1B	31	72	8	17	5	2	0	7	0	.236
1952	Escogido	DMSL	1B	-	129	17	38	-	-	-	2	15	.295
1953	Cibaenas	DMSL	1B	-	166	24	54	-	-	-	11	1	.325
1954	Del Rio	BGST	1B	140	563	85	194	31	12	12	93	15	.345
1954	Port Arthur	BGST	1B	65	247	47	76	12	6	3	31	3	.308
1956	Tijunan-Nogales	AZMX	1B	36	142	17	37	8	0	4	21	1	.261
42-3	Almendares	CWL	1B	1	1	0	0	0	0	0	0	0	.000
46-7	Marianao	CWL	1B	50	113	11	28	2	1	0	10	2	.248
47-8	Marianao	CWL	1B	47	170	18	43	5	1	0	8	2	.253
48-9	Marianao	CWL	1B	61	207	20	65	11	4	1	18	5	.314
49-0	Marianao	CWL	1B	63	227	26	75	16	5	0	31	6	.330
50-1	Marianao	CWL	1B	70	257	36	88	12	4	1	29	6	.342
51-2	Marianao	CWL	1B	55	205	23	61	12	5	1	21	1	.298
52-3	Marianao	CWL	1B	64	245	32	77	16	2	4	32	2	.314
53-4	Havana, Marianao	CWL	1B	71	291	41	92	15	3	5	35	3	.316
54-5	Cienfuegos	CWL	1B	57	189	25	56	10	5	0	17	1	.296
55-6	Cienfuegos	CWL	1B	-	100	-	31	-	-	0	11	-	.310

Year	Club	League	Pos	G	AB	R	H	2B	3B	HR	RBI	SB	BA

Joseph Clifford Caffie. Born February 14, 1931 at Ramer, AL. 5'10 1/2", 180 lbs. BL TR

Year	Club	League	Pos	G	AB	R	H	2B	3B	HR	RBI	SB	BA
1950	Cleveland	NAL	OF	18	69	4	14	2	1	0	1	1	.203
1951	Duluth	NORL	OF	96	375	56	116	24	7	4	52	22	.309
1951	Harrisburg	INST	OF	29	94	17	19	2	3	1	4	2	.202
1952	Duluth	NORL	OF	120	**500**	**105**	**171**	34	**18**	10	98	25	**.342**
1953	Indianapolis	AA	OF	49	173	19	40	9	2	4	13	2	.231
1953	Reading	EAST	OF	94	371	68	119	16	10	7	64	22	.321
1954	Indianapolis	AA	OF	42	118	19	34	5	0	3	10	8	.288
1955	Indianapolis	AA	OF	46	122	12	29	3	2	0	8	4	.238
1955	Syracuse	INT	OF	74	283	38	74	8	1	4	22	24	.261
1956	Buffalo	INT	OF	128	483	84	150	16	6	8	46	19	.311
1956	Cleveland	AL	OF	12	38	7	13	0	0	0	1	3	.342
1956	Spokane	PCL	OF	19	47	5	11	3	0	0	2	2	.234
1957	Buffalo	INT	OF	108	440	69	145	33	5	8	41	7	**.330**
1957	Cleveland	AL	OF	32	89	14	24	2	1	3	10	0	.270
1958	Buffalo	INT	OF	151	603	89	178	**39**	5	9	48	14	.295
1959	Buffalo	INT	OF	37	139	23	38	8	1	7	17	0	.273
1959	St. Paul	AA	OF	74	226	26	58	9	4	4	25	6	.257
1960	Montreal, Miami	INT	OF	80	206	21	45	11	0	4	24	4	.218
1961	Charlotte	SATL	OF	43	137	22	31	3	0	2	11	2	.226
1961	Wilson	CARO	OF	31	105	17	28	8	1	2	15	0	.267
57-8	Almendares	CWL	OF	-	104	7	23	4	1	0	3	0	.221

Roy Campanella. Born November 19, 1921 at Philadelphia, PA. Died June 26, 1993 at Woodland Hillds, CA. 5'9 1/2", 205 lbs. BR TR

Year	Club	League	Pos	G	AB	R	H	2B	3B	HR	RBI	SB	BA
1937	Baltimore	NNL	C	-	-	-	-	-	-	-	-	-	
1938	Baltimore	NNL	C	2	3	-	-	-	-	-	-	-	.000
1939	Baltimore	NNL	C	16	46	-	13	1	0	1	-	0	.283
1940	Baltimore	NNL	C	26	82	-	25	2	1	5	-	1	.305
1941	Baltimore	NNL	C	23	68	-	25	7	2	3	-	1	.368
1942	Baltimore	NNL	C	30	111	-	33	4	3	1	-	1	.297
1942	Monterrey	MEX	C	20	81	15	24	6	2	2	15	2	.296
1943	Monterrey	MEX	C	90	342	**74**	99	24	5	12	54	4	.289
1944	Baltimore	NNL	C	45	175	36	64	19	4	3	24	6	.366
1945	Baltimore	NNL	C	43	146	34	51	8	2	5	36	1	.349
1946	Nashua	NENG	C	113	396	74	115	19	8	13	96	16	.290
1947	Montreal	INT	C	135	440	64	120	25	3	13	75	7	.273
1948	Brooklyn	NL	C	93	279	32	72	11	3	9	45	3	.258
1948	St. Paul	AA	C OF	35	123	31	40	5	2	13	39	0	.325
1949	Brooklyn	NL	C	130	456	65	125	22	2	22	82	3	.274
1950	Brooklyn	NL	C	126	437	70	123	19	3	31	89	1	.281
1951	Brooklyn	NL	C	143	505	90	164	33	1	33	108	1	.325
1952	Brooklyn	NL	C	128	468	73	126	18	1	22	97	8	.269
1953	Brooklyn	NL	C	144	519	103	162	26	3	41	142	4	.312
1954	Brooklyn	NL	C	111	397	43	82	14	3	19	51	1	.207
1955	Brooklyn	NL	C	123	446	81	142	20	1	32	107	2	.318
1956	Brooklyn	NL	C	124	388	39	85	6	1	20	73	1	.219
1957	Brooklyn	NL	C	103	330	31	80	9	0	13	62	1	.242
40-1	Caguas	PRWL	C	-	171	36	45	-	-	8	-	-	.263
41-2	Caguas	PRWL	C	-	156	22	46	11	2	0	18	-	.295
43-4	Marianao	CWL	C	-	128	15	34	9	3	0	27	2	.266
44-5	Santurce	PRWL	C	-	85	20	25	4	1	1	14	-	.294
46-7	San Juan	PRWL	C	-	45	8	10	-	-	2	7	-	.222

Joe Campini. Born May 11, 1923 at East Wareham, MA. 5'10", 191 lbs. BL TR

Year	Club	League	Pos	G	AB	R	H	2B	3B	HR	RBI	SB	BA
1948	Baltimore	NNL	C	-	-	-	-	-	-	-	-	-	
1949	Bangor-Berwick	NATL	C	29	104	14	28	1	1	0	8	1	.269
1950	Watertown	BORD	C	19	49	8	13	4	0	0	5	0	.265

Avelino Canizares. Born November 10, 1919 at Havana, Cuba. 5'7", 140 lbs. BR TR

Year	Club	League	Pos	G	AB	R	H	2B	3B	HR	RBI	SB	BA
1944	Tampico	MEX	SS	73	295	49	90	13	4	1	21	14	.305
1945	Cleveland	NAL	SS	55	226	53	71	11	7	3	31	6	.314
1946	Torreon	MEX	SS	90	383	72	114	16	5	2	32	18	.298
1947	San Luis Potosi	MEX	SS	113	427	93	120	16	6	1	33	24	.281
1948	Monterrey, San Luis	MEX	SS	72	289	40	78	10	3	1	18	14	.270
1950	Sherbrooke	PROV	SS 2B OF	98	343	69	101	18	0	0	37	12	.294
1952	Keokuk	III	SS 3B	65	239	35	53	7	4	1	25	8	.222
1954	Mexico City	MEX	SS	74	307	47	75	8	2	4	26	10	.244
1955	Saltillo	CMEX	SS	18	59	19	20	2	1	0	5	-	.339
1956	Durango	CMEX	SS 2B	98	421	77	127	28	7	2	53	16	.302

Year	Club	League	Pos	G	AB	R	H	2B	3B	HR	RBI	SB	BA
1957	Mexicali	AZMX	SS 3B	123	514	120	155	26	8	8	55	25	.302
1958	Mexicali	AZMX	SS 3B	109	465	110	167	27	4	3	39	17	.359
42-3	Cienfuegos,Almend.	CWL	SS	8	9	-	-	-	-	-	-	0	.000
43-4	Almendares	CWL	SS	46	169	19	48	4	1	1	29	1	.284
44-5	Almendares	CWL	SS	47	176	29	41	6	1	1	20	4	.233
45-6	Almendares	CWL	SS	56	220	33	60	8	1	1	19	6	.273
46-7	Almendares	CWL	SS	66	254	47	66	8	5	0	13	7	.260
47-8	Alacranes	CWL	SS	87	368	53	114	12	5	0	19	9	.310
48-9	Almendares	CWL	SS	63	239	27	60	6	2	0	23	7	.251
49-0	Almendares	CWL	SS	35	106	15	21	2	0	0	5	0	.198
50-1	Almendares	CWL	SS	11	13	5	2	1	0	0	2	2	.154
51-2	Almendares	CWL	SS	37	115	16	31	3	2	0	5	1	.270
52-3	Almend.,Cienfuegos	CWL	SS	30	27	4	4	0	0	0	0	0	.148
53-4	Cienfuegos	CWL	SS	35	43	9	11	0	0	0	1	1	.256

Paulino "Paul" Casanova y Ortiz. Born December 21, 1941 at Colon, Cuba. 6'4", 180 lbs. BR TR

Year	Club	League	Pos	G	AB	R	H	2B	3B	HR	RBI	SB	BA
1960	Indianapolis	NAL	C	-	-	-	-	-	-	-	-	-	
1960	Minot	NORL	C	10	6	4	0	0	0	0	0	1	.000
1962	San Antonio	TEX	PH OF	2	1	0	0	0	0	0	0	0	.000
1963	Geneva	NYP	C	94	329	40	86	18	4	7	34	1	.261
1964	Geneva	NYP	C	120	480	98	156	27	2	19	99	11	.325
1965	Burlington	CARO	C	142	506	62	145	25	5	8	76	3	.287
1965	Washington	AL	C	5	13	2	4	0	0	0	3	0	.308
1966	Washington	AL	C	122	429	45	109	16	5	13	44	1	.254
1966	York	EAST	C	5	19	5	4	0	0	0	3	1	.211
1967	Washington	AL	C	141	528	47	131	19	1	9	53	1	.248
1968	Buffalo	INT	C	24	84	10	23	1	0	2	8	0	.274
1968	Washington	AL	C	96	322	19	63	6	0	4	25	0	.196
1969	Washington	AL	C	124	379	26	82	9	2	4	37	0	.216
1970	Washington	AL	C	104	328	25	75	17	3	6	30	0	.229
1971	Washington	AL	C	94	311	19	63	9	1	5	26	0	.203
1972	Atlanta	NL	C	49	136	8	28	3	0	2	10	0	.206
1973	Atlanta	NL	C	82	236	18	51	7	0	7	18	0	.216
1974	Atlanta	NL	C	42	104	5	21	0	0	0	8	0	.202

William Walker "Ready" Cash. Born February 21, 1919 at Round Oak, GA. 6'1 1/2", 195 lbs. BR TR

Year	Club	League	Pos	G	AB	R	H	2B	3B	HR	RBI	SB	BA
1943	Philadelphia	NNL	C	22	80	-	20	4	3	0	-	0	.250
1944	Philadelphia	NNL	C	41	131	18	37	7	2	1	18	6	.282
1945	Philadelphia	NNL	C	35	119	10	29	2	1	0	8	2	.244
1946	Philadelphia	NNL	C	41	131	13	31	5	-	1	18	4	.237
1947	Philadelphia	NNL	C	-	156	25	43	11	-	1	-	0	.276
1948	Philadelphia	NNL	C	-	-	-	-	-	-	-	-	-	
1949	Philadelphia	NAL	C	52	168	24	45	-	-	-	-	-	.268
1950	Mexico City	MEX	C	62	226	34	70	16	2	4	39	10	.310
1950	Philadelphia	NAL	C	-	-	-	-	-	-	-	-	-	
1951	Granby	PROV	C OF	105	321	56	95	21	2	16	54	9	.296
1952	Superior	NORL	C	-	-	-	-	-	-	-	-	-	
1952	Waterloo	III	C	38	127	20	29	4	1	2	20	1	.228
1953	Cibaenas	DMSL	C	-	89	16	32	-	-	0	21	0	.360
1954	Cibaenas	DMSL	C	-	108	15	33	-	-	0	19	1	.306
47-8	Marianao, Almend.	CWL	C	-	224	23	48	10	2	1	24	5	.214

Ernest Joseph Chretian. BR TR

Year	Club	League	Pos	G	AB	R	H	2B	3B	HR	RBI	SB	BA
1949	Kansas City	NAL	OF	-	-	-	-	-	-	-	-	-	
1950	KC, Philadelphia	NAL	OF 3B INF	33	99	16	24	3	0	1	16	1	.242
1953	Lake Charles	GCL	UTIL	22	56	6	13	2	0	0	3	1	.232
1954	Tallahassee	FLIN	UTIL	10	28	1	4	0	0	0	0	1	.143

James Buster Clarkson. Born March 13, 1913 at Hopkins, SC. Died January 18, 1989 at Jeanette, PA. 5'11", 200 lbs. BR TR

Year	Club	League	Pos	G	AB	R	H	2B	3B	HR	RBI	SB	BA
1937	Pittsburgh	NNL	SS	-	-	-	-	-	-	-	-	-	
1938	Pittsburgh	NNL	SS	-	-	-	-	-	-	-	-	-	
1939	Toledo	NNL	SS	5	19	-	8	0	0	0	-	0	.421
1940	Newark, Ind..	NNL	SS	-	89	-	39	3	1	8	-	-	.438
1940	Nuevo Laredo	MEX	SS	19	80	12	27	4	3	1	13	1	.338
1941	Tampico	MEX	SS	82	326	67	109	23	3	19	83	7	.334
1942	Newark, Phil.	NNL		31	114	-	41	11	0	2	-	2	.360
1946	Philadelphia	NNL	3B SS	38	146	26	45	7	2	2	34	8	.308
1946	Vera Cruz	MEX	SS	37	131	29	39	8	1	9	32	7	.298
1947	Philadelphia	NNL		-	-	-	-	-	-	-	-	-	
1947	Vera Cruz	MEX	SS	112	390	75	118	19	7	17	68	20	.303

Year	Club	League	Pos	G	AB	R	H	2B	3B	HR	RBI	SB	BA
1948	St. Jean	PROV	3B	80	279	93	112	12	-	**29**	93	16	.401
1949	Philadelphia	NAL	3B SS	56	192	32	60	-	-	-	-	-	.313
1950	Milwaukee	AA	3B	59	205	34	62	11	1	7	33	0	.302
1950	Philadelphia, Balt.	NAL	SS 3B	33	108	21	32	10	1	4	18	8	.296
1951	Milwaukee	AA	SS	97	283	52	97	12	4	5	49	6	.343
1952	Boston	NL	SS 3B	14	25	3	5	0	0	0	1	0	.200
1952	Milwaukee	AA	SS 3B	74	242	49	77	14	2	12	68	10	.318
1953	Dallas	TEX	3B SS	137	445	91	147	32	1	18	87	11	.330
1954	Beaumont, Dallas	TEX	3B SS	157	543	109	176	21	2	**42**	135	7	.324
1955	Los Angeles	PCL	3B	100	316	40	93	8	0	13	46	1	.294
1956	Des Moines	WEST	3B	60	205	45	57	11	0	13	50	3	.278
1956	Los Angeles	PCL	3B	8	11	2	3	1	0	0	0	0	.273
1956	Tulsa	TEX	3B	48	137	24	35	4	0	5	19	3	.255
40-1	Mayaquez	PRWL	UTL	-	-	**48**	-	-	-	-	-	-	
41-2	Mayaquez	PRWL	UTL	-	-	-	-	-	-	-	-	**18**	
46-7	Caguas, Guayama	PRWL	UTL	-	172	43	60	-	-	13	51	-	.349
47-8	Alacranes	CUBA	UTL	-	106	12	21	5	0	1	14	1	.198
48-9	Ponce	PRWL	UTL	-	149	41	46	7	1	8	36	8	.309
49-0	Ponce	PRWL	UTL	-	269	57	77	16	6	13	56	-	.286
50-1	Santurce	PRWL	UTL	-	-	-	-	-	-	-	62	-	
51-2	Santurce	PRWL	UTL	-	-	-	-	-	-	4	28	6	-
52-3	Santurce	PRWL	UTL	-	-	-	-	-	-	**18**	-	-	
53-4	Santurce	PRWL	UTL	-	175	-	49	-	-	3	25	-	.280
54-5	Santurce	PRWL	UTL	-	240	-	76	-	-	15	**61**	-	.317

Nathaniel "Sweetwater" Clifton. Born October 13, 1922 at England, AR. Died September 2, 1990 in Chicago, IL. 6'6", 221 lbs. BL TR

Year	Club	League	Pos	G	AB	R	H	2B	3B	HR	RBI	SB	BA
1949	Chicago	NAL	1B	-	-	-	-	-	-	-	-	-	
1949	Dayton	CENT	1B	73	264	36	85	19	5	11	53	1	.322
1949	Pittsfield	CAAM	1B	24	80	10	22	2	1	3	10	0	.275
1950	Wilkes-Barre	EAST	1B	120	427	70	130	27	7	9	86	4	.304
1958	Detroit	NAL	1B	10	35	4	10	2	0	0	5	0	.286

Jose L. Colas. Born in Cuba. BR TR

Year	Club	League	Pos	G	AB	R	H	2B	3B	HR	RBI	SB	BA
1946	Vera Cruz San Luis	MEX	OF	79	291	32	82	8	8	3	35	6	.282
1947	Memphis	NAL	OF	-	-	-	-	-	-	-	-	-	
1948	Memphis	NAL	OF	61	242	40	75	10	1	5	37	7	.310
1949	Memphis	NAL	OF	65	219	30	54	-	-	-	-	-	.247
1950	Memphis	NAL	OF	63	228	27	61	10	2	3	38	4	.268
1951	Memphis	NAL	OF	-	-	-	-	-	-	-	-	-	
1952	Memphis	NAL	OF	-	-	-	-	-	-	-	-	-	
1952	Scranton	EAST	OF	13	46	3	7	0	0	0	0	0	.152
1954	Mt. Vernon	MOV	OF 2B 3B	67	269	38	64	13	0	9	43	8	.238
48-9	Cienfuegos	CWL	OF	30	33	2	2	0	0	0	1	0	.061

Eugene Marvin "Gene" Collins. Born January 7, 1925 at Kansas City, MO. 5'8", 168 lbs. BL TL

Year	Club	League	Pos	G	AB	R	H	2B	3B	HR	RBI	SB	BA
1947	Kansas City	NAL	P OF	-	-	-	-	-	-	-	-	-	
1948	Kansas City	NAL	P OF	18	37	7	9	2	1	0	2	0	.243
1949	Kansas City	NAL	P OF	26	77	13	23	-	-	-	-	-	.299
1950	Kansas City	NAL	P OF	72	242	33	55	8	4	3	37	3	.227
1951	Kansas City	NAL	OF P	-	181	38	65	-	8	3	39	-	.359
1951	Waterloo	III	OF P	25	59	9	9	4	0	1	4	0	.153
1952	Colorado Springs	WEST	OF P	-	-	-	-	-	-	-	-	-	
1952	Superior	NORL	OF P	31	120	19	32	4	3	3	22	3	.267
1952	Wisconsin Rapids	WISC	OF P	79	310	47	88	17	5	6	57	6	.284
1953	Colorado Springs	WEST	OF P	-	-	-	-	-	-	-	-	-	
1953	Escogido	DMSL	OF	-	7	0	2	0	0	0	-	-	.286
1953	Superior	NORL	OF P	18	51	6	10	1	0	0	4	3	.196
1955	Aguila	MEX	OF P	73	241	56	81	10	4	13	36	2	.336
1956	Aguila	MEX	OF P	99	366	53	101	17	4	9	49	4	.276
1957	Aguila	MEX	OF P	81	287	41	79	12	2	7	35	4	.275
1958	Poza Rica	MEX	OF P	105	395	73	128	26	4	17	63	8	.324
1959	Poza Rica	MEX	OF P 1B	122	430	67	121	22	4	7	46	8	.281
1960	Poza Rica	MEX	OF P	103	353	62	112	26	3	13	50	5	.317
1961	Pz Rica, Mex City	MEX	OF 1B	127	454	75	127	23	5	16	86	5	.280
48-9	Caguas	PRWL	P	-	-	-	-	-	-	-	-	-	
49-0	San Juan	PRWL	P	-	-	-	-	-	-	-	-	-	
58-9	Pampero	VENZ	OF P	28	104	9	37	9	2	0	17	1	.356

Year	Club	League	Pos	G	AB	R	H	2B	3B	HR	RBI	SB	BA

Thomas R. Cooper. Born 1927. 5'11", 175 lbs. BB TR

Year	Club	League	Pos	G	AB	R	H	2B	3B	HR	RBI	SB	BA
1947	Kansas City	NAL	OF C 1B	-	-	-	-	-	-	-	-	-	
1948	Kansas City	NAL	1B OF	49	182	31	49	7	3	2	21	1	.269
1949	Kansas City	NAL	C OF	29	95	6	12	-	-	-	-	-	.126
1950	Kansas City	NAL	C OF	60	204	32	57	13	3	7	35	4	.279
1951	Kansas City	NAL	C	-	-	-	-	-	-	-	-	-	
1952	Kansas City	NAL	C 1B	-	-	-	-	-	-	-	-	-	
1953	Kansas City	NAL	C OF	66	228	30	64	16	1	4	34	13	.281
1953	Schenectady	EAST	C	29	52	4	10	1	0	0	5	0	.192
1954	Three Rivers	PROV	C	19	44	6	10	0	1	0	7	1	.227
1957	Schenectady	EAST	C	14	16	0	0	0	0	0	0	0	.000

Alejandro "Alex" Crespo. Born February 26, 1915 at Guira de Melena, Cuba. 6'1", 206 lbs. BR TR

Year	Club	League	Pos	G	AB	R	H	2B	3B	HR	RBI	SB	BA
1940	New York	NNL	OF	21	79	-	22	-		-	-	0	.278
1941	Torreon	MEX	OF 2B	104	418	90	151	**36**	14	9	86	9	.361
1942	Torreon	MEX	OF	61	238	39	79	18	4	2	50	12	.332
1943	Torreon	MEX	OF	87	356	65	118	**31**	**13**	6	**70**	11	.331
1944	Nuevo Laredo	MEX	OF 3B 1B	91	377	65	119	21	10	9	83	9	.316
1945	Nuevo Laredo	MEX	OF C 1B	90	366	84	114	21	10	8	79	10	.311
1946	New York	NNL	OF	29	107	24	36	4	2	2	16	0	.336
1947	Puebla	MEX	OF C	123	478	64	140	26	7	8	**96**	10	.293
1948	Puebla	MEX	OF	82	331	48	103	17	5	5	55	8	.311
1950	Gavilanes	VENZ	OF	-	-	-	-	-	-	-	-	-	
1950	Vera Cruz	MEX	OF	20	78	7	25	4	0	2	14	1	.321
1951	Vera Cruz	MEX	OF C	54	216	31	65	14	2	2	32	1	.301
1952	Cibaenas	DMSL	OF	**54**	**210**	**34**	60	-	-	-	27	3	.286
1953	Cibaenas	DMSL	OF	-	216	39	69	-	7	-	28	3	.319
1954	Licey	DMSL	OF	-	159	19	49	-	-	-	30	4	.308
1955	Charlotte	SATL	OF	35	118	10	30	9	0	3	20	2	.254
1955	Hobbs	LGHN	OF 1B	87	343	66	111	24	0	16	65	3	.324
39-0	Cienfuegos	CWL	OF	-	177	36	60	-	-	-	28	7	.339
40-1	Cienfuegos	CWL	OF	-	198	22	57	-	-	-	29	15	.288
41-2	Cienfuegos	CWL	OF	-	177	19	41	12	1	1	14	7	.232
42-3	Cienfuegos	CWL	OF	-	187	28	63	-	-	-	24	3	.337
43-4	Cienfuegos	CWL	OF	-	208	30	54	-	-	-	24	3	.260
44-5	Cienfuegos	CWL	OF	-	199	19	59	-	-	1	29	4	.296
45-6	Cienfuegos	CWL	OF	64	242	30	72	13	5	1	35	2	.298
46-7	Cienfuegos	CWL	OF	52	173	19	42	4	3	2	30	2	.243
47-8	Alacranes,Cuba	CWL	OF	89	351	48	95	19	6	2	53	14	.271
48-9	Cienfuegos	CWL	OF	59	224	27	73	10	3	4	40	3	.326
49-0	Cienfuegos	CWL	OF	65	209	20	51	7	1	4	30	2	.244
50-1	Cienfuegos Havana	CWL	OF	64	234	26	56	11	2	5	39	3	.239
51-2	Havana	CWL	OF	57	158	29	40	4	3	4	31	0	.253
52-3	Havana	CWL	OF	36	94	10	25	5	1	1	7	0	.266
53-4	Marianao	CWL	OF	28	50	6	8	0	0	0	2	0	.160

George Daniel Crowe. Born March 22, 1921 at Whiteland, IN. 6'2", 210 lbs. BL TL

Year	Club	League	Pos	G	AB	R	H	2B	3B	HR	RBI	SB	BA
1947	New York	NNL	1B OF	-	141	25	43	4	0	2	-	1	.305
1948	New York	NNL	1B	-	-	-	-	-	-	-	-	-	
1949	New York	NAL	1B	-	-	-	-	-	-	-	-	-	
1949	Pawtucket	NENG	1B	123	466	89	165	29	11	12	**106**	13	.354
1950	Hartford	EAST	1B	**139**	524	**122**	**185**	**43**	7	24	122	10	**.353**
1951	Milwaukee	AA	1B	150	557	105	**189**	**41**	7	24	**119**	2	.339
1952	Boston	NL	1B	73	217	25	56	13	1	4	20	0	.258
1952	Milwaukee	AA	1B	27	94	19	33	8	1	6	29	1	.351
1953	Milwaukee	NL	1B	47	42	6	12	2	0	2	6	0	.286
1954	Toledo	AA	1B	**154**	589	100	197	38	3	**34**	128	7	.334
1955	Milwaukee	NL	1B	104	303	41	85	12	4	15	55	1	.281
1956	Cincinnati	NL	1B	77	144	22	36	2	1	10	23	0	.250
1957	Cincinnati	NL	1B	133	494	71	134	20	1	31	92	1	.271
1958	Cincinnati	NL	1B	111	345	31	95	12	5	7	61	1	.275
1959	St. Louis	NL	1B	77	103	14	31	6	0	8	29	0	.301
1960	St. Louis	NL	1B	73	72	5	17	3	0	4	13	0	.236
1961	Charleston	INT	1B	76	144	8	34	6	0	3	20	0	.236
1961	St. Louis	NL	PH	7	7	0	1	0	0	0	0	0	.143
50-1	Caguas	PRWL	1B	-	285	74	**107**	-	7	11	69	-	**.375**
51-2	San Juan	PRWL	1B	-	182	-	72	**23**	-	9	**70**	-	**.396**
53-4	Cienfuegos	CWL	1B	-	75	3	12	2	0	1	10	0	.160
54-5	Santurce	PRWL	1B	-	-	-	-	-	-	12	-	-	

Year	Club	League	Pos	G	AB	R	H	2B	3B	HR	RBI	SB	BA

Raymond Emmett "Hooks" Dandridge. Born August 31, 1913 at Richmond, VA. Died February 12, 1994 at Palm Bay, FL. 5'7", 175 lbs. BR TR

Year	Club	League	Pos	G	AB	R	H	2B	3B	HR	RBI	SB	BA
1933	Detroit, Nashville	NNL	SS	11	38	-	8	1	2	0	-	0	.211
1934	Newark	NNL	3B	29	110	-	48	5	2	0	-	0	.436
1935	Newark	NNL	3B	44	137	-	45	11	3	0	-	0	.328
1936	Newark	NNL	3B	31	103	-	31	4	0	1	-	1	.301
1937	Newark	NNL	3B	25	96	-	34	3	1	1	-	0	.354
1938	Newark	NNL	3B	14	52	-	21	-	-	-	-	0	.404
1940	Vera Cruz	MEX	2B	27	127	27	44	8	3	1	27	6	.346
1941	Vera Cruz	MEX	2B	101	430	94	158	32	5	8	86	12	.367
1942	Newark	NNL	3B 2B	25	85	-	14	1	-	-	-	-	.165
1942	Vera Cruz	MEX	SS	35	142	27	44	7	1	4	37	8	.310
1943	Vera Cruz	MEX	2B	90	370	67	**131**	24	4	8	**70**	17	.354
1944	Newark	NNL	INF	50	**203**	**38**	75	15	5	2	21	8	.369
1945	Mexico City	MEX	SS 2B	83	344	67	126	29	4	1	58	20	.366
1946	Mexico City	MEX	SS 2B OF	98	**418**	79	135	24	0	7	51	24	.323
1947	Mexico City	MEX	SS	122	514	90	**169**	24	6	2	65	23	.329
1948	New York	NNL	3B	-	-	-	-	-	-	-	-	-	
1948	Vera Cruz	MEX	SS	88	369	63	**136**	24	3	3	33	13	**.369**
1949	Minneapolis	AA	3B 2B	99	398	60	144	22	5	6	64	4	.362
1949	New York	NAL	3B	-	-	-	-	-	-	-	-	-	
1950	Minneapolis	AA	3B 2B	150	**627**	106	**195**	24	1	11	80	6	.311
1951	Minneapolis	AA	3B	107	423	59	137	24	1	8	61	1	.324
1952	Minneapolis	AA	3B	145	618	86	180	27	1	10	68	3	.291
1953	Sacramento,Oakland	PCL	2B 3B	87	254	32	68	10	1	0	13	1	.268
1954	Escogido	DMSL	SS	50	178	21	50	8	0	1	18	0	.281
1955	Bismark	NDL	3B	-	328	-	118	-	-	-	-	-	.360
37-8	Alamendares	CWL	3B	57	228	26	66	5	2	1	27	**11**	.289
38-9	Cuba	CWL	3B	45	182	18	58	9	9	1	30	3	.319
39-0	Cienfuegos	CWL	3B	28	116	15	36	4	1	1	11	1	.310
40-1	Cienfuegos	CWL	3B	40	158	16	29	2	2	0	15	4	.184
41-2	Santurce	PRWL	INF	-	104	30	30	2	1	1	9	-	.288
45-6	Marianao	CWL	3B	46	173	24	55	5	2	-	13	2	.318
46-7	Marianao	CWL	3B	3	8	0	1	1	0	0	0	0	.125
46-7	Oriente	CUBA	3B	25	103	18	37	8	3	0	10	4	.359
47-8	Cuba	CWL	3B	17	67	11	14	2	1	0	4	3	.209
48-9	Obregon	MXWL	3B	47	189	21	60	11	3	0	37	6	.317
49-0	Marianao	CWL	3B	74	**318**	40	84	15	3	2	28	10	.264
50-1	Marianao	CWL	3B	65	273	38	83	12	1	2	24	3	.304
51-2	Marianao	CWL	3B	54	221	30	64	8	2	3	16	2	.290
52-3	Marianao	CWL	3B	72	**305**	36	85	12	1	1	21	4	.279
53-4	Santurce	PRWL	INF	60	228	22	53	-	-	1	23	2	.232

Johnny Howard Davis. Born February 6, 1917 at Ashland, VA. Died November 17, 1982 at Ft. Lauderdale, FL. 6'2", 200 lbs. BR TR

Year	Club	League	Pos	G	AB	R	H	2B	3B	HR	RBI	SB	BA
1940	Newark	NNL	OF-	-	-	-	-	-	-	-	-	-	
1941	Newark	NNL	OF	13	48	-	9	0	0	1	-	1	.188
1942	Newark	NNL	OF P	15	42	-	17	1	2	2	-	1	.405
1943	Newark	NNL	OF P	-	118	-	36	4	0	3	-	-	.305
1944	Newark	NNL	OF P	51	154	28	53	10	1	4	30	1	.344
1945	Newark	NNL	OF P	38	138	28	44	**14**	3	6	34	1	.319
1946	Newark	NNL	OF P	45	159	31	54	9	0	**8**	40	3	.340
1947	Newark	NNL	OF P	80	262	52	69	13	-	13	-	3	.263
1948	Newark	NNL	OF	-	-	-	-	-	-	-	-	-	
1948	Vera Cruz	MEX	OF P	36	76	11	19	3	1	1	22	-	.250
1949	Houston	NAL	OF	66	262	36	60	-	-	**14**	-	-	.229
1950	Houston	NAL	OF P	-	-	-	-	-	-	-	-	-	
1950	Pastora	VENZ	OF	-	-	-	-	-	-	-	-	-	
1951	Drummondville	PROV	OF	120	421	106	146	28	1	31	116	2	.347
1952	Escogido	DMSL	P	-	28	4	6	0	0	0	5	-	.214
1952	San Diego	PCL	OF	61	167	26	44	9	1	6	36	1	.263
1953	Ft. Lauderdale	FLIN	OF	140	514	117	165	18	2	35	136	6	.321
1954	Escogido	DMSL	OF P	-	104	17	32	-	-	-	20	2	.308
1954	Montgomery	SATL	OF	40	133	27	35	4	-	8	25	1	.263
45-6	San Juan	PRWL	P OF	-	116	-	29	-	-	-	20	0	.250
46-7	Matanzas	CUBA	OF	-	109	12	26	-	-	-	-	-	.239
47-8	Cienfuegos	CWL	OF	-	188	17	57	5	4	0	19	4	.303
47-8	Mayaquez	PRWL	P OF	-	-	-	-	-	-	11	-	-	
48-9	Mayaquez	PRWL	OF	-	-	-	-	-	-	-	51	-	

Year	Club	League	Pos	G	AB	R	H	2B	3B	HR	RBI	SB	BA
49-0	Mayaquez	PRWL	P OF	-	-	-	-	-	-	9	51	-	
51-2	Mayaquez	PRWL	OF	-	-	-	-	-	-	**9**	-	-	

Lorenzo "Piper" Davis. Born July 3, 1917 at Piper, AL. 6'3", 187 lbs. BR TR

Year	Club	League	Pos	G	AB	R	H	2B	3B	HR	RBI	SB	BA
1942	Birmingham	NAL	INF	2	4	0	0	0	0	0	-	0	.000
1943	Birmingham	NAL	SS	-	57	-	22	9	1	1	-	1	.386
1944	Birmingham	NAL	2B	64	253	40	38	3	3	2	-	7	.150
1945	Birmingham	NAL	1B	58	211	36	66	10	7	3	33	7	.313
1946	Birmingham	NAL	2B	4	11	-	3	0	1	0	-	0	.273
1947	Birmingham	NAL	1B	56	228	52	82	1	-	2	-	-	.360
1948	Birmingham	NAL	2B	76	295	63	104	19	8	7	**69**	6	.353
1949	Birmingham	NAL	2B	82	299	63	113	-	-	-	-	-	.378
1950	Birmingham	NAL	2B 1B	42	149	36	57	10	2	3	28	4	.383
1950	Jalisco	MEX	1B	30	116	29	33	4	3	6	15	6	.284
1950	Scranton	EAST	2B SS	15	63	6	21	4	0	3	10	0	.333
1951	Oakland	PCL	2B OF	79	289	38	77	16	1	4	35	5	.266
1951	Ottawa	INT	2B 1B	78	278	18	73	10	3	3	32	7	.263
1952	Oakland	PCL	2B 3B OF	122	399	57	122	24	6	8	44	1	.306
1953	Oakland	PCL	2B 1B OF	174	670	90	193	39	8	13	97	1	.288
1954	Oakland	PCL	2B OF	120	365	43	105	19	2	9	59	3	.288
1955	Oakland, San Fran.	PCL	3B OF	126	369	39	90	19	1	6	41	1	.244
1956	Los Angeles	PCL	3B OF	64	152	19	48	9	-	6	24	1	.316
1957	Ft. Worth	TEX	1B 3B OF	87	219	11	47	10	2	2	20	-	.215
1957	Los Angeles	PCL	PH	2	2	0	1	0	0	0	0	0	.500
1958	Ft. Worth	TEX	1B 3B OF	82	220	23	62	9	1	2	36	3	.282
47-8	Caguas	PRWL	INF	-	188	-	57	5	4	10	49	4	.303
48-9	Caguas	PRWL	INF	-	-	-	-	-	-	8	66	-	
49-0	Ponce	PRWL	INF	-	304	52	89	14	8	3	59	-	.293
51-2	Caguas-Guayama	PRWL	INF		-	-	-	-	-	-	-	-	

Robert Lomax "Butch" Davis. BL TR

Year	Club	League	Pos	G	AB	R	H	2B	3B	HR	RBI	SB	BA
1946	Atlanta	NSL	OF	-	-	-	-	-	-	-	-	-	
1947	Baltimore	NNL	OF	-	306	62	**104**	17	-	2	-	27	.340
1949	Baltimore	NAL	OF	75	280	49	104	-	-	-	-	-	.371
1950	Baltimore	NAL	OF	-	-	-	-	-	-	-	-	-	
1950	Winnipeg	MADK	OF	42	171	-	78	-	-	4	38	-	.456
1951	Albany	EAST	OF	37	140	18	49	11	2	5	30	0	.350
1951	Winnipeg	MADK	OF	50	212	-	86	-	-	7	53	-	.406
1952	Scranton	EAST	OF	38	156	25	40	7	3	3	9	1	.256
1952	Toledo, Charleston	AA	OF	77	257	28	82	13	3	4	35	1	.319
47-8	Cienfuegos	CWL	OF	-	188	17	57	5	4	0	19	4	.303

Leon Day. Born October 30, 1916 at Alexandria, VA. 5'10", 180 lbs. BR TR

Year	Club	League	Pos	G	AB	R	H	2B	3B	HR	RBI	SB	BA
1934	Baltimore	NNL	P	-	-	-	-	-	-	-	-	-	
1935	Brooklyn	NNL	P	11	29	-	7	3	0	-	-	-	.241
1936	Newark	NNL	P	6	11	-	3	0	0	0	-	0	.273
1937	Newark	NNL	P	20	50	8	16	2	0	0	-	0	.320
1938	Newark	NNL	OF P	-	-	-	-	-	-	-	-	-	
1939	Newark	NNL	P	10	28	-	8	0	2	0	-	0	.286
1940	Vera Cruz	MEX	P OF	14	47	6	14	4	1	1	11	0	.298
1941	Newark	NNL	P OF	30	122	-	41	10	5	2	-	1	.336
1942	Newark	NNL	P OF	-	100	-	31	4	1	-	-	1	.310
1943	Newark	NNL	P	-	54	-	11	2	1	1	-	0	.204
1946	Newark	NNL	P	21	49	12	23	3	1	1	13	0	.469
1947	Mexico City	MEX	P OF 2B	56	128	26	46	7	3	0	14	1	.359
1948	Mexico City	MEX	P OF 2B	56	115	23	31	4	3	4	30	2	.270
1949	Baltimore	NAL	OF P	57	181	29	49	-	-	-	-	-	.271
1950	Baltimore	NAL	OF	12	39	6	7	1	0	0	5	2	.179
1950	Winnipeg	MADK	OF P	31	108	-	35	-	-	-	14	-	.324
1951	Toronto	INT	P	20	27	5	7	1	0	0	1	0	.259
1952	Scranton	EAST	P PH	73	102	8	32	4	1	0	12	1	.314
1953	Edmonton	WINT	P	44	70	10	16	6	1	0	6	0	.229
37-8	Almendares	CWL	P	-	-	-	-	-	-	-	-	-	
39-0	Aquadilla	PRWL	P OF	-	177	27	48	8	5	3	36	13	.271
40-1	Aquadilla	PRWL	P OF	-	-	-	-	-	-	-	-	-	
41-2	Aquadilla	PRWL	P	-	-	-	-	-	-	-	-	-	
47-8	Santiago	CWL	P	-	-	-	-	-	-	-	-	-	
49-0	Santurce	PRWL	P	-	-	-	-	-	-	-	-	-	

Year	Club	League	Pos	G	AB	R	H	2B	3B	HR	RBI	SB	BA

Lawrence Eugene "Larry" Doby. Born December 13, 1924 at Camden, SC. 6'1", 180 lbs. BL TR

Year	Club	League	Pos	G	AB	R	H	2B	3B	HR	RBI	SB	BA
1942	Newark	NNL	2B 3B	26	92	-	36	4	1	1	-	2	.391
1943	Newark	NNL	2B	23	85	-	24	1	1	2	-	1	.282
1946	Newark	NNL	2B	43	170	41	58	8	5	7	31	7	.341
1947	Cleveland	AL	INF	29	32	3	5	1	0	0	2	0	.156
1947	Newark	NNL	2B	41	162	-	67	16	-	14	-	-	.414
1948	Cleveland	AL	OF	121	439	83	132	23	9	14	66	9	.301
1949	Cleveland	AL	OF	147	547	106	153	25	3	24	85	10	.280
1950	Cleveland	AL	OF	142	503	110	164	25	5	25	102	8	.326
1951	Cleveland	AL	OF	134	447	84	132	27	5	20	69	4	.295
1952	Cleveland	AL	OF	140	519	**104**	143	26	8	**32**	104	5	.276
1953	Cleveland	AL	OF	149	513	92	135	18	5	29	102	3	.263
1954	Cleveland	AL	OF	153	577	94	157	18	4	**32**	**126**	3	.272
1955	Cleveland	AL	OF	131	491	91	143	17	5	26	75	2	.291
1956	Chicago	AL	OF	140	504	89	135	22	3	24	102	0	.268
1957	Chicago	AL	OF	119	416	57	120	27	2	14	79	2	.288
1958	Cleveland	AL	OF	89	247	41	70	10	1	13	45	0	.283
1959	Detroit, Chicago	AL	OF	39	113	6	26	4	2	0	12	1	.230
1959	San Diego	PCL	OF	9	27	2	6	0	1	0	3	-	.222
1962	Chunichi	JAP	OF	72	240	27	54	9	1	10	35	-	.225
46-7	San Juan	PRWL	OF	-	152	27	53	-	-	12	42	-	.349

Jesse Warren Douglas. Born March 27, 1916 at Longview, TX. BB TR

Year	Club	League	Pos	G	AB	R	H	2B	3B	HR	RBI	SB	BA
1938	New York	NNL	SS	-	-	-	-	-	-	-	-	-	
1940	Kansas City	NAL	2B	-	-	-	-	-	-	-	-	-	
1941	Birmingham	NAL	INF	-	36	-	14	2	1	0	-	-	.389
1942	Birmingham	NAL	INF	-	-	-	-	-	-	-	-	-	
1944	Chicago	NAL	INF	62	232	39	65	9	7	0	-	14	.280
1945	Chicago	NAL	INF	64	254	39	77	11	7	2	30	4	.303
1946	Mex City, Mont.	MEX	3B 2B OF	79	326	51	88	9	6	0	32	11	.270
1947	Mexico City	MEX	2B	114	465	61	106	11	3	0	43	15	.228
1949	Chicago	NAL	INF	**93**	331	57	95	-	-	-	-	-	.287
1950	Chicago	NAL	3B 2B	46	169	44	56	8	7	1	21	12	.331
1951	Colorado Springs	WEST	3B 2B	72	290	47	76	8	4	0	21	11	.262
1951	New Orleans	NAL	3B	-	-	-	-	-	-	-	-	-	
1952	Winnipeg	MADK	3B	-	-	-	-	-	-	-	-	-	
1953	Brandon	MADK	2B	53	206	-	52	-	-	2	25	-	.252
1954	Yucatan	MEX	2B	23	89	10	28	2	3	0	10	3	.315
1956	Mexicali	AZMX	2B	48	180	31	58	13	-	0	35	7	.322
1958	Yakima	NWL	3B 2B	9	29	4	6	0	0	0	2	-	.207

Claro Duany. Born August 12, 1917 at Caibarien, Santiago, Cuba. 6'2", 215 lbs. BL TL

Year	Club	League	Pos	G	AB	R	H	2B	3B	HR	RBI	SB	BA
1944	New York	NNL	OF	28	80	16	24	7	1	2	11	0	.300
1945	Monterrey	MEX	OF	93	373	78	140	**31**	4	9	**100**	10	**.375**
1946	Monterrey	MEX	OF	85	313	62	114	27	4	10	64	2	**.364**
1947	New York	NNL	OF	-	182	31	54	12	-	7	-	1	.297
1948	Sherbrooke	PROV	OF	-	209	49	81	17	0	23	77	-	.388
1949	Sherbrooke	PROV	OF	-	355	55	103	18	0	22	**99**	-	.290
1950	Aguila	MEX	OF 1B	28	93	17	26	7	0	6	28	2	.280
1950	Pastora	VENZ	OF	-	-	-	-	-	-	-	-	-	
1951	Mexico City	MEX	OF	25	97	14	28	3	1	2	16	2	.289
1951	Sherbrooke	PROV	OF	107	374	79	126	23	1	23	88	5	.337
1952	Tampa-Havana	FLIN	OF	105	342	45	83	13	2	13	61	1	.243
1953	Escogido	DMSL	OF	-	39	2	5	-	-	-	4	0	.128
42-3	Almendares	CWL	OF	-	30	2	4	-	-	-	1	0	.133
43-4	Havana, Almendares	CWL	OF	-	88	11	24	-	-	-	6	2	.273
44-5	Marianao, Almend.	CWL	OF	-	162	25	55	-	-	3	22	1	.340
45-6	Marianao	CWL	OF	59	208	21	60	8	0	4	32	2	.288
46-7	Havana	CWL	OF	29	106	10	39	7	0	1	15	0	.368
47-8	Marianao	CWL	OF	74	267	32	80	21	4	4	40	1	.300
48-9	Marianao	CWL	OF	59	197	25	48	9	1	9	38	0	.244
49-0	Marianao	CWL	OF	72	230	36	63	18	2	7	40	5	.274
50-1	Marianao	CWL	OF	61	175	21	55	10	1	2	27	4	.314
51-2	Marianao	CWL	OF	58	189	20	52	11	2	6	28	0	.275
52-3	Cienfuegos	CWL	OF	30	38	4	7	-	-	1	6	0	.184
54-5	Cienfuegos	CWL	OF	5	6	0	0	0	0	0	0	0	.000

Luscious Luke Easter. Born August 4, 1914 at Jonestown, MS. Died March 29, 1979 at Euclid, OH. 6'4 1/2", 240 lbs. BL TR

Year	Club	League	Pos	G	AB	R	H	2B	3B	HR	RBI	SB	BA
1947	Homestead	NNL	OF	-	219	46	68	11	-	10	-	1	.311
1948	Homestead	NNL	OF	58	215	-	78	22	8	13	-	-	.363

Year	Club	League	Pos	G	AB	R	H	2B	3B	HR	RBI	SB	BA
1949	Cleveland	AL	OF	21	45	6	10	3	0	0	2	0	.222
1949	San Diego	PCL	1B	80	273	56	99	23	0	25	92	1	.363
1950	Cleveland	AL	1B OF	141	540	96	151	20	4	28	107	0	.280
1951	Cleveland	AL	1B	128	486	65	131	12	5	27	103	0	.270
1952	Cleveland	AL	1B	127	437	63	115	10	3	31	97	1	.263
1952	Indianapolis	AA	1B	14	50	13	17	2	0	6	12	1	.340
1953	Cleveland	AL	1B	68	211	26	64	9	0	7	31	0	.303
1954	Cleveland	AL	PH	6	6	0	1	0	0	0	0	0	.167
1954	Ottawa	INT	1B	66	230	49	80	10	-	15	48	1	.348
1954	San Diego	PCL	1B	56	198	43	55	8	1	13	42	1	.278
1955	Charleston	AA	1B	144	477	78	135	25	5	30	102	1	.283
1956	Buffalo	INT	1B	145	483	75	148	20	3	**35**	**106**	0	.306
1957	Buffalo	INT	1B	154	534	87	149	27	2	**40**	**128**	0	.279
1958	Buffalo	INT	1B	148	502	89	154	33	0	38	109	1	.307
1959	Buffalo, Rochester	INT	1B	143	478	68	125	32	2	22	76	0	.262
1960	Rochester	INT	1B	115	275	36	83	12	1	14	57	0	.302
1961	Rochester	INT	1B	82	203	24	59	13	1	10	51	0	.291
1962	Rochester	INT	1B	93	249	39	70	11	1	15	60	0	.281
1963	Rochester	INT	1B	77	188	20	51	8	1	6	35	0	.271
1964	Rochester	INT	PH	10	10	0	2	0	0	0	1	0	.200
47-8	Venezuela	VENZ	OF	-	-	-	-	-	-	8	-	-	
48-9	Mayaquez	PRWL	1B	-	249	**81**	100	**27**	**9**	**14**	80	15	.402
55-6	San Juan, Ponce	PRWL	1B	-	191	31	58	7	1	**17**	40	-	.304

William "Benny" Felder. Born 1925. 5'10", 170 lbs. BR TR

Year	Club	League	Pos	G	AB	R	H	2B	3B	HR	RBI	SB	BA
1946	Newark	NNL	INF	-	-	-	-	-	-	-	-	-	
1947	Newark	NNL	INF	-	-	-	-	-	-	-	-	-	
1952	Key West	FINT	INF	77	245	13	43	5	1	1	14	2	.176
1953	Pampa	WTNM	2B 3B	128	522	113	157	32	6	5	73	15	.301
1954	Artesia	LGHN	3B	23	95	18	28	3	0	2	18	2	.295
1954	Pampa	WTNM	SS 2B	95	377	62	114	21	4	6	69	3	.302

Wilmer Leon "Red" Fields. Born August 2, 1922 at Manassas, VA. 6'3", 215 lbs. BR TR

Year	Club	League	Pos	G	AB	R	H	2B	3B	HR	RBI	SB	BA
1940	Homestead	NNL	P	1	2	0	1	0	0	0	0	0	.500
1941	Homestead	NNL	P	-	-	-	-	-	-	-	-	-	
1942	Homestead	NNL	P 3B	1	4	-	1	0	0	0	-	-	.250
1946	Homestead	NNL	P OF 3B	12	30	6	7	1	2	0	3	0	.233
1947	Homestead	NNL	P 3B	14	49	4	14	2	0	0	-	0	.286
1948	Homestead	NNL	P OF	47	148	-	46	-	-	-	-	-	.311
1949	Homestead	ANL	OF	-	-	-	-	-	-	-	-	-	
1950	Homestead	NAL	OF	-	-	-	-	-	-	-	-	-	
1952	Toronto	INT	OF P	51	167	24	48	10	1	2	13	-	.287
1953	Oriente	DMSL	OF P	-	107	15	42	-	-	0	19	2	.393
1958	Mex City, Mont.	MEX	3B	25	88	10	33	2	0	7	35	0	.375
47-8	Mayaquez	PRWL	OF P	-	184	-	58	-	-	5	44	0	.315
48-9	Mayaquez	PRWL	P OF 3B	-	325	-	108	-	-	11	**88**	1	.332
49-0	Mayaquez	PRWL	P 3B OF	-	279	-	91	-	-	6	-	0	.326
50-1	Mayaquez	PRWL	OF	-	279	-	90	-	-	-	-	0	.323
51-2	Caracas	VENZ	OF	52	207	**48**	72	**21**	2	8	**45**	2	**.348**

Pedro Formenthal. Born April 19, 1915 at Baguanos, Cuba. 5'11", 200 lbs. BL TL

Year	Club	League	Pos	G	AB	R	H	2B	3B	HR	RBI	SB	BA
1943	Tampico	MEX	OF	90	324	58	101	21	8	4	29	11	.312
1944	Vera Cruz	MEX	OF	88	330	81	114	24	9	5	73	14	.345
1945	Vera Cruz	MEX	OF	91	312	72	113	19	10	7	58	22	.362
1946	San Luis	MEX	OF	35	125	35	48	15	3	3	20	11	.384
1949	Memphis	NAL	OF	84	296	56	101	-	-	-	-	-	.341
1950	Memphis	NAL	OF	23	72	20	19	5	0	0	9	4	.264
1951	Cibaenas	DMSL	OF	-	108	34	35	-	-	13	31	8	.324
1952	Oriente	DMSL	OF	-	165	25	48	-	-	-	24	4	.291
1953	Oriente	DMSL	OF	-	109	17	29	-	-	-	11	1	.266
1954	Havana	INT	OF	77	266	36	78	6	2	13	41	2	.293
1955	Havana	INT	OF	127	358	47	105	16	5	8	55	3	.293
42-3	Cienfuegos	CWL	OF	-	65	8	15	-	-	-	5	0	.231
43-4	Cienfuegos	CWL	OF	-	108	22	42	-	-	-	20	3	.389
44-5	Cienfuegos	CWL	OF	-	107	20	27	-	-	2	11	1	.252
45-6	Havana	CWL	OF	62	227	31	64	13	2	3	15	4	.282
46-7	Havana	CWL	OF	67	204	34	50	6	6	0	19	8	.245
47-8	Havana	CWL	OF	76	266	39	62	8	7	4	23	2	.233
48-9	Havana	CWL	OF	68	229	38	66	11	3	2	24	3	.288
49-0	Havana	CWL	OF	75	295	51	99	11	5	6	40	6	.336

Year	Club	League	Pos	G	AB	R	H	2B	3B	HR	RBI	SB	BA
50-1	Havana	CWL	OF	73	272	42	68	7	6	8	38	4	.250
51-2	Havana	CWL	OF	71	256	47	65	11	4	9	46	5	.254
52-3	Havana	CWL	OF	73	261	50	88	18	3	10	57	6	.337
53-4	Havana, Marianao	CWL	OF	64	233	25	60	8	2	5	32	5	.258
54-5	Havana	CWL	OF	45	137	24	40	5	0	7	32	-	.292

Raul Galata y Capote. Born 1930 in Cuba. 5'9", 170 lbs. BL TL

Year	Club	League	Pos	G	AB	R	H	2B	3B	HR	RBI	SB	BA
1949	Indianapolis	NAL	P	-	-		-	-		-	-	-	
1950	Indianapolis	NAL	P	30	67	6	21	2	1	0	13	0	.313
1951	Indianapolis	NAL	P	-	-	-	-	-	-	-	-	0	
1951	Monterrey	MEX	P OF	37	75	8	19	2	3	0	5	0	.253
1952	Monterrey	MEX	P OF	4	8	0	1	0	0	0	1	0	.125
1953	Indianapolis	NAL	P OF	-	-	-	-	-	-	-	-	-	
1953	Mex City, Aguila	MEX	P 1B	65	188	41	47	9	1	4	22	3	.250
1954	Aguila	MEX	P 1B	65	195	39	61	13	-	6	24	7	.313
1955	Aguila	MEX	P OF	52	111	21	34	4	-	6	14	1	.306
1956	Aguila	MEX	P 1B OF	87	171	17	34	4	2	1	18	1	.199
1957	Aguila	MEX	P OF	63	101	21	28	6	0	2	12	1	.277
1958	Chihuanua	AZMX	P 1B	28	100	19	31	4	0	4	18	0	.310
1958	Yucatan, Poza Rica	MEX	P PH	9	6	0	1	0	0	0	0	0	.167
1959	Monterrey	MEX	OF P	32	48	8	13	2	0	1	2	0	.271
1960	Monterrey	MEX	OF P	110	262	50	70	12	2	7	36	0	.267
1961	Monterrey	MEX	1B OF P	102	310	43	71	5	1	8	41	1	.229
1962	Monterrey	MEX	P PH	8	1	0	0	0	0	0	0	0	.000
1963	Monterrey	MEX	OF P	53	141	26	41	8	0	2	11	1	.291
1964	Puerto Mexican	MXSE	P OF 1B	64	161	14	44	9	2	0	14	0	.273
49-0	Ponce	PRWL	P	-	-	-	-	-	-	-	-	-	
50-1	Magallanes	VENZ	P	-	-	-	-	-	-	-	-	-	

Silvio Garcia. Born October 11, 1914 at Limonar, Cuba. 6', 195 lbs. BR TR

Year	Club	League	Pos	G	AB	R	H	2B	3B	HR	RBI	SB	BA
1937	Ciudad Trujillo	DOM	SS	31	128	26	38	14	1	-	20	-	.297
1937	Pastora	VENZ	SS	-	-	-	-	-	-	-	-	-	
1938	Vera Cruz	MEX	SS P	45	175	38	61	9	2	4	27	10	.349
1940	New York	NNL	INF	-	-	-	-	-	-	-	-	-	
1941	Mexico City	MEX	2B	101	434	102	**159**	29	11	5	68	15	.366
1942	Mexico City	MEX	2B	85	349	75	127	19	4	11	**83**	21	.364
1943	Mexico City	MEX	SS	86	356	49	107	16	2	5	61	7	.301
1944	Mex.City, Vera Cruz	MEX	SS	89	373	73	117	25	3	11	83	**31**	.314
1945	Vera Cruz	MEX	3B	91	386	70	135	21	7	15	86	**40**	.350
1946	New York	NNL	SS	39	144	21	46	6	5	2	15	10	.319
1947	New York	NNL	SS	-	219	37	71	11	-	3	-	10	.324
1948	Mexico City	MEX	SS	66	271	42	80	13	1	1	32	6	.295
1949	Sherbrooke	PROV	3B	-	400	59	126	30	-	4	76	20	.315
1950	Sherbrooke	PROV	3B	106	411	78	150	29	4	**21**	**116**	19	**.365**
1951	Sherbrooke	PROV	3B	123	495	101	168	34	1	12	82	14	.339
1952	Havana	FLIN	3B	114	428	45	121	22	0	3	40	9	.283
1952	Licey	DMSL	SS	-	35	9	10	-	-	-	4	0	.286
1953	Cibaenas	DMSL	SS	-	107	15	42	-	-	-	20	2	.393
31-2	Havana	CWL	SS	20	66	13	17	2	2	-	5	0	.258
34-5	Marianao	CWL	SS P	28	96	5	18	1	1	1	7	1	.188
35-6	Marianao	CWL	SS	-	131	13	36	-	-	-	16	-	.275
36-7	Marianao	CWL	P SS	54	188	33	44	-	-	-	23	3	.234
37-8	Marianao	CWL	SS P	41	156	25	46	-	-	-	19	10	.295
38-9	Almendares	CWL	SS P	-	140	17	41	-	-	-	16	2	.293
39-0	Ponce	PRWL	P	-	124	17	37	8	3	1	24	7	.298
40-1	Santa Clara	CWL	SS	-	175	24	55	-	-	-	20	9	.314
41-2	Cienfuegos	CWL	SS	46	171	24	60	5	0	4	19	6	.351
42-3	Cienfuegos	CWL	SS	-	175	26	53	-	-	-	24	7	.303
43-4	Cienfuegos	CWL	SS	-	170	28	56	-	-	-	14	3	.329
44-5	Cienfuegos	CWL	SS P	-	173	24	44	-	-	-	21	3	.254
45-6	Cienfuegos	CWL	SS	63	215	24	62	13	4	2	23	4	.288
46-7	Matanzas	CWL	SS P	40	160	22	55	10	2	1	25	23	.344
47-8	Cienfuegos	CWL	SS	60	216	33	63	10	6	1	23	3	.292
48-9	Cienfuegos	CWL	SS	40	132	9	33	4	2	1	18	0	.250
49-0	Cienfuegos	CWL	SS	55	173	25	45	8	1	1	7	6	.260
50-1	Cienfuegos	CWL	3B	62	239	40	83	13	1	5	36	17	.347
51-2	Cienfuegos	CWL	SS	59	207	21	48	11	3	1	21	4	.232
52-3	Marianao	CWL	SS	72	281	29	76	12	4	1	30	4	.270
53-4	Marianao,Almend.	CWL	SS	31	64	4	11	0	0	1	9	1	.172

Year	Club	League	Pos	G	AB	R	H	2B	3B	HR	RBI	SB	BA
Horace T. Garner. Born 1925. 6'3", 200 lbs. BR TR													
1949	Indianapolis	NAL	OF	-	-	-	-	-	-	-	-	-	
1951	Eau Claire	NORL	OF	117	409	109	147	30	6	15	96	44	.359
1952	Evansville	III	OF	112	381	89	121	9	10	23	107	12	.318
1953	Jacksonville	SATL	OF	120	426	79	130	25	5	15	71	12	.305
1954	Jacksonville	SATL	OF	94	288	54	83	14	2	7	47	2	.288
1955	Jacksonville	SATL	OF	123	425	67	125	11	4	18	77	8	.294
1956	Augusta	SATL	OF	31	115	23	33	6	-	1	9	2	.287
1956	Evansville	III	OF	85	314	59	111	23	4	13	91	6	.354
1957	Evansville	III	OF	108	383	69	128	20	4	20	100	4	.334
1958	Cedar Rapids	III	OF	109	377	69	118	23	0	27	79	7	.313
1959	Cedar Rapids	III	OF	97	317	65	98	18	3	17	75	0	.309
1961	Cedar Rapids	III	PH	1	1	0	0	0	0	0	0	0	.000
Alphonso Gerrard. BR TR													
1945	New York	NNL	OF	27	93	9	24	5	0	0	5	2	.258
1946	San Luis	MEX	INF	40	153	16	40	7	1	0	7	4	.261
1947	New York, Ind..	NNL	INF	-	39	2	5	0	0	0	-	0	.128
1948	Chicago	NAL	INF	45	183	20	48	6	3	0	22	5	.262
1949	Indianapolis	NAL	INF	17	65	9	23	-	-	-	-	-	.354
1950	Kingston	COL	OF	55	189	36	63	7	2	2	27	10	.333
1950	Pittsfield	CAAM	OF	45	151	23	39	9	4	1	19	4	.258
1951	Three Rivers	PROV	OF	117	412	51	139	8	6	1	55	22	.337
1952	T.R., Granby	PROV	OF	108	406	61	123	13	3	0	46	17	.303
1953	Escogido	DMSL	OF	-	85	11	24	-	-	-	5	9	.282
44-5	Santurce	PRWL	INF	-	91	-	30	-	-	-	-	12	.330
46-7	Santurce	PRWL	SS	-	134	25	42	-	-	-	8	-	.313
53-4	Santurce	PRWL	OF	-	117	-	33	-	-	-	9	-	.282
54-5	Santurce	PRWL	OF	-	161	-	54	-	-	-	18	-	.335
Joshua Gibson Jr. Born August 11, 1930 at Pittsburgh, PA lbs. BR TR													
1948	Youngstown			8	23	-	3	-	-	-	-	-	.130
1949	Homestead	NAA	3B	-	-	-	-	-	-	-	-	-	
1950	Homestead		UTL	-	-	-	-	-	-	-	-	-	
1951	Farnham	PROV	3B	68	187	35	43	8	0	2	20	20	.230
James William "Junior" Gilliam. Born October 17, 1928 at Nashville, TN. Died October 8, 1978 at Inglewood, CA. 5'10 1/2", 175 lbs. BB TR													
1946	Baltimore	NNL	2B INF OF	-	9	-	1	-	-	-	-	-	.111
1947	Baltimore	NNL	2B	71	257	47	65	10	-	0	-	9	.253
1948	Baltimore	NNL	2B	-	-	-	-	-	-	-	-	-	
1949	Baltimore	NAL	2B	88	326	**94**	98	-	**13**	-	-	-	.301
1950	Baltimore	NAL	2B	42	162	38	43	10	5	2	25	13	.265
1951	Baltimore	NAL	2B	-	-	-	-	-	-	-	-	-	
1951	Montreal	INT	2B 3B OF	152	565	**117**	162	22	9	7	73	15	.287
1952	Montreal	INT	2B 3B OF	151	561	**111**	169	39	9	9	112	18	.301
1953	Brooklyn	NL	2B	151	605	125	168	31	17	6	63	21	.278
1954	Brooklyn	NL	2B OF	146	607	107	171	28	8	13	52	8	.282
1955	Brooklyn	NL	2B OF	147	538	110	134	20	8	7	40	15	.249
1956	Brooklyn	NL	2B OF	153	594	102	178	23	8	6	43	21	.300
1957	Brooklyn	NL	2B OF	149	617	89	154	26	4	2	37	26	.250
1958	Los Angeles	NL	OF 2B 3B	147	555	81	145	25	5	2	43	18	.261
1959	Los Angeles	NL	3B 2B	145	553	91	156	18	4	3	34	23	.282
1960	Los Angeles	NL	3B 2B	151	557	96	138	20	2	5	40	12	.248
1961	Los Angeles	NL	3B 2B OF	144	439	74	107	26	3	4	32	8	.244
1962	Los Angeles	NL	2B 3B OF	160	588	83	159	24	1	4	43	17	.270
1963	Los Angeles	NL	2B 3B	148	525	77	148	27	4	6	49	19	.282
1964	Los Angeles	NL	3B 2B OF	116	334	44	76	8	3	2	27	4	.228
1965	Los Angeles	NL	3B 2B OF	111	372	54	104	19	4	4	39	9	.280
1965	Los Angeles	NL	3B 2B 1B	88	235	30	51	9	0	1	16	2	.217
48-9	Almendares	CWL	PH	1	1	0	0	0	0	0	0	0	.000
51-2	Santurce	PRWL	2B	-	-	**63**	-	-	-	-	-	-	
52-3	Santurce	PRWL	2B	-	-	**55**	-	-	-	-	-	-	
Granville A. "Happy" or "Rock" Gladstone. Born January 26, 1925 in Panama. 5'11", 170 lbs. BR TR													
1950	Indianapolis	NAL	OF	64	192	40	46	6	**13**	4	23	9	.240
1951	Portland	PCL	OF	90	161	31	37	6	1	1	14	2	.230
1952	Portland	PCL	OF	10	42	10	11	2	1	3	8	0	.262
1952	Victoria	WINT	OF	143	550	81	162	40	6	15	126	19	.295
1953	Portland	PCL	OF	69	244	21	60	9	1	5	33	-	.246

Year	Club	League	Pos	G	AB	R	H	2B	3B	HR	RBI	SB	BA
1953	Victoria	WINT	OF	85	310	72	108	23	2	19	93	5	.348
1954	Portland	PCL	OF	123	392	47	86	11	4	10	54	3	.219
1955	Eugene	NWL	OF	98	352	76	106	22	6	11	88	12	.301
1956	St. Paul	AA	OF	130	393	71	109	22	2	12	59	5	.277
1957	St. Paul	AA	OF	83	254	34	64	15	3	3	32	3	.252
1958	Mexico City	MEX	OF	80	304	58	89	16	3	12	47	5	.293
1959	Amarillo	TEX	OF	3	5	0	0	0	0	0	0	0	.000
53-4		PANA	OF	-	117	-	36	-	-	4	27	-	.308
58-9	Azucareros	PANA	OF	-	136	-	37	-	-	1	24	-	.272

Stanley Glenn. Born September 19, 1926 at Wachatreague, VA. 6'3", 197 lbs. BR TR

Year	Club	League	Pos	G	AB	R	H	2B	3B	HR	RBI	SB	BA
1943	Philadelphia	NNL	C	-	-	-	-	-	-	-	-	-	
1944	Philadelphia	NNL	C	-	-	-	-	-	-	-	-	-	
1945	Philadelphia	NNL	C	7	19	3	4	2	0	0	2	0	.211
1946	Philadelphia	NNL	C	-	-	-	-	-	-	-	-	-	
1947	Philadelphia	NNL	C	-	97	5	20	1	-	-	-	-	.206
1948	Philadelphia	NNL	C	-	-	-	-	-	-	-	-	-	
1949	Philadelphia	NAL	C	46	166	22	34	-	-	-	-	-	.205
1950	Hartford	EAST	C	20	58	8	15	5	0	1	10	0	.259
1950	Philadelphia	NAL	C	27	97	4	22	6	1	4	7	0	.227
1951	Hartford	EAST	C	109	334	23	72	14	0	1	32	0	.216
1952	Hartford	EAST	C	12	29	5	8	2	0	0	3	0	.276
1952	Quebec City	PROV	C OF	75	234	33	58	10	1	5	27	6	.248
1953	Quebec City	PROV	C 1B	110	375	69	103	20	3	16	90	1	.275

Rene Gonzalez. Born 1923 in Cuba. 6'2", 206 lbs. BR TR

Year	Club	League	Pos	G	AB	R	H	2B	3B	HR	RBI	SB	BA
1947	San Luis, Vera Cruz	MEX	1B	96	323	53	102	19	6	6	43	9	.316
1948	Tampico, Mex City	MEX	1B	81	303	42	94	17	4	6	51	4	.310
1949	San Luis	MEX	1B	80	311	72	111	22	3	12	72	15	.357
1950	New York	NAL	1B	32	129	22	39	8	1	4	21	3	.302
1951	San Luis	MEX	1B	79	297	76	96	21	3	21	**79**	4	.323
1952	Aquila	MEX	1B	81	316	83	117	19	4	**21**	84	9	**.370**
1953	Aquila	MEX	1B	69	271	58	93	20	4	9	63	0	**.343**
1954	Aguila	MEX	1B	79	315	64	113	16	2	**21**	77	5	.359
1955	Aguila	MEX	1B	99	395	59	132	21	1	16	79	4	.334
1956	N.Laredo, Monterry	MEX	1B OF	113	381	44	98	15	1	19	71	2	.257
48-9	Almendares	CWL	1B	30	52	3	13	2	1	1	9	0	.250
50-1		VENZ	1B	-	-	-	-	**18**	-	**10**	56	-	
57-8	Oriental	NICR	1B	-	159	-	54	-	-	6	25	-	.340

William "Willie" Grace. Born June 30, 1919 at Memphis TN. 6', 170 lbs. BB TR

Year	Club	League	Pos	G	AB	R	H	2B	3B	HR	RBI	SB	BA
1942	Cinc.-Cleveland	NAL	OF	-	-	-	-	-	-	-	-	-	
1943	Cleveland	NAL	OF	-	-	-	-	-	-	-	-	-	
1944	Cleveland	NAL	OF	56	177	27	42	7	0	1	-	3	.237
1945	Cleveland	NAL	OF	32	112	14	26	5	0	0	13	1	.232
1946	Cleveland	NAL	OF	59	226	-	69	-	-	1	-	3	.305
1947	Cleveland	NAL	OF	-	256	38	77	-	-	-	-	-	.301
1948	Cleveland	NAL	OF	78	307	42	99	15	3	0	45	5	.322
1949	Louisville	NAL	OF	76	244	22	54	-	-	-	-	-	.221
1950	Cleveland, Houston	NAL	OF	55	198	20	54	6	4	0	21	4	.273
1951	Erie	MATL	OF	120	488	86	146	14	5	2	53	12	.299

Napoleon "Nap" Gulley. Born August 29, 1924 at Huttig, AR. 6', 170 lbs. BL TL

Year	Club	League	Pos	G	AB	R	H	2B	3B	HR	RBI	SB	BA
1943	Cleveland	NAL		-	-	-	-	-	-	-	-	-	
1945	Cleveland	NAL		-	-	-	-	-	-	-	-	-	
1947	Newark	NNL	P	6	26	2	10	2	-	0	-	0	.385
1948	Tampico	MEX		-	-	-	-	-	-	-	-	-	
1949	San Luis, MC	MEX	P	10	8	1	3	0	-	1	3	-	.375
1950	Visalia	CALF	OF	106	383	73	112	22	4	14	83	7	.292
1951	Visalia	CALF	OF	123	427	67	123	27	3	13	88	3	.288
1952	Visalia	CALF	OF	103	393	74	131	43	6	8	82	7	.333
1953	Victoria	WINT	OF	28	89	19	24	6	-	4	23	2	.270
1954	Visalia	CALF	OF	124	446	77	141	27	5	14	81	12	.316
1955	Spokane	NWL	OF	127	479	88	173	26	2	18	126	11	.361
1956	Spokane	NWL	OF	71	263	41	83	19	3	3	35	5	.316

Samuel Hairston. Born January 20, 1920 at Crawford, MS. 5'11", 195 lbs. BR TR

Year	Club	League	Pos	G	AB	R	H	2B	3B	HR	RBI	SB	BA
1945	Cinc.-Indianapolis	NAL	C	52	165	29	47	5	5	-	20	3	.285
1946	Indianapolis	NAL	C	-	-	-	-	-	-	-	-	-	
1947	Indianapolis	NAL	C	67	255	41	92	-	1^	-	-	-	.361

Year	Club	League	Pos	G	AB	R	H	2B	3B	HR	RBI	SB	BA
1948	Indianapolis	NAL	C 3B 1B	76	285	54	91	18	5	4	36	6	.319
1949	Indianapolis	NAL	C	91	342	58	105	-	-	-	-	-	.307
1950	Colorado Springs	WEST	C	38	133	18	38	5	1	1	28	2	.286
1950	Indianapolis	NAL	C	70	236	55	100	23	1	**17**	**71**	5	**.424**
1951	Chicago	AL	C	4	5	1	2	1	0	0	1	0	.400
1951	Colorado Springs	WEST	C	15	54	15	21	6	1	0	13	0	.389
1951	Sacramento	PCL	C PH	68	190	15	48	14	1	0	18	3	.253
1952	Colorado Springs	WEST	C	134	503	89	159	29	3	12	98	1	.316
1953	Colorado Springs	WEST	C	143	535	84	166	42	6	8	102	3	.310
1954	Charleston	AA	C	139	481	47	129	18	8	1	60	5	.268
1955	Colorado Springs	WEST	C	142	546	107	191	38	4	6	91	2	.350
1956	Colorado Springs	WEST	C	123	453	82	144	38	0	8	69	3	.318
1957	Indianapolis	AA	C	89	264	27	67	15	5	1	35	0	.254
1958	Indianapolis	AA	C	17	31	2	10	2	1	0	6	0	.323
1958	San Antonio	TEX	C	74	217	17	59	12	3	3	31	0	.272
1959	Charleston	SATL	C	120	427	60	141	21	2	10	63	0	.330
1960	Charleston	SATL	C	45	160	17	42	8	0	3	21	1	.263
50-1	Vargas	VENZ	C	40	163	29	62	15	1	0	34	0	.380
56-7	Puebla	MXWL	C	-	318	-	115	-	-	6	60	-	.362

George William Handy. Born 1924. 5'6", 175 lbs. BL TR

Year	Club	League	Pos	G	AB	R	H	2B	3B	HR	RBI	SB	BA
1946	Memphis	NAL	INF	-	-	-	-	-	-	-	-	-	
1947	Memphis	NAL	INF	61	227	37	74	-	-	-	-	-	.326
1949	Bridgeport	COL	2B	126	529	115	183	22	6	22	104	25	.346
1949	Houston	NAL	INF	-	-	-	-	-	-	-	-	-	
1950	Bridgeport	COL	2B	36	136	25	37	6	0	2	22	-	.272
1950	St. Hyacinthe	PROV	2B	74	270	53	95	11	4	5	60	14	.352
1951	St. Hyacinthe	PROV	2B	121	456	78	152	17	6	13	72	8	.333
1952	Keokuk	III	2B	53	201	45	61	9	2	6	25	4	.303
1952	Miami Beach	FLIN	2B	45	136	18	36	5	1	3	7	3	.265
1953	Ft.Lauderdale	FLIN	2B OF	130	500	93	157	32	3	13	94	5	.314
1954	Montgomery	SATL	3B	107	333	51	102	19	0	2	40	2	.306
1955	Norfolk	PIED	3B	62	231	47	77	13	0	6	43	3	.333
1955	Winston-Salem	CARO	3B	9	24		5	-	-	-	-	-	.208

Walter Hardy. Born 1927. 5'11", 165 lbs. BR TR

Year	Club	League	Pos	G	AB	R	H	2B	3B	HR	RBI	SB	BA
1945	New York	NNL	2B SS	22	62	8	8	2	0	0	4	0	.129
1946	New York	NNL	2B SS	34	121	7	26	1	1	0	7	4	.215
1947	New York	NNL	2B SS	-	163	12	26	3	-	0	-	1	.160
1948	New York	NNL	2B SS	-	-	-	-	-	-	-	-	-	
1949	New York	NAL	2B SS	38	135	22	36	-	-	-	-	-	.267
1950	New York	NAL	2B SS	32	127	18	32	6	4	-	13	1	.252
1950	St. Jean	PROV	SS	23	80	6	16	1	0	1	9	1	.200
1951	St. Jean	PROV	SS	107	379	52	95	20	1	6	50	1	.251
1955	St. Jean	PROV	SS	110	424	61	117	19	2	4	45	8	.276

Charles Byron Harmon. Born April 23, 1924 at Washington, IN. 6'2", 175 lbs. BR TR

Year	Club	League	Pos	G	AB	R	H	2B	3B	HR	RBI	SB	BA
1947	Gloversville	CAAM	OF	64	200	24	54	10	1	-	20	6	.270
1947	Indianapolis	NAL	OF	-	-	-	-	-	-	-	-	-	
1949	Gloversville	CAAM	OF	14	51	3	11	1	2	0	7	0	.216
1949	Olean	PONY	OF 3B	31	134	20	47	12	1	1	21	0	.351
1950	Olean	PONY	3B SS 1B	**125**	**551**	125	**206**	**47**	10	22	**139**	17	.374
1951	Olean	PONY	2B	113	467	107	175	**37**	10	15	**143**	24	.375
1952	Burlington	III	3B OF	**124**	479	97	**153**	34	6	5	71	**43**	.319
1953	Tulsa	TEX	3B RF	143	566	86	176	24	11	14	83	24	.311
1954	Cincinnati	NL	3B 1B	94	286	39	68	7	3	2	25	7	.238
1955	Cincinnati	NL	3B OF 1B	96	198	31	50	6	3	5	28	9	.253
1956	Cinc., St. Louis	NL	OF 3B 1B	33	19	4	0	0	0	0	0	1	.000
1956	Omaha	AA	OF	58	242	50	87	17	6	10	49	4	.360
1957	St. Louis, Phil.	NL	OF 3B 1B	66	89	16	23	2	2	0	6	8	.258
1958	Miami	INT	OF 3B	36	126	12	26	2	2	0	11	4	.206
1958	St. Paul	AA	OF 3B	38	143	18	41	4	2	0	9	1	.287
1959	Charleston	AA	OF	20	65	9	15	3	1	4	11	0	.231
1959	Salt Lake City	PCL	OF	118	449	64	139	22	9	7	90	9	.310
1960	Salt Lake City	PCL	OF	136	415	57	119	15	7	4	35	10	.287
1961	Hawaii	PCL	UTL	7	23	3	4	0	0	0	1	1	.174
53-4	Ponce	PRWL	3B	70	269	36	88	5	7	1	23	9	.327
55-6		PRWL	3B	-	278	-	82	-	-	5	26	-	.295

Year	Club	League	Pos	G	AB	R	H	2B	3B	HR	RBI	SB	BA

William Harrell. Born July 18, 1928 at Norristown, PA. 6'1 1/2", 180 lbs. BR TR

Year	Club	League	Pos	G	AB	R	H	2B	3B	HR	RBI	SB	BA
1951	Birmingham	NAL	SS	-	-	-	-	-	-	-	-	-	
1952	Cedar Rapids	III	3B	55	206	38	67	16	3	5	35	14	.325
1952	Reading	EAST	3B	5	9	2	2	0	0	0	0	0	.222
1953	Reading	EAST	SS OF 3B	141	515	89	170	21	10	4	84	33	.330
1954	Indianapolis	AA	3B SS OF	134	453	70	139	23	5	5	59	10	.307
1955	Cleveland	AL	SS	13	19	2	8	0	0	0	1	1	.421
1955	Indianapolis	AA	SS OF 3B	149	581	99	159	30	8	9	60	7	.274
1956	Indianapolis	AA	OF SS	135	455	76	127	18	10	7	56	14	.279
1957	Cleveland	AL	INF	22	57	6	15	1	1	1	5	3	.263
1957	San Diego	PCL	SS	117	467	56	129	18	0	6	42	5	.276
1958	Cleveland	AL	INF	101	229	36	50	4	0	7	19	12	.218
1959	Rochester	INT	INF	142	564	80	150	27	9	17	69	5	.266
1960	Rochester	INT	3B	150	564	86	165	24	9	15	78	7	.293
1961	Boston	AL	INF	37	37	10	6	2	0	0	1	0	.162
1962	Seattle	PCL	OF SS	128	459	71	135	22	8	17	78	10	.294
1963	Seattle, Portland	PCL	3B	149	541	66	145	26	8	10	52	9	.268
1964	Seattle	PCL	INF	131	468	61	119	20	4	14	57	10	.254
1965	Toronto	INT	2B OF	51	135	17	39	5	2	3	16	2	.289
1966	Toronto	INT	3B	33	81	7	14	2	0	2	6	0	.173
56-7	Ponce	PRWL	SS	69	276	46	75	10	7	4	32	5	.272
57-8	Santurce	PRWL	SS	-	208	-	66	-	-	4	28	-	.317

J.C. Hartman. Born April 15, 1934 at Cottonton, AL. 6', 175 lbs. BR TR

Year	Club	League	Pos	G	AB	R	H	2B	3B	HR	RBI	SB	BA
1955	Kansas City	NAL	SS	-	-	-	-	-	-	-	-	-	
1956	Magic Valley	PION	SS	132	508	63	139	25	3	0	52	12	.274
1959	San Antonio	TEX	SS	142	545	80	150	17	3	5	48	13	.275
1960	San Antonio	TEX	SS	143	581	94	170	24	3	3	49	17	.293
1961	Houston	AA	SS	144	599	64	155	19	3	6	53	7	.259
1962	Houston	NL	SS	51	148	11	33	5	0	0	5	1	.223
1962	Oklahoma City	AA	SS	90	388	54	126	12	2	4	40	9	.325
1963	Houston	NL	SS	39	90	2	11	1	0	0	3	1	.122
1963	San Antonio	TEX	SS	67	278	60	85	11	4	3	24	2	.306
1964	Hawaii	PCL	SS	84	301	30	79	10	3	2	26	2	.262
1964	San Antonio	TEX	SS	49	183	24	42	5	0	0	12	2	.230
1965	Amarillo	TEX	3B	17	68	7	16	3	0	1	4	0	.235
1965	Oklahoma City	PCL	3B	82	216	30	54	7	1	2	17	3	.250
1966	Amarillo	TEX	2B	71	264	39	77	11	2	5	20	13	.292
1966	Oklahoma City	PCL	SS 2B	41	133	15	34	2	0	0	6	3	.256
1967	Amarillo	TEX	INF	24	83	17	22	2	1	1	9	2	.265
1967	Denver	PCL	INF	107	353	47	109	10	5	0	37	10	.309

Joe Henry. BB TR

Year	Club	League	Pos	G	AB	R	H	2B	3B	HR	RBI	SB	BA
1950	Memphis	NAL	2B	48	183	30	52	4	4	0	15	5	.284
1951	Memphis	NAL	2B	-	-	-	-	-	-	-	-	-	
1952	Canton	MOV	3B	89	343	68	104	15	4	0	43	5	.303
1952	Memphis	NAL	2B	-	-	-	-	-	-	-	-	-	
1953	Mt. Vernon	MOV	3B	92	363	60	100	12	4	3	30	8	.275
1954	Mt. Vernon	MOV	2B 3B	30	106	20	29	6	1	1	16	1	.274
1958	Detroit	NAL	3B	41	109	12	31	2	-	3	15	1	.284

Ramon Napoleon Heredia. Born 1917 in Cuba. 6', 200 lbs. BR TR

Year	Club	League	Pos	G	AB	R	H	2B	3B	HR	RBI	SB	BA
1939	New York	NNL	SS 2B	-	-	-	-	-	-	-	-	-	
1940	New York	NNL	3B	25	101	-	24	-	-	-	-	-	.238
1941	New York	NNL	3B	5	21	-	9	-	-	-	-	-	.429
1942	Monterrey	MEX	3B	89	343	48	96	20	4	0	49	9	.280
1943	Monterrey	MEX	3B	75	257	18	66	13	3	0	46	3	.257
1944	Monterrey	MEX	3B	91	343	40	81	9	4	2	34	2	.236
1945	Monterrey	MEX	3B	70	267	50	84	21	2	3	62	4	.315
1945	New York	NNL	3B	-	-	-	-	-	-	-	-	-	
1946	Monterrey	MEX	3B	87	330	38	99	16	2	1	38	3	.300
1947	Vera Cruz	MEX	3B	64	182	19	46	4	1	1	23	0	.253
1949	Vera Cruz	MEX	3B	86	323	26	86	20	2	1	65	5	.266

Juan Francisco "Pancho" Herrera y Villavicencio. Born June 16, 1934 at Santiago, Cuba. 6'3", 220 lbs. BR TR

Year	Club	League	Pos	G	AB	R	H	2B	3B	HR	RBI	SB	BA
1953	Kansas City	NAL	1B	75	268	53	75	10	3	6	43	3	.280
1954	Kansas City	NAL	1B	62	241	44	79	16	7	13	48	8	.328
1955	Schenectady	EAST	OF 3B	109	377	64	116	20	6	19	79	-	.308
1955	Syracuse	INT	1B OF	18	46	7	14	0	1	2	8	-	.304
1956	Schenectady	EAST	1B OF	131	476	68	136	24	0	14	88	-	.286

Year	Club	League	Pos	G	AB	R	H	2B	3B	HR	RBI	SB	BA
1957	Miami	INT	1B 2B 3B	154	566	77	173	25	6	17	93	-	.306
1958	Miami	INT	1B	121	436	72	123	17	3	20	66	-	.282
1958	Philadelphia	NL	3B 1B	29	63	5	17	3	0	1	6	-	.270
1959	Buffalo	INT	1B 3B	151	569	104	**187**	42	3	**37**	**128**	-	.329
1960	Philadelphia	NL	1B 2B	145	512	61	144	26	6	17	71	-	.281
1961	Philadelphia	NL	1B	126	400	56	103	17	2	13	51	-	.258
1962	Buffalo	INT	1B	143	509	93	150	25	0	**32**	**108**	-	.295
1963	Columbus	INT	1B	140	422	52	98	8	3	22	58	-	.232
1964	Columbus	INT	1B	138	454	69	140	20	4	21	70	-	.308
1965	Columbus	INT	1B	143	508	71	146	19	2	**21**	72	-	.287
1966	Columbus, Syracuse	INT	1B 2B	129	423	45	109	12	3	15	57	-	.258
1967	Dallas-Ft. Worth	TEX	1B 2B	22	59	4	13	2	1	0	5	-	.220
1967	Reynosa	MEX	1B 2B	69	149	21	39	5	0	8	30	1	.262
1968	Carmen	MXSE	1B	83	286	52	88	12	1	22	67	-	.308
1968	Miami	FLST	1B 2B	31	80	14	27	6	2	4	20	-	.338
1969	Carmen	MXSE	1B	114	380	87	125	16	1	**39**	**106**	-	.329
1969	Miami	FLST	1B	39	128	21	38	2	1	4	21	-	.297
1970	Carmen	MXSE	1B	50	157	32	56	9	1	10	36	-	.357
1970	Saltillo	MEX	1B	32	86	13	25	4	1	3	12	1	.291
1972	Key West	FLST	1B	89	218	39	62	12	3	11	46	-	.284
1974	Tampico	MEX	1B	6	15	1	5	0	0	0	4	-	.333

Samuel Hill. Born 1929?. 6'2", 180 lbs. BL TR

Year	Club	League	Pos	G	AB	R	H	2B	3B	HR	RBI	SB	BA
1937	Detroit	NNL	OF	-	-	-	-	-	-	-	-	-	
1947	Chicago	NAL	OF	-	-	-	-	-	-	-	-	-	
1948	Chicago	NAL	OF	68	281	61	88	16	2	6	32	4	.313
1950	Winnipeg	MADK	RF	43	163	-	34	-	-	0	15	-	.209
1951	Winnipeg	MADK	RF	55	247	-	72	-	-	3	26	-	.291
1952	Carman	MADK	OF	-	-	-	-	-	-	-	-	-	
1952	Memphis	NAL	OF	-	-	-	-	-	-	-	-	-	
1954	Williamsport	EAST	OF	141	529	62	144	22	9	12	83	6	.272
1957	Charlotte	SATL	OF	12	33	9	9	1	0	2	9	0	.273
1957	Duluth-Superior	NORL	OF	107	407	77	127	17	2	8	62	3	.312
1958	Duluth-Superior	NORL	OF	28	98	15	26	2	1	1	18	2	.265
1958	Memphis	NAL	OF	27	88	11	20	3	-	1	18	^	.227

David Taylor Hoskins. Born August 3, 1925 at Greenwood, MS. Died April 2, 1970 in Flint, MI. 6'1", 180 lbs. BL TR

Year	Club	League	Pos	G	AB	R	H	2B	3B	HR	RBI	SB	BA
1944	Homestead	NNL	P OF	40	141	23	50	7	4	2	27	1	.355
1945	Homestead	NNL	P OF	41	169	29	47	8	2	2	16	4	.278
1946	Homestead	NNL	P OF	33	96	17	25	4	2	0	2	0	.260
1948	Grand Rapids	CENT	OF	46	173	44	68	10	4	6	23	4	.393
1949	Grand Rapids	CENT	P	-	-	-	-	-	-	-	-	-	
1949	Louisville	NAL	OF P	58	210	30	64	-	-	-	-	-	.305
1950	Dayton	CENT	OF P	66	151	24	48	11	3	5	31	2	.318
1951	Wilkes-Barre	EAST	OF P	77	196	22	56	5	1	2	31	2	.286
1952	Dallas	TEX	P OF	62	128	16	42	7	0	0	12	0	.328
1953	Cleveland	AL	P PH	38	58	10	15	2	0	1	9	0	.259
1954	Cleveland	AL	P	15	8	2	0	0	0	0	0	0	.000
1954	Indianapolis	AA	P	7	14	0	5	0	0	0	0	0	.357
1955	Indianapolis	AA	P OF	74	117	19	27	5	3	2	18	1	.231
1956	San Diego	PCL	P PH	55	67	6	16	3	0	1	7	0	.239
1957	Louisville	AA	P PH	45	66	9	15	2	0	2	12	0	.227
1958	Dallas	TEX	P PH	62	121	17	27	4	1	0	13	0	.223
1959	Dallas, Houston	AA	P PH	41	77	11	26	3	2	0	12	0	.338
1959	Spokane	PCL	P PH	15	25	3	6	0	0	0	3	0	.240
1960	Montreal	INT	P PH	16	15	0	1	1	0	0	2	0	.067
1960	Poza Rica	MEX	P PH	24	48	1	15	0	0	0	6	0	.313
55-6	Gavilanes	VENZ	P	-	-	-	-	-	-	-	-	-	
56-7	Gavilanes	VENZ	P OF	-	96	-	31	-	-	-	10	-	.323
58-9	Gavilanes	VENZ	P	-	-	-	-	-	-	-	-	-	

Elston Gene "Ellie" Howard. Born February 23, 1929 at St. Louis, MO. Died December 14, 1980 in New York City, NY. 6'2", 196 lbs. BR TR

Year	Club	League	Pos	G	AB	R	H	2B	3B	HR	RBI	SB	BA
1948	Kansas City	NAL	OF C 1B	24	99	22	28	8	3	2	22	1	.283
1949	Kansas City	NAL	OF C 1B	85	307	41	83	-	-	-	-	-	.270
1950	Kansas City	NAL	OF	48	188	36	60	13	5	3	43	0	.319
1950	Muskegon	CENT	OF	54	184	22	52	6	2	9	42	0	.283
1953	Kansas City	AA	OF C	139	497	58	142	22	9	10	70	3	.286
1954	Toronto	INT	C OF	138	497	78	164	21	**16**	22	109	2	.330
1955	New York	AL	OF C	97	279	33	81	8	7	10	43	0	.290

Year	Club	League	Pos	G	AB	R	H	2B	3B	HR	RBI	SB	BA
1956	New York	AL	OF C	98	290	35	76	8	3	5	34	0	.262
1957	New York	AL	OF C 1B	110	356	33	90	13	4	8	44	2	.253
1958	New York	AL	C OF 1b	103	376	45	118	19	5	11	66	1	.314
1959	New York	AL	OF 1B C	125	443	59	121	24	6	18	73	0	.273
1960	New York	AL	C OF	107	323	29	79	11	3	6	39	3	.245
1961	New York	AL	C 1B	129	446	64	155	17	5	21	77	0	.348
1962	New York	AL	C	136	494	63	138	23	5	21	91	1	.279
1963	New York	AL	C	135	487	75	140	21	6	28	85	0	.287
1964	New York	AL	C	150	550	63	172	27	3	15	84	1	.313
1965	New York	AL	C 1B OF	110	391	38	91	15	1	9	45	0	.233
1966	New York	AL	C 1B	126	410	38	105	19	2	6	35	0	.256
1967	New York, Boston	AL	C 1B	108	315	22	56	9	0	4	28	0	.178
1968	Boston	AL	C	71	203	22	49	4	0	5	18	1	.241
54-5	San Juan	PRWL	C	-	121	-	45	-	-	7	24	-	.372

Leonard Hunt. Born in 1929. 5'9", 170 lbs. BL TL

Year	Club	League	Pos	G	AB	R	H	2B	3B	HR	RBI	SB	BA
1949	Kansas City	NAL	OF	33	111	20	35	-	-	-	-	-	.315
1950	Kansas City	NAL	OF	-	-	-	-	-	-	-	-	-	
1950	Springfield	MOV	OF	69	247	64	82	14	12	4	25	18	.332
1951	Kansas City	NAL	OF	-	-	-	-	-	-	-	-	-	
1953	Texarkana	BGST	OF	129	454	71	142	20	9	7	70	11	.313
1954	Augusta	SATL	OF	77	283	54	92	16	11	2	39	4	.325
1954	Tyler	BGST	OF	13	54	14	21	6	1	1	16	1	.389
1956	Aberdeen	NORL	OF	100	356	83	113	26	6	12	52	6	.317
1957	Aberdeen	NORL	OF	15	55	7	14	2	0	0	2	0	.255

Cowan F. "Bubba" Hyde. Born April 10, 1908 at Pontotoc, MS. 5'8 1/2", 155 lbs. BR TR

Year	Club	League	Pos	G	AB	R	H	2B	3B	HR	RBI	SB	BA
1927	Memphis	NNL	OF	-	-	-	-	-	-	-	-	-	
1930	Birmingham	NNL	OF	-	-	-	-	-	-	-	-	-	
1937	Cinc., Ind.	NAL	OF	-	-	-	-	-	-	-	-	-	
1938	Memphis	NAL	OF	-	-	-	-	-	-	-	-	-	
1939	Memphis	NAL	OF	-	-	-	-	-	-	-	-	-	
1940	Memphis	NAL	OF	-	-	-	-	-	-	-	-	-	
1940	Santa Rosa	MEX	OF	11	49	10	15	4	-	1	5	4	.306
1941	Memphis	NAL	OF	-	28	-	10	-	-	-	-	-	.357
1942	Memphis	NAL	OF	16	67	-	21	4	1	-	0	0	.313
1943	Memphis	NAL	OF	-	42	-	17	2	1	-	0	0	.405
1944	Memphis	NAL	OF	66	245	37	68	11	5	2	-	14	.278
1945	Memphis	NAL	OF	39	152	17	39	9	1	0	8	5	.257
1946	Memphis	NAL	OF	-	-	-	-	-	-	-	-	-	
1947	Memphis	NAL	OF	-	-	-	-	-	-	-	-	-	
1948	Memphis	NAL	OF	73	252	43	69	9	7	1	28	11	.274
1949	Bridgeport	COL	OF	25	98	13	32	6	0	1	23	4	.327
1949	Memphis	NAL	OF	-	-	-	-	-	-	-	-	-	
1950	Chicago, Memphis	NAL	OF	17	72	16	21	4	2	0	8	7	.292
1950	Elmwood	MADK	OF	33	143	-	45	-	-	-	5	-	.315
1951	Chicago	NAL	OF	-	-	-	-	-	-	-	-	-	
1951	Elmwood	MADK	OF	30	132	-	46	-	-	2	10	-	.348
1951	Farnham	PROV	OF	15	57	5	11	3	0	0	5	2	.193
1952	Winnipeg	MADK	OF	-	-	-	-	-	-	-	-	-	
1953	Brandon	MADK	OF	62	271	-	79	-	-	0	30	-	.292

Monford Merrill "Monte" Irvin. Born February 25, 1919 at Columbia, AL. 6'2", 195. BR TR

Year	Club	League	Pos	G	AB	R	H	2B	3B	HR	RBI	SB	BA
1937	Newark	NNL	SS	-	-	-	-	-	-	-	-	-	
1938	Newark	NNL	OF SS	-	-	-	-	-	-	-	-	-	
1939	Newark	NNL	3B OF	22	72	-	29	4	-	3	-	1	.403
1940	Newark	NNL	SS OF	36	133	-	48	8	5	4	-	3	.361
1941	Newark	NNL	OF SS	30	108	-	41	9	1	5	-	2	.380
1942	Newark	NNL	OF	8	32	-	17	6	4	2	-	1	.531
1942	Vera Cruz	MEX	2B	63	237	74	94	17	6	**20**	79	11	**.397**
1945	Newark	NNL	OF	5	18	5	4	1	0	1	3	0	.222
1946	Newark	NNL	SS OF	43	157	33	**63**	**14**	3	7	**44**	6	.401
1947	Newark	NNL	OF SS	81	287	70	91	18	-	**14**	-	19	.317
1948	Newark	NNL	OF	42	135	-	43	-	-	-	-	-	.319
1949	Jersey City	INT	OF	63	204	55	76	18	5	9	52	14	.373
1949	New York	NL	OF INF	36	76	7	17	3	2	0	7	0	.224
1950	Jersey City	INT	OF	18	51	28	26	4	1	10	33	2	.510
1950	New York	NL	OF 1B 3B	110	374	61	112	19	5	15	66	3	.299
1951	New York	NL	OF 1B	151	558	94	174	19	11	24	**121**	12	.312
1952	New York	NL	OF	46	126	10	39	2	1	4	21	0	.310

Year	Club	League	Pos	G	AB	R	H	2B	3B	HR	RBI	SB	BA
1953	New York	NL	OF	124	444	72	146	21	5	21	97	2	.329
1954	New York	NL	OF INF	135	432	62	113	13	3	19	64	7	.262
1955	Minneapolis	AA	OF	75	250	57	88	21	1	14	52	2	.352
1955	New York	NL	OF	51	150	16	38	7	1	1	17	3	.253
1956	Chicago	NL	OF	111	339	44	92	13	3	15	50	1	.271
1957	Los Angeles	PCL	OF	4	10	1	3	0	0	1	2	0	.300
40-1	San Juan	PRWL	SS	-	159	31	59	-	-	2	-	-	.371
41-2	San Juan	PRWL	SS	-	158	32	47	18	5	4	26	-	.297
44-5	San Juan	PRWL	OF	-	108	-	41	-	-	-	-	-	.380
45-6	San Juan	PRWL	OF	-	155	34	57	11	3	3	31	2	.368
46-7	San Juan	PRWL	OF	-	142	26	55	-	-	11	41	-	.387
47-8	Almendares	CWL	OF	29	99	14	24	2	1	1	8	5	.242
48-9	Almendares	CWL	OF	72	259	52	71	14	6	10	53	19	.274

Isiah "Ike" Jackson. Born in 1927. 6'1", 210 lbs. BR TR

Year	Club	League	Pos	G	AB	R	H	2B	3B	HR	RBI	SB	BA
1951	Kansas City	NAL	OF C	-	-	-	-	-	-	-	-	-	
1952	Kansas City	NAL	OF C	-	-	-	-	-	-	-	-	-	
1953	Carlsbad	LGHN	C	122	490	105	190	28	12	18	101	3	.388
1953	Kansas City	NAL	C	-	-	-	-	-	-	-	-	-	
1954	Carlsbad	LGHN	1B C	136	561	141	215	48	10	26	153	11	.383
1955	Carlsbad	LGHN	C 1B	125	482	95	144	36	6	12	91	4	.299
1956	Midland	SWL	C OF	135	539	102	187	38	6	31	138	5	.347

Samuel "Jet" Jethroe. Born January 20, 1922 at East St. Louis, IL. 6'1", 178 lbs. BB TR

Year	Club	League	Pos	G	AB	R	H	2B	3B	HR	RBI	SB	BA
1942	Cinc.-Clev	NAL	OF	-	97	-	43	6	1	0	-	1	.443
1942	Cinc.-Clev	NAL	OF	25	98	-	28	8	4	2	-	^	.286
1944	Cleveland	NAL	OF	68	275	55	97	14	2	2	-	18	.353
1945	Cleveland	NAL	OF	56	214	61	84	10	10	3	37	21	.393
1946	Cleveland	NAL	OF	62	226	54	70	-	-	6	-	20	.310
1947	Cleveland	NAL	OF	70	306	90	108	35	10	7	-	52	.353
1948	Cleveland	NAL	OF	47	186	61	55	13	4	5	30	29	.296
1948	Montreal	INT	OF	76	292	52	94	19	11	1	25	18	.322
1949	Montreal	INT	OF	153	635	154	207	34	19	17	83	89	.326
1950	Boston	NL	OF	141	582	100	159	28	8	18	58	35	.273
1951	Boston	NL	OF	148	572	101	160	29	10	18	65	35	.280
1952	Boston	NL	OF	151	608	79	141	23	7	13	58	28	.232
1953	Toledo	INT	OF	145	543	137	168	32	10	28	74	27	.309
1954	Pittsburgh	NL	OF	2	1	0	0	0	0	0	0	0	.000
1954	Toronto	INT	OF	154	593	113	181	36	8	21	84	23	.305
1955	Toronto	INT	OF	145	485	88	127	16	4	16	66	24	.262
1956	Toronto	INT	OF	149	567	105	163	25	4	19	68	22	.287
1957	Toronto	INT	OF	130	451	83	125	16	6	15	39	24	.277
1958	Toronto	INT	OF	68	184	20	43	11	-	2	18	5	.234
44-5	San Juan	PRWL	OF	-	161	37	55	-	7	1	27	-	.342
45-6	Vargas	VENZ	OF	-	-	-	-	-	5	-	-	11	
46-7	San Juan	PRWL	OF	-	39	-	13	-	-	-	2	-	.333
47-8	Almendares	CWL	OF	75	305	53	94	12	10	1	18	22	.308
48-9	Almendares	CWL	OF	64	260	52	71	9	5	5	31	32	.273
54-5	Cienfuegos	CWL	OF	25	98	21	27	1	2	4	13	6	.276

Ernest D. Johnson. Born 1931. 6'3", 165 lbs. BL TR

Year	Club	League	Pos	G	AB	R	H	2B	3B	HR	RBI	SB	BA
1949	Kansas City	NAL	OF	-	-	-	-	-	-	-	-	-	
1950	Kansas City	NAL	OF	-	-	-	-	-	-	-	-	-	
1953	Kansas City	NAL	OF	67	260	43	77	12	5	11	43	7	.296
1954	Thetford Mines	PROV	OF 1B	88	285	38	82	12	2	9	54	1	.288
1955	Macon	SATL	OF	30	110	11	32	6	1	0	15	2	.291
1955	Magic Valley	PION	OF	99	384	63	112	19	6	10	61	8	.292
1956	Des Moines	WEST	OF	134	566	100	180	32	6	8	67	5	.318
1957	Des Moines	WEST	OF	147	590	89	177	23	7	9	68	6	.300
1958	Sioux City	WEST	OF	130	533	83	164	24	6	15	92	15	.308
1959	Charleston	SATL	OF	107	339	42	90	12	1	10	43	3	.265

Louis Brown "Sweet Lou" Johnson. Born September 22, 1933 at Lexington, KY. 5'11", 170 lbs. BR TR

Year	Club	League	Pos	G	AB	R	H	2B	3B	HR	RBI	SB	BA
1953	Olean	PONY	OF	45	165	25	32	6	1	3	18	6	.194
1954	Lexington	MTST	OF	59	231	49	63	12	2	1	21	17	.273
1954	Pampa	WTNM	OF	23	90	16	29	5	0	2	11	4	.322
1955	Clinton	MOV	OF	24	80	13	19	2	5	1	12	5	.238
1955	Kansas City	NAL	OF	-	-	-	-	-	-	-	-	-	

Year	Club	League	Pos	G	AB	R	H	2B	3B	HR	RBI	SB	BA
1955	St. Jean	PROV	OF	4	10	5	3	1	1	0	2	0	.300
1956	Ponca City	SOON	OF	110	423	88	125	14	11	11	75	33	.296
1957	Burlington	III	OF	87	274	43	67	17	2	6	42	22	.245
1958	Burlington	III	OF	18	60	11	7	0	0	3	7	4	.117
1958	Paris	MIDW	OF	105	395	**103**	144	23	7	15	77	**35**	**.365**
1959	Lancaster	EAST	OF	97	361	54	114	13	11	9	63	4	.316
1959	San Antonio	TEX	OF	30	113	17	37	3	4	2	25	1	.327
1960	Chicago	NL	OF	34	68	6	14	2	1	0	1	13	.206
1960	Houston	AA	OF	103	409	54	118	23	6	12	58	3	.289
1961	Los Angeles	AL	OF	1	0	0	0	0	0	0	0	0	
1961	Toronto	INT	OF	146	510	93	146	22	18	13	64	**21**	.286
1962	Milwaukee	NL	OF	61	117	22	33	4	5	2	13	6	.282
1962	Toronto	INT	OF	90	341	56	108	15	10	8	40	6	.317
1963	Denver	PCL	OF	12	46	4	6	3	0	0	3	1	.130
1963	Toronto, Syracuse	INT	OF	123	473	90	140	22	9	15	71	14	.296
1964	Spokane	PCL	OF	153	589	93	**193**	29	5	18	70	23	.328
1965	Los Angeles	NL	OF	131	468	57	121	24	1	12	58	15	.259
1965	Spokane	PCL	OF	15	61	10	19	4	1	4	11	4	.311
1966	Los Angeles	NL	OF	152	526	71	143	20	2	17	73	8	.272
1967	Los Angeles	NL	OF	104	330	39	89	14	1	11	41	4	.270
1968	Chicago	NL	OF	62	205	14	50	14	3	1	14	3	.244
1968	Cleveland	AL	OF	65	202	25	52	11	1	5	23	6	.257
1969	California	AL	OF	67	133	10	27	8	0	0	9	5	.203
63-4		OCC	OF	-	55	-	15	-	-	3	10	-	.273
63-4		PANA	OF	-	105	-	31	-	-	3	18	-	.295
64-5		PRWL	OF	-	237	-	81	-	-	6	41	-	**.342**

Edrick "Leon" Kellman. Born 1927 in Panama. 5'11", 165 lbs. BR TR

Year	Club	League	Pos	G	AB	R	H	2B	3B	HR	RBI	SB	BA
1946	Cleveland	NAL	3B C P	58	192	-	57	12	2	3	35	-	.297
1947	Cleveland	NAL	3B	-	216	46	66	-	-	-	54	-	.306
1948	Cleveland	NAL	3B 2B	73	264	49	81	17	4	2	31	13	.307
1949	Louisville	NAL	3B	79	280	31	71	-	-	-	-	-	.254
1950	Memphis	NAL	3B	65	234	44	77	12	2	2	34	9	.329
1951	Vera Cruz	MEX	C 3B SS	75	271	58	79	9	2	10	48	1	.292
1952	Ind., Memphis	NAL	3B OF	-	-	-	-	-	-	-	-	-	
1952	Licey	DMSL	3B	-	14	1	1	0	0	0	0	1	.071
1953	Memphis	NAL	3B	-	-	-	-	-	-	-	-	-	
1953	Nuevo Laredo	MEX	C	79	276	47	74	14	3	3	43	7	.268
1954	Nuevo Laredo	MEX	C	73	255	74	91	15	5	13	61	8	.357
1955	Nuevo Laredo	MEX	C	100	351	80	118	23	3	8	65	3	.336
1956	N.Laredo, Yucatan	MEX	C 3B	101	296	50	88	11	2	8	41	3	.297
1957	Yucatan	MEX	C	104	333	46	103	19	2	5	57	3	.309
1958	Yucatan, Mex.City	MEX	C	34	104	16	29	3	3	1	11	0	.279
45-6	General Electric	PANA	3B	41	135	26	50	9	1	2	26	3	.370
46-7	General Electric	PANA	3B	41	149	26	41	11	3	1	22	4	.275
47-8	CPR	PANA	3B	42	123	33	36	8	3	2	16	7	.293
48-9	Spur Cola	PANA	3B	38	129	23	46	9	0	1	30	4	.357
49-0	Spur Cola	PANA	3B	29	95	12	20	3	1	3	15	3	.211
50-1	Spur Cola	PANA	3B	40	134	29	46	12	1	2	26	10	.343
51-2	Spur Cola	PANA	3B	29	91	11	25	4	3	3	18	1	.275
52-3	Spur Cola	PANA	3B	34	112	20	34	7	2	5	29	0	.304
53-4	Spur Cola	PANA	C	36	102	11	26	7	0	1	22	0	.255
54-5	Spur Cola	PANA	C	24	39	3	5	1	0	1	2	0	.128

John Irvin Kennedy. Born November 23, 1934 at Sumter, SC. 5'10", 175 lbs. BR TR

Year	Club	League	Pos	G	AB	R	H	2B	3B	HR	RBI	SB	BA
1953	St. Cloud	NORL	2B	125	496	93	130	30	7	3	42	33	.262
1954	Birmingham	NAL	SS 3B	76	289	69	79	13	5	4	35	16	.273
1955	Birmingham	NAL	3B SS	-	-	-	-	-	-	-	-	-	
1957	High-Point,Thomas.	CARO	3B SS	120	441	73	119	26	2	19	81	23	.270
1957	Philadelphia	NL	3B	5	2	1	0	0	0	0	0	0	.000
1958	Tulsa	TEX	INF	110	364	55	82	12	3	6	35	15	.225
1959	Des Moines	III	SS	88	281	50	64	10	2	3	41	15	.228
1960	Asheville	SATL	UTL	104	317	34	78	13	0	8	44	7	.246
1961	Jacksonville	SATL		1	4	0	1	0	0	0	0	0	.250

Walter Fenner "Buck" Leonard. Born September 8, 1907 At Rocky Mount, NC. 5'10", 185 lbs. BL TL

Year	Club	League	Pos	G	AB	R	H	2B	3B	HR	RBI	SB	BA
1934	Homestead	NNL	1B	9	35	-	14	1	0	2	-	0	.400
1935	Homestead	NNL	1B	39	151	-	51	14	2	2	-	0	.338
1936	Homestead	NNL	1B	5	21	-	5	1	0	3	-	0	.238
1937	Homestead	NNL	1B	14	54	-	18	1	0	2	-	0	.333

Year	Club	League	Pos	G	AB	R	H	2B	3B	HR	RBI	SB	BA
1938	Homestead	NNL	1B	18	58	-	20	-	0	4	-	0	.345
1939	Homestead	NNL	1B	25	69	-	22	2	0	4	-	0	.319
1940	Homestead	NNL	1B	52	175	-	67	15	3	**8**	-	2	.383
1941	Homestead	NNL	1B	37	116	-	37	4	5	6	-	2	.319
1942	Homestead	NNL	1B	20	79	-	14	4	0	0	-	3	.177
1943	Homestead	NNL	1B	-	187	-	56	11	11	3	-	0	.299
1944	Homestead	NNL	1B	48	161	32	51	11	6	**7**	30	1	.317
1945	Homestead	NNL	1B	40	144	29	54	9	4	6	25	1	.375
1946	Homestead	NNL	1B	37	118	28	38	5	4	5	37	2	.322
1947	Homestead	NNL	1B	31	105	31	43	11	-	7	-	1	.410
1948	Homestead	NNL	1B	47	157	-	62	-	-	**13**	-	-	**.395**
1949	Homestead	BAA	1B	-	-	-	-	-	-	-	-	-	
1950	Homestead		1B	-	-	-	-	-	-	-	-	-	
1951	Torreon	MEX	1B	83	273	64	88	19	1	14	64	5	.322
1952	Torreon	MEX	1B	86	295	50	96	15	1	8	71	12	.325
1953	Portsmouth	PIED	1B	10	33	5	11	2	0	0	4	1	.333
1953	Torreon	MEX	1B	58	190	39	63	20	2	5	38	4	.332
1955	Durango	CMEX	1B	62	218	46	68	14	3	13	60	-	.312
36-7	Marianao	CWL	1B	-	171	26	52	3	1	1	19	4	.304
40-1	Mayaquez	PRWL	1B	-	118	45	46	**17**	0	**8**	-	-	.390
48-9	Marianao	CWL	1B	30	65	9	15	4	0	2	18	0	.231

Edward Locke. Born 1923. 5'11", 181 lbs. BL TR

Year	Club	League	Pos	G	AB	R	H	2B	3B	HR	RBI	SB	BA
1943	Cincinnati	NAL		-	-	-	-	-	-	-	-	-	
1944	Kansas City	NAL	P	20	37	4	11	2	0	0	-	-	.297
1945	Kansas City	NAL		-	-	-	-	-	-	-	-	0	
1945	Tampico	MEX		-	-	-	-	-	-	-	-	-	
1948	Chicago	NAL		-	-	-	-	-	-	-	-	-	
1949	KC, New York	NAL		-	-	-	-	-	-	-	-	-	
1950	New York	NAL		-	-	-	-	-	-	-	-	-	
1950	Springfield	MOV	P OF	44	148	34	43	5	8	0	18	2	.291
1951	Kansas City	NAL		-	-	-	-	-	-	-	-	-	
1951	Mexico City	MEX		-	-	-	-	-	-	-	-	-	
1952	Vancouver	WINT	P OF PH	98	257	30	68	11	9	2	42	0	.265
1953	Amarillo	WTNM	P OF	82	280	59	103	15	4	17	74	0	.368
1953	Yakima	WINT	P PH	21	44	5	12	2	1	0	5	0	.273
1954	Amarillo	WTNM	P OF	109	357	62	111	27	1	12	68	0	.311
1955	Amarillo	WTNM	P OF	20	65	12	22	2	2	5	23	0	.338
1955	Artesia	LGHN	P OF	83	245	50	87	21	6	11	50	0	.355
1956	Monterrey	MEX	P PH	33	62	6	14	2	1	1	5	1	.226
1956	Victoria	BGST	P OF	29	58	7	17	2	1	1	8	2	.293
1957	Monterrey	MEX	P PH	52	109	10	29	1	2	1	9	0	.266
1958	Monterrey	MEX	P PH	43	108	9	21	6	0	0	11	0	.194
1959	Monterrey	MEX	P PH	47	110	7	36	4	0	1	15	0	.327
1967	Monterrey	MEX		-	-	-	-	-	-	-	-	-	
56-7		MXWL		-	-	-	-	-	-	-	-	-	
57-8		MXWL		-	-	-	-	-	-	-	-	-	

Lester Lockett. Born March 25, 1912 at Princeton, IN. 5' 10", 185 lbs. BR TR

Year	Club	League	Pos	G	AB	R	H	2B	3B	HR	RBI	SB	BA
1937	St. Louis	NAL	SS	-	-	-	-	-	-	-	-	-	
1938	Birmingham	NAL	SS	2	5	0	0	0	0	0	-	0	.000
1940	Cincinnati	NAL	OF	-	-	-	-	-	-	-	-	-	
1941	Birmingham	NAL	3B	20	67	-	22	3	0	1	-	0	.328
1942	Birmingham, Chicago	NAL	3B 2B	15	54	-	17	-	2	0	-	0	.315
1943	Birmingham	NAL	LF	-	76	-	31	5	4	2	-	0	.408
1944	Birmingham	NAL	OF	57	191	35	49	8	4	0	-	3	.257
1945	Birmingham	NAL	OF	61	229	40	70	11	2	3	30	8	.306
1946	Birmingham	NAL	3B OF	3	14	-	2	1	1	0	-	0	.143
1947	Baltimore	NNL	OF 3B	76	278	43	87	11	0	1	-	4	.313
1948	Baltimore	NNL	LF	71	277	-	107	-	-	-	-	-	.386
1949	Baltimore	NAL	OF	-	-	-	-	-	-	-	-	-	
1950	Chicago	NAL	OF	31	103	29	31	7	0	2	13	9	.301
1951	Farnham	PROV	OF	33	129	14	28	5	0	1	21	2	.217
1952	Winnipeg	MADK	OF	-	-	-	-	-	-	-	-	-	
1953	Carman	MADK	OF	56	232	-	77	-	-	1	30	-	.332
1953	Torreon	MEX	OF	8	37	7	13	3	1	0	13	-	.351

Bernell "Chick" Longest. BL TR

Year	Club	League	Pos	G	AB	R	H	2B	3B	HR	RBI	SB	BA
1946	Chicago	NAL	2B	-	-	-	-	-	-	-	-	-	
1947	Chicago	NAL	2B	-	-	-	-	-	-	-	-	-	

Year	Club	League	Pos	G	AB	R	H	2B	3B	HR	RBI	SB	BA
1951	Jalisco	MEX	UTL	13	44	7	14	1	1	0	7	2	.318
1952	Carman	MADK	UTL	-	-	-	-	-	-	-	-	-	
1953	Carman	MADK	UTL	57	221	-	71	-	-	6	40	-	.321
1955	Burlington	PROV	OF	38	152	17	52	4	1	1	20	2	.342

Benjamin "Benny" Lott. Born in 1927. 5'11", 167 lbs. BR TR

Year	Club	League	Pos	G	AB	R	H	2B	3B	HR	RBI	SB	BA
1949	New York	NAL	SS	-	-	-	-	-	-	-	-	-	
1950	Indianapolis, NY	NAL	3B	62	237	43	72	11	3	9	39	5	.304
1951	Colorado Springs	WEST	2B	15	55	14	19	3	-	3	14	4	.345
1951	Indianapolis	NAL	3B	-	-	44	-	17		9	-	-	
1951	Waterloo	III	3B OF	26	92	21	28	6	2	4	15	5	.304
1952	Oriente	DMSL	3B	-	179	32	44	-	-	0	30	13	.246
1953	Carman	MADK	3B	37	136	-	41	-	-	1	21	-	.301
1953	Escogido	DMSL	3B	-	25	-	3	-	0	-	1	-	.120
1953	Tulsa	TEX	UTIL	12	33	5	10	2	0	0	0	0	.303
1955	San Angelo	LGHN	OF 3B	110	402	95	110	15	3	16	72	19	.274

Louis Louden. Born August 19, 1919 at West Point, VA. Died August 31, 1989 in Newark, NJ. 5'10", 172 lbs. BR TR

Year	Club	League	Pos	G	AB	R	H	2B	3B	HR	RBI	SB	BA
1942	New York	NNL	OF C	-	-	-	-	-	-	-	-	-	
1943	New York	NNL	C	26	86	-	24	4	0	0	-	-	.279
1944	New York	NNL	C	31	113	14	30	4	1	6	14	1	.265
1945	New York	NNL	C	24	81	9	20	6	1	1	10	0	.247
1946	New York	NNL	C	32	116	21	29	5	0	0	16	2	.250
1947	New York	NNL	C	-	131	21	38	7	-	3	-	1	.290
1948	New York	NNL	C	-	-	-	-	-	-	-	-	-	
1949	New York	NAL	C	40	143	20	35	-	-	-	-	-	.245
1950	New York	NAL	C	28	103	15	32	2	4	1	16	1	.311
1951	Jalisco	MEX	C	17	49	9	11	4	0	0	9	1	.224
1952	Winnipeg	MADK	C	-	-	-	-	-	-	-	-	-	
1953	Winnipeg	MADK	C	65	274	-	69	-	-	2	32	-	.252
1957	El Paso	SWL	C	24	72	12	14	1	0	0	15	0	.194
47-8	Ponce	PRWL	C	-	168	32	51	9	3	2	36	-	.304
50-1	Cienfuegos	CWL	C	11	18	1	4	1	0	0	0	0	.222

Everett Marcell. Born September 1, 1916 at New Orleans, LA. Died 1990 in Los Angeles, CA. 6'2", 190 lbs. BR TR

Year	Club	League	Pos	G	AB	R	H	2B	3B	HR	RBI	SB	BA
1939	Kansas City	NAL	C	-	-	-	-	-	-	-	-	-	
1940	Homestead	NNL	C	-	-	-	-	-	-	-	-	-	
1941	New York	NNL	C	-	-	-	-	-	-	-	-	-	
1947	Baltimore	NNL	C	-	35	5	8	0	0	0	-	1	.229
1950	Farnham	PROV	C	89	294	41	80	10	1	7	42	3	.272

Luis Angel "Canena" Marquez y Sanchez. Born October 28, 1925 at Aguadilla, PR. Died March 1, 1988 in Aguadilla, PR. 5'10 1/2", 179 lbs. BR TR

Year	Club	League	Pos	G	AB	R	H	2B	3B	HR	RBI	SB	BA
1945	New York	NNL	OF	-	-	-	-	-	-	1	13	3	.309
1946	Balt., Homestead	NNL	OF	22	81	14	25	3	0	1	13	29	
1947	Homestead	NNL	OF	-	230	50	96	15	-	5	-	29	.417
1948	Homestead	NNL	OF	-	-	-	-	-	-	-	-	-	
1949	Newark	INT	OF	18	69	13	17	3	0	1	6	3	.246
1949	Portland	PCL	OF	132	511	87	150	26	7	4	46	32	.294
1950	Portland	PCL	OF	194	775	136	241	41	19	9	86	38	.311
1951	Boston	NL	OF	68	122	19	24	5	1	0	11	4	.197
1952	Milwaukee	AA	OF	136	521	100	180	38	10	14	99	24	.345
1953	Toledo	AA	OF	130	510	77	149	28	3	13	81	37	.292
1954	Chicago, Pittsburgh	NL	OF	31	21	5	2	0	0	0	0	3	.095
1954	Toledo	AA	OF	58	229	46	76	18	1	8	36	7	.332
1955	Portland	PCL	OF	112	381	60	119	24	1	8	57	5	.312
1955	Toledo	AA	IF	21	75	10	18	6	1	2	8	0	.240
1956	Portland	PCL	OF	155	602	122	207	27	10	25	110	18	.344
1957	Portland	PCL	OF	167	610	92	169	31	6	31	85	13	.277
1958	Portland	PCL	OF	109	335	43	89	13	6	8	42	2	.266
1959	Dallas	AA	OF	142	510	80	176	24	4	18	78	14	.345
1960	Dallas-Ft. Worth	AA	OF	144	469	57	124	30	3	3	30	6	.264
1961	Dallas-Ft. Worth	AA	OF	18	43	5	9	3	1	0	3	0	.209
1961	Williamsport	EAST	OF	19	54	10	14	1	1	1	7	1	.259
1962	Poza Rica	MEX	OF	126	460	94	164	28	4	21	91	9	.357
1963	Poza Rica	MEX	OF	118	401	67	126	19	3	20	72	8	.314
45-6	Aquadilla	PRWL	OF	-	-	-	-	-	10	-	-	-	
46-7	Aquadilla	PRWL	OF	-	224	69	78	27	-	14	-	27	.348
47-8	Aquadilla	PRWL	OF	-	-	-	-	-	-	-	-	20	
48-9	Aquadilla	PRWL	OF	-	-	-	108	-	-	-	-	29	

Year	Club	League	Pos	G	AB	R	H	2B	3B	HR	RBI	SB	BA
49-0	Aquadilla	PRWL	OF	-	233	56	73	-	10	-	-	23	.313
51-2	San Juan	PRWL	OF	-	275	42	73	-	3	8	29	23	.265
52-3	San Juan	PRWL	OF	-	288	-	88	-	-	3	34	-	.306
53-4	Mayaquez	PRWL	OF	-	282	**51**	94	-	-	5	43	**32**	.333
54-5	Mayaquez	PRWL	OF	-	165	-	60	-	10	5	21	28	.364
55-6	Ponce	PRWL	OF	-	191	32	47	12	3	3	18	5	.246
56-7	Ponce,Mayaquez	PRWL	OF	73	256	**56**	70	12	1	9	38	11	.273
57-8	Ponce	PRWL	OF	62	209	37	65	**15**	**7**	9	40	5	.311
58-9	Ponce	PRWL	OF	63	220	40	68	14	4	7	34	4	.309
59-0	Ponce	PRWL	OF	56	173	24	44	10	1	5	19	5	.254
60-1	Ponce	PRWL	OF	41	79	11	17	6	1	0	6	3	.215
61-2	Ponce	PRWL	OF	12	12	0	1	1	0	0	1	0	.083

Willie Howard Mays. Born May 6, 1931 at Westfield, AL. 5'10 1/2", 170 lbs. BR TR

Year	Club	League	Pos	G	AB	R	H	2B	3B	HR	RBI	SB	BA
1948	Birmingham	NAL	OF	25	84	10	22	3	0	1	7	1	.262
1949	Birmingham	NAL	OF	75	270	63	84	-	-	-	-	-	.311
1950	Birmingham	NAL	OF	27	106	22	35	7	2	4	28	2	.330
1950	Trenton	INST	OF	81	306	50	108	20	8	4	55	7	.353
1951	Minneapolis	AA	OF	35	149	38	71	18	3	8	30	5	.477
1951	New York	NL	OF	121	464	59	127	22	5	20	68	7	.274
1952	New York	NL	OF	34	127	17	30	2	4	4	23	4	.236
1954	New York	NL	OF	151	565	119	195	33	**13**	41	110	8	**.345**
1955	New York	NL	OF	152	580	123	185	18	**13**	51	127	24	.319
1956	New York	NL	OF	152	578	101	191	27	8	36	84	**40**	.330
1957	New York	NL	OF	152	585	112	195	26	**20**	35	97	**38**	.333
1958	San Francisco	NL	OF	152	600	**121**	208	33	11	29	96	31	.347
1959	San Francisco	NL	OF	151	575	125	180	43	5	34	104	**27**	.313
1960	San Francisco	NL	OF	153	595	107	**190**	29	12	29	103	25	.319
1961	San Francisco	NL	OF	154	572	129	**176**	32	3	40	123	18	.308
1962	San Francisco	NL	OF	162	621	130	189	36	5	**49**	141	18	.304
1963	San Francisco	NL	OF SS	157	596	115	187	32	7	38	103	8	.314
1964	San Francisco	NL	OF INF	157	578	121	171	21	9	**47**	111	19	.296
1965	San Francisco	NL	OF	157	558	118	177	21	3	**52**	112	9	.317
1966	San Francisco	NL	OF	152	552	99	159	29	4	37	103	5	.288
1967	San Francisco	NL	OF	141	486	83	128	22	2	22	70	6	.263
1968	San Francisco	NL	OF 1B	148	498	84	144	20	5	23	79	12	.289
1969	San Francisco	NL	OF 1B	117	403	64	114	17	3	13	58	6	.283
1970	San Francisco	NL	OF 1B	139	478	94	139	15	2	28	83	5	.291
1971	San Francisco	NL	OF 1B	136	417	82	113	24	5	18	61	23	.271
1972	S.F., New York	NL	OF 1B	88	244	35	61	11	1	8	22	4	.250
1973	New York	NL	OF 1B	66	209	24	44	10	0	6	25	1	.211
54-5	Santurce	PRWL	OF	-	172	63	68	15	**7**	12	33	10	**.395**

Clinton H. "Butch" McCord Jr.. Born November 2, 1925 at Nashville, TN. 5'10", 168 lbs. BL TL

Year	Club	League	Pos	G	AB	R	H	2B	3B	HR	RBI	SB	BA
1947	Baltimore	NNL	1B OF	-	-	-	-	-	-	-	-	-	
1948	Baltimore	NNL	1B OF	-	-	-	-	-	-	-	-	-	
1949	Baltimore	NAL	1B	55	182	29	49	-	-	-	-	-	.269
1950	Baltimore, Chicago	NAL	OF	31	106	19	39	1	-	1	14	5	.368
1951	Paris	MOV	1B	121	476	132	173	38	12	16	118	22	.363
1952	Paris	MOV	1B	119	482	123	189	40	15	15	109	20	.392
1953	Denver	WEST	1B	101	299	39	84	19	2	5	39	3	.281
1954	Denver	WEST	1B OF	85	246	43	88	18	4	6	61	4	.358
1955	Richmond	INT	1B	139	462	49	119	18	9	4	52	4	.258
1956	Columbus	INT	1B	147	488	62	134	23	3	8	52	0	.275
1957	Louisville	AA	1B	140	554	73	148	30	9	7	55	3	.267
1958	Macon	SATL	1B	137	501	70	153	37	2	10	81	8	.305
1959	Victoria	TEX	1B	136	526	83	157	27	6	10	57	1	.298
1960	St. Paul	AA	1B	17	56	2	15	0	1	1	6	0	.268
1960	Victoria	TEX	1B	117	420	61	126	19	1	7	56	3	.300
1961	Victoria, Ardmore	TEX	1B	53	172	20	49	10	0	0	15	0	.285

Terris "The Great" McDuffie. Born July 22, 1910 at Mobile, AL. Died in New York City, NY. 6'2", 200 lbs. BR TR

Year	Club	League	Pos	G	AB	R	H	2B	3B	HR	RBI	SB	BA
1930	Birmingham	NNL	OF	61	186	-	54	10	2	3	-	16	.290
1932	Balt. Cubans, Bach.	NNL	OF	11	33	-	11	0	0	0	-	0	.333
1940	Santa Rosa	MEX	P	10	25	4	10	3	0	0	5	0	.400
1941	Homestead	NNL	P	2	7	-	2	-	-	-	-	-	.286
1943	Torreon	MEX	P	28	70	3	21	4	0	0	9	0	.300

Year	Club	League	Pos	G	AB	R	H	2B	3B	HR	RBI	SB	BA
Clyde McNeal. Born December 15, 1928. 6', 185 lbs. BR TR													
1945	Chicago	NAL	SS	-	-	-	-	-	-	-	-	-	
1946	Chicago	NAL	SS	-	-	-	-	-	-	-	-	-	
1947	Chicago	NAL	SS	-	-	-	-	-	-	-	-	-	
1948	Chicago	NAL	2B	72	263	33	66	18	4	5	33	5	.251
1949	Chicago	NAL	2B	85	286	52	76	-	-	-	-	-	.266
1950	Chicago	NAL	SS	42	168	38	48	13	3	5	18	20	.286
1953	Elmira	EAST	3B SS	133	472	61	130	35	7	9	70	9	.275
1954	Montreal	INT	SS 2B 3B	4	8	0	1	0	0	0	0	0	.125
1954	Newport News	PIED	SS 2B 3B	75	259	53	80	19	2	10	53	13	.309
1955	Monterrey	MEX	INF	12	37	10	10	1	0	0	7	3	.270
1955	Newport News	PIED	SS	60	212	51	57	10	0	12	46	4	.269
1955	Pueblo	WEST	3B	33	81	11	16	3	0	2	9	4	.198
1956	Cedar Rapids	III	2B 3B	116	452	86	137	18	1	27	89	12	.303
1957	Cedar Rapids	III	2B	1	1	0	0	0	0	0	0	0	.000
1957	Pueblo	WEST	2B 3B	19	54	7	10	3	0	1	5	0	.185
Saturnino Orestes Armas "Minnie" Minoso y Arrieta. Born November 29, 1922 at Havana Cuba. 5'10", 175. BR TR													
1945	New York	NNL	3B	-	-	-	-	-	-	-	-	-	
1946	New York	NNL	3B	33	123	22	32	7	3	3	16	1	.260
1947	New York	NNL	3B	55	228	56	67	14	0	3	-	7	.294
1948	Dayton	CENT	3B 2B	11	40	14	21	7	1	1	8	6	.525
1948	New York	NNL	3B	-	-	-	-	-	-	-	-	-	
1949	Cleveland	AL	OF	9	16	2	3	0	0	1	1	0	.188
1949	San Diego	PCL	OF	137	532	99	158	19	7	22	75	13	.297
1950	San Diego	PCL	3B OF SS	169	599	130	203	40	10	20	115	30	.339
1951	Cleveland, Chicago	AL	OF 3B 1B SS	146	530	112	173	34	**14**	10	76	31	.326
1952	Chicago	AL	OF 3B SS	147	569	96	160	24	9	13	61	22	.281
1953	Chicago	AL	OF 3B	151	556	104	174	24	8	15	104	25	.313
1954	Chicago	AL	OF 3B	153	568	119	182	29	**13**	19	116	18	.320
1955	Chicago	AL	OF 3B	139	517	79	149	26	7	10	70	19	.288
1956	Chicago	AL	OF 3B 1B	151	545	106	172	29	**11**	21	88	12	.316
1957	Chicago	AL	OF 3B	153	568	96	176	**36**	5	12	103	18	.310
1958	Cleveland	AL	OF 3B	149	556	94	168	25	2	24	80	14	.302
1959	Cleveland	AL	OF	148	570	92	172	32	0	21	92	8	.302
1960	Chicago	AL	OF	**154**	591	89	**184**	32	4	20	105	17	.311
1961	Chicago	AL	OF	152	540	91	151	28	3	14	82	9	.280
1962	St. Louis	NL	OF	39	97	14	19	5	0	1	10	4	.196
1963	Washington	AL	OF 3B	109	315	38	72	12	2	4	30	8	.229
1964	Chicago	AL	OF	30	31	4	7	0	0	1	5	0	.226
1964	Indianapolis	PCL	OF 3B	52	178	22	47	11	0	4	26	6	.264
1965	Jalisco	MEX	OF 3B 1B	134	469	**106**	169	**35**	10	14	82	7	.360
1966	Jalisco	MEX	1B	107	376	70	131	18	1	6	45	6	.348
1967	Jalisco	MEX	1B OF	13	37	5	9	1	2	0	3	1	.243
1967	Orizara	MXSE	1B OF 3B	36	100	20	35	7	3	5	19	3	.350
1968	Jalisco	MEX	1B	22	54	9	16	5	1	2	13	1	.296
1968	Puerto Mexico	MXSE	1B OF 3B	56	145	30	53	17	2	4	23	2	.366
1969	Jalisco	MEX	1B OF 3B	36	103	18	33	3	1	2	14	0	.320
1969	Puerto Mexico	MXSE	1B OF	74	193	33	58	10	2	2	32	6	.301
1970	Torreon	MEX	1B	40	47	6	22	6	0	2	17	0	.468
1971	Torreon	MEX	1B 2B	112	336	37	106	15	2	6	57	5	.315
1972	Torreon	MEX	1B	121	425	48	121	24	1	12	63	5	.285
1973	Torreon	MEX	1B OF	120	407	50	108	15	1	12	83	10	.265
1976	Chicago	AL	DH PH	3	8	0	1	0	0	0	0	0	.125
1980	Chicago	AL	PH	2	2	0	0	0	0	0	0	0	.000
45-6	Marianao	CWL	OF	37	143	14	42	7	2	0	13	5	.294
46-7	Marianao	CWL	OF	64	253	36	63	9	5	0	20	7	.249
47-8	Marianao	CWL	OF	70	270	43	77	15	13	1	36	7	.285
48-9	Marianao	CWL	OF	69	260	42	69	8	5	4	27	9	.265
50-1	Marianao	CWL	OF	66	252	54	81	12	6	4	41	10	.321
51-2	Marianao	CWL	OF	42	144	19	39	6	1	2	10	1	.271
52-3	Marianao	CWL	OF	71	266	67	87	9	5	13	42	13	.327
53-4	Marianao	CWL	OF	47	176	25	52	9	3	9	36	2	.295
55-6	Marianao	CWL	OF	64	252	47	69	10	3	8	35	8	.274
56-7	Marianao	CWL		50	218	40	68	13	3	7	38	0	**.312**
57-8	Marianao	CWL	OF	58	238	37	60	9	1	8	34	3	.252
58-9	Marianao	CWL		55	233	33	60	8	1	5	25	6	.258
59-0	Marianao	CWL	OF	45	169	25	39	3	2	4	23	4	.231
60-1	Marianao	CWL	OF	35	128	12	32	7	1	1	12	1	.250

Year	Club	League	Pos	G	AB	R	H	2B	3B	HR	RBI	SB	BA
Lee Moody. BR TR													
1944	Kansas City	NAL	1B OF	48	171	15	43	7	3	1	-	2	.251
1945	Kansas City	NAL	1B OF	45	169	21	55	12	3	0	27	3	.325
1946	KC, Birmingham	NAL	OF	-	-	-	-	-	-	-	-	-	
1947	KC, Birmingham	NAL	OF	-	-	-	-	-	-	-	-	-	
1950	Cairo	KITT	OF	38	140	17	39	2	5	0	14	1	.279
1951	Three Rivers	PROV	1B OF	60	219	18	53	4	0	0	16	2	.242
Euthumn "Eudie" Napier. Born January 3, 1915 at Cleveland, OH. 5'9", 190 lbs. BL TR													
1946	Homestead	NNL	C	-	-	-	-	-	-	-	-	-	
1947	Homestead	NNL	C	-	119	15	34	3	-	2	-	2	.286
1948	Homestead	NNL	C	-	-	-	-	-	-	-	-	-	
1950	Homestead		C	-	-	-	-	-	-	-	-	-	
1951	Farnham	PROV	C	93	319	47	91	14	1	8	42	4	.285
Charles Lenard "Charlie" Neal. Born January 30, 1931 at Longview, TX. 5'10", 165 lbs. BR TR													
1949	Atlanta	NSL	INF	-	-	-	-	-	-	-	-	-	
1950	Hornell	PONY	INF	119	402	96	121	23	5	11	83	32	.301
1951	Lancaster	INST	2B	136	502	**114**	162	18	**24**	12	86	**22**	.323
1952	Elmira	EAST	2B	126	418	50	103	16	6	2	69	10	.246
1953	Newport News	PIED	2B SS	124	444	83	135	24	12	5	74	24	.304
1954	St. Paul	AA	2B	146	585	101	159	25	13	18	66	20	.272
1955	Montreal	INT	2B	145	558	111	153	29	**14**	16	75	13	.274
1956	Brooklyn	NL	2B SS	62	136	22	39	5	1	2	14	2	.287
1957	Brooklyn	NL	INF	128	448	62	121	13	7	12	62	11	.270
1958	Los Angeles	NL	2B SS	140	473	87	120	9	6	22	65	7	.254
1959	Los Angeles	NL	2B SS	151	616	103	177	30	**11**	19	83	17	.287
1960	Los Angeles	NL	2B SS	139	477	60	122	23	2	8	40	5	.256
1961	Los Angeles	NL	2B	108	341	40	80	6	1	10	48	3	.235
1962	New York	NL	INF	136	508	59	132	14	9	11	58	2	.260
1963	New York, Cinc..	NL	INF	106	317	28	67	13	1	3	21	2	.211
Richard Newberry. Born in 1926. 5'8", 165 lbs. BR TR													
1947	Chicago	NAL	SS	-	-	-	-	-	-	-	-	-	
1951	Duluth	NORL	2B	121	494	97	143	26	12	9	66	30	.289
1952	Duluth	NORL	2B	122	488	101	150	21	15	2	58	36	.307
1953	Duluth	NORL	2B	124	500	120	163	20	10	5	93	15	.326
1954	Duluth	NORL	2B 3B	94	367	70	121	23	4	5	51	12	.330
Donald "Newk" Newcombe. Born June 14, 1926 at Madison, NJ. 6'4", 220 lbs. BL TR													
1944	Newark	NNL	P	10	13	-	3	0	0	0	1	0	.231
1945	Newark	NNL	P	20	50	6	10	-	0	0	5	2	.200
1946	Nashua	NENG	P	43	74	10	23	5	3	2	14	0	.311
1947	Nashua	NENG	P	48	107	14	29	6	0	0	18	0	.271
1948	Montreal	INT	P	42	68	6	18	4	0	1	12	0	.265
1949	Brooklyn	NL	P	39	96	8	22	4	0	0	10	0	.229
1949	Montreal	INT	P	-	-	-	-	-	-	-	-	-	
1950	Brooklyn	NL	P	40	97	8	24	3	1	1	8	0	.247
1951	Brooklyn	NL	P	40	103	11	23	3	1	0	8	0	.223
1954	Brooklyn	NL	P	31	47	6	15	1	0	0	4	0	.319
1955	Brooklyn	NL	P	57	117	18	42	9	1	7	23	1	.359
1956	Brooklyn	NL	P	52	111	13	26	6	0	2	16	1	.234
1957	Brooklyn	NL	P	34	74	8	17	2	0	1	9	0	.230
1958	Los Angeles, Cinc.	NL	P	50	72	11	26	1	0	1	9	0	.361
1959	Cincinnati	NL	P	61	105	10	32	2	0	3	21	0	.305
1960	Cincinnati	NL	P	24	36	0	5	1	0	0	1	0	.139
1960	Cleveland	AL	P	24	20	1	6	1	0	0	1	0	.300
1961	Spokane	PCL	P PH	41	62	5	14	1	0	1	7	0	.226
1962	Chunichi	JAP	OF 1B	81	279	34	73	23	0	12	43	-	.262
46-7	Matanzas	CWL	P	-	-	-	-	-	-	-	-	-	
48-9	Marianao,Almend.	CWL	P	11	12	4	4	0	0	0	2	0	.333
Rafael Miguel "Ray" Noble y Magee. Born March 15, 1919 at Central Hatillo, Cuba. 5' 11 1/2", 205 lbs. BR TR													
1945	New York	NNL	C	16	33	1	3	0	0	0	2	0	.091
1946	New York	NNL	C	-	-	-	-	-	-	-	-	-	
1947	New York	NNL	C	-	83	22	27	10	-	-	-	3	.325
1948	New York	NNL	C	-	-	-	-	-	-	-	-	-	
1949	Jersey City	INT	C	67	189	33	49	6	1	7	29	1	.259
1950	New York	NAL	C	-	-	-	-	-	-	-	-	-	
1950	Oakland	PCL	C	110	345	58	109	23	3	15	76	4	.316

Year	Club	League	Pos	G	AB	R	H	2B	3B	HR	RBI	SB	BA
1951	New York	NL	C	55	141	26	33	6	-	5	26	1	.234
1952	New York	NL	C	6	5	0	0	0	0	0	0	0	.000
1952	Oakland	PCL	C	104	366	54	109	12	3	12	60	2	.298
1953	Minneapolis	AA	C	29	111	21	34	5	0	4	21	2	.306
1953	New York	NL	C	46	97	15	20	0	1	4	14	1	.206
1954	Havana	INT	C	125	409	46	117	25	1	7	61	0	.286
1955	Havana	INT	C	123	363	46	92	16	2	10	51	1	.253
1956	Columbus	INT	C	132	396	43	91	12	0	13	64	0	.230
1957	Buffalo	INT	C	118	363	49	91	14	0	21	62	0	.251
1958	Buffalo	INT	C	127	424	59	114	20	2	20	72	0	.269
1959	Houston	INT	C	138	415	53	122	21	0	15	68	0	.294
1960	Houston	INT	C	92	208	18	57	6	1	6	21	0	.274
1961	Houston	INT	C	5	4	0	1	0	0	0	0	0	.250
42-3	Havana	CWL	C	3	3	0	0	0	0	0	0	0	.000
46-7	Cienfuegos	CWL	C	42	86	10	23	1	1	2	16	0	.267
47-8	Cienfuegos	CWL	C	70	250	37	73	8	7	5	35	4	.292
48-9	Cienfuegos	CWL	C	60	177	21	45	7	4	4	23	3	.254
49-0	Cienfuegos	CWL	C	39	90	18	21	4	2	2	12	0	.233
50-1	Cienfuegos	CWL	C	59	212	26	57	10	3	4	28	0	.269
51-2	Cienfuegos	CWL	C	65	237	32	76	10	1	7	39	2	.321
52-3	Cienfuegos	CWL	C	69	240	30	62	7	4	7	34	2	.258
53-4	Cienfuegos	CWL	C	60	203	29	57	12	0	10	39	1	.281
54-5	Cienfuegos	CWL	C	65	216	32	55	6	1	9	35	0	.255
57-8	Cienfuegos	CWL	C	-	226	-	58	-	-	5	21	-	.257

Pedro Pages. Born in Cuba. BB TL

Year	Club	League	Pos	G	AB	R	H	2B	3B	HR	RBI	SB	BA
1939	New York	NNL	1B	-	-	-	-	-	-	-	-	-	
1940	Mexico City	MEX	1B	78	314	80	94	27	4	3	38	23	.299
1941	Tampico	MEX	1B	98	400	77	115	22	0	3	48	12	.288
1942	Puebla	MEX	OF	81	312	68	114	18	8	3	47	**30**	.365
1943	Puebla	MEX	OF	84	323	57	114	29	8	4	44	10	.353
1944	Puebla	MEX	OF 1B	90	372	80	129	20	11	5	78	15	.347
1945	Puebla	MEX	OF	92	335	78	90	18	7	3	56	25	.269
1946	Puebla	MEX	OF 1B	97	382	83	113	24	8	3	50	11	.296
1947	New York	NNL	OF	-	181	31	43	8	-	1	-	5	.238
1950	Gavilanes	VENZ	OF	-	-	-	-	-	-	-	-	-	
1950	Vera Cruz	MEX	OF	19	72	13	17	2	1	0	3	2	.236
1951	Sherbrooke	PROV	OF 1B	112	405	56	99	15	2	2	34	16	.244
48-9	Marianao	CWL	OF	58	147	16	30	2	0	0	14	2	.204
50-1	Cienfuegos	CWL	OF	60	184	32	44	5	3	1	14	3	.239

Jonathan Clyde Parris. Born September 11, 1926 at Panama City, Panama. 5'8", 170 lbs. BR TR

Year	Club	League	Pos	G	AB	R	H	2B	3B	HR	RBI	SB	BA
1946	New York	NNL	3B	27	103	13	22	3	1	1	9	0	.214
1947	New York	NNL	3B	-	187	22	46	7	-	1	-	3	.246
1948	New York	NNL	3B	-	-	-	-	-	-	-	-	-	
1949	Louisville	NAL	3B	-	-	-	-	-	-	-	-	-	
1951	St. Jean	PROV	2B 3B	66	252	50	74	12	0	16	44	3	.294
1952	Pueblo	WEST	3B 2B	113	382	64	107	18	2	13	56	9	.280
1953	Miami	FLIN	3B	132	476	70	136	22	10	6	94	11	.286
1954	Elmira	EAST	3B	133	504	65	158	**40**	11	11	**90**	2	.313
1955	Montreal	INT	3B	140	509	72	147	19	4	16	89	7	.289
1956	Montreal	INT	3B	152	552	92	177	37	0	17	78	3	**.321**
1957	Montreal	INT	3B	45	160	17	38	5	0	7	21	1	.238
1958	Montreal	INT	3B OF	153	550	72	165	32	6	10	93	11	.300
1959	Montreal	INT	3B	142	509	71	152	32	0	23	90	5	.299
1960	Dallas-Ft. Worth	AA	3B	30	109	12	34	6	0	2	10	0	.312
1960	Monterrey	MEX	3B	60	220	33	67	7	2	5	37	2	.305
1960	Toronto	INT	3B	17	53	10	11	3	0	1	4	1	.208
45-6	General Electric	PANA	3B	40	146	25	39	4	1	6	26	3	.267
46-7	General Electric	PANA	3B	34	141	30	50	12	4	5	42	4	.355
47-8	Chesterfield	PANA	3B	43	153	30	40	11	0	3	15	9	.261
48-9	C.N.	PANA	3B	36	139	29	49	6	4	5	37	8	.353
49-0	Chesterfield	PANA	3B	2	7	0	1	0	0	0	1	0	.143
50-1	C.N.	PANA	3B	38	141	20	40	9	3	3	18	1	.284
51-2	C.N.	PANA	3B	36	136	16	37	7	0	5	18	3	.272
52-3	C.N.	PANA	3B	34	125	22	41	9	0	2	14	2	.328
53-4	Chesterfield	PANA	3B	33	131	20	45	8	2	6	25	0	.344
54-5	Chesterfield	PANA	3B	40	149	24	49	10	1	2	23	2	.329
56-7	Chesterfield	PANA	3B	-	104	-	31	-	-	6	15	-	.298

Year	Club	League	Pos	G	AB	R	H	2B	3B	HR	RBI	SB	BA
58-9	Cerveza	PANA	3B	-	153	-	50	-	-	6	21	-	.327
59-0	Comercios	PANA	3B	-	122	-	53	-	-	7	21	-	**.434**

Roy Partlow. Born in 1912. Died April 19, 1987 in Cherry Hill, NJ. 6', 180 lbs. BR TL

Year	Club	League	Pos	G	AB	R	H	2B	3B	HR	RBI	SB	BA
1943	Vera Cruz	MEX	OF P	34	103	13	30	7	1	1	10	0	.291
1945	Philadelphia	NNL	P OF	30	73	8	19	0	0	0	4	0	.260
1946	Montreal	INT	P	10	13	3	2	0	0	0	2	0	.154
1946	Three Rivers	CAAM	P	23	47	11	19	5	0	0	9	3	.404
1947	Philadelphia	NNL	P	15	45	5	10	0	-	1	-	0	.222
1950	Granby		P	36	36	5	10	2	0	0	3	0	.278
39-0	San Juan	PRWL	P OF	-	131	28	48	6	2	1	22	2	.366
40-1	San Juan	PRWL	P OF	-	122	-	54	-	-	-	-	-	.443
45-6	Ponce	PRWL	P OF	-	84	11	22	5	2	0	11	2	.262
46-7	Santurce	PRWL	OF P	-	126	23	45	-	-	-	22	-	.357

Gabriel Patterson. BR TR

Year	Club	League	Pos	G	AB	R	H	2B	3B	HR	RBI	SB	BA
1941	New York	NNL	OF	-	-	-	-	-	-	-	-	-	
1943	New York	NNL	OF	-	-	-	-	-	-	-	-	-	
1945	Pittsburgh	USL	OF	-	-	-	-	-	-	-	-	-	
1946	Pittsburgh	USL	OF	-	-	-	-	-	-	-	-	-	
1947	NY, Home., Phil.	NNL	OF	-	71	17	21	2	-	3	-	4	.296
1948	New York	NNL	OF	-	-	-	-	-	-	-	-	-	
1950	Homestead		OF	-	-	-	-	-	-	-	-	-	
1951	Butler	MATL	OF	31	89	13	30	6	2	1	15	5	.337

Leonard Curtis Pearson. Born May 23, 1918 at Akron, OH. Died 1984 in Newark, NJ. 6'1 1/2", 200 lbs. BR TR

Year	Club	League	Pos	G	AB	R	H	2B	3B	HR	RBI	SB	BA
1937	Newark	NNL	OF 1B	49	174	27	44	11	4	4	-	5	.253
1937	St. Louis	NAL	OF	-	-	-	-	-	-	-	-	-	
1938	Newark	NNL	OF	8	16	-	10	0	0	1	-	1	.625
1939	Newark	NNL	OF 3B	17	64	-	16	0	0	0	-	0	.250
1940	Newark	NNL	3B OF	-	199	-	63	6	2	6	-	3	.317
1941	Newark	NNL	OF 3B	20	65	-	21	1	0	4	-	-	.323
1942	Newark	NNL	OF 1B	31	112	-	33	7	0	5	-	0	.295
1943	Newark	NNL	1B	26	95	-	30	5	3	5	-	2	.316
1944	Newark	NNL	3B 1B OF	48	172	31	56	11	2	2	**37**	3	.326
1945	Newark	NNL	1B	33	123	23	38	8	5	2	26	6	.309
1946	Newark	NNL	1B 3B	45	**184**	38	55	10	3	5	41	21	.299
1947	Newark	NNL	OF 1B	80	313	64	91	19	-	10	-	10	.291
1948	Newark	NNL	1B	-	6	-	4	3	0	1	-	0	.667
1949	Baltimore	NAL	OF 1B	90	331	53	110	-	-	-	-	-	.332
1950	Baltimore	NAL	1B OF	-	-	-	-	-	-	-	-	-	
1950	Milwaukee	AA	1B	63	223	29	68	10	2	4	24	0	.305
1951	Hartford	EAST	1B	125	456	56	124	24	-	10	69	1	.272
1951	Milwaukee	AA	1B	5	9	0	1	0	0	0	1	0	.111
1953	Drummondville	PROV	1B	76	280	45	82	13	1	16	58	1	.293
39-0	Humacao	PRWL	OF	-	-	-	-	-	-	-	-	-	
40-1	Caguas	PRWL	OF	-	-	-	-	-	-	-	27	-	
41-2	Caguas	PRWL	OF	-	-	-	-	-	-	-	-	-	
46-7	Havana	CWL	1B	70	**265**	25	68	14	1	2	**45**	8	.257
47-8	Havana	CWL	1B	81	**338**	37	96	6	2	5	49	3	.284
48-9	Havana	CWL	1B	73	**301**	44	77	13	1	5	**54**	5	.256
49-0	Havana	CWL	1B	69	280	42	76	**19**	0	11	**55**	0	.271
50-1	Almendares	CWL	1B	39	115	12	23	2	1	5	15	0	.200

Maurice Peatros. Born in 1930. 5'11", 210 lbs. BL TL

Year	Club	League	Pos	G	AB	R	H	2B	3B	HR	RBI	SB	BA
1945	Pittsburgh	USL	1B	-	-	-	-	-	-	-	-	-	
1947	Homestead	NNL	1B	-	-	-	-	-	-	-	-	-	
1949	Geneva	BORD	OF	16	53	5	11	2	0	0	4	2	.208
1950	Fargo-Moorhead	NORL	1B	87	285	56	90	12	5	1	52	8	.316
1951	Erie	MATL	1B	121	472	103	141	27	10	3	57	11	.299
1952	Magic Valley	PION	1B	132	469	86	135	26	2	4	75	9	.288
1953	Drummondville	PROV	1B OF	36	124	27	36	3	1	2	17	-	.290

Fernando Diaz Pedroso. Born May 30, 1924 at Marianao, Cuba. 5'11 1/2", 175 lbs. BR TR

Year	Club	League	Pos	G	AB	R	H	2B	3B	HR	RBI	SB	BA
1945	New York	NNL	3B	27	103	10	30	4	3	0	11	1	.291
1946	New York	NNL	OF	39	162	26	34	6	1	2	14	10	.210
1947	New York	NNL	OF	-	-	-	-	-	-	-	-	-	
1948	New York	NNL	OF	-	-	-	-	-	-	-	-	-	
1949	New York	NAL	OF	47	193	35	55	-	-	-	-	-	.285

Year	Club	League	Pos	G	AB	R	H	2B	3B	HR	RBI	SB	BA
1950	New York	NAL	OF	34	138	22	35	6	5	1	22	4	.254
1951	Vera Cruz, N.L.	MEX	OF	78	309	56	103	15	4	3	47	13	.333
1952	Cibaeano	DMSL	OF	-	209	30	57	-	-	-	20	9	.273
1954	Nuevo Laredo	MEX	OF	80	352	72	116	13	5	14	80	5	.330
1955	Nuevo Larado	MEX	OF	96	411	86	136	20	2	17	79	5	.331
1956	Mexico City	MEX	OF	120	464	70	160	27	9	3	66	8	.345
1957	Mexico City	MEX	OF	117	465	69	155	19	5	8	89	3	.333
1958	Mexico City	MEX	OF	73	251	32	72	12	6	3	28	2	.287
43-4	Cienfuegos	CWL	OF	-	26	3	6	-	-	-	2	0	.231
44-5	Marianao	CWL	OF	-	41	5	10	-	-	-	-	2	.244
44-5	Ponce	PRWL	OF	-	61	-	22	-	-	-	-	0	.361
45-6	Marianao	CWL	OF	27	50	2	14	2	1	0	6	0	.280
45-6	Ponce	PRWL	2B	-	95	27	35	7	4	3	18	7	**.368**
46-7	Ponce	PRWL	2B	-	256	35	89	-	-	12	35	**19**	.348
47-8	Ponce	PRWL	2B	-	238	53	86	11	3	13	58	-	.361
48-9	Ponce	PRWL	2B	-	169	41	45	12	4	7	23	7	.266
49-0	Marianao	CWL	OF	13	24	2	7	3	0	0	1	1	.292
49-0	San Juan	PRWL	OF	-	258	-	73	-	-	4	41	-	.283
50-1	Marianao, Havana	CWL	OF	32	24	6	5	-	-	-	1	3	.208
51-2	Havana	CWL	OF	56	147	25	39	7	1	1	21	1	.265
52-3	Marianao	CWL	OF	38	68	12	16	1	0	1	5	2	.235
53-4	Almendares	CWL	OF	25	36	3	7	1	0	0	4	1	.194
54-5	Havana	CWL	OF	28	34	6	6	1	0	0	0	3	.176
57-8	Oriental	NICR	OF	-	178	-	52	-	-	2	21	-	.292

Nathaniel "Nate" Peeples. Born June 29, 1926 at Memphis, TN. 6'2", 180 lbs. BR TR

Year	Club	League	Pos	G	AB	R	H	2B	3B	HR	RBI	SB	BA
1949	Kansas City	NAL	OF	-	-	-	-	-	-	-	-	-	
1950	KC, Indianapolis	NAL	C OF	55	182	39	55	5	3	3	30	20	.302
1951	Elmira	EAST	OF	74	274	55	69	14	2	5	29	24	.252
1951	Indianapolis, KC	NAL	OF C	-	-	-	18	-	-	-	27	-	
1952	Elmira	EAST	OF	12	47	11	12	3	1	2	7	3	.255
1952	Santa Barbara	CALF	OF	108	373	82	122	15	4	14	72	52	.327
1953	Keokuk, Evansville	III	OF	90	308	73	102	17	1	15	65	36	.331
1953	Pueblo	WEST	OF C	11	34	4	8	1	0	3	5	2	.235
1954	Atlanta	SOU		2	4	0	0	0	0	0	0	0	.000
1954	Jacksonville	SATL	OF C	94	288	54	83	14	2	7	47	11	.288
1955	Evansville	III	OF	55	200	40	65	8	2	9	40	13	.325
1955	Jacksonville	SATL	OF	40	100	13	27	2	1	3	16	3	.270
1956	Austin	TEX	OF	66	170	17	34	8	2	3	26	8	.200
1956	Jacksonville	SATL	OF	58	200	24	53	5	2	5	27	3	.265
1957	Corpus Christi	BGST	OF	124	455	116	143	22	6	25	99	31	.314
1958	Austin	TEX	OF	140	471	80	122	16	2	21	75	23	.259
1959	Austin, San Anton.	TEX	OF	90	278	49	71	9	0	8	48	9	.255
1959	Louisville	AA	OF	12	20	5	7	1	0	2	7	0	.350
1960	Mexico City	MEX	OF	2	7	0	3	0	0	0	0	0	.429

Charles "Mule" Peete. Born February 22, 1929 at Franklin, VA. Died November 27, 1956 in Caracas, Venezuela. 5'9 1/2", 190 lbs. BL TR

Year	Club	League	Pos	G	AB	R	H	2B	3B	HR	RBI	SB	BA
1950	Brandon	MADK	OF	33	127	-	-	-	-	2	14	-	.000
1950	Indianapolis	NAL	OF	31	84	11	18	2	2	2	8	1	.214
1953	Portsmouth	PIED	OF	125	461	68	127	21	9	4	56	4	.275
1954	Portsmouth	PIED	OF	140	**546**	92	**170**	25	9	17	79	10	.311
1955	Omaha	AA	OF	99	309	55	98	20	4	9	63	5	.317
1955	Rochester	INT	OF	31	75	10	21	4	1	1	10	3	.280
1956	Omaha	AA	OF	116	417	84	146	28	6	16	63	3	**.350**
1956	St. Louis	NL	OF	23	52	3	10	2	2	0	6	-	.192
55-6	Cienfuegos	CWL	OF	-	39	5	5	1	0	0	3	-	.128

James Edward Pendleton. Born January 7, 1924 at St. Charles, MO. 6', 190 lbs. BR TR

Year	Club	League	Pos	G	AB	R	H	2B	3B	HR	RBI	SB	BA
1948	Chicago	NAL	SS	75	302	52	91	11	9	6	47	4	.301
1949	St. Paul	AA	SS OF	105	347	83	95	9	5	6	39	27	.274
1950	St. Paul	AA	SS	145	571	105	171	25	**19**	10	98	25	.299
1951	St. Paul	AA	SS	143	564	**116**	170	18	13	21	79	14	.301
1952	Montreal	INT	SS	151	**595**	87	173	24	14	11	92	14	.291
1953	Milwaukee	NL	SS OF	120	251	48	75	12	4	7	27	6	.299
1954	Milwaukee	NL	OF	71	173	20	38	3	1	1	16	2	.220
1955	Milwaukee	NL	OF SS 3B	8	10	0	0	0	0	0	0	0	.000
1955	Toledo	AA	OF	95	368	42	100	15	6	9	59	8	.272
1956	Milwaukee	NL	INF	14	11	0	0	0	0	0	0	0	.000
1956	Wichita	AA	OF SS	69	253	37	73	15	5	12	43	3	.289

Year	Club	League	Pos	G	AB	R	H	2B	3B	HR	RBI	SB	BA
1957	Pittsburgh	NL	OF 3B SS	46	59	9	18	1	1	0	9	0	.305
1958	Columbus	INT	OF	123	490	73	153	21	8	14	68	3	.312
1958	Pittsburgh	NL	PH	3	3	0	1	0	0	0	0	0	.333
1959	Cincinnati	NL	OF 3B SS	65	113	13	29	2	0	3	9	3	.257
1960	Jersey City	INT	OF	152	590	73	**178**	28	9	16	88	3	.302
1961	Jersey City	INT	OF	134	460	69	140	**33**	6	12	61	5	.304
1962	Houston	NL	OF 3B SS1B	117	321	30	79	12	2	8	36	0	.246
1963	Oklahoma City	PCL	UTILITY	21	54	6	12	3	0	1	6	0	.222
1963	San Antonio	TEX	OF	86	306	41	84	15	4	9	57	0	.275
49-0	Magallanes	VENZ	SS	41	155	47	60	12	3	7	24	6	**.387**
50-1	Magallanes	VENZ	SS	-	-	-	-	**18**	**5**	-	-	-	
52-3	Cienfuegos	CWL	SS	-	227	33	66	9	3	6	30	4	.291

Arthur David "Art" or "Superman" Pennington. Born May 18, 1923 at Memphis, TN. 5'11", 185 lbs. BB TR

Year	Club	League	Pos	G	AB	R	H	2B	3B	HR	RBI	SB	BA
1940	Chicago	NAL	1B OF	-	-	-	-	-	-	-	-	-	
1941	Chicago	NAL	1B OF	-	-	-	-	-	-	-	-	-	
1942	Chicago	NAL	OF	-	65	-	12	3	1	1	-	0	.185
1943	Chicago	NAL	OF	-	62	-	12	1	3	2	-	1	.194
1944	Chicago	NAL	OF	46	157	35	47	6	3	4	37	4	.299
1945	Chicago	NAL	OF	**68**	234	48	84	**16**	1	5	24	18	.359
1946	Chicago	NAL	OF	-	-	-	-	-	-	-	-	-	
1946	Mont.VC, Puebla	MEX	1B OF	80	290	40	91	14	3	5	48	8	.314
1947	Puebla	MEX	1B OF	123	437	86	127	10	10	5	50	6	.291
1948	Puebla	MEX	1B OF	84	276	48	83	18	8	4	42	12	.301
1949	Chicago	NAL	OF	57	201	39	70	-	-	-	-	-	.348
1949	Portland	PCL	OF	20	53	7	11	1	0	0	2	1	.208
1949	Salem	WINT	OF	18	65	15	20	3	0	2	16	3	.308
1950	Chicago	NAL	OF	43	146	40	54	10	2	6	28	14	.370
1951	Chicago	NAL	OF	-	-	-	-	-	-	-	-	-	
1952	Keokuk	III	OF	116	427	126	149	17	10	20	89	24	.349
1953	Cibaenas	DMSL	OF	-	48	12	11	-	-	-	12	1	.229
1953	Keokuk, Ced. Rap.	III	OF	64	225	45	74	13	1	4	31	10	.329
1954	Cedar Rapids	III	OF	119	423	88	146	22	6	16	79	11	.345
1958	St.Petersburg	FLST	OF	128	419	94	142	26	7	8	93	12	.339
1959	Modesto	CAL	OF 1B	108	359	62	92	18	5	10	65	14	.256
47-8	Leones	CWL		-	77	6	18	3	1	0	10	1	.234

Alonzo Thomas Perry. Born April 14, 1923 at Birmingham, AL. Deceased. 6'3", 200 lbs. BL TR

Year	Club	League	Pos	G	AB	R	H	2B	3B	HR	RBI	SB	BA
1940	Homestead	NNL	P	-	-	-	-	-	-	-	-	-	
1946	Birmingham	NAL	P	-	-	-	-	-	-	-	-	-	
1946	Homestead	NNL	P	-	-	-	-	-	-	-	-	-	
1947	Birminghamm	NAL	P	-	-	-	-	-	-	-	-	-	
1948	Birmingham	NAL	P 1B	31	80	7	26	4	0	2	12	1	.325
1949	Birmingham	NAL	P	-	-	-	-	-	-	-	-	-	
1949	Oakland	PCL	1B OF	12	15	0	3	0	0	0	4	0	.200
1950	Birmingham	NAL	1B OF	73	294	**80**	92	14	7	14	64	18	.313
1951	Brandon	PROV	1B	-	-	-	-	-	-	-	-	-	
1951	Licey	DMSL	1B	25	90	27	36	4	1	**9**	32	10	.400
1951	Syracuse	INT	1B	9	18	3	5	0	0	0	3	0	.278
1952	Licey	DMSL	1B	45	162	29	53	9	1	**11**	38	5	.327
1953	Licey	DMSL	1B	56	**229**	40	67	11	4	**11**	**53**	**16**	.293
1954	Licey	DMSL	1B	42	146	**29**	49	11	1	8	29	6	**.336**
1955	Mexico City	MEX	1B	92	365	76	137	24	**15**	21	**122**	5	.375
1956	Mexico City	MEX	1B	123	451	**103**	**177**	**33**	**13**	**28**	118	10	**.392**
1957	Mexico City	MEX	1B	121	466	**96**	**164**	32	6	22	**107**	15	.352
1958	Mexico City	MEX	1B	115	417	93	152	30	4	22	85	5	.365
1959	Mexico City	MEX	1B	127	459	93	153	29	9	12	94	7	.333
1962	Monterrey	MEX	1B	124	468	91	149	28	5	16	**105**	4	.318
1963	Monterrey	MEX	1B	130	496	96	175	27	6	17	90	5	.353
48-9	Mayaquez	CWL	P 1B	-	-	76	100	24	-	-	64	-	
49-0	Mayaquez	CWL	1B	-	213	-	71	-	-	-	-	-	.333
54-5	Ponce	PRWL	1B	22	83	5	18	4	1	1	13	2	.217
55-6	Licey	DOML	1B	53	209	29	68	**13**	6	3	31	2	.325
56-7	Licey	DOML	1B	46	159	19	40	7	1	0	19	2	.252
57-8	Licey	DOML	1B	51	202	18	**67**	8	2	3	23	1	**.332**
58-9	Escogido	DOML	1B	**60**	233	27	63	9	2	4	27	0	.270

Alfred Charles Pinkston. Born October 22, 1917 at Newbern, AL. Died March, 1981 at New Orleans, LA. 6'5", 225 lbs. BL TR

Year	Club	League	Pos	G	AB	R	H	2B	3B	HR	RBI	SB	BA
1936	St. Louis	NAL	1B	-	-	-	-	-	-	-	-	-	
1951	Farnham	PROV	OF	123	465	67	140	32	6	15	72	21	.301

Year	Club	League	Pos	G	AB	R	H	2B	3B	HR	RBI	SB	BA
1952	St. Hyacinthe	PROV	OF 1B	125	480	103	173	34	4	**30**	**121**	18	**.360**
1953	Ottawa	INT	OF	45	101	9	20	6	0	1	9	0	.198
1953	Williamsport	EAST	OF	70	278	47	92	15	4	10	47	5	.331
1954	Savannah	SATL	OF	136	500	100	**180**	33	4	27	102	9	.360
1955	Columbus	INT	OF	71	227	38	68	13	2	8	34	1	.300
1956	Columbia, Jacksonv.	SATL	OF	77	263	36	77	15	4	4	31	2	.293
1956	Columbus	INT	OF	12	22	1	4	1	0	0	1	0	.182
1957	Amarillo	WEST	OF	141	554	104	206	41	6	23	**133**	2	.372
1958	Amarillo	WEST	OF	148	606	114	**204**	**44**	5	24	126	3	.337
1959	Mexico City	MEX	OF	140	534	**114**	**197**	34	11	13	97	7	**.369**
1960	Mexico City	MEX	OF	138	567	110	**225**	41	11	26	**144**	4	**.397**
1961	Aguila	MEX	OF	109	406	79	152	26	4	13	86	4	**.374**
1962	Aguila	MEX	OF	123	451	75	**172**	33	8	8	87	5	**.381**
1963	Aguila	MEX	OF	113	394	61	145	34	1	20	91	1	.368
1964	Aguila	MEX	OF	136	475	86	**173**	32	5	17	89	0	.364
1965	Aguila	MEX	OF	120	406	49	140	27	0	11	65	0	.345

David Pope. Born June 17, 1925 at Talladega, AL. 5'10 1/2", 170 lbs. BL TR

Year	Club	League	Pos	G	AB	R	H	2B	3B	HR	RBI	SB	BA
1946	Homestead	NNL	OF	-	-	-	-	-	-	-	-	-	
1948	Farnham	PROV	OF	-	313	-	113	-	-	23	72	-	.361
1949	Farnham	PROV	OF	-	304	-	93	-	-	19	77	-	.306
1950	Wilkes-Barre	EAST	OF	120	403	74	108	13	**18**	8	71	7	.268
1951	Wilkes-Barre	EAST	OF	138	512	**113**	158	27	**13**	15	95	8	.309
1952	Cleveland	AL	OF	12	34	9	10	1	1	1	4	0	.294
1952	Indianapolis	AA	OF	126	475	77	167	29	7	13	79	4	**.352**
1953	Indianapolis	AA	OF	154	600	101	172	33	**14**	24	88	3	.287
1954	Cleveland	AL	OF	60	102	21	30	2	1	4	13	2	.294
1955	Clev., Baltimore	AL	OF	121	326	38	86	13	4	7	52	5	.264
1956	Balt., Cleveland	AL	OF	37	89	7	20	3	1	0	4	0	.225
1956	Indianapolis	AA	OF	100	367	66	111	18	9	25	76	4	.302
1957	San Diego	PCL	OF	129	460	74	144	21	6	18	83	8	.313
1958	San Diego	PCL	OF	142	545	88	172	31	7	19	96	11	.316
1959	Toronto	INT	OF	129	455	62	125	30	3	16	69	5	.275
1960	Houston	AA	OF	135	498	61	138	33	5	12	62	9	.277
1961	Toronto	INT	OF	30	50	8	12	2	0	2	5	0	.240
51-2	San Juan	PRWL	OF	-	111	-	29	-	-	2	17	-	.261
52-3	San Juan	PRWL	OF	-	18	-	9	-	-	0	5	-	.500
53-4	Gavilanes	VENZ	OF	78	275	57	95	**22**	**6**	9	52	12	**.345**
54-5	Santa Maria	VENZ	OF	-	171	**32**	55	-	**6**	5	25	-	.322

Lawrence Glenn Hope Raines. Born March 9, 1930 at St. Albans, WV. Died January 28, 1978 in Lansing, MI. 5'10 1/2", 165 lbs. BR TR

Year	Club	League	Pos	G	AB	R	H	2B	3B	HR	RBI	SB	BA
1951	Chicago	NAL	SS	-	-	-	-	-	-	-	-	-	
1952	Chicago	NAL	SS	-	-	-	-	-	-	-	-	-	
1953	Hankyu	JAP	SS	120	503	92	144	21	16	8	49	61	.286
1954	Hankyu	JAP	SS	137	546	96	184	38	8	18	96	45	.337
1955	Indianapolis	AA	INF	17	47	3	11	3	1	0	3	0	.234
1955	Reading	EAST	SS 3B	91	324	61	108	17	8	7	43	24	.333
1956	Indianapolis	AA	SS 2B	148	563	105	174	19	**14**	10	66	**22**	.309
1957	Cleveland	AL	INF OF	96	244	39	64	14	0	2	16	5	.262
1958	Cleveland	AL	2B	7	9	1	0	0	0	0	0	0	.000
1958	San Diego	PCL	SS	144	532	78	161	32	9	5	65	14	.303
1959	Toronto	INT	SS 2B	146	589	79	167	23	7	4	43	32	.284
1960	Indianapolis	AA	2B SS	144	558	78	149	27	6	12	47	46	.267
1961	Indianapolis	AA	2B OF	52	138	16	29	9	1	0	15	3	.210
1961	Syracuse	INT	2B	32	120	16	26	2	0	1	9	5	.217
1962	Hankyu	JAP	INF	73	218	21	55	6	1	5	27	8	.252
56-7	Almendares	CWL	INF	-	165	16	42	2	4	4	21	0	.255
57-8	Ponce	PRWL	INF	6	21	2	1	0	1	0	1	0	.048
60-1	Rapinos	OCC	INF	-	199	-	56	-	-	5	19	-	.281

Fleming "Buddy" Reedy, Sr. Born 1929. 5'11", 165 lbs. BL TR

Year	Club	League	Pos	G	AB	R	H	2B	3B	HR	RBI	SB	BA
1950	Baltimore	NAL	OF 2B	38	137	29	41	9	5	1	26	5	.299
1951	Baltimore	NAL	3B	-	233	65	8	-	-	5	56	-	.343
1952	Lincoln	WEST	OF 2B	154	565	92	159	27	9	4	61	15	.281
1953	Savannah	SATL	OF	139	513	73	123	22	7	2	52	9	.240
1954	Lancaster	PIED	OF	137	514	96	160	29	9	5	76	18	.311
1955	Lancaster	PIED	OF 3B	119	371	75	120	27	11	4	54	15	.323
1956	Columbia	SATL	OF	138	478	77	141	27	13	4	57	11	.295
1957	Columbia	SATL	OF	133	453	61	120	16	7	1	53	7	.265

Year	Club	League	Pos	G	AB	R	H	2B	3B	HR	RBI	SB	BA
1958	Albany	EAST	OF 3B	125	406	61	124	25	10	6	64	6	.305
1959	Albany	EAST	OF	139	525	85	165	35	12	8	86	4	.314
1960	Sioux City	III	OF	134	505	86	136	21	4	8	78	11	.269
1961	Sarasota	FLST	OF	137	439	107	138	18	12	2	69	42	.314
1962	Daytona Beach	FLST	OF 1B	67	250	50	64	11	7	3	25	23	.256
1962	Minot	NORL	OF	58	190	34	52	7	2	0	21	20	.274

John Franklin "Hoss" Ritchey. Born January 5, 1923 at San Diego, CA. 5'9", 180 lbs. BL TR

Year	Club	League	Pos	G	AB	R	H	2B	3B	HR	RBI	SB	BA
1947	Chicago	NAL	C	58	176	42	67	-	-	-	-	-	.381
1948	San Diego	PCL	C	103	217	35	70	10	2	4	44	2	.323
1949	San Diego	PCL	C	112	327	29	84	10	1	3	35	12	.257
1950	Portland	PCL	C	107	241	32	65	8	4	2	46	1	.270
1951	Portland	PCL	C	1	3	0	-	-	-	-	-	-	.000
1951	Vancouver	WINT	C	137	451	91	156	26	5	7	86	20	.346
1952	Vancouver	WINT	C	137	443	96	152	24	8	2	76	27	.343
1953	Sacramento	PCL	C	147	454	62	132	18	8	5	55	10	.291
1954	Sacramento	PCL	C	94	283	24	77	6	2	-	23	5	.272
1955	San Francisco	PCL	C	130	375	52	107	15	1	6	41	10	.285
1956	Syracuse	INT	C	19	54	6	10	2	-	-	7	-	.185
48-9	Magallanes	VENZ	C	-	-	30	-	14	-	-	-	-	

Curtis Benjamin "Curt" Roberts. Born August 16, 1929 at Pineland, TX. Died November 14, 1969 in Oakland, CA. 5'8", 165. BR TR

Year	Club	League	Pos	G	AB	R	H	2B	3B	HR	RBI	SB	BA
1947	Kansas City	NAL	2B	-	-	-	-	-	-	-	-	-	
1948	Kansas City	NAL	2B	63	249	33	66	19	-	1	37	3	.265
1949	Kansas City	NAL	2B	83	294	32	81	-	-	-	-	-	.276
1950	Kansas City	NAL	2B SS	60	231	43	69	15	4	1	24	2	.299
1951	Denver	WEST	2B	132	459	80	129	24	5	5	53	10	.281
1952	Denver	WEST	2B	129	503	99	141	25	4	3	38	15	.280
1953	Denver	WEST	2B	151	587	126	171	32	2	12	70	17	.291
1954	Pittsburgh	NL	2B	134	496	47	115	18	7	1	36	6	.232
1955	Hollywood	PCL	2B	123	452	79	145	22	3	8	49	17	.321
1955	Pittsburgh	NL	2B	6	17	1	2	1	0	0	0	0	.118
1956	Columbus	AA	2B	87	325	50	104	17	0	8	35	0	.320
1956	Pittsburgh	NL	2B	31	62	6	11	5	2	0	4	1	.177
1956	Williamsport	EAST	2B	11	37	5	11	1	1	1	7	0	.297
1957	Denver	AA	2B	147	572	115	174	36	7	10	81	23	.304
1958	Denver	AA	2B	138	544	93	162	33	5	11	60	7	.298
1959	Richmond, Montreal	INT	2B	138	500	84	148	34	1	11	56	11	.296
1960	Montreal	INT	2B	6	26	3	8	1	0	1	5	1	.308
1960	Spokane	PCL	2B	120	472	76	137	24	2	2	45	9	.290
1961	Spokane	PCL	2B	91	371	55	114	18	3	4	28	1	.307
1962	Omaha	AA	2B	142	542	62	138	22	6	8	65	3	.255
1963	Lynchburg	SATL	3B 2B	109	334	43	95	10	1	3	43	6	.284
55-6	Cienfuegos	CWL	2B	-	268	36	71	10	5	2	21	6	.265
56-7	Cienfuegos	CWL	2B	-	292	38	72	7	1	5	32	-	.247
59-0	Escogido	DOML	2B	-	249	-	70	-	-	3	18	-	.281
60-1	Comercios	PANA	2B	-	140	-	38	-	-	1	13	-	.271
63-4	Leon	NICR	2B	-	233	34	66	-	-	-	21	-	.283

John Roosevelt "Jackie" Robinson. Born January 31, 1919 at Cairo, GA. Died October 24, 1972 in Stamford, CT. 5'11 1/2", 195 lbs. BR TR

Year	Club	League	Pos	G	AB	R	H	2B	3B	HR	RBI	SB	BA
1945	Kansas City	NAL	SS	47	163	36	63	14	4	5	23	13	.387
1946	Montreal	INT	2B	124	444	113	155	25	8	3	66	40	.349
1947	Brooklyn	NL	1B	151	590	125	175	31	5	12	48	29	.297
1948	Brooklyn	NL	2B 1B 3B	147	574	108	170	38	8	12	85	22	.296
1949	Brooklyn	NL	2B	156	593	122	203	38	12	16	124	37	.342
1950	Brooklyn	NL	2B	144	518	99	170	39	4	14	81	12	.328
1951	Brooklyn	NL	2B	153	548	106	185	33	7	19	88	25	.338
1952	Brooklyn	NL	2B	149	510	104	157	17	3	19	75	24	.308
1953	Brooklyn	NL	INF OF	136	484	109	159	34	7	12	95	17	.329
1954	Brooklyn	NL	INF OF	124	386	62	120	22	4	15	59	7	.311
1955	Brooklyn	NL	INF OF	105	317	51	81	6	2	8	36	12	.256
1956	Brooklyn	NL	INF OF	117	357	61	98	15	2	10	43	12	.275

Hector Antonio "Hec" Rodriguez y Ordenana. Born june 13, 1920 at Villa Alquizar, Cuba. 5'8", 165 lbs. BR TR

Year	Club	League	Pos	G	AB	R	H	2B	3B	HR	RBI	SB	BA
1943	Mexico City	MEX	3B	90	395	68	127	19	4	0	34	22	.322
1944	New York	NNL	3B	34	130	29	31	3	3	0	8	8	.238
1945	Tampico	MEX	3B	92	374	70	122	13	14	0	47	17	.326
1946	Tampico	MEX	3B	99	412	78	132	11	8	3	32	29	.320

Year	Club	League	Pos	G	AB	R	H	2B	3B	HR	RBI	SB	BA
1947	Tampico	MEX	3B	123	504	91	147	13	8	1	51	**36**	.292
1948	Tampico,Vera Cruz	MEX	3B	87	338	63	96	15	6	2	41	12	.284
1949	Torreon	MEX	3B	76	320	40	91	6	5	0	40	1	.284
1950	Gavilanes	VENZ	3B	-	-	-	-	-	-	-	-	-	
1950	Vera Cruz	MEX	3B	20	85	17	28	2	2	1	12	4	.329
1951	Montreal	INT	3B	153	609	105	184	28	10	8	95	26	.302
1951	San Luis Potosi	MEX	3B	62	253	51	78	7	0	5	30	0	.308
1952	Chicago	AL	3B	124	407	55	108	14	0	1	40	7	.265
1952	SLP, Mex Cty, Mont.	MEX	3B	72	280	36	71	10	4	2	27	1	.254
1953	Syracuse	INT	3B SS	148	527	90	159	21	7	4	62	12	.302
1954	Toronto	INT	SS 3B	147	535	105	164	22	3	4	43	8	.307
1955	Toronto	INT	SS	146	560	99	162	31	8	9	57	7	.289
1956	Toronto	INT	SS	150	524	73	143	17	3	4	40	8	.273
1957	Toronto	INT	SS	147	528	53	152	19	7	2	62	2	.288
1958	Toronto	INT	SS 3B	128	456	54	104	11	2	3	34	5	.228
1959	Toronto	INT	SS 3B OF	132	414	48	106	16	3	6	30	3	.256
1960	San Diego	PCL	SS	134	446	52	117	9	3	0	42	8	.262
1961	San Diego	PCL	3B SS	100	300	33	88	15	3	0	33	3	.293
1962	Mexico City	MEX	3B SS	96	321	37	89	18	7	0	29	5	.277
1963	Mexico City	MEX	SS 3B	113	379	45	111	16	4	3	54	3	.293
1964	Campeche	MXSE	SS	88	320	38	89	9	**9**	1	37	8	.278
1965	San Luis Potosi	MXCT	Manager	-	-	-	-	-	-	-	-	-	
1966	Tabasco	MXSE	3B	30	95	11	30	4	3	0	16	0	.316
42-3	Almendares	CWL	3B	43	161	16	39	3	4	0	14	3	.242
43-4	Almendares	CWL	3B	46	193	30	42	4	3	0	11	4	.218
44-5	Almendares	CWL	3B	54	205	29	50	3	5	0	25	4	.244
45-6	Almendares	CWL	3B	65	240	24	55	3	2	0	19	1	.229
46-7	Almendares	CWL	3B	59	203	32	58	4	2	1	24	15	.286
47-8	Alaeranes	CWL	3B	92	343	34	98	13	10	1	50	19	.286
48-9	Almendares	CWL	3B	66	240	27	59	4	4	0	33	14	.246
49-0	Almendares	CWL	3B	76	277	40	72	4	9	1	36	6	.260
50-1	Almendares	CWL	3B	72	289	32	87	11	4	3	50	3	.301
51-2	Almendares	CWL	3B	70	279	32	75	6	6	1	29	9	.269
52-3	Almendares	CWL	3B	70	268	43	79	10	5	1	26	3	.295
53-4	Almendares	CWL	3B	66	252	30	73	13	2	1	34	3	.290
54-5	Almendares	CWL	3B	71	266	28	74	10	4	0	43	4	.278
59-0	Havana	CWL	3B	-	204	-	60	-	-	-	13	-	.294

Carlos Santiago. Born 1928. 5'11", 170 lbs. BR TR

Year	Club	League	Pos	G	AB	R	H	2B	3B	HR	RBI	SB	BA
1945	New York	NNL	INF	-	-	-	-	-	-	-	-	-	
1946	New York	NNL	INF	-	-	-	-	-	-	-	-	-	
1947	Stamford	COL	SS	-	-	-	-	-	-	-	-	-	
1948	Stamford	COL	2B 3B	91	343	54	92	10	2	4	41	16	.268
1949	Stamford	COL	SS	111	395	65	116	13	4	4	50	7	.294
1950	Farnham	PROV	2B	44	164	15	32	7	0	2	21	6	.195
1950	Poughkeepsie	COL	SS	62	226	58	77	12	4	11	41	3	.341
1953	St. Petersburg	FLIN	SS	133	465	61	122	13	6	8	64	6	.262
1954	CH., Petersburg	PIED	SS	29	105	13	28	6	0	2	12	2	.267
1954	Lincoln	WEST	SS	12	43	7	10	0	0	0	4	0	.233
1954	Tallahassee	FLIN	SS	66	254	45	74	17	2	2	27	1	.291
1955	Mexico City	MEX	SS	67	234	36	58	6	1	6	30	4	.248
58-9	San Juan	PRWL	INF	-	31	-	6	-	-	0	1	-	.194

Patricio Athelstan Scantlebury. Born November 11, 1917 at Gatun, Canal Zone. Died May 24, 1991 at Glen Ridge, NJ. 6'1", 185 lbs. BL TL

Year	Club	League	Pos	G	AB	R	H	2B	3B	HR	RBI	SB	BA
1944	New York	NNL	P	-	-	-	-	-	-	-	-	-	
1945	New York	NNL	P	13	16	3	8	2	1	0	2	0	.500
1946	New York	NNL	P	23	36	5	11	1	-	0	3	0	.306
1947	New York	NNL	P	17	41	7	15	2	-	0	0	-	.366
1948	New York	NNL	P	-	-	-	-	-	-	-	-	-	
1949	New York	NAL	P	22	54	6	18	-	-	-	-	-	.333
1950	New York	NAL	P	11	29	7	13	1	2	2	16	0	.448
1951	Vera Cruz	MEX	P OF	58	164	26	50	8	4	3	27	4	.305
1953	Texarkana	BGST	P UTL	75	167	33	44	10	0	5	24	2	.263
1954	Dallas	TEX	P UTL	75	133	18	40	9	0	0	11	0	.301
1954	Havana	INT	P	3	3	0	0	0	0	0	0	0	.000
1955	Havana	INT	P PH	51	68	7	9	3	0	0	7	0	.132
1956	Cincinnati	NL	P	8	3	0	0	0	0	0	0	0	.000
1956	Havana	INT	P	20	33	2	5	-	1	0	5	0	.152
1956	Seattle	PCL	P	14	29	5	11	3	1	0	3	0	.379

Year	Club	League	Pos	G	AB	R	H	2B	3B	HR	RBI	SB	BA
1957	Havana	INT	P PH	69	111	10	25	4	3	0	3	1	.225
1958	Toronto	INT	P PH	47	90	8	16	3	0	0	6	1	.178
1959	Toronto	INT	P PH	68	77	13	25	4	0	2	5	0	.325
1960	Toronto	INT	P PH	54	17	0	3	0	0	0	0	0	.176
1961	Toronto	INT	P	46	14	3	4	2	0	0	0	0	.286
46-7	Ponce	PRWL	P	-	-	-	-	-	-	-	-	-	
47-8	Almendares	CWL		-	-	-	-	-	-	-	-	-	

Joseph Scott. Born June 15, 1918 at Shreveport, LA. 5'11', 175 lbs. BL TL

Year	Club	League	Pos	G	AB	R	H	2B	3B	HR	RBI	SB	BA
1947	Birmingham	NAL	1B	-	-	-	-	-	-	-	-	-	
1948	Birmingham	NAL	1B	68	255	47	50	14	2	3	40	2	.196
1949	Birmingham	NAL	1B	76	298	38	71	-	-	-	-	-	.238
1950	Chicago	NAL	1B	39	133	14	30	7	3	1	34	4	.226
1950	Farnham	PROV	1B OF	106	381	89	119	22	2	8	44	28	.312
1951	Farn., St. Hyacin.	PROV	OF 1B	113	402	89	106	25	2	4	38	25	.264

William C. "Bonnie" Serrell. Born March 9, 1922 at Dallas TX. 5'11", 160 lbs. BL TR

Year	Club	League	Pos	G	AB	R	H	2B	3B	HR	RBI	SB	BA
1941	Chicago	NAL	UTL	1	4	0	1	0	0	0	0	0	.250
1942	Kansas City	NAL	UTL	-	141	-	53	6	3	2	-	0	.376
1943	Kansas City	NAL	UTL	-	126	-	34	10	5	3	-	1	.270
1944	Kansas City	NAL	UTL	53	190	32	61	4	2	1	-	6	.321
1945	Kansas City	NAL	1B	-	-	-	-	-	-	-	-	-	
1945	Tampico	MEX	2B	71	281	49	88	12	7	4	65	6	.313
1946	Tampico	MEX	2B	90	345	40	94	11	3	3	50	9	.272
1947	Tampico	MEX	2B 1B OF	126	519	67	137	23	12	3	58	19	.264
1948	San Luis, Vera Cruz	MEX	2B OF	85	345	57	101	21	2	11	52	15	.293
1949	Kansas City	NAL	INF	89	348	55	98	-	-	-	-	-	.282
1950	Kansas City	NAL	1B 2B	68	259	44	82	8	6	3	39	16	.317
1951	Kansas City	NAL	OF INF	-	-	-	-	-	-	-	-	-	
1951	San Francisco	PCL	2B	62	169	20	41	11	1	-	15	3	.243
1951	Yakima	WINT	2B	43	179	31	54	6	6	3	30	9	.302
1952	Escogido	DMSL		-	42	2	6	-	-	-	2	-	.143
1952	Nuevo Laredo	MEX	INF	44	184	30	68	8	4	1	35	6	.370
1953	Nuevo Laredo	MEX	2B	79	338	55	109	15	9	5	53	4	.322
1954	Nuevo Laredo	MEX	2B	80	360	79	126	33	9	5	55	4	.350
1955	Nuevo Laredo	MEX	2B	93	397	82	134	18	8	6	52	3	.338
1956	Nuevo Laredo	MEX	2B	107	432	52	141	17	4	5	51	20	.326
1957	N.L., Monterrey	MEX	1B 2B	88	338	49	101	15	8	1	46	4	.299
1958	Nogales-Juarez	AZMX	3B 2B	100	418	100	157	31	7	20	90	5	.376
45-6	Marianao	CWL	3B	-	237	23	59	14	3	2	29	2	.249
46-7	Marianao	CWL	3B	-	16	2	4	0	0	0	0	0	.250
46-7	Matanzas	CUBA	3B	-	89	19	29	-	-	-	-	-	.326
49-0	Ponce	PRWL	2B	-	294	51	85	11	9	1	31	-	.289
57-8		MXPC	INF	-	151	-	40	-	-	5	19	-	.265

Harry Leon "Suitcase" Simpson. Born December 3, 1925 at Atlanta, GA. Died April 3, 1979 in Akron, OH. 6'1 1/2', 175 lbs. BL TR

Year	Club	League	Pos	G	AB	R	H	2B	3B	HR	RBI	SB	BA
1946	Philadelphia	NNL	OF	33	99	18	24	2	2	3	13	1	.242
1947	Philadelphia	NNL	OF	-	135	13	33	5	-	1	-	1	.244
1948	Philadelphia	NNL	OF	-	-	-	-	-	-	-	-	-	
1949	Wilkes-Barre	EAST	OF	139	522	125	159	27	16	31	120	5	.305
1950	San Diego	PCL	OF	178	697	121	225	41	19	33	156	2	.323
1951	Cleveland	AL	OF 1B	122	332	51	76	7	0	7	24	6	.229
1952	Cleveland	AL	OF 1B	146	545	66	145	21	10	10	65	5	.266
1953	Cleveland	AL	OF 1B	82	242	25	55	3	1	7	22	0	.227
1954	Indianapolis	AA	OF 1B	100	330	50	93	19	5	12	58	1	.282
1955	Cleveland, KC	AL	OF 1B	115	397	43	119	16	7	5	52	3	.300
1956	Kansas City	AL	OF 1B	141	543	76	159	22	11	21	105	2	.293
1957	KC, New York	AL	OF 1B	125	403	51	109	16	9	13	63	1	.270
1958	New York, KC	AL	1B OF	102	263	22	67	9	2	7	33	0	.255
1959	KC, Chicago	AL	OF 1B	46	89	6	18	5	1	3	15	0	.202
1959	Pittsburgh	NL	OF	9	15	3	4	2	0	0	2	0	.267
1960	San Diego	PCL	OF 1B	95	284	38	63	11	5	8	40	3	.222
1961	San Diego	PCL	OF 1B	146	515	82	156	23	6	24	105	3	.303
1962	Indianapolis	AA	OF	132	444	74	124	17	2	19	79	1	.279
1963	Indianapolis	AA	OF	11	34	5	13	2	1	-	7	0	.382
1963	Mexico City	MEX	1B	92	329	70	110	15	2	21	71	1	.334
1964	Mexico City	MEX	OF 1B	137	428	83	131	19	4	14	69	0	.306
48-9	San Juan	PRWL	OF	-	109	-	35	-	-	2	17	-	.321

Year	Club	League	Pos	G	AB	R	H	2B	3B	HR	RBI	SB	BA
54-5	Marianao	CWL	OF	35	132	13	28	10	0	1	8	-	.212
63-4		NICR		-	202	35	61	-	-	-	32	-	.302

Alphonse Eugene "Al" or "Fuzzy" Smith. Born February 7, 1928 at Kirkwood, MO. 6' 1/2", 189 lbs. BR TR

Year	Club	League	Pos	G	AB	R	H	2B	3B	HR	RBI	SB	BA
1946	Cleveland	NAL	3B	-	-	-	-	-	-	-	-	-	
1947	Cleveland	NAL	SS	-	214	38	61	-	-	-	-	-	.285
1948	Cleveland	NAL	OF	58	217	44	65	9	8	3	39	10	.300
1948	Wilkes-Barre	EAST	OF 3B	68	231	37	73	8	8	1	30	5	.316
1949	Wilkes-Barre	EAST	3B	139	521	112	162	27	17	12	82	11	.311
1950	San Diego	PCL	OF 3B 2B	104	326	73	81	13	4	10	50	11	.248
1951	San Diego	PCL	OF	25	89	16	25	5	2	3	10	1	.281
1952	Indianapolis	AA	OF 3B	136	455	80	131	26	12	20	69	10	.288
1953	Cleveland	AL	OF 3B	47	150	28	36	9	0	3	14	2	.240
1953	Indianapolis	AA	3B	86	313	72	104	20	7	18	75	9	.332
1954	Cleveland	AL	OF 3B	131	481	101	135	29	6	11	50	2	.281
1955	Cleveland	AL	OF 3B	154	607	**123**	186	27	4	22	77	11	.306
1956	Cleveland	AL	OF 3B	141	526	87	144	26	5	16	71	6	.274
1957	Cleveland	AL	3B OF	135	507	78	125	23	5	11	49	12	.247
1958	Chicago	AL	OF	139	480	61	121	23	5	12	58	3	.252
1959	Chicago	AL	OF	129	472	65	112	16	4	17	55	7	.237
1960	Chicago	AL	OF	142	536	80	169	31	3	12	72	8	.315
1961	Chicago	AL	3B OF	147	532	88	148	29	4	28	93	4	.278
1962	Chicago	AL	3B OF	142	511	62	149	23	8	16	82	3	.292
1963	Baltimore	AL	OF 3B	120	368	45	100	17	1	10	39	9	.272
1964	Cleveland, Boston	AL	OF 3B	90	187	25	33	5	1	6	16	0	.176
51-2	Ponce	PRWL	OF	64	242	54	71	9	5	**9**	33	10	.293
52-3	Ponce	PRWL	OF	-	210	39	56	15	7	4	28	-	.267
53-4	Ponce	PRWL	OF	60	206	41	53	6	1	5	19	-	.257

George Cornelius Smith. Born July 7, 1937 at St.Petersburg, FL. Died June 15, 1987 at St. Petersburg, FL. 5'10", 170 lbs. BR TR

Year	Club	League	Pos	G	AB	R	H	2B	3B	HR	RBI	SB	BA
1955	St. Petersburg	FLST	SS	2	9	0	1	0	0	0	0	0	.111
1956	Indianapolis	NAL	SS	-	-	-	-	-	-	-	-	-	
1957	Indianapolis	NAL	SS	-	-	-	-	-	-	-	-	-	
1958	Durham	CARO	2B	83	300	40	68	9	2	4	24	2	.227
1959	Duluth-Superior	NORL	2B	107	384	61	91	8	5	3	30	8	.237
1959	Durham	CARO	2B	11	42	4	10	0	0	0	2	1	.238
1960	Knoxville	SATL	2B	41	116	19	27	5	3	1	12	2	.233
1961	Knoxville	SATL	3B 2B	104	406	66	102	11	7	5	36	8	.251
1962	Denver	AA	2B	5	18	5	7	2	0	0	0	0	.389
1962	Knoxville	SATL	OF INF	118	445	90	130	15	8	2	45	14	.292
1963	Detroit	AL	2B	52	171	16	37	8	2	0	17	4	.216
1963	Syracuse	INT	2B	111	418	50	94	17	5	6	36	4	.225
1964	Detroit	AL	2B	5	7	1	2	0	0	0	2	1	.286
1964	Syracuse	INT	2B SS	151	596	82	159	24	8	6	48	10	.267
1965	Detroit	AL	INF	32	53	6	5	0	0	1	1	0	.094
1965	Syracuse	INT	2B SS	91	352	58	91	14	6	4	25	9	.259
1966	Boston	AL	2B SS	128	403	41	86	19	4	8	37	4	.213
1967	Phoenix	PCL	2B	46	120	12	24	5	1	1	9	1	.200
1968	Buffalo	INT	2B	22	77	13	25	6	0	1	7	2	.325
1968	Oklahoma City	PCL	2B	11	43	6	8	1	0	0	1	0	.186

John Ford Smith. Born January 9, 1919 at Phoenix, AZ. Died February 26, 1983 in Phoenix, AZ. 6'1", 198 lbs. BB TR

Year	Club	League	Pos	G	AB	R	H	2B	3B	HR	RBI	SB	BA
1944	Chicago	NAL	OF P	46	156	23	59	6	4	1	-	7	.378
1945	Chicago	NAL	OF P	68	251	35	76	6	3	1	35	2	.303
1948	KC, New York			24	59	8	17	5	1	0	11	0	.288
1952	Phoenix	AZTX	P	48	140	18	51	12	1	2	34	0	.364

Milton Smith. Born March 27, 1929 at Columbus, GA. 5'10", 165 lbs. BR TR

Year	Club	League	Pos	G	AB	R	H	2B	3B	HR	RBI	SB	BA
1949	Philadelphia	NAL	2B	26	88	8	18	-	-	-	-	-	.205
1950	Philadelphia	NAL	2B	41	156	25	35	3	3	0	11	7	.224
1951	Philadelphia	NAL	2B	-	-	-	-	-	-	-	-	-	
1952	Lewiston	WINT	SS 3B	146	538	126	171	33	12	12	73	42	.318
1952	San Diego	PCL	PH	1	1	0	0	0	0	0	0	0	.000
1953	Salem	WINT	3B	56	202	51	79	10	7	7	51	14	.391
1953	San Diego	PCL	3B	55	144	20	39	5	1	3	10	1	.271
1954	San Diego	PCL	3B OF	131	388	61	114	22	5	9	51	14	.294
1955	Cincinnati	NL	3B 2B	36	102	15	20	3	1	3	8	2	.196
1955	San Diego	PCL	3B	108	414	89	140	35	9	9	65	10	.338
1956	Seattle	PCL	3B 2B	145	516	72	141	28	13	9	58	15	.273
1957	Omaha	AA	3B 2B	145	516	88	136	27	12	8	70	9	.264

Year	Club	League	Pos	G	AB	R	H	2B	3B	HR	RBI	SB	BA
1958	Toronto	INT	3B 2B OF	130	439	72	124	22	9	3	32	6	.282
1959	Sacramento	PCL	3B 2B	133	482	71	131	23	8	6	51	7	.272
1960	Sacramento	PCL	3B	140	510	65	130	22	9	5	51	5	.255
1961	Hawaii	PCL	2B 3B OF	70	234	27	56	10	1	7	30	4	.239
1961	Tri-Cities	NWL	2B 3B	39	138	28	49	12	2	1	21	7	.355
55-6	Cienfuegos	CWL	2B	-	225	42	56	10	5	5	18	5	.249
57-8	Marianao	CWL	2B	-	241	40	77	10	4	5	39	5	**.320**
58-9	Marianao	CWL	2B	-	239	22	56	7	2	1	19	9	.234
59-0	Estrellas	DOM	2B	-	230	-	66	-	-	1	21	-	.287
60-1	Cervbalboa	PANA	2B	-	136	-	38	-	-	1	17	-	.279

Quincy Smith. Born 1921. 5'10 1/2", 171 lbs. BB TR

Year	Club	League	Pos	G	AB	R	H	2B	3B	HR	RBI	SB	BA
1943	Cleveland	NAL	OF	-	-	-	-	-	-	-	-	-	
1945	Birmingham	NAL	OF	20	67	15	19	2	1	0	2	1	.284
1946	Birmingham	NAL	OF	-	-	-	-	-	-	-	-	-	
1949	Belleville	MOV	OF	100	383	82	107	21	9	6	56	18	.279
1950	Vincenes	MOV	OF	114	450	91	141	30	7	8	75	22	.313
1951	Centralia-Paris	MOV	OF	120	506	126	155	35	14	8	105	36	.306
1952	Paris	MOV	OF	117	483	124	153	31	10	11	65	30	.317
1953	Paris	MOV	OF	117	443	94	139	32	10	7	65	49	.314
1954	Paris	MOV	OF	85	319	59	93	16	5	5	52	19	.292

Theolic "Fireball" Smith. Born May 19, 1914 at St. Louis, MO. 5'11 1/2", 170 lbs. BB TR

Year	Club	League	Pos	G	AB	R	H	2B	3B	HR	RBI	SB	BA
1940	Mexico City	MEX	P OF	80	291	55	106	22	4	3	53	4	.364
1941	Mexico City	MEX	OF P	93	327	65	93	10	6	1	38	4	.284
1942	Mexico City	MEX	OF P	73	270	54	80	12	1	0	25	5	.296
1944	Mexico City	MEX	P OF	87	271	35	81	5	2	1	26	5	.299
1945	Mexico City	MEX	P OF	73	251	47	72	11	7	2	42	1	.287
1946	Mexico City	MEX	P OF	77	236	33	66	6	3	3	31	4	.280
1947	Mexico City	MEX	P OF 1B	67	149	24	43	5	2	1	20	2	.289
1948	Mexico City	MEX	P OF	54	105	17	29	4	4	0	14	1	.276
38-9	Almendares	CWL	OF P	-	79	11	30	1	0	0	9	1	.380

Willie Smith. Born February 11, 1939 at Anniston, AL. 6', 182 lbs. BL TL

Year	Club	League	Pos	G	AB	R	H	2B	3B	HR	RBI	SB	BA
1958	Birmingham	NAL	P	15	24	3	11	1	2	0	9	0	.458
1959	Birmingham	NAL	P OF	-	-	-	-	-	-	-	-	-	
1960	Duluth-Superior	NORL	P OF	44	91	6	27	2	0	1	10	0	.297
1961	Knoxville	SATL	P OF	68	115	9	25	2	1	1	12	0	.217
1962	Knoxville	SATL	P OF	71	147	23	40	7	1	1	14	1	.272
1963	Detroit	AL	P	17	8	2	1	0	0	0	0	0	.125
1963	Syracuse	INT	P	50	79	10	30	4	1	1	13	0	.380
1964	Los Angeles	AL	OF P	118	359	46	108	14	6	11	51	7	.301
1964	Syracuse	INT	P	2	3	1	2	0	0	1	1	0	.667
1965	California	AL	OF 1B	136	459	52	120	14	9	14	57	9	.261
1966	California	AL	OF	90	195	18	36	3	2	1	20	1	.185
1967	Cleveland	AL	OF 1B	21	32	0	7	2	0	0	2	0	.219
1967	Portland	PCL	1B OF P	119	413	60	121	29	5	17	56	2	.293
1968	Chicago	NL	OF 1B P	55	142	13	39	8	2	5	25	0	.275
1968	Cleveland	AL	1B P OF	33	42	1	6	2	0	0	3	0	.143
1969	Chicago	NL	OF 1B	103	195	21	48	9	1	9	25	1	.246
1970	Chicago	NL	1B OF	87	167	15	36	9	1	5	24	2	.216
1971	Cincinnati	NL	1B	31	55	3	9	2	0	1	4	0	.164
1971	Indianapolis	AA	1B OF	77	259	50	91	15	3	8	43	1	.351

Sylvester Snead. BR TR

Year	Club	League	Pos	G	AB	R	H	2B	3B	HR	RBI	SB	BA
1941	Kansas City	NAL	OF	-	-	-	-	-	-	-	-	-	
1943	Cinc.-Ind.	NAL	OF	-	27	-	5	2	0	0	-	0	.185
1946	New York	NNL	OF	19	66	6	16	3	0	0	3	5	.242
1950	Elmwood	MADK	UTL	47	162	-	41	-	-	1	15	-	.253
1951	Drum., St. Hyacin.	PROV	C 1B	31	69	6	12	3	0	0	2	1	.174

Herbert Souell. Born February 5, 1913 at West Monroe, LA. BB TR

Year	Club	League	Pos	G	AB	R	H	2B	3B	HR	RBI	SB	BA
1940	Kansas City	NAL	3B	-	-	-	-	-	-	-	-	-	
1941	Kansas City	NAL	3B	-	-	-	-	-	-	-	-	-	
1942	Kansas City	NAL	3B	-	121	-	33	4	-	-	-	0	.273
1943	Kansas City	NAL	3B	-	103	-	32	3	0	-	-	1	.311
1944	Kansas City	NAL	3B	57	205	26	50	6	4	1	-	8	.244
1945	Kansas City	NAL	3B	46	177	34	49	5	4	-	22	14	.277
1946	Kansas City	NAL	3B	-	-	-	-	-	-	-	-	-	
1946	San Luis	MEX	3B	12	47	3	9	1	0	0	6	0	.191

Year	Club	League	Pos	G	AB	R	H	2B	3B	HR	RBI	SB	BA
1947	Kansas City	NAL	3B	-	-	-	-	-	-	-	-	-	
1948	Kansas City	NAL	3B	69	298	68	90	11	8	5	36	9	.302
1949	Kansas City	NAL	3B	88	**380**	53	97	-	-	-	-	-	.255
1950	Kansas City	NAL	3B	68	286	49	86	17	4	1	34	71	.301
1951	Carman	MADK	3B	59	212	-	65	-	-	7	39	-	.307
1951	Kansas City	NAL	3B	-	-	-	-	-	-	-	-	-	
1952	Carman	MADK	3B	-	-	-	-	-	-	-	-	-	
1952	Spokane	WINT	3B	20	72	12	19	1	1	0	10	2	.264
1952	Tucson-Chihuahua	AZMX	3B	91	367	58	109	16	8	1	51	18	.297
1953	Carman	MADK	3B	72	318	-	96	-	-	5	39	-	.302
47-8	Ponce	PRWL	3B	-	252	44	87	11	0	3	25	-	.345

Edward Steele. Born August 8, 1915 at Selma, AL. 5'10", 195 lbs. BL TR

Year	Club	League	Pos	G	AB	R	H	2B	3B	HR	RBI	SB	BA
1941	Birmingham	NAL	OF	-	-	-	-	-	-	-	-	-	
1942	Birmingham	NAL	OF	-	-	-	-	-	-	-	-	-	
1943	Birmingham	NAL	OF	-	-	-	-	-	-	-	-	-	
1944	Birmingham	NAL	OF	61	218	47	66	13	8	4	-	9	.303
1945	Birmingham	NAL	OF	57	196	41	69	10	4	1	27	11	.352
1946	Birmingham	NAL	OF	-	-	-	-	-	-	-	-	-	
1947	Birmingham	NAL	OF	-	-	-	-	-	-	-	-	-	
1948	Birmingham	NAL	OF	72	260	71	78	15	5	8	46	10	.300
1949	Birmingham	NAL	OF	85	**304**	68	96	-	-	-	-	-	.316
1950	Birmingham	NAL	OF	71	245	57	75	21	5	4	51	15	.306
1951	Birmingham	NAL	OF	-	184	42	68	-	-	5	33	-	.370
1952	Birmingham	NAL	OF	-	-	-	-	-	-	-	-	-	
1952	Denver	WEST	OF	47	142	26	36	7	1	0	18	5	.254
1952	Hollywood	PCL	OF	22	61	11	13	3	0	2	10	1	.213
1953	Detroit	NAL	OF	14	48	8	7	1	1	0	6	0	.146
1955	Detroit	NAL	OF	-	-	-	-	-	-	-	-	-	
1958	Detroit	NAL	OF	17	22	5	6	2	1	1	2	0	.273

Lonnie Summers. Born August 2, 1915 at Davis, OK. 6', 210 lbs. BR TR

Year	Club	League	Pos	G	AB	R	H	2B	3B	HR	RBI	SB	BA
1938	Baltimore	NNL	C	-	-	-	-	-	-	-	-	-	
1940	Tam., SR, NL, VC, Chi.	MEX	P C	95	372	58	116	23	13	5	65	2	.312
1941	Tampico	MEX	C P	28	117	19	35	9	4	4	27	1	.299
1943	Chicago	NAL	C	-	-	-	-	-	-	-	-	-	
1946	Tampico	MEX	C OF	39	147	20	45	11	0	4	24	0	.306
1947	Tampico	MEX	C OF	120	440	45	119	23	4	2	44	0	.270
1948	Chicago	NAL	C	-	-	-	-	-	-	-	-	-	
1948	Tampico, Mex.City	MEX	C OF	66	176	24	51	9	3	4	15	2	.290
1949	Chicago	NAL	C	81	296	56	90	-	-	-	-	-	.304
1949	Mexico City	MEX	C	8	27	6	10	3	0	3	13	0	.370
1950	Pastora	VENZ	C	-	-	-	-	-	-	-	-	-	
1951	Chicago	NAL	1B C OF	-	-	-	-	-	-	-	-	-	
1952	San Diego	PCL	C	125	340	31	82	21	2	7	57	2	.241
1953	Lincoln	WEST	C	13	46	5	7	2	0	0	2	0	.152
1953	Oklahoma City	TEX	C	12	25	2	4	1	0	0	-	0	.160
1953	San Diego	PCL	C	43	88	6	14	2	0	1	7	0	.159
1954	Yakima	WINT	C	119	414	63	129	20	3	14	80	3	.312
1956	Yakima	NWL	C	3	12	0	4	0	0	0	0	0	.333
49-0	Ponce	PRWL	C	-	67	10	17	2	1	0	5	0	.254

Earl Taborn. Born July 21, 1922 at Carrie Mills, IL. 5'11", 170 lbs. BR TR

Year	Club	League	Pos	G	AB	R	H	2B	3B	HR	RBI	SB	BA
1946	Kansas City	NAL	C	-	-	-	-	-	-	-	-	-	
1947	Kansas City	NAL	C	-	-	-	-	-	-	-	-	-	
1948	Kansas City	NAL	C	63	226	26	68	13	1	0	27	2	.301
1949	Kansas City	NAL	C	-	-	-	-	-	-	-	-	-	
1949	Newark	INT	C	33	97	6	24	5	1	0	6	0	.247
1950	Kansas City	NAL	C	24	87	18	30	6	1	4	25	2	.345
1951	Kansas City	NAL	C	-	-	-	-	-	-	-	-	-	
1951	Mexico City	MEX	C OF P	82	314	56	78	9	0	8	61	5	.248
1952	Aguila	MEX	C P	88	315	44	88	14	0	7	70	4	.279
1953	Aguila	MEX	C	76	264	47	78	7	4	6	30	6	.295
1954	Aguila	MEX	C	13	46	15	14	2	0	5	10	1	.304
1954	Oriente	DMSL	C	-	135	18	30	-	-	0	27	3	.222
1955	Aguila	MEX	C	96	342	60	99	12	3	15	65	3	.289
1956	Aguila	MEX	C	120	377	57	105	13	5	12	66	4	.279
1957	Nuevo Laredo	MEX	C	104	331	66	104	8	1	**27**	69	5	.314
1958	Nuevo Laredo	MEX	C	112	383	69	105	13	0	17	58	5	.274
1959	Mexico City	MEX	C	18	56	7	13	1	0	2	6	1	.232

Year	Club	League	Pos	G	AB	R	H	2B	3B	HR	RBI	SB	BA
1960	Aguila	MEX	C	81	192	28	53	7	0	5	27	0	.276
1961	Puebla	MEX	C	66	187	22	50	10	0	2	26	0	.267
49-0	Santurce	PRWL	C	-	-	-	-	-	-	-	-	-	

Joe Cephus Taylor. Born March 2, 1926 at Chapman, AL. 6'1", 185 lbs. BR TR

Year	Club	League	Pos	G	AB	R	H	2B	3B	HR	RBI	SB	BA
1949	Chicago	NAL	C	-	-	-	-	-	-	-	-	-	
1950	Chicago	NAL	C	-	-	-	-	-	-	-	-	-	
1950	Winnipeg	MADK	C	34	114	-	27	-	-	3-	15	-	.237
1951	Chicago	NAL	C OF	-	-	-	-	-	-	-	-	-	
1951	Farnham	PROV	OF	43	172	25	62	9	1	10	29	1	.360
1952	St. Hyacinthe	PROV	OF	120	483	102	149	35	4	25	112	16	.308
1953	Ottawa	INT	OF	70	243	42	76	16	3	7	45	4	.313
1953	Williamsport	EAST	OF	78	284	38	92	9	2	10	44	14	.324
1954	Ottawa	INT	OF	131	462	71	149	24	4	23	79	4	.323
1954	Philadelphia	AL	OF	18	58	5	13	1	1	1	8	0	.224
1955	Columbus, Toronto	INT	OF	55	203	44	58	10	1	12	38	2	.286
1955	Portland	PCL	OF	73	271	38	80	18	4	10	55	2	.295
1956	Seattle	PCL	OF	150	484	79	126	32	0	24	89	5	.260
1957	Cincinnati	NL	OF	33	107	14	28	7	0	4	9	0	.262
1957	Seattle	PCL	OF	115	394	70	120	15	4	22	72	3	.305
1958	Baltimore	AL	OF	36	77	11	21	4	0	2	9	0	.273
1958	Omaha	AA	OF	43	148	28	40	10	0	10	34	4	.270
1958	St. Louis	NL	OF	18	23	2	7	3	0	1	3	0	.304
1959	Baltimore	AL	OF	14	32	2	5	1	0	1	2	0	.156
1959	Vancouver	PCL	OF	110	401	70	117	25	2	23	77	10	.292
1960	Seattle	PCL	OF	145	526	104	153	26	7	30	94	7	.291
1961	San Diego	PCL	OF	132	441	69	118	22	4	26	74	-	.268
1962	Hawaii, Vancouver	PCL	OF	109	353	35	87	15	0	13	37	2	.246
1963	Puebla, Mex City	MEX	OF	122	418	82	129	23	3	19	76	4	.309
53-4		PANA	OF	-	113	-	43	-	-	7	22	-	.381
53-4	San Juan	PRWL	OF	-	124	-	24	-	-	5	20	-	.194
54-5	San Juan	PRWL	OF	-	138	-	36	-	-	6	16	-	.261

Henry Curtis Thompson. Born December 8, 1925 at Oklahoma City, OK. Died September 30, 1969 in Fresno, CA. 5'9 1/2", 174 lbs. BL TR

Year	Club	League	Pos	G	AB	R	H	2B	3B	HR	RBI	SB	BA
1943	Kansas City	NAL	OF	-	70	-	22	6	1	2	-	1	.314
1945	Kansas City	NAL	2B	5	6	-	1	0	0	0	-	0	.167
1946	Kansas City	NAL	2B	8	27	-	6	0	0	4	0	2	.222
1947	Kansas City	NAL	INF	48	189	54	65	3	2	2	-	0	.344
1947	St. Louis	AL	2B	27	78	10	20	1	1	0	5	2	.256
1948	Kansas City	NAL	INF OF	70	267	75	100	20	8	11	58	20	.375
1949	Jersey City	INT	SS OF	68	230	53	68	14	3	14	37	11	.296
1949	New York	NL	2B 3B	75	275	51	77	10	4	9	34	5	.280
1950	New York	NL	3B OF	148	512	82	148	17	6	20	91	8	.289
1951	Minneapolis	AA	3B OF SS	14	53	18	18	2	0	7	13	5	.340
1951	New York	NL	3B	87	264	37	62	8	4	8	33	1	.235
1952	New York	NL	OF 3B 2B	128	423	67	110	13	9	17	67	4	.260
1953	New York	NL	3B 2B OF	114	388	80	117	15	8	24	74	6	.302
1954	New York	NL	3B 2B OF	136	448	76	118	18	1	26	86	3	.263
1955	New York	NL	3B 2B OF	135	432	65	106	13	1	17	63	2	.245
1956	New York	NL	3B OF SS	83	183	24	43	9	0	8	29	2	.235
1957	Minneapolis	AA	OF	78	222	32	54	5	0	2	19	4	.243
46-7	Havana	CWL	3B	64	225	40	72	6	6	4	32	5	.320
47-8	Havana	CWL	3B	80	299	48	95	11	10	1	50	13	.318
48-9	Havana	CWL	3B	70	265	60	85	14	8	7	44	19	.321
57-8	Ponce	PRWL	3B	3	8	0	1	0	0	0	1	0	.125

Robert Burns Thurman. Born May 14, 1917 at Wichita, KS. 6'1", 200 lbs. BL TL

Year	Club	League	Pos	G	AB	R	H	2B	3B	HR	RBI	SB	BA
1946	Homestead	NNL	P OF	21	49	5	20	1	1	2	16	0	.408
1947	Homestead	NNL	OF P	46	157	29	53	7	-	6	-	3	.338
1948	Homestead	NNL	OF P	55	206	-	71	-	-	-	-	-	.345
1949	Kansas City	NAL	OF	64	219	47	78	-	-	-	-	13	.356
1949	Newark	INT	OF	59	221	37	70	11	2	6	33	4	.317
1950	Springfield	INT	OF	145	465	68	125	26	7	12	78	5	.269
1951	San Francisco	PCL	OF	104	379	63	104	12	10	13	63	11	.274
1952	San Francisco	PCL	OF	116	393	60	110	19	4	9	52	9	.280
1953	Escogido	DMSL	OF	-	104	24	30	-	-	0	21	2	.288
1954	Escogido	DMSL	OF	-	140	29	42	-	-	11	34	2	.300
1955	Cincinnati	NL	OF	82	152	19	33	2	3	7	22	0	.217
1956	Cincinnati	NL	OF	80	139	25	41	5	2	8	22	0	.295

Year	Club	League	Pos	G	AB	R	H	2B	3B	HR	RBI	SB	BA
1957	Cincinnati	NL	OF	74	190	38	47	4	2	16	40	0	.247
1957	Seattle	PCL	OF	28	104	17	30	2	0	8	13	0	.288
1958	Cincinnati	NL	OF	94	178	23	41	7	4	4	20	1	.230
1959	Cincinnati	NL	PH	4	4	1	1	0	0	0	2	0	.250
1959	Omaha	AA	OF 1B	73	214	20	53	8	2	5	24	1	.248
1959	Seattle	PCL	OF	31	92	10	22	3	1	1	11	1	.239
1960	Charleston	AA	OF P	97	307	34	84	19	4	10	42	1	.274
1960	Seattle	PCL	OF	11	19	4	4	0	0	1	3	0	.211
1961	Charlotte	SATL	OF	21	75	13	20	2	0	4	16	0	.267
47-8	Santurce	PRWL	OF	-	248	-	**102**	-	-	**9**	-	-	.411
48-9	Santurce	PRWL	OF	-	-	-	-	-	-	**18**	65	-	
49-0	Santurce	PRWL	OF	-	303	**69**	107	19	-	13	57	25	.353
50-1	Santurce	PRWL	OF	-	-	-	**112**	**22**	-	-	66	-	
51-2	Santurce	PRWL	OF	-	190	-	58	17	**8**	4	35	3	.305
52-3	Santurce	PRWL	OF	-	-	-	-	-	-	13	-	-	
53-4	Santurce	PRWL	OF	-	302	-	85	-	-	5	35	-	.281
54-5	Santurce	PRWL	OF	-	229	-	74	-	-	14	60	-	.323
55-6	Santurce	PRWL		-	187	-	65	-	-	11	47	-	.348
56-7	Santurce	PRWL	OF	-	-	-	-	-	-	10	-	-	
57-8	Santurce	PRWL	OF	-	239	-	63	-	**8**	10	36	-	.264
59-0	Ponce	PRWL	OF P	25	84	10	22	3	1	3	11	2	.262

Robert Lee "Bill" Trice. Born August 28, 1926 at Newton, GA. Died September 16, 1988 in Wierton, WV. 6'2 1/2", 190 lbs. BR TR

Year	Club	League	Pos	G	AB	R	H	2B	3B	HR	RBI	SB	BA
1951	Farnham	PROV	P OF 3B	70	194	27	46	9	1	2	12	4	.237
1952	St. Hyacinthe	PROV	P OF	88	300	62	89	13	5	1	39	16	.297
1953	Ottawa	INT	P OF	56	106	21	27	5	0	4	16	0	.255
1953	Philadelphia	AL	P	3	7	2	1	1	0	0	1	0	.143
1954	Ottawa	INT	P PH	22	47	8	14	2	0	4	10	0	.298
1954	Philadelphia	AL	P	20	42	6	12	3	0	1	5	0	.286
1955	Columbus	INT	P PH	30	38	5	7	1	1	1	6	0	.184
1955	Kansas City	AL	P	4	3	0	2	0	0	0	0	0	.667
1955	Savannah	SATL	P PH	20	34	3	6	1	1	0	1	0	.176
1956	Mexico City	MEX	OF P 3B	78	180	33	52	5	1	7	27	1	.289
1957	Mexico City	MEX	OF P	58	133	31	34	4	0	7	24	0	.256
1958	Mexico City	MEX	1B OF P	70	176	29	39	5	3	7	24	8	.222

Quincy Thomas Trouppe. Born December 25, 1912 at Dublin, GA. Died August 10, 1993 at Crevecoeur, MO. 6'2 1/2", 215 lbs. BB TR

Year	Club	League	Pos	G	AB	R	H	2B	3B	HR	RBI	SB	BA
1930	St. Louis	NNL	OF C	-	-	-	-	-	-	-	-	-	
1931	St. Louis	NNL	C OF	-	-	-	-	-	-	-	-	-	
1932	KC, Det., Home.		C OF	-	-	-	-	-	-	-	-	-	
1933	Chicago	NNL	C OF	-	-	-	-	-	-	-	-	-	
1934	Kansas City		C OF	-	-	-	-	-	-	-	-	-	
1935	KC, Chicago		C OF	-	-	-	-	-	-	-	-	-	
1936	Kansas City		C OF	-	-	-	-	-	-	-	-	-	
1938	Indianapolis	NAL	C OF	-	-	-	-	-	-	-	-	-	
1939	Monterrey	MEX	C 2B SS OF	38	137	33	42	11	3	4	18	7	.307
1939	St. Louis	NAL	C	-	-	-	-	-	-	-	-	-	
1940	Monterrey	MEX	3B	76	276	67	93	25	7	6	67	9	.337
1941	Monterrey	MEX	C 3B	98	363	73	111	25	4	9	67	9	.306
1942	Mexico City	MEX	C	70	269	69	98	**27**	5	12	57	20	.364
1943	Mexico City	MEX	C	76	276	51	83	18	3	12	42	5	.301
1944	Mexico City	MEX	C 3B 1B OF	57	197	32	47	12	1	7	35	4	.239
1945	Cleveland	NAL	C OF	50	159	29	39	6	6	1	23	5	.245
1946	Cleveland	NAL	C OF	55	179	-	56	-	-	5	-	-	.313
1947	Cleveland	NAL	C OF	49	142	34	50	-	-	-	-	-	.352
1948	Chicago	NAL	C OF	52	152	38	52	10	2	10	29	2	.342
1949	Drummondville	PROV	C OF	-	209	-	59	-	-	5	30	-	.282
1949	New York	NAL	C	-	-	-	-	-	-	-	-	-	
1950	Jalisco	MEX	C 3B	67	206	39	58	10	0	8	38	3	.282
1951	Jalisco	MEX	C	63	177	41	45	6	5	3	26	2	.254
1952	Cleveland	AL	C	6	10	1	1	0	0	0	0	0	.100
1952	Indianapolis	AA	C	84	205	39	53	7	2	8	40	0	.259
41-2	Guayama	PRWL	C	-	-	-	-	-	**10**	-	**57**	-	
44-5	Marianao	CWL	C	-	63	11	20	2	3	1	14	1	.317
44-5	San Juan	PRWL	C	-	40	-	11	-	-	1	4	-	.275
47-8	Caguas	PRWL	C	-	-	-	-	20	-	-	-	-	
49-0	Marianao	CWL	C	-	129	18	33	6	2	3	13	2	.256
50-1	Marianao	CWL	C	40	115	17	25	5	1	1	10	-	.217

Year	Club	League	Pos	G	AB	R	H	2B	3B	HR	RBI	SB	BA
James C. "Jim" Tugerson. Born 1923 at Florence Villa, FL. 6'4", 194 lbs. BR TR													
1952	Indianapolis	NAL	P	-	63	15	22	-	-	5	18	-	.349
1953	Knoxville	MTST	P 1B	81	182	46	56	8	1	5	35	4	.308
Robert Turner. Born in 1927. BR TR													
1946	Kansas City	NAL	C	-	-	-	-	-	-	-	-	-	
1949	Berwick	NATL	C	12	27	4	7	0	0	1	5	0	.259
1949	Kingston	COL	C	3	0	0	0	0	0	0	0	0	
1950	Houston	NAL	C	-	-	-	-	-	-	-	-	-	
1952	Porterville	SWIN	C	50	170	19	45	8	3	0	30	3	.265
1953	Carman	MADK	C	54	201	-	41	-	-	1	33	-	.204
Guillermo Vargas. Born in 1919. 5'11", 140 lbs. BR TR													
1949	New York	NAL	OF	35	123	10	34	-	-	-	-	-	.276
1950	Nuevo Laredo	MEX	OF	35	126	7	31	4	0	0	10	2	.246
1952	Drummondville	PROV	OF	120	444	76	125	15	6	3	-	4	.282
Gilbert Varona. Born in Cuba. BR TR													
1950	Memphis	NAL	1B	22	71	12	15	2	0	0	7	0	.211
1951	Memphis	NAL	1B	-	-	-	-	-	-	-	-	-	
1952	Memphis	NAL	1B	-	-	-	-	-	-	-	-	-	
1953	Nuevo Laredo	MEX	1B	10	37	4	9	0	0	0	4	0	.243
1954	Del Rio	BGST	1B	13	34	3	6	2	0	0	1	0	.176
1954	Memphis	NAL	1B	74	276	58	74	9	6	7	35	13	.268
1955	Memphis	NAL	1B	-	-	-	-	-	-	-	-	-	
Orlando Varona. Born December 8, 1926 at Havana, Cuba. 6', 170 lbs. BR TR													
1948	Memphis	NAL	SS 3B	52	142	14	25	6	1	0	13	2	.176
1949	Memphis	NAL	SS	82	310	37	70	-	-	-	-	-	.226
1950	Memphis	NAL	SS	74	300	65	82	15	4	0	28	7	.273
1951	Memphis	NAL	SS	-	-	-	-	-	-	-	-	-	
1952	Memphis	NAL	SS	-	-	-	-	-	-	-	-	-	
1952	Tampa	FLIN	SS	44	147	12	31	3	2	0	17	0	.211
1953	Monterrey	MEX	SS	75	315	42	85	16	2	0	27	5	.270
1954	Abilene	WTNM	2B SS	127	507	85	141	24	4	6	61	9	.278
1955	Memphis	NAL	SS	-	-	-	-	-	-	-	-	-	
50-1	Havana	CWL	SS	6	2	1	0	0	0	0	0	0	.000
51-2	Havana	CWL	SS	49	149	18	32	2	0	3	16	-	.215
52-3	Havana	CWL	SS	27	45	4	8	0	0	0	1	-	.178
53-4	Havana	CWL	SS	25	28	1	7	0	0	0	1	-	.250
Armando Vasquez. Born August 20, 1922 at Guines, Cuba. 5'8", 160 lbs. BL TL													
1944	Cinc.-Ind.	NAL	1B	56	184	25	44	3	3	0	-	7	.239
1945	Cinc.-Ind.	NAL	1B	42	134	16	33	5	3	0	10	2	.246
1948	New York	NNL	1B	-	-	-	-	-	-	-	-	-	
1950	Brandon	MADK	1B	47	193	-	47	-	-	1	27	-	.244
1951	Brandon	MADK	1B	57	201	-	42	-	-	3	36	-	.209
1952	Brandon	MADK	1B	-	-	-	-	-	-	-	-	-	
1952	Indianapolis	NAL	1B	-	-	-	-	-	-	-	-	-	
1954	Thibodaux	Evag	1B	34	108	19	28	8	0	0	14	2	.259
Luis Villodas. Born 1922 at Ponce, PR. 6'2", 200 lbs. BR TR													
1946	Baltimore	NNL	C	26	62	12	17	6	2	1	9	-	.274
1947	Baltimore	NNL	C	-	76	8	17	-	-	-	-	-	.224
1951	Cibaenas	DMSL	C	-	156	19	54	-	-	-	25	2	**.346**
1952	Cibaenas	DMSL	C	-	180	15	48	-	5	-	28	-	.267
1954	Borger, Alb.	WTNM	C	132	477	83	169	40	3	9	79	1	.354
1955	Abilene	WTNM	C	28	113	24	37	11	2	1	24	2	.327
45-6	Mayaquez	PRWL	C	-	40	-	16	-	-	-	-	-	.400
53-4	Ponce	PRWL	C P	27	51	4	6	1	-	-	1	-	.118
54-5	San Juan	PRWL	C	-	39	-	13	0	0	2	7	-	.333
55-6	San Juan	PRWL	C	-	26	-	5	0	0	0	6	-	.192
Archie V. Ware. Born June 19, 1918 at Greenville, FL. 5'9", 160 lbs. BL TL													
1940	Chicago	NAL	1B	-	-	-	-	-	-	-	-	-	
1942	Cinc.-Cleveland	NAL	1B	-	-	-	-	-	-	-	-	-	
1943	Cleveland	NAL	1B	-	80	-	23	2	3	0	-	-	.288
1944	Cleveland	NAL	1B	**71**	255	33	68	7	4	1	-	4	.267
1945	Cleveland	NAL	1B	56	215	42	64	7	3	1	39	7	.298
1946	Cleveland	NAL	1B	-	-	-	-	-	-	-	-	-	

Year	Club	League	Pos	G	AB	R	H	2B	3B	HR	RBI	SB	BA
1947	Cleveland	NAL	1B	73	284	64	99	-	-	-	-	-	.349
1948	Cleveland	NAL	1B	77	307	50	107	23	2	0	29	2	.349
1949	Louisville	NAL	1B	77	279	37	63	-	-	-	-	-	.226
1950	Indianapolis	NAL	1B	83	325	52	90	14	3	0	23	3	.277
1951	Farnham	PROV	1B	122	439	67	113	10	1	6	48	7	.257
1951	Indianapolis	NAL	1B	-	-	-	-	-	-	-	-	-	
1952	Lewiston	WINT	1B	15	42	9	12	1	0	0	6	0	.286

Charles "Charlie" White. Born August 12, 1928 at Kingston, NC. 5'11", 196 lbs. BL TR

Year	Club	League	Pos	G	AB	R	H	2B	3B	HR	RBI	SB	BA
1950	Philadelphia	NAL	3B C	38	129	16	33	4	0	0	13	5	.256
1951	Toronto	INT	3B	60	230	31	65	10	2	4	27	5	.283
1951	Winnipeg	MADK	3B	-	-	-	-	-	-	-	-	-	
1952	Toronto	INT	C 3B	72	123	7	32	9	0	2	13	0	.260
1953	San Antonio	TEX	C 3B	108	358	30	98	23	1	4	46	5	.274
1954	Milwaukee	NL	C	50	93	14	22	4	0	1	8	0	.237
1955	Milwaukee	NL	C	12	30	3	7	1	0	0	4	0	.233
1955	Rochester	INT	C	45	116	19	24	3	0	2	14	3	.207
1956	Wichita	AA	C	87	226	28	63	16	2	6	39	1	.279
1957	Vancouver	PCL	C	100	318	38	88	14	4	1	48	1	.277
1958	Vancouver	PCL	C	119	351	38	102	18	3	2	38	4	.291
1959	Vancouver	PCL	C	50	139	18	38	7	2	1	16	1	.273
1960	Vancouver	PCL	C	118	336	36	87	16	2	3	46	0	.259
1961	Vanc., Portland	PCL	C	95	272	31	73	14	1	2	37	1	.268
1962	Hawaii	PCL	C	82	248	39	64	11	0	6	23	2	.258
1963	Hawaii	PCL	C	56	156	12	36	7	0	1	14	0	.231
1965	Vancouver	PCL	C	8	6	0	0	0	0	0	0	0	.000
60-1	Cerv., Balboa	PANA	C	-	128	-	40	-	-	1	19	-	.313

James Eugene Wilkes. Born October 1, 1925 at Philadelphia, PA. 5'6", 150 lbs. BL TL

Year	Club	League	Pos	G	AB	R	H	2B	3B	HR	RBI	SB	BA
1945	Newark	NNL	OF	15	41	9	13	0	1	0	6	2	.317
1946	Newark	NNL	OF	42	147	25	40	4	2	2	21	3	.272
1947	Newark	NNL	OF	-	278	48	65	11	-	2	-	5	.234
1949	Houston	NAL	OF	66	256	42	65	-	-	-	-	-	.254
1950	Elmira	EAST	OF	36	135	16	38	3	0	0	14	1	.281
1950	Houston	NAL	OF	39	156	33	31	4	1	4	15	7	.199
1950	Three Rivers	CAAM	OF	34	122	22	22	8	2	1	11	15	.180
1951	Elmira	EAST	OF	10	11	0	3	0	0	0	3	1	.273
1951	Lancaster	INST	OF	105	389	65	90	11	5	2	32	17	.231
1952	Great Falls	PION	OF	9	17	4	4	2	1	0	-	2	.235
1952	Indianapolis	NAL	OF	-	292	63	95	-	-	5	34	43	.325

Jesse Harold Williams. Born June 22, 1913 at Henderson, TX. Died February 27, 1990 in Kansas City, MO. BR TR

Year	Club	League	Pos	G	AB	R	H	2B	3B	HR	RBI	SB	BA
1939	Kansas City	NAL	3B OF	-	-	-	-	-	-	-	-	-	
1940	Kansas City	NAL	SS	-	-	-	-	-	-	-	-	-	
1941	Kansas City	NAL	SS	-	69	-	16	2	4	0	-	0	.232
1942	Kansas City	NAL	SS	-	50	-	13	5	0	0	-	0	.260
1943	Kansas City	NAL	SS	-	87	-	25	4	2	1	-	0	.287
1944	Kansas City	NAL	SS	41	135	18	35	6	3	0	-	8	.259
1945	Kansas City	NAL	SS	49	198	35	50	7	1	1	12	8	.253
1946	Kansas City	NAL	SS	-	-	-	-	-	-	-	-	-	
1946	San Luis	MEX	SS	96	386	50	107	16	6	3	44	16	.277
1949	Indianapolis	NAL	SS	80	311	52	74	-	-	-	-	-	.238
1950	Indianapolis	NAL	SS	-	-	-	-	-	-	-	-	-	
1951	Kansas City	NAL	SS	-	-	-	-	-	-	-	-	27	
1951	Nuevo Laredo	MEX	SS	1	1	0	0	0	0	0	0	0	.000
1952	Vancouver	PCL	SS 3B	126	474	73	119	18	4	0	42	20	.251
1954	Beaumont	TEX	SS	8	6	0	1	0	0	0	0	0	.167
1954	Oriente	DMSL		-	67	16	18	-	-	-	8	2	.269
46-7	Almendares	CWL	SS	-	121	11	32	4	1	1	11	2	.264
48-9	San Juan	PRWL	SS	-	92	-	19	-	-	-	7	-	.207

Johnny Williams. Born 1916 at Shreveport, LA. 6'2", 208 lbs. BR TR

Year	Club	League	Pos	G	AB	R	H	2B	3B	HR	RBI	SB	BA
1944	Ind.-Cinc.	NAL	P OF	20	41	1	10	0	0	0	-	0	.244
1945	Cinc.-Ind.	NAL	P OF	32	50	2	15	3	0	0	1	0	.300
1948	Indianapolis	NAL	P OF	29	59	3	11	4	0	0	5	0	.186
1954	Ind.-Louis	NAL	SS OF	48	188	32	23	6	3	2	48	7	.188
1954	Oriente	DMSL		-	67	16	18	-	-	-	8	2	.269
1958	Birmingham	NAL	OF	31	115	30	41	6	2	4	27	0	.357

Year	Club	League	Pos	G	AB	R	H	2B	3B	HR	RBI	SB	BA
Leonard Williams. Born 1928. 5'10", 185 lbs. BR TR													
1950	Indianapolis	NAL	1B INF	-	-	-	-	-	-	-	-	-	
1951	Indianapolis	NAL	1B	-	-	-	-	-	-	14	-	-	
1952	Hartford	EAST	1B SS	109	367	61	93	20	1	16	64	13	.253
1953	Evansville	III	2B	130	494	99	151	15	14	24	95	5	.306
1954	Evansville	III	OF	101	330	62	89	13	2	12	57	4	.270
1954	Jacksonville	SATL	OF	9	17	-	5	-	-	-	-	-	.294
1955	Evansville	III	OF INF	108	383	85	119	25	5	17	68	4	.311
1956	Boise	PION	3B	77	293	63	103	17	1	24	93	3	.352
1957	Topeka	WEST	OF 3B 1B	141	534	119	169	27	5	43	113	4	.316
1958	Charlotte	SATL	OF	86	283	54	83	11	4	5	34	4	.293
1958	Ft. Worth	TEX	OF	12	41	6	7	1	1	0	2	0	.171
1959	Lancaster	EAST	OF	16	56	2	9	1	0	1	3	0	.161
57-8	Willard	COLB	OF	-	217	-	68	-	-	14	52	-	.313
Leroy Williams. Born 1928. 5'9 1/2", 169 lbs. BR TR													
1947	Newark	NNL	SS	-	-	-	-	-	-	-	-	-	
1948	Newark	NNL	SS	-	-	-	-	-	-	-	-	-	
1950	Kansas City	NAL	SS	18	65	14	20	1	2	1	9	2	.308
1950	Springfield	MOV	SS 2B	69	261	55	73	18	6	7	63	15	.280
Marvin Williams. Born February 12, 1923 at Houston, TX. 6', 195 lbs. BR TR													
1943	Philadelphia	NNL	2B	-	-	-	-	-	-	-	-	-	
1944	Philadelphia	NNL	2B	40	154	30	52	8	3	4	32	2	.338
1945	Mexico City	MEX	2B	51	221	53	80	18	6	10	51	7	.362
1945	Philadelphia	NNL	2B	15	56	15	22	1	3	4	13	1	.393
1947	Pastora	VENZ	2B	-	-	-	-	-	-	-	-	-	
1948	Mexico City	MEX	2B 1B	78	302	69	99	13	11	14	57	8	.328
1949	Jalisco	MEX	2B	3	12	4	7	1	0	1	4	0	.583
1949	Philadelphia	NAL	OF	-	-	-	-	-	-	-	-	-	
1950	Cleveland	NAL	2B	22	84	14	21	4	1	0	10	1	.250
1950	Sacramento	PCL	2B	38	120	18	30	4	1	6	21	3	.250
1951	Mexico City	MEX	INF OF	80	296	58	95	18	5	12	64	8	.321
1952	Chihuahua	AZTX	2B 3B	117	397	136	159	27	9	45	131	10	.401
1953	Laredo	GCL	OF	23	86	14	24	7	3	3	14	0	.279
1953	Mexico City	MEX	2B	40	153	37	57	12	3	2	29	11	.373
1954	Vancouver	PCL	2B	119	456	114	164	32	9	20	90	15	.360
1955	Columbia	SATL	3B	97	351	70	115	18	7	16	84	1	.328
1955	Seattle	PCL	1B 2B	35	117	20	27	6	2	5	22	1	.231
1956	Tulsa	TEX	INF OF	144	534	102	172	36	7	26	111	1	.322
1957	Tulsa	TEX	INF OF	134	466	53	118	23	3	8	76	2	.253
1958	Tulsa	TEX	1B	144	524	76	154	33	3	19	88	2	.294
1959	Mexico City	MEX	1B OF	109	378	76	117	14	2	29	109	1	.310
1959	Victoria	TEX	PH	5	5	2	2	0	0	1	2	0	.400
1960	Vict.,San Ant.	Tex	1B 3B OF	94	297	52	83	13	2	17	54	0	.279
1961	Vict., Rio Grd.Vall	TEX	3B 1B	116	354	55	98	16	2	10	71	2	.277
4405	Ponce	PRWL	2B	-	90	17	34	-	-	1	13	-	.378
46-7		VENZ	SS	-	-	29	-	13	-	-	41	-	
47-8	Leones	CUBA	2B	-	42	5	12	1	-	-	4	2	.286
49-0	Ponce	PRWL	2B	-	183	31	44	8	1	2	25	-	.240
57-8	Vera Cruz	MXWL	2B	-	232	-	77	-	-	11	57	-	.332
Willie C. "Curley" Williams. Born May 25, 1925 at Holy Hill, SC. 5'11 1/2", 176 lbs. BL TR													
1945	Newark	NNL	SS	25	87	20	29	5	1	6	11	6	.333
1947	Newark	NNL	SS	-	200	36	43	7	-	2	-	3	.215
1948	Newark	NNL	SS	-	-	-	-	-	-	-	-	-	
1949	Houston	NAL		53	210	34	61	-	-	-	-	-	.290
1950	Houston	NAL	SS	65	250	59	73	15	5	8	32	2	.292
1951	Colorado Springs	WEST	SS	20	64	17	19	2	1	4	19	0	.297
1951	New Orleans	NAL	SS	-	262	58	92	-	-	11	62	-	.351
1952	Scranton	EAST	SS 2B	66	228	33	61	8	4	5	30	5	.268
1952	Toledo, Charleston	AA	3B	36	128	16	30	3	2	2	14	0	.234
1953	Carman	MADK	SS	57	199	-	57	-	-	12	40	-	.286
1953	Licey	DMSL	INF	-	37	7	4	-	-	0	3	-	.108
1954	Birmingham	NAL	SS OF	77	241	47	68	17	2	12	58	6	.282
Arthur Lee "Artie" Wilson. Born October 28, 1920 at Springfield, AL. 5'11', 162 lbs. BL TR													
1944	Birmingham	NAL	SS	65	266	51	92	9	6	0	-	17	.346
1945	Birmingham	NAL	SS	63	249	51	90	8	2	3	23	17	.361
1946	Birmingham	NAL	SS	2	4	0	0	0	0	0	0	0	.000

Year	Club	League	Pos	G	AB	R	H	2B	3B	HR	RBI	SB	BA
1947	Birmingham	NAL	SS	53	212	42	79	-	-	-	-	-	.373
1948	Birmingham	NAL	SS	76	**333**	78	**134**	19	8	2	41	10	**.402**
1949	San Diego,Oakland	PCL	SS	165	607	129	211	19	9	0	37	47	.348
1950	Oakland	PCL	SS	196	**848**	**168**	**264**	27	17	1	48	31	.311
1951	Minneapolis	AA	INF OF	17	59	12	23	2	1	2	13	0	.390
1951	New York	NL	SS 2B 1B	19	22	2	4	0	0	0	1	2	.182
1951	Oakland	PCL	SS	81	349	39	89	8	1	0	22	6	.255
1951	Ottawa	INT	OF	2	7	2	2	1	0	0	0	1	.286
1952	Seattle	PCL	SS	160	683	95	**216**	15	8	1	59	25	.316
1953	Seattle	PCL	SS	177	638	80	212	23	**14**	2	76	9	.332
1954	Seattle	PCL	SS 2B 1B	163	660	92	222	24	**16**	0	50	20	.336
1955	Portland	PCL	2B 1B	155	616	88	189	20	2	2	23	12	.307
1956	Portland, Seattle	PCL	INF	101	273	33	80	9	4	0	25	6	.293
1957	Sacramento	PCL	2B	75	315	34	83	10	6	0	17	3	.263
1962	Kennewick	NWL	2B	14	42	7	9	0	0	0	2	1	.214
1962	Portland	PCL	2B 3B	25	55	3	9	0	1	0	2	0	.164
47-8	Mayaquez	CWL	SS	-	252	66	**102**	-	-	-	-	-	.405
48-9	Mayaquez	PRWL	SS	-	338	69	**126**	-	-	3	-	9	.373
49-0	Mayaquez	CWL	SS	-	262	52	87	-	-	-	53	-	.332
50-1	Marianao	CWL	SS	65	232	21	56	10	1	5	33	2	.241

Robert Wilson. Born February 22, 1925 at Dallas, TX. Died April 23, 1985 in Dallas, TX. 5'11", 197 lbs. BR TR

Year	Club	League	Pos	G	AB	R	H	2B	3B	HR	RBI	SB	BA
1947	Newark	NNL	3B OF	-	163	32	45	2	-	2	-	1	.276
1948	Newark	NNL	OF	-	-	-	-	-	-	-	-	-	
1949	Houston	NAL	OF	59	256	40	90	-	-	-	-	-	.352
1950	Elmira	EAST	3B	65	251	35	75	15	5	4	39	3	.299
1950	Houston	NAL	3B	38	156	33	56	12	2	5	27	3	.359
1951	Elmira	EAST	3B	131	492	87	154	26	2	8	60	14	.313
1952	St. Paul	AA	3B	**154**	626	90	209	31	9	13	117	7	.334
1953	St. Paul	AA	3B	147	575	70	182	32	5	12	77	8	.317
1954	Montreal	INT	3B	106	396	64	121	25	4	9	61	4	.306
1954	Oakland	PCL	3B	56	220	27	62	12	0	4	33	3	.282
1955	Montreal	INT	OF	150	**599**	94	**190**	**41**	10	9	85	10	.317
1956	Montreal	INT	OF	140	571	83	175	**43**	3	12	90	14	.306
1957	Montreal	INT	OF	140	528	63	153	30	2	8	57	11	.290
1958	Los Angeles	NL	OF	3	5	0	1	0	0	0	0	0	.200
1958	St. Paul	AA	OF	74	252	26	88	20	1	2	42	2	.349
1959	Montreal, Toronto	INT	OF 3B	145	511	67	166	30	1	17	72	2	.325
1960	Dallas-Ft. Worth	AA	OF	22	67	9	15	6	0	1	6	0	.224
1960	Toronto	INT	OF 3B	28	88	10	20	1	0	1	8	2	.227
49-0	Mayaquez	CWL	OF	-	270	-	89	-	-	-	57	-	.330
52-3	Cienfuegos	CWL	3B	-	225	28	61	7	2	5	22	1	.271
53-4	Ponce	PRWL	3B OF	55	193	21	45	10	-	1	17	2	.233
55-6	Leone	DOM	OF	-	207	-	**69**	-	-	-	-	-	**.333**
56-7	Caracas	VENZ	OF	45	180	27	63	14	2	4	33	2	**.350**

Lester Witherspoon. Born 1927. 6'1", 190 lbs. BB TR

Year	Club	League	Pos	G	AB	R	H	2B	3B	HR	RBI	SB	BA
1948	Indianapolis	NAL	OF	-	-	-	-	-	-	-	-	-	
1949	Homestead, Ind.		OF	-	-	-	-	-	-	-	-	-	
1950	Indianapolis	NAL	P OF	-	-	-	-	-	-	-	-	-	
1952	Porterville	SWIN	OF 1B	93	369	105	134	27	14	16	95	17	.363
1952	San Diego	PCL	OF	7	13	1	2	0	0	0	2	0	.154
1953	Salem	WINT	OF 1B	120	408	74	135	27	7	4	71	14	.331
1954	Lakeland	FLST	OF	70	257	54	85	14	4	5	58	8	.331
1954	West Palm Beach	FLST	OF	11	38	6	2	0	0	1	1	1	.053
1955	Texas City	BGST	3B 1B	114	406	63	123	20	11	14	72	6	.303

Parnell Woods. Born February 26, 1912 at Birmingham, AL. Died July 23, 1977 at Cleveland, OH. 5'9", 170.BR TR

Year	Club	League	Pos	G	AB	R	H	2B	3B	HR	RBI	SB	BA
1936	Birmingham	NAL	3B	2	6	-	1	0	0	0	-	0	.167
1937	Birmingham	NAL	3B 2B	23	93	-	25	1	3	5	-	-	.269
1938	Birmingham	NAL	3B	14	43	-	11	1	1	1	-	1	.256
1939	Cleveland, Jackson.	NAL	3B	21	67	-	23	1	3	0	-	1	.343
1940	Cleveland, Birm.	NAL	3B	16	66	-	21	2	0	0	-	0	.318
1941	Jacksonville	NAL	3B	4	11	-	1	0	0	0	-	2	.091
1942	Cincinnati, Jacks.	NAL	3B	0	35	-	12	1	1	1	-	0	.343
1943	Cleveland	NAL	3B	-	59	-	17	2	1	0	-	1	.288
1944	Cleveland	NAL	3B	62	217	28	70	10	6	1	-	11	.323
1945	Cleveland	NAL	3B	53	2^9	36	70	11	3	0	37	16	.335
1949	Louisville	NAL	3B	-	-	-	-	-	-	-	-	-	
1949	Oakland	PCL	3B	40	91	14	25	3	2	2	15	4	.275

Year	Club	League	Pos	G	AB	R	H	2B	3B	HR	RBI	SB	BA
1950	Memphis	NAL	3B	24	46	8	8	3	-	1	5	-	.174
1951	Chicago	NAL	3B	-	152	34	57	21	-	3	23	-	.325
39-0	Ponce	PRWL	SS 3B	-	156	31	42	4	1	0	15	10	.269
46-7	Venezuela	VENZ	3B	36	144	28	51	**13**	3	1	17	7	.354
47-8	Santiago	CUBA	3B	-	62	5	16	1	1	0	5	0	.258

Burnis "Bill" Wright. Born June 6, 1914 at Milan, TN. 6'4", 225 lbs. BB TR

Year	Club	League	Pos	G	AB	R	H	2B	3B	HR	RBI	SB	BA
1932	Nashville	NSL	OF	12	40	-	12	1	1	0	-	2	.300
1933	Nashville	NNL	OF	21	78	-	19	2	2	0	-	0	.244
1934	Nashville	NNL	OF	12	50	-	6	0	1	3	-	2	.120
1935	Columbus	NNL	OF	21	82	-	20	1	0	2	-	4	.244
1936	Washington	NNL	OF	21	74	-	25	2	5	1	-	2	.338
1937	Washington	NNL	OF	31	100	-	41	4	2	7	-	-	.410
1938	Baltimore	NNL	OF	35	174	73	55	11	10	7	27	19	.316
1939	Baltimore	NNL	OF	27	99	-	40	1	3	3	-	2	.404
1940	Mex City, Santa Rosa	MEX	OF	87	350	94	126	**30**	10	8	67	29	.360
1941	Mexico City	MEX	OF	100	387	98	151	25	9	17	85	**26**	**.390**
1942	Baltimore	NNL	OF	44	163	-	5	8	2	1	-	2	.031
1943	Mexico City	MEX	OF	88	352	65	129	25	5	**13**	**70**	21	**.366**
1944	Mexico City	MEX	OF	87	334	59	112	24	7	10	60	14	.335
1945	Baltimore	NNL	OF	44	165	34	62	12	5	3	31	5	.376
1946	Mexico City	MEX	OF	85	316	47	95	11	8	5	52	17	.301
1947	Mexico City	MEX	OF	79	249	36	76	10	4	3	38	13	.305
1948	Monterrey	MEX	OF	66	258	47	86	16	3	0	32	12	.333
1949	Torreon, Mex City	MEX	OF	74	293	48	81	14	3	7	43	3	.276
1950	Mexico City	MEX	OF	63	248	32	75	10	1	2	31	5	.302
1951	Mex City, N.L.	MEX	OF	30	104	23	38	10	2	2	25	2	.365
1952	Orizaba	MXSE	OF	-	129	-	43	-	-	-	-	-	.333
1955	Aquascalientes	MXCT	OF	68	250	49	75	12	3	3	40	6	.300
1956	Aquascalientes	MXCT	OF	79	297	48	102	8	3	8	45	7	.343
41-2	San Juan	PRWL	OF	-	157	-	44	-	-	4	27	-	.280

James Zapp. Born April 18, 1924 at Nashville, TN. 6'3", 232 lbs. BR TR

Year	Club	League	Pos	G	AB	R	H	2B	3B	HR	RBI	SB	BA
1948	Birmingham	NAL	OF	61	221	36	53	11	5	1	26	1	.240
1950	Baltimore	NAL	OF	-	-	-	-	-	-	-	-	-	
1951	Baltimore	NAL	OF	-	-	-	-	-	-	-	-	-	
1952	Paris	MOV	OF	122	467	85	154	31	9	20	136	7	.330
1953	Danville	MOV	OF	11	42	11	12	3	0	1	10	0	.286
1953	Lincoln	WEST	OF	3	7	-	1	-	-	-	-	-	.143
1954	Big Springs	LGHN	OF	90	341	76	99	18	1	32	86	5	.290
1955	Big Springs	LGHN	OF 1B	89	334	74	104	15	0	29	90	4	.311
1955	Port Arthur	BGST	OF	39	129	20	37	7	1	8	29	0	.287

Willard Brown is congratulated after hitting a homerun by Joe Greene, the catcher is Josh Gibson.
National Baseball Library, Cooperstown, NY

1945-46 All Cubans team; standing from the left: Raul Diaz, Santos Amaro, Silvio Garcia, Virgilio Arteaga, Cleveland Clark, Jose Fernandez, Luis Tiant SR, Isidore Leon, and Pedro Formenthal. In front: Minnie Minoso, Fernando Diaz Pedroso, Rogelio Linares, Euislic Caberra, Felix Castaneda, and Raul Alenagro.
Luis Munoz Collection

A truly great player, Alonzo Perry.
Luis Munoz Collection

Year	Club	League	G	IP	W	L	H	R	ER	BB	SO	ERA

Career Statistics by Individual Pitchers

Daniel Robert Bankhead. Born May 3, 1920 at Empire, AL. Died May 2, 1976 in Houston, TX., 6'1", 184 lbs. BR TR

Year	Club	League	G	IP	W	L	H	R	ER	BB	SO	ERA
1940	Birmingham	NAL	1	6	1	0	3	1	1	2	5	1.50
1941	Birmingham	NAL	-	-	6	1	-	-	-	-	-	-
1942	Birmingham	NAL	-	-	-	-	-	-	-	-	-	-
1946	Memphis	NAL	-	-	5	2	-	-	-	-	-	-
1947	Brooklyn	NL	4	10	0	0	15	8	8	8	6	7.20
1947	Memphis	NAL	-	-	4	4	-	-	-	-	-	-
1948	Nashua	NENG	31	203	**20**	6	120	63	53	**128**	**143**	2.35
1948	St. Paul	AA	6	35	4	0	34	15	14	18	22	3.60
1949	Montreal	INT	38	249	20	6	192	118	104	**170**	**176**	3.76
1950	Brooklyn	NL	41	129	9	4	119	84	79	88	96	5.51
1951	Brooklyn	NL	7	14	0	1	27	24	24	14	9	15.43
1951	Montreal	INT	10	46	2	6	50	26	20	26	16	3.91
1952	Escogido	DMSL	3	17	0	2	-	-	4	-	-	2.12
1952	Montreal	INT	5	13	0	1	14	11	10	11	7	6.92
1953	Drummondville	PROV	47	45	-	-	46	-	-	26	-	-
1953	Monterrey	MEX	2	10	1	0	3	1	1	0	12	0.90
1954	Monterrey	MEX	7	34	2	2	36	25	21	31	22	5.56
1955	Monterrey, Aguila	MEX	5	8	0	1	18	8	8	5	6	9.00
1956	Aguila, Mex. City	MEX	4	6	1	0	7	2	2	4	3	3.00
1957	Aquascalientes	CMEX	8	30	2	2	35	26	21	22	24	6.30
1959	Aguila	MEX	2	-	-	-	-	-	-	-	-	-
1960	Puebla	MEX	16	48	5	2	39	30	24	27	34	4.50
1961	Puebla	MEX	21	49	8	2	57	35	28	21	33	5.14
1962	Puebla	MEX	47	113	9	6	110	59	51	59	65	4.06
1963	Puebla	MEX	29	62	2	5	66	45	36	31	27	5.23
1964	Leon	MXCT	13	30	4	1	29	14	14	12	24	4.20
1966	Reynosa	MEX	6	19	1	0	20	15	10	10	11	4.74
41-2	Mayaquez	PRWL	-	-	7	8	-	-	-	81	74	-
46-7	Caguas	PRWL	-	-	12	8	-	-	-	-	**179**	-
48-9	Caguas	PRWL	-	144	9	8	-	-	59	73	119	3.69
49-0	Caguas	PRWL	-	160	10	8	-	-	46	82	**133**	2.59
51-2	Santurce	PRWL	12	70.1	7	1	-	31	29	49	38	3.71
62-3	Ponce, Aguas.	PRWL	17	39.1	3	0	-	9	8	14	22	1.83

Frank Barnes. Born August 26, 1928 at Longwood, MS., 6'1", 185 lbs. BR TR

Year	Club	League	G	IP	W	L	H	R	ER	BB	SO	ERA
1949	Kansas City	NAL	23	131	8	6	119	63	55	76	90	3.78
1950	Kansas City	NAL	16	112	9	4	94	44	30	43	85	2.41
1950	Muskegon	CENT	15	105	8	4	73	36	26	54	82	2.23
1951	Muskegon	CENT	25	176	15	6	141	80	63	111	152	3.22
1951	Toronto	INT	2	1	0	1	2	5	5	8	1	45.00
1952	Scranton	EAST	17	99	7	3	90	35	22	60	62	2.00
1952	Toronto	INT	1	2	0	0	1	0	0	0	4	0.00
1953	Oriente	DMSL	14	88	5	8	-	-	38	-	-	3.89
1954	Toronto	INT	30	147	9	8	132	80	69	102	118	4.22
1955	Charleston	AA	4	5	0	2	14	-	17	10	6	30.60
1955	Oklahoma City	TEX	13	69	4	3	57	32	29	33	61	3.78
1955	Toronto	INT	14	40	2	2	38	-	16	18	37	3.60
1956	Minn., Omaha	AA	25	154	13	5	144	63	58	71	96	3.39
1956	Toronto	INT	4	10	0	0	12	-	9	14	5	8.10
1957	Omaha	AA	31	205	12	10	153	66	55	93	165	**2.41**
1957	St. Louis	NL	3	10	0	1	13	5	5	9	5	4.50
1958	Omaha	AA	18	122	7	6	101	39	35	50	115	2.58
1958	St. Louis	NL	8	19	1	1	19	16	16	16	17	7.58
1959	Omaha	AA	29	160	15	12	158	65	51	66	119	2.87
1960	Rochester	INT	1	6	1	0	5	2	2	3	4	3.00
1960	San Diego	PCL	24	122	5	10	113	60	44	49	92	3.25
1960	St. Louis	NL	4	8	0	1	8	5	3	9	8	3.38
1961	San Diego, Port.	PCL	30	114	8	7	125	63	60	53	86	4.74
1962	Reynosa	MEX	30	80	3	4	76	40	35	39	44	3.94
1963	Reynosa	MEX	13	91	8	3	95	40	34	32	85	3.36
1964	Reynosa	MEX	25	191	14	10	163	68	57	51	174	2.69
1965	Reynosa	MEX	25	177	13	5	152	41	31	34	125	**1.58**
1965	Seattle	PCL	2	5	0	0	10	11	11	4	7	19.80
1966	Reynosa	MEX	26	197	17	8	154	58	46	31	145	2.10

Year	Club	League	G	IP	W	L	H	R	ER	BB	SO	ERA
1967	Reynosa	MEX	12	78	6	5	72	29	22	19	66	2.54
56-7	San Juan	PRWL	-	80	6	2	-	-	38	50	53	4.28

Dave Barnhill. Born October 30, 1914 at Greenville, NC. Died January 8, 1983 at Miami, FL., 5'7", 155 lbs. BB TR

Year	Club	League	G	IP	W	L	H	R	ER	BB	SO	ERA
1938	Jacksonville	NAL	2	9	1	0	8	-	-	-	-	-
1939	Ethiopian		-	-	-	-	-	-	-	-	-	-
1940	Ethiopian		3	13	2	0	5	-	-	-	20	-
1941	New York	NNL	16	124	9	6	92	-	-	25	71	-
1942	New York	NNL	11	89	4	7	77	44	-	16	43	-
1943	New York	NNL	17	129	11	3	88	46	-	25	55	-
1944	New York	NNL	6	46	4	1	33	-	-	13	12	-
1945	New York	NNL	5	23	1	3	29	-	-	9	21	-
1946	New York	NNL	12	76	8	3	71	-	-	29	40	-
1947	New York	NNL	7	47	4	0	39	-	-	-	35	-
1948	New York	NNL	2	18	2	0	9	-	-	-	9	-
1949	Minneapolis	AA	28	144	7	10	154	100	92	82	91	5.75
1949	New York	NAL	-	-	4	1	-	-	-	-	-	-
1950	Minneapolis	AA	27	140	11	3	124	68	56	48	128	3.60
1951	Minneapolis	AA	33	105	6	5	96	56	52	47	59	4.46
1952	Miami Beach	FINT	28	181	13	8	125	35	24	71	93	1.19
1953	Ft. Lauderdale	FINT	4	-	1	1	-	-	-	-	-	-
40-1	Humacao	PRWL	-	-	-	-	-	-	-	-	**193**	-
47-8	Marianao	CWL	26	187	10	8	157	-	47	60	**122**	2.26
48-9	Marianao	CWL	25	174.2	**13**	8	156	-	55	60	79	2.83
49-0	Marianao	CWL	3	24	0	3	24	-	13	8	10	4.88

Joseph Black. Born February 8, 1924 at Plainfield, NJ., 6'2", 209 lbs. BR TR

Year	Club	League	G	IP	W	L	H	R	ER	BB	SO	ERA
1943	Baltimore	NNL	-	-	-	-	-	-	-	-	-	-
1944	Baltimore	NNL	9	59	3	3	58	-	-	19	27	-
1945	Baltimore	NNL	1	7	0	1	6	-	-	2	3	-
1946	Baltimore	NNL	**20**	102	4	9	100	-	-	**45**	49	-
1947	Baltimore	NNL	**26**	148	9	**9**	174	-	-	-	78	-
1948	Baltimore	NNL	21	-	10	5	117	-	-	36	90	-
1949	Baltimore	NNL	23	155	11	7	164	85	67	44	64	3.89
1950	Baltimore	NAL	13	94	8	3	87	48	39	23	56	3.73
1951	Montreal	INT	26	110	7	9	106	53	47	37	49	3.85
1951	St. Paul	AA	9	60	4	3	44	19	15	24	35	2.25
1952	Brooklyn	NL	56	142	15	4	102	40	34	41	85	2.15
1953	Brooklyn	NL	34	73	6	3	74	46	43	27	42	5.30
1954	Brooklyn	NL	5	7	0	0	11	9	9	5	3	11.57
1954	Montreal	INT	31	185	12	10	182	82	74	61	94	3.60
1955	Brook., Cinc.	NL	38	118	6	2	121	63	53	30	63	4.04
1956	Cincinnati	NL	32	62	3	2	61	31	31	25	27	4.50
1957	Seattle	PCL	10	-	1	1	-	-	-	-	-	-
1957	Tulsa	TEX	4	-	0	0	-	-	-	-	-	-
1957	Washington	AL	7	13	0	1	22	11	10	1	2	6.92
47-8	Magallanes	VENZ	-	-	-	-	-	-	-	-	-	-
51-2	Cienfuegos	CWL	16	91.2	5	7	101	-	44	46	41	4.32
52-3	Cienfuegos	CWL	27	163.1	**15**	6	124	-	44	51	78	**2.42**

Ramon "El Professor" Bragana. Born May 11, 1909 at Havana, Cuba. Deceased., 5'10", 175 lbs. BR TR

Year	Club	League	G	IP	W	L	H	R	ER	BB	SO	ERA
1928	Cuban Stars	ECL	-	-	-	-	-	-	-	-	-	-
1930	Cuban Stars		-	-	-	-	-	-	-	-	-	-
1935	New York	NNL	-	-	-	-	-	-	-	-	-	-
1938	Agrario	MEX	16	124.2	8	5	114	-	34	32	69	2.45
1939	Anahuac	MEX	21	146	8	6	116	-	40	52	78	2.47
1940	Vera Cruz	MEX	37	233.2	16	8	236	-	67	80	144	**2.58**
1941	Vera Cruz	MEX	30	184.1	13	8	215	-	103	106	79	5.03
1942	Vera Cruz	MEX	38	265	22	10	288	-	110	116	136	3.74
1943	Vera Cruz	MEX	39	278.2	17	16	291	-	100	88	123	3.23
1944	Vera Cruz	MEX	45	325.1	30	8	336	-	119	149	144	3.29
1945	Vera Cruz	MEX	40	258	15	16	276	-	130	126	62	4.53
1946	Vera Cruz	MEX	37	224	9	16	257	-	91	72	89	3.66
1947	Cleveland	NAL	-	-	-	-	-	-	-	-	-	-
1947	Vera Cruz	MEX	42	**279**	18	12	294	-	108	112	90	3.48
1948	Vera Cruz	MEX	31	202.2	12	9	188	-	69	72	55	3.06
1949	Vera Cruz	MEX	33	171.2	8	10	184	94	76	92	84	3.98
1950	Vera Cruz	MEX	30	172	10	9	192	-	63	68	49	3.30
1951	Vera Cruz	MEX	27	163.2	9	6	186	-	77	80	66	4.23
1952	Jalisco, Monterrey	MEX	26	139.2	7	12	143	72	65	55	28	4.19

Year	Club	League	G	IP	W	L	H	R	ER	BB	SO	ERA
1953	Monterrey	MEX	23	113.2	7	6	93	55	41	64	37	3.25
1954	Mexico City	MEX	1	3	0	0	2	0	0	1	1	0.00
1955	Yucatan, Vera Cruz	MEX	26	91	2	5	103	57	47	41	38	4.65
36-7	Gavilanes	VENZ	-	-	-	-	-	-	-	-	-	-
53-4		MEX	24	108	7	6	-	-	-	63	37	-

Ollie Brantley. Born 1932 at Lexon, AR. 6'2 1/2", 178 lbs. BR TR

Year	Club	League	G	IP	W	L	H	R	ER	BB	SO	ERA
1950	Memphis	NAL	-	-	-	-	-	-	-	-	-	-
1951	Memphis	NAL	-	-	-	-	-	-	-	-	-	-
1952	Memphis	NAL	-	-	-	-	-	-	-	-	-	-
1953	Memphis	NAL	-	-	-	-	-	-	-	-	-	-
1954	Waterloo	III	3	-	1	1	-	-	-	-	-	-
1955	Bisbee	AZMX	49	157	10	11	180	126	105	65	124	6.02
1956	Waterloo	III	36	114	7	9	125	60	49	49	70	3.87
1957	Eugene	NWL	42	**264**	**22**	15	243	124	107	98	166	3.65
1958	Colorado Springs	WEST	39	193	15	6	201	96	73	54	126	3.40
1959	Charleston	SATL	46	198	12	11	207	96	86	64	121	3.91
1960	Charleston	SATL	27	143	7	9	142	66	58	43	91	3.65
1960	San Diego	PCL	3	5	0	0	4	1	1	4	0	1.80
1961	Columbia	SATL	18	66	4	5	74	35	28	13	31	3.82
1961	Topeka	III	8	35	2	1	34	21	15	12	30	3.86
1962	Bismark, Manitoba	NORL	38	109	7	2	111	48	34	30	99	2.81
1963	Bismark, Manitoba	NORL	43	76	7	6	76	35	34	20	64	4.03
1964	Bismark, Manitoba	NORL	31	60	6	3	39	12	10	23	52	1.50
1965	Orlando	FLST	**61**	144	15	8	113	33	26	21	105	1.63
1966	Wisconsin Rapids	MIDW	56	91	5	6	87	36	27	18	70	2.67
1967	Wisconsin Rapids	MIDW	37	48	8	2	53	19	15	9	30	2.81
1968	Wilson	CARO	31	71	2	3	81	35	26	13	38	3.30
1969	Orlando	FLST	22	24	5	1	32	14	13	4	13	4.88

Eugene Bremmer. Born June 16, 1915 at New Orleans, LA. 5'8", 160 lbs. BR TR

Year	Club	League	G	IP	W	L	H	R	ER	BB	SO	ERA
1937	Cincinnati	NAL	4	36	4	0	25	-	-	-	13	-
1938	Memphis	NAL	4	21	1	1	19	-	-	-	4	-
1939	Memphis	NAL	6	42	0	5	37	-	-	17	9	-
1939	Monterrey	MEX	7	34.2	1	2	31	12	12	23	11	3.12
1940	Memphis	NAL	7	53	5	2	20	-	-	16	10	-
1942	Cleveland	NAL	6	36	5	1	27	-	-	-	-	-
1943	Cleveland	NAL	11	84	8	2	55	-	-	-	-	-
1944	Cleveland	NAL	20	113	10	6	109	-	36	34	44	2.87
1945	Cleveland	NAL	15	96	8	4	78	33	26	17	30	2.44
1946	Cleveland	NAL	2	8	1	0	7	-	-	1	2	-
1947	Cleveland	NAL	-	-	1	0	-	-	-	-	-	-
1948	Cleveland	NAL	10	67	3	5	95	53	27	26	22	3.63
1949	Cedar Rapids	III	11	-	-	-	-	-	-	-	-	-

Chester Arthur "Chet" Brewer. Born January 14, 1907 at Leavenworth, KA. Died March 26, 1990 in Whittier, CA. 6'4", 176 lbs. BB TR

Year	Club	League	G	IP	W	L	H	R	ER	BB	SO	ERA
1925	Kansas City	NNL	9	20	1	0	21	-	-	16	11	-
1926	Kansas City	NNL	16	110	12	1	72	-	-	40	63	-
1927	Kansas City	NNL	20	103	8	7	98	-	-	38	46	-
1928	Kansas City	NNL	19	135	7	9	130	-	-	27	51	-
1929	Kansas City	NNL	24	167	17	3	124	-	-	35	83	-
1930	Kansas City	NNL	17	145	8	8	150	-	-	35	85	-
1931	Kansas City	NNL	4	31	2	2	14	-	-	-	-	-
1932	KC, Washington		7	45	5	1	32	-	-	7	13	-
1933	Kansas City		-	-	-	-	-	-	-	-	-	-
1934	Kansas City		-	-	-	-	-	-	-	-	-	-
1935	Kansas City	NAL	3	25	0	1	16	-	-	-	-	-
1936	New York	NNL	12	86	4	6	64	-	-	25	40	-
1937	Kansas City	NAL	2	9	1	1	1	-	-	-	-	-
1938	Tampico	MEX	22	182.1	17	5	124	-	38	53	153	1.88
1939	Philadelphia	NNL	-	-	-	-	-	-	-	-	-	-
1939	Tampico	MEX	26	176.1	12	7	129	-	49	48	122	2.50
1940	Kansas City	NAL	-	-	-	-	-	-	-	-	-	-
1941	Phil., KC	NAL	15	99	3	9	79	-	-	-	-	-
1942	Cleveland	NAL	-	-	5	1	-	-	-	-	-	-
1943	Cleveland	NAL	-	-	10	3	-	-	-	-	-	-
1944	Mexico City	MEX	28	146.1	3	12	181	-	83	73	42	5.10
1946	Cleve, Chi	NAL	10	51.1	4	6	31	-	25	-	-	4.41
1947	Cleveland	NAL	21	147	12	6	137	58	49	29	81	3.00

Year	Club	League	G	IP	W	L	H	R	ER	BB	SO	ERA
1948	Cleveland	NAL	15	95	5	5	118	61	34	19	55	3.22
1952	Riverside, Porterv.	SWIN	24	96	6	5	102	56	36	47	59	3.38
1952	Visalia	CAL	7	48	1	4	63	40	29	25	31	5.44
30-1	Havana	CWL	6	-	2	2	-	-	-	-	-	-
37-8	Aguilas	DOM	-	-	2	3	-	-	-	-	-	-
47-8	Caguas	PRWL	-	-	7	6	-	-	-	-	-	-

Marshall Bridges. Born June 2, 1931 at Jackson, MS. Died September 3, 1990 in Jackson, MS. 6'1", 165 BB TL

Year	Club	League	G	IP	W	L	H	R	ER	BB	SO	ERA
1951	Memphis	NAL	-	-	-	-	-	-	-	-	-	-
1952	Memphis	NAL	-	-	-	-	-	-	-	-	-	-
1953	Sioux City	WEST	4	6	0	0	9	-	6	7	8	9.00
1954	Memphis	NAL	9	66	6	2	65	37	32	31	74	4.37
1955	Amarillo	AZMX	21	139	14	1	129	83	72	97	177	4.66
1955	Beaumont	TEX	8	21	0	2	23	-	13	16	15	5.57
1956	Austin	TEX	1	6	0	0	5	-	2	3	4	3.00
1956	Topeka	WEST	39	**242**	**18**	11	208	129	105	**154**	**213**	3.90
1957	Sacramento	PCL	30	207	12	16	210	122	104	96	104	4.52
1958	Sacramento	PCL	35	232	**16**	11	206	108	95	**111**	**205**	3.69
1959	Rochester	INT	11	66	3	3	51	28	26	40	64	3.55
1959	St. Louis	NL	27	76	6	3	67	38	26	37	76	3.08
1960	St. Louis, Cinc.	NL	34	57	6	2	47	18	15	23	53	2.37
1961	Cincinnati	NL	13	21	0	1	26	19	18	11	17	7.71
1961	Jersey City	INT	15	100	6	8	99	45	39	38	86	3.51
1962	New York	AL	52	72	8	4	49	30	25	48	66	3.13
1963	New York	AL	23	33	2	0	27	18	14	30	35	3.82
1964	Toronto	INT	17	41	1	3	36	19	18	25	40	3.95
1964	Washington	AL	17	30	0	3	37	22	19	17	16	5.70
1965	Hawaii	PCL	5	7	2	0	1	0	0	0	6	0.00
1965	Washington	AL	40	57	1	2	62	26	17	25	39	2.68
1966	Hawaii	PCL	48	64	2	2	51	24	18	20	44	2.53
1967	Hawaii	PCL	9	8	1	0	5	4	4	8	5	4.50

Barney Brown. BL TL

Year	Club	League	G	IP	W	L	H	R	ER	BB	SO	ERA
1931	Cuban Stars		-	-	-	-	-	-	-	-	-	-
1932	Cuban Stars		-	-	-	-	-	-	-	-	-	-
1936	New York	NNL	-	-	-	-	-	-	-	-	-	-
1937	New York, Phil.	NNL	-	-	-	-	-	-	-	-	-	-
1938	New York	NNL	-	-	-	-	-	-	-	-	-	-
1939	New York	NNL	-	-	-	-	-	-	-	-	-	-
1939	Vera Cruz	MEX	23	173.1	16	5	138	-	48	33	141	2.49
1940	Vera Cruz	MEX	29	175	16	7	206	-	78	56	113	4.01
1941	Vera Cruz	MEX	28	173.2	**16**	5	183	-	76	60	78	3.94
1942	Philadelphia	NNL	-	-	-	-	-	-	-	-	-	-
1943	Philadelphia	NNL	-	-	4	3	-	-	-	-	-	-
1944	Philadelphia	NNL	-	-	-	-	-	-	-	-	-	-
1945	Mexico City	MEX	24	137.1	6	8	170	-	69	72	56	4.52
1945	Philadelphia	NNL	5	29	3	1	26	-	-	8	19	-
1946	Philadelphia	NNL	12	93	8	4	79	-	-	15	52	-
1947	Philadelphia	NNL	13	62	2	8	82	-	-	-	16	-
1948	Philadelphia	NNL	-	-	-	-	-	-	-	-	-	-
1949	Philadelphia	NAL	12	78	1	8	93	48	39	30	38	4.50
1950	Torreon	MEX	30	213.2	12	10	198	-	66	86	**157**	2.78
1951	Torreon	MEX	32	230	15	12	245	-	80	94	98	3.13
1952	Brandon	MADK	-	-	-	-	-	-	-	-	-	-
1952	Escogido	DMSL	5	29.2	3	1	-	-	7	-	-	2.12
1952	Torreon	MEX	12	83	3	6	94	-	43	50	40	4.66
1953	Brandon	MADK	-	-	-	-	-	-	-	-	-	-
1954	Cibaenas	DMSL	4	13	0	1	-	-	8	-	-	5.54
35-6	Marianao	CWL	9	-	3	4	-	-	-	-	-	-
36-7	Marianao	CWL	19	-	7	9	-	-	-	-	-	-
37-8	Havana	CWL	4	-	0	1	-	-	-	-	-	-
38-9	Havana	CWL	24	-	6	9	-	-	-	-	-	-
41-2	Guayama	PRWL	-	-	16	6	-	-	-	-	-	-
46-7	San Juan	PRWL	-	166	16	5	-	-	23	-	-	1.25
47-8	Ponce	PRWL	-	47.2	2	4	-	-	25	28	17	4.72

Year	Club	League	G	IP	W	L	H	R	ER	BB	SO	ERA

Raymond Brown. Born February 23, 1908 at Ashland Grove, OH. Died in Dayton, OH. 6'1", 195 lbs. BB TR

Year	Club	League	G	IP	W	L	H	R	ER	BB	SO	ERA
1931	Indianapolis	NNL	-	-	-	-	-	-	-	-	-	-
1932	Detroit, Home.	EWL	15	91	7	5	63	-	-	-	-	-
1933	Homestead	NNL	8	47	6	1	41	-	-	5	18	-
1934	Homestead	NNL	3	26	2	1	13	-	-	-	-	-
1935	Homestead	NNL	18	120	12	3	82	-	-	34	45	-
1936	Homestead	NNL	2	9	0	1	9	-	-	-	4	-
1937	Homestead	NNL	6	41	3	2	31	-	-	-	-	-
1938	Homestead	NNL	9	36	7	0	28	-	-	-	-	-
1939	Homestead	NNL	6	48	4	1	34	-	-	-	-	-
1940	Homestead	NNL	32	240	24	4	178	75	-	36	63	-
1941	Homestead	NNL	22	147	13	6	128	47	-	37	42	-
1942	Homestead	NNL	17	114	12	4	78	35	-	30	39	-
1943	Homestead	NNL	8	47	4	1	41	24	-	13	17	-
1944	Homestead	NNL	20	125	11	3	116	-	-	21	38	-
1945	Homestead	NNL	7	46	4	2	55	-	-	9	17	-
1946	Tampico	MEX	31	204	13	9	199	-	80	93	93	3.53
1947	Tampico	MEX	28	194.2	10	12	190	-	70	92	47	3.24
1948	Tampico, Vera Cruz	MEX	28	153	13	4	132	-	55	65	55	3.24
1949	Mexico City	MEX	32	231.1	15	11	226	110	83	92	118	3.23
1950	Sherbrooke	PROV	-	-	-	-	-	-	-	-	-	-
1951	Sherbrooke	PROV	28	174	11	10	158	85	64	63	104	3.31
1953	Thetford Mines	PROV	2	-	1	0	-	-	-	-	-	-
36-7	Santa Clara	CWL	26	-	**21**	4	-	-	-	-	-	-
37-8	Santa Clara	CWL	20	-	**12**	5	-	-	-	-	-	-
38-9	San Juan	PRWL	-	-	7	0	-	-	-	16	28	-
38-9	Santa Clara	CWL	22	-	11	7	-	-	-	-	-	-
39-0	San Juan	PRWL	-	60	7	0	-	-	7	22	38	**1.05**
40-1	Santurce	PRWL	-	-	-	-	-	-	-	-	115	-
41-2	Ponce	PRWL	18	150	12	4	-	-	30	65	91	**1.80**
44-5	San Juan	PRWL	-	65	3	4	-	-	18	-	-	2.49
45-6	Almend., Marianao	CWL	18	-	2	3	-	-	-	-	-	-
47-8	Santiago	CWL	3	-	0	1	-	-	-	-	-	-

Ernest Burke. Born June 26, 1924 at Havre de Grace, MD. 6'1", 180 lbs. BL TR

Year	Club	League	G	IP	W	L	H	R	ER	BB	SO	ERA
1949	Pough., Kingston	WL	-	-	-	-	-	-	-	-	-	-
1950	St. Jean	PROV	-	-	15	3	-	-	-	-	-	-
1951	St. Jean	PROV	-	-	8	8	-	-	-	-	-	-

Harry T. Butts. BR TL

Year	Club	League	G	IP	W	L	H	R	ER	BB	SO	ERA
1949	Indianapolis	NAL	14	69	2	8	86	52	40	33	36	5.22
1950	Indianapolis	NAL	25	142	8	8	130	93	71	79	107	4.50
1951	Indianapolis	NAL	-	65	6	1	-	-	-	-	49	-
1951	Oriente	DMSL	11	66	4	1	-	35	27	-	-	3.68
1952	Vancouver	WINT	4	16	0	2	14	13	12	12	10	6.75
1953	Portsmouth, Richm.	PIED	28	121	3	15	119	96	80	120	87	5.95
49-0	San Juan	PRWL	-	4.1	0	1	-	-	6	5	3	12.47

Luis Raul Cabrera. Born in Cuba. BR TR

Year	Club	League	G	IP	W	L	H	R	ER	BB	SO	ERA
1944	Ind.-Cinc.	NAL	-	-	-	-	-	-	-	-	-	-
1945	Puebla	MEX	36	204	6	16	225	-	103	79	57	4.54
1946	Mex. City, VeraCruz	MEX	40	137	8	9	157	-	80	49	50	5.26
1948	Indianapolis	NAL	14	103	8	5	92	41	32	22	66	2.80
1949	Bristol	COL	14	83	11	1	57	20	13	38	57	1.41
1950	Bristol	COL	11	61	3	3	66	35	29	27	50	4.28
1950	St. Jean	PROV	17	107	7	6	112	54	52	44	81	4.37
1951	Escogido	DMSL	5	20	1	3	-	19	16	-	-	7.20
1951	St. Jean	PROV	15	87	2	8	91	53	48	38	39	4.97
39-0	Santurce	PRWL	25	176	8	14	-	-	77	74	61	3.94
40-1	Santurce	PRWL	-	-	10	8	-	-	-	-	116	-
41-2	Santurce	PRWL	-	-	13	8	-	-	-	-	-	-
42-3	Santurce	PRWL	-	-	16	0	-	-	-	-	-	-
43-4	Santurce	PRWL	-	-	13	7	-	-	-	-	-	-
44-5	Santurce	PRWL	-	-	13	10	-	-	-	-	**81**	-
45-6	Santurce	PRWL	-	-	-	-	-	-	-	-	**75**	-
46-7		PRWL	-	-	-	-	-	-	-	-	-	-
47-8		PRWL	-	-	-	-	-	-	-	-	-	-
48-9	Santurce	PRWL	-	-	10	8	-	-	-	-	-	-
49-0	Santurce	PRWL	-	-	7	3	-	-	-	-	-	-

Year	Club	League	G	IP	W	L	H	R	ER	BB	SO	ERA

Vibert Ernesto "Webbo" Clarke. Born June 8, 1928 at Colon, Panama. Died June 14, 1970 at Cristobel, Canal Zone. 6', 165 lbs. BL TL

Year	Club	League	G	IP	W	L	H	R	ER	BB	SO	ERA
1946	Cleveland	NAL	-	-	-	-	-	-	-	-	-	-
1947	Cleveland	NAL	16	102	11	2	118	54	46	44	75	4.06
1948	Cleveland	NAL	20	130	8	9	129	77	53	54	72	3.67
1949	Louisville	NAL	23	108	4	10	117	79	54	63	33	4.50
1950	Memphis	NAL	25	**166**	13	10	**184**	99	55	73	105	2.98
1951	Memphis	NAL	-	-	-	-	-	-	-	-	-	-
1952	Memphis	NAL	-	-	-	-	-	-	-	-	-	-
1953	Memphis	NAL	-	-	-	-	-	-	-	-	-	-
1953	Nuevo Laredo	MEX	22	151.1	8	10	132	79	63	121	75	3.75
1955	Charlotte	SATL	33	**262**	16	12	260	116	99	109	145	3.40
1955	Washington	AL	7	21	0	0	17	11	11	14	9	4.71
1956	Charlotte	SATL	16	80	3	10	87	51	39	48	44	4.39
1956	Louisville	AA	16	103	4	10	116	70	56	40	44	4.89
1957	Dallas	TEX	8	-	1	1	-	-	-	-	-	-
1957	Minneapolis	AA	21	80	3	5	85	42	39	38	22	4.39
1957	Springfield	EAST	12	55	3	6	59	49	40	42	37	6.55
62-3		PANA	-	41	2	2	-	-	9	-	-	1.98
63-4		PANA	-	61	4	2	-	-	-	-	24	-

Eugene "Gene" Collins. Born January 7, 1925 at Kansas City, MO. 5'8", 168 lbs. BL TL

Year	Club	League	G	IP	W	L	H	R	ER	BB	SO	ERA
1948	Kansas City	NAL	17	93	9	3	53	38	24	57	97	2.32
1949	Kansas City	NAL	18	117	8	9	87	56	44	80	**131**	3.38
1950	Kansas City	NAL	3	20	3	0	7	5	2	19	20	0.90
1951	Kansas City	NAL	-	74	7	1	-	-	-	-	117	-
1951	Waterloo	III	25	77	7	2	45	37	28	93	71	3.27
1952	Colorado Springs	WEST	-	-	1	2	-	-	-	-	-	-
1952	Superior	NORL	-	-	1	0	-	-	-	-	-	-
1953	Colorado Springs	WEST	-	-	1	1	-	-	-	-	-	-
1953	Escogido	DMSL	4	13.1	0	2	-	-	12	-	-	8.10
1953	Superior	NORL	-	-	2	2	-	-	-	-	-	-
1955	Aguila	MEX	26	111	7	5	121	76	57	104	82	4.62
1956	Aguila	MEX	4	17	0	1	7	10	6	17	21	3.18
1957	Aguila	MEX	3	-	0	1	-	-	-	-	-	-
1958	Poza Rica	MEX	8	64	5	3	40	24	22	53	47	3.09
1959	Poza Rica	MEX	9	49	2	4	58	36	30	44	45	5.51
1960	Poza Rica	MEX	3	-	0	1	-	-	-	-	-	-
48-9	Caguas	PRWL	-	-	10	9	-	-	-	-	**157**	-
49-0	San Juan	PRWL	-	21	0	2	-	-	17	34	19	7.29
58-9	Pampero	VENZ	-	-	-	-	-	-	-	-	-	-

Johnny Howard Davis. Born February 6, 1917 at Ashland, VA. Died November 17, 1982 at Ft. Lauderdale, FL. 6'2", 217 lbs. BR TR

Year	Club	League	G	IP	W	L	H	R	ER	BB	SO	ERA
1940	Newark	NNL	1	-	0	1	-	-	-	-	-	-
1942	Newark	NNL	-	-	-	-	-	-	-	-	-	-
1943	Newark	NNL	-	-	-	-	-	-	-	-	-	-
1944	Newark	NNL	-	-	3	3	-	-	-	-	-	-
1945	Newark	NNL	-	-	1	0	-	-	-	-	-	-
1946	Newark	NNL	-	-	1	1	-	-	-	-	-	-
1947	Newark	NNL	6	40	2	2	43	-	-	-	34	-
1948	Vera Cruz	MEX	21	117.1	6	10	118	-	52	92	87	3.99
1950	Houston	NAL	1	9	1	0	6	4	4	4	7	4.00
1950	Pastora	VENZ	-	-	-	-	-	-	-	-	-	-
1952	Escogido	DMSL	4	27	3	1	-	-	8	-	-	2.67
1954	Escogido	DMSL	1	1	0	1	-	5	5	-	-	45.00
45-6	San Juan	PRWL	-	100	7	4	-	-	26	57	57	2.34
47-8	Mayaquez	PRWL	-	-	12	7	-	-	-	-	100	-
48-9	Mayaquez	PRWL	-	-	-	-	-	-	-	-	-	-
49-0	Mayaquez	PRWL	-	-	10	9	-	-	-	-	-	-

Leon Day. Born October 30, 1916 at Alexandria, VA. 5'10", 180 lbs. BR TR

Year	Club	League	G	IP	W	L	H	R	ER	BB	SO	ERA
1934	Baltimore	NNL	-	-	-	-	-	-	-	-	-	-
1935	Brooklyn	NNL	12	79	9	2	60	-	-	7	38	-
1936	Newark	NNL	7	34	3	4	28	-	-	4	24	-
1937	Newark	NNL	8	55	6	0	36	-	-	-	16	-
1938	Newark	NNL	-	-	-	-	-	-	-	-	-	-
1939	Newark	NNL	17	113	12	4	98	-	-	11	16	-
1940	Vera Cruz	MEX	9	67	6	0	61	-	24	26	29	3.22
1941	Newark	NNL	2	14.2	1	1	14	10	-	6	4	-

Year	Club	League	G	IP	W	L	H	R	ER	BB	SO	ERA
1942	Newark	NNL	9	74	7	1	39	14	-	18	65	-
1943	Newark	NNL	10	46	4	3	44	30	-	10	27	-
1946	Newark	NNL	19	**141**	**13**	4	97	-	-	34	**83**	-
1947	Mexico City	MEX	28	178.2	10	11	169	-	82	131	81	4.13
1948	Mexico City	MEX	23	132.2	8	9	133	-	64	46	31	4.34
1949	Baltimore	NAL	14	105	7	5	110	52	39	25	51	3.34
1950	Winnipeg	MADK	-	-	-	-	-	-	-	-	-	-
1951	Toronto	INT	14	40	1	1	33	-	7	28	20	1.58
1952	Scranton	EAST	45	161	13	9	151	73	61	81	82	3.41
1953	Edmonton	WINT	23	93	5	5	114	59	50	55	56	4.84
37-8	Almendares	CWL	16	-	7	3	-	-	-	-	-	-
39-0	Aquadilla	PRWL	25	207	12	11	-	-	50	70	186	2.17
40-1	Aquadilla	PRWL	-	-	10	6	-	-	-	-	149	-
41-2	Aquadilla	PRWL	-	-	12	9	-	-	-	-	**168**	-
47-8	Santiago	CWL	3	-	1	1	-	-	-	-	-	-
49-0	Santurce	PRWL	-	-	-	-	-	-	-	-	-	-

Lino Donoso y Galeta. Born September 23, 1922 at Havana, Cuba. Died October 13, 1990 in Vera Cruz, Mexico. 5'11", 160 lbs. BL TL

Year	Club	League	G	IP	W	L	H	R	ER	BB	SO	ERA
1947	New York	NNL	19	105	8	2	93	-	-	-	82	-
1948	Gavilanes	VENZ	-	-	-	-	-	-	-	-	-	-
1949	Gavilanes	VENZ	-	-	-	-	-	-	-	-	-	-
1949	New York	NAL	-	-	-	-	-	-	-	-	-	-
1950	Aguila	MEX	30	207	12	11	176	-	52	89	151	2.26
1951	Aguila	MEX	43	260.2	14	14	237	-	74	102	**197**	2.55
1952	Aguila	MEX	42	264.1	18	11	210	-	73	100	**235**	2.49
1953	Aguila	MEX	37	205.1	17	9	177	65	51	74	**160**	2.24
1954	Hollywood	PCL	46	205	19	8	175	60	54	51	141	2.37
1955	Hollywood	PCL	15	58	4	3	57	24	21	13	42	3.26
1955	Pittsburgh	NL	25	95	4	6	106	58	56	35	38	5.31
1956	Hollywood	PCL	14	46	2	2	57	30	26	11	19	5.09
1956	Mexico City	MEX	16	93	6	4	93	38	30	24	49	2.90
1956	Pittsburgh	NL	3	1.2	0	0	2	0	0	1	1	0.00
1957	Columbus	INT	11	38	1	2	39	24	20	20	18	4.74
1957	Mexico City	MEX	24	112	8	2	109	53	32	27	59	2.57
1958	Juarez	AZMX	40	234	16	**14**	247	109	83	49	231	3.19
1958	Mexico City	MEX	1	-	0	1	-	-	-	-	4	-
1959	Aguila	MEX	43	212	16	10	216	90	67	41	151	2.84
1960	Aguila	MEX	37	175	13	9	198	95	81	60	94	4.17
1961	Aguila	MEX	32	160	10	6	194	93	86	55	86	4.84
1962	Aguila	MEX	22	100	4	7	91	45	35	37	48	3.15
46-7	Camag.	CUBA	7	37	1	2	29	-	11	25	23	2.68
46-7	Marianao	CWL	10	26	1	2	26	-	14	17	11	4.85
47-8	Marianao	CWL	14	48	3	3	51	-	26	23	42	4.88
48-9	Marianao	CWL	20	68.2	3	4	72	-	21	40	31	2.75
49-0	Marianao, Almend.	CWL	11	8.2	0	0	15	-	-	8	3	-
54-5	Almendares	CWL	31	91.1	4	3	72	-	32	35	52	3.15
57-8		MXWL	-	101	4	7	103	-	-	-	-	-

Wilmer Leon "Red" Fields. Born August 2, 1922 at Manassas, VA. 6'3", 215 lbs. BR TR

Year	Club	League	G	IP	W	L	H	R	ER	BB	SO	ERA
1940	Homestead	NNL	2	3.2	0	1	2	2	-	0	2	-
1941	Homestead	NNL	-	-	13	5	-	-	-	-	-	-
1942	Homestead	NNL	-	-	15	3	-	-	-	-	-	-
1946	Homestead	NNL	9	55	6	1	47	-	-	23	25	-
1947	Homestead	NNL	12	57	4	4	58	-	-	-	39	-
1948	Homestead	NNL	10	73	7	1	46	-	-	12	31	-
1949	Homestead	BAA	-	-	-	-	-	-	-	-	-	-
1950	Homestead		-	-	-	-	-	-	-	-	-	-
1952	Toronto	INT	-	-	-	-	-	-	-	-	-	-
1953	Oriente	DMSL	11	67	2	7	-	-	29	-	-	3.90
1958	Mex. City, Monterrey	MEX	1	-	0	0	-	-	-	-	-	-
47-8	Mayaquez	PRWL	-	136	6	6	-	-	69	73	87	4.57
48-9	Mayaquez	PRWL	-	-	10	4	-	-	-	-	-	-
49-0	Mayaquez	PRWL	-	-	8	7	-	-	-	-	-	-

Willy Gaines. Born 1931. 6', 190 lbs. BR TR

Year	Club	League	G	IP	W	L	H	R	ER	BB	SO	ERA
1950	Philadelphia	NAL	12	81	5	3	76	41	30	32	57	3.33
1951	Philadelphia	NAL	-	-	-	-	-	-	-	-	-	-
1952	Philadelphia	NAL	-	-	-	-	-	-	-	-	-	-
1952	Porterville	SWIN	11	31	0	1	49	43	28	17	25	8.13

Year	Club	League	G	IP	W	L	H	R	ER	BB	SO	ERA
1953	Indianapolis	NAL	21	146	8	8	153	85	69	38	68	4.25
1954	Indianapolis	NAL	18	112	7	6	117	67	48	52	71	3.86
1955	Indianapolis	NAL	-	-	-	-	-	-	-	-	-	-

Raul Galata y Capote. Born 1930 in Cuba. 5'9", 170 lbs. BL TL

Year	Club	League	G	IP	W	L	H	R	ER	BB	SO	ERA
1949	Indianapolis	NAL	-	-	-	-	-	-	-	-	-	-
1950	Indianapolis	NAL	28	145	11	6	128	67	47	78	**120**	2.92
1951	Indianapolis	NAL	-	-	-	-	-	-	-	-	-	-
1951	Monterrey	MEX	24	136	7	7	123	76	64	97	95	4.24
1952	Monterrey	MEX	2	9	0	1	7	9	6	9	5	6.00
1953	Indianapolis	NAL	-	-	-	-	-	-	-	-	-	-
1953	Mex. City,Aguila	MEX	14	98.1	4	6	103	-	41	69	58	3.75
1954	Aguila	MEX	31	193.2	12	11	203	-	93	110	**118**	4.32
1955	Aguila	MEX	27	162	14	8	167	81	67	85	98	3.72
1956	Aguila	MEX	34	156	5	12	153	83	63	104	93	3.63
1957	Aguila	MEX	45	214	10	14	251	151	108	**136**	117	4.54
1958	Chihuanua	AZMX	14	110	12	2	86	49	31	67	83	2.54
1958	Yucatan, Poza Rica	MEX	4	-	0	1	-	-	-	-	-	-
1959	Monterrey	MEX	4	6	0	0	8	6	4	6	2	6.00
1960	Monterrey	MEX	32	136	7	8	127	75	64	93	64	4.24
1961	Monterrey	MEX	13	53	2	4	50	22	18	32	33	3.06
1962	Monterrey	MEX	3	6	0	1	9	5	5	4	3	7.50
1963	Monterrey	MEX	2	3	0	0	5	3	2	2	1	6.00
1964	Puerto Mexican	MXSL	27	161	8	13	160	85	62	63	119	3.47
49-0	Ponce	PRWL	2	17.2	1	1	-	-	9	15	6	4.58
50-1	Magallanes	VENZ	-	-	-	-	-	-	-	-	-	-

Silvio Garcia. Born October 11, 1914 at Limonar, Cuba. 6', 195 lbs. BR TR

Year	Club	League	G	IP	W	L	H	R	ER	BB	SO	ERA
1937	Pastora	VENZ	-	-	-	-	-	-	-	-	-	-
1938	Vera Cruz	MEX	13	112.1	10	2	80	-	21	28	88	1.68
1941	Mexico City	MEX	1	-	-	-	-	-	-	-	-	-
1944	Mex. City, Vera Cruz	MEX	1	1.2	0	0	0	0	0	0	0	0.00
1945	Vera Cruz	MEX	1	.2	0	0	0	0	0	0	0	0.00
34-5	Marianao	CWL	6	33.1	1	2	-	-	9	-	-	2.43
35-6	Marianao	CWL	5	-	1	3	-	-	-	-	-	-
36-7	Marianao	CWL	15	-	10	2	-	-	-	-	-	-
37-8	Marianao	CWL	1	-	0	1	-	-	-	-	-	-
38-9	Almendares	CWL	7	-	1	4	-	-	-	-	-	-
39-0	Ponce	PRWL	16	150	10	6	-	-	22	48	98	**1.32**
44-5	Cienfuegos	CWL	2	-	0	0	-	-	-	-	-	-
46-7	Matanzas	CWL	3	3	0	0	3	0	0	2	3	0.00

Welda Gibson. Born 1929, BB TR

Year	Club	League	G	IP	W	L	H	R	ER	BB	SO	ERA
1949	Houston	NAL	13	56	3	4	73	33	23	22	29	3.70
1950	Houston	NAL	20	115	4	12	166	101	83	39	49	6.50
1955	Oklahoma City	TEX	5	-	0	0	-	-	-	-	-	-
1955	Yuma	AZMX	19	112	6	5	128	82	65	40	60	5.22
1956	Victoria	BGST	9	-	0	0	-	-	-	-	-	-
1957	Hobbs	SWL	2	-	0	0	-	-	-	-	-	-
1957	Tucson	AZMX	4	-	0	0	-	-	-	-	-	-

Stanley Glenn. Born September 19, 1926 at Wachatreague, VA. 6'3", 197 lbs. BR TR

Year	Club	League	G	IP	W	L	H	R	ER	BB	SO	ERA
1944	Philadelphia	NNL	8	47	3	3	45	-	-	23	17	-

William Henry "Bill" or "Booster" Greason. Born September 3, 1924 at Atlanta, GA. 5'10", 170 lbs. BR TR

Year	Club	League	G	IP	W	L	H	R	ER	BB	SO	ERA
1948	Birmingham	NAL	14	90	6	4	85	47	33	38	66	3.30
1949	Birmingham	NAL	26	158	7	13	179	108	**95**	**84**	107	5.41
1950	Birmingham	NAL	19	142	9	6	108	53	38	72	106	2.41
1950	Jalisco	MEX	14	93.2	10	1	76	-	36	76	52	3.46
1951	Birmingham	NAL	-	-	-	-	-	-	-	-	-	-
1951	Jalisco	MEX	7	28.1	1	4	30	-	25	37	23	7.94
1952	Oklahoma City	TEX	11	80	9	1	53	21	19	26	57	2.14
1953	Oklahoma City	TEX	37	249	16	13	206	116	100	**162**	193	3.61
1954	Columbus	AA	34	191	10	13	172	101	87	99	110	4.10
1954	St. Louis	NL	3	4	0	1	8	8	6	4	2	13.50
1955	Houston	TEX	34	240	17	11	222	124	111	110	160	4.16
1956	Houston	TEX	27	154	10	6	149	86	80	87	80	4.68
1956	Rochester	INT	5	-	2	1	-	-	-	-	-	-
1957	Rochester	INT	36	126	5	6	105	54	48	72	97	3.43
1958	Rochester	INT	38	162	7	10	152	90	72	93	125	4.00

Year	Club	League	G	IP	W	L	H	R	ER	BB	SO	ERA
1959	Rochester	INT	23	58	2	1	72	37	36	30	44	5.59
50-1	Marianao	CWL	7	-	2	2	-	-	-	-	-	-
53-4	Santurce	PRWL	-	180	12	10	-	-	-	-	107	-
54-5	Santurce	PRWL	-	107	8	2	-	-	-	-	45	-
55-6	Santurce	PRWL	-	87	6	4	-	-	30	-	41	3.10
57-8	Santurce	PRWL	-	163	12	6	-	-	50	-	100	2.76

Robert Lee Griffith. Born October 1, 1912 at Liberty, TN. Died November 8, 1977 in Indianapolis, IN. 6'2", 215 lbs. BL TR

Year	Club	League	G	IP	W	L	H	R	ER	BB	SO	ERA
1934	Nashville	NNL	-	-	-	-	-	-	-	-	-	-
1935	Columbus	NNL	-	-	-	-	-	-	-	-	-	-
1936	Washington	NNL	-	-	-	-	-	-	-	-	-	-
1937	Washington	NNL	-	-	-	-	-	-	-	-	-	-
1938	Baltimore	NNL	-	-	-	-	-	-	-	-	-	-
1939	Cordoba	MEX	9	60.1	6	1	74	-	32	15	40	4.77
1940	Nuevo Laredo	MEX	15	86.1	7	6	90	-	46	33	56	4.80
1941	Baltimore	NNL	-	-	-	-	-	-	-	-	-	-
1942	New York	NNL	-	-	-	-	-	-	-	-	-	-
1943	New York	NNL	-	-	-	-	-	-	-	-	-	-
1946	New York	NNL	10	43	2	3	53	-	-	16	10	-
1947	New York	NNL	17	79	2	9	123	-	-	-	52	-
1948	New York	NNL	-	-	-	-	-	-	-	-	-	-
1949	Philadelphia	NAL	14	105	9	3	108	32	27	19	50	**2.31**
1950	Mexico City	MEX	38	198	11	11	196	-	83	105	100	3.77
1951	Granby	PROV	15	80	6	5	89	49	39	30	31	4.39
1951	Philadelphia	NAL	-	-	-	-	-	-	-	-	-	-
1952	Indianapolis	NAL	-	-	-	-	-	-	-	-	-	-
1952	Oriente	DMSL	9	48	2	3	-	-	33	-	-	6.19
37-8	Santa Clara	CWL	**24**	-	**13**	6	-	-	-	-	-	-
38-9	Havana	CWL	11	-	4	5	-	-	-	-	-	-
46-7	Aquadilla	PRWL	-	-	-	-	-	-	-	-	-	-

Napoleon "Nap" Gulley. Born August 29, 1924 at Huttig, AR. 6', 170 lbs. BL TL

Year	Club	League	G	IP	W	L	H	R	ER	BB	SO	ERA
1943	Cleveland	NAL	1	-	0	1	-	-	-	-	-	-
1945	Cleveland	NAL	3	6	0	1	8	8	-	5	1	-
1947	Newark	NNL	6	34	2	4	30	-	-	-	24	-
1948	Tampico	MEX	2	6.1	0	1	9	-	3	4	7	4.27
1949	San Luis, Mex. City	MEX	10	15.1	0	1	11	20	19	30	5	11.15

David William "Bill" Harvey. Born March 23, 1908 at Clarksdale, MS. Died March 3, 1989 in Baltimore, MD. 5'8 1/2", 176 lbs. BL TL

Year	Club	League	G	IP	W	L	H	R	ER	BB	SO	ERA
1932	Memphis, Monroe	NSL	-	-	-	-	-	-	-	-	-	-
1933	Clev., Pitts., Memph.		-	-	-	-	-	-	-	-	-	-
1935	Pittsburgh	NNL	-	-	-	-	-	-	-	-	-	-
1936	Pittsburgh	NNL	-	-	-	-	-	-	-	-	-	-
1937	Pittsburgh	NNL	-	-	-	-	-	-	-	-	-	-
1938	Pittsburgh	NNL	-	-	-	-	-	-	-	-	-	-
1939	Toledo	NNL	-	-	-	-	-	-	-	-	-	-
1940	Indianapolis	NNL	-	-	-	-	-	-	-	-	-	-
1940	Monterrey, Tampico	MEX	21	128.1	7	9	136	78	69	64	62	4.84
1941	Tampico	MEX	11	58	2	7	78	-	49	44	17	7.60
1942	Baltimore	NNL	-	-	2	1	-	-	-	-	-	-
1943	Baltimore	NNL	-	-	-	-	-	-	-	-	-	-
1944	Baltimore	NNL	12	38	3	2	51	-	-	7	17	-
1945	Baltimore	NNL	3	13	1	1	14	-	-	3	2	-
1950	Youngstown	MATL	34	94	5	10	96	82	68	96	44	6.51

Jehosie "Jay" Heard. Born January 17, 1920 at Atlanta, GA. 5'7 1/2", 147 lbs. BL TL

Year	Club	League	G	IP	W	L	H	R	ER	BB	SO	ERA
1946	Birmingham	NAL	-	-	-	-	-	-	-	-	-	-
1947	Birmingham	NAL	-	-	-	-	-	-	-	-	-	-
1948	Birmingham	NAL	12	33	6	1	48	25	-	14	18	-
1949	Houston	NAL	23	132	10	6	126	50	35	28	84	2.39
1950	Houston	NAL	24	160	8	9	165	89	60	40	89	3.38
1951	New Orleans	NAL	-	203	**17**	6	-	-	-	-	**163**	-
1952	Portland	PCL	1	1	0	0	0	0	0	2	0	0.00
1952	Victoria	WINT	44	269	20	12	219	108	88	122	**216**	2.94
1953	Portland	PCL	40	226	16	12	203	97	80	92	85	3.19
1954	Baltimore	AL	2	3	0	0	6	5	5	3	2	15.00
1954	Portland	PCL	19	87	3	3	85	38	33	26	47	3.41
1955	Charleston	AA	21	58	1	3	71	44	35	22	36	5.43
1955	Seattle	PCL	14	76	5	7	66	33	33	36	44	3.91

Year	Club	League	G	IP	W	L	H	R	ER	BB	SO	ERA
1955	Tulsa	TEX	9	72	6	2	62	23	17	21	37	2.13
1956	Havana	INT	17	62	3	5	65	39	34	31	36	4.94
1956	Tulsa	TEX	31	119	7	10	139	75	64	46	68	4.84
1957	Havana	INT	19	-	-	-	-	-	-	-	-	-
1958	Memphis	NAL	2	-	0	0	-	-	-	-	-	-
49-0	San Juan	PRWL	-	4.1	0	1	-	-	2	2	1	4.16
52-3	Caracas	VENZ	-	-	-	-	-	-	-	-	-	-
53-4	Magallanes	VENZ	-	-	-	-	-	-	-	-	-	-
56-7		COLB	-	139	7	7	114	-	-	-	-	-

Lenial Hooker. Born June 28, 1919. 6' 1/2", 169 lbs. BR TR

Year	Club	League	G	IP	W	L	H	R	ER	BB	SO	ERA
1940	Newark	NNL	9	18	1	5	10	2	-	5	3	-
1941	Newark	NNL	5	25	3	1	-	13	-	-	-	-
1942	Newark	NNL	-	-	-	-	-	-	-	-	-	-
1943	Newark	NNL	-	-	5	3	-	-	-	-	-	-
1944	Newark	NNL	17	119	8	9	116	-	-	46	46	-
1945	Newark	NNL	12	84	5	7	90	-	-	10	22	-
1945	Vera Cruz	MEX	12	52.1	2	5	70	-	38	44	18	6.54
1946	Newark	NNL	10	50	3	4	53	-	-	14	20	-
1947	Newark	NNL	17	82	3	7	84	-	-	-	30	-
1948	Newark	NNL	-	-	-	-	-	-	-	-	-	-
1949	Houston	NAL	-	-	-	-	-	-	-	-	-	-
1950	Drummondville	PROV	21	139	11	6	138	60	39	48	60	2.53
1951	Drummondville	PROV	28	190	10	9	193	105	80	58	66	3.79
46-7	Havana	CUBA	3	-	0	1	-	-	-	-	-	-

David Taylor Hoskins. Born August 3, 1925 at Greenwood, MS. Died April 2, 1970 in Flint, MI. 6'1", 180 lbs. BL TR

Year	Club	League	G	IP	W	L	H	R	ER	BB	SO	ERA
1944	Homestead	NNL	-	-	-	-	-	-	-	-	-	-
1945	Homestead	NNL	3	9	2	0	11	-	-	4	5	-
1946	Homestead	NNL	-	-	-	-	-	-	-	-	-	-
1949	Grand Rapids	CENT	1	5	0	0	8	3	3	2	2	5.40
1949	Louisville	NAL	-	-	-	-	-	-	-	-	-	-
1950	Dayton	CENT	3	14	0	2	16	10	10	10	12	6.43
1951	Wilkes-Barre	EAST	11	60	5	1	56	28	24	31	35	3.60
1952	Dallas	TEX	35	**280**	**22**	10	237	77	66	70	128	2.12
1953	Cleveland	AL	26	113	9	3	102	57	50	38	55	3.98
1954	Cleveland	AL	14	27	0	1	29	10	9	10	9	3.00
1954	Indianapolis	AA	4	29	1	3	26	-	19	12	15	5.90
1955	Indianapolis	AA	37	171	8	10	194	112	93	58	67	4.89
1956	San Diego	PCL	46	158	7	11	159	94	81	63	87	4.61
1957	Louisville	AA	40	148	9	11	176	99	83	47	74	5.05
1958	Dallas	TEX	31	246	17	8	250	102	87	49	121	3.18
1959	Dallas, Houston	AA	27	155	7	9	174	88	74	27	53	4.30
1959	Spokane	PCL	8	51	2	2	46	18	14	11	21	2.47
1960	Montreal	INT	12	42	0	2	49	26	25	6	13	5.36
1960	Poza Rica	MEX	16	96	7	5	104	50	43	32	18	4.03
55-6	Gavilanes	VENZ	-	-	-	-	-	-	-	-	-	-
56-7	Gavilanes	VENZ	-	**167**	**14**	5	-	-	-	-	107	-
58-9	Gavilanes	VENZ	-	158	**12**	7	-	-	-	-	86	-

Willie "Ace" Hutchinson. BR TR

Year	Club	League	G	IP	W	L	H	R	ER	BB	SO	ERA
1939	Memphis	NAL	-	-	-	-	-	-	-	-	-	-
1940	Memphis	NAL	-	-	1	0	-	-	-	-	-	-
1941	Memphis, KC	NAL	-	-	1	0	-	-	-	-	-	-
1942	Memphis	NAL	-	-	3	3	-	-	-	-	-	-
1943	Memphis	NAL	-	-	0	6	-	-	-	-	-	-
1944	Memphis	NAL	**26**	144	6	10	138	-	51	42	79	3.19
1946	Memphis	NAL	-	-	-	-	-	-	-	-	-	-
1947	Memphis	NAL	-	-	-	-	-	-	-	-	-	-
1947	Tampico	MEX	36	169.1	6	11	148	-	73	108	105	3.88
1949	Memphis	NAL	18	144	8	8	160	91	61	60	87	3.81
1950	Memphis	NAL	5	30	1	2	26	15	9	14	20	2.70
1953	Danville	MOV	10	63	4	2	61	31	26	15	35	3.71

Clifford "Connie" Johnson. Born December 27, 1922 At Stone Mountain, GA. 6'4", 198 lbs. BR TR

Year	Club	League	G	IP	W	L	H	R	ER	BB	SO	ERA
1940	Ind., KC	NAL	-	-	-	-	-	-	-	-	-	-
1941	Kansas City	NAL	4	-	2	2	-	-	-	-	-	-
1942	Kansas City	NAL	3	-	3	0	-	-	-	-	-	-
1946	Kansas City	NAL	13	85	9	3	-	-	-	-	-	-
1947	Kansas City	NAL	3	10	1	1	5	-	-	-	-	-

Year	Club	League	G	IP	W	L	H	R	ER	BB	SO	ERA
1948	Kansas City	NAL	7	33	2	2	42	31	-	18	19	-
1949	Kansas City	NAL	-	-	-	-	-	-	-	-	-	-
1950	Kansas City	NAL	14	112	11	2	98	34	27	23	70	2.17
1951	St. Hyacinthe	PROV	38	250	15	14	225	118	90	112	**172**	3.24
1952	Colorado Springs	WEST	30	248	18	9	215	104	93	103	**233**	3.38
1953	Charleston	AA	15	102	6	6	92	50	41	50	86	3.62
1953	Chicago	AL	14	61	4	4	55	27	24	38	44	3.54
1954	Toronto	INT	34	201	17	8	187	91	83	86	145	3.72
1955	Chicago	AL	17	99	7	4	95	40	38	52	72	3.45
1955	Toronto	INT	16	121	12	2	107	51	41	40	86	3.05
1956	Chicago, Baltimore	AL	31	196	9	11	176	84	75	69	136	3.44
1957	Baltimore	AL	35	242	14	11	212	93	86	66	177	3.20
1958	Baltimore	AL	26	118	6	9	116	58	51	32	68	3.89
1959	Vancouver	PCL	48	111	8	4	109	45	39	35	61	3.16
1960	Vancouver	PCL	1	1	0	1	6	3	3	0	0	27.00
1961	Puebla	MEX	3	-	1	0	-	-	-	-	-	-
54-5	Marianao	CWL	31	174.2	12	11	175	-	64	84	**126**	3.30

Paul Henry Jones. Born in 1929. 6'3", 223 lbs. BR TR

Year	Club	League	G	IP	W	L	H	R	ER	BB	SO	ERA
1949	Louisville	NAL	24	106	2	11	123	89	72	57	73	6.11
1950	Cleveland	NAL	9	40	0	5	58	43	36	18	26	8.10
1951	Flint	CENT	29	179	3	19	231	165	136	101	91	6.84
1952	Vancouver	WINT	19	94	4	6	87	46	36	44	52	3.45
1958	Memphis	NAL	2	-	0	1	-	-	-	-	-	-

Samuel "Toothpick Sam" Jones. Born December 14, 1925 at Stewartsville, OH. Died November 5, 1971 in Morgantown, WV. 6'4", 200 lbs. BR TR

Year	Club	League	G	IP	W	L	H	R	ER	BB	SO	ERA
1946	Homestead	NNL	-	-	-	-	-	-	-	-	-	-
1947	Cleveland	NAL	10	70	4	2	67	44	37	40	47	4.76
1948	Cleveland	NAL	22	143	9	8	140	106	78	63	**112**	4.91
1950	Wilkes-Barre	EAST	30	219	17	8	164	90	66	127	**169**	2.71
1951	Cleveland	AL	2	9	0	1	4	2	2	5	4	2.00
1951	San Diego	PCL	40	**267**	16	13	179	98	82	175	246	2.76
1952	Cleveland	AL	14	36	2	3	38	30	29	37	28	7.25
1952	Indianapolis	AA	5	35	4	0	28	13	12	18	24	3.09
1953	Indianapolis	AA	31	187	10	12	160	86	69	115	118	3.32
1954	Indianapolis	AA	35	199	15	8	155	98	83	129	178	3.75
1955	Chicago	NL	36	242	14	**20**	175	118	110	**185**	198	4.09
1956	Chicago	NL	33	189	9	14	155	93	82	**115**	176	3.90
1957	St. Louis	NL	28	183	12	9	164	77	73	71	154	3.59
1958	St. Louis	NL	35	250	14	13	204	95	80	**107**	225	2.88
1959	San Francisco	NL	50	271	**21**	15	232	99	85	**109**	209	**2.82**
1960	San Francisco	NL	39	234	18	14	200	112	83	91	190	3.19
1961	San Francisco	NL	37	128	8	8	134	72	64	57	105	4.50
1962	Detroit	AL	30	81	2	4	77	39	33	35	73	3.67
1963	St. Louis	NL	11	11	2	0	15	12	11	5	8	9.00
1963	Toronto, Atlanta	INT	43	84	9	4	62	31	24	34	100	2.57
1964	Baltimore	AL	7	10	0	0	5	3	3	5	6	2.70
1964	Columbus	INT	52	82	7	6	54	23	16	37	89	1.76
1965	Columbus	INT	58	77	12	4	67	27	26	33	65	3.04
1966	Columbus	INT	45	64	7	3	51	22	21	19	62	2.95
1967	Columbus	INT	46	66	7	8	58	38	29	22	50	3.95
51-2	San Juan	PRWL	-	168	13	5	-	-	47	94	**140**	2.52
53-4	Gavilanes	VENZ	-	-	-	-	-	-	-	-	-	-
54-5	Santurce	PRWL	-	157	**14**	4	-	-	33	-	**171**	1.89
64-5	Boer	NICR	-	45	2	0	-	-	18	-	46	3.60

Cecil Kaiser. BL TL

Year	Club	League	G	IP	W	L	H	R	ER	BB	SO	ERA
1945	Homestead	NNL	-	-	-	-	-	-	-	-	-	-
1946	San Luis	MEX	33	149.1	6	12	171	-	83	47	56	5.00
1947	Homestead	NNL	-	-	-	-	-	-	-	-	-	-
1948	Homestead	NNL	-	-	-	-	-	-	-	-	-	-
1949	Homestead	BAA	-	-	-	-	-	-	-	-	-	-
1951	Farnham	PROV	33	216	14	13	230	112	95	48	70	3.96
1952	Licey	DMSL	9	42.2	1	3	-	-	6	-	-	1.27
1952	Tampa	FINT	-	-	2	2	-	-	-	-	-	-
45-6	Havana, Marianao	CWL	15	-	3	3	-	-	-	-	-	-
49-0	Caguas, Guayama	PRWL	-	-	**13**	2	-	-	-	-	-	-

Year	Club	League	G	IP	W	L	H	R	ER	BB	SO	ERA

James Harding "Lefty" LaMarque. Born July 29, 1920 at Potosi, MO. 6'2", 182 lbs. BL TL

Year	Club	League	G	IP	W	L	H	R	ER	BB	SO	ERA
1942	Kansas City	NAL	-	-	1	1	-	-	-	-	-	-
1944	Kansas City	NAL	8	44	2	3	48	-	22	18	27	4.50
1945	Kansas City	NAL	12	83	8	2	75	43	28	23	70	3.04
1946	Kansas City	NAL	-	-	-	-	-	-	-	-	-	-
1947	Kansas City	NAL	19	133	12	2	141	66	56	43	99	3.79
1948	Kansas City	NAL	25	**170**	**15**	5	128	50	37	44	109	**1.96**
1949	Kansas City	NAL	27	**196**	13	7	**187**	89	67	39	96	3.08
1950	Kansas City	NAL	16	119	6	7	105	57	43	29	53	3.25
1951	Kansas City	NAL	-	-	-	-	-	-	-	-	-	-
1951	Mexico City	MEX	46	233.1	**19**	6	279	-	108	93	72	4.17
46-7	Havana	CWL	21	-	7	6	-	-	-	-	-	-
47-8	Havana	CWL	32	-	11	7	-	-	-	-	-	-

Rufus Lewis. Born December 13, 1919 at Hattiesburg, MS. 6'1", 180 lbs. BR TR

Year	Club	League	G	IP	W	L	H	R	ER	BB	SO	ERA
1936	Pittsburgh	NNL	-	-	-	-	-	-	-	-	-	-
1937	Pittsburgh	NNL	-	-	-	-	-	-	-	-	-	-
1946	Newark	NNL	11	72	6	1	54	-	-	21	44	-
1947	Newark	NNL	23	147	11	6	129	-	-	-	99	-
1948	Newark	NNL	-	-	-	-	-	-	-	-	-	-
1949	Houston	NAL	18	133	7	9	144	78	51	34	104	3.45
1950	Houston	NAL	3	3	0	0	-	-	-	-	-	-
1950	Mexico City	MEX	19	124.1	5	8	120	-	53	71	69	3.84
1951	Mex.City, Vera Cruz	MEX	28	147	10	9	131	-	56	76	105	3.43
1952	Chihuahua	AZTX	27	183	8	15	220	135	100	71	136	4.92
1952	Mexico City	MEX	5	20.2	0	1	25	-	13	12	13	5.66
47-8	Havana	CWL	30	151	11	6	125	-	40	62	75	2.38
48-9	Havana	CWL	25	125	8	5	118	-	44	74	64	3.17

Edward Locke. Born 1923. 5'11", 181 lbs. BL TR

Year	Club	League	G	IP	W	L	H	R	ER	BB	SO	ERA
1943	Cincinnati	NAL	-	-	-	-	-	-	-	-	-	-
1944	Kansas City	NAL	11	45	3	3	33	-	19	19	29	3.80
1945	Kansas City	NAL	6	33	2	3	44	24	-	16	18	-
1945	Tampico	MEX	9	38	1	2	40	-	17	35	10	4.03
1948	Chicago	NAL	13	69	2	4	80	42	38	20	36	4.96
1949	KC, New York	NAL	-	-	-	-	-	-	-	-	-	-
1950	New York	NAL	-	-	-	-	-	-	-	-	-	-
1950	Springfield	MOV	25	139	10	8	111	64	44	96	124	2.85
1951	Kansas City	NAL	-	-	-	-	-	-	-	-	-	-
1951	Mexico City	MEX	15	64.1	0	5	67	-	34	44	33	4.76
1952	Vancouver	WINT	42	209	11	13	211	102	80	85	142	3.44
1953	Amarillo	WTNM	37	226	21	7	236	139	106	51	114	4.22
1953	Yakima	WINT	9	-	1	5	-	-	-	-	-	-
1954	Amarillo	WTNM	49	267	24	15	307	183	142	66	211	4.79
1955	Amarillo	WTNM	10	47	3	4	64	47	37	18	32	7.09
1955	Artesia	LGHN	38	211	20	7	216	104	88	41	150	3.75
1956	Monterrey	MEX	28	132	6	11	130	54	38	39	59	2.59
1956	Victoria	BGST	15	68	6	2	71	39	34	24	70	4.50
1957	Monterrey	MEX	43	256	**18**	12	226	99	91	56	125	**3.20**
1958	Monterrey	MEX	40	**267**	**19**	16	263	113	100	57	144	3.37
1959	Monterrey	MEX	43	278	21	14	276	123	110	57	146	3.56
1967	Monterrey	MEX	36	185	10	13	221	95	73	51	72	3.55
56-7		MXWL	-	194	18	6	200	-	-	-	-	-
57-8		MXWL	-	**221**	**19**	7	187	-	-	-	-	-

Raul Lopez. Born 1923 in Cuba. 5'11", 154 lbs. BL TL

Year	Club	League	G	IP	W	L	H	R	ER	BB	SO	ERA
1948	New York	NNL	-	-	-	-	-	-	-	-	-	-
1949	New York	NAL	-	-	-	-	-	-	-	-	-	-
1950	Jersey City	INT	16	63	2	7	73	57	46	70	34	6.57
1950	New York	NAL	1	10	0	1	12	8	5	5	11	4.50
1951	Oakland	PCL	4	6	0	2	13	17	15	12	3	22.50
1951	Ottawa	INT	19	78	2	8	86	49	43	46	60	4.96
1952	Sioux City	WEST	2	2	0	0	-	-	-	-	-	-
1953	Havana	FLIN	8	-	2	4	-	-	-	-	-	-

Henry "Hank" Mason. Born June 19, 1931 at Marshall, MO. 6', 185 lbs. BR TR

Year	Club	League	G	IP	W	L	H	R	ER	BB	SO	ERA
1951	Kansas City	NAL	-	-	-	-	-	-	-	-	-	-
1952	Kansas City	NAL	-	-	-	-	-	-	-	-	-	-
1954	Kansas City	NAL	14	97	5	7	85	57	45	50	69	4.18
1955	Schenectady	EAST	39	175	14	9	124	60	57	89	166	2.93

Year	Club	League	G	IP	W	L	H	R	ER	BB	SO	ERA
1955	Syracuse	INT	4	-	0	0	-	-	-	-	-	-
1956	Schenectady	EAST	34	205	15	11	144	68	52	59	176	2.28
1957	Miami	INT	35	69	4	5	60	35	31	39	45	4.04
1958	Miami	INT	42	100	4	2	92	36	34	37	60	3.06
1958	Philadelphia	NL	1	5	0	0	7	7	6	2	3	10.80
1959	Buffalo	INT	41	125	12	3	119	51	45	37	82	3.24
1960	Buffalo	INT	41	115	2	5	125	70	64	45	70	5.01
1960	Philadelphia	NL	3	5.1	0	0	9	6	6	5	3	10.13
1961	Buffalo	INT	4	10	0	2	11	7	7	3	8	6.30
1961	Hawaii	PCL	14	74	4	7	83	57	48	29	37	5.84
1961	Williamsport	EAST	9	58	5	1	51	19	18	15	30	2.79
1962	Hawaii	PCL	3	6	0	1	11	7	7	4	1	10.50

Walter McCoy. Born February 20, 1923 at Los Angeles, CA. 5'11", 172 lbs. BR TR

Year	Club	League	G	IP	W	L	H	R	ER	BB	SO	ERA
1945	Chicago	NAL	20	120	9	6	97	69	46	64	95	3.45
1946	Chicago	NAL	-	-	-	-	-	-	-	-	-	-
1947	Chicago	NAL	-	-	-	-	-	-	-	-	-	-
1948	Chicago	NAL	-	-	-	-	-	-	-	-	-	-
1949	Visalia	CALF	8	46	2	2	58	42	34	38	50	6.65
1950	Sacramento	PCL	5	26	0	4	26	23	18	18	9	6.23
1951	Licey	DMSL	3	11	1	2	-	9	8	-	-	6.55
1951	Tijuana	SWIN	6	36	1	5	47	26	19	15	10	4.75
1952	Tijuana	SWIN	9	68	5	2	78	46	32	31	40	4.24
1954	Nuevo Laredo	MEX	3	19.1	1	2	14	-	8	17	9	3.72
1955	Nuevo Laredo	MEX	2	3	0	0	8	9	7	5	1	21.00

Booker Taliaferro McDaniels. Born in 1912 at Morrilton, AR. Died December 12, 1974 in Kansas City, MO. 6'2", 195 lbs. BR TR

Year	Club	League	G	IP	W	L	H	R	ER	BB	SO	ERA
1940	Kansas City	NAL	-	-	-	-	-	-	-	-	-	-
1941	Kansas City	NAL	-	-	3	0	-	-	-	-	-	-
1942	Kansas City	NAL	-	-	7	0	-	-	-	-	-	-
1943	Kansas City	NAL	-	-	9	1	-	-	-	-	-	-
1944	Kansas City	NAL	12	54	2	5	51	-	20	19	47	3.33
1945	Kansas City	NAL	21	101	6	3	95	40	34	17	78	3.03
1946	San Luis	MEX	45	234.1	14	18	217	-	85	176	**171**	3.26
1947	Kansas City	NAL	-	-	-	-	-	-	-	-	-	-
1947	Vera Cruz	MEX	39	242.2	14	14	226	-	92	161	**127**	3.41
1948	San Luis, Mex. City	MEX	33	173.1	12	12	183	-	89	**106**	91	4.62
1949	Kansas City	NAL	9	53	4	2	49	20	16	15	28	2.72
1949	Los Angeles	PCL	18	113	8	9	123	60	53	59	60	4.22
1950	Los Angeles	PCL	37	68	3	4	72	52	49	44	43	6.49
1951	Licey	DMSL	1	3.2	0	1	-	2	2	-	-	4.90
1951	Mexico City	MEX	12	45.1	1	2	50	-	26	31	11	5.16
1952	Kansas City	NAL	-	-	-	-	-	-	-	-	-	-
45-6	Marianao	CWL	26	-	9	7	-	-	-	-	-	-
46-7	Marianao	CWL	3	-	0	2	-	-	-	-	-	-
46-7	Oriente	CUBA	3	-	3	0	-	-	-	-	-	-
47-8	Santiago, Alac.	CWL	17	-	3	5	-	-	-	-	-	-
49-0	Ponce	PRWL	-	52.1	2	5	-	-	29	15	24	4.99

Terris "The Great" McDuffie. Born July 22, 1910 at Mobile, AL. Died in New York City, NY. 6'2", 200 lbs. BR TR

Year	Club	League	G	IP	W	L	H	R	ER	BB	SO	ERA
1935	Newark, Brooklyn	NNL	1	5	0	0	10	-	-	1	3	-
1936	Newark	NNL	5	16	2	2	10	-	-	6	6	-
1937	Newark	NNL	11	79	7	3	54	-	-	5	9	-
1938	Newark, New York	NNL	17	108	11	3	86	-	-	5	19	-
1939	New York	NNL	9	54	5	3	44	-	-	6	9	-
1940	Philadelphia	NNL	9	47	5	3	34	-	-	5	7	-
1940	Santa Rosa	MEX	8	39.2	0	4	66	-	40	12	25	9.07
1941	Homestead	NNL	4	18	1	3	10	-	-	2	1	-
1942	Philadelphia	NNL	-	-	5	3	-	-	-	-	-	-
1943	Torreon	MEX	28	189.1	9	11	194	-	66	66	105	3.14
1944	Newark	NNL	25	90	5	6	98	-	-	21	33	-
1945	Newark	NNL	4	39	2	1	44	-	-	12	13	-
1945	Nuevo Laredo	MEX	6	26.2	1	4	33	-	18	12	19	6.07
1946	Torreon	MEX	15	75.1	4	4	93	-	42	25	44	5.02
1947	Vera Cruz	MEX	22	126.2	7	10	118	-	52	51	45	3.69
1950	Gavilanes	VENZ	-	-	-	-	-	-	-	-	-	-
1951	Gavilanes	VENZ	-	-	-	-	-	-	-	-	-	-
1952	Cibaenas	DMSL	17	140	12	3	-	-	28	-	-	1.80
1953	Cibaenas	DMSL	17	124.1	8	4	-	-	35	-	-	2.53
1954	Dallas	TEX	14	71	3	4	57	31	24	25	35	3.04

Year	Club	League	G	IP	W	L	H	R	ER	BB	SO	ERA
1954	Oriente	DMSL	6	25.2	1	2	-	-	14	-	-	4.91
37-8	Havana	CWL	5	-	0	3	-	-	-	-	-	-
40-1	Cienfuegos, Almen.	CWL	21	-	7	6	-	-	-	-	-	-
41-2	San Juan	PRWL	-	76	5	5	-	-	28	15	45	3.32
44-5	Cienfuegos	CWL	20	138	7	6	121	-	36	68	43	2.35
45-6	Havana	CWL	23	-	1	3	-	-	-	14	17	-
46-7	Havana	CWL	14	40.1	3	3	33	-	9	22	22	2.01
47-8	Leones	CUBA	28	170.2	9	12	166	-	56	68	61	2.95
50-1	Almendares	CWL	9	51	5	2	57	-	17	7	27	3.00
52-3	Marianao	CWL	15	99.2	5	8	94	-	33	22	19	2.98

Gready "Lefty" McKinnis. Born October 11, 1913 at Bullock County, AL. 6'2", 170 lbs. BR TL

Year	Club	League	G	IP	W	L	H	R	ER	BB	SO	ERA
1941	Birmingham	NAL	-	-	4	1	-	-	-	-	-	-
1942	Birmingham	NAL	-	-	2	5	-	-	-	-	-	-
1943	Birmingham	NAL	-	-	6	4	-	-	-	-	-	-
1944	Chicago	NAL	13	78	6	6	80	-	28	28	38	3.23
1945	Chicago	NAL	18	109	6	5	87	34	31	24	91	2.56
1949	Chicago	NAL	31	142	12	7	117	52	37	20	99	2.35
1952	Oriente	DMSL	12	55	0	8	-	-	25	-	-	4.09
1952	Tampa	FLIN	11	73	3	5	70	37	26	40	35	3.21
1953	Tampa	FLIN	13	-	1	4	-	-	-	-	-	-
1955	St. Petersburg	FLST	28	112	5	8	137	78	57	54	81	4.58

Henry Joseph "Hank" Miller. Born July 17, 1917 at Glenolden, PA. Died August 30, 1972 in Philadelphia, PA. 6' 1/2", 178 lbs. BR TR

Year	Club	League	G	IP	W	L	H	R	ER	BB	SO	ERA
1939	Philadelphia	NNL	-	-	-	-	-	-	-	-	-	-
1940	Philadelphhia	NNL	-	-	-	-	-	-	-	-	-	-
1941	Philadelphia	NNL	-	-	-	-	-	-	-	-	-	-
1943	Philadelphia	NNL	-	-	-	-	-	-	-	-	-	-
1944	Philadelphia	NNL	9	64	5	3	68	-	-	24	41	-
1945	Philadelphia	NNL	6	39	2	4	49	-	-	15	15	-
1946	Philadelphia	NNL	-	-	-	-	-	-	-	-	-	-
1947	Philadelphia	NNL	20	132	9	3	138	-	-	-	86	-
1948	Philadelphia	NNL	-	-	-	-	-	-	-	-	-	-
1949	Philadelphia	NAL	13	93	6	4	79	36	31	32	57	3.00
1950	Torreon	MEX	29	190	8	11	147	-	15	136	141	0.71
1951	San Diego	PCL	6	9	0	0	27	15	14	19	12	14.00
48-9	Cienfuegos	CWL	3	-	0	1	-	-	-	-	-	-

Nathaniel "Nate" Moreland. Born in 1917. 6'1", 195 lbs. BR TL

Year	Club	League	G	IP	W	L	H	R	ER	BB	SO	ERA
1940	Baltimore	NNL	4	-	2	1	-	-	-	-	-	-
1941	Tampico	MEX	36	223.1	16	12	219	-	91	116	74	3.67
1944	Tampico	MEX	49	234.1	8	16	229	-	91	152	58	3.50
1945	Baltimore	NNL	1	4	0	1	9	-	-	1	0	-
1945	Kansas City	NAL	1	8	0	1	11	6	-	0	6	-
1946	Monterrey	MEX	15	66.1	2	6	68	25	22	25	15	2.99
1947	El Centro	SUN	42	241	20	12	267	161	116	68	154	4.33
1948	El Centro	SUN	43	260	17	15	300	191	143	100	164	4.95
1949	El Centro	SUN	28	179	13	10	198	128	98	82	108	4.93
1950	El Cent., Mexicali	SUN	20	112	13	3	92	59	37	52	87	2.97
1951	Mexicali	SWIN	32	221	14	13	232	139	101	103	119	4.11
1952	Mexicali	SWIN	22	136	5	10	131	66	47	38	88	3.11
1953	Mexicali	AZMX	41	267	20	13	303	172	127	70	142	4.28
1954	Mexicali	AZMX	49	228	22	11	238	133	98	76	112	3.87
1955	Mexicali	AZMX	37	171	11	9	201	101	76	49	95	4.00
1956	Cananea	AZMX	41	209	17	8	243	155	105	69	92	4.52

Pedro Naranjo. Born in 1932. 5'10 1/2", 180 lbs. BL TL

Year	Club	League	G	IP	W	L	H	R	ER	BB	SO	ERA
1950	Indianapolis	NAL	3	7	0	1	9	6	5	3	0	6.43
1951	Indianapolis	NAL	-	-	-	-	-	-	-	-	-	-
1952	Decatur	MOV	29	201	13	10	188	77	52	62	157	2.33
1953	Decatur	MOV	10	54	3	6	57	35	28	27	32	4.67
1953	Paris	BGST	17	80	2	8	91	63	54	51	45	6.08
1954	San Angelo	LGHN	2	-	0	1	-	-	-	-	-	-
1954	Thibodaux	EVAG	5	-	2	2	-	-	-	-	-	-
1954	Detroit Stars	NAL	3	10	0	1	10	4	2	2	4	1.80

James "Jimmy" Newberry. Born in 1922 at Birmingham, AL. 5'7", 170 lbs. BB TR

Year	Club	League	G	IP	W	L	H	R	ER	BB	SO	ERA
1943	Birmingham	NAL	-	-	1	3	-	-	-	-	-	-
1944	Birmingham	NAL	12	67	4	5	66	-	24	18	34	3.22

Year	Club	League	G	IP	W	L	H	R	ER	BB	SO	ERA
1945	Birmingham	NAL	21	94	5	3	100	35	32	30	42	3.06
1946	Birmingham	NAL	-	-	-	-	-	-	-	-	-	-
1947	Birmingham	NAL	-	-	-	-	-	-	-	-	-	-
1948	Birmingham	NAL	**31**	157	14	5	158	52	38	30	**112**	2.18
1949	Birmingham	NAL	9	46	4	2	49	26	20	9	11	3.91
1950	Birmingham	NAL	6	51	4	1	47	19	16	13	31	2.82
1951	Licey	DMSL	2	2.2	0	1	-	-	8	-	-	26.97
1952	Hankyu	JAP	36	206	11	10	-	-	74	-	-	3.23
1954	Abilene	WTNM	21	79	2	6	95	62	53	33	48	6.04
1955	Amarillo	WTNM	7	-	0	3	-	-	-	-	-	-
1955	Big Spring	LGHN	5	32	1	4	33	29	16	7	30	4.50
1955	Port Arthur	BGST	33	124	6	4	146	86	69	46	51	5.01
1956	El Paso	SWL	5	-	0	1	-	-	-	-	-	-

Donald "Newk" Newcombe. Born June 14, 1926 at Madison, N.J. 6'4", 220 lbs. BL TR

Year	Club	League	G	IP	W	L	H	R	ER	BB	SO	ERA
1944	Newark	NNL	14	48	1	3	53	-	-	24	27	-
1945	Newark	NNL	15	115	8	4	102	-	-	55	78	-
1946	Nashua	NENG	26	155	14	4	109	40	38	79	104	2.21
1947	Nashua	NENG	29	223	**19**	6	180	94	72	116	**186**	2.91
1948	Montreal	INT	37	189	17	6	151	83	66	106	144	3.14
1949	Brooklyn	NL	38	244.1	17	8	223	89	86	73	149	3.17
1949	Montreal	INT	5	34	2	2	21	12	10	16	27	2.65
1950	Brooklyn	NL	40	267.1	19	11	258	120	110	75	130	3.70
1951	Brooklyn	NL	40	272	20	9	235	115	99	91	**164**	3.28
1954	Brooklyn	NL	29	144.1	9	8	158	81	73	49	82	4.55
1955	Brooklyn	NL	34	233.2	20	5	222	103	83	38	143	3.20
1956	Brooklyn	NL	38	268	**27**	7	219	101	91	46	139	3.06
1957	Brooklyn	NL	28	198.2	11	12	199	86	77	33	90	3.49
1958	Los Angeles, Cinc.	NL	31	167.2	7	13	212	98	87	36	69	4.67
1959	Cincinnati	NL	30	222	13	8	216	87	78	27	100	3.16
1960	Cincinnati	NL	16	83	4	6	99	48	42	14	36	4.55
1960	Cleveland	AL	20	54	2	3	61	28	26	8	27	4.33
1961	Spokane	PCL	25	147	9	8	204	90	81	15	76	4.96
46-7	Matanzas	CWL	-	-	-	-	-	-	-	-	-	-
48-9	Marianao, Almend.	CWL	9	-	1	4	-	-	-	-	-	-

Alexander Newkirk. BL, TR

Year	Club	League	G	IP	W	L	H	R	ER	BB	SO	ERA
1946	New York	NNL	14	91	4	8	102	-	-	32	37	-
1947	New York	NNL	17	86	2	**9**	108	-	-	-	37	-
1948	New York	NNL	-	-	-	-	-	-	-	-	-	-
1949	New York	NAL	9	67	5	2	62	33	30	26	28	4.03
1950	St. Jean	PROV	10	56	3	2	53	24	22	18	21	3.54
1951	St. Jean, Granby	PROV	27	189	7	12	171	112	77	85	54	3.67

Fernando Alberto "Al" Osorio. Born November 21, 1929 in Panama. 6'1", 165 lbs. BR TR

Year	Club	League	G	IP	W	L	H	R	ER	BB	SO	ERA
1948	Pastora	VENZ	-	-	-	-	-	-	-	-	-	-
1949	Louisville	NAL	22	94	3	7	118	66	45	28	30	4.31
1950	Ventura	CALF	28	133	9	6	150	88	73	54	80	4.94
1951	Denver	WEST	48	119	5	3	120	58	46	37	64	3.48
1952	Denver	WEST	40	227	**20**	6	210	92	82	64	95	3.25
1953	Denver	WEST	30	186	12	9	174	79	70	50	106	3.39
1953	Hollywood	PCL	6	-	0	0	-	-	-	-	-	-
1954	Minneapolis	AA	14	33	1	0	46	20	17	5	19	4.64
1955	Johnstown	EAST	34	172	6	16	221	119	91	44	90	4.76
1956	Albuquerque	WEST	34	92	3	5	93	44	38	34	70	3.72
1956	Johnstown	EAST	3	-	0	1	-	-	-	-	-	-
1957	Albuquerque	WEST	54	157	10	8	182	95	84	70	116	4.82
1958	Monterrey	MEX	16	74	4	4	81	37	35	13	41	4.26
1958	San Antonio	TEX	17	76	4	5	99	41	34	19	47	4.03
1959	Mexico City	MEX	8	58	6	2	59	19	19	8	21	2.95
1959	San Antonio	TEX	32	71	3	3	89	46	32	17	30	4.06
1960	Monterrey	MEX	40	213	14	7	269	124	103	46	101	4.35
1961	Mexico City	MEX	25	135	6	8	159	91	71	38	53	4.73
1962	Mex. City, Aguila	MEX	28	57	4	3	63	37	30	22	25	4.74
1963	Aguila	MEX	35	190	8	14	224	116	99	38	109	4.69
1964	Aguila	MEX	26	172	15	5	154	57	49	24	103	**2.56**
1965	Aguila	MEX	31	186	11	14	217	106	90	49	89	4.35
1966	Aguila	MEX	20	142	14	5	130	41	33	20	52	2.09
1967	Aguila	MEX	27	205	14	10	200	68	65	14	93	2.85
1968	Aguila	MEX	27	189	13	8	194	70	59	23	79	2.81

Year	Club	League	G	IP	W	L	H	R	ER	BB	SO	ERA
1969	Aguila	MEX	28	196	14	4	182	60	54	25	79	2.48
1970	Aguila	MEX	20	133	10	7	149	44	42	26	42	2.84
1971	Aguila	MEX	25	171	13	7	214	84	78	31	41	4.11
1972	Aguila	MEX	15	97	4	6	87	36	31	14	44	2.88
56-7		PANA	-	45	4	1	-	-	7	-	-	1.40
59-0		PANA	-	78	0	3	-	-	20	-	-	2.31
62-3		PANA	-	67	6	3	-	-	17	-	-	2.28
63-4		PANA	-	64	4	6	-	-	-	-	34	-
64-5		PANA	-	67	7	2	-	-	23	-	-	3.-9
65-6		PANA	-	97	6	6	-	-	-	-	44	-
66-7		PANA	-	44	3	1	-	-	-	-	13	-

Leroy Robert "Satchel" Paige. Born July 7, 1906 at Mobile, AL. Died June 8, 1982 in Kansas City, MO. 6'3 1/2", 180 lbs. BR TR

Year	Club	League	G	IP	W	L	H	R	ER	BB	SO	ERA
1927	Birmingham	NNL	20	93	8	3	63	34	-	19	80	-
1928	Birmingham	NNL	26	120	12	4	107	41	-	19	112	-
1929	Birmingham	NNL	31	196	11	11	191	114	-	39	184	-
1930	Birm., Balt.	NNL	18	120	11	4	92	38	-	15	86	-
1931	Cleveland, Pitts.	NNL	12	60.1	5	5	36	30	-	4	23	-
1932	Pittsburgh	EWL	29	181	14	8	92	77	-	13	109	-
1933	Pittsburgh	NNL	13	95	5	7	39	39	-	10	57	-
1934	Pittsburgh	NNL	20	154	13	3	85	34	-	21	97	-
1935	Pittsburgh, KC		2	7	0	0	-	-	-	-	10	-
1936	Pittsburgh, KC		9	70	7	2	54	21	-	11	59	-
1937	Ciudad Trujillo	DOML	-	-	8	2	-	-	-	-	-	-
1937	St. Louis	NAL	3	26	1	2	22	-	-	6	11	-
1938	Agrario	MEX	3	19.1	1	1	28	-	11	12	7	5.12
1940	Kansas City	NAL	2	12	1	1	10	6	-	-	15	-
1941	Kansas City	NAL	13	67	7	1	38	14	-	6	61	-
1942	Kansas City	NAL	20	100	8	5	68	32	-	12	78	-
1943	Kansas City, Memph.	NAL	24	88	9	10	80	48	-	16	54	-
1944	Kansas City	NAL	13	77.2	5	5	47	-	11	8	70	1.27
1945	Kansas City	NAL	13	68	3	5	65	-	-	12	48	-
1946	Phil., KC		9	38	5	1	22	-	-	2	23	-
1947	Kansas City	NAL	2	11	1	1	5	-	-	-	-	-
1948	Cleveland	AL	21	73	6	1	61	21	20	25	45	2.47
1949	Cleveland	AL	31	83	4	7	70	29	28	33	54	3.04
1950	KC, Philadelphia	NAL	8	26	1	2	28	17	15	7	23	5.19
1951	Chicago	NAL	-	-	-	-	-	-	-	-	-	-
1951	St. Louis	AL	23	62	3	4	67	39	33	29	48	4.79
1952	St. Louis	AL	46	138	12	10	116	51	47	57	91	3.07
1953	St. Louis	AL	57	117	3	9	114	51	46	39	51	3.54
1955	Kansas City	NAL	-	-	-	-	-	-	-	-	-	-
1956	Miami	INT	27	111	11	4	101	29	23	28	79	1.86
1957	Miami	INT	40	119	10	8	98	35	32	11	76	2.42
1958	Miami	INT	28	110	10	10	94	44	36	15	40	2.95
1961	Portland	PCL	5	25	0	0	28	12	8	5	19	2.88
1965	Kansas City	AL	1	3	0	0	1	0	0	0	1	0.00
1966	Peninsula	CARO	1	2	0	0	5	2	2	0	0	9.00
29-0	Santa Clara	CWL	15	-	6	5	-	-	-	-	-	-
39-0	Guayama	PRWL	24	205	**19**	3	-	-	44	54	**208**	1.93
47-8	Santurce	PRWL	-	40	0	3	-	-	11	13	26	2.48

Roy Partlow. Born in 1912. Died April 19, 1987 at Cherry Hill, N.J. 6', 180 lbs. BR TL

Year	Club	League	G	IP	W	L	H	R	ER	BB	SO	ERA
1934	Memphis		-	-	-	-	-	-	-	-	-	-
1937	Cincinnati	NAL	-	-	-	-	-	-	-	-	-	-
1938	Homestead	NNL	-	-	-	-	-	-	-	-	-	-
1939	Homestead	NNL	-	-	-	-	-	-	-	-	-	-
1940	Vera Cruz	MEX	6	20.2	0	1	29	-	20	20	20	8.71
1941	Homestead	NNL	-	-	-	-	-	-	-	-	-	-
1942	Homestead	NNL	4	-	3	0	-	-	-	-	-	-
1943	Homestead	NNL	-	-	-	-	-	-	-	-	-	-
1943	Vera Cruz	MEX	17	95.1	6	9	128	-	62	56	50	5.85
1945	Philadelphia	NNL	17	99	7	4	99	-	-	36	83	-
1946	Montreal	INT	10	29	2	0	26	18	18	16	19	5.59
1946	Three Rivers	CAAM	14	95	10	1	94	42	34	33	78	3.22
1947	Philadelphia	NNL	15	91	4	7	98	-	-	-	55	-
1948	Philadelphia	NNL	-	-	-	-	-	-	-	-	-	-
1949	Homestead	BAA	-	-	-	-	-	-	-	-	-	-
1950	Granby	PROV	-	-	-	-	-	-	-	-	-	-
1950	Homestead		-	-	-	-	-	-	-	-	-	-

Year	Club	League	G	IP	W	L	H	R	ER	BB	SO	ERA
1950	San Luis Potosi	MEX	6	31.2	1	3	39	-	23	19	22	6.54
1951	Escogido	DMSL	5	47	5	0	-	13	3	-	-	0.57
1951	Granby	PROV	-	-	-	-	-	-	-	-	-	-
39-0	San Juan	PRWL	16	145	11	4	-	-	24	54	139	1.49
39-0	Santa Clara	CWL	13	-	7	4	-	-	-	-	-	-
40-1	San Juan	PRWL	-	141	8	9	-	-	41	-	-	2.62
44-5	San Juan	PRWL	-	52	3	2	-	-	27	-	-	4.67
45-6	Ponce	PRWL	-	112.1	6	3	-	-	38	40	67	3.04

Alonzo Thomas Perry. Born April 14, 1923 at Birmingham, AL. Deceased. 6'3", 200 lbs. BL TR

Year	Club	League	G	IP	W	L	H	R	ER	BB	SO	ERA
1940	Homestead	NNL	-	-	-	-	-	-	-	-	-	-
1946	Birmingham	NAL	-	-	-	-	-	-	-	-	-	-
1946	Homestead	NNL	7	34	2	2	35	-	-	22	16	-
1947	Birmingham	NAL	-	-	-	-	-	-	-	-	-	-
1948	Birmingham	NAL	18	120	10	2	145	80	63	33	59	4.73
1949	Birmingham	NAL	24	133	12	4	124	61	51	31	61	3.45
1950	Birmingham	NAL	3	9	0	1	18	15	8	9	3	8.00
1951	Licey	DMSL	2	3.2	0	1	-	3	1	-	-	2.45
48-9	Mayaquez	CWL	-	-	11	4	-	-	-	-	-	-

William Pope. Born December 14, 1918 at Birmingham, AL. 6'3", 230 lbs. BR TR

Year	Club	League	G	IP	W	L	H	R	ER	BB	SO	ERA
1946	Pittsburgh	USL	-	-	-	-	-	-	-	-	-	-
1947	Homestead	NNL	17	97	6	7	98	-	-	-	64	-
1948	Homestead	NNL	-	-	-	-	-	-	-	-	-	-
1950	Farnham	PROV	8	72	3	5	62	29	19	23	52	2.38
1950	Jalisco	MEX	16	96	5	8	97	-	42	67	51	3.94
1951	St. Hyacinthe	PROV	39	225	12	11	206	113	85	104	145	3.40
1952	Colorado Springs	WEST	23	159	12	5	166	64	53	33	102	3.00
1953	Colorado Springs	WEST	31	232	16	12	221	104	87	82	167	3.38
1954	Charleston	AA	31	128	4	11	154	85	75	40	71	5.27
1955	Colorado Springs	WEST	29	181	13	8	194	91	70	52	111	3.48

Andrew "Pullman" Porter. Born March 7, 1911 at Little Rock, AK. 6'3 1/2", 190 lbs. BR TR

Year	Club	League	G	IP	W	L	H	R	ER	BB	SO	ERA
1932	Nash., Louis., Clev.	NSL	-	-	-	-	-	-	-	-	-	-
1933	Nashville	NNL	-	-	-	-	-	-	-	-	-	-
1934	Nashville	NNL	-	-	-	-	-	-	-	-	-	-
1935	Columbus	NNL	-	-	-	-	-	-	-	-	-	-
1936	Washington	NNL	-	-	-	-	-	-	-	-	-	-
1937	Washington	NNL	-	-	-	-	-	-	-	-	-	-
1938	Baltimore	NNL	-	-	-	-	-	-	-	-	-	-
1939	Baltimore	NNL	-	-	-	-	-	-	-	-	-	-
1939	Tampico	MEX	22	146	10	7	117	-	37	35	111	2.28
1940	Nuevo Laredo	MEX	**42**	**296**	21	14	268	-	110	**125**	**232**	3.34
1941	Mexico City	MEX	37	**235.1**	11	**16**	261	-	117	116	**133**	4.47
1942	Baltimore	NNL	-	-	8	0	-	-	-	-	-	-
1942	Vera Cruz	MEX	19	103.1	5	8	125	-	65	81	47	5.66
1943	Baltimore	NNL	-	-	-	-	-	-	-	-	-	-
1943	Vera Cruz	MEX	3	3.1	0	0	17	-	10	7	0	27.03
1944	Baltimore	NNL	8	43	3	1	54	-	-	19	14	-
1945	Baltimore	NNL	11	82	8	0	82	-	-	18	30	-
1946	Baltimore	NNL	9	60	2	4	72	-	-	16	31	-
1946	Nuevo Laredo	MEX	9	38.2	2	2	50	-	22	24	13	5.12
1947	Newark	NNL	-	-	-	-	-	-	-	-	-	-
1948	Indianapolis	NAL	12	77	4	5	101	47	40	21	54	4.68
1949	Indianapolis	NAL	20	139	10	6	143	66	56	30	61	3.63
1950	Indianapolis	NAL	3	17	2	0	15	9	7	5	6	3.71
1952	Porterville	SWIN	12	78	3	5	92	58	37	35	47	4.27
39-0	Santa Clara	CWL	9	-	3	4	-	-	-	-	-	-
40-1	Almendares	CWL	14	-	6	5	-	-	-	-	-	-

William Henry Powell. Born May 8, 1919 at West Birmingham, AL. 6'2 1/2", 195 lbs. BL TR

Year	Club	League	G	IP	W	L	H	R	ER	BB	SO	ERA
1946	Birmingham	NAL	-	-	-	-	-	-	-	-	-	-
1947	Birmingham	NAL	10	70	5	0	55	27	23	25	34	2.96
1948	Birmingham	NAL	19	130	11	3	133	63	55	40	103	3.81
1949	Birmingham	NAL	**32**	182	11	11	189	86	73	56	124	3.61
1950	Birmingham	NAL	26	162	**15**	4	164	79	54	68	110	3.00
1951	Colorado Springs	WEST	33	188	14	8	189	125	98	107	157	4.69
1951	Sacramento	PCL	5	9	0	1	6	8	7	13	6	7.00
1952	Birmingham	NAL	-	-	-	-	-	-	-	-	-	-
1952	Toledo, Charleston	AA	31	175	5	15	205	127	99	88	88	5.09

Year	Club	League	G	IP	W	L	H	R	ER	BB	SO	ERA
1953	Charleston	AA	33	215	14	9	187	92	73	85	121	3.06
1954	Toronto, Havana	INT	31	151	10	8	145	89	71	97	76	4.23
1955	Charleston	AA	31	131	3	10	152	88	75	58	59	5.15
1955	Havana	INT	13	46	3	4	55	31	27	27	17	5.28
1956	San Antonio	TEX	16	47	1	3	52	34	30	45	19	5.74
1956	Savannah	SATL	25	175	8	12	153	73	61	80	71	3.14
1957	Nuevo Laredo	MEX	17	84	3	7	82	56	37	62	52	3.96
1957	Savannah	SATL	3	-	2	0	-	-	-	-	-	-
1958	Knoxville	SATL	**70**	141	7	8	127	67	58	57	58	3.70
1959	Asheville	SATL	1	-	0	0	-	-	-	-	-	-
1961	Charlotte	SATL	16	23	1	1	30	21	15	13	15	6.22
49-0	Marianao	CWL	10	-	1	4	-	-	-	-	-	-
52-3	Cienfuegos	CWL	11	-	3	2	-	-	-	-	-	-

Albert Webber Preston. Born June 26, 1926 at New York City, NY. Died September 21, 1979 in New York City, NY. 6'1", 170 lbs. BR TR

Year	Club	League	G	IP	W	L	H	R	ER	BB	SO	ERA
1943	New York	NNL	-	-	-	-	-	-	-	-	-	-
1946	New York	NNL	-	-	-	-	-	-	-	-	-	-
1947	New York	NNL	-	-	-	-	-	-	-	-	-	-
1947	Stamford	COL	10	51	2	3	53	39	26	41	36	4.59
1949	New York		-	-	-	-	-	-	-	-	-	-
1950	Baltimore	NAL	2	5	0	0	-	-	-	-	-	-
1951	Escogido	DMSL	3	17.1	1	2	-	7	6	-	-	3.12
1952	Chicago	NAL	-	-	-	-	-	-	-	-	-	-

James Arthur Proctor. Born September 9, 1935 at Brandywine, MD. 6', 165 lbs. BR TR

Year	Club	League	G	IP	W	L	H	R	ER	BB	SO	ERA
1955	Indianapolis	NAL	-	-	-	-	-	-	-	-	-	-
1955	West Palm Beach	FLST	5	7	0	0	-	-	-	-	-	-
1956	Augusta	SATL	29	126	8	7	119	46	38	35	79	2.71
1956	Terre Haute	III	6	39	3	1	-	-	-	11	25	-
1957	Augusta	SATL	13	80	7	2	50	16	14	23	63	1.58
1957	Charleston	AA	31	94	7	6	96	47	37	27	62	3.54
1958	Lancaster	EAST	1	0	0	0	0	0	0	1	0	-
1959	Detroit	AL	2	2.2	0	1	8	5	5	3	0	16.85
1959	Knoxville	SATL	28	181	15	5	139	52	44	55	131	2.19
1960	Victoria	TEX	29	191	15	8	182	87	83	77	98	3.91
1961	Houston	AA	6	25	0	4	27	12	12	9	10	4.32
1962	Salt Lake City	PCL	34	100	3	7	109	66	54	54	51	4.86
1963	Salt Lake City	PCL	8	26	1	1	26	15	13	10	20	4.50

William Ricks. BR TR

Year	Club	League	G	IP	W	L	H	R	ER	BB	SO	ERA
1944	Philadelphia	NNL	19	**121**	**10**	4	106	-	-	40	**74**	-
1945	Philadelphia	NNL	12	58	1	4	59	-	-	14	32	-
1946	Philadelphia	NNL	10	50	1	3	42	-	-	25	16	-
1947	Philadelphia	NNL	-	-	-	-	-	-	-	-	-	-
1948	Philadelphia	NNL	-	-	-	-	-	-	-	-	-	-
1949	Philadelphia	NAL	16	89	4	8	91	51	39	44	60	3.94
1950	Philadelphia	NAL	3	19	1	1	25	10	6	5	11	2.84
1951	Granby	PROV	28	124	8	8	135	69	58	70	54	4.21

Ray "Not Sugar" Robinson. 6'2 1/2", 205 lbs. BR TR

Year	Club	League	G	IP	W	L	H	R	ER	BB	SO	ERA
1941	Newark	NNL	-	-	-	-	-	-	-	-	-	-
1942	Cinc.-Cleveland	NAL	-	-	-	-	-	-	-	-	-	-
1947	Philadelphia	NNL	-	-	-	-	-	-	-	-	-	-
1955	Aberdeen	NORL	13	55	5	3	49	24	21	30	36	3.44
1955	Thetford Mines	PROV	2	-	0	1	-	-	-	-	-	-
1956	Texas City	BGST	39	205	8	**18**	218	142	98	95	127	4.30

Antonio Ruiz. BR TR

Year	Club	League	G	IP	W	L	H	R	ER	BB	SO	ERA
1944	Cinc., Ind.	NAL	18	127	10	4	140	-	39	11	34	2.76
1946	Torreon	MEX	4	22	1	1	18	-	10	6	2	4.09
1950	Juarez	AZTX	-	-	-	-	-	-	-	-	-	-
1951	Tucson	SWIN	32	180	10	9	190	86	72	70	76	3.60
1952	Juarez	AZTX	4	12	0	2	18	13	9	6	3	6.75
1952	Odessa	LGHN	2	6.1	0	1	11	8	8	4	0	11.37

Year	Club	League	G	IP	W	L	H	R	ER	BB	SO	ERA

Wilfredo Salas. Born in Cuba, Deceased. BR TR

Year	Club	League	G	IP	W	L	H	R	ER	BB	SO	ERA
1946	Torreon	MEX	22	112	7	7	86	-	28	55	72	2.25
1947	S.L., Mex. City, VR	MEX	41	158.1	5	13	146	-	79	96	79	4.49
1948	New York	NNL	-	-	-	-	-	-	-	-	-	-
1949	Torreon	MEX	39	201.2	11	13	176	120	86	151	158	3.84
1950	Pastora	VENZ	-	-	-	-	-	-	-	-	-	-
1951	Monterrey	MEX	31	186.1	14	6	164	65	56	108	126	2.70
1952	Escogido	DMSL	5	25.2	2	2	-	-	10	-	-	3.51
1952	Monterrey	MEX	14	88.1	5	4	65	42	25	55	45	2.55
1953	Monterrey	MEX	35	200.1	10	10	180	97	79	93	137	3.55
1954	Monterrey	MEX	19	114.2	6	10	121	68	55	54	65	4.32
1955	Aguila	MEX	10	46	5	2	37	25	19	17	32	3.72
1956	Aguila	MEX	28	139	9	8	152	61	49	58	79	3.17

Jose Guillermo "Pants" Santiago y Guzman. Born September 4, 1928 at Coamo, PR., 5'10", 178 lbs. BR TR

Year	Club	League	G	IP	W	L	H	R	ER	BB	SO	ERA
1947	New York	NNL	-	-	-	-	-	-	-	-	-	-
1948	New York	NNL	-	-	-	-	-	-	-	-	-	-
1949	Dayton	CENT	37	211	16	12	153	74	61	85	**233**	2.60
1950	Wilkes-Barre	EAST	36	141	12	7	118	58	51	80	107	3.26
1951	San Diego	PCL	12	40	1	5	53	34	30	23	23	6.75
1951	Wilkes-Barre	EAST	28	187	**21**	5	149	51	33	65	129	**1.59**
1952	Dallas	TEX	25	178	14	7	154	68	56	45	92	2.83
1953	Dallas	TEX	31	187	13	11	170	83	71	77	161	3.42
1954	Cleveland	AL	1	2	0	0	0	1	0	2	1	0.00
1954	Escogido	DMSL	8	59.1	3	3	-	-	20	-	-	3.03
1954	Indianapolis	AA	1	.1	0	1	2	4	3	0	1	81.82
1955	Cleveland	AL	17	33	2	0	31	11	9	14	19	2.45
1955	Indianapolis	AA	25	96	5	3	88	48	44	48	66	4.13
1956	Columbus	INT	11	-	1	4	-	-	-	-	-	-
1956	Kansas City	AL	9	22	1	2	36	26	20	17	9	8.18
1957	Buffalo, Havana	INT	21	100	4	7	95	55	48	44	63	4.32
1958	Havana	INT	19	76	4	7	103	49	42	35	48	4.97
1958	San Antonio	TEX	14	78	7	5	69	32	29	20	63	3.35
1959	San Antonio	TEX	38	212	14	9	205	92	73	60	121	3.10
46-7	Ponce	PRWL	-	105	8	2	-	-	36	42	60	3.09
47-8	Ponce	PRWL	-	138.2	10	8	-	-	58	52	91	3.76
48-9	Ponce	PRWL	-	131	9	10	-	58	46	69	87	3.16
49-0	Ponce	PRWL	-	147	11	8	-	-	48	51	101	2.94
50-1	Ponce	PRWL	-	140.2	11	6	-	-	42	46	111	2.69
51-2	Ponce	PRWL	-	159	10	9	-	66	59	50	119	3.34
52-3	Ponce	PRWL	-	113	7	5	-	-	26	33	70	2.07
53-4	Ponce	PRWL	20	118	9	3	-	-	31	37	63	2.36
54-5	Ponce	PRWL	-	99.2	4	9	-	55	41	21	56	3.70
55-6	San Juan	PRWL	-	79	5	6	-	-	32	28	29	3.65
56-7	San Juan	PRWL	-	114	5	9	90	-	27	-	-	2.13
57-8	San Juan	PRWL	-	112	8	6	-	-	28	-	41	2.25
59-0	San Juan	PRWL	-	91	4	7	-	-	25	-	49	2.47
62-3	Ponce	PRWL	-	5	0	1	-	-	2	1	4	3.60

Patricio Athelstan Scantlebury. Born November 11, 1917 at Gatun, Canal Zone. Died May 24, 1991 in Glen Ridge, NJ. 6'1", 185 lbs. BL TL

Year	Club	League	G	IP	W	L	H	R	ER	BB	SO	ERA
1944	New York	NNL	6	23	1	4	36	-	-	7	15	-
1945	New York	NNL	7	32	1	2	44	-	-	11	16	-
1946	New York	NNL	13	57	5	2	64	-	-	16	25	-
1947	New York	NNL	17	70	10	5	77	-	-	-	21	-
1948	New York	NNL	-	-	-	-	-	-	-	-	-	-
1949	New York	NAL	15	115	7	5	120	54	45	15	37	3.52
1950	New York	NAL	8	64	5	3	69	31	28	21	21	3.94
1951	Vera Cruz	MEX	29	181	13	11	188	-	84	104	102	4.18
1953	Texarkana	BGST	39	286	**24**	11	314	135	107	69	**177**	3.37
1954	Dallas	TEX	41	258	18	13	255	136	118	102	168	4.12
1954	Havana	INT	-	-	-	-	-	-	-	-	-	-
1955	Havana	INT	40	147	13	9	108	41	31	51	76	**1.90**
1956	Cincinnati	NL	6	19	0	1	24	14	14	5	10	6.63
1956	Havana	INT	17	105	5	5	101	42	30	34	62	2.57
1956	Seattle	PCL	10	62	4	2	72	30	23	14	34	3.34
1957	Havana	INT	43	209	12	15	190	95	80	56	111	3.44
1958	Toronto	INT	32	207	15	9	203	98	89	52	133	3.87
1959	Toronto	INT	57	167	12	5	158	63	57	59	96	3.07
1960	Toronto	INT	53	106	7	5	85	37	31	28	60	2.63

Year	Club	League	G	IP	W	L	H	R	ER	BB	SO	ERA
1961	Toronto	INT	46	76	2	4	54	33	29	30	60	3.43
46-7	Ponce	PRWL	-	-	-	-	-	-	-	-	-	-
47-8	Almendares	CWL	24	140	10	6	122	-	29	44	57	1.86

Fred Shepard. BR TR

Year	Club	League	G	IP	W	L	H	R	ER	BB	SO	ERA
1945	Birmingham	NAL	-	-	-	-	-	-	-	-	-	-
1946	Birmingham	NAL	-	-	-	-	-	-	-	-	-	-
1947	Stamford	COL	-	-	-	-	-	-	-	-	-	-
1948	Stamford	COL	13	45	1	2	53	44	32	32	10	6.40

John Ford Smith. Born January 9, 1919 at Phoenix, AZ. Died February 26, 1983 in Phoenix, AZ., 6'1", 198 lbs. BB TR

Year	Club	League	G	IP	W	L	H	R	ER	BB	SO	ERA
1939	Ind., Chicago	NAL	-	-	-	-	-	-	-	-	-	-
1940	Indianapolis	NAL	-	-	-	-	-	-	-	-	-	-
1941	Kansas City	NAL	-	-	1	1	-	-	-	-	-	-
1942	Chicago	NAL	-	-	-	-	-	-	-	-	-	-
1944	Chicago	NAL	-	-	-	-	-	-	-	-	-	-
1945	Chicago	NAL	2	8	0	1	12	7	-	1	3	-
1946	KC, New York		-	-	-	-	-	-	-	-	-	-
1947	KC, New York		9	63	7	2	59	22	18	20	29	2.57
1948	KC, New York		18	133	10	5	127	67	39	36	86	2.64
1949	Jersey City	INT	31	154	10	8	142	84	71	106	78	4.15
1949	New York	NAL	-	-	-	-	-	-	-	-	-	-
1950	Jersey City	INT.	12	45	2	3	41	22	17	40	20	3.40
1950	New York		-	-	-	-	-	-	-	-	-	-
1951	Drummondville	PROV	29	179	16	8	153	67	59	67	104	2.97
1952	Phoenix	AZTX	20	152	13	4	154	87	66	70	97	3.91
1953	Phoenix	AZTX	33	199	11	14	255	153	125	84	141	5.65
1954	El Paso	AZTX	16	81	9	3	73	38	32	54	61	3.56
1954	Escogido	DMSL	2	15.1	0	0	-	-	-	-	-	-
47-8	Caguas	PRWL	-	-	**13**	-	-	-	-	-	-	-
48-9	Santurce	PRWL	-	-	**13**	-	-	-	-	-	-	-
49-0	Havana	CWL	19	103	8	6	78	-	32	57	52	2.80

Theolic "Fireball" Smith. Born May 19, 1914 at St. Louis, MO., 5'11 1/2", 170 lbs. BB TR

Year	Club	League	G	IP	W	L	H	R	ER	BB	SO	ERA
1936	Pittsburgh	NNL	-	-	-	-	-	-	-	-	-	-
1938	Pittsburgh	NNL	-	-	-	-	-	-	-	-	-	-
1939	Toledo, St. Louis	NAL	-	-	-	-	-	-	-	-	-	-
1940	Mexico City	MEX	30	219	19	9	193	-	97	88	111	3.99
1941	Mexico City	MEX	32	207	**16**	8	209	-	115	131	73	5.00
1942	Mexico City	MEX	26	198.2	13	11	210	-	92	111	77	4.17
1943	Cleveland	NAL	-	-	7	5	-	-	-	-	-	-
1944	Mexico City	MEX	43	255.2	16	15	281	-	118	136	86	4.15
1945	Kansas City	NAL	-	-	-	-	-	-	-	-	-	-
1945	Mexico City	MEX	38	235	15	**16**	247	-	125	123	69	4.79
1946	Mexico City	MEX	28	179	11	10	172	-	75	93	83	3.77
1947	Mexico City	MEX	40	269.1	**22**	10	264	-	83	93	117	2.77
1948	Chicago	NAL	8	25	1	1	20	16	-	27	20	-
1948	Mexico City	MEX	31	176	9	11	220	-	83	61	59	4.24
1949	Chicago, KC	NAL	16	87	4	5	87	56	49	44	53	5.07
1950	Pastora	VENZ	-	-	-	-	-	-	-	-	-	-
1951	Chicago	NAL	-	139	15	2	116	45	-	38	89	-
1952	San Diego	PCL	35	147	9	10	135	64	53	60	75	3.24
1953	San Diego	PCL	39	185	13	16	185	101	93	80	84	4.52
1954	San Diego	PCL	24	83	3	2	80	43	37	32	36	4.01
1955	San Diego	PCL	7	-	2	1	-	-	-	-	-	-
38-9	Almendares	CWL	16	-	5	**9**	-	-	-	-	-	-
47-8	Leones	CUBA	3	-	-	-	-	-	-	-	-	-
49-0	Magallanes	VENZ	-	-	-	-	-	-	-	-	-	-

Willie Smith. Born February 11, 1939 at Anniston, AL., 6', 182 lbs. BL TL

Year	Club	League	G	IP	W	L	H	R	ER	BB	SO	ERA
1958	Birmingham	NAL	10	54	6	2	43	16	16	19	58	2.67
1960	Duluth-Superior	NORL	20	140	10	6	105	57	46	105	143	2.96
1961	Knoxville	SATL	30	211	13	11	162	99	75	93	153	3.20
1962	Knoxville	SATL	25	120	10	7	103	58	48	61	94	3.60
1963	Detroit	AL	11	21.2	1	0	24	13	11	13	16	4.57
1963	Syracuse	INT	19	145	14	2	129	37	34	41	92	2.11
1964	Los Angeles	AL	15	31.2	1	4	34	13	10	10	20	2.84
1964	Syracuse	INT	1	6	0	1	8	4	3	1	3	4.50

Year	Club	League	G	IP	W	L	H	R	ER	BB	SO	ERA
1967	Portland	PCL	5	12	2	0	9	2	1	5	12	0.75
1968	Chicago	NL	1	2.2	0	0	0	0	0	0	2	0.00
1968	Cleveland	AL	2	5	0	0	2	0	0	1	1	0.00

Othello Strong, BB TR

Year	Club	League	G	IP	W	L	H	R	ER	BB	SO	ERA
1949	Chicago	NAL	-	-	-	-	-	-	-	-	-	-
1950	Chicago	NAL	17	117	5	8	133	79	66	51	54	5.08
1951	Chicago	NAL	-	-	-	-	-	-	-	-	-	-
1952	Chicago	NAL	-	-	-	-	-	-	-	-	-	-
1953	Danville	MOV	10	59	3	2	45	18	13	22	29	1.98

Robert Burns Thurman. Born May 14, 1917 at Wichita, KS., 6'1", 200 lbs. BL TL

Year	Club	League	G	IP	W	L	H	R	ER	BB	SO	ERA
1946	Homestead	NNL	9	34	1	2	37	· -	-	18	21	-
1947	Homestead	NNL	5	11	0	2	14	-	-	0	4	-
1948	Homestead	NNL	11	81	6	4	-	-	-	33	40	-
1953	Escogido	DMSL	5	31	1	1	-	-	11	-	-	3.19
49-0	Santurce	PRWL	-	-	5	3	-	-	-	-	-	-
59-0	Ponce	PRWL	3	6	0	0	-	-	-	4	5	-

Robert Lee "Bill" Trice. Born August 28, 1926 at Newton, GA. Died September 16, 1988 in Wierton, WV., 6'2 1/2", 190 lbs. BR TR

Year	Club	League	G	IP	W	L	H	R	ER	BB	SO	ERA
1948	Homestead	NNL	-	-	-	-	-	-	-	-	-	-
1949	Homestead	ANL	-	-	-	-	-	-	-	-	-	-
1950	Farnham	PROV	-	-	5	3	-	-	-	-	-	-
1950	Homestead		-	-	-	-	-	-	-	-	-	-
1951	Farnham	PROV	23	152	7	12	172	104	87	67	61	5.15
1952	St. Hyacinthe	PROV	24	152	**16**	3	162	75	59	29	68	3.49
1953	Ottawa	INT	38	229	**21**	10	207	90	79	84	57	3.10
1953	Philadelphia	AL	3	23	2	1	25	14	14	4	6	5.48
1954	Ottawa	INT	13	117	4	8	113	58	42	35	26	3.23
1954	Philadelphia	AL	219	119	7	8	146	86	74	48	22	5.60
1955	Columbus	INT	15	58	2	4	66	35	30	18	8	4.66
1955	Kansas City	AL	4	10	0	0	14	13	10	6	2	9.00
1955	Savannah	SATL	11	63	3	5	63	40	35	18	23	5.00
1956	Mexico City	MEX	18	81	3	4	79	36	20	53	30	2.22
1957	Mexico City	MEX	14	83	7	5	105	54	52	40	34	5.64
1958	Mexico City	MEX	25	114	4	6	111	63	54	49	32	4.26

James C. "Jim" Tugerson. Born 1923 at Florence Villa, FL., 6'4", 194 lbs. BR TR

Year	Club	League	G	IP	W	L	H	R	ER	BB	SO	ERA
1951	Indianapolis, KC	NAL	-	128	10	5	-	-	-	-	67	-
1952	Indianapolis	NAL	-	83	8	2	-	-	-	-	60	-
1952	Oriente	DMSL	9	52	3	4	-	-	21	-	-	3.63
1953	Knoxville	MTST	**46**	**330**	**29**	11	**306**	168	136.	122	**286**	3.71
1954	Artesia	LGHN	14	84	9	1	54	21	14	28	89	1.50
1954	Dallas	TEX	32	190	9	14	187	95	84	78	107	3.98
1955	Dallas	TEX	38	220	9	12	201	87	78	81	156	3.19
1956	Amarillo	WEST	27	154	11	6	169	110	97	58	132	5.67
1956	Dallas	TEX	9	-	0	2	-	-	-	-	-	-
1958	Dallas	TEX	34	238	14	13	220	100	88	73	**199**	3.33
1959	Dallas	AA	35	136	5	12	129	68	53	55	69	3.51

Roberto Enrique Vargas. Born May 29, 1929 at Santurce, PR., 5'11", 175 lbs. BL TL

Year	Club	League	G	IP	W	L	H	R	ER	BB	SO	ERA
1948	Chicago	NAL	18	99	6	8	90	50	34	29	70	3.09
1950	Jalisco	MEX	30	140	7	8	123	-	52	107	90	3.33
1951	Lakeland	FLIN	40	244	18	8	232	102	73	126	157	2.69
1952	Reading	EAST	36	180	13	10	135	66	55	79	99	2.75
1953	Escogido	DMSL	23	147	10	8	-	-	46	-	-	2.82
1954	Reading	EAST	31	154	12	13	123	60	50	57	87	2.92
1955	Milwaukee	NL	25	25	0	0	39	25	24	14	13	8.64
1956	Wichita	AA	40	103	6	5	120	71	61	50	60	5.33
1957	Montreal	INT	37	93	5	8	88	45	36	35	46	3.48
1958	Macon	SATL	30	126	9	4	104	31	25	46	97	**1.79**
1958	Victoria	TEX	3	2	0	1	-	-	-	4	0	-
1959	Houston	AA	9	-	0	0	-	-	-	-	-	-
1959	Montreal	INT	6	-	0	1	-	-	-	-	-	-
1959	Poza Rica	MEX	21	152	13	3	138	49	43	39	103	**2.55**
1960	Poza Rica	MEX	31	190	13	13	180	82	75	65	79	3.55
1961	Poza Rica	MEX	18	88	6	8	128	62	51	40	39	5.22
47-8	Caguas	PRWL	-	-	-	-	-	-	-	-	-	-
48-9	Caguas	PRWL	-	-	11	7	-	-	-	-	-	-

Year	Club	League	G	IP	W	L	H	R	ER	BB	SO	ERA
49-0	Caguas	PRWL	36	-	-	-	-	-	-	-	-	-
50-1	Caguas	PRWL	-	-	10	1	-	-	-	-	-	-
51-2	Caguas	PRWL	-	-	3	2	-	-	-	-	-	-
52-3	Caguas	PRWL	-	-	-	-	-	-	-	-	-	-
53-4	Caguas	PRWL	-	-	-	-	-	-	-	-	-	-
54-5	Caguas	PRWL	-	149	12	6	-	-	-	-	62	-
55-6	Caguas	PRWL	-	-	-	-	-	-	-	-	-	-
56-7	Caguas	PRWL	-	-	10	6	-	-	-	-	-	-
57-8	Caguas	PRWL	-	-	-	-	-	-	-	-	-	-
58-9	Caguas	PRWL	-	-	-	-	-	-	-	-	-	-
59-0	Caguas	PRWL	-	73	5	2	-	-	23	-	37	2.84

George T. "Little" Walker. Born February 5, 1915 at Waco, TX. Died August 19, 1967 in Waco, TX., 6', 180 lbs. BR TR

Year	Club	League	G	IP	W	L	H	R	ER	BB	SO	ERA
1937	Homestead	NNL	-	-	-	-	-	-	-	-	-	-
1938	Homestead	NNL	-	-	-	-	-	-	-	-	-	-
1939	Kansas City	NAL	-	-	-	-	-	-	-	-	-	-
1940	Kansas City	NAL	-	-	-	-	-	-	-	-	-	-
1941	Kansas City	NAL	-	-	-	-	-	-	-	-	-	-
1942	Kansas City	NAL	-	-	-	-	-	-	-	-	-	-
1943	Kansas City	NAL	-	-	-	-	-	-	-	-	-	-
1945	Kansas City	NAL	-	-	-	-	-	-	-	-	-	-
1950	Kansas City	NAL	18	132	12	3	115	43	29	19	67	**1.98**
1951	Kansas City	NAL	-	-	-	-	-	-	-	-	-	-
1952	Kansas City	NAL	-	-	-	-	-	-	-	-	-	-
1952	Tucson	AZMX	1	.3	0	0	1	1	1	1	0	27.27
1953	Tyler	BGST	41	98	5	1	93	35	28	30	60	2.57

Roy Horace Welmaker. Born December 6, 1913 at Atlanta, GA., 6', 200 lbs. BB TL

Year	Club	League	G	IP	W	L	H	R	ER	BB	SO	ERA
1932	Atlanta	NSL	-	-	-	-	-	-	-	-	-	-
1937	Homestead	NNL	-	-	-	-	-	-	-	-	-	-
1938	Homestead	NNL	-	-	-	-	-	-	-	-	-	-
1939	Philadelphia	NNL	-	-	-	-	-	-	-	-	-	-
1940	Philadelphia	NNL	3	-	0	1	-	-	-	-	-	-
1940	Torreon	MEX	24	142	9	8	150	-	62	66	83	3.92
1941	Torreon	MEX	**40**	225	11	16	269	-	132	111	131	5.27
1942	Homestead	NNL	3	-	2	1	-	-	-	-	-	-
1944	Homestead	NNL	3	27	3	0	30	-	-	9	14	-
1945	Homestead	NNL	**19**	**143**	**12**	4	**129**	-	-	**36**	75	-
1949	Wilkes-Barre	EAST	35	**254**	22	12	229	99	69	118	151	2.44
1950	San Diego	PCL	47	213	16	10	226	117	101	107	143	4.27
1951	San Diego, Hollyw.	PCL	29	87	3	4	95	50	46	47	50	4.76
1952	Hollyw., Portland	PCL	36	116	4	8	114	54	43	41	72	3.34
1953	Portl., Hollywood	PCL	33	90	4	2	105	56	41	32	49	4.10

Ladd White. BL TR

Year	Club	League	G	IP	W	L	H	R	ER	BB	SO	ERA
1948	Indianapolis	NAL	-	-	-	-	-	-	-	-	-	-
1949	Leavenworth	WEAS	19	96	3	9	106	73	55	56	64	5.16
1950	Drummondville	PROV	35	179	9	12	216	137	75	96	78	3.77

Johnny Williams. Born 1916 at Shreveport, LA., 6'2", 208 lbs. BR TR

Year	Club	League	G	IP	W	L	H	R	ER	BB	SO	ERA
1944	Ind.-Cinc.	NAL	15	90	6	4	72	-	20	24	43	2.00
1945	Cinc.-Ind.	NAL	23	95	5	6	96	54	40	18	47	3.79
1946	Indianapolis	NAL	-	-	-	-	-	-	-	-	-	-
1947	Indianapolis	NAL	-	-	-	-	-	-	-	-	-	-
1948	Indianapolis	NAL	15	98	3	7	106	70	55	44	39	5.05
1951	Chicago	NAL	-	-	-	-	-	-	-	-	-	-
1951	Elmira	EAST	31	168	8	10	113	59	48	133	103	2.57
1952	Chicago	NAL	-	-	-	-	-	-	-	-	-	-
1952	Elmira	PONY	7	-	0	1	-	-	-	-	-	-
1952	Hornell	PONY	32	198	13	9	134	83	47	139	215	2.14
1955	Birmingham, Ind.	NAL	-	-	-	-	-	-	-	-	-	-
46-7	Cienfuegos	CWL	1	-	0	1	-	-	-	-	-	-
46-7	Matanzas	CUBA	8	-	2	2	-	-	-	-	-	-
47-8	San Juan	PRWL	-	16	0	2	-	-	11	5	5	6.19

Samuel C. Williams. Born 1923., 6'1", 155 lbs. BL TR

Year	Club	League	G	IP	W	L	H	R	ER	BB	SO	ERA
1941	Birmingham	NAL	1	7	1	0	5	4	-	3	6	-
1947	Birmingham	NAL	-	-	-	-	-	-	-	-	-	-
1948	Birmingham	NAL	12	84	6	3	84	46	30	13	51	3.21
1949	Birmingham	NAL	21	146	8	6	150	64	52	36	60	3.21

Year	Club	League	G	IP	W	L	H	R	ER	BB	SO	ERA
1950	Birmingham	NAL	22	151	13	7	161	82	64	44	60	3.81
1951	Jalisco	MEX	26	134	5	10	134	-	59	62	34	3.97
1952	Birmingham	NAL	-	-	-	-	-	-	-	-	-	-
1952	Licey	DMSL	13	52	1	6	-	-	22	-	-	3.83
1953	Pampa	WTNM	52	281	25	12	338	206	163	124	142	5.22
1954	Oklahoma City	TEX	11	-	0	3	-	-	-	-	-	-
1954	Pampa	WTNM	33	182	15	10	242	134	94	53	84	4.65
1955	Eugene	NWL	25	132	9	7	124	65	50	46	90	3.41
1956	San Jose	CALF	28	203	15	9	189	86	70	52	121	3.10
1957	Aguila	MEX	36	169	8	8	162	98	87	58	83	4.63
1958	Poza Rica	MEX	22	145	9	11	176	94	84	39	57	5.21

Alfred G. "Apples" Wilmore. Born November 15, 1924 at Philadelphia, PA., 6'1", 180 lbs. BR TR

Year	Club	League	G	IP	W	L	H	R	ER	BB	SO	ERA
1947	Philadelphia	NNL	-	-	-	-	-	-	-	-	-	-
1948	Baltimore	NNL	-	-	-	-	-	-	-	-	-	-
1949	Baltimore	NAL	22	122	10	7	109	70	54	66	60	3.98
1950	Baltimore	NAL	13	88	6	4	75	47	41	58	50	4.19
50-1	Cienfuegos	CWL	9	-	1	1	-	-	-	-	-	-

Sam Woods. Born 1922., 6'2", 205 lbs. BR TR

Year	Club	League	G	IP	W	L	H	R	ER	BB	SO	ERA
1946	Cleveland	NAL	-	-	-	-	-	-	-	-	-	-
1948	Memphis	NAL	22	109	4	6	117	62	46	38	53	3.80
1949	Memphis	NAL	26	123	1	8	185	**117**	81	38	52	5.93
1950	Memphis	NAL	24	144	10	6	170	90	65	51	84	4.06
1951	AC	DMSL	11	66	5	5	-	34	22	-	-	3.02
1952	Memphis	NAL	-	-	-	-	-	-	-	-	-	-
1953	Memphis	NAL	24	128	8	9	139	74	54	34	79	3.80
1954	Memphis	NAL	4	15	0	1	14	11	8	9	11	4.80
1955	Pampa	WTNM	33	165	10	11	219	132	108	89	113	5.89
1956	Pampa	SWL	42	199	14	10	251	143	114	59	119	5.16
1957	Plainview	SWL	14	70	4	4	124	77	65	19	57	8.36
1957	Tucson, Las Vegas	AZMX	13	80	3	7	106	63	47	44	61	5.29
1957	Yakima	NWL	5	-	0	1	-	-	-	-	-	-

John Richard Wright Sr.. Born November 28, 1916 at New Orleans, LA. Died May 10, 1990 in Jackson, MS., 5'11", 172 lbs. BR TR

Year	Club	League	G	IP	W	L	H	R	ER	BB	SO	ERA
1937	Newark	NNL	-	-	-	-	-	-	-	-	-	-
1938	Newark	NNL	-	-	-	-	-	-	-	-	-	-
1939	Toledo	NNL	-	-	-	-	-	-	-	-	-	-
1940	Indianapolis	NNL	-	-	-	-	-	-	-	-	-	-
1941	Homestead	NNL	-	-	-	-	-	-	-	-	-	-
1942	Homestead	NNL	10	49	1	2	52	24	-	11	20	-
1943	Homestead	NNL	-	-	-	-	-	-	-	-	-	-
1944	Homestead	NNL	1	7	1	0	7	5	-	-	-	-
1945	Homestead	NNL	3	25	3	0	14	-	-	3	6	-
1946	Montreal	INT	2	-	0	0	-	-	-	-	-	-
1946	Three Rivers	CAAM	32	154	12	8	174	88	71	58	105	4.15
1947	Homestead	NNL	17	102	8	4	95	-	-	-	70	-
1948	Homestead	NNL	-	-	-	-	-	-	-	-	-	-
1948	Pastora	VENZ	-	-	-	-	-	-	-	-	-	-
1949	Gavilanes	VENZ	-	-	-	-	-	-	-	-	-	-
1950	San Luis, VeraCruz	MEX	36	241	13	14	195	-	75	132	147	2.80
1951	Torreon,N.L.	MEX	37	211	14	14	171	-	81	144	111	3.46
1952	Escogido	DMSL	20	144	10	5	-	-	33	-	-	2.07
1953	Escogido	DMSL	13	82	4	9	-	-	15	-	-	1.64
1954	Cibaenas	DMSL	10	40	0	7	-	-	22	-	-	4.95
1954	Indianapolis	NAL	5	40	3	1	34	16	15	9	29	3.38

John Thomas Wyatt. Born April 19, 1935 at Chicago, IL., 5'11 1/2", 200 lbs. BR TR

Year	Club	League	G	IP	W	L	H	R	ER	BB	SO	ERA
1953	Indianapolis	NAL	-	-	-	-	-	-	-	-	-	-
1954	Hannibal	MOV	31	156	12	11	160	102	88	62	107	5.08
1955	Indianapolis	NAL	-	-	-	-	-	-	-	-	-	-
1956	El Paso	SWL	17	63	4	3	58	32	29	34	58	4.14
1956	Jacksonville	SATL	2	6	0	0	6	5	5	4	1	7.50
1956	Pocatello	PION	11	58	2	8	85	73	57	47	43	8.84
1959	Albany	EAST	19	47	1	6	58	33	29	24	44	5.55
1959	Sioux City	III	26	74	4	4	66	34	28	36	89	3.41
1960	Dallas-Ft. Worth	AA	10	38	1	2	39	26	22	25	29	5.21
1960	Monterrey	MEX	14	79	4	6	79	50	40	49	55	4.56
1960	Sioux City	III	4	32	2	2	28	14	13	21	31	3.66

Year	Club	League	G	IP	W	L	H	R	ER	BB	SO	ERA
1961	Kansas City	AL	5	7	0	0	8	3	2	4	6	2.46
1961	Portsmouth	SATL	52	101	9	3	87	45	35	49	91	3.12
1962	Kansas City	AL	59	125	10	7	121	66	62	80	106	4.46
1963	Kansas City	AL	63	92	6	4	83	37	32	43	81	3.13
1964	Kansas City	AL	**81**	128	9	8	111	53	51	52	74	3.59
1965	Kansas City	AL	65	89	2	6	78	36	32	53	70	3.25
1966	KC, Boston	AL	61	95	3	7	78	41	39	43	88	3.68
1967	Boston	AL	60	93	10	7	71	30	27	39	68	2.60
1968	Boston, NY, Detroit	AL	37	49	2	4	42	19	15	26	42	2.74
1969	Oakland	AL	4	8	0	1	8	5	5	6	5	5.40

Quincy Trouppe and Sam "The Jet" Jethroe.
Quincy Trouppe

Londell Jamerson and Elston Howard.
Jamerson Family

Bob Thurman.
Robert Thurman

Bibliography

This is the most comprehensive and complete bibliographical listing of Negro Leagues material ever made available. We have attempted to include every book, magazine, newspaper and publication which has Negro Leagues-related material. Because of the tremendous amount of material written on players like Jackie Robinson and Roy Campanella, only selected publications relating to their Negro Leagues careers are included. We have not indexed newpaper stories from the African-American press. We feel the researcher would do better to read the entire paper for an appreciation of the period and the impact of segregation.

We realize that because of the enormous resurgence in popularity of the Negro Leagues that this section will be incomplete as it goes to print. Future editions will be updated.

1941 Season
Bolton, Todd. "Before the Game Was Color Blind." *The National Pastime* #11, 6-1-1992, 65-66.
19th Century BB
Kleinknecht, Merl. "Blacks in 19th Century Organized Baseball." *Baseball Research Journal* #6, 1-1-1977, 118-127.
Malloy, Jerry. "Out At Home." *The National Pastime*, 1-1-1983, 14-28.
Marable, William Manning. "Black Athletes in White Men's Games. "1880-1920." *Maryland Historian*, Fall, 1-1-1973, 143-149.
Murphy, Miriam B. "Black Baseball Heroes of '09." *Beehive History* #7, 1-1-1981, 25-27.
Pietrusza, Dave. "Robinson's Breakthrough Not First." *USA Today Baseball Weekly*, 2-10-1993, 28.
Reiss, Steven A. "Professional Sunday Baseball: A Study in Reform, 1892-1934." *Maryland Historian*, Fall, 9-1-1973, 95-108.
Savoie, Mark. "Drawing the Line: The Trails of African-American Baseball Players in the International League." *Nine: Journal of Baseball History*, Spring, 3-1-1992, 42-60.
Zuckerman, Stull & Eyler. "Black Athlete in Post Bellum 19th Century." *Physical Educator* #29, 10-1-1972, 142-146.
Aaron, Hank
Wheeler, Lonnie & Aaron, Hank. *I Had A Hammer: The Hank Aaron Story*. Harper Collins, 3-1-1991, 333 pages.
Algona Brownies
Kemp, David & Wildin, Roger. "The Algona Brownies, Champs of the West." *Baseball Research Journal* #17, 1-1-1988, 76-79.

All-Star Games

Clark, James C. "All-Star Players Made Two Dollars A Game." *Orlando Sentinel*, 2-23-1990.

Gelman, Steve. "You Could Almost Have a Negro All-Star Game." *Sport*, 2-1-1960, 48-49.

Kleinknecht, Merl. "East Meets West in Negro Games." *Baseball Research Journal #1*, 1-1-1972, 78-79.

Levy, Scott J. "The Birth of Baseball's (Other) All-Star Game at Comiskey Park, part 2." *Chicago Tribune*, 1-1-1991, 30.

All-Star Team

Kerkhoff, Blair. "Players and Writers Vote for Negro League All-Timers." *Kansas City Star*, 5-23-1993, C5.

Allen, Newt

Dixon, Phil. "Newt Allen, Great Star of the Monarchs Dies in Cincinnati." *Kansas City Call*, 6-17-1988, 12.

Kleinknecht, Merl. "Newt Allen." *Biographical Dictionary of American Sports: Baseball,* D. Porter, Greenwood Press. 1-1-1987, 6,7.

Lester, Larry. "Newt Allen." *The Ballplayers, Arbor House, William Morrow.* Arbor House, William Morrow. 1-1-1990, 13.

Alston, Tom

Kelley, Brent. "Tom Alston: The First Black Redbird." *Sports Collectors Digest*, 10-30-1992, 159,161.

Anderson, Andy

Baker, Andrew. "Andrew Anderson, Catcher for Satchel Paige, Dies." *Syracuse Post-Standard*, 7-26-1989.

Baker, Andrew. "Musician Andrew Anderson Played Pro Baseball 20 Years." *Syracuse Post-Standard*, 7-24-1989.

Anson, Cap

"Cap Anson." *Old Tyme Baseball News*, 7-1-1988, 3.

Argos Giants

Kovach, John. "It Was A Year The Giants Came to Argos." *Southbend Tribune*, 8-13-1989.

Articles of Incorporatio

Burnes, Brian. "Charter of Negro League to be Shown at Ceremony." *Kansas City Star*, 6-5-1993, C2.

Ashford, Emmett

McGuff, Joe. "Emmett Ashford." *Baseball Digest*, 7-1-1980, 64-65.

Rosenbaum, A. "Colored Ump with Color." *Baseball Digest*, 12-1-1965, 57-59.

Ashland Museum

"Kentucky Musuem Recalls Black Baseball Mountain Life." *Southern Living*, 16.

Ashland Reunion

Anderson, Bruce. "Time Worth Remembering." *Sports Illustrated*, 7-6-1981, 46.

Atlanta Black Crackers

Joyce, Allan Emory. "The Atlanta Black Crackers." Emory University, 1-1-1975, thesis

Joyce, Kuhn & West. "The Atlanta Black Crackers" (cassettes). *WRGF Living Atlanta Project*, 1-1-1978.

Jubera, Drew. "In A League of their Own." *Atlanta Journal & Constitution*, 2-2-1990, C1, C4.

Rogers, Prentis. "Black Crackers Didn't Have the Park But Had the People." *Atlanta Daily World*, 7-2-1978, 7.

Schwartz, Michael. "Honoring the Pioneers of the Negro Leagues." *Atlanta Constitution*, 8-11-1991, F1, F8.

Awkard, Russell

Buckley, Taylor. "The Name is Awkard, with one W." *USA Today*, 7-15-1993, 2C

Bacharach Giants

Reynolds, Frankie. "The Bacharach Giants." *Colored Baseball & Sports Monthly*, 10-1-1934, 12.

Baker, Gene

"Most Important Negro in Baseball." Ebony, 5-1-1956, 100-104.

Ballparks

Benson, Michael. *Ballparks of North America*. McFarland & Co., 1-1-1989.

Lowry, Philip J. *Green Cathedrals*. SABR, 1-1-1986, 91-121.

Lowry, Philip J. *Green Cathedrals II*. Meckler, 1-1-1992.

Baltimore Black Sox

Bready, James H. *The Home Team: Baltimore Baseball*. Private Publication, 1-1-1984, 108-9.

Holway, J. & Holloway, Crush. "Baseball with Baltimore's Black Sox." *Baltimore Sun Magazine*, 7-11-1971.

Holway, John. "Baltimore's Great Black Ball Team." *Baltimore Sun Magazine*, 8-28-1977.

Windhauser, John. "Baltimore Black Sox and the Baltimore Elite Giants." *Sports Encyclopedia of North America*, Vol 3, 1-1-1990.

Baltimore Elite Giants

Brelsford, Karen. "Negro League: Blackball before Jackie." *Columbus Flier*, 10-10-1985, 97-100.

Glauber, Bill. "Elite Giants: Great Players, Even Greater Personalities." *Baltimore Sun*, 4-30-1990, C1, C6.

Glauber, Bill. "Elite Giants: The Pride of Baltimore Baseball History." *Baltimore Sun*, 4-29-1990, C1, C12.

Glauber, Bill. "Search for Giants A Real Treasure Hunt." *Baltimore Sun*, 4-29-1990, C13.

Leffler, Robert V. "Boom & Bust: The Elite Giants and Black Baseball in Baltimore, 1936-1951." *Maryland Historical Magazine*, Summer, 6-1-1992, 171-86.

Riley, James A. "Baltimore Baseball Nobody Knows." *1993 All-Star Game Program*, 7-13-1993, 94-95,97,99,101,103,105.

Baltimore Teams

Leffler, Robert V. "The History of Black Baseball in Baltimore from 1913 to 1951." Morgan State College, 1-1-1974, thesis, 132 pages.

Bankhead, Dan

Maher, Edward G. "Dan Bankhead." *The Ballplayers, Arbor House, William Morrow.* 1-1-1990, 45.

Bankhead, Sam

"Bankhead, Doby, Campy, Robinson." *Our World*, 4-1-1948, 46.

Plott, Bill. "Sam Bankhead." *The Ballplayers, Arbor House, William Morrow.* 1-1-1990, 45.

Banks, Ernie

Simms, Gregory. "Ernie Banks Recalls His Days in the Old Negro Leagues." *Jet*, 2-10-1977, 54-55.

Barnhill, Dave

Holway, John. "Blackballed, Dave Barnhill." *Miami Herald Topic Magazine*, 1-1-1982, 17-19.

Riley, James A. "David Barnhill." *Baseball Research Journal #10*, 1-1-1981, 56-59.

Barnstorming

Kaplan, Jim. "Bittersweet Barnstorming." *Sports Illustrated*, 2-16-1981, 45+

Beckwith, John

Brennan, Gerald E. "John Beckwitch." *Biographical Dictionary of American Sports: Baseball*, D. Porter, Greenwood Press. 1-1-1987, 29,30.

Holway, John. "The Black Bomber Named Beckwith." *Baseball Research Journal #5*, 1-1-1976, 100-103.

Bell, Cool Papa

"Cool Papa Bell Living Reminder of Country's Past." *Richmond Times Dispatch*, 2-11-1990.

"Daguerreotypes." *The Sporting News*, 1-1-1990, 23-24.

"Speedy Bell Latest to Join Hall from old Negro Leagues." *Jet*, 2-28-1974, 52.

"Struggles of Black Players told by 'Cool Papa' Bell." *Jet*, 8-29-1974, 53.

"Whatever Happened to Cool Papa Bell?" Ebony, 3-1-1974, 162.

Bankes, James. "Baseball's Cool Papa Bell." *Sports History*, 3-1-1990, 38-43.

Bankes, James. "Flying Feet: The Life & Times of Cool Papa Bell, The Fastest Runner BB Has." *Baseball History*, Fall, 1-1-1986, 39-58.

Banks, James. "How Fast was Cool Papa Bell?." *The National Pastime*, 1-1-1982, 10-12.

Banks, Jim & Zeech, Mary. "Travlin' Man." *St. Louis American*, 8-1-1982, 54-57.

Borst, William. "James Cool Papa Bell." *The Ballplayers, Arbor House, William Morrow*. 1-1-1990, 63,64.

Broeg, Bob. "Cool Papa Gives A Helping Hand." *Baseball Research Journal #20*, 10-1-1991, 38.

Broeg, Bob. "Interview with Cool Papa Bell." *The Sporting News*, 5-26-1973.

Bryan, Bill. "Con Men Take Mementos From 'Cool Papa' Bell." *St. Louis Post-Dispatch*, 4-6-1990, 1,14.

Butch, John. "And the Best of Them All Was Cool Papa." *Clarion-Ledger (MS)*, 7-8-1990, 5D

Callahan, Tom. "So Fast Only Time Could Catch Him." *Washington Post*, 3-10-1991, C3.

Coates, John M. "Cool Papa Bell, the Black Ty Cobb." *Baseball Digest*, 12-1-1973, 53-56.

Coates, John M. "Historically Speaking: James Bell." *Black Sports*, 10-1-1973, 10-11.

Dixon, Phil. "Cool Papa Bell: A Legend in His Own Time." *St. Louis American*, 3-31-1991.

Drees, Jack & Mullen, Jim C. *Where Is He Now?*. Jonathan David Publications, 1-1-1973, 18-21.

Fiffer, Steve. "Don't Look Back." *The World of Baseball: Speed, Redefinition Books*, 1-1-1990, 108-111.

Fink, David. "Cool Papa: He Rings a Bell for Nostalgia." *Pittsburgh Post Gazette*, 1-26-1976, 10.

Green, Paul. "Baseball and James Bell." *Sports Collectors Digest*, 4-29-1983, 24.

Heaphy, Leslie. "James Thomas "Cool Papa" Bell." *Sports Encyclopedia of North America*, vol 5, 1-1-1993, 220-22.

Holway, John. "How to Score from First on a Sacrifice." *American Heritage*, 8-1-1970, 30-36.

Honig, Donald. *Baseball When the Grass Was Real*. Coward, McCann and Geohegan, 1-1-1975, 165-177.

Johnson, Lloyd. "Baseball's Dream Teams." *Gallery Books*, 1-1-1990, 61,77,79,81.

Kindred, David. "He Was Fast, Crafty and Humble, but, above all, Papa was Cool." *National Sports Daily*, 3-15-1991, 2.

Kram, Mark. "No Place in the Shade: Cool Papa Bell of the Old Negro Leagues." *Sports Illustrated*, 8-20-1973, 68-73, 77-78.

Lawes, Rick. "Before Brock, Before Rickey, a legendary Bell." *USA Today Baseball Weekly*, 4-5-1991, 5.

Levy, Scott J. "Tricky Ball: Cool Papa Bell & Life in the Negro Leagues." *Gateway Heritage*, Spring, 1-1-1989, 26-35.

Martin, Douglas D. "James Bell." *Biographical Dictionary of American Sports: Baseball*, D. Porter, Greenwood Press. 1-1-1987, 31,32.

McCarron, John. "Legendary Baseball Player Finally Can Feel Safe at Home." *Chicago Tribune*, 3-7-1990.

Mendelson, Abby. "They Called Him 'Cool'." *Baseball Magazine*, 6-1-1980, 25-27.

Pearson, Richard. "James 'Cool Papa' Bell, Baseball Legend, Dies." *Washington Post*, 3-9-1991, B4.

Pierce, Charles. "Thieves of Time." *National Sports Daily*, 5-10-1990, 30-33.

Bell, Julian

Byrd, Ben. "Byrd's Eye View." *Knoxville Journal*, 2-11-1987.

Bell, Mackey & Paige

Holway, John. "Cool Papa, Biz and Satch." *LA Weekly*, 5-15-1992, 41-42.

Benson, Gene

"Gene Benson: Baseball Pioneer." *Old Tyme Baseball News*, Spring, 4-1-1990, 6-7.

Holway, John. "Black Star of Philadelphia: Gene Benson." *Black Diamonds, Meckler Books*. 1-1-1989, 70-88.

Holway, John. "What I Taught Bob Feller About Pitching." *Philadelphia Inquirer Magazine*, 1-1-1981, 26-30.

Kelley, William G. "Flashback: Gene Benson." *Phillie Sport*, 6-1-1990, 64, 59-60.

Kleinknecht, Merl. "Gene Benson." *The Ballplayers, Arbor House, William Morrow*. 1-1-1990, 69.

Beverly, Charlie

Farmer, Neal. "'Fireball' Beverly Mulls Lost Chance." *Houston Chronicle*, 7-1-1992, 1C, 8C.

Biot, Charles

Forman, Ross. "Great Outfielder in the Negro Leagues." *Sports Collectors Digest*, 6-26-1992, 90.

Birmingham Black Barons

Cary, Tim. "Slidin' & Ridin': At home and on the Road with the 1948 Birmingham Black Barons." *Alabama Heritage*, Fall, 1-1-1986, 20-49.

Black, Joe

Black, Joe. *Ain't Nobody Better Than You: An Autobiography of Joe Black*. Ironwood Lithographers, 1-1-1983, 255 pages.

Forman, Ross. "Joe Black's Philosophy - 'Live and Learn'." *Sports Collectors Digest*, 4-9-1993, 130-131.

Lewis, Allen. "Joe Black Had No Regrets." *Baseball Digest*, 3-1-1964, 65-67.

Blair, Garnett
Smith, Shelley. "Remembering Their Game." *Sports Illustrated*, 7-6-1992, 83.
Bolden, Ed
Wilson, Rollo W. "Ed Bolden's Hilldale Club Was Tops." *Pittsburgh Courier Magazine*, 4-14-1951, 11.
Bostock Sr., Lyman
Forman, Ross. "Ex-Negro Leaguer Now Makes Bats For a Living." *Sports Collectors Digest*, 10-16-1992, 124.
Young, A.S. "Doc". "Baseball's Unspoiled Millionaire." *Sepia*, 5-1-1978, 68-70.
Boyd, Bob
Kelley, Brent. "SCD Visits with Bob 'The Rope' Boyd." *Sports Collectors Digest*, 6-21-1991, 200,201.
Boyd, Willie James
Long, Shepard C. "Dennis Oil Can Boyd." *The Ballplayers, Arbor House, William Morrow.* 1-1-1990, 102.
Brewer, Chet
Ellenbecker, Phil. "Brewer: Cooperstown Bound?." *Leavenworth Times*, 8-30-1987, 8A
Etkin, Jack. "Chet Brewer." *Innings Ago, Normandy Square Publications,* 1-1-1987, 46-51.
Holway, John. "Chet Brewer: Just as Good as Satchel?." *The Sporting News*, 11-28-1983, 56.
Holway, John. "Papa Chet: Chet Brewer." *Black Diamonds, Meckler Books.* 1-1-1989, 18-38.
Holway, John. "Papa Chet: Monarch of Los Angeles: An Interview with Chet Brewer." *Baseball History*, Spring, 1-1-1986, 52-69.
Lester, Larry. "Chet Brewer." *The Ballplayers, Arbor House, William Morrow.* 1-1-1990, 112.
Maly, Ron & Holway, John. "Baseball's Great Brewer Joins Register Hall." *Des Moines Sun Register*, 4-1-1984.
Rae, Lorne W. "It Was a Real Baseball." *Saskatchewan History*, 1-1-1991, 16-20.
Bridges, Marshall
Butch, John. "Bridges Was Among the Fortunate Ones." *Clarion-Ledger (MS)*, 7-8-1990, 4D
Brooklyn Dodgers
"Baseball's Most Colorful Team." *Ebony* #15, 7-1-1960, 103-7.
"Safe At First." *Our Sports*, 1-1-1946, 10.
Hepburn, Dave. "The Jackpot Boys." *Our World*, 9-1-1948, 30-33.
Hepburn, Dave. "What Now, You Bums?." *Our World*, 5-1-1947, 28-30.
Brooklyn Royal Giants
"Royal Giants Play Games Friday." *Japan Times*, 3-31-1927.
Brown, Larry
Grabar, Phil. "Larry Brown." *The Ballplayers, Arbor House, William Morrow.* 1-1-1990, 124.
Brown, W. & Beverly, B.
Olafson, Steve. "Field of Broken Dreams." *Houston Post Staff*, 8-24-1991, A1,A19.
Brown, Willard
Cottrol, Bob. "Historically Speaking: Willard Brown." *Black Sports*, 3-1-1975, 50,51.
Cottrol, Bob. "Willard Brown, He lasted only Six Weeks, but He was Among the first Blacks in the majors." *Black Sports* #4, 3-1-1975, 50-51.

Etkin, Jack. "Willard Brown." *Innings Ago, Normandy Square Publications,* 1-1-1987, 100-105.
Floto, James. "Willard Brown." *Diamond Angle*, V4, #2, 2-1-1993, 29-30.
Holway, John. "Ese Hombre: Willard "Home Run" Brown." *Black Diamonds, Meckler Books.* 1-1-1989, 107-118.
Kleinknecht, Merl. "Willard Brown." *Biographical Dictionary of American Sports: Baseball ,* D. Porter, Greenwood Press. 1-1-1987, 55,56.
Lester, Larry. "Willard Brown." *The Ballplayers, Arbor House, William Morrow.* 1-1-1990, 126.
Bruce, Clarence
"Clarence Bruce, was Homestead Grays Player." *Pittsburgh Post Gazette*, 1-23-1990, 10.
Bruton, Billy
O'Connell, T.S. "Age Never Slowed This Speedster Down." *Sports Collectors Digest*, 6-21-1991, 184-185.
Bryant, Allen "Lefty"
Etkin, Jack. "Lefty Bryant." *Innings Ago, Normandy Square Publications,* 1-1-1987, 130-137.
Tolmon, Rosetta. "Allen "Sports" Bryant Remembers the Monarchs." *Kansas City Call*, 6-15-1984, 36.
Buckner, George
Phelps, Howard. "George Buckner." *The Half Century*, 4-1-1919, 8.
Burbage, Buddy
"K.O. ""Buddy" Burbage, Former Negro League Star dead at 84." *Jet*, 9-25-1989.
St. George, Donna. "Burbage Was a Ballplayer." *Philadelphia Inquirer*, 9-2-1989, D9.
Burt, Thomas
Knepler, Mike. "He Rubbed Shoulders With the Greats of the Game." *Virginian Pilot*, 8-19-1991, C1, C3.
Bushwicks
Eisen, Robert. "Dexter Park and the Bushwicks, Part 1." *Times Weekly (LI)*, 9-19-1991.
Eisen, Robert. "Dexter Park and the Bushwicks, Part 2." *Times Weekly (LI)*, 9-26-1991.
Byrd, Bill
Green, Paul. "Bill Byrd." *Forgotten Fields*, Parker Publications. 1-1-1984, 156-162.
Holway, John. "The Original Baltimore Byrd." *Baseball Research Journal* #19, 9-1-1991, 23-27.
Plott, Bill. "Bill Byrd." *The Ballplayers, Arbor House, William Morrow.* 1-1-1990, 143-44.
Riley, James A. "Bill Byrd: Baseball's Black Spitballer." *Old Tyme Baseball News*, Fall, 9-1-1989, 14.
Campanella, Roy
"Baseball's Best Catcher." *Ebony*, 6-1-1950, 50-54.
"Big Man from Nicetown." *Time*, 8-8-1955, 50-55.
"Biography of Roy Campanella." *Current Biography*, NY: H.W. Wilson Co. 1-1-1953, 105-108.
"Everybody's Hero." *Ebony*, 8-1-1959, 25-32.
Roy Campanella—Baseball Hero. Fawcett Publication, 1-1-1950, Comic Book
"The Man Roy Campanella." *Black Sports* #1, 11-1-1972, 24-25.
"Whatever Happened to Roy Campanella?" *Ebony*, 4-1-1972, 154.

Blauvelt, Harry. "Dodgers' Catching Great As Courageous As They Came." *USA Today*, 6-28-1993, 3C

Campanella, Roy. *It's Good to Be Alive*. Little, Brown, 1-1-1959, 306 pages.

Fimrite, Ron. "Triumph of the Spirit." *Sports Illustrated*, 9-24-1990, 95-105.

Green, Paul. "Interview with Roy Campanella." *Sports Collectors Digest*, 8-5-1983, 96-110.

Greenfield, Steve. "Roy Campanella." *The Ballplayers, Arbor House, William Morrow*. 1-1-1990, 149-50.

Haag, Ken. "Campy: A Great Player, A Great Human Being." *Sports Collectors Digest*, 7-23-1993, 60-61.

Harris, Scott. "Thanks, Campy—A Most Valuable Player." *Times Valley Edition (Chatsworth, CA)*, 6-27-1993, B1,B7.

Holmes, Tommy. "Doin What Comes Naturally." *Sport Life*, 6-1-1952, 15-17.

Honig, Donald. "Roy Campanella." *The Greatest Catchers of All-Time*, Crown Publishers, 1-1-1991, 63-68.

May, Julian. *Brave Man of Baseball*. Crestwood House, Mankato, MN, 1-1-1974.

Meany, Thomas. "King of the Catchers." *Negro Digest*, 10-1-1950, 13.

Murray, Tom, Editors. *Sport Magazine's All-Time All-Stars*. New American Library, 1-1-1977, 316-22.

Pearson, Richard. "Famed Dodgers Catcher Roy Campanella Dies." *Washington Post*, 6-28-1993, D8.

Shapiro, Milton J. *The Roy Campanella Story*. Julian Messner, 1-1-1958, Book, 193 pages.

Solomon, Alan. "Truly A Hall of Famer." *Chicago Tribune*, 6-28-1993, 3.

Weir, Tom. "Campy's Leadership Crushed Myths." *USA Today*, 6-28-1993, 3C

Young, A.S. "Doc". "Campanella." *Ebony*, 4-1-1955, 91-97.

Campy, Newk, Robinson

"Brooklyn's 3 Brown Bums." *Our World*, 9-1-1946, 51-53.

Canadian Baseball

Clifton, Merritt. "Disorganized Baseball, the Provincial League from LaRoque to Les Expos." *Samisdat*, 1-1-1982.

Carr, George

Kavanagh, Jack. "George Carr." *The Ballplayers, Arbor House, William Morrow.* 1-1-1990, 160.

Carter, Marlin

Mills, Prentice. "Marlin Carter: Texas Gold." *Black Ball News*, V1, #4, 12-1-1992, 2-11.

Chandler, Happy

Green, Paul. "Interview with Happy Chandler." *Sports Collectors Digest*, 11-25-1983, 29,50.

Holway, John. "A Vote for Chandler: An Ignored Pioneer." *New York Times*, 3-1-1981.

Holway, John. "Happy Chandler on the Road to the Hall of Fame." *New York Times*, 3-14-1982.

Marx, Jeffrey. "Happy's Vote of Confidence." *Sports Heritage*, May-Jun, 5-1-1987, 21-25.

Charleston, Oscar

"Committee Names O. "Charleston to Shrine." *The Sporting News*, 2-21-1976, 45.

"Daguerreotypes." *The Sporting News*, 1-1-1990, 53-54.

"Tales of Negro League Revived as Charleston Gets Hall of Fame Nod." *Jet*, 9-9-1976, 49.

Brennan, Gerald E. "Oscar Charleston." *Biographical Dictionary of American Sports: Baseball*, D. Porter, Greenwood Press. 1-1-1987, 87,89.

Clark, D. & Holway, J. "Charleston No. "1 Star of 1921 Negro League." *Baseball Research Journal #14*, 1-1-1985, 63-70.

Holway, John. "Historically Speaking . . . Oscar Charleston." *Black Sports*, 3-1-1976, 18-20, 50-51, 56, 59.

Holway, John. "Oscar Charleston." *Black Sports #7*, 7-1-1977, 50-53.

Holway, John. "Oscar Charleston: Was Cobb "The White Charleston?" *Blackball Stars: Negro League Pioneers*, Meckler Books. 1-1-1988, 96-124.

Kleinknecht, Merl. "Oscar Charleston." *The Ballplayers, Arbor House, William Morrow. Arbor House, William Morrow.* 1-1-1990, 179-80.

Malarcher, Dave. "Oscar Charleston." *Baseball Research Journal #7*, 1-1-1978, 68.

Malarcher, Dave. "Poem." *Baseball Research Journal #7*, 1-1-1978, 68.

Chicago American Giants

Levy, Scott J. "Chicago's Forgotten Giants of Negro League Baseball." *Chicago Cubs Magazine Scoreboard*, V9, #3, 1-1-1990, 34-35, 39-42.

Chicago Giants

Leland, Frank. *Frank Leland's Chicago Giants Base Ball Club*. Fraternal Printing Co., 1-1-1911, book, 13 pages.

Cincinnati Teams

Erardi, John. "Baseball '93: The Negro Leagues & Cincinnati." *Cincinnati Enquirer*, 4-5-1993, C17-C23.

Wheeler, Lonnie & Baskin, John. "In the Shadows: Cincinnati's Black Baseball Players." *Queen City Heritage*, Summer, 1-1-1988, 13-19.

Wheeler, Lonnie & Baskin, John. *The Cincinnati Game*. Orange Frazer Press, Wilmington, OH, 1-1-1988.

Claxton, Jimmy

Weiss, William J. "The First Negro in 20th Century Organized Baseball." *Baseball Research Journal #8*, 1-1-1979, 31-34.

Cleage, Pete

Byrd, Ben. "Pete Cleage Recalls Days of the Knoxville Giants." *Knoxville Journal*, 6-28-1977, 10.

West, Marvin. "Early Blacks Could Have Made It: Cleage Relives the Old Days." *Knoxville News Sentinel*, 7-13-1975, D4.

Cleveland Buckeyes

Cheeks, Dwayne. "The Cleveland Buckeyes Remembered: Played Second Fiddle to Tribe Until Demise." *Cleveland Plain Dealer*, 1-18-1982, 8d

Jedick, Peter. "League Park." *SABR*, 1-1-1990, 20-22.

Kleinknecht, Merl. "Cleveland in the Black Major Leagues." *Baseball Research Journal*, 1-1-1990, 16-17.

Kleinknecht, Merl. "Erie Has Unique Association With Old Negro Baseball Loop." *Erie Weekender*, 10-16-1982.

Lammers, Bill. "Champions of A Forgotten League." *Cleveland Plain Dealer Magazine*, 6-14-1992, 10-11,14-15.

Cockrell, Phil

Plott, Bill. "Phil Cockrell." *The Ballplayers, Arbor House, William Morrow.* 1-1-1990, 205.

Cohen, Jim

Steadman, John. "Clowns Could Put On Show, But Talent Wasn't A Baseball Joke, Cohen Recalls." *The Evening Sun,* Washington DC. 3-31-1993, D1.

Coimbre, Pancho

Alvelo, Luis. "Rememberanza del Pundonorso." *Puerto Rico Illustrado,* 11-4-1990, 8-9.

Collectibles

"Negro Leaguers Cite Exploitation." *USA Today,* 8-13-1991, 2C

Craft, David. "Former Negro Leaguers Gather at Chicago Card Show." *Sports Collectors Digest,* 3-29-1991, 52.

Forman, Ross. "Negro League Stars Collect New Fans." *USA Today Baseball Weekly,* 6-28-1991, 45.

Forman, Ross. "New Cards to Make Debut at Negro League Forum." *USA Today Baseball Weekly,* 10-25-1991.

Hoekstra, Dave. "Linking Once and Future Fans with Series of Baseball Cards." *Chicago Sun-Times,* 3-29-1992, E5.

McAllister, Karen. "Back to the Future: Armed with History and Color, The Negro Leagues Take the Field." *Team Leader,* 7-19-1993, 11.

Obojoski, Robert. "Negro League Poster Sells for $2,650." *Sports Collectors Digest,* 7-16-1988, 39-40.

Rawlins, Elvin. "Collectibles from the Negro Leagues." *Sports Collectors Digest,* 10-29-1982, 60-66.

Crowe, George

"The Majors May Meet Crowe." *Sport Life,* 6-1-1952, 48-49+

Crutchfield, Jimmie

Forman, Ross. "Jimmie Crutchfield, Walking, Talking Baseball History." *Sports Collectors Digest,* 9-4-1992, 144-46.

Hewitt, Brian. "Blacks' Beautiful Baseball." *Chicago Sun-Times,* 6-21-1991, 92.

Hoekstra, Dave. "Two 'Giants' Remember Days of Black Baseball." *Chicago Sun-Times,* 1-30-1992, 1,40.

Miller, John. "Jimmie Crutchfield." *The Ballplayers, Arbor House, William Morrow.* 1-1-1990, 239.

Shulruff, Lawrence. "People." *Modern Maturity—AARP,* 4-1-1992, 12.

Smith, Shelley. "Remembering Their Game." *Sports Illustrated,* 7-6-1992, 80-81.

Sutton, William A. "Jimmie Crutchfield." *Biographical Dictionary of American Sports: Baseball,* D. Porter, Greenwood Press. 1-1-1987, 127.

Cuban Baseball

Bjarkman, Peter C. "Cuban Blacks in the Majors Before Jackie Robinson." *The National Pastime* #12, 7-1-1992, 58-63.

Figueredo, Jorge S. "Winter in Cuba." *The National Pastime* #11, 6-1-1992, 59-60.

Holway, John. "Cuba's Baseball Greats Stifled by Politics." *USA Today Baseball Weekly,* 7-22-1992, 44.

Jeansonne, John. "Beisbol, Cuba: A Land of Rought-Cut Diamonds." *New York Newsday,* 8-11-1991, 12,16.

Onigman, Mark. "Historically Speaking: Beisbol Cubanos." *Black Sports,* 4-1-1978, 40-43.

Torres, Angel. *La Historia del Beisbol Cubano, 1878-1976.* Los Angeles, CA, 1-1-1976, 191 pages.

Cuban Giants

Johnson, James Weldon. *Black Manhattan.* 1-1-1930, 62-65.

Old Timer's Diary. "Colored Baseball Origin and Scope." *Colored Baseball & Sports Monthly,* 10-1-1934, 16.

Vincent, Ted. *Mudville's Revenge, The Rise and Fall of American Sport.* Seaview Books, 8-1-1981, 115-116, 184.

Cuban Stars

"Cuban Stars Baseball Team." *The Half Century,* 10-1-1919, 8.

Cuban X Giants

Malloy, Jerry. "The Cubans' Last Stand." *The National Pastime* #11, 6-1-1992, 11-12.

Cumberland Cubs

Mastrangelo, Mike. "John Brown's 1921 Cumberland Cubs Remembered." *Cumberland Sunday Times News,* 11-19-1989, B4-5.

Dandridge, Ray

"Batter Up In Mexico." *Our World,* 8-1-1947, 25-29.

"Daguerreotypes." *The Sporting News,* 1-1-1990, 71-72.

"Newark's Unsung Baseball Hero: Ray Dandridge." *Metro Newark,* 1-2-1985, 28-29.

Appel, Alfred & Goldblatt, Andrew. *Yesterday's Heroes.* William Morrow & Company, 1-1-1988, 100-3.

Crepeau, Richard. "Baseball Immortality . ". "Ray Dandridge." *Baseball History,* Winter, 1-1-1987, 63-64.

Davidoff, T. "Nicholas. "Big Call from the Hall." *Sports Illustrated,* 7-6-1987, 100-3.

Durso, Joe. "Hall of Fame Doors Open for Dandridge." *New York Times,* 3-4-1987.

Forman, Ross. "Ray Dandridge Active on Card Show Circuit." *Sports Collectors Digest,* 10-2-1992, 197.

Green, Paul. "There's No One Better at Third." *Sports Collectors Digest,* 9-2-1983, 54-55, 58,60,62,64,70.

Hogan, Lawrence D. "The Invisible Men of History." *New York Times,* 10-7-1984.

Holway, John. "Dandy at Third: Ray Dandridge." *The National Pastime,* 1-1-1982, 7-11.

Holway, John. "Historically Speaking: Ray Dandridge." *Black Sports,* 9-1-1977, 52-55.

Holway, John. "Ray Dandridge: Dandy at Third." *Blackball Stars: Negro League Pioneers,* 1-1-1988, 353-374.

Leusner, Donna. "Essex Freeholders Bestow Honor on Veteran Black Baseball Player." *Newark Star-Ledger,* 7-25-1985, 38.

May, Roy. "Hall of Fame Taps ex-Buffalonian." *Buffalo News,* 3-4-1987, D1-D3.

Perry, Claudia. "Ray Dandridge: Church Hill Lots to Hall of Fame." *Richmond Times-Dispatch,* 7-26-1987, D1,D4.

Riley, James A. *Dandy, Day & the Devil: A Trilogy of Negro League Biographies.* TK Publishers, 1-1-1987, book, 153 pages.

Riley, James A. "Ray Dandridge." *The Ballplayers, Arbor House, William Morrow.* 1-1-1990, 249-50.

Ruck, Rob. "Ray Dandridge." *Biographical Dictionary of American Sports: Baseball,* D. Porter, Greenwood Press. 1-1-1987, 132-3.

Smith, Deborah. "New Hall of Famer, Ray Dandridge Saluted." *New Jersey Afro-American,* 8-8-1987, 6.

Strother, Shelby. "Hall of Fame Wasn't Dandridge Dream." *Detroit News,* 9-11-1987.

Vecsey, George. "Ray Dandridge, the Hall of Fame & Fences." *New York Times*, 5-1-1987, S3.

Volgenau, Gerald. "Arthritis Slows Dandridge, But Not His Memory." *Detroit Free Press*, 2-23-1990, 1D, 7D

Davis, Fritz

Newberry, Kevin. "Ahead of His Time: Otis "Fritz" Davis." *Houston Post*, 7-11-1992, B1, B6.

Davis, Johnny

Holway, John. "Cherokee: Johnny Davis." *Black Diamonds, Meckler Books.* 1-1-1989, 156-167.

Riley, James A. "Johnny Davis." *Baseball Research Journal #11*, 1-1-1982, 36-39.

Davis, Piper

Holway, John. "Piper Davis." *Baseball History 4*, 1-1-1991, 62-74.

Plott, Bill. "Piper Davis." *The Ballplayers, Arbor House, William Morrow.* 1-1-1990, 258.

Riley, James A. "Piper Davis, Willie Mays' Mentor." *Old Tyme Baseball News*, V4, N1, 1-1-1992, 13.

Riley, James A. "The Man Who Made Mays." *The Diamond*, 7-1-1993, 34-38, 46,50,

Rosengarten, Theodore. "Reading the Hops: Recollections of Lorenzo "Piper" Davis and the NBL." *Southern Exposure*, Sum-Fall, 1-1-1977, 62-79.

Scarbinsky, Kevin. "Born Too Soon." *Birmingham News*, 7-19-1987, 1C, 8C

Smith, Shelley. "Remembering Their Game." *Sports Illustrated*, 7-6-1992, 92.

Davis, Saul

Bone, Jack. "Saul Davis: A Model for Dealing with Conflicts." *Minot (ND) Daily News*, 12-22-1991, E3.

Flagstad, Carl O. "Davis Keeps Busy as He Reaches 90." *Minot (ND) Daily News*, 2-22-1991, A8.

Flagstad, Carl O. "Davis Talks About Baseball's Good Old Days." *Minot (ND) Daily News*, 12-11-1991, B-4.

Day, Leon

"O's Plan Leon Day Day." *Baltimore Afro-American*, 9-19-1992.

Baxter, Terry. "Leon Day." *Biographical Dictionary of American Sports: Baseball*, D. Porter, Greenwood Press. 1-1-1987, 141-2.

Bolton, Todd. "Day Unfairly Snubbed by Hall of Fame." *The Baltimore Herald-Mail*, 6-27-1992, D14.

Bolton, Todd. "Hall of Fame Hopefuls: Leon Day." *Discover Greatness—NLBM Yearbook*, 6-1-1993, 6.

Bolton, Todd. "Leon Day: The Living Void At Cooperstown." *Baltimore Afro-American*, 2-16-1991.

Coutros, Pete. "Day Waits for Call to Hall." *New York Post*, 1-31-1992, 70.

Floto, James. "Leon Day to the Hall?, Pro and Con." *Diamond Angle*, winter, 1-1-1992, 31-32.

Gilbert, Ray. "Local Baseball Legend Waits for Next Year." *Baltimore Afro-American*, 3-28-1992, A6.

Ginsburg, David. "Baltimore's Day Had Hall of Fame Numbers." *Daily Mail (Baltimore)*, 9-25-1992, B1.

Hines, Rick. "Leon Day: the Man Cooperstown Forgot." *Sports Collectors Digest*, 3-13-1992, 70-71.

Holway, John. "Leon Day: A Great Day for Cooperstown." *Blackball Stars: Negro League Pioneers*, Meckler Books. 1-1-1988, 344-352.

Holway, John. "One Day at a Time." *Baseball Research Journal #12*, 1-1-1983, 137-143.

Keyser, Tom. "It's Day's Turn to Throw Again." *Baltimore Sun*, 9-24-1992, 1D, 6D

Kubatko, Roch Eric. "Maryland Honors Day, Star in the Negro Leagues." *Baltimore Sun*, 5-19-1992, 5B

Mani, Thomas E. "Black Baseball—And a Day That Should Live in Fame." *Pentagram*, 2-20-1992, 29,31.

Miller, Jason. "Negro League Remembered." *The Towerlight*, 2-27-1992, 9,13.

Riley, James A. "Baltimore's Living Legend." *1993 All-Star Game Program*, 7-13-1993, 99.

Riley, James A. *Dandy, Day & the Devil: A Trilogy of Negro League Biographies*. TK Publishers, 1-1-1988, Book, 55-100.

Riley, James A. "Forgotten Heroes: Leon Day." *Old Tyme Baseball News*, Spring, 3-1-1989, 4.

Riley, James A. "Leon Day." *The Ballplayers, Arbor House, William Morrow.* 1-1-1990, 261.

Smith, Shelley. "Remembering Their Game." *Sports Illustrated*, 7-6-1992, 82.

Steadman, John. "Integration Couldn't Catch up with Day's Best Fastball, Either." *The (Baltimore) Evening Sun*, 3-2-1992, D2.

Steadman, John. "Negro Leagues Sew Up Some New Fans." *The (Baltimore) Evening Sun*, 3-1-1993.

Stuckey, Tom. "Negro League Pitcher Honored." *Daily Mail (Baltimore)*, 5-10-1992.

Tiano, Charles. *Great Ballplayers Snubbed by Hall*. Woodstock (NY), 1-1-1989.

DeMoss, Bingo

Brennan, Gerald E. "Bingo DeMoss." *Biographical Dictionary of American Sports: Baseball*, D. Porter, Greenwood Press. 1-1-1987, 144.

Miller, John. "Bingo DeMoss." *The Ballplayers, Arbor House, William Morrow.* 1-1-1990, 267-68.

Denver Post Tournament

Melrose, Frances. "Black Baseball Team Threw 1st Colorado Pitch in '30s." *Rocky Mountain News*, 6-23-1991, 9.

Renfroe, Chico. "Sports of the World." *Atlanta Daily World*, 4-2-1991, 5.

Detroit Stars

Bak, Richard, Editor. "Cobb Would Have Caught It." *The Golden Age of Baseball in Detroit*, Wayne State University Press, 1-1-1992.

Cantor, George. "Stars of the Past." *Detroit News*, 9-16-1992, 1A,12A

Dials, Lou

Agostini, Ron. "You Should've Seen Him." *Modesto Bee*, 8-20-1989, C1,C10.

Clark, Dick. "Lou Dials." *The Ballplayers, Arbor House, William Morrow.* 1-1-1990, 272.

Dials, Lou. *Life in the Negro Leagues*. Self-published, 1-1-1987.

Herron, Gary. "A Brief Interview with Former Negro League Star, Lou Dials." *Sports Collectors Digest*, 8-17-1990, 110.

Horowitz, Mikhail. "Baseball Turns On Dials, Cooperstown still Possible." *Freeman's Journal (Kingston, NY)*, 8-16-1987, 29.

Kaye, Allan. "The Great Lou Dials." *Baseball Card News*, 8-1-1987, 14-16.

Newhouse, Dave. "Dials Had All the Right Numbers." *The Tribune (Oakland, CA)*, 11-9-1989, D1, D6.

Smith, John. "At 82, Dials Words Span Decades of Sense." *Las Vegas Journal*, 6-30-1986, 1C, 4C

Stutz, Howard. "Lou Dials Says He Could Have Preceded Jackie Robinson." *Las Vegas Sun*, 1-5-1986, 2C

Dihigo, Martin & Lloyd, Pop

Broeg, Bob. "Broeg on Baseball: Lloyd and Dihigo Had Talent to Burn." *The Sporting News*, 3-19-1977, 38.

Dihigo, Martin

"Daguerreotypes." *The Sporting News*, 1-1-1990, 79-80.

Broeg, Bob. "Historically Speaking: Martin (El Maestro) DiHigo." *The Sporting News*, 3-1-1977.

Coates, J. & Kleinknecht, M. "Historically Speaking: Martin Dihigo." *Black Sports #2*, 11-1-1973, 13-14.

Holway, John. "Martin Dihigo: El Maestro." *Blackball Stars: Negro League Pioneers*, 1-1-1988, 344-352.

Miller, John. "Martin Dihigo." *The Ballplayers, Arbor House, William Morrow.* 1-1-1990, 275-76.

Porter, David L. "Martin Dihigo." *Biographical Dictionary of American Sports: Baseball* , D. Porter, Greenwood Press. 1-1-1987, 147-8.

Dismukes, Dizzy

Clifton, Merritt. "William Dizzy Dismukes." *The Ballplayers, Arbor House, William Morrow.* 1-1-1990, 279.

Dixon, Rap

Suchsdorf, A.D. "Rap Dixon." *Biographical Dictionary of American Sports: Baseball* , D. Porter, Greenwood Press. 1-1-1987, 150-1.

Williams, Edith. "Rap Dixon." *The Ballplayers, Arbor House, William Morrow.* 1-1-1990, 280.

Doby, Larry

De Vries, Jack. "Doby's Historic Career is Second to None." *USA Today Baseball Weekly*, 7-1-1992, 35.

Hepburn, Dave. "Larry Doby Story." *Our World*, 5-1-1949, 29-31.

Kleinknecht, Merl. "Larry Doby." *Biographical Dictionary of American Sports: Baseball* , D. Porter, Greenwood Press. 1-1-1987, 151-2.

Moore, Joseph Thomas. *Pride Against Prejudice.* Praeger Publications, 1-1-1988, book, 195 pages.

Slear, Tom. "Larry Doby hit for his own Triple Crown in 1947—Dignity,_" *Sports History*, 1-1-1989, 54,56.

Smith, Red. "Larry Doby, Manager in Waiting." *New York Times*, 9-30-1974.

Spink, J.G. "Taylor. "Doby's Play Makes Eagles Scream." *The Sporting News*, 10-20-1948, 2.

Young, A.S. "Doc". "Black Athletes in the Golden Age of Sports, Ebony, 2-1-1969, 66-74.

Donaldson, John

Lester, Larry. "John Donaldson." *The Ballplayers, Arbor House, William Morrow.* 1-1-1990, 285.

Drake, Bill "Plunk"

Holway, John. "Historically Speaking: Bill Drake, the Man Who Taught Satchel the Hestitation Pitch." *Black Sports*, 6-1-1974, 40-41.

Duncan, Frank

Grabar, Phil. "Frank Duncan." *The Ballplayers, Arbor House, William Morrow.* 1-1-1990, 297.

Holway, John. "Historically Speaking: Frank Duncan, the Complete Catcher." *Black Sports #3*, 12-1-1973, 22-23,54.

Durham Black Sox

Morris, Ron. "Baseball, Hotdogs Durham Black Sox." *Durham Morning Herald*, 4-12-1990, B1, B5.

East-West Game

Brown, Larry. "Comments on East-West Game." *Colored Baseball & Sports Monthly*, 10-1-1934, 14.

Cattau, Daniel. "Baseball Strikes Out With Black Fans." *Chicago Reporter*, 4-1-1991, 1,6-9,13.

Irvin, Monte. "The Time of A Lifetime." *Sports Illustrated*, 7-19-1993, 106.

Tramell, Nat. "Baseball Classic—East vs. "West." *Colored Baseball & Sports Monthly*, 10-1-1934, 6.

Vanderberg, Bob. "Sox Footnote Provides Rich Anecdote." *Chicago Tribune*, 9-23-1990, Sec 3, p2.

Easter, Luke

"He Carries the Mail for Billy." *Jet*, 4-19-1979, 54-55.

"Luke Easter." *Our World*, 4-1-1950.

Cattau, Daniel. "Luke Easter: The First Black Major Leaguer from St. Louis." *St. Louis Post-Dispatch Magazine*, 4-5-1992, 8-13.

Cattau, Daniel. "So, Maybe There Really is such a thing as 'The Natural'." *Smithsonian*, 8-1-1991, 117-127.

Fowley, Kim. "Luke Easter." *Cult Baseball Players*, Simon & Schuster, 1-1-1990, 308-311.

Goodrich, James. "Luke Easter—King of Swat." *Negro Digest*, 8-1-1950, 3-8.

Overfield, Joseph M. "Easter's Charisma, Remarkable Slugging Captivated Fans." *Baseball Research Journal #13*, 1-1-1984, 14-16.

Easterling, Howard

Kleinknecht, Merl. "Howard Easterling." *The Ballplayers, Arbor House, William Morrow.* 1-1-1990, 304.

Elster, Jess

Harms, Richard. "Play Ball—A Local Legend." *Grand Times (MI)*, 4-1-1992, 20.

Ethiopian Clowns

"Ethiopian Clowns." *Toledo*, 8-27-1943, 7.

Evans, Bill

Holway, John. "Historically Speaking: Bill Evans, Rifle-Armed Infielder of the Homestead Grays." *Black Sports #12*, 1-1-1975, 52-56.

Evans, Chin

Miller, Jeff. "An All-Star for All Ages." *Palm Peach Post (Florida)*, 7-13-1992, 1C, 3C

Riley, James A. "Felix 'Chin' Evans." *Old Tyme Baseball News*, 1990, Vol 2 #6, 17.

Ewing, Buck

Black Sports, 6-1-1973, 30-31.

Amedio, Steve. "Ewing Split His Career with Negro League, Mohawk Giants." *Schenectady Sunday Gazette*, 5-12-1991, D5.

Long, Allen. "Historically Speaking: Buck Ewing." *Black Sports*, 6-1-1973, 30-31.

Reagles, Walter. "William Monroe Ewing." *The Schenectadian (New York)*, 11-1-1933.

Exhibits

Hirsch, Rod. "Negro Baseball Recalled in New Museum Exhibit." *Antique Week*, 3-13-1989.

Marquis, Cecilia A. "'Bums, Heroes' Exhibit Covers 153 Years of Baseball History." *Arizona Republic*, 3-1-1992, B1.

Murphy, Ed. "Exhibit in Dover to Focus on Baseball in Delaware." *The News Journal*, 3-3-1990, B5.

Pajerowski, Denise. "Show Honors Delaware Baseball." *The News Journal*, 3-2-1990.

Taylor, Ted. "Black Baseball Exhibit Honors Black Baseball Pioneers." *Sports Collectors Digest*, 1-1-1981.

Farrell, Luther

Holway, John. "Red Grier and Luther Farrell: The First Series No-Hitters." *Blackball Stars: Negro League Pioneers*, Meckler Books. 1-1-1988, 283-292.

Fernandez, Rodolfo

Coffey, Wayne. "The Forgotten Ones: The Cuban Flavor." *New York Daily News*, 8-12-1991, 38.

Forman, Ross. "SCD Visits with Negro Leaguer Rodolfo Fernandez." *Sports Collectors Digest*, 10-2-1992, 197.

Ritter, Almon S. "Life As A Cuban Ballplayer." *Old Tyme Baseball News*, V4, N1, 1-1-1992, 25.

Fields, Wilmer

Baskervill, Bil. "Manassas' Fields Would Have Made It In Majors." *Manassas Journal Messenger*, 1-19-1990.

Edison, Ted. "Fields' Dreams Chronicled for Upcoming Autobiography." *Manassas Journal Messenger*, 9-14-1991.

Fields, Wilmer. *My Life the Negro Leagues*. Meckler Publishing, 1-1-1992, Book, 191 pages.

Holway, John. "I Never Will Forget It." *Washington Star Sportsweek*, 8-22-1971.

Holway, John. "The Big Red Gray: Wilmer Fields." *Black Diamonds, Meckler Books*. 1-1-1989, 168-181.

Perry, Claudia. "A Good Life: Fields Remembers Playing in Negro and Latin Leagues." *Richmond Times-Dispatch*, 7-26-1987, D4.

Foster, Rube

"Daguerreotypes." *The Sporting News*, 1-1-1990, 93-94.

"Yesterday in Negro History." *Jet*, 12-10-1964, 11.

Brennan, Gerald E. "Rube Foster." *Biographical Dictionary of American Sports: Baseball*, D. Porter, Greenwood Press. 1-1-1987, 188-90.

Broeg, Bob. "Mize, Foster to Enter Hall." *The Sporting News*, 3-1-1981, 32.

Floto, James. "Profile—Rube Foster." *Diamond Angle*, V4, #2, 2-1-1993, 21-23.

Holway, John. "Andrew 'Rube' Foster." *Black Sports*, 11-1-1977, 58-60.

Holway, John. "Rube Foster and the League." *Chicago Sun-Times*, 3-29-1981, 25.

Holway, John. "Rube Foster: The Father of Black Baseball." *Pretty Pages*, 1-1-1981, book, 28 pages.

Holway, John. "Rube Foster: The Father of Black Baseball." *Blackball Stars: Negro League Pioneers*, Meckler Books. 1-1-1988, 8-35.

Holway, John. "Rube Foster: Father of the Black Game." *The Sporting News*, 1-1-1981, 19-20.

Kleinknecht, Merl. "Rube Foster." *The Ballplayers, Arbor House, William Morrow*. 1-1-1990, 352-53.

Madden, Bill. "At Long Last, Mize is in Hall of Fame." *New York Daily News*, 3-12-1981.

Malloy, Jerry. "Rube Foster and Black Baseball in Chicago." *Baseball in Chicago*, 1-1-1986, 24-27.

Peterson, Robert. "Rube Foster: Best of Black Managers." *Sport*, 5-1-1975, 38-40.

Phelps, Howard. "Andrew 'Rube' Foster." *The Half Century*, 3-1-1919, 8.

Streur, Russell. "Rube Foster, Father of Negro League Baseball." *Sports Collectors Digest*, 2-8-1991, 186.

Whitehead, Charles E. *A Man & His Diamonds: A Story of the Great Andrew Rube Foster*. Vintage Press, 1-1-1982, book, 186 pages.

Young, A.S. "Doc". "Baseball's Hall of Fame: How Bob Gibson and Rube Foster Made It." *Sepia*, 6-1-1981, 38.

Young, Frank. "More About Foster's Baseball Team." *The Half Century*, 6-1-1919, 8, 13.

Young, Frank A. "Rube Foster—The Master Mind of Baseball." *Abbott's Monthly*, 11-1-1930, 42-49,93.

Foster, Willie

Holway, John. "Hall of Fame Hopeful: Willie Foster." *Discover Greatness—NLBM Yearbook*, 6-1-1993, 4.

Holway, John. "Historically Speaking: Bill Foster." *Black Sports*, 3-1-1974, 58-59,62.

Lester, Larry. "Bill Foster." *The Ballplayers, Arbor House, William Morrow*. 1-1-1990, 350-51.

Fowler, Bud

"Acclaim on Fowler." *Sporting Life*, 4-11-1988, 1.

"Fowler Released." *Binghamton Leader*, 7-5-1987, 4.

Chalk, Ocania. "The First Pioneer." *Discover Greatness—NLBM Yearbook*, 6-1-1993, 28.

Davids, L. "Robert. "Bio of Bud Fowler." *Nineteenth Century Stars*, 1-1-1989, 48.

Peterson, Robert. "John Fowler." *Biographical Dictionary of American Sports: Baseball*, D. Porter, Greenwood Press. 1-1-1987, 213-4.

Shogren, Elizabeth. "Bud Fowler: First Black in Organized Baseball." *Stripes Magazine*, 8-27-1987.

Tholkes, Bob. "Bud Fowler, Black Pioneer and the 1884 Stillwaters." *Baseball Research Journal #15*, 1-1-1986, 11-13.

White, Richard. "Baseball's John Fowler: The 1887 Season in Binghamton, NY." *Afro-Americans in N.Y. Life & History*, #16, 1-1-1992, 7-17.

Gaines, A.S.

Holtzman, Jerome. "Don't Forget These Comiskey Stars." *Chicago Tribune*, 9-27-1990, Sec. 4, 11.

Gaines, Jonas

"Negro Baseball Players in Japan." *Ebony*, 10-1-1953, 101-102, 105-8.

Gardner, Jelly

Holway, John. "Historically Speaking: Jelly Gardner, He Could Bunt for a 2 Base Hit." *Black Sports*, 9-1-1974, 58-60.

Miller, John. "Floyd Jelly Gardner." *The Ballplayers, Arbor House, William Morrow.* 1-1-1990, 377.

General

"A Catcher talks about a Catcher." *Negro History Bulletin*, 12-1-1954, 71.

"Baseball Jumps into its 2nd Century." *Sepia*, 6-1-1969, 60-62.

"Baseball's Million Dollar Rookies." *Our World*, 4-1-1953.

"Baseball's Murderers' Row." *Our World*, 8-1-1951.

"Baseball's New Look." *Our World*, 6-1-1949.

"Baseball's Young Turks." *Sepia*, 9-1-1966, 59-60.

"End of An Era for Negroes in Baseball." *Ebony*, 6-1-1961, 36-40.

"Historically Speaking: The Negro Baseball Leagues." *Black Sports*, 5-1-1971, 74.

"It's Great to Be Traded." *Ebony*, 10-1-1959, 46-48.

"National Negro Ball Loop Discusses Plans for '36 Race." *Philadelphia Evening Ledger*, 1-27-1936.

"New York State Bars Jim Crow." *Crisis*, 4-1-1945, 98-99.

"Place in the Sun: Negro Players." *Time*, 5-14-1951, 91-93.

"Play Ball." *Sporting Life*, 4-20-1987, 1.

"SABR Survey of the Best Negro Players." *Baseball Research Journal #2*, 1-1-1973, 51-53.

"Sports: Negro Ball Players." *Negro History Bulletin*, 2-1-1955, 120-22.

"The Colored Leagues." *Sporting Life*, 5-18-1987, 6.

"The Future of Negroes in Big League Baseball." *Ebony*, 10-1-1962, 34-39.

"The Indifference Line." *Sports Illustrated*, 6-18-1990, 14.

"The Negro Comes of Age in Baseball." *Ebony* #14, 6-1-1959, 41-46.

"The Negroes Role in Baseball." *Sepia*, 4-1-1968, 10-14.

"Top 10 Negro Rookies." *Our World*, 4-1-1951.

Agostini, Ron. "You Should Have Seen Him." *The Modesto Bee*, 8-20-1990, C9-10.

Alexander, Charles. *Our Game, An American Baseball Hy.* Henry Holt & Co., Inc., 1-1-1991.

Allbaugh, Dave. "Ohioans." *Ohio Magazine*, 8-1-1990, 11-12,88.

Allhoff, Fred. "Thunder over Kansas City." *Liberty*, 9-17-1938, 4-8.

Arata, Oliver S. "The Colored Athlete in Professional Baseball." *Baseball Magazine* #42, 5-1-1929, 553-556.

Ashe, Arthur. *A Hard Road to Glory: The History of African-American Athlete.* Warner Publisher—3 Volumes, 1-1-1988, I-194 II-497 III-571.

Ashe, Arthur. "Taking the Hard Road with Black Athletes." *New York Times*, 11-13-1988, 11.

Banker, Stephen. "Black Diamonds." *Black Collegian*, 2-1-1979, 30,32,34.

Banker, Stephen. *Black Diamonds: An Oral History of Negro Baseball* (cassettes). Princeton, N.J. Video Education Corp., 1-1-1978.

Banks, Stephen. *The 150 Years of Baseball.* Publica's International, 1-1-1989, 194-201,248-9,196,218,.

Barber, Walter (Red). *1947, When All Hell Broke Loose In Baseball.* Doubleday & Co., 1-1-1982, book, 367 pages.

Bardolph, Richard. *The Negro Vanguard.* Vintage Press, 1-1-1939, book

Barnett, James. "Welcome to the Journey." *Kansas City Call*, 8-30—9-5 1991.

Blake, Mike. *The Minor Leagues: A Celebration of the LIttle Show.* Winwood Press (New York), 1-1-1991, 80-98.

Blanchard, Jon Todd. "Negro Leagues Set Stage to Majors." *Freeman's Journal (Kingston, NY)*, Summer, 7-1-1990, 20-21.

Bledsoe, Theodore. "Black Dominance of Sports: Strictly From Hungar." *Sport in Contemporary Society: Anthology*, St. Martin's Press, 1-1-1979, 358-365.

Bogira, Steve. "Blackball Reader." *Chicago Free Weekly*, 6-12-1987, 16-26, 30-43.

Bontemp, Arna W. *Famous Negro Athletes.* Dodd, Mead & Co., 1-1-1964, 81-92,71-80,57-70.

Bowman, John & Zoss Joel. *The Pictorial History of Baseball.* Gallery Books, 1-1-1990, 50-53.

Boyle, Robert. "The Private World of the Negro Ball Player." *Sports Illustrated*, 3-21-1960, 16-19,74-80,82,84.

Brace, George Edwards. "The Evolution of Baseball." *Old Tyme Baseball News*, 2-1-1989, 4.

Bradley, John. "Blacksox Coach Contemplate the End of the Long Season." *Washington Post*, 7-30-1984, D8.

Brigham, Bob. "Black Diamonds." *Diamond Angle*, Spring, 5-1-1991, 16.

Brosnan, Jim. "A Good Pitch is Better than a Wild Swing." *National Review*, 6-1-1962, 446-488.

Brower, William A. "Time for Baseball to Erase the Blackball." *Opportunity*, 6-1-1942, 164-167.

Brown, David. "The Negro in Baseball." *Negro History Bulletin*, 12-1-1951, 51-52.

Butch, John. "Stolen Bases." *Clarion-Ledger (MS)*, 7-8-1990, 1D, 4D

Cattau, Daniel. "Forgotten Champions." *Washington Post Magazine*, 6-3-1990, 22-30.

Cavanaugh, Jack. "Negro Leagues Get Their Due in Updated Baseball Encyclopedia." *National Sports Daily*, 5-20-1990, 37.

Chadwick, Bruce. *When the Game Was Black and White.* Abbeville Press, 12-1-1992, book, 191 pages.

Chalk, Ocania. *Black College Sports.* Dodd, Mead & Co., 1-1-1976, 1-69.

Chalk, Ocania. *Pioneers of Black Sport.* Dodd, Mead & Co., 1-1-1975, 3-82.

Clay, G.D. "Basking in 'Show Time' Negro League Stars love to pitch their history." *New York Newsday*, 8-18-1991.

Cleveland, Rick. "At Least One Old-Timer Still Takes His Cuts." *Clarion-Ledger (MS)*, 7-10-1990, 1C

Coates, John M. "Many Old Negro League Stars Around." *Baseball Research Journal #1*, 1-1-1972, 69-71.

Coffey, Wayne. "The Forgotten Ones: Proud to Play." *New York Daily News*, 8-11-1991, 62-63.

Coffey, Wayne. "The Forgotten Ones: The Legacy Lives." *New York Daily News*, 8-13-1991, 69.

Cohen, Haskell. "Ace of Diamonds." *Negro Digest*, 7-1-1944, 31-33.

Collier, Gene. "Black Baseball Leagues: Keeping Your Mouth Shut." *Philadelphia Journal*, 1-27-1981, D1, D6.

Conrads, David. "A Natural." *Kansas City Live*, 2-1-1992, 43-46.

Conrads, David. "Negro Leaguers Loved Careers, Lifestyle." *USA Today Baseball Weekly*, 6-28-1991, 48.

Conrads, David. "Reseeing the Rich History of Black Baseball." *Christian Science Monitor*, 2-8-1991, 14.

Cook, Ron. "Greatness Touched Negro Leagues." *Pittsburgh Press*, 9-9-1988, D1, D6.

Cooper, Michael L. *Playing America's Game: The Story of Negro League Baseball*. Lodestar Books, 1-1-1993.

Cope, Myron. "The Frustration of the Negro Athlete." *Sport*, 1-1-1966, 24-25+

Cox, James A. "The Birth of the Negro Leagues." *The World of Baseball: Lively Ball*, Refinition Books. 1-1-1990, 138-39.

Craft, David. "Negro Leaguers Desire Place in Game's History." *Sports Collectors Digest*, 6-21-1991, 84,85.

Craft, David. *The Negro Leagues: 40 Years of Black Professional Baseball in Words and Pictures*. Crescent, 4-1-1993, 112 pages.

Croce, Bob. "They Also Played." *Albany Times Union*, 7-1-1990, D1, D10.

Cummiskey, Joe. "Baseball's Biggest Drawing Card." *Negro Digest*, 8-1-1944, 69-70.

Daniel, Daniel M. "Negro Baseball." *Baseball Magazine* #86, 4-1-1951, 373-375+

Davidson, Craig. *There Was Always Sun Shining Someplace*, (Video). 1-1-1984.

Davis, Lenwood & Daniels, Belinda. *Black Athletes in the US: Bibliography of books, articles, etc. "1800-1981*. NY. Greenwood Press, 1-1-1981, book, 265 pages.

Davis, Jeff. "Negro League's Glory Still Big Hit in Player's Memory." *Binghamton Press & Sun Bull.*, 4-5-1987.

Davis, John P. *The American Negro Reference Book*. Prentice Hall, 1-1-1966, 797-81.

Dixon, Phil & Hannigan, Pat. *The Negro Baseball Leagues: A Photographic History*. Amereon House, 7-1-1992, Book, 329 pages.

Donaghy, Jim. "Negro League Stars Honored in New York." *New York Daily News*, 6-3-1992.

Donnelly, Joe. "A Moving Tribute." *Long Island Newsday*, 7-2-1993, 159.

Donough, John. ""Giants" Looks at Other Half of Baseball's History." *Chicago Tribune TV Week*, 1-26-1992, 5,7.

Editor. "Nationally Televised Game Includes Tickets to Negro League Players." *Birmingham World*, 5-29-1992, 9,12.

Editor. "Old Negro Baseball Leagues Make Comeback." *Capitol Spotlight* #38, 5-14-1992, 1,12.

Edwards, Harry. "Review Essay on Invisible Men and Baseball's Great Experiment." *Journal of Sport & Social Issues*, vol 9, 9-1-1985, 41-43.

Epstein, Theo. "Negro League Players Faced Incredible Obstacles." *Orioles Gazette*, 7-8-1993, 28,69.

Erickson, Arden. "Remembering the Giants." *Elkhart Truth*, 1-1-1989, 1,4.

Erickson, Arden. "We Borrowed Our Bats and Gloves." *Elkhart Truth*, 7-18-1989.

Federal Writer's Project. *Baseball in Old Chicago*. A.C. McClurg and Co, 1-1-1939, book

Floto, James. "Tales of the Negro Leagues." *Diamond Angle*, winter, 1-1-1992, 9-13.

Floto, James. "The Black Leagues, Part I." *Diamond Angle*, winter, 2-1-1990, 5,6.

Floto, James. "The Black Leagues, Part II." *Diamond Angle*, spring, 4-1-1990, 2,5,6.

Foreman, T.E. *Discrimination Against the Negro in America in American Athletics*. Fresno State University, 1-1-1957, thesis.

Frank, Stanley. "No Diamond Dimout." *Negro Digest*, 7-1-1943, 17-18.

Furlong, William B. "A Negro Ballplayer's Life Today." *Sport*, 5-1-1962, 38-39+

Gardner, R. & Shortelle D. *The Forgotten Players*. Walker and Company, 1-1-1993, 120 pages.

Garvey, Amy. "N.J.'s Negro Baseball History Detailed in Paper, Book." *Suburban News (NJ)*, 6-30-1991, 2.

Glauber, Bill. "With Color Line Broken, Negro Leagues Break Down." *Baltimore Sun*, 5-1-1990, E1, E5.

Goldman, Marty. *If Only You Was White: Sixty Years of Baseball Apartheid*. 5-22-1981, thesis, 103 pages. College Unknown.

Goldstein, Richard. *Superstars and Screwballs: 100 Years of Brooklyn Baseball*. Dutton , 1-1-1991, 243-251, 252-265.

Gross, Milton. "Will the Yankees Hire a Negro Player?." *Our Sports*, 7-1-1953, 9-10,58.

Guttman, Allen. *A Whole New Ball Game*. University of North Carolina Press, 1-1-1988, 121-22, 125-30.

Hall, John. "Hall of Shame." *Los Angeles Times*, 2-28-1974.

Hardwick, Leon Herbert. *Blacks in Baseball*. Pilot Historical Assn., 1-1-1980, book, 173 pages.

Harlow, Alvin F. "Unrecognized Stars." *Esquire*, 9-1-1938, 75,119-20.

Harold, Larry. "The Glory Days of Black Baseball." *Dallas Life Magazine*, 1-19-1986, 26-29.

Harwell, Ernie. "Found: A Popular Umpire." *Negro Digest*, 2-1-1944, 10.

Heaphy, Leslie. "Baseball, Black (Negro) League (1920-1960)." *Sports Encyclopedia of North America*, Vol 3, 3-1-1990, 107-123, 138-39.

Heaphy, Leslie. *The Growth & Decline of the Negro Leagues*. University of Toledo, 1-1-1989, thesis, 224 pages.

Henderson, Edwin. *The Negro in Sports*. Associated Press, 1-1-1939, 507 pages.

Hoekstra, Dave. "Old Negro Leagues Star Gather at Rosemont Show." *Chicago Sun-Times*, 2-25-1991, 108.

Hoekstra, Dave. "Play Ball—In Their Memories." *Chicago Sun-Times*, 2-25-1991.

Hogan, Lawrence D. "Stealing Home." *Courier-Post Forum (Camden, NJ)*, 2-20-1983, 1,14.

Holway, John. "Baseball Blackout." *Washington Post*, 4-4-1993, C1,C3.

Holway, John. "Before You Could Say Jackie Robinson: Black Players." *Look*, 7-13-1971, 46-50.

Holway, John. *Blackball Stars: The Pioneers*. Meckler Publishing, 1-1-1988, book, 400 pages.

Holway, John. "Blacks, 268, Whites 168." *Los Angeles Times*, 9-16-1975.

Holway, John. "Cool Papa, Biz and Satch." *LA Weekly*, 5-15-1992, 41-42.

Holway, John. "Negro Leagues History Told in Film Tonight." *Washington Post*, 7-7-1983, D5.

Holway, John. "Stats Shine on Stars of Negro Leagues." *USA Today Baseball Weekly*, 6-14-1991, 48.

Holway, John & Leonard, Buck. "A Gallery of Greats in Baseball's 'Other' League." *Washington Star Sportsweek*, 9-8-1970.

Honig, Donald. *Baseball America, the Heroes of the Game.* Macmillan, 1-1-1985, 248-50.

Hoose, Phillip M. *Necessities, Racial Barriers in American Sports.* Random House, 1-1-1989, 123-37.

Hoskins, Alan. "Negro League Stars Appreciated." *Kansas City Kansan*, 11-24-1991, 7A

Howard, Bill &Gat, Dimitri V. . *Some Are Called Clowns.* Thomas Y. Crowell, 1-1-1974.

Hruby, Dan. "Majors, not Minors, at Peak." *San Jose Mercury News*, 6-9-1967.

Hutchinson, G. *Black Athletes' Contribution Towards Social Change in the U.S.: the Black Athlete in Baseball.* U.S. International University, thesis., 1-1-1977, 114-53.

Hyland, Mike. "Astounding Tales, Negro League History Remains Vivid." *Richmond News Reader*, 5-9-1988.

Irvin, Monte. "This is Where the Negro Ballplayer Stands Today." *Sport*, 4-1-1957, 25-27.

Izenberg, Jerry. "Black Baseball Had its Pride and Pros." *New York Post*, 2-21-1989.

Jablow, Paul. "How They Played the Game Before Jackie Robinson." *Philadelphia Inquirer*, 1-16-1981.

John, Butch. "If There Was A Pasture, You Had Baseball." *Clarion-Ledger (MS)*, 7-9-1990, 1C, 3C

John, Butch. "Leagues Were Formed To Train, Entertain." *Clarion-Ledger (MS)*, 7-10-1990, 1C, 5C

John, Butch. "Negro Leagues: The Stories Are Still Big Winners." *Clarion-Ledger (MS)*, 7-8-1990, 1A, 5A

John, Butch. "Teams are Losing Money, Players." *Clarion-Ledger (MS)*, 7-10-1990.

Johnson, Chuck. "Vincent Lauds Contribution Negro League Players Made." *USA Today*, 8-13-1991, 1C

Johnson, Ernest E. "Legislation in the 79th Congress." *Crisis*, 1-1-1945, 9,30.

Johnson, Lloyd. *Baseball's Dream Teams.* Gallery Books, 1-1-1990, 36,62-4,67-9,74,79,81,88.

Jones, Wally & Washington, Jim. *Black Champions Challenge American Sports.* David McKay & Co., 1-1-1972, 9-11,29-31,38-9,62-7,96-102.

Jordan, Larry. "Black Markets and Future Superstars: An Instrumental Approach to Opportunity in Sport.." *Journal of Black Studies*, 1-1-1981, 289-306.

Katz, Lee Michael. "Baseball was a Nasty Business for a Blackman." *Washington Post*, 6-5-1983, C3.

Kaufman, Michelle. "Negro Leagues Found Respect on Rough Road." *Detroit Free Press*, 2-3-1990, 1D, 6D

Kelly, Frederic. "Of Greatness Confined to a Harsher Time." *Philadelphia Inquirer*, 8-11-1978, 4c

Kenney, Kirk. "Negro League Stars Recalls a Bygone Era." *San Diego Union*, 7-15-1989, C1.

Kimok, William M. "Black Baseball in New York States Capitol District, 1907-1950." *Afro-American in New York Life & History* #16, 10-1-1992, 41-74.

Kirsch, George B. "Baseball Spectators, 1855-70." *Baseball History*, Fall, 9-1-1987, 4-20.

Kleinknecht, Merl. "History of Negro League Baseball." *The Ballplayers, Arbor House, William Morrow.* 1-1-1990, 788.

Knisley, Michael. "Life in the Negro Leagues." *Denver Post*, 6-27-1982, 6E

Kountze, Mabray "Doc". *50 Sports Years Along Memory Lane.* Mystic Valley Press, 1-1-1979, book

Kovach, John. *Readers! Tales from South Bend Baseball Past.* Greenstocking Press, 1-1-1991, 80 pages.

Kram, Mark. "It Seemed Like it Happened in another Century." *Baltimore News American*, 8-9-1981, 2e

Kriegel, Mark. "Baseball's Black Eye." *New York Post*, 6-3-1992.

Lacey, Marc. "Baseball Star Who was Denied Gets Belated Recognition." *Los Angeles Times*, 7-15-1990, B1, B12.

Lacy, Sam. "Major Leaguers Outclassed in Mexican Baseball." *Afro-American*, 7-20-1946, 1.

Lamar, Hal. "Sports of the World." *Atlanta Daily World*, 6-27-1980, 5.

Leavy, Walter. "Baseball's Unknown Superstars." *Ebony*, 6-1-1982, 72-3,76-7.

Lester, Larry. "Above the White Foul Lines." *Emphasis '91*, V XXXIX, 6-1-1991, 22-23.

Lester, Larry. "Discover Greatness: Negro Leagues Baseball Museum Yearbook." *Negro Leagues Baseball Museum*, 6-1-1993, 32 pages.

Lester, Larry. "Touring Negro League Exhibit Kicks Off with Ground Breaking Ceremony." *Silhouettes*, Summer, 7-1-1993, 1-6.

Letters to the Editor. "Negro Players in Major League Baseball." *Crisis*, 4-1-1937, 112.

Levin, Doran P. "PIttsburgh Recalls a Neglected Title." *New York Times*, 9-12-1988.

Levine, Harris. *The Ultimate Baseball Book*, Houghton-Mifflin. 1-1-1979, 20,58-9,148,177-9,223.

Levy, Scott J. "Chicago's Forgotten Giants of Negro League Baseball, part I." *Chicago Tribune*, 1-1-1991, 31.

Levy, Scott J. *Lily Dippers, Sockamayocks, and the Blue Goose: Black Baseball and the Color Line.* Washington University, 5-1-1989, thesis, 161 pages.

Lewis, Greg. *Blackball, How Some of the Best Baseball Players_Frozen Out of History.* Image Sports, San Francisco, 4-8-1990, 22-28.

Light, Ivan. "Numbers Gambling Among Blacks." *American Sociological Review*, 12-1-1977, 892-904.

Littlefield, Bill. "A Real World Series at Last?." *World Monitor*, 11-1-1988, 84-86.

Lockwood, Wayne. "Sports." *San Diego Union*, 7-16-1989, H1.

Lowe, Frederick H. "The Thrill of Victory." *NorthStar News and Analysis*, 8-1-1991, 12-13.

Maisel, Bob. "Old-Timers Game Dusts Off Memories of Gibson, Blair & Many More." *Baltimore Sun*, 4-30-1990, C2, C6.

Manley, Effa. "Negro Baseball Isn't Dead." *Our World*, 8-1-1948, 27-28.

Manley, Effa & Hardwick, L. *Negro Baseball_Before Integration.* Adams Press, 1-1-1976, book, 129pages.

Masin, Herman L. "Baseball, the Great Americanizer." *Scholastic*, 5-3-1950, 10-11.

Mazer, Bill. *Bill Mazer's Amazin' Baseball Book*. Zebra Books, 1-1-1991, 191,133,184,131,26,189.

McAlpin, Harry. "The Post War Response of the Negro Press." *Opportunity*, Apr-Jun, 4-1-1945, 70-71,118.

McDonnell, Patrick. "Remembering Their League and Their Own." *Los Angeles Times*, 2-14-1993, B1, B13.

McKinney, Gordon B. "Negro Prof. Baseball Players in the Upper South in the Gilded Age." *Journal of Sport History*, Winter#3, 1-1-1976, 273-280.

Meacham, Jody. "Black Baseball Spanned Almost a Century." *San Jose Mercury News*, 2-25-1991, 1C

Mills, Prentice. "The People's Game: A Recollections of Negro Leagues Baseball Fans." *Black Ball News*, V1, #6, 6-1-1993, 2-16.

Monroe, Al. "Panic is Seen Within the Ranks of Organized Basebll." *Abbott's Monthly*, 8-1-1932, 16-17, 48.

Monroe, Al. "The Big League." *Abbott's Monthly*, 4-1-1933, 6-8, 38-39.

Monroe, Al. "What is the Matter with Baseball?." *Abbott's Monthly*, 4-1-1932, 26-29, 60-61.

Moran, Malcolm. "A Busride Back to the Negro Leagues." *New York Times*, 6-5-1989, 43.

Morse, George G. "Iron Men of Baseball." *Negro Digest*, 9-1-1946, 23-26.

Murray, Jim. "The Really Free Agents." *Los Angeles Times*, 12-5-1976.

Murray, Ken. "Out of Shadows, Into Spotlight." *Baltimore Sun*, 7-10-1993, 1C, 9C

Muskat, Currie. "Black Stars are Honored." *USA Today Baseball Weekly*, 5-6-1992, 3.

Myrick, Clarina. "The Unsung Champions: Baseball Players in the Black Leagues." *Negro Heritage* #21, 11-1-1981, 44-46.

Naison, Mark. "Lefties & Rights: The Communist Party & Sport during the Great Depression." *Sport in America New History Perspective*, 1-1-1985.

Nakamura, David. "Bo Jackson Gives His Thanks to Negro League Players." *Washington Post*, 7-11-1993, D9.

Neel, Richard Lee. *America's Game in Middletown, USA: Baseball in Muncie, Indiana, 1876-1953*. Ball State University,1-1-1989, dissertation.

Nelson, Robert L. "The Negro in Athletes." *Service Bureau for Intercultural Educ.*, 1-1-1940.

Neugeboren, Jay. "My Life and Death in the Negro American Baseball League: A Slave Narrative." *Massachussets Review*, Summer, 6-1-1973, 545-66.

O'Keeffe, Kevin. "Negro League Still Seeking Deserved Recognition." *San Antonio Express-News*, 8-6-1991, 2B

Oleksak, Michael & Mary Adams. *Beisbol: Latin America's and the Grand Old Game*. Masters Press, Grand Rapids, MI, 1-1-1991.

Olsen, Jack. "The Black Athlete." *Sports Illustrated*, 7-1-1968, 15-27,19-31,30-43,284.

Olsen, Jack. *The Black Athlete: A Shameful Story*. Time-Life Books, 1-1-1968, book

Orr, Jack. *The Black Athlete: His Story in American History*. Pyramid Books, 1-1-1970, book, 157 pages.

Ostenby, Peter Marshall. *Other Games, Other Glory: The Memphis Red Sox and the Trauma of Integration, 1948-1955*. Univeristy of North Carolina, 1-1-1989, thesis

Overmyer, James E. "Minorities Have Never Occupied Baseball's Tower Suite." *New York Times*, 2-23-1992.

Owen, Charles A. "Remember Griffith Stadium? So Do These Guys/." *The Sentinel*, 6-3-1981.

Paglia, Bernice & Hogan, Larry. "On the Shoulders of Giants." *Courier News (Bridgewater, NJ)*, 3-13-1991.

Papalas, A. "Lil' Rastus Cobb's Good Luck Charm." *Baseball Research Journal* #11, 1-1-1984, 69-70.

Pavelic, B.J. & DiClerico, J. "Glory in the Shadows: The Negro Leagues Flourish in New Jersey." *The Jersey Game*. Rutgers University Press, 1-1-1991, 133-159.

Peterson, Robert. "Men Who Changed Baseball." *Boy's Life*, 8-1-1972, 14-17.

Peterson, Robert. *Only The Ball Was White*. Video, 1-1-1981.

Peterson, Robert. *Only the Ball Was White*. Prentice Hall, 1-1-1970, 406 pages.

Peterson, Robert. "Only the Ball Was White, Part I." *Pittsburgh Press*, 7-26-1970, 4-6,15.

Peterson, Robert. "Only the Ball Was White, Part II." *Pittsburgh Press*, 8-2-1970, 4-6,15.

Peterson, Robert. "This Was Negro Baseball." *Sport & Society: An Anthology*, 1-1-1973, 3-15.

Phelon, W. A. "The Negro Ball Players." *Sacramento Union*, 9-2-1910.

Phelps, Howard. "A Cup of Dew Drops." *The Half Century*, 9-1-1919, 8.

Phelps, Howard. "Colored Women Play Ball." *The Half Century*, 8-1-1919, 8.

Phelps, Howard. "George Buckner." *The Half Century*, 4-1-1919, 8.

Phelps, Howard. "Inter-racial Baseball Should Come to Fruition." *The Half Century*, 4-1-1919, 8.

Phelps, Howard. "Memories of Champions." *The Half Century*, 6-1-1919, 8.

Phillips, John C. "Blacks and Baseball." *Harper's*, 5-1-1984, 35+

Phillips, John C. "Leagues Apart." *TDC*, 7-1-1992, 33-40.

Porter, David L. *Biographical Dictionary of American Sports: Baseball*. Greenwood Press, 1-1-1987.

Powers, James Joseph A. *Baseball Personalities, the Most Colorful Figures of All Time*. R. Field, 1-1-1949, 320.

Rader, Benjamin G. *Baseball: A History of America's Game*. University of Illinois Press, 1-1-1992, 141-154.

Rader, Benjamin G. *American Sports from the Age of Folk Games to the Age of Televised Sports*. Prentice Hall, 2nd ed., 1-1-1990, 170-71.

Redmond, D.E. "It Happened in Harlingen: Negro In the Little League Team." *Christian Century*, 2-10-1954, 175-76.

Reid, Zachary. "The Other Side of the Line." *Tuff Stuff*, 9-1-1992, 66-70.

Retort, Robert. *Pictorial Negro League Legends Album*. R.D. Retort Enterprises, 1-1-1992, 260 pages.

Richardson, Andrew. *A Retrospective Look at the Negro Leagues & Professional Negro Baseball Players*. San Jose State University, 1-1-1980, thesis.

Riley, James A. "A Hot Time in the Old Town: A Cooperstown Diary." *Old Tyme Baseball News*, 9-1-1992, 18,19,23,32.

Riley, James A. "President Bush Hits a Homer / Negro League Players Honored at the White House." *Old Tyme Baseball News*, V 4, #2, 4-1-1992, 20.

Riley, James A. *The All-Time, All-Stars of Black Baseball*. TK Publishers, 1-1-1983, book, 305 pages.

Rogosin, Donn. *Black Baseball: The Life in the Negro Leagues*. University of Texas at Austin, 1-1-1981, dissertation.

Rogosin, Donn. *Invisible Men: Life in Baseball's Negro Leagues*. Atheneum, 1-1-1983, book, 283 pages.

Rosenblatt, Aaron. "Negroes in Baseball: The Failure of Success." *Transaction*, 9-1-1966, 51-53.

Rowland, Debran. "Black Baseball Pioneers Honored." *New Pittsburgh Courier*, 11-30-1988, A1, A3.

Ruck, Rob. *Sandlot Seasons: Sports in Black Pittsburgh*. University of Illinois Press, 1-1-1986, 238 pages.

Ruck, Rob. *The Tropic of Baseball: Baseball in the Dominican Republic*. Meckler, 1-1-1991, 205 pages.

Rust, Edna & Art. *Illustrated History of the Black Athlete*. Doubleday & Co., 1-1-1985, book, 435 pages.

Rust, Jr., Art. *Get That Nigger Off the Field*. Delacorte, 1-1-1976, book, 228 pages.

Rust, Jr., Art. *Recollections of a Baseball Junkie*. Morrow, 1-1-1973, book, 244 pages.

Salvo, Patrick. "Black Baseball in the Movies." *Sepia*, 6-1-1976, 42-46.

Santa Maria, Michael. "One Strike and You're Out!." *American Visions*, 4-1-1990, 16-21.

Scully, Gerald W. "Discrimination: The Case of Baseball." *Gov't & the Sports Business*, 1-1-1974, 221-273.

Seidler, Mitch. "Professor Recalls Days When Only the Ball Was White." *Newark Star-Ledger*, 8-21-1988, Section 4, p 27.

Semler, James. "Qualifying a Colored Team in Majors." *Colored Baseball & Sports Monthly*, 10-1-1934, 13.

Seymour, Harold. *Baseball: The Early Years*. Oxford, 1-1-1960, 42,83,334-35.

Seymour, Harold. *Baseball: The Golden Years*. Oxford, 1-1-1971.

Seymour, Harold. *Baseball: The Peoples Game*. Oxford, 1-1-1990, 531-609.

Sierwood, John. "Baseball's Invisible Men: Life in the Negro Leagues." *Harlem Weekly*, 7-28-1983.

Skipper, James K. Jr. "Nicknames, Folkheroes and Assimilation: Black League BB Players, 1884-1950." *Educ. "Journal of Sport Behavior*, 6-1-1985, 100-12.

Skipper James K. Jr. *Baseball Nicknames: A Dictionary of Origins and Meanings*. McFarland and Company, 1-1-1992, 335-336.

Smith, Claire. "They Played on Diamonds When It Was Really Tough." *Patriot News (Harrisburg, PA)*, 8-18-1991, D1,D2.

Smith, Wendell. "Baseball on Diplomatic Rocks." *Negro Digest*, 4-1-1943, 71-72.

Southwell, David. "Negro League Stars Harbor No Ill Will About Lost Chances." *Chicago Sun-Times*, 11-25-1991, 100.

Spink, Al. "The Colored Gentlemen of America Propose to Organize & Maintain a Little M.L." *Spink Sport Stories*, Volume 1, 1-1-1921, 362-3.

Sullivan, Neil J. *The Minors: The Struggle and the Triumph of Baseball's Poor Relation from 1816 to Present*. St. Martin's Press, 1-1-1990, 186-207.

Taylor, Tony. "Touching All The Bases: The History of Integration in Professional Baseball in Shreveport." *North Louisiana Hist. Assoc. Journal*, 1-1-1984, 23-29.

Thorn, J. & Holway, J. *The Pitcher*. Prentice Hall, 1-1-1987, book, 324 pages.

Throwbridge, Matt. "White Sox Honor Players, Learn Negro League History." *USA Today Baseball Weekly*, 5-4-1992, 6C

Tobin, Richard L. "Sports as an Integrator." *Saturday Review* #28, 1-1-1967, 32.

Trouppe, Quincy. *20 Years Too Soon*. Sands Enterprises, 1-1-1977, book, 285 pages.

Turkin, Hy. "Brown Supermen." *Ebony*, 1-1-1946, 6-8.

Turkin, Hy. "Foul Bawl." *Negro Digest*, 2-1-1945, 35-36.

Tygiel, Jules. "Black Ball." *Total Baseball*. Warner Books, 1-1-1989, 548-562.

Tygiel, Jules. "The Negro Leagues." *OAH Magazine of History*, Summer, 6-1-1992, 24-27.

Various. "Negro Baseball Yearbooks." *Negro Baseball Yearbooks*, 1945/46, 12-1-1945, ?

Veeck, Bill. "Are There Too Many Negroes in Baseball?." *Ebony*, 8-1-1960, 25-31.

Voigt, David Quentin. *Baseball: An Illustrated History*. Penn State University Press, 1-1-1987, 195-207.

Warren, Tim. "A Tribute to Blacks in Baseball (an interview with John Holway)." *Washington Star*, 4-23-1976.

Wartzman, Rick. "Negro League Ball Players Feted." *Pittsburgh Journal*, 9-14-1988.

Weaver, Bill L. "The Black Press & the Assault on Professional Baseball's Color Line." *Phylon*. 12-1-1979, 303-17.

Webber, H.R. & Brown, O. "Play Ball." *Crisis*, 5-1-1938, 136-37.

Weir, Tom. "Black Goes to Bat for Old-Timers." *USA Today*, 3-4-1991, 3C

West, Norris. "Shutout: The Stars of the Negro Baseball Leagues." *Toledo Magazine*, 8-2-1987, 6-7,10,12,14.

White, Sol. *History of Coloured Baseball*. H. Walter Schlicter, 1-1-1907.

Whiteside, Larry. "A Joyful Win for the Negro Leagues." *Boston Globe*, 8-18-1991, A19, A22.

Wiggins, David K. "From Plantation to Playing Field: Historical Writings on the Black Athlete in American Sport." *Research Quarterly For Exercise & Sport*, 6-1-1982, 101-116.

Williams, Joseph. "Even After Four Decades Baseball Memories Clear." *Richmond Times Dispatch*, 8-30-1984.

Wilson, Kendall. "Baseball Greats Recall Pains of Bigotry." *Philadelphia Tribune*, 1-27-1981.

Winterich, J.T. "Playing Ball: Negroes in Organized Baseball." *Saturday Review of Literature*, 11-24-1945, 12.

Young, A.S. "Doc". "A Baseball History Lesson." *Sepia* #27, 7-1-1978, 62-66.

Young, A.S. "Doc". "A View from the Press Box." *LA Weekly*, 12-4-1992, 29-30.

Young, A.S. "Doc". "Baseball's Top 10 All-Time Black Stars." *Sepia*, 6-1-1971, 26-33.

Young, A.S. "Doc". *Great Negro Baseball Stars and How They Made the Major Leagues*. A.S. Barnes, 1-1-1953, book, 248 pages.

Young, A.S. "Doc". *Negro First in Sports*. Johnson Publishing Co., 1-1-1963, book, 301 pages.

Young, A.S. "Doc". "The Black Athlete Makes His Mark." *Ebony*, 5-1-1969, 110-120.

Ziegel, Vic. "Listen to This, Owners." *New York Daily News*, 6-2-1992, 47.

Zoss, Joel & Bowman, John. *Diamonds in the Rough*. Macmillan, 1-1-1989, 101-2, 135-58, 159-95.

Gibson, Josh & Paige, Satchel

"White Rascism Kept Them Out of Big Leagues." *Jet*, 7-22-1971, 48-49.

Lester, Larry. "Satch vs. Josh." *National Pastime*, 6-1-1993, 30-33.

Rogosin, Donn. "Satch vs. Josh—Classic Duel was a Lark." *The Sporting News*, 7-18-1981, 48.

Gibson, Josh

"Daguerreotypes." *The Sporting News*, 1-1-1990, 103-4.

"Hero of the Thirties." *Black Sports*, 4-1-1971, 6+

"Josh Gibson." *Dictionary of American Biographies*, Supp. "#4, 327-328.

"Josh Gibson, Buck Leonard in Baseball's Hall of Fame." *Jet* #42, 8-24-1972, 51.

"Josh Gibson: Greatest Slugger of 'Em All." *Ebony* #27, 5-1-1972, 45-53.

"Josh the Basher." *Time* #42, 7-19-1943, 75-76.

"Picture of Josh Gibson." *Sepia*, 10-1-1975, 55.

"The Brown Bomber of Baseball." *Sport*, 8-1-1942.

Bowen, Robert T. "Josh Gibson." *Biographical Dictionary of American Sports: Baseball* , D. Porter, Greenwood Press. 1-1-1987, 213-4.

Brashler, William. *Josh Gibson: A Life in the Negro Leagues*. Harper & Row, 1-1-1978, book, 201 pages.

Brashler, William. "Looking for Josh Gibson: Negro Leagues." *Esquire* #89, 2-1-1978, 104-108+

Burnes, Robert L. "This Was Josh Gibson." *Baseball Digest* #26, 2-1-1967, 83-85.

Campanella w/ Ed Linn. "The Best Catcher I Ever Saw." *Sport*, 11-1-1954, 35,70-72.

Cheeks, Dwayne. "Bias Denied Josh Gibson his place Among the Immortals." *Baseball Digest* #41, 5-1-1982, 40-48.

Cohen, Haskell. "Josh Gibson." *Negro Digest*, 7-1-1944, 31.

Holway, John. *Josh and Satch*. Meckler Publishing, 11-1-1991, 238 pages.

Holway, John. "Josh Gibson — Baseball's Forgotten Great." *Washington Post Potomac Magazine*, 2-8-1970, 11-13.

Holway, John. "Josh Gibson: An Uncrowned King." *The World of Baseball: The Power Game*, Refinition Books. 1-1-1990, 168-69.

Holway, John. "Josh Gibson: Greatest Slugger of them All." *Baseball Digest*, 3-1-1971, 62-69.

Honig, Donald. "Josh Gibson." *The Greatest Catchers of All-Time*, Crown Publishers, 1-1-1991, 51-53.

Ikan, Ronald. "Lament for Josh Gibson." *Sport*, 9-1-1972, 36,41.

Johnson, Lloyd. *Baseball's Dream Teams*. Gallery Books, 1-1-1990, 61,65,67,69,83,88-90.

Lloyd, Lewis. "Longest Homer." *Pittsburgh Post Gazette*, 7-24-1979, 17.

Miller, John. "Josh Gibson." *The Ballplayers, Arbor House, William Morrow*. 1-1-1990, 389-90.

Minks, Benton. *100 Greatest Hitters*. Crescent Books, 1-1-1988, 40.

Peterson, Robert. "Josh." *The Armchair Book of Baseball*, NY: Scribner's, 1-1-1985, 239-248.

Peterson, Robert. "Josh Gibson was the Equal of Babe Ruth, But.." *New York Times Magazine*, 4-11-1971, 12+

Peterson, Robert. *Josh: In How I Would Pitch to Babe Ruth*. Playboy Press, 1-1-1974, 797-803.

Vaughn, Gerald F. "Mexico's Year of Josh Gibson." *The National Pastime* #11, 6-1-1992, 55-56.

Gibson, Jr., Josh

Craft, David. "The Legend's Son Still Had to Prove Himself." *Sports Collectors Digest*, 6-21-1991, 98,99.

Giles, George

Coates, John. "George Giles." *Black Sports*, 1-1-1974, 58-59.

Craft, David. "The Negro Leagues' Other Great First Baseman." *Sports Collectors Digest*, 6-21-1991, 112,113.

Editor. "They Too Played the Game: George Giles." *One More Inning*, 12-1-1991.

Hartsock, Andrew. "Baseball Player's Death Signals End of Era in History of Sport." *Lawrence Journal-World*, 3-6-1992, 5B

Harvey, Denise R. "A Baseball Memoir George Giles: A Young Man's Dream, A Nation's Shame." *Manhattan Mercury (Kansas)*, 5-27-1984, D1,D4.

Holway, John. "The Black Terry: George Giles." *Black Diamonds*, Meckler Books. 1-1-1989, 55-69.

Lester, Larry. "George Giles." *The Ballplayers, Arbor House, William Morrow*. 1-1-1990, 391.

Giles, George & Brian

Finnegan, Bob. "Baseball Runs in their Bloodlines." *Kansas City Star*, 6-28-1990, D1, D6.

Gilliam, Junior

Clifton, Merritt. "James Junior Gilliam." *The Ballplayers, Arbor House, William Morrow*. 1-1-1990, 392.

Wiesbrusch, John. "Gilliam Recalls Tough Times in Negro Leagues." *Baseball Digest* #28, 6-1-1969, 38-41.

Grace, Willie

Smith, Shelley. "Remembering Their Game." *Sports Illustrated*, 7-6-1992, 91.

Grand Rapids Black Sox

Bond, Gary. "Exhibit Spotlights Black Baseball History in GR." *Grand Rapids Press*, 1993. C1-2.

Grant, Charlie

Miller, John. "Charlie Grant." *The Ballplayers, Arbor House, William Morrow*. 1-1-1990, 406.

Riley, James A. "When A Barrier Almost Was Broken." *1993 All-Star Game Program*, 7-13-1993, 105.

Grant, Frank

Malloy, Jerry. "Bio on Frank Grant." *Nineteenth Century Stars*, Society for American Baseball Research. 1-1-1989, 54.

Malloy, Jerry. "Frank Grant." *The Ballplayers, Arbor House, William Morrow*. 1-1-1990, 407.

Overmyer, Frank. "Frank Grant." *Baseball History 4*, 1-1-1991, 24-38.

Overmyer, James E. "The Unhappy Odyssey of a Great Ballplayer." *Berkshire Eagle*, 2-5-1990.

Peterson, Robert. "Frank Grant." *Biographical Dictionary of American Sports: Baseball*, D. Porter, Greenwood Press. 1-1-1987, 221.

Gray, Chester

"Catching Satchel, Rooming with Jackie." *Detroit Free Press*, 10-1-1991.

Greason, William

Garrison, Greg. "It's A New Ballgame." *Birmingham News*, 3-26-1993, 1h,2h

Great Lakes Teams

"Great Lakes Negro Baseball Team." *Crestline Advocate (OH)*, 9-6-1944.

Malloy, Jerry. "Black Bluejackets." *The National Pastime*, 1-1-1985, 72-77.

Green, Pumpsie

Cooper, Tony. "Ending Baseball's All-White Bastion in Boston." *San Francisco Chronicle*, 2-23-1993.

Greene, Joe

Holway, John. "I Was Satchel's Catcher." *Journal of Popular Culture*, Summer, 1-1-1972, 157-170.

Greenlee, Gus

Holway, John. "Cum Posey and Gus Greenlee: The Long Gray Line." *Blackball Stars: Negro League Pioneers*, Meckler Books. 1-1-1988, 299-326.

Kleinknecht, Merl. "Gus Greenlee." *The Ballplayers, Arbor House, William Morrow.* 1-1-1990, 411-12.

Ruck, Rob. "Gus Greenlee." *Biographical Dictionary of American Sports: Baseball*, D. Porter, Greenwood Press. 1-1-1987, 223-4.

Grier, Red

Holway, John. "Red Grier and Luther Farrell: The First Series No-Hitters." *Blackball Stars: Negro League Pioneers, Meckler Books.* 1-1-1988, 283-292.

Hall of Fame

"Black Baseball's History to be Preserved in Hall." *Winston-Salem Journal*, 11-7-1980.

"Hall to Stay Open to Negro Stars." *Winston-Salem Journal*, 9-4-1977.

"Negro League Hall of Famers." *USA Today*, 3-4-1987, 9C

"Negro Leagues Hall of Famers." *USA Today*, 4-4-1987, 9C

Appel & Goldblatt. *Baseball's Best, The Hall of Fame Gallery.* McGraw-Hill, 1-1-1980, 29,71,175,224,230,263,310,411.

Astor, Gerald. *The Baseball Hall of Fame 50th Anniversary Book.* Prentice Hall, 1-1-1988, 203-13,94-99,24,52.

Bates, Ken. "Ex-Negro Leaguer is Hall Material." *Baltimore Sun*, 2-20-1983.

Cress, Doug. "Negro Leagues Don't Get Invitations." *Washington Post*, 7-1-1984, B6.

Editor. "Place for Ex-Negro Stars in Shrine." *The Sporting News*, 2-13-1971, 30.

Holway, John. "Baseball Hall a Mockery of Itself if Doors are Shut on Black Greats." *Washington Post*, 7-31-1977.

Holway, John. "Baseball Hall of Fame about to Induct All-White Slate." *Los Angeles Times*, 7-16-1978.

Holway, John. "Baseball Hall of Fame May Terminate Black Committee." *Washington Post*, 8-10-1975.

Holway, John. "Black Stars Await Hall Ruling." *Los Angeles Herald-Examiner*, 8-1-1977.

Holway, John. "Cold Outside Hall for Surviving Stars of Negro Leagues." *Washington Post*, 2-11-1979.

Holway, John. "Hall Must Revise Negro League Committee." *USA Today Baseball Weekly*, 5-6-1992, 66.

Holway, John. "Hall of Fame Off Limits to Black Vets." *Washington Star*, 7-20-1980.

Holway, John. "Hall of Fame's Black Unit is Facing Ax." *New York Daily World Sports*, 8-5-1975.

Holway, John. "Shutting Door on Negro Leagues Stars." *New York Times*, 7-31-1977.

Holway, John. "Still Hoping for Their Spots in Cooperstown." *New York Times*, 3-9-1980, Sect. "5, S2.

LaPointe, Joe. "Pressure Builds to Enshrine Negro Leaguers." *Detroit Free Press*, 7-30-1962.

Lester, Larry. "Cooperstown Roll Call." *Silhouettes*, Spring, 4-1-1992, 1-4.

Mills, Prentice. "The Hall of Fame Game II." *Black Ball News*, V1, #6, 6-1-1993, 21-23.

Rapaport, Ron. "Hall of Fame Cheats Blacks." *Chicago Sun-Times*, 2-22-1985, 119.

Reidenbaugh, Lowell. *Baseball's Hall of Fame, Cooperstown: Where Baseball Legends Live Forever.* Arlington House, 2nd ed., 1-1-1986, 24,43,59,82,93,123,145.

Rogosin, Donn. "Honoring Black Ball Players—The Tortuous Road to Cooperstown." *North American Society for Sport History*, 8th, 1-1-1980, 29-30.

Smith, Red. "The Outcasts of Cooperstown." *New York Times*, Jul-Aug, 7-1-1977.

Steele, David. "Negro Leaguers Seek Entry Into Hall." *USA Today Baseball Weekly*, 8-16-1991, 17.

Terrell, Stanley. "Cooperstown Covers A Base." *Newark Star-Ledger*, 8-27-1991.

Wolf, Mark. "Hall Should Recognize More Negro Leaguers." *San Jose Mercury News*, 2-25-1991, 5C

Harmon, Charles

Lammar, C.L. "The Man: Chuck Harmon." *Black Sports*, 1-1-1974, 12-13.

Harris, Jim

Harlow, Alvin F. "Names, Games Are Still Vivid for this Fill-in." *Harrisburg Sun-Patriot News*, 8-18-1991, D1.

Harris, Vic

Holway, John. "Vic Harris Managed Homestead Grays." *Washington Afro-American Dawn Magazine*, 3-8-1975, 12.

Kleinknecht, Merl. "Vic Harris." *Biographical Dictionary of American Sports: Baseball*, D. Porter, Greenwood Press. 1-1-1987, 243-4.

Plott, Bill. "Vic Harris." *The Ballplayers, Arbor House, William Morrow.* 1-1-1990, 449.

Harvey, Bob

Forman, Ross. "Bob Harvey Recalls Negro League Days." *Sports Collectors Digest*, 6-21-1991, 108.

Welsh, Jonathan D. "Race Line Clouded His Season In Sun." *The Montclair Times*, 5-23-1991, A1, A10.

Hayes, Thomas

Church, Roberta & Walter, Ron. "Thomas H. "Hayes, 1863-1949 Businessman." *Nineteenth Century Memphis Families*, 1-1-1987, 40-41.

Hamilton, G.P. "The Bright Side of Memphis." 1-1-1908, 277-278.

Haynes, Sammie

Curran, Ron. "The Negro Leagues Revisited." *LA Weekly*, 4-3-1992, 18-19,26-28.

Libman, Gary. "In A Special League." *Los Angeles Times*, 4-3-1992, E1,E8 (PT I), E2,E6 (PT II)

Schubert, Mary. "Transcending Segregation: Negro Leaguer Recounts Days as a Catcher." *Santa Clarita Daily News*, 3-6-1993, 1,4.

Heard, Jehosie

Glauber, Bill. "His Stay Was Brief, But Jehosie Heard Broke Color Barrier with Orioles in 1954." *Baltimore Sun*, 4-29-1990, C13.

Higgins, Williams

Hamilton, G.P. "The Bright Side of Memphis." 1-1-1908, 109.

Hill, Jim

Barrett, D. & Delehanty, E. "Albany Twilight League 50th Anniversity Commemorative Yearbook." *Albany, New York*, 1-1-1980, 23.

Hill, Jimmy

Frey, Bonnie. "Negro National League All-Star Dies." *Sarasota Herald-Tribune*, 6-4-1993.

Hill, Pete

Baxter, Terry. "Pete Hill." *Biographical Dictionary of American Sports: Baseball*, D. Porter, Greenwood Press. 1-1-1987, 255-56.

Lester, Larry. "Pete Hill." *The Ballplayers*, Arbor House, William Morrow. 1-1-1990, 473-74.

Phelps, Howard. "The Passing of Pete Hill." *The Half Century*, 5-1-1919, 8.

Riley, James A. "Pete Hill: The Greatest Black Outfielder of the Deadball Era." *Old Tyme Baseball News*, V3, #5, 9-1-1991, 9,31.

Hilldale Club

Jacobson, Steve. "Playing for a Dream." *Newsday*, 6-3-1992, 15.

Lanctot, Neil. "Fair Dealing and Clean Playing: Ed Bolden and the Hilldale Club, 1910-1932." *Pennsylvania Magazine*, 4-1-1993, 1-48.

Holland, Bill

Holway, John. "Bill Holland." *Black Sports*, 5-1-1976, 22-23+,59,61.

Holway, John. "Bill Holland." *New York Folklore Quarterly*, 297-313.

Homestead Grays

Holway, John. "Honoring the Homestead Grays." *Pittsburgh Post Gazette*, 9-10-1988, 8.

Jeffries, Eddie. "Pirates to Honor 40th Anniversary of Grays Final Negro League Title." *Pittsburgh Courier*, 9-7-1988, C-3.

Levin, Doug P. "Pittsburgh Recalls A Neglected Title." *New York Times*, 9-12-1988.

Miner, Curtis. "Homestead: The Story of a Steel Town." *Historical Society of Western Penna.*, 1-1-1989, 48-50, 55.

Smith, Chet, ed. *Pittsburgh and Western Pennsylvania Sports Hall of Fame.* Wolfson Publishing Company, 1-1-1969, 44-45.

House of David

Kirshenbaum, Jerry. "The Hairest Team of All." *Sports Illustrated*, 4-13-1970, 104-6.

Sculley, Francis X. "Do You Remember the House of David?." *Leatherstocking Journal*, Summer, 1-1-1980, 13-15.

Howard, Elston

"The First Black Yankee—Howard." *Our World*, 4-1-1955.

Hubbard, Jesse

Holway, John. "Historically Speaking: Jesse Hubbard." *Black Sports* #4, 2-1-1974, 18-20.

Hughes, Sammy T.

Baxter, Terry. "Sammy T. "Hughes." *Biographical Dictionary of American Sports: Baseball*, D. Porter, Greenwood Press. 1-1-1987, 269-70.

Hyde, Cowan 'Bubba'

Forman, Ross. "'Bubba' Hyde discusses baseball career." *Sports Collectors Digest*, 6-21-1991, 102,103.

Idlett, Leroy "Kid"

"Obituary." *Kansas City Star*, 5-18-1991, D8.

Indianapolis ABCs

Debono, Paul. "Black Ball: Negro League Locals Etched Their Names in Baseball History." *Indianapolis New Times*, 4-1-1991, 6-7.

Guthrie, Wayne. "City Had Super Team in ABC's." *Indianapolis News*, 4-14-1975.

Indianapolis Clowns

"Baseball's Comedy Kings." *Ebony*, 9-1-1959, 67-70.

"The Funny Men of Baseball." *Sepia*, 8-1-1965, 60-64.

Heward, B. & Dimitri V. *Some Are Called Clowns: A Season with the Last of the Great Barnstorming Teams*. Thomas Crowell & Co., 1-1-1974, book, 354 pages.

Integration

"Integration Didn't Include Baseball Executives." *Baseball America*, 7-25-1990, 4.

Clifton, Merritt. "Quebec Loop Broke Color Line in 1935." *Baseball Research Journal* #13, 1-1-1984, 67-68.

Dodson, Daniel. "The Integration of Negroes in Baseball." *Journal of Educational Sociology*, 10-1-1954, 73-82.

Haley, Alex. "Baseball in a Segregated Town." *Sport*, 7-1-1961, 20-21, 73-75.

Hepburn, Dave. "Baseball's New Look." *Our World*, 6-1-1949, 48-53.

Jennings, S.E. "As American As Hot Dogs, Apple Pie and Chevrolet—The Desegregation of Little League BB." *Journal of American Culture*, 1-1-1981, 81-91.

Kleinknecht, Merl. "Integration of Baseball After World War II." *Baseball Research Journal* #12, 1-1-1983, 100-106.

Mogull, R.G. "Salary Discrimination in Major League Baseball." *Review of Black Political Economy*, Spring, 1975, 269-79.

Ruck, Rob. "Loss of the Negro Leagues was part of the Price for Integration." *Bill Mazeroski's Baseball '93*, 1-1-1993.

Sherwood, John. "Recalling Days of Baseball Apartheid." *The Journal (Washington, DC)*, 2-16-1990, B1, B8.

Wiggins, David K. "The Pittsburgh Courier-Journal & the Campaign to Include Blacks in Org. Baseball." *Journal of Sport History* #10, 1-1-1983, 5-29.

Interviews

Etkin, Jack. *Innings Ago: Recollections by Kansas City Ballplayers of their Days in the Game.* Normandy Square Pub., 1-1-1987, book, 201 pages.

Green, Paul. *Forgotten Fields*. Parker Publications, 1-1-1984, book, 238 pages.

Holway, John. *Voices From the Great Black Baseball Leagues*. Dodd, Mead & Co., 1-1-1975, book, 363 pages.

Inventions

Thomas, Ron. "Black Innovations Enriched Baseball." *Des Moines Sunday Register*, 3-28-1993, 9D

Thomas, Ron. "Tinkering with the Game." *San Francisco Chronicle*, 2-25-1993, C1, C7.

Iowa Baseball

Beran, Janice A. "Diamonds in Iowa: Blacks, Buxton, and Baseball." *Journal of Negro History #89*, Sum,Fall, 6-1-1990, 81-95.

Irvin, Monte

"Daguerreotypes." *The Sporting News*, 1-1-1990, 133-34.

"Monte Irvin." *Our World*, 5-1-1952.

"The Man: Monte Irvin." *Black Sports*, 7-21-1971, 21.

Appel & Goldblatt. *Yesterday's Heroes*. William Morrow & Company, 1-1-1988, 134-38.

Forman, Ross. "Baseball HOFer goes to bat for former Negro players." *Sports Collectors Digest*, 3-22-1991, 64.

Green, Paul. "Interview with Monte Irvin." *Sports Collectors Digest*, 9-16-1983, 42-50.

Green, Paul. "Monte Irvin." *Forgotten Fields*, Parker Publications. 1-1-1984, 220-227.

Huard, Kevin. "SCD Interviews Hall of Fame Great Monte Irvin." *Sports Collectors Digest*, 3-22-1991, 80-82.

Martin, Douglas D. "Monte Irvin." *Biographical Dictionary of American Sports: Baseball*, D. Porter, Greenwood Press. 1-1-1987, 273-74.

Riley, James A. "Monte Irvin." *The Ballplayers, Arbor House, William Morrow.* 1-1-1990, 510-11.

True, Frank C. "Baseball's Giant Killers." *Negro Digest*, 7-1-1951, 58-62.

Jackman, Will

Stout, Glenn. "Diamonds Aren't Forever." *Boston Magazine*, 1-1-1986, 92-97.

Jackson, Martinez

Forman, Ross. "Martinez Jackson: Reggie's Father Discusses 'Mr. October'." *Sports Collectors Digest*, 2-19-1993, 174-5.

Japanese Baseball

Sayama, Kazuo. "A Black Team in Japan." *Baseball Research Journal #16*, 1-1-1987, 85-88.

Jenkins, Fats

Miller, John. "Fats Jenkins." *The Ballplayers, Arbor House, William Morrow.* 1-1-1990, 523.

Jethroe, Sam & Walker, Moses Fleetwood

Blaha, Tom. "Ohio Baseball Hall of Fame Inducts Five." *Sports Collectors Digest*, 9-27-1991, 24.

Jethroe, Sam

"Baseball's Fastest Player." *Ebony*, 10-1-1950, 55-58.

"Sam Jethroe." *Our World*, 6-1-1950.

Editor. "He Carries The Mail for Billy." *Sporting Life*, 5-1-1951, 54,55.

Haag, Ken. "'The Jet' Could Fly Like the Wind." *Sports Collectors Digest*, 6-11-1993, 50.

Hirshberg, Al. "Jethroe and the Sophomore Jinx." *Negro Digest*, 8-1-1951, 34-44.

Kleinknecht, Merl. "Hall of Fame Hopefuls: Sam Jethroe." *Discover Greatness—NLBM Yearbook*, 6-1-1993, 8.

Lester, L. & Eckhouse, M. "Sam Jethroe." *The Ballplayers, Arbor House, William Morrow.* 1-1-1990, 525-26.

Obojoski, Robert. "Sam 'The Jet' Jethroe's Career Remembered." *Sports Collectors Digest*, 9-27-1991, 100.

Overfield, Joseph M. "The Richards-Jethroe Caper: Fact or Fiction?." *Baseball Research Journal #16*, 33-35.

Johnson, Byron "Mex"

Johnson, Scott. "Satchel, Buck and Me." *New Odyssey*, Fall, 9-1-1992, 19-21.

Johnson, Chappie

Hart, Larry. *Schenectady's Golden Era, 1880 and 1930*. Old Dorp Books, 1-1-1974, 63-65.

Plott, Bill. "Chappie Johnson." *The Ballplayers, Arbor House, William Morrow.* 1-1-1990, 529.

Johnson, Connie

Etkin, Jack. "Connie Johnson." *Innings Ago*, Normandy Square Publications, 1-1-1987, 146-157.

Kelley, Brent. "Connie Johnson Remembers His Pitching Days." *Sports Collectors Digest*, 6-15-1990, 260-63.

Johnson, Grant

Grabar, Phil. "Grant Johnson." *The Ballplayers, Arbor House, William Morrow.* 1-1-1990, 532.

Riley, James A. "Grant Johnson." *Biographical Dictionary of American Sports: Baseball*, D. Porter, Greenwood Press. 1-1-1987, 286-74.

Johnson, Judy

"Daguerreotypes." *The Sporting News*, 1-1-1990, 143.

Baxter, Terry. "Judy Johnson." *Biographical Dictionary of American Sports: Baseball*, D. Porter, Greenwood Press. 1-1-1987, 289-90.

Bolton, Todd. "Judy Johnson." *The Ballplayers, Arbor House, William Morrow.* 1-1-1990, 533-35.

Cobourn, Tom. "Johnson Treated Everybody Right." *News Journal (Delaware)*, 6-16-1989.

Editor. "Judy Johnson Dies." *Pittsburgh Press*, 6-16-1989, 12.

Green, Paul. "Baseball and William 'Judy' Johnson." *Sports Collectors Digest*, 9-2-1983, 54-70.

Harvin, Al. "Historically Speaking: Judy Johnson." *Black Sports*, 4-1-1975, 52-54,60.

Harvin, Al. "Recognize Me Now." *Black Sports*, 6-1-1973, 32-33.

Holway, John. "Judy Johnson: The Man Named Judy." *Blackball Stars: Negro League Pioneers, Meckler Books.* 1-1-1988, 150-166.

Holway, John. "Judy Johnson: A True Hot Corner Hotshot." *Baseball Research Journal #15*, 1-1-1986, 62-64.

Hughes, David. "Johnson Finally Recognized in Print." *Wilmington News-Journal (DE)*, 6-15-1990, C1, C3.

Hunt, Donald. "Local Black Shortstop Remembers the Way We Were." *Sport*, 9-1-1972, 36-41.

Izenberg, Jerry. "Footsteps to Remember." *Newark Star-Ledger*, 1-10-1989.

Johnson, Lloyd. *Baseball's Dream Teams*. Gallery Books, 1-1-1990, 60,74.

Katzman, Izzy. "Johnson Raps Baseball Color Line." *Wilmington News-Journal (DE)*, 11-10-1979.

Katzman, Izzy & Soulsman, Gary. "Hall of Famer Judy Johnson Dies." *News Journal (Delaware)*, 6-16-1989.

Kerrane & Grossinger. *Baseball Diamonds*. Anchor Books, 1-1-1980, 200-7.

Lang, Jack. "Johnson, "Black Traynor" Elected to Shrine." *The Sporting News*, 3-1-1975, 34.

Minks, Benton. *100 Greatest Hitters*. Crescent Books, 1-1-1988, 5-9.

Newton, J.E. "William Judy Johnson: Delaware's Folk Hero of the Diamond." *Negro History Bulletin*, Fall, 1-1-1980, 91+

Zabitka, Matt. "Judy Johnson Had to Wait for Honors He Richly Deserved." *News Journal (Delaware)*, 1-1-1990.

Johnson, Wm. "Big C"

Holway, John. "Travels with "Big C" Johnson." *Black Sports*, 1-1-1977, 10,11.

Pace, Jack. "William "Big C" Johnson." *Colored Baseball & Sports Monthly*, 10-1-1934, 19.

Jones, Sam

"'Toothpick' Jones Laid to Rest in West Virginia." *Jet*, 11-25-1971, 52-53.

Jones, Slim

Pace, Jack. "Slim Jones." *Colored Baseball & Sports Monthly*, 10-1-1934, 19.

Williams, Edith. "Slim Jones." *The Ballplayers, Arbor House, William Morrow.* 1-1-1990, 543.

Kansas City Monarchs

Basenfelder, Don. "Paige is hero as KC Wins Flag Here." *Philadelphia Record*, 9-30-1942.

Bruce, Janet. *The Kansas City Monarchs: Champions of Black Baseball*. University Press of Kansas, 1-1-1985, 176 pages.

Campbell, Janet Bruce. "Beyond the Box Score: The Kansas City Monarchs." *History News*, 3-1-1992, 6-11.

Chaudhuri, Nupur. "We All Seem Like Brothers and Sisters." *Kansas History*, winter, 1-1-1991, 270-288.

Dixon, Phil. "Baseball in Kansas City." *Kansas City Call*, 7-27-1989, 14.

Holway, John. "K.C.'s Mighty Monarchs." *Missouri Life*, Mar-Jun, 3-1-1975, 83-89.

Young, William & Nathan. "The Story of the Kansas City Monarchs." *Your Kansas City and Mine*, Self-published, 1-1-1950, 68-70, 127-28.

Kemp, James "Gabby"

Renfroe, Chico. "This and That in Sports." *Atlanta Daily World*, 6-15-1978, 8.

Kimbro, Henry

Plott, Bill. "Henry Kimbro." *The Ballplayers, Arbor House, William Morrow.* 1-1-1990, 569.

Smith, Shelley. "Remembering Their Game." *Sports Illustrated*, 7-6-1992, 85.

Klep, Eddie

Feldman, Jay. "He Was Out of His League." *Sports Illustrated*, 6-8-1987.

Lacy, Sam

"Black Sports Writers Broke Journalism Barrier." *Houston Herald-Mail*, 8-25-1991.

Dominguez, Alex. "First Black Baseball Writer Blazed Trail for Others to Follow." *Chicago Sun-Times*, 11-3-1991, 20.

Fimrite, Ron. "Sam Lacy: Black Crusader." *Sports Illustrated*, 1-1-1990.

Judge, Mark G. "Writing the Good Fight." *Washington City Paper*, 5-17-1991, 28-30.

LaMarque, Jim

Etkin, Jack. "Jim LaMarque." *Innings Ago, Normandy Square Publications*, 1-1-1987, 164-175.

Smith, Shelley. "Remembering Their Game." *Sports Illustrated*, 7-6-1992, 88.

Landis, Judge

"Landis' decree on Negroes in Baseball & letters to the Editor." *Sport*, 10-1-1942.

Latin American Baseball

Costas, Rafael. *Enciclopedia Beisbol Ponces Leones, 1938-1987*. Dominican Republic, 1-1-1988.

Small, Collie. "Baseball's Improbable Imports." *Saturday Evening Post*, 8-2-1952, 28-29+

Leonard, Buck

"Daguerreotypes." *The Sporting News*, 1-1-1990, 163-64.

"Three Blacks Enshrined in the Hall of Fame for Baseball and Football." *Jet*, 2-24-1972, 56.

Carney, Gene. "Buck." *Diamond Angle*, V4, #2, 2-1-1993, 20.

Carr, A.J. "At Age 40, Leonard Belted 42 HR's." *The Sporting News*, 3-4-1972, 24.

Gergen, Joe. "Buck Walks to the Hall, and it was a Long Haul." , 2-9-1972.

Green, Paul. "Baseball and Buck Leonard." *Sports Collectors Digest*, 3-18-1983, 82+

Green, Paul. "Buck Leonard." *Forgotten Fields*, Parker Publications. 1-1-1984, 149-155.

Holway, John. "Lost Stars in Baseball's Firmament." *Washington Star Sportsweek*, 8-30-1970.

Holway, John & Leonard, Buck. "Buck Leonard, Lou Gehrig of Black Baseball." *The Sporting News*, 3-4-1972, 19,24.

Jacobs, Barry. "Buck Leonard." *Baseball America*, 6-1-1983, 5.

Johnson, Lloyd. *Baseball's Dream Teams*. Gallery Books, 1-1-1990, 61,67,69.

McKinstry, D. Scott. "Buck Leonard—A Monument of Hope." *Old Tyme Baseball News*, 2-1-1989, 2.

Minks, Benton. *100 Greatest Hitters*. Crescent Books, 1-1-1988, 5-9.

Riley, James A. "Buck Leonard." *The Ballplayers, Arbor House, William Morrow.* 1-1-1990, 617-18.

Sisti, Mark. "For the Love of the Game." *Legend Sports*, 11-1-1992, 67-69.

Smith, Jr., Leverett T. "Buck Leonard." *Biographical Dictionary of American Sports: Baseball*, D. Porter, Greenwood Press. 1-1-1987, 330-32.

Smith, Shelley. "Remembering Their Game." *Sports Illustrated*, 7-6-1992, 90.

Van Blair, Rick. "Buck Leonard: The Black Lou Gehrig." *Sports Collectors Digest*, 8-2-1991, 120, 121.

Lincoln Giants

Babcock, Mike. "City's Baseball Fans Colorblind in 1890." *Lincoln Sunday Journal-Star*, 7-26-1992.

Lloyd, Pop

"Daguerreotypes." *The Sporting News*, 1-1-1990, 164-66.

"John Henry "Pop" Lloyd." *Black Sports*, 12-1-1972, 48.

Argote-Freyre, Frank. "Field Named for Ace Player Falls to Disrepair." *Asbury Park Press*, 9-8-1991, AA1, AA4.

Bontemps, David. "Committee to Launch Drive to Restore Pop Lloyd Field." *Atlantic City Press*, 10-10-1991, D3.

DePalma, Anthony. "About New Jersey." *New York Times*, 4-26-1992, 17.

Editorial. "Atlantic City's 'Pop' Lloyd Park, Keep the Promise." *The Press (Atlantic City, NJ)*, 4-10-1991, A12.

Hogan, Lawrence D. "Two Groups Seek to Honor State's Black Athletic Heritage." *New Jersey Historical Commission Newslet #23*, 2-1-1992, 1,3.

Holway, J. & Kleinknecht, M. "John Henry Pop Lloyd." *Biographical Dictionary of American Sports: Baseball*, D. Porter, Greenwood Press. 1-1-1987, 333-34.

Holway, John. "John Henry Lloyd: The Black Wagner." *Blackball Stars: Negro League Pioneers, Meckler Books*. 1-1-1988, 36-49.

Johnson, Lloyd. *Baseball's Dream Teams*. Gallery Books, 1-1-1990, 25,34-36.

Lester, Larry. "John Henry Pop Lloyd." *The Ballplayers, Arbor House, William Morrow*. 1-1-1990, 626-27.

Levitt, M. & Edwards, D. "Historically Speaking: John Henry (Pop) Lloyd." *Black Sports #2*, 4-1-1973, 48-49.

Minks, Benton. *100 Greatest Hitters*. Crescent Books, 1-1-1988, 60.

Weinert, Joe. "Tawdry Monument to a Baseball Great." *The Press (Atlantic City, NJ)*, 4-8-1991, D1-D3.

Wilson, Rollo W. "J.H.Lloyd: Our Greatest Diamond Star of All Time?." *Pittsburgh Courier Magazine*, 1-13-1951, 11.

Lord Baltimores/Mutuals

"Baltimore's Colored Club." *Sporting Life*, 1887, 4-27-1987, 6.

Lundy, Richard

Holway, John. "Dick Lundy: King Richard." *Blackball Stars: Negro League Pioneers, Meckler Books*. 1-1-1988, 135-142.

Kleinknecht, Merl. "Richard Lundy." *Biographical Dictionary of American Sports: Baseball*, D. Porter, Greenwood Press. 1-1-1987, 338-39.

Tramell, Nat. "The Greatest Manager in the East." *Colored Baseball & Sports Monthly*, 10-1-1934, 7.

Williams, Edith. "Dick Lundy." *The Ballplayers, Arbor House, William Morrow*. 1-1-1990, 645.

Luque, Dolf

Bjarkman, Peter C. "First Hispanic Star?." *Baseball Research Journal #19*, 3-1-1991, 28-32.

Lyons, Jimmy

Grabar, Phil. "Jimmie Lyons." *The Ballplayers, Arbor House, William Morrow*. 1-1-1990, 645.

Riley, James A. "Jimmy Lyons." *Biographical Dictionary of American Sports: Baseball*, D. Porter, Greenwood Press. 1-1-1987, 342-43.

Mackey, Biz

Barbier, Larry. "Do You Remember Biz Mackey?." *Negro Digest*, 2-1-1951, 35-36.

Holway, John. "Biz Mackey: Artist in a Face Mask." *Blackball Stars: Negro League Pioneers, Meckler Books*. 1-1-1988, 217-235.

Lacy, Sam. "Hall of Fame Hopefuls: Raleigh "Biz" Mackey." *Discover Greatness—NLBM Yearbook*, 6-1-1993, 10.

Lester, Larry. "Biz Mackey." *The Ballplayers, Arbor House, William Morrow*. 1-1-1990, 649-50.

Martin, Douglas D. "Biz Mackey." *Biographical Dictionary of American Sports: Baseball*, D. Porter, Greenwood Press. 1-1-1987, 362-63.

Malarcher, Dave

Kleinknecht, Merl. "Dave Malarcher." *The Ballplayers, Arbor House, William Morrow*. 1-1-1990, 657-58.

Young, A.S. "Doc". "A Baseball History Lesson." *Sepia*, 7-1-1978, 62-66.

Manley, Effa

Burley, Dan. "The Mother of Negro Baseball." *Sepia*, 8-1-1959, 51-54.

Hecht, Harry. "Woman with a Mission." *New York Post*, 9-15-1975.

Kisner, Ronald E. "White Widow of Baseball League Pioneer Writes Book About Saga." *Jet*, 3-3-1977, 46-48.

Lester, Larry. "Effa Manley." *The Ballplayers, Arbor House, William Morrow*. 1-1-1990, 661.

Manley, Effa. "Baseball Leagues Spend Half Million." *Baltimore Afro-American*, 7-26-1941.

Rogosin, Donn. "Queen of the Negro Leagues." *Sportscape*, Summer, 6-1-1981.

Spink, C.C. "Johnson. "A Furious Woman." *The Sporting News*, 6-20-1977.

Young, A.S. "Doc". "Fair Lady of Baseball Decides to Call It Quits." *Cleveland Call*, 2-23-1948.

Manning, Max

Argote-Freyre, Frank. "When Color, Not Talent, Mattered." *Asbury Park Press*, 9-8-1991, AA1, AA4.

DeLuca, Joseph C. "Max Manning South Jersey's Pitching Ace." *South Jersey Magazine*, Spring, 4-1-1992, 7,8.

Holway, John. "Black Eagle: Max Manning." *Black Diamonds, Meckler Books*. 1-1-1989, 119-130.

Stadnicki, Michael A. "Max Manning: Still Pitching for the Negro Leagues." *Sports Collectors Digest*, 12-11-1992, 180.

Marcelle, Oliver

Clark, Nancy. "The Boys of Summer: Even Oliver Will be Here in Spirit." *Denver Magazine*, 9-1-1991, 1.

Miller, John. "Oliver Marcelle." *The Ballplayers, Arbor House, William Morrow*. 1-1-1990, 666.

Patty, Mike. "Riverside Grave Memorial to Honor 'Ghost' Marcelle." *Rocky Mountain News*, 6-1-1991, E3.

Riley, James A. "Oliver Marcelle." *Biographical Dictionary of American Sports: Baseball*, D. Porter, Greenwood Press. 1-1-1987, 378.

Van De Voorde, Andy. "Ghost Story: A Denver Sports Sleuth Goes Beyond the Grave to Honor A Baseball Legend." *Westword—(Denver, CO)*, 7-9-1991, 4,6.

Maritoba-Dakota League

Craw, Don. *A Short History of the Maritobe-Dakota League.*, 3-24-1982, 1-18.

Marquez, Luis

"Luis Marquez." *Our World*, 5-1-1951.

Marshall, Willard

Editor. "Two Days in the life of Willard Marshall." *One More Inning*, 12-1-1991.

Mathews, Fran
Curran, Ron. "The Negro Leagues Revisited." *LA Weekly*, 4-3-1992, 18-19,26-28.
Mathis, Verdell
Forman, Ross. "Lefty Mathis Fared Well Against Hero." *Sports Collectors Digest*, 6-21-1991, 108.
Grabar, Phil. "Verdell Mathis." *The Ballplayers*, Arbor House, William Morrow. 1-1-1990, 683.
Holway, John. "The Mighty Giant Killer." *Commercial Appeal Magazine*, 1-1-1970.
Holway, John. "When Red Sox Were Black: Verdell Mathis." *Black Diamonds, Meckler Books.* 1-1-1989, 147-155.
Mills, Prentice. "Verdell Mathis: King of the Hill." *Black Ball News*, V1, #3, 9-1-1992, 2-11.
Mays, Willie
"Mays' Cover Story." *Our World*, 6-1-1955.
"Willie Mays." *Our World*, 9-1-1952.
Editor. "The Amazing Willie Mays." *Ebony*, 9-1-1958, 45-52.
Floto, James. "Profile—Willie Mays." *Diamond Angle*, winter, 1-1-1992, 14-19.
Holway, John. "The Discoverer of Willie Mays." *Sports Quarterly Presents BB Extra*, Summer, 6-1-1972, 40-44.
Holway, John. "They Made Me Survive, Mays Says (at Negro League Reunion)." *The Sporting News*, 7-18-1981, 48.
Mays, W. & Einstein, Charles. *Born to Play Ball*. Putnam, 1-1-1955, book, 176 pages.
McClellan, Dan
Plott, Bill. "Dan McClellan." *The Ballplayers*, Arbor House, William Morrow. 1-1-1990, 699.
McDonald, Webster
Holway, John. "Historically Speaking: Webster McDonald." *Black Sports*, 5-1-1974, 54-55.
Welsh, John. "Mac Was a Hero." *Times (St. Cloud, MN)*, Spring, 3-1-1991, 1A, 3A
McDuffie, Terris
Plott, Bill. "Terris McDuffie." *The Ballplayers*, Arbor House, William Morrow. 1-1-1990, 707.
McNair, Hurley
Lester, Larry. "Hurley McNair." *The Ballplayers*, Arbor House, William Morrow. 1-1-1990, 722.
Mellix, Ralph "Lefty"
Rosensweet, Alvin. "Ralph "Lefty" Mellix Dies, Renowned Negro Pitcher." *Pittsburgh Post Gazette*, 3-26-1985, 10.
Memphis Red Sox
Neill, Kenneth. "The Memphis Red Sox." *Memphis Magazine*, 6-1-1979, 36-43.
Mendez, Jose
Holway, John. "Cuba's Black Diamond." *Baseball Research Journal* #10, 1-1-1981, 139-145.
Holway, John. "Jose Mendez: Cuba's Black Diamond." *Blackball Stars: Negro League Pioneers, Meckler Books.* 1-1-1988, 50-60.
Miller, John. "Jose Mendez." *The Ballplayers*, Arbor House, William Morrow. 1-1-1990, 730.
Mexican Baseball
"Batter Up in Mexico." *Our World*, 8-1-1947, 26-29.
Agundis, Teodulo Manuel. "El Verdadero Jorge Pasqual." *Mexico*, 1-1-1956, 119-188.

Cisneros, Pedro Treio. "Enciclopedia del Beisbol Mexicano." *REDSA*, 1-1-1992, 702 pages.
Crichton, Kyle. "Hot Tamali Circuit, Part 1." *Collier's*, 6-22-1946.
Crichton, Kyle. "Hot Tamali Circuit, Part 2." *Collier's*, 8-29-1946.
Lacy, Sam. "Ten Sepia Stars in Mexican Classic." *Afro-American*, 7-20-1946, 1.
Vaughn, Gerald F. "George Hausmann Recalls the Mexican League of 1946-47." *Baseball Research Journal*, 3-1-1991, 59-63.
Miami Giants
Tramell, Nat. "Florida Team Clicks in East." *Colored Baseball & Sports Monthly*, 10-1-1934, 16.
Miles, John Mule
Colaw, Captain Becky. "In the Game." *Airman: Magazine of America's Air Force*, 2-1-1993, 38-41.
Mineola Black Spiders
Sherrington, Kevin. "Barnstorming Black Spiders Found Their Home on the Road." *Black Ball News*, V1, #4, 12-1-1992, 14-20.
Minor Leagues
Hoie, Robert C. "Riverside-Ensenada-Porterville: An All-Negro Minor League Team." *Baseball Research Journal* #8, 1-1-1979, 61-64.
Plott, Bill. "The Colored Base Ballists." *Baseball Research Journal* #4, 1-1-1974, 91-95.
Minoso, Minnie
"Minnie Minoso." *Black Sports*, 12-1-1977, 30.
"Minnie Minoso Lands Job with ball team in Mexico." *Jet*, 5-16-1974, 52.
"Whatever Happened to Minnie Minoso?." *Ebony*, 7-1-1978, 58-60.
Hoffman, J.C. "Minnie's What you say hokay!" *Colliers*, 4-5-1952, 56-59.
Holway, John. "Minoso, Oliva, Others." *The Sporting News*, 6-6-1983, 20.
Lindberg, Richard C. "Minoso By Any Other Name." *The National Pastime* #12, 7-1-1992, 55-57.
Minoso, Minnie. *Extra Innings: My Life in Baseball*. Regency, 1-1-1983, Book, 202 pages.
Mortenson, Tom. "Minnie Minoso." *Cult Baseball Players*, Simon & Schuster, 1-1-1990, 235-240.
Smith, Wendell. "The Guy Who Makes 'Go-Go' White Sox Go!." *Our Sports*, 7-1-1953, 16-19,72.
Mohawk Giants
Hart, Larry. *Schenectady's Golden Era, 1880—1930*. Old Dorp Books, 1-1-1974, 63-65.
Monroe, Bill
Kleinknecht, Merl. "Bill Monroe." *The Ballplayers*, Arbor House, William Morrow. 1-1-1990, 753.
Moore, C.L.
Robinson, Henry. "Ex-Coach C.L. "Moore Dies." *Asheville Citizen-Times*, 11-19-1992, 1D, 5D
Moore, Dobie
Holway, John. "Dobie Moore." *Baseball Research Journal* #11, 1-1-1982, 168-173.
Holway, John. "Dobie Moore: The Black Cat." *Blackball Stars: Negro League Pioneers, Meckler Books.* 1-1-1988, 191-199.

Lester, Larry. "Dobie Moore." *The Ballplayers, Arbor House, William Morrow.* 1-1-1990, 756.

Moore, James "Red"

Renfroe, Chico. "This and That in Sports." *Atlanta Daily World,* 6-15-1978, 8.

Moss, Porter

Erardi, John. "Porter Moss Was 'The Best of it All'." *Cincinnati Enquirer,* 4-5-1993, C18.

N.Y. Black Yankees

"Batter-Up! Bigger and Better." *Our Sports,* 6-1-1946, 28-29.

"Black Diamonds in the Rough." *Flash,* 9-1-1941.

Daiuto, Alfred. "Remembering Rosebank Pioneers." *Staten Island Register,* 5-11-1989, 15.

Newark Dodgers

Tramell, Nat. "The Newark Baseball Club." *Colored Baseball & Sports Monthly,* 10-1-1934, 10-11.

Newark Eagles

"Newark Eagles." *Our World,* 9-1-1947, 41-44.

"The Eagle Forgotten." *Newark Star-Ledger,* 2-22-1988.

Newcombe, Don

"Biography of Don Newcombe." *Current Biography,* NY: H.W. Wilson Co. 1-1-1957, 399-401.

"Don Newcombe." *Our World,* 5-1-1950.

"Pitcher Don Newcombe." *Jet,* 3-25-1976, 48-49.

Creamer, Robert. "Conversation Piece: Subject, Don Newcombe." *Sports Illustrated* #3, 8-22-1955, 28-30.

Green, Paul. "Interview with Don Newcombe." *Sports Collectors Digest,* 6-21-1985, 152-182.

Young, A.S. "Doc". "Don Newcombe." *Ebony,* 4-1-1976, 54-56.

Night Baseball

Holway, John & Leonard, Buck. "Grays Brought Night Baseball to Washington." *The Sporting News,* 3-11-1972, 27-28.

Lowry, Philip J. "The Night the Lights Didn't Go Out in Georgia." *Baseball History,* Winter, 9-1-1986, 46-62.

Zang, David. "A Dress Rehearsal for Night Baseball." *Cinc. Historical Society Bulletin,* Spring, 4-1-1981, 109-112.

Noble, Ray

Clifton, Merritt. "Ray Noble." *The Ballplayers, Arbor House, William Morrow.* 1-1-1990, 810.

O'Kelley, James Stretch

Moore, Terence. "Negro League Heroes Are Legacy of O'Kelley." Atlanta Constitution. 6-12-1991, E-3.

O'Neil, Buck

"Vice-Prexy Says O'Neil May Head Cubs Eventually." *Ebony,* 8-1-1962, 29-30+

Bhonslay, Marianne. "A Hard Road to Glory." *Team Leader,* 7-19-1993, 15-19.

Burnes, Brian. "Buck O'Neil: A Star From A Royal Era." *Kansas City Star Magazine,* 3-15-1981, 14-18.

Burnett, James. "Welcome to the Journey." *Kansas City Call,* 8-30-1991.

Editor. "Buck O'Neil to Receive Nostalgia Award at Baseball Dinner, Jan. 18." *Kansas City Call,* 1-17-1992, 11.

Etkin, Jack. "Buck O'Neil." *Innings Ago, Normandy Square Publications,* 1-1-1987, 2-13.

Etkin, Jack. "In More Ways than One, O'Neil Holds Special Spot." *Kansas City Star,* 9-8-1991, S-2.

Etkin, Jack. "Scout's deeds Lure Them Back." *Kansas City Star,* 11-13-1991, D1, D7.

Hill, Jr., Clarence E. "Former Chief, Ex-Monarchs winners of Pioneer Awards." *Kansas City Star,* 7-27-1991.

Hockaday, Laura R. "Baseball Has Changed A Lot in 53 Years." *Kansas City Star,* 11-24-1991, F4.

Holway, John. "An American Monarch: John "Buck" O'Neil." *Black Diamonds, Meckler Books.* 1-1-1989, 89-106.

Hoskins, Alan. "O'Neil Deserving of Spot in Baseball Hall of Fame." *Kansas City Kansan,* 11-17-1991.

Johnson, Chuck. "Black Players Carved Niche in History." *USA Today,* 8-9-1991, 1,2.

Jones, Carmen. "Baseball Great John "Buck" O'Neil Roasts the Roasters At Gala." *Kansas City Call,* 12-13-1991, 9, 19.

Jones, Carmen. "Birthday Bash Held for John "Buck" O'Neil." *Kansas City Call,* 11-22-1991, 5, 18.

Kaegel, Dick. "O'Neil Touches All With Usual Good Will." *Kansas City Times,* 10-1-1989.

Lester, Larry. "John "Buck" O'Neil." *The Ballplayers, Arbor House, William Morrow.* 1-1-1990, 827.

Riley, James A. "The Dean of the Monarchs." *Old Tyme Baseball News,* V4, #6, 12-1-1992, 31.

Smith, Shelley. "Remembering Their Game." *Sports Illustrated,* 7-6-1992, 84.

Twyman, Gib. "O'Neil is a KC Treasure." *Kansas City Star,* 1-19-1992, S-1.

Wheelock, Sean D. "So Alive!." *The New Times,* 11-21-1991, 16.

Oms, Alexandro

Kleinknecht, Merl. "Alexandro Oms." *The Ballplayers, Arbor House, William Morrow.* 1-1-1990, 827.

Owens, William

Carpenter, Dan. "Bill Owens Remembers When Only the Ball Was White." *Indianapolis Star,* 8-15-1991.

Debono, Paul. "The Negro Leagues Major Part of Baseball History." *Indianapolis New Times,* 1-1-1993.

Ownership

"Blacks' Owning Team Unrealistic." *Journal & Sentinel,* 2-15-1970.

Pa. Red Caps

Bryant, Mel. "Pennsylvania Red Caps." *Colored Baseball & Sports Monthly,* 10-1-1934, 15.

Tramell, Nat. "Longest Game of the 1934 Season." *Colored Baseball & Sports Monthly,* 10-1-1934, 17.

Page Fence Giants

Bak, Richard. "Swinging With the Page Fence Giants." *Detroit Monthly,* 4-1-1993, 23.

Powers, Thomas E. "The Page Fence Giants Play Ball." *The Chronicle: The Quarterly Magazine of H.E.,* Spring, 3-1-1983, 14-19.

Page, Ted

Grabar, Phil. "Ted Page." *The Ballplayers, Arbor House, William Morrow.* 1-1-1990, 839.

Holway, John. "The Homestead Grays and other Highlights of Baseball's Dark Ages." *Pittsburgh Renaissance,* 4-1-1974, 21-22.

Leonard, Vince. "Nephew Says Ted Page Batted 1.000 when he found someone in a Squeeze." *Pittsburgh Post Gazette,* 12-4-1984, 4.

Paige, Satchel

"Actor Satch, Ageless Hurler Plays Cavalary Sergeant." *Ebony* #7, 12-1-1959, 109-110,112,114.

"Biography of Satchel Paige." *Current Biography Yearbook*, NY: H.W. Wilson Co. 1-1-1952, 458-460.

"Black Hall of Famers Get Special Berth, Satchel Paige First In." *Jet*, 2-25-1971, 52-53.

"Braves Activate Satchel Paige." *Kansas City Times*, 8-13-1968.

"Daguerreotypes." *The Sporting News*, 1-1-1990, 226-27.

"Paige vs. 1965 Red Sox." *New York Times*, 8-3-1968, 12:2.

"Satch Makes the Big Leagues." *Life*, 7-26-1948, 49-50+

"Satchel Paige in Hall of Fame; Wants a Manager's Job." *Jet*, 8-26-1971, 50-52.

"Satchel Paige Pitches His Best Game for Title Down in Old San Domingo." *Kansas City Times*, 3-26-1943.

"Satchel the Great." *Time*, 7-19-1948, 56-57.

"Satchelfoots." *Time*, 6-1-1940, 44.

"Slow: Satchel Paige." *New Yorker*, 9-1-1952, 32-33.

"The Brainiest Man in Baseball: Leroy 'Satchel' Paige is One of the National Game's ...." *Ebony*, 8-1-1952, 26-28,30-34.

"The Fabulous Satchel Paige." *Our World*, 11-1-1948, 38-40.

Anderson, Dave. "Looking Back at Satchel." *New York Times*, 6-10-1982, 29.

Barrett, D. & Delehanty, E. *Albany Twilight League 50th Anniversary Commemorative Yearbook*. Albany, New York, 1-1-1980, 57.

Berger, Wally & Snyder, George. "An Encounter with the Great Satchel Paige." *Diamond Angle*, winter, 1-1-1991, 17-19.

Brown, George F. "Satchel Paige Tells the World..'You Don't Have to Get Old'." *Sepia*, 12-1-1961, 51-54.

Bryson, Bill. "Clubhouse was Satchel's Bullpen." *Baseball Digest*, 7-1-1961, 89-90.

Burnes, Brian. "It Ain't Restful: The Legend Rambles On." *Boston Phoenix*, 7-15-1993, 8-9,14-16.

Cobbledick, Gordon. "Old Satch: He's Really Got It." *Sport*, 12-1-1948, 32-35,73.

Cobbledick, Gordon. "Satch a Natch for the Hall of Fame." *Baseball Digest*, 10-1-1952, 31-35.

Cohane, Tim. "Ancient Satchel." *Look*, 4-7-1953, 65-66.

Creamer, Robert. "Fine Paige out of History." *Sports Illustrated*, 6-1-1981, 55.

Cummiskey, Joe. "Baseball's Biggest Drawing Card." *Negro Digest*, 8-1-1944, 69-70.

Daley, Arthur. "Satch Proved Self in Brief Role." *Baseball Digest*, 5-1-1950, 55-57.

Dokes, David. "Looking Back on Satchel Paige." *Great Moments in Sports-Baseball Mag.*, 5-1-1988, 6-10.

Donovan, Richard E. "The Fabulous Satchel Paige." *Collier's*, 5-30-1953, 20-24,54-59,62+

Donovan, Richard E. "The Fabulous Satchel Paige." *The Fireside Book of Baseball* 1-1-1956, 75-95.

Durso, Joe. "Satchel Paige, Black Pitching Star is Dead at 75." *New York Times*, 6-9-1982, 48.

Editor. "Law Tells Satch—'Win or Jail'." *Ebony*, 9-1-1958, 77-78,80,82.

Editorial. "Satchel." *New York Times*, 6-10-1982, A30.

Einstein, Charles. *The Baseball Reader—Satchel Paige*. Bonanza Books, 1-1-1984, 68-101.

Fitzgerald, Ed. "Let's Get Old Satch into the Hall of Fame." *Sport*, 11-1-1952, 16-17,71.

Floto, James. "Profile #14—Satchel Paige." *Diamond Angle*, winter, 1-1-1991, 12-17.

Fox, William Price, Jr. "A Conversation with Satchel Paige." *Holiday*, 8-1-1965, 18,24-26,28.

Gietschier, Steven P. "The Short, Sweet Indian Summer of Satchel Paige." *Timeline*, 4-1-1989, 44-53.

Grady, Sandy. "The Return of Satchel Paige." *Baseball Digest*, 10-1-1968, 32-35.

Greenfield, Steven. "Satchel Paige." *The Ballplayers*, Arbor House, William Morrow. 1-1-1990, 839-41.

Gutskey, Earl. "Satchel Paige Breaks His Own Rule and Looks Back." *Baseball Digest*, 3-1-1980, 78-83.

Harrison, Roscoe. "Satchel Paige Runs for Missouri Legislature." *Jet*, 8-8-1968, 50-54.

Herskowitz, Mickey. "Paige Near the End of the Book." *Baseball Digest*, 4-1-1964, 46-49.

Holway, John. *Josh and Satch*. Meckler Publishing, 11-1-1991, 238 pages.

Holway, John. "Paige Helped Change Baseball and the World." *Washington Post*, 6-13-1982.

Holway, John. "Paige's Four-Day Rider Does Job." *Washington Post*, 7-7-1991, D3.

Holway, John. "Satch's Fast Ball was Elusive as a Shadow." *Baltimore Sun Magazine*, 6-27-1982, C4,C5.

Holway, John. "Satchel Paige." *TV Guide*, 5-30-1981, 30-32.

Johnson, Lloyd. *Baseball's Dream Teams*. Gallery Books, 1-1-1990, 15,60,63,64,67,88.

Jones, Carmen. "Monument Honors Satchel Paige, Wife." *Kansas City Call*, 8-10-1989, 1,4.

Kerrane, Kevin. "Satchel Paige." *The World of Baseball: The Hurlers*, Redefinition Books. 1-1-1990, 108-9.

Lardner, Rex. "Sports Hall of Fame: The Ageless Satchel Paige." *Sport*, 1-1-1969, 44-47.

Lebovitz, Hal. "Pitchin' Man." *Cleveland News*, 1-1-1948, book, 96 pages.

Lebovitz, Hal. "The Day Old Satch Made the Majors." *Sport*, 9-1-1957, 70-74.

Lewis, Allen. "For Satchel It Was Always in the Bag." *Baseball Digest*, 8-1-1960, 10.

Lewis, Franklin. "Fast or Not, It's Still Satchmo." *Baseball Digest*, 10-1-1951, 35-37.

Lewis, Lloyd. "Hesitation Ball." *Negro Digest*, 11-1-1944, 37-38.

Lipmann, David L. "Maybe I'll Pitcher Forever." *Negro Digest*, 11-1-1944, 37-38.

Lipsyte, Robert. "A Little Rusted Up." *Book of Sports Legends*, Times Books, Random House, 1-1-1991, 242-244.

Lloyd, Lewis. "Satchel Paige." *It Takes All Kinds*, 1-1-1947, 177-84.

Manning, Max. "Satchel Paige." *Cult Baseball Players*, Simon & Schuster, 1-1-1990, 301-7.

Mehl, Ernest. "My Biggest Baseball Day." *Negro Digest*, 5-1-1943, 7-10.

Mills, Prentice. "Satchel Paige: The Great Integrator of the Game." *Black Ball News*, V1, #2, 6-1-1992, 2-8.

O'Neil, John "Buck". "Unforgettable Satchel Paige." *Reader's Digest*, 4-1-1984, 89-93.

Otto, S. & Otto, J.S. "I Played Against Satchel for Three Seasons: Blacks & Whites in the Twilight Leagues." *Journal of Popular Culture*, Spring, 4-1-1974, 797-803.

Paige, Leroy & Lipman, David. *Maybe I'll Pitch Forever*. Doubleday, 1-1-1962, book, 285 pages.

Powers, Jimmy. "Satchel Paige." *Baseball Personalities*, Rudolph Field Publisher. 1-1-1949, 283-288.

Rae, Lorne W. "It Was A Real Baseball." *Saskatchewan History*, 1-1-1991, 16-20.

Reasons, George. *They Had A Dream*, Vol. 3, 1-1-1901, 47.

Reece, L.V. "Satchel and His Fellow Monarchs." *Sportland*, Summer, 6-1-1946, 19-22.

Rubin, Robert. *Satchel Paige, All-Time Baseball Great*. Putnam, 1-1-1974, book, 157 pages.

Ruck, Rob. "Satchel Paige." *Biographical Dictionary of American Sports: Baseball*, D. Porter, Greenwood Press. 1-1-1987, 435-37.

Shane, T. "Satchel Man." *Reader's Digest*, 6-1-1949, 39-42.

Shirley, David. *Satchel Paige: Baseball Great*. Chelsea House, 3-1-1993, 100 pages.

Silverman, Al. "Satchel Paige Sounds Off." *Sport*, 11-1-1972, 44-46.

Stainback, Barry. "Dang! Nobody Like Hitting His Ole Trouble Ball." *Panorama I*, 9-1-1980, 82-85.

Stann, Francis. "Satchel Paige: Hall of Famer." *Baseball Digest*, 1-1-1972, 78-80.

Stewart, D.F. "Dedication Held for Paige Academy." *Kansas City Call*, 10-11-1991, 1.

Tramell, Nat. "Leroy "Satchel" Paige." *Colored Baseball & Sports Monthly*, 10-1-1934, 3.

Vecchione, Joseph J. "Satchel Paige, 1906-1982." *Book of Sports Legends*, 1-1-1991, 239-242.

Walburn, Lee. "Satchel Might Be Gaining on Us." *Atlanta*, 8-1-1980, 79+

Wheatley, Tom. "Who Was Satch Paige and Why do They Still Talk About Him?." *Beckett Monthly*, 9-1-1989, 75-77.

Wolf, Al. "A Bookful in a Paige." *Baseball Digest*, 4-1-1954, 65-67.

Woodward, Stanley. "Satchel's Ambition." *Negro Digest*, 8-1-1943, 41-43.

Young, Andrew S. "A Black Athlete in the Golden Age of Sports." *Ebony*, 3-1-1969, 122-132.

Parrott, Harold

Scott, Gil. "Rap with Harold Parrott." *Black Sports*, 7-1-1976, 34-37.

Parsons, Ellwood

Allbaugh, Dave. "Ohioans." *Ohio Magazine*, 8-1-1990, 11-12,88.

Patterson, Pat

Kleinknecht, Merl. "Pat Patterson." *The Ballplayers, Arbor House, William Morrow*. 1-1-1990, 848.

Peete, Charles (Mule)

"Charley "Mule" Peete." *Black Sports*, 8-1-1975, 58-59,61.

Petway, Bruce

"Bruce Petway." *Half Century*, 6-1-1919, 8.

Plott, Bill. "Bruce Petway." *The Ballplayers, Arbor House, William Morrow*. 1-1-1990, 861.

Philadelphia Pythians

Reed, Harry A. "Not By Protest Alone: Afro-American Activists and the Pythian BB club of Phil. "1867-1869." *The Western Journal of Black Studies*, 1-1-1985, 144-150.

Philadelphia Stars

"Philadelphia Stars—Greatest Defensive Club in East." *Colored Baseball & Sports Monthly*, 10-1-1934, 18.

Historical Society of Penna. "Philadelphia's Baseball History." *Historical Society of Pennsylvania*, 2-24-1990, 84 pages.

Pigg, Leonard

Forman, Ross. "Leonard Pigg Still Enjoys Game of Baseball." *Sports Collector Digest*, 10-2-1992, 196.

Pittsburgh Crawfords

Bankes, Jim. *The Pittsburgh Crawfords: The Lives and Times of Black Baseball's Most Exciting Team*. Brown and Company, 6-1-1991, 162 pages.

Ruck, Rob. "Baseball in its Heyday." *Pittsburgh Magazine*, 2-1-1993, 36-39, 56-58.

Ruck, Rob. "Black Sandlot Baseball: The Pittsburgh Crawfords." *Western Pennsylvania Historical Review*, 1-1-1983, 49-68.

Ruck, Rob. "Kings on the Hill." *Pittsburgh Magazine*, 12-1-1985, 23,24.

Santa Maria, Michael. "King of the Hill." *American Visions*, 6-1-1991, 20-24.

Tramell, Nat. "The Pittsburgh Crawfords." *Colored Baseball & Sports Monthly*, 10-1-1934, 2-3.

Playoffs

Tramell, Nat. "The Four Team Doubleheader." *Colored Baseball & Sports Monthly*, 10-1-1934, 8-9.

Poles, Spottswood

Bayerd, Wayde. "Baseball's Black Ty Cobb." *Winchester Star (VA)*, 7-14-1990, D1, D6.

Bayerd, Wayde. "His Nephew Remembers." *Winchester Star (VA)*, 7-14-1990, D1, D6.

Holway, John. "Old-Timer Poles Ranks with Best Players Ever." *Washington Times*, 8-13-1986.

Holway, John. "Spottswood Poles." *Baseball Research Journal #4*, 1-1-1975, 66-68.

Miller, John. "Spottswood Poles." *The Ballplayers, Arbor House, William Morrow*. 1-1-1990, 876.

Riley, James A. "Spots Poles." *Biographical Dictionary of American Sports: Baseball*, D. Porter, Greenwood Press. 1-1-1987, 451-52.

Porter, Andy

Curran, Ron. "The Negro Leagues Revisited." *LA Weekly*, 4-3-1992, 18-19,26-28.

Porter, Merle

Curran, Ron. "The Negro Leagues Revisited." *LA Weekly*, 4-3-1992, 18-19,26-28.

Portsmouth Stadium

Brinkley, Robin. "Stadium is Going, but Memories Remain." *Virginian Pilot*, 7-1-1992, C5.

Posey, Cum

Baxter, Terry. "Cumberland Posey." *Biographical Dictionary of American Sports: Baseball*, D. Porter, Greenwood Press. 1-1-1987, 452-54.

Holway, John. "Cum Posey and Gus Greenlee: The Long Gray Line." *Blackball Stars: Negro League Pioneers, Meckler Books.* 1-1-1988, 299-326.

Powell, Dick

Glauber, Bill. "Powell's Records, Memory Are Key to Historic Past." *Baltimore Sun,* 4-29-1990, C13.

Riley, James A. "An Executive and A Fan." *1993 All-Star Game Program,* 7-13-1993, 103.

Powell, Jake

Crepeau, Richard. "Jake Powell Incident and the Press: A Study in Black & White." *Baseball History,* Summer, 6-1-1986, 32-46.

Crepeau, Richard. "Jake Powell Incident and the Press: A Study in Black and White." *North American Society for Sport Hist.,* No. "8, 1-1-1980.

Powell, Willie

Clark, D. & Holway, J. "Willie Powell: An American Giant." *The National Pastime,* Winter, 9-1-1985, 28-34.

Holway, John. "An American Giant: Ernest "Willie" Powell." *Black Diamonds, Meckler Books.* 1-1-1989, 39-54.

Puerto Rican Baseball

Alvelo, Luis. "The Golden Age of Puerto Rican Ball." *The National Pastime #11,* 6-1-1992, 57-58.

Racism

"MacPhail Declares Rickey Lied on Veto of Negroes in Majors." *Philadelphia Evening Bulletin,* 2-21-1948, 11.

"White Racism Kept Them Out of Big Leagues; Says They Are Not Bitter." *Jet,* 7-22-1971, 48-49.

Elliott, Jeffrey. "Its Time to Finish Taking the Racism out of Pro Baseball." *Sepia,* 12-1-1977, 28-33.

Farmer, Jr., Greene. *Social Implicaton of Black Professional Baseball in the United States.* U.S. International University, Ph.D., 1-1-1975, dissertation.

Finston, Mark. "Hall of Shame: Baseball's Color Line." *Newark Star-Ledger,* 8-17-1988.

Freischlag, J. & Strom, B. "Dimensions of Racial Discrimination in Organized Baseball." *Review of Sport and Leisure,* 1-1-1978, 42-53.

Gwartney, J. & Hawroth, C. "Employer Costs and Discrimination: The Case of Baseball." *Journal of Political Economics,* 1-1-1974, 873-881.

Hicks, J.H. "St. Louis: Is it the Toughest Town for Negro Baseball Players?." *Crisis,* 10-1-1950, 573-76.

Lieberman, Herman. "Radicals Fought the Color Bar." *New York Times,* 1-14-1990.

Lowenfish, Lee E. "Sport, Race & the Baseball Bus: The Jackie Robinson Story Revisited." *Arena,* Spring, 4-1-1978, 2-16.

Loy, J.W. & Elvogue, J.F. "Racial Segregation in American Sport." *International Review of Sport Sociology,* 1-1-1970, 5-23.

Meacham, Jody. "Racism, California Had Racial Problems, Too." *San Jose Mercury News,* 2-22-1991, 1D

Nabil, P.A. *Emergence & Arrival of the Afro-American in the National Game: His Participation in Sport.* Ball State University, 1-1-1989, thesis.

Parker, Rob. "Where Are All the Black Faces." *YSB (Young Sisters & Brothers),* 5-1-1993, 36-39,41.

Pascal, A.H. & Rapping, L.A. "Racial Discrimination in Organized Baseball." *RAND Memorandum,* RM-6227, 1-1-1970, 53 pages.

Riess, Steven A. "Race & Ethnicity in American Baseball, 1900-1919." *Journal of Ethnic Studies,* Winter, 1-1-1977, 39-55.

Robinson, Alan. "Blacks Broke Back of Baseball's racial Barrier." *Chicago Sun-Times,* 10-16-1988, 18-19.

Smith, Red. "From Jim Crow to Cooperstown." *New York Times,* 2-14-1978.

Staples, Brent. "Where Are the Black Fans?." *New York Times Magazine,* 5-17-1987, 25-34,56.

Starr, Mark & Barrett, Todd. "Baseball's Black Problem." *Newsweek,* 7-19-1993, 56-57.

Young, A.S. "Doc". "The Black Athlete in the Golden Age of Sports: Stereotypes, Prejudices, etc." *Ebony,* 6-1-1969, 114-124.

Radcliffe, Alex

Kleinknecht, Merl. "Alex Radcliffe." *The Ballplayers, Arbor House, William Morrow.* 1-1-1990, 890.

Radcliffe, Ted

"Double Duty On the Move." *Chicago Sun-Times,* 3-11-1990, 6.

Cantor, George. "Stars of the Past." *Detroit News,* 9-16-1992, 1A, 12A

Holway, John. "Better Than the Majors." *Chicago Sun-Times Midwest Magazine,* 7-11-1971.

Kovach, John. "Radcliffe Recounts Days of Old Negro Leagues." *Tri County News,* 5-25-1990, 2.

Kovach, John. "The Legendary Double Duty." *Tri County News,* 5-18-1990, 2.

Miller, John. "Ted Radcliffe." *The Ballplayers, Arbor House, William Morrow.* 1-1-1990, 890.

Post, Paul. "Double Duty Radcliffe Has Fond Memories." *Sports Collectors Digest,* 3-5-1993.

Royko, Mike. "Safe At Home Would Suit Former Catcher." *Chicago Tribune,* 11-20-1989, 3.

Smith, Shelley. "Remembering Their Game." *Sports Illustrated,* 7-6-1992, 89.

Whiteside, Larry. "Catching a Negro League Legend by the Tale." *Boston Globe,* 8-20-1991.

Redding & Wms. "Joe

Holway, John. *Smokey Joe and the Cannonball.* Capital Press, 1-1-1983, book, 37 pages.

Redding, Cannonball

Evers, John L. "Richard Cannonball Redding." *Biographical Dictionary of American Sports: Baseball ,* D. Porter, Greenwood Press. 1-1-1987, 465-66.

Holway, John. "Dick Redding: The Cannonball." *Blackball Stars: Negro League Pioneers, Meckler Books.* 1-1-1988, 79-87.

Holway, John. "The Cannonball, Dick Redding." *Baseball Research Journal #9,* 1-1-1980, 99-103.

Miller, John. "Richard Cannonball Redding." *The Ballplayers, Arbor House, William Morrow.* 1-1-1990, 896-97.

Reed, Percy

Howard, Allen. "Little Umpire Stood Among The Giants." *Cincinnati Enquirer,* 1-21-1992, F

Renfroe, Chico

"Negro League's Renfroe Dies." *USA Today,* 9-4-1991, 2C

Barnett, James. "'Chico' Renfroe, Former Monarch, Dies in Atlanta." *Kansas City Call*, 9-13-1991, 14.

Reunion

"Atlanta Fans Honor Baseball's Negro League." *Columbus (GA) Ledger-Enquirer*, 6-5-1989.

"Negro Baseball League to Stage Second Reunion." *New York Times*, 6-22-1980, S12.

"Negro League Stars Celebrate Reunion at Hall of Fame." *Jet*, 9-2-1991, 46.

Ainslie, Peter. "In Kentucky: Memories of Black Baseball." *Time*, 8-1-1981, 4-5.

Anderson, B. "Time Worth Remembering." *Sports Illustrated* #55, 7-6-1981, 46-47.

Anderson, Dave. "Here's A Soda for Buck Leonard." *New York Times*, 6-1-1992, C5.

Associated Press. "No Bitterness at Negro League Reunion." *Salt Lake Tribune*, 8-13-1991, C2.

Babington, C. & Nakamura, D. "Baltimore's Time to Shine." *Washington Post*, 7-13-1993, A1,A7.

Bryant, Howard. "Stars From Old Negro Leagues Get Their Due at Ballpark." *Oakland Tribune*, 6-19-1993, D4.

Editor. "Chicago's Comiskey Park Fetes Negro League Stars." *Jet*, 5-18-1992, 52-53.

Forman, Ross. "Memories Abundant at NLBPA Card Show." *Sports Collectors Digest*, 8-7-1992, 172-175.

Holway, John. "Negro League Reunion: Paige and Pals." *Washington Post*, 6-28-1981.

Hutchinson, David. "Negro League Alumni Recall a Rich Legacy." *Washington Times*, 9-1-1991, D1, D3.

Nicholson, Collie J. "Seventy-Five Surviving Negro Leaguers Attend Reunion." *Kansas City Call*, 8-30-1991, 14.

Smith, Claire. "A Ring is Nice, But a Pension Would Be Better." *New York Times*, 8-14-1991.

Smith, Claire. "Belated Tribute to Baseball's Negro Leagues." *New York Times*, 8-23-1991, A1, B9.

Smith, Claire. "Rejoicing, Urgently, For Times Long Gone." *New York Times*, 8-12-1991.

Terry, Mike. "Pride of the Negro Leagues." *Emerge*, 11-1-1991, 56.

Tingley, Ken. "Black Stars Memories Fond." *Ashland (KY) Daily Independent*, 7-5-1979, 15.

Richardson, Gene

"Player of the Year: San Diego Schoolboy is Big League Prospect." *Ebony*, 9-1-1946, 45.

Richmond Giants

Perry, Claudia. "Richmond Giants: Long Days, Low Pay, Back Door." *Richmond Times Dispatch*, 2-28-1988, D1, D6.

Rickey, Branch

"Branch Rickey Discusses The Negro in Baseball Today." *Ebony* #12, 5-1-1957, 38-44.

Cohane, Tim. "A Branch Grows in Brooklyn." *Look*, 3-19-1946.

Dexter, Charles. "Branch Rickey to the Rescue." *The Star Weekly*, 2-3-1951, 4.

Holway, John. "Integration Not Rickey's Real Goal." *Washington Post*, 7-5-1986.

Laney, Al. "Negro Players Seeking Dodger tryouts Catch Rickey's Guard Down." *Philadelphia Evening Bulletin*, 2-8-1945.

Polner, Murray. *Branch Rickey: A Biography*. Atheneum, 1-1-1982, book

Robinson, Jackie

"An Interview with Jackie Robinson." *Black Sports*, 8-1-1977, 8-11,39,60,62.

"Are They Ganging-Up on Jackie?." *Our World*, 8-1-1954, 42-46.

"Baseball Review." *Our World*, 9-1-1948, 46.

"Baseball: Batting At Robinson." *Newsweek*, 5-19-1947, 88.

"Biography of Jackie Robinson." *Current Biography*, NY: H.W. Wilson Co. 1-1972, 469.

"Biography of Jackie Robinson." *Current Biography Yearbook*, NY: H.W. Wilson Co. 1-1-1947, 544-547.

"Branch Breaks the Ice: Brooklyn signed J. Robinson, Negro Shortstop." *Time* #46, 11-5-1945, 77.

"Branch Rickey did for BB what a Million Sporting_" *Sports History*, 1-1-1989, 6.

"Branch Rickey Discusses the Negro In Baseball Today." *Jet* #43, 11-9-1972, 46-48.

"Brooklyn Dodgers sign first Negro to Play for Organized Baseball." *Life* #19, 11-26-1945, 133-34.

"Buttoned Lip." *Newsweek*, 4-21-1947, 88.

"Can Jackie Make the Hall of Fame." *Negro History Bulletin*, 10-1-1953, 6.

"Does the Best Team Win?." *Quick News Weekly*, 4-10-1950.

"Friends Recall Jackie Robinson." *Jet* #43, 11-16-1972, 51-57.

"From First to Fame: Jackie Robinson." *Ebony* #17, 10-1-1962, 85-86.

"Good Citizens Make Good Communities." *Scholastic*, 12-13-1950, 5.

"Hot-Stove League." *Time*, 2-6-1950, 69.

"Hurray for Jackie Robinson." *Negro History Bulletin* #18, 1-1-1955, 93.

"Jackie Can Play First Base and Bat Too, But_". *Our World*, 5-1-1947, 28-30.

Jackie Robinson—Baseball Hero. Fawcett Publication, 1-1-1949, comic

"Jackie Robinson Goes in Training." *Our World*, 3-1-1950.

"Jackie Robinson Pitching." *Newsweek*, 8-1-1949, 18-19.

"Jackie Robinson Scores Big in Business." *Sepia* #15, 6-1-1966, 52-56.

"Jackie Robinson's Double Play." *Life* #28, 5-8-1950, 129-132.

"Jackie Robinson, Mr. Baseball." *Our World*, 4-1-1952, 15-18.

"Jackie Robinson, the first Black Man to Play Major League Baseball." *Washington Post Magazine*, 4-12-1987, 34A

"Jackie Robinson: A Man for All Seasons." *Crisis*, 12-1-1972, 345-349.

"Jackie Takes a Bride." *Our World*, 5-1-1946.

"Laurels and Leverage." *Time*, 11-28-1949, 40.

"Negroes Are Americans." *Life*, 8-1-1949, 22-3.

"Negroes Are Americans." *Survey*, 8-1-1949, 410.

"No Help Wanted." *Time*, 8-1-1949, 10.

"Portrait of Jackie Robinson." *Life*, 4-21-1947, 100.

"Portrait of Jackie Robinson." *Life*, 4-28-1947, 37.

"Riches for A Rookie." *Time*, 11-24-1947, 54.

"Robinson Crosses Line in Daytona Beach." *Orlando Sentinel*, 9-16-1990, C-16.

"Robinson For Merit." *Newsweek*, 8-22-1947, 80.

"Robinson Photos." *Our World*, 5-1-1947.

"Robinson Replies to Robeson and Others." *Christian Century*, 8-3-1949, 908.

"Rookie." *New Republic*, 5-19-1947, 9-10.

"Rookie of the Year." *Time*, 9-22-1947, 70-76.

"Safe at First." *Our World*, 9-1-1946, 10.

"Safe At First?." *Time*, 4-21-1947, 55.

"South Seeks Jackie." *Newsweek*, 4-19-1948, 82.

"Stamp Honors Robinson Feats." *New York Times*, 6-16-1982, 27.

"Success: Brooklyn Dodgers' Second Baseman as Television-Set Salesman." *New Yorker*, 1-7-1950, 20.

"The Jackie Robinson Story." *Ebony*, 6-1-1950, 87-91.

"The Jackie Robinson Story is Filmed." *Color*, 7-1-1950.

"The Jackpot Boys." *Our World*, 9-1-1948, 30.

"The World Series." *Quick News Weekly*, 10-6-1952.

"Wait Til Next Year." *Ebony*, 9-1-1960, 89-94.

"Will Jackie Robinson Crack Up?." *Ebony*, 9-1-1951, 23-28.

"Wright-Jackie Picture." *Our World*, 10-1-1946.

Allen, Harold C. "Jackie Robinson." *Great Black Americans*, Pendulum Press, 1-1-1971, 97-126.

Allen, Lee & Meany, Thomas. "Kings of the Diamond." *Immortals of Baseball*, Putnam Publishing, 1-1-1965, book, 130-133.

Allen, Maury. *Jackie Robinson: A Life Remembered*. Franklin Watts, 1-1-1987, book, 260 pages.

Anderson, Dave. "Jackie Loved Playing in St. Louis." *New York Times*, 10-24-1985, 24.

Anderson, Dave. "Jackie Robinson, First Black in Major League Dies." *New York Times*, 10-25-1972.

Barber, Walter (Red). "Lead Off Man? (Book Review of Tygiel's Greatest Experiment)." *New Republic*, 7-4-1983, 28-31.

Benjamin, Peter. "Then and Now." *New York Times Magazine*, 4-15-1962, 84-86.

Bergman, Peter M. *The Chronological History of the Negro*. Harper & Row, 1-1-1969, 394.

Berkow, Ira. "Dixie Walker Recalls Robinson Breakthrough." *New York Times*, 12-10-1981, 29.

Berkow, Ira. "Jackie Robinson! Who's That?." *New York Times*, 12-10-1989, S3.

Bims, Hamilton J. "Black America Says 'Goodbye, Jackie.'" *Ebony* #28, 12-1-1972, 173-4+

Bogle, Donald. *Toms, Coons, Mulattoes*. Viking Press, 7-1-1973, 184-185.

Bonner, Mary G. "Jackie Robinson." *Baseball Rookies Who Made Good*, 1-1-1954, 131-139.

Bowen, C.D. "A Quarter Century: Its Human Triumphs." *Look* #25, 12-5-1961, 97-98.

Brenner, Keith. "Jackie Robinson, American Hero." *All Time Baseball Greats*, 11-1-1990, 23-26.

Brockenbury, L.I. "Tales of Two Brothers Jack and Mack Robinson." *Sepia*, 10-1-1962, 66-72.

Broeg, Bob. "Jackie Robinson." *Super Stars of Baseball / TSN*, 1-1-1971, book, 201-8.

Broom, Larry. "The Jackie Robinson Case." *Sport & Society: An Anthology*, 1-1-1973, 235-240.

Brosnan, Jim. *Great Rookies of the Major Leagues*. Random House, 1-1-1966, book, 9-25.

Brubaker, J. "Small Beginning." *New Republic*, 6-9-1947, 38.

Burchard, S.H. "Jackie Robinson." *Book of Baseball Greats*, 1-1-1983, 36-39.

Butler, Hal. "Jackie Robinson." *Sports Heroes Who Wouldn't Quit*. Julian Messner, 1973, 43-53.

Cable, Dale. *Jackie Robinson and the Integration of Organized Baseball*. Allegheny College, 1-1-1979, thesis

Campbell, Bob. "Jackie Robinson Inspires New Play." *Newark Star-Ledger*, 3-2-1990, 41,64.

Cope, Myron. "Jackie Robinson." *Great American Athletes of the 20th C*, 1-1-1966, 124-127.

Cosell, Howard. "Great Moments in Sports: Jackie Breaks the Barrier." *Sport* #31, 6-1-1961, 78-91.

Cosell, Howard. *Jackie Taught Us All*. Pocket Books, 1-1-1973, 83-96.

Creamer, Robert. "Perspective." *Sports Illustrated*, 11-1-1982, 99-100.

Curvin, Robert. "Remembering Jackie Robinson." *New York Times Magazine*, Sec. "6, 4-4-1982, 46+

Daley, Arthur. "Between Two Putouts." *Baseball Digest* #16, 3-1-1957, 72-75.

Daley, Arthur. "Jackie Robinson." *Sports of The Times*, 1-1-1959, 113-115.

Dennis, R. Ethel. *Black People of America*. Readers Press, 1-1-1970, 317-318.

Dexter, Charles. *Baseball Has Done It*. Lippincott Co., 1-1-1964, book

Dougherty, Bill. "The Jackie Robinson of Today." *Baseball Digest* #10, 7-1-1951, 25-28.

Douglass, Gualterio. "Se Espera Que Invitenal Circuito Mexicano." *Excelsior*, 3-6-1946, 14.

Dowling, Tom. "Jackie Robinson 25 Years Later." *Baseball Digest* #31, 3-1-1972, 72-75.

Duckett, Alfred. "The American Family Robinson." *Sepia*, 1-1-1973, 28-34.

Durslag, Melvin. "Leo Durocher and Jackie Robinson." *TV Guide* #12, 7-24-1965, 12-13.

Editor. "A Day in the Life of Jackie Robinson." *Ebony*, 8-1-1958, 90-94.

Epstein, Samuel & Sue. *Jackie Robinson: Baseball's Gallant Fighter*. Garrard Publishing Company, 1-1-1974, 96pages.

Flynn, James J. "Jackie Robinson." *Negroes of Achievement in Modern America*, NY: Dodd, Mead, 1-1-1970, 121-137, 267-68.

Frommer, Harvey. *Rickey and Robinson: The Men Who Broke Baseball's Color Barrier*. Macmillan, 1-1-1982, book

Gallagher, Tom. "Jackie Robinson." *The Ballplayers, Arbor House, William Morrow.* 1-1-1990, 927-29.

Gaven, Michael. "Jackie Robinson's Sore Arm." *Baseball Digest* #7, 1-1-1948, 37-39.

Goren, Herb. "Are they Giving Jackie Robinson the Works?." *Baseball Digest* #14, 9-1-1955, 77-82.

Goren, Herb. "Do the Dodgers Miss Jackie Robinson." *Baseball Digest* #16, 8-1-1957, 51-55.

Goren, Herb. "Jackie Robinson Himself Now." *Baseball Digest* #7, 10-1-1948, 65-69.

Goudl, Paul. "Rickey No Tightwad, Sincere in Breaking Color Line." *Brooklyn Eagle*, 6-28-1953.

Grimsley, Will. "Jackie Robinson: Breaker of the Color Line." *101 Great Athletes,* Bonanaza Books, 1-1-1987, 249-51.

Gross, Milton. "The Emancipation of Jackie Robinson." *Sport,* 10-1-1951, 11-15, 80-85.

Gross, Milton. "Why They Boo Jackie Robinson." *Sport* #14, 2-1-1953, 10-13, 94-97.

Gutman, Bill. *Famous Baseball Stars: Jackie Robinson.* Dodd, Mead & Co., 1-1-1973, 124-137.

Head, John. "Great Granddaddy verus Jackie Robinson." *Southern Exposure,* Fall, 9-1-1979, 14-18.

Hewitt, Brian. "An Untold Story: Jackie Robinson & a Kid's Heart." *Chicago Sun-Times,* 4-5-1987.

Hollander, Zander. *Great American Athletes of the 20th Century.* Random House, 1-1-1966, 124-27.

Hughes, Langston. "Jackie Robinson." *Famous American Negroes,* NY: Dodd, Mead, 1-1-1954, 139-144.

Johnson, Spencer. "Value of Courage: The Story of Jackie Robinson." *The Story of Jackie Robinson,* 1-1-1977, 66 pages.

Kahn, Roger. *A Season in the Sun.* Harper & Row, 1-1-1960, 137-54.

Kahn, Roger. "Jackie Robinson." *Sport* #71, 12-1-1971, 64-87.

Kahn, Roger. "The Ten Years of Jackie Robinson." *Sport* #20, 10-1-1955, 12-13+

Kelley, William G. "Jackie Robinson and the Press." *Journalism Quarterly,* Spring, 4-1-1976, 137-9.

Kisner, R.E. & Thompson, M.C. "Troubles Cease for Robinson after 53 Years." *Jet* #43, 11-9-1972, 48-59.

Kuenster, John. "Jackie Robinson: His National Impact Was Greater Than Ruth's." *Baseball Digest* #35, 7-1-1976, 15-20.

Lardner, John. "Pee Wee Reese and Robinson: Team Within A Team." *New York Times Magazine,* 9-18-1949, 17+

Libby, Bill. "Jackie Robinson." *Heroes of the Hot Corner,* 1-1-1972, 83-85.

Lincoln, C.E. "A Conversation with Clyde Sukeforth." *Baseball Research Journal* #16, 1-1-1991, 72-73.

Lowenfish, Lew. "Sport, Race and the Baseball Business: The Jackie Robinson Story Revisted." *Arena Review II,* spring, 1-1-1978, 2-16.

Mann, Arthur. "24 Letterman." *Negro Digest,* 5-1-1946, 31-35.

Mann, Arthur. "Jackie an Immortal, Mr. Rickey Knows." *Newsday,* 6-28-1962.

Mann, Arthur. "Say Jack Robinson: Meet the Dodgers' Newest Recruit." *Collier's,* 3-2-1946, 67-68.

Mann, Arthur. *The Jackie Robinson Story.* Grosset, 1-1-1957, 120 pages.

Mann, Arthur. "Truth About the Jackie Robinson Case." *Saturday Evening Post,* 5-13-1950, 19-21, 36.

Marsh, I.T. & Ehre, Edward. *30 Years, Best Sports Stories.* E.P. Dutton and Co., 1-1-1955, 27-31.

Maxwell, Jocko. "Robinson's the Name for 1947." *Baseball Digest,* 4-10-1946, 57-58.

Meany, Thomas. "Does Jackie Robinson belong in the Hall of Fame." *Sport* #24, 11-1-1957, 24-25, 61-63.

Meany, Thomas. "Jackie Robinson." *Baseball's Best,* 1-1-1964, 160-168.

Meany, Thomas. "Jackie Robinson." *Baseball's Greatest Players,* 1-1-1953, 194-204.

Meany, Thomas. "Jackie's One of the Gang." *Sport* #7, 8-1-1949, 24-28.

Meany, Thomas. "Jackie's One of the Gang Now." *Negro Digest,* 11-1-1949, 11-17.

Meany, Thomas. "What Chance Has Jackie Robinson." *Sport* #2, 1-1-1947, 12-15.

Metcalf, George R. *Black Profiles: Jackie Robinson.* McGraw-Hill, 1-1-1968, 143-167.

Morse, A.D. "Jackie Wouldn't Have Gotten to 1st Base without the Determined Mothering of a Quiet Woman." *Better Homes and Gardens,* 5-1-1950, 226.

Olsen, James T. "Jackie Robinson: Pro Ball's First Black Star." *Creative Education,* 1-1-1974, 29 pages.

Orr, Jack. "Jackie Robinson: Symbol of the Revolution." *Sport* #29, 2-1-1960, 52-59.

Ostler, Scott. "A Day of Little Challenges." *The Sporting News, Best Sports Stories,* 1-1-1988, 87-91.

Oursler, Fulton. "Rookie of the Year." *Reader's Digest,* 2-1-1948, 34-38.

Oursler, Fulton. "Why I Know There is a God." *St. Louis Glove-Democrat,* 9-15-1950, 67-84.

Palant, Miriam. "Sweats, Shouts and Tears." *New York Post,* 5-14-1950, 24.

Pollack, J.K. "Meet a Family Named Robinson." *Parent's Magazine* #30, 10-1-1955, 46-47+

Reese, Harold (Pee Wee). "Baseball is a Different Game Now." *Collier's,* 8-19-1955, 38,40-41.

Rice, Grantland. "The Emancipation of Jackie Robinson." *Sport* #11, 10-1-1951, 12-15.

Ritter, Lawrence. "Jackie Robinson Breaks the Color Barrier." *The Story of Baseball,* William Morrow, 1-1-1983, 43-58.

Robinson & Down, Fred. "20 Years Later." *Sports All-Stars 1967 Baseball,* 1-1-1967, 42-49.

Robinson & Duckett, Alfred. *Break-through to the Big Leagues: The Story of Jackie Robinson.* 1-1-1965, 178 pages.

Robinson & Lorimer, L. T. "The Guts Not to Fight Back." *Breaking In,* 1-1-1974, 173-198.

Robinson, J. & Peale, Norman. "Trouble Ahead Needn't Bother You." *Faith Made Them Champions,* Guidepost Associates, 1-1-1955, 238-241.

Robinson, J. & Smith, Wendell. "Jackie Robinson's First Spring Training." *The American Sporting Experience,* 1-1-1984, 365-370.

Robinson, Jackie. "A Kentucky Colonel (Pee Wee Reese) Kept Me in Baseball." *Look* #19, 2-8-1955, 82-84+

Robinson, Jackie. *Baseball Has Done It.* Lippincott, 1-1-1964, 216 pages.

Robinson, Jackie. *I Never Had It Made.* G. P. Putnam, 1-1-1972, 287 pages.

Robinson, Jackie. "My Own Story." *Ebony,* 6-1-1948, 19-24.

Robinson, Jackie. "Now I Know Why They Boo Me." *Look* #19, 1-25-1955, 23-28.

Robinson, Jackie. "The Best Advice I Ever Had." *Reader's Digest,* Jan-Jun, 5-1-1958, 214-216.

Robinson, Jackie. "The Most Unforgettable Character I've Met." *Reader's Digest,* 10-1-1961, 97-102.

Robinson, Jackie. "What's Wrong With Negro Baseball." *Ebony,* 6-1-1948, 16-18.

Robinson, Jackie. "Why I'm Quitting Baseball." *Look* #21, 1-22-1957, 91-92.

Robinson, Mack. "My Brother Jackie." *Ebony*, 7-1-1957, 75-82.

Robinson, Rachel. "I live with a Hero." *Negro Digest*, 6-1-1951, 3-14.

Robinson, Sharon A. "Remembering Jackie Robinson." *Essence* #17, 4-1-1987, 49.

Roeder, B. & Cousins, R. "All-Star Second Baseman." *Saturday Review of Literature*, 7-15-1950, 10.

Roeder, Bill. *Jackie Robinson*. A.S. Barnes, 1-1-1950, 183 pages.

Rosenthal, Harold. "Are Robby's Rough Days Over?." *Negro Digest*, 9-1-1950, 19.

Rothe, Emil H. "Jackie Robinson's Major League Debut." *Baseball Digest* #31, 12-1-1972, 82-88.

Rowan, Carl T. & Robinson, Jackie. *Wait 'Til Next Year: The LIfe Story of Jackie Robinson*. Random House, 1-1-1960, 339 pages.

Russo, Neal. "Robinson Discovered at 14." *Baseball Digest* #18, 10-1-1959, 52-55.

Schoor, Gene. *Jackie Robinson, Baseball Hero*. NY: Putnam, 1-1-1958, 187 pages.

Shapiro, Milton J. *Jackie Robinson of the Brooklyn Dodgers*. Julian Messner, 1-1-1973, 192 pages.

Sheed, Wilfred. "And Playing Second Base for Brooklyn: Jackie Robinson." *Esquire*, 12-1-1983, 82-86.

Sher, Jack. "Jackie Robinson: The Great Experiment." *Sport* #5, 10-1-1948, 30-33+

Shorto, Russell. *Jackie Robinson and the Breaking of the Color Barrier*. Millbrook Press, 1-1-1991, 32 pages.

Simons, Williams. "Jack Robinson and the American Mind: Journalistic Perceptions of the Reintegration of BB." *Journal of Sport History*, Spring, 3-1-1985, 39-64.

Slater, Jack. "Jackie Robinson Was a Prince, A Knight." *Jet* #43, 11-9-1972, 55.

Smith, Red. "Jackie Robinson." *The Best of Red Smith*, Franklin Watts, 1-1-1963, 65-69.

Smith, Robert. *Heroes of Baseball*. World Publishing Company, 1-1-1952, 213-24.

Smith, Ronald A. "Paul Robeson-Jackie Robinson Saga and a Political Collision." *Journal of Sport History*, Summer, 6-1-1979, 5-27.

Smith, Wendell. "The Jackie Robinson I Knew." *Baseball Digest* #32, 1-1-1973, 27-30.

Smith, Wendell & Robinson, J. *My Own Story*. Greenberg, 1-1-1948, 172 pages.

Staff. "Negro on the Farm." *Newsweek*, 11-5-1945, 94-5.

Steele, David. "Times Wasn't Right for Robinson to Join Sox." *USA Today Baseball Weekly*, 8-16-1991, 31.

Stone, Sgt. "Bob. "Jackie Robinson, Pathfinder." *Baseball Digest* #5, 2-1-1946, 19-20.

Stratton, Madeline R. "Jackie Robinson." *Negroes Who Helped Build America*, Boston: Ginn, 1-1-1965, 144-154.

Thompson, M. "Cordell. "Jackie Robinson: The Man and the Legacy He Leaves." *Jet* #43, 11-16-1972, 12-18, 52-57.

Thorn, John & Tygiel, Jules. "The Signing of Jackie Robinson." *Sport* #79, 6-1-1988, 65-70.

Toppin, Edgar A. *Biographical Historical of Blacks*, NY: McKay, 1971, 401-404.

Turkin, Hy. "No BlackBall for Black Jackie." *Negro Digest*, 3-1-1946, 41-43.

Tygiel, Jules. *Baseball's Great Experiment: Jackie Robinson & His Legacy*. Oxford, 1-1-1983, 392 pages.

Tygiel, Jules. "Beyond the Point (Color Line) of No Return." *Sports Illustrated*, 6-20-1983, 40-43, 62-67.

Tygiel, Jules. "The Court Martial of Jackie Robinson." *American Heritage*, 9-1-1984, 34-39.

Vass, George. "Jackie Robinson." *Champions of Sports: Adventures in Courage*, 1-1-1970, Chapter 2.

Waldman, Frank. "Jackie Robinson." *Famous American Athletes of Today*, Boston: Page, 11th ser, 1-1-1949, 237-257.

Washburn, Pat. "New York Newspapers & Robinson's First Season." *Journalism Quarterly*, Winter, 9-1-1981, 640-644.

White, Al. "Five Years Later: Negroes in Big League Baseball." *Our World*, 10-1-1950, 53-55.

Wolitzer, Hilma. "Jackie Robinson." *Cult Baseball Players, Simon & Schuster*, 1990, 208-212.

Wormley, Stanton L. *Many Shades of Black*, NY: William Morrow, 1969, 213-214.

Young, A.S. "Doc". "Black Athlete in the Golden Age of Sports." *Ebony* #24, 11-1-1968, 152-4+, 126-8+

Young, A.S. "Doc". "Fortieth Anniversary — On Jackie Robinson." *Ebony* #42, 5-1-1987, 66-68, 70.

Young, A.S. "Doc". "I Remember Jackie." *Sepia* #26, 4-1-1977, 64-72.

Young, A.S. "Doc". "The Jackie Robinson Era." *Ebony* #11, 11-1-1955, 152-56.

Robinson, Neil

Plott, Bill. "Neil Robinson." *The Ballplayers, Arbor House, William Morrow*. 1-1-1990, 930.

Rogan, Bullet

Holway, J. & Kleinknecht, M. "Wilber Bullet Rogan." *Biographical Dictionary of American Sports: Baseball*, D. Porter, Greenwood Press. 1-1-1987, 482-83.

Holway, John. *Bullet Joe and the Monarchs*. Capital Press, 1-1-1984.

Holway, John. "Joe Rogan: Bullet Joe." *Blackball Stars: Negro League Pioneers, Meckler Books*. 1-1-1988, 167-190.

Lester, Larry. "Wilber Bullet Rogan." *The Ballplayers, Arbor House, William Morrow*. 1-1-1990, 932-33.

Malloy, Jerry. "Hall of Fame Hopefuls: Wilber "Bullet" Rogan." *Discover Greatness—NLBM Yearbook*, 6-1-1993, 12.

Rogers, Nat

"Nat Rogers, 52-Year-old Manager of Knox Giants, Still a Great Slugger." *Knoxville Times*, 5-26-1946.

Holway, John. "Get a Man on Second, Ol' Nat Would Bring Him Home." *Black Sports*, 1-1-1975, 40-41.

Saddler, William Bubble

Zabitka, Matt. "Delaware City Names Park After Negro League Star." *News Journal (Delaware)*, 1-1-1992.

Salmon, Harry

Holway, John. "Historically Speaking: Harry Salmon, Black Diamond of the Coal Mines." *Black Sports*, 11-1-1974, 52-53.

Santop, Louis

Holway, J. & Kleinknecht, M. "Louis Santop." *Biographical Dictionary of American Sports: Baseball*, D. Porter, Greenwood Press. 1-1-1987, 500.

Holway, John. "Louis Santop, The Big Bertha." *Baseball Research Journal #8*, 1-1-1979, 93-97.

Holway, John. "Louis Santop: The Big Bertha." *Blackball Stars: Negro League Pioneers, Meckler Books.* 1-1-1988, 88-95.

Miller, John. "Louis Santop." *The Ballplayers, Arbor House, William Morrow.* 1-1-1990, 963.

Satch & Josh

Rogosin, Donn. "Satch vs. Josh." *The Sporting News*, 7-18-1981.

Lester, Larry & O'Neil, John. "Satch vs. Josh. The National Pastime, Society for American Baseball Research, Winter, 1992, 30-33.

Scales, George

Holway, John. "Historically Speaking: George Scales: The Rifle Arm of Negro Professional Baseball." *Black Sports*, 5-1-1973, 32-33.

Lester, Larry. "George Scales." *The Ballplayers, Arbor House, William Morrow.* 1-1-1990, 965.

Scantlebury, Pat

"Patricio Scantlebury, Baseball Player, 73." *Newark Star-Ledger*, 5-27-1991.

Rives, Bill. "Husky Pat Pulls Load as Dallas Hill Workhorse." *The Sporting News*, 8-11-1954, 33.

Scott, Joe

Williams, Larry. "Batting 1.000." *Commerical Appeal* (Memphis), 6-1-1991, A16.

Seay, Dickie

"Richard Seay." *Colored Baseball & Sports Monthly*, 10-1-1934, 20.

Smallwood, Woody

Brigham, Bob. "The Disarmed Rifle, Woody Smallwood." *Diamond Angle*, winter, 1-1-1992, 22-23.

Smith, Al

"Al Smith." *Ebony*, 10-1-1960, 85-88,92.

Hines, Rick. "He Took A Beer Bath in the '59 Series." *Sports Collectors Digest*, 6-21-1991, 188.

Smith, Chino

Holway, John. "Charlie "Chino" Smith." *Baseball Research Journal #7*, 1-1-1978, 63-67.

Holway, John. "Chino Smith: Black Fist, Black Bat." *Blackball Stars: Negro League Pioneers, Meckler Books.* 1-1-1988, 293-298.

Miller, John. "Chino Smith." *The Ballplayers, Arbor House, William Morrow.* 1-1-1990, 1011.

Riley, James A. "Chino Smith." *Biographical Dictionary of American Sports: Baseball*, D. Porter, Greenwood Press. 1-1-1987, 519.

Smith, Hilton

Baxter, Terry. "Hilton Smith." *Biographical Dictionary of American Sports: Baseball*, D. Porter, Greenwood Press. 1-1-1987, 520-21.

Holway, John. "Hilton Smith Remembers." *The Armchair Book of Baseball*, NY: Scribner's, 1-1-1987, 165-176.

Kleinknecht, Merl. "Hilton Smith." *The Ballplayers, Arbor House, William Morrow.* 1-1-1990, 1013.

St. Louis Black Bronchos

Debono, Paul. "1910: The St. Louis Black Bronchos." *American Visions*, 6-1-1993, 26-27.

St. Louis Stars

Pietrusza, David. "Night Baseball Comes to St. Louis." *National Pastime*, 6-1-1992.

Tiemann, Bob. "St. Louis Wins 1930 Series in Seven Games." *SABR 22 Convention Program*, 6-25-1992, 48-51.

Stamford Team

McGreal, Jim. "Stamford Team Fielded Six Black Players." *Baseball Research Journal #13*, 1-1-1984, 45-48.

Stearnes, Turkey

Bak, Richard. "After Words." *Detroit Monthly*, 5-1-1989, 124.

Bak, Richard. "Black Diamonds." *Michigan: The Magazine*, 4-5-1987, 92-107.

Bak, Richard. "Black Diamonds, Chapter 3." *The Golden Age of Baseball in Detroit*, 1-1-1991, 92-107.

Clark, Dick. "Hall of Fame Hopefuls: Norman "Turkey" Stearnes." *Discover Greatness—NLBM Yearbook*, 6-1-1993, 9.

Clark, Dick. "Norman Turkey Stearnes." *The Ballplayers, Arbor House, William Morrow.* 1-1-1990, 1039-40.

Holway, John. "Historically Speaking: Turkey Stearnes 'A Humdinger of a Hitter.'" *Black Sports*, 7-1-1976, 48-54,56.

Holway, John. "I Never Counted My Homers Unless They Won Games." *Detroit News Magazine*, 8-15-1971, 384.

Holway, John. "Norman 'Turkey' Stearnes: "I Never Counted My Homers." *Blackball Stars: Negro League Pioneers, Meckler Books.* 1-1-1988, 248-265.

Holway, John. "Turkey Stearnes." *Black Sports*, 5-1-1976, 48+

LaPointe, Joe. "Negro League Star Turkey Stearnes (obit)." *Detroit Free Press*, 9-6-1979.

Martin, Douglas D. "Norman Turkey Stearnes." *Biographical Dictionary of American Sports: Baseball*, D. Porter, Greenwood Press. 1-1-1987, 533-34.

Stephens, Jake

Holway, John. "Country Jake: Paul "Jake" Stephens." *Black Diamonds, Meckler Books.* 1-1-1989, 1-17.

Stewart, Charles W.

Howard, Allen. *Cincinnati Enquirer*, 5-21-1992, C6.

Stone, Toni

"Lady Ball Player." *Ebony*, 7-1-1953, 48-50,52-3.

"Speaking of People." *Ebony*, 9-1-1950, 4.

"Toni Stone—female baseball player." *Our World*, 7-1-1953.

Dallas, Bill. "Female Players Here July 19 in Negro League Twin Bill." *Philadelphia Evening Bulletin*, 7-7-1953.

Editor. "Black Woman Was Alone in Own League." *USA Today*, 7-2-1992, 2C

Editor. "Female Player Remembered by Major League Baseball." *Jet*, 6-1-1992, 50.

Forman, Ross. "Marcenia 'Toni' Stone: Veteran of Negro Leagues." *Sports Collectors Digest*, 8-7-1992, 177.

Gregorich, Barbara. "1954: Toni Stone." *American Visions*, 6-1-1993, 27.

Gregorich, Barbara. *Women At Play: The Story of Women in Baseball*. Harcourt & Brace, 3-1-1993, 169-171, 173-76.

Smith, Wendell. "First Woman Signed to Baseball Contract." *Our Sports*, 5-1-1953, 16-18.

Thomas, Ron. "Baseball's 'Intruder' Loved Game." *San Francisco Chronicle*, 8-23-1991.

Weaver, Mike. "Female Player Was A Minority of One." *San Jose Mercury News*, 8-11-1991, 1D, 3D

Stovey, George

Malloy, Jerry. "George Washington Stovey." *19th Century Stars, Society for American Baseball Research, Volume 2*, 1-1-1993.

Miller, John. "George Stovey." *The Ballplayers, Arbor House, William Morrow*. 1-1-1990, 1052.

Streeter, Sam

Holway, John. "Sam Streeter: Smartest Pitcher in Negro Leagues." *Baseball Research Journal #13*, 1-1-1984, 71-72.

Plott, Bill. "Sam Streeter." *The Ballplayers, Arbor House, William Morrow*. 1-1-1990, 1055.

Sukeforth, Clyde

Honig, Donald. *Baseball When the Grass Was Real*. Coward, McCann and Geohegan, 1-1-1975, 179-191.

Lincoln, C.E. "A Conversation with Clyde Sukeforth." *Baseball Research Journal #16*, 1-1-1991, 72-73.

Summers, Lonnie

Curran, Ron. "The Negro Leagues Revisited." *LA Weekly*, 4-3-1992, 18-19,26-28.

Suttles, Mule

Holway, John. "Hall of Fame Hopefuls: Mule Suttles." *Discover Greatness—NLBM Yearbook*, 6-1-1993, 4.

Holway, John. "Mule Suttles: "Kick, Mule." *Blackball Stars: Negro League Pioneers, Meckler Books*. 1-1-1988, 266-282.

Holway, John. "Not All Stars were White (Mules Suttles' All-Star Homerun)." *The Sporting News*, 7-1-1983, All-Star Special

Kleinknecht, Merl. "George Mule Suttles." *Biographical Dictionary of American Sports: Baseball*, D. Porter, Greenwood Press. 1-1-1987, 542-43.

Plott, Bill. "George Mule Suttles." *The Ballplayers, Arbor House, William Morrow*. 1-1-1990, 1062.

Sweatt, George

Holway, John. "George Sweatt: 'No Sweat' Would take Two Strikes, Then Tear Cover off Ball." *Black Sports*, 9-1-1975, 49,55,58.

Sykes, Doc

Carter, Dan T. *A Tragedy of the American South*. Oxford, 1-1-1969, 201.

Glauber, Bill. "Doc Sykes Was A Pitcher & Fighter Against Bigotry." *Baltimore Sun*, 4-29-1990, C7.

Taylor, Ben

"Circling the Wagons for Old Black Leaguer." *Washington Afro-American*, 9-28-1991, A15.

Bolton, Todd. "Hall of Fame Hopefuls: Ben Taylor." *Discover Greatness—NLBM Yearbook*, 6-1-1993, 7.

Editor. "Ben Taylor: Memorial Dedicated Negro League Great." *Washington Sun*, 4-2-1992, 17.

Editor. "Memorial Marker to Dedicate Old Time Star." *Dawn Magazine*, 3-28-1992.

Editor. "Taylor Gets Memorial." *USA Today Baseball Weekly*, 4-1-1992, 2.

Forman, Ross. "Negro League Group to Honor Deceased Star." *USA Today*, 4-1-1992.

Greczyn, Mary. "Honored in Death." *Greenville News*, 4-7-1992, 1D, 4D

Kerzel, Pat. "Error Is Corrected As Negro Leaguer Gets Grave Marker." *Arbutus Times*, 4-8-1992, 6.

Martin, Douglas D. "Ben Taylor." *Biographical Dictionary of American Sports: Baseball*, D. Porter, Greenwood Press. 1-1-1987, 548.

Miller, John. "Ben Taylor." *The Ballplayers, Arbor House, William Morrow*. 1-1-1990, 1070.

Taylor, C.I.

Holway, John. "Taylor Made for the Diamond." *Indianapolis Star Magazine*, 8-26-1973, 48, 50-52.

Kleinknecht, Merl. "Charles I. Taylor." *Biographical Dictionary of American Sports: Baseball*, D. Porter, Greenwood Press. 1-1-1987, 548-49.

Overfield, Joseph M. "C.I. Taylor." *The Ballplayers, Arbor House, William Morrow*. 1-1-1990, 1070.

Taylor, Candy Jim

Brown, Larry. "Candy Jim Taylor." *Colored Baseball & Sports Monthly*, 10-1-1934, 14.

Kleinknecht, Merl. "Candy Jim Taylor." *The Ballplayers, Arbor House, William Morrow*. 1-1-1990, 1070-71.

Taylor, Johnny

Fernandez, Angel. "Fue' Contratado el Pitcher Johnny Taylor." *Excelsior*, 2-23-1946, 46.

Holway, John. "Schoolboy Johnny Taylor." *Baseball Research Journal #16*, 36-44.

Holway, John. "Taylor Made for the Diamond." *Indianapolis Star Magazine*, 8-26-1973, 48,50-2.

Smith, George. "Hartford's Johnny Taylor Was Just Born Too Soon." *Hartford Courant*, 7-25-1976, sec C, p1.

Thomas, Clint

Baxter, Terry. "Clint Thomas." *Biographical Dictionary of American Sports: Baseball*, D. Porter, Greenwood Press. 1-1-1987, 552-53.

Kleinknecht, Merl. "Clint Thomas." *The Ballplayers, Arbor House, William Morrow*. 1-1-1990, 1080.

Whiteford, Mike. "Black DiMaggio Deserves a Niche." 7-14-1985, 2D

Thompson, Hank

"Hank Thompson: My Pick for Stardom." *Our World*, 9-1-1950.

Chapin, Dwight. "Henry Thompson Looks Back to the Glory Days." *Baseball Digest*, 9-1-1969, 45-49.

True, Frank C. "Baseball's Giant Killers." *Negro Digest*, 7-1-1951, 58-62.

Thurman, Bob

Obojoski, Robert. "SCD Profiles Former Reds Outfielder—Bob Thurman." *Sports Collectors Digest*, 10-11-1991, 210.

Tiant, Sr., Luis

Holway, John. "Will the Real Luis Tiant (Sr.) Stand Up." *Baseball Digest*, 2-1-1976, 74-78.

Lester, Larry. "Louis Tiant, Sr." *The Ballplayers, Arbor House, William Morrow*. 1-1-1990, 1088.

Yanthakos, Harry. "Luis Tiant Dares to Dream." *Black Sports*, 8-1-1975, 42-45.

Tinker, Harold

Ruck, Rob. "Harold Tinker: He Played with the Best on the Hill. " A Baseball Legend Looks Back." *Pittsburgh Magazine*, 8-1-1991, 29-31.

Torriente, Cristobal

Figueredo, Jorge S. "Nov. 4, 1920: The Day Torriente Outclassed Ruth." *Baseball Research Journal* #11, 1-1-1982, 130-131.

Holway, John. "The One-Man team—Cristobal Torriente." *Baseball Historical Review*, 1-1-1974, 72-74.

Miller, John. "Cristobal Torriente." *The Ballplayers, Arbor House, William Morrow.* 1-1-1990, 1097.

Trent, Ted

Grabar, Phil. "Ted Trent." *The Ballplayers, Arbor House, William Morrow.* 1-1-1990, 1100.

Tramell, Nat. "Theodore Trent." *Colored Baseball & Sports Monthly*, 10-1-1934, 9.

Trouppe, Quincy

Bennett, Chuck. "Remembering the Negro Leagues." *Sports Collectors Digest*, 7-21-1989, 154,56.

Elliott, Jeffrey. "Quincy Trouppe: Portrait of a Super Star Negro League Player." *Negro History Bulletin*, 3-1-1978, 804-7.

Forman, Ross. "Former All-Star Catcher Just Missed Majors." *Sports Collectors Digest*, 6-21-1991, 160,161.

Kleinknecht, Merl. "Quincy Trouppe." *The Ballplayers, Arbor House, William Morrow.* 1-1-1990, 1101.

Trouppe, Quincy. *20 Years Too Soon.* S and S Enterprises, 1-1-1977, book 285 pages.

Trouppe, Quincy. "Quincy Trouppe; Baseball Great and Catcher to Satchel Paige, Comments:." *Sepia*, 12-1-1977, 28-33.

United States League

"U.S. Negro League is Launched with Brown Dodgers in Brooklyn." *New York Times*, 5-8-1945.

Cohen, Leonard. "The Sports Parade." *New York Post*, 5-8-1945, 30.

Various

Shatzkin, Mike & Charlton, Jim. *The Ballplayers.* Arbor House, 1-1-1990, 1225 pages.

Vasquez, Armando

Coffey, Wayne. "Almost War-bound, Due to Pal Satchel." *New York Daily News*, 8-21-1991, 38.

Craft, David. "Former Negro Leaguer Armando Vazquez Profiled." *Sports Collectors Digest*, 6-21-1991, 110.

Kriegel, Mark. "His Time Came A Bit Too Soon." *New York Post*, 12-24-1991, 46.

Verona Black Sox

Butch, John. "Teams Are Losing Money, Players." *Clarion-Ledger (MS)*, 7-10-1990, 5C

Walker, Edsall

Amedio, Steve. "My, Those Were Some Times." *Schenectady Sunday Gazette*, 5-12-1991, D1,D5.

Goudrea, Mike. "Profile—Edsall Walker." *Metroland (Albany, NY)*, 6-14-1990, 13.

Jochnowitz, Jay. "Ex-Negro League Star Honored in Albany Ceremony." *Albany Times Union*, 7-2-1990, B1, B7.

Post, Paul. "Edsall Walker Remembers the Grays." *Sports Collectors Digest*, 6-21-1991, 104, 105.

Walker, Leonard "Bo"

Eckberg, John. "Former Ballplayer Gets Major-League Help." *Cincinnati Enquirer*, 9-18-1992.

Eckberg, John. "Pros Should Pinch-Hit for Ex-Players." *Cincinnati Enquirer*, 8-14-1992.

Walker, Moses Fleetwood

"A Belated Honor." *Oberlin News-Tribune*, 10-23-1990.

"Fleetwood Walker: The First Black Player in Major League Baseball." *Black Sports* #1, 11-1-1971, 48-49.

"Openers: No Matter How They Tell Jackie's Story, Fleet Was First." *The Sporting News*, 10-29-1990, 6.

"Two African Americans Inducted into Ohio Baseball Hall of Fame." *Toledo Journal*, 8-28-1991, 26.

Appleby, John. "Alumnus Was First Black Major Leaguer." *Oberlin Observer*, 10-25-1990.

Blaha, Tom. "Fleet Finally Gets His Recognition." *Touching All the Bases*, v1, no.3, 9-1-1991, 1,3.

Bolton, Todd. "Blacks Played in Majors Long Before Robinson." *The Herald-Mail*, 6-27-1992, D14.

Bowman, Larry. "Moses Fleetwood Walker: The 1st Black Major League BB Player." *Baseball History*, Premier, 1-1-1989, 61-74.

Brewer, William K. "Barehanded Catcher." *Negro Digest*, 10-1-1951, 85-87.

Cheeks, Dwayne. "Moses Walker in Majors Long Before Robinson." *Cleveland Plain Dealer*, 6-7-1975, 5D

Craig, Pete. "Oberlinian Was First Negro Star in Big Leagues." *Oberlin News-Tribune*, 12-28-1945.

Craig, Pete. "The Scoreboard." *Oberlin News-Tribune*, 12-28-1945.

Enrietto, John. "Better (66 Years) Late Than Never: Baseball Legend Fleetwood Walker finally Receive Dues." *Steubenville Herald-Star (Ohio)*, 10-19-1990.

Giancaterino, Randy. "1884: Moses Fleetwood Walker." *American Visions*, 6-1-1993, 25-26.

Hill, Bob. "Oberlin Club Honors Walker as First Black Major Leaguer." *Cleveland Plain Dealer*, 10-14-1990, 14-B

Hill, Bob. "Walker Recognition Rights A Wrong." *Cleveland Plain Dealer*, 10-14-1990, 1B, 10B

Hobson, Geoff. "Syracuse Had Black Player on 1888 Team." *Syracuse Herald American*, 6-21-1987.

Jacobs, Dan. "Oberlin's Black Baseball Player Honored." *Morning Journal (Lorain County, Ohio)*, 10-19-1990.

Jewell, Thomas. "'Fleet' Walker To Get Hall of Fame Honor." *Wheeling Intelligencer*, 8-14-1991, 1,7.

Jewell, Thomas. "Man of Many Firsts Get Recognition: Fleet Walker Receives Long-Awaited Headstone." *Wheeling Intelligencer*, 10-19-1990, 1,3.

Kinsey, Daniel C. "The History of Physical Education in Oberlin College, 1833—1890." date unknown. *Oberlin College, Master Thesis*

Lankiewicz, Donald. "Fleet Walker in the Twilight Zone." *Journal of the Cincinnati Hist. Society* #50, 6-1-1992, 2-11.

Linweber, Ralph. *The Toledo Baseball Guide of the Mud Hens.* Rossford, 1-1-1944, 7,14.

Luse, Vern. "Letter to the Editors." *The National Pastime*, Spring, 4-1-1985, 87-88.

Malloy, Jerry. "Bio on Moses Walker." *Nineteenth Century Stars,*

1-1-1989, 131.

Malloy, Jerry. "Out at Home: Baseball Draws the Color Line, 1887." *The National Pastime*, Fall, 9-1-1982, 14-28.

Matheney, Timothy Michael. *Heading for Home: Moses Fleetwood Walker's Encounter With Racism in America.* Princeton University, 1-1-1989, 103 pages. thesis.

Miller, Glen. "Moses Gets His Due: New Stone Marks Grave of First Black in Majors." *Chronicle Telegram (Oberlin)*, 10-19-1990.

Nutt, Amy. "An All-but-Forgotten First." *Sports Illustrated*, 6-15-1992.

Pluto, Terry. "When It Was a Whole Different Ballgame." *The Beacon (Akron, Ohio)* #19, 9-16-1991, 4-6,10-11.

Porter, Tana Mosier. "Bootleg Baseball." *Greater Toledo Magazine*, 5-1-1985, 26-27, 56.

Shults, Frederick David. *The History and Philosophy of Athletics for Men at Oberlin College.* Indiana University, 1-1-1967, dissertation

Walker, Moses Fleetwood. "Family File." *Jefferson County Historical Association.*

Walker, Moses Fleetwood. *Our Home Colony: A Treatise on the Past, Present and Future of the Negro Race in America.* Herald Printing Co., 1-1-1908.

Weiss, William J. "The First Negro in 20th Organized Baseball." *Insiders Baseball*, 1-1-1983, 58-60.

Wheeler, Lonnie. "Hounded out of Baseball." *Ohio Magazine*, 5-1-1993, 22-26, 53-55.

Williams, Nudie E. "Footnote to Trivia: Moses Fleetwood Walker & the All-American Dream." *Journal of American Culture*, Summer, 6-1-1988, 65-72.

Wittke, Carl. "Oberlinian Was First Negro in Major Leagues." *Oberlin News-Tribune*, 11-14-1946, 4.

Wolfe, Don. "First Black Big Leaguer to Get Grave Marker." *Toledo Blade*, 10-17-1990.

Warfield, Frank

Williams, Edith. "Frank Warfield." *The Ballplayers, Arbor House, William Morrow.* 1-1-1990, 1145.

Webb, Tweed

Feldman, Jay. "'I've Seen Them All': Tweed Webb, Baseball Historian." *St. Louis Limelight*, 9-1-1989.

Wells, Willie

Floto, James. "Willie Wells." *Diamond Angle*, V4, #2, 2-1-1993, 30.

Holway, John B. "Willie Wells, A Devil of an Infielder." *Black Sports*, 8-1-1973, 10-11,51.

Kelso, John. "Willie Wells: It Was A Good Time." *Austin American-Statesman*, 1-2-1977, A1, A16.

Riley, James A. *Dandy, Day & the Devil: A Trilogy of Negro League Biographies.* TK Publishers, 1-1-1988, 101-146.

Riley, James A. "Hall of Fame Hopefuls: Willie Wells." *Discover Greatness—NLBM Yearbook*, 6-1-1993, 13.

Riley, James A. "Willie Wells." *The Ballplayers, Arbor House, William Morrow.* 1-1-1990, 1156-57.

Ruck, Rob. "Willie Wells." *Biographical Dictionary of American Sports: Baseball*, D. Porter, Greenwood Press. 1-1-1987, 599-600.

Walker, Jackie. "Willie "Devil" Wells." *Black Sports*, 6-1-1975, 52,54.

Ward, Pamela. "Group Goes to Bat with Campaign to Honor Baseball Legend Wells." *Austin American-Statesman*, 1-2-1977, A1, A9.

West Coast Baseball

Washington, Wayne. "Fields of Forgotten Dreams, part 1." *San Jose Mercury News*, 2-24-1991, 1D, 8D-9D

Washington, Wayne. "Fields of Forgotten Dreams, part 2." *San Jose Mercury News*, 2-25-1991, 1C, 4C

White, Chaney

Bergen, Phil. "Chaney White." *The Ballplayers, Arbor House, William Morrow.* 1-1-1990, 1162-63.

White, Sol

Holway, John. "Sol White: White on Blackball." *Blackball Stars: Negro League Pioneers, Meckler Books.* 1-1-1988, 1-7.

Malloy, Jerry. "Bio on Sol White." *Nineteenth Century Stars*, 1-1-1989, 136.

Miller, John. "Sol White." *The Ballplayers, Arbor House, William Morrow.* 1-1-1990, 1166.

White, Sol. *Sol White's Official Baseball Guide or History of Colored Baseball.* Camden House, 1-1-1984, 128 pages.

Wickware, Frank

Keetz, Frank. "When 'The Big Train' Met 'The Red Ant'." *Baseball Research Journal #20*, 10-1-1991, 63-65.

Miller, John. "Frank Wickware." *The Ballplayers, Arbor House, William Morrow.* 1-1-1990, 1169.

Wilkinson, J.L.

Holway, J. & Kleinknecht, M. "James L. Wilkinson." *Biographical Dictionary of American Sports: Baseball*, D. Porter, Greenwood Press. 1-1-1987, 608-9.

Holway, John. "J.L. Wilkinson: The Gift of Light." *Blackball Stars: Negro League Pioneers, Meckler Books.* 1-1-1988, 327-343.

Lester, Larry. "J.L. Wilkinson." *The Ballplayers, Arbor House, William Morrow.* 1-1-1990, 1171-72.

Williams, Charlie

Tramell, Nat. "Charles 'Lefty' Williams." *Colored Baseball & Sports Monthly*, 10-1-1934, 13.

Williams, Jesse

Etkin, Jack. "Ex-Monarch Remained Strong to the End." *Kansas City Star*, 2-28-1990.

Etkin, Jack. "Jesse Williams." *Innings Ago, Normandy Square Publications*, 1-1-1987, 68-77.

Williams, Smokey Joe

"Rube and Smokey Joe: Black Baseball Greats." *Dawn Magazine*, 9-1-1977, 12-14+

Chalk, Ocania. "Hall of Fame Hopefuls: Smokey Joe Williams." *Discover Greatness—NLBM Yearbook*, 6-1-1993, 11.

Coates, John M. "Smokey Joe Williams." *Baseball Historical Review*, 1-1-1973, 46-47.

Coates, John M. "Smokey Joe Williams." *Baseball Research Journal #2*, 1-1-1973, 54-56.

Holway, J. & Kleinknecht, M. "Smokey Joe Williams." *Biographical Dictionary of American Sports: Baseball*, D. Porter, Greenwood Press. 1-1-1987, 611-12.

Holway, John. "Joe Williams: Smokey Joe." *Blackball Stars: Negro League Pioneers, Meckler Books.* 1-1-1988, 61-78.

Miller, John. "Smokey Joe Williams." *The Ballplayers, Arbor House, William Morrow.* 1-1-1990, 1177-78.

Wilmore, Apples

Hines, Rick. "An Interview with Al 'Apples' Wilmore." *Sports Collectors Digest*, 11-20-1992, 160-161.

Wilson, Artie

Cooper, Tony. "Breaking the PCL Color Barrier." *San Francisco Chronicle*, 3-1-1993.

Forman, Ross. "Negro League great Artie Wilson profiled." *Sports Collectors Digest*, 1-29-1993, 76-77.

Wilson, Jud

Holway, J. & Kleinknecht, M. "Jud Wilson." *Biographical Dictionary of American Sports: Baseball*, D. Porter, Greenwood Press. 1-1-1987, 619-20.

Holway, John. "Jud 'Boojum' Wilson." *Baltimore Sun Magazine*, 6-24-1979, 19-23.

Holway, John. "Jud Wilson: Boojum." *Blackball Stars: Negro League Pioneers, Meckler Books*. 1-1-1988, 200-216.

Williams, Edith. "Jud Wilson." *The Ballplayers, Arbor House, William Morrow*. 1-1-1990, 1187.

Wilson, Tom

Hendrix, Tom. "I Remember Tom." *Black Music*, 1-1-1983, 15 pages.

Mills, Prentice. "Southern Stars: Dixie's Contributions to the Negro Leagues." *Black Ball News*, V1, #2, 6-1-1992, 9-16.

Winters, Nip

Grabar, Phil. "Nip Winters." *The Ballplayers, Arbor House, William Morrow*. 1-1-1990, 1192.

Holway, John. "How I Struck out Babe Ruth and Beat Lefty Grove." *Columbia History Magazine (Washington, DC)*, 1971, 1-1-1970, 752-757.

Woods, Parnell

Kleinknecht, Merl. "Parnell Woods." *The Ballplayers, Arbor House, William Morrow*. 1-1-1990, 1197.

World Series

Renfroe, Chico. "The Last of the Truly Great Negro World Series, Part I." *Atlanta Daily World*, 4-14-1977, 9.

Wright, Bill

Craft, David. "'Wild Bill' Was the Wright man for the Job." *Sports Collectors Digest*, 6-21-1991, 86,87.

Miller, John. "Bill Wright." *The Ballplayers, Arbor House, William Morrow*. 1-1-1990, 1202.

Riley, James A. "Wild Bill Wright: A Mexican League Legend Comes Home." *Old Tyme Baseball News*, 6-1-1991, V3, I3, 17.

Smith, Shelley. "Remembering Their Game." *Sports Illustrated*, 7-6-1992, 86.

Wright, Johnny

Bell, Don. "The Wright Stuff." *MVP Magazine: Best Sport Stories of 1986*, 1-1-1986, 260-71.

Wright, Johnny & Jackie Robinson

"May Bar Negroes." *Erie Daily Times*, 3-22-1946, 23.

Yancey, Bill

Tramell, Nat. "The Dr. Jekyl and Mr. Hyde of Athletics." *Colored Baseball & Sports Monthly*, 10-1-1934, 4.

Yokeley, Laymon

Holway, John. "I Remember Pitching Six No-Hitters for the Black Sox." *Baltimore Sun Magazine*, 7-19-1970.

Courier's All-Time All-Stars

The *Pittsburgh Courier*, the widely circulating black weekly that had followed the Negro Leagues from their beginnings and covered the fall of the color line in the majors, selected an All-Time All-Star team in 1952. The 19 men on the first team included nine men eventually inducted into the Baseball Hall of Fame, and there were three members of the Hall on the second squad.

	First Team	*Second Team*
1B	Buck Leonard*	Ben Taylor
2B	Jackie Robinson*	Bingo DeMoss
SS	John Henry Lloyd*	Willie Wells
3B	Oliver Marcelle	Judy Johnson*
LF	Monte Irvin*	Pete Hill
CF	Oscar Charleston*	Cool Papa Bell*
RF	Cristobal Torriente	Chino Smith
C	Josh Gibson*	Roy Campanella*
	Biz Mackey	Bruce Petway
P	Joe Williams, Dave Brown, Satchel Paige*, Dick Redding, Bullet Rogan, Nip Winters, John Donaldson Dizzy Dismukes, Bill Foster, Don Newcombe	
Utl	Martin Dihigo*	John Beckwith
	Sam Bankhead	Newt Allen
Mgr	Rube Foster*	Cum Posey
Coach	Dizzy Dismukes	C.I. Taylor
	Danny McClellan	Dave Malarcher

* Member, Baseball Hall of Fame

—Clark

"Double Duty"

The famous writer Damon Runyon began his long career in New York writing sports, and although the white-owned newspapers paid little attention to black baseball in the 1930s, Runyon would frequent Negro League games. As historian Donn Rogosin recounts in his book, *Invisible Men*, at a doubleheader in 1932 even the experienced Runyon was fascinated with the Pittsburgh Crawford who caught Satchel Paige's first game shutout, and then took the mound in the second game to pitch his own shutout. Runyon wrote about what he had seen, and gave Ted "Double Duty" Radcliffe the nickname he carries to this day.

Newspapers

and

Sportswriters

On March 16, 1827, New York residents Rev. Samuel Cornish and John Brown Russwurm published the first black newspaper in America. In tune with the racial climate of the times, it was called *Freedom's Journal.*

The editorial in that first edition signified the need for the black press stating: "…We wish to plead our own cause. Too long have others spoken for us. Too long has the public been deceived by misrepresentation in things which concern us dearly.…"

With this concept in mind the black press was born. Bias in the white daily newspapers had created a need for a vehicle to report on the other professional baseball teams of our National Pastime—the Negro Leagues. As legendary insurance entrepreneur A.G. Gaston, of Birmingham, once said, "Successful businesses are founded on needs."

In 1928, the Scott Brothers, William and Cornelius, launched the *Atlanta Daily World*, the first successful black daily. And earlier in 1909, P. Bernard Young, Sr., started the *Norfolk Journal & Guide*. Young avoided the sensationalism prominent in many newspapers, and emphasized accuracy. His *Journal and Guide* received respect as a high quality newspaper. Press aficionado referred to it as *The New York Times* of the black press.

This section does not include every newspaper with Negro League data, but it is a geographical listing of daily and weekly papers, some white, but mostly black, that carried regular information about the Negro Leagues. Most of the newspapers are or were minority owned enterprises catering to an African-American audience. The white newspapers included here have traditionally featured noteworthy coverage on the subject.

The *Pittsburgh Courier* and the *Chicago Defender* carried the most detailed information. The *Defender* focused on games and players from the Midwest, while the *Courier* tended to emphasize players and games played along the Eastern seaboard.

In 1905, Robert S. Abbott, from Georgia, pitched the first *Chicago Defender* for five cents a copy. Within fifteen years, the *Defender*'s national circulation rose to more than 200,000 copies a week. This paper, like the *Afro-American*, became a sort of chain. Issues were published in several cities, with different local news, but with the same national coverage.

Lawyer Robert Lee Vann, from North Carolina, along with five men, started the *Pittsburgh Courier* in 1910. Thirty-five years later the *Courier* had a national circulation of 300,000.

Other papers with the extensive coverage were the *New York Amsterdam News*, the *Indianapolis Freeman*, the *Baltimore Afro-American*, and the *Kansas City Call*.

The black press was blessed with many gifted writers. Listed below are twenty-two of the most influential African-American writers on Negro Leagues baseball during its heyday. These men, like their ballplaying counterparts, struggled for recognition and respect in their field. We hope that someday they will receive their just due.

Sam Lacy.
Sam Lacy

Joe Bostic—*New York Peoples Voice*
St. Clair Bourne—*New York Age, New York Amsterdam News*
Art Carter—*Afro-American*
William Clark—*New York Age*
Romeo Dougherty—*New York Amsterdam News*
Al Dunmore—*Pittsburgh Courier*
Leon Herbert Hardwick—*Afro-American*
Mal Goode—*Pittsburgh Courier*
Cal J. Jacox—*Norfolk Journal & Guide*
John J. Johnson—*Kansas City Call*
Mabray "Doc" Kountze—*Boston Chronicle*
Sam Lacy—*Afro-American*
Alvin Moses—*New York Age*
Al Monroe—*Abbott's Monthly*
Ric Roberts—*Atlanta World*
Wendell Smith—*Pittsburgh Courier, Chicago HeraldAmerican*
Al Sweeney—*Washington Tribune, Afro-American*
Chester Washington—*Pittsburgh Courier, Los Angeles Wave*
Normal "Tweed" Webb—*St. Louis Argus*
Rollo Wilson—*Philadelphia Tribune*
A.S. "Doc" Young—*Chicago Defender, Los Angeles Sentinel*
Frank "Fay" Young—*Chicago Defender*

Revealing editorials were written by the following players:
William "Dizzy" Dismukes
Andrew "Rube" Foster
Cumberland Posey
Ben Taylor
C.I. Taylor

Special mention for their books on the subject.
Ocania Chalk
Edwin B. Henderson

Newspapers that Regularly Carried Information about Negro Leagues Baseball

City	Newspaper
Alabama	
Birmingham	*Age Herald*
Birmingham	*Ledger*
Birmingham	*News*
Birmingham	*Post*
Birmingham	*World*
Birmingham	*Reporter*
Mobile	*Weekly Press*

City	Newspaper		City	Newspaper

California
- Los Angeles — *California Eagle*
- Los Angeles — *New Age Dispatch*
- Los Angeles — *Sentinel*
- Los Angeles — *Times*
- Los Angeles — *Wave*

Colorado
- Denver — *Democrat*
- Denver — *Post*
- Denver — *Rocky Mountain News*
- Denver — *Star*

District of Columbia
- Washington — *Afro-American*
- Washington — *Bee*
- Washington — *Daily News*
- Washington — *Post*
- Washington — *Tribune*

Delaware
- Wilmington — *Journal*

Florida
- Miami — *Florida Courier*
- Miami — *Times*
- Orlando — *Florida Sun & Mirror*

Georgia
- Albany — *Southwest Georgian*
- Atlanta — *Age*
- Atlanta — *Inquirer*
- Atlanta — *Daily World*
- Atlanta — *Independent*
- Atlanta — *Post*
- Atlanta — *Voice*
- Augusta — *Colored American*
- Augusta — *News*
- Augusta — *Union*
- Columbus — *Chronicle*
- Macon — *Sentinel*
- Macon — *Times*
- Savannah — *Tribune*

Hawaii
- Honolulu — *Star Bulletin*

Illinois
- Chicago — *American Sports Weekly*
- Chicago — *Blade*
- Chicago — *Broad Ax*
- Chicago — *Collyer's Eye*
- Chicago — *Conservator*
- Chicago — *Daily Journal*
- Chicago — *Daily News*
- Chicago — *Defender* (City Edition)
- Chicago — *Defender* (National Edition)
- Chicago — *Enterprise*
- Chicago — *Evening Post*
- Chicago — *Herald American*
- Chicago — *Inter-Ocean*
- Chicago — *Journal*
- Chicago — *Plaindealer*
- Chicago — *Sun Times*
- Chicago — *Times*
- Chicago — *Tribune*
- Chicago — *Whip*
- Chicago — *World*

Indiana
- Indianapolis — *Freeman*
- Indianapolis — *News*
- Indianapolis — *Star*
- Indianapolis — *Ledger*
- Indianapolis — *Recorder*
- Indianapolis — *World*

Iowa
- Des Moines — *Algona Advance*
- Des Moines — *Algona Upper Des Moines*
- Des Moines — *Iowa Bystander*
- Des Moines — *Upper Des Moines Republican*
- Dubuque — *Daily Times*
- Sioux City — *Journal*

Kansas
- Independence — *Daily Reporter*
- Kansas City — *Advocate* (Independent Negro)
- Kansas City — *Daily American*
- Kansas City — *Evening Star*
- Kansas City — *Kansan*
- Parsons — *Parson Weekly Blade*
- Topeka — *Herald*
- Topeka — *Plaindealer*
- Wichita — *Evening Eagle Beacon*
- Wichita — *Eagle*

Kentucky
- Louisville — *Defender*

Louisiana
- New Orleans — *Black Data Weekly*
- New Orleans — *Louisiana Weekly*
- New Orleans — *Republican Courier*
- New Orleans — *Southern Republican*
- New Orleans — *Tribune*
- New Orleans — *Weekly Louisianian*
- Shreveport — *Sun*

Maryland
- Annapolis — *Negro Appeal*
- Baltimore — *Afro-American*
- Baltimore — *Commonwealth*
- Baltimore — *Evening News*
- Baltimore — *News Post*
- Baltimore — *Sun*
- Baltimore — *Weekly Herald*

Massachusetts
- Boston — *Chronicle*
- Boston — *Globe*
- Boston — *Post*

Michigan
- Adrian — *Weekly Times*
- Adrian — *Daily Times & Expositor*
- Detroit — *Contender*
- Detroit — *Free Press*
- Detroit — *Leader*
- Detroit — *Michigan Chronicle*
- Detroit — *Plaindealer*
- Detroit — *State News*
- Detroit — *Times*
- Detroit — *Tribune*
- Grand Rapids — *Democrat*
- Grand Rapids — *Press*
- Grand Rapids — *State News*

City	Newspaper	City	Newspaper
Minnesota		New York	*Herald Tribune*
Minneapolis	*National Accounts*	New York	*Journal American*
Minneapolis	*Star*	New York	*Long Island Daily Press*
Minneapolis	*Twin City*	New York	*Met*
St. Paul	*Dispatch*	New York	*Negro World*
St. Paul	*Mirror Press*	New York	*Mercury*
St. Paul	*Recorder*	New York	*Sun*
Missouri		New York	*News*
Kansas City	*American*	New York	*People's Voice*
Kansas City	*American Citizen*	New York	*Post*
Kansas City	*Call*	New York	*Spirit of the Times*
Kansas City	*Journalist*	New York	*The Sporting Times*
Kansas City	*Liberator*	New York	*Times*
Kansas City	*Missouri Messenger*	New York	*Tribune*
Kansas City	*Rising Sun*	New York	*Weekly Advocate*
Kansas City	*Star*	New York	*World Telegram*
Kansas City	*Sun*	Rochester	*Democrat and Chronicle*
Kansas City	*Times*	**North Carolina**	
St. Louis	*American*	Charlotte	*Post*
St. Louis	*Argus*	Durham	*Carolina Times*
St. Louis	*Globe Democrat*	Raleigh	*Carolinian*
St. Louis	*Independent Clarion*	Wilmington	*Journal*
St. Louis	*Independent News*	**North Dakota**	
St. Louis	*Post Dispatch*	Bismarck	*Tribune*
Nebraska		**Ohio**	
Lincoln	*Nebraska State Journal*	Cincinnati	*Enquirer*
Omaha	*Bee*	Cincinnati	*Journal*
Omaha	*Enterprise*	Cincinnati	*Weekly Enquirer*
Omaha	*Monitor*	Cleveland	*Advocate*
Omaha	*Star*	Cleveland	*Afro-American*
New Jersey		Cleveland	*Call & Post*
Atlantic City	*Evening News*	Cleveland	*Full Express*
Atlantic City	*Press*	Cleveland	*Gazette*
Newark	*Afro-American*	Cleveland	*Journal*
Newark	*Evening News*	Cleveland	*Plain Dealer*
Newark	*New Jersey Herald News*	Columbus	*Call & Post*
Newark	*Call*	Columbus	*Citizen*
Newark	*Star Ledger*	Columbus	*Dispatch*
New York		Columbus	*Ohio State Journal*
Babylon	*South Side Signal*	Dayton	*Daily Journal*
Binghamton	*Daily Leader*	Dayton	*Daily News*
Brooklyln	*Daily Eagle*	Toledo	*Blade*
Brooklyn	*American*	**Oklahoma**	
Buffalo	*American*	Crescent	*Crescent City Times*
Buffalo	*Criterion*	Enid	*Daily Eagle*
Frankfurt	*Evening Telegram*	Enid	*Morning News*
Long Island	*Daily Press*	Langston	*City Herald*
New York	*Age*	Muskogee	*Scimeter*
New York	*Amsterdam News*	Muskogee	*Watchman Lantern*
New York	*Baseball Tribune*	Oklahoma City	*Black Dispatch*
New York	*Black Monitor*	Oklahoma City	*Daily Oklahoman*
New York	*Clipper*	Okmulgee	*Daily Times*
New York	*Colored American*	Ponca City	*Times*
New York	*Daily Mirror*	Tonkawa	*Tonkawa News* (Salt Fork)
New York	*Daily News*	Tulsa	*Daily World*
New York	*Daily Worker*	Tulsa	*Oklahoma Eagle*
New York	*Dispatch*	Tulsa	*Sun*
New York	*Freedom's Journal*	Tulsa	*Tribune*
New York	*Globe*		

City	Newspaper
Pennsylvania	
Homestead	*Daily Messenger*
Norristown	*Daily Herald*
Philadelphia	*Afro-American*
Philadelphia	*American*
Philadelphia	*Daily Evening Bulletin*
Philadelphia	*Daily News*
Philadelphia	*Evening Item (City Item)*
Philadelphia	*Evening Ledger*
Philadelphia	*Independent*
Philadelphia	*Inquirer*
Philadelphia	*North American*
Philadelphia	*Old Fellow's Journal*
Philadelphia	*Public Ledger*
Philadelphia	*Record*
Philadelphia	*The Item*
Philadelphia	*The Sporting Life*
Philadelphia	*Tribune*
Pittsburgh	*American*
Pittsburgh	*Courier*
Pittsburgh	*Daily Worker*
Pittsburgh	*Press*
Pittsburgh	*Record*
Pittsburgh	*Politician*
Pittsburgh	*Post Gazette*
Pittsburgh	*Sun Telegraph*
York	*Gazette & Daily*
York	*Gazette*
South Carolina	
	South Carolina Journal & Guide
South Dakota	
Alexandria	*Journal*
Sioux Falls	*Argus Leader*
Tennessee	
Chattanooga	*Daily Times*
Chattanooga	*Defender*
Knoxville	*Flashlight Herald*
Memphis	*Buff City News*
Memphis	*Commercial Appeal*
Memphis	*Free Speech*
Memphis	*World*
Nashville	*Globe*
Texas	
Dallas	*Informer*
Dallas	*Item*
Dallas	*Weekly*
Fort Worth	*Hornet*
Houston	*Defender*
Houston	*Informer*
Houston	*Independent*
Houston	*Observer*
Houston	*Western Star*
Tyler	*Morning Telegraph*
Waco	*Messenger*
Virginia	
Norfolk	*Journal & Guide*
Richmond	*Afro-American*
Roanoke	*Tribune*

City	Newspaper
Wisconsin	
Milwaukee	*Enterprise Blade*
Canada	
Guelph, Ontario	*Herald*
Cuba	
Havana	*La Lucha*
Japan	
Tokyo	*Japan Times & Mail*

Sources: *American Newspapers*, W. Gregory.
Union List of Newspapers , Available in many academic libraries.

   (The true value of these newpapers was actually demonstrated by the active research of the members of the Negro Leagues Committee of SABR and others interested in the Negro Leagues.)

Oscar Charleston.
Anna Bradley

Reference Books

Listed below are books that have information vital to researchers and educators. This list does not include *all* books with pertinent information about the Negro Leagues. We have selected these books because we think they are most valuable to the serious student of Negro baseball history.

Allen, Maury. *Jackie Robinson: A Life Remembered*. New York, NY: Franklin Watts, 1987 (OP)

Alvarez, Mark. *The Official Baseball Hall of Fame Story of Jackie Robinson*. New York, NY: Little Simon, 1990 (OP).

Ashe, Arthur. *A Hard Road to Glory: The History of the AfricanAmerican Athlete*. New York: Amistad Books, 1988, Volumes 1 & 2. Reprinted Amistad Books, 1993

Bankes, James. *The Pittsburgh Crawfords: The Lives and Times of Black Baseball's Most Exciting Team!* Dubuque, IL: William Brown Publishers, 1991.

Barber, Red. 1947, *When All Hell Broke Loose in Baseball*. Garden City, NY: Doubleday & Co., 1982 (OP). Reprint. 1993

Black, Joe. *Ain't Nobody Better Than You*. Scottsdale, AZ: Ironwood Lithographers, 1983 (OP).

Brashler, William. *Josh Gibson: A Life in the Negro Leagues*. New York, NY: Harper and Row, 1978 (OP).

Bruce, Janet. *The Kansas City Monarchs: Champions of Black Baseball*. Lawrence, KS: University of Kansas Press, 1985.

Campanella, Roy. *It's Good To Be Alive*. Boston, MA: Little, Brown and Company, 1959 (OP).

Chadwick, Bruce. *When the Game was Black and White: The Illustrated History of Baseball's Negro Leagues*. New York, NY: Abbeville Press, 1992

Chalk, Ocania. *Black College Sports*. New York, NY: Dodd, Mead & Company, 1976 (OP).

_____. *Pioneers of Black Sports*. New York, NY: Dodd, Mead & Company, 1975 (OP).

Charlton, Jim & Shatzkin, Mike. *The Ballplayers*. New York, NY: William Morrow, 1990.

Cooper, Michael. *Playing America's Game: The Story of Negro League Baseball*. New York, NY: Lodestar Books, 1993

Craft, David. *The Negro Leagues: 40 Years of Black Professional Baseball in Words and Pictures*. Avenel, NJ: Crescent Books, 1993.

Dexter, Charles & Robinson, Jackie. *Baseball Has Done It*. New York, NY: J.B. Lippincott, 1964 (OP).

Dials, Lou. *Life in the Negro Leagues*. Self Published. 1978 (OP).

Dixon, Phil S. & Hannigan, Patrick. *The Negro Baseball Leagues: A Photographic History, 1867-1955*. Mattituck, NY: Amereon House, (1992).

Duckett, Alfred & Robinson, Jackie. *I Never Had It Made*. New York, NY: G.P. Putnam's Sons, 1972 (OP).

Etkin, Jack. *Innings Ago (Recollections by Kansas City Ballplayers)*. Kansas City, MO: Normandy Square Publications, 1987.

Fields, Wilmer. *My Life in the Negro Leagues*. Westport, CT: Meckler Books, 1992.

Frommer, Harvey. *Rickey & Robinson: The Men Who Broke Baseball's Color Barrier*. New York, NY: Collier-Macmillan Publishers, 1982 (OP).

Gardner, Robert & Shortelle, Dennis. *The Forgotten Players: The Story of Black Baseball in America*. New York, NY: Walker and Company, 1993.

Hardwick, Leon Herbert. *Blacks in Baseball*. Los Angeles, CA: Pilot Historical Association, 1980 (OP).

Hardwick, Leon & Manley, Effa. *Negro Baseball... Before Integration* (paperback). Chicago, IL: Adam Press, 1976 (OP).

Henderson, Edwin Bancroft. *The Negro in Sports*. Washington, DC: Associated Publishers, 1939 (OP). Reprinted, 1949. (OP).

Holway, John B. *Black Diamonds: Life in the Negro Leagues from the Men Who Lived It*. Westport, CT: Meckler Books, 1989. Reprint. New York, NY: Stadium Books, 1991.

_____. *Blackball Stars: Negro League Pioneers*. Westport, CT: Meckler Books, 1988. Reprint. New York, NY: Carroll & Graf Publishers, 1992.

_____. *Bullet Joe and the Monarchs*. Washington, DC: Capital Press, 1984 (OP).

_____. *Josh and Satch: The Life and Times of Josh Gibson and Satchel Paige*. Westport: Meckler Books, 1991. Reprint. Carrol & Graf Publishers, 1992.

_____. *The Father of Black Baseball: Rube Foster*. Washington, DC: Pretty Pages, 1981 (OP).

_____. *Smokey Joe and the Cannonball*. Washington, DC: Capital Press, 1983 (OP).

_____. *Voices from the Great Black Baseball Leagues*. New York, NY: Dodd, Mead Company, 1975 (OP). Reprinted, New York, NY: Decapo Press, 1993.

Humphrey, Kathryn Long. *Satchel Paige*. New York, NY: Franklin Watts, 1988.

Kountze, Mabray "Doc". *50 Sports Years Along Memory Lane*. Medford, MA: Mystic Valley Press, 1979 (OP).

Lebovitz, Hal with Satchel Paige. *Satchel Paige's Own Story: Pitchin' Man* (paperback). Self published, 1948 (OP).

O'Connor, Jim. *Jackie Robinson and the Story of All-Black Baseball*. New York, NY: Random House, 1989 (OP).

Paige, LeRoy "Satchel" (as told to David Lipman). *Maybe I'll Pitch Forever*. Garden City, NY: Doubleday & Company, 1961 (OP). Reprint by University of Nebraska, 1993.

Moore, Joseph Thomas. *Pride Against Prejudice: The Biography of Larry Doby*. New York, NY: Praeger Publishers, (1988).

Overmyer, James E. *Newark Eagles*. Scarecrow Books, 1993.

Peterson, Robert. *Only The Ball Was White: A History of Legendary Black Players and All-Black Professional Teams*. Englewood Cliffs, NJ: Prentice-Hall Publishers, 1970. Reprint. New York, NY: McGraw-Hill, 1984, Oxford University Press, 1992.

Porter, David L. *Biographical Dictionary of American Sports: Baseball*. Westport, CO: Greenwood Press, 1987.

Retort, Robert D. *Pictorial Negro League Legends Album*. New Castle, PA: Commercial Printing, 1992.

Riley, James A. *All-Time, All-Stars of Black Baseball*. Cocoa, FL: TK Publishers, 1983 (OP).

_____. *Dandy, Day and the Devil: a Trilogy of Negro League Baseball*. Cocoa, FL: TK Publishers, 1987.

Robinson, Jackie. *My Own Story*. New York, NY: Greenberg, 1948 (OP).

Rogosin, Donn. *Invisible Men: Life in the Negro Leagues*. New York: Atheneum, 1983.

Rowan, Carl T. (with Jackie Robinson). *Wait till Next Year: The Life Story of Jackie Robinson*. New York: Random House, 1960 (OP).

Rubin, Robert. *Satchel Paige, All-Time Baseball Great* (OP) 1974.

Ruck, Rob. *Sandlot Seasons: Black Sport in Pittsburgh*. Urbana: University of Illinois Press, 1987. Reprint, 1993.

Ruck, Rob. *The Tropic of Baseball: Baseball in the Dominican Republic*. Westport, CT: Meckler Publishing, 1991, New York, Carroll & Graf, 1993

Rust, Art, Jr. *Get That Nigger Off The Field: An Oral History of Black Ballplayers from the Negro Leagues to the Present*. 1976 (OP). Reprint. Brooklyn Book Mail Services, 1992.

Shapiro, Milton J. *The Roy Campanella Story*. New York, NY: Julian Messner, 1958 (OP).

Shirley, David. *Satchel Paige: Baseball Great*. New York, NY: Chelsea House Publishers, 1993.

Trouppe, Quincy. *Twenty Years Too Soon*. Los Angeles, CA: Sands Enterprises, 1977 (OP).

Tygiel, Jules. *Baseball's Great Experiment: Jackie Robinson & His Legacy*. New York, NY: Oxford Press, 1983. Reprint 1993.

Wheeler, Lonnie. *I Had A Hammer: The Hank Aaron Story*. New York, NY: Harper Collins, 1991.

White, Sol. *Sol White's Official Baseball Guide: History of Colored Baseball*. Philadelphia, PA: H. Walter Schlichter, 1907. Reprint, Columbia, SC: Camden House, 1984.

Whitehead, Charles A. *Man and His Diamonds: The Story of Rube Foster*. New York, NY: Vantage Press, 1980 (OP).

Young, A.S. "Doc". *Great Negro Baseball Stars and How They Made the Major Leagues*. New York, NY: A.S. Barnes, 1953 (OP).

_____. *Negro First in Sports*. Chicago, IL: Johnson Publishing Co., 1963.

The Midnight Game

In the mid 1930s the Pittsburgh Crawfords and the Homestead Grays squared off in the earliest start for a game in baseball history, with the first pitch thrown at midnight. Crawfords owner Gus Greenlee had become so disgusted with the loss of lucrative Sunday night playing dates caused by a Pennsylvania "blue law" ending Sunday games at 6:59 p.m. that he decided to make a point by scheduling a game at his Greenlee Field for midnight Monday morning.

Theses

and

Dissertations

Negro Leagues

Cable, Dale, "Jackie Robinson and the Integration of Organized Baseball," Unpublished Master Thesis, Allegheny College, Meadville, Pennsylvania, 1979.

Farmer, Greene, Jr., "Social Implications of Black Professional Baseball in the United States." Doctoral Dissertation, United States International University, San Diego, California, 1975.

Goldman, Marty, "If Only You Was White: Sixty Years of Baseball Apartheid." Unpublished Thesis, College Unknown, (BL-3376.82), 1981.

Harvey, John Albert, "The Role of American Negroes in Organized Baseball." Unpublished Doctoral Dissertation, Columbia University, New York, New York, 1961.

Heaphy, Leslie A., "The Growth and Decline of the Negro Leagues," Unpublished Master Thesis, University of Toledo, Toledo, Ohio, 1989.

Joyce, Allan E., "The Atlanta Black Crackers." Unpublished Master Thesis, Emory University, Atlanta, Georgia, 1975.

Kinsey, Daniel C., "The History of Physical Education in Oberlin College, 1833-1890," Unpublished Master Thesis, Oberlin College, Oberlin, Ohio, date unknown. [Moses Fleetwood Walker]

Leffler, Robert V. Jr., "History of Black Baseball in Baltimore from 1913 to 1951," Unpublished Master Thesis, Morgan State University, Baltimore, Maryland, 1974.

Levy, Scott Jarman, "Lily Dippers, Sockamayocks, and the Blue Goose: Black Baseball and the Color Line," Unpublished Master Thesis, Washington University, St. Louis, Missouri, 1989.

Matheney, Timothy Michael, "Heading for Home: Moses Fleetwood Walker's Encounter with Racism in America," Unpublished Master Thesis, Princeton University, Princeton, New Jersey, 1989.

Ostenby, Peter Marshall, "Other Games, Other Glory: The Memphis Red Sox and the Trauma of Integration, 1948-1955," Unpublished Master Thesis, University of North Carolina, Chapel Hill, North Carolina, 1989.

Richardson, Andrew, "A Retrospective Look at the Negro Leagues and Professional Negro Baseball Players," Unpublished Master Thesis, San Jose State University, San Jose, California, 1980.

Rogosin, William Donn, "Black Baseball: The Life in the Negro League," Doctoral Dissertation, University of Texas, Austin, Texas, 1981. (DAI 35, No. 94, 3005-A)

Sheingold, Peter, M., "In Black and White: Sam Lacy's Campaign to Integrate Baseball," Partial Fulfillment for Bachelor of Arts Degree in American History, Hampshire College, Amherst, Massachusetts, 1992.

Shortelle, Dennis, P., "They Also Played," Unpublished Master Thesis, Wesleyan University, Middletown, Connecticut, 1985.

Shults, Frederick David, "The History and Philosophy of Athletics for Men at Oberlin College," Doctoral dissertation, Indiana University, South Bend, Indiana, 1967. [Moses Fleetwood Walker]

Related Theses and Dissertations

Anderson, Torben, "Race Discrimination by Major League Baseball Fans," Unpublished Doctoral Dissertation, University of Washington, Seattle, Washington, 1988.

Coursey, Leon, M., "The Life of Edwin Bancroft Henderson and His Professional Contributions to Physical Education," Unpublished dissertation, Ohio State University, Columbus, Ohio, 1971.

Ellman, Tracy D., "The Influence of Race/Ethnicity in the Salary Arbitration Process in Major League Baseball," Unpublished Master Thesis, Illinois State University, Normal, Illinois, 1991.

Foreman, T.E., "Discrimination Against the Negro in American Athletics," Unpublished Master Thesis, Fresno State College, Fresno, California, 1957.

Hutchinson, G., "Black Athletes' Contribution Towards Social Change in the United States," Unpublished Doctoral Dissertation, United States International University, San Diego, California, 1977.

Mendonca, Lenny, "Racial Discrimination in Major League Baseball," Unpublished Senior Honors Thesis, College Unknown, 1983.

Nabil, P.A., "Emergence and Arrival of the Afro-American in the National Game: His Participation in Sport in General and Baseball in Particular as a Positive Mechanism for Socio-Economic Mobility in American Society," Unpublished Doctoral Dissertation, University of Illinois-Urbana-Champagne, Champagne, Illinois, 1979.

Neal, Richard Lee, "America's Game in Middletown, USA: Baseball in Muncie, Indiana, 1876-1953," Doctoral Dissertation, Ball State University, Muncie, Indiana, 1989.

Pascal, Anthony H. and Rapping, Leonard A., "Racial Discrimination in Organized Baseball," RAND Memorandum RM-6227-RC. Santa Monica, California, Rand Corporation, 1970, 53 pages.

Pride, Armistead S. "A Register and History of Negro Newspapers in the United States, 1827-1950," Doctoral Dissertation, Northwestern University, Evanston, Illinois, 1950. 426 pages. Pride found more than 2700 newspapers in his search.

Yetman, N.R. and Eitzen, D.S., "Black Americans in Sports: Unequal Opportunity for Equal Ability," W.N. Widmeyer, Editor, "Physical Activity and the Social Sciences." New: MSS Information Corporation, 1976, pages 206-228. Reprinted for the Civil Rights Digest, August, 1972, pages 21-34.

Wiggins, David K. "Sport & Popular Pastimes in the Plantation Community: The Slave Experience," Doctoral Dissertation, University of Maryland, College Park, Maryland, 1979.

A Song for the Heroes

Andy Razaf, the popular song lyricist from New York (his motto was "a song without words is a frame without a picture"), was a friend of Abe and Effa Manley, the owners of the Newark Eagles, and a Negro baseball enthusiast. Just before a 1945 game between a team of black players organized by the Eagles and a squad of white major leaguers, he sent Effa Manley the following song lyrics, to be read to the players as a pep talk:

> **To Our Negro Ball Players**
> *(facing Major Leaguers Sunday)*
>
> Get in there and go to town
> Bat those Jim Crow fences down,
> Demonstrate what you can do,
> Prove you're "Big-time" players too.
> Put your heart in every play
> For Sunday is your "Judgement Day"
> Every word and act of yours
> May either close or open doors!
> Is the Negro player fit?
> Can he pitch, field, think and hit?
> Has he guts and dignity?
> And does he use diplomacy?
> Can he smile and do his stuff
> When he finds the going rough?
> To these questions, you're the key;
> Boys, what will your answer be?
>   —*Eagle team files*

Abe and Effa Manley
Negro Leagues Baseball Museum

Black Stars

On The

Silver Screen

Documentaries

American Giants: Legends of the Negro Leagues, by WGN-TV, 1992. Narrated by Morgan Freeman.

Behind the White Lines: The Negro Baseball Leagues, by CNN Sports, 1991. Narrated by Tom Kirtland.

Biography: Jackie Robinson, 1989. narrated by Peter Graves.

Colored Champions on Parade, produced by William Alexander, date unknown.

Colored Champions of Sport, produced by Harry M. Popkin and distributed by Alfred N. Sack Amusement Enterprise, date unknown.

Greatest Sports Legends: Jackie Robinson, produced by Sports Legend Video, Inc., date unknown. Narrated by Ken Howard.

Hard Road to Glory, by Arthur Ashe, 1989. Narrated by James Earl Jones.

The History of Great Black Baseball Players, produced by Melvin B. Bergman and William M. Speckin. Directed by Bud Morgan and distributed by Fries Home Video, 1990. Narrated by Ernie Banks.

Kings on the Hill: Baseball's Forgotten Men, produced by Rob Ruck and Molly Youngling, 1993. Music by Nathan Davis. Narrated by Ossie Davis.

Major League Baseball Magazine: The Negro Leagues, by Major League Baseball Properties, 1989.

Not In Our League: The Negro Baseball Leagues, by Group W Television, Inc., WJZ-TV Baltimore, 1993. Narrated by Al Sanders.

Only The Ball Was White, by WTTW-TV Chicago, 1980. Narrated by Paul Winfield.

The Heart and Soul of Baseball: The Kansas City Monarchs, by ABC-TV, 1991. Narrated by Mike Mahoney.

The Long Summers of Lou Dials, by David E. Carter, date unknown. Narrated by Dave Diles.

There Was Always Sun Shining Someplace: Life in the Negro Baseball Leagues, by Refocus Films Productions, 1984. Narrated by James Earl Jones.

This Is Your Life: Leroy 'Satchel' Paige, by Ralph Edwards Productions, 1972. Ralph Edwards, host.

Safe at Home Plate, produced by Conne Ward-Cameron and Toni Lee for WPBA Atlanta Public Television, 1994. Narrated by Charlie Pride.

Movies

As the World Rolls On (1921), with Jack Johnson and Blanche Thompson. Jack Johnson plays himself, as he assists Joe Walker, a physically weak young man, who learns physical fitness and the art of self-defense from the former heavyweight champion. Walker eventually wins the love of Polly, played by Blanche Thompson. This film has footage of a game between the Kansas City Monarchs and the Detroit Stars. Produced by Andlauer Productions/Elk Photo Plays, it is a silent, black and white, 5600 foot film.

The Ballad of Satchel Paige (1949), by Richard Durham. An NBC production, it is also called Destination Freedom.

The Court Martial of Jackie Robinson (1990), produced by Turner Pictures, Inc. This film stars Andre Braughter as Jackie Robinson and Stan Shaw as Joe Louis. It traces Robinson's college days, along with highlights and lowlights of his military career, plus his days with the Kansas City Monarchs. Ruby Dee, who had played Jackie's wife in The Jackie Robinson Story in 1950, stars as his mother in this made-for-cable TV movie.

Don't Look Back: The Story of Leroy 'Satchel' Paige (1981), with Louis Gossett, Jr. (Satchel Paige), Beverly Todd (Lahoma Brown Paige), Ernie Barnes (Josh Gibson), Clifton Davis (Cool Papa Bell) and Jim Davis (J.L. Wilkinson). The slender Gossett does an admirable job in portraying Satchel Paige in this made-for-TV movie. The movie was adapted from the book *Maybe I'll Pitch Forever*. Satchel Paige served as a technical consultant. Produced by TBA/Saties/Triseme Productions in color, 98 minutes in length. Directed by Richard A. Colla.

It's Good to Be Alive: The Story of Roy Campanella (1974), with Paul Winfield, Rube Dee and Louis Gossett, Jr. This made-for-TV movie tells the story of former Baltimore Elite Giant and Brooklyn Dodger Roy Campanella's life after his career-ending automobile accident in 1958. Winfield plays Campanella, with Dee as his wife, Ruthie, while Gossett plays the never-quit therapist (Sam Brockington). Produced by Larry Harmon Pictures/Metromedia in color, 100 minutes in length. Directed by Michael Landon.

The Jackie Robinson Story (1950), with Jackie Robinson and Ruby Dee This movie debuted soon after Robinson won the National League's Most Valuable Player Award. An excellent biography of Robinson, who plays himself surprisingly well, while Rube Dee stars as his supportive wife, Rachel.

Produced by Jewel Productions/Eagle-Lion, this film is in black and white and is 76 minutes in length. Author Arthur Mann served as technical advisor.

The Kid from Cleveland (1950), with Satchel Paige and the Cleveland Indians. Bill Veeck gives a superb performance in this sentimental journey to rehabilitate Johnny Barrows as their new batboy. The film was produced by Republic Films in black and white. It is 89 minutes in length. Paige makes frequent appearances throughout the film.

The Wonderful Country (1959) with Robert Mitchum and Julie London. Satchel Paige portrays a U.S. Cavalry sergeant in this movie filmed on location in Durango, Mexico. Paige gave an outstanding performance, but was never asked to act again.

Leroy "Satchel" Paige.
Pamela Paige O'Neal